Michael Flemmin

Readings in Database Systems

Edited by
Michael Stonebraker
University of California, Berkeley

MORGAN KAUFMANN PUBLISHERS, INC.
SAN MATEO, CALIFORNIA

Acquisitions Editor *Bruce Spatz*
Permissions and Coordinating Editor *Shirley Jowell*
Production Manager *Shirley Jowell*
Copy Editor *Lori Windsor*
Cover Designer *Rick Van Genderen*
Typesetter *Technically Speaking Publications*

Library of Congress Cataloging Publication is Available
88-12742
ISBN 0-934613-65-6

Morgan Kaufmann Publishers, Inc.
Editorial Office: 2929 Campus Drive, San Mateo, California 94403
Order to: P.O. Box 50490, Palo Alto, California 94305

Printed in the United States of America

92 91 90 89 88 5 4 3 2 1

Contents

Acknowledgments

A.E. Abbadi, D. Skeen and F. Cristian. (1985) "An Efficient, Fault-Tolerant Protocol for Replicated Data Management," *Proceedings (1985) SIGACT-SIGMOD Conference* pp. 215-229. All rights reserved. Reprinted by permission of ACM and the author.

Anon et A. (1985) "A Measure of Transaction Processing Power," Reprinted from Datamation 1985. © by Chaners Publishing Co.

M.M. Astrahan, P.G. Selinger, D.D. Chamberlin, R.A. Lorie, and T.G. Price. (1979) "Access Path Selection in a Relational Database Management System," *Proceedings (1979) SIGMOD Conference* pp. 23-34. All rights reserved. Reprinted by permission of ACM and the author.

M.M. Astrahan, M.W. Blasgen, D.D. Chamberlin, K.P. Eswaran, J.N. Gray, P.P. Griffiths, W.F. King, R.A. Lorie, P.R. McJones, J.W. Mehl, G.R. Putzolu, I.L. Traiger, B.W. Wade, and V. Watson. (1976) "System R: Relational Approach to Database Management," *ACM Transactions on Database Systems* 1(2): 97-137. All rights reserved. Reprinted by permission of ACM and the author.

F. Bancilhon and R. Ramakrishnan. (1986) "An Amateur's Introduction to Recursive Query Processing Strategies," *Proceedings (1984) SIGMOD*, pp. 16-52. All rights reserved. Reprinted by permission of ACM and the author.

J. Banerjee, Hong-Tai Chou, J.F. Garza, W. Kim, D. Woelk, and N. Ballou, MCC and Hyoung-Joo Kim. (1987) "Data Model Issues for Object-Oriented Applications," *ACM Transactions on Office Information Systems* 5(1): 3-26. All rights reserved. Reprinted by permission of ACM and the author.

R. Bayer and M. Scholnick. (1977) "Concurrency of Operations on B-Trees," *Acta Informatica*. Reprinted with permission of the publisher and the author.

M.J. Carey, D. Frank, M. Muralkrishna, D.J. DeWitt, G. Graefe, J.E. Richardson, and E.J. Shekita. (1986) "The Architecture of the EXODUS Extensible DBMS," *Proceedings of Object-Oriented Database Workshop* pp. 52-65. All rights reserved. Reprinted by permission of ACM and the author.

D.D. Chamberlin, M.M. Astrahan, M.W. Blasgen, J.N. Gray, W.F. King, B.G. Lindsay, R. Lorie, J.W. Mehl, T.G. Price, F. Putzolu, and R.A. Yost. (1981) "A History and Evaluation of System R," *Communications of the ACM,* 24(10): 632-646. All rights reserved. Reprinted by permission of ACM and the author.

H. Chou and D.J. DeWitt. (1985) "An Evaluation of Buffer Management Strategies for Relational Database Systems," *Proceedings 11th International on Very Large Databases*. Reprinted with permission of the publisher and the author.

G. Copeland and D. Maier. (1984) "Making Smalltalk a Database System," *Proceedings (1984) SIGMOD Conference* pp. 316-325. All rights reserved. Reprinted by permission of ACM and the author.

E.F. Codd. (1970) "A Relational Model of Data for Large Shared Data Banks," *Communications of the ACM* 13(6): 377-387. All rights reserved. Reprinted by permission of ACM and the author.

E.F. Codd. (1979) "Extending the Database Relational Model to Capture More Meaning," *ACM Transactions on Database Systems* 4(4): 397-434. All rights reserved. Reprinted by permission of ACM and the author.

D.J. DeWitt, G. Graefe, K.B. Kumer, R.H. Gerber, M.L. Heytens, and M. Muralikrishna. (1986) "Gamma: A High Performance Dataflow Database Machine," *Proceedings 12th International on Very Large Databases*. Reprinted with permission of the publisher and the author.

J.N. Gray, R.A. Lorie, G.R. Putzolu, and I.L. Traiger. "Granularity of Locks and Degrees of Consistency in a Shared Data Base," *IFIP Working Conference on Modeling of Data Base Management Systems* pp. 1-29. All rights reserved. Reprinted by permission of ACM and the author.

J. Gray. (1981) "The Transaction Concept: Virtues and Limitations," *Lecture Notes in Computer Science, Conference Proceedings*, Netherlands. All rights reserved. Reprinted by permission of ACM and the author.

A. Guttman. (1984) "R-Trees: A Dynamic Index Structure for Spatial Searching," *Proceedings (1984) SIGMOD Conference* pp. 47-57. All rights reserved. Reprinted by permission of ACM and the author.

H. Hammer and D. McLeod. (1981) "Database Description with SDM: A Semantic Database Model," *ACM Transactions on Database Systems* 6(3): 351-386. All rights reserved. Reprinted by permission of ACM and the author.

T. Haerder and A. Reuter. (1983) "Principles of Transaction-Oriented Database Recovery," *Computing Surveys* 15(4): 287-318. All rights reserved. Reprinted by permission of ACM and the author.

W. Kim. (1984) "Highly Available Systems for Database Applications," *Computing Surveys* 16(1): 71-98. All rights reserved. Reprinted by permission of ACM and the author.

H.T. Kung and John T. Robinson. (1981) "On Optimistic Methods for Concurrency Control," *ACM Transactions on Database Systems* 6(2): 213-226. All rights reserved. Reprinted by permission of ACM and the author.

W. Litwin. (1980) "Linear Hashing: A New Tool for File and Table Addressing," *Proceedings 6th International on Very Large Databases*. Reprinted with permission of the publisher and the author.

L.F. Mackert and G.M. Lohman. (1986) "R* Optimizer Validation and Performance Evaluation for Distributed Queries," *Proceedings 12th International on Very Large Databases*. Reprinted with permission of the publisher and the author.

J. Nievergelt, H. Hinterberger, and K.C. Sevcik. (1984) "The Grid File: An Adaptable, Symmetric Multikey File Structure," *ACM Transactions on Database Systems* 9(1): 38-71. All rights reserved. Reprinted by permission of ACM and the author.

P. Pin-Shan Chen. (1976) "The Entity-Relationship Model — Toward a Unified View of Data," *ACM Transactions on Database Systems* 1(1): 9-36. All rights reserved. Reprinted by permission of ACM and the author.

T.R. Rogers and R.G.G. Cattell. (1987) "Entity-Relationship Database User Interfaces," *Proceedings of the ER Institute*. Reprinted with permission of the ER Institute, Baton Rouge, Louisiana.

L.A. Rowe. (1985) "Fill-in-the-Form Programming," *Proceedings 11th International on Very Large Databases*, Stockholm, Sweden. Reprinted with permission of the publisher and the author.

J.W. Schmidt. (1977) "Some High Level Language Constructs for Data of Type Relation," *ACM Transactions on Database Systems* 2(3): 247-261. All rights reserved. Reprinted by permission of ACM and the author.

D.W. Shipman. (1981) "The Functional Data Language DAPLEX," *ACM Transactions on Database Systems* 6(1): 140-173. All rights reserved. Reprinted by permission of ACM and the author.

D. Skeen. (1981) "Nonblocking Commit Protocols," *Proceedings (1981) SIGMOD Conference* pp. 132-141. All rights reserved. Reprinted by permission of ACM and the author.

M. Stonebraker. (1981) "Operating System Support for Database Management," *Communications of the ACM* 24(7): 412-418. All rights reserved. Reprinted by permission of ACM and the author.

M. Stonebraker. (1980) "Retrospection on a Database System," *ACM Transactions on Database Systems* 5(2): 225-240. All rights reserved. Reprinted by permission of ACM and the author.

M. Stonebraker, E. Wong, P. Kreps, and G. Held. (1976) "Design and Implementation of INGRES," *ACM Transactions on Database Systems* 1(3): 189-222. All rights reserved. Reprinted by permission of ACM and the author.

M. Stonebraker. (1987) "The Design of the Postgres Storage System," *Readings 13th International on Very Large Databases,* Brighton, England. Reprinted with permission of the publisher and the author.

M. Stonebraker, E. Hanson and Chin-Heng Hong. (1987) "The Design of the Postgres Rules System", *International Conference on Data Engineering* pp. 356-374. © 1987 IEEE. Reprinted, with permission, from Proceedings of the International Conference on Data Engineering.

M. Stonebraker. (1986) "Inclusion of New Types in Relational Data Base Systems," *Proceedings of IEEE/Data Engineering* pp. 262-269. © 1986 IEEE. Reprinted, with permission, from Proceedings of the International Conference on Data Engineering.

R. Williams, D. Daniels, L. Haas, G. Lapis, B. Lindsay, P. Pg, R. Obermark, P. Selinger, A. Walker, P. Wilms, and R. Yost. (1981) "An Overview of the Architecture." Reprinted with permission of the publisher and the author.

C. Zoniolo. (1983) "The Database Language GEM," *Proceedings (1983) SIGMOD Conference* pp. 297-218.

Preface

The purpose of this collection is to assemble significant research contributions so they are easily accessible to anyone interested in database research. It is appropriate for use as an introduction for students or professionals from industry, and as a reference volume to anyone active in database systems. This set of readings represents what I perceive to be the most important papers in the database area. It is intended to serve as a core of material that any DBMS professional should be familiar with. Moreover, any industrial practioner or graduate student who wishes to be current on the important research themes would be well advised to read these papers.

To facilitate its use as a text for classroom or independent reading, I have included an introduction to each chapter. These introductions summarize the comments I make during lectures in my graduate course and discuss the papers in the broader context of database research. They are included as an aid to students and instructors alike. In each introduction I have strived to be as controversial as possible, to maximize the opportunity for discussion, and to encourage the independent reader to critically evaluate research results.

I have been teaching a graduate level course in database management for several years at the University of California. The course is typically taught to first- and second-year graduate students. Students take an undergraduate introduction to databases as a prerequisite. Because there has never been a text appropriate to the course, I have always organized it around a collection of readings from the literature. However, the effort required to maintain and distribute this material is significant, and there are numerous restrictions on use of copyrighted papers. These points have motivated me to prepare *Readings in Database Systems* as a more readily available, and convenient format for this essential information.

I have selected the papers in this volume by first evaluating the quality of research in each and its potential for lasting importance. I tried to select papers that were both seminal in nature and accessible to a reader who has a basic familiarity with database systems. This often resulted in situations where I had two or more papers to chose from. In such cases, I selected what I felt was the best or which discussed the broadest variety of issues. In other areas, such as the relationship of logic programming to databases, the research is very complex. In these cases I selected the most accessible paper. There were several topics such as database design, data dictionaries, and protection, where I couldn't find any papers that were appropriate within the context of this volume. In these cases, I reluctantly excluded some otherwise important topics from the collection.

After the initial selection I made further modifications to achieve better balance among the various topics and corrected some of my initial prejudices. In this regard, I was assisted greatly by the following reviewers whose candid feedback was instrumental in broadening the content and usefulness of this volume:

Dr. Dina Bitton, University of Illinois;
Dr. Umeshwar Dayal, Computer Corp. of America;
Dr. David DeWitt, University of Wisconsin;
Dr. James Gray, Tandem Computers;
Dr. Henry Korth, University of Texas;
Dr. Hector Garcia-Molian, Princeton University;
Dr. Timos Sellis, University of Maryland.

I would like to thank them for their time and effort in this endeavor. I plan to revise this collection of readings every couple of years, so that it remains current with the material needed by students and professionals as a fundamental survey and reference in Database Systems. Reader suggestions for changes or additions to this collection may be sent to the publisher—a reply form is included at the end of this book.

Berkeley, Ca.
April 1, 1988

Chapter 1

The Roots

1.1 Introduction

The first five papers in this book represent the "roots" of relational database systems. Of course Ted Codd gets most of the credit for focusing attention on the relational model of data with his pioneering paper in CACM in June 1970, which I have chosen to be the kickoff article in this volume (1.2). This paper started a heated controversy in all ACM SIGFIDET (now SIGMOD) meetings from 1971 onward between two collections of people. Loosely speaking on one side were members of the COBOL/CODASYL camp, who had recently written their proposal for a standard network database system. This document, referred to as "the DBTG Report" [DBTG71], suggested a network data model containing records and sets with a syntax closely aligned with COBOL and a low-level navigational interface. Perhaps the best nontechnical exposition of the point of view of the DBTG camp is the 1973 Turing Award paper [BACH73] written by Charlie Bachman, the main developer of IDS, a Honeywell DBMS written in the 1960s, from which the DBTG Report borrowed heavily. On the other side were Ted Codd and virtually all academic researchers lauding the merits of the relational model.

The positions of the two camps were approximately the following:

COBOL/CODASYL Camp:

1. The relational model is too mathematical. No mere mortal programmer will be able to understand your newfangled languages.
2. Even if you can get programmers to learn your new languages, you won't be able to build an efficient implementation of them.
3. On-line transaction-processing applications want to do record-oriented operations.

Relational camp:

1. Nothing as complicated as the DBTG proposal can possibly be the right way to do data management.
2. Any set-oriented query is too hard to program using the DBTG data manipulation language.
3. The CODASYL model has no formal underpinning with which to define the semantics of the complex operations in the model.

This argument came to a head at the 1975 ACM/SIGMOD Conference in Ann Arbor, Michigan where Ted Codd and two seconds squared off against Charlie Bachman and two seconds in what was publicized as "The Great Debate."

The debate was significant in that it highlighted once again that neither camp could talk in terms the other could understand. Codd gave a formal treatment of how the CODASYL people could best make the semantics of their model less arbitrary. Bachman then argued that the CODASYL model was almost no different than the relational model. Both talks and the resulting discussion left the audience more confused than ever.

In the latter half of the 1970s the two camps began to understand each other and the discussion became more focused. At the same time, however, interest in CODASYL systems began to decline based, in my opinion, on two events of the late 1970s. First, easier-to-use relational languages such as QUEL [HELD75] and SQL [CHAM76] were devised to blunt the criticism that earlier relational languages (specifically Codd's relational calculus [CODD71] and algebra [CODD72]) were too mathematical. Second, prototype relational systems began to appear and prove that implementations could be done with reasonable efficiency.

The two most widely used prototypes were System R and INGRES, and they helped shape a fair amount of the history that followed. Under the able direction of Frank King, a group of about 15 researchers at the IBM Research Laboratory in San Jose built System R from about 1974 to 1978. Although it was a significant effort by a large group of people, the influence of Jim Gray, Franco Putzolu, and Irv Traiger on the lower half of the system (the RSS level) is noteworthy, while the RDS level shows the influence of Mort Astrahan, Don Chamberlin, and Pat Selinger. Fifty miles away a pickup team of Berkeley students built INGRES under the direction of myself and Eugene Wong from 1973 to 1977. The next two papers in this section present the status of these two systems in 1976 (1.3, 1.4). After both systems were more or less finished, excellent retrospectives were written by both groups on the good and bad points of their designs. The final two papers in this section present these retrospections (1.5, 1.6).

I wish to use the rest of this introduction to make a collection of comments about these prototypes. The reader of the "before" and "after" versions should carefully note what each group admitted to screwing up (e.g., poor integration between the RDS and RSS in System R and the compile time structure in INGRES). The INGRES system was constructed as an interpreter because of inexperience on the part of the designers. In System R links and images exist at the RSS level but the RDS level does not allow users to take advantage of them. The apparent reason is that System R development was done by two teams. The RSS team was further ahead, and its facilities were defined first. According to Jim Gray, links were put into the RSS in case they would be required at some future time to support a DBTG or IMS interface. The RDS group decided later not to use links and images in their initial implementation because they made the query optimization problem harder.

Both retrospections are less than completely candid about their failures. For example the recovery management scheme in System R based on shadow pages was declared a failure in another paper [GRAY81]. The absence of hashing is also widely regarded as a substantial mistake. In addition, achieving good performance seemed to require wizardry in the setting of system parameters [DEWI87]. Finally, System R paid little attention to presentation services and gave the end user only a very primitive query capability called the User Friendly Interface (UFI).

On the other hand, the INGRES designers do not point out several shortcuts they took. They used the UNIX file system even though there is no way to guarantee crash recovery services in this environment. The System R designers elected to write their own file system when faced with an unusable file manager. Moreover, they chose simplistic implementations for both locking and crash recovery that were clearly naive.

One should also observe what facilities are discussed in the "before" paper that the "after" paper is notably silent about (e.g., triggers in System R). One also should notice the dominance of the 16-bit architecture of the PDP-11 on the INGRES system and the amount of effort that was expended to deal with it. This pain and suffering has vanished outside the low end of the personal computer world a scant ten years later.

Another comment is the tremendous commercial significance that these systems (especially System R) have had over the years. Kapali Eswaren left the System R project to form his own company, ESVAL, which built a commercial version of System R. Later, the ESVAL code became the basis for both the Hewlett-Packard ALLBASE system and IDMS/SQL from Cullinet. Larry Ellison started Oracle Corp and independently implemented the published external specifications for System R. Lastly, with some rewriting, DB 2 and SQL/DS are derivatives of the original System R prototype.

On the INGRES side of the ledger, Relational Technology and Computer Associates both commercially exploited the public domain University of California prototype. Bob Epstein left the INGRES project in 1979 to join Britton-Lee and help build the IDM software. More recently he joined a second-generation offspring, Sybase, to build another relational system focused on the transaction-processing marketplace.

As a result much of the current commercial landscape shows the influence of these systems. In general this influence is very positive. For example, the query-optimization architecture and compilation techniques of System R are generally praised and form the basis for the algorithms in most commercial systems. The cleanliness of QUEL and the query modification algorithms for views, protection, and integrity control get good marks for INGRES.

However, some of the legacy is less exemplary. For example, because of the position of IBM, the programming level interface between PL1 and SQL will be an intergalactic standard for a very long time. Unfortunately SQL and its embedding are not very elegant, and Date clearly explains [DATE85] in the language mistakes that were made. Secondly, neither INGRES nor System R was particularly faithful to the relational model. Both systems allow one to perpetrate the cardinal sin, to create a relation with duplicate tuples in it. Moreover, System R would carefully retain the correct number of duplicates during join processing, so a willing user could build semantics into the number of duplicate records. This was one of the "features" of the DBTG data model that relational advocates most despised. Both systems failed to implement the notion of domains or even primary keys. Hence, current commercial systems are generally lacking in these areas.

I want to comment on two little-known facts that might have dramatically altered the events of the last several years. First, IBM initially attempted to build an SQL interface on top of IMS. This project, code-named Eagle, would have allowed DL/1 and SQL to be used interchangeably to express DBMS commands for a single database. This effort was abandoned in the late 1970s because of semantic difficulties in building an SQL to DL/1 translator. Then IBM decided to build a separate relational system. However, they still had a choice of which approach to convert into a production system. Besides System R there were available prototypes for QBE [ZLOO75] and UDL [DATE76]. Although QBE was designed as an end user interface and would be very difficult to call from PL/1, UDL offered a number of advantages over SQL, including a clean coupling with PL/1. A very different collection of events would have unfolded if IBM had chosen to exploit one of the other competitors.

I want to close this section with another suggestion for additional reading. It appears that Ted Codd has been designated "the keeper of the faith" and has the individual initiative to redefine the relational model whenever appropriate. Hence, one can think of four different versions of the model:

1. Defined by the 1970 CACM paper
2. Defined by Codd's 1981 Turing award paper [CODD82]
3. Defined by Codd's 12 rules and scoring system [CODD85]
4. In preparation [CODD87]

The interested reader is advised to read all four and consider the evolution of the model over time.

References

[BACH73] Bachman, C., "The Programmer as Navigator," CACM, Nov. 1973.

[CHAM76] Chamberlin, D. et al., "SEQUEL 2: A Unified Approach to Data Definition, Manipulation and Control," IBM Journal of Research and Development, Nov. 1976.

[CODD71] Codd, E., "A Data Base Sublanguage Founded on the Relational Calculus," Proc. 1971 ACM-SIGFIDET Workshop on Data Description, Access and Control, San Diego, Calif., Nov. 1971.

[CODD72] Codd, E., "Relational Completeness of Data Base Sublanguages," Courant Computer Science Symposium 6, Prentice-Hall, Englewood Cliffs, N.J., May 1972.

[CODD82] Codd, E., "Relational Database: A Practical Foundation for Productivity," CACM, Feb. 1982.

[CODD85] Codd, E., "Is Your DBMS Really Relational," Computer World, Oct. 14, 1985.

[CODD87] Codd, E., private communication.

[DATE76] Date, C., "An Architecture for High-Level Language Database Extensions," Proc. 1976 ACM-SIGMOD Conference on Management of Data, San Jose, Calif., June 1976.

[DATE85] Date, C., "A Critique of SQL," SIGMOD RECORD, Jan. 1985.

[DBTG71] Data Base Task Group, "April 1971 Report," available from ACM.

[DEWI87] Dewitt, D. et al, "A Single-User Performance Evaluation of the Terradata Database Machine," MCC Technical Report, DB-081-87, Mar. 1987.

[GRAY81] Gray, J. et al., "The Recovery Manager of the System R Database Manager," ACM Computing Surveys, June 1981.

[HELD75] Held, G. et al., "INGRES — A Relational Data Base System," Proc. 1975 National Computer Conference, Anaheim, Calif., June 1975.

[ZLOO75] Zloof, M., "Query by Example," Proc. 1975 National Computer Conference, Anaheim, Ca., June 1975.

A Relational Model of Data for Large Shared Data Banks

E. F. Codd
IBM Research Laboratory, San Jose, California

Future users of large data banks must be protected from having to know how the data is organized in the machine (the internal representation). A prompting service which supplies such information is not a satisfactory solution. Activities of users at terminals and most application programs should remain unaffected when the internal representation of data is changed and even when some aspects of the external representation are changed. Changes in data representation will often be needed as a result of changes in query, update, and report traffic and natural growth in the types of stored information.

Existing noninferential, formatted data systems provide users with tree-structured files or slightly more general network models of the data. In Section 1, inadequacies of these models are discussed. A model based on *n*-ary relations, a normal form for data base relations, and the concept of a universal data sublanguage are introduced. In Section 2, certain operations on relations (other than logical inference) are discussed and applied to the problems of redundancy and consistency in the user's model.

KEY WORDS AND PHRASES: data bank, data base, data structure, data organization, hierarchies of data, networks of data, relations, derivability, redundancy, consistency, composition, join, retrieval language, predicate calculus, security, data integrity
CR CATEGORIES: 3.70, 3.73, 3.75, 4.20, 4.22, 4.29

1. Relational Model and Normal Form

1.1. Introduction

This paper is concerned with the application of elementary relation theory to systems which provide shared access to large banks of formatted data. Except for a paper by Childs [1], the principal application of relations to data systems has been to deductive question-answering systems. Levein and Maron [2] provide numerous references to work in this area.

In contrast, the problems treated here are those of *data independence*—the independence of application programs and terminal activities from growth in data types and changes in data representation—and certain kinds of *data inconsistency* which are expected to become troublesome even in nondeductive systems.

The relational view (or model) of data described in Section 1 appears to be superior in several respects to the graph or network model [3, 4] presently in vogue for non-inferential systems. It provides a means of describing data with its natural structure only—that is, without superimposing any additional structure for machine representation purposes. Accordingly, it provides a basis for a high level data language which will yield maximal independence between programs on the one hand and machine representation and organization of data on the other.

A further advantage of the relational view is that it forms a sound basis for treating derivability, redundancy, and consistency of relations—these are discussed in Section 2. The network model, on the other hand, has spawned a number of confusions, not the least of which is mistaking the derivation of connections for the derivation of relations (see remarks in Section 2 on the "connection trap").

Finally, the relational view permits a clearer evaluation of the scope and logical limitations of present formatted data systems, and also the relative merits (from a logical standpoint) of competing representations of data within a single system. Examples of this clearer perspective are cited in various parts of this paper. Implementations of systems to support the relational model are not discussed.

1.2. Data Dependencies in Present Systems

The provision of data description tables in recently developed information systems represents a major advance toward the goal of data independence [5, 6, 7]. Such tables facilitate changing certain characteristics of the data representation stored in a data bank. However, the variety of data representation characteristics which can be changed *without logically impairing some application programs* is still quite limited. Further, the model of data with which users interact is still cluttered with representational properties, particularly in regard to the representation of collections of data (as opposed to individual items). Three of the principal kinds of data dependencies which still need to be removed are: ordering dependence, indexing dependence, and access path dependence. In some systems these dependencies are not clearly separable from one another.

1.2.1. *Ordering Dependence.* Elements of data in a data bank may be stored in a variety of ways, some involving no concern for ordering, some permitting each element to participate in one ordering only, others permitting each element to participate in several orderings. Let us consider those existing systems which either require or permit data elements to be stored in at least one total ordering which is closely associated with the hardware-determined ordering of addresses. For example, the records of a file concerning parts might be stored in ascending order by part serial number. Such systems normally permit application programs to assume that the order of presentation of records from such a file is identical to (or is a subordering of) the stored ordering. Those application programs which take advantage of the stored ordering of a file are likely to fail to operate correctly if for some reason it becomes necessary to replace that ordering by a different one. Similar remarks hold for a stored ordering implemented by means of pointers.

It is unnecessary to single out any system as an example, because all the well-known information systems that are marketed today fail to make a clear distinction between order of presentation on the one hand and stored ordering on the other. Significant implementation problems must be solved to provide this kind of independence.

1.2.2. *Indexing Dependence.* In the context of formatted data, an index is usually thought of as a purely performance-oriented component of the data representation. It tends to improve response to queries and updates and, at the same time, slow down response to insertions and deletions. From an informational standpoint, an index is a redundant component of the data representation. If a system uses indices at all and if it is to perform well in an environment with changing patterns of activity on the data bank, an ability to create and destroy indices from time to time will probably be necessary. The question then arises: Can application programs and terminal activities remain invariant as indices come and go?

Present formatted data systems take widely different approaches to indexing. TDMS [7] unconditionally provides indexing on all attributes. The presently released version of IMS [5] provides the user with a choice for each file: a choice between no indexing at all (the hierarchic sequential organization) or indexing on the primary key only (the hierarchic indexed sequential organization). In neither case is the user's application logic dependent on the existence of the unconditionally provided indices. IDS [8], however, permits the file designers to select attributes to be indexed and to incorporate indices into the file structure by means of additional chains. Application programs taking advantage of the performance benefit of these indexing chains must refer to those chains by name. Such programs do not operate correctly if these chains are later removed.

1.2.3. *Access Path Dependence.* Many of the existing formatted data systems provide users with tree-structured files or slightly more general network models of the data. Application programs developed to work with these systems tend to be logically impaired if the trees or networks are changed in structure. A simple example follows.

Suppose the data bank contains information about parts and projects. For each part, the part number, part name, part description, quantity-on-hand, and quantity-on-order are recorded. For each project, the project number, project name, project description are recorded. Whenever a project makes use of a certain part, the quantity of that part committed to the given project is also recorded. Suppose that the system requires the user or file designer to declare or define the data in terms of tree structures. Then, any one of the hierarchical structures may be adopted for the information mentioned above (see Structures 1–5).

Structure 1. Projects Subordinate to Parts

File	*Segment*	*Fields*
F	PART	part #
		part name
		part description
		quantity-on-hand
		quantity-on-order
	PROJECT	project #
		project name
		project description
		quantity committed

Structure 2. Parts Subordinate to Projects

File	*Segment*	*Fields*
F	PROJECT	project #
		project name
		project description
	PART	part #
		part name
		part description
		quantity-on-hand
		quantity-on-order
		quantity committed

Structure 3. Parts and Projects as Peers
Commitment Relationship Subordinate to Projects

File	*Segment*	*Fields*
F	PART	part #
		part name
		part description
		quantity-on-hand
		quantity-on-order
G	PROJECT	project #
		project name
		project description
	PART	part #
		quantity committed

Structure 4. Parts and Projects as Peers
Commitment Relationship Subordinate to Parts

File	*Segment*	*Fields*
F	PART	part #
		part description
		quantity-on-hand
		quantity-on-order
	PROJECT	project #
		quantity committed
G	PROJECT	project #
		project name
		project description

Structure 5. Parts, Projects, and
Commitment Relationship as Peers

File	*Segment*	*Fields*
F	PART	part #
		part name
		part description
		quantity-on-hand
		quantity-on-order
G	PROJECT	project #
		project name
		project description
H	COMMIT	part #
		project #
		quantity committed

Now, consider the problem of printing out the part number, part name, and quantity committed for every part used in the project whose project name is "alpha." The following observations may be made regardless of which available tree-oriented information system is selected to tackle this problem. If a program P is developed for this problem assuming one of the five structures above—that is, P makes no test to determine which structure is in effect—then P will fail on at least three of the remaining structures. More specifically, if P succeeds with structure 5, it will fail with all the others; if P succeeds with structure 3 or 4, it will fail with at least 1, 2, and 5; if P succeeds with 1 or 2, it will fail with at least 3, 4, and 5. The reason is simple in each case. In the absence of a test to determine which structure is in effect, P fails because an attempt is made to exceute a reference to a nonexistent file (available systems treat this as an error) or no attempt is made to execute a reference to a file containing needed information. The reader who is not convinced should develop sample programs for this simple problem.

Since, in general, it is not practical to develop application programs which test for all tree structurings permitted by the system, these programs fail when a change in structure becomes necessary.

Systems which provide users with a network model of the data run into similar difficulties. In both the tree and network cases, the user (or his program) is required to exploit a collection of user access paths to the data. It does not matter whether these paths are in close correspondence with pointer-defined paths in the stored representation—in IDS the correspondence is extremely simple, in TDMS it is just the opposite. The consequence, regardless of the stored representation, is that terminal activities and programs become dependent on the continued existence of the user access paths.

One solution to this is to adopt the policy that once a user access path is defined it will not be made obsolete until all application programs using that path have become obsolete. Such a policy is not practical, because the number of access paths in the total model for the community of users of a data bank would eventually become excessively large.

1.3. A Relational View of Data

The term *relation* is used here in its accepted mathematical sense. Given sets $S_1, S_2, \cdots, S_n$ (not necessarily distinct), R is a relation on these n sets if it is a set of n-tuples each of which has its first element from S_1, its second element from S_2, and so on.[1] We shall refer to S_j as the jth *domain* of R. As defined above, R is said to have *degree n*. Relations of degree 1 are often called *unary*, degree 2 *binary*, degree 3 *ternary*, and degree n *n-ary*.

For expository reasons, we shall frequently make use of an array representation of relations, but it must be remembered that this particular representation is not an essential part of the relational view being expounded. An array which represents an n-ary relation R has the following properties:

(1) Each row represents an n-tuple of R.
(2) The ordering of rows is immaterial.
(3) All rows are distinct.
(4) The ordering of columns is significant—it corresponds to the ordering $S_1, S_2, \cdots, S_n$ of the domains on which R is defined (see, however, remarks below on domain-ordered and domain-unordered relations).
(5) The significance of each column is partially conveyed by labeling it with the name of the corresponding domain.

The example in Figure 1 illustrates a relation of degree 4, called *supply*, which reflects the shipments-in-progress of parts from specified suppliers to specified projects in specified quantities.

supply	*(supplier*	*part*	*project*	*quantity)*
	1	2	5	17
	1	3	5	23
	2	3	7	9
	2	7	5	4
	4	1	1	12

Fig. 1. A relation of degree 4

One might ask: If the columns are labeled by the name of corresponding domains, why should the ordering of columns matter? As the example in Figure 2 shows, two columns may have identical headings (indicating identical domains) but possess distinct meanings with respect to the relation. The relation depicted is called *component*. It is a ternary relation, whose first two domains are called *part* and third domain is called *quantity*. The meaning of *component* (x, y, z) is that part x is an immediate component (or subassembly) of part y, and z units of part x are needed to assemble one unit of part y. It is a relation which plays a critical role in the parts explosion problem.

component	*(part*	*part*	*quantity)*
	1	5	9
	2	5	7
	3	5	2
	2	6	12
	3	6	3
	4	7	1
	6	7	1

Fig. 2. A relation with two identical domains

It is a remarkable fact that several existing information systems (chiefly those based on tree-structured files) fail to provide data representations for relations which have two or more identical domains. The present version of IMS/360 [5] is an example of such a system.

The totality of data in a data bank may be viewed as a collection of time-varying relations. These relations are of assorted degrees. As time progresses, each n-ary relation may be subject to insertion of additional n-tuples, deletion of existing ones, and alteration of components of any of its existing n-tuples.

[1] More concisely, R is a subset of the Cartesian product $S_1 \times S_2 \times \cdots \times S_n$.

In many commercial, governmental, and scientific data banks, however, some of the relations are of quite high degree (a degree of 30 is not at all uncommon). Users should not normally be burdened with remembering the domain ordering of any relation (for example, the ordering *supplier*, then *part*, then *project*, then *quantity* in the relation *supply*). Accordingly, we propose that users deal, not with relations which are domain-ordered, but with *relationships* which are their domain-unordered counterparts.[2] To accomplish this, domains must be uniquely identifiable at least within any given relation, without using position. Thus, where there are two or more identical domains, we require in each case that the domain name be qualified by a distinctive *role name*, which serves to identify the role played by that domain in the given relation. For example, in the relation *component* of Figure 2, the first domain *part* might be qualified by the role name *sub*, and the second by *super*, so that users could deal with the relationship *component* and its domains—*sub.part super.part, quantity*—without regard to any ordering between these domains.

To sum up, it is proposed that most users should interact with a relational model of the data consisting of a collection of time-varying relationships (rather than relations). Each user need not know more about any relationship than its name together with the names of its domains (role qualified whenever necessary).[3] Even this information might be offered in menu style by the system (subject to security and privacy constraints) upon request by the user.

There are usually many alternative ways in which a relational model may be established for a data bank. In order to discuss a preferred way (or normal form), we must first introduce a few additional concepts (active domain, primary key, foreign key, nonsimple domain) and establish some links with terminology currently in use in information systems programming. In the remainder of this paper, we shall not bother to distinguish between relations and relationships except where it appears advantageous to be explicit.

Consider an example of a data bank which includes relations concerning parts, projects, and suppliers. One relation called *part* is defined on the following domains:

(1) part number
(2) part name
(3) part color
(4) part weight
(5) quantity on hand
(6) quantity on order

and possibly other domains as well. Each of these domains is, in effect, a pool of values, some or all of which may be represented in the data bank at any instant. While it is conceivable that, at some instant, all part colors are present, it is unlikely that all possible part weights, part names, and part numbers are. We shall call the set of values represented at some instant the *active domain* at that instant.

Normally, one domain (or combination of domains) of a given relation has values which uniquely identify each element (n-tuple) of that relation. Such a domain (or combination) is called a *primary key*. In the example above, part number would be a primary key, while part color would not be. A primary key is *nonredundant* if it is either a simple domain (not a combination) or a combination such that none of the participating simple domains is superfluous in uniquely identifying each element. A relation may possess more than one nonredundant primary key. This would be the case in the example if different parts were always given distinct names. Whenever a relation has two or more nonredundant primary keys, one of them is arbitrarily selected and called *the* primary key of that relation.

A common requirement is for elements of a relation to cross-reference other elements of the same relation or elements of a different relation. Keys provide a user-oriented means (but not the only means) of expressing such cross-references. We shall call a domain (or domain combination) of relation R a *foreign key* if it is not the primary key of R but its elements are values of the primary key of some relation S (the possibility that S and R are identical is not excluded). In the relation *supply* of Figure 1, the combination of *supplier, part, project* is the primary key, while each of these three domains taken separately is a foreign key.

In previous work there has been a strong tendency to treat the data in a data bank as consisting of two parts, one part consisting of entity descriptions (for example, descriptions of suppliers) and the other part consisting of relations between the various entities or types of entities (for example, the *supply* relation). This distinction is difficult to maintain when one may have foreign keys in any relation whatsoever. In the user's relational model there appears to be no advantage to making such a distinction (there may be some advantage, however, when one applies relational concepts to machine representations of the user's set of relationships).

So far, we have discussed examples of relations which are defined on simple domains—domains whose elements are atomic (nondecomposable) values. Nonatomic values can be discussed within the relational framework. Thus, some domains may have relations as elements. These relations may, in turn, be defined on nonsimple domains, and so on. For example, one of the domains on which the relation *employee* is defined might be *salary history*. An element of the salary history domain is a binary relation defined on the domain *date* and the domain *salary*. The *salary history* domain is the set of all such binary relations. At any instant of time there are as many instances of the *salary history* relation in the data bank as there are employees. In contrast, there is only one instance of the *employee* relation.

The terms attribute and repeating group in present data base terminology are roughly analogous to simple domain

[2] In mathematical terms, a relationship is an equivalence class of those relations that are equivalent under permutation of domains (see Section 2.1.1).

[3] Naturally, as with any data put into and retrieved from a computer system, the user will normally make far more effective use of the data if he is aware of its meaning.

and nonsimple domain, respectively. Much of the confusion in present terminology is due to failure to distinguish between type and instance (as in "record") and between components of a user model of the data on the one hand and their machine representation counterparts on the other hand (again, we cite "record" as an example).

1.4. Normal Form

A relation whose domains are all simple can be represented in storage by a two-dimensional column-homogeneous array of the kind discussed above. Some more complicated data structure is necessary for a relation with one or more nonsimple domains. For this reason (and others to be cited below) the possibility of eliminating nonsimple domains appears worth investigating.[4] There is, in fact, a very simple elimination procedure, which we shall call normalization.

Consider, for example, the collection of relations exhibited in Figure 3 (a). *Job history* and *children* are nonsimple domains of the relation *employee*. *Salary history* is a nonsimple domain of the relation *job history*. The tree in Figure 3 (a) shows just these interrelationships of the nonsimple domains.

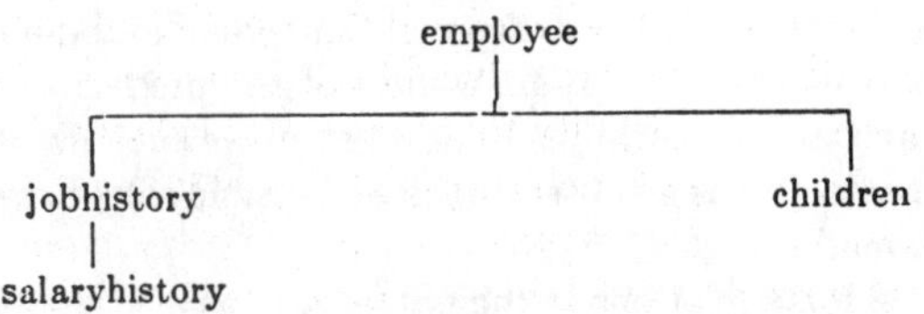

employee (*man#*, name, birthdate, jobhistory, children)
jobhistory (*jobdate*, title, salaryhistory)
salaryhistory (*salarydate*, salary)
children (*childname*, birthyear)

Fig. 3(a). Unnormalized set

employee′ (*man#*, name, birthdate)
jobhistory′ (*man#*, *jobdate*, title)
salaryhistory′ (*man#*, *jobdate*, *salarydate*, salary)
children′ (*man#*, *childname*, birthyear)

Fig. 3(b). Normalized set

Normalization proceeds as follows. Starting with the relation at the top of the tree, take its primary key and expand each of the immediately subordinate relations by inserting this primary key domain or domain combination. The primary key of each expanded relation consists of the primary key before expansion augmented by the primary key copied down from the parent relation. Now, strike out from the parent relation all nonsimple domains, remove the top node of the tree, and repeat the same sequence of operations on each remaining subtree.

The result of normalizing the collection of relations in Figure 3 (a) is the collection in Figure 3 (b). The primary key of each relation is italicized to show how such keys are expanded by the normalization.

[4] M. E. Sanko of IBM, San Jose, independently recognized the desirability of eliminating nonsimple domains.

If normalization as described above is to be applicable, the unnormalized collection of relations must satisfy the following conditions:

(1) The graph of interrelationships of the nonsimple domains is a collection of trees.

(2) No primary key has a component domain which is nonsimple.

The writer knows of no application which would require any relaxation of these conditions. Further operations of a normalizing kind are possible. These are not discussed in this paper.

The simplicity of the array representation which becomes feasible when all relations are cast in normal form is not only an advantage for storage purposes but also for communication of bulk data between systems which use widely different representations of the data. The communication form would be a suitably compressed version of the array representation and would have the following advantages:

(1) It would be devoid of pointers (address-valued or displacement-valued).

(2) It would avoid all dependence on hash addressing schemes.

(3) It would contain no indices or ordering lists.

If the user's relational model is set up in normal form, names of items of data in the data bank can take a simpler form than would otherwise be the case. A general name would take a form such as

$$R(g).r.d$$

where R is a relational name; g is a generation identifier (optional); r is a role name (optional); d is a domain name. Since g is needed only when several generations of a given relation exist, or are anticipated to exist, and r is needed only when the relation R has two or more domains named d, the simple form $R.d$ will often be adequate.

1.5. Some Linguistic Aspects

The adoption of a relational model of data, as described above, permits the development of a universal data sublanguage based on an applied predicate calculus. A first-order predicate calculus suffices if the collection of relations is in normal form. Such a language would provide a yardstick of linguistic power for all other proposed data languages, and would itself be a strong candidate for embedding (with appropriate syntactic modification) in a variety of host languages (programming, command- or problem-oriented). While it is not the purpose of this paper to describe such a language in detail, its salient features would be as follows.

Let us denote the data sublanguage by R and the host language by H. R permits the declaration of relations and their domains. Each declaration of a relation identifies the primary key for that relation. Declared relations are added to the system catalog for use by any members of the user community who have appropriate authorization. H permits supporting declarations which indicate, perhaps less permanently, how these relations are represented in storage. R permits the specification for retrieval of any subset of data from the data bank. Action on such a retrieval request is subject to security constraints.

The universality of the data sublanguage lies in its descriptive ability (not its computing ability). In a large data bank each subset of the data has a very large number of possible (and sensible) descriptions, even when we assume (as we do) that there is only a finite set of function subroutines to which the system has access for use in qualifying data for retrieval. Thus, the class of qualification expressions which can be used in a set specification must have the descriptive power of the class of well-formed formulas of an applied predicate calculus. It is well known that to preserve this descriptive power it is unnecessary to express (in whatever syntax is chosen) every formula of the selected predicate calculus. For example, just those in prenex normal form are adequate [9].

Arithmetic functions may be needed in the qualification or other parts of retrieval statements. Such functions can be defined in H and invoked in R.

A set so specified may be fetched for query purposes only, or it may be held for possible changes. Insertions take the form of adding new elements to declared relations without regard to any ordering that may be present in their machine representation. Deletions which are effective for the community (as opposed to the individual user or subcommunities) take the form of removing elements from declared relations. Some deletions and updates may be triggered by others, if deletion and update dependencies between specified relations are declared in R.

One important effect that the view adopted toward data has on the language used to retrieve it is in the naming of data elements and sets. Some aspects of this have been discussed in the previous section. With the usual network view, users will often be burdened with coining and using more relation names than are absolutely necessary, since names are associated with paths (or path types) rather than with relations.

Once a user is aware that a certain relation is stored, he will expect to be able to exploit[5] it using any combination of its arguments as "knowns" and the remaining arguments as "unknowns," because the information (like Everest) is there. This is a system feature (missing from many current information systems) which we shall call (logically) *symmetric exploitation* of relations. Naturally, symmetry in performance is not to be expected.

To support symmetric exploitation of a single binary relation, two directed paths are needed. For a relation of degree n, the number of paths to be named and controlled is n factorial.

Again, if a relational view is adopted in which every n-ary relation ($n > 2$) has to be expressed by the user as a nested expression involving only binary relations (see Feldman's LEAP System [10], for example) then $2n - 1$ names have to be coined instead of only $n + 1$ with direct n-ary notation as described in Section 1.2. For example, the 4-ary relation *supply* of Figure 1, which entails 5 names in n-ary notation, would be represented in the form

$$P\ (supplier,\ Q\ (part,\ R\ (project,\ quantity)))$$

in nested binary notation and, thus, employ 7 names.

A further disadvantage of this kind of expression is its asymmetry. Although this asymmetry does not prohibit symmetric exploitation, it certainly makes some bases of interrogation very awkward for the user to express (consider, for example, a query for those parts and quantities related to certain given projects via Q and R).

[5] Exploiting a relation includes query, update, and delete.

1.6. Expressible, Named, and Stored Relations

Associated with a data bank are two collections of relations: the *named set* and the *expressible set*. The named set is the collection of all those relations that the community of users can identify by means of a simple name (or identifier). A relation R acquires membership in the named set when a suitably authorized user declares R; it loses membership when a suitably authorized user cancels the declaration of R.

The expressible set is the total collection of relations that can be designated by expressions in the data language. Such expressions are constructed from simple names of relations in the named set; names of generations, roles and domains; logical connectives; the quantifiers of the predicate calculus;[6] and certain constant relation symbols such as $=$, $>$. The named set is a subset of the expressible set—usually a very small subset.

Since some relations in the named set may be time-independent combinations of others in that set, it is useful to consider associating with the named set a collection of statements that define these time-independent constraints. We shall postpone further discussion of this until we have introduced several operations on relations (see Section 2).

One of the major problems confronting the designer of a data system which is to support a relational model for its users is that of determining the class of stored representations to be supported. Ideally, the variety of permitted data representations should be just adequate to cover the spectrum of performance requirements of the total collection of installations. Too great a variety leads to unnecessary overhead in storage and continual reinterpretation of descriptions for the structures currently in effect.

For any selected class of stored representations the data system must provide a means of translating user requests expressed in the data language of the relational model into corresponding—and efficient—actions on the current stored representation. For a high level data language this presents a challenging design problem. Nevertheless, it is a problem which must be solved—as more users obtain concurrent access to a large data bank, responsibility for providing efficient response and throughput shifts from the individual user to the data system.

[6] Because each relation in a practical data bank is a finite set at every instant of time, the existential and universal quantifiers can be expressed in terms of a function that counts the number of elements in any finite set.

2. Redundancy and Consistency

2.1. Operations on Relations

Since relations are sets, all of the usual set operations are applicable to them. Nevertheless, the result may not be a relation; for example, the union of a binary relation and a ternary relation is not a relation.

The operations discussed below are specifically for relations. These operations are introduced because of their key role in deriving relations from other relations. Their principal application is in noninferential information systems—systems which do not provide logical inference services—although their applicability is not necessarily destroyed when such services are added.

Most users would not be directly concerned with these operations. Information systems designers and people concerned with data bank control should, however, be thoroughly familiar with them.

2.1.1. *Permutation.* A binary relation has an array representation with two columns. Interchanging these columns yields the converse relation. More generally, if a permutation is applied to the columns of an n-ary relation, the resulting relation is said to be a *permutation* of the given relation. There are, for example, $4! = 24$ permutations of the relation *supply* in Figure 1, if we include the identity permutation which leaves the ordering of columns unchanged.

Since the user's relational model consists of a collection of relationships (domain-unordered relations), permutation is not relevant to such a model considered in isolation. It is, however, relevant to the consideration of stored representations of the model. In a system which provides symmetric exploitation of relations, the set of queries answerable by a stored relation is identical to the set answerable by any permutation of that relation. Although it is logically unnecessary to store both a relation and some permutation of it, performance considerations could make it advisable.

2.1.2. *Projection.* Suppose now we select certain columns of a relation (striking out the others) and then remove from the resulting array any duplication in the rows. The final array represents a relation which is said to be a *projection* of the given relation.

A selection operator π is used to obtain any desired permutation, projection, or combination of the two operations. Thus, if L is a list of k indices[7] $L = i_1, i_2, \cdots, i_k$ and R is an n-ary relation ($n \geq k$), then $\pi_L(R)$ is the k-ary relation whose jth column is column i_j of R ($j = 1, 2, \cdots, k$) except that duplication in resulting rows is removed. Consider the relation *supply* of Figure 1. A permuted projection of this relation is exhibited in Figure 4. Note that, in this particular case, the projection has fewer n-tuples than the relation from which it is derived.

2.1.3. *Join.* Suppose we are given two binary relations, which have some domain in common. Under what circumstances can we combine these relations to form a ternary relation which preserves all of the information in the given relations?

The example in Figure 5 shows two relations R, S, which are joinable without loss of information, while Figure 6 shows a join of R with S. A binary relation R is *joinable* with a binary relation S if there exists a ternary relation U such that $\pi_{12}(U) = R$ and $\pi_{23}(U) = S$. Any such ternary relation is called a *join* of R with S. If R, S are binary relations such that $\pi_2(R) = \pi_1(S)$, then R is joinable with S. One join that always exists in such a case is the *natural join* of R with S defined by

$$R*S = \{(a, b, c): R(a, b) \wedge S(b, c)\}$$

where $R(a, b)$ has the value *true* if (a, b) is a member of R and similarly for $S(b, c)$. It is immediate that

$$\pi_{12}(R*S) = R$$

and

$$\pi_{23}(R*S) = S.$$

Note that the join shown in Figure 6 is the natural join of R with S from Figure 5. Another join is shown in Figure 7.

Π_{31}(*supply*)	(*project*	*supplier*)
	5	1
	5	2
	1	4
	7	2

Fig. 4. A permuted projection of the relation in Figure 1

R	(*supplier*	*part*)	S	(*part*	*project*)
	1	1		1	1
	2	1		1	2
	2	2		2	1

Fig. 5. Two joinable relations

R*S	(*supplier*	*part*	*project*)
	1	1	1
	1	1	2
	2	1	1
	2	1	2
	2	2	1

Fig. 6. The natural join of R with S (from Figure 5)

U	(*supplier*	*part*	*project*)
	1	1	2
	2	1	1
	2	2	1

Fig. 7. Another join of R with S (from Figure 5)

Inspection of these relations reveals an element (element 1) of the domain *part* (the domain on which the join is to be made) with the property that it possesses more than one relative under R and also under S. It is this ele-

[7] When dealing with relationships, we use domain names (role-qualified whenever necessary) instead of domain positions.

ment which gives rise to the plurality of joins. Such an element in the joining domain is called a *point of ambiguity* with respect to the joining of R with S.

If either $\pi_{21}(R)$ or S is a function,[8] no point of ambiguity can occur in joining R with S. In such a case, the natural join of R with S is the only join of R with S. Note that the reiterated qualification "of R with S" is necessary, because S might be joinable with R (as well as R with S), and this join would be an entirely separate consideration. In Figure 5, none of the relations R, $\pi_{21}(R)$, S, $\pi_{21}(S)$ is a function.

Ambiguity in the joining of R with S can sometimes be resolved by means of other relations. Suppose we are given, or can derive from sources independent of R and S, a relation T on the domains *project* and *supplier* with the following properties:

$$(1)\ \pi_1(T) = \pi_2(S),$$

$$(2)\ \pi_2(T) = \pi_1(R),$$

$$(3)\ T(j, s) \rightarrow \exists p(R(S, p)\ \wedge\ S(p, j)),$$

$$(4)\ R(s, p) \rightarrow \exists j(S(p, j)\ \wedge\ T(j, s)),$$

$$(5)\ S(p, j) \rightarrow \exists s(T(j, s)\ \wedge\ R(s, p)),$$

then we may form a three-way join of R, S, T; that is, a ternary relation such that

$$\pi_{12}(U) = R, \qquad \pi_{23}(U) = S, \qquad \pi_{31}(U) = T.$$

Such a join will be called a *cyclic 3-join* to distinguish it from a *linear 3-join* which would be a quaternary relation V such that

$$\pi_{12}(V) = R, \qquad \pi_{23}(V) = S, \qquad \pi_{34}(V) = T.$$

While it is possible for more than one cyclic 3-join to exist (see Figures 8, 9, for an example), the circumstances under which this can occur entail much more severe constraints

R (s	p)
1	a
2	a
2	b

S (p	j)
a	d
a	e
b	d
b	e

T (j	s)
d	1
d	2
e	2
e	2

Fig. 8. Binary relations with a plurality of cyclic 3-joins

U (s	p	j)
1	a	d
2	a	e
2	b	d
2	b	e

U′ (s	p	j)
1	a	d
2	a	d
2	a	e
2	b	d
2	b	e

Fig. 9. Two cyclic 3-joins of the relations in Figure 8

than those for a plurality of 2-joins. To be specific, the relations R, S, T must possess points of ambiguity with respect to joining R with S (say point x), S with T (say y), and T with R (say z), and, furthermore, y must be a relative of x under S, z a relative of y under T, and x a relative of z under R. Note that in Figure 8 the points $x = a$; $y = d$; $z = 2$ have this property.

The natural linear 3-join of three binary relations R, S, T is given by

$$R{*}S{*}T = \{(a, b, c, d){:}R(a, b)\ \wedge\ S(b, c)\ \wedge\ T(c, d)\}$$

where parentheses are not needed on the left-hand side because the natural 2-join ($*$) is associative. To obtain the cyclic counterpart, we introduce the operator γ which produces a relation of degree $n - 1$ from a relation of degree n by tying its ends together. Thus, if R is an n-ary relation ($n \geq 2$), the *tie* of R is defined by the equation

$$\gamma(R) = \{(a_1, a_2, \cdots, a_{n-1}){:}R(a_1, a_2, \cdots, a_{n-1}, a_n)\ \wedge\ a_1 = a_n\}.$$

We may now represent the natural cyclic 3-join of R, S, T by the expression

$$\gamma(R{*}S{*}T).$$

Extension of the notions of linear and cyclic 3-join and their natural counterparts to the joining of n binary relations (where $n \geq 3$) is obvious. A few words may be appropriate, however, regarding the joining of relations which are not necessarily binary. Consider the case of two relations R (degree r), S (degree s) which are to be joined on p of their domains ($p < r$, $p < s$). For simplicity, suppose these p domains are the last p of the r domains of R, and the first p of the s domains of S. If this were not so, we could always apply appropriate permutations to make it so. Now, take the Cartesian product of the first r-p domains of R, and call this new domain A. Take the Cartesian product of the last p domains of R, and call this B. Take the Cartesian product of the last s-p domains of S and call this C.

We can treat R as if it were a binary relation on the domains A, B. Similarly, we can treat S as if it were a binary relation on the domains B, C. The notions of linear and cyclic 3-join are now directly applicable. A similar approach can be taken with the linear and cyclic n-joins of n relations of assorted degrees.

2.1.4. *Composition.* The reader is probably familiar with the notion of composition applied to functions. We shall discuss a generalization of that concept and apply it first to binary relations. Our definitions of composition and composability are based very directly on the definitions of join and joinability given above.

Suppose we are given two relations R, S. T is a *composition* of R with S if there exists a join U of R with S such that $T = \pi_{13}(U)$. Thus, two relations are composable if and only if they are joinable. However, the existence of more than one join of R with S does not imply the existence of more than one composition of R with S.

Corresponding to the natural join of R with S is the

[8] A function is a binary relation, which is one-one or many-one, but not one-many.

natural composition[9] of R with S defined by

$$R \cdot S = \pi_{13}(R * S).$$

Taking the relations R, S from Figure 5, their natural composition is exhibited in Figure 10 and another composition is exhibited in Figure 11 (derived from the join exhibited in Figure 7).

R·S	*(project*	*supplier)*
	1	1
	1	2
	2	1
	2	2

FIG. 10. The natural composition of R with S (from Figure 5)

T	*(project*	*supplier)*
	1	2
	2	1

FIG. 11. Another composition of R with S (from Figure 5)

When two or more joins exist, the number of distinct compositions may be as few as one or as many as the number of distinct joins. Figure 12 shows an example of two relations which have several joins but only one composition. Note that the ambiguity of point c is lost in composing R with S, because of unambiguous associations made via the points a, b, d, e.

R	*(supplier*	*part)*	S	*(part*	*project)*
	1	a		a	g
	1	b		b	f
	1	c		c	f
	2	c		c	g
	2	d		d	g
	2	e		e	f

FIG. 12. Many joins, only one composition

Extension of composition to pairs of relations which are not necessarily binary (and which may be of different degrees) follows the same pattern as extension of pairwise joining to such relations.

A lack of understanding of relational composition has led several systems designers into what may be called the *connection trap*. This trap may be described in terms of the following example. Suppose each supplier description is linked by pointers to the descriptions of each part supplied by that supplier, and each part description is similarly linked to the descriptions of each project which uses that part. A conclusion is now drawn which is, in general, erroneous: namely that, if all possible paths are followed from a given supplier via the parts he supplies to the projects using those parts, one will obtain a valid set of all projects supplied by that supplier. Such a conclusion is correct only in the very special case that the target relation between projects and suppliers is, in fact, the natural composition of the other two relations—and we must normally add the phrase "for all time," because this is usually implied in claims concerning path-following techniques.

[9] Other writers tend to ignore compositions other than the natural one, and accordingly refer to this particular composition as *the* composition—see, for example, Kelley's "General Topology."

2.1.5. *Restriction.* A subset of a relation is a relation. One way in which a relation S may act on a relation R to generate a subset of R is through the operation *restriction* of R by S. This operation is a generalization of the restriction of a function to a subset of its domain, and is defined as follows.

Let L, M be equal-length lists of indices such that $L = i_1, i_2, \cdots, i_k$, $M = j_1, j_2, \cdots, j_k$ where $k \leqq$ degree of R and $k \leqq$ degree of S. Then the L, M restriction of R by S denoted $R_L|_M S$ is the maximal subset R' of R such that

$$\pi_L(R') = \pi_M(S).$$

The operation is defined only if equality is applicable between elements of $\pi_{i_h}(R)$ on the one hand and $\pi_{j_h}(S)$ on the other for all $h = 1, 2, \cdots, k$.

The three relations R, S, R' of Figure 13 satisfy the equation $R' = R_{(2,3)}|_{(1,2)}S$.

R	*(s*	*p*	*j)*	S	*(p*	*j)*	R′	*(s*	*p*	*j)*
	1	a	A		a	A		1	a	A
	2	a	A		c	B		2	a	A
	2	a	B		b	B		2	b	B
	2	b	A							
	2	b	B							

FIG. 13. Example of restriction

We are now in a position to consider various applications of these operations on relations.

2.2. REDUNDANCY

Redundancy in the named set of relations must be distinguished from redundancy in the stored set of representations. We are primarily concerned here with the former. To begin with, we need a precise notion of derivability for relations.

Suppose θ is a collection of operations on relations and each operation has the property that from its operands it yields a unique relation (thus natural join is eligible, but join is not). A relation R is *θ-derivable* from a set S of relations if there exists a sequence of operations from the collection θ which, for all time, yields R from members of S. The phrase "for all time" is present, because we are dealing with time-varying relations, and our interest is in derivability which holds over a significant period of time. For the named set of relationships in noninferential systems, it appears that an adequate collection θ_1 contains the following operations: projection, natural join, tie, and restriction. Permutation is irrelevant and natural composition need not be included, because it is obtainable by taking a natural join and then a projection. For the stored set of representations, an adequate collection θ_2 of operations would include permutation and additional operations concerned with subsetting and merging relations, and ordering and connecting their elements.

2.2.1. *Strong Redundancy.* A set of relations is *strongly redundant* if it contains at least one relation that possesses a projection which is derivable from other projections of relations in the set. The following two examples are intended to explain why strong redundancy is defined this way, and to demonstrate its practical use. In the first example the collection of relations consists of just the following relation:

employee (serial #, name, manager#, managername)

with *serial#* as the primary key and *manager#* as a foreign key. Let us denote the active domain by Δ_t, and suppose that

$$\Delta_t(manager\#) \subset \Delta_t(serial\#)$$

and

$$\Delta_t(managername) \subset \Delta_t(name)$$

for all time t. In this case the redundancy is obvious: the domain *managername* is unnecessary. To see that it is a strong redundancy as defined above, we observe that

$$\pi_{34}(employee) = \pi_{12}(employee)_1|_1\pi_3(employee).$$

In the second example the collection of relations includes a relation S describing suppliers with primary key $s\#$, a relation D describing departments with primary key $d\#$, a relation J describing projects with primary key $j\#$, and the following relations:

$$P(s\#, d\#, \cdots), \qquad Q(s\#, j\#, \cdots), \qquad R(d\#, j\#, \cdots),$$

where in each case $\cdots$ denotes domains other than $s\#$, $d\#$, $j\#$. Let us suppose the following condition C is known to hold independent of time: supplier s supplies department d (relation P) if and only if supplier s supplies some project j (relation Q) to which d is assigned (relation R). Then, we can write the equation

$$\pi_{12}(P) = \pi_{12}(Q) \cdot \pi_{21}(R)$$

and thereby exhibit a strong redundancy.

An important reason for the existence of strong redundancies in the named set of relationships is user convenience. A particular case of this is the retention of semi-obsolete relationships in the named set so that old programs that refer to them by name can continue to run correctly. Knowledge of the existence of strong redundancies in the named set enables a system or data base administrator greater freedom in the selection of stored representations to cope more efficiently with current traffic. If the strong redundancies in the named set are directly reflected in strong redundancies in the stored set (or if other strong redundancies are introduced into the stored set), then, generally speaking, extra storage space and update time are consumed with a potential drop in query time for some queries and in load on the central processing units.

2.2.2. *Weak Redundancy.* A second type of redundancy may exist. In contrast to strong redundancy it is not characterized by an equation. A collection of relations is *weakly redundant* if it contains a relation that has a projection which is not derivable from other members but is at all times a projection of *some* join of other projections of relations in the collection.

We can exhibit a weak redundancy by taking the second example (cited above) for a strong redundancy, and assuming now that condition C does not hold at all times. The relations $\pi_{12}(P)$, $\pi_{12}(Q)$, $\pi_{12}(R)$ are complex[10] relations with the possibility of points of ambiguity occurring from time to time in the potential joining of any two. Under these circumstances, none of them is derivable from the other two. However, constraints do exist between them, since each is a projection of some cyclic join of the three of them. One of the weak redundancies can be characterized by the statement: for all time, $\pi_{12}(P)$ is *some* composition of $\pi_{12}(Q)$ with $\pi_{21}(R)$. The composition in question might be the natural one at some instant and a nonnatural one at another instant.

Generally speaking, weak redundancies are inherent in the logical needs of the community of users. They are not removable by the system or data base administrator. If they appear at all, they appear in both the named set and the stored set of representations.

2.3. Consistency

Whenever the named set of relations is redundant in either sense, we shall associate with that set a collection of statements which define all of the redundancies which hold independent of time between the member relations. If the information system lacks—and it most probably will—detailed semantic information about each named relation, it cannot deduce the redundancies applicable to the named set. It might, over a period of time, make attempts to *in*duce the redundancies, but such attempts would be fallible.

Given a collection C of time-varying relations, an associated set Z of constraint statements and an instantaneous value V for C, we shall call the state (C, Z, V) *consistent* or *inconsistent* according as V does or does not satisfy Z. For example, given stored relations R, S, T together with the constraint statement "$\pi_{12}(T)$ is a composition of $\pi_{12}(R)$ with $\pi_{12}(S)$", we may check from time to time that the values stored for R, S, T satisfy this constraint. An algorithm for making this check would examine the first two columns of each of R, S, T (in whatever way they are represented in the system) and determine whether

(1) $\pi_1(T) = \pi_1(R)$,

(2) $\pi_2(T) = \pi_2(S)$,

(3) for every element pair (a, c) in the relation $\pi_{12}(T)$ there is an element b such that (a, b) is in $\pi_{12}(R)$ and (b, c) is in $\pi_{12}(S)$.

There are practical problems (which we shall not discuss here) in taking an instantaneous snapshot of a collection of relations, some of which may be very large and highly variable.

It is important to note that consistency as defined above is a property of the instantaneous state of a data bank, and is independent of how that state came about. Thus, in particular, there is no distinction made on the basis of whether a user generated an inconsistency due to an act of omission or an act of commission. Examination of a simple

[10] A binary relation is complex if neither it nor its converse is a function.

example will show the reasonableness of this (possibly unconventional) approach to consistency.

Suppose the named set C includes the relations S, J, D, P, Q, R of the example in Section 2.2 and that P, Q, R possess either the strong or weak redundancies described therein (in the particular case now under consideration, it does not matter which kind of redundancy occurs). Further, suppose that at some time t the data bank state is consistent and contains no project j such that supplier 2 supplies project j and j is assigned to department 5. Accordingly, there is no element (2, 5) in $\pi_{12}(P)$. Now, a user introduces the element (2, 5) into $\pi_{12}(P)$ by inserting some appropriate element into P. The data bank state is now inconsistent. The inconsistency could have arisen from an act of omission, if the input (2, 5) is correct, and there does exist a project j such that supplier 2 supplies j and j is assigned to department 5. In this case, it is very likely that the user intends in the near future to insert elements into Q and R which will have the effect of introducing $(2, j)$ into $\pi_{12}(Q)$ and $(5, j)$ in $\pi_{12}(R)$. On the other hand, the input (2, 5) might have been faulty. It could be the case that the user intended to insert some other element into P—an element whose insertion would transform a consistent state into a consistent state. The point is that the system will normally have no way of resolving this question without interrogating its environment (perhaps the user who created the inconsistency).

There are, of course, several possible ways in which a system can detect inconsistencies and respond to them. In one approach the system checks for possible inconsistency whenever an insertion, deletion, or key update occurs. Naturally, such checking will slow these operations down. If an inconsistency has been generated, details are logged internally, and if it is not remedied within some reasonable time interval, either the user or someone responsible for the security and integrity of the data is notified. Another approach is to conduct consistency checking as a batch operation once a day or less frequently. Inputs causing the inconsistencies which remain in the data bank state at checking time can be tracked down if the system maintains a journal of all state-changing transactions. This latter approach would certainly be superior if few nontransitory inconsistencies occurred.

2.4. Summary

In Section 1 a relational model of data is proposed as a basis for protecting users of formatted data systems from the potentially disruptive changes in data representation caused by growth in the data bank and changes in traffic. A normal form for the time-varying collection of relationships is introduced.

In Section 2 operations on relations and two types of redundancy are defined and applied to the problem of maintaining the data in a consistent state. This is bound to become a serious practical problem as more and more different types of data are integrated together into common data banks.

Many questions are raised and left unanswered. For example, only a few of the more important properties of the data sublanguage in Section 1.4 are mentioned. Neither the purely linguistic details of such a language nor the implementation problems are discussed. Nevertheless, the material presented should be adequate for experienced systems programmers to visualize several approaches. It is also hoped that this paper can contribute to greater precision in work on formatted data systems.

Acknowledgment. It was C. T. Davies of IBM Poughkeepsie who convinced the author of the need for data independence in future information systems. The author wishes to thank him and also F. P. Palermo, C. P. Wang, E. B. Altman, and M. E. Senko of the IBM San Jose Research Laboratory for helpful discussions.

Received September, 1969; revised February, 1970

REFERENCES

1. Childs, D. L. Feasibility of a set-theoretical data structure—a general structure based on a reconstituted definition of relation. Proc. IFIP Cong., 1968, North Holland Pub. Co., Amsterdam, p. 162–172.
2. Levein, R. E., and Maron, M. E. A computer system for inference execution and data retrieval. *Comm. ACM 10*, 11 (Nov. 1967), 715–721.
3. Bachman, C. W. Software for random access processing. *Datamation* (Apr. 1965), 36–41.
4. McGee, W. C. Generalized file processing. In *Annual Review in Automatic Programming 5*, 13, Pergamon Press, New York, 1969, pp. 77–149.
5. Information Management System/360, Application Description Manual H20-0524-1. IBM Corp., White Plains, N. Y., July 1968.
6. GIS (Generalized Information System), Application Description Manual H20-0574. IBM Corp., White Plains, N. Y., 1965.
7. Bleier, R. E. Treating hierarchical data structures in the SDC time-shared data management system (TDMS). Proc. ACM 22nd Nat. Conf., 1967, MDI Publications, Wayne, Pa., pp. 41–49.
8. IDS Reference Manual GE 625/635, GE Inform. Sys. Div., Pheonix, Ariz., CPB 1093B, Feb. 1968.
9. Church, A. *An Introduction to Mathematical Logic I*. Princeton U. Press, Princeton, N.J., 1956.
10. Feldman, J. A., and Rovner, P. D. An Algol-based associative language. Stanford Artificial Intelligence Rep. AI-66, Aug. 1, 1968.

System R: Relational Approach to Database Management

M. M. ASTRAHAN, M. W. BLASGEN, D. D. CHAMBERLIN,
K. P. ESWARAN, J. N. GRAY, P. P. GRIFFITHS,
W. F. KING, R. A. LORIE, P. R. MCJONES, J. W. MEHL,
G. R. PUTZOLU, I. L. TRAIGER, B. W. WADE, AND V. WATSON

IBM Research Laboratory

System R is a database management system which provides a high level relational data interface. The system provides a high level of data independence by isolating the end user as much as possible from underlying storage structures. The system permits definition of a variety of relational views on common underlying data. Data control features are provided, including authorization, integrity assertions, triggered transactions, a logging and recovery subsystem, and facilities for maintaining data consistency in a shared-update environment.

This paper contains a description of the overall architecture and design of the system. At the present time the system is being implemented and the design evaluated. We emphasize that System R is a vehicle for research in database architecture, and is not planned as a product.

Key Words and Phrases: database, relational model, nonprocedural language, authorization, locking, recovery, data structures, index structures
CR categories: 3.74, 4.22, 4.33, 4.35

CONTENTS

1. INTRODUCTION

The relational model of data was introduced by Codd [7] in 1970 as an approach toward providing solutions to various problems in database management. In particular, Codd addressed the problems of providing a data model or view which is divorced from various implementation considerations (the data independence problem) and also the problem of providing the database user with a very high level, nonprocedural data sublanguage for accessing data.

To a large extent, the acceptance and value of the relational approach hinges on the demonstration that a system can be built which can be used in a real environment to solve real problems and has performance at least comparable to today's existing systems. The purpose of this paper is to describe the overall architecture and design aspects of an experimental prototype database management system called System R, which is currently being implemented and evaluated at the IBM San Jose Research Laboratory. At the time of this writing, the design has been completed and major portions of the system are implemented and running. However, the overall system is not completed. We plan a complete performance evaluation of the system which will be available in later papers.

The System R project is not the first implementation of the relational approach [12, 30]. On the other hand, we know of no other relational system which provides a complete database management capability—including application programming as well as query capability, concurrent access support, system recovery, etc. Other relational systems have focused on, and demonstrated, feasibility of techniques for solving various specific problems. For example, the IS/1 system [22] demonstrated the feasibility of supporting the relational algebra [8] and also developed optimization techniques for evaluating algebraic expressions [29]. Techniques for optimization of the relational algebra have also been developed by Smith and Chang at the University of Utah [27]. The extended relational memory (XRM) system [19] developed at the IBM Cambridge Scientific Center has been used as a single user access method by other relational systems [2]. The SEQUEL prototype [1] was originally developed as a single-user system to demonstrate the feasibility of supporting the SEQUEL [5] language. However, this system has been extended by the IBM Cambridge Scientific Center and the MIT Sloan School Energy Laboratory to allow a simple type of concurrency and is being used as a component of the Generalized Management Information System (GMIS) [9] being developed at MIT for energy related applications. The INGRES project [16] being developed at the University of California, Berkeley, has demonstrated techniques for the decomposition of relational expressions in the QUEL language into "one-variable

Authors' address: IBM Research Laboratory, San Jose, CA 95193.

queries." Also, this system has investigated the use of query modification [28] for enforcing integrity constraints and authorization constraints on users. The problem of translating a high level user language into lower level access primitives has also been studied at the University of Toronto [21, 26].

Architecture and System Structure

We will describe the overall architecture of System R from two viewpoints. First, we will describe the system as seen by a single transaction, i.e. a monolithic description. Second, we will investigate its multiuser dimensions. Figure 1 gives a functional view of the system including its major interfaces and components.

The Relational Storage Interface (RSI) is an internal interface which handles access to single tuples of base relations. This interface and its supporting system, the Relational Storage System (RSS), is actually a complete storage subsystem in that it manages devices, space allocation, storage buffers, transaction consistency and locking, deadlock detection, backout, transaction recovery, and system recovery. Furthermore, it maintains indexes on selected fields of base relations, and pointer chains across relations.

The Relational Data Interface (RDI) is the external interface which can be called directly from a programming language, or used to support various emulators and other interfaces. The Relational Data System (RDS), which supports the RDI, provides authorization, integrity enforcement, and support for alternative views of data. The high level SEQUEL language is embedded within the RDI, and is used as the basis for all data definition and manipulation. In addition, the RDS maintains the catalogs of external names, since the RSS uses only system generated internal names. The RDS contains an optimizer which chooses an appropriate access path for any given request from among the paths supported by the RSS.

Fig. 1. Architecture of System R

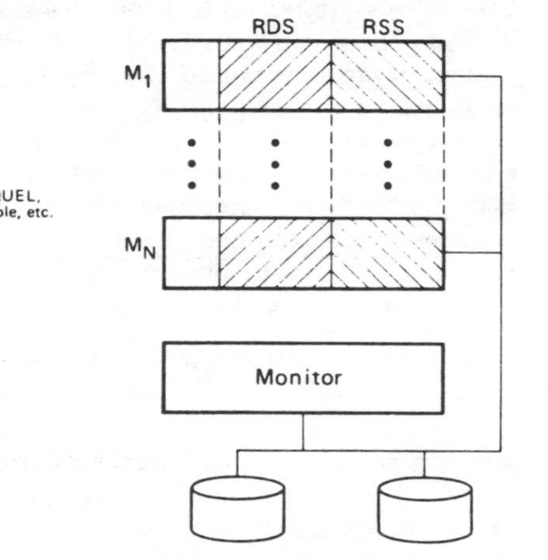

Fig. 2. Use of virtual machines in System R

The current operating system environment for this experimental system is VM/370 [18]. Several extensions to this virtual machine facility have been made [14] in order to support the multiuser environment of System R. In particular, we have implemented a technique for the selective sharing of read/write virtual memory across any number of virtual machines and for efficient communication among virtual machines through processor interrupts. Figure 2 illustrates the use of many virtual machines to support concurrent transactions on shared data. For each logged-on user there is a dedicated *database machine*. Each of these database machines contains all code and tables needed to execute all data management functions; that is, services are not reserved to a centralized machine.

The provision for many database machines, each executing shared, reentrant code and sharing control information, means that the database system need not provide its own multitasking to handle concurrent transactions. Rather, one can use the host operating system to multithread at the level of virtual machines. Furthermore, the operating system can take advantage of multiprocessors allocated to several virtual machines, since each machine is capable of providing all data management services. A single-server approach would eliminate this advantage, since most processing activity would then be focused on only one machine.

In addition to the database machines, Figure 2 also illustrates the Monitor Machine, which contains many system administrator facilities. For example, the Monitor Machine controls logon authorization and initializes the database machine for each user. The Monitor also schedules periodic checkpoints and maintains usage and performance statistics for reorganization and accounting purposes.

In Sections 2 and 3 we describe the main components of System R: the Relational Data System and the Relational Storage System.

2. THE RELATIONAL DATA SYSTEM

The Relational Data Interface (RDI) is the principal external interface of System R. It provides high level, data independent facilities for data retrieval, manipulation, definition, and control. The data definition facilities of the RDI allow a variety of alternative relational views to be defined on common underlying data. The Relational Data System (RDS) is the subsystem which implements the RDI. The RDS contains an optimizer which plans the execution of each RDI command, choosing a low cost access path to data from among those provided by the Relational Storage System (RSS).

The RDI consists of a set of operators which may be called from PL/I or other host programming languages. (See Appendix I for a list of these operators.) All the facilities of the SEQUEL data sublanguage [5] are available at the RDI by means of the RDI operator called SEQUEL. (A Backus-Naur Form (BNF) syntax for SEQUEL is given in Appendix II.) The SEQUEL language can be supported as a stand-alone interface by a simple program, written on top of the RDI, which handles terminal communications. (Such a stand-alone SEQUEL interface, called the User-Friendly Interface, or UFI, is provided as a part of System R.) In addition, programs may be written on top of the RDI to support other relational interfaces, such as Query by Example [31], or to simulate nonrelational interfaces.

Host Language Interface

The facilities of the RDI are basically those of the SEQUEL data sublanguage, which is described in [5] and in Appendix II. Several changes have been made to SEQUEL since the earlier publication of the language; they are described below.

The illustrative examples used in this section are based on the following database of employees and their departments:

```
EMP(EMPNO, NAME, DNO, JOB, SAL, MGR)
DEPT(DNO, DNAME, LOC, NEMPS)
```

The RDI interfaces SEQUEL to a host programming language by means of a concept called a *cursor*. A cursor is a name which is used at the RDI to identify a set of tuples called its *active set* (e.g. the result of a query) and furthermore to maintain a position on one tuple of the set. The cursor is associated with a set of tuples by means of the RDI operator SEQUEL; the tuples may then be retrieved, one at a time, by the RDI operator FETCH.

Some host programs may know in advance exactly the degree and data types of the tuples they wish to retrieve. Such a program may specify, in its SEQUEL call, the program variables into which the resulting tuples are to be delivered. The program must first give the system the addresses of the program variables to be used by means of the RDI operator BIND. In the following example, the host program identifies variables *X* and *Y* to the system and then issues a query whose results are to be placed in these variables:

```
CALL BIND('X', ADDR(X));
CALL BIND('Y', ADDR(Y));
CALL SEQUEL(C1,  'SELECT NAME:X,  SAL:Y
                  FROM EMP
                  WHERE JOB = ''PROGRAMMER''');
```

The SEQUEL call has the effect of associating the cursor C1 with the set of tuples which satisfy the query and positioning it just before the first such tuple. The optimizer is invoked to choose an access path whereby the tuples may be materialized. However, no tuples are actually materialized in response to the SEQUEL call. The materialization of tuples is done as they are called for, one at a time, by the FETCH operator. Each call to FETCH delivers the next tuple of the active set into program variables *X* and *Y*, i.e. NAME to *X* and SAL to *Y*:

```
CALL FETCH(C1);
```

A program may wish to write a SEQUEL predicate based on the contents of a program variable—for example, to find the programmers whose department number matches the contents of program variable *Z*. This facility is also provided by the RDI BIND operator, as follows:

```
CALL BIND('X', ADDR(X));
CALL BIND('Y', ADDR(Y));
CALL BIND('Z', ADDR(Z));
CALL SEQUEL(C1,  'SELECT NAME:X, SAL:Y
                  FROM EMP
                  WHERE JOB = ''PROGRAMMER''
                  AND DNO = Z');
CALL FETCH(C1);
```

Some programs may not know in advance the degree and data types of the tuples to be returned by a query. An example of such a program is one which supports an interactive user by allowing him to type in queries and display the results. This type of program need not specify in its SEQUEL call the variables into which the result is to be delivered. The program may issue a SEQUEL query, followed by the DESCRIBE operator which returns the degree and data types. The program then specifies the destination of the tuples in its FETCH commands. The following example illustrates these techniques:

```
CALL SEQUEL(C1,  'SELECT *
                  FROM EMP
                  WHERE DNO = 50');
```

This statement invokes the optimizer to choose an access path for the given query and associates cursor *C*1 with its active set.

```
CALL DESCRIBE(C1, DEGREE, P);
```

P is a pointer to an array in which the description of the active set of *C*1 is to be returned. The RDI returns the degree of the active set in DEGREE, and the data types and lengths of the tuple components in the elements of the array. If the array (which contains an entry describing its own length) is too short to hold the description of a tuple, the calling program must allocate a larger array and make another call to DESCRIBE.

Having obtained a description of the tuples to be returned, the calling program may proceed to allocate a structure to hold the tuples and may specify the location of this structure in its FETCH command:

```
CALL FETCH(C1, Q);
```

Q is a pointer to an array of pointers which specify where the individual components of the tuple are to be delivered. If this "destination" parameter is present in a FETCH command, it overrides any destination which may have been specified in the SEQUEL command which defined the active set of *C*1.

A special RDI operator OPEN is provided as a shorthand method to associate a cursor with an entire relation. For example, the command

```
CALL OPEN(C1, 'EMP');
```

is exactly equivalent to

```
CALL SEQUEL(C1, 'SELECT * FROM EMP');
```

The use of OPEN is slightly preferable to the use of SEQUEL to open a cursor on a relation, since OPEN avoids the use of the SEQUEL parser.

A program may have many cursors active at the same time. Each cursor remains active until an RDI operator CLOSE or KEEP is issued on it. CLOSE simply deactivates a cursor. KEEP causes the tuples identified by a cursor to be copied to form a new permanent relation in the database, having some specified relation name and field names.

The RDI operator FETCH_HOLD is included for the support of interfaces which provide for explicit locking. FETCH_HOLD operates in exactly the same way as FETCH except that it also acquires a "hold" on the tuple returned, which prevents other users from updating or deleting it until it is explicitly released or until the holding transaction has ended. A tuple may be released by the RELEASE operator, which takes as a parameter a cursor positioned on the tuple to be released. If no cursor is furnished, the RELEASE operator releases all tuples currently held by the user.

Query Facilities

In this section we describe only the most significant changes made to the SEQUEL query facilities since their original publication [5]. The changes correct certain deficiencies in the original syntax and facilitate the interfacing of SEQUEL with a host programming language. One important change deals with the handling of block labels. The following example, illustrating the original version of SEQUEL, is taken from [5]. (For simplicity, "CALL SEQUEL(...)" has been deleted from the next several examples.)

Example 1(a). List names of employees who earn more than their managers.

```
B1: SELECT NAME
    FROM   EMP
    WHERE  SAL >
           SELECT SAL
           FROM   EMP
           WHERE  EMPNO = B1.MGR
```

Experience has shown that this block label notation has three disadvantages:

(1) It is not possible to select quantities from the inner block, such as: "For all employees who earn more than their manager, list the employee's name and his manager's name."

(2) Since the query is asymmetrically expressed, the optimizer is biased toward making an outer loop for the first block and an inner loop for the second block. Since this may not be the optimum method for interpreting the query, the optimization process is made difficult.

(3) Human factors studies have shown that the block label notation is hard for nonprogrammers to learn [24, 25].

Because of these disadvantages, the block label notation has been replaced by the following more symmetrical notation, which allows several tables to be listed in the FROM clause and optionally referred to by variable names.

Example 1(b). For all employees who earn more than their managers, list the employee's name and his manager's name.

```
SELECT X.NAME, Y.NAME
FROM   EMP X, EMP Y
WHERE  X.MGR = Y.EMPNO
AND    X.SAL > Y.SAL
```

Example 1(b) illustrates the SEQUEL notation for the JOIN operator of the relational algebra. The tables to be joined are listed in the FROM clause. A variable name may optionally be associated with each table listed in the FROM clause (e.g. *X* and *Y* above). The criterion for joining rows is given in the WHERE clause (in this case, *X*.MGR = *Y*.EMPNO). Field names appearing in the query may stand alone (if unambiguous) or may be qualified by a table name (e.g. EMP.SAL) or by a variable (e.g. *X*.SAL).

In the earlier report [5], the WHERE clause is used for two purposes: it serves both to qualify individual tuples (e.g. "List the employees who are clerks") and to qualify groups of tuples (e.g. "List the departments having more than ten employees"). This ambiguity is now eliminated by moving group qualifying predicates to a separate HAVING clause. Queries are processed in the following order:

(1) Tuples are selected by the WHERE clause;

(2) Groups are formed by the GROUP BY clause;

(3) Groups are selected which satisfy the HAVING clause, as shown in the example below.

Example 2. List the DNOs of departments having more than ten clerks.

```
SELECT DNO
FROM   EMP
WHERE  JOB = 'CLERK'
GROUP BY DNO
HAVING COUNT(*) > 10
```

Two more query features have been added to the ones described in [5]. The first allows the user to specify a value ordering for his query result.

Example 3 (Ordering). List all the employees in Dept. 50, ordered by their salaries.

```
SELECT *
FROM   EMP
WHERE  DNO = 50
ORDER BY SAL
```

The other new feature, which is useful primarily to host language users of the RDI, allows a query to qualify tuples by comparing them with the current tuple of some active cursor:

Example 4 (Cursor reference). Find all the employees in the department indicated by cursor *C*5.

```
SELECT *
FROM   EMP
WHERE  DNO = DNO OF CURSOR C5 ON DEPT
```

The evaluation of this reference to the content of cursor *C*5 occurs when the query is executed (by a SEQUEL call). Thereafter, moving the cursor *C*5 does not affect the set of tuples defined by the query. The optional phrase "ON DEPT" indicates to the optimizer that it can expect the cursor *C*5 to be positioned on a tuple of the DEPT table. This information may be useful in selecting an access path for the query.

Since elimination of duplicates from a query result is an expensive process and is not always necessary, the RDS does not eliminate duplicates unless explicitly requested to do so. For example, "SELECT DNO, JOB FROM EMP" may return duplicate DNO, JOB pairs, but "SELECT UNIQUE DNO, JOB FROM EMP" will return only unique pairs. Similarly, "SELECT AVG(SAL) FROM EMP" allows duplicate salary values to participate in the average, while "SELECT COUNT (UNIQUE JOB) FROM EMP" returns the count only of different job types in the EMP relation.

Data Manipulation Facilities

The RDI facilities for insertion, deletion, and update of tuples are also provided via the SEQUEL data sublanguage. SEQUEL can be used to manipulate either one tuple at a time or a set of tuples with a single command. The current tuple of a particular cursor may be selected for some operation by means of the special predicate CURRENT TUPLE OF CURSOR. The values of a tuple may be set equal to constants, or to new values computed from their old values, or to the contents of a program variable suitably identified by a BIND command. These facilities will be illustrated by a series of examples. Since no result is returned to the calling program in these examples, no cursor name is included in the calls to SEQUEL.

Example 5 (Set oriented update). Give a 10 percent raise to all employees in Dept. 50.

```
CALL SEQUEL('UPDATE EMP
            SET SAL = SAL × 1.1
            WHERE DNO = 50');
```

Example 6 (Individual update).

```
CALL BIND('PVSAL', ADDR(PVSAL));
CALL SEQUEL('UPDATE EMP
            SET SAL = PVSAL
            WHERE CURRENT TUPLE OF CURSOR C3');
```

Example 7 (Individual insertion). This example inserts a new employee tuple into EMP. The new tuple is constructed partly from constants and partly from the contents of program variables.

```
CALL BIND('PVEMPNO', ADDR(PVEMPNO));
CALL BIND('PVNAME', ADDR(PVNAME));
CALL BIND('PVMGR' ADDR(PVMGR));
CALL SEQUEL('INSERT INTO EMP:
            (PVEMPNO, PVNAME, 50, ''TRAINEE'', 8500, PVMGR)');
```

An insertion statement in SEQUEL may provide only some of the values for the new tuple, specifying the names of the fields which are provided. Fields which are not provided are set to the null value. The physical position of the new tuple in storage is influenced by the "clustering" specification made on associated RSS access paths (see below).

Example 8 (Set oriented deletion). Delete all employees who work for departments in Evanston.

```
CALL SEQUEL('DELETE EMP
            WHERE DNO =
                SELECT DNO
                FROM   DEPT
                WHERE LOC = ''EVANSTON''');
```

The SEQUEL assignment statement allows the result of a query to be copied into a new permanent or temporary relation in the database. This has the same effect as a query followed by the RDI operator KEEP.

Example 9 (Assignment). Create a new table UNDERPAID consisting of names and salaries of programmers who earn less than $10,000.

```
CALL SEQUEL('UNDERPAID(NAME, SAL) ←
        SELECT  NAME, SAL
        FROM    EMP
        WHERE   JOB = ''PROGRAMMER''
        AND     SAL < 10,000');
```

The new table UNDERPAID represents a snapshot taken from EMP at the moment the assignment was executed. UNDERPAID then becomes an independent relation and does not reflect any later changes to EMP.

Data Definition Facilities

System R takes a unified approach to data manipulation, definition, and control. Like queries and set oriented updates, the data definition facilities are invoked by means of the RDI operator SEQUEL. Many of these facilities have been described in [4] and [15].

The SEQUEL statement CREATE TABLE is used to create a new base (i.e. physically stored) relation. For each field of the new relation, the field name and data type are specified.[1] If desired, it may be specified at creation time that null values are not permitted in one or more fields of the new relation. A query executed on the relation will deliver its results in system determined order (which depends upon the access path which the optimizer has chosen), unless the query has an ORDER BY clause. When a base relation is no longer useful, it may be deleted by issuing a DROP TABLE statement.

System R currently relies on the user to specify not only the base tables to be stored but also the RSS access paths to be maintained on them. (Database design facilities to automate and adapt some of these decisions are also being investigated.) Access paths include images and binary links,[2] described in Section 3. They may be specified by means of the SEQUEL verbs CREATE and DROP. Briefly, images are value orderings maintained on base relations by the RSS, using multilevel index structures. The index structures associate a value with one or more Tuple Identifiers (*TID*s). A *TID* is an internal address which allows rapid access to a tuple, as discussed in Section 3. Images provide associative and sequential access on one or more fields which are called the *sort fields* of the image. An image may be declared to be UNIQUE, which forces each combination of sort field values to be unique in the relation. At most one image per relation may have the *clustering* property, which causes tuples whose sort field values are close to be physically stored near each other.

Binary links are access paths in the RSS which link tuples of one relation to

[1] The data types of INTEGER, SMALL INTEGER, DECIMAL, FLOAT, and CHARACTER (both fixed and varying length) are supported.

[2] Unary links, described in Section 3, are used for internal system purposes only, and are not exposed at the RDI.

related tuples of another relation through pointer chains. In System R, binary links are always employed in a value dependent manner: the user specifies that each tuple of Relation 1 is to be linked to the tuples in Relation 2 which have matching values in some field(s), and that the tuples on the link are to be ordered in some value dependent way. For example, a user may specify a link from DEPT to EMP by matching DNO, and that EMP tuples on the link are to be ordered by JOB and SAL. This link is maintained automatically by the system. By declaring a link frem DEPT to EMP on matching DNO, the user implicitly declares this to be a one-to-many relationship (i.e. DNO is a key of DEPT). Any attempts to define links or to insert or update tuples in violation of this rule will be refused. Like an image, a link may be declared to have the *clustering* property, which causes each tuple to be physically stored near its neighbor in the link.

It should be clearly noted that none of the access paths (images and binary links) contain any logical information other than that derivable from the data values themselves. This is in accord with the relational data model, which represents all information as data values. The RDI user has no explicit control over the placement of tuples in images and links (unlike the "manual sets" of the DBTG proposal [6]). Furthermore, the RDI user may not explicitly use an image or link for access to data; all choices of access path are made automatically by the optimizer.

The query power of SEQUEL may be used to define a view as a relation derived from one or more other relations. This view may then be used in the same ways as a base table: queries may be written against it, other views may be defined on it, and in certain circumstances described below, it may be updated. Any SEQUEL query may be used as a view definition by means of a DEFINE VIEW statement. Views are dynamic windows on the database, in that updates made to base tables immediately become visible via the views defined on these base tables. Where updates to views are supported, they are implemented in terms of updates to the underlying base tables. The SEQUEL statement which defines a view is recorded in a system maintained catalog where it may be examined by authorized users. When an authorized user issues a DROP VIEW statement, the indicated view and all other views defined in terms of it disappear from the system for this user and all other users.

If a modification is issued against a view, it can be supported only if the tuples of the view are associated one-to-one with tuples of an underlying base relation. In general, this means that the view must involve a single base relation and contain a key of that relation; otherwise, the modification statement is rejected. If the view satisfies the one-to-one rule, the WHERE clause of the SEQUEL modification statement is merged into the view definition; the result is optimized and the indicated update is made on the relevant tuples of the base relation.

Two final SEQUEL commands complete the discussion of the data definition facility. The first is KEEP TABLE, which causes a temporary table (created, for example, by assignment) to become permanent. (Temporary tables are destroyed when the user who created them logs off.) The second command is EXPAND TABLE, which adds a new field to an existing table. All views, images, and links defined on the original table are retained. All existing tuples are interpreted as having null values in the expanded fields until they are explicitly updated.

Data Control Facilities

Data control facilities at the RDI have four aspects: transactions, authorization, integrity assertions, and triggers.

A transaction is a series of RDI calls which the user wishes to be processed as an atomic act. The meaning of "atomic" depends on the level of consistency specified by the user, and is explained in Section 3. The highest level of consistency, Level 3, requires that a user's transactions appear to be serialized with the transactions of other concurrent users. The user controls transactions by the RDI operators BEGIN__TRANS and END__TRANS. The user may specify save points within a transaction by the RDI operator SAVE. As long as a transaction is active, the user may back up to the beginning of the transaction or to any internal save point by the operator RESTORE. This operator restores all changes made to the database by the current transaction, as well as the state of all cursors used by this transaction. No cursors may remain active (open) beyond the end of a transaction. The RDI transactions are implemented directly by RSI transactions, so the RDI commands BEGIN__TRANS, END__TRANS, SAVE, and RESTORE are passed through to the RSI, with some RDS bookkeeping to permit the restoration of its internal state.

The System R approach to authorization is described in [15]. System R does not require a particular individual to be the database administrator, but allows each user to create his own data objects by executing the SEQUEL statements CREATE TABLE and DEFINE VIEW. The creator of a new object receives full authorization to perform all operations on the object (subject, of course, to his authorization for the underlying tables, if it is a view). The user may then grant selected capabilities for his object to other users by the SEQUEL statement GRANT. The following capabilities may be independently granted for each table or view: READ, INSERT, DELETE, UPDATE (by fields), DROP, EXPAND, IMAGE specification, LINK specification, and CONTROL (the ability to specify assertions and triggers on the table or view). For each capability which a user possesses for a given table, he may optionally have GRANT authority (the authority to further grant or revoke the capability to/from other users).

System R relies primarily on its view mechanism for read authorization. If it is desired to allow a user to read only tuples of employees in Dept. 50, and not to see their salaries, then this portion of the EMP table can be defined as a view and granted to the user. No special statistical access is distinguished, since the same effect (e.g. ability to read only the average salary of each department) can be achieved by defining a view. To make the view mechanism more useful for authorization purposes, the reserved word USER is always interpreted as the user-id of the current user. Thus the following SEQUEL statement defines a view of all those employees in the same department as the current user:

```
DEFINE VIEW VEMP AS:
       SELECT *
       FROM   EMP
       WHERE  DNO =
              SELECT DNO
              FROM   EMP
              WHERE  NAME = USER
```

The third important aspect of data control is that of integrity assertions. The System R approach to data integrity is described in [10]. Any SEQUEL predicate may be stated as an assertion about the integrity of data in a base table or view. At the time the assertion is made (by an ASSERT statement in SEQUEL), its truth is checked; if true, the assertion is automatically enforced until it is explicitly dropped by a DROP ASSERTION statement. Any data modification, by any user, which violates an active integrity assertion is rejected. Assertions may apply to individual tuples (e.g. "No employee's salary exceeds $50,000") or to sets of tuples (e.g. "The average salary of each department is less than $20,000"). Assertions may describe permissible *states* of the database (as in the examples above) or permissible *transitions* in the database. For this latter purpose the keywords OLD and NEW are used in SEQUEL to denote data values before and after modification, as in the example below.

Example 10 (Transition assertion). Each employee's salary must be non-decreasing.

```
ASSERT ON UPDATE TO EMP: NEW SAL ≥ OLD SAL
```

Unless otherwise specified, integrity assertions are checked and enforced at the end of each transaction. Transition assertions compare the state before the transaction began with the state after the transaction concluded. If some assertion is not satisfied, the transaction is backed out to its beginning point. This permits complex updates to be done in several steps (several calls to SEQUEL, bracketed by BEGIN_TRANS and END_TRANS), which may cause the database to pass through intermediate states which temporarily violate one or more assertions. However, if an assertion is specified as IMMEDIATE, it cannot be suspended within a transaction, but is enforced after each data modification (each RDI call). In addition, "integrity points" within a transaction may be established by the SEQUEL command ENFORCE INTEGRITY. This command allows a user to guard against having a long transaction completely backed out. In the event of an integrity failure, the transaction is backed out to its most recent integrity point.

The fourth aspect of data control, triggers, is a generalization of the concept of assertions. A trigger causes a prespecified sequence of SEQUEL statements to be executed whenever some triggering event occurs. The triggering event may be retrieval, insertion, deletion, or update of a particular base table or view. For example, suppose that in our example database, the NEMPS field of the DEPT table denotes the number of employees in each department. This value might be kept up to date automatically by the following three triggers (as in assertions, the keywords OLD and NEW denote data values before and after the change which invoked the trigger):

```
DEFINE TRIGGER EMPINS
      ON INSERTION OF EMP:
           (UPDATE  DEPT
            SET     NEMPS = NEMPS + 1
            WHERE   DNO = NEW EMP.DNO)
DEFINE TRIGGER EMPDEL
      ON DELETION OF EMP:
           (UPDATE DEPT
            SET     NEMPS = NEMPS - 1
            WHERE   DNO = OLD EMP.DNO)
DEFINE TRIGGER EMPUPD
      ON UPDATE OF EMP:
           (UPDATE  DEPT
            SET     NEMPS = NEMPS - 1
            WHERE   DNO = OLD EMP.DNO;
            UPDATE  DEPT
            SET     NEMPS = NEMPS + 1
            WHERE   DNO = NEW EMP.DNO)
```

The RDS automatically maintains a set of catalog relations which describe the other relations, views, images, links, assertions, and triggers known to the system. Each user may access a set of views of the system catalogs which contain information pertinent to him. Access to catalog relations is made in exactly the same way as other relations are accessed (i.e. by SEQUEL queries). Of course, no user is authorized to modify the contents of a catalog directly, but any authorized user may modify a catalog indirectly by actions such as creating a table. In addition, a user may enter comments into his various catalog entries by means of the COMMENT statement (see syntax in Appendix II).

The Optimizer

The objective of the optimizer is to find a low cost means of executing a SEQUEL statement, given the data structures and access paths available. The optimizer attempts to minimize the expected number of pages to be fetched from secondary storage into the RSS buffers during execution of the statement. Only page fetches made under the explicit control of the RSS are considered. If necessary, the RSS buffers will be pinned in real memory to avoid additional paging activity caused by the VM/370 operating system. The cost of CPU instructions is also taken into account by means of an adjustable coefficient, H, which is multiplied by the number of tuple comparison operations to convert to equivalent page accesses. H can be adjusted according to whether the system is compute-bound or disk access-bound.

Since our cost measure for the optimizer is based on disk page accesses, the physical clustering of tuples in the database is of great importance. As mentioned earlier, each relation may have at most one clustering image, which has the property that tuples near each other in the image ordering are stored physically near each other in the database. To see the importance of the clustering property, imagine that we wish to scan over the tuples of a relation in the order of some image, and that the number of RSS buffer pages is much less than the number of pages used to store the relation. If the image is not the clustering image, the locations of the tuples will be independent of each other and in general a page will have to be fetched from disk for each tuple. On the other hand, if the image is the clustering image, each disk page will contain several (usually at least 20) adjacent tuples, and the number of page fetches will be reduced by a corresponding factor.

The optimizer begins by classifying the given SEQUEL statement into one of several statement types, according to the presence of various language features such as join and GROUP BY. Next the optimizer examines the system catalogs to find the set of images and links which are pertinent to the given statement. A rough decision procedure is then executed to find the set of "reasonable" methods of executing the statement. If there is more than one "reasonable" method, an expected cost formula is evaluated for each method and the minimum-cost method is chosen. The parameters of the cost formulas, such as relation cardinality and number of tuples per page, are obtained from the system catalogs.

We illustrate this optimization process by means of two example queries. The first example involves selection of tuples from a single relation, and the second involves joining two relations together according to a matching field. For simplicity we consider only methods based on images and relation scans. (A relation scan in the RSS accesses each of the pages in a data segment in turn (see Section 3), and selects those tuples belonging to the given relation.) Consideration of links involves a straightforward extension of the techniques we will describe.

Example 11 will be used to describe the decision process for a query involving a single relation:

Example 11. List the names and salaries of programmers who earn more than $10,000.

```
SELECT NAME, SAL
FROM   EMP
WHERE  JOB = 'PROGRAMMER'
AND    SAL > 10,000
```

In planning the execution of this example, the optimizer must choose whether to access the EMP relation via an image (on JOB, SAL or some other field) or via a relation scan. The following parameters, available in the system catalogs, are taken into account:

- R relation cardinality (number of tuples in the relation)
- D number of data pages occupied by the relation
- T average number of tuples per data page (equal to R/D)
- I image cardinality (number of distinct sort field values in a given image)
- H coefficient of CPU cost ($1/H$ is the number of tuple comparisons which are considered equivalent in cost to one disk page access).

An image is said to "match" a predicate if the sort field of the image is the field which is tested by the predicate. For example, an image on the EMP relation ordered by JOB (which we will refer to as an "image on EMP.JOB") would match the predicate JOB = 'PROGRAMMER' in Example 11. In order for an image to match a predicate, the predicate must be a simple comparison of a field with a value. More complicated predicates, such as EMP.DNO = DEPT.DNO, cannot be matched by an image.

In the case of a simple query on a single relation, such as Example 11, the optimizer compares the available images with the predicates of the query, in order to determine which of the following eight methods are available:

Method 1: Use a clustering image which matches a predicate whose comparison-operator is '='. The expected cost to retrieve all result tuples is $R/(T \times I)$ page accesses (R/I tuples divided by T tuples per page).

Method 2: Use a clustering image which matches a predicate whose comparison operator is not '='. Assuming half the tuples in the relation satisfy the predicate, the expected cost is $R/(2 \times T)$.

Method 3: Use a nonclustering image which matches a predicate whose comparison operator is '='. Since each tuple requires a page access, the expected cost is R/I.

Method 4: Use a nonclustering image which matches a predicate whose comparison-operator is not '='. Expected cost to retrieve all result tuples is $R/2$.

Method 5: Use a clustering image which does not match any predicate. Scan the image and test each tuple against all predicates. Expected cost is $(R/T) + H \times R \times N$, where N is the number of predicates in the query.

Method 6: Use a nonclustering image which does not match any predicate. Expected cost is $R + H \times R \times N$.

Method 7: Use a relation scan where this relation is the only one in its segment. Test each tuple against all predicates. Expected cost is $(R/T) + H \times R \times N$.

Method 8: Use a relation scan where there are other relations sharing the segment. Cost is unknown, but greater than $(R/T) + H \times R \times N$, because some pages may be fetched which contain no tuples from the pertinent relation.

The optimizer chooses a method from this set according to the following rules:

1. If Method 1 is available, it is chosen.
2. If exactly one among Methods 2, 3, 5, and 7 is available, it is chosen. If more than one method is available in this class, the expected cost formulas for these methods are evaluated and the method of minimum cost is chosen.
3. If none of the above methods are available, the optimizer chooses Method 4, if available; else Method 6, if available; else Method 8. (Note: Either Method 7 or Method 8 is always available for any relation.)

As a second example of optimization, we consider the following query, which involves a join of two relations:

Example 12. List the names, salaries, and department names of programmers located in Evanston.

```
SELECT NAME, SAL, DNAME
FROM   EMP, DEPT
WHERE  EMP.JOB = 'PROGRAMMER'
AND    DEPT.LOC = 'EVANSTON'
AND    EMP.DNO = DEPT.DNO
```

Example 12 is an instance of a join query type, the most general form of which involves restriction, projection, and join. The general query has the form:

> Apply a given restriction to a relation R, yielding R1, and apply a possibly different restriction to a relation S, yielding S1. Join R1 and S1 to form a relation T, and project some fields from T.

To illustrate the optimization of join-type queries, we will consider four possible methods for evaluating Example 12:

Method 1 (use images on join fields): Perform a simultaneous scan of the image on DEPT.DNO and the image on EMP.DNO. Advance the DEPT scan to obtain the next DEPT where LOC is 'EVANSTON'. Advance the EMP scan and fetch all the EMP tuples whose DNO matches the current DEPT and whose JOB is 'PROGRAMMER'. For each such matching pair of DEPT, EMP tuples, place the NAME, SAL, and DNAME fields into the output. Repeat until the image scans are completed.

Method 2 (sort both relations): Scan EMP and DEPT using their respective clustering images and create two files W1 and W2. W1 contains the NAME, SAL, and DNO fields of tuples from EMP which have JOB = 'PROGRAMMER'. W2 contains the DNO and DNAME fields of tuples from DEPT whose location is 'EVANSTON'. Sort W1 and W2 on DNO. (This process may involve repeated passes over W1 and W2 if they are too large to fit the available main memory buffers.) The resulting sorted files are scanned simultaneously and the join is performed.

Method 3 (multiple passes): DEPT is scanned via its clustering image, and the DNO and DNAME fields (a subtuple) of those DEPT tuples which have LOC = 'EVANSTON' are inserted into a main memory data structure called W. If space in main memory is available to insert a subtuple (say S), it is inserted. If there is no space and if S.DNO is less than the current highest DNO value in W, the subtuple with the highest DNO in W is deleted and S inserted. If there is no room for S and the DNO in S is greater than the highest DNO in W, S is discarded. After completing the scan of DEPT, EMP is scanned via its clustering image and a tuple E of EMP is obtained. If E.JOB = 'PROGRAMMER', then W is checked for the presence of the E.DNO. If present, E is joined to the appropriate subtuple in W. This process is continued until all tuples of EMP have been examined. If any DEPT subtuples were discarded, another scan of DEPT is made to form a new W consisting of subtuples with DNO value greater than the current highest. EMP is scanned again and the process repeated.

Method 4 (*TID* algorithm): Using the image on EMP.JOB, obtain the *TID*s of tuples from EMP which satisfy the restriction JOB = 'PROGRAMMER'. Sort them and store the *TID*s in a file W1. Do the same with DEPT, using the image on DEPT.LOC and testing for LOC = 'EVANSTON', yielding a *TID* file W2. Perform a simultaneous scan over the images on DEPT.DNO and EMP.DNO, finding the *TID* pairs of tuples whose DNO values match. Check each pair (*TID*1, *TID*2) to see if *TID*1 is present in W1 and *TID*2 is in W2. If they are, the tuples are fetched and joined and the NAME, SAL, and DNAME fields placed into the output.

These methods should be considered as illustrative of the techniques considered by the optimizer. The optimizer will draw from a larger set of methods, including methods which use links to carry out the join.

A method cannot be applied unless the appropriate access paths are available. For example, Method 4 is applicable only if there are images on EMP.DNO and EMP.JOB, as well as on DEPT.DNO and DEPT.LOC. In addition, the performance of a method depends strongly on the clustering of the relations with respect to the access paths. We will consider how the optimizer would choose among these four methods in four hypothetical situations. These choices are made on the basis of cost formulas which will be detailed in a later paper.

Situation 1: There are clustering images on both EMP.DNO and DEPT.DNO, but no images on EMP.JOB or DEPT.LOC. In this situation, Method 1 is always chosen.

Situation 2: There are unclustered images on EMP.DNO and DEPT.DNO, but no images on EMP.JOB or DEPT.LOC. In this case, Method 3 is chosen if the entire working file W fits into the main memory buffer at once; otherwise Method 2 is chosen. It is interesting to note that the unclustered images on DNO are never used in this situation.

Situation 3 :There are clustering images on EMP.DNO and DEPT.DNO, and unclustered images on EMP.JOB and DEPT.LOC. In this situation, Method 4 is always chosen.

Situation 4: There are unclustered images on EMP.DNO, EMP.JOB, DEPT.DNO, and DEPT.LOC. In this situation, Method 3 is chosen if the entire working file W fits into the main memory buffer. Otherwise, Method 2 is chosen if more than one tuple per disk page is expected to satisfy the restriction predicates. In the remaining cases, where the restriction predicates are very selective, Method 4 should be used.

After analyzing any SEQUEL statement, the optimizer produces an Optimized Package (OP) containing the parse tree and a plan for executing the statement. If the statement is a query, the OP is used to materialize tuples as they are called for by the FETCH command (query results are materialized incrementally whenever possible). If the statement is a view definition, the OP is stored in the form of a Pre-Optimized Package (POP) which can be fetched and utilized whenever an access is made via the specified view. If any change is made to the structure of a base table or to the access paths (images and links) maintained on it, the POPs of all views defined on that base table are invalidated, and each view must be reoptimized from its defining SEQUEL code to form a new POP.

When a view is accessed via the RDI operators OPEN and FETCH, the POP for the view can be used directly to materialize the tuples of the view. Often, however, a query or another view definition will be written in terms of an existing view. If the query or view definition is simple (e.g. a projection or restriction), it can sometimes be *composed* with the existing view (i.e. their parse trees can be merged and optimized together to form a new OP for the new query or view). In more complex cases the new statement cannot be composed with the existing view definition. In these cases the POP for the existing view is treated as a formula for materializing tuples. A new OP is formed for the new statement which treats the existing view as a table from which tuples can be fetched in only one way: by interpreting the existing POP. Of course, if views are cascaded on other views in several levels, there may be several levels of POPs in existence, each level making reference to the next.

Modifying Cursors

A number of issues are raised by the use of the insertion, deletion, and update facilities of System R. When a modification is made to one of the tuples in the active set of a cursor, the modification may change the ordinal position of the tuple or even disqualify it entirely from the active set. It should be noted here that a user operating at Level 3 consistency is automatically protected against having his cursors affected by the modifications of other users. However, even in Level 3 consistency, a user may make a modification which affects one of his own active cursors.

If the cursor in question is open on a base relation, the case is simple: the modification is done and immediately becomes visible via the cursor. Let us consider a case in which the cursor is not on a base relation, but rather on the result of a SEQUEL query. Suppose the following query has been executed:

```
SELECT *
FROM   EMP
WHERE DNO = 50
ORDER BY SAL
```

If the system has no image ordered on SAL, it may execute this query by finding the employees where DNO = 50 and sorting them by SAL to create an ordered list of answer tuples. Along with this list, the system will keep a list of the base relations from which the list was derived (in this case, only EMP). The effect resembles that of performing a DBTG KEEP verb [6] on the underlying base relations: if any tuple in an underlying relation is modified, the answer list is marked "potentially invalid." Now any fetch from this list will return a warning code since the tuple returned may not be up to date. If the calling program wishes to guarantee accuracy of its results, it must close its cursor and reevaluate the query when this warning code is received.

Simulation of Nonrelational Data Models

The RDI is designed in such a way that programs can be written on top of it to simulate "navigation oriented" database interfaces. These interfaces are often characterized by collections of records connected in a hierarchic [17] or network [6] structure, and by the concept of establishing one or more "current positions" within the structure (e.g. the currency indicators of DBTG). In general our strategy will be to represent each record type as a relation and to represent information about ordering and connections between records in the form of explicit fields in the corresponding relations. In this way all information inserted into the database via the "navigational" interface (including information about orderings and connections) is available to other users who may be using the underlying relations directly. One or more "current positions" within the database may then be simulated by means of one or more RDI cursors.

We will illustrate this simulation process by means of an example. Suppose we wish to simulate the database structure shown in Figure 3, and wish to maintain a "current position" in the structure. The hierarchical connections from DEPT to

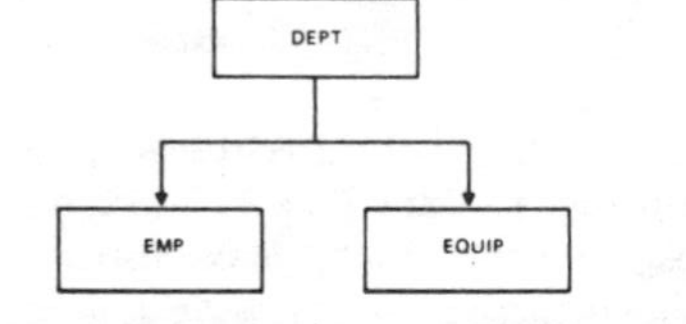

FIG. 3. Example of a hierarchic data structure

EMP and from DEPT to EQUIP may be unnamed in a hierarchic system such as IMS [17], or they may represent named set types in a network oriented system such as DBTG [6].

At database definition time, a relation is created to simulate each record type. The DEPT relation must have a sequence-number field to represent the ordering of the DEPT records. The EMP and EQUIP relations must have, in addition to a sequence-number field, one or more fields which uniquely identify their "parent" or "owner" records (let us assume the key of DEPT is DNO). If a record had several "owners" in different set types, several "owner's key" fields would have to appear in the corresponding relation.

Also at database definition time, a view definition is entered into the system which will represent the "currently visible" tuples of each relation at any point in time. The view definitions for our example are given below:

```
DEFINE VIEW VDEPT AS
       SELECT *
       FROM   DEPT
       ORDER BY ⟨sequence field⟩
DEFINE VIEW VEMP AS
       SELECT *
       FROM   EMP
       WHERE  DNO = DNO OF CURSOR C1 ON DEPT
       ORDER BY ⟨sequence field⟩
DEFINE VIEW VEQUIP AS
       SELECT *
       FROM   EQUIP
       WHERE  DNO = DNO OF CURSOR C1 ON DEPT
       ORDER BY ⟨sequence field⟩
```

The definitions of VEMP and VEQUIP call for tuples of EMP and EQUIP which have the same DNO as cursor $C1$; furthermore they promise that, when these views are used, cursor $C1$ will be active on the DEPT relation. These view definitions are parsed and optimized, and stored in the form of POPs. During this optimization process, any direct physical support for the hierarchy (such as a link from DEPT to EMP by matching DNO) will be discovered.

At run time, when a position is to be established on a DEPT record, the cursor $C1$ is opened on the view VDEPT. If the "current position" then moves downward to an EMP record, the view VEMP is opened. The exact subset of EMP tuples made available by this view opening depends on the location of the cursor $C1$ in the "parent" relation. If the "current position" moves upward again to DEPT, the view VEMP is closed, to be reopened later as needed. Any insertion, deletion, or update operations issued against the hierarchy are simulated by SEQUEL INSERT, DELETE, and UPDATE operations on the corresponding relations, with appropriate sequence-number and parent-key values generated, if necessary, by the simulator program. At the end of the transaction, all cursors are closed.

Following this general plan, it is expected that hierarchic oriented or network oriented interfaces can be simulated on top of the RDI. It should be particularly noted that no parsing or optimization is done in response to a command to move the "current position"; the system merely employs the POP for the view which was optimized at database definition time. For any connections which are given direct physical support in the form of a binary link, the optimizer will take advantage of the link to provide good performance. The system is also capable of simulating connections which have no direct physical support, since the optimizer will automatically find an appropriate access path.

3. THE RELATIONAL STORAGE SYSTEM

This section is concerned with the Relational Storage System or RSS, the database management subsystem which provides underlying support for System R. The RSS supports the RSI which provides simple, tuple-at-a-time operators on base relations. Operators are also supported for data recovery, transaction management, and data definition. (A list of all RSI operators can be found in Appendix III.) Calls to the RSI require explicit use of data areas called segments and access paths called images and links, along with the use of RSS-generated, numeric identifiers for data segments, relations, access paths, and tuples. The RDS handles the selection of efficient access paths to optimize its operations, and maps symbolic relation names to their internal RSS identifiers.

In order to facilitate gradual database integration and retuning of access paths, the RSI has been designed so that new stored relations or new indexes can be created at any time, or existing ones destroyed, without quiescing the system and without dumping and reloading the data. One can also add new fields to existing relations, or add or delete pointer chain paths across existing relations. This facility, coupled with the ability to retrieve any subset of fields in a tuple, provides a degree of data independence at a low level of the system, since existing programs which execute RSI operations on tuples will be unaffected by the addition of new fields.

As a point of comparison, the RSS has many functions which can be found in other systems, both relational and nonrelational, such as the use of index and pointer chain structures. The areas which have been emphasized and extended in the RSS include dynamic definition of new data types and access paths, as described above, dynamic binding and unbinding of disk space to data segments, multipoint recovery for in-process transactions, a novel and efficient technique for system checkpoint and restart, multiple levels of isolation from the actions of other concurrent users, and automatic locking at the level of segments, relations, and single tuples. The next several subsections describe all of these RSS functions and include a sketch of the implementation.

Segments

In the RSS, all data is stored in a collection of logical address spaces called *segments*, which are employed to control physical clustering. Segments are used for storing user data, access path structures, internal catalog information, and intermediate results generated by the RDS. All the tuples of any relation must reside within a single segment chosen by the RDS. However, a given segment may contain several relations. A special segment is dedicated to the storage of transaction logs for backing out the changes made by individual transactions.

Several types of segments are supported, each with its own combination of functions and overhead. For example, one type is intended for storage of shared data, and has provisions for concurrent access, transaction backout, and recovery of the segment's contents to a previous state. Another segment type is intended for low overhead storage of temporary relations, and has no provision for either concurrent access or segment recovery. A maximum length is associated with each segment; it is chosen by a user during initialization of the system.

The RSS has the responsibility for mapping logical segment spaces to physical extents on disk storage, and for supporting segment recovery. Within the RSS, each segment consists of a sequence of equal-sized *pages*, which are referenced and formatted by various components of the RSS. Physical page slots in the disk extents are allocated to segments dynamically upon first reference, by checking and modifying bit maps associated with the disk extents. Physical page slots are freed when access path structures are destroyed or when the contents of a segment are destroyed. This dynamic allocation scheme allows for the definition of many large sized segments, to accommodate large intermediate results and growing databases. Facilities are provided to cluster pages on physical media so that sequential or localized access to segments can be handled efficiently.

The RSS maintains a page map for each segment, which is used to map each segment page to its location on disk. Such a map is maintained as a collection of equal-sized *blocks*, which are allocated statically. A page request is handled by allocating space within a main memory buffer shared among all concurrent users. In fact two separate buffers are managed, one for the page map blocks and one for the segment pages themselves. Both pages and blocks are fixed in their buffer slots until they are explicitly freed by RSS components. Freeing a page makes it available for replacement, and when space is needed the buffer manager replaces whichever freed page was least recently requested.

The RSS provides a novel technique to handle segment recovery, by associating with each recoverable segment *two* page maps, called current and backup. When the OPEN_SEGMENT operator is issued, to make the segment available for processing, these page maps have identical entries. When a component of the RSS later requests access to a page, with intent to update (after suitable locks have been acquired), the RSS checks whether this is the first update to the page since the OPEN or since the last SAVE_SEGMENT operation. If so, a new page slot is allocated nearby on disk, the page is accessed from its original disk location, and the current page map is then modified to point to the new page slot. When the page is later replaced from the buffer, it will be directed to the new location, while the backup page and backup page map are left intact.

When the SAVE_SEGMENT operator is issued, the disk pages bound to segments are brought up to date by storing through all buffer pages which have been updated. Both page maps are then scanned, and any page which has been modified since the last save point has its old page slot released. Finally the backup page map entries are set equal to the current page map entries, and the cycle is complete.

With this technique, the RESTORE_SEGMENT operation is relatively simple, since the backup page map points to a complete, consistent copy of the segment. The current page map is simply set equal to the backup one, and newly allocated page slots are released. The SAVE_SEGMENT and RESTORE_SEGMENT functions are useful for recovering a previous version of private data, and also for support of system checkpoint and restart, as explained below. However, the effect of restoring a segment of public data segment may be to undo changes made by several transactions, since each of them may have modified data since the segment was last saved. An entirely different mechanism is therefore used to back out only those changes made by a single transaction, and is explained below.

Note that our recovery scheme depends on the highly stylized management of two page maps per segment, and on our ability to control when pages are stored through from main memory to disk. These particular requirements led to the decision to handle our own storage management and I/O for RSS segments, rather than relying on the automatic paging of virtual memory in the operating system.

Relations

The main data object of the RSS is the n-ary *relation*, which consists of a time-varying number of tuples, each containing n fields. A new relation can be defined at any time within any segment chosen by the RDS. An existing relation and its associated access path structures can be dropped at any time, with all storage space made reusable. Even after a relation is defined and loaded, new fields may be added on the right, without a database reload and without immediate modification to existing tuples.

Two field types are supported: fixed length and variable length. For both field types, a special protocol is used at the RSI to generate an undefined value. This feature has a number of uses, but a particularly important one is that when the user adds new fields to an existing relation, values for those fields in each existing tuple are treated as undefined until they are explicitly updated.

Operators are available to INSERT and DELETE single tuples, and to FETCH and UPDATE any combination of fields in a tuple. One can also fetch a sequence of tuples along an access path through the use of an RSS cursor or *scan*. Each scan is created by the RSS for fetching tuples on a particular access path through execution of the OPEN_SCAN operator. The tuples along the path may then be accessed by a sequence of NEXT operations on that scan. The access paths which are supported include a value determined ordering of tuples through use of an image, an RDS determined ordering of tuples through use of a link (see below for discussions of images and links), and an RSS determined ordering of tuples in a relation. For all of these access paths the RDS may attach a search argument to each NEXT operation. The search argument may be any disjunctive normal form expression where each atomic expression has the form ⟨field number, operator, value⟩. The value is an explicit byte string provided by the RDS, and the operator is '=', '≠', '<', '>', '≤', or '≥'.

Associated with every tuple of a relation is a *tuple identifier* or *TID*. Each tuple identifier is generated by the RSS, and is available to the RDS as a concise and efficient means of addressing tuples. *TID*s are also used within the RSS to refer to tuples from index structures, and to maintain pointer chains. However, they are not intended for end users above the RDS, since they may be reused by the RSS after tuple deletions and are reassigned during database reorganization.

The RSS stores and accesses tuples within relations, and maintains pointer chains to implement the links described below. Each tuple is stored as a contiguous sequence of field values within a single page. Field lengths are also included for variable length fields. A prefix is stored with the tuple for use within the RSS. The prefix contains such information as the relation identifier, the pointer fields (*TID*s) for link structures, the number of stored data fields, and the number of pointer fields. These numbers are employed to support dynamic creation of new fields and links to existing relations, without requiring immediate access or modification to the existing tuples. Tuples are found only on pages which have been reserved as data pages. Other pages within the segment are reserved for the storage of index or internal catalog entries. A given data page may contain tuples from more than one relation, so that extra page accesses can be avoided when tuples from different relations are accessed together. When a scan is executed on a relation (rather than an image or link), an internal scan is generated on all nonempty data pages within the segment containing that relation. Each such data page is touched once, and the prefix of each tuple within the page is checked to see if it belongs to the relation.

The implementation of tuple identifier access is a hybrid scheme, similar to one used in such systems as IDS [11] and RM [20], which combines the speed of a byte address pointer with the flexibility of indirection. Each tuple identifier is a concatenation of a page number within the segment, along with a byte offset from the bottom of the page. The offset denotes a special entry or "slot" which contains the byte location of the tuple in that page. This technique allows efficient utilization of space within data pages, since space can be compacted and tuples moved with only local changes to the pointers in the slots. The slots themselves are never moved from their positions at the bottom of each data page, so that existing *TID*s can still be employed to access the tuples. In the rare case when a tuple is updated to a longer total value and insufficient space is available on its page, an overflow scheme is provided to move the tuple to another page. In this case the *TID* points to a tagged overflow record which is used to reference the other page. If the tuple overflows again, the original overflow record is modified to point to the newest location. Thus, a tuple access via a *TID* almost always involves a single page access, and never involves more than two page accesses (plus possible accesses to the page map blocks).

In order to tune the database to particular environments, the RSS accepts hints for physical allocation during INSERT operations, in the form of a tentative *TID*. The new tuple will be inserted in the page associated with that *TID*, if sufficient space is available. Otherwise, a nearby page is chosen by the RSS. Use of this facility enables the RDS to cluster tuples of a given relation with respect to some criterion such as a value ordering on one or more fields. Another use would be to cluster tuples of one relation near particular tuples of another relation, because of matching values in some of the fields. This clustering rule would result in high performance for relational join operations, as well as for the support of hierarchical and network applications.

Images

An *image* in the RSS is a logical reordering of an n-ary relation with respect to values in one or more sort fields. Images combined with scans provide the ability to scan relations along a value ordering, for low level support of simple views. More importantly, an image provides associative access capability. The RDS can rapidly fetch a tuple from an image by keying on the sort field values. The RDS can also open a scan at a particular point in the image, and retrieve a sequence of tuples or subtuples with a given range of sort values. Since the image contains all the tuples and all the fields in a relation, the RDS can employ a disjunctive normal form search argument during scanning to further restrict the set of tuples which is returned. This facility is especially useful for situations where SEQUEL search predicates involve several fields of a relation, and at least one of them has image support.

A new image can be defined at any time on any combination of fields in a relation. Furthermore, each of the fields may be specified as ascending or descending. Once defined, an image is maintained automatically by the RSS during all INSERT, DELETE, and UPDATE operations. An image can also be dropped at any time.

The RSS maintains each image through the use of a multipage index structure. An internal interface is used for associative or sequential access along an image, and also to delete or insert index entries when tuples are deleted, inserted, or updated. The parameters passed across this interface include the sort field values along with the *TID* of the given tuple. In order to handle variable length, multifield indexes efficiently, a special encoding scheme is employed on the field values so that the resulting concatenation can be compared against others for ordering and search. This encoding eliminates the need for costly padding of each field and slow field-by-field comparison.

Each index is composed of one or more pages within the segment containing the relation. A new page can be added to an index when needed as long as one of the pages within the segment is marked as available. The pages for a given index are organized into a balanced hierarchic structure, in the style of B-trees [3] and of Key Sequenced Data Sets in IBM's VSAM access method [23]. Each page is a node within the hierarchy and contains an ordered sequence of index entries. For nonleaf nodes, an entry consists of a ⟨sort value, pointer⟩ pair. The pointer addresses another page in the same structure, which may be either a leaf page or another nonleaf page. In either case the target page contains entries for sort values less than or equal to the given one. For the leaf nodes, an entry is a combination of sort values along with an ascending list of *TID*s for tuples having exactly those sort values. The leaf pages are chained in a doubly linked list, so that sequential access can be supported from leaf to leaf.

Links

A *link* in the RSS is an access path which is used to connect tuples in one or two relations. The RDS determines which tuples will be on a link and determines their relative position, through explicit CONNECT and DISCONNECT operations. The RSS maintains internal pointers so that newly connected tuples are linked to previous and next twins, and so that previous and next twins are linked to each other when a tuple is disconnected. A link can be scanned using a sequence of OPEN SCAN and NEXT operations, with the optional search arguments described above.

A unary link involves a single relation and provides a partially defined ordering of tuples. Unary links can be used to maintain tuple ordering specifications which are not supported by the RSS (i.e. not value ordered). Another use is to provide an efficient access path through all tuples of a relation without the time overhead of an internal page scan.

The more important access path is a binary link, which provides a path from single tuples (parents) in one relation to sequences of tuples (children) in another relation. The RDS determines which tuples will be children under a given parent, and the relative order of children under a given parent, through the CONNECT and DISCONNECT operators. Operators are then available to scan the children of a parent or go directly from a child to its parent along a given link. In general, a tuple in the parent relation may have no children, and a tuple in the child relation may have no parent. Also, tuples in a relation may be parents and/or children in an arbitrary number of different links. The only restriction is that a given tuple can appear only once within a given link. Binary links are similar to the notion of an owner coupled set with manual membership found in the DBTG specifications for a network model of data [6].

The main use of binary links in System R is to connect child tuples to a parent based on value matches in one or more fields. With such a structure the RDS can access tuples in one relation, say the Employee relation, based on matching the Department Number field in a tuple of the Department relation. This function is especially important for supporting relational join operations, and also for supporting navigational processing through hierarchical and network models of data. The link provides direct access to the correct Employee tuples from the Department tuple (and vice versa), while use of an image may involve access to several pages in the index. A striking advantage is gained over images when the child tuples have been clustered on the same page as the parent, so that no extra pages are touched using the link, while three or more pages may be touched in a large index.

Another important feature of links is to provide reasonably fast associative access to a relation without the use of an extra index. In the above example, if the Department relation has an image on Department Number, then the RDS can gain associative access to Employee tuples for a given value of Department Number by using the Department relation image and the binary link—even if the Department tuple is not being referenced by the end user.

Links are maintained in the RSS by storing *TID*s in the prefix of tuples. New links can be defined at any time. When a new link is defined for a relation, a portion of the prefix is assigned to hold the required entries. This operation does not require access to any of the existing tuples, since new prefix space for an existing tuple is formatted only when the tuple is connected to the link. When necessary, the prefix length is enlarged through the normal mechanisms used for updates and new data fields. An existing link can be dropped at any time. When this occurs, each tuple in the corresponding relation(s) is accessed by the RSS, in order to invalidate the existing prefix entries and make the space available for subsequent link definitions.

Transaction Management

A *transaction* at the RSS is a sequence of RSI calls issued in behalf of one user. It also serves as a unit of consistency and recovery, as will be discussed below. In general, an RSS transaction consists of those calls generated by the RDS to execute all RDI operators in a single System R transaction, including the calls required to perform such RDS internal functions as authorization, catalog access, and integrity checking. An RSS transaction is marked by the START_TRANS and

END_TRANS operators. Various resources are assigned to transactions by the RSS, using the locking techniques described below. Also, a transaction recovery scheme is provided which allows a transaction to be incrementally backed out to any intermediate save point. This multipoint recovery function is important in applications involving relatively long transactions when backup is required because of errors detected by the user or RDS, because of deadlock detected by the RSS, or because of long periods of inactivity or system congestion detected by the Monitor.

A transaction save point is marked using the SAVE_TRANS operator, which returns a save point number for subsequent reference. In general, a save point may be generated by any one of the layers above the RSS. An RDI user may mark a save point at a convenient place in his transaction in order to handle backout and retry. The RDS may mark a save point for each new set oriented SEQUEL expression, so that the sequence of RSI calls needed to support the expression can be backed out for automatic retry if any of the RSI calls fails to complete.

Transaction recovery occurs when the RDS or Monitor issues the RESTORE_TRANS operator, which has a save point number as its input parameter, or when the RSS initiates the procedure to handle deadlock. The effect is to undo all the changes made by that transaction to recoverable data since the given save point. Those changes include all the tuple and image modifications caused by INSERT, DELETE, and UPDATE operations, all the link modifications caused by CONNECT and DISCONNECT operations, and even all the declarations for defining new relations, images, and links. In order to aid the RDS in continuing the transaction, all scan positions on recoverable data are automatically reset to the tuples they were pointing to at the time of the save. Finally, all locks on recoverable data which have been obtained since the given save point are released.

The transaction recovery function is supported through the maintenance of time ordered lists of log entries, which record information about each change to recoverable data. The entries for each transaction are chained together, and include the old and new values of all modified recoverable objects along with the operation code and object identification. Modifications to index structures are not logged, since their values can be determined from data values and index catalog information.

At each transaction save point, special entries are stored containing the state of all scans in use by the transaction, and the identity of the most recently acquired lock. During transaction recovery, the log entries for the transaction are read in last-in-first-out order. Special routines are employed to undo all the listed modifications back to the recorded save point, and also to restore the scans and release locks acquired after the save point.

The log entries themselves are stored in a dedicated segment which is used as a ring buffer. This segment is treated as a simple linear byte space with entries spanning page boundaries. Entries are also archived to tape to support audits and database reconstruction after system failure.

Concurrency Control

Since System R is a concurrent user system, locking techniques must be employed to solve various synchronization problems, both at the logical level of objects like relations and tuples and at the physical level of pages.

At the *logical* level, such classic situations as the "lost update" problem must be handled to insure that two concurrent transactions do not read the same value and then try to write back an incremented value. If these transactions are not synchronized, the second update will overwrite the first, and the effect of one increment will be lost. Similarly, if a user wishes to read only "clean" or committed data, not "dirty" data which has been updated by a transaction still in progress and which may be backed out, then some mechanism must be invoked to check whether the data is dirty. For another example, if transaction recovery is to affect only the modifications of a single user, then mechanisms are needed to insure that data updated by some ongoing transaction, say T1, is not updated by another, say T2. Otherwise, the backout of transaction T1 will undo T2's update and thus violate our principle of isolated backout.

At the *physical* level of pages, locking techniques are required to insure that internal components of the RSS give correct results. For example, a data page may contain several tuples with each tuple accessed through its tuple identifier, which requires following a pointer within the data page. Even if no logical conflict occurs between two transactions, because each is accessing a different relation or a different tuple in the same relation, a problem could occur at the physical level if one transaction follows a pointer to a tuple on some page while the other transaction updates a second tuple on the same page and causes a data compaction routine to reassign tuple locations.

One basic decision in establishing System R was to handle both logical and physical locking requirements within the RSS, rather than splitting the functions across the RDS and RSS subsystems. Physical locking is handled by setting and holding locks on one or more pages during the execution of a single RSI operation. Logical locking is handled by setting locks on such objects as segments, relations, *TIDs*, and key value intervals and holding them until they are explicitly released or to the end of the transaction. The main motivation for this decision is to facilitate the exploration of alternative locking techniques. (One particular alternative has already been included in the RSS as a tuning option, whereby the finest level of locking in a segment can be expanded to an entire page of data, rather than single tuples. This option allows pages to be locked for both logical and physical purposes, by varying the duration of the lock.) Other motivations are to simplify the work of the RDS and to develop a complete, concurrent user RSS which can be tailored to future research applications.

Another basic decision in formulating System R was to automate all of the locking functions, both logical and physical, so that users can access shared data and delegate some or all lock protocols to the system. For situations detected by the end user or RDS where locking large aggregates is desirable, the RSS also supports operators for placing explicit share or exclusive locks on entire segments or relations.

In order to provide reasonable performance for a wide spectrum of user requirements, the RSS supports multiple levels of consistency which control the isolation of a user from the actions of other concurrent users (see also [13]). When a transaction is started at the RSI, one of three consistency levels must be specified. (These same consistency levels are also reflected at the RDI.) Different consistency levels may be chosen by different concurrent transactions. For all of these levels, the RSS guarantees that any data modified by the transaction is not modified by any other until the given transaction ends. This rule is essential to our transaction recovery scheme, where the backout of modifications by one transaction does not affect modifications made by other transactions.

The differences in consistency levels occur during read operations. Level 1 consistency offers the least isolation from other users, but causes the lowest overhead and lock contention. With this level, dirty data may be accessed, and one may read different values for the same data item during the same transaction. It is clear that execution with Level 1 consistency incurs the risk of reading data values that violate integrity constraints, and that in some sense never appeared if the transaction which set the data values is later backed out. On the other hand, this level may be entirely satisfactory for gathering statistical information from a large database when exact results are not required. The HOLD option can be used during read operations to insure against lost updates or dirty data values.

In a transaction with Level 2 consistency, the user is assured that every item read is clean. However, no guarantee is made that subsequent access to the same item will yield the same values or that associative access will yield the same item. At this consistency level it is possible for another transaction to modify a data item any time after the given Level 2 transaction has read it. A second read by the given transaction will then yield the new value, since the item will become clean again when the other transaction terminates. Transactions running at Level 2 consistency still require use of the HOLD option during read operations preceding updates, to insure against lost updates.

For the highest consistency level, called Level 3, the user sees the logical equivalent of a single user system. Every item read is clean, and subsequent reads yield the same values, subject of course to updates by the given user. This repeatability feature applies not only to a specific item accessed directly by tuple identifier, but even to sequences of items and to items accessed associatively. For example, if the RDS employs an image on the Employee relation, ordered by Employee Name, to find all employees whose names start with 'B', then the same answer will occur every time within the same transaction. Thus, the RDS can effectively lock a set of items defined by a SEQUEL predicate and obtained by any search strategy, against insertions into or deletions from the set. Similarly, if the RDS employs an image to access the unique tuple where Name = 'Smith', and no such tuple exists, then the same nonexistence result is assured for subsequent accesses.

Level 3 consistency eliminates the problem of lost updates, and also guarantees that one can read a logically consistent version of any collection of tuples, since other transactions are logically serialized with the given one. As an example of this last point, consider a situation where two or more related data items are periodically updated, such as the mean and variance of a sequence of temperature measurements. With Level 3 consistency, a reader is assured of reading a consistent pair—rather than, say, a new variance and an old mean. Although one could use the HOLD option to handle this particular problem, many such associations may not be understood in a more complex database environment, even by relatively experienced programmers.

The RSS components set locks automatically in order to guarantee the logical functions of these various consistency levels. For example, in certain cases the RSS must set locks on tuples, such as when they have been inserted or updated. Similarly, in certain cases the RSS must set locks on index values or ranges of index values, even when the values are not currently present in the index—such as in handling the case of 'Smith' described above. In both of these cases the RSS must also acquire physical locks on one or more pages, which are held at least during the execution of each RSI operation, in order to insure that data and index pages are accessed and maintained correctly.

The RSS employs a single lock mechanism to synchronize access to all objects. This synchronization is handled by a set of procedures in every activation of the RSS, which maintains a collection of queue structures called *gates* in shared, read/write memory. Some of these gates are numbered and are associated by convention with such resources as the table of buffer contents, or the availability of the database for processing. However, in order to handle locks on a potentially huge set of objects like the tuples themselves, the RSS also includes a named gate facility. Internal components can request a lock by giving an eight-character name for the object, using such names as a tuple identifier, index value, or page number. If the named resource is already locked it will have a gate. If not, then a named gate will be allocated from a special pool of numbered gates. The named gate will be deallocated when its queue becomes empty.

An internal request to lock an object has several parameters: the name of the object, the mode of the lock (such as shared, exclusive, or various other modes mentioned below), and an indication of lock duration, so that the RSS can quickly release all locks held for a single RSI call, or all locks held for the entire transaction. The duration of a lock is also used for scheduling purposes, such as to select a transaction for backout when deadlock is detected.

The choice of lock duration is influenced by several factors, such as the type of action requested by the user and the consistency level of the transaction. If a tuple is inserted or updated by a transaction at any consistency level, then an exclusive lock must be held on the tuple (or some superset) until the transaction has ended. If a tuple is deleted, then an exclusive lock must be held on the *TID* of that tuple for the duration of the transaction, in order to guarantee that the deletion can be undone correctly during transaction backout. For any of these cases, as well as for the ones described below, an additional lock is typically set on the page itself to prevent conflict of transactions at the physical level. However, these page locks are released at the end of the RSI call.

In the case of a transaction with Level 3 consistency, share locks must be maintained on all tuples and index values which are read, for the duration of the transaction, to insure repeatability. For transactions with Level 2 consistency, read accesses require a share lock with immediate duration. Such a lock request is enqueued behind earlier exclusive lock requests so that the user is assured of reading clean data. The lock is then released as soon as the request has been granted, since reads do not have to be repeatable. Finally, for transactions with Level 1 consistency, no locks are required for read purposes, other than short locks on pages to insure that the read operation is correct.

Data items can be locked at various granularities, to insure that various applications run efficiently. For example, locks on single tuples are effective for transactions which access small amounts of data, while locks on entire relations or even entire segments are more reasonable for transactions which cause the RDS to access large amounts of data. In order to accommodate these differences, a dynamic lock hierarchy protocol has been developed so that a small number of locks can be used to lock both few and many objects [13]. The basic idea of the scheme is that separate locks are associated with each granularity of object, such as segment, relation, and tuple. If the RDS requests a lock on an entire segment in share or exclusive mode, then every tuple of every relation in the segment is implicitly locked in the same mode. If the RDS requests a lock on a single relation, say in exclusive mode, but does not wish exclusive access to the entire segment, then the RSS first generates an automatic request for a lock in *intent-exclusive* mode on the segment, before requesting an exclusive lock on the relation. This intent-exclusive lock is compatible with other intent locks but incompatible with share and exclusive locks. The same protocol is extended to include locks on individual tuples, through automatic acquisition of intent locks on the segment and relation, before a lock is acquired on the tuple in share or exclusive mode.

Since locks are requested dynamically, it is possible for two or more concurrent activations of the RSS to deadlock. The RSS has been designed to check for deadlock situations when requests are blocked, and to select one or more victims for backout if deadlock is detected. The detection is done by the Monitor, on a periodic basis, by looking for cycles in a user-user matrix. The selection of a victim is based on the relative ages of transactions in each deadlock cycle, as well as on the durations of the locks. In general the RSS selects the youngest transaction whose lock is of short duration, i.e. being held for the duration of a single RSI call, since the partially completed call can easily be undone. If none of the locks in the cycle are of short duration, then the youngest transaction is chosen. This transaction is then backed out to the save point preceding the offending lock request, using the transaction recovery scheme described above. (To simplify the code, special provisions are made for transactions which need locks and are already backing up.)

System Checkpoint and Restart

The RSS provides functions to recover the database to a consistent state in the event of a system crash. By a consistent state we mean a set of data values which would result if a set of transactions had been completed, and no other transactions were in progress. At such a state all image and link pointers are correct at the RSS level, and more importantly all user defined integrity assertions on data values are valid at the RDS level, since the RDS guarantees all integrity constraints at transaction boundaries.

In the RSS, special attention has been given to reduce the need for complete database dumps from disk to tape to accomplish a system checkpoint. The database dump technique has several difficulties. Since the time to copy the database to tape may be long for large databases, checkpoints may be taken infrequently, such as overnight or weekly. System restart is then a time consuming process, since many database changes must be reconstructed from the system log to restore a recent database state. In addition, before the checkpoint is performed, all ongoing transactions must first be completed. If any of these are long, then no new transactions are allowed to initiate until the long one is completed and the database dump is taken.

In the RSS, two system recovery mechanisms have been developed to alleviate these difficulties. The first mechanism uses disk storage to recover in the event of a "soft" failure which causes the contents of main memory to be lost; it is oriented toward frequent checkpoints and rapid recovery. The second mechanism uses tape storage to recover in the relatively infrequent case that disk storage is destroyed; it is oriented toward less frequent checkpoints. In both mechanisms, checkpoints can be made while transactions are still in progress.

The disk oriented recovery mechanism is heavily dependent on the segment recovery functions described above, and also on the availability of transaction logs. The Monitor Machine has the responsibility for scheduling checkpoints, based on parameters set during system startup. When a checkpoint is required, the Monitor quiesces all activity within the RSS at a point of physical consistency: transactions may still be in progress, but may not be executing an RSI operation. The technique for halting RSS activity is to acquire a special RSS lock in exclusive mode, which every activation of the RSS code acquires in share mode before executing an RSI operation, and releases at the end of the operation. The Monitor then issues the SAVE_SEGMENT operator to bring disk copies of all relevant segments up to date. Finally, the RSS lock is released and transactions are allowed to resume.

When a soft failure occurs, the RESTORE_SEGMENT operator is used to restore the contents of all saved segments. Recall that the restore function is a relatively simple one involving the setting of current page map values equal to the backup page map values and the releasing of pages allocated since the save point. The log segment, which is saved more frequently than normal data segments, is effectively saved at the end of each transaction, and contains "after" values as well as "before" values of modified data. Therefore transactions completing after the last database save, but before the last log save, can be redone automatically. In addition, the transaction logs are used to back out transactions which were incomplete at the checkpoint and cannot be redone, in order that a consistent database state is reached.

Our tape oriented recovery scheme is an extension of the above one. In order to recover in the event of lost disk data, some technique is required to get a sufficient copy of data and log information to tape. The technique we have chosen is to have the Monitor schedule certain checkpoints as "long" rather than standard short ones. A long checkpoint performs the usual segment save operations described above, but also initiates a process which copies the saved pages from disk to tape. Thus the checkpoint to tape is incremental.

4. SUMMARY AND CONCLUSION

We have described the overall architecture of System R and also the two main components: the Relational Data System (RDS) and the Relational Storage System (RSS). The RSS is a concurrent user, data management subsystem which provides underlying support for System R. The Relational Storage Interface (RSI) has operations at the single tuple level, with automatic maintenance of an arbitrary number of value orderings, called *images*, based on values in one or more fields. Images are implemented through the use of multilevel index structures. The

RSS also supports efficient navigation from tuples in one relation to tuples in another, through the maintenance of pointer chain structures called *links*. Images and links, along with physical scans through RSS pages, constitute the access path primitives which the RDS employs for efficient support of operators on the relational, hierarchical, and network models of data. Furthermore, to facilitate gradual integration of data and changing performance requirements, the RSS supports dynamic addition and deletion of relations, indexes, and links, with full space reclamation, and the addition of new fields to existing relations—all without special utilities or database reorganization.

Another important aspect of the RSS is full support of concurrent access in a multiprocessor environment, through the use of gate structures in shared, read/write memory. Several levels of consistency are provided to control the interaction of each user with others. Also locks are set automatically within the RSS, so that even unsophisticated users can write transactions without explicit lock protocols or file open protocols. These locks are set on various granularities of data objects, so that various types of application environments can be accommodated.

In the area of recovery, transaction backout is provided to any one of an arbitrary number of user specified save points, to aid in the recovery of long application programs. Backout may also be initiated by the RSS during automatic detection of deadlock. A new recovery scheme is provided at the system level, so that both checkpoint and restart operations can be performed efficiently.

The RDS supports the Relational Data Interface (RDI), the external interface of System R, and provides the user with a consistent set of facilities for data retrieval, manipulation, definition, and control. The RDI is designed as a set of operators which may be called directly from a host program. It is expected that programs will be written on top of the RDI to implement various stand-alone relational interfaces and other, possibly nonrelational, interfaces.

The most important component of the RDS is the optimizer, which makes plans for efficient execution of high level operations using the RSS access path primitives. Of great importance in optimizing queries is the method by which tuples are arranged in physical storage. The RDS provides the RSS with clustering hints during insert operations, so that the tuples of a relation are physically clustered according to some value ordering, or placed near associated tuples along a binary link. Given the cluster properties of stored relations, the optimizer uses an access path strategy with the main emphasis on reducing the number of I/O operations between main memory and on-line, direct access storage.

In addition to the optimizer, the RDS contains components for various other functions. The authorization component allows the creator of a relation or view to grant or revoke various capabilities. The integrity system automatically enforces assertions about database values, which are entered through SEQUEL commands. A similar mechanism is employed to trigger one or more database actions when a given action is detected. The SEQUEL language may also be used to define any query as a named view. The access plan to materialize this view is selected by the optimizer, and can be stored away as a Pre-Optimized Package (POP) for subsequent execution. POPs are especially important for the support of transactions which are run repetitively, since they avoid much of the overhead usually associated with a high level of data independence.

APPENDIX I. RDI OPERATORS

Square brackets [ ] are used below to indicate optional parameters.

```
Operators for data definition and manipulation:

    SEQUEL ( [ <cursor name>,] <any SEQUEL statement> )

    FETCH ( <cursor name> [, <pointers to I/O locations>] )

    FETCH_HOLD ( <cursor name> [, <pointers to I/O locations> ] )

    OPEN ( <cursor name>, <name of relation or view> )

    CLOSE ( <cursor name> )

    KEEP ( <cursor name>, <new relation name>,

           <list of new field names> )

    DESCRIBE ( <cursor name>, <degree>, <pointers to I/O

               locations> )

    BIND ( <program variable name>, <program variable address> )


Operators on transactions and locks:

    BEGIN_TRANS ( <transaction id>, <consistency level> )

    END_TRANS

    SAVE ( <save point name> )

    RESTORE ( <save point name> )

    RELEASE ( <cursor name> )
```

APPENDIX II. SEQUEL SYNTAX

The following is a shortened version of the BNF syntax for SEQUEL. It contains several minor ambiguities and generates a number of constructs with no semantic support, all of which are (hopefully) missing from our complete, production syntax. Square brackets [ ] are used to indicate optional constructs.

```
statement  ::=  query
              | dml-statement
              | ddl-statement
              | control-statement

dml-statement  ::=  assignment
                  | insertion
                  | deletion
                  | update

query  ::=  query-expr [ ORDER BY  ord-spec-list ]

assignment  ::=  receiver <- query-expr

receiver  ::=  table-name [ ( field-name-list ) ]

insertion  ::=  INSERT  INTO  receiver  :  insert-spec

insert-spec  ::=  query-expr
                | literal
                | constant

field-name-list  ::=  field-name
                    | field-name-list  ,  field-name
```

```
deletion  ::=  DELETE table-name [ var-name ]  [ where-clause ]

update  ::=  UPDATE  table-name [ var-name ] set-clause-list
               [ where-clause ]

where-clause  ::=  WHERE  boolean
                 | WHERE  CURRENT [ TUPLE ] OF
                      [ CURSOR ] cursor-name

set-clause-list  ::=  set-clause
                    | set-clause-list  ,  set-clause

set-clause  ::=  SET  field-name  =  expr
               | SET  field-name  =  ( query-expr )

query-expr  ::=  query-block
               | query-expr  set-op  query-block
               | ( query-expr )

set-op  ::=  INTERSECT  |  UNION  |  MINUS

query-block  ::=  select-clause  FROM  from-list
                     [ WHERE boolean ]
                     [ GROUP BY  field-spec-list
                        [ HAVING boolean ] ]

select-clause  ::=  SELECT [ UNIQUE ] sel-expr-list
                  | SELECT [ UNIQUE ] *

sel-expr-list  ::=  sel-expr
                  | sel-expr-list  ,  sel-expr

sel-expr  ::=  expr [ : host-location ]
             | var-name  .  *  |  table-name     *

from-list  ::=  table-name [ var-name ]
              | from-list  ,  table-name [ var-name ]

field-spec-list  ::=  field-spec
                    | field-spec-list  ,  field-spec

ord-spec-list  ::=  field-spec [ direction ]
                  | ord-spec-list  ,  field-spec [ direction ]

direction  ::=  ASC  |  DESC

boolean  ::=  boolean-term
            | boolean  OR  boolean-term

boolean-term  ::=  boolean-factor
                 | boolean-term  AND  boolean-factor

boolean-factor  ::=  [ NOT ] boolean-primary

boolean-primary  ::=  predicate
                    | ( boolean )

predicate  ::=  expr  comparison  expr
              | expr  BETWEEN  expr  AND  expr
              | expr  comparison  table-spec
              | < field-spec-list >  =  full-table-spec
              | < field-spec-list >  [ IS ]  IN  full-table-spec
              | IF  predicate  THEN  predicate
              | SET ( field-spec-list )  comparison
                      full-table-spec
              | SET ( field-spec-list )  comparison
                      SET ( field-spec-list )
              | table-spec  comparison  full-table-spec

full-table-spec  ::=  table-spec
                    | ( entry  )
                    | constant

table-spec  ::=  query-block
               | ( query-expr )
               | literal

expr  ::=  arith-term
         | expr  add-op  arith-term
```

```
arith-term  ::=  arith-factor
               | arith-term  mult-op  arith-factor

arith-factor  ::=  [ add-op ] primary

primary  ::=  [ OLD | NEW ]  field-spec
            | set-fn  ( [ UNIQUE ] expr )
            | COUNT  (  *  )
            | constant
            | (  expr  )

field-spec  ::=  field-name
               | table-name  .  field-name
               | var-name  .  field-name

comparison  ::=  comp-op
               | CONTAINS
               | DOES NOT CONTAIN
               | [  IS  ]  IN
               | [  IS  ]  NOT IN

comp-op  ::=  =  | ¬=  |  >  |  >=  |  <  |  <=

add-op  ::=  +  |  -

mult-op  ::=  *  |  /

set-fn  ::=  AVG  |  MAX  |  MIN  |  SUM  |  COUNT  |  identifier

literal  ::=  (  lit-tuple-list  )
            | ( entry-list )
            | lit-tuple

lit-tuple-list  ::=  lit-tuple
                   | lit-tuple-list  ,  lit-tuple

lit-tuple  ::=  <  entry  >
              | <  entry-list  >

entry-list  ::=  entry  ,  entry
               | entry-list  ,  entry

entry  ::=  [ constant ]

constant  ::=  quoted-string
             | number
             | host-location
             | NULL
             | USER
             | DATE
             | field-name  OF CURSOR  cursor-name
                  [ ON  table-name ]

table-name  ::=  name

image-name  ::=  name

link-name  ::=  name

asrt-name  ::=  name

trig-name  ::=  name

name  ::=  [ creator  . ] identifier

creator  ::=  identifier

user-name  ::=  identifier

field-name  ::=  identifier

var-name  ::=  identifier

cursor-name  ::=  identifier

host-location  ::=  identifier

integer  ::=  number
```

```
ddl-statement  ::=  create-table
                 |  expand-table
                 |  keep-table
                 |  create-image
                 |  create-link
                 |  define-view
                 |  drop
                 |  comment

create-table  ::=  CREATE  [ perm-spec ]  [ share-spec ]  TABLE
                       table-name  :  field-defn-list

perm-spec  ::=  PERMANENT  |  TEMPORARY

share-spec  ::=  SHARED  |  PRIVATE

field-defn-list  ::=  field-defn
                   |  field-defn-list  ,  field-defn

field-defn  ::=  field-name  ( type [ , NONULL ] )

type  ::=  CHAR  ( integer )
        |  CHAR ( * )
        |  INTEGER
        |  SMALLINT
        |  DECIMAL ( integer , integer )
        |  FLOAT

expand-table  ::=  EXPAND  TABLE  table-name  ADD
                         FIELD  field-defn

keep-table  ::=  KEEP  TABLE  table-name

create-image  ::=  CREATE  [ image-mod-list ]  IMAGE  image-name
                       ON  table-name  ( ord-spec-list )

image-mod-list  ::=  image-mod
                  |  image-mod-list  image-mod

image-mod  ::=  UNIQUE
             |  CLUSTERING

create-link  ::=  CREATE  [ CLUSTERING ]  LINK  link-name
                    FROM  table-name ( field-name-list )
                    TO  table-name ( field-name-list )
                    [ ORDER BY ord-spec-list ]

define-view  ::=  DEFINE  [ perm-spec ]  VIEW  table-name
                [ ( field-name-list ) ]  AS  query

drop  ::=  DROP  system-entity  name

comment  ::=  COMMENT ON  system-entity  name  :  quoted-string
           |  COMMENT ON FIELD  table-name . field-name
                   :  quoted-string

system-entity  ::=  TABLE  |  VIEW  |  ASSERTION
                 |  TRIGGER  |  IMAGE  |  LINK

control-statement  ::=  asrt-statement
                     |  enforcement
                     |  define-trigger
                     |  grant
                     |  revoke

asrt-statement  ::=  ASSERT  asrt-name [ IMMEDIATE ]
                         [ ON asrt-condition ]  :  boolean

asrt-condition  ::=  action-list
                  |  table-name  [ var-name ]

action-list  ::=  action
               |  action-list  ,  action

action  ::=  INSERTION OF  table-name [ var-name ]
          |  DELETION OF  table-name [ var-name ]
          |  UPDATE OF  table-name [ var-name ]
                 [ ( field-name-list ) ]

enforcement  ::=  ENFORCE  INTEGRITY
               |  ENFORCE ASSERTION  asrt-name

define-trigger  ::=  DEFINE TRIGGER  trig-name
                       ON trig-condition  :  ( statement-list )

trig-condition  ::=  action
                  |  READ OF  table-name [ var-name ]

statement-list  ::=  statement
                  |  statement-list  ;  statement

grant  ::=  GRANT [ auth ] table-name  TO  user-list
                   [ WITH GRANT OPTION ]

auth  ::=  ALL RIGHTS ON
        |  operation-list  ON
        |  ALL BUT  operation-list  ON

user-list  ::=  user-name
             |  user-list  ,  user-name
             |  PUBLIC

operation-list  ::=  operation
                  |  operation-list  ,  operation

operation  ::=  READ
             |  INSERT
             |  DELETE
             |  UPDATE [ ( field-name-list ) ]
             |  DROP
             |  EXPAND
             |  IMAGE
             |  LINK
             |  CONTROL

revoke  ::=  REVOKE [ operation-list ON ] table-name
                 FROM  user-list
```

APPENDIX III. RSI OPERATORS

The RSI operators are oriented toward the use of formatted control blocks. Rather than explain the detailed conventions of these control blocks, we list below an approximate but hopefully readable form for the operators. Square brackets [ ] are used to indicate optional parameters.

```
Operators on segments:

   OPEN_SEGMENT ( <segid> )

   CLOSE_SEGMENT ( <segid> )

   SAVE_SEGMENT ( <segid> )

   RESTORE_SEGMENT ( <segid> )


Operators on transactions and locks:

   START_TRANS ( <consistency level> )

   END_TRANS

   SAVE_TRANS, RETURNS ( <saveid> )

   RESTORE_TRANS ( <saveid> )

   LOCK_SEGMENT ( <segid>, <mode: SHARE or EXCLUSIVE or SIX> )

   LOCK_RELATION ( <segid>, <relid>, <mode, as above> )

   RELEASE_TUPLE ( <segid>, <tid> )
```

```
Operators on tuples and scans:

    FETCH ( <segid>, <relid>, <identifier: tid or scanid or imageid,
            key values>, <field list>, <pointers to I/O locations>
            [, HOLD] )
    INSERT ( <segid>, <relid>, <pointers to I/O locations>
             [, <nearby tid> ] ),   RETURNS ( <tid> )
    DELETE ( <segid>, <relid>, <identifier, as above> )
    UPDATE ( <segid>, <relid>, <identifier, as above>,
             <field list>, <pointers to I/O locations> )
    OPEN_SCAN ( <segid>, <path: relid or imageid or linkid>,
                <start-point: key values for image, or tid for link,
                or scanid for link> ),
                  RETURNS ( <scanid> )
    NEXT ( <segid>, <scanid>, <field list>, <pointers to I/O locations>
           [, <search argument>] [, HOLD] )
    CLOSE ( <segid>, <scanid> )
    PARENT ( <child segid>, <linkid>, <identifier for new tuple, as
             above>, <field list>, <pointers to I/O locations>
             [, HOLD] )
    CONNECT ( <child segid>, <linkid>, <identifier for new tuple, as
              above>, <neighbor relid>, <neighbor tid>,
              <location: BEFORE or AFTER> )
    DISCONNECT ( <child segid>, <linkid>, <identifier for child, as
                 above> )

Operators for data definition:

    CREATE ( <segid>, <object type: REL or IMAGE or LINK >, <specs> ),
             RETURNS ( <object identifier: relid or imageid or linkid> )
    DESTROY ( <segid>, <object identifier, as above> )
    CHANGE ( <segid>, <object identifier, as above>,
             <new specs> )
    READSPEC ( <segid>, <object identifier, as above>,
               <pointer to I/O location> )
```


ACKNOWLEDGMENTS

The authors wish to acknowledge many helpful discussions with E.F. Codd, originator of the relational model of data, and with L.Y. Liu, manager of the Computer Science Department of the IBM San Jose Research Laboratory. We also wish to acknowledge the extensive contributions to System R of Phyllis Reisner, whose human factors experiments (reported in [24, 25]) have resulted in significant improvements in the SEQUEL language.

REFERENCES

1. ASTRAHAN, M.M., AND CHAMBERLIN, D.D. Implementation of a structured English query language. *Comm. ACM 18*, 10 (Oct. 1975), 580–588.
2. ASTRAHAN, M.M., AND LORIE, R.A. SEQUEL-XRM: A relational system. Proc. ACM Pacific Conf., San Francisco, Calif., April 1975, pp. 34–38.
3. BAYER, R., AND MCCREIGHT, E.M. Organization and maintenance of large ordered indexes. *Acta Informatica 1* (1972), 173–189.
4. BOYCE, R.F., AND CHAMBERLIN, D.D. Using a structured English query language as a data definition facility. Res. Rep. RJ 1318, IBM Res. Lab., San Jose, Calif., Dec. 1973.
5. CHAMBERLIN, D.D., AND BOYCE, R.F. SEQUEL: A structured English query language. Proc. ACM SIGFIDET Workshop, Ann Arbor, Mich., May 1974, pp. 249–264.
6. CODASYL DATA BASE TASK GROUP. April 1971 Rep. (Available from ACM, New York.)
7. CODD, E.F. A relational model of data for large shared data banks. *Comm. ACM 13*, 6 (June 1970), 377–387.
8. CODD, E.F. Relational completeness of data base sublanguages. In *Courant Computer Science Symposia, Vol. 6: Data Base Systems*, G. Forsythe, Ed., Prentice-Hall, Engelwood Cliffs, N.J., 1971, pp. 65–98.
9. DONOVAN, J.J., FESSEL, R., GREENBERG, S.S., AND GUTENTAG, L.M. An experimental VM/370 based information system. Proc. Internat. Conf. on Very Large Data Bases, Framingham, Mass., Sept. 1975, pp. 549–553. (Available from ACM, New York.)
10. ESWARAN, K.P., AND CHAMBERLIN, D.D. Functional specifications of a subsystem for data base integrity. Proc. Internat. Conf. on Very Large Data Bases, Framingham, Mass., Sept. 1975, pp. 48–68. (Available from ACM, New York.)
11. Feature analysis of generalized data base management systems. CODASYL Systems Committee Tech. Rep., May 1971. (Available from ACM, New York.)
12. GOLDSTEIN, R.C., AND STRNAD, A.L. The MACAIMS data management system. Proc. ACM SIGFIDET Workshop on Data Description and Access, Houston, Tex., Nov. 1970, pp. 201–229.
13. GRAY, J.N., LORIE, R.A., PUTZOLU, G.R., AND TRAIGER, I.L. Granularity of locks and degrees of consistency in a shared data base. Proc. IFIP Working Conf. on Modelling of Data Base Management Systems, Freudenstadt, Germany, Jan. 1976, pp. 695–723.
14. GRAY, J.N., AND WATSON, V. A shared segment and inter-process communication facility for VM/370. Res. Rep. RJ 1579, IBM Res. Lab., San Jose, Calif., Feb. 1975.
15. GRIFFITHS, P.P., AND WADE, B.W. An authorization mechanism for a relational data base system. Proc. ACM SIGMOD Conf., Washington, D.C., June 1976 (to appear).
16. HELD, G.D., STONEBRAKER, M.R., AND WONG, E. INGRES: A relational data base system. Proc. AFIPS 1975 NCC, Vol. 44, AFIPS Press, Montvale, N.J., pp. 409–416.
17. Information Management System, General Information Manual. IBM Pub. No. GH20-1260, IBM Corp., White Plains, N.Y., 1975.
18. Introduction to VM/370. Pub. No. GC20-1800, IBM Corp., White Plains, N.Y., Jan. 1975.
19. LORIE, R.A. XRM—An extended (*n*-ary) relational memory. IBM Scientific Center Rep. G320-2096, Cambridge, Mass., Jan. 1974.
20. LORIE, R.A., AND SYMONDS, A.J. A relational access method for interactive applications. In *Courant Computer Science Symposia, Vol. 6: Data Base Systems*, G. Forsythe, Ed., Prentice-Hall, Engelwood Cliffs, N.J., 1971, pp. 99–124.
21. MYLOPOULOS, J., SCHUSTER, S.A., AND TSICHRITZIS, D. A multi-level relational system. Proc. AFIPS 1975 NCC, Vol. 44, AFIPS Press, Montvale, N.J., pp. 403–408.
22. NOTLEY, M.G. The Peterlee IS/1 System. IBM UK Scientific Center Rep. UKSC-0018, March 1972.
23. Planning for Enhanced VSAM under OS/VS. Pub. No. GC26-3842, IBM Corp., White Plains, N.Y., 1975.
24. REISNER, P. Use of psychological experimentation as an aid to development of a query language. Res. Rep. RJ 1707, IBM Res. Lab., San Jose, Calif., Jan. 1976.
25. REISNER, P., BOYCE, R.F., AND CHAMBERLIN, D.D. Human factors evaluation of two data base query languages: SQUARE and SEQUEL. Proc. AFIPS 1975 NCC, Vol. 44, AFIPS Press, Montvale, N.J., pp. 447–452.

26. SCHMID, H.A., AND BERNSTEIN, P.A. A multi-level architecture for relational data base systems. Proc. Internat. Conf. on Very Large Data Bases, Framingham, Mass., Sept. 1975, pp. 202–226. (Available from ACM, New York.)
27. SMITH, J.M., AND CHANG, P.Y. Optimizing the performance of a relational algebra database interface. *Comm. ACM 18*, 10 (Oct. 1975), 568–579.
28. STONEBRAKER, M. Implementation of integrity constraints and views by query modification. Proc. ACM SIGMOD Conf., San Jose, Calif., May 1975, pp. 65–78.
29. TODD, S. PRTV: An efficient implementation for large relational data bases. Proc. Internat. Conf. on Very Large Data Bases, Framingham, Mass., Sept. 1975, pp. 554–556. (Available from ACM, New York.)
30. WHITNEY, V.K.M. RDMS: A relational data management system. Proc. Fourth Internat. Symp. on Computer and Information Sciences, Miami Beach, Fla., Dec. 1972, pp. 55–66.
31. ZLOOF, M.M. Query by Example. Proc. AFIPS 1975 NCC, Vol. 44, AFIPS Press, Montvale, N.J., pp. 431–437.

Received November 1975; revised February 1976

The Design and Implementation of INGRES

MICHAEL STONEBRAKER, EUGENE WONG, AND PETER KREPS
University of California, Berkeley
and
GERALD HELD
Tandem Computers, Inc.

The currently operational (March 1976) version of the INGRES database management system is described. This multiuser system gives a relational view of data, supports two high level nonprocedural data sublanguages, and runs as a collection of user processes on top of the UNIX operating system for Digital Equipment Corporation PDP 11/40, 11/45, and 11/70 computers. Emphasis is on the design decisions and tradeoffs related to (1) structuring the system into processes, (2) embedding one command language in a general purpose programming language, (3) the algorithms implemented to process interactions, (4) the access methods implemented, (5) the concurrency and recovery control currently provided, and (6) the data structures used for system catalogs and the role of the database administrator.

Also discussed are (1) support for integrity constraints (which is only partly operational), (2) the not yet supported features concerning views and protection, and (3) future plans concerning the system.

Key Words and Phrases: relational database, nonprocedural language, query language, data sublanguage, data organization, query decomposition, database optimization, data integrity, protection, concurrency
CR Categories: 3.50, 3.70, 4.22, 4.33, 4.34

1. INTRODUCTION

INGRES (Interactive Graphics and Retrieval System) is a relational database system which is implemented on top of the UNIX operating system developed at Bell Telephone Laboratories [22] for Digital Equipment Corporation PDP 11/40, 11/45, and 11/70 computer systems. The implementation of INGRES is primarily programmed in C, a high level language in which UNIX itself is written. Parsing is done with the assistance of YACC, a compiler-compiler available on UNIX [19].

This research was sponsored by Army Research Office Grant DAHCO4-74-G0087, the Naval Electronic Systems Command Contract N00039-76-C-0022, the Joint Services Electronics Program Contract F44620-71-C-0087, National Science Foundation Grants DCR75-03839 and ENG74-06651-A01, and a grant from the Sloan Foundation.

Authors' addresses: M. Stonebraker and E. Wong, Department of Electrical Engineering and Computer Sciences, University of California, Berkeley, Berkeley, CA 94720; P. Kreps, Department of Computer Science and Applied Mathematics, Building 50B, Lawrence Berkeley Laboratories, University of California, Berkeley, Berkeley, CA 94720; G. Held, Tandem Computers, Inc., Cupertino, CA 95014.

The advantages of a relational model for database management systems have been extensively discussed in the literature [7, 10, 11] and hardly require further elaboration. In choosing the relational model, we were particularly motivated by (a) the high degree of data independence that such a model affords, and (b) the possibility of providing a high level and entirely procedure free facility for data definition, retrieval, update, access control, support of views, and integrity verification.

1.1 Aspects Described in This Paper

In this paper we describe the design decisions made in INGRES. In particular we stress the design and implementation of: (a) the system process structure (see Section 2 for a discussion of this UNIX notion); (b) the embedding of all INGRES commands in the general purpose programming language C; (c) the access methods implemented; (d) the catalog structure and the role of the database administrator; (e) support for views, protection, and integrity constraints; (f) the decomposition procedure implemented; (g) implementation of updates and consistency of secondary indices; (h) recovery and concurrency control.

In Section 1.2 we briefly describe the primary query language supported, QUEL, and the utility commands accepted by the current system. The second user interface, CUPID, is a graphics oriented, casual user language which is also operational [20, 21] but not discussed in this paper. In Section 1.3 we describe the EQUEL (Embedded QUEL) precompiler, which allows the substitution of a user supplied C program for the "front end" process. This precompiler has the effect of embedding all of INGRES in the general purpose programming language C. In Section 1.4 a few comments on QUEL and EQUEL are given.

In Section 2 we describe the relevant factors in the UNIX environment which have affected our design decisions. Moreover, we indicate the structure of the four processes into which INGRES is divided and the reasoning behind the choices implemented.

In Section 3 we indicate the catalog (system) relations which exist and the role of the database administrator with respect to all relations in a database. The implemented access methods, their calling conventions, and, where appropriate, the actual layout of data pages in secondary storage are also presented.

Sections 4, 5, and 6 discuss respectively the various functions of each of the three "core" processes in the system. Also discussed are the design and implementation strategy of each process. Finally, Section 7 draws conclusions, suggests future extensions, and indicates the nature of the current applications run on INGRES.

Except where noted to the contrary, this paper describes the INGRES system operational in March 1976.

1.2 QUEL and the Other INGRES Utility Commands

QUEL (QUEry Language) has points in common with Data Language/ALPHA [8], SQUARE [3], and SEQUEL [4] in that it is a complete query language which frees the programmer from concern for how data structures are implemented and what algorithms are operating on stored data [9]. As such it facilitates a considerable degree of data independence [24].

The QUEL examples in this section all concern the following relations.

```
EMPLOYEE (NAME, DEPT, SALARY, MANAGER, AGE)
DEPT     (DEPT, FLOOR#)
```

A QUEL interaction includes at least one RANGE statement of the form

```
RANGE OF variable-list IS relation-name
```

The purpose of this statement is to specify the relation over which each variable ranges. The variable-list portion of a RANGE statement declares variables which will be used as arguments for tuples. These are called *tuple variables*.

An interaction also includes one or more statements of the form

```
Command [result-name](target-list)
        [WHERE Qualification]
```

Here Command is either RETRIEVE, APPEND, REPLACE, or DELETE. For RETRIEVE and APPEND, result-name is the name of the relation which qualifying tuples will be retrieved into or appended to. For REPLACE and DELETE, result-name is the name of a tuple variable which, through the qualification, identifies tuples to be modified or deleted. The target-list is a list of the form

```
result-domain = QUEL Function. . . .
```

Here the result-domains are domain names in the result relation which are to be assigned the values of the corresponding functions.

The following suggest valid QUEL interactions. A complete description of the language is presented in [15].

Example 1.1. Compute salary divided by age-18 for employee Jones.

```
RANGE OF E IS EMPLOYEE
RETRIEVE INTO W
(COMP = E.SALARY/(E.AGE-18))
WHERE E.NAME = "Jones"
```

Here E is a tuple variable which ranges over the EMPLOYEE relation, and all tuples in that relation are found which satisfy the qualification E.NAME = "Jones." The result of the query is a new relation W, which has a single domain COMP that has been calculated for each qualifying tuple.

If the result relation is omitted, qualifying tuples are written in display format on the user's terminal or returned to a calling program.

Example 1.2. Insert the tuple (Jackson,candy,13000,Baker,30) into EMPLOYEE.

```
APPEND TO EMPLOYEE(NAME = "Jackson", DEPT = "candy",
   SALARY = 13000, MGR = "Baker", AGE = 30)
```

Here the result relation EMPLOYEE is modified by adding the indicated tuple to the relation. Domains which are not specified default to zero for numeric domains and null for character strings. A shortcoming of the current implemenation is that 0 is not distinguished from "no value" for numeric domains.

Example 1.3. Fire everybody on the first floor.

```
RANGE OF E IS EMPLOYEE
RANGE OF D IS DEPT
DELETE E WHERE  E.DEPT = D.DEPT
           AND  D.FLOOR# = 1
```

Here E specifies that the EMPLOYEE relation is to be modified. All tuples are to be removed which have a value for DEPT which is the same as some department on the first floor.

Example 1.4. Give a 10-percent raise to Jones if he works on the first floor.

```
RANGE OF E IS EMPLOYEE
RANGE OF D IS DEPT
REPLACE E(SALARY = 1.1*E.SALARY)
WHERE  E.NAME = "Jones"  AND
       E.DEPT = D.DEPT AND D.FLOOR# = 1
```

Here E.SALARY is to be replaced by 1.1*E.SALARY for those tuples in EMPLOYEE where the qualification is true.

In addition to the above QUEL commands, INGRES supports a variety of utility commands. These utility commands can be classified into seven major categories.

(a) Invocation of INGRES:

```
INGRES data-base-name
```

This command executed from UNIX "logs in" a user to a given database. (A database is simply a named collection of relations with a given database administrator who has powers not available to ordinary users.) Thereafter the user may issue all other commands (except those executed directly from UNIX) within the environment of the invoked database.

(b) Creation and destruction of databases:

```
CREATEDB data-base-name

DESTROYDB data-base-name
```

These two commands are called from UNIX. The invoker of CREATEDB must be authorized to create databases (in a manner to be described presently), and he automatically becomes the database administrator. DESTROYDB successfully destroys a database only if invoked by the database administrator.

(c) Creation and destruction of relations:

```
CREATE relname(domain-name IS format, domain-name IS format, . . .)

DESTROY relname
```

These commands create and destroy relations within the current database. The invoker of the CREATE command becomes the "owner" of the relation created. A user may only destroy a relation that he owns. The current formats accepted by INGRES are 1-, 2-, and 4-byte integers, 4- and 8-byte floating point numbers, and 1- to 255-byte fixed length ASCII character strings.

(d) Bulk copy of data:

```
COPY relname(domain-name IS format, domain-name IS format, . . . ) direction "file-
   name"

PRINT relname
```

The command COPY transfers an entire relation to or from a UNIX file whose name is "filename." Direction is either TO or FROM. The format for each domain is a description of how it appears (or is to appear) in the UNIX file. The relation relname must exist and have domain names identical to the ones appearing in the COPY command. However, the formats need not agree and COPY will automatically convert data types. Support is also provided for dummy and variable length fields in a UNIX file.

PRINT copies a relation onto the user's terminal, formatting it as a report. In this sense it is stylized version of COPY.

(e) Storage structure modification:

MODIFY relname TO storage-structure ON (key1, key2, . . .)

INDEX ON relname IS indexname(key1, key2, . . .)

The MODIFY command changes the storage structure of a relation from one access method to another. The five access methods currently supported are discussed in Section 3. The indicated keys are domains in relname which are concatenated left to right to form a combined key which is used in the organization of tuples in all but one of the access methods. Only the owner of a relation may modify its storage structure.

INDEX creates a secondary index for a relation. It has domains of key1, key2, . . . , pointer. The domain "pointer" is the unique identifier of a tuple in the indexed relation having the given values for key1, key2, ... An index named AGEINDEX for EMPLOYEE might be the following binary relation (assuming that there are six tuples in EMPLOYEE with appropriate names and ages).

	Age	Pointer
	25	identifier for Smith's tuple
	32	identifier for Jones's tuple
AGEINDEX	36	identifier for Adams's tuple
	29	identifier for Johnson's tuple
	47	identifier for Baker's tuple
	58	identifier for Harding's tuple

The relation indexname is in turn treated and accessed just like any other relation, except it is automatically updated when the relation it indexes is updated. Naturally, only the owner of a relation may create and destroy secondary indexes for it.

(f) Consistency and integrity control:

INTEGRITY CONSTRAINT is qualification

INTEGRITY CONSTRAINT LIST relname

INTEGRITY CONSTRAINT OFF relname

INTEGRITY CONSTRAINT OFF (integer, . . . , integer)

RESTORE data-base-name

The first four commands support the insertion, listing, deletion, and selective deletion of integrity constraints which are to be enforced for all interactions with a relation. The mechanism for handling this enforcement is discussed in Section 4. The last command restores a database to a consistent state after a system crash. It must be executed from UNIX, and its operation is discussed in Section 6. The RESTORE command is only available to the database administrator.

(g) Miscellaneous:

HELP [relname or manual-section]

SAVE relname UNTIL expiration-date

PURGE data-base-name

HELP provides information about the system or the database invoked. When called with an optional argument which is a command name, HELP returns the appropriate page from the INGRES reference manual [31]. When called with a relation name as an argument, it returns all information about that relation. With no argument at all, it returns information about all relations in the current database.

SAVE is the mechanism by which a user can declare his intention to keep a relation until a specified time. PURGE is a UNIX command which can be invoked by a database administrator to delete all relations whose "expiration-dates" have passed. This should be done when space in a database is exhausted. (The database administrator can also remove any relations from his database using the DESTROY command, regardless of who their owners are.)

Two comments should be noted at this time.

(a) The system currently accepts the language specified as QUEL_1 in [15]; extension is in progress to accept QUEL_n. (b) The system currently does not accept views or protection statements. Although the algorithms have been specified [25, 27], they are not yet operational. For this reason no syntax for these statements is given in this section; however the subject is discussed further in Section 4.

1.3 EQUEL

Although QUEL alone provides the flexibility for many data management requirements, there are applications which require a customized user interface in place of the QUEL language. For this as well as other reasons, it is often useful to have the flexibility of a general purpose programming language in addition to the database facilities of QUEL. To this end, a new language, EQUEL (Embedded QUEL), which consists of QUEL embedded in the general purpose programming language C, has been implemented.

In the design of EQUEL the following goals were set: (a) The new language must have the full capabilities of both C and QUEL. (b) The C program should have the capability for processing each tuple individually, thereby satisfying the qualification in a RETRIEVE statement. (This is the "piped" return facility described in Data Language/ALPHA [8].)

With these goals in mind, EQUEL was defined as follows:

(a) Any C language statement is a valid EQUEL statement.
(b) Any QUEL statement (or INGRES utility command) is a valid EQUEL statement as long as it is prefixed by two number signs (##).
(c) C program variables may be used anywhere in QUEL statements except as

command names. The declaration statements of C variables used in this manner must also be prefixed by double number signs.

(d) RETRIEVE statements without a result relation have the form

```
RETRIEVE (target-list)
        [WHERE qualification]
##{
C-block
##}
```

which results in the C-block being executed once for each qualifying tuple.

Two short examples illustrate EQUEL syntax.

Example 1.5. The following program implements a small front end to INGRES which performs only one query. It reads in the name of an employee and prints out the employee's salary in a suitable format. It continues to do this as long as there are names to be read in. The functions READ and PRINT have the obvious meaning.

```
main( )
{
## char EMPNAME[20];
## int SAL;
while (READ(EMPNAME))
        {
##      RANGE OF X IS EMP
##      RETRIEVE (SAL = X.SALARY)
##      WHERE X.NAME = EMPNAME
            ##{
            PRINT("The salary of", EMPNAME, "is", SAL);
            ##}
        }
}
```

In this example the C variable *EMPNAME* is used in the qualification of the QUEL statement, and for each qualifying tuple the C variable *SAL* is set to the appropriate value and then the PRINT statement is executed.

Example 1.6. Read in a relation name and two domain names. Then for each of a collection of values which the second domain is to assume, do some processing on all values which the first domain assumes. (We assume the function PROCESS exists and has the obvious meaning.) A more elaborate version of this program could serve as a simple report generator.

```
main( )
{
## int VALUE;
## char RELNAME[13], DOMNAME[13], DOMVAL[80];
## char DOMNAME  2[13];
READ(RELNAME);
READ(DOMNAME);
READ(DOMNAME  2);
## RANGE OF X IS RELNAME
while (READ(DOMVAL))
        {
##          RETRIEVE (VALUE = X.DOMNAME)
##              WHERE X.DOMNAME  2 = DOMVAL
                ##{
                PROCESS(VALUE);
                ##}
        }
}
```

Any RANGE declaration (in this case the one for X) is assumed by INGRES to hold until redefined. Hence only one RANGE statement is required, regardless of the number of times the RETRIEVE statement is executed. Note clearly that anything except the name of an INGRES command can be a C variable. In the above example *RELNAME* is a C variable used as a relation name, while *DOMNAME* and *DOMNAME* 2 are used as domain names.

1.4 Comments on QUEL and EQUEL

In this section a few remarks are made indicating differences between QUEL and EQUEL and selected other proposed data sublanguages and embedded data sublanguages.

QUEL borrows much from Data Language/ALPHA. The primary differences are: (a) Arithmetic is provided in QUEL; Data Language/ALPHA suggests reliance on a host language for this feature. (b) No quantifiers are present in QUEL. This results in a consistent semantic interpretation of the language in terms of functions on the crossproduct of the relations declared in the RANGE statements. Hence, QUEL is considered by its designers to be a language based on functions and not on a first order predicate calculus. (c) More powerful aggregation capabilities are provided in QUEL.

The latest version of SEQUEL [2] has grown rather close to QUEL. The reader is directed to Example 1(b) of [2], which suggests a variant of the QUEL syntax. The main differences between QUEL and SEQUEL appear to be: (a) SEQUEL allows statements with no tuple variables when possible using a block oriented notation. (b) The aggregation facilities of SEQUEL appear to be different from those defined in QUEL.

System R [2] contains a proposed interface between SEQUEL and PL/1 or other host language. This interface differs substantially from EQUEL and contains explicit cursors and variable binding. Both notions are implicit in EQUEL. The interested reader should contrast the two different approaches to providing an embedded data sublanguage.

2. THE INGRES PROCESS STRUCTURE

INGRES can be invoked in two ways: First, it can be directly invoked from UNIX by executing INGRES database-name; second, it can be invoked by executing a program written using the EQUEL precompiler. We discuss each in turn and then comment briefly on why two mechanisms exist. Before proceeding, however, a few details concerning UNIX must be introduced.

2.1 The UNIX Environment

Two points concerning UNIX are worthy of mention in this section.

(a) The UNIX file system. UNIX supports a tree structured file system similar to that of MULTICS. Each file is either a directory (containing references to descendant files in the file system) or a data file. Each file is divided physically into 512-byte blocks (pages). In response to a read request, UNIX moves one or more pages from secondary memory to UNIX core buffers and then returns to the user the actual byte string desired. If the same page is referenced again (by the same or another user) while it is still in a core buffer, no disk I/O takes place.

It is important to note that UNIX pages data from the file system into and out of system buffers using a "least recently used" replacement algorithm. In this way the entire file system is managed as a large virtual store.

The INGRES designers believe that a database system should appear as a user job to UNIX. (Otherwise, the system would operate on a nonstandard UNIX and become less portable.) Moreover the designers believe that UNIX should manage the system buffers for the mix of jobs being run. Consequently, INGRES contains no facilities to do its own memory management.

(b) The UNIX process structure. A process in UNIX is an address space (64K bytes or less on an 11/40, 128K bytes or less on an 11/45 or 11/70) which is associated with a user-id and is the unit of work scheduled by the UNIX scheduler. Processes may "fork" subprocesses; consequently a parent process can be the root of a process subtree. Furthermore, a process can request that UNIX execute a file in a descendant process. Such processes may communicate with each other via an interprocess communication facility called "pipes." A pipe may be declared as a one direction communication link which is written into by one process and read by a second one. UNIX maintains synchronization of pipes so no messages are lost. Each process has a "standard input device" and a "standard output device." These are usually the user's terminal, but may be redirected by the user to be files, pipes to other processes, or other devices.

Last, UNIX provides a facility for processes executing reentrant code to share procedure segments if possible. INGRES takes advantage of this facility so the core space overhead of multiple concurrent users is only that required by data segments.

2.2 Invocation from UNIX

Issuing INGRES as a UNIX command causes the process structure shown in Figure 1 to be created. In this section the functions in the four processes will be indicated. The justification of this particular structure is given in Section 2.4.

Process 1 is an interactive terminal monitor which allows the user to formulate, print, edit, and execute collections of INGRES commands. It maintains a workspace with which the user interacts until he is satisfied with his interaction. The contents of this workspace are passed down pipe A as a string of ASCII characters when execution is desired. The set of commands accepted by the current terminal monitor is indicated in [31].

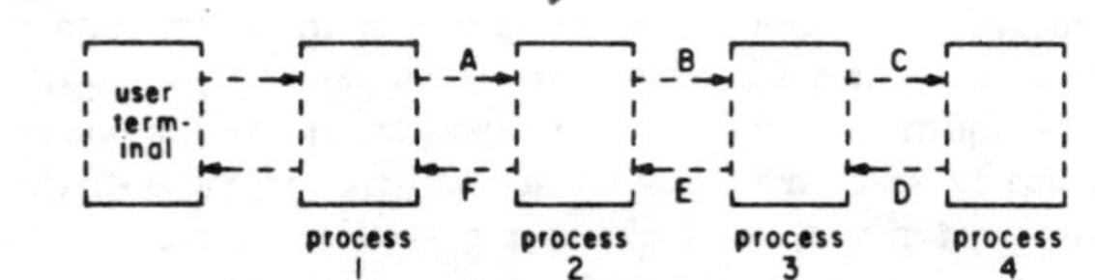

Fig. 1. INGRES process structure

As noted above, UNIX allows a user to alter the standard input and output devices for his processes when executing a command. As a result the invoker of INGRES may direct the terminal monitor to take input from a user file (in which case he runs a "canned" collection of interactions) and direct output to another device (such as the line printer) or file.

Process 2 contains a lexical analyzer, a parser, query modification routines for integrity control (and, in the future, support of views and protection), and concurrency control. Because of size constraints, however, the integrity control routines are not in the currently released system. When process 2 finishes, it passes a string of tokens to process 3 through pipe B. Process 2 is discussed in Section 4.

Process 3 accepts this token string and contains execution routines for the commands RETRIEVE, REPLACE, DELETE, and APPEND. Any update is turned into a RETRIEVE command to isolate tuples to be changed. Revised copies of modified tuples are spooled into a special file. This file is then processed by a "deferred update processor" in process 4, which is discussed in Section 6.

Basically, process 3 performs two functions for RETRIEVE commands. (a) A multivariable query is *decomposed* into a sequence of interactions involving only a single variable. (b) A one-variable query is executed by a one-variable query processor (OVQP). The OVQP in turn performs its function by making calls on the access methods. These two functions are discussed in Section 5; the access methods are indicated in Section 3.

All code to support utility commands (CREATE, DESTROY, INDEX, etc.) resides in process 4. Process 3 simply passes to process 4 any commands which process 4 will execute. Process 4 is organized as a collection of overlays which accomplish the various functions. Some of these functions are discussed in Section 6.

Error messages are passed back through pipes D, E, and F to process 1, which returns them to the user. If the command is a RETRIEVE with no result relation specified, process 3 returns qualifying tuples in a stylized format directly to the "standard output device" of process 1. Unless redirected, this is the user's terminal.

2.3 Invocation from EQUEL

We now turn to the operation of INGRES when invoked by code from the precompiler.

In order to implement EQUEL, a translator (precompiler) was written to convert an EQUEL program into a valid C program with QUEL statements converted to appropriate C code and calls to INGRES. The resulting C program is then compiled by the normal C compiler, producing an executable module. Moreover, when an EQUEL program is run, the executable module produced by the C compiler is used as the front end process in place of the interactive terminal monitor, as noted in Figure 2.

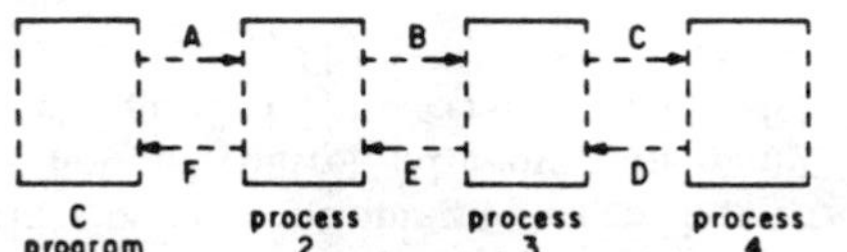

Fig. 2. The forked process structure

During execution of the front end program, database requests (QUEL statements in the EQUEL program) are passed through pipe A and processed by INGRES. Note that unparsed ASCII strings are passed to process 2; the rationale behind this decision is given in [1]. If tuples must be returned for tuple at a time processing, then they are returned through a special data pipe set up between process 3 and the C program. A condition code is also returned through pipe F to indicate success or the type of error encountered.

The functions performed by the EQUEL translator are discussed in detail in [1].

2.4 Comments on the Process Structure

The process structure shown in Figures 1 and 2 is the fourth different process structure implemented. The following considerations suggested this final choice:

(a) Address space limitations. To run on an 11/40, the 64K address space limitation must be adhered to. Processes 2 and 3 are essentially their maximum size; hence they cannot be combined. The code in process 4 is in several overlays because of size constraints.

Were a large address space available, it is likely that processes 2, 3, and 4 would be combined into a single large process. However, the necessity of 3 "core" processes should not degrade performance substantially for the following reasons.

If one large process were resident in main memory, there would be no necessity of swapping code. However, were enough real memory available (~300K bytes) on a UNIX system to hold processes 2 and 3 and all overlays of process 4, no swapping of code would necessarily take place either. Of course, this option is possible only on an 11/70.

On the other hand, suppose one large process was paged into and out of main memory by an operating system and hardware which supported a virtual memory. It is felt that under such conditions page faults would generate I/O activity at approximately the same rate as the swapping/overlaying of processes in INGRES (assuming the same amount of real memory was available in both cases).

Consequently the only sources of overhead that appear to result from multiple processes are the following: (1) Reading or writing pipes require system calls which are considerably more expensive than subroutine calls (which could be used in a single-process system). There are at least eight such system calls needed to execute an INGRES command. (2) Extra code must be executed to format information for transmission on pipes. For example, one cannot pass a pointer to a data structure through a pipe; one must linearize and pass the whole structure.

(b) Simple control flow. The grouping of functions into processes was motivated by the desire for simple control flow. Commands are passed only to the right; data and errors only to the left. Process 3 must issue commands to various overlays in process 4; therefore, it was placed to the left of process 4. Naturally, the parser must precede process 3.

Previous process structures had a more complex interconnection of processes. This made synchronization and debugging much harder.

The structure of process 4 stemmed from a desire to overlay little-used code in a single process. The alternative would have been to create additional processes 5, 6, and 7 (and their associated pipes), which would be quiescent most of the time. This would have required added space in UNIX core tables for no real advantage.

The processes are all synchronized (i.e. each waits for an error return from the next process to the right before continuing to accept input from the process to the left), simplifying the flow of control. Moreover, in many instances the various processes *must* be synchronized. Future versions of INGRES may attempt to exploit parallelism where possible. The performance payoff of such parallelism is unknown at the present time.

(c) Isolation of the front end process. For reasons of protection the C program which replaces the terminal monitor as a front end must run with a user-id different from that of INGRES. Otherwise it could tamper directly with data managed by INGRES. Hence, it must be either overlayed into a process or run in its own process. The latter was chosen for efficiency and convenience.

(d) Rationale for two process structures. The interactive terminal monitor could have been written in EQUEL. Such a strategy would have avoided the existence of two process structures which differ only in the treatment of the data pipe. Since the terminal monitor was written prior to the existence of EQUEL, this option could not be followed. Rewriting the terminal monitor in EQUEL is not considered a high priority task given current resources. Moreover, an EQUEL monitor would be slightly slower because qualifying tuples would be returned to the calling program and then displayed rather than being displayed directly by process 3.

3. DATA STRUCTURES AND ACCESS METHODS

We begin this section with a discussion of the files that INGRES manipulates and their contents. Then we indicate the five possible storage structures (file formats) for relations. Finally we sketch the access methods language used to interface uniformly to the available formats.

3.1 The INGRES File Structure

Figure 3 indicates the subtree of the UNIX file system that INGRES manipulates. The root of this subtree is a directory made for the UNIX user "INGRES." (When

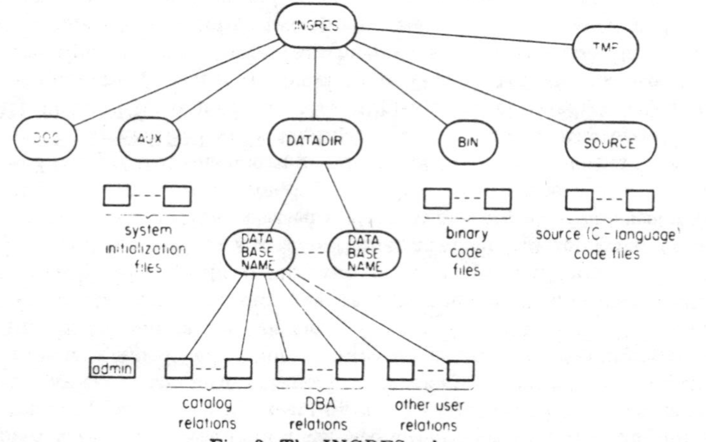

Fig. 3. The INGRES subtree

the INGRES system is initially installed such a user must be created. This user is known as the "superuser" because of the powers available to him. This subject is discussed further in [28].) This root has six descendant directories. The AUX directory has descendant files containing tables which control the spawning of processes (shown in Figures 1 and 2) and an authorization list of users who are allowed to create databases. Only the INGRES superuser may modify these files (by using the UNIX editor). BIN and SOURCE are directories indicating descendant files of respectively object and source code. TMP has descendants which are temporary files for the workspaces used by the interactive terminal monitor. DOC is the root of a subtree with system documentation and the reference manual. Last, there is a directory entry in DATADIR for each database that exists in INGRES. These directories contain the database files in a given database as descendants.

These database files are of four types:

(a) Administration file. This contains the user-id of the database administrator (DBA) and initialization information.

(b) Catalog (system) relations. These relations have predefined names and are created for every database. They are owned by the DBA and constitute the system catalogs. They may be queried by a knowledgeable user issuing RETRIEVE statements; however, they may be updated only by the INGRES utility commands (or directly by the INGRES superuser in an emergency). (When protection statements are implemented the DBA will be able to selectively restrict RETRIEVE access to these relations if he wishes.) The form and content of some of these relations will be discussed presently.

(c) DBA relations. These are relations owned by the DBA and are shared in that any user may access them. When protection is implemented the DBA can "authorize" shared use of these relations by inserting protection predicates (which will be in one of the system relations and may be unique for each user) and deauthorize use by removing such predicates. This mechanism is discussed in [28].

(d) Other relations. These are relations created by other users (by RETRIEVE INTO W or CREATE) and are *not shared*.

Three comments should be made at this time.

(a) The DBA has the following powers not available to ordinary users: the ability to create shared relations and to specify access control for them; the ability to run PURGE; the ability to destroy any relations in his database (except the system catalogs).

This system allows "one-level sharing" in that only the DBA has these powers, and he cannot delegate any of them to others (as in the file systems of most time sharing systems). This strategy was implemented for three reasons: (1) The need for added generality was not perceived. Moreover, added generality would have created tedious problems (such as making revocation of access privileges nontrivial). (2) It seems appropriate to entrust to the DBA the duty (and power) to resolve the policy decision which must be made when space is exhausted and some relations must be destroyed or archived. This policy decision becomes much harder (or impossible) if a database is not in the control of one user. (3) Someone must be entrusted with the policy decision concerning which relations are physically stored and which are defined as "views." This "database design" problem is best centralized in a single DBA.

(b) Except for the single administration file in each database, every file is treated as a relation. Storing system catalogs as relations has the following advantages: (1) Code is economized by sharing routines for accessing both catalog and data relations. (2) Since several storage structures are supported for accessing data relations quickly and flexibly under various interaction mixes, these same storage choices may be utilized to enhance access to catalog information. (3) The ability to execute QUEL statements to examine (and patch) system relations where necessary has greatly aided system debugging.

(c) Each relation is stored in a separate file, i.e. no attempt is made to "cluster" tuples from *different* relations which may be accessed together on the same or on a nearby page.

Note clearly that this clustering is analogous to DBTG systems in declaring a record type to be accessed via a set type which associates records of that record type with a record of a different record type. Current DBTG implementations usually attempt to physically cluster these associated records.

Note also that clustering tuples from one relation in a given file has obvious performance implications. The clustering techniques of this nature that INGRES supports are indicated in Section 3.3.

The decision not to cluster tuples from different relations is based on the following reasoning. (1) UNIX has a small (512-byte) page size. Hence it is expected that the number of tuples which can be grouped on the same page is small. Moreover, logically adjacent pages in a UNIX file are *not necessarily* physically adjacent. Hence clustering tuples on "nearby" pages has no meaning in UNIX; the next logical page in a file may be further away (in terms of disk arm motion) than a page in a different file. In keeping with the design decision of *not* modifying UNIX, these considerations were incorporated in the design decision not to support clustering. (2) The access methods would be more complicated if clustering were supported. (3) Clustering of tuples only makes sense if associated tuples can be linked together using "sets" [6], "links" [29], or some other scheme for identifying clusters. Incorporating these access paths into the decomposition scheme would have greatly increased its complexity.

It should be noted that the designers of System R have reached a different conclusion concerning clustering [2].

3.2 System Catalogs

We now turn to a discussion of the system catalogs. We discuss two relations in detail and indicate briefly the contents of the others.

The RELATION relation contains one tuple for every relation in the database (including all the system relations). The domains of this relation are:

relid	the name of the relation.
owner	the UNIX user-id of the relation owner; when appended to relid it produces a unique file name for storing the relation.
spec	indicates one of five possible storage schemes or else a special code indicating a virtual relation (or "view").
indexd	flag set if secondary index exists for this relation. (This flag and the following two are present to improve performance by avoiding catalog lookups when possible during query modification and one variable query processing.)

protect	flag set if this relation has protection predicates.
integ	flag set if there are integrity constraints.
save	scheduled lifetime of relation.
tuples	number of tuples in relation (kept up to date by the routine "closer" discussed in the next section).
atts	number of domains in relation.
width	width (in bytes) of a tuple.
prim	number of primary file pages for this relation.

The ATTRIBUTE catalog contains information relating to individual domains of relations. Tuples of the ATTRIBUTE catalog contain the following items for each domain of every relation in the database:

relid	name of relation in which attribute appears.
owner	relation owner.
domain_name	domain name.
domain_no	domain number (position) in relation. In processing interactions INGRES uses this number to reference this domain.
offset	offset in bytes from beginning of tuple to beginning of domain.
type	data type of domain (integer, floating point, or character string).
length	length (in bytes) of domain.
keyno	if this domain is part of a key, then "keyno" indicates the ordering of this domain within the key.

These two catalogs together provide information about the structure and content of each relation in the database. No doubt items will continue to be added or deleted as the system undergoes further development. The first planned extensions are the minimum and maximum values assumed by domains. These will be used by a more sophisticated decomposition scheme being developed, which is discussed briefly in Section 5 and in detail in [30]. The representation of the catalogs as relations has allowed this restructuring to occur very easily.

Several other system relations exist which provide auxiliary information about relations. The INDEX catalog contains a tuple for every secondary index in the database. Since secondary indices are themselves relations, they are independently cataloged in the RELATION and ATTRIBUTE relations. However, the INDEX catalog provides the association between a primary relation and its secondary indices and records which domains of the primary relation are in the index.

The PROTECTION and INTEGRITY catalogs contain respectively the protection and integrity predicates for each relation in the database. These predicates are stored in a partially processed form as character strings. (This mechanism exists for INTEGRITY and will be implemented in the same way for PROTECTION.) The VIEW catalog will contain, for each virtual relation, a partially processed QUEL-like description of the view in terms of existing relations. The use of these last three catalogs is described in Section 4. The existence of any of this auxiliary information for a given relation is signaled by the appropriate flag(s) in the RELATION catalog.

Another set of system relations consists of those used by the graphics subsystem to catalog and process maps, which (like everything else) are stored as relations in the database. This topic has been discussed separately in [13].

3.3 Storage Structures Available

We will now describe the five storage structures currently available in INGRES. Four of the schemes are keyed, i.e. the storage location of a tuple within the file is a function of the value of the tuple's key domains. They are termed "hashed," "ISAM," "compressed hash," and "compressed ISAM." For all four structures the key may be any ordered collection of domains. These schemes allow rapid access to specific portions of a relation when key values are supplied. The remaining nonkeyed scheme (a "heap") stores tuples in the file independently of their values and provides a low overhead storage structure, especially attractive in situations requiring a complete scan of the relation.

The nonkeyed storage structure in INGRES is a randomly ordered sequential file. Fixed length tuples are simply placed sequentially in the file in the order supplied. New tuples added to the relation are merely appended to the end of the file. The unique tuple identifier for each tuple is its byte-offset within the file. This mode is intended mainly for (a) very small relations, for which the overhead of other schemes is unwarranted; (b) transitional storage of data being moved into or out of the system by COPY; (c) certain temporary relations created as intermediate results during query processing.

In the remaining four schemes the key-value of a tuple determines the page of the file on which the tuple will be placed. The schemes share a common "page-structure" for managing tuples on file pages, as shown in Figure 4.

A tuple must fit entirely on a single page. Its unique tuple identifier (TID) consists of a page number (the ordering of its page in the UNIX file) plus a line number. The line number is an index into a line table, which grows upward from the bottom of the page, and whose entries contain pointers to the tuples on the page. In this way the physical arrangement of tuples on a page can be reorganized without affecting TIDs.

Initially the file contains all its tuples on a number of primary pages. If the relation grows and these pages fill, overflow pages are allocated and chained by pointers

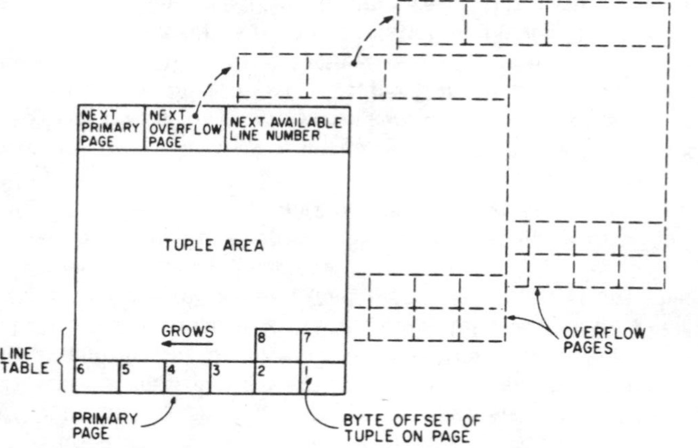

Fig. 4. Page layout for keyed storage structures

to the primary pages with which they are associated. Within a chained group of pages no special ordering of tuples is maintained. Thus in a keyed access which locates a particular primary page, tuples matching the key may actually appear on any page in the chain.

As discussed in [16], two modes of key-to-address transformation are used—randomizing (or "hashing") and order preserving. In a "hash" file tuples are distributed randomly throughout the primary pages of the file according to a hashing function on a key. This mode is well suited for situations in which access is to be conditioned on a specific key value.

As an order preserving mode, a scheme similar to IBM's ISAM [18] is used. The relation is sorted to produce the ordering on a particular key. A multilevel directory is created which records the high key on each primary page. The directory, which is static, resides on several pages following the primary pages within the file itself. A primary page and its overflow pages are *not* maintained in sort order. This decision is discussed in Section 4.2. The "ISAM-like" mode is useful in cases where the key value is likely to be specified as falling within a range of values, since a near ordering of the keys is preserved. The index compression scheme discussed in [16] is currently under implementation.

In the above-mentioned keyed modes, fixed length tuples are stored. In addition, both schemes can be used in conjunction with data compression techniques [14] in cases where increased storage utilization outweighs the added cost of encoding and decoding data during access. These modes are known as "compressed hash" and "compressed ISAM."

The current compression scheme suppresses blanks and portions of a tuple which match the preceding tuple. This compression is applied to each page independently. Other schemes are being experimented with. Compression appears to be useful in storing variable length domains (which must be declared their maximum length). Padding is then removed during compression by the access method. Compression may also be useful when storing secondary indices.

3.4 Access Methods Interface

The Access Methods Interface (AMI) handles all actual accessing of data from relations. The AMI language is implemented as a set of functions whose calling conventions are indicated below. A separate copy of these functions is loaded with each of processes 2, 3, and 4.

Each access method must do two things to support the following calls. First, it must provide some linear ordering of the tuples in a relation so that the concept of "next tuple" is well defined. Second, it must assign to each tuple a unique tuple-id (TID).

The nine implemented calls are as follows:

(a) OPENR(descriptor, mode, relation_name)

Before a relation may be accessed it must be "opened." This function opens the UNIX file for the relation and fills in a "descriptor" with information about the relation from the RELATION and ATTRIBUTE catalogs. The descriptor (storage for which must be declared in the calling routine) is used in subsequent calls on AMI routines as an input parameter to indicate which relation is involved. Consequently, the AMI data accessing routines need not themselves check the system catalogs for the description of a relation. "Mode" specifies whether the relation is being opened for update or for retrieval only.

(b) GET(descriptor, tid, limit_tid, tuple, next_flag)

This function retrieves into "tuple," a single tuple from the relation indicated by "descriptor." "Tid" and "limit_tid" are tuple identifiers. There are two modes of retrieval, "scan" and "direct." In "scan" mode GET is intended to be called successively to retrieve all tuples within a range of tuple-ids. An initial value of "tid" sets the low end of the range desired and "limit_tid" sets the high end. Each time GET is called with "next-flag" = TRUE, the tuple following "tid" is retrieved and its tuple-id is placed into "tid" in readiness for the next call. Reaching "limit_tid" is indicated by a special return code. The initial settings of "tid" and "limit_tid" are done by calling the FIND function. In "direct" mode ("next_flag" = FALSE), GET retrieves the tuple with tuple-id = "tid."

(c) FIND(descriptor, key, tid, key_type)

When called with a negative "key-type," FIND returns in "tid" the lowest tuple-id on the lowest page which could possibly contain tuples matching the key supplied. Analogously, the highest tuple-id is returned when "key-type" is positive. The objective is to restrict the scan of a relation by eliminating tuples from consideration which are known from their placement not to satisfy a given qualification.

"Key-type" also indicates (through its absolute value) whether the key, if supplied, is an EXACTKEY or a RANGEKEY. Different criteria for matching are applied in each case. An EXACTKEY matches only those tuples containing exactly the value of the key supplied. A RANGEKEY represents the low (or high) end of a range of possible key values and thus matches any tuple with a key value greater than or equal to (or less than or equal to) the key supplied. Note that only with an order preserving storage structure can a RANGEKEY be used to successfully restrict a scan.

In cases where the storage structure of the relation is incompatible with the "key-type," the "tid" returned will be as if no key were supplied (that is, the lowest or highest tuple in the relation). Calls to FIND invariably occur in pairs, to obtain the two tuple-ids which establish the low and high ends of the scan done in subsequent calls to GET.

Two functions are available for determining the access characteristics of the storage structure of a primary data relation or secondary index, respectively.

(d) PARAMD(descriptor, access_characteristics_structure)

(e) PARAMI(index-descriptor, access_characteristics_structure)

The "access-characteristics-structure" is filled in with information regarding the type of key which may be utilized to restrict the scan of a given relation. It indicates whether exact key values or ranges of key values can be used, and whether a partially specified key may be used. This determines the "key-type" used in a subsequent call to FIND. The ordering of domains in the key is also indicated. These two functions allow the access optimization routines to be coded independently of the specific storage structures currently implemented.

Other AMI functions provide a facility for updating relations.

(f) INSERT(descriptor, tuple)

The tuple is added to the relation in its "proper" place according to its key value and the storage mode of the relation.

(g) REPLACE(descriptor, tid, new_tuple)

(h) DELETE(descriptor, tid)

The tuple indicated by "tid" is either replaced by new values or deleted from the relation altogether. The tuple-id of the affected tuple will have been obtained by a previous GET.

Finally, when all access to a relation is complete it must be closed:

(i) CLOSER(descriptor)

This closes the relation's UNIX file and rewrites the information in the descriptor back into the system catalogs if there has been any change.

3.5 Addition of New Access Methods

One of the goals of the AMI design was to insulate higher level software from the actual functioning of the access methods, thereby making it easier to add different ones. It is anticipated that users with special requirements will take advantage of this feature.

In order to add a new access method, one need only extend the AMI routines to handle the new case. If the new method uses the same page layout and TID scheme, only FIND, PARAMI, and PARAMD need to be extended. Otherwise new procedures to perform the mapping of TIDs to physical file locations must be supplied for use by GET, INSERT, REPLACE, and DELETE.

4. THE STRUCTURE OF PROCESS 2

Process 2 contains four main components:

(a) a lexical analyzer;
(b) a parser (written in YACC [19]);
(c) concurrency control routines;
(d) query modification routines to support protection, views, and integrity control (at present only partially implemented).

Since (a) and (b) are designed and implemented along fairly standard lines, only (c) and (d) will be discussed in detail. The output of the parsing process is a tree structured representation of the input query used as the internal form in subsequent processing. Furthermore, the qualification portion of the query has been converted to an equivalent Boolean expression in conjunctive normal form. In this form the query tree is then ready to undergo what has been termed "query modification."

4.1 Query Modification

Query modification includes adding integrity and protection predicates to the original query and changing references to virtual relations into references to the appropriate physical relations. At the present time only a simple integrity scheme has been implemented.

In [27] algorithms of several levels of complexity are presented for performing integrity control on updates. In the present system only the simplest case, involving single-variable, aggregate free integrity assertions, has been implemented, as described in detail in [23].

Briefly, integrity assertions are entered in the form of QUEL qualification clauses to be applied to interactions updating the relation over which the variable in the assertion ranges. A parse tree is created for the qualification and a representation of this tree is stored in the INTEGRITY catalog together with an indication of the relation and the specific domains involved. At query modification time, updates are checked for any possible integrity assertions on the affected domains. Relevant assertions are retrieved, rebuilt into tree form, and grafted onto the update tree so as to AND the assertions with the existing qualification of the interaction.

Algorithms for the support of views are also given in [27]. Basically a view is a virtual relation defined in terms of relations which physically exist. Only the view definition will be stored, and it will be indicated to INGRES by a DEFINE command. This command will have a syntax identical to that of a RETRIEVE statement. Thus legal views will be those relations which it is possible to materialize by a RETRIEVE statement. They will be allowed in INGRES to support EQUEL programs written for obsolete versions of the database and for user convenience.

Protection will be handled according to the algorithm described in [25]. Like integrity control, this algorithm involves adding qualifications to the user's interaction. The details of the implementation (which is in progress) are given in [28], which also includes a discussion of the mechanisms being implemented to physically protect INGRES files from tampering in any way other than by executing the INGRES object code. Last, [28] distinguishes the INGRES protection scheme from the one based on views in [5] and indicates the rationale behind its use.

In the remainder of this section we give an example of query modification at work.

Suppose at a previous point in time all employees in the EMPLOYEE relation were under 30 and had no manager recorded. If an EQUEL program had been written for this previous version of EMPLOYEE which retrieved ages of employees coded into 5 bits, it would now fail for employees over 31.

If one wishes to use the above program without modification, then the following view must be used:

```
RANGE OF E IS EMPLOYEE
DEFINE OLDEMP (E.NAME, E.DEPT, E.SALARY, E.AGE)
WHERE   E.AGE < 30
```

Suppose that all employees in the EMPLOYEE relation must make more than $8000. This can be expressed by the integrity constraint:

```
RANGE OF E IS EMPLOYEE
INTEGRITY CONSTRAINT IS E.SALARY > 8000
```

Last, suppose each person is only authorized to alter salaries of employees whom he manages. This is expressed as follows:

```
RANGE OF E IS EMPLOYEE
PROTECT EMPLOYEE FOR ALL (E.SALARY; E.NAME)
WHERE   E.MANAGER = *
```

The * is a surrogate for the logon name of the current UNIX user of INGRES. The semicolon separates updatable from nonupdatable (but visible) domains.

Suppose Smith through an EQUEL program or from the terminal monitor issues the following interaction:

```
RANGE OF L IS OLDEMP
REPLACE L(SALARY = .9*L.SALARY)
WHERE  L.NAME = "Brown"
```

This is an update on a view. Hence the view algorithm in [27] will first be applied to yield:

```
RANGE OF E IS EMPLOYEE
REPLACE E(SALARY = .9*E.SALARY)
WHERE  E.NAME = "Brown"
AND  E.AGE < 30
```

Note Brown is only in OLDEMP if he is under 30. Now the integrity algorithm in [27] must be applied to ensure that Brown's salary is not being cut to as little as $8000. This involves modifying the interaction to:

```
RANGE OF E IS EMPLOYEE
REPLACE E(SALARY = .9*E.SALARY)
WHERE  E.NAME = "Brown"
   AND  E.AGE < 30
   AND  .9*E.SALARY > $8000
```

Since .9*E.SALARY will be Brown's salary after the update, the added qualification ensures this will be more than $8000.

Last, the protection algorithm of [28] is applied to yield:

```
RANGE OF E IS EMPLOYEE
REPLACE E(SALARY = .9*E.SALARY)
WHERE  E.NAME = "Brown"
   AND  E.AGE < 30
   AND  .9*E.SALARY > $8000
   AND  E.MANAGER = "Smith"
```

Notice that in all three cases more qualification is ANDed onto the user's interaction. The view algorithm must in addition change tuple variables.

In all cases the qualification is obtained from (or is an easy modification of) predicates stored in the VIEW, INTEGRITY, and PROTECTION relations. The tree representation of the interaction is simply modified to AND these qualifications (which are all stored in parsed form).

It should be clearly noted that only one-variable, aggregate free integrity assertions are currently supported. Moreover, even this feature is not in the released version of INGRES. The code for both concurrency control and integrity control will not fit into process 2 without exceeding 64K words. The decision was made to release a system with concurrency control.

The INGRES designers are currently adding a fifth process (process 2.5) to hold concurrency and query modification routines. On PDP 11/45s and 11/70s that have a 128K address space this extra process will not be required.

4.2 Concurrency Control

In any multiuser system provisions must be included to ensure that multiple concurrent updates are executed in a manner such that some level of data integrity can be guaranteed. The following two updates illustrate the problem.

```
      RANGE OF E IS EMPLOYEE
U1    REPLACE E(DEPT = "toy")
        WHERE E.DEPT = "candy"

      RANGE OF F IS EMPLOYEE
U2    REPLACE F(DEPT = "candy")
        WHERE F.DEPT = "toy"
```

If U1 and U2 are executed concurrently with no controls, some employees may end up in each department and the particular result may not be repeatable if the database is backed up and the interactions reexecuted.

The control which must be provided is to guarantee that some database operation is "atomic" (occurs in such a fashion that it *appears* instantaneous and before or after any other database operation). This atomic unit will be called a "transaction."

In INGRES there are five basic choices available for defining a transaction:

(a) something smaller than one INGRES command;
(b) one INGRES command;
(c) a collection of INGRES commands with no intervening C code;
(d) a collection of INGRES commands with C code but no system calls;
(e) an arbitrary EQUEL program.

If option (a) is chosen, INGRES could not guarantee that two concurrently executing update commands would give the same result as if they were executed sequentially (in either order) in one collection of INGRES processes. In fact, the outcome could fail to be repeatable, as noted in the example above. This situation is clearly undesirable.

Option (e) is, in the opinion of the INGRES designers, impossible to support. The following transaction could be declared in an EQUEL program.

```
BEGIN TRANSACTION
    FIRST QUEL UPDATE
    SYSTEM CALLS TO CREATE AND DESTROY FILES
    SYSTEM CALLS TO FORK A SECOND COLLECTION OF INGRES PROCESSES
        TO WHICH COMMANDS ARE PASSED
    SYSTEM CALLS TO READ FROM A TERMINAL
    SYSTEM CALLS TO READ FROM A TAPE
    SECOND QUEL UPDATE (whose form depends on previous two system calls)
END TRANSACTION
```

Suppose T1 is the above transaction and runs concurrently with a transaction T2 involving commands of the same form. The second update of each transaction may well conflict with the first update of the other. Note that there is no way to tell a priori that T1 and T2 conflict, since the form of the second update is not known in advance. Hence a deadlock situation can arise which can only be resolved by aborting one transaction (an undesirable policy in the eyes of the INGRES designers) or attempting to back out one transaction. The overhead of backing out through the intermediate system calls appears prohibitive (if it is possible at all).

Restricting a transaction to have no system calls (and hence no I/O) cripples the power of a transaction in order to make deadlock resolution possible. This was judged undesirable.

For example, the following transaction requires such system calls:

BEGIN TRANSACTION
QUEL RETRIEVE to find all flights on a particular day from San Francisco to Los Angeles with space available.
Display flights and times to user.
Wait for user to indicate desired flight.
QUEL REPLACE to reserve a seat on the flight of the user's choice.
END TRANSACTION

If the above set of commands is not a transaction, then space on a flight may not be available when the REPLACE is executed even though it was when the RETRIEVE occurred.

Since it appears impossible to support multi-QUEL statement transactions (except in a crippled form), the INGRES designers have chosen Option (b), one QUEL statement, as a transaction.

Option (c) can be handled by a straightforward extension of the algorithms to follow and will be implemented if there is sufficient user demand for it. This option can support "triggers" [2] and may prove useful.

Supporting Option (d) would considerably increase system complexity for what is perceived to be a small generalization. Moreover, it would be difficult to enforce in the EQUEL translator unless the translator parsed the entire C language.

The implementation of (b) or (c) can be achieved by physical locks on data items, pages, tuples, domains, relations, etc. [12] or by predicate locks [26]. The current implementation is by relatively crude physical locks (on domains of a relation) and avoids deadlock by not allowing an interaction to proceed to process 3 until it can lock all required resources. Because of a problem with the current design of the REPLACE access method call, all domains of a relation must currently be locked (i.e. a whole relation is locked) to perform an update. This situation will soon be rectified.

The choice of avoiding deadlock rather than detecting and resolving it is made primarily for implementation simplicity.

The choice of a crude locking unit reflects our environment where core storage for a large lock table is not available. Our current implementation uses a LOCK relation into which a tuple for each lock requested is inserted. This entire relation is physically locked and then interrogated for conflicting locks. If none exist, all needed locks are inserted. If a conflict exists, the concurrency processor "sleeps" for a fixed interval and then tries again. The necessity to lock the entire relation and to sleep for a fixed interval results from the absence of semaphores (or an equivalent mechanism) in UNIX. Because concurrency control can have high overhead as currently implemented, it can be turned off.

The INGRES designers are considering writing a device driver (a clean extension to UNIX routinely written for new devices) to alleviate the lack of semaphores. This driver would simply maintain core tables to implement desired synchronization and physical locking in UNIX.

The locks are held by the concurrency processor until a termination message is received on pipe E. Only then does it delete its locks.

In the future we plan to experimentally implement a crude (and thereby low CPU overhead) version of the predicate locking scheme described in [26]. Such an approach may provide considerable concurrency at an acceptable overhead in lock table space and CPU time, although such a statement is highly speculative.

To conclude this section, we briefly indicate the reasoning behind not sorting a page and its overflow pages in the "ISAM-like" access method. This topic is also discussed in [17].

The proposed device driver for locking in UNIX must at least ensure that read-modify-write of a single UNIX page is an atomic operation. Otherwise, INGRES would still be required to lock the whole LOCK relation to insert locks. Moreover, any proposed predicate locking scheme could not function without such an atomic operation. If the lock unit is a UNIX page, then INGRES can insert and delete a tuple from a relation by holding only one lock at a time if a primary page and its overflow page are unordered. However, maintenance of the sort order of these pages may require the access method to lock more than one page when it inserts a tuple. Clearly deadlock may be possible given concurrent updates, and the size of the lock table in the device driver is not predictable. To avoid both problems these pages remain unsorted.

5. PROCESS 3

As noted in Section 2, this process performs the following two functions, which will be discussed in turn:

(a) Decomposition of queries involving more than one variable into sequences of one-variable queries. Partial results are accumulated until the entire query is evaluated. This program is called DECOMP. It also turns any updates into the appropriate queries to isolate qualifying tuples and spools modifications into a special file for deferred update.

(b) Processing of single-variable queries. The program is called the one-variable query processor (OVQP).

5.1 DECOMP

Because INGRES allows interactions which are defined on the crossproduct of perhaps several relations, efficient execution of this step is of crucial importance in searching as small a portion of the appropriate crossproduct space as possible. DECOMP uses three techniques in processing interactions. We describe each technique, and then give the actual algorithm implemented followed by an example which illustrates all features. Finally we indicate the role of a more sophisticated decomposition scheme under design.

(a) Tuple substitution. The basic technique used by DECOMP to reduce a query to fewer variables is tuple substitution. One variable (out of possibly many) in the query is selected for substitution. The AMI language is used to scan the relation associated with the variable one tuple at a time. For each tuple the values of domains in that relation are substituted into the query. In the resulting modified query, all previous references to the substituted variable have now been replaced by values (constants) and the query has thus been reduced to one less variable. Decomposition is repeated (recursively) on the modified query until only one variable remains, at which point the OVQP is called to continue processing.

(b) One-variable detachment. If the qualification Q of the query is of the form

$Q_1(V_1)$ AND $Q_2(V_1, \ldots, V_n)$

for some tuple variable V_1, the following two steps can be executed:

(1) Issue the query
RETRIEVE INTO W (TL[V_1])
WHERE $Q_1[V_1]$

Here TL[V_1] are those domains required in the remainder of the query. Note that this is a one-variable query and may be passed directly to OVQP.

(2) Replace R_1, the relation over which V_1 ranges, by W in the range declaration and delete $Q_1[V_1]$ from Q.

The query formed in step 1 is called a "one-variable, detachable subquery," and the technique for forming and executing it is called "one-variable detachment" (OVD). This step has the effect of reducing the size of the relation over which V_1 ranges by restriction and projection. Hence it may reduce the complexity of the processing to follow.

Moreover, the opportunity exists in the process of creating new relations through OVD, to choose storage structures, and particularly keys, which will prove helpful in further processing.

(c) Reformatting. When a tuple variable is selected for substitution, a large number of queries, each with one less variable, will be executed. If (b) is a possible operation after the substitution for some remaining variable V_1, then the relation over which V_1 ranges, R_1, can be reformatted to have domains used in $Q_1(V_1)$ as a key. This will expedite (b) each time it is executed during tuple substitution.

We can now state the complete decomposition algorithm. After doing so, we illustrate all steps with an example.

Step 1. If the number of variables in the query is 0 or 1, call OVQP and then return; else go on to step 2.

Step 2. Find all variables, $\{V_1, \ldots, V_n\}$, for which the query contains a one-variable clause. Perform OVD to create new ranges for each of these variables. The new relation for each variable V_i is stored as a hash file with key K_i chosen as follows:

2.1. For each j select from the remaining multivariable clauses in the query the collection, C_{ij}, which have the form $V_i \cdot d_i = V_j \cdot d_j$, where d_i, d_j are domains of V_i and V_j.

2.2. From the key K_i to be the concatenation of domains $d_{i1}, d_{i2}, \ldots$ of V_i appearing in clauses in C_{ij}.

2.3. If more than one j exists, for which C_{ij} is nonempty, one C_{ij} is chosen arbitrarily for forming the key. If C_{ij} is empty for all j, the relation is stored as an unsorted table.

Step 3. Choose the variable V_s with the smallest number of tuples as the next one for which to perform tuple substitution.

Step 4. For each tuple variable V_j for which C_{js} is nonnull, reformat if necessary the storage structure of the relation R_j over which it ranges so that the key of R_j is the concatenation of domains $d_{j1}, \ldots$ appearing in C_{js}. This ensures that when the clauses in C_{js} become one-variable after substituting for V_s, subsequent calls to OVQP to restrict further the range of V_j will be done as efficiently as possible.

Step 5. Iterate the following steps over all tuples in the range of the variable selected in step 3 and then return:

5.1. Substitute values from tuple into query.

5.2. Invoke decomposition algorithm recursively on a copy of resulting query which now has been reduced by one variable.

5.3. Merge the results from 5.2 with those of previous iterations.

We use the following query to illustrate the algorithm:

```
RANGE OF E, M IS EMPLOYEE
RANGE OF D IS DEPT
RETRIEVE (E.NAME)
WHERE  E.SALARY    > M.SALARY   AND
       E.MANAGER   = M.NAME     AND
       E.DEPT      = D.DEPT     AND
       D.FLOOR#    = 1          AND
       E.AGE       > 40
```

This request is for employees over 40 on the first floor who earn more than their manager.

LEVEL 1

Step 1. Query is not one variable.

Step 2. Issue the two queries:

```
RANGE OF D IS DEPT
RETRIEVE INTO T1(D.DEPT)                                          (1)
WHERE  D.FLOOR# = 1

RANGE OF E IS EMPLOYEE
RETRIEVE INTO T2(E.NAME, E.SALARY, E.MANAGER, E.DEPT)             (2)
WHERE E.AGE > 40
```

T1 is stored hashed on DEPT; however, the algorithm must choose arbitrarily between hashing T2 on MANAGER or DEPT. Suppose it chooses MANAGER. The original query now becomes:

```
RANGE OF D IS T1
RANGE OF E IS T2
RANGE OF M IS EMPLOYEE
RETRIEVE (E.NAME)
WHERE  E.SALARY    > M.SALARY   AND
       E.MANAGER   = M.NAME     AND
       E.DEPT      = D.DEPT
```

Step 3. Suppose T1 has smallest cardinality. Hence D is chosen for substitution.

Step 4. Reformat T2 to be hashed on DEPT; the guess chosen in step 2 above was a poor one.

Step 5. Iterate for each tuple in T1 and then quit:

5.1 Substitute value for D. DEPT yielding

```
RANGE OF E IS T1
RANGE OF M IS EMPLOYEE
RETRIEVE (E.NAME)
WHERE  E.SALARY > M.SALARY      AND
       E.MANAGER = M.NAME       AND
       E.DEPT      = value
```

5.2. Start at step 1 with the above query as input (Level 2 below).

5.3. Cumulatively merge results as they are obtained.

LEVEL 2

Step 1. Query is not one variable.

Step 2. Issue the query

```
RANGE OF E IS T2
RETRIEVE INTO T3 (E.NAME, E.SALARY, E.NAME)        (3)
WHERE  E.DEPT = value
```

T3 is constructed hashed on MANAGER. T2 in step 4 in Level 1 above is reformatted so that this query (which will be issued once for each tuple in T1) will be done efficiently by OVQP. Hopefully the cost of reformatting is small compared to the savings at this step. What remains is

```
RANGE OF E IS T3
RANGE IF M IS EMPLOYEE
RETRIEVE (E.NAME)
WHERE  E.SALARY    > M.SALARY  AND
       E.MANAGER = M.NAME
```

Step 3. T3 has less tuples than EMPLOYEE; therefore choose T3.

Step 4. [unnecessary]

Step 5. Iterate for each tuple in T3 and then return to previous level:

5.1. Substitute values for E.NAME, E.SALARY, and E.MANAGER, yielding

```
RANGE OF M IS EMPLOYEE
RETRIEVE (VALUE 1)                                 (4)
WHERE  Value2 > M.SALARY  AND
       Value3 = M.NAME
```

5.2. Start at step 1 with this query as input (Level 3 below).

5.3. Cumulatively merge results as obtained.

LEVEL 3

Step 1. Query has one variable; invoke OVQP and then return to previous level.

The algorithm thus decomposes the original query into the four prototype, one-variable queries labeled (1)–(4), some of which are executed repetitively with different constant values and with results merged appropriately. Queries (1) and (2) are executed once, query (3) once for each tuple in T1, and query (4) the number of times equal to the number of tuples in T1 times the number of tuples in T3.

The following comments on the algorithm are appropriate.

(a) OVD is almost always assured of speeding processing. Not only is it possible to choose the storage structure of a temporary relation wisely, but also the cardinality of this relation may be much less than the one it replaces as the range for a tuple variable. It only fails if little or no reduction takes place and reformatting is unproductive.

It should be noted that a temporary relation is created rather than a list of qualifying tuple-id's. The basic tradeoff is that OVD must copy qualifying tuples but can remove duplicates created during the projection. Storing tuple-id's avoids the copy operation at the expense of reaccessing qualifying tuples and retaining duplicates. It is clear that cases exist where each strategy is superior. The INGRES designers have chosen OVD because it does not appear to offer worse performance than the alternative, allows a more accurate choice of the variable with the smallest range in step 3 of the algorithm above, and results in cleaner code.

(b) Tuple substitution is done when necessary on the variable associated with the smallest number of tuples. This has the effect of reducing the number of eventual calls on OVQP.

(c) Reformatting is done (if necessary) with the knowledge that it will usually replace a collection of complete sequential scans of a relation by a collection of limited scans. This almost always reduces processing time.

(d) It is believed that this algorithm efficiently handles a large class of interactions. Moreover, the algorithm does not require excessive CPU overhead to perform. There are, however, cases where a more elaborate algorithm is indicated. The following comment applies to such cases.

(e) Suppose that we have two or more strategies ST_0, ST_1, ..., ST_n, each one being better than the previous one but also requiring a greater overhead. Suppose further that we begin an interaction on ST_0 and run it for an amount of time equal to a fraction of the estimated overhead of ST_1. At the end of that time, by simply counting the number of tuples of the first substitution variable which have already been processed, we can get an estimate for the total processing time using ST_0. If this is significantly greater than the overhead of ST_1, then we switch to ST_1. Otherwise we stay and complete processing the interaction using ST_0. Obviously, the procedure can be repeated on ST_1 to call ST_2 if necessary, and so forth.

The algorithm detailed in this section may be thought of as ST_0. A more sophisticated algorithm is currently under development [30].

5.2 One-Variable Query Processor (OVQP)

This module is concerned solely with the efficient accessing of tuples from a single relation given a particular one-variable query. The initial portion of this program, known as STRATEGY, determines what key (if any) may be used profitably to access the relation, what value(s) of that key will be used in calls to the AMI routine FIND, and whether access may be accomplished directly through the AMI to the storage structure of the primary relation itself or if a secondary index on the relation should be used. If access is to be through a secondary index, then STRATEGY must choose which *one* of possibly many indices to use.

Tuples are then retrieved according to the access strategy selected and are processed by the SCAN portion of OVQP. These routines evaluate each tuple against the qualification part of the query, create target list values for qualifying tuples, and dispose of the target list appropriately.

Since SCAN is relatively straightforward, we discuss only the policy decisions made in STRATEGY.

First STRATEGY examines the qualification for clauses which specify the value of a domain, i.e. clauses of the form

V.domain op constant

or

constant op *V*.domain

where "op" is one of the set {=, <, >, ≤, ≥}. Such clauses are termed "simple" clauses and are organized into a list. The constants in simple clauses will determine the key values input to FIND to limit the ensuing scan.

Obviously a nonsimple clause may be equivalent to a simple one. For example, E.SALARY/2 = 10000 is equivalent to E.SALARY = 20000. However, recognizing and converting such clauses requires a general algebraic symbol manipulator. This issue has been avoided by ignoring all nonsimple clauses.

STRATEGY must select one of two accessing strategies: (a) issuing two AMI FIND commands on the primary relation followed by a sequential scan of the relation (using GET in "scan" mode) between the limits set, or (b) issuing two AMI FIND commands on some index relation followed by a sequential scan of the index between the limits set. For each tuple retrieved the "pointer" domain is obtained; this is simply the tuple-id of a tuple in the primary relation. This tuple is fetched (using GET in "direct" mode) and processed.

To make the choice, the access possibilities available must be determined. Keying information about the primary relation is obtained using the AMI function PARAMD. Names of indices are obtained from the INDEX catalog and keying information about indices is obtained with the function PARAMI.

Further, a compatability between the available access possibilities and the specification of key values by simple clauses must be established. A hashed relation requires that a simple clause specify equality as the operator in order to be useful; for combined (multidomain) keys, all domains must be specified. ISAM structures, on the other hand, allow range specifications; additionally, a combined ISAM key requires only that the most significant domains be specified.

STRATEGY checks for such a compatability according to the following priority order of access possibilities: (1) hashed primary relation, (2) hashed index, (3) ISAM primary relation, (4) ISAM index. The rationale for this ordering is related to the expected number of page accesses required to retrieve a tuple from the source relation in each case. In the following analysis the effect of overflow pages is ignored (on the assumption that the four access possibilities would be equally affected).

In case (1) the key value provided locates a desired source tuple in one access via calculation involving a hashing function. In case (2) the key value similarly locates an appropriate index relation tuple in one access, but an additional access is required to retrieve the proper primary relation tuple. For an ISAM-structured scheme a directory must be examined. This lookup itself incurs at least one access but possibly more if the directory is multilevel. Then the tuple itself must be accessed. Thus case (3) requires at least two (but possibly more) total accesses. In case (4) the use of an index necessitates yet another access in the primary relation, making the total at least three.

To illustrate STRATEGY, we indicate what happens to queries (1)–(4) from Section 5.1.

Suppose EMPLOYEE is an ISAM relation with a key of NAME, while DEPT is hashed on FLOOR#. Moreover a secondary index for AGE exists which is hashed on AGE, and one for SALARY exists which uses ISAM with a key of SALARY.

Query (1): One simple clause exists (D.FLOOR# = 2). Hence Strategy (a) is applied against the hashed primary relation.

Query (2): One simple clause exists (E.AGE > 40). However, it is not usable to limit the scan on a hashed index. Hence a complete (unkeyed) scan of EMPLOYEE is required. Were the index for AGE an ISAM relation, then Strategy (b) would be used on this index.

Query (3): One simple clause exists and T1 has been reformatted to allow Strategy (a) against the hashed primary relation.

Query (4): Two simple clauses exist (value2 > M.SALARY; value3 = M.NAME). Strategy (a) is available on the hashed primary relation, as is Strategy (b) for the ISAM index. The algorithm chooses Strategy (a).

6. UTILITIES IN PROCESS 4

6.1 Implementation of Utility Commands

We have indicated in Section 1 several database utilities available to users. These commands are organized into several overlay programs as noted previously. Bringing the required overlay into core as needed is done in a straightforward way.

Most of the utilities update or read the system relations using AMI calls. MODIFY contains a sort routine which puts tuples in collating sequence according to the concatenation of the desired keys (which need not be of the same data type). Pages are initially loaded to approximately 80 percent of capacity. The sort routine is a recursive N-way merge-sort where N is the maximum number of files process 4 can have open at once (currently eight). The index building occurs in an obvious way. To convert to hash structures, MODIFY must specify the number of primary pages to be allocated. This parameter is used by the AMI in its hash scheme (which is a standard modulo division method).

It should be noted that a user who creates an empty hash relation using the CREATE command and then copies a large UNIX file into it using COPY creates a very inefficient structure. This is because a relatively small default number of primary pages will have been specified by CREATE, and overflow chains will be long. A better strategy is to COPY into an unsorted table so that MODIFY can subsequently make a good guess at the number of primary pages to allocate.

6.2 Deferred Update and Recovery

Any updates (APPEND, DELETE, REPLACE) are processed by writing the tuples to be added, changed, or modified into a temporary file. When process 3 finishes, it calls process 4 to actually perform the modifications requested and any updates to secondary indices which may be required as a final step in processing. Deferred update is done for four reasons.

(a) Secondary index considerations. Suppose the following QUEL statement is executed:

```
RANGE OF E IS EMPLOYEE
REPLACE E(SALARY = 1.1•E.SALARY)
WHERE  E.SALARY > 20000
```

Suppose further that there is a secondary index on the salary domain and the primary relation is keyed on another domain.

OVQP, in finding the employees who qualify for the raise, will use the secondary index. If one employee qualifies and his tuple is modified and the secondary index updated, then the scan of the secondary index will find his tuple a second time since it has been moved forward. (In fact, his tuple will be found an arbitrary number of times.) Either secondary indexes cannot be used to identify qualifying tuples when range qualifications are present (a rather unnatural restriction), or secondary indices must be updated in deferred mode.

(b) Primary relation considerations. Suppose the QUEL statement

```
RANGE OF E, M IS EMPLOYEE
REPLACE E(SALARY = .9*E.SALARY)
Where  E.MGR     = M.NAME  AND
       E.SALARY > M.SALARY
```

is executed for the following EMPLOYEE relation:

NAME	SALARY	MANAGER
Smith	10K	Jones
Jones	8K	
Brown	9.5K	Smith

Logically Smith should get the pay cut and Brown should not. However, if Smith's tuple is updated before Brown is checked for the pay cut, Brown will qualify. This undesirable situation must be avoided by deferred update.

(c) Functionality of updates. Suppose the following QUEL statement is executed:

```
RANGE OF E, M IS EMPLOYEE
REPLACE E(SALARY = M.SALARY)
```

This update attempts to assign to each employee the salary of every other employee, i.e. a single data item is to be replaced by multiple values. Stated differently, the REPLACE statement does not specify a function. In certain cases (such as a REPLACE involving only one tuple variable) functionality is guaranteed. However, in general the functionality of an update is data dependent. This nonfunctionality can only be checked if deferred update is performed.

To do so, the deferred update processor must check for duplicate TIDs in REPLACE calls (which requires sorting or hashing the update file). This potentially expensive operation does not exist in the current implementation, but will be optionally available in the future.

(d) Recovery considerations. The deferred update file provides a log of updates to be made. Recovery is provided upon system crash by the RESTORE command. In this case the deferred update routine is requested to destroy the temporary file if it has not yet started processing it. If it has begun processing, it reprocesses the entire update file in such a way that the effect is the same as if it were processed exactly once from start to finish.

Hence the update is "backed out" if deferred updating has not yet begun; otherwise it is processed to conclusion. The software is designed so the update file can be optionally spooled onto tape and recovered from tape. This added feature should soon be operational.

If a user from the terminal monitor (or a C program) wishes to stop a command he can issue a "break" character. In this case all processes reset except the deferred update program, which recovers in the same manner as above.

All update commands do deferred update; however the INGRES utilities have not yet been modified to do likewise. When this has been done, INGRES will recover from all crashes which leave the disk intact. In the meantime there can be disk-intact crashes which cannot be recovered in this manner (if they happen in such a way that the system catalogs are left inconsistent).

The INGRES "superuser" can checkpoint a database onto tape using the UNIX backup scheme. Since INGRES logs all interactions, a consistent system can always be obtained, albeit slowly, by restoring the last checkpoint and running the log of interactions (or the tape of deferred updates if it exists).

It should be noted that deferred update is a very expensive operation. One INGRES user has elected to have updates performed directly in process 3, cognizant that he must avoid executing interactions which will run incorrectly. Like checks for functionality, direct update may be optionally available in the future. Of course, a different recovery scheme must be implemented.

7. CONCLUSION AND FUTURE EXTENSIONS

The system described herein is in use at about fifteen installations. It forms the basis of an accounting system, a system for managing student records, a geodata system, a system for managing cable trouble reports and maintenance calls for a large telephone company, and assorted other smaller applications. These applications have been running for periods of up to nine months.

7.1 Performance

At this time no detailed performance measurements have been made, as the current version (labeled Version 5) has been operational for less than two months. We have instrumented the code and are in the process of collecting such measurements.

The sizes (in bytes) of the processes in INGRES are indicated below. Since the access methods are loaded with processes 2 and 3 and with many of the utilities, their contribution to the respective process sizes has been noted separately.

access methods (AM)	11K
terminal monitor	10K
EQUEL	30K + AM
process 2	45K + AM
process 3 (query processor)	45K + AM
utilities (8 overlays)	160K + AM

7.2 User Feedback

The feedback from internal and external users has been overwhelmingly positive. In this section we indicate features that have been suggested for future systems.

(a) Improved performance. Earlier versions of INGRES were very slow; the current version should alleviate this problem.

(b) Recursion. QUEL does not support recursion, which must be tediously programmed in C using the precompiler; recursion capability has been suggested as a desired extension.

(c) Other language extensions. These include user defined functions (especially counters), multiple target lists for a single qualification statement, and if-then-else control structures in QUEL; these features may presently be programmed, but only very inefficiently, using the precompiler.

(d) Report generator. PRINT is a very primitive report generator and the need for augmented facilities in this area is clear; it should be written in EQUEL.

(e) Bulk copy. The COPY routine fails to handle easily all situations that arise.

7.3 Future Extensions

Noted throughout the paper are areas where system improvement is in progress, planned, or desired by users. Other areas of extension include: (a) a multicomputer system version of INGRES to operate on distributed databases; (b) further performance enhancements; (c) a higher level user language including recursion and user defined functions; (d) better data definition and integrity features; and (e) a database administrator advisor.

The database administrator advisor program would run at idle priority and issue queries against a statistics relation to be kept by INGRES. It could then offer advice to a DBA concerning the choice of access methods and the selection of indices. This topic is discussed further in [16].

ACKNOWLEDGMENT

The following persons have played active roles in the design and implementation of INGRES: Eric Allman, Rick Berman, Jim Ford, Angela Go, Nancy McDonald, Peter Rubinstein, Iris Schoenberg, Nick Whyte, Carol Williams, Karel Youssefi, and Bill Zook.

REFERENCES

1. ALLMAN, E., STONEBRAKER, M., AND HELD, G. Embedding a relational data sublanguage in a general purpose programming language. Proc. Conf. on Data, SIGPLAN Notices (ACM) *8*, 2 (1976), 25–35.
2. ASTRAHAN, M. M., ET AL. System R: Relational approach to database management. *ACM Trans. on Database Systems 1*, 2 (June 1976), 97–137.
3. BOYCE, R., ET AL. Specifying queries as relational expessions: SQUARE. Rep. RJ 1291, IBM Res. Lab., San Jose, Calif., Oct. 1973.
4. CHAMBERLIN, D., AND BOYCE, R. SEQUEL: A structured English query language. Proc. 1974 ACM-SIGMOD Workshop on Data Description, Access and Control, Ann Arbor, Mich., May 1974, pp. 249–264.
5. CHAMBERLIN, D., GRAY, J.N., AND TRAIGER, I.L. Views, authorization and locking in a relational data base system. Proc. AFIPS 1975 NCC, Vol. 44, AFIPS Press, Montvale, N.J., May 1975, pp. 425–430.
6. Comm. on Data Systems Languages. CODASYL Data Base Task Group Rep., ACM, New York, 1971.
7. CODD, E.F. A relational model of data for large shared data banks. *Comm. ACM 13*, 6 (June 1970), 377–387.
8. CODD, E.F. A data base sublanguage founded on the relational calculus. Proc. 1971 ACM-SIGFIDET Workshop on Data Description, Access and Control, San Diego, Calif., Nov. 1971, pp. 35–68.
9. CODD, E.F. Relational completeness of data base sublanguages. Courant Computer Science Symp. 6, May 1971, Prentice-Hall, Englewood Cliffs, N.J., pp. 65–90.
10. CODD, E.F., AND DATE, C.J. Interactive support for non-programmers, the relational and network approaches. Proc. 1974 ACM-SIGMOD Workshop on Data Description, Access and Control, Ann Arbor, Mich., May 1974.
11. DATE, C.J., AND CODD, E.F. The relational and network approaches: Comparison of the application programming interfaces. Proc. 1974 ACM-SIGMOD Workshop on Data Description, Access and Control, Vol. II, Ann Arbor, Mich., May 1974, pp. 85–113.
12. GRAY, J.N., LORIE, R.A., and PUTZOLU, G.R. Granularity of Locks in a Shared Data Base. Proc. Int. Conf. of Very Large Data Bases, Framingham, Mass., Sept. 1975, pp. 428–451. (Available from ACM, New York.)
13. GO, A., STONEBRAKER, M., AND WILLIAMS, C. An approach to implementing a geo-data system. Proc. ACM SIGGRAPH/SIGMOD Conf. for Data Bases in Interactive Design, Waterloo, Ont., Canada, Sept. 1975, pp. 67–77.
14. GOTTLIEB, D., ET AL. A classification of compression methods and their usefulness in a large data processing center. Proc. AFIPS 1975 NCC, Vol. 44, AFIPS Press, Montvale, N.J., May 1975, pp. 453–458.
15. HELD, G.D., STONEBRAKER, M., AND WONG, E. INGRES—A relational data base management system. Proc. AFIPS 1975 NCC, Vol. 44, AFIPS Press, Montvale, N.J., 1975, pp. 409–416.
16. HELD, G.D. Storage Structures for Relational Data Base Management Systems. Ph.D. Th., Dep. of Electrical Eng. and Computer Science, U. of California, Berkeley, Calif., 1975.
17. HELD, G., AND STONEBRAKER, M. *B*-trees re-examined. Submitted to a technical journal.
18. IBM CORP. OS ISAM logic. GY28-6618, IBM Corp., White Plains, N.Y., 1966.
19. JOHNSON, S.C. YACC, yet another compiler-compiler. UNIX Programmer's Manual, Bell Telephone Labs, Murray Hill, N.J., July 1974.
20. MCDONALD, N., AND STONEBRAKER, M. Cupid—The friendly query language. Proc. ACM-Pacific-75, San Francisco, Calif., April 1975, pp. 127–131.
21. MCDONALD, N. CUPID: A graphics oriented facility for support of non-programmer interactions with a data base. Ph.D. Th., Dep. of Electrical Eng. and Computer Science, U. of California, Berkeley, Calif., 1975.
22. RITCHIE, D.M., AND THOMPSON, K. The UNIX Time-sharing system. *Comm. ACM 17*, 7 (July 1974), 365–375.
23. SCHOENBERG, I. Implementation of integrity constraints in the relational data base management system, INGRES. M.S. Th., Dep. of Electrical Eng. and Computer Science, U. of California, Berkeley, Calif., 1975.
24. STONEBRAKER, M. A functional view of data independence. Proc. 1974 ACM-SIGFIDET Workshop on Data Description, Access and Control, Ann Arbor, Mich., May 1974.
25. STONEBRAKER, M., AND WONG, E. Access control in a relational data base management system by query modification. Proc. 1974 ACM Nat. Conf., San Diego, Calif., Nov. 1974, pp. 180–187.
26. STONEBRAKER, M. High level integrity assurance in relational data base systems. ERI Mem. No. M473, Electronics Res. Lab., U. of California, Berkeley, Calif., Aug. 1974.
27. STONEBRAKER, M. Implementation of integrity constraints and views by query modification. Proc. 1975 SIGMOD Workshop on Management of Data, San Jose, Calif., May 1975, pp. 65–78.
28. STONEBRAKER, M., AND RUBINSTEIN, P. The INGRES protection system. Proc. 1976 ACM National Conf., Houston, Tex., Oct. 1976 (to appear).
29. TSICHRITZIS, D. A network framework for relational implementation. Rep. CSRG-51, Computer Systems Res. Group, U. of Toronto, Toronto, Ont., Canada, Feb. 1975.
30. WONG, E., AND YOUSSEFI, K. Decomposition—A strategy for query processing. *ACM Trans. on Database Systems 1*, 3 (Sept. 1976), 223–241 (this issue).
31. ZOOK, W., ET AL. INGRES—Reference manual, 5. ERL Mem. No. M585, Electronics Res. Lab., U. of California, Berkeley, Calif., April 1976.

Received January 1976; revised April 1976

A History and Evaluation of System R

Donald D. Chamberlin
Morton M. Astrahan
Michael W. Blasgen
James N. Gray
W. Frank King
Bruce G. Lindsay
Raymond Lorie
James W. Mehl
Thomas G. Price
Franco Putzolu
Patricia Griffiths Selinger
Mario Schkolnick
Donald R. Slutz
Irving L. Traiger
Bradford W. Wade
Robert A. Yost

IBM Research Laboratory
San Jose, California

SUMMARY: System R, an experimental database system, was constructed to demonstrate that the usability advantages of the relational data model can be realized in a system with the complete function and high performance required for everyday production use. This paper describes the three principal phases of the System R project and discusses some of the lessons learned from System R about the design of relational systems and database systems in general.

1. Introduction

Throughout the history of information storage in computers, one of the most readily observable trends has been the focus on data independence. C.J. Date [27] defined data independence as "immunity of applications to change in storage structure and access strategy." Modern database systems offer data independence by providing a high-level user interface through which users deal with the information content of their data, rather than the various bits, pointers, arrays, lists, etc. which are used to represent that information. The system assumes responsibility for choosing an appropriate internal representation for the information; indeed, the representation of a given fact may change over time without users being aware of the change.

The relational data model was proposed by E.F. Codd [22] in 1970 as the next logical step in the trend toward data independence. Codd observed that conventional database systems store information in two ways: (1) by the contents of records stored in the database, and (2) by the ways in which these records are connected together. Different systems use various names for the connections among records, such as links, sets, chains, parents, etc. For example, in Figure 1(a), the fact that supplier Acme supplies bolts is represented by connections between the relevant part and supplier records. In such a system, a user frames a question, such as "What is the lowest price for bolts?", by writing a program which "navigates" through the maze of connections until it arrives at the answer to the question. The user of a "navigational" system has the burden (or opportunity) to specify exactly how the query is to be processed; the user's algorithm is then embodied in a program which is dependent on the data structure that existed at the time the program was written.

Relational database systems, as proposed by Codd, have two important properties: (1) all information is

---

Key words and phrases: database management systems, relational model, compilation, locking, recovery, access path selection, authorization
CR Categories: 3.50, 3.70, 3.72, 4.33, 4.6
Authors' address: D. D. Chamberlin et al., IBM Research Laboratory, 5600 Cottle Road, San Jose, California 95193.

represented by data values, never by any sort of "connections" which are visible to the user; (2) the system supports a very high-level language in which users can frame requests for data without specifying algorithms for processing the requests. The relational representation of the data in Figure 1(a) is shown in Figure 1(b). Information about parts is kept in a PARTS relation in which each record has a "key" (unique identifier) called PARTNO. Information about suppliers is kept in a SUPPLIERS relation keyed by SUPPNO. The information which was formerly represented by connections between records is now contained in a third relation, PRICES, in which parts and suppliers are represented by their respective keys. The question "What is the lowest price for bolts?" can be framed in a high-level language like SQL [16] as follows:

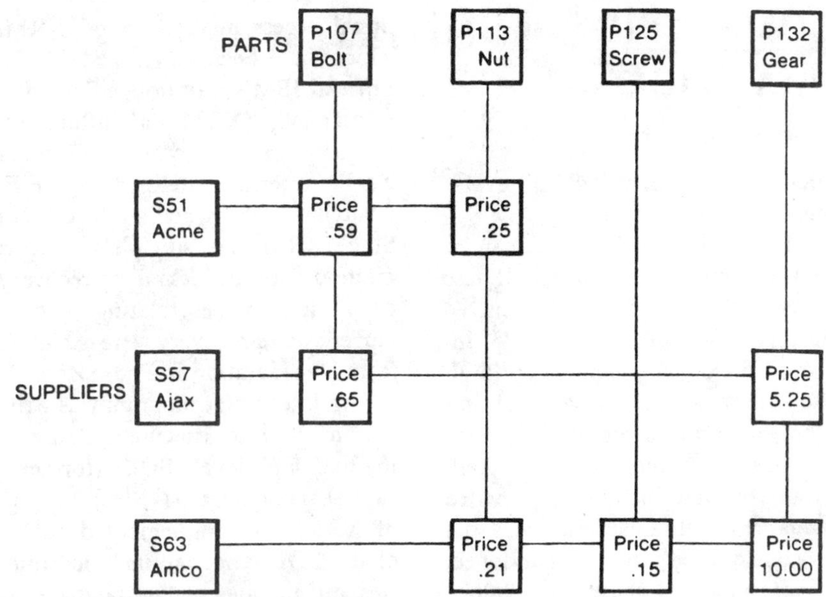

Fig. 1(a). A "Navigational" Database.

```
SELECT MIN(PRICE)
FROM   PRICES
WHERE  PARTNO IN
       (SELECT PARTNO
        FROM   PARTS
        WHERE  NAME = 'BOLT');
```

A relational system can maintain whatever pointers, indices, or other access aids it finds appropriate for processing user requests, but the user's request is not framed in terms of these access aids and is therefore not dependent on them. Therefore, the system may change its data representation and access aids periodically to adapt to changing requirements without disturbing users' existing applications.

Since Codd's original paper, the advantages of the relational data model in terms of user productivity and data independence have become widely recognized. However, as in the early days of high-level programming languages, questions are sometimes raised about whether or not an automatic system can choose as efficient an algorithm for processing a complex query as a trained programmer would. System R is an experimental system constructed at the San Jose IBM Research Laboratory to demonstrate that a relational database system can incorporate the high performance and complete function required for everyday production use.

The key goals established for System R were:

(1) To provide a high-level, nonnavigational user interface for maximum user productivity and data independence.

(2) To support different types of database use including programmed transactions, ad hoc queries, and report generation.

(3) To support a rapidly changing database environment, in which tables, indexes, views, transactions, and other objects could easily be added to and removed from the database without stopping the system.

(4) To support a population of many concurrent users, with mechanisms to protect the integrity of the database in a concurrent-update environment.

(5) To provide a means of recovering the contents of the database to a consistent state after a failure of hardware or software.

(6) To provide a flexible mechanism whereby different views of stored data can be defined and various users can be authorized to query and update these views.

(7) To support all of the above functions with a level of performance comparable to existing lower-function database systems.

Throughout the System R project, there has been a strong commitment to carry the system through to an operationally complete prototype

PARTS

PARTNO	NAME
P107	Bolt
P113	Nut
P125	Screw
P132	Gear

SUPPLIERS

SUPPNO	NAME
S51	Acme
S57	Ajax
S63	Amco

PRICES

PARTNO	SUPPNO	PRICE
P107	S51	.59
P107	S57	.65
P113	S51	.25
P113	S63	.21
P125	S63	.15
P132	S57	5.25
P132	S63	10.00

Fig. 1(b). A Relational Database.

COMPUTING PRACTICES

which could be installed and evaluated in actual user sites.

The history of System R can be divided into three phases. "Phase Zero" of the project, which occurred during 1974 and most of 1975, involved the development of the SQL user interface [14] and a quick implementation of a subset of SQL for one user at a time. The Phase Zero prototype, described in [2], provided valuable insight in several areas, but its code was eventually abandoned. "Phase One" of the project, which took place throughout most of 1976 and 1977, involved the design and construction of the full-function, multiuser version of System R. An initial system architecture was presented in [4] and subsequent updates to the design were described in [10]. "Phase Two" was the evaluation of System R in actual use. This occurred during 1978 and 1979 and involved experiments at the San Jose Research Laboratory and several other user sites. The results of some of these experiments and user experiences are described in [19–21]. At each user site, System R was installed for experimental purposes only, and not as a supported commercial product.[1]

This paper will describe the decisions which were made and the lessons learned during each of the three phases of the System R project.

2. Phase Zero: An Initial Prototype

Phase Zero of the System R project involved the quick implementation of a subset of system functions. From the beginning, it was our intention to learn what we could from this initial prototype, and then scrap the Phase Zero code before construction of the more complete version of System R. We decided to use the relational access method called XRM, which had been developed by R. Lorie at IBM's Cambridge Scientific Center [40]. (XRM was influenced, to some extent, by the "Gamma Zero" interface defined by E.F. Codd and others at San Jose [11].) Since XRM is a single-user access method without locking or recovery capabilities, issues relating to concurrency and recovery were excluded from consideration in Phase Zero.

An interpreter program was written in PL/I to execute statements in the high-level SQL (formerly SEQUEL) language [14, 16] on top of XRM. The implemented subset of the SQL language included queries and updates of the database, as well as the dynamic creation of new database relations. The Phase Zero implementation supported the "subquery" construct of SQL, but not its "join" construct. In effect, this meant that a query could search through several relations in computing its result, but the final result would be taken from a single relation.

The Phase Zero implementation was primarily intended for use as a standalone query interface by end users at interactive terminals. At the time, little emphasis was placed on issues of interfacing to host-language programs (although Phase Zero could be called from a PL/I program). However, considerable thought was given to the human factors aspects of the SQL language, and an experimental study was conducted on the learnability and usability of SQL [44].

One of the basic design decisions in the Phase Zero prototype was that the system catalog, i.e., the description of the content and structure of the database, should be stored as a set of regular relations in the database itself. This approach permits the system to keep the catalog up to date automatically as changes are made to the database, and also makes the catalog information available to the system optimzer for use in access path selection.

The structure of the Phase Zero interpreter was strongly influenced by the facilities of XRM. XRM stores relations in the form of "tuples," each of which has a unique 32-bit "tuple identifier" (TID). Since a TID contains a page number, it is possible, given a TID, to fetch the associated tuple in one page reference. However, rather than actual data values, the tuple contains pointers to the "domains" where the actual data is stored, as shown in Figure 2. Optionally, each domain may have an "inversion," which associates domain values (e.g., "Programmer") with the TIDs of tuples in which the values appear. Using the inversions, XRM makes it easy to find a list of TIDs of tuples which contain a given value. For example, in Figure 2, if inversions exist on both the JOB and LOCATION domains, XRM provides commands to create a list of TIDs of employees who are programmers, and another list of TIDs of employees who work in Evanston. If the SQL query calls for programmers who work in Evanston, these TID lists can be intersected to obtain the list of TIDs of tuples which satisfy the query, before any tuples are actually fetched.

The most challenging task in constructing the Phase Zero prototype was the design of optimizer algorithms for efficient execution of SQL statements on top of XRM. The design of the Phase Zero optimizer is given in [2]. The objective of the optimizer was to minimize the number of tuples fetched from the database in processing a query. Therefore, the optimizer made extensive use of inversions and often manipulated TID lists before beginning to fetch tuples. Since the TID lists were potentially large, they were stored as temporary objects in the database during query processing.

The results of the Phase Zero implementation were mixed. One strongly felt conclusion was that it is a very good idea, in a project the size of System R, to plan to throw away the initial implementation. On the positive side, Phase Zero demonstrated the usability of the SQL language, the feasibility of creating new tables and inversions "on the fly"

[1] The System R research prototype later evolved into SQL/Data System, a relational database management product offered by IBM in the DOS/VSE operating system environment.

and relying on an automatic optimizer for access path selection, and the convenience of storing the system catalog in the database itself. At the same time, Phase Zero taught us a number of valuable lessons which greatly influenced the design of our later implementation. Some of these lessons are summarized below.

(1) The optimizer should take into account not just the cost of fetching tuples, but the costs of creating and manipulating TID lists, then fetching tuples, then fetching the data pointed to by the tuples. When these "hidden costs" are taken into account, it will be seen that the manipulation of TID lists is quite expensive, especially if the TID lists are managed in the database rather than in main storage.

(2) Rather than "number of tuples fetched," a better measure of cost would have been "number of I/Os." This improved cost measure would have revealed the great importance of clustering together related tuples on physical pages so that several related tuples could be fetched by a single I/O. Also, an I/O measure would have revealed a serious drawback of XRM: Storing the domains separately from the tuples causes many extra I/Os to be done in retrieving data values. Because of this, our later implementation stored data values in the actual tuples rather than in separate domains. (In defense of XRM, it should be noted that the separation of data values from tuples has some advantages if data values are relatively large and if many tuples are processed internally compared to the number of tuples which are materialized for output.)

(3) Because the Phase Zero implementation was observed to be CPU-bound during the processing of a typical query, it was decided the optimizer cost measure should be a weighted sum of CPU time and I/O count, with weights adjustable according to the system configuration.

(4) Observation of some of the applications of Phase Zero convinced us of the importance of the "join" formulation of SQL. In our subsequent implementation, both "joins" and "subqueries" were supported.

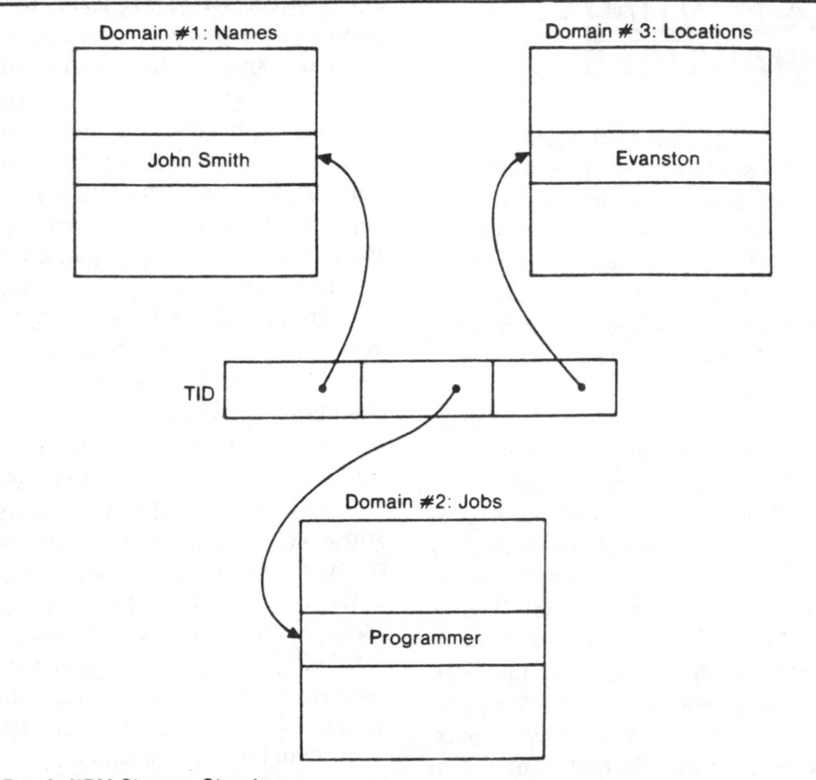

Fig. 2. XRM Storage Structure.

(5) The Phase Zero optimizer was quite complex and was oriented toward complex queries. In our later implementation, greater emphasis was placed on relatively simple interactions, and care was taken to minimize the "path length" for simple SQL statements.

3. Phase One: Construction of a Multiuser Prototype

After the completion and evaluation of the Phase Zero prototype, work began on the construction of the full-function, multiuser version of System R. Like Phase Zero, System R consisted of an access method (called RSS, the Research Storage System) and an optimizing SQL processor (called RDS, the Relational Data System) which runs on top of the RSS. Separation of the RSS and RDS provided a beneficial degree of modularity; e.g., all locking and logging functions were isolated in the RSS, while all authorization and access path selection functions were isolated in the RDS. Construction of the RSS was underway in 1975 and construction of the RDS began in 1976. Unlike XRM, the RSS was originally designed to support multiple concurrent users.

The multiuser prototype of System R contained several important subsystems which were not present in the earlier Phase Zero prototype. In order to prevent conflicts which might arise when two concurrent users attempt to update the same data value, a locking subsystem was provided. The locking subsystem ensures that each data value is accessed by only one user at a time, that all the updates made by a given transaction become effective simultaneously, and that deadlocks between users are detected and resolved. The security of the system was enhanced by view and authorization subsystems. The view subsystem permits users to define alternative views of the database (e.g., a view of the employee file in which salaries are deleted or aggregated by department).

COMPUTING PRACTICES

The authorization subsystem ensures that each user has access only to those views for which he has been specifically authorized by their creators. Finally, a recovery subsystem was provided which allows the database to be restored to a consistent state in the event of a hardware or software failure.

In order to provide a useful host-language capability, it was decided that System R should support both PL/I and Cobol application programs as well as a standalone query interface, and that the system should run under either the VM/CMS or MVS/TSO operating system environment. A key goal of the SQL language was to present the same capabilities, and a consistent syntax, to users of the PL/I and Cobol host languages and to ad hoc query users. The imbedding of SQL into PL/I is described in [16]. Installation of a multiuser database system under VM/CMS required certain modifications to the operating system in support of communicating virtual machines and writable shared virtual memory. These modifications are described in [32].

The standalone query interface of System R (called UFI, the User-Friendly Interface) is supported by a dialog manager program, written in PL/I, which runs on top of System R like any other application program. Therefore, the UFI support program is a cleanly separated component and can be modified independently of the rest of the system. In fact, several users improved on our UFI by writing interactive dialog managers of their own.

The Compilation Approach

Perhaps the most important decision in the design of the RDS was inspired by R. Lorie's observation, in early 1976, that it is possible to compile very high-level SQL statements into compact, efficient routines in System/370 machine language [42]. Lorie was able to demonstrate that SQL statements of arbitrary complexity could be decomposed into a relatively small collection of machine-language "fragments," and that an optimizing compiler could assemble these code fragments from a library to form a specially tailored routine for processing a given SQL statement. This technique had a very dramatic effect on our ability to support application programs for transaction processing. In System R, a PL/I or Cobol program is run through a preprocessor in which its SQL statements are examined, optimized, and compiled into small, efficient machine-language routines which are packaged into an "access module" for the application program. Then, when the program goes into execution, the access module is invoked to perform all interactions with the database by means of calls to the RSS. The process of creating and invoking an access module is illustrated in Figures 3 and 4. All the overhead of parsing, validity checking, and access path selection is removed from the path of the executing program and placed in a separate preprocessor step which need not be repeated. Perhaps even more important is the fact that the running program interacts only with its small, special-purpose access module rather than with a much larger and less efficient general-purpose SQL interpreter. Thus, the power and ease of use of the high-level SQL language are combined with the execution-time efficiency of the much lower level RSS interface.

Since all access path selection decisions are made during the preprocessor step in System R, there is the possibility that subsequent changes in the database may invalidate the decisions which are embodied in an access module. For example, an index selected by the optimizer may later be dropped from the database. Therefore, System R records with each access module a list of its "dependencies" on database objects such as tables and indexes. The dependency list is stored in the form of a regular relation in the system catalog. When the structure of the database changes (e.g., an index is dropped), all affected access modules are marked "invalid." The next time an invalid access module is invoked, it is regenerated from its original SQL statements, with newly optimized access paths. This process is completely transparent to the System R user.

SQL statements submitted to the interactive UFI dialog manager are processed by the same optimizing compiler as preprocessed SQL statements. The UFI program passes the ad hoc SQL statement to System R with a special "EXECUTE" call. In response to the EXECUTE call, System R parses and optimizes the SQL statement and translates it into a machine-language routine. The routine is indistinguishable from an access module and is executed immediately. This process is described in more detail in [20].

RSS Access Paths

Rather than storing data values in separate "domains" in the manner of XRM, the RSS chose to store data values in the individual rcords of the database. This resulted in records becoming variable in length and longer, on the average, than the equivalent XRM records. Also, commonly used values are represented many times rather than only once as in XRM. It was felt, however, that these disadvantages were more than offset by the following advantage: All the data values of a record could be fetched by a single I/O.

In place of XRM "inversions," the RSS provides "indexes," which are associative access aids implemented in the form of B-Trees [26]. Each table in the database may have anywhere from zero indexes up to an index on each column (it is also possible to create an index on a combination of columns). Indexes make it possible to scan the table in order by the indexed values, or to directly access the records which match a particular value. Indexes are maintained automatically by the RSS in the event of updates to the database.

The RSS also implements "links," which are pointers stored

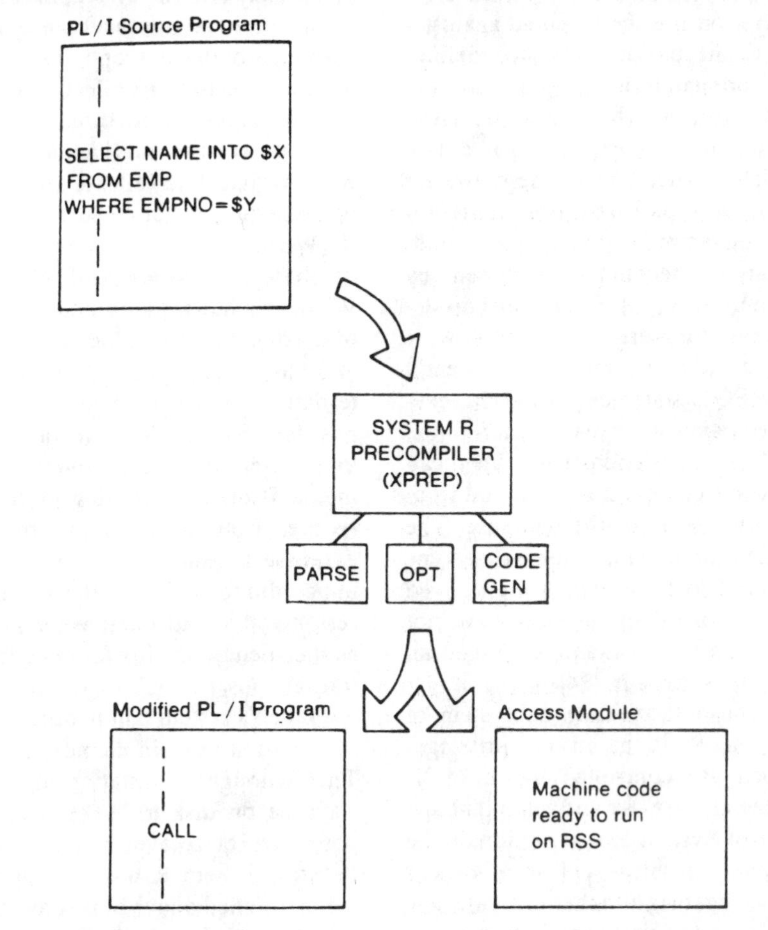

Fig. 3. Precompilation Step.

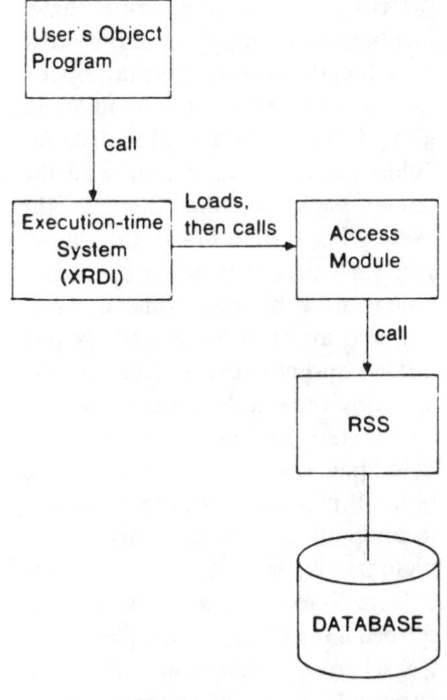

Fig. 4. Execution Step.

with a record which connect it to other related records. The connection of records on links is not performed automatically by the RSS, but must be done by a higher level system.

The access paths made available by the RSS include (1) index scans, which access a table associatively and scan it in value order using an index; (2) relation scans, which scan over a table as it is laid out in physical storage; (3) link scans, which traverse from one record to another using links. On any of these types of scan, "search arguments" may be specified which limit the records returned to those satisfying a certain predicate. Also, the RSS provides a built-in sorting mechanism which can take records from any of the scan methods and sort them into some value order, storing the result in a temporary list in the database. In System R, the RDS makes extensive use of index and relation scans and sorting. The RDS also utilizes links for internal purposes but not as an access path to user data.

The Optimizer

Building on our Phase Zero experience, we designed the System R optimizer to minimize the weighted sum of the predicted number of I/Os and RSS calls in processing an SQL statement (the relative weights of these two terms are adjustable according to system configuration). Rather than manipulating TID lists, the optimizer chooses to scan each table in the SQL query by means of only one index (or, if no suitable index exists, by means of a relation scan). For example, if the query calls for programmers who work in Evanston, the optimizer might choose to use the job index to find programmers and then examine their locations; it might use the location index to find Evanston employees and examine their jobs; or it might simply scan the relation and examine the job and location of all employees. The choice would be based on the optimizer's estimate of both the clustering and selectivity properties of each index, based on statistics stored in the system catalog. An index is considered highly selective if it has a large ratio of distinct key values to total entries. An index is considered to have the clustering property if the key order of the index corresponds closely to the ordering of records in physical storage. The clustering property is important because when a record is fetched via a clustering index, it is likely that other records with the same key will be found on the same page, thus minimizing the number of page fetches. Because of the importance of clustering, mechanisms were provided for loading data in value order and preserving the value ordering when new records are inserted into the database.

The techniques of the System R optimizer for performing joins of two or more tables have their origin in a study conducted by M. Blasgen and

K. Eswaran [7]. Using APL models, Blasgen and Eswaran studied ten methods of joining together tables, based on the use of indexes, sorting, physical pointers, and TID lists. The number of disk accesses required to perform a join was predicted on the basis of various assumptions for the ten join methods. Two join methods were identified such that one or the other was optimal or nearly optimal under most circumstances. The two methods are as follows:

Join Method 1: Scan over the qualifying rows of table A. For each row, fetch the matching rows of table B (usually, but not always, an index on table B is used).

Join Method 2: (Often used when no suitable index exists.) Sort the qualifying rows of tables A and B in order by their respective join fields. Then scan over the sorted lists and merge them by matching values.

When selecting an access path for a join of several tables, the System R optimizer considers the problem to be a sequence of binary joins. It then performs a tree search in which each level of the tree consists of one of the binary joins. The choices to be made at each level of the tree include which join method to use and which index, if any, to select for scanning. Comparisons are applied at each level of the tree to prune away paths which achieve the same results as other, less costly paths. When all paths have been examined, the optimizer selects the one of minimum predicted cost. The System R optimizer algorithms are described more fully in [47].

Views and Authorization

The major objectives of the view and authorization subsystems of System R were power and flexibility. We wanted to allow any SQL query to be used as the definition of a view. This was accomplished by storing each view definition in the form of an SQL parse tree. When an SQL operation is to be executed against a view, the parse tree which defines the operation is merged with the parse tree which defines the view, producing a composite parse tree which is then sent to the optimizer for access path selection. This approach is similar to the "query modification" technique proposed by Stonebraker [48]. The algorithms developed for merging parse trees were sufficiently general so that nearly any SQL statement could be executed against any view definition, with the restriction that a view can be updated only if it is derived from a single table in the database. The reason for this restriction is that some updates to views which are derived from more than one table are not meaningful (an example of such an update is given in [24]).

The authorization subsystem of System R is based on privileges which are controlled by the SQL statements GRANT and REVOKE. Each user of System R may optionally be given a privilege called RESOURCE which enables him/her to create new tables in the database. When a user creates a table, he/she receives all privileges to access, update, and destroy that table. The creator of a table can then grant these privileges to other individual users, and subsequently can revoke these grants if desired. Each granted privilege may optionally carry with it the "GRANT option," which enables a recipient to grant the privilege to yet other users. A REVOKE destroys the whole chain of granted privileges derived from the original grant. The authorization subsystem is described in detail in [37] and discussed further in [31].

The Recovery Subsystem

The key objective of the recovery subsystem is provision of a means whereby the database may be recovered to a consistent state in the event of a failure. A consistent state is defined as one in which the database does not reflect any updates made by transactions which did not complete successfully. There are three basic types of failure: the disk media may fail, the system may fail, or an individual transaction may fail. Although both the scope of the failure and the time to effect recovery may be different, all three types of recovery require that an alternate copy of data be available when the primary copy is not.

When a media failure occurs, database information on disk is lost. When this happens, an image dump of the database plus a log of "before" and "after" changes provide the alternate copy which makes recovery possible. System R's use of "dual logs" even permits recovery from media failures on the log itself. To recover from a media failure, the database is restored using the latest image dump and the recovery process reapplies all database changes as specified on the log for completed transactions.

When a system failure occurs, the information in main memory is lost. Thus, enough information must always be on disk to make recovery possible. For recovery from system failures, System R uses the change log mentioned above plus something called "shadow pages." As each page in the database is updated, the page is written out in a new place on disk, and the original page is retained. A directory of the "old" and "new" locations of each page is maintained. Periodically during normal operation, a "checkpoint" occurs in which all updates are forced out to disk, the "old" pages are discarded, and the "new" pages become "old." In the event of a system crash, the "new" pages on disk may be in an inconsistent state because some updated pages may still be in the system buffers and not yet reflected on disk. To bring the database back to a consistent state, the system reverts to the "old" pages, and then uses the log to redo all committed transactions and to undo all updates made by incomplete transactions. This aspect of the System R recovery subsystem is described in more detail in [36].

When a transaction failure occurs, all database changes which have been made by the failing transaction must be undone. To accomplish this, System R simply processes the change log backwards removing all changes made by the transaction. Unlike media and system recovery which both require that System R be reinitialized, transaction recovery takes place on-line.

The Locking Subsystem

A great deal of thought was given to the design of a locking subsystem which would prevent interference among concurrent users of System R. The original design involved the concept of "predicate locks," in which the lockable unit was a database property such as "employees whose location is Evanston." Note that, in this scheme, a lock might be held on the predicate LOC = 'EVANSTON', even if no employees currently satisfy that predicate. By comparing the predicates being processed by different users, the locking subsystem could prevent interference. The "predicate lock" design was ultimately abandoned because: (1) determining whether two predicates are mutually satisfiable is difficult and time-consuming; (2) two predicates may appear to conflict when, in fact, the semantics of the data prevent any conflict, as in "PRODUCT = AIRCRAFT" and "MANUFACTURER = ACME STATIONERY CO."; and (3) we desired to contain the locking subsystem entirely within the RSS, and therefore to make it independent of any understanding of the predicates being processed by various users. The original predicate locking scheme is described in [29].

The locking scheme eventually chosen for System R is described in [34]. This scheme involves a hierarchy of locks, with several different sizes of lockable units, ranging from individual records to several tables. The locking subsystem is transparent to end users, but acquires locks on physical objects in the database as they are processed by each user. When a user accumulates many small locks, they may be "traded" for a larger lockable unit (e.g., locks on many records in a table might be traded for a lock on the table). When locks are acquired on small objects, "intention" locks are simultaneously acquired on the larger objects which contain them. For example, user A and user B may both be updating employee records. Each user holds an "intention" lock on the employee table, and "exclusive" locks on the particular records being updated. If user A attempts to trade her individual record locks for an "exclusive" lock at the table level, she must wait until user B ends his transaction and releases his "intention" lock on the table.

4. Phase Two: Evaluation

The evaluation phase of the System R project lasted approximately 2½ years and consisted of two parts: (1) experiments performed on the system at the San Jose Research Laboratory, and (2) actual use of the system at a number of internal IBM sites and at three selected customer sites. At all user sites, System R was installed on an experimental basis for study purposes only, and not as a supported commercial product. The first installations of System R took place in June 1977.

General User Comments

In general, user response to System R has been enthusiastic. The system was mostly used in applications for which ease of installation, a high-level user language, and an ability to rapidly reconfigure the database were important requirements. Several user sites reported that they were able to install the system, design and load a database, and put into use some application programs within a matter of days. User sites also reported that it was possible to tune the system performance after data was loaded by creating and dropping indexes without impacting end users or application programs. Even changes in the database tables could be made transparent to users if the tables were read-only, and also in some cases for updated tables.

Users found the performance characteristics and resource consumption of System R to be generally satisfactory for their experimental applications, although no specific performance comparisons were drawn. In general, the experimental databases used with System R were smaller than one 3330 disk pack (200 Megabytes) and were typically accessed by fewer than ten concurrent users. As might be expected, interactive response slowed down during the execution of very complex SQL statements involving joins of several tables. This performance degradation must be traded off against the advantages of normalization [23, 30], in which large database tables are broken into smaller parts to avoid redundancy, and then joined back together by the view mechanism or user applications.

The SQL Language

The SQL user interface of System R was generally felt to be successful in achieving its goals of simplicity, power, and data independence. The language was simple enough in its basic structure so that users without prior experience were able to learn a usable subset on their first sitting. At the same time, when taken as a whole, the language provided the query power of the first-order predicate calculus combined with operators for grouping, arithmetic, and built-in functions such as SUM and AVERAGE.

Users consistently praised the uniformity of the SQL syntax across the environments of application programs, ad hoc query, and data definition (i.e., definition of views). Users who were formerly required to learn inconsistent languages for these purposes found it easier to deal with the single syntax (e.g., when debugging an application program by querying the database to observe its effects). The single syntax also enhanced communication among different functional organizations (e.g., between database administrators and application programmers).

While developing applications using SQL, our experimental users made a number of suggestions for extensions and improvements to the language, most of which were implemented during the course of the project. Some of these suggestions are summarized below:

(1) Users requested an easy-to-use syntax when testing for the existence or nonexistence of a data item, such as an employee record whose department number matches a given department record. This facility was implemented in the form of a special "EXISTS" predicate.

(2) Users requested a means of seaching for character strings whose contents are only partially known, such as "all license plates beginning with NVK." This facility was implemented in the form of a special "LIKE" predicate which searches for "patterns" that are allowed to contain "don't care" characters.

(3) A requirement arose for an application program to compute an SQL statement dynamically, submit the statement to the System R optimizer for access path selection, and then execute the statement repeatedly for different data values without reinvoking the optimizer. This facility was implemented in the form of PREPARE and EXECUTE statements which were made available in the host-language version of SQL.

(4) In some user applications the need arose for an operator which Codd has called an "outer join" [25]. Suppose that two tables (e.g., SUPPLIERS and PROJECTS) are related by a common data field (e.g., PARTNO). In a conventional join of these tables, supplier records which have no matching project record (and vice versa) would not appear. In an "outer join" of these tables, supplier records with no matching project record would appear together with a "synthetic" project record containing only null values (and similarly for projects with no matching supplier). An "outer-join" facility for SQL is currently under study.

A more complete discussion of user experience with SQL and the resulting language improvements is presented in [19].

The Compilation Approach

The approach of compiling SQL statements into machine code was one of the most successful parts of the System R project. We were able to generate a machine-language routine to execute any SQL statement of arbitrary complexity by selecting code fragments from a library of approximately 100 fragments. The result was a beneficial effect on transaction programs, ad hoc query, and system simplicity.

In an environment of short, repetitive transactions, the benefits of compilation are obvious. All the overhead of parsing, validity checking, and access path selection are removed from the path of the running transaction, and the application program interacts with a small, specially tailored access module rather than with a larger and less efficient general-purpose interpreter program. Experiments [38] showed that for a typical short transaction, about 80 percent of the instructions were executed by the RSS, with the remaining 20 percent executed by the access module and application pro-

Example 1:

```
SELECT SUPPNO, PRICE
FROM   QUOTES
WHERE  PARTNO = '010002'
AND MINQ<=1000 AND MAXQ>=1000;
```

Operation	CPU time (msec on 168)	Number of I/Os
Parsing	13.3	0
Access Path Selection	40.0	9
Code Generation	10.1	0
Fetch answer set (per record)	1.5	0.7

Example 2:

```
SELECT ORDERNO,ORDERS.PARTNO,DESCRIP,DATE,QTY
FROM   ORDERS,PARTS
WHERE  ORDERS.PARTNO = PARTS.PARTNO
AND    DATE BETWEEN '750000' AND '751231'
AND    SUPPNO = '797';
```

Operation	CPU time (msec on 168)	Number of I/Os
Parsing	20.7	0
Access Path Selection	73.2	9
Code Generation	19.3	0
Fetch answer set (per record)	8.7	10.7

Fig. 5. Measurements of Cost of Compilation.

gram. Thus, the user pays only a small cost for the power, flexibility, and data independence of the SQL language, compared with writing the same transaction directly on the lower level RSS interface.

In an ad hoc query environment the advantages of compilation are less obvious since the compilation must take place on-line and the query is executed only once. In this environment, the cost of generating a machine-language routine for a given query must be balanced against the increased efficiency of this routine as compared with a more conventional query interpreter. Figure 5 shows some measurements of the cost of compiling two typical SQL statements (details of the experiments are given in [20]). From this data we may draw the following conclusions:

(1) The code generation step adds a small amount of CPU time and no I/Os to the overhead of parsing and access path selection. Parsing and access path selection must be done in any query system, including interpretive ones. The additional instructions spent on code generation are not likely to be perceptible to an end user.

(2) If code generation results in a routine which runs more efficiently than an interpreter, the cost of the code generation step is paid back after fetching only a few records. (In Example 1, if the CPU time per record of the compiled module is half that of an interpretive system, the cost of generating the access module is repaid after seven records have been fetched.)

A final advantage of compilation is its simplifying effect on the system architecture. With both ad hoc queries and precanned transactions being treated in the same way, most of the code in the system can be made to serve a dual purpose. This ties in very well with our objective of supporting a uniform syntax between query users and transaction programs.

Available Access Paths

As described earlier, the principal access path used in System R for retrieving data associatively by its value is the B-tree index. A typical index is illustrated in Figure 6. If we assume a fan-out of approximately 200 at each level of the tree, we can index up to 40,000 records by a two-level index, and up to 8,000,000 records by a three-level index. If we wish to begin an associative scan through a large table, three I/Os will typically be required (assuming the root page is referenced frequently enough to remain in the system buffers, we need an I/O for the intermediate-level index page, the "leaf" index page, and the data page). If several records are to be fetched using the index scan, the three start-up I/Os are relatively insignificant. However, if only one record is to be fetched, other access techniques might have provided a quicker path to the stored data.

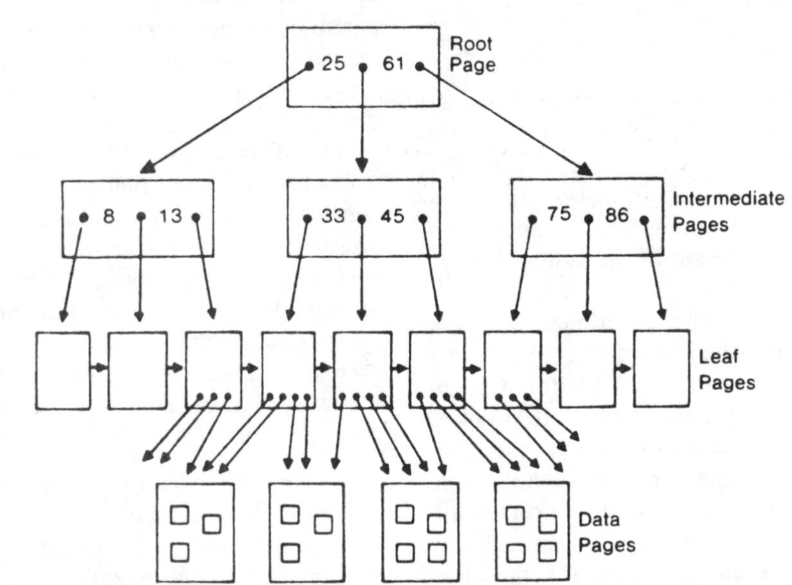

Fig. 6. A B-Tree Index.

Two common access techniques which were not utilized for user data in System R are hashing and direct links (physical pointers from one record to another). Hashing was not used because it does not have the convenient ordering property of a B-tree index (e.g., a B-tree index on SALARY enables a list of employees ordered by SALARY to be retrieved very easily). Direct links, although they were implemented at the RSS level, were not used as an access path for user data by the RDS for a twofold reason. *Essential links* (links whose semantics are not known to the system but which are connected directly by users) were rejected because they were inconsistent with the nonnavigational user interface of a relational system, since they could not be used as access paths by an automatic optimizer. *Nonessential links* (links which connect records to other records with matching data values) were not implemented because of the difficulties in automatically maintaining their connections. When a record is updated, its connections on many links may need to be updated as well, and this may involve many "subsidiary queries" to find the other records which are involved in these connections. Problems also arise relating to records which have no matching partner record on the link, and records whose link-controlling data value is null.

In general, our experience showed that indexes could be used very efficiently in queries and transactions which access many records, but that hashing and links would have enhanced the performance of "canned transactions" which access only a few records. As an illustration of this problem, consider an inventory application which has two tables: a PRODUCTS table, and a much larger PARTS table which contains data on the individual parts used for each product. Suppose a given transaction needs to find the price of the heating element in a particular toaster. To execute this transaction, System R might require two I/Os to traverse a two-level index to find the toaster record, and three more I/Os to traverse another three-level index to find the heating element record. If access paths based on hashing and direct links were available, it might be possible to find the toaster record in one I/O via hashing, and the heating element record in one more I/O via a link. (Additional I/Os would be required in the event of hash collisions or if the toaster parts records occupied more than one page.) Thus, for this very simple transaction hashing and links might reduce the number of I/Os from five to three, or even two. For transactions which retrieve a large set of records, the additional I/Os caused by indexes compared to hashing and links are less important.

The Optimizer

A series of experiments was conducted at the San Jose IBM Research Laboratory to evaluate the success of the System R optimizer in choosing among the available access paths for typical SQL statements. The results of these experiments are reported in [6]. For the purpose of the experiments, the optimizer was modified in order to observe its behavior. Ordinarily, the optimizer searches through a tree of path choices, computing estimated costs and pruning the tree until it arrives at a single preferred access path. The optimizer was modified in such a way that it could be made to generate the complete tree of access paths, without pruning, and to estimate the cost of each path (cost is defined as a weighted sum of page fetches and RSS calls). Mechanisms were also added to the system whereby it could be forced to execute an SQL statement by a particular access path and to measure the actual number of page fetches and RSS calls incurred. In this way, a comparison can be made between the optimizer's predicted cost and the actual measured cost for various alternative paths.

In [6], an experiment is described in which ten SQL statements, including some single-table queries and some joins, are run against a test database. The database is artificially generated to conform to the two basic assumptions of the System R optimizer: (1) the values in each column are uniformly distributed from some minimum to some maximum value; and (2) the distribution of values of the various columns are independent of each other. For each of the ten SQL statements, the ordering of the predicted costs of the various access paths was the same as the ordering of the actual measured costs (in a few cases the optimizer predicted two paths to have the same cost when their actual costs were unequal but adjacent in the ordering).

Although the optimizer was able to correctly order the access paths in the experiment we have just described, the magnitudes of the predicted costs differed from the measured costs in several cases. These discrepancies were due to a variety of causes, such as the optimizer's inability to predict how much data would remain in the system buffers during sorting.

The above experiment does not address the issue of whether or not a very good access path for a given SQL statement might be overlooked because it is not part of the optimizer's repertoire. One such example is known. Suppose that the database contains a table T in which each row has a unique value for the field SEQNO, and suppose that an index exists on SEQNO. Consider the following SQL query:

```
SELECT * FROM T WHERE SEQNO IN
(15, 17, 19, 21);
```

This query has an answer set of (at most) four rows, and an obvious method of processing it is to use the SEQNO index repeatedly: first to find the row with SEQNO = 15, then SEQNO = 17, etc. However, this access path would not be chosen by System R, because the optimizer is not presently structured to consider multiple uses of an index within a single query block. As we gain more experience with access path selection, the optimizer may grow to encompass this and other access paths which have so far been omitted from consideration.

Views and Authorization

Users generally found the System R mechanisms for defining views and controlling authorization to be powerful, flexible, and convenient. The following features were considered to be particularly beneficial:

(1) The full query power of SQL is made available for defining new views of data (i.e., any query may be defined as a view). This makes it possible to define a rich variety of views, containing joins, subqueries, aggregation, etc., without having to learn a separate "data definition language." However, the view mechanism is not completely transparent to the end user, because of the restrictions described earlier (e.g., views involving joins of more than one table are not updateable).

(2) The authorization subsystem allows each installation of System R to choose a "fully centralized policy" in which all tables are created and privileges controlled by a central administrator; or a "fully decentralized policy" in which each user may create tables and control access to them; or some intermediate policy.

During the two-year evaluation of System R, the following suggestions were made by users for improvement of the view and authorization subsystems:

(1) The authorization subsystem could be augmented by the concept of a "group" of users. Each group would have a "group administrator" who controls enrollment of new members in the group. Privileges could then be granted to the group as a whole rather than to each member of the group individually.

(2) A new command could be added to the SQL language to change the ownership of a table from one user to another. This suggestion is more difficult to implement than it seems at first glance, because the owner's name is part of the fully qualified name of a table (i.e., two tables owned by Smith and Jones could be named SMITH.PARTS and JONES.PARTS). References to the table SMITH.PARTS might exist in many places, such as view definitions and compiled programs. Finding and changing all these references would be difficult (perhaps impossible, as in the case of users' source programs which are not stored under System R control).

(3) Occasionally it is necessary to reload an existing table in the database (e.g., to change its physical clustering properties). In System R this is accomplished by dropping the old table definition, creating a new table with the same definition, and reloading the data into the new table. Unfortunately, views and authorizations defined on the table are lost from the system when the old definition is dropped, and therefore they both must be redefined on the new table. It has been suggested that views and authorizations defined on a dropped table might optionally be held "in abeyance" pending reactivation of the table.

The Recovery Subsystem

The combined "shadow page" and log mechanism used in System R proved to be quite successful in safeguarding the database against media, system, and transaction failures. The part of the recovery subsystem which was observed to have the greatest impact on system performance was the keeping of a shadow page for each updated page. This performance impact is due primarily to the following factors:

(1) Since each updated page is written out to a new location on disk, data tends to move about. This limits the ability of the system to cluster related pages in secondary storage to minimize disk arm movement for sequential applications.

(2) Since each page can potentially have both an "old" and "new" version, a directory must be maintained to locate both versions of each page. For large databases, the directory may be large enough to require a paging mechanism of its own.

(3) The periodic checkpoints which exchange the "old" and "new" page pointers generate I/O activity and consume a certain amount of CPU time.

A possible alternative technique for recovering from system failures would dispense with the concept of shadow pages, and simply keep a log of all database updates. This design would require that all updates be written out to the log before the updated page migrates to disk from the system buffers. Mechanisms could be developed to minimize I/Os by retaining updated pages in the buffers until several pages are written out at once, sharing an I/O to the log.

The Locking Subsystem

The locking subsystem of System R provides each user with a choice of three levels of isolation from other users. In order to explain the three levels, we define "uncommitted data" as those records which have been updated by a transaction that is still in progress (and therefore still subject to being backed out). Under no circumstances can a transaction, at any isolation level, perform updates on the uncommitted data of another transaction, since this might lead to lost updates in the event of transaction backout.

The three levels of isolation in System R are defined as follows:

Level 1: A transaction running at Level 1 may read (but not update) uncommitted data. Therefore, successive reads of the same record by a Level-1 transaction may not give consistent values. A Level-1 transaction does not attempt to acquire any locks on records while reading.

Level 2: A transaction running at Level 2 is protected against reading uncommitted data. However, successive reads at Level 2 may still yield inconsistent values if a second transaction updates a given record and then terminates between the first and second reads by the Level-2 transaction. A Level-2 transaction locks each record before reading it to make sure it is committed at the time of the read, but then releases the lock immediately after reading.

Level 3: A transaction running at Level 3 is guaranteed that successive reads of the same record will yield the same value. This guarantee is enforced by acquiring a lock on each record read by a Level-3 transaction and holding the lock until the end of the transaction. (The lock acquired by a Level-3 reader is a "share" lock which permits other users to read but not update the locked record.)

It was our intention that Isolation Level 1 provide a means for very quick scans through the database when approximate values were acceptable, since Level-1 readers acquire no locks and should never need to wait for other users. In practice, however, it was found that Level-1 readers did have to wait under certain circumstances while the physical consistency of the data was suspended (e.g., while indexes or pointers were being adjusted). Therefore, the potential of Level 1 for increasing system concurrency was not fully realized.

It was our expectation that a tradeoff would exist between Isolation Levels 2 and 3 in which Level 2 would be "cheaper" and Level 3 "safer." In practice, however, it was observed that Level 3 actually involved less CPU overhead than Level 2, since it was simpler to acquire locks and keep them than to acquire locks and immediately release them. It is true that Isolation Level 2 permits a greater degree of access to the database by concurrent readers and updaters than does Level 3. However, this increase in concurrency was not observed to have an important effect in most practical applications.

As a result of the observations described above, most System R users ran their queries and application programs at Level 3, which was the system default.

The Convoy Phenomenon

Experiments with the locking subsystem of System R identified a problem which came to be known as the "convoy phenomenon" [9]. There are certain high-traffic locks in System R which every process requests frequently and holds for a short time. Examples of these are the locks which control access to the buffer pool and the system log. In a "convoy" condition, interaction between a high-traffic lock and the operating system dispatcher tends to serialize all processes in the system, allowing each process to acquire the lock only once each time it is dispatched.

In the VM/370 operating system, each process in the multiprogramming set receives a series of small "quanta" of CPU time. Each quantum terminates after a preset amount of CPU time, or when the process goes into page, I/O, or lock wait. At the end of the series of quanta, the process drops out of the multiprogramming set and must undergo a longer "time slice wait" before it once again becomes dispatchable. Most quanta end when a process waits for a page, an I/O operation, or a low-traffic lock. The System R design ensures that no process will ever hold a high-traffic lock during any of these types of wait. There is a slight probability, however, that a process might go into a long "time slice wait" while it is holding a high-traffic lock. In this event, all other dispatchable processes will soon request the same lock and become enqueued behind the sleeping process. This phenomenon is called a "convoy."

In the original System R design, convoys are stable because of the protocol for releasing locks. When a process *P* releases a lock, the locking subsystem grants the lock to the first waiting process in the queue (thereby making it unavailable to be reacquired by *P*). After a short time, *P* once again requests the lock, and is forced to go to the end of the convoy. If the mean time between requests for the high-traffic lock is 1,000 instructions, each process may execute only 1,000 instructions before it drops to the end of the convoy. Since more than 1,000 instructions are typically used to dispatch a process, the system goes into a "thrashing" condition in which most of the cycles are spent on dispatching overhead.

The solution to the convoy problem involved a change to the lock release protocol of System R. After the change, when a process *P* releases a lock, all processes which are enqueued for the lock are made dispatchable, but the lock is not granted to any particular process. Therefore, the lock may be regranted to process *P* if it makes a subsequent request. Process *P* may acquire and release the lock many times before its time slice is exhausted. It is highly probable that process *P* will not be holding the lock when it goes into a long wait. Therefore, if a convoy should ever form, it will most likely evaporate as soon as all the members of the convoy have been dispatched.

Additional Observations

Other observations were made during the evaluation of System R and are listed below:

(1) When running in a "canned transaction" environment, it would be helpful for the system to include a data communications front end to handle terminal interactions, priority scheduling, and logging and restart at the message level. This facility was not included in the System R design. Also, space would be saved and the working set reduced if several users executing the same "canned transaction" could share a common access module. This would require the System R code generator to produce reentrant code. Approximately half the space occupied by the multiple copies of the access module could be saved by this method, since the other half consists of working storage which must be duplicated for each user.

(2) When the recovery subsystem attempts to take an automatic checkpoint, it inhibits the processing of new RSS commands until all users have completed their current RSS command; then the checkpoint is taken and all users are allowed to proceed. However, certain RSS commands potentially involve long operations, such as sorting a file. If these "long" RSS operations were made interruptible, it would avoid any delay in performing checkpoints.

(3) The System R design of automatically maintaining a system catalog as part of the on-line database was very well liked by users, since it permitted them to access the information in the catalog with exactly the same query language they use for accessing other data.

5. Conclusions

We feel that our experience with System R has clearly demonstrated the feasibility of applying a relational database system to a real production environment in which many concurrent users are performing a mixture of ad hoc queries and repetitive transactions. We believe that the high-level user interface made possible by the relational data model can have a dramatic positive effect on user productivity in developing new applications, and on the data independence of queries and programs. System R has also demonstrated the ability to support a highly dynamic database environment in which application requirements are rapidly changing.

In particular, System R has illustrated the feasibility of compiling a very high-level data sublanguage, SQL, into machine-level code. The result of this compilation technique is that most of the overhead cost for implementing the high-level language is pushed into a "precompilation" step, and performance for canned transactions is comparable to that of a much lower level system. The compilation approach has also proved to be applicable to the ad hoc query environment, with the result that a unified mechanism can be used to support both queries and transactions.

The evaluation of System R has led to a number of suggested improvements. Some of these improvements have already been implemented and others are still under study. Two major foci of our continuing research program at the San Jose laboratory are adaptation of System R to a distributed database environment, and extension of our optimizer algorithms to encompass a broader set of access paths.

Sometimes questions are asked about how the performance of a relational database system might compare to that of a "navigational" system in which a programmer carefully hand-codes an application to take advantage of explicit access paths. Our experiments with the System R optimizer and compiler suggest that the relational system will probably approach but not quite equal the performance of the navigational system for a particular, highly tuned application, but that the relational system is more likely to be able to adapt to a broad spectrum of unanticipated applications with adequate performance. We believe that the benefits of relational systems in the areas of user productivity, data independence, and adaptability to changing circumstances will take on increasing importance in the years ahead.

Acknowledgments

From the beginning, System R was a group effort. Credit for any success of the project properly belongs to the team as a whole rather than to specific individuals.

The inspiration for constructing a relational system came primarily from E. F. Codd, whose landmark paper [22] introduced the relational model of data. The manager of the project through most of its existence was W. F. King.

In addition to the authors of this paper, the following people were associated with System R and made important contributions to its development:

M. Adiba	M. Mresse
R.F. Boyce	J.F. Nilsson
A. Chan	R.L. Obermarck
D.M. Choy	D. Stott Parker
K. Eswaran	D. Portal
R. Fagin	N. Ramsperger
P. Fehder	P. Reisner
T. Haerder	P.R. Roever
R.H. Katz	R. Selinger
W. Kim	H.R. Strong
H. Korth	P. Tiberio
P. McJones	V. Watson
D. McLeod	R. Williams

References

1. Adiba, M.E., and Lindsay, B.G. Database snapshots. IBM Res. Rep. RJ2772, San Jose, Calif., March 1980.

2. Astrahan, M.M., and Chamberlin, D.D. Implementation of a structured English query language. *Comm. ACM 18*, 10 (Oct. 1975), 580–588.

3. Astrahan, M.M., and Lorie, R.A. SEQUEL-XRM: A Relational System. Proc. ACM Pacific Regional Conf., San Francisco, Calif., April 1975, p. 34.

4. Astrahan, M.M., et al. System R: A relational approach to database management. *ACM Trans. Database Syst. 1*, 2 (June 1976) 97–137.

5. Astrahan, M.M., et al. System R: A relational data base management system. *IEEE Comptr. 12*, 5 (May 1979), 43–48.

6. Astrahan, M.M., Kim, W., and Schkolnick, M. Evaluation of the System R access path selection mechanism. Proc. IFIP Congress, Melbourne, Australia, Sept. 1980, pp. 487–491.

7. Blasgen, M.W., Eswaran, K.P. Storage and access in relational databases. *IBM Syst. J. 16*, 4 (1977), 363–377.

8. Blasgen, M.W., Casey, R.G., and Eswaran, K.P. An encoding method for multifield sorting and indexing. *Comm. ACM 20*, 11 (Nov. 1977), 874–878.

9. Blasgen, M., Gray, J., Mitoma, M., and Price, T. The convoy phenomenon. *Operating Syst. Rev. 13*, 2 (April 1979), 20–25.

10. Blasgen, M.W., et al. System R: An architectural overview. *IBM Syst. J. 20*, 1 (Feb. 1981), 41–62.

11. Bjorner, D., Codd, E.F., Deckert, K.L., and Traiger, I.L. The Gamma Zero N-ary relational data base interface. IBM Res. Rep. RJ1200, San Jose, Calif., April 1973.

12. Boyce, R.F., and Chamberlin, D.D. Using a structured English query language as a data definition facility. IBM Res. Rep. RJ1318, San Jose, Calif., Dec. 1973.

13. Boyce, R.F., Chamberlin, D.D., King, W.F., and Hammer, M.M. Specifying queries as relational expressions: The SQUARE data sublanguage. *Comm. ACM 18*, 11 (Nov. 1975), 621–628.

14. Chamberlin, D.D., and Boyce, R.F. SEQUEL: A structured English query language. Proc. ACM-SIGMOD Workshop on Data Description, Access, and Control, Ann Arbor, Mich., May 1974, pp. 249–264.

15. Chamberlin, D.D., Gray, J.N., and Traiger, I.L. Views, authorization, and locking in a relational database system. Proc. 1975 Nat. Comptr. Conf., Anaheim, Calif., pp. 425–430.

16. Chamberlin, D.D., et al. SEQUEL 2: A unified approach to data definition, manipulation, and control. *IBM J. Res. and Develop. 20*, 6 (Nov. 1976), 560–575 (also see errata in Jan. 1977 issue).

17. Chamberlin, D.D. Relational database management systems. *Comptng. Surv. 8*, 1 (March 1976), 43–66.

18. Chamberlin, D.D., et al. Data base system authorization. In *Foundations of Secure Computation*, R. Demillo, D. Dobkin, A. Jones, and R. Lipton, Eds., Academic Press, New York, 1978, pp. 39–56.

19. Chamberlin, D.D. A summary of user experience with the SQL data sublanguage. Proc. Internat. Conf. Data Bases, Aberdeen, Scotland, July 1980, pp. 181–203 (also IBM Res. Rep. RJ2767, San Jose, Calif., April 1980).

20. Chamberlin, D.D., et al. Support for repetitive transactions and ad-hoc queries in System R. *ACM Trans. Database Syst. 6*, 1 (March 1981), 70–94.

21. Chamberlin, D.D., Gilbert, A.M., and Yost, R.A. A history of System R and SQL/data system (presented at the Internat. Conf. Very Large Data Bases, Cannes, France, Sept. 1981).

22. Codd, E.F. A relational model of data for large shared data banks. *Comm. ACM 13*, 6 (June 1970), 377–387.

23. Codd, E.F. Further normalization of the data base relational model. In *Courant Computer Science Symposia, Vol. 6: Data Base Systems*, Prentice-Hall, Englewood Cliffs, N.J., 1971, pp. 33–64.

24. Codd, E.F. Recent investigations in relational data base systems. Proc. IFIP Congress, Stockholm, Sweden, Aug. 1974.

25. Codd, E.F. Extending the database relational model to capture more meaning. *ACM Trans. Database Syst. 4*, 4 (Dec. 1979), 397–434.

26. Comer, D. The ubiquitous B-Tree. *Comptng. Surv. 11*, 2 (June 1979), 121–137.

27. Date, C.J. *An Introduction to Database Systems*. 2nd Ed., Addison-Wesley, New York, 1977.

28. Eswaran, K.P., and Chamberlin, D.D. Functional specifications of a subsystem for database integrity. Proc. Conf. Very Large Data Bases, Framingham, Mass., Sept. 1975, pp. 48–68.

29. Eswaran, K.P., Gray, J.N., Lorie, R.A., and Traiger, I.L. On the notions of consistency and predicate locks in a database system. *Comm. ACM 19*, 11 (Nov. 1976), 624–633.

30. Fagin, R. Multivalued dependencies and a new normal form for relational databases. *ACM Trans. Database Syst. 2*, 3 (Sept. 1977), 262–278.

31. Fagin, R. On an authorization mechanism. *ACM Trans. Database Syst. 3*, 3 (Sept. 1978), 310–319.

32. Gray, J.N., and Watson, V. A shared segment and inter-process communication facility for VM/370. IBM Res. Rep. RJ1579, San Jose, Calif., Feb. 1975.

33. Gray, J.N., Lorie, R.A., and Putzolu, G.F. Granularity of locks in a large shared database. Proc. Conf. Very Large Data Bases, Framingham, Mass., Sept. 1975, pp. 428–451.

34. Gray, J.N., Lorie, R.A., Putzolu, G.R., and Traiger, I.L. Granularity of locks and degrees of consistency in a shared data base. Proc. IFIP Working Conf. Modelling of Database Management Systems, Freudenstadt, Germany, Jan. 1976, pp. 695–723 (also IBM Res. Rep. RJ1654, San Jose, Calif.).

35. Gray, J.N. Notes on database operating systems. In *Operating Systems: An Advanced Course*, Goos and Hartmanis, Eds., Springer-Verlag, New York, 1978, pp. 393–481 (also IBM Res. Rep. RJ2188, San Jose, Calif.).

36. Gray, J.N., et al. The recovery manager of a data management system. IBM Res. Rep. RJ2623, San Jose, Calif., June 1979.

37. Griffiths, P.P., and Wade, B.W. An authorization mechanism for a relational database system. *ACM Trans. Database Syst. 1*, 3 (Sept. 1976), 242–255.

38. Katz, R.H., and Selinger, R.D. Internal comm., IBM Res. Lab., San Jose, Calif., Sept. 1978.

39. Kwan, S.C., and Strong, H.R. Index path length evaluation for the research storage system of System R. IBM Res. Rep. RJ2736, San Jose, Calif., Jan. 1980.

40. Lorie, R.A. XRM—An extended (N-ary) relational memory. IBM Tech. Rep. G320-2096, Cambridge Scientific Ctr., Cambridge, Mass., Jan. 1974.

41. Lorie, R.A. Physical integrity in a large segmented database. *ACM Trans. Database Syst. 2*, 1 (March 1977), 91–104.

42. Lorie, R.A., and Wade, B.W. The compilation of a high level data language. IBM Res. Rep. RJ2598, San Jose, Calif., Aug. 1979.

43. Lorie, R.A., and Nilsson, J.F. An access specification language for a relational data base system. *IBM J. Res. and Develop. 23*, 3 (May 1979), 286–298.

44. Reisner, P., Boyce, R.F., and Chamberlin, D.D. Human factors evaluation of two data base query languages: SQUARE and SEQUEL. Proc. AFIPS Nat. Comptr. Conf., Anaheim, Calif., May 1975, pp. 447–452.

45. Reisner, P. Use of psychological experimentation as an aid to development of a query language. *IEEE Trans. Software Eng. SE-3*, 3 (May 1977), 218–229.

46. Schkolnick, M., and Tiberio, P. Considerations in developing a design tool for a relational DBMS. Proc. IEEE COMPSAC 79, Nov. 1979, pp. 228–235.

47. Selinger, P.G., et al. Access path selection in a relational database management system. Proc. ACM SIGMOD Conf., Boston, Mass., June 1979, pp. 23–34.

48. Stonebraker, M. Implementation of integrity constraints and views by query modification. Tech. Memo ERL-M514, College of Eng., Univ. of Calif. at Berkeley, March 1975.

49. Strong, H.R., Traiger, I.L., and Markowsky, G. Slide Search. IBM Res. Rep. RJ2274, San Jose, Calif., June 1978.

50. Traiger, I.L., Gray J.N., Galtieri, C.A., and Lindsay, B.G. Transactions and consistency in distributed database systems. IBM Res. Rep. RJ2555, San Jose, Calif., June 1979.

Retrospection on a Database System

MICHAEL STONEBRAKER
University of California at Berkeley

This paper describes the implementation history of the INGRES database system. It focuses on mistakes that were made in progress rather than on eventual corrections. Some attention is also given to the role of structured design in a database system implementation and to the problem of supporting nontrivial users. Lastly, miscellaneous impressions of UNIX, the PDP-11, and data models are given.

Key Words and Phrases: relational databases, nonprocedural languages, recovery, concurrency, protection, integrity
CR Categories: 3.50, 3.70, 4.22, 4.33, 4.34

1. INTRODUCTION

This paper was written in response to several requests to know what really happened in the INGRES database management system project [22] and why. To the extent that it contains practical wisdom for other implementation projects, it serves its purpose. To the extent that it is a self-righteous defense of the existing design, the author apologizes in advance.

It may be premature to write such a document, since INGRES has only been fully operational for three years and user experience is still somewhat limited. Hence the ultimate jury, real users, has not yet made a full report. The reason for reporting now is that we have reached a turning point. Until late 1978, the goal was to make INGRES "really work," i.e., efficiently, reliably, and without surprises (bugs) for users. There are now only marginal returns to pursuing that goal. Consequently, the project is taking new directions, which are discussed below.

This paper is organized as follows. In Section 2 we trace the history of the project through its various phases and highlight the more significant events that took place. Then, in Section 3, we discuss several lessons that we had to learn the hard way. Section 4 takes a critical look at the current design of INGRES and discusses some of the mistakes. Next, Section 5 consists of an assortment of random comments. Lastly, Section 6 outlines the future plans of the project.

2. HISTORY

The project can be roughly decomposed into three periods: (1) the early times—March 1973–June 1974; (2) the first implementation—June 1974–September 1975; (3) making it really work—September 1975–present. We discuss each period in turn.

2.1 The Early Times

The project began in 1973 when Eugene Wong and I agreed to read and discuss literature relating to relational databases. From the beginning we were both enthusiastic about an implementation. It did not faze either one of us that we possessed no experience whatsoever in leading a nontrivial implementation effort. In fact, neither of us had ever written a sizable computer program.

Our first task was to find a suitable machine environment for an implementation. It quickly become clear that no machine to which we had access was appropriate for an interactive database system. Through various mechanisms (mainly engineered by Eugene Wong and Pravin Varaiya) we obtained about $90,000 for hardware. The liability that we obtained was a commitment to write a geodata system for the Urban Economics Group led by Pravin Varaiya and Roland Artle.

Our major concerns in selecting hardware were in obtaining large (50 or 100 megabytes at the time) disks and a decent software environment. After studying the UNIX [18], I was convinced that we should use UNIX and buy whatever hardware we could afford to make it run. We placed a hardware order in February of 1974 and had a system in September of the same year.

We decided to offer a seminar running from September 1973 to June 1974 in which a design would be pursued. Somewhat symbiotically the seminar split into two groups: One group, led by Gene, would plan the user language; the other group, led by me, would plan the support system. The language group converged quickly on the retrieval portion of the data sublanguage QUEL. It was loosely based on DSL/Alpha [5] but had no notion of quantifiers.

As soon as UNIX was chosen, my group laid out the system catalogs (data dictionary) and the access method interface. Initially, we considered a nonrelational structure for the catalogs, as that would make them somewhat more efficient. However it quickly became clear that providing a specialized access facility for the system catalogs involved code duplication and would ruin the possibility of using QUEL to query the system catalogs. The latter feature would, in essence, provide a data dictionary system for free. Hence the system catalogs became simply more relational data for the system to manage.

An idea from the very start had been to have several implementations of the access method interface. Each would have the same calling conventions for simplicity and would function interchangeably. We were committed to the relational principle that users see nothing of the underlying storage structure. Hence no provisions were made to allow a user to access a lower level of the system (as is done in some other database systems).

The INGRES project was sponsored by the U.S. Air Force Office of Scientific Research under Grant 78-3596, the U.S. Army Research Office under Grant DAAG-29-G-0245, the Naval Electronics Systems Command under Contract N00039-78-G-0013, and the National Science Foundation under Grant MCS75-03839-AD1.
Author's address: Department of Electrical Engineering and Computer Science, University of California, Berkeley, CA 94720.

During the winter of 1974 a lot of effort went into the tactics we would use for "solving" QUEL commands (query processing). The notion of tuple substitution [25] as a strategy for decomposing QUEL commands into simpler commands in QUEL itself was developed at this time. This notion of decomposition strongly influenced the resulting design. For example, having a level in the system that corresponded to the "one-variable query processor" occurred because decomposition required it.

In summary, the salient features of INGRES at the time were

(1) QUEL retrieval was defined;
(2) an integrated data dictionary was proposed;
(3) multiple implementations of the access methods were suggested;
(4) a "pure" relational system was agreed on;
(5) decomposition was developed.

This first period ended with the delivery in June 1974 of a PDP-11, which could be used on an interim basis for code development. Hence we could begin inplementing before our own machine arrived. The project was organized as a chief programmer team of four persons under the direction of Gerry Held. This same organizational structure remains today.

2.2 The First Implementation

We expected to exploit the natural parallelism which multiple UNIX processes allow. Hence decomposition would be a process to run in parallel with the one-variable query processor (OVQP). The utilities (e.g., to create relations, destroy them, and modify their storage structure) would be several overlays, but nobody was exactly sure where they would go. By this time we had decided to take protection seriously and realized that a database administrator (DBA) was an appropriate concept. He or she would own all the physical UNIX files in which relations for a given database were stored. In addition, the INGRES object code would use the "set user id" facility of UNIX so that it would run on behalf of any user with an effective user id of the DBA. This was the only way we could see to guarantee that nobody (except the DBA) could touch a database except by executing INGRES. Any less restrictive scheme would allow tampering with the database by other programs, which we thought undesirable.

Because the terminal monitor allowed the user to edit files directly, we had to protect the rest of INGRES from it. Hence it had to be a separate process. The notion of query modification for protection, integrity control, and views was developed during this time. It would be implemented with the parser, but no thought was given to the form of this module. During the summer of 1974 the process structure changed several times. Moreover, no one could coherently check any code because everyone needed the access methods as part of his code, and they did not work yet.

About this time another version of QUEL, which included updates and more general aggregates, was developed. This version survives today except for the keyword syntax, which was changed in early 1975.

By the end of the summer we had some access method code, some routines to access the data dictionary (to create and destroy relations, for example), and a terminal monitor, along with pieces of DECOMP and OVQP. In September the department arranged to invite Ken Thompson (the creator of UNIX in conjunction with Dennis Ritchie) to Berkeley for a two-week visit. Ken was instrumental in getting UNIX to run on the INGRES machine and introduced us to YACC [14] as a parser generator.

In January of 1975 we invited Ted Codd to come to Berkeley in early March to see a demonstration of INGRES. The final two weeks before his visit everyone worked night and day so that we would have something to show him. What we demonstrated was a very "buggy" system with the following characteristics:

(1) The access methods "sort of" worked. Retrieves worked on all five implementations of the access methods (heap, hash, compressed hash, index, and compressed index). However, only heaps could be updated without fear of disaster.
(2) Decomposition was implemented by brute force.
(3) A primitive database load program existed, but few other services existed.
(4) All the messy interprocess problems had been ignored. For example, there was no way to reset INGRES so that it would stop executing the current command and be ready to do something new. Instead "reset" simply killed all of the INGRES processes and returned the user to the operating system command language interpreter.
(5) There were many bugs. For example, Boolean operators sometimes worked incorrectly. The average function applied to a relation with no tuples produced a weird response, etc.

At this point it became clear that the punctuation-oriented syntax for QUEL was horrible, and it was scrapped in favor of a keyword-oriented approach. The designers of SEQUEL [4] saw this important point sooner than we did. This was the last significant change made to the user language.

During this period we spent a lot of time discussing the pros and cons of dynamic directory facilities (e.g., B-treelike structures) and static directories (e.g., ISAM). The basic issue was whether the index levels in a keyed sequential access method were read-only or not. At the time we opted for static directories and wrote the paper "B-Trees Re-examined" [13]. This is one of the mistakes discussed in Section 4.

Lastly, it became clear that we needed a coupling to a host language. Moreover, C was the only possible candidate, since it alone allowed interprocess communication; a fact essential for INGRES operation. As a result, we began work on a preprocessor EQUEL [1], to allow convenient access to INGRES from C.

The end of this initial implementation period occurred when we acquired a user. Through Ken Thompson, to whom a tape of an early system had been sent, and through a group at Bell Laboratories in Holmdel, Dan Gielan of New York Telephone Co. become interested in using our system. After using our machine for a trial period, he obtained his own and set about tailoring INGRES to his environment and fixing its flaws (many bugs, bad performance, no concurrency control, no recovery, shaky physical protection, EQUEL barely usable). In a sense, during the next year he was duplicating much of the effort at Berkeley, and the two systems quickly and radically diverged.

The following issues were resolved during this period:

(1) QUEL syntax for updates was specified;
(2) the final syntax and semantics of QUEL were defined;
(3) protection was figured out;
(4) EQUEL was designed;
(5) concurrency control and recovery loomed on the horizon as big issues, and initial discussions on these subjects were started.

2.3 Making It Really Work

The current phase of INGRES development began during the latter part of 1975. At this time the system "more or less" worked. There were lots of bugs, and it was increasingly difficult to get them out. The system had performance problems due to convoluted and inefficient code everywhere. The code was also in bad shape. It had been constructed haphazardly by several people, not all of whom were still with the project. Each had his own coding style, way of naming variables, and library of common routines. In short, the system was unmaintainable.

The objective of the current phase was to make the system efficient, reliable, and *maintainable*. At the time we did not realize that this amounted to a total rewrite. We began to operate with more so-called "controls." No longer was there arbitrary tampering with the "current" copy of the code; rudimentary testing procedures were constructed, and rigid coding conventions were enforced. We began to operate more like a production software house and less like a freewheeling, unstructured operation.

During the current phase, concurrency control and recovery were seriously addressed. We took a long time to decide whether to take concurrency control seriously and write a sophisticated locking subsystem (such as the one in System R [8, 9]), or to do a quick and dirty subsystem using either coarse physical locks (say on files or collections of files) or predicate locks [7]. We also gave considerable thought to the size of a transaction. Should it be larger than one QUEL statement? If so, the simple strategy of demanding all needed resources in advance and avoiding deadlock was not possible.

Eventually it was decided to base the transaction size largely on simplicity. Once one QUEL statement was selected as the atomic operation for concurrency control and recovery, our hunch was that coarse physical locking would be best. This was later verified by simulation experiments [16, 17].

Recovery code was postponed as long as possible because it involved major changes to the utilities. All QUEL statements went through a "deferred update" facility, which made recovery from soft crashes (i.e., the disk remains intact) easy if a QUEL statement was being executed. The more difficult problem was to survive crashes while the utilities were running. Each utility performed its own manipulation of the system catalogs in addition to other functions. Leaving the system catalogs in a consistent state required being able to back up or run forward each command. The basic idea was to create an algorithm which would pass the system catalogs once (or at most twice), find all the inconsistencies regardless of what commands were running, and take appropriate action. Creating such a program required ironclad protocols on how the utilities were to manipulate the system catalogs. Installing such protocols was a lot of work, most of it in the utilities, which by this time everyone regarded as boring code in enormous volume.

The parser had finally become so top-heavy from patches that it was rewritten from scratch. Decomposition was improved, and the system became progressively faster. In addition, the system was instrumented (no performance hooks were built in from the start). As a result we caught several serious performance botches. Elaborate tracing facilities were retrofitted to allow a decent debugging environment. In short, the entire system was rewritten.

During this time we also started to support a user community. There are currently some 100 users—all requesting better documentation, more features, and better performance. These became a serious time drain on the project.

Some of our early users appeared to be contemplating selling our software. We had taken no initial precautions to safeguard our rights to the code. It became necessary to prepare a license form and to pull everyone's lawyers into the act. This became a headache that could not easily be deflected, but which made technically supporting users look easy by comparison.

3. LESSONS

In this section some of the lessons that were learned from the INGRES project are discussed.

3.1 Goals

Our goals expanded several times (always when we were in danger of achieving the previous collection). Thus we added features which had not been thought about in the initial design (such as concurrency control and recovery) and began worrying about distributed databases (which had *never* been even talked about earlier). The effect of this goal expansion was to force us to rewrite a lot of INGRES, in some cases more than once.

3.2 Structured Design

The current wave of structured programming enthusiasts suggests the following implementation plan. Starting with the overall problem, one successively refines it until one has a tree structure of subproblems. Each level in such a tree serves as a "virtual machine" and hides its internal details from higher level machines. We encountered several problems in attempting to follow this seemingly sound advice. We discuss four of them.

(a) Use of structured design presumes that one knows what he is doing from the outset. There were many times we were confused with regard to how to proceed. In all cases we chose to do *something* as opposed to doing *nothing*, feeling that this was the most appropriate way to discover what we should have done. This philosophy caused several virtual machines to be dead wrong. Whenever this happened, a lot of redesign was inevitable. One example is the access method interface. This level was designed before it was completely understood how optimization concerning restricting scans of relations would be handled. It turned out that the interface chosen initially was ultimately not what we needed.

(b) We have had to contend with a 64K address space limitation. Initially we did not have a good understanding of how large various modules would be. On more than one occasion we ran out of space in a process which forced us into the unpleasant task of restructuring the code on space considerations alone. Moreover, since interprocess communication is not fast, we could not always structure code in the "natural" way because of performance problems.
(c) There was a strong temptation not to think out all of the details in advance. Because the design leaders had many other responsibilities, we often operated in a mode of "plan the general strategy and rough out the attack." In the subsequent detailed design, flaws would often be uncovered which we had not thought of, and corrective action would have to be taken. Often, major redesigns were the result.
(d) It was sometimes necessary to violate the information hiding of the virtual machines for performance reasons. For example, there is a utility which loads indexed sequential (ISAM-like) files and builds the directory structure. It is not reasonable to have the utility create an empty file and then add records one at a time through the access method. This strategy would result in a directory structure with unacceptable performance because of bad balance. Rather, one must sort the records, then physically lay them out on the disk, and then, as a final step, build the directory. Hence the program which loads ISAM files must know the physical structure of the ISAM access method. When this structure changed (and it did several times), the ISAM loader had to be changed.

All of these problems created a virtually constant rewrite/maintenance job of huge magnitude. In four years there were between two and five incarnations of all pieces of the system. Roughly speaking, we have rewritten a major portion of the system each year since the project began. Only now is code beginning to have a longer lifetime.

Earlier, there was hesitation on the part of the implementors to document code because it might have a short lifetime. Therefore documentation was almost nonexistent until recently.

3.3 Coding Conventions

To learn the necessity of this task was a very important lesson to us. As mentioned earlier, the equivalent of one total rewrite resulted from our initial failure in this area. We found that pieces of code which had a nontrivial lifetime were unmaintainable except by the original writer. Also, every time we gave someone responsibility for a new module, it would be rewritten according to the individual's personal standards (allegedly to clean up the other person's bad habits). This process never converges, and only coding conventions stop it.

3.4 User Support

There are lessons which we have learned about users in three areas.

3.4.1 *Serious Users.* There have been a few serious users (5–10). All are extremely bold and forward-looking people who have exercised our system extensively before committing themselves to use it. All of these users first chose UNIX (which says something about their not being a random sample of users) and then obtained INGRES.

Most have made modifications to personalize INGRES to their needs, viewed us as a collection of goofy academicians, and been pretty skeptical that our code was any good. All have been very concerned about support, future enhancements, and how much longer our research grants would last.

All have developed end-user facilities using EQUEL and given us a substantial wish list of features. The following list is typical:

(1) The system is too slow (especially for trivial interactions).
(2) The system is too slow for very large databases (whatever this means).
(3) Protection, integrity constraints, and concurrency control are missing (true for earlier versions).
(4) The EQUEL interface is not particularly friendly.
(5) The system should have partial string-matching capabilities, a data type of "bit," and a macro facility. (The wish list of such features is almost unbounded.)

Surprisingly, nobody has ever complained about the crash recovery facilities. Also, a concurrency control scheme consisting of locking the whole database would be an acceptable alternative for most of our users.

The biggest problem that these users have faced is the problem of understanding some 500,000 bytes of source code, most of it free of documentation (other than comments in the code).

The merits of INGRES that most of these users claim, rest on the following:

(1) The system is easy to use after a minor amount of training. The "start-up" cost is much lower than for other systems.
(2) The high-level language allows applications to be constructed incredibly fast, as much as ten times faster than originally anticipated.

The short coding cycle allowed at least one user to utilize a novel approach to application design. The conventional approach is to construct a specification of the application by interacting with the end user. Then programmers go into their corner to implement the specifications. A long time later they emerge with a system, and the users respond that it is not really what they wanted. Then the rounds of retrofitting begin.

The novel approach was to do application specification and coding in parallel. In other words, the application designer interacted with end users to ascertain their needs and then coded what they wanted. In a few days he returned with a working prototype (which of course was not quite what they had in mind). Then the design cycle iterated. The important point is that end users were in the design loop and their needs were met in the design process. Only the ability to write database applications quickly and economically allowed this to happen.

3.4.2 *Casual Users.* There are about 90 more "casual" users. We hear less from these people. Most are universities who use the system in teaching and research applications. These users are less disgruntled with performance and unconcerned about support.

3.4.3 *Performance Decisions*. Users are not always able to make crucial performance decisions correctly. For example, the INGRES system catalogs are accessed very frequently and in a predictable way. There are clear instructions concerning how the system catalogs should be physically structured (they begin as heaps and should be hashed when their size becomes somewhat stable). Even so, some users fail to hash them appropriately. Of course, the system continues to run; it just gets slower and slower. We have finally removed this particular decision from the user's domain entirely. It makes me a believer in automatic database design (e.g., [11])!

4. FLAT OUT MISTAKES

In this section we discuss what we believe to be the major mistakes in the current implementation.

4.1 Interpreted Code

The current prototype interprets QUEL statements even when these statements come from a host language program. An interpreter is reasonable when executing ad hoc interactions. However the EQUEL interface processes interactions from a host language program as if they were ad hoc statements. Hence parsing and finding an execution strategy are done at run time, interaction by interaction.

The problem is that most interactions from host languages are simple and done repetitively. (For example, giving a 10 percent raise to a collection of employee names read in from a terminal amounts to a single parameterized update inside a WHILE statement.) The current prototype has a fixed overhead per interaction of about 400 milliseconds (400,000 instructions). Hence throughput for simple statements is limited by this fixed overhead to about 2.5 interactions per second. Parsing at compile time would reduce this fixed overhead somewhat.

At least as serious is the fact that the interpreter consumes a lot of space. The "working set" for an EQUEL program is about 150 kbytes plus the program. For systems with a limited amount of main memory this presents a terrible burden. A compiled EQUEL would take up much less space (at least for EQUEL programs with fewer than ten interactions per program). Moreover, a compiled EQUEL could run as fewer processes, saving us some interprocess communication overhead. This issue is further discussed in Section 4.3.

The interpreter was built with ad hoc interactions in mind. Only recently did we realize the importance of a programming language interface. Now we are slowly converting INGRES to be alternatively compiled and interpreted. We were clearly naive in this respect.

4.2 Validity Checking

This mistake is related to the previous one. When an interaction is received from a terminal or an application program, it is parsed at run time. Moreover (and at a very high cost), the system catalogs are interrogated to validate that the relation exists, that the domains exist, that the constants to which the domains are being compared are of the correct type or are converted correctly, etc. This costs perhaps 100 milliseconds of the 400-milliseconds fixed overhead, and no effort has been made to minimize its impact. This makes the "do nothing" overhead high and, from a performance viewpoint, is the really expensive component of interpretation.

4.3 Process Problems

The "do nothing" overhead is greatly enlarged by our problems with a 16-bit address space. The current system runs as five processes (and the experimental system at Berkeley as six), and processing the "nothing" interaction requires that the flow of control go through eight processes. This necessitates formatting eight messages, calling the UNIX scheduler eight times, and invoking the interprocess message system (pipes) eight times. This generates about 150–175 milliseconds of the 400 milliseconds of fixed overhead.

In addition, code cannot be shared between processes. Hence the access methods must appear in every process. This causes wasted space and duplicated code. Moreover, some of the interprocess messages are the internal form of QUEL commands. As such, we require a routine to linearize a tree-structured object to pass through a pipe and the inverse of the routine to rebuild the tree in the recipient process. This is considerably more difficult than a procedure call passing as an argument a pointer to the tree. Again, the result is extra complexity, extra code, and lower performance.

Besides this performance problem, in the previous section it was noted that the process structure has changed several times because of space considerations. As a result, a considerable amount of energy has gone into designing new process structures, writing the code which correctly "spawns" the right run-time environment, and handling user interrupts correctly.

In retrospect, we had no idea how serious the performance problems associated with being forced to run multiple processes would be. It would have been clearly advantageous to choose a 32-bit machine for development; however, there was no affordable candidate to be obtained at the time we started. Also, perhaps we should have relaxed the 64K address limitation once we obtained a PDP-11/70 (which has a 128K limitation). This would have cut the number of processes somewhat. However, many of our 100 users have 11/34s or 11/40s and we were reluctant to cut them off. Lastly, we could have opted for less complexity in the code. However, to effectively cut the number of processes and the resulting overhead, the system would have to be reduced by at least a factor of 2. It is not clear that an interesting system could be written within such a constraint. The bottom line is that this has been an enormous problem, but one for which we see no obvious solution other than to buy a PDP-11/780 and correct the situation now that a 32-bit machine which can run our existing code is available.

4.4 Access Methods

Very early the decision was made not to write our own file system to get around UNIX performance (as System R elected to do for VM/370 [2]). Instead, we would simply build access methods on top of the existing file system.

The reasoning behind this decision was to avoid duplicating operating system functions. Also, exporting our code would have been more difficult if it contained its own file system. Lastly, we underestimated the severity of the performance degradation that the UNIX file system contributes to INGRES when it is processing large queries. This topic is further discussed in [12]. In retrospect, we probably should have written our own file system.

The other problem with the access methods concerns whether they are I/O bound. Our initial assumption was that it would never take INGRES more than 30 milliseconds to process a 512-byte page. Since it takes UNIX about this long to fetch a page from the disk, INGRES would always be I/O bound for systems with a single-disk controller (the usual case for PDP-11 environments). Although INGRES is sometimes I/O bound, there are significant cases where it is CPU bound [12].

The following three situations are bad mistakes when INGRES is CPU bound:

(a) An entire 512-byte page is always searched even if one is looking only for one tuple (i.e., a hash bucket is a UNIX page).
(b) A tuple may be moved in main memory one more time than is strictly necessary.
(c) A whole tuple is manipulated, rather than just desired fields.

Although we have corrected points (b) and (c), point (a) is fundamental to our design and is a mistake.

4.5 Static Directories

INGRES currently supports an indexing access method with a directory structure which is built at load time and never modified thereafter. The arguments in favor of such a structure are presented in [13]. However, we would implement a dynamic directory (as in B-trees) if the decision were made again. Two considerations have influenced the change in our thinking.

The database administrator has the added burden of periodically rebuilding a static directory structure. Also, he can achieve better performance if he indicates to INGRES a good choice for how full to load data pages initially. In the previous section we indicated that database administrators often had trouble with performance decisions, and we now believe that they should be relieved of all possible choices. Dynamic directories do not require periodic maintenance.

The second fundamental problem with static directories is that buffer requirements are not predictable. In order to achieve good performance, INGRES buffers file system pages in user space when advantageous. However, when overflow pages are present in a static directory structure, INGRES should buffer all of them. Since address space is so limited, a fixed buffer size is used and performance degrades severely when it is not large enough to hold all overflow pages. On the other hand, dynamic directories have known (and nearly constant) buffering requirements.

4.6 Decomposition

Although decomposition [25] is an elegant way to process queries and is easy to implement and optimize, there is one important case which it cannot handle. For a two-variable query involving an equijoin, it is sometimes best to sort both relations on the join field and then merge the results to identify qualifying tuples [3]. Consequently, it would be desirable for us to add this as a tactic to apply when appropriate. This would require modifying the decomposition process to look for a special case (which is not very hard) and, in addition, restructuring the INGRES process structure (since query processing is in two UNIX processes, and this would necessarily alter the interface between them). Again, the address space issue rears its ugly head!

4.7 Protection

It appears much cleaner to protect "views" as in [10] rather than base relations as in [19, 21]. It appears that sheer dogma on my part prevented us from correcting this.

4.8 Lawyers

I would be strongly tempted to put INGRES into the public domain and delete our interactions with all attorneys (ours and everyone else's). Whatever revenue the University of California derives from license fees may well not compensate for the extreme hassle which licensing has caused us. Great insecurity and our egos drove us to force others to recognize our legal position. This was probably a big mistake.

4.9 Usability

Insufficient attention has been paid to the INGRES user interface. We have learned much about "human factors" during the project and have corrected many of the botches. However, there are several which remain. Perhaps the most inconvenient is that updates are "silent." In other words, INGRES performs an update and then responds a "done." It never gives an indication of the tuples that were modified, added, or deleted (or even how many there were). This "feature" has been soundly criticized by almost everyone.

5. COMMENTS

This section contains a collection of comments about various things which do not fit easily into the earlier sections.

5.1 UNIX

As a program development tool, we feel that UNIX has few equals. We especially like the notion of the command processor; the notion of pipes; the ability to treat pipes, terminals, and files interchangeably; the ability to spawn subprocesses; and the ability to fork the command interpreter as a subprocess from within a user program. UNIX supports these features with a pleasing syntax, very few "surprises," and most unnecessary details (e.g., blocking factors for the file system) remain hidden.

The use of UNIX has certainly expedited our project immeasurably. Hence we would certainly choose it again as an operating system.

The problems which we have encountered with UNIX have almost all been associated with the fact that it was envisioned as a general-purpose time-sharing system for small machines and not as a support system for database applications.

Hence there is no concurrency control and no crash recovery for the file system. Also, the file system does not support large files (16 Mbytes is the current limit) and uses a small (512 bytes) page size. Moreover, the method used to map logical pages to physical ones is not very efficient. In general, it appears that the performance of the file system for our application could be dramatically improved.

5.2 The PDP-11

Other than the address space problems with a PDP-11, I have only two other comments regarding the hardware. First, there is no notion of "undefined" as a value for numeric data types supported by the hardware. Allowing such a notion in INGRES would require taking some legal bit pattern and by fiat making it equal undefined. Then we would have to inspect every arithmetic operation to see if the chosen pattern happened inadvertently. This could be avoided by simple hardware support (such as found on CDC 6000 machines).

Second there is no machine instruction which can move a string in main memory. Consequently, data pages are moved in main memory one word at a time inside a loop. This is a source of considerable inefficiency.

5.3 Data Models

There has been a lot of debate over the efficiency of the various data models. In fact, a major criticism of the relational model has been its (alleged) inefficiency.

There are (at least) two ways to compare the performance of database systems.

(a) The overhead for small transactions. This is a reasonable measure of how many transactions per second can be done in a typical commerical environment.
(b) The cost of a given big query.

It should be evident that (a) has nothing to do with the data model used (at least in a PDP-11 environment). It is totally an issue of the cost of the operating system, system calls, environment switches, data validity costs, etc. In fact, if INGRES were a network-oriented system and ran as five processes, it would also execute 2.5 transactions per second.

The cost of a big query is somewhat data model dependent. However, even here this cost is extremely sensitive to the cost of a system call, the operating system decisions concerning buffering and scheduling, the cost of shuffling output around and formatting it for printing, and the extent to which clever tuning has been done. In addition, the design of a database management system is often very sensitive to the features (and quirks) of the operating system on which it is constructed. (At least INGRES is.) These are probably much more important in determining performance than what data model is used.

In summary, I would allege that a comparison of two systems using different data models would result primarily in a test of the underlying operating system and the implementation skill (or man-years allowed) of the designers and only secondarily in a test of the data models.

6. INGRES PROJECT PLANS

INGRES appears to be at least potentially commercially viable. However a commercial version would require, at least

(1) someone to market it;
(2) much better documentation;
(3) someone willing to guarantee maintenance (whether or not we do it, the University of California will not promise to fix bugs);
(4) a pile of boring utilities (e.g., a report generator, a tie into some communications facilities, and access to the system from languages other than C).

Even so, we would not have a good competitive position because UNIX is not supported and because no Cobol exists for UNIX.

There has been a clear decision on the part of the major participants not to create a commercial product (although that decision is often reexamined). On the other hand, the project cannot simply announce that it has accomplished its goals and close shop. Hence we have gone through a (sometimes painful) process of self-examination to decide "what next." Here are our current plans.

6.1 Distributed INGRES

We are well into designing a distributed database version of INGRES which will run on a network of PDP-11s. The idea here is to hide the details of location of data from the users and fool them into thinking that a large unified database system exists [6, 23].

6.2 A Distributed Database Machine

This is a variant on a distributed database system in which we attempt only to improve performance. It has points in common with "back end machines" and depends on customizing nodes to improve performance [24].

6.3 A New Database Programming Language

Obviously, starting with C and an existing database language QUEL and attempting to glue them together into a composite language is rather like interfacing an apple to a pancake. It would clearly be desirable to start from scratch and design a good language. Initial thoughts on this language are presented in [15].

6.4 A Data Entry Facility

An application designer must write EQUEL programs to support his customized interface. The portion of such programs that can be attributed to the database system has shrunk to near zero (by the high-level language facilities of QUEL). Hence we are left with transactions that have virtually no database code and are entirely what might be called "screen definition, formatting, and data entry." We are designing a facility to help in this area.

6.5 Improved Integrity Control

Currently, INGRES is not very smart in this area. Other than integrity constraints [20] (which do something but not as much as might be desired), we have no systematic means to assist users with integrity/validation problems. We are investigating what can be done in this area.

It is pretty clear that all of the above will require substantial changes in the current software. Hence we can remain busy for a seemingly arbitrary amount of time. This will clearly continue until we get tired or are again in danger of meeting our goals.

ACKNOWLEDGMENT

The INGRES project has been directed by Profs. Eugene Wong and Larry Rowe in addition to myself. The role of chief programmer has been filled by Gerald Held, Peter Kreps, Eric Allman, and Robert Epstein. The following persons worked on the project at various times; Richard Berman, Ken Birman, James Ford, Paula Hawthorn, Randy Katz, Nancy MacDonald, Marc Meyer, Daniel Ries, Peter Rubinstein, Polly Siegel, Michael Ubell, Nick Whyte, Carol Williams, John Woodfill, Karel Youseffi, and William Zook.

REFERENCES

1. ALLMAN, E., HELD, G., AND STONEBRAKER, M. Embedding a data manipulation language in a general purpose programming language. Proc. ACM SIGPLAN SIGMOD Conf. on Data Abstractions, Salt Lake City, Utah, March 1976, pp. 25–35.
2. ASTRAHAN, M.M., ET AL. System R: Relational approach to database management. *ACM Trans. Database Syst. 1*, 2 (June 1976), 97-137.
3. BLASGEN, M., AND ESWARAN, K. Storage and access in relational data base systems. *IBM Syst. J.* (Dec. 1977), 363–377.
4. CHAMBERLIN, D.D., AND BOYCE, R.F. SEQUEL: A structured English query language. Proc. ACM SIGFIDET Workshop on Data Description, Access and Control, Ann Arbor, Mich., May 1974, pp. 249–264.
5. CODD, E.F. A database sublanguage founded on the relational calculus. Proc. ACM SIGFIDET Workshop on Data Description, Access and Control, San Diego, Calif., Nov. 1971, pp. 35–68.
6. EPSTEIN, R., STONEBRAKER, M., AND WONG, E. Query processing in a distributed data base system. Proc. ACM SIGMOD Conf. on Management of Data, Austin, Tex., May 1978, pp. 169–180.
7. ESWARAN, K.P., GRAY, J.N., LORIE, R.A., AND TRAIGER, I.L. The notions of consistency and predicate locks in a database system. *Comm. ACM 19*, 11 (Nov. 1976), 624–633.
8. GRAY, J.N., LORIE, R.A., PUTZOLU, G.R., AND TRAIGER, I.L. Granularity of locks and degrees of consistency in a shared data base. Res. Rep. RJ 1849, IBM Research Lab., San Jose, Calif., July 1976.
9. GRAY, J. Notes on data base operating systems. Res. Rep. RJ 2188, IBM Research Lab., San Jose, Calif., Feb. 1978.
10. GRIFFITHS, P.P., AND WADE, B.W. An authorization mechanism for a relational database system. *ACM Trans. Database Syst. 1*, 3 (Sept. 1976), 242–255.
11. HAMMER, M., AND CHAN, I. Index selection in a self adaptive data base system. Proc. ACM SIGMOD Conf. on Management of Data, Washington, D.C., June 1976, pp. 1–8.
12. HAWTHORN, P., AND STONEBRAKER, M. Use of technological advances to enhance data base management system performance. Memo No. 79-5, Electronics Res. Lab., U. of California, Berkeley, Calif., Jan. 1979.
13. HELD, G., AND STONEBRAKER, M. B-trees re-examined. *Comm. ACM 21*, 2 (Feb. 1978), 139–143.
14. JOHNSON, S. YACC—yet another compiler-compiler. Comptr. Sci. Tech. Rep. No. 32, Bell Telephone Laboratories, Murray Hill, N. J., July 1975.
15. PRENNER, C., AND ROWE, L. Programming languages for relational data base systems. Proc. Nat. Comptr. Conf., Anaheim, Calif., June 1978, pp. 849–855.
16. RIES, D.R., AND STONEBRAKER, M. Effects of locking granularity in a database management system. *ACM Trans. Database Syst. 2*, 3 (Sept. 1977), 233–246.
17. RIES, D.R., AND STONEBRAKER, M.R. Locking granularity revisted. *ACM Trans. Database Syst. 4*, 2 (June 1979), 210–227.
18. RITCHIE, D.M., AND THOMPSON, K. The UNIX time-sharing system. *Comm. ACM 17*, 7 (July 1974), 365–375.
19. STONEBRAKER, M.R., AND WONG, E. Access control in a relational data base management system by query modification. Proc. ACM Ann. Conf., San Diego, Calif., Nov. 1974, pp. 180–187.
20. STONEBRAKER, M. Implementation of integrity constraints and views by query modification. Proc. ACM SIGMOD Conf. on Management of Data, San Jose, Calif., May 1975, pp. 65–78.
21. STONEBRAKER, M., AND RUBINSTEIN, P. The INGRES protection system. Proc. ACM Ann. Conf., Houston, Tex., Nov. 1976, pp. 80–84.
22. STONEBRAKER, M., WONG, E., AND KREPS, P. The design and implementation of INGRES. *ACM Trans. Database Syst. 1*, 3 (Sept. 1976), 189–222.
23. STONEBRAKER, M. Concurrency control, crash recovery and consistency of multiple copies of data in a distributed data base system. Proc. 3rd Berkeley Workshop on Distributed Data Bases and Computer Networks, San Francisco, Calif., Aug. 1978, pp. 235–258.
24. STONEBRAKER, M. MUFFIN: A distributed data base machine. Proc. First Int. Conf. on Distributed Computing Systems, Huntsville, Ala., Oct. 1979, pp. 459–469.
25. WONG, E., AND YOUSEFFI, K. Decomposition—a strategy for query processing. *ACM Trans. Database Syst. 1*, 3 (Sept. 1976), 223–241.

Received January 1979; revised September 1979; accepted September 1979

Chapter 2

Relational Implementation Techniques

2.1 Introduction

Any data manager consists of the following modules:

1. Scanner and parser
2. Authentication
3. Query modification routines for views and integrity control
4. Query optimizer
5. Run-time system
6. Access methods
7. Buffer manager
8. Transaction support code
9. Interface to the operating system

In this collection of papers we concentrate on items 4, 7, 8 and 9. Item 1 is standard programming language material, and a reader interested in techniques in this area is referred to a text on parsing such as "the red dragon book" [AHO86]. The output of the parser is a "parse tree," which corresponds to the user command. Query modification routines to support view processing and integrity control transform this parse tree into another one, which will then be executed. A reader interested in query modification should read [STON75] for further information on the algorithms involved. The query optimizer accepts a parse tree and outputs a "query plan." This plan is typically a tree-structured data structure whose nodes contain directives concerning what steps to take (e.g., merge—join the two relations specified by the two subtrees beneath this node). Some systems compile this query plan into a machine language program, which is then directly executed by the hardware. A description of this approach is contained in [LORI79]. Other systems compile expression evaluation for individual records (e.g., age > 40 and salary < 1000) but interpret the rest of the plan data structure, [RTI86]. The general wisdom that has evolved is that compiling to machine code is not worth it. That is, the additional 10-20 percent in efficiency is not worth the extra hassle and dependence on a specific machine platform that it entails.

The query plan, whether represented as machine code or as a data structure, must make calls on the access methods. This is a collection of routines that allow a user to obtain the next record; get a record matching a unique key; and delete, replace, or insert a given record. Current data managers implement hashing and/or B-trees as their underlying access methods. For a summary of hashing one should consult the "bible" [KNUT73]. A good discussion of B-trees is presented in [COME79]. For business data-processing applications, these access methods are nearly universal. The only improvement that may find its way into commercial systems in the future is extendible hashing, which is considered in Section 9. For nonbusiness data-processing applications, a variety of new access methods may be appropriate. We will have papers on two such methods appropriate to spatial objects in Section 9.

At the bottom of the system, the access methods must fetch data pages from the file system. At the moment, all data managers have a buffer pool in application data space that is internal to the data manager. Hence, the run-time system looks first in the buffer pool to see if the required page is already in main memory. If so, it is accessed directly without further overhead. If the page is not present in main memory, the run-time system schedules a read to get it, reserves a page frame in the buffer pool to hold the incoming page, and tosses a page out of main memory to make room if necessary.

Lastly, all commercial data managers must support transaction management. This means correctly interleaving concurrent user interactions and recovering from system crashes by either finishing or backing out transactions that are in progress at the time of the crash.

In this section we concentrate on query optimization, transaction management, the operating system interface, and buffer management. First, we present what is widely regarded as the optimizer "bible," namely the System R approach presented by Pat Selinger (2.2). All commercial optimizers use some variant of her algorithms. See, for example, [KOOI82] for one variant. There are only a few comments that I want to make at this time. First, the Selinger optimizer suggests exhaustive search over all possible plans. The original INGRES optimizer [WONG76] used a hill climbing "greedy algorithm" and did not perform as well in practice. Hence, the conventional wisdom is that exhaustive search is the way to go. However, the interested reader should read [GRAE87] for evidence that hill climbing may be a better idea than originally thought.

Second, there is a big issue concerning how good the statistics should be. Selinger suggests very primitive statistics extended by some "rules of thumb" (such as the selectivity of a restriction clause is 1/10 if you don't have any better information). There is conflicting evidence about how much help better statistics might be. The evidence in [EPST80, MACK86] suggests that bad selectivity estimates can be devastating. However, [KUMA87] indicates that the plan space is fairly flat and wide selectivity excursions can be tolerated before a bad plan is selected. Readers are encouraged to examine the above papers and come to their own conclusions.

The third comment is that current commercial optimizers are at the limit of complexity with which humans can deal. Hence there has to be a way to reduce algorithm complexity in future optimizers. One approach is to convert optimizers to be rule-driven modules that use expert system construction techniques. Several authors are investigating this approach, including [GRAE87, LOHM87, ROSE86]. Another approach is to assume that giant amounts of main memory will alter the problem to one that is much easier to solve. This approach is explored in [STON88, KRIS84].

The second theme of this section is transaction management. The seminal work in this area is the 1975 paper by Jim Gray (2.3) which contains a good presentation of two-phase dynamic locking and degrees of consistency. For completeness, I have also included the original paper on optimistic methods (2.4). There have been a plethora of simulation studies that compare dynamic locking to alternate concurrency control schemes including optimistic methods (e.g., [CARE84, TAY84, AGRA85]). The net result of these studies is that dynamic locking wins except when unrealistic assumptions are made, such as the existence of an arbitrary number of processors. Hence, **all** commercial systems use dynamic locking as the method of choice. For a good treatment of the various other alternatives, the reader is directed to [BERN87].

Only a few embellishments on dynamic locking algorithms have been shown to make any sense. First, it is reasonable for read transactions to access the database as of a time in the recent past. This allows such a transaction to set no locks as explained in [CHAN82]. This allows readers to set no locks, increases parallelism, and has been implemented commercially by at least one vendor. The second embellishment concerns "hot spots" in data bases. In high transaction rate systems there are often records that many transactions wish to read or write. The ultimate hot spot is a one-record database. In order to do a large number of transactions per second to a one-record database, some new technique must be used. One possibility is to use some form of escrow transactions, as discussed in [ONEI86] and implemented in IMS Fast Path [DATE84]. The third embellishment is that increased parallelism can be obtained in B-trees if a special (non-two-phase) locking protocol is used for physical index pages. The protocol for these special cases is discussed in the fourth paper in this section (2.5).

The last concurrency control paper is another one by Jim Gray that discusses shortcomings of the transaction model (2.6). The limitations discussed in this paper have now become widely recognized but no new theory of concurrency control has been constructed to deal with them. The reader interested in initial steps in this direction is directed to [GARC87, KIM83]. Anyone who invents a more comprehensive theory of transactions will hit a research "home run."

Crash recovery is the second required service performed by any transaction manager. The very readable paper by Haerder and Reuter (2.7) presents the possible options. They categorize the techniques into:

- Atomic versus not atomic
- Force versus no force
- Steal versus no steal

Loosely, *atomic* means a shadow page recovery scheme while *not atomic* represents an update-in-place algorithm. *Force* represents the technique of forcing dirty data pages from the buffer pool when a transaction commits. *No force* is the converse. Lastly, *steal* connotes the possibility that dirty data pages will be written to disk prior to end of transaction, while *no steal* is the opposite. Although Haerder and Reuter discuss the subject as if there are a collection of reasonable techniques, in fact, most commercial systems use

- Not atomic
- No force
- Steal

The basic reasoning is that atomic writing of pages would require that the DBMS use shadow page techniques. As discussed in [GRAY81], use of this technique was one of the major mistakes of System R that had to be corrected in DB2. It and all other commercial system do "update in place." This essentially entails that writes to the disk are not atomic. Second, a DBMS will go vastly slower if it forces pages at commit time. Hence, nobody takes *force* seriously. Also, *no steal* requires enough buffer space to hold the updates of the largest transaction. Because *batch* transactions are still quite common, no commercial system is willing to make this assumption.

Lastly, most DBMSs do some logical logging to control the size of the physical log. At one extreme is pure physical logging whereby the before and after images of each changed bit are recorded in the log. Inserting a record into a B-tree index will thereby cause about half the bits on the corresponding page to be changed and result in a large log record. To avoid this cost, virtually all commercial systems place an "event" into the log of the form "key XXXX inserted onto page YYY." Hence, an insert operation to a relation with one index would result in two events being placed into the log, one for the data insert and one for the index insert. Some systems even compress the log to a single event in this case.

One can get the impression that crash recovery is complex and difficult to implement. Additionally, the code is hard to debug because one has to test it on failed databases. Lastly, it must work reliably; otherwise the client cannot recover the database. If the client is important enough and the database is central to the business, this failure could be front page news. Obviously crash recovery is a software engineering problem, a lot of code that is hard to debug and must work. There seem to be only two ways to deal with this problem. First, one could invent a new storage organization that makes crash recovery easier. This is explored in [STON87], which is included in Section 9 (9.5). The second tactic would be to abdicate crash recovery to the operating system.

The next paper in this section explores the interaction between operating systems and data managers and basically points out that traditional operating systems do not do anything that a DBMS approves of (2.8). In addition to the points mentioned in that paper, I wish to discuss two matters. Several current operating systems have taken over or are proposing to take over transaction management and free the DBMS of that burden. This matter is analyzed in [KUMA87b], and the viability of this approach seems uncertain at best, if based on physical logging.

The second point concerns large systems. If one has 1000 terminals in a large system, all running the DBMS, a DBMS process for each user will die in overhead. Such a system will have to manage 1000 DBMS processes, plus a like number probably executing user application programs. Not only will the operating system die trying to schedule all these tasks, but also the resulting system will be a memory hog. The reason is that each DBMS process will statically allocate data structures to hold the current query plan, the current parse tree, etc. If a server process is used, these data structures can be shared resulting in lower memory requirements, and also the operating system is freed from the burden of managing a large number of tasks. Hence, **all** high-performance DBMSs use a single server process or a collection of server processes for each CPU. Furthermore, ultra-high-performance systems also use a server processes to run the application programs. Hence, so-called transaction monitors on IBM systems such as CICS are executing as a single process and running application programs on behalf of a variety of users. As a result, both the DBMS and the transaction server are implementing small operating systems entirely in user space, together with control blocks for various users and a scheduler to manage running tasks. This sorry state of affairs means that each subsystem must implement a fairly complete operating system in user space.

One can only cry out in the wilderness and plead for better operating system services. Specifically, most operating systems are coded with "time-sharing" users in mind. This focus was probably appropriate for the mix of work that required operating system services in the 1970s. However, the importance of networking software and data managers in the 1980s and 1990s should not be underestimated. It would probably be appropriate for the needs of these two clients to receive greater attention in the future. I would advocate directing **all** operating system services toward the needs of these software systems, at the expense of other users.

The final paper in this section discusses buffer management (2.9). It argues convincingly that one should not use traditional LRU as a replacement algorithm. Hence, commercial systems tend to use much more complex strategies. A similar point of view is contained in [SACC86].

References

[AGRA85] Agrawal, R. et al., "Models for Studying Concurrency Control Performance: Alternatives and Implications," Proc. 1985 ACM-SIGMOD Conference on Management of Data, Austin, Tex., June 1985.

[AHO86] Aho, A. et al., "Compilers: Principles, Techniques and Tools," Addison-Wesley, Reading, Mass., 1986.

[BERN87] Bernstein, P. et al., "Concurrency Control and Recovery in Database Systems," Addison-Wesley, Reading, Mass., 1987.

[CARE84] Carey, M., and Stonebraker, M., "The Performance of Concurrency Control Algorithms for DBMSs," Proc. 1984 VLDB Conference, Singapore, Aug. 1984.

[CHAN82] Chan, A. et al., "The Implementation of an Integrated Concurrency Control and Recovery Scheme," Proc. 1982 ACM-SIGMOD Conference on Management of Data, Orlando, Fla., June 1982.

[COME79] Comer, D., "The Ubiquitous B-Tree," Computing Surveys, June 1979.

[DATE84] Date, C., "An Introduction to Database Systems (3d Edition)," Addison-Wesley, Reading, Mass., 1984.

[EPST80] Epstein, R., and Stonebraker, M., "Analysis of Distributed Database Processing Strategies," Proc. 1980 VLDB Conference, Montreal, Can., Oct. 1980.

[GARC87] Garcia-Molina, H., and Salem, K., "Sagas," Princeton University, Dept. of Computer Science, Princeton, N.J., CS-TR-070-87, Jan. 1987.

[GRAE87] Graefe, G., and Dewitt, D., "The EXODUS Optimizer Generator," Proc. 1987 ACM-SIGMOD Conference on Management of Data, San Francisco, Calif., May 1987.

[GRAY81] Gray, J. et al., "The Recovery Manager of the System R Database Manager," Computing Surveys, June 1981.

[KIM83] Kim, W. et al., "Nested Transactions for Engineering Design Databases," IBM Research, San Jose, Calif., RJ3934, June 1983.

[KNUT73] Knuth, D., "The Art of Computer Programming, Vol. 3, Sorting and Searching" Addison-Wesley, Reading, Mass., 1973.

[KOOI82] Kooi, R., and Frankforth, D., "Query Optimization in INGRES," IEEE Database Engineering, Sept. 1982.

[KRIS84] Krishnamurthy, R., and Morgan, S., "Query Processing on Personal Computers: A Pragmatic Approach," Proc. 1984 VLDB Conference, Singapore, Aug. 1984.

[KUMA87] Kumar, A., and Stonebraker, M., "The Effect of Join Selectivities on Optimal Nesting Order," SIGMOD Record, Mar. 1987.

[KUMA87b] Kumar, A., and Stonebraker, M., "Performance Evaluation of an Operating System Transaction Manager," Proc. 1987 VLDB Conference, Brighton, Eng., Sept. 1987.

[LORI79] Lorie, R., and Wade, B., "The Compilation of a High Level Data Language," IBM Research, San Jose, Calif., RJ2598, Aug. 1979.

[LOHM87] Lohman, G., "Grammar-like Functional Rules for Representing Query Optimization Alternatives," IBM Research, San Jose, Calif., RJ5992, Dec. 1987.

[MACK86] Mackert, L., and Lohman, G., "R* Optimizer Validation and Performance Evaluation for Local Queries," Proc. 1986 ACM-SIGMOD Conference on Management of Data, Washington, D.C., June 1986.

[ONEI86] O'Neil, P., "The Escrow Transactional Method," ACM-TODS, Dec. 1986.

[ROSE86] Rosenthal, A., and Helman, P., "Understanding and Extending Transformation-Based Optimizers," IEEE Database Engineering, Dec. 1986.

[RTI86] Relational Technology, Inc., "INGRES Reference Manual, Version 5.0," Alameda, Calif., 1986.

[SACC86] Sacco, G., and Schkolnick, M., "Buffer Management in Relational Database Systems," ACM-TODS, Dec. 1986.

[STON75] Stonebraker, M., "Implementation of Views and Integrity Constraints by Query Modification," Proc. 1975 ACM-SIGMOD Conference on Management of Data, San Jose, Calif., May 1975.

[STON87] Stonebraker, M., "The POSTGRES Storage System," Proc. 1987 VLDB Conference, Brighton, Eng., Sept. 1987.

[STON88] Stonebraker, M. et al., "The Design of XPRS," Electronics Research Laboratory, University of California, Berkeley, Calif., M88/07, Feb. 1988.

[TAY84] Tay, Y., and Sufi, R., "Choice and Performance in Locking in Databases," Proc. 1984 VLDB Conference, Singapore, Aug. 1984.

[WONG76] Wong, E., and Youseffi, K., "Decomposition—A Strategy for Query Processing," ACM-TODS, Sept. 1976.

Access Path Selection in a Relational Database Management System

P. Griffiths Selinger
M. M. Astrahan
D. D. Chamberlin
R. A. Lorie
T. G. Price

IBM Research Division, San Jose, California 95193

ABSTRACT: In a high level query and data manipulation language such as SQL, requests are stated non-procedurally, without reference to access paths. This paper describes how System R chooses access paths for both simple (single relation) and complex queries (such as joins), given a user specification of desired data as a boolean expression of predicates. System R is an experimental database management system developed to carry out research on the relational model of data. System R was designed and built by members of the IBM San Jose Research Laboratory.

1. Introduction

System R is an experimental database management system based on the relational model of data which has been under development at the IBM San Jose Research Laboratory since 1975 <1>. The software was developed as a research vehicle in relational database, and is not generally available outside the IBM Research Division.

This paper assumes familiarity with relational data model terminology as described in Codd <7> and Date <8>. The user interface in System R is the unified query, data definition, and manipulation language SQL <5>. Statements in SQL can be issued both from an on-line casual-user-oriented terminal interface and from programming languages such as PL/I and COBOL.

In System R a user need not know how the tuples are physically stored and what access paths are available (e.g. which columns have indexes). SQL statements do not require the user to specify anything about the access path to be used for tuple retrieval. Nor does a user specify in what order joins are to be performed. The System R optimizer chooses both join order and an access path for each table in the SQL statement. Of the many possible choices, the optimizer chooses the one which minimizes "total access cost" for performing the entire statement.

This paper will address the issues of access path selection for queries. Retrieval for data manipulation (UPDATE, DELETE) is treated similarly. Section 2 will describe the place of the optimizer in the processing of a SQL statement, and section 3 will describe the storage component access paths that are available on a single physically stored table. In section 4 the optimizer cost formulas are introduced for single table queries, and section 5 discusses the joining of two or more tables, and their corresponding costs. Nested queries (queries in predicates) are covered in section 6.

2. Processing of an SQL statement

A SQL statement is subjected to four phases of processing. Depending on the origin and contents of the statement, these phases may be separated by arbitrary intervals of time. In System R, these arbitrary time intervals are transparent to the system components which process a SQL statement. These mechanisms and a description of the processing of SQL statements from both programs and terminals are further discussed in <2>. Only an overview of those processing steps that are relevant to access path selection will be discussed here.

The four phases of statement processing are parsing, optimization, code generation, and execution. Each SQL statement is sent to the parser. where it is checked for correct syntax. A query block is represented by a SELECT list, a FROM list, and a WHERE tree, containing, respectively the list of items to be retrieved, the table(s) referenced, and the boolean combination of simple predicates specified by the user. A single SQL statement may have many query blocks because a predicate may have one operand which is itself a query.

If the parser returns without any errors detected, the OPTIMIZER component is called. The OPTIMIZER accumulates the names of tables and columns referenced in the query and looks them up in the System R catalogs to verify their existence and to retrieve information about them.

The catalog lookup portion of the OPTIMIZER also obtains statistics about the referenced relations, and the access paths available on each of them. These will be used later in access path selection. After catalog lookup has obtained the datatype and length of each column, the OPTIMIZER rescans the SELECT-list and WHERE-tree to check for semantic errors and type compatibility in both expressions and predicate comparisons.

Finally the OPTIMIZER performs access path selection. It first determines the evaluation order among the query blocks in the statement. Then for each query block, the relations in the FROM list are processed. If there is more than one relation in a block, permutations of the join order and of the method of joining are evaluated. The access paths that minimize total cost for the block are chosen from a tree of alternate path choices. This minimum cost solution is represented by a structural modification of the parse tree. The result is an execution plan in the Access Specification Language (ASL) <10>.

After a plan is chosen for each query block and represented in the parse tree, the CODE GENERATOR is called. The CODE GENERATOR is a table-driven program which translates ASL trees into machine language code to execute the plan chosen by the OPTIMIZER. In doing this it uses a relatively small number of code templates, one for each type of join method (including no join). Query blocks for nested queries are treated as "subroutines" which return values to the predicates in which they occur. The CODE GENERATOR is further described in <9>.

During code generation, the parse tree is replaced by executable machine code and its associated data structures. Either control is immediately transfered to this code or the code is stored away in the database for later execution, depending on the origin of the statement (program or terminal). In either case, when the code is ultimately executed, it calls upon the System R internal storage system (RSS) via the storage system interface (RSI) to scan each of the physically stored relations in the query. These scans are along the access paths chosen by the OPTIMIZER. The RSI commands that may be used by generated code are described in the next section.

3. <u>The Research Storage System</u>

The Research Storage System (RSS) is the storage subsystem of System R. It is responsible for maintaining physical storage of relations, access paths on these relations, locking (in a multi-user environment), and logging and recovery facilities. The RSS presents a tuple-oriented interface (RSI) to its users. Although the RSS may be used independently of System R, we are concerned here with its use for executing the code generated by the processing of SQL statements in System R, as described in the previous section. For a complete description of the RSS, see <1>.

Relations are stored in the RSS as a collection of tuples whose columns are physically contiguous. These tuples are stored on 4K byte pages; no tuple spans a page. Pages are organized into logical units called segments. Segments may contain one or more relations, but no relation may span a segment. Tuples from two or more relations may occur on the same page. Each tuple is tagged with the identification of the relation to which it belongs.

The primary way of accessing tuples in a relation is via an RSS scan. A scan returns a tuple at a time along a given access path. OPEN, NEXT, and CLOSE are the principal commands on a scan.

Two types of scans are currently available for SQL statements. The first type is a segment scan to find all the tuples of a given relation. A series of NEXTs on a segment scan simply examines all pages of the segment which contain tuples from <u>any</u> relation, and returns those tuples belonging to the given relation.

The second type of scan is an index scan. An index may be created by a System R user on one or more columns of a relation, and a relation may have any number (including zero) of indexes on it. These indexes are stored on separate pages from those containing the relation tuples. Indexes are implemented as B-trees <3>, whose leaves are pages containing sets of (key, identifiers of tuples which contain that key). Therefore a series of NEXTs on an index scan does a sequential read along the leaf pages of the index, obtaining the tuple identifiers matching a key, and using them to find and return the data tuples to the user in key value order. Index leaf pages are chained together so that NEXTs need not reference any upper level pages of the index.

In a segment scan, all the non-empty pages of a segment will be touched, regardless of whether there are any tuples from the desired relation on them. However, each page is touched only once. When an entire relation is examined via an index scan, each page of the index is touched only once, but a data page may be examined more than once if it has two tuples on it which are not "close" in the index ordering. If the tuples are inserted into segment pages in the index ordering, and if this physical proximity corresponding to index key value is maintained, we say that the index is <u>clustered</u>. A clustered index has the property that not only each index page, but also each data page containing a tuple from that relation will be touched only once in a scan on that index.

An index scan need not scan the entire relation. Starting and stopping key values may be specified in order to scan only those tuples which have a key in a range of index values. Both index and segment scans may optionally take a set of predicates, called search arguments (or SARGS), which are applied to a tuple before it is returned to the RSI caller. If the tuple satisfies the predicates, it is returned; otherwise the scan continues until it either finds a tuple which satisfies the SARGS or exhausts the segment or the specified index value range. This reduces cost by eliminating the overhead of making RSI calls for tuples which can be efficiently rejected within the RSS. Not all predicates are of the form that can become SARGS. A <u>sargable predicate</u> is one of the form (or which can be put into the form) "column comparison-operator value". SARGS are expressed as a boolean expression of such predicates in disjunctive normal form.

4. <u>Costs for single relation access paths</u>

In the next several sections we will describe the process of choosing a plan for evaluating a query. We will first describe the simplest case, accessing a single relation, and show how it extends and generalizes to 2-way joins of relations, n-way joins, and finally multiple query blocks (nested queries).

The OPTIMIZER examines both the predicates in the query and the access paths available on the relations referenced by the query, and formulates a cost prediction for each access plan, using the following cost formula:

COST = PAGE FETCHES + W * (RSI CALLS).

This cost is a weighted measure of I/O (pages fetched) and CPU utilization (instructions executed). W is an adjustable weighting factor between I/O and CPU. RSI CALLS is the predicted number of tuples returned from the RSS. Since most of System R's CPU time is spent in the RSS, the number of RSI calls is a good approximation for CPU utilization. Thus the choice of a minimum cost path to process a query attempts to minimize total resources required.

During execution of the type-compatibility and semantic checking portion of the OPTIMIZER, each query block's WHERE tree of predicates is examined. The WHERE tree is considered to be in conjunctive normal form, and every conjunct is called a <u>boolean factor</u>. Boolean factors are notable because every tuple returned to the user must satisfy every boolean factor. An index is said to match a boolean factor if the boolean factor is a sargable predicate whose referenced column is the index key; e.g., an index on SALARY matches the predicate 'SALARY = 20000'. More precisely, we say that a predicate or set of predicates <u>matches</u> an index access path when the predicates are sargable and the columns mentioned in the predicate(s) are an initial substring of the set of columns of the index key. For example, a NAME, LOCATION index matches NAME = 'SMITH' AND LOCATION = 'SAN JOSE'. If an index matches a boolean factor, an access using that index is an efficient way to satisfy the boolean factor. Sargable boolean factors can also be efficiently satisfied if they are expressed as search arguments. Note that a boolean factor may be an entire tree of predicates headed by an OR.

During catalog lookup, the OPTIMIZER retrieves statistics on the relations in the query and on the access paths available on each relation. The statistics kept are the following:

For each relation T,
- NCARD(T), the cardinality of relation T.
- TCARD(T), the number of pages in the segment that hold tuples of relation T.
- P(T), the fraction of data pages in the segment that hold tuples of relation T.
  P(T) = TCARD(T) / (no. of non-empty pages in the segment).

For each index I on relation T,
- ICARD(I), number of distinct keys in index I.
- NINDX(I), the number of pages in index I.

These statistics are maintained in the System R catalogs, and come from several sources. Initial relation loading and index creation initialize these statistics. They are then updated periodically by an UPDATE STATISTICS command, which can be run by any user. System R does not update these statistics at every INSERT, DELETE, or UPDATE because of the extra database operations and the locking bottleneck this would create at the system catalogs. Dynamic updating of statistics would tend to serialize accesses that modify the relation contents.

Using these statistics, the OPTIMIZER assigns a <u>selectivity factor</u> 'F' for each boolean factor in the predicate list. This selectivity factor very roughly corresponds to the expected fraction of tuples which will satisfy the predicate. TABLE 1 gives the selectivity factors for different kinds of predicates. We assume that a lack of statistics implies that the relation is small, so an arbitrary factor is chosen.

TABLE 1 SELECTIVITY FACTORS

```
column = value
        F = 1 / ICARD(column index) if there is an index on column
        This assumes an even distribution of tuples among the index key
        values.
        F = 1/10    otherwise

column1 = column2
        F = 1/MAX(ICARD(column1 index), ICARD(column2 index))
            if there are indexes on both column1 and column2
        This assumes that each key value in the index with the smaller
        cardinality has a matching value in the other index.
        F = 1/ICARD(column-i index) if there is only an index on column-i
        F = 1/10    otherwise

column > value (or any other open-ended comparison)
        F = (high key value - value) / (high key value - low key value)
        Linear interpolation of the value within the range of key values
        yields F if the column is an arithmetic type and value is known at
        access path selection time.
        F = 1/3 otherwise (i.e. column not arithmetic)
        There is no significance to this number, other than the fact that
        it is less selective than the guesses for equal predicates for
        which there are no indexes, and that it is less than 1/2.  We
        hypothesize that few queries use predicates that are satisfied by
        more than half the tuples.

column BETWEEN value1 AND value2
        F = (value2 - value1) / (high key value - low key value)

        A ratio of the BETWEEN value range to the entire key value range is
        used as the selectivity factor if column is arithmetic and both
        value1 and value2 are known at access path selection.
        F = 1/4 otherwise
        Again there is no significance to this choice except that it is
        between the default selectivity factors for an equal predicate and
        a range predicate.

column IN (list of values)
        F = (number of items in list) * (selectivity factor for column =
        value)
        This is allowed to be no more than 1/2.

columnA IN subquery
        F = (expected cardinality of the subquery result) /
            (product of the cardinalities of all the relations in the
        subquery's FROM-list).
        The computation of query cardinality will be discussed below.
        This formula is derived by the following argument:
        Consider the simplest case, where subquery is of the form "SELECT
        columnB FROM relationC ...". Assume that the set of all columnB
        values in relationC contains the set of all columnA values.  If all
        the tuples of relationC are selected by the subquery, then the
        predicate is always TRUE and F = 1.  If the tuples of the subquery
        are restricted by a selectivity factor F', then assume that the set
        of unique values in the subquery result that match columnA values
        is proportionately restricted, i.e. the selectivity factor for the
        predicate should be F'.  F' is the product of all the subquery's
        selectivity factors, namely (subquery cardinality) / (cardinality
        of all possible subquery answers).  With a little optimism, we can
        extend this reasoning to include subqueries which are joins and
        subqueries in which columnB is replaced by an arithmetic expression
        involving column names.  This leads to the formula given above.

(pred expression1) OR (pred expression2)
        F = F(pred1) + F(pred2) - F(pred1) * F(pred2)
```

(pred1) AND (pred2)
F = F(pred1) * F(pred2)
Note that this assumes that column values are independent.

NOT pred
F = 1 - F(pred)

Query cardinality (QCARD) is the product of the cardinalities of every relation in the query block's FROM list times the product of all the selectivity factors of that query block's boolean factors. The number of expected RSI calls (RSICARD) is the product of the relation cardinalities times the selectivity factors of the <u>sargable</u> boolean factors, since the sargable boolean factors will be put into search arguments which will filter out tuples without returning across the RSS interface.

Choosing an optimal access path for a single relation consists of using these selectivity factors in formulas together with the statistics on available access paths. Before this process is described, a definition is needed. Using an index access path or sorting tuples produces tuples in the index value or sort key order. We say that a tuple order is an <u>interesting order</u> if that order is one specified by the query block's GROUP BY or ORDER BY clauses.

For single relations, the cheapest access path is obtained by evaluating the cost for each available access path (each index on the relation, plus a segment scan). The costs will be described below. For each such access path, a predicted cost is computed along with the ordering of the tuples it will produce. Scanning along the SALARY index in ascending order, for example, will produce some cost C and a tuple order of SALARY (ascending). To find the cheapest access plan for a single relation query, we need only to examine the cheapest access path which produces tuples in each "interesting" order and the cheapest "unordered" access path. Note that an "unordered" access path may in fact produce tuples in some order, but the order is not "interesting". If there are no GROUP BY or ORDER BY clauses on the query, then there will be no interesting orderings, and the cheapest access path is the one chosen. If there are GROUP BY or ORDER BY clauses, then the cost for producing that interesting ordering must be compared to the cost of the cheapest unordered path <u>plus</u> the cost of sorting QCARD tuples into the proper order. The cheapest of these alternatives is chosen as the plan for the query block.

The cost formulas for single relation access paths are given in TABLE 2. These formulas give index pages fetched plus data pages fetched plus the weighting factor times RSI tuple retrieval calls. W is the weighting factor between page fetches and RSI calls. Some situations give several alternative formulas depending on whether the set of tuples retrieved will fit entirely in the RSS buffer pool (or effective buffer pool per user). We assume for clustered indexes that a page remains in the buffer long enough for every tuple to be retrieved from it. For non-clustered indexes, it is assumed that for those relations not fitting in the buffer, the relation is sufficiently large with respect to the buffer size that a page fetch is required for every tuple retrieval.

TABLE 2 COST FORMULAS

<u>SITUATION</u>	<u>COST</u> (<u>in pages</u>)
Unique index matching an equal predicate	1 + 1 + W
Clustered index I matching one or more boolean factors	F(preds) * (NINDX(I) + TCARD) + W * RSICARD
Non-clustered index I matching one or more boolean factors	F(preds) * (NINDX(I) + NCARD) + W * RSICARD or F(preds) * (NINDX(I) + TCARD) + W * RSICARD if this number fits in the System R buffer
Clustered index I not matching any boolean factors	(NINDX(I) + TCARD) + W * RSICARD
Non-clustered index I not matching any boolean factors	(NINDX(I) + NCARD) + W * RSICARD or (NINDX(I) + TCARD) + W * RSICARD if this number fits in the System R buffer
Segment scan	TCARD/P + W * RSICARD

5. Access path selection for joins

In 1976, Blasgen and Eswaran <4> examined a number of methods for performing 2-way joins. The performance of each of these methods was analyzed under a variety of relation cardinalities. Their evidence indicates that for other than very small relations, one of two join methods were always optimal or near optimal. The System R optimizer chooses between these two methods. We first describe these methods, and then discuss how they are extended for n-way joins. Finally we specify how the join order (the order in which the relations are joined) is chosen. For joins involving two relations, the two relations are called the outer relation, from which a tuple will be retrieved first, and the inner relation, from which tuples will be retrieved, possibly depending on the values obtained in the outer relation tuple. A predicate which relates columns of two tables to be joined is called a join predicate. The columns referenced in a join predicate are called join columns.

The first join method, called the nested loops method, uses scans, in any order, on the outer and inner relations. The scan on the outer relation is opened and the first tuple is retrieved. For each outer relation tuple obtained, a scan is opened on the inner relation to retrieve, one at a time, all the tuples of the inner relation which satisfy the join predicate. The composite tuples formed by the outer-relation-tuple / inner-relation-tuple pairs comprise the result of this join.

The second join method, called merging scans, requires the outer and inner relations to be scanned in join column order. This implies that, along with the columns mentioned in ORDER BY and GROUP BY, columns of equi-join predicates (those of the form Table1.column1 = Table2.column2) also define "interesting" orders. If there is more than one join predicate, one of them is used as the join predicate and the others are treated as ordinary predicates. The merging scans method is only applied to equi-joins, although in principle it could be applied to other types of joins. If one or both of the relations to be joined has no indexes on the join column, it must be sorted into a temporary list which is ordered by the join column.

The more complex logic of the merging scan join method takes advantage of the ordering on join columns to avoid rescanning the entire inner relation (looking for a match) for each tuple of the outer relation. It does this by synchronizing the inner and outer scans by reference to matching join column values and by "remembering" where matching join groups are located. Further savings occur if the inner relation is clustered on the join column (as would be true if it is the output of a sort on the join column). "Clustering" on a column means that tuples which have the same value in that column are physically stored close to each other so that one page access will retrieve several tuples.

N-way joins can be visualized as a sequence of 2-way joins. In this visualization, two relations are joined together, the resulting composite relation is joined with the third relation, etc. At each step of the n-way join it is possible to identify the outer relation (which in general is composite) and the inner relation (the relation being added to the join). Thus the methods described above for two way joins are easily generalized to n-way joins. However, it should be emphasized that the first 2-way join does not have to be completed before the second 2-way join is started. As soon as we get a composite tuple for the first 2-way join, it can be joined with tuples of the third relation to form result tuples for the 3-way join, etc. Nested loop joins and merge scan joins may be mixed in the same query, e.g. the first two relations of a three-way join may be joined using merge scans and the composite result may be joined with the third relation using a nested loop join. The intermediate composite relations are physically stored only if a sort is required for the next join step. When a sort of the composite relation is not specified, the composite relation will be materialized one tuple at a time to participate in the next join.

We now consider the order in which the relations are chosen to be joined. It should be noted that although the cardinality of the join of n relations is the same regardless of join order, the cost of joining in different orders can be substantially different. If a query block has n relations in its FROM list, then there are n factorial permutations of relation join orders. The search space can be reduced by observing that that once the first k relations are joined, the method to join the composite to the k+1-st relation is independent of the order of joining the first k; i.e. the applicable predicates are the same, the set of interesting orderings is the same, the possible join methods are the same, etc. Using this property, an efficient way to organize the search is to find the best join order for successively larger subsets of tables.

A heuristic is used to reduce the join order permutations which are considered. When possible, the search is reduced by consideration only of join orders which have join predicates relating the inner relation to the other relations already participating in the join. This means that in joining relations t1,t2,...,tn only those orderings ti1,ti2,...,tin are examined in which for all j (j=2,...,n) either
(1) tij has at least one join predicate

with some relation tik, where k < j, or (2) for all k > j, tik has no join predicate with ti1,ti2,...,or ti(j-1). This means that all joins requiring Cartesian products are performed as late in the join sequence as possible. For example, if T1,T2,T3 are the three relations in a query block's FROM list, and there are join predicates between T1 and T2 and between T2 and T3 on different columns than the T1-T2 join, then the following permutations are not considered:

T1-T3-T2
T3-T1-T2

To find the optimal plan for joining n relations, a tree of possible solutions is constructed. As discussed above, the search is performed by finding the best way to join subsets of the relations. For each set of relations joined, the cardinality of the composite relation is estimated and saved. In addition, for the unordered join, and for each interesting order obtained by the join thus far, the cheapest solution for achieving that order and the cost of that solution are saved. A solution consists of an ordered list of the relations to be joined, the join method used for each join, and a plan indicating how each relation is to be accessed. If either the outer composite relation or the inner relation needs to be sorted before the join, then that is also included in the plan. As in the single relation case, "interesting" orders are those listed in the query block's GROUP BY or ORDER BY clause, if any. Also every join column defines an "interesting" order. To minimize the number of different interesting orders and hence the number of solutions in the tree, equivalence classes for interesting orders are computed and only the best solution for each equivalence class is saved. For example, if there is a join predicate E.DNO = D.DNO and another join predicate D.DNO = F.DNO, then all three of these columns belong to the same order equivalence class.

The search tree is constructed by iteration on the number of relations joined so far. First, the best way is found to access each single relation for each interesting tuple ordering and for the unordered case. Next, the best way of joining any relation to these is found, subject to the heuristics for join order. This produces solutions for joining pairs of relations. Then the best way to join sets of three relations is found by consideration of all sets of two relations and joining in each third relation permitted by the join order heuristic. For each plan to join a set of relations, the order of the composite result is kept in the tree. This allows consideration of a merge scan join which would not require sorting the composite. After the complete solutions (all of the relations joined together) have been found, the optimizer chooses the cheapest solution which gives the required order, if any was specified. Note that if a solution exists with the correct order, no sort is performed for ORDER BY or GROUP BY, unless the ordered solution is more expensive than the cheapest unordered solution plus the cost of sorting into the required order.

The number of solutions which must be stored is at most 2**n (the number of subsets of n tables) times the number of interesting result orders. The computation time to generate the tree is approximately proportional to the same number. This number is frequently reduced substantially by the join order heuristic. Our experience is that typical cases require only a few thousand bytes of storage and a few tenths of a second of 370/158 CPU time. Joins of 8 tables have been optimized in a few seconds.

<u>Computation of costs</u>

The costs for joins are computed from the costs of the scans on each of the relations and the cardinalities. The costs of the scans on each of the relations are computed using the cost formulas for single relation access paths presented in section 4.

Let C-outer(path1) be the cost of scanning the outer relation via path1, and N be the cardinality of the outer relation tuples which satisfy the applicable predicates. N is computed by:

N = (product of the cardinalities of all relations T of the join so far) * (product of the selectivity factors of all applicable predicates).

Let C-inner(path2) be the cost of scanning the inner relation, applying all applicable predicates. Note that in the merge scan join this means scanning the contiguous group of the inner relation which corresponds to one join column value in the outer relation. Then the cost of a nested loop join is

C-nested-loop-join(path1,path2)=
C-outer(path1) + N * C-inner(path2)

The cost of a merge scan join can be broken up into the cost of actually doing the merge plus the cost of sorting the outer or inner relations, if required. The cost of doing the merge is

C-merge(path1,path2)=
C-outer(path1) + N * C-inner(path2)

For the case where the inner relation is sorted into a temporary relation none of the single relation access path formulas in section 4 apply. In this case the inner scan is like a segment scan except that the merging scans method makes use of the fact that the inner relation is sorted so that it is not necessary to scan the entire inner relation looking for a match. For this case we use the following formula for the cost of the inner scan.

C-inner(sorted list) =
TEMPPAGES/N + W*RSICARD

where TEMPPAGES is the number of pages

required to hold the inner relation. This formula assumes that during the merge each page of the inner relation is fetched once.

It is interesting to observe that the cost formula for nested loop joins and the cost formula for merging scans are essentially the same. The reason that merging scans is sometimes better than nested loops is that the cost of the inner scan may be much less. After sorting, the inner relation is clustered on the join column which tends to minimize the number of pages fetched, and it is not necessary to scan the entire inner relation (looking for a match) for each tuple of the outer relation.

The cost of sorting a relation, C-sort(path), includes the cost of retrieving the data using the specified access path, sorting the data, which may involve several passes, and putting the results into a temporary list. Note that prior to sorting the inner table, only the local predicates can be applied. Also, if it is necessary to sort a composite result, the entire composite relation must be stored in a temporary relation before it can be sorted. The cost of inserting the composite tuples into a temporary relation before sorting is included in C-sort(path).

EMP

NAME	DNO	JOB	SAL
SMITH	50	12	8500
JONES	50	5	15000
DOE	51	5	9500

DEPT

DNO	DNAME	LOC
50	MFG	DENVER
51	BILLING	BOULDER
52	SHIPPING	DENVER

JOB

JOB	TITLE
5	CLERK
6	TYPIST
9	SALES
12	MECHANIC

```
SELECT  NAME, TITLE, SAL, DNAME
FROM    EMP, DEPT, JOB
WHERE   TITLE='CLERK'
AND     LOC='DENVER'
AND     EMP.DNO=DEPT.DNO
AND     EMP.JOB=JOB.JOB
```

"Retrieve the name, salary, job title, and department name of employees who are clerks and work for departments in Denver."

Figure 1. JOIN example

<u>Example of tree</u>

We now show how the search is done for the example join shown in Fig. 1. First we find all of the reasonable access paths for single relations with only their local predicates applied. The results for this example are shown in Fig. 2. There are three access paths for the EMP table: an index on DNO, an index on JOB, and a segment scan. The interesting orders are DNO and JOB. The index on DNO provides the tuples in DNO order and the index on JOB provides the tuples in JOB order. The segment scan access path is, for our purposes, unordered. For this example we assume that the index on JOB is the cheapest path, so the segment scan path is pruned. For the DEPT relation there are two access paths, an index on DNO and a segment scan. We assume that the index on DNO is cheaper so the segment scan path is pruned. For the JOB relation there are two access paths, an index on JOB and a segment scan. We assume that the segment scan path is cheaper, so both paths are saved. The results just described are saved in the search tree as shown in Fig. 3. In the figures, the notation C(EMP.DNO) or C(E.DNO) means the cost of scanning EMP via the DNO index, applying all predicates which are applicable given that tuples from the specified set of relations have already been fetched. The notation Ni is used to represent the cardinalities of the different partial results.

Next, solutions for pairs of relations are found by joining a second relation to the results for single relations shown in Fig. 3. For each single relation, we find access paths for joining in each second relation for which there exists a predicate connecting it to the first relation. First we consider access path selection for nested loop joins. In this example we assume that the EMP-JOB join is cheapest by accessing JOB on the JOB index. This is

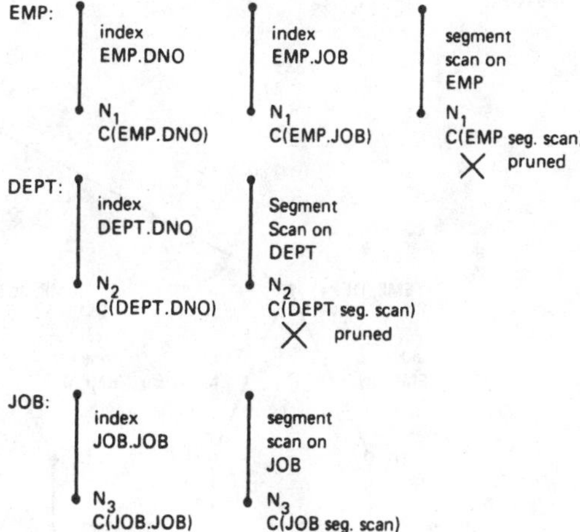

Figure 2.

likely since it can fetch directly the tuples with matching JOB (without having to scan the entire relation). In practice the cost of joining is estimated using the formulas given earlier and the cheapest path is chosen. For joining the EMP relation to the DEPT relation we assume that the DNO index is cheapest. The best access path for each second-level relation is combined with each of the plans in Fig. 3 to form the nested loop solutions shown in Fig. 4.

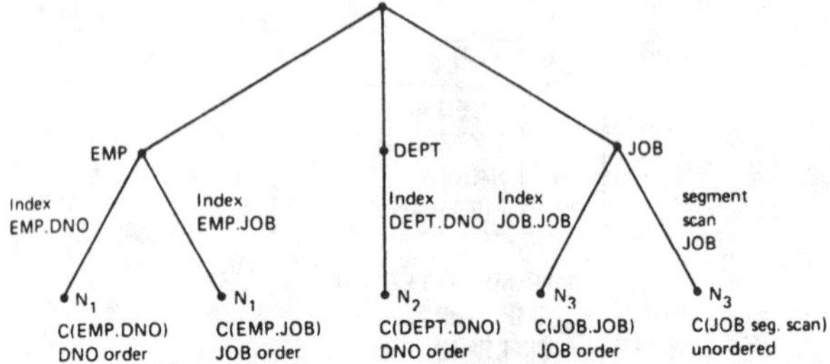

Figure 3. Search tree for single relations

Next we generate solutions using the merging scans method. As we see on the left side of Fig. 3, there is a scan on the EMP relation in DNO order, so it is possible to use this scan and the DNO scan on the DEPT relation to do a merging scans join, without any sorting. Although it is possible to do the merging join without sorting as just described, it might be cheaper to use the JOB index on EMP, sort on DNO, and then merge. Note that we never consider sorting the DEPT table because the cheapest scan on that table is already in DNO order.

For merging JOB with EMP, we only consider the JOB index on EMP since it is the cheapest access path for EMP regardless of order. Using the JOB index on JOB, we can merge without any sorting. However, it might be cheapter to sort JOB using a relation scan as input to the sort and then do the merge.

Referring to Fig. 3, we see that the access path chosen for the the DEPT relation is the DNO index. After accessing DEPT via this index, we can merge with EMP using the DNO index on EMP, again without any sorting. However, it might be cheaper to sort EMP first using the JOB index as input to the sort and then do the merge. Both of these cases are shown in Fig. 5.

As each of the costs shown in Figs. 4 and 5 are computed they are compared with the cheapest equivalent solution (same tables and same result order) found so far, and the cheapest solution is saved. After this pruning, solutions for all three relations are found. For each pair of relations, we find access paths for joining in the remaining third relation. As before we will extend the tree using nested loop joins and merging scans to join the third relation. The search tree for three relations is shown in Fig. 6. Note that in one case both the composite relation and the table being added (JOB) are sorted. Note also that for some of the cases no sorts are performed at all. In these cases, the composite result is materialized one tuple at a time and the intermediate composite relation is never stored. As before, as each of the costs are computed they are compared with the cheapest solu-

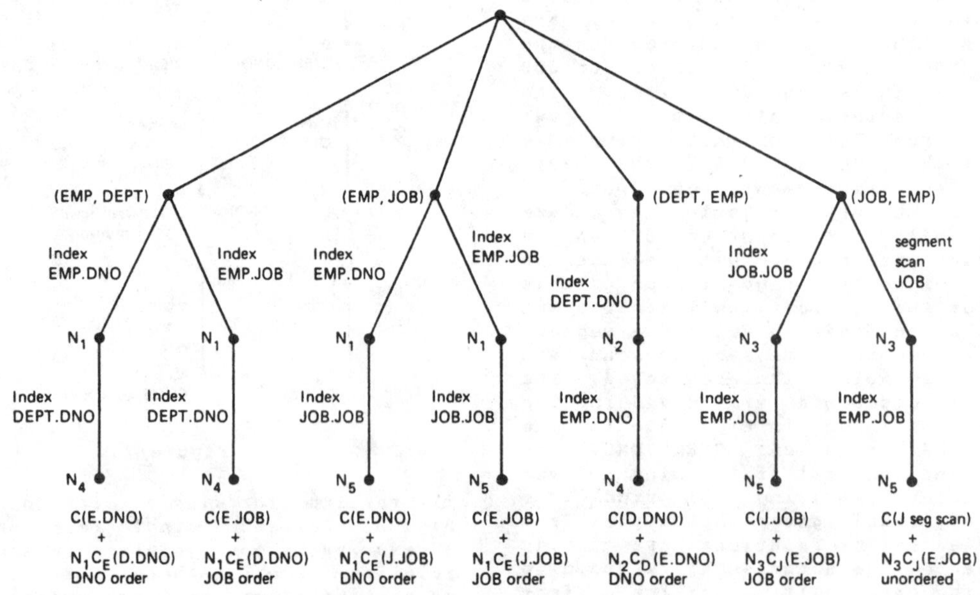

Figure 4. Extended search tree for second relation (nested loop join)

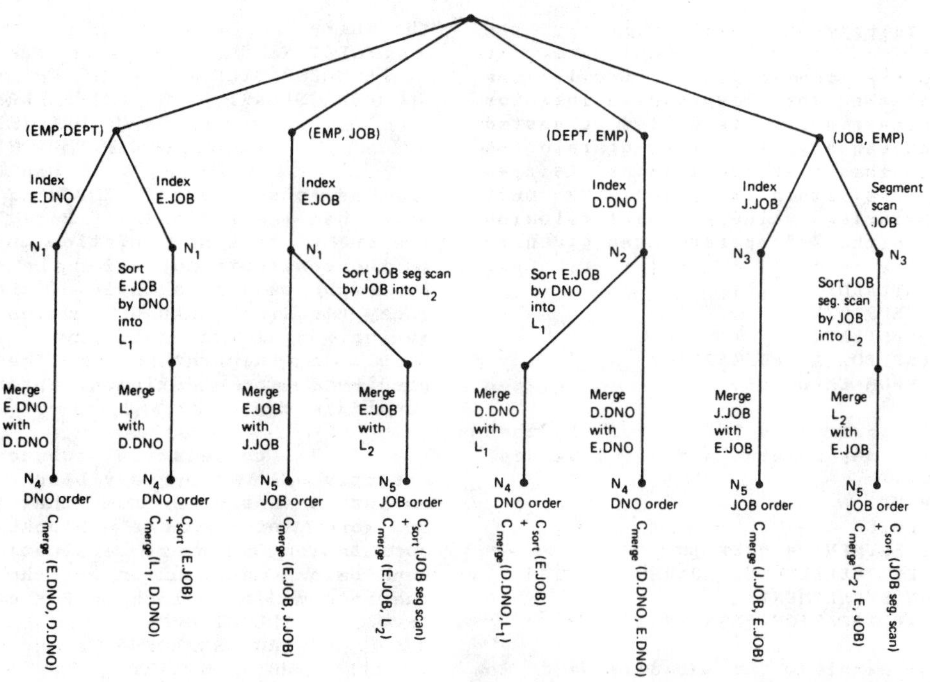

Figure 5. Extended search tree for second relation (merge join)

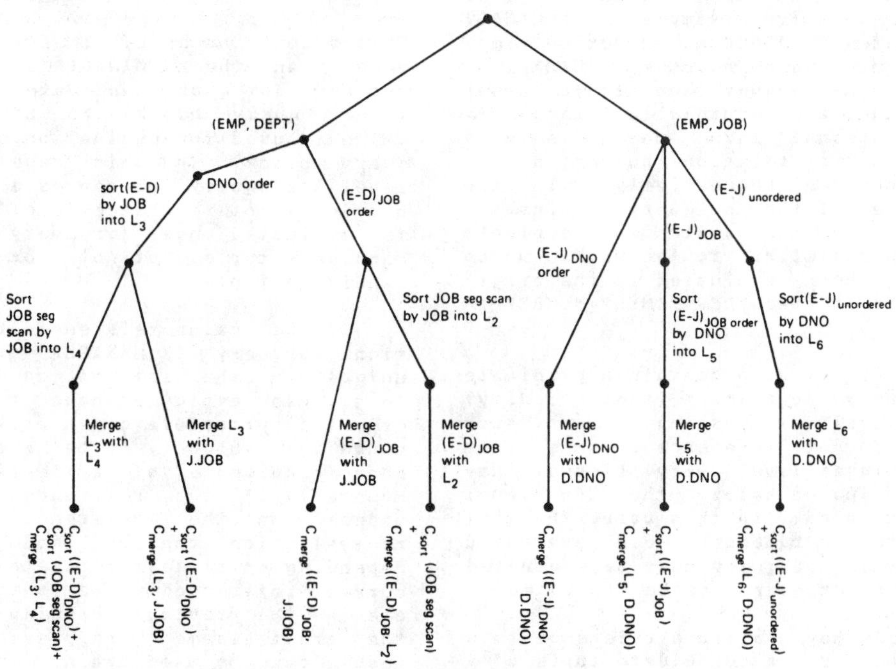

Figure 6. Extended search tree for third relation

6. Nested Queries

A query may appear as an operand of a predicate of the form "expression operator query". Such a query is called a Nested Query or a Subquery. If the operator is one of the six scalar comparisons (=, ¬=, >, >=, <, <=), then the subquery must return a single value. The following example using the "=" operator was given in section 2:

```
SELECT NAME
FROM EMPLOYEE
WHERE SALARY =
   (SELECT AVG(SALARY)
    FROM EMPLOYEE)
```

If the operator is IN or NOT IN then the subquery may return a set of values. For example:

```
SELECT NAME
FROM EMPLOYEE
WHERE DEPARTMENT_NUMBER IN
    (SELECT DEPARTMENT_NUMBER
     FROM DEPARTMENT
     WHERE LOCATION='DENVER')
```

In both examples, the subquery needs to be evaluated only once. The OPTIMIZER will arrange for the subquery to be evaluated before the top level query is evaluated. If a single value is returned, it is incorporated into the top level query as though it had been part of the original query statement; for example, if AVG(SAL) above evaluates to 15000 at execution time, then the predicate becomes "SALARY = 15000". If the subquery can return a set of values, they are returned in a temporary list, an internal form which is more efficient than a relation but which can only be accessed sequentially. In the example above, if the subquery returns the list (17,24) then the predicate is evaluated in a manner similar to the way in which it would have been evaluated if the original predicate had been DEPARTMENT_NUMBER IN (17,24).

A subquery may also contain a predicate with a subquery, down to a (theoretically) arbitrary level of nesting. When such subqueries do not reference columns from tables in higher level query blocks, they are all evaluated before the top level query is evaluated. In this case, the most deeply nested subqueries are evaluated first, since any subquery must be evaluated before its parent query can be evaluated.

A subquery may contain a reference to a value obtained from a candidate tuple of a higher level query block (see example below). Such a query is called a <u>correlation</u> subquery. A correlation subquery must in principle be re-evaluated for each candidate tuple from the referenced query block. This re-evaluation must be done before the correlation subquery's parent predicate in the higher level block can be tested for acceptance or rejection of the candidate tuple. As an example, consider the query:

```
SELECT NAME
FROM EMPLOYEE X
WHERE SALARY > (SELECT SALARY
                FROM EMPLOYEE
                WHERE EMPLOYEE_NUMBER=
                      X.MANAGER)
```

This selects names of EMPLOYEE's that earn more than their MANAGER. Here X identifies the query block and relation which furnishes the candidate tuple for the correlation. For each candidate tuple of the top level query block, the MANAGER value is used for evaluation of the subquery. The subquery result is then returned to the "SALARY >" predicate for testing acceptance of the candidate tuple.

If a correlation subquery is not directly below the query block it references but is separated from that block by one or more intermediate blocks, then the correlation subquery evaluation will be done before evaluation of the highest of the intermediate blocks. For example:

```
level 1   SELECT NAME
          FROM EMPLOYEE X
          WHERE SALARY >
level 2         (SELECT SALARY
                 FROM EMPLOYEE
                 WHERE EMPLOYEE_NUMBER =
level 3                (SELECT MANAGER
                        FROM EMPLOYEE
                        WHERE EMPLOYEE_NUMBER =
                              X.MANAGER))
```

This selects names of EMPLOYEE's that earn more than their MANAGER's MANAGER. As before, for each candidate tuple of the level-1 query block, the EMPLOYEE.MANAGER value is used for evaluation of the level-3 query block. In this case, because the level 3 subquery references a level 1 value but does not reference level 2 values, it is evaluated once for every new level 1 candidate tuple, but not for every level 2 candidate tuple.

If the value referenced by a correlation subquery (X.MANAGER above) is not unique in the set of candidate tuples (e.g., many employees have the same manager), the procedure given above will still cause the subquery to be re-evaluated for each occurrence of a replicated value. However, if the referenced relation is ordered on the referenced column, the re-evaluation can be made conditional, depending on a test of whether or not the current referenced value is the same as the one in the previous candidate tuple. If they are the same, the previous evaluation result can be used again. In some cases, it might even pay to sort the referenced relation on the referenced column in order to avoid re-evaluating subqueries unnecessarily. In order to determine whether or not the referenced column values are unique, the OPTIMIZER can use clues like NCARD > ICARD, where NCARD is the relation cardinality and ICARD is the index cardinality of an index on the referenced column.

7. Conclusion

The System R access path selection has been described for single table queries, joins, and nested queries. Evaluation work on comparing the choices made to the "right" choice is in progress, and will be described in a forthcoming paper. Preliminary results indicate that, although the costs predicted by the optimizer are often not accurate in absolute value, the true optimal path is selected in a large majority of cases. In many cases, the ordering among the estimated costs for all paths considered is precisely the same as that among the actual measured costs.

Furthermore, the cost of path selection is not overwhelming. For a two-way join, the cost of optimization is approximately equivalent to between 5 and 20 database retrievals. This number becomes even more insignificant when such a path selector is placed in an environment such as System R, where application programs are compiled once and run many times. The cost of optimization is amortized over many runs.

The key contributions of this path selector over other work in this area are the expanded use of statistics (index cardinality, for example), the inclusion of CPU utilization into the cost formulas, and the method of determining join order. Many queries are CPU-bound, particularly merge joins for which temporary relations are created and sorts performed. The concept of "selectivity factor" permits the optimizer to take advantage of as many of the query's restriction predicates as possible in the RSS search arguments and access paths. By remembering "interesting ordering" equivalence classes for joins and ORDER or GROUP specifications, the optimizer does more bookkeeping than most path selectors, but this additional work in many cases results in avoiding the storage and sorting of intermediate query results. Tree pruning and tree searching techniques allow this additional bookkeeping to be performed efficiently.

More work on validation of the optimizer cost formulas needs to be done, but we can conclude from this preliminary work that database management systems can support non-procedural query languages with performance comparable to those supporting the current more procedural languages.

Cited and General References

<1> Astrahan, M. M. et al. System R: Relational Approach to Database Management. ACM Transactions on Database Systems, Vol. 1, No. 2, June 1976, pp. 97-137.

<2> Astrahan, M. M. et al. System R: A Relational Database Management System. To appear in Computer.

<3> Bayer, R. and McCreight, E. Organization and Maintenance of Large Ordered Indices. Acta Informatica, Vol. 1, 1972.

<4> Blasgen, M.W. and Eswaran, K.P. On the Evaluation of Queries in a Relational Data Base System. IBM Research Report RJ1745, April, 1976.

<5> Chamberlin, D.D., et al. SEQUEL2: A Unified Approach to Data Definition, Manipulation, and Control. IBM Journal of Research and Development, Vol. 20, No. 6, Nov. 1976, pp. 560-575.

<6> Chamberlin, D.D., Gray, J.N., and Traiger, I.L. Views, Authorization and Locking in a Relational Data Base System. ACM National Computer Conference Proceedings, 1975, pp. 425-430.

<7> Codd, E.F. A Relational Model of Data for Large Shared Data Banks. ACM Communications, Vol. 13, No. 6, June, 1970, pp. 377-387.

<8> Date, C.J. An Introduction to Data Base Systems, Addison-Wesley, 1975.

<9> Lorie, R.A. and Wade, B.W. The Compilation of a Very High Level Data Language. IBM Research Report RJ2008, May, 1977.

<10> Lorie, R.A. and Nilsson, J.F. An Access Specification Language for a Relational Data Base System. IBM Research Report RJ2218, April, 1978.

<11> Stonebraker, M.R., Wong, E., Kreps, P., and Held, G.D. The Design and Implementation of INGRES. ACM Trans. on Database Systems, Vol. 1, No. 3, September, 1976, pp. 189-222.

<12> Todd, S. PRTV: An Efficient Implementation for Large Relational Data Bases. Proc. International Conf. on Very Large Data Bases, Framingham, Mass., September, 1975.

<13> Wong, E., and Youssefi, K. Decomposition - A Strategy for Query Processing. ACM Transactions on Database Systems, Vol. 1, No. 3 (Sept. 1976) pp. 223-241.

<14> Zloof, M.M. Query by Example. Proc. AFIPS 1975 NCC, Vol. 44, AFIPS Press, Montvale, N.J., pp. 431-437.

Granularity of Locks and Degrees of Consistency in a Shared Data Base

J.N. Gray
R.A. Lorie
G.R. Putzolu
I.L. Traiger

IBM Research Laboratory
San Jose, California

ABSTRACT: In the first part of the paper the problem of choosing the granularity (size) of lockable objects is introduced and the related tradeoff between concurrency and overhead is discussed. A locking protocol which allows simultaneous locking at various granularities by different transactions is presented. It is based on the introduction of additional lock modes besides the conventional share mode and exclusive mode. A proof is given of the equivalence of this protocol to a conventional one.

In the second part of the paper the issue of consistency in a shared environment is analyzed. This discussion is motivated by the realization that some existing data base systems use automatic lock protocols which insure protection only from certain types of inconsistencies (for instance those arising from transaction backup), thereby automatically providing a limited degree of consistency. Four degrees of consistency are introduced. They can be roughly characterized as follows: degree 0 protects others from your updates, degree 1 additionally provides protection from losing updates, degree 2 additionally provides protection from reading incorrect data items, and degree 3 additionally provides protection from reading incorrect relationships among data items (i.e. total protection). A discussion follows on the relationships of the four degrees to locking protocols, concurrency, overhead, recovery and transaction structure.

Lastly, these ideas are related to existing data management systems.

I. GRANULARITY OF LOCKS:

An important problem which arises in the design of a data base management system is choosing the lockable units, i.e. the data aggregates which are atomically locked to insure consistency. Examples of lockable units are areas, files, individual records, field values, intervals of field values, etc.

The choice of lockable units presents a tradeoff between concurrency and overhead, which is related to the size or granularity of the units themselves. On the one hand, concurrency is increased if a fine lockable unit (for example a record or field) is chosen. Such unit is appropriate for a "simple" transaction which accesses few records. On the other hand a fine unit of locking would be costly for a "complex" transaction which accesses a large number of records. Such a transaction would have to set/reset a large number of locks, hence incurring too many times the computational overhead of accessing the lock subsystem, and the storage overhead of representing a lock in memory. A coarse lockable unit (for example a file) is probably convenient for a transaction which accesses many records. However, such a coarse unit discriminates against transactions which only want to lock one member of the file. From this discussion it follows that it would be desirable to have lockable units of different granularities coexisting in the same system.

In the following a lock protocol satisfying these requirements will be described. Related implementation issues of scheduling,granting and converting lock requests are not discussed. They were covered in a companion paper [1].

Hierarchical locks:

We will first assume that the set of resources to be locked is organized in a hierarchy. Note that the concept of hierarchy is used in the context of a collection of resources and has nothing to do with the data model used in a data base system. The hierarchy of Figure 1 may be suggestive. We adopt the notation that each level of the hierarchy is given a node type which is a generic name for all the node instances of that type. For example, the data base has nodes of type area as its immediate descendants, each area in turn has nodes of type file as its immediate descendants and each file has nodes of type record as its immediate descendants in the hierarchy. Since it is a hierarchy each node has a unique parent.

Figure 1. A sample lock hierarchy.

Each node of the hierarchy can be locked. If one requests exclusive access (X) to a particular node, then when the request is granted, the requestor has exclusive access to that node and implicitly to each of its descendants. If one requests shared access (S) to a particular node, then when the request is granted, the requestor has shared access to that node and implicitly to each descendant of that node. These two access modes lock an entire subtree rooted at the requested node.

Our goal is to find some technique for implicitly locking an entire subtree. In order to lock a subtree rooted at node R in share or exclusive mode it is important to prevent share or exclusive locks on the ancestors of R which would implicitly lock R and its descendants. Hence a new access mode, intention mode (I), is introduced. Intention mode is used to "tag" (lock) all ancestors of a node to be locked in share or exclusive mode. These tags signal the fact that locking is being done at a "finer" level and prevent implicit or explicit exclusive or share locks on the ancestors.

The protocol to lock a subtree rooted at node R in exclusive or share mode is to lock all ancestors of R in intention mode and to lock node R in exclusive or share mode. So for example using Figure 1, to lock a particular file one should obtain intention access to the data base, to the area containing the file and then request exclusive (or share) access to the file itself. This implicitly locks all records of the file in exclusive (or share) mode.

Access modes and compatibility:

We say that two lock requests for the same node by two different transaction are compatible if they can be granted concurrently. The mode of the request determines its compatibility with requests made by other transactions. The three modes: X, S and I are incompatible with one another but distinct S requests may be granted together and distinct I requests may be granted together.

The compatibilities among modes derive from their semantics. Share mode allows reading but not modification of the corresponding resource by the requestor and by other transactions. The semantics of exclusive mode is that the grantee may read and modify the resource and no other transaction may read or modify the resource while the exclusive lock is set. The reason for dichotomizing share and exclusive access is that several share requests can be granted concurrently (are compatible) whereas an exclusive request is not compatible with any other request. Intention mode was introduced to be incompatible with share and exclusive mode (to prevent share and exclusive locks). However, intention mode is compatible with itself since two transactions having intention access to a node will explicitly lock descendants of the node in X, S or I mode and thereby will either be compatible with one another or will be scheduled on the basis of their requests at the finer level. For example, two transactions can be concurrently granted the data base and some area and some file in intention mode. In this case their explicit locks on records in the file will resolve any conflicts among them.

The notion of intention mode is refined to <u>intention share mode</u> (IS) and <u>intention exclusive mode</u> (IX) for two reasons: the intention share mode only requests share or intention share locks at the lower nodes of the tree (i.e. never requests an exclusive lock below the intention share node). Since read-only is a common form of access it will be profitable to distinguish this for greater concurrency. Secondly, if a transaction has an intention share lock on a node it can convert this to a share lock at a later time, but one cannot convert an intention exclusive lock to a share lock on a node (see [1] for a discussion of this point).

We recognize one further refinement of modes, namely <u>share and intention exclusive mode</u> (SIX). Suppose one transaction wants to read an entire subtree and to update particular nodes of that subtree. Using the modes provided so far it would have the options of: (a) requesting exclusive access to the root of the subtree and doing no further locking or (b) requesting intention exclusive access to the root of the subtree and explicitly locking the lower nodes in intention, share or exclusive mode. Alternative (a) has low concurrency. If only a small fraction of the read nodes are updated then alternative (b) has high locking overhead. The correct access mode would be share access to the subtree thereby allowing the transaction to read all nodes of the subtree without further locking <u>and</u> intention exclusive access to the subtree thereby allowing the transaction to set exclusive locks on those nodes in the subtree which are to be updated and IX or SIX locks on the intervening nodes. Since this is such a common case, SIX mode is introduced for this purpose. It is compatible with IS mode since other transactions requesting IS mode will explicitly lock lower nodes in IS or S mode thereby avoiding any updates (IX or X mode) produced by the SIX mode transaction. However SIX mode is not compatible with IX, S, SIX or X mode requests. An equivalent approach would be to consider only four modes (IS,IX,S,X), but to assume that a transaction can request both S and IX lock privileges on a resource.

Table 1 gives the compatibility of the request modes, where for completeness we have also introduced the <u>null mode</u> (NL) which represents the absence of requests of a resource by a transaction.

	NL	IS	IX	S	SIX	X
NL	YES	YES	YES	YES	YES	YES
IS	YES	YES	YES	YES	YES	NO
IX	YES	YES	YES	NO	NO	NO
S	YES	YES	NO	YES	NO	NO
SIX	YES	YES	NO	NO	NO	NO
X	YES	NO	NO	NO	NO	NO

Table 1. Compatibilities among access modes.

To summarize, we recognize six modes of access to a resource:

NL: Gives no access to a node i.e. represents the absence of a request of a resource.

IS: Gives <u>intention share</u> access to the requested node and allows the requestor to lock descendant nodes in S or IS mode. (It does <u>no</u> implicit locking.)

IX: Gives <u>intention exclusive</u> access to the requested node and allows the requestor to <u>explicitly</u> lock descendants in X, S, SIX, IX or IS mode. (It does <u>no</u> implicit locking.)

S: Gives <u>share</u> access to the requested node and to all descendants of the requested node without setting further locks. (It implicitly sets S locks on all descendants of the requested node.)

SIX: Gives <u>share</u> and <u>intention exclusive</u> access to the requested node. In particular it implicitly locks all descendants of the node in share mode and allows the requestor to explicitly lock descendant nodes in X, SIX or IX mode.

X: Gives <u>exclusive</u> access to the requested node and to all descendants of the requested node without setting further locks. (It implicitly sets X locks on all descendants.) (Locking lower nodes in S or IS mode would give no increased access.)

IS mode is the weakest non-null form of access to a resource. It carries fewer privileges than IX or S modes. IX mode allows IS, IX, S, SIX and X mode locks to be set on descendant nodes while S mode allows read only access to all descendants of the node without further locking. SIX mode carries the privileges of S and of IX mode (hence the name SIX). X mode is the most privileged form of access and allows reading and writing of all descendants of a node without further locking. Hence the modes can be ranked in the partial order (lattice) of privileges shown in Figure 2. Note that it is not a total order since IX and S are incomparable.

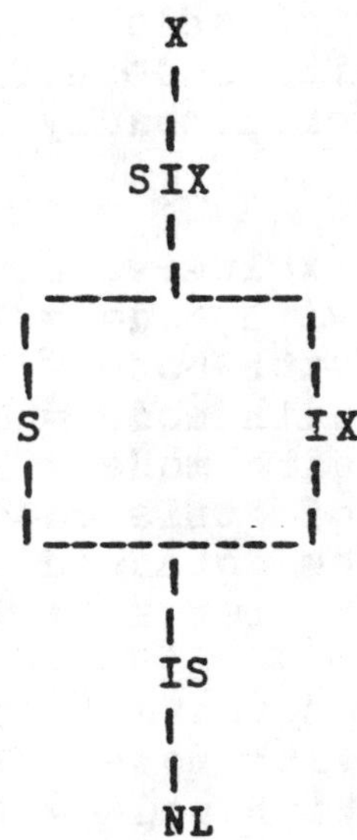

Figure 2. The partial ordering of modes by their privileges.

<u>Rules for requesting nodes</u>:

The implicit locking of nodes will not work if transactions are allowed to leap into the middle of the tree and begin locking nodes at random. The implicit locking implied by the S and X modes depends on all transactions obeying the following protocol:

(a) Before requesting an S or IS lock on a node, all ancestor nodes of the requested node must be held in IX or IS mode by the requestor.

(b) Before requesting an X, SIX or IX lock on a node, all ancestor nodes of the requested node must be held in SIX or IX mode by the requestor.

(c) Locks should be released either at the end of the transaction (in any order) or in leaf to root order. In particular, if locks are not held to end of transaction, one should not hold a lower lock after releasing its ancestor.

To paraphrase this, <u>locks are requested root to leaf, and released leaf to root</u>. Notice that leaf nodes are never requested in intention mode since they have no descendants.

<u>Several examples</u>:

It may be instructive to give a few examples of hierarchical request sequences:

```
To lock record R for read:
 lock data-base               with mode = IS
 lock area containing R       with mode = IS
 lock file containing R       with mode = IS
 lock record R                with mode = S
```

Don't panic, the transaction probably already has the data base, area and file lock.

```
To lock record R for write-exclusive access:
 lock data-base               with mode = IX
 lock area containing R       with mode = IX
 lock file containing R       with mode = IX
 lock record R                with mode = X
```

Note that if the records of this and the previous example are distinct, each request can be granted simultaneously to different transactions even though both refer to the same file.

```
To lock a file F for read and write access:
 lock data-base               with mode = IX
 lock area containing F       with mode = IX
 lock file F                  with mode = X
```

Since this reserves exclusive access to the file, if this request uses the same file as the previous two examples it or the other transactions will have to wait.

```
To lock a file F for complete scan and occasional update:
 lock data-base               with mode = IX
 lock area containing F       with mode = IX
 lock file F                  with mode = SIX
```

Thereafter, particular records in F can be locked for update by locking records in X mode. Notice that (unlike the previous example) this transaction is compatible with the first example. This is the reason for introducing SIX mode.

```
To quiesce the data base:
lock data base with mode = X.
```

Note that this locks everyone else out.

Directed acyclic graphs of locks:

The notions so far introduced can be generalized to work for directed acyclic graphs (DAG) of resources rather than simply hierarchies of resources. A tree is a simple DAG. The key observation is that to implicitly or explicitly lock a node, one should lock _all_ the parents of the node in the DAG and so by induction lock all ancestors of the node. In particular, to lock a subgraph one must implicitly or explicitly lock all ancestors of the subgraph in the appropriate mode (for a tree there is only one parent). To give an example of a non-hierarchical structure, imagine the locks are organized as in Figure 3.

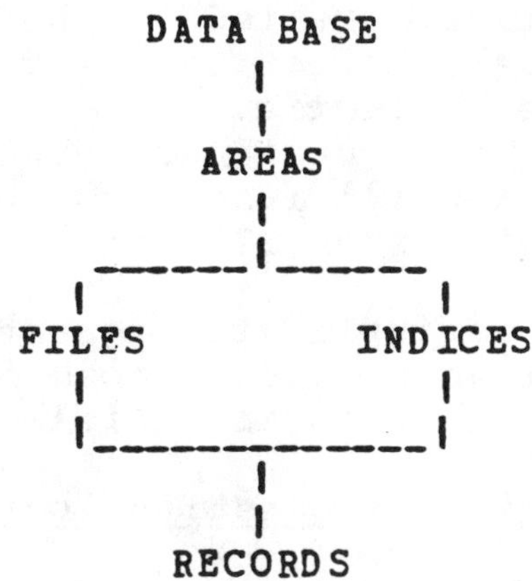

Figure 3. A non-hierarchical lock graph.

We postulate that areas are "physical" notions and that files, indices and records are logical notions. The data base is a collection of areas. Each area is a collection of files and indices. Each file has a corresponding index in the same area. Each record belongs to some file and to its corresponding index. A record is comprised of field values and some field is indexed by the index associated with the file containing the record. The file gives a sequential access path to the records and the index gives an associative access path to the records based on field values. Since individual fields are never locked, they do not appear in the lock graph.

```
To write a record R in file F with index I:
 lock data base              with mode = IX
 lock area containing F      with mode = IX
 lock file F                 with mode = IX
 lock index I                with mode = IX
 lock record R               with mode = X
```

Note that <u>all</u> paths to record R are locked. Alternaltively, one could lock F and I in exclusive mode thereby implicitly locking R in exclusive mode.

To give a more complete explanation we observe that a node can be locked <u>explicitly</u> (by requesting it) or <u>implicitly</u> (by appropriate explicit locks on the ancestors of the node) in one of five modes: IS, IX, S, SIX, X. However, the definition of implicit locks and the protocols for setting explicit locks have to be extended as follows:

A node is <u>implicitly granted in S</u> mode to a transaction if <u>at least one</u> of its parents is (implicitly or explicitly) granted to the transaction in S, SIX or X mode. By induction that means that at least one of the node's ancestors must be explicitly granted in S, SIX or X mode to the transaction.

A node is <u>implicitly granted in X</u> mode if <u>all</u> of its parents are (implicitly or explicitly) granted to the transaction in X mode. By induction, this is equivalent to the condition that all nodes in some cut set of the collection of all paths leading from the node to the roots of the graph are explicitly granted to the transaction in X mode and all ancestors of nodes in the cut set are explicitly granted in IX or SIX mode.

From Figure 2, a node is implicitly granted in IS mode if it is implicitly granted in S mode, and a node is implicitly granted in IS, IX, S and SIX mode if it is implicitly granted in X mode.

<u>The protocol for explicitly requesting locks on a DAG</u>:

(a) Before requesting an S or IS lock on a node, one should request at least one parent (and by induction a path to a root) in IS (or greater) mode. As a consequence none of the ancestors along this path can be granted to another transaction in a mode incompatible with IS.

(b) Before requesting IX, SIX or X mode access to a node, one should request all parents of the node in IX (or greater) mode. As a consequence all ancestors will be held in IX (or greater mode) and cannot be held by other transactions in a mode incompatible with IX (i.e. S, SIX, X).

(c) Locks should be released either at the end of the transaction (in any order) or in leaf to root order. In particular, if locks are not held to the end of transaction, one should not hold a lower lock after releasing its ancestors.

To give an example using Figure 3, a sequential scan of all records in file F need not use an index so one can get an implicit share lock on each record in the file by:

```
lock data base               with mode = IS
lock area containing F       with mode = IS
lock file F                  with mode = S
```

This gives implicit S mode access to all records in F. Conversely, to read a record in a file via the index I for file F, one need not get an implicit or explicit lock on file F:

```
lock data base                with mode = IS
lock area containing R        with mode = IS
lock index I                  with mode = S
```

This again gives implicit S mode access to all records in index I (in file F). In both these cases, <u>only one path was locked for reading</u>.

But to insert, delete or update a record R in file F with index I one must get an implicit or explicit lock on all ancestors of R.

The first example of this section showed how an explicit X lock on a record is obtained. To get an implicit X lock on all records in a file one can simply lock the index and file in X mode, or lock the area in X mode. The latter examples allow bulk load or update of a file without further locking since all records in the file are implicitly granted in X mode.

<u>Proof of equivalence of the lock protocol</u>.

We will now prove that the described lock protocol is equivalent to a conventional one which uses only two modes (S and X), and which locks only atomic resources (leaves of a tree or a directed graph).

Let G = (N,A) be a finite (directed) <u>graph</u> where N is the set of nodes and A is the set of arcs. G is assumed to be without circuits (i.e. there is no non-null path leading from a node n to itself). A node p is a <u>parent</u> of a node n and n is a <u>child</u> of p if there is an arc from p to n. A node n is a <u>source</u> (<u>sink</u>) if n has no parents (no children). Let SI be the set of sinks of G. An <u>ancestor</u> of node n is any node (including n) in a path from a source to n. A <u>node-slice</u> of a sink n is a collection of nodes such that each path from a source to n contains at least one of these nodes.

We also introduce the set of lock modes M = {NL,IS,IX,S,SIX,X} and the compatibility matrix C : MxM->{YES,NO} described in Table 1. We will call c : mxm->{YES,NO} the restriction of C to m = {NL,S,X}.

A <u>lock-graph</u> is a mapping L : N->M such that:

(a) if L(n) ∈ {IS,S} then either n is a source or there exists a parent p of n such that L(p) ∈ {IS,IX,S,SIX,X}. By induction there exists a path from a source to n such that L takes only values in {IS,IX,S,SIX,X} on it. Equivalently L is not equal to NL on the path.

(b) if L(n) ∈ {IX,SIX,X} then either n is a root or for all parents p1...pk of n we have L(pi) ∈ {IX,SIX,X} (i=1...k). By induction L takes only values in {IX,SIX,X} on all the ancestors of n.

The interpretation of a lock-graph is that it gives a map of the explicit locks held by a particular transaction observing the six state lock protocol described above. The notion of projection of a lock-graph is now introduced to model the set of implicit locks on atomic resources correspondingly acquired by a transaction.

The <u>projection</u> of a lock-graph L is the mapping l: SI->m constructed as follows:

(a) l(n)=X if there exist a node-slice {n1...ns} of n such that L(ni)=X (i=1...ns).

(b) l(n)=S if (a) is not satisfied and there exist an ancestor a of n such that L(a) ∈ {S,SIX,X}.

(c) l(n)=NL if (a) and (b) are not satisfied.

Two lock-graphs L1 and L2 are said to be <u>compatible</u> if C(L1(n),L2(n))=YES for all n ∈ N. Similarly two projections l1 and l2 are compatible if c(l1(n),l2(n))=YES for all n ∈ SI.

We are now in a position to prove the following <u>Theorem</u>:

If two lock-graphs L1 and L2 are compatible then their projections l1 and l2 are compatible.In other words if the explicit locks set by two transactions are not conflicting then also the three-state locks implicitely acquired are not conflicting.

<u>Proof</u>: Assume that l1 and l2 are incompatible. We want to prove that L1 and L2 are incompatible. By definition of compatibility there must exist a sink n such that l1(n)=X and l2(n) ∈ {S,X} (or vice versa). By definition of projection there must exist a node-slice {n1...ns} of n such that L1(n1)=...=L1(ns)=X. Also there must exist an ancestor n0 of n such that L2(n0) ∈ {S,SIX,X}. From the definition of lock-graph there is a path P1 from a source to n0 on which L2 does not take the value NL.

If P1 intersects the node-slice at ni then L1 and L2 are incompatible since L1(ni)=X which is incompatible with the non null value of L2(ni). Hence the theorem is proved.

Alternatively there is a path P2 from n0 to the sink n which intersects the node-slice at ni. From the definition of lock-graph L1 takes a value in {IX,SIX,X} on all ancestors of ni. In particular L1(n0) ∈ {IX,SIX,X}. Since L2(n0) ∈ {S,SIX,X} we have C(L1(n0),L2(n0))=NO. Q.E.D.

<u>Dynamic lock graphs</u>:

Thus far we have pretended that the lock graph is static. However, examination of Figure 3 suggests otherwise. Areas, files and indices are dynamically created and destroyed, and of course records are continually inserted, updated, and deleted. (If the data base is only read, then there is no need for locking at all.)

The lock protocol for such operations is nicely demonstrated by the implementation of <u>index interval locks</u>. Rather than being forced to lock entire indices or individual records, we would like to be able to lock all records with a certain index value; for example, lock all records in the bank account file with the location field equal to Napa. Therefore, the index is partitioned into lockable key value intervals. Each indexed record "belongs" to a particular index interval and all records in a file with the same field value on an indexed field will belong to the same key value interval (i.e. all Napa accounts will belong to the same interval). This new structure is depicted in Figure 4.

DATA BASE

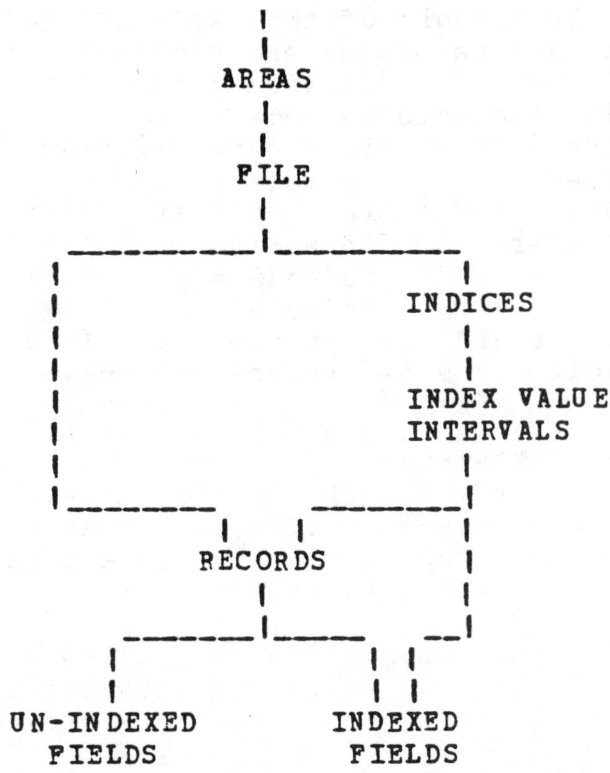

Figure 4. The lock graph with key interval locks.

The only subtle aspect of Figure 4 is the dichotomy between indexed and un-indexed fields and the fact that a key value interval is the parent of both the record and its indexed fields. Since the field value and record identifier (data base key) appear in the index, one can read the field directly (i.e. without touching the record). Hence a key value interval is a parent of the corresponding field values. On the other hand, the index "points" via record identifiers to all records with that value and so is a parent of all records with that field value.

Since Figure 4 defines a DAG, the protocol of the previous section can be used to lock the nodes of the graph. However, it should be extended as follows. When an indexed field is updated, it and its parent record move from one index interval to another. So for example when a Napa account is moved to the St. Helena branch, the account record and its location field "leave" the Napa interval of the location index and "join" the St. Helena index interval. When a new record is inserted it "joins" the interval containing the new field value and also it "joins" the file. Deletion removes the record from the index interval and from the file.

The lock protocol for changing the parents of a node is:

(d) Before moving a node in the lock graph, the node must be implicitly or explicitly granted in X mode in both its old and its new position in the graph. Further, the node must not be moved in such a way as to create a cycle in the graph.

So to carry out the example of this section, to move a Napa bank account to the St. Helena branch one would:

```
 lock data base                 in mode = IX
 lock area containg accounts    in mode = IX
 lock accounts file             in mode = IX
 lock location index            in mode = IX
 lock Napa interval             in mode = IX
 lock St. Helena interval       in mode = IX
 lock record                    in mode = IX
 lock field                     in mode = X.
```

Alternatively, one could get an implicit lock on the field by requesting explicit X mode locks on the record and index intervals.

II. DEGREES OF CONSISTENCY:

The data base consists of entities which are known to be structured in certain ways. This structure is best thought of as assertions about the data. Examples of such assertions are:

'Names is an index for Telephone_numbers.'

'The value of Count_of_x gives the number of employees in department x.'

The data base is said to be consistent if it satisfies all its assertions [2]. In some cases, the data base must become temporarily inconsistent in order to transform it to a new consistent state. For example, adding a new employee involves several atomic actions and the updating of several fields. The data base may be inconsistent until all these updates have been completed.

To cope with these temporary inconsistencies, sequences of atomic actions are grouped to form transactions. Transactions are the units of consistency. They are larger atomic actions on the data base which transform it from one consistent state to a new consistent state. Transactions preserve consistency. If some action of a transaction fails then the entire transaction is 'undone' thereby returning the data base to a consistent state. Thus transactions are also the units of recovery. Hardware failure, system error, deadlock, protection violations and program error are each a source of such failure. The system may enforce the consistency assertions and undo a transaction which tries to leave the data base in an inconsistent state.

If transactions are run one at a time then each transaction will see the consistent state left behind by its predecessor. But if several transactions are scheduled concurrently then locking is required to insure that the inputs to each transaction are consistent.

Responsibility for requesting and releasing locks can be either assumed by the user or delegated to the system. User controlled locking results in potentially fewer locks due to the user's knowledge of the semantics of the data. On the other hand, user controlled locking requires difficult and potentially unreliable application programming. Hence the approach taken by some data base systems is to use automatic lock protocols which insure protection from general types of inconsistencies, while still relying on the user to protect himself against other sources of inconsistencies. For example, a system may automatically lock updated records but not records which are read. Such a system prevents lost updates arising from transaction backup. Still, the user should explicitly lock records in a read-update sequence to insure that the read value does not change before the actual update. In other words, a user is guaranteed a limited automatic degree of consistency. This degree of consistency may be system wide or the system may provide options to select it (for instance a lock protocol may be associated with a transaction or with an entity).

We now present several _equivalent_ definitions of four consistency degrees:

Informal definition of consistency:

An output (write) of a transaction is _committed_ when the transaction abdicates the right to 'undo' the write thereby making the new value available to all other transactions. Outputs are said to be _uncommitted_ or _dirty_ if they are not yet committed by the writer. Concurrent execution raises the problem that reading or writing other transactions' dirty data may yield inconsistent data.

Using this notion of dirty data, the degrees of consistency may be defined as:

Definition 1:

Degree 3: Transaction T _sees degree 3 consistency_ if:
- (a) T does not overwrite dirty data of other transactions.
- (b) T does not commit any writes until it completes all its writes (i.e. until the end of transaction (EOT)).
- (c) T does not read dirty data from other transactions.
- (d) Other transactions do not dirty any data read by T before T completes.

Degree 2: Transaction T _sees degree 2 consistency_ if:
- (a) T does not overwrite dirty data of other transactions.
- (b) T does not commit any writes before EOT.
- (c) T does not read dirty data of other transactions.

Degree 1: Transaction T _sees degree 1 consistency_ if:
- (a) T does not overwrite dirty data of other transactions.
- (b) T does not commit any writes before EOT.

Degree 0: Transaction T _sees degree 0 consistency_ if:
- (a) T does not overwrite dirty data of other transactions.

Note that if a transaction sees a high degree of consistency then it also sees all the lower degrees.

These definitions have implications for transaction recovery. Transactions are dichotomized as _recoverable transactions_ which can be undone without affecting other transactions, and _unrecoverable transactions_ which cannot be undone because they have committed data to other transactions and to the external world. Unrecoverable transactions cannot be undone without cascading transaction backup to other transactions and to the external world (e.g. 'unprinting' a message is usually impossible). If the system is to undo individual transactions without cascading backup to other transactions then none of the transaction's writes can be committed before the end of the transaction. Otherwise some other transaction could further update the entity thereby making it impossible to perform transaction backup without propagating backup to the subsequent transaction.

Degree 0 consistent transactions are unrecoverable because they commit outputs before the end of transaction. If all transactions see at least degree 0 consistency, then any transaction which is at least degree 1 consistent is recoverable because it does not commit writes before the end of the transaction. For this reason, many data base systems require that all transactions see at least degree 1 consistency in order to guarantee that all transactions are recoverable.

Degree 2 consistency isolates a transaction from the uncommitted data of other transactions. With degree 1 consistency a transaction might read uncommitted values which are subsequently updated or are undone.

Degree 3 consistency isolates the transaction from dirty relationships among entities. For example, a degree 2 consistent transaction may read two different (committed) values if it reads the same entity twice. This is because a transaction which updates the entity could begin, update and end in the interval of time between the two reads. More elaborate kinds of anomalies due to concurrency are possible if one updates an entity after reading it or if more than one entity is involved (see example below). Degree 3 consistency completely isolates the transaction from inconsistencies due to concurrency.

To give an example which demonstrates the application of these several degrees of consistency, imagine a process control system in which some transaction is dedicated to reading a gauge and periodically writing batches of values into a list. Each gauge reading is an individual entity. For performance reasons, this transaction sees degree 0 consistency, committing all gauge readings as soon as they enter the data base. This transaction is not recoverable (can't be undone). A second transaction is run periodically which reads all the recent gauge readings, computes a mean and variance and writes these computed values as entities in the data base. Since we want these two values to be consistent with one another, they must be committed together (i.e. one cannot commit the first before the second is written). This allows transaction undo in the case that it aborts after writing only one of the two values. Hence this statistical summary transaction should see degree 1. A third transaction which reads the mean and writes it on a display sees degree 2 consistency. It will not read a mean which might be 'undone' by a backup. Another transaction which reads both the mean and the variance must see degree 3 consistency to insure that the mean and variance derive from the same computation (i.e. the same run which wrote the mean also wrote the variance).

Lock protocol definition of consistency:

Whether an instantiation of a transaction sees degree 0, 1, 2 or 3 consistency depends on the actions of other concurrent transactions. Lock protocols are used by a transaction to guarantee itself a certain degree of consistency independent of the behavior of other transactions (so long as all transactions at least observe the degree 0 protocol).

The degrees of consistency can be operationally defined by the lock protocols which produce them. A transaction locks its inputs to guarantee their consistency and locks its outputs to mark them as dirty (uncommitted). Degrees 0, 1 and 2 are important because of the efficiencies implicit in these protocols. Obviously, it is cheaper to lock less.

Locks are dichotomized as share mode locks which allow multiple readers of the same entity and exclusive mode locks which reserve exclusive access to an entity. Locks may also be characterized by their duration: locks held for the duration of a single action are called short duration locks while locks held to the end of the transaction are called long duration locks. Short duration locks are used to mark or test for dirty data for the duration of an action rather than for the duration of the transaction.

The lock protocols are:

Definition 2:

Degree 3: transaction T observes degree 3 lock protocol if:
 (a) T sets a long exclusive lock on any data it dirties.
 (b) T sets a long share lock on any data it reads.

Degree 2: transaction T observes degree 2 lock protocol if:
 (a) T sets a long exclusive lock on any data it dirties.
 (b) T sets a (posibly short) share lock on any data it reads.

Degree 1: transaction T observes degree 1 lock protocol if:
 (a) T sets a long exclusive lock on any data it dirties.

Degree 0: transaction T observes degree 0 lock protocol if:
 (a) T sets a (possibly short) exclusive lock on any data it dirties.

The lock protocol definitions can be stated more tersly with the introduction of the following notation. A transaction is well formed with respect to writes (reads) if it always locks an entity in exclusive (shared or exclusive) mode before writing (reading) it. The transaction is well formed if it is well formed with respect to reads and writes.

A transaction is two phase (with respect to reads or updates) if it does not (share or exclusive) lock an entity after unlocking some entity. A two phase transaction has a growing phase during which it acquires locks and a shrinking phase during which it releases locks.

Definition 2 is too restrictive in the sense that consistency will not require that a transaction hold all locks to the EOT (i.e. the EOT is the shrinking phase); rather the constraint that the transaction be two phase is adaquate to insure consistency. On the other hand, once a transaction unlocks an updated entity, it has committed that entity and so cannot be undone without cascading backup to any transactions which may have subsequently read the entity. For that reason, the shrinking phase is usually deferred to the end of the transaction so that the transaction is always recoverable and so that all updates are committed together. The lock protocols can be redefined as:

Definition 2':

Degree 3: T is well formed
and T is two phase.

Degree 2: T is well formed
and T is two phase with respect to writes.

Degree 1: T is well formed with respect to writes
and T is two phase with respect to writes.

Degree 0: T is well formed with respect to writes.

All transactions are <u>required</u> to observe the degree 0 locking protocol so that they do not update the uncommitted updates of others. Degrees 1, 2 and 3 provide increasing system-guaranteed consistency.

<u>Consistency of schedules</u>:

The definition of what it means for a transaction to see a degree of consistency was originally given in terms of dirty data. In order to make the notion of dirty data explicit it is necessary to consider the execution of a transaction in the context of a set of concurrently executing transactions. To do this we introduce the notion of a schedule for a set of transactions. A schedule can be thought of as a history or audit trail of the actions performed by the set of transactions. Gven a schedule the notion of a particular entity being dirtied by a particular transaction is made explicit and hence the notion of seeing a certain degree of consistency is formalized. These notions may then be used to connect the various definitions of consistency and show their equivalence.

The system directly supports <u>entities</u> and <u>actions</u>. Actions are categorized as <u>begin</u> actions, <u>end</u> actions, <u>share lock</u> actions, <u>exclusive lock</u> actions, <u>unlock</u> actions, <u>read</u> actions, and <u>write</u> actions. An end action is presumed to unlock any locks held by the transaction but not explicitly unlocked by the transaction. For the purposes of the following definitions, share lock actions and their corresponding unlock actions are additionally considered to be read actions and exclusive lock actions and their corresponding unlock actions are additionally considered to be write actions.

A transaction is any sequence of actions beginning with a begin action and ending with an end action and not containing other begin or end actions.

Any (sequence preserving) merging of the actions of a set of transactions into a single sequence is called a schedule for the set of transactions.

A schedule is a history of the order in which actions are executed (it does not record actions which are undone due to backup). The simplest schedules run all actions of one transaction and then all actions of another transaction,... Such one-transaction-at-a-time schedules are called serial because they have no concurrency among transactions. Clearly, a serial schedule has no concurrency induced inconsistency and no transaction sees dirty data.

Locking constrains the set of allowed schedules. In particular, a schedule is legal only if it does not schedule a lock action on an entity for one transaction when that entity is already locked by some other transaction in a conflicting mode.

An initial state and a schedule completely define the system's behavior. At each step of the schedule one can deduce which entity values have been committed and which are dirty: if locking is used, updated data is dirty until it is unlocked.

Since a schedule makes the definition of dirty data explicit, one can apply Definition 1 to define consistent schedules:

Definition 3:

A transaction runs at degree 0 (1, 2 or 3) consistency in schedule S if T sees degree 0 (1, 2 or 3) consistency in S.
If all transactions run at degree 0 (1,2 or 3) consistency in schedule S then S is said to be a degree 0 (1, 2 or 3) consistent schedule.

Given these definitions one can show:

Assertion 1:
(a) If each transaction observes the degree 0 (1, 2 or 3) lock protocol (Definition 2) then any legal schedule is degree 0 (1, 2 or 3) consistent (Definition 3) (i.e, each transaction sees degree 0 (1, 2 or 3) consistency in the sense of Definition 1).
(b) Unless transaction T observes the degree 1 (2 or 3) lock protocol then it is possible to define another transaction T'

which does observe the degree 1 (2 or 3) lock protocol such that T and T' have a legal schedule S but T does not run at degree 1 (2 or 3) consistency in S.

Assertion 1 says that if a transaction observes the lock protocol definition of consistency (Definition 2) then it is assured of the informal definition of consistency based on committed and dirty data (Definition 1). Unless a transaction actually sets the locks prescribed by degree 1 (2 or 3) consistency one can construct transaction mixes and schedules which will cause the transaction to run at (see) a lower degree of consistency. However, in particular cases such transaction mixes may never occur due to the structure or use of the system. In these cases an apparently low degree of locking may actually provide degree 3 consistency. For example, a data base reorganization usually need do no locking since it is run as an off-line utility which is never run concurrently with other transactions.

<u>Assertion 2</u>:
If each transaction in a set of transactions at least observes the degree 0 lock protocol and if transaction T observes the degree 1 (2 or 3) lock protocol then T runs at degree 1 (2 or 3) consistency (Definitions 1, 3) in any legal schedule for the set of transactions.

Assertion 2 says that each transaction can choose its degree of consistency so long as all transactions observe at least degree 0 protocols. Of course the outputs of degree 0, 1 or 2 consistent transactions may be degree 0, 1 or 2 consistent (i.e. inconsistent) because they were computed with potentially inconsistent inputs. One can imagine that each data entity is tagged with the degree of consistency of its writer. A transaction must beware of reading entities tagged with degrees lower than the degree of the transaction.

<u>Dependencies among transactions</u>:

One transaction is said to depend on another if the first takes some of its inputs from the second. The notion of dependency is defined differently for each degree of consistency. These dependency relations are completely defined by a schedule and can be useful in discussing consistency and recovery.

Each schedule defines three <u>relations</u>: <, << and <<< on the set of transactions as follows. Suppose that transaction T performs action a on entity e at some step in the schedule and that transaction T' performs action a' on entity e at a later step in the schedule. Further suppose that T does not equal T'. Then:

T <<< T' if a is a write action and a' is a write action
or a is a write action and a' is a read action
or a is a read action and a' is a write action

T << T' if a is a write action and a' is a write action

or a is a write action and a' is a read action

T < T' if a is a write action and a' is a write action

The following table is a notationally convenient way of seeing these definitions:

```
<<<  :  W->W  |  W->R  |  R->W

<<   :  W->W  |  W->R

<    :  W->W
```

meaning that (for example) T <<< T' if T writes (W) something later read (R) by T' or written (W) by T' or T reads (R) something later written (W) by T'.

Let <* be the transitive closure of <, then define:
BEFORE1(T) = {T'| T' <* T}
AFTER1(T) = {T'| T <* T'}.

The sets BEFORE2, AFTER2, BEFORE3 and AFTER3 are defined analogously for << and <<<.

The obvious interpretation for this is that each BEFORE set is the set of transactions which contribute inputs to T and each AFTER set is the set of transactions which take their inputs from T (where the ordering only considers dependencies induced by the corresponding consistency degree).

If some transaction is both before T and after T in some schedule then no serial schedule could give such results. In this case concurrency has introduced inconsistency. On the other hand, if all relevant transactions are either before or after T (but not both) then T will see a consistent state (of the corresponding degree). If all transactions dichotomize others in this way then the relation <* (<<* or <<<*) will be a partial order and the whole schedule will give degree 1 (2 or 3) consistency. This can be strengthened to:

<u>Assertion 3</u>:
A schedule is degree 1 (2 or 3) consistent if and only if the relation <* (<<* or <<<*) is a partial order.

The <, << and <<< relations are variants of the dependency sets introduced in [2]. In that paper only degree 3 consistency is introduced and Assertion 3 was proved for that case. In particular such a schedule is equivalent to the serial schedule obtained by running the transactions one at a time in <<< order. The proofs of [2] generalize fairly easily to handle assertion 1 in the case of degree 1 or 2 consistency.

Consider the following example:

```
T1 LOCK    A
```

```
T1 READ    A
T1 UNLOCK  A
T2 LOCK    A
T2 WRITE   A
T2 LOCK    B
T2 WRITE   B
T2 UNLOCK  A
T2 UNLOCK  B
T1 LOCK    B
T1 WRITE   B
T1 UNLOCK  B
```

In this schedule T2 gives B to T1 and T2 updates A after T1 reads A so T2<T1, T2<<T1, T2<<<T1 and T1<<<T2. The schedule is degree 2 consistent but not degree 3 consistent. It runs T1 at degree 2 consistency and T2 at degree 3 consitency.

It would be nice to define a transaction to see degree 1 (2 or 3) consistency if and only if the BEFORE and AFTER sets are disjoint in some schedule. However, this is not restrictive enough, rather one must require that the before and after sets be disjoint in all schedules in order to state Definition 1 in terms of dependencies. Further, there seems to be no natural way to define the dependencies of degree 0 consistency. Hence the principal application of the dependency definition is as a proof technique and for discussing schedules and recovery issues.

Relationship to transaction backup and system recovery:

As mentioned previously, system wide degree 1 consistency allows transaction backup and system recovery without lost updates. (i.e. without affecting updates of transactions which are not being backed up). The transaction is unrecoverable after its first commit of an update (unlock) and so although degree 1 does not require it, the shrinking phase is usually deferred to the end of transaction so that the transaction is recoverable.

Given any current state and a time ordered log of the updates of transactions, one can return to a consistent state by un-doing any incomplete transactions (uncommitted updates). Given a checkpoint at time T0 and a log which records old and new values of entities up to time T0+e, one can construct the most recent consistent state by undoing all updates which were made before time T0 but were not yet committed at time T0+e; and by redoing all updates which were made and committed in the interval T0 to T0+e. If the schedule (log) is degree 0 consistent then the actions can be re-done LOG order (skipping uncommitted updates). If the schedule (log) is degree 1 consistent then the actions can be sorted by transaction in <* order and recovery performed with the sorted log. The outcome of this process will be a state reflecting all the changes made by all transactions which completed before the log stopped.

However, degree 1 consistent transactions may read uncommitted (dirty) data. Transaction and system recovery may undo uncommitted updates. So if the degree 1 consistent transaction is re-run (i.e. re-executed by the system) in the absence of the undone transactions it may produce entirely different results than would be obtained if the transaction were blindly re-done (from the updates recorded in the log). If the system is degree 2 consistent then no transaction reads uncommitted data. So if the completed transactions are re-done in log order but in the absence of some undone (incomplete) transactions they will give exactly the same results as were obtained in the presence of the undone transactions. In particular, if the transactions were re-run in the order specified by the log but in the absence of the undone transactions the same consistent state would result.

ISSUE	DEGREE 0	DEGREE 1	DEGREE 2	DEGREE 3
COMMITTED DATA	WRITES ARE COMMITTED IMMEDIATELY	WRITES ARE COMMITTED AT EOT	SAME	SAME
DIRTY DATA	YOU DON'T UPDATE DIRTY DATA	0 AND NO ONE ELSE UPDATES YOUR DIRTY DATA	0,1 AND YOU DON'T READ DIRTY DATA	0,1,2 AND NO ONE ELSE DIRTIES DATA YOU READ
LOCK PROTOCOL	SET SHORT EXCL. LOCKS ON ANY DATA YOU WRITE	SET LONG EXCL. LOCKS ON ANY DATA YOU WRITE	1 AND SET SHORT SHARE LOCKS ON ANY DATA YOU READ	1 AND SET LONG SHARE LOCKS ON ANY DATA YOU READ
TRANSACTION STRUCTURE see [1]	WELL FORMED WRT WRITES	(WELL FORMED AND 2 PHASE) WRT WRITES	WELL FORMED (AND 2 PHASE WRT WRITES)	WELL FORMED AND TWO PHASE
CONCURRENCY	GREATEST: ONLY WAIT FOR SHORT WRITE LOCKS	GREAT: ONLY WAIT FOR WRITE LOCKS	MEDIUM: ALSO WAIT FOR READ LOCKS	LOWEST: ANY DATA TOUCHED IS LOCKED TO EOT
OVERHEAD	LEAST: ONLY SET SHORT WRITE LOCKS	SMALL: ONLY SET WRITE LOCKS	MEDIUM: SET BOTH KINDS OF LOCKS BUT NEED NOT STORE SHORT LOCKS	HIGHEST: SET AND STORE BOTH KINDS OF LOCKS
TRANSACT-ION BACKUP	CAN NOT UNDO WITHOUT CASCADING TO OTHERS	UN-DO INCOMPLETE TRANSACTIONS IN ANY ORDER	SAME	SAME
PROTECTION PROVIDED	LETS OTHERS RUN HIGHER CONSISTENCY	0 AND CAN'T LOSE WRITES	0,1 AND CAN'T READ BAD DATA ITEMS	0,1,2 AND CAN'T READ BAD DATA RELATIONSHIPS
SYSTEM RECOVERY TECHNIQUE	APPLY LOG IN ORDER OF ARRIVAL	APPLY LOG IN < ORDER	SAME AS 1: BUT RESULT IS SAME AS SOME SCHEDULE	RERUN TRANSACTIONS IN <<< ORDER
DEPENDENCIES	none	W->W	W->W W->R	W->W W->R R->W
ORDERING	NONE	< IS AN ORDERING OF THE TRANS-ACTIONS	<< IS AN ORDERING OF THE TRANS-ACTIONS	<<< IS AN ORDERING OF THE TRANS-ACTIONS

Table 2. Summary of consistency degrees.

III. LOCK HIERARCHIES AND DEGREES OF CONSISTENCY IN EXISTING SYSTEMS:

IMS/VS with the program isolation feature [3] has a two level lock hierarchy: segment types (sets of records), and segment instances (records) within a segment type. Segment types may be locked in EXCLUSIVE (E) mode (which corresponds to our exclusive (X) mode) or in EXPRESS READ (R), RETRIEVE (G), or UPDATE (U) (each of which correspond to our notion of intention (I) mode) [3 page 3.18-3.27]. Segment instances can be locked in share or exclusive mode. Segment type locks are requested at transaction initiation, usually in intention mode. Segment instance locks are dynamically set as the transaction proceeds. In addition IMS/VS has user controlled share locks on segment instances (the *Q option) which allow other read requests but not other *Q or exclusive requests. IMS/VS has no notion of S or SIX locks on segment types (which would allow a scan of all members of a segment type concurrent with other readers but without the overhead of locking each segment instance). Since IMS/VS does not support S mode on segment types one need not distinguish the two intention modes IS and IX (see the section introducing IS and IX modes). In general, IMS/VS has a notion of intention mode and does implicit locking but does not recognize all the modes described here. It uses a static two level lock tree.

IMS/VS with the program isolation feature basically provides degree 2 consistency. Hovever degree 1 consistency can be obtained on a segment type basis in a PCB (view) by specifying the EXPRESS READ option for that segment. Similarly degree 3 consistency can be obtained by specifying the EXCLUSIVE option. IMS/VS also has the user controlled share locks discussed above which a program can request on selected segment instances to obtain additional consistency over the degree 1 or 2 consistency provided by the system.

IMS/VS without the program isolation feature (and also the previous version of IMS namely IMS/2) doesn't have a lock hierarchy since locking is done only on a segment type basis. It provides degree 1 consistency with degree 3 consistency obtainable for a segment type in a view by specifying the EXCLUSIVE option. User controlled locking is also provided on a limited basis via the HOLD option.

DMS 1100 has a two level lock hierarchy [4]: areas and pages within areas. Areas may be locked in one of seven modes when they are OPENed: EXCLUSIVE RETRIEVAL (which corresponds to our notion of exclusive mode), PROTECTED UPDATE (which corresponds to our notion of share and intention exclusive mode), PROTECTED RETRIEVAL (which we call share mode), UPDATE (which corresponds to our intention exclusive mode), and RETRIEVAL (which is our intention share mode). Given this transliteration, the compatibility matrix displayed in Table 1 is identical to the compatibility matrix of DMS 1100 [4, page 3.59]. However, DMS 1100 sets only exclusive locks on pages within areas (short term share locks are invisibly set during internal pointer following). Further, even if a transaction locks an area in exclusive mode, DMS 1100 continues to set exclusive locks (and internal share locks) on the pages in the area, despite the fact that an exclusive lock on an area precludes reads or updates of the area by other transactions. Similar observations apply to the DMS 1100 implementation of S and SIX modes. In general, DMS 1100 recognizes all the modes described here and uses intention modes to detect conflicts but does not utilize implicit locking. It uses a static two level lock tree.

DMS 1100 provides level 2 consistency by setting exclusive locks on the modified pages and and a temporary lock on the page corresponding to the page which is "current of run unit". The temporary lock is released when the "current of run unit" is moved. In addition a run-unit can obtain additional locks via an explicit KEEP command.

The ideas presented were developed in the process of designing and implementing an experimental data base system at the IBM San Jose Research Laboratory. (We wish to emphasize that this system is a vehicle for research in data base architecture, and does not indicate plans for future IBM products.) A subsystem which provides the modes of locks herein described, plus the necessary logic to schedule requests and conversions, and to detect and resolve deadlocks has been implemented as one component of the data manager. The lock subsystem is in turn used by the data manager to automatically lock the nodes of its lock graph (see Figure 5). Users can be unaware of these lock protocols beyond the verbs "begin transaction" and "end transaction".

The data base is broken into several storage areas. Each area contains a set of relations (files), their indices, and their tuples(records) along with a catalog of the area. Each tuple has a unique tuple identifier (data base key) which can be used to quickly (directly) address the tuple. Each tuple identifier maps to a set of field values. All tuples are stored together in an area-wide heap to allow physical clustering of tuples from different relations. The unused slots in this heap are represented by an area-wide pool of free tuple identifiers (i.e. identifiers not allocated to any relation). Each tuple "belongs" to a unique relation, and all tuples in a relation have the same number and type of fields. One may construct an index on any subset of the fields of a relation. Tuple identifiers give fast direct access to tuples, while indices give fast associative access to field values and to their corresponding tuples. Each key value in an index is made a lockable object in order to solve the problem of "phantoms" [1] without locking the entire index. We do not explicitly lock individual fields or whole indices so those nodes appear in Figure 5 only for pedagogical reasons. Figure 5 gives only the "logical" lock graph, there is also a graph for physical page locks and for other low level resources.

As can be seen, Figure 5 is not a tree. Heavy use is made of the techniques mentioned in the section on locking DAG's. For example, one can read via tuple identifier without setting any index locks but to lock a field for update its tuple identifier and the old and new index key values covering the updated field must be locked in X mode. Further, the tree is not static, since data base keys are dynamically allocated to relations; field values dynamically enter, move around in, and leave index value intervals when records are inserted, updated and deleted; relations and indices are dynamically created and destroyed within areas; and areas are dynamically allocated. The implementation of such operations observes the lock protocol presented in the section on dynamic graphs: When a node changes parents, all old and new parents must be held (explicitly or implicitly) in intention exclusive mode and the node to be moved must be held in exclusive mode.

The described system supports concurrently consistency degrees 1,2 and 3 which can be specified on a transaction basis. In addition share locks on individual tuples can be acquired by the user.

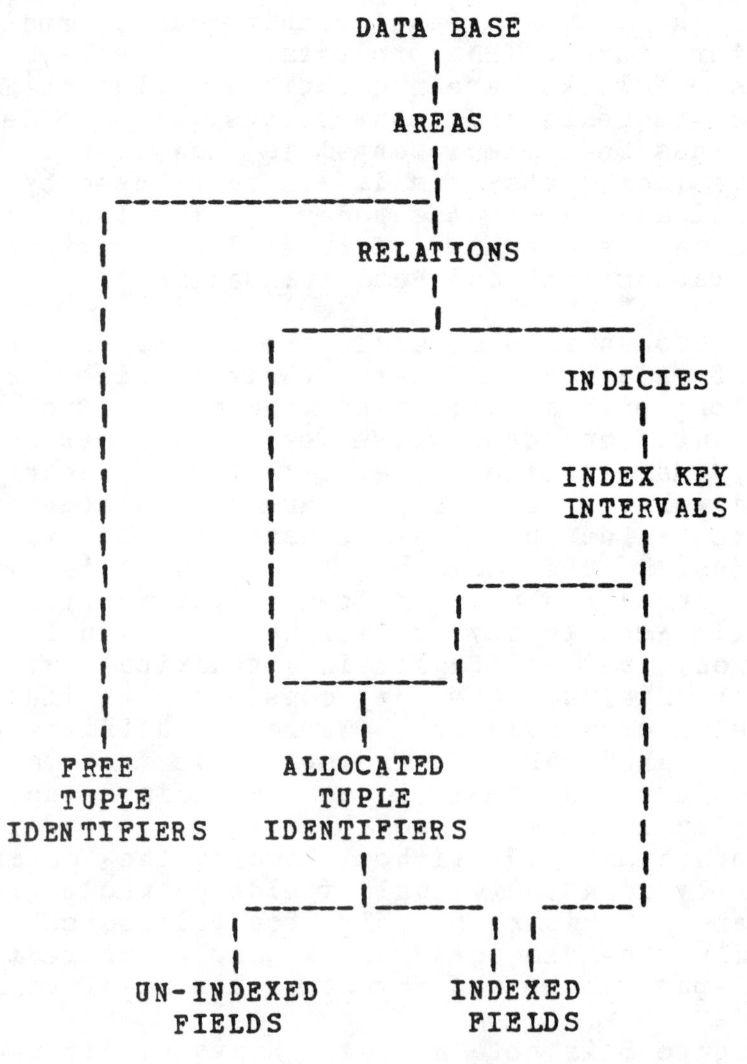

Figure 5. A lock graph.

ACKNOWLEDGMENT

We gratefully acknowledge many helpful discussions with Phil Macri, Jim Mehl and Brad Wade on how locking works in existing systems and how these results might be better presented. We are especially indebted to Paul McJones in this regard.

REFERENCES

[1] J.N. Gray, R.A. Lorie, G.R. Putzolu, "Granularity of Locks in a Shared Data Base," Proceedings of the International Conference on Very Large Data Bases, Boston, Mass., September 1975.

[2] K.P. Eswaran, J.N. Gray, R.A. Lorie, I.L. Traiger, On the Notions of Consistency and Predicate Locks, Technical Report RJ.1487, IBM Research Laboratory, San Jose, Ca., Nov. 1974.

[3] Information Management System Virtual Storage (IMS/VS). System Application Design Guide, Form No. SH20-9025-2, IBM Corp., 1975.

[4] UNIVAC 1100 Series Data Management System (DMS 1100). ANSI COBOL Field Data Manipulation Language. Order No. UP7908-2, Sperry Rand Corp., May 1973.

On Optimistic Methods for Concurrency Control

H.T. KUNG and JOHN T. ROBINSON
Carnegie-Mellon University

Most current approaches to concurrency control in database systems rely on locking of data objects as a control mechanism. In this paper, two families of nonlocking concurrency controls are presented. The methods used are "optimistic" in the sense that they rely mainly on transaction backup as a control mechanism, "hoping" that conflicts between transactions will not occur. Applications for which these methods should be more efficient than locking are discussed.

Key Words and Phrases: databases, concurrency controls, transaction processing
CR Categories: 4.32, 4.33

1. INTRODUCTION

Consider the problem of providing shared access to a database organized as a collection of objects. We assume that certain distinguished objects, called the roots, are always present and access to any object other than a root is gained only by first accessing a root and then following pointers to that object. Any sequence of accesses to the database that preserves the integrity constraints of the data is called a *transaction* (see, e.g., [4]).

If our goal is to maximize the throughput of accesses to the database, then there are at least two cases where highly concurrent access is desirable.

(1) The amount of data is sufficiently great that at any given time only a fraction of the database can be present in primary memory, so that it is necessary to swap parts of the database from secondary memory as needed.
(2) Even if the entire database can be present in primary memory, there may be multiple processors.

In both cases the hardware will be underutilized if the degree of concurrency is too low.

However, as is well known, unrestricted concurrent access to a shared database will, in general, cause the integrity of the database to be lost. Most current approaches to this problem involve some type of locking. That is, a mechanism is provided whereby one process can deny certain other processes access to some portion of the database. In particular, a lock may be associated with each node of the directed graph, and any given process is required to follow some locking protocol so as to guarantee that no other process can ever discover any lack of integrity in the database temporarily caused by the given process.

The locking approach has the following inherent disadvantages.

(1) Lock maintenance represents an overhead that is not present in the sequential case. Even read-only transactions (queries), which cannot possibly affect the integrity of the data, must, in general, use locking in order to guarantee that the data being read are not modified by other transactions at the same time. Also, if the locking protocol is not deadlock-free, deadlock detection must be considered to be part of lock maintenance overhead.
(2) There are no general-purpose deadlock-free locking protocols for databases that always provide high concurrency. Because of this, some research has been directed at developing special-purpose locking protocols for various special cases. For example, in the case of B-trees [1], at least nine locking protocols have been proposed [2, 3, 9, 10, 13].
(3) In the case that large parts of the database are on secondary memory, concurrency is significantly lowered whenever it is necessary to leave some congested node locked (a congested node is one that is often accessed, e.g., the root of a tree) while waiting for a secondary memory access.
(4) To allow a transaction to abort itself when mistakes occur, locks cannot be released until the end of the transaction. This may again significantly lower concurrency.
(5) Most important for the purposes of this paper, *locking may be necessary only in the worst case.* Consider the following simple example: The directed graph consists solely of roots, and each transaction involves one root only, any root equally likely. Then if there are n roots and two processes executing transactions at the same rate, locking is *really* needed (if at all) every n transactions, on the average.

In general, one may expect the argument of (5) to hold whenever (a) the number of nodes in the graph is very large compared to the total number of nodes involved in all the running transactions at a given time, and (b) the probability of modifying a congested node is small. In many applications, (a) and (b) are designed to hold (see Section 6 for the B-tree application).

Research directed at finding deadlock-free locking protocols may be seen as an attempt to lower the expense of concurrency control by eliminating transaction backup as a control mechanism. In this paper we consider the converse problem, that of eliminating locking. We propose two families of concurrency controls that do not use locking. These methods are "optimistic" in the sense that they rely for efficiency on the hope that conflicts between transactions will not occur. If (5) does hold, such conflict will be rare. This approach also has the advantage that it is completely general, applying equally well to any shared directed graph structure and associated access algorithms. Since locks are not used, it is deadlock-free (however, starvation is a possible problem, a solution for which we discuss).

This research was supported in part by the National Science Foundation under Grant MCS 78-236-76 and the Office of Naval Research under Contract N00014-76-C-0370.

Authors' address: Department of Computer Science, Carnegie-Mellon University, Pittsburgh, PA 15213.

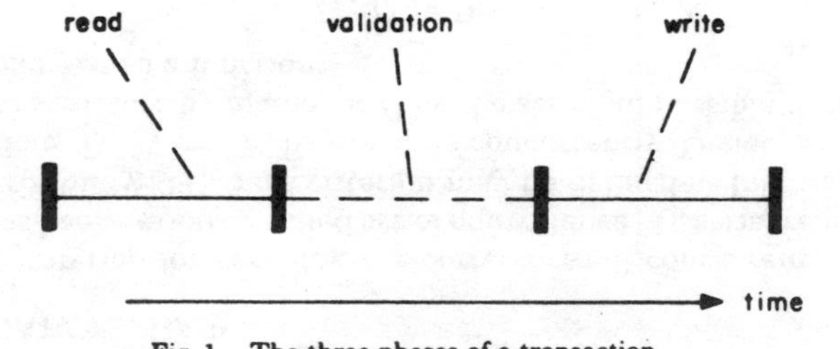

Fig. 1. The three phases of a transaction.

It is also possible using this approach to avoid problems (3) and (4) above. Finally, if the transaction pattern becomes query dominant (i.e., most transactions are read-only), then the concurrency control overhead becomes almost totally negligible (a partial solution to problem (1)).

The idea behind this optimistic approach is quite simple, and may be summarized as follows.

(1) Since reading a value or a pointer from a node can never cause a loss of integrity, reads are completely unrestricted (however, returning a result from a query is considered to be equivalent to a write, and so is subject to validation as discussed below).
(2) Writes are severely restricted. It is required that any transaction consist of two or three phases: a *read phase*, a *validation phase*, and a possible *write phase* (see Figure 1). During the read phase, all writes take place on local copies of the nodes to be modified. Then, if it can be established during the validation phase that the changes the transaction made will not cause a loss of integrity, the local copies are made global in the write phase. In the case of a query, it must be determined that the result the query would return is actually correct. The step in which it is determined that the transaction will not cause a loss of integrity (or that it will return the correct result) is called *validation*.

If, in a locking approach, locking is only necessary in the worst case, then in an optimistic approach validation will fail also only in the worst case. If validation does fail, the transaction will be backed up and start over again as a new transaction. Thus a transaction will have a write phase only if the preceding validation succeeds.

In Section 2 we discuss in more detail the read and write phases of transactions. In Section 3 a particularly strong form of validation is presented. The correctness criteria used for validation are based on the notion of serial equivalence [4, 12, 14]. In the next two sections concurrency controls that rely on the serial equivalence criteria developed in Section 3 for validation are presented. The family of concurrency controls in Section 4 have serial final validation steps, while the concurrency controls of Section 5 have completely parallel validation, at however higher total cost. In Section 6 we analyze the application of optimistic methods to controlling concurrent insertions in B-trees. Section 7 contains a summary and a discussion of future research.

2. THE READ AND WRITE PHASES

In this section we briefly discuss how the concurrency control can support the read and write phases of user-programmed transactions (in a manner invisible to the user), and how this can be implemented efficiently. The validation phase will be treated in the following three sections.

We assume that an underlying system provides for the manipulation of objects of various types. For simplicity, assume all objects are of the same type. Objects are manipulated by the following procedures, where n is the name of an object, i is a parameter to the type manager, and v is a value of arbitrary type (v could be a pointer, i.e., an object name, or data):

create	create a new object and return its name.
delete(n)	delete object n.
read(n, i)	read item i of object n and return its value.
write (n, i, v)	write v as item i of object n.

In order to support the read and write phases of transactions we also use the following procedures:

copy(n)	create a new object that is a copy of object n and return its name.
exchange($n1$, $n2$)	exchange the names of objects $n1$ and $n2$.

The concurrency control is invisible to the user; transactions are written as if the above procedures were used directly. However, transactions are required to use the syntactically identical procedures *tcreate*, *tdelete*, *tread*, and *twrite*. For each transaction, the concurrency control maintains sets of object names accessed by the transaction. These sets are initialized to be empty by a *tbegin* call. The body of the user-written transaction is in fact the read phase mentioned in the introduction; the subsequent validation phase does not begin until after a *tend* call. The procedures *tbegin* and *tend* are shown in detail in Sections 4 and 5. The semantics of the remaining procedures are as follows:

```
tcreate = (
  n := create;
  create set := create set ∪ {n};
  return n)

twrite(n, i, v) = (
  if n ∈ create set
      then write(n, i, v)
  else if n ∈ write set
      then write(copies[n], i, v)
  else (
      m := copy(n);
      copies[n] := m;
      write set := write set ∪ {n};
      write(copies[n], i, v)))

tread(n, i) = (
  read set := read set ∪ {n};
  if n ∈ write set
      then return read(copies[n], i)
```

```
    else
        return read(n, i))
tdelete(n) = (
    delete set := delete set ∪ {n}).
```

Above, *copies* is an associative vector of object names, indexed by object name. We see that in the read phase, no global writes take place. Instead, whenever the first write to a given object is requested, a copy is made, and all subsequent writes are directed to the copy. This copy is potentially global but is inaccessible to other transactions during the read phase by our convention that all nodes are accessed only by following pointers from a root node. If the node is a root node, the copy is inaccessible since it has the wrong name (all transactions "know" the global names of root nodes). It is assumed that no root node is created or deleted, that no dangling pointers are left to deleted nodes, and that created nodes become accessible by writing new pointers (these conditions are part of the integrity criteria for the data structure that each transaction is required to individually preserve).

When the transaction completes, it will request its validation and write phases via a *tend* call. If validation succeeds, then the transaction enters the write phase, which is simply

```
for n ∈ write set do exchange(n, copies[n]).
```

After the write phase all written values become "global," all created nodes become accessible, and all deleted nodes become inaccessible. Of course some cleanup is necessary, which we do not consider to be part of the write phase since it does not interact with other transactions:

```
(for n ∈ delete set do delete(n);
 for n ∈ write set do delete(copies[n])).
```

This cleanup is also necessary if a transaction is aborted.

Note that since objects are virtual (objects are referred to by name, not by physical address), the *exchange* operation, and hence the write phase, can be made quite fast: essentially, all that is necessary is to exchange the physical address parts of the two object descriptors.

Finally, we note that the concept of two-phase transactions appears to be quite valuable for recovery purposes, since at the end of the read phase, all changes that the transaction intends to make to the data structure are known.

3. THE VALIDATION PHASE

A widely used criterion for verifying the correctness of concurrent execution of transactions has been variously called serial equivalence [4], serial reproducibility [11], and linearizability [14]. This criterion may be defined as follows.

Let transactions $T_1, T_2, \ldots, T_n$ be executed concurrently. Denote an instance of the shared data structure by d, and let D be the set of all possible d, so that each T_i may be considered as a function:

$$T_i : D \rightarrow D.$$

If the initial data structure is d_{initial} and the final data structure is d_{final}, the concurrent execution of transactions is correct if some permutation π of $\{1, 2, \ldots, n\}$ exists such that

$$d_{\text{final}} = T_{\pi(n)} \circ T_{\pi(n-1)} \circ \cdots \circ T_{\pi(2)} \circ T_{\pi(1)}(d_{\text{initial}}), \tag{1}$$

where "$\circ$" is the usual notation for functional composition.

The idea behind this correctness criterion is that, first, each transaction is assumed to have been written so as to individually preserve the integrity of the shared data structure. That is, if d satisfies all integrity criteria, then for each T_i, $T_i(d)$ satisfies all integrity criteria. Now, if d_{initial} satisfies all integrity criteria and the concurrent execution of $T_1, T_2, \ldots, T_n$ is serially equivalent, then from (1), by repeated application of the integrity-preserving property of each transaction, d_{final} satisfies all integrity criteria. Serial equivalence is useful as a correctness criterion since it is in general much easier to verify that (a) each transaction preserves integrity and (b) every concurrent execution of transaction is serially equivalent than it is to verify directly that every concurrent execution of transactions preserves integrity. In fact, it has been shown in [7] that serialization is the weakest criterion for preserving consistency of a concurrent transaction system, even if complete syntactic information of the system is available to the concurrency control. However, if semantic information is available, then other approaches may be more attractive (see, e.g., [6, 8]).

3.1 Validation of Serial Equivalence

The use of validation of serial equivalence as a concurrency control is a direct application of eq. (1) above. However, in order to verify (1), a permutation π must be found. This is handled by *explicitly* assigning each transaction T_i a unique integer *transaction number* $t(i)$ during the course of its execution. The meaning of transaction numbers in validation is the following: there must exist a serially equivalent schedule in which transaction T_i comes before transaction T_j whenever $t(i) < t(j)$. This can be guaranteed by the following validation condition: for each transaction T_j with transaction number $t(j)$, and for all T_i with $t(i) < t(j)$; one of the following three conditions must hold (see Figure 2):

(1) T_i completes its write phase before T_j starts its read phase.
(2) The write set of T_i does not intersect the read set of T_j, and T_i completes its write phase before T_j starts its write phase.
(3) The write set of T_i does not intersect the read set *or* the write set of T_j, and T_i completes its read phase before T_j completes its read phase.

Condition (1) states that T_i actually completes before T_j starts. Condition (2) states that the writes of T_i do not affect the read phase of T_j, and that T_i finishes writing before T_j starts writing, hence does not overwrite T_j (also, note that T_j cannot affect the read phase of T_i). Finally, condition (3) is similar to condition (2) but does not require that T_i finish writing before T_j starts writing; it simply requires that T_i not affect the read phase *or* the write phase of T_j (again note that T_j cannot affect the read phase of T_i, by the last part of the condition). See [12] for a set of similar conditions for serialization.

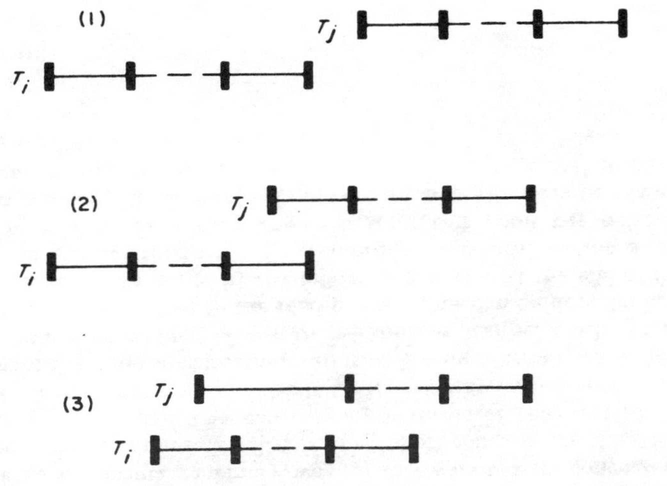

Fig. 2. Possible interleaving of two transactions.

3.2 Assigning Transaction Numbers

The first consideration that arises in the design of concurrency controls that explicitly assign transaction numbers is the question: how should transaction numbers be assigned? Clearly, they should somehow be assigned in order, since if T_i completes before T_j starts, we *must* have $t(i) < t(j)$. Here we use the simple solution of maintaining a global integer counter *tnc* (transaction number counter); when a transaction number is needed, the counter is incremented, and the resulting value returned. Also, transaction numbers must be assigned somewhere before validation, since the validation conditions above require knowledge of the transaction number of the transaction being validated. On first thought, we might assign transaction numbers at the beginning of the read phase; however, this is not optimistic (hence contrary to the philosophy of this paper) for the following reason. Consider the case of two transactions, T_1 and T_2, starting at roughly the same time, assigned transaction number n and $n + 1$, respectively. Even if T_2 completes its read phase much earlier than T_1, before being validated T_2 must wait for the completion of the read phase of T_1, since the validation of T_2 in this case relies on knowledge of the write set of T_1 (see Figure 3). In an optimistic approach, we would like for transactions to be validated immediately if at all possible (in order to improve response time). For these and similar considerations we assign transaction numbers at the end of the read phase. Note that by assigning transaction numbers in this fashion the last part of condition (3), that T_i complete its read phase before T_j completes its read phase if $t(i) < t(j)$, is automatically satisfied.

3.3 Some Practical Considerations

Given this method for assigning transaction numbers, consider the case of a transaction T that has an arbitrarily long read phase. When this transaction is

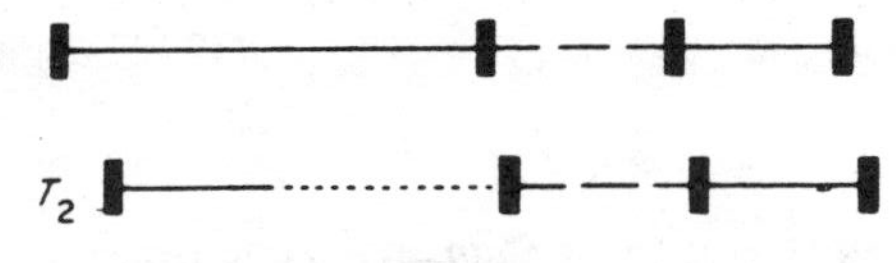

Fig. 3. Transaction 2 waits for transaction 1 in ....

validated, the write sets of all transactions that completed their read phase before T but had not yet completed their write phase at the start of T must be examined. Since the concurrency control can only maintain finitely many write sets, we have a difficulty (this difficulty does not arise if transaction numbers are assigned at the beginning of the read phase). Clearly, if such transactions are common, the assignment of transaction numbers described above is unsuitable. Of course, we take the optimistic approach and assume such transactions are very rare; still, a solution is needed. We solve this problem by only requiring the concurrency control to maintain some finite number of the most recent write sets where the number is large enough to validate almost all transactions (we say write set a is more recent than write set b if the transaction number associated with a is greater than that associated with b). In the case of transactions like T, if old write sets are unavailable, validation fails, and the transaction is backed up (probably to the beginning). For simplicity, we present the concurrency controls of the next two sections as if potentially infinite vectors of write sets were maintained; the above convention is understood to apply.

One last consideration must be mentioned at this point, namely, what should be done when validation fails? In such a case the transaction is aborted and restarted, receiving a new transaction number at the completion of the read phase. Now a new difficulty arises: what should be done in the case in which validation repeatedly fails? Under our optimistic assumptions this should happen rarely, but we still need some method for dealing with this problem when it does occur. A simple solution is the following. Later, we will see that transactions enter a short critical section during *tend*. If the concurrency control detects a "starving" transaction (this could be detected by keeping track of the number of times validation for a given transaction fails), the transaction can be restarted, but without releasing the critical section semaphore. This is equivalent to write-locking the entire database, and the "starving" transaction will run to completion.

4. SERIAL VALIDATION

In this section we present a family of concurrency controls that are an implementation of validation conditions (1) and (2) of Section 3.1. Since we are not using condition (3), the last part of condition (2) implies that write phases must be serial. The simplest way to implement this is to place the assignment of a transaction number, validation, and the subsequent write phase all in a critical section. In the following, we bracket the critical section by "⟨" and "⟩." The concurrency control is as follows:

```
tbegin = (
  create set := empty;
  read set := empty;
  write set := empty;
  delete set := empty;
  start tn := tnc)

tend = (
  (finish tn := tnc;
   valid := true;
  for t from start tn + 1 to finish tn do
      if (write set of transaction with transaction number t intersects read set)
        then valid := false;
  if valid
      then ((write phase); tnc := tnc + 1; tn := tnc));
  if valid
      then (cleanup)
      else (backup)).
```

In the above, the transaction is assigned a transaction number via the sequence *tnc* := *tnc* + 1; *tn* := *tnc*. An optimization has been made in that transaction numbers are assigned only if validation is successful. We may imagine that the transaction is "tentatively" assigned a transaction number of *tnc* + 1 with the statement *finish tn* := *tnc*, but that if validation fails, this transaction number is freed for use by another transaction. By condition (1) of Section 3.1, we need not consider transactions that have completed their write phase before the start of the read phase of the current transaction. This is implemented by reading *tnc* in *tbegin*; since a "real" assignment of a transaction number takes place only after the write phase, it is guaranteed at this point that all transactions with transaction numbers less than or equal to *start tn* have completed their write phase.

The above is perfectly suitable in the case that there is one CPU and that the write phase can usually take place in primary memory. If the write phase often cannot take place in primary memory, we probably want to have concurrent write phases, unless the write phase is still extremely short compared to the read phase (which may be the case). The concurrency controls of the next section are appropriate for this. If there are multiple CPUs, we may wish to introduce more potential parallelism in the validation step (this is only necessary for efficiency if the processors cannot be kept busy with read phases, that is, if validation is not extremely short as compared to the read phase). This can be done by using the solution of the next section, or by the following method. At the end of the read phase, we immediately read *tnc* before entering the critical section and assign this value to *mid tn*. It is then known that at this point the write sets of transactions *start tn* + 1, *start tn* + 2, . . . , *mid tn* must certainly be examined in the validation step, and this can be done outside the critical section. The concurrency control is thus

```
tend := (
  mid tn := tnc;
  valid := true;
  for t from start tn + 1 to mid tn do
  if (write set of transaction with transaction number t intersects read set)
      then valid := false;
 (finish tn := tnc;
  for t from mid tn + 1 to finish tn do
      if (write set of transaction with transaction number t intersects read set)
        then valid := false;
  if valid
      then ((write phase); tnc := tnc + 1; tn := tnc));
  if valid
      then (cleanup)
      else (backup)).
```

The above optimization can be carried out a second time: at the end of the preliminary validation step we read *tnc* a third time, and then, still outside the critical section, check the write sets of those transactions with transaction numbers from *mid tn* + 1 to this most recent value of *tnc*. Repeating this process, we derive a family of concurrency controls with varying numbers of stages of validation and degrees of parallelism, all of which however have a final indivisible validation step and write phase. The idea is to move varying parts of the work done in the critical section outside the critical section, allowing greater parallelism.

Until now we have not considered the question of read-only transactions, or queries. Since queries do not have a write phase, it is unnecessary to assign them transaction numbers. It is only necessary to read *tnc* at the end of the read phase and assign its value to *finish tn*; validation for the query then consists of examining the write sets of the transactions with transaction numbers *start tn* + 1, *start tn* + 2, . . . , *finish tn*. This need not occur in a critical section, so the above discussion on multiple validation stages does not apply to queries. This method for handling queries also applies to the concurrency controls of the next section. Note that for query-dominant systems, validation will often be trivial: It may be determined that *start tn* = *finish tn*, and validation is complete. For this type of system an optimistic approach appears ideal.

5. PARALLEL VALIDATION

In this section we present a concurrency control that uses all three of the validation conditions of Section 3.1, thus allowing greater concurrency. We retain the optimization of the previous section, only assigning transaction numbers after the write phase if validation succeeds. As in the previous solutions, *tnc* is read at the beginning and the end of the read phase; transactions with transactions numbers *start tn* + 1, *start tn* + 2, . . . , *finish tn* all may be checked under condition (2) of Section 3.1. For condition (3), we maintain a set of transaction ids *active* for transactions that have completed their read phase but have not yet completed their write phase. The concurrency control is as follows (*tbegin* is as in the previous section):

```
tend = (
  (finish tn := tnc;
   finish active := (make a copy of active);
   active := active ∪ {id of this transaction});
   valid := true;
```

```
for t from start tn + 1 to finish tn do
    if (write set of transaction with transaction number t intersects read set)
        then valid := false;
for i ∈ finish active do
    if (write set of transaction T_i intersects read set or write set)
        then valid := false;
if valid
    then (
        (write phase);
        (tnc := tnc + 1;
         tn := tnc;
         active := active—{id of this transaction});
        (cleanup))
    else (
        (active := active—{id of transaction});
        (backup))).
```

In the above, at the end of the read phase *active* is the set of transactions that have been assigned "tentative" transaction numbers less than that of the transaction being validated. Note that modifications to *active* and *tnc* are placed together in critical sections so as to maintain the invariant properties of *active* and *tnc* mentioned above. Entry to the first critical section is equivalent to being assigned a "tentative" transaction number.

One problem with the above is that a transaction in the set *finish active* may invalidate the given transaction, even though the former transaction is itself invalidated. A partial solution to this is to use several stages of preliminary validation, in a way completely analogous to the multistage validation described in the previous section. At each stage, a new value of *tnc* is read, and transactions with transaction numbers up to this value are checked. The final stage then involves accessing *active* as above. The idea is to reduce the size of *active* by performing more of the validation before adding a new transaction id to *active*.

Finally, a solution is possible where transactions that have been invalidated by a transaction in *finish active* wait for that transaction to either be invalidated, and hence ignored, or validated, causing backup (this possibility was pointed out by James Saxe). However, this solution involves a more sophisticated process communication mechanism than the binary semaphore needed to implement the critical sections above.

6. ANALYSIS OF AN APPLICATION

We have previously noted that an optimistic approach appears ideal for query-dominant systems. In this section we consider another promising application, that of supporting concurrent index operations for very large tree-structured indexes. In particular, we examine the use of an optimistic method for supporting concurrent insertions in B-trees (see [1]). Similar types of analysis and similar results can be expected for other types of tree-structured indexes and index operations.

One consideration in analyzing the efficiency of an optimistic method is the expected size of read and write sets, since this relates directly to the time spent in the validation phase. For B-trees, we naturally choose the objects of the read and write sets to be the pages of the B-tree. Now even very large B-trees are only a few levels deep. For example, let a B-tree of order m contain N keys. Then if $m = 199$ and $N \leq 2 \times 10^8 - 2$, the depth is at most $1 + \log_{100}(N + 1)/2) < 5$. Since insertions do not read or write more than one already existing node on a given level, this means that for B-trees of order 199 containing up to almost 200 million keys, the size of a read or write set of an insertion will never be more than 4. Since we are able to bound the size of read and write sets by a small constant, we conclude that validation will be fast, the validation time essentially being proportional to the degree of concurrency.

Another important consideration is the time to complete the validation and write phases as compared to the time to complete the read phase (this point was mentioned in Section 4). B-trees are implemented using some paging algorithm, typically least recently used page replaced first. The root page and some of the pages on the first level are normally in primary memory; lower level pages usually need to be swapped in. Since insertions always access a leaf page (here, we call a page on the lowest level a leaf page), a typical insertion to a B-tree of depth d will cause $d - 1$ or $d - 2$ secondary memory accesses. However, the validation and write phases should be able to take place in primary memory. Thus we expect the read phase to be orders of magnitude longer than the validation and write phases. In fact, since the "densities" of validation and write phases are so low, we believe that the serial validation algorithms of Section 4 should give acceptable performance in most cases.

Our final and most important consideration is determining how likely it is that one insertion will cause another concurrent insertion to be invalidated. Let the B-tree be of order m (m odd), have depth d, and let n be the number of leaf pages. Now, given two insertions I_1 and I_2, what is the probability that the write set of I_1 intersects the read set of I_2? Clearly this depends on the size of the write set of I_1, and this is determined by the degree of splitting. Splitting occurs only when an insertion is attempted on an already full page, and results in an insertion to the page on the next higher level. Lacking theoretical results on the distribution of the number of keys in B-tree pages, we make the conservative assumption that the number of keys in any page is uniformly distributed between $(m - 1)/2$ and $m - 1$ (this is a conservative assumption since it predicts storage utilization of 75 percent, but theoretical results do exist for storage utilization [15], which show that storage utilization is about 69 percent—since nodes are on the average emptier than our assumption implies, this suggests that the probability of splitting we use is high). We also assume that an insertion accesses any path from root to leaf equally likely. With these assumptions we find that the write set of I_1 has size i with probability

$$p_s(i) = \left(\frac{2}{m+1}\right)^{i-1}\left(1 - \frac{2}{m+1}\right)$$

Given the size of the write set of I_1, an upper bound on the probability that the read set of I_2 intersects the subtree written by I_1 is easily derived by assuming the maximal number of pages in the subtree, and is

$$p_I(i) < \frac{m^{i-1}}{n}.$$

Combining these, we find the probability of conflict p_C satisfies

$$p_C = \sum_{1 \le i \le d} p_s(i) p_I(i)$$

$$< \frac{1}{n}\left(1 - \frac{2}{m+1}\right) \sum_{1 \le i \le d} \left(\frac{2m}{m+1}\right)^{i-1}$$

For example, if $d = 3$, $m = 199$, and $n = 10^4$, we have $p_C < 0.0007$. Thus we see that it is very rare that one insertion would cause another concurrent insertion to restart for large B-trees.

7. CONCLUSIONS

A great deal of research has been done on locking approaches to concurrency control, but as noted above, in practice two control mechanisms are used: locking and backup. Here we have begun to investigate solutions to concurrency control that rely almost entirely on the latter mechanism. We may think of the optimistic methods presented here as being orthogonal to locking methods in several ways.

(1) In a locking approach, transactions are controlled by having them wait at certain points, while in an optimistic approach, transactions are controlled by backing them up.

(2) In a locking approach, serial equivalence can be proved by partially ordering the transactions by first access time for each object, while in an optimistic approach, transactions are ordered by transaction number assignment.

(3) The major difficulty in locking approaches is deadlock, which can be solved by using backup; in an optimistic approach, the major difficulty is starvation, which can be solved by using locking.

We have presented two families of concurrency controls with varying degrees of concurrency. These methods may well be superior to locking methods for systems where transaction conflict is highly unlikely. Examples include query-dominant systems and very large tree-structured indexes. For these cases, an optimistic method will avoid locking overhead, and may take full advantage of a multiprocessor environment in the validation phase using the parallel validation techniques presented. Some techniques are definitely needed for determining all instances where an optimistic approach is better than a locking approach, and in such cases, which type of optimistic approach should be used.

A more general problem is the following: Consider the case of a database system where transaction conflict is rare, but not rare enough to justify the use of any of the optimistic approaches presented here. Some type of generalized concurrency control is needed that provides "just the right amount" of locking versus backup. Ideally, this should vary as the likelihood of transaction conflict in the system varies.

REFERENCES

1. Bayer, R., and McCreight, E. Organization and maintenance of large ordered indexes. *Acta Inf. 1*, 3 (1972), 173–189.
2. Bayer, R., and Schkolnick, M. Concurrency of operations on B-trees. *Acta Inf. 9*, 1 (1977), 1–21.
3. Ellis, C. S. Concurrency search and insertion in 2-3 trees. *Acta Inf. 14*, 1 (1980), 63–86.
4. Eswaran, K. P., Gray, J. N., Lorie, R. A., and Traiger, I. L. The notions of consistency and predicate locks in a database system. *Commun. ACM 19*, 11 (Nov. 1976), 624–633.
5. Gray, J. Notes on database operating systems. In *Lecture Notes in Computer Science* 60: *Operating Systems*, R. Bayer, R. M. Graham, and G. Seegmuller, Eds. Springer-Verlag, Berlin, 1978, pp. 393–481.
6. Kung, H. T., and Lehman, P. L. Concurrent manipulation of binary search trees. *ACM Trans. Database Syst. 5*, 3 (Sept. 1980), 354–382.
7. Kung, H. T., and Papadimitriou, C. H. An optimality theory of concurrency control for databases. In *Proc. ACM SIGMOD 1979 Int. Conf. Management of Data*, May 1979, pp. 116–126.
8. Lamport, L. Towards a theory of correctness for multi-user data base systems. Tech. Rep. CA-7610-0712, Massachusetts Computer Associates, Inc., Wakefield, Mass., Oct. 1976.
9. Lehman, P. L., and Yao, S. B. Efficient locking for concurrent operations on B-trees. Submitted for publication.
10. Miller, R. E., and Snyder, L. Multiple access to B-trees. Presented at Proc. Conf. Information Sciences and Systems, Johns Hopkins Univ., Baltimore, Md., Mar. 1978.
11. Papadimitriou, C. H., Bernstein, P. A., and Rothnie, J. B. Computational problems related to database concurrency control. In *Conf. Theoretical Computer Science*, Univ. Waterloo, 1977, pp. 275–282.
12. Papadimitriou, C. H. Serializability of concurrent updates. *J. ACM 26*, 4 (Oct. 1979), 631–653.
13. Samadi, B. B-trees in a system with multiple users. *Inf. Process. Lett. 5*, 4 (Oct. 1976), 107–112.
14. Stearns, R. E., Lewis, P. M., II, and Rosenkrantz, D. J. Concurrency control for database systems. In *Proc. 7th Symp. Foundations of Computer Science*, 1976, pp. 19–32.
15. Yao, A. On random 2-3 trees. *Acta Inf. 2*, 9 (1978), 159–170.

Received May 1979; revised July 1980; accepted September 1980

Concurrency of Operations on *B*-Trees

R. Bayer* and M. Schkolnick

IBM Research Laboratory, San José, CA 95193, USA

Summary. Concurrent operations on *B*-trees pose the problem of insuring that each operation can be carried out without interfering with other operations being performed simultaneously by other users. This problem can become critical if these structures are being used to support access paths, like indexes, to data base systems. In this case, serializing access to one of these indexes can create an unacceptable bottleneck for the entire system. Thus, there is a need for locking protocols that can assure integrity for each access while at the same time providing a maximum possible degree of concurrency. Another feature required from these protocols is that they be deadlock free, since the cost to resolve a deadlock may be high.

Recently, there has been some questioning on whether *B*-tree structures can support concurrent operations. In this paper, we examine the problem of concurrent access to *B*-trees. We present a deadlock free solution which can be tuned to specific requirements. An analysis is presented which allows the selection of parameters so as to satisfy these requirements.

The solution presented here uses simple locking protocols. Thus, we conclude that B-trees can be used advantageously in a multi-user environment.

1. Introduction

In this paper, we examine the problem of concurrent access to indexes which are maintained as *B*-trees. This type of organization was introduced by Bayer and McCreight [2] and some variants of it appear in Knuth [10] and Wedekind [13]. Performance studies of it were restricted to the single user environment. Recently, these structures have been examined for possible use in a multi-user (concurrent) environment. Some initial studies have been made about the feasibility of their use in this type of situation [1, 6], and [11].

An accessing schema which achieves a high degree of concurrency in using the index will be presented. The schema allows dynamic tuning to adapt its performance to the profile of the current set of users. Another property of the schema is that it is deadlock free. This is achieved by providing a set of strict locking protocols which must be followed by each process accessing an index. The properties of the locks and the protocols together guarantee that deadlocks cannot arise. Furthermore, the schema is shown to be a generalization of several methods used in earlier attempts to achieve concurrent operations in *B*-trees.

In Section 2, we define terms which will be used in the paper. Then in Section 3, we introduce the problem and some basic solutions to it. In Section 4, we present the general schema to be studied. In Section 5, the schema is shown to be deadlock free. Section 6 contains a quantitative analysis of the schema. Using the results of this analysis, tuning parameters can be selected to optimize the performance of the schema. Finally, Section 7 briefly discusses some extensions to the schema.

* *Permanent address*: Institut für Informatik der Technischen Universität München, Arcisstr. 21, D-8000 München 2, Germany (Fed. Rep.)

2. Definitions

We assume the reader is familiar with *B*-trees ([2, 10]). In the sequel we will be using the variant known as B^*-tree [13]. A B^*-tree with parameter k is a tree structure for storing entries. An *entry* is a pair (entry key, associated information). The keys are linearly ordered, the associated information is of no interest in this paper. B^*-trees have the following properties:

1) All entries are stored on leaf nodes. Each leaf node contains a number μ of entries.

2) All paths from the root to a leaf node have the same length.

3) All nonleaf nodes contain a number of elements: $p_0, r_1, p_1, r_2, p_2, \ldots, r_\mu, p_\mu$, where the p_i's are pointers to immediate descendants of this node and the r_i's are elements which can be compared with the keys in the entries. They are called *reference keys*. All keys in the subtree pointed to by p_{i-1} are less than the reference key r_i and all keys in the subtree pointed to by p_i are greater than or equal to the reference key r_i.

4) The number μ referred to in 1 and 3, may vary from node to node but satisfies $k \leqq \mu \leqq 2k$ for all nodes except for the root, where $1 \leqq \mu \leqq 2k$.

We will say that a node in a B^*-tree is at a *level i* if the path from that node to a leaf contains i nodes. Because of property 2, this number is well defined for all nodes. The level of the root is said to be the height of the tree. We will use $\ell(n)$ to denote the level of node n and $\hbar$ to denote the height of the tree.

An example of a B^*-tree with $\hbar=3$ and $k=2$ is shown in Figure 1. Entries on the leaf nodes are shown as parenthesized objects. The value in parentheses is the entry key. Nodes have been given labels in order to refer to them.

The operations to be performed on these structures will be of three kinds: A *search* for a given key, an *insertion* of a given entry, and a *deletion* of an entry with a given key. A process executing the first operation is said to be a *reader*. A process executing the second or third operation is said to be an *updater*. Note that a search does not result in a modification of the tree. If an insertion (respectively a deletion) is attempted and the key to be inserted (deleted) is (is not) found

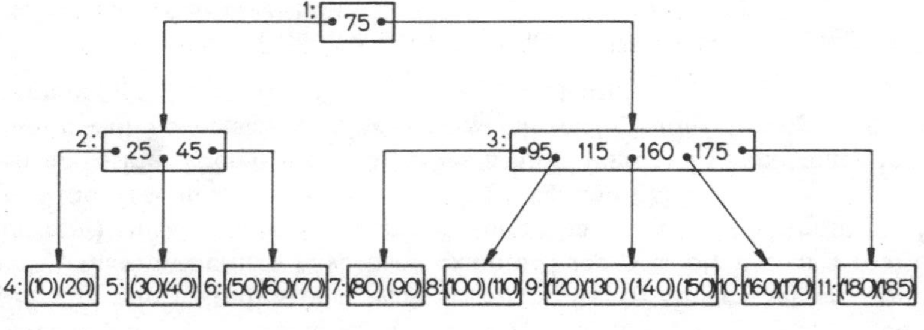

Fig. 1. A B^*-tree with $\hbar = 3$, $k = 2$

in a leaf node then the insertion (deletion) is said to be *unsuccessful*. A successful operation done by an updater results in a modification of the tree. We assume the reader is familiar with the way these modifications affect the tree structure. We will use the following important fact: When an updater attempts an insertion (deletion) and scans node *n*, it can easily check a sufficient condition on *n* that any ancestors will not be affected by the insertion (deletion). If the condition is satisfied, *n* will be known as *safe*; otherwise, *n* is said to be *unsafe*.

In a B^*-tree, the criterion for determining safeness of a node is very simple: on insertions, a node is safe if the number μ is less than $2k$. On deletions, a node is safe if the number μ is greater than k. For example, a process trying to insert the key (186) in the tree shown in Figure 1 would first scan the root (node 1) and it would determine it is safe. It would then branch to node 3. Since for this node $\mu = 2k$, it would determine this node is unsafe, i.e., it cannot tell whether its ancestors, in this case node 1, would be affected by the insertion. Finally, it would move on to node 11 which it would determine to be safe, i.e., neither node 3 nor node 1 will be affected by the insertion. (In what follows, we will not worry about changing the unsafeness status of node 3 to being safe.)

The fact that we can determine safeness of a node is the feature of a B^*-tree that is used in all solutions described in this paper. In fact, any other tree structure for which the same property can be established can be accessed concurrently using the protocols described here. Examples of these are prefix *B*-trees [4] and enciphered *B*-trees [3].

3. Basic Solutions

In a multiuser environment, concurrent access of processes to an index structure must be supported. The problem of concurrent access is that of allowing a maximum number of processes to operate on the tree without impairing the correctness of their operations.

A simple-minded solution for the problem of concurrent access would be to strictly serialize all updaters, by requiring each updater to gain exclusive control of the tree – e.g., by placing an exclusive lock on the whole tree – before it begins accessing it, thus, preventing all other updaters and readers from altering or reading the index while the specific update takes place. Readers, on the other hand, could access the structure concurrently with other readers. Clearly this simple mechanism can only be used if the level of activity is rather low.

Fig. 2. Compatibility graph for locks: Solutions 1 and 2

We will now present three solutions to the problem of concurrent access in a B^*-tree. For each solution we will give a protocol for both readers and updaters. All solutions use locks on the nodes of the tree. These locks are granted by a scheduler upon request by a process. We will assume that, except as noted in Solution 3, the scheduler services these requests in a FIFO order. This order is maintained by having one service queue for every node in the tree. A process requesting a lock on a node will be placed at the end of the queue for that node and the scheduler will service processes that are at the beginning of the queues.

Solution 1. This solution is essentially the one presented by Metzger [11]. It is derived from the simple-minded solution when the fact that safeness of a node can be established is used. The solution uses two types of locks: a *read* lock, or ρ-lock, and an *exclusive* lock, or ξ-lock. A node cannot simultaneously be locked with a ρ-lock and a ξ-lock. In fact, these locks satisfy the compatibility relation shown in Figure 2.

An edge between any two nodes in a compatibility graph means that two *different* processes may simultaneously hold these locks on the same node. The absence of an edge indicates that two different processes cannot hold these locks simultaneously on a node. These constraints are enforced by the lock scheduler.

The protocol for readers is as follows:

```
             0) Place ρ-lock on root;
             1) Get root and make it the current node;
main loop:   2) While current node is not a leaf node do
                {Exactly one ρ-lock is held by process}
                begin
                   3) Place ρ-lock on appropriate son of current node;
                   4) Release ρ-lock on current node;
                   5) Get son of current node and make it current;
                end mainloop
```

By executing this protocol, a reader would scan the B^*-tree, starting at the root and moving down towards a leaf node.

The protocol for an updater is as follows:

```
             0) Place ξ-lock on root;
             1) Get root and make it the current node;
main loop:   2) While current node is not a leaf node do
                {number of ξ-locks held ≧ 1}
```

```
begin
    3) Place ξ-lock on appropriate son of current node;
    4) Get son and make it the current node;
    5) If current node is safe
       then release all locks held on ancestors of current node
end
```

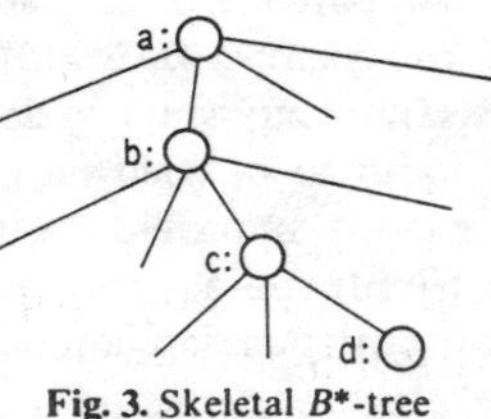

Fig. 3. Skeletal B^*-tree

As an example of how this last protocol would work, consider an update on the node d of the (skeletal) B^*-tree shown in Figure 3. Assume that, for this update, nodes a, b, and d are safe and c is not. Before execution of the mainloop, a ξ-lock would be placed on node a and this node would be scanned.

Then the following sequence of events would take place.

i) [Step 3] A ξ-lock is requested on node b.
ii) [Step 4] After ξ-lock is granted, node b is retrieved.
iii) [Step 5] Since node b is safe, the ξ-lock on node a is released, thereby, allowing other updaters or readers to access node a.
iv) [Step 3] A ξ-lock is requested on node c.
v) [Step 4] After ξ-lock is granted, node c is retrieved.
vi) [Step 5] Since node c is unsafe, the ξ-lock on node b is kept.
vii) [Step 3] A ξ-lock is requested on node d.
viii) [Step 4] After ξ-lock is granted, node d is retrieved.
ix) [Step 5] Since node d is safe, the ξ-locks on nodes b and c can be released.

This solution has the advantage of requiring only a simple protocol to achieve a reasonable gain in concurrency over the simple minded solution described at the beginning of this section. However, it suffers from the fact that updaters first ξ-lock the root of a subtree when updating this subtree (and thus preventing all other accesses to this subtree) even when, as it happens most of the time, the update will have no effect on this root. In the above example, the entire tree remained ξ-locked while node b was being retrieved and examined (a slow process). In turn, the subtree rooted at b had a ξ-lock on its root while both nodes c and d were retrieved and examined to find that node b would not be modified as a result of the update.

To achieve higher concurrency one may let updaters behave like readers in the upper part of the tree. This leads to the next solution.

Solution 2. This solution is a variant of one used by one of the authors in the design of an interactive data base system [12]. It uses the same locks as in Solution 1. The protocol for a reader is also as in Solution 1. Updaters however, have a different protocol, as follows:

```
            0) Place ρ-lock on root;
            1) Get root and make it the current node;
main loop:  2) While current node is not a leaf node do
               begin
                 3) If son is not a leaf node
                    then place ρ-lock on appropriate son
                    else place ξ-lock on appropriate son;
                 4) Release lock on current node;
                 5) Get son and make it the current node
               end mainloop;
            6) {A leaf node has been reached}
               If current node is unsafe
               then release all locks and repeat access to the tree, this time
                    using the protocol for an updater as in Solution 1;
```

By following this protocol, updaters will proceed down the tree as if they were readers until they are about to go to a leaf node. At this point, they ξ-lock the leaf node in order to make the update. However, if it is found that the update would affect nodes higher in the tree, all the analysis done so far would be lost and the update must be retried (note that this only involves the release of one lock and the time lost in scanning the tree). There is no actual modification done to any node which would have to be restored.

The protocol shown works for trees of height greater than one but it is a simple matter to accommodate for this case, so from now one we assume all of our trees have heights greater than one.

Solution 2 achieves high concurrency by allowing both readers and updaters to share all higher levels of the tree. It is only when the update is to be performed on an unsafe leaf that the updater adopts the protocol of the previous solution and thus prevents concurrency as occurred in that solution. Since this only happens roughly once every k updates done to the tree it is a very infrequent action, for typical uses of B^*-trees is with a large k [2].

If the time spent in the unsuccessful analysis or the interference with readers becomes critical, as would be for example, on a very deep tree, then Solution 3 is more attractive.

Solution 3. This solution uses three types of locks, a ρ-lock, an α-lock, and a ξ-lock. The compatibility graph is shown in Figure 4. In this diagram, a new type of edge is shown by a directed broken line from the α node to the ξ node. This means that the α-lock can be converted into a ξ-lock.

Conversion from one type of lock to another type is taken to be a basic (or atomic) operation which happens in one step. To request a conversion from one type of lock to another, a process has to hold a lock of the first type on a node. When making a request for a conversion, a process will be placed *at the beginning* of the queue for the node in question (thus, these conversion requests are serviced before any other requests). If the conversion is granted the process now holds a lock of the second type on this node. If the conversion requests a lock incompatible with a lock placed by another process then the conversion is not granted

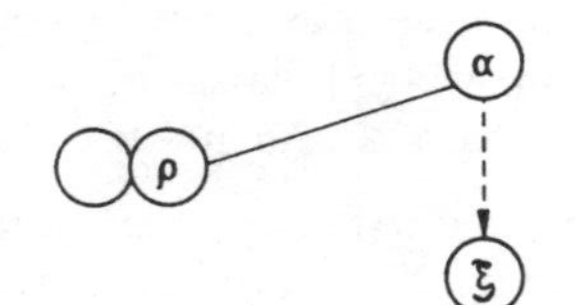

Fig. 4. Compatibility and convertibility graph for locks: Solution 3

and the requesting process is placed on a wait status at the beginning of the queue for that node.

For the three types of locks as defined for Solution 3, the only time a conversion (from α-lock to ξ-lock) fails is when another process holds a ρ lock on the resource on which a conversion is being attempted. (Note that a ρ-lock is the only type of lock which is compatible with an α-lock.) An attempt to convert this α-lock into a ξ-lock will be delayed until the ρ-lock on the resource is released since the ξ-lock is incompatible with the ρ-lock.

Readers use the same protocol as in Solution 1. Updaters now use the following protocol:

```
            0) Place an α-lock on the root;
            1) Get the root and make it the current node;
main loop:  2) While current node is not a leaf node do
               {number of α-locks held ≧ 1}
               begin
                 3) Place an α-lock on appropriate son of current node;
                 4) Get son and make it the current node;
                 5) If current node is safe
                    then release all locks held on ancestors of current node
               end mainloop;
            6) {A leaf node has been reached. At this time we can determine
               if update can be successfully completed.}
               If the update will be successful
               then convert, top-down, all α-locks into ξ-locks;
```

Using this protocol, an updater descends the tree as in Solution 1 but using α-locks instead of ξ-locks. This has the advantage of allowing readers to share the nodes on which an updater has placed its α-locks, thus increasing concurrency. On the other hand, all nodes that need to be modified as a result of the update, are locked exclusively after Step 6. Thus, the analysis phase need not be repeated, as occurred in Solution 2. Moreover, ξ-locks are placed only on those nodes that will be modified, thus readers are prevented from examining only the minimal possible set of nodes.

The main disadvantage of this solution is that, as in Solution 1, one updater may temporarily block other updaters from scanning a node, even if this node will not be affected by the update. Also, there is overhead time spent in doing lock conversions.

Although the α-lock on the leaf node needs to be converted to a ξ-lock everytime the update can be successfully completed, conversion of locks in higher nodes occurs as infrequently as the repetition of analysis in Solution 2, a very small proportion of time. Note that the required α to ξ conversion on the leaf node could be eliminated by changing the protocol to set up a ξ-lock directly on a leaf node, instead of an α-lock. If the update affects higher nodes still held with α-locks, then as will be seen in the generalized solution, the ξ-lock on the leaf must first be converted to an α-lock and then the α- to ξ-lock conversion can be made. Thus, the very frequent operation of converting the α-lock on the leaf to a ξ-lock can be replaced by a slightly more complicated protocol and the infrequent conversion of a ξ-lock on a leaf to an α-lock. A new conversion property among locks is needed, namely ξ-locks must be convertible into α-locks.

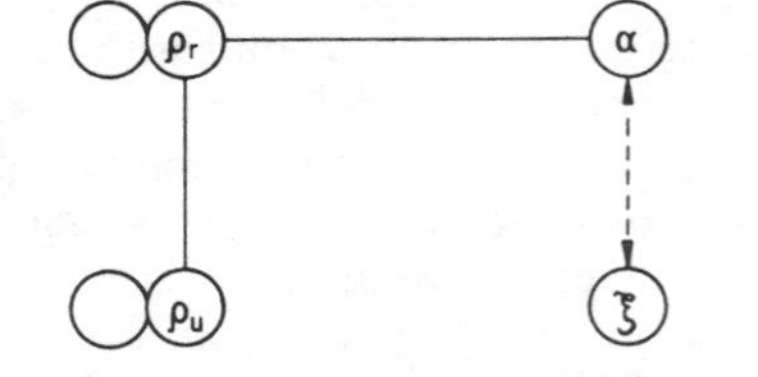

Fig. 5. Compatibility and convertibility graph for locks: Generalized solution

4. A Generalized Solution

In the previous section, we presented three solutions to the problem of deadlock free concurrent operations on *B*-trees. We observed that these solutions were complimentary in the sense that each had advantages over the other in certain situations. Thus, none of them was a best solution in all possible cases. This suggests that a combined solution may be more suitable. In this section, we present such a generalized solution.

There are 4 locks needed in this approach. A ρ_r-lock, a ρ_u-lock, an α-lock, and a ξ-lock. Their compatibility-convertibility diagram is shown in Figure 5. Note that, as mentioned already in the remarks following Solution 3, there is a need for conversion from α to ξ and from ξ to α.

The protocol for a reader is as in Solution 1, with ρ_r replacing ρ. The protocol for an updater is given below. As can be observed, there are two parameters Ρ and Ξ. Intuitively, these stand for the maximum number of levels in the tree on which an updater may place ρ_u-locks and ξ-locks respectively. A variable *H* is introduced which has as its value, the current value of the height $\hbar$ of the tree. In an implementation of a *B**-tree the value $\hbar$ can be stored in a directory entry together with a pointer to the root of the tree. The variable *H* then refers to this entry and the root of the tree is considered a descendant of *H*.

Protocol for an updater:

```
begin
  {Let variable H always contain the height ℏ of the tree, ℏ ≧ 0}
  procedure process son of current;
```

```
begin     get son of current;
          current:=son of current;
          if current is safe
          then remove locks on all ancestors of current;
end;
0) If P≠0 then place ρu-lock on H else place α-lock on H;
   current:=H; {root=son of H};
1) Ξ̄:=min {h, Ξ};
   P̄:=min {P, h−Ξ̄};
   ᾱ:=h−Ξ̄−P̄;
2) for L:=1 step 1 until P̄ do
      begin place a ρu-lock on son of current;
            release ρu-lock on current;
            get son of current;
            current:=son of current
      end;
3) for L:=1 step 1 until ᾱ do
      begin place an α-lock on son of current;
            process son of current;
      end;
4) for L:=1 step 1 until Ξ̄ do
      begin place a ξ-lock on son of current;
            process son of current;
      end;
5) if ρu-lock still held
   then begin release all locks;
              P=0; Ξ=0;
              repeat protocol and exit.
      end;
6) if α-locks still held
   then begin 6a): convert top-down all ξ to α;
              6b): convert top-down all α to ξ;
      end;
7) MODIFY: modify all nodes with ξ-locks, requesting additional ξ-locks
           for overflows, underflows, splits and merges as necessary;
8) release all locks;
end;
```

After Step 6 of this protocol is executed, the updater can proceed with the actual change. This is done in Step 7. All nodes in the locked subpath are locked with ξ-locks. The rules for insertion and deletion on B^*-trees determines whether additional ξ-locks will be acquired. This happens when attempting an overflow (or underflow) into a brother. This situation is shown in Figure 6. Assume that, at the end of Step 6, nodes b and c are held with ξ-locks and an update operation is to be performed on node c. Nodes d and e are immediate brothers of c. Since b has a ξ-lock we know that the update on c will propagate up to b. An overflow (or underflow) operation is then attempted into one of d or e. To do this, a ξ-lock is requested on d and when granted, an attempt is made to combine c and d together. (If this is not possible, an attempt to combine c and e is made.) After the required modifications at this level have been completed, node b is updated. Note that node b is safe (since there is no lock on node a) so after it is modified, the update terminates.

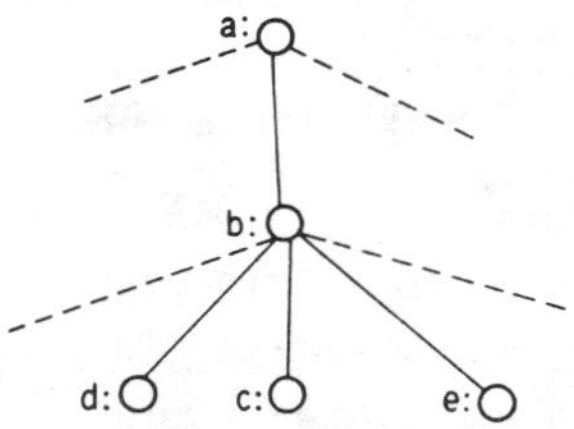

a: b: c: d: e:

Fig. 6. Example of update

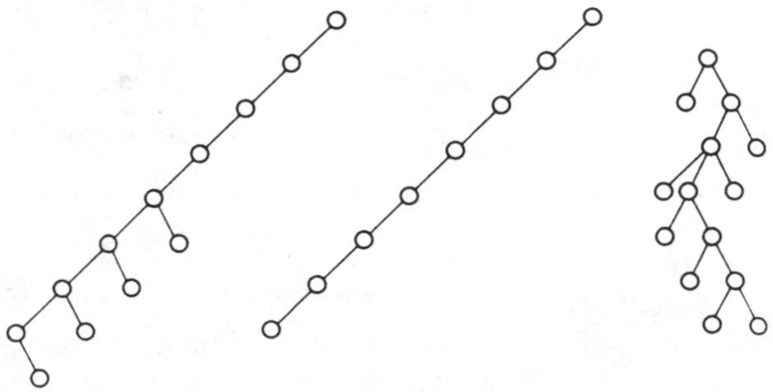

(a) (b) (c)

Fig. 7. Combs

The following observations follow directly from the protocols:

Observation 1. All nodes which are locked by a process form a comb. (A comb of a tree is a subtree with the following restriction: if a node has more than one subtree as descendants, only one of them can have more than one node.) Examples of combs are shown if Figure 7.

Observation 2. If a process holds a ρ_r, ρ_u, or α-locks, then its comb is reduced to a path (as in Fig. 7b). Let this path be $(p_1, p_2, \ldots, p_n)$. Then

a) The process has not been granted any α to ξ conversions. In this case, there are integers j, k, with $0 \leqq j \leqq k \leqq n$ such that all nodes $p_1, p_2, \ldots, p_j$ have ρ_r-locks (if a reader, in this case $j=k=n$) or ρ_u-locks (if an updater), all nodes $p_{j+1}, \ldots, p_k$ have α-locks and all nodes $p_{k+1}, \ldots, p_n$ have ξ-locks.

b) The process has been granted α to ξ lock conversions. Then it no longer holds ρ_u-locks, p_n is a leaf node and there is an integer k such that $1 \leqq k \leqq n$, $p_1, \ldots, p_k$ have ξ-locks and $p_{k+1}, \ldots, p_n$ have α-locks.

In the following sections we will examine these protocols more closely. We will show that they are deadlock free and will analyze the amount of concurrency they provide.

5. Deadlock Freeness of the Generalized Solution

In this section we will show that the generalized solution is deadlock free. As can be observed, the protocols for this solution are combinations of protocols for Solutions 1, 2, and 3. In fact, the main loop of each of these solutions can be obtained from the generalized solution by appropriate choices of the parameters P and Ξ (this will be done in Section 6) and by identifying both ρ_r and ρ_u locks with

Fig. 8. Example of deadlock

the ρ lock. Since each one of Solutions 1, 2, and 3 can be shown to be deadlock free, it would appear that a solution as presented in Section 4 but with just 3 locks, a ρ-lock (instead of a ρ_r and a ρ_u-lock), an α-lock and a ξ-lock could be also shown to be deadlock free (the ρ-lock would be compatible with itself and an α-lock but not with a ξ-lock). Thus a simpler generalized solution would be obtained. This turns out not to be the case as shown by the following example:

Example. Consider a tree as in Figure 8a, where node c is unsafe and all other nodes shown are safe.

Assume $P=2$, $\Xi=1$. An updater, U_1 on node c
would: set up a ρ-lock on a and get node a;
set up a ρ-lock on b; release ρ-lock on a; get b;

Now, other updaters can enter the tree through node a and go down towards node d. As a result of successive updates along this path, node a may split and a new root e be created as in Figure 8b.

A second updater U_2 may now want to update node c.
He would then: set up a ρ-lock on node e; get node e;
set up a ρ-lock on node a; release ρ-lock on e; get a;
set up an α-lock on b (this would be granted since the only other lock on b, which is held by U_1, is a ρ-lock, compatible with α);
get b;
since b is safe, release ρ-lock on a;
get ξ-lock on node c; get node c since node c is unsafe, no locks are released;
At this point, U_2 would begin converting its ξ-locks into α-locks:
Convert ξ-locks in node c into an α-lock.
Then, the α-locks would be converted into ξ-locks:
Convert α-lock in node b into a ξ-lock;

This last conversion would be blocked since there is another process, U_1, holding a ρ-lock on b which is incompatible with a ξ-lock. Thus U_2 could not proceed. But U_1 is now also blocked since it would try to set up a ξ-lock on node c next. This request cannot be granted since another process, U_2, holds an α-lock which is incompatible with a ξ-lock. Thus, U_1 and U_2 are in a deadlock situation.

Forcing a read lock requested by an updater to be incompatible with an α-lock, as is done in the generalized solution by distinguishing between the ρ_r and ρ_u locks, resolves the above problem. In fact, as we now proceed to show, it makes this solution deadlock free. We first introduce some definitions:

Definition 1. A lock request on a node is said to be *pending* until granted by the scheduler.

Definition 2. Given two processes U and V, we say that U *waits on* V, denoted $U \vdash V$, if U has a pending request to lock a node on which V has a lock incompatible with the one U is requesting.

Definition 3. A process is called a *c*-process if it has a pending request for a lock conversion.

Definition 4. If a process U has a pending lock request on a node n then n is said to be the *critical node* of U. If U is not requesting a lock or the request was granted then U does not have a critical node.

Definition 5. The *critical level* of a process U, denoted by $\lambda(U)$ is the level of its critical node, if U has one, or 0 otherwise.

Our intent is to show that the given locking protocol is deadlock free. Intuitively, this means that any given process using these protocols to request locks will not be forever prevented from completing its task because of the existence of other locks placed by other processes. We must, however, be careful not to include the lock scheduler as an interfering process. In fact, a lock scheduler can arbitrarily produce deadlock situations by consistently failing to service a given process request, thus preventing it from completing its task. We then request that the scheduler have the following properties:

a) It shouldn't grant incompatible lock requests (or conversions) since this would create a situation inconsistent with the attributes of the locks.

b) It should grant lock conversion requests on a node before any other requests on that node. Note that since both α and ξ locks are incompatible among themselves, there can be at most one lock conversion request on any given node. Granting the unique lock conversion possible on a node before other requests eliminates the possibilities of trivial deadlock situations.

c) It should be fair in servicing requests, i.e., there should be a finite number of requests granted by the scheduler before a given request is finally granted. Servicing a request which doesn't result in an incompatible lock to be placed in a node should result in granting the requested lock.

There are many lock schedulers satisfying these restrictions and we have chosen one using a FIFO model to illustrate our protocols. Any other scheduler satisfying a), b), and c) will also result in a deadlock free operation.

Now we present a series of lemmas, all of which follow from the observations on the protocols made at the end of the previous section.

Lemma 1. If a process V holds a ρ_r or ρ_u-lock on a node m then

$\lambda(V) < \ell(m)$.

(Recall that $\ell(m)$ is the level of node m.)

Proof. Follows directly from observation 2a. □

Lemma 2. If a process V holds a ξ-lock on a node m then either
2a) $\lambda(V) < \ell(m)$ or
2b) $\lambda(V) \geqq \ell(m)$ and V also holds a ξ-lock on the father of m.

Proof. We use observation 2. If V has not requested α to ξ conversions then Case 2a applies (Steps 0 through 5 of the protocol). In Step 6a) since a ξ to α conversion is always granted then $\lambda(V)=0$. In Step 6b), α to ξ conversion is top down, and $\lambda(V)<$level of any node on which V holds a ξ-lock. Thus, $\lambda(V)<\ell(m)$. If, on the other hand, V has been granted all α to ξ conversions then V holds a comb made up of nodes all of which are ξ-locked and V is performing the actual update on some node in Step 7. If $\lambda(V)\geqq\ell(m)$ it means that V is acquiring a ξ-lock on a node q to perform an overflow (or underflow) or split (or merge) operation. But in this case, V holds a ξ-lock on the father r of q. Since all nodes held with ξ-locks by V form a comb, if $\lambda(V)\geqq\ell(m)$ it means that m is a descendant of r, and V holds a ξ-lock on the father of m. This completes the proof of Lemma 2. □

Lemma 3. If a process V holds an α-lock on a node m then either

3a) $\lambda(V)<\ell(m)$ or

3b) $\lambda(V)=\ell(m)$ and V is attempting an α to ξ conversion on node m or

3c) $\lambda(V)>\ell(m)$ and V is attempting an α to ξ conversion and has an α-lock on the father of m.

Proof. Assume $\lambda(V)\geqq\ell(m)$. Since V holds an α-lock, observation 2 applies. Thus, if $\lambda(V)=\ell(m)$, V must be attempting an α to ξ conversion on m while if $\lambda(V)>\ell(m)$, V must be attempting an α to ξ conversion on an ancestor of m, and since all nodes locked by V form a path, holds an α-lock on a father of m.

This proves the lemma. □

Lemmas 1, 2, and 3 are now used to prove Lemma 4. This is the key lemma in proving deadlock freeness of the generalized solution.

Lemma 4. If U, V are processes and $U\vdash V$ then either

4a) $\lambda(U)>\lambda(V)$ or

4b) $\lambda(U)=\lambda(V)$, V is a c-process and U is not a c-process.

Proof. Let $U\vdash V$ and let m be the critical node for U. Thus $\lambda(U)=\ell(m)$. We consider 3 cases.

Case 1. If V holds a ρ_u or ρ_r lock on m, then by Lemma 1,

$$\lambda(U)=\ell(m)>\lambda(V)$$

and Case 4a) of Lemma 4 holds.

Case 2. If V holds a ξ-lock on m, Lemma 2 applies. Thus, either $\lambda(V)<\ell(m)$ and the lemma holds or $\lambda(V)\geqq\ell(m)$. But this last case is not possible for then V would hold a ξ-lock on the father of m also, which means that U could not have any locks set up on the father of m and so it could not be attempting to acquire a lock on m. Clearly, U could not be attempting a conversion either since V has a ξ-lock on m.

Case 3. If V holds an α-lock on m, Lemma 3 applies. Thus, either $\lambda(V)<\ell(m)$ (and we are done) or $\lambda(V)\geqq\ell(m)$. If $\lambda(V)=\ell(m)$, we know V is attempting an α- to ξ-conversion on node m. But since no two processes can be attempting a conversion simultaneously on the same node (they would both have to hold α-locks on the node which is not possible) we get that U cannot be a c-process. Finally, if $\lambda(V)>\ell(m)$ then V holds α-locks on both m and its parent. We already saw that U cannot be attempting a conversion on node m since V has an α-lock on it. Thus, U must be attempting to acquire a new lock on m. But to do this it must have a lock on a parent of m. If U were a reader then U would not be waiting to get a ρ_r-lock on m. Thus U has to be an updater. But this cannot happen since any lock U holds on a parent of m is incompatible with α. This concludes the proof of the lemma. □

Lemma 4 allows us to show:

Theorem. The generalized solution is deadlock free.

Proof. Assume to the contrary that a deadlock exists. Then, there exist processes $U_1, U_2, \ldots, U_k$ such that

$$U_1\vdash U_2\vdash U_3\vdash \cdots \vdash U_{k-1}\vdash U_k\vdash U_1 \qquad (*)$$

and there is no way to grant any pending locks in the chain. Note that since $U_1\vdash U_1$ cannot happen, $k\geqq 2$ and so, there are at least three processes U_1, U_2, U_3 with $U_1\vdash U_2\vdash U_3$ and $U_2\neq U_1$, $U_2\neq U_3$.

By Lemma 4, $\lambda(U_1)\geqq\lambda(U_2)$ with $\lambda(U_1)=\lambda(U_2)$ if U_2 is a c-process. On the other hand, $\lambda(U_2)\geqq\lambda(U_3)$ with $\lambda(U_2)=\lambda(U_3)$ only if U_2 is not a c-process. Thus $\lambda(U_1)>\lambda(U_3)$.

The above result implies that in (*) we have $\lambda(U_1)>\lambda(U_1)$ a contradiction. Thus, the theorem holds. □

6. Selection of P and Ξ

As presented in Section 4 the generalized solution depends on the parameters P and Ξ.

By varying these parameters, many different concurrency patterns can be obtained.

For example, if $P=0$, $\Xi=h$ Steps 2 and 3 of the protocol would not be executed and Step 4 essentially reduces this solution to Solution 1. Note that setting up Ξ to h is not possible since one does not know in advance how high the tree is. But it is easy to define a way of simulating the protocol for the generalized solution to work as if one knew what h was before accessing the tree. Also, in order to get Solution 1, one has to change ρ_r to ρ, but clearly this is no problem either since α-locks are not present so that the locks ρ_r and ξ in the generalized solution can be mapped to the ρ and ξ-lock respectively of Solution 1. In the sequel, when saying that the generalized solution reduces to one of Solution 1, 2, or 3 we mean it modulo these types of changes.

If we let $P=h-1$ and $\Xi=1$ then we get Solution 2 (in this case, the retry would have to have $P=0$, $\Xi=h$). Finally, setting $P=0$, $\Xi=0$ one gets Solution 3. As was mentioned in Section 3 each one of these solutions has advantages and disadvantages over the other. A proper choice of P and Ξ will *tune* the generalized solution to yield the best performance for a given application. In what follows we show a model of access with an analysis of the relevant components of the cost of a solution. Expressions for these components will be obtained from which

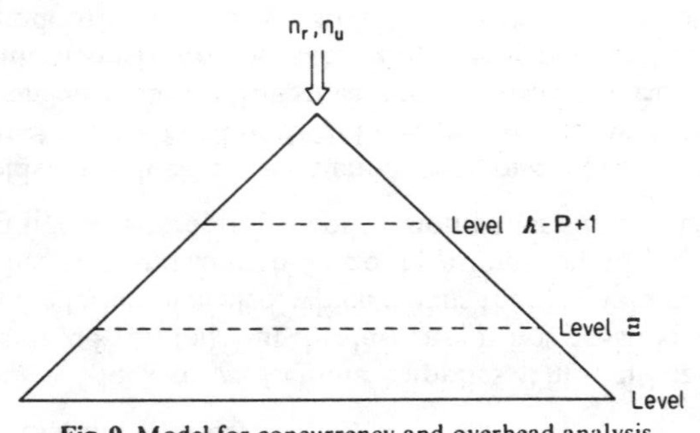

Fig. 9. Model for concurrency and overhead analysis

suitable values of P and Ξ can be chosen. We will assume that all readers and updaters access the structure using the same P and Ξ (as will be explained below, this may not be the case, but helps to evaluate a strategy).

There are two main components in the cost of a given solution. One is the time spent by processes waiting for locks to be removed before they can proceed. The second one is the time overhead due to placing locks on the nodes, converting locks, or repeating part of an analysis.

Assume a tree as in Figure 9, and a given number n_r of readers and n_u of updaters. The updaters will place ρ_u-locks from level h down to level $h-\text{P}+1$. From level $h-\text{P}$ down to $\Xi+1$ they will place α-locks and finally, for the last Ξ levels, they will place ξ-locks.

Now, in the upper P levels there are no conflicts, since updaters and readers use compatible ρ_u and ρ_r locks. But in level $h-\text{P}$, the updaters set up α-locks which are incompatible among themselves. Thus, at this level, some updaters will have to wait for other updaters.

Let v_i denote the number of nodes of the tree at level i. We will assume that each updater has equal probability $\frac{1}{v_i}$ of scanning each node at level i when traversing the tree from the root to a leaf node. Then, since there are n_u updaters, the expected number of nodes which are visited by the n_u updaters at level $h-\text{P}$ is given by

$$\Phi(h-\text{P}, n_u)=v_{h-\text{P}}\left(1-\left(1-\frac{1}{v_{h-\text{P}}}\right)^{n_u}\right).$$

To obtain this expression, note that $\left(1-\frac{1}{v_{h-\text{P}}}\right)^{n_u}$ is the probability that a given node will not be scanned by any of the n_u updaters. Thus, $1-\left(1-\frac{1}{v_{h-\text{P}}}\right)^{n_u}$ gives the probability that a given node will be scanned by at least one updater. The expected number of nodes which will be scanned by at least one updater is then $\Phi(h-\text{P}, n_u)$.

This expression also gives the expected number of updaters that will proceed down the tree (from level $h-\text{P}$) without waiting for an α-lock to be granted. Thus, the expected number of updaters that will wait is given by:

$$W_u=n_u-\Phi(v_{h-\text{P}}, n_u).$$

The $\Phi(h-\text{P}, n_u)$ updaters that can proceed downwards from level $h-\text{P}$ will do so without interfering with each other. When they get to level Ξ they may interact with readers. Assuming the updaters acquire the ξ-locks before the readers request ρ_r-locks (this will give a worst case value for the quantity being computed), the expected number of readers that wait is:

$$W_r=\begin{cases} n_r\dfrac{\Phi(h-\text{P}, n_u)}{v_\Xi} & (\text{if } \Xi\neq 0)\\ 0 & (\text{if } \Xi=0).\end{cases}$$

W_u and W_r together give a measure of the number of processes that will have to wait when accessing the tree. Besides this component of the cost of a (P, Ξ) solution there is the overhead cost involved. This cost has three subcomponents. One is given by the fact that, after scanning the tree from the root to the leaf, a process may find that all his processing has to be repeated (this happens if in Step 5 of the protocol an updater finds that it still holds a ρ_u-lock). We will measure this component by computing Q, the expected number of nodes per updater that are scanned again to repeat an analysis. The second subcomponent is C_ξ, the expected number of ξ-locks that an updater will convert into α-locks. Finally, the third subcomponent is C_α, the expected number of α-locks that an updater will convert into ξ-locks.

To compute Q, we will assume that all updaters are performing insertions. In this case, one out of k updaters will, on the average, cause a split of a node at the leaf level which propagates up the tree; one out of k^2 updaters will, on the average, cause a split of a node at level 2 which will propagate up the tree, and so on. Thus, we consider the probability that an updater will *modify* a node at level i or above to be $\left(\frac{1}{k}\right)^{i-1}$.

An updater will repeat his analysis if it causes a node at level $h-\text{P}+1$ or above to be modified. Since when this happens, h nodes will be scanned again, we have that

$$Q=\begin{cases} h\cdot\left(\frac{1}{k}\right)^{h-\text{P}} & \text{if P}\neq 0\\ 0 & \text{if P}=0.\end{cases}$$

(Note that if P=0, there is no retry involved.)

To compute C_ξ we note that an updater will convert ξ-locks into α-locks whenever it reaches Step 5 of the protocol and discovers it holds an α-lock, but not a ρ_u-lock. This, in turn happens only if the update will modify nodes at a level $\Xi+1$ or higher, but lower than level $h-\text{P}+1$. The number of locks to be modified in this case is always Ξ. Thus,

$$C_\xi=\begin{cases} \Xi\cdot\left[\left(\frac{1}{k}\right)^{\Xi}-\left(\frac{1}{k}\right)^{h-\text{P}}\right] & \text{if } h>\text{P}+\Xi\\ 0 & \text{otherwise}.\end{cases}$$

Finally, to compute C_α, we note that if the update will modify nodes exactly up to a level i, $\Xi+1 \leq i \leq h-\mathrm{P}$ then i α-locks are converted into ξ-locks. Thus, if $h > \mathrm{P}+\Xi$

$$C_\alpha = \sum_{i=\Xi+1}^{h-\mathrm{P}} i \cdot \left[\left(\frac{1}{k}\right)^{i-1} - \left(\frac{1}{k}\right)^{i}\right]$$

$$= \frac{k-1}{k} \sum_{i=\Xi+1}^{h-\mathrm{P}} i \left(\frac{1}{k}\right)^{i-1}.$$

Clearly, if $h \leq \mathrm{P}+\Xi$ no α-locks are placed in the first place so $C_\alpha = 0$.

In Table 1, we give values for these 5 components for various choices of h, k, n_r, and n_u. Notice that W_u and W_r are shown in two columns, a high and a low. This is because the actual number of nodes at level i, v_i can fluctuate according to:

$$v_h = 1$$

$$2 \leq v_{h-1} \leq 2k+1$$

$$2(k+1)^{h-i-1} \leq v_i \leq (2k+1)^{h-i} \qquad i \leq h-2.$$

The high value is obtained when using the upper bound for v_i and the low value is obtained when using the lower bound for v_i.

From Table 1, we can choose values of P and Ξ which will guarantee an average performance prescribed in advance. For example, a concurrency of more than 50% of the updaters and more than 99% of the readers would be possible, in the case $h=5$, $k=10$, $n_u=30$, $n_r=70$ by choosing $\Xi=1$, $\mathrm{P}=2$. The average number of nodes that are scanned again after a retry by an updater is 0.005 and the number of lock conversions per updater is on the average, 0.099 for ξ to α conversion and 0.207 for α to ζ conversion.

For $h=3$, $k=100$ good concurrency levels are achieved with $\Xi=1$ and $\mathrm{P}=1$ or 2. In the latter case, there is an increase in the number of nodes that are accessed before a retry which is compensated by reducing to 0 the number of lock conversions.

We have shown how to select the parameters P and Ξ to obtain a given level of concurrency. This assumes that all updaters use the update protocol with the same values of P and Ξ. But there is nothing that prevents an updater from using its own P and Ξ. By doing this, an updater may use information he has gathered on previous accesses to further contribute to an increase in concurrency. For example, an updater that accesses an index to perform an insertion on a leaf node he has visited recently and found to be very far from full could choose $\mathrm{P}=h-1$ and $\Xi=1$ and be almost guaranteed not to perform a retry while at the same time allowing for maximum concurrency with other processes. (If the updater had found the node almost full on a previous access, it may use $\mathrm{P}=h-2$, $\Xi=1$ to insure that even a split to level 2 would not cause a retry and still allow for high concurrency!)

The fact that each updater may use its own parameters P and Ξ gives the generalized solution an added flexibility while at the same time preserving deadlock freeness of the schema. In fact, in proving deadlock freeness in Section 5, no assumptions where made as to the values for P and Ξ each updater might choose.

Table 1

			$n_u=5$	$n_r=95$	$h=5$	$k=10$		
Ξ	P	W_u low	W_u high	W_r low	W_r high	Q	C_ξ	C_α
0	0	4.00	4.00	0.00	0.00	0.0000	0.0000	1.1110
0	1	3.06	0.45	0.00	0.00	0.0005	0.0000	1.1106
0	2	0.43	0.02	0.00	0.00	0.0050	0.0000	1.1070
0	3	0.04	0.00	0.00	0.00	0.0500	0.0000	1.0800
0	4	0.00	0.00	0.00	0.00	0.5000	0.0000	0.9000
1	0	4.00	4.00	0.04	0.00	0.0000	0.1000	0.2110
1	1	3.06	0.45	0.07	0.00	0.0005	0.0999	0.2106
1	2	0.43	0.02	0.16	0.00	0.0050	0.0990	0.2070
1	3	0.04	0.00	0.18	0.00	0.0500	0.0900	0.1800
1	4	0.00	0.00	0.18	0.00	0.5000	0.0000	0.0000
2	0	4.00	4.00	0.39	0.01	0.0000	0.0200	0.0310
2	1	3.06	0.45	0.76	0.05	0.0005	0.0198	0.0306
2	2	0.43	0.02	1.79	0.05	0.0050	0.0180	0.0270
2	3	0.04	0.00	1.95	0.05	0.0500	0.0000	0.0000
3	0	4.00	4.00	4.32	0.22	0.0000	0.0030	0.0040
3	1	3.06	0.45	8.37	0.98	0.0005	0.0027	0.0036
3	2	0.43	0.02	19.72	1.07	0.0050	0.0000	0.0000
4	0	4.00	4.00	47.50	4.52	0.0000	0.0004	0.0004
4	1	3.06	0.45	92.03	20.57	0.0005	0.0000	0.0000
5	0	4.00	4.00	95.00	95.00	0.0000	0.0000	0.0000

			$n_u=5$	$n_r=95$	$h=3$	$k=100$		
Ξ	P	W_u low	W_u high	W_r low	W_r high	Q	C_ξ	C_α
0	0	4.00	4.00	0.00	0.00	0.0000	0.0000	1.0101
0	1	3.06	0.05	0.00	0.00	0.0003	0.0000	1.0098
0	2	0.05	0.00	0.00	0.00	0.0300	0.0000	0.9900
1	0	4.00	4.00	0.47	0.00	0.0000	0.0100	0.0201
1	1	3.06	0.05	0.91	0.01	0.0003	0.0099	0.0198
1	2	0.05	0.00	2.33	0.01	0.0300	0.0000	0.0000
2	0	4.00	4.00	47.50	0.47	0.0000	0.0002	0.0003
2	1	3.06	0.05	92.03	2.34	0.0003	0.0000	0.0000
3	0	4.00	4.00	95.00	95.00	0.0000	0.0000	0.0000

			$n_u=5$	$n_r=95$	$h=2$	$k=1000$		
Ξ	P	W_u low	W_u high	W_r low	W_r high	Q	C_ξ	C_α
0	0	4.00	4.00	0.00	0.00	0.0000	0.0000	1.0010
0	1	3.06	0.00	0.00	0.00	0.0020	0.0000	0.9990
1	0	4.00	4.00	47.50	0.05	0.0000	0.0010	0.0020
1	1	3.06	0.00	92.03	0.24	0.0020	0.0000	0.0000
2	0	4.00	4.00	95.00	95.00	0.0000	0.0000	0.0000

7. Extensions to Sequential Readers

In some uses of B^*-trees to support indexes, the nodes of the tree can also belong to sequential data structures. A common situation would be that of readers performing sequential scans through a sequence of nodes at the same level in

Table 1 (continued)

			$n_u=30$	$n_r=70$	$k=5$	$k=10$		
Ξ	P	W_u low	W_u high	W_r low	W_r high	Q	C_ξ	C_α
0	0	29.00	29.00	0.00	0.00	0.0000	0.0000	1.1110
0	1	28.00	13.86	0.00	0.00	0.0005	0.0000	1.1106
0	2	13.45	0.97	0.00	0.00	0.0050	0.0000	1.1070
0	3	1.73	0.05	0.00	0.00	0.0500	0.0000	1.0800
0	4	0.16	0.00	0.00	0.00	0.5000	0.0000	0.9000
1	0	29.00	29.00	0.03	0.00	0.0000	0.1000	0.2110
1	1	28.00	13.86	0.05	0.01	0.0005	0.0999	0.2106
1	2	13.45	0.97	0.44	0.01	0.0050	0.0990	0.2070
1	3	1.73	0.05	0.74	0.01	0.0500	0.0900	0.1800
1	4	0.16	0.00	0.78	0.01	0.5000	0.0000	0.0000
2	0	29.00	29.00	0.29	0.01	0.0000	0.0200	0.0310
2	1	28.00	13.86	0.58	0.12	0.0005	0.0198	0.0306
2	2	13.45	0.97	4.79	0.22	0.0050	0.0180	0.0270
2	3	1.73	0.05	8.18	0.23	0.0500	0.0000	0.0000
3	0	29.00	29.00	3.18	0.16	0.0000	0.0030	0.0040
3	1	28.00	13.86	6.36	2.56	0.0005	0.0027	0.0036
3	2	13.45	0.97	52.66	4.61	0.0050	0.0000	0.0000
4	0	29.00	29.00	35.00	3.33	0.0000	0.0004	0.0004
4	1	28.00	13.86	70.00	53.80	0.0005	0.0000	0.0000
5	0	29.00	29.00	70.00	70.00	0.0000	0.0000	0.0000

			$n_u=30$	$n_r=70$	$k=3$	$k=100$		
Ξ	P	W_u low	W_u high	W_r low	W_r high	Q	C_ξ	C_α
0	0	29.00	29.00	0.00	0.00	0.0000	0.0000	1.0101
0	1	28.00	2.07	0.00	0.00	0.0003	0.0000	1.0098
0	2	2.06	0.01	0.00	0.00	0.0300	0.0000	0.9900
1	0	29.00	29.00	0.35	0.00	0.0000	0.0100	0.0201
1	1	28.00	2.07	0.69	0.05	0.0003	0.0099	0.0198
1	2	2.06	0.01	9.68	0.05	0.0300	0.0000	0.0000
2	0	29.00	29.00	35.00	0.35	0.0000	0.0002	0.0003
2	1	28.00	2.07	70.00	9.73	0.0003	0.0000	0.0000
3	0	29.00	29.00	70.00	70.00	0.0000	0.0000	0.0000

			$n_u=30$	$n_r=70$	$k=2$	$k=1000$		
Ξ	P	W_u low	W_u high	W_r low	W_r high	Q	C_ξ	C_α
0	0	29.00	29.00	0.00	0.00	0.0000	0.0000	1.0010
0	1	28.00	0.22	0.00	0.00	0.0020	0.0000	0.9990
1	0	29.00	29.00	35.00	0.03	0.0000	0.0010	0.0020
1	1	28.00	0.22	70.00	1.04	0.0020	0.0000	0.0000
2	0	29.00	29.00	70.00	70.00	0.0000	0.0000	0.0000

the tree. The ideas developed in the protocols presented in Section 4 can also be adapted to allow sequential read accesses concurrently with random read and update accesses. We will briefly discuss how this can be done for one case. The reader will then quickly see how these concepts could be used in other situations.

Consider the very frequent case of readers accessing the nodes of the tree following a path from the root down, with the additional freedom of allowing a left to right scan of some adjacent nodes to be made at the same level of the tree. Thus, a reader could, for example, start at the root, follow a downward path to a node, move right on adjacent nodes at the same level to another node then continue down the tree.

A similar analysis to that done in Lemmas 1, 2, and 3 would show that no deadlocks could occur by allowing such traversals, except for one case. This occurs when an updater, having locked with ξ-locks all nodes that will be modified, begins to perform the actual modifications and discovers that an overflow or underflow exists and wishes to scan the left brother q of a node p (on which it holds a ξ-lock) to see if there is room to accommodate for this overflow or underflow. Instead of acquiring a ξ-lock on q, as indicated in Step 7 of the protocol for the generalized solution, the updating process would then have to:

1) convert the ξ-lock on p to an α-lock;

2) place a ξ-lock on q;

3) Examine node q. If it can be used to accommodate the overflow or underflow, convert the α-lock on p to a ξ-lock and perform the operation; otherwise, release the ξ-lock on q and convert the α-lock on p to a ξ-lock; {Examination of the right brother would not require any changes to our original protocol}.

It can be shown that with this modification, the new protocols are still deadlock free.

Other modes of traversals by readers can also be accommodated using the ideas presented here.

8. Conclusions and Implementation Considerations

In this paper we have examined several solutions to the problem of concurrency in indexes implemented as B^*-trees. A generalized solution has been presented which allows tuning the access to these structures to optimize concurrency of operations. Furthermore, this solution has been shown to be deadlock free. This shows that with proper locking techniques, B^*-trees support easy and highly concurrent access to indexes.

When implementing B^*-trees with the provision for parallel operations some structuring concept should be chosen, which allows to consider a B^*-tree together with the operations and their lockprotocols as one conceptual unit. Several such concepts, most of them related to the Simula classes, have been offered in the literature, but they usually ignore the problem of parallel operations, assuming that these units will be used by one sequential process only. This automatically results in a serial application of operations.

To deal with parallel (from an external point of view) operations the concept of a Monitor has been introduced [5, 7]. Monitors, however, deal with external parallelism essentially by enforcing internally a serialization of operations. Unfortunately this means that a Monitor would cancel exactly the effect we are trying to achieve.

In the Operating Systems Project BSM at the Technical University in Munich a structuring concept called *Manager* was developed [8, 9]. *Managers* deal with parallel external operations but allow in a carefully controlled way also internal parallelism of operations. It seems that Managers would be a suitable structuring concept for implementing the solutions presented in this paper.

Acknowledgements. Mike Blasgen participated in the initial discussions that lead to the generalized solution presented here. His ideas about locking in B^*-trees as implemented in System R [1] and his cooperation with the authors are sincerely appreciated.

References

1. Astrahan, M.M., et al.: System R: Relational approach to database management. ACM Transactions on Database Systems **1**, 97–137 (1976)
2. Bayer, R., McCreight, E.: Organization and maintenance of large ordered indexes. Acta Informat. **1**, 173–189 (1972)
3. Bayer, R., Metzger, J.: On the Encypherment of Search Trees and Random Access Files. ACM Transactions on Database Systems **1**, 37–52 (1976)
4. Bayer, R., Unterauer, K.: Prefix *B*-trees. IBM Research Report RJ 1796, San Jose, Calif., 1976. ACM Transactions on Database Systems **2**, 11–26 (1977)
5. Brinch Hansen, P.: A programming methodology for operating system design. IFIP Congress 1974, Stockholm, pp. 394–397. Amsterdam: North Holland 1974
6. Held, G., Stonebraker, M.: *B*-trees reexamined. ERL, College of Engineering, Univ. of California, Berkeley, Calif., Memo. ♯ERL-M528, July 2, 1975
7. Hoare, C.A.R.: Monitors: An operating system structuring concept. Comm. ACM **17**, 549–557 (1974)
8. Jammel, A., Stiegler, H.: Verwalter, eine Methode der rekursiven Prozeßzerlegung. Leibniz-Rechenzentrum der Bayerischen Akademie der Wissenschaften, LRZ Internschrift 7604/1, München, 1976
9. Jammel, A., Stiegler, H.: Managers versus Monitors. Submitted to: IFIP Congress (1977)
10. Knuth, D.E.: The art of computer programming, Vol. 3. Sorting and searching. Reading, Mass.: Addison-Wesley 1972
11. Metzger, J.K.: Managing simultaneous operations in large ordered indexes. Technische Universität München, Institut für Informatik, TUM-Math. Report, 1975
12. Schkolnick, M.: Initial specifications for DFMAS. Unpublished document, May 1975
13. Wedekind, H.: On the selection of access paths in a data base system (J.W. Klimbie, K.L. Koffeman, eds.), Data base management, pp. 385–397. Amsterdam: North-Holland 1974

Received June 10, 1976

The Transaction Concept: Virtues and Limitations

Jim Gray

Tandem Computers Incorporated
19333 Vallco Parkway
Cupertino Ca. 95014

ABSTRACT: A transaction is a transformation of state which has the properties of atomicity (all or nothing), durability (effects survive failures) and consistency (a correct transformation). The transaction concept is key to the structuring of data management applications. The concept seems to have applicability to programming systems in general. This paper restates the transaction concepts and attempts to put several implementation approaches in perspective. It then describes some areas which require further study: (1) the integration of the transaction concept with the notion of abstract data type, (2) some techniques to allow transactions to be composed of sub-transactions, and (3) handling transactions which last for extremely long times (days or months).

CONTENTS

INTRODUCTION: What is a transaction?

The transaction concept derives from contract law. In making a contract, two or more parties negotiate for a while and then make a deal. The deal is made binding by the joint signature of a document or by some other act (as simple as a handshake or nod). If the parties are rather suspicious of one another or just want to be safe they appoint an intermediary (usually called an escrow officer) to coordinate the commitment of the transaction.

The Christian wedding ceremony gives a good example of such a contract. The bride and groom "negotiate" for days or years and then appoint a minister to conduct the marriage ceremony. The minister first asks if anyone has any objections to the marriage; he then asks the bride and groom if they agree to the marriage. If they both say "I do", he pronounces them man and wife.

Of course, a contract is simply an agreement. Individuals can violate it if they are willing to break the law. But legally, a contract (transaction) can only be annulled if it was illegal in the first place. Adjustment of a bad transaction is done via further compensating transactions (including legal redress).

The transaction concept emerges with the following properties:

- Consistency: the transaction must obey legal protocols.
- Atomicity: it either happens or it does not; either all are bound by the contract or none are.
- Durability: once a transaction is committed, it cannot be abrogated.

A GENERAL MODEL OF TRANSACTIONS

Translating the transaction concept to the realm of computer science, we observe that most of the transactions we see around us (banking, car rental, or buying groceries) may be reflected in a computer as transformations of a system state.

A system state consists of records and devices with changeable values. The system state includes assertions about the values of records and about the allowed transformations of the values. These assertions are called the system consistency constraints.

The system provides actions which read and transform the values of records and devices. A collection of actions which comprise a consistent transformation of the state may be grouped to form a transaction. Transactions preserve the system consistency constraints -- they obey the laws by transforming consistent states into new consistent states.

Transactions must be atomic and durable: either all actions are done and the transaction is said to commit, or none of the effects of the transaction survive and the transaction is said to abort.

These definitions need slight refinement to allow some actions to be ignored and to account for others which cannot be undone. Actions on entities are categorized as:

unprotected: the action need not be undone or redone if the transaction must be aborted or the entity value needs to be reconstructed.
protected: the action can and must be undone or redone if the transaction must be aborted or if the entity value needs to be reconstructed.
real: once done, the action cannot be undone.

Operations on temporary files and transmission of intermediate messages are examples of unprotected actions. Conventional database and message operations are examples of protected actions. Transaction commitment and operations on real devices (cash dispensers and airplane wings) are examples of real actions.

Each transaction is defined to have exactly one of two outcomes: committed or aborted. All protected and real actions of committed transactions persist, even in the presence of failures. On the other hand, none of the effects of protected and real actions of an aborted transaction are ever visible to other transactions.

Once a transaction commits, its effects can only be altered by running further transactions. For example, if someone is underpaid, the corrective action is to run another transaction which pays an additional sum. Such post facto transactions are called compensating transactions.

A simple transaction is a linear sequence of actions. A complex transaction may have concurrency within a transaction; the initiation of one action may depend on the outcome of a group of actions. Such transactions seem to have transactions nested within them, although the effects of the nested transactions are only visible to other parts of the transaction (see Figure 1).

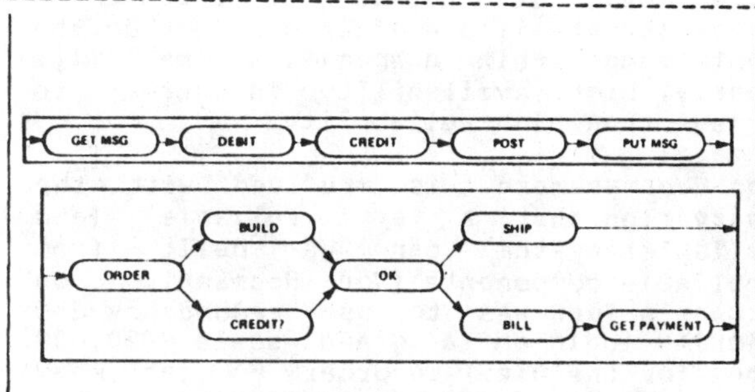

Figure 1. Two transactions. T1 is a simple sequence of actions. T2 is a more complex transaction which demonstrates parallelism and nesting within a transaction.

NonStop (TM): Making failures rare

One way to get transaction atomicity and durability is to build a perfect system which never fails. Suppose you built perfect hardware which never failed and software which did exactly what it was supposed to do. Your system would be very popular and all transactions would always be successful. But the system would fail occasionally, because the people who adapted your system to their environment would make some mistakes (application programming errors) and the people who operated the system would make some mistakes (data entry and procedural errors). Even with very careful management, the system would fail every few months or years and at least one transaction in 100 would fail due to data-entry error or authorization error [Japan].

One may draw two conclusions from this:

1. You don't have to make a perfect system, one that fails once every thousand years is good enough to please most customers.
2. Even if the system is perfect, some transactions will abort because of data-entry error, insufficient funds, operator cancelation, or timeout.

This section discusses techniques for "almost perfect" systems and explains their relationship to transaction processing.

Imperfection comes in several flavors. A system may fail because of a design error or because of a device failure. The error may become visible to a user or redundant checks may detect the failure.

A system is unreliable if it does the wrong thing (does not detect the error). A system is unavailable if it does not do the right thing within a specified time limit. Clearly, high availability is harder to achieve than high reliability.

John Von Neumann is credited with the observation that a very reliable (and available) system can be built from unreliable components [Von Neumann]. Von Neumann's idea was to use redundancy and majority logic on a grand scale (20,000 wires for one wire) in order to get mean times to failure measured in decades. Von Neumann was thinking in terms of neurons and vacuum tubes which have mean times to failures measured in days and which are used in huge quantities (millions or billions) in a system. In addition, Von Neumann's model was flat so that any failure in a chain broke the whole chain.

Fortunately, computer systems do not need redundancy factors of 20,000 in order to get very long mean times to failure. Unlike Von Neumann's nerve nets, computer systems are hierarchically composed of modules and each module is self-checked so that it either operates correctly or detects its failure and does nothing. Such modules are called fail-fast. Fail-fast computer modules such as processors and memories achieve mean times to failure measured in months. Since relatively few modules make up a system (typically less than 100), very limited redundancy is needed to improve the system reliability.

Consider the simple case of disks. A typical disk fails about once a year. Failures arise from bad spots on the disk, physical failure of the spindle or electronic failure of the path to the disk. It takes about an hour to fix a disk or get a spare disk to replace it. If the disks are duplexed (mirrored) and if they fail independently then the pair will both be down about once every three thousand years. More realistic analysis gives a mean time to failure of 800 years. So a system with eight pairs of disks would have an unavailable disk pair about once a century. Without mirroring the same system would have an unavailable disk about eight times a year.

Although duplexed disks have been used since the late sixties [Heistand] we have been slow to generalize from this experience to the observation that:

* Mean time to failures of modules are measured in months.
* Modules can be made fail-fast: either they work properly or they fail to work.
* Spare modules give the appearance of mean time to repair measured in seconds or minutes.
* Duplexing such modules gives mean times to failure measured in centuries.

The systematic application of these ideas to both hardware and software produces highly reliable and highly available systems.

High availability requires rethinking many concepts of system design. Consider for example, the issue of system maintenance: one must be able to plug components into the system while it is operating. At the hardware level this requires Underwriters Laboratory Approval that there are no high voltages around and requires that components tolerate high power drains and surges and, and, and,... At the software level this means that there is no "SYSGEN" and that any program or data structure can be replaced while the system is operating. These are major departures from most current system designs.

Commercial versions of systems which provide continuous service are beginning to appear in the marketplace. Perhaps the best known art the Tandem systems. Tandem calls its approach to high availability NonStop (a Tandem trademark). Their systems typically have mean times to failure between one and ten years. At the hardware level, modules and paths are duplexed and all components are designed for reliable and fail-fast operation [Katzman]. At the software level, the system is structured as a message-based operating system in which each process may have a backup process which continues the work of the primary process should the primary process or its supporting hardware fail [Bartlett1], [Bartlett2]. Alsberg proposed a related technique [Alsberg].

It is not easy to build a highly available system. Given such a system, it is non-trivial to program fault-tolerant applications unless other tools are provided: takeover by the backup process when the primary process fails is delicate. The backup process must somehow continue the computation where it left off without propagating the failure to other processes.

One strategy for writing fault-tolerant applications is to have the primary process "checkpoint" its state to the backup process prior to each operation. If the primary fails, the backup process picks up the conversation where the primary left off. Resynchronizing the requestor and server processes in such an event is very subtle.

Another strategy for writing fault-tolerant software is to collect all the processes of a computation together as a transaction and to reset them all to the initial transaction state in case of a failure. In the event of a failure, the transaction is undone (to a save point or to the beginning) and continued from that point by a new process. The backout and restart facilities provided by transaction management free the application programmer from concerns about failures or process pairs.

The implementors of the transaction concept must use the primitive process-pair mechanism and must deal with the subtleties of NonStop; but thereafter, all programmers may rely on the transaction mechanism and hence may easily write fault-tolerant software [Borr]. Programs in such a system look no different from programs in a conventional system except that they contain the verbs BEGIN-TRANSACTION, COMMIT-TRANSACTION and ABORT-TRANSACTION.

Use of the transaction concept allows the application programmer to abort the transaction in case the input data or system state looks bad. This feature comes at no additional cost because the mechanism to undo a transaction is already in place.

In addition, if transactions are implemented with logging, then the transaction manager may be used to reconstruct the system state from an old state plus the log. This provides transaction durability in the presence of multiple failures.

In summary, NonStop (TM) techniques can make computer systems appear to have failure rates measured in decades or centuries. In practice, systems have failure rates measured in months or years because of operator error (about one per year) and application program errors (several per year) [Japan]. These now become the main limit of system reliability rather than the software or hardware supplied by the manufacturer.

This section showed the need for the transaction concept to ease the implementation of fault-tolerant applications. There are two apparently different approaches to implementing the transaction concept: time-domain addressing and logging plus locking. The following sections explain these two approaches and contrast them.

To give a preview of the two techniques, logging clusters the current state of all objects together and relegates old versions to a history file called a log. Time domain addressing clusters the complete history (all versions) of each object with the object. Each organization will be seen to have some unique virtues.

UPDATE IN PLACE: A poison apple?

When book-keeping was done with clay tablets or paper and ink, accountants developed some clear rules about good accounting practices. One of the cardinal rules is double-entry bookkeeping so that calculations are self checking, thereby making them fail-fast. A second rule is that one never alters the books; if an error is made, it is annotated and a new compensating entry is made in the books. The books are thus a complete history of the transactions of the business.

The first computer systems obeyed these rules. The book-keeping entries were represented on punched cards or on tape as records. A run would take in the old master and the day's activity, represented as records on punched cards. The result was a new master. The old master was never updated. This was due in part to good accounting practices but also due to the technical aspects of cards and tape: writing a new tape was easier than re-writing the old tape.

The advent of direct access storage (disks and drums) changed this. It was now possible to update only a part of a file. Rather than copying the whole disk whenever one part was updated, it became attractive to update just the parts that changed in order to construct the new master. Some of these techniques, notably side files and differential files [Severence] did not update the old master and hence followed good accounting techniques. But for performance reasons, most disk-based systems have been seduced into updating the data in-place.

TIME-DOMAIN ADDRESSING: one solution

Update-in-place strikes many systems designers as a cardinal sin: it violates traditional accounting practices which have been observed for hundreds of years. There have been several proposals for systems in which objects are never altered, rather an object is considered to have a time history and object addresses become <name,time>

rather than simply name. In such a system, an object is not "updated", it is "evolved" to have some additional information. Evolving an object consists of creating a new value and appending it as the current (as of this time) value of the object. The old value continues to exist and may be addressed by specifying any time within the time interval that value was current. Such systems are called "time-domain addressing" or "version-oriented systems". (Some call them immutable object systems but I think that is a misnomer since objects do change values with time.)

Davies and Bjork proposed an implementation for time-domain addressing as "general ledger" in which each entity had a time sequence of values [Davies], [Bjork]. Their system not only kept these values but also kept the chain of dependencies so that if an error was discovered, the compensating transaction could run and the new value could be propagated to each transaction that depended on the erroneous data. The internal book-keeping and expected poor performance of such a system discouraged most who have looked at it. Graham Wood at University of Newcastle showed that the dependency information grows exponentially [Wood].

Dave Reed has made the most complete proposal for a transaction system based on time-domain addressing [Reed1]. In Reed's proposal an entity E has a set of values Vi each of which is valid for a time period: For example the entity E and its value history might be denoted by:

E: <V0,[T0,T1)>, <V1,[T1,T2)>, <V2,[T2,*)>

meaning that E had value V0 from time T0 up to T1, at time T1 it got value V1 and at time T2 it got value V2 which is the current value. Each transaction is assigned a unique time of execution and all of its reads and writes are interpreted with respect to that time. A transaction at time T3 reading entity E gets the value of the entity at that time. In the example above, if T3>T2 then the value V2 will be made valid for the period [T2,T3). A transaction at time T3 writing value V3 to entity E starts a new time interval:

E: <V0,[T0,T1)>,<V1,[T1,T2)>,<V2,[T2,T3)>, <V3,[T3,*)>

If T2 >= T3 then the transaction is aborted because it is attempting to rewrite history.

The writes of the transaction all depend upon a commit record. At transaction commit, the system validates (makes valid) all of the updates of the transaction. At transaction abort the system invalidates all of the updates. This is done by setting the state of the commit record to commit or abort and then broadcasting the transaction outcome.

This is a simplified description of Reed's proposal. The full proposal has many other features including a nested transaction mechanism. In addition, Reed does not use "real" time but rather "pseudo-time" in order to avoid the difficulties of implementing a global clock. See [Reed2] and [Svobodova] for a very understandable presentations of this proposal.

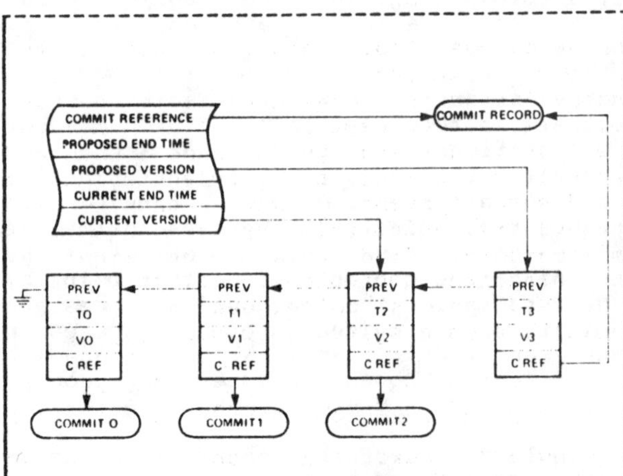

Figure 2. Representation of versions of object E. Three committed versions and one proposed version are shown. When version V3 is committed or aborted, the commit record and object header will be updated. Adapted from [Svobodova].

Reed observes that this proposal is a unified solution to both the concurrency control problem and the reliability problem. In addition, the system allows applications the full power of time domain addressing. One can easily ask questions such as "What did the books look like at year-end?"

There are some problems with time-domain addressing proposals.

(1) Reads are writes: reads advance the clock on an object and therefore update its header. This may increase I/O activity.
(2) Waits are aborts: In most cases a locking system will cause conflicts to result in one process waiting for another. In time-domain systems, conflicts abort the writer. This may preclude long-running "batch" transactions which do many updates.
(3) Timestamps force a single granularity: reading a million records updates a million timestamps. A simple lock hierarchy allows sequential (whole file) and direct (single record) locking against the same data (at the same time.)

(4) Real operations and pseudo-time: If one reads or writes a real device, it is read at some real time or written at some real time (consider the rods of a nuclear reactor, or an automated teller machine which consumes and dispenses money). It is unclear how real time correlates with pseudo-time and how writes to real devices are modeled as versions.

As you can see from this list, not all the details of implementing a time domain addressing system have been worked out. Certainly the concept is valid. All but the last issue are performance issues and may well be solved by people trying to build such systems. Many people are enthusiastic about this approach, and they will certainly find ways to eliminate or ameliorate these problems. In particular, Dave Reed and his colleagues at MIT are building such a system [Svobodova].

LOGGING AND LOCKING: another solution

Logging and locking are an alternative implementation of the transaction concept. The legendary Greeks, Ariadne and Theseus invented logging. Ariadne gave Theseus a magic ball of string which he unraveled as he searched the Labyrinth for the Minotaur. Having slain the Minotaur, Theseus followed the string back to the entrance (rather than remaining lost in the Labyrinth). This string was his log allowing him to undo the process of entering the Labyrinth. But the Minotaur was not a protected object so its death was not undone by Theseus' exit.

Hansel and Gretel copied Theseus' trick as they wandered into the woods in search of berries. They left behind a trail of crumbs which would allow them to retrace their steps (by following the trail backwards) and would allow their parents to find them by following the trail forwards. This was the first undo and redo log. Unfortunately, a bird ate the crumbs and caused the first log failure.

The basic idea of logging is that every undoable action must not only do the action but must also leave behind a string, crumb or undo log record which allows the operation to be undone. Similarly, every redoable action must not only do the operation but must also generate a redo log record which allows the operation to be redone. Based on Hansel's and Gretel's experiences, these log records should be made out of strong stuff (not something a bird would eat). In computer terms, the records should be kept in stable storage-- usually implemented by keeping the records on several non-volatile devices, each with independent failure modes. Occasionally, a stable copy of each object should be recorded so that the current state may be reconstructed from the old state.

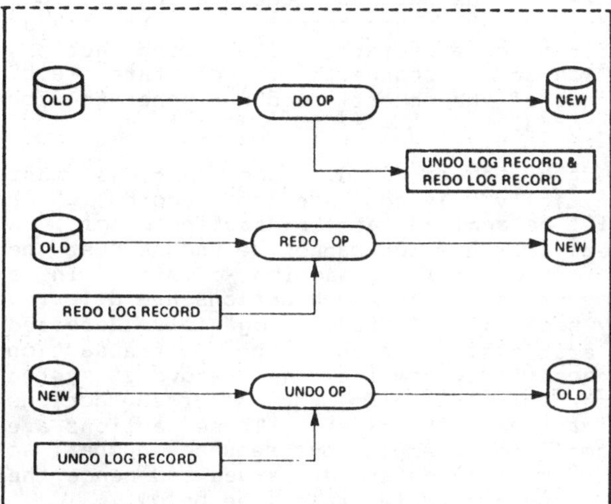

Figure 3. The DO-UNDO-REDO protocol. The execution of each protected action generates a log record which allows the action to be undone or redone. Unprotected actions need not generate log records. Actions which are not undoable (called real actions) use a related but slightly different protocol (see next figure).

The log records for database operations are very simple. They have the form:

NAME OF TRANSACTION:
PREVIOUS LOG RECORD OF THIS TRANSACTION:
NEXT LOG RECORD OF THIS TRANSACTION:
TIME:
TYPE OF OPERATION:
OBJECT OF OPERATION:
OLD VALUE:
NEW VALUE:

The old and new values can be complete copies of the object, but more typically they just encode the changed parts of the object. For example, an update of a field of a record of a file generally records the names of the file, record and field along with the old and new field values rather than logging the old and new values of the entire file or entire record.

The log records of a transaction are threaded together. In order to undo a transaction one undoes each action in its log. This technique may be used both for transaction abort issued by the program and for cleaning up after incomplete (uncommitted) transactions in case of a system problem such as deadlock or hardware failure.

In the event that the current state of an object is lost, one may reconstruct the current state from an old state in stable storage by using the redo log to redo all recent committed actions on the old state.

Some actions need not generate log records. Actions on unprotected objects (e.g. writing on a scratch file), and actions which do not change the object state (e.g. reads of the object) need not generate log records.

On the other hand, some actions must initially only generate log records which will be applied at transaction commit. A real action which cannot be undone must be deferred until transaction commit. In a log-based system, such actions are deferred by keeping a redo log of deferred operations. When the transaction successfully commits, the recovery system uses this log to do the deferred actions (for the first time). These actions are named (for example by sequence number) so that duplicates are discarded and hence the actions are restartable (see below).

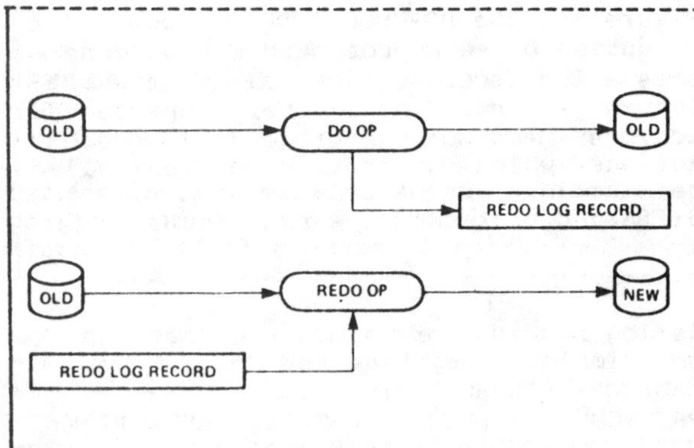

Figure 4. Real actions (ones that cannot be undone) must be deferred until commit. The logging approach to this is to apply the redo log of deferred operations as part of commit completion.

Another detail is that the undo and redo operations must be restartable, that is if the operation is already undone or redone, the operation should not damage or change the object state. The need for restartability comes from the need to deal with failures during undo and redo processing. Restartability is usually accomplished with version numbers (for disk pages) and with sequence numbers (for virtual circuits or sessions). Essentially, the undo or redo operation reads the version or sequence number and does nothing if it is the desired number. Otherwise it transforms the object and the sequence number.

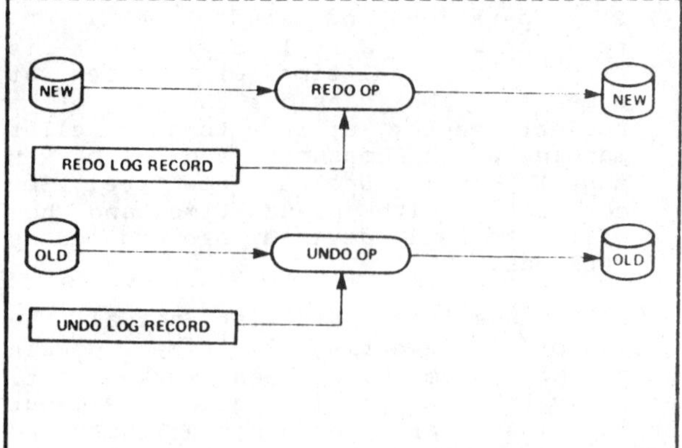

Figure 5: UNDO and REDO must be restartable, that is if the action has already happened, they must not alter the object.

In a log-based scheme, transaction commit is signaled by writing the commit record to the log. If the transaction has contributed to multiple logs then one must be careful to assure that the commit appears either in all logs or in none of the logs. Multiple logs frequently arise in distributed systems (since there are generally one or more logs per node) but also arise in central systems.

The simplest strategy to make commit an atomic action is to allow only the active node of the transaction to decide to commit or abort (all other participants are slaves and look to the active node for the commit or abort decision). Rosenkrantz, Sterns and Lewis describe such a scheme [Rosenkrantz].

It is generally desirable to allow each participant in a transaction to unilaterally abort the transaction prior to the commit. If this happens, all other participants must also abort. The two-phase commit protocol is intended to minimize the time during which a node is not allowed to unilaterally abort a transaction. It is very similar to the wedding ceremony in which the minister asks "Do you?" and the participants say "I do" (or "No way!") and then the minister says "I now pronounce you", or "The deal is off". At commit, the two-phase commit protocol gets agreement from each participant that the transaction is prepared to commit. The participant abdicates the right to unilaterally abort once it says "I do" to the prepare request. If all agree to commit, then the commit coordinator broadcasts the commit message. If unanimous consent is not achieved, the transaction aborts. Many variations on this protocol are known (and probably many more will be published).

If transactions run concurrently, one transaction might read the outputs (updates or messages) of another transaction. If the first transaction aborts, then undoing it requires undoing the updates or messages read by the second transaction. This in turn requires undoing the second transaction. But the second transaction may have already committed and so cannot be undone. To prevent this dilemma, real and protected updates (undoable updates) of a transaction must be hidden from other transactions until the transaction commits. To assure that reading two related records or rereading the same record will give consistent results, one must also stabilize records which a transaction reads and keep them constant until the transaction commits. Otherwise a transaction could reread a record and get two different answers [Eswaran].

There appear to be many ways of achieving this input stability and hiding outputs. But they all seem to boil down to the following ideas:

* A transaction has a set of inputs "I".
* A transaction has a set of outputs "O".
* Other transactions may read "I" but must not read or write "O".

Some schemes try to guess the input and output sets in advance and do set intersection (or predicate intersection) at transaction scheduling time to decide whether this transaction might conflict with some already executing transactions. In such cases, initiation of the new transaction is delayed until it does not conflict with any running transaction. IMS/360 seems to have been the first to try this scheme, and it has been widely rediscovered. It has not been very successful. IMS abandoned predeclaration (called "intent scheduling") in 1973 [Obermarck].

A simpler and more efficient scheme is to lock an object when it is accessed. This technique dynamically computes the I and O sets of the transaction. If the object is already locked, then the requestor waits. Multiple readers can be accommodated by distinguishing two lock modes: one indicating update access and another indicating read access. Read locks are compatible while update locks are not.

An important generalization is to allow locks at multiple granularities. Some transactions want to lock thousands of records while others only want to lock just a few. A solution is to allow transactions to issue a lock as a single predicate which covers exactly the records they want locked. Testing for lock conflict involves evaluating or testing membership in such predicates [Eswaran]. This is generally expensive. A compromise is to pick a fixed set of predicates, organize them into a directed acyclic graph and lock from root to leaf. This is a compromise between generality and efficiency [Gray1].

If a transaction T waits for a transaction T which is waiting for T, both transactions will be stalled forever in deadlock. Deadlock is rare, but it must be dealt with. Deadlock must be detected (by timeout or by looking for cycles in the who-waits-for-whom graph), a set of victims must be selected and they must be aborted (using the log) and their locks freed [Gray1], [Beeri]. In practice waits seem to be rare (one transaction in 1000 [Beeri]) and deadlocks seem to be miracles. But it appears that deadlocks per second rise as the square of the degree of multiprogramming and as the fourth power of transaction size [Gray3], indicating that deadlocks may be a problem in the future as we see large transactions or many concurrent transactions.

SUMMARY

The previous sections discussed apparently different approaches to implementing the transaction concept: time-domain addressing and logging. It was pointed out that to make log operations restartable, the object or object fragments are tagged with version numbers. Hence, most logging schemes contain a form of time-domain addressing.

If each log record is given a time stamp, then a log can implement time-domain addressing. If Gretel had written a time on each crumb, then we could find out where they were at a certain time by following the crumbs until the desired time interval was encountered. Logging systems write the old value out to the log and so do not really discard old values. Rather, the log is a time-domain addressable version of the state and the disk contains the current version of the state.

Time-domain addressing schemes "garbage collect" old versions into something that looks very much like a log and they use locks to serialize the update of the object headers [Svobodova].

I conclude from this that despite the external differences between time domain addressing and logging schemes, they are more similar than different in their internal structure. There appear to be difficulties in implementing time-domain addressing. Arguing by analogy, Dave Reed asserts that every locking and logging trick has an analogous trick for time-domain addressing. If this is true, both schemes are viable implementations of transactions.

LIMITATIONS OF KNOWN TECHNIQUES

The transaction concept was adopted to ease the programming of certain applications. Indeed, the transaction concept is very effective in areas such as airlines reservation, electronic funds transfer or car rental. But each of these applications has simple transactions of short duration.

I see the following difficulties with current transaction models:

1. Transactions cannot be nested inside transactions.
2. Transactions are assumed to last minutes rather than weeks.
3. Transactions are not unified with programming languages.

NESTED TRANSACTIONS

Consider implementing a travel agent system. A transaction in such a system consists of:

1. Customer calls the travel agent giving destination and travel dates.
2. Agent negotiates with airlines for flights.
3. Agent negotiates with car rental companies for cars.
4. Agent negotiates with hotels for rooms.
5. Agent receives tickets and reservations.
6. Agent gives customer tickets and gets credit card number.
7. Agent bills credit card.
8. Customer uses tickets.

Not infrequently, the customer cancels the trip and the agent must undo the transaction.

The transaction concept as described thus far crumbles under this example. Each interaction with other organizations is a transaction with that organization (is an atomic, consistent durable transformation). The agent cannot unilaterally abort an interaction after it completes, rather the agent must run a compensating transaction to reverse the previous transaction (e.g., cancel reservation). The customer thinks of this whole scenario as a single transaction. The agent views the fine structure of the scenario, treating each step as an action. The airlines and hotels see only individual actions but view them as transactions. This example makes it clear that actions may be transactions at the next lower level of abstraction.

An approach to this problem which seems to offer some help is to view a transaction as a collection of:

* actions on unprotected objects
* protected actions which may be undone or redone
* real actions which may be deferred but not undone
* nested transactions which may be undone by invoking compensating transactions.

Nested transactions differ from protected actions because their effects are visible to the outside world prior to the commit of the parent transaction.

When a nested transaction is run, it returns as a side effect the name and parameters of the compensating transaction for the nested transaction. This information is kept in a log of the parent transaction and is invoked if the parent is undone. This log needs to be user-visible (part of the database) so that the user and application can know what has been done and what needs to be done or undone. In most applications, a transaction already has a compensating transaction so generating the compensating transaction (either coding it or invoking it) is not a major programming burden. If all else fails, the compensating transaction might just send a human the message "Help, I can't handle this".

This may not seem very satisfying, but it is better than the entirely manual process which is in common use today. At least in this proposal, the recovery system keeps track of what the transaction has done and what must be done to undo it.

At present, application programmers implement such applications using a technique called a "scratchpad" (in IMS) and a "transaction work area" in CICS. The application programmer keeps the transaction state (his own log) as a record in the database. Each time the transaction becomes active, it reads its scratchpad. This reestablishes the transaction state. The transaction either advances and inserts the new scratchpad in the database or aborts and uses the scratchpad as a log of things to undo. In this instance, the application programmer is implementing nested transactions. It is a general facility that should be included in the host transaction management system.

Some argue that nested transactions are not transactions. They do have some of the transaction properties:

Consistent transformation of the state,
Either all actions commit or are undone by compensation.
Once committed, cannot be undone.

They use the BEGIN, COMMIT and ABORT verbs. But they do not have the property of atomicity; others can see the uncommitted updates of nested transactions. These updates may subsequently be undone by compensation.

LONG-LIVED TRANSACTIONS

A second problem with the travel agent example is that transactions are suddenly long-lived. At present the largest airlines and banks have about 10,000 terminals and about 100 active transactions at any instant. These transactions live for a second or two and are gone forever. Now suppose that transactions with lifetimes of a few days or weeks appear. This is not uncommon in applications such as travel, insurance, government, and electronic mail. There will be thousands of concurrent transactions. At least in database applications, the frequency of deadlock goes up with the square of the multiprogramming level and the fourth power of the transaction size [Gray3]. You might think this is a good argument against locking and for time-domain addressing. Time-domain addressing has the same problem.

Again, the solution I see to this problem is to accept a lower degree of consistency [Gray2] so that only "active" transactions hold locks. This will mean that the updates of uncommitted transactions are visible to other transactions. This in turn means that the UNDO and REDO operations of one transaction will have to commute with the DO operations of others. (I.e. if transaction T1 updates entity E and then T2 updates entity E and then T1 aborts, the update of T2 should not be undone.) If some object is only manipulated with additions and subtractions, and if the log records the delta rather than the old and new value, then UNDO an REDO may be made to commute with DO. IMS Fast Path uses the fact that plus and minus commute to reduce lock contention. No one knows how far this trick can be generalized.

A minor problem with long-running transactions is that current systems tend to abort them at system restart. When only 100 transactions are active and people are waiting at terminals to resubmit them this is conceivable (but not nice). When 10,000 transactions are lost at system restart then the old approach of discarding them all at restart is inconceivable. Active transactions may be salvaged across system restarts by using transaction save points: a transaction declares a save point and the transaction (program and data) is reset to its most recent save point in the event of a system restart.

INTEGRATION WITH PROGRAMMING LANGUAGES

How should the transaction concept be reflected in programming languages? The proposal I favor is providing the verbs BEGIN, SAVE, COMMIT and ABORT. Whenever a new object type and its operations are defined, the protected operations on that type must generate undo and redo log records as well as acquiring locks if the object is shared. The type manager must provide UNDO and REDO procedures which will accept the log records and reconstruct the old and new version of the object. If the operation is real, then the operation must be deferred and the log manager must invoke the type manager to actually do the operation at commit time. If the operation is a nested transaction, the operation must put the name of the compensating transaction and the input to the compensating transaction in the undo log. In addition, the type manager must participate in system checkpoint and restart or have some other approach to handling system failures and media failures.

I´m not sure that this idea will work in the general case and whether the concept of transaction does actually generalize to non-EDP areas of programming. The performance of logging may be prohibitive. However, the transaction concept has been very convenient in the database area and may be applicable to some parts of programming beyond conventional transaction processing. Brian Randell and his group at Newcastle have a proposal in this area [Randell]. The artificial inteligence languages such as Interlisp support backtracking and an UNDO-REDO facility. Barbara Liskov has been exploring the idea of adding transactions to the language Clu and may well discover a new approach.

SUMMARY

Transactions are not a new idea, they go back thousands of years. The idea of a transformation being consistent, atomic and durable is simple and convenient. Many implementation techniques are known and we have practical experience with most of them. However, our concept of transaction and the implementation techniques we have are inadequate to the task of many applications. They cannot handle nested transactions, long-lived transactions and they may not fit well into conventional programming systems.

We may be seeing the Peter Principle in operation here: "every good idea is generalized to its level of inapplicability". But I believe that the problems I have outlined here (long-lived and nested transactions) must be solved.

I am optimistic that the transaction concept provides a convenient abstraction for structuring applications. People implementing such applications are confronted with these problems and have adopted expedient solutions. One contribution of this paper is to abstract these problems and to sketch generalizations of techniques in common use which address the problems. I expect that these general techniques will allow both long-lived and nested transactions.

ACKNOWLEDGMENTS

This paper owes an obvious debt to the referenced authors. In addition, the treatment of nested and long-lived transactions grows from discussions with Andrea Borr, Bob Good, Jerry Held, Pete Homan, Bruce Lindsay, Ron Obermarck and Franco Putzolu. Wendy Bartlett, Andrea Borr, Dave Gifford and Paul McJones made several contributions to the presentation.

REFERENCES

[Alsberg] Alsberg, P.A., J.D. Day, "A principle for Resilient Sharing of Distributed Resources", Proc. 2nd Int. Conf. on Software Engineering, IEEE 1976.

[Bartlett1] Bartlett, J.F., "A NonStop Operating System", Eleventh Hawaii International Conference on System Sciences, 1978.

[Bartlett2] Bartlett, J.F., "A NonStop Kernel", Proceedings of Eighth Symposium on Operating Systems Principles, ACM, 1981. (also Tandem TR 81.4).

[Beeri] Beeri, C., R. Obermarck, "A Resource Class Independent Deadlock Detectio Algorithm", IBM RJ-3077 (38123). 1981.

[Bernstein] Bernstein, P.A., D.W. Shipman, J.B. Rothnie, Concurrency Control in a System fo Distributed Databases (SDD-1), ACM TODS V. 5, No. 1, 1980.

[Borr] Borr, A.J., "Transaction Monitoring in Encompass: Reliable Distributed Transaction Processing", Proceedings of Very Large Database Conference, 1981. (also Tandem TR 81.3).

[Davies and Bjork] Davies C.T., Bjork L.A. private communication 1972.

[Bjork] Bjork, L.A., C.T. Davies, "The Semantics of the Preservation and Recovery of Integrity in a Data System", IBM TR-02.540, 1972.

[Eswaran] Eswaran K.E., J.N. Gray, R.A. Lorie, I.L. Traiger, "On the Notions of Consistency and Predicate Locks", CACM V. 19, No. 11, 1976.

[Gray1] Gray, J., "Notes on Database Operating Systems", Operating Systems - An Advanced Course, Springer Verlag Lecture Notes in Computer Science, V. 60, 1978.

[Gray2] Gray, J., "A Transaction Model", Automata Languages and Programming, Springer Verlag Lecture Notes in Computer Science, V. 80, 1980.

[Gray3] Gray, J., P. Homan, H. Korth, R. Obermarck, "A Strawman Analysis of Deadlock Frequency" To be published in SIGOPS Review.

[Heistand] Heistand, R.E., "Airlines Control Program System, Concepts and Facilities" IBM form number GH20-1473-1, 1975.

[Japan] Papers from the Tutorial on Reliable Business Systems in Japan, AFIPS Press, 1978.

[Katzman] Katzman, J.A., "A Fault-Tolerant Computing System", Eleventh Hawaii International Conference on System Sciences, 1978.

[Obermarck] Obermarck R., "IMS/VS Program Isolation Feature" IBM RJ2879 (36435), 1980.

[Randell] Randell, B., "System Structure for Fault Tolerance", IEEE Trans. on Software Engineering, V. 1, No. 2, 1975.

[Reed1] Reed, D.P., "Naming and Synchronization in a Decentralized System", MIT/LCS TR-205, 1978.

[Reed2] Reed, D.P., "Implementing Atomic Actions on Decentralized Data", Proc. Seventh ACM/SIGOPS Symposium on Operating Systems Principles, 1979.

[Rosenkrantz] Rosenkrantz, D.J., R.D. Stearns, P.M. Lewis, "System Level Concurrency Control for Database Systems", ACM TODS, V. 3, No. 2, 1977.

[Severence] Severence, D.G., G.M. Loman, "Differential Files: Their Application to Maintenance of Large Databases", ACM TODS V. 1, No. 3, 1976.

[Svobodova] Svobodova, L. "Management of Object Histories in the Swallow Repository", MIT/LCS TR-243, 1980.

[Von Neumann] Von Neumann, J. "Probabilistic Logics and the Synthesis of Reliable Organisms From Unreliable Components", Automata Studies Princeton University Press, 1956.

[Wood] Wood, W.G., "Recovery Control of Communicating Processes in a Distributed System", U. Newcastle upon Tyne TR-158, 1980.

Principles of Transaction-Oriented Database Recovery

THEO HAERDER

Fachbereich Informatik, University of Kaiserslautern, West Germany

ANDREAS REUTER[1]

IBM Research Laboratory, San Jose, California 95193

In this paper, a terminological framework is provided for describing different transaction-oriented recovery schemes for database systems in a conceptual rather than an implementation-dependent way. By introducing the terms materialized database, propagation strategy, and checkpoint, we obtain a means for classifying arbitrary implementations from a unified viewpoint. This is complemented by a classification scheme for logging techniques, which are precisely defined by using the other terms. It is shown that these criteria are related to all relevant questions such as speed and scope of recovery and amount of redundant information required. The primary purpose of this paper, however, is to establish an adequate and precise terminology for a topic in which the confusion of concepts and implementational aspects still imposes a lot of problems.

Categories and Subject Descriptors: D.4.5 [**Operating Systems**]: Reliability—*fault tolerance*; H.1.0 [**Models and Principles**]: General; H.2.2 [**Database Management**]: Physical Design—*recovery and restart*; H.2.4 [**Database Management**]: Systems—*transaction processing*; H.2.7 [**Database Management**]: Database Administration—*logging and recovery*

General Terms: Databases, Fault Tolerance, Transactions

CONTENTS

INTRODUCTION

Database technology has seen tremendous progress during the past ten years. Concepts and facilities that evolved in the single-user batch environments of the early days have given rise to efficient multiuser database systems with user-friendly interfaces, distributed data management, etc. From a scientific viewpoint, database systems today are established as a mature discipline with well-approved methods and technology. The methods and technology of such a discipline should be well represented in the literature by systematic surveys of the field. There are, in fact, a number of recent publications that attempt to summarize what is known about different aspects of database management [e.g., Astrahan et al. 1981; Stonebraker 1980; Gray et al. 1981; Kohler 1981; Bernstein and Goodman 1981; Codd 1982]. These papers fall into two categories: (1) descriptions of innovative prototype systems and (2) thorough analyses of special problems and their solutions, based on a clear methodological and terminological framework. We are contributing to the second category in the field of database recovery. In particular, we are establishing a systematic framework for establishing and evaluating the basic concepts for fault-tolerant database operation.

The paper is organized as follows. Section 1 contains a short description of what recovery is expected to accomplish and which notion of consistency we assume. This involves introducing the transaction, which has proved to be the major paradigm for synchronization and recovery in advanced database systems. This is also the most important difference between this paper and Verhofstadt's survey, in which techniques for file recovery are described without using a particular notion of consistency [Verhofstadt 1978]. Section 2 provides an implementational model for database systems, that is, a mapping hierarchy of data types. Section 3 introduces the key concepts of our framework, describing the database states after a crash, the type of log information required, and additional measures for facilitating recovery. Crash recovery is demonstrated with three sample implementation techniques. Section 4 applies concepts addressed in previous sections on media recovery, and Section 5 summarizes the scope of our taxonomy.

1. DATABASE RECOVERY: WHAT IT IS EXPECTED TO DO

Understanding the concepts of database recovery requires a clear comprehension of two factors:

- the type of failure the database has to cope with, and
- the notion of consistency that is assumed as a criterion for describing the state to be reestablished.

Before beginning a discussion of these factors, we would like to point out that the contents of this section rely on the description of failure types and the concept of a transaction given by Gray et al. [1981].

1.1 What Is a Transaction?

It was observed quite early that manipulating data in a multiuser environment requires some kind of isolation to prevent uncontrolled and undesired interactions. A user (or process) often does things when working with a database that are, up to a certain point in time, of tentative or preliminary value. The user may read some data and modify others before finding out that some of the initial input was wrong, invalidating everything that was done up to that point. Consequently, the user wants to remove what he or she has done from the system. If other users (or processes) have already seen the "dirty data" [Gray et al. 1981] and made decisions based upon it, they obviously will encounter difficulties. The following questions must be considered:

- How do they get the message that some of their input data has disappeared, when it is possible that they have already finished their job and left the terminal?
- How do they cope with such a situation? Do they also throw away what they have done, possibly affecting others in turn? Do they reprocess the affected parts of their program?

[1] Permanent address: Fachbereich Informatik, University of Kaiserslautern, West Germany.

```
FUNDS_TRANSFER: PROCEDURE;
  $BEGIN_TRANSACTION;
  ON ERROR DO;                                        /*in case of error*/
    $RESTORE_TRANSACTION;                             /*undo all work*/
    GET INPUT MESSAGE;                                /*reacquire input*/
    PUT MESSAGE ('TRANSFER FAILED');                  /*report failure*/
    GO TO COMMIT;
    END;
  GET INPUT MESSAGE;                                  /*get and parse input*/
  EXTRACT ACCOUNT_DEBIT, ACCOUNT_CREDIT,
      AMOUNT FROM MESSAGE;
  $UPDATE ACCOUNTS                                    /*do debit*/
    SET BALANCE = BALANCE – AMOUNT
      WHERE ACCOUNTS NUMBER = ACCOUNTS_DEBIT;
  $UPDATE ACCOUNTS                                    /*do credit*/
    SET BALANCE = BALANCE + AMOUNT
      WHERE ACCOUNTS NUMBER = ACCOUNTS_CREDIT;
  $INSERT INTO HISTORY                                /*keep audit trail*/
      (DATE, MESSAGE);
  PUT MESSAGE ('TRANSFER DONE');                      /*report success*/
 COMMIT:                                              /*commit updates*/
$COMMIT_TRANSACTION;
  END;                                                /*end of program*/
```

Figure 1. Example of a transaction program. (From Gray et al. [1981].)

These situations and dependencies have been investigated thoroughly by Bjork and Davies in their studies of the so-called "spheres of control" [Bjork 1973; Davies 1973, 1978]. They indicate that data being operated by a process must be isolated in some way that lets others know the degree of reliability provided for these data, that is,

- Will the data be changed without notification to others?
- Will others be informed about changes?
- Will the value definitely not change any more?

This ambitious concept was restricted to use in database systems by Eswaran et al. [1976] and given its current name, the "transaction." The transaction basically reflects the idea that the activities of a particular user are isolated from all concurrent activities, but restricts the degree of isolation and the length of a transaction. Typically, a transaction is a short sequence of interactions with the database, using operators such as FIND a record or MODIFY an item, which represents one meaningful activity in the user's environment. The standard example that is generally used to explain the idea is the transfer of money from one account to another. The corresponding transaction program is given in Figure 1.

The concept of a transaction, which includes all database interactions between $BEGIN_TRANSACTION and $COMMIT_TRANSACTION in the above example, requires that all of its actions be executed *indivisibly*: Either all actions are properly reflected in the database or nothing has happened. No changes are reflected in the database if at any point in time before reaching the $COMMIT_TRANSACTION the user enters the ERROR clause containing the $RESTORE_TRANSACTION. To achieve this kind of indivisibility, a transaction must have four properties:

Atomicity. It must be of the all-or-nothing type described above, and the user must, whatever happens, know which state he or she is in.

Consistency. A transaction reaching its normal end (EOT, end of transaction), thereby committing its results, preserves the consistency of the database. In other words, each successful transaction by definition commits only legal results. This condition is necessary for the fourth property, durability.

```
BEGIN      BEGIN      BEGIN
READ       READ       READ
WRITE      WRITE      WRITE
READ       READ       READ
  :          :          :
WRITE      ABORT      ⇐SYSTEM ABORTS
COMMIT                  TRANSACTION
```

Figure 2. Three possible outcomes of a transaction. (From Gray et al. [1981].)

Isolation. Events within a transaction must be hidden from other transactions running concurrently. If this were not the case, a transaction could not be reset to its beginning for the reasons sketched above. The techniques that achieve isolation are known as *synchronization*, and since Gray et al. [1976] there have been numerous contributions to this topic of database research [Kohler 1981].

Durability. Once a transaction has been completed and has committed its results to the database, the system must guarantee that these results survive any subsequent malfunctions. Since there is no sphere of control constituting a set of transactions, the database management system (DBMS) has no control beyond transaction boundaries. Therefore the user must have a guarantee that the things the system says have happened have actually happened. Since, by definition, each transaction is correct, the effects of an inevitable incorrect transaction (i.e., the transaction containing faulty data) can only be removed by countertransactions.

These four properties, atomicity, consistency, isolation, and durability (ACID), describe the major highlights of the transaction paradigm, which has influenced many aspects of development in database systems. We therefore consider the question of whether the transaction is supported by a particular system to be the ACID test of the system's quality.

In summary, a transaction can terminate in the three ways illustrated in Figure 2. It is hoped that the transaction will reach its commit point, yielding the all case (as in the all-or-nothing dichotomy). Sometimes the transaction detects bad input or other violations of consistency, preventing a normal termination, in which case it will reset all that it has done (abort). Finally, a transaction may run into a problem that can only be detected by the system, such as time-out or deadlock, in which case its effects are aborted by the DBMS.

In addition to the above events occurring during normal execution, a transaction can also be affected by a system crash. This is discussed in the next section.

1.2 Which Failures Have to Be Anticipated

In order to design and implement a recovery component, one must know precisely which types of failures are to be considered, how often they will occur, how much time is expected for recovery, etc. One must also make assumptions about the reliability of the underlying hardware and storage media, and about dependencies between different failure modes. However, the list of anticipated failures will never be complete for these reasons:

- For each set of failures that one can think of, there is at least one that was forgotten.
- Some failures are extremely rare. The cost of redundancy needed to cope with them may be so high that it may be a sensible design decision to exclude these failures from consideration. If one of them does occur, however, the system will not be able to recover from the situation automatically, and the database will be corrupted. The techniques for handling this catastrophe are beyond the scope of this paper.

We shall consider the following types of failure:

Transaction Failure. The transaction of failure has already been mentioned in the previous section. For various reasons, the transaction program does not reach its normal commit and has to be reset back to its beginning, either at its own request or on behalf of the DBMS. Gray indicates that 3 percent of all transactions terminate abnormally, but this rate is not likely to be a constant [Gray et al. 1981]. From our own experiences with different application databases, and from Gray's result [Effelsberg et al. 1981; Gray 1981], we can conclude that

- Within one application, the ratio of transactions that abort themselves is rather constant, depending only on the amount of incorrect input data, the quality of consistency checking performed by the transaction program, etc.
- The ratio of transactions being aborted by the DBMS, especially those caused by deadlocks, depends to a great extent on the degree of parallelism, the granularity of locking used by the DBMS, the logical schema (there may be hot spot data, or data that are very frequently referenced by many concurrent transactions), and the degree of interference between concurrent activities (which is, in turn, very application dependent).

For our classification, it is sufficient to say that transaction failures occur *10–100 times per minute*, and that recovery from these failures must take place within the time required by the transaction for its regular execution.

System Failure. The system failures that we are considering can be caused by a bug in the DBMS code, an operating system fault, or a hardware failure. In each of these cases processing is terminated in an uncontrolled manner, and we assume that the contents of main memory are lost. Since database-related secondary (nonvolatile) storage remains unaffected, we require that a recovery take place in the same amount of time that would have been required for the execution of all interrupted transactions. If one transaction is executed within the order of 10 milliseconds to 1 second, the recovery should take no more than a few minutes. A system failure is assumed to occur *several times a week*, depending on the stability of both the DBMS and its operational environment.

Media Failure. Besides these more or less normal failures, we have to anticipate the loss of some or all of the secondary storage holding the database. There are several causes for such a problem, the most common of which are

- bugs in the operating system routines for writing the disk,
- hardware errors in the channel or disk controller,
- head crash,
- loss of information due to magnetic decay.

Such a situation can only be overcome by full redundancy, that is, by a copy of the database and an audit trail covering what has happened since then.

Magnetic storage devices are usually very reliable, and recovery from a media failure is not likely to happen more often than *once or twice a year.* Depending on the size of a database, the media used for storing the copy, and the age of the copy, recovery of this type will take on the order of 1 hour.

1.3 Summary of Recovery Actions

As we mentioned in Section 1.1, the notion of consistency that we use for defining the targets of recovery is tied to the transaction paradigm, which we have encapsulated in the "ACID principle." According to this definition, a database is consistent *if and only if* it contains the results of successful transactions. Such a state will hereafter be called *transaction consistent* or *logically consistent.* A transaction, in turn, must not see anything but effects of complete transactions (i.e., a consistent database in those parts that it uses), and will then, by definition, create a consistent update of the database. What does that mean for the recovery component?

Let us for the moment ignore transactions being aborted during normal execution and consider only a system failure (a crash). We might then encounter the situation depicted in Figure 3. Transactions T1, T2, and T3 have committed before the crash, and therefore will survive. Recovery after a system failure must ensure that the effects of all successful transactions are actually reflected in the database. But what is to be done with T4 and T5? Transactions have been defined to be atomic; they either succeed or disappear as though they had never been entered. There is therefore no choice about what to do after a system failure; the effects of all incomplete transactions must be removed from the database. Clearly, a recovery component adhering to these principles will produce a transaction-consistent database. Since *all* successful transactions have contributed to the database state, it will be the *most recent* transaction-consistent state. We now can distinguish four recovery actions coping with different situations [Gray 1978]:

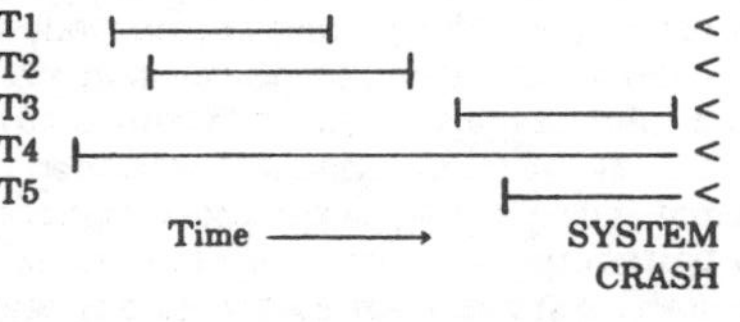

Figure 3. Scenario for discussing transaction-oriented recovery. (From Gray et al. [1981].)

Transaction UNDO. If a transaction aborts itself or must be aborted by the system during normal execution, this will be called "transaction UNDO." By definition, UNDO removes all effects of this transaction from the database and does not influence any other transaction.

Global UNDO. When recovering from a system failure, the effects of all incomplete transactions have to be rolled back.

Partial REDO. When recovering from a system failure, since execution has been terminated in an uncontrolled manner, results of complete transactions may not yet be reflected in the database. Hence they must be repeated, if necessary, by the recovery component.

Global REDO. Gray terms this recovery action "archive recovery" [Gray et al. 1981]. The database is assumed to be physically destroyed; we therefore must start from a copy that reflects the state of the database some days, weeks, or months ago. Since transactions are typically short, we need not consider incomplete transactions over such a long time. Rather we have to supplement the copy with the effects of all transactions that have committed since the copy was created.

With these definitions we have introduced the transaction as the *only unit of recovery* in a database system. This is an ideal condition that does not exactly match reality. For example, transactions might be nested, that is, composed of smaller subtransactions. These subtransactions also are atomic, consistent, and isolated—but they are not durable. Since the results of subtransactions are removed whenever the enclosing transaction is undone, durability can only be guaranteed for the highest transaction in the composition hierarchy. A two-level nesting of transactions can be found in System R, in which an arbitrary number of save points can be generated inside a transaction [Gray et al. 1981]. The database and the processing state can be reset to any of these save points by the application program.

Another extension of the transaction concept is necessary in fields like CAD. Here the units of consistent state transitions, that is, the design steps, are so long (days or weeks) that it is not feasible to treat them as indivisable actions. Hence these *long* transactions are consistent, isolated, and durable, but they are not atomic [Gray 1981]. It is sufficient for the purpose of our taxonomy to consider "ideal" transactions only.

2. THE MAPPING HIERARCHY OF A DBMS

There are numerous techniques and algorithms for implementing database recovery, many of which have been described in detail by Verhofstadt [1978]. We want to reduce these various methods to a small set of basic concepts, allowing a simple, yet precise classification of all reasonable implementation techniques; for the purposes of illustration, we need a basic model of the DBMS architecture and its hardware environment. This model, although it contains many familiar terms from systems like INGRES, System R, or those of the CODASYL [1973, 1978] type, is in fact a rudimentary database architecture that can also be applied to unconventional approaches like CASSM or DIRECT [Smith and Smith 1979], although this is not our purpose here.

2.1 The Mapping Process: Objects and Operations

The model shown in Table 1 describes the major steps of dynamic abstraction from the level of physical storage up to the user

Table 1. Description of the DB-Mapping Hierarchy

Level of abstraction	Objects	Auxiliary mapping data
Nonprocedural or algebraic access	Relations, views tuples	Logical schema description
Record-oriented, navigational access	Records, sets, hierarchies, networks	Logical and physical schema description
Record and access path management	Physical records, access paths	Free space tables, DB-key translation tables
Propagation control	Segments, pages	Page tables, Bloom filters
File management	Files, blocks	Directories, VTOCs, etc.

interface. At the bottom, the database consists of some billions of bits stored on disk, which are interpreted by the DBMS into meaningful information on which the user can operate. With each level of abstraction (proceeding from the bottom up), the objects become more complex, allowing more powerful operations and being constrained by a larger number of integrity rules. The uppermost interface supports one of the well-known data models, whether relational, networklike, or hierarchical.

Note that this mapping hierarchy is virtually contained in each DBMS, although for performance reasons it will hardly be reflected in the module structure. We shall briefly sketch the characteristics of each layer, with enough detail to establish our taxonomy. For a more complete description see Haerder and Reuter [1983].

File Management. The lowest layer operates directly on the bit patterns stored on some nonvolatile, direct access device like a disk, drum, or even magnetic bubble memory. This layer copes with the physical characteristics of each storage type and abstracts these characteristics into fixed-length blocks. These blocks can be read, written, and identified by a (relative) block number. This kind of abstraction is usually done by the data management system (DMS) of a normal general-purpose operating system.

Propagation[2] *Control.* This level is not usually considered separately in the current database literature, but for reasons that will become clear in the following sections we strictly distinguish between *pages* and *blocks*. A page is a fixed-length partition of a linear address space and is mapped into a physical block by the propagation control layer. Therefore a page can be stored in different blocks during its lifetime in the database, depending on the strategy implemented for propagation control.

Access Path Management. This layer implements mapping functions much more complicated than those performed by subordinate layers. It has to maintain all physical object representations in the database (records, fields, etc.), and their related access paths (pointers, hash tables, search trees, etc.) in a *potentially unlimited* linear virtual address space. This address space, which is divided into fixed-length pages, is provided by the upper interface of the supporting layer. For performance reasons, the partitioning of data into pages is still visible on this level.

Navigational Access Layer. At the top of this layer we find the operations and objects that are typical for a procedural data manipulation language (DML). Occurrences of record types and members of sets are handled by statements like STORE, MODIFY, FIND NEXT, and CONNECT [CODASYL 1978]. At this interface, the user navigates one record at a time through a hierarchy, through a network, or along logical access paths.

Nonprocedural Access Layer. This level provides a nonprocedural interface to the database. With each operation the user can handle sets of results rather than single records. A relational model with high-level query languages like SQL or QUEL is a convenient example of the abstraction achieved by the top layer [Chamberlin 1980; Stonebraker et al. 1976].

On each level, the mapping of higher objects to more elementary ones requires additional data structures, some of which are shown in Table 1.

[2] This term is introduced in Section 2.4; its meaning is not essential to the understanding of this paragraph.

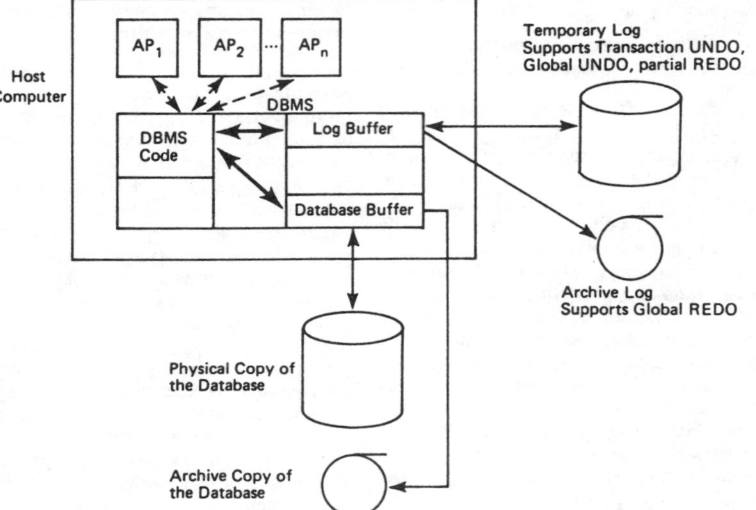

Figure 4. Storage hierarchy of a DBMS during normal mode of operation.

2.2 The Storage Hierarchy: Implementational Environment

Both the number of redundant data required to support the recovery actions described in Section 1 and the methods of collecting such data are strongly influenced by various properties of the different storage media used by the DBMS. In particular, the dependencies between volatile and permanent storage have a strong impact on algorithms for gathering redundant information and implementing recovery measures [Chen 1978]. As a descriptional framework we shall use a storage hierarchy, as shown in Figure 4. It closely resembles the situation that must be dealt with by most of today's commercial database systems.

The host computer, where the application programs and DBMS are located, has a main memory, which is usually volatile.[3] Hence we assume that the contents of the database buffer, as well as the contents of the output buffers to the log files, are lost whenever the DBMS terminates abnormally. Below the volatile main memory there is a two-level hierarchy of permanent copies of the database. One level contains an on-line version of the database in direct access memory; the other contains an archive copy as a provision against loss of the on-line copy. While both are functionally situated on the same level, the on-line copy is almost always up-to-date, whereas the archive copy can contain an old state of the database. Our main concern here is database recovery, which, like all provisions for

[3] In some real-time applications main memory is supported by a battery backup. It is possible that in the future mainframes will have some stable buffer storage. However, we are not cohsidering these conditions here.

fault tolerance, is based upon redundancy. We have mentioned one type of redundancy: the archive copy, kept as a starting point for reconstruction of an up-to-date on-line version of the database (global REDO). This is discussed in more detail in Section 4. To support this, and other recovery actions introduced in Section 1, two types of log files are required:

Temporary Log. The information collected in this file supports crash recovery; that is, it contains information needed to reconstruct the most recent database (DB) buffer. Selective transaction UNDO requires random access to the log records. Therefore we assume that the temporary log is located on disk.

Archive Log. This file supports global REDO after a media failure. It depends on the availability of the archive copy and must contain all changes committed to the database after the state reflected in the archive copy. Since the archive log is always processed in sequential order, we assume that the archive log is written on magnetic tape.

2.3 Different Views of a Database

In Section 2.1, we indicated that the database looks different at each level of abstraction, with each level using different objects and interfaces. But this is not what we mean by "different views of a database" in this section. We have observed that the process of abstraction really begins at Level 3, up to which there is only a more convenient representation of data in external storage. At this level, abstraction is dependent on which pages actually establish the linear address space, that is, which block is read when a certain page is referenced. In the event of a failure, there are different possibilities for retrieving the contents of a page. These possibilities are denoted by different views of the database:

The *current database* comprises all objects accessible to the DBMS during normal processing. The current contents of all pages can be found on disk, except for those pages that have been recently modified. Their new contents are found in the DB buffer. The mapping hierarchy is completely correct.

The *materialized database* is the state that the DBMS finds at restart after a crash *without* having applied any log information. There is no buffer. Hence some page modifications (even of successful transactions) may not be reflected in the on-line copy. It is also possible that a new state of a page has been written to disk, but the control structure that maps pages to blocks has not yet been updated. In this case, a reference to such a page will yield the old value. This view of the database is what the recovery system has to transform into the most recent logically consistent current database.

The *physical database* is composed of all blocks of the on-line copy containing page images—current or obsolete. Depending on the strategy used on Level 2, there may be different values for one page in the physical database, none of which are necessarily the current contents. This view is not normally used by recovery procedures, but a salvation program would try to exploit all information contained therein.

With these views of a database, we can distinguish three types of update operations—all of which explain the mapping function provided by the propagation control level. First, we have the *modification of page contents* caused by some higher level module. This operation takes place in the DB buffer and therefore affects only the current database. Second, there is the *write* operation, transferring a modified page to a block on disk. In general, this affects only the physical database. If the information about the block containing the new page value is stored in volatile memory, the new contents will not be accessible after a crash; that is, it is not yet part of the materialized database. The operation that makes a previously written page image part of the materialized database is called *propagation*. This operation writes the updated control structures for mapping pages to blocks in a safe, nonvolatile place, so that they are available after a crash.

If pages are always written to the same block (the so-called "update-in-place" operation, which is done in most commercial DBMS), writing implicitly is the equivalent of propagation. However, there is an important difference between these operations if a page can be stored in different blocks. This is explained in the next section.

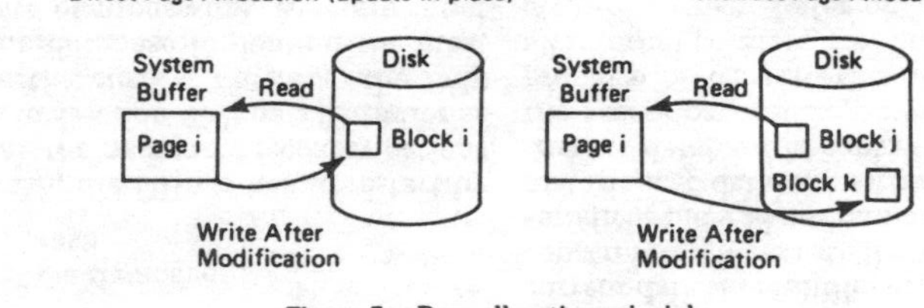

Figure 5. Page allocation principles.

2.4 Mapping Concepts for Updates

In this section, we define a number of concepts related to the operation of mapping changes in a database from volatile to nonvolatile storage. They are directly related to the views of a database introduced previously. The key issue is that each modification of a page (which changes the current database) takes place in the database buffer and is allocated to *volatile* storage. In order to save this state, the corresponding page must be brought to nonvolatile storage, that is, to the physical database. Two different schemes for accomplishing this can be applied, as sketched in Figure 5.

With *direct page allocation*, each page of a segment is related to exactly one block of the corresponding file. Each output of a modified page causes an update in place. By using an *indirect page allocation* scheme, each output is directed to a new block, leaving the old contents of the page unchanged. It provides the option of holding *n* successive versions of a page. The moment when a younger version definitively replaces an older one can be determined by appropriate (consistency-related) criteria; it is no longer bound to the moment of writing. This update scheme has some very attractive properties in case of recovery, as is shown later on. Direct page allocation leaves no choice as to when to make a new version part of the materialized database; the output operation destroys the previous image. Hence in this case writing and propagating coincide.

There is still another important difference between direct and indirect page allocation schemes, which can be characterized as follows:

- In *direct* page allocation, each single propagation (physical write) is interruptable by a system crash, thus leaving the materialized, and possibly the physical, database in an inconsistent state.
- In *indirect* page allocation, there is always a way back to the old state. Hence propagation of an arbitrary set of pages can be made uninterruptable by system crashes. References to such algorithms will be given.

On the basis of this observation, we can distinguish two types of propagation strategies:

ATOMIC. Any set of modified pages can be propagated as a unit, such that either all or none of the updates become part of the materialized database.

¬ATOMIC. Pages are written to blocks according to an update-in-place policy. Since no set of pages can be written indivisibly (even a single write may be interrupted somewhere in between), propagation is vulnerable to system crashes.

Of course, many details have been omitted from Figure 5. In particular, there is no hint of the techniques used to make propagation take place atomically in case of indirect page mapping. We have tried to illustrate aspects of this issue in Figure 6. Figure 6 contains a comparison of the current and the materialized database for the update-in-place scheme and three different implementations of indirect page mapping allowing for ATOMIC propagation. Figure 6b refers to the well-known shadow page

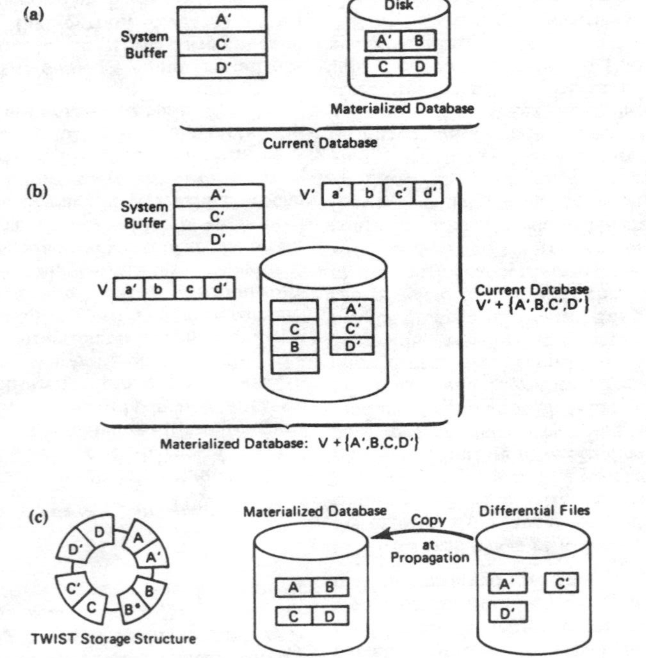

Figure 6. Current versus materialized database in ¬ATOMIC (a) and ATOMIC (b and c) propagation.

mechanism [Lorie 1977]. The mapping of page numbers to block numbers is done by using page tables. These tables have one entry per page containing the block number where the page contents are stored. The *shadow pages*, accessed via the shadow page Table V, preserve the old state of the materialized database. The current version is defined by the current page Table V′. Before this state is made stable (propagated), all changed pages are written to their new blocks, and so is the current page table. If this fails, the database will come up in its old state. When all pages have been written related to the new state, ATOMIC propagation takes place by changing one record on disk (which now points to V′ rather than V) in a way that cannot be confused by a system crash. Thus the problem of indivisibly propagating a set of pages has been reduced to safely updating one record, which can be done in a simple way. For details, see Lorie [1977].

There are other implementations for ATOMIC propagation. One is based on maintaining two recent versions of a page. For each page access, both versions have to be read into the buffer. This can be done with minimal overhead by storing them in adjacent disk blocks and reading them with chained I/O. The latest version, recognized by a time stamp, is kept in the buffer; the other one is immediately discarded. A modified page replaces the older version on disk. ATOMIC propagation is accomplished by incrementing a special counter that is related to the time stamps in the pages. Details can be found in Reuter [1980]. Another approach to ATOMIC propagation has been introduced under the name "differential files" by Severance and Lohman [1976]. Modified pages are written to a separate (differential) file. Propagating these updates to the main database is not ATOMIC in itself, but once all modifications are written to the differential file, propagation can be repeated as often as wished. In other words, the process of copying modified pages into the materialized database can be made to appear ATOMIC. A variant of this technique, the "intention list," is described by Lampson and Sturgis [1979] and Sturgis et al. [1980].

Thus far we have shown that arbitrary sets of pages can be propagated in an ATOMIC manner using indirect page allocation. In the next section we discuss how these sets of pages for propagation should be defined.

3. CRASH RECOVERY

In order to illustrate the consequences of the concepts introduced thus far, we shall present a detailed discussion of crash recovery. First, we consider the state in which a database is left when the system terminates abnormally. From this we derive the type of redundant (log) information required to reestablish a transaction-consistent state, which is the overall purpose of DB recovery. After completing our classification scheme, we give examples of recovery techniques in currently available database systems. Finally, we present a table containing a qualitative evaluation of all instances encompassed by our taxonomy (Table 4).

Note that the results in this section also apply to transaction UNDO—a much simpler case of global UNDO, which applies when the DBMS is processing normally and no information is lost.

3.1 State of the Database after a Crash

After a crash, the DBMS has to restart by applying all the necessary recovery actions described in Section 1. The DB buffer is lost, as is the *current database*, the only view of the database to contain the most recent state of processing. Assuming that the on-line copy of the database is intact, there are the *materialized database* and the *temporary log file* from which to start recovery. We have not discussed the contents of the log files for the reason that the type and number of log data to be written during normal processing are dependent upon the state of the materialized database after a crash. This state, in turn, depends upon which method of page allocation and propagation is used.

In the case of direct page allocation and ¬ATOMIC propagation, each write operation affects the materialized database. The decision to write pages is made by the *buffer manager* according to buffer capacity at points in time that appear arbitrary. Hence the state of the materialized database after a crash is unpredictable: When recent modifications are reflected in the materialized database, it is not possible (without further provisions) to know which pages were modified by complete transactions (whose contents must be reconstructed by partial REDO) and which pages were modified by incomplete transactions (whose contents must be returned to their previous state by global UNDO). Further possibilities for providing against this situation are briefly discussed in Section 3.2.1.

In the case of indirect page allocation and ATOMIC propagation, we know much more about the state of the materialized database after crash. ATOMIC propagation is indivisible by any type of failure, and therefore we find the materialized database to be exactly in the state produced by the most recent successful propagation. This state may still be inconsistent in that not all updates of complete transactions are visible, and some effects of incomplete transactions are. However, ATOMIC propagation ensures that a set of related pages is propagated in a safe manner by restricting propagation to points in time when the current database fulfills certain consistency constraints. When these constraints are satisfied, the updates can be mapped to the materialized database all at once. Since the current database is consistent in terms of the access path management level—where propagation occurs—this also ensures that all internal pointers, tree structures, tables, etc. are correct. Later on, we also discuss schemes that allow for transaction-consistent propagation.

The state of the materialized database after a crash can be summarized as follows:

¬*ATOMIC Propagation.* Nothing is known about the state of the materialized database; it must be characterized as "chaotic."

ATOMIC Propagation. The materialized database is in the state produced by the most recent propagation. Since this is bound by certain consistency constraints, the materialized database will be consistent (but not necessarily up-to-date) at least up to the third level of the mapping hierarchy.

In the case of ¬ATOMIC propagation, one cannot expect to read valid images for all pages from the materialized database after a crash; it is inconsistent on the propagation level, and all abstractions on higher levels will fail. In the case of ATOMIC propagation, the materialized database is consistent at least on Level 3, thus allowing for the execution of operations on Level 4 (DML statements).

3.2 Types of Log Information to Support Recovery Actions

The temporary log file must contain all the information required to transform the materialized database "as found" into the most recent transaction-consistent state (see Section 1). As we have shown, the materialized database can be in more or less defined states, may or may not fulfill consistency constraints, etc. Hence the number of log data will be determined by what is contained in the materialized database at the beginning of restart. We can be fairly certain of the contents of the materialized database in the case of ATOMIC propagation, but the result of ¬ATOMIC schemes have been shown to be unpredictable. There are, however, additional measures to somewhat reduce the degree of uncertainty resulting from ¬ATOMIC propagation, as discussed in the following section.

3.2.1 Dependencies between Buffer Manager and Recovery Component

3.2.1.1 Buffer Management and UNDO Recovery Actions. During the normal mode of operation, modified pages are written to disk by some replacement algorithm managing the database buffer. Ideally, this happens at points in time determined solely by buffer occupation and, from a consistency perspective, seem to be arbitrary. In general, even dirty data, that is, pages modified by incomplete transactions, may be written to the physical database. Hence the UNDO operations described earlier will have to recover the contents of both the materialized database and the external storage media. The only way to avoid this requires that the buffer manager be modified to prevent it from writing or propagating dirty pages under all circumstances. In this case, UNDO could be considerably simplified:

- If no dirty pages are propagated, global UNDO becomes virtually unnecessary that is, if there are no dirty data in the materialized database.
- If no dirty pages are written, transaction UNDO can be limited to main storage (buffer) operations.

The major disadvantage of this idea is that very large database buffers would be required (e.g., for long batch update transactions), making it generally incompatible with existing systems. However, the two different methods of handling modified pages introduced with this idea have important implications with UNDO recovery. We shall refer to these methods as:

STEAL. Modified pages may be written and/or propagated at any time.

¬*STEAL.* Modified pages are kept in buffer at least until the end of the transaction (EOT).

The definition of STEAL can be based on either writing or propagating, which are not discriminated in ¬ATOMIC schemes. In the case of ATOMIC propagation both variants of STEAL are conceivable, and each would have a different impact on UNDO recovery actions; in the case of ¬STEAL, no logging is required for UNDO purposes.

3.2.1.2 Buffer Management and REDO Recovery Actions. As soon as a transaction commits, all of its results must survive any subsequent failure (*durability*). Committed updates that have not been propagated to the materialized database would definitely be lost in case of a system crash, and so there must be enough redundant information in the log file to reconstruct these results during restart (partial REDO). It is conceivable, however to avoid this kind of recovery by the following technique.

During Phase 1 of EOT processing all pages modified by this transaction are propagated to the materialized database; that is, their writing *and* propagation are enforced. Then we can be sure that either the transaction is complete, which means that all of its results are safely recorded (no partial REDO), or in case of a crash, some updates are not yet written, which means that the transaction is not successful and must be rolled back (UNDO recovery actions).

Thus we have another criterion concerning buffer handling, which is related to the necessity of REDO recovery during restart:

FORCE. All modified pages are written and propagated during EOT processing.

¬*FORCE.* No propagation is triggered during EOT processing.

The implications with regard to the gathering of log data are quite straightforward in the case of FORCE. No logging is required for *partial REDO*; in the case of ¬FORCE such information is required. While FORCE avoids partial REDO, there must still be some REDO-log information for *global REDO* to provide against loss of the on-line copy of the database.

3.2.2 Classification of Log Data

Depending on which of the write and propagation schemes introduced above are being implemented, we will have to collect log information for the purpose of

- removing invalid data (modifications effected by incomplete transactions) from the materialized database and
- supplementing the materialized database with updates of complete transactions that were not contained in it at the time of crash.

In this section, we briefly describe what such log data can look like and when such data are applicable to the crash state of the materialized database.

Table 2. Classification Scheme for Log Data

	State	Transition
Logical	—	Actions (DML statements)
Physical	Before images After images	EXOR differences

Log data are redundant information, collected for the sole purpose of recovery from a crash or a media failure. They do not undergo the mapping process of the database objects, but are obtained on a certain level of the mapping hierarchy and written directly to nonvolatile storage, that is, the log files. There are two different, albeit not fully orthogonal, criteria for classifying log data. The first is concerned with the *type* of objects to be logged. If some part of the physical representation, that is, the bit pattern, is written to the log, we refer to it as *physical logging*; if the operators and their arguments are recorded on a higher level, this is called *logical logging*. The second criterion concerns whether the *state* of the database—before or after a change—or the *transition* causing the change is to be logged. Table 2 contains some examples for these different types of logging, which are explained below.

Physical State Logging on Page Level. The most basic method, which is still applied in many commercial DBMSs, uses the page as the unit of log information. Each time a part of the linear address space is changed by some modification, insertion, etc., the whole page containing this part of the linear address space is written to the log. If UNDO logging is required, this will be done before the change takes place, yielding the so-called *before image*. For REDO purposes, the resulting page state is recorded as an *after image*.

Physical Transition Logging on Page Level. This logging technique is based also on pages. However, it does not explicitly record the old and new *states* of a page; rather it writes the *difference between them* to the log. The function used for computing the "difference" between two bit strings is the exclusive-or, which is both commutative and associative as required by the recovery algorithm. If this difference is applied to the old state of a page, again using the exclusive-or, the new state will result. On the other hand, applying it to the new state will yield the old state. There are some problems in the details of this approach, but these are beyond the scope of the paper.

The two methods of page logging that we have discussed can be compared as follows:

- Transition logging requires only one log entry (the difference), whereas state logging uses both a before image and an after image. If there are multiple changes applied to the same page during one transaction, transition logging can express these either by successive differences or by one accumulated difference. With state logging, the first before image and the last after image are required.
- Since there are usually only a small number of data inside a page affected by a change, the exclusive-or difference will contain long strings of 0's, which can be removed by well-known compression techniques. Hence transition logging can potentially require much less space than does state logging.

Physical State Logging on Access Path Level. Physical logging can also be applied to the objects of the access path level, namely, physical records, access path structures, tables, etc. The log component has to be aware of these storage structures and record only the changed entry, rather than blindly logging the whole page around it. The advantage of this requirement is obvious: By logging only the physical objects actually being changed, space requirements for log files can be drastically reduced. One can save even more space by exploiting the fact that most access path structures consist of fully redundant information. For example, one can completely reconstruct a B*-tree from the record occurrences to which it refers. In itself, this type of reconstruction is certainly too expensive to become a standard method for crash recovery. But if only the modifications in the records are logged, after a crash the corresponding B* tree can be recovered consistently, provided that an appropriate write discipline has been observed for the pages containing the tree. This principle, stating that changed nodes must be written bottom up, is a special case of the "careful replacement" technique explained in detail by Verhofstadt [1978]. For our taxonomy it makes no difference whether the principle is applied or not.

Transition Logging on the Access Path Level. On the access path level, we are dealing with the entries of storage structures, but do not know how they are related to each other with regard to the objects of the database schema. This type of information is maintained on higher levels of the mapping hierarchy. If we look only at the physical entry representation (*physical* transition logging), state transition on this level means that a physical record, a table entry, etc. is *added* to, *deleted* from, or *modified* in a page. The arguments pertaining to these operations are the entries themselves, and so there is little difference between this and the previous approach. In the case of physical state logging on the access path level, we placed the physical address together with the entry representation. Here we place the operation code and object identifier with the same type of argument. Thus physical transition logging on this level does not provide anything essentially different.

We can also consider *logical* transition logging, attempting to exploit the syntax of the storage structures implemented on this level. The logical addition, a new record occurrence, for example, would include all the redundant table updates such as the record id index, the free space table, etc., each of which was explicitly logged with the physical schemes. Hence we again have a potential saving of log space. However, it is important to note that the logical transitions on this level generally affect *more than one page*. If they (or their inverse operators for UNDO) are to be applied during recovery, we must be sure that all affected pages have the same state in the materialized database. This is not the case with direct page allocation, and using the more expensive indirect schemes cannot be justified by the comparatively few benefits yielded by logical transition logging on the access path level. Hence logical transition logging on this level can generally be ruled out, but will become more attractive on the next higher level.

TRANSACTION LOG

TRANSACTION DESCRIPTOR ⇒ RECORD ID, OLDVAL, NEWVAL

Figure 7. Logical transition logging as implemented in System R. (From Gray et al. [1981].)

Logical Logging on the Record-Oriented Level. At one level higher, it is possible to express the changes performed by the transaction program in a very compact manner by simply recording the update DML statements with their parameters. Even if a nonprocedural query language is being used above this level, its updates will be decomposed into updates of single records or tuples equivalent to the single-record updates of procedural DB languages. Thus logging on this level means that only the INSERT, UPDATE, and DELETE operations, together with their record ids and attribute values, are written to the log. The mapping process discerns which entries are affected, which pages must be modified, etc. Thus recovery is achieved by reexecuting some of the previously processed DML statements. For UNDO recovery, of course, the inverse DML statement must be executed, that is, a DELETE to compensate an INSERT and vice versa, and an UPDATE returned to the original values. These inverse DML statements must be generated automatically as part of the regular logging activity, and for this reason this approach is not viable for network-oriented DBMSs with information-bearing interrecord relations. In such cases, it can be extremely expensive to determine, for example, the inverse for a DELETE. Details can be found in Reuter [1981].

System R is a good example of a system with logical logging on the record-oriented level. All update operations performed on the tuples are represented by one generalized modification operator, which is not explicitly recorded. This operator changes a tuple identified by its tuple identifier (TID) from an old value to a new one, both of which are recorded. Inserting a tuple entails modifying its initial null value to the given value, and deleting a tuple entails the inverse transition. Hence the log contains the information shown in Figure 7.

Logical transition logging obviously requires a materialized database that is consistent up to Level 3; that is, it can only be combined with ATOMIC propagation schemes. Although the number of log data written are very small, recovery will be more expensive than that in other schemes, because it involves the reprocessing of some DML statements, although this can be done more cheaply than the original processing.

Table 3 is a summation of the properties of all logging techniques that we have described under two considerations: What is the cost of collecting the log data during normal processing? and, How expensive is recovery based on the respective type of log information? Of course, the entries in the table are only very rough qualitative estimations; for more detailed quantitative analysis see Reuter [1982].

Writing log information, no matter what type, is determined by two rules:

- UNDO information must be written to the log file *before* the corresponding updates are propagated to the materialized database. This has come to be known as the "write ahead log" (WAL) principle [Gray 1978].
- REDO information must be written to the temporary and the archive log file *before* EOT is acknowledged to the transaction program. Once this is done, the system must be able to ensure the transaction's durability.

We return to different facets of these rules in Section 3.4.

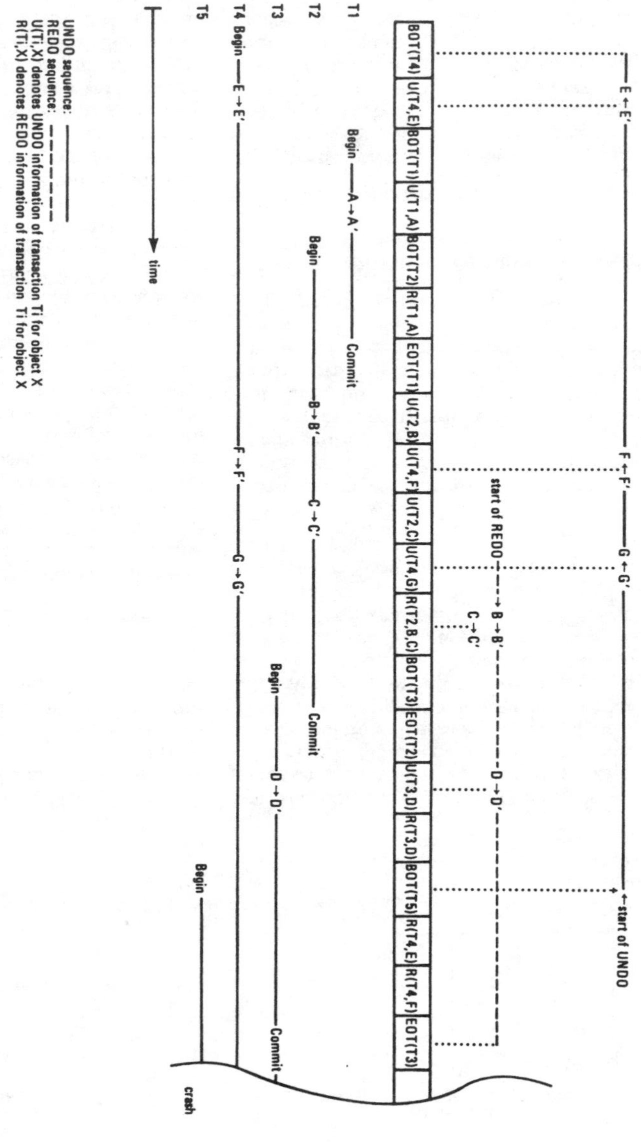

UNDO sequence: ———
REDO sequence: - - - - - -
U(Ti,X) denotes UNDO information of transaction Ti for object X
R(Ti,X) denotes REDO information of transaction Ti for object X

Figure 8. A crash recovery scenario.

Table 3. Qualitative Comparison of Various Logging Techniques[a]

Logging technique	Level no.	Expenses during normal processing	Expenses for recovery operations
Physical state	2	High	Low
Physical transition	2	Medium	Low
Physical state	3	Low	Low
Logical transition	4	Very low	Medium

[a] Costs are basically measured in units of physical I/O operations. Recovery in this context means crash recovery.

3.3 Examples of Recovery Techniques

3.3.1 *Optimization of Recovery Actions by Checkpoints*

An appropriate combination of redundancy provided by log protocols and mapping techniques is basically all that we need for implementing transaction-oriented database recovery as described in Section 1. In real systems, however, there are a number of important refinements that reduce the amount of log data required and the costs of crash recovery. Figure 8 is a very general example of crash recovery. In the center, there is the temporary log containing UNDO and REDO information and special entries notifying the begin and end of a transaction (BOT and EOT, respectively). Below the temporary log, the transaction history preceding the crash is shown, and above it, recovery processing for global UNDO and partial REDO is related to the log entries. We have not assumed a specific propagation strategy.

There are two questions concerning the costs of crash recovery:

- In the case of the materialized DB being modified by incomplete transactions, to what extent does the log have to be processed for UNDO recovery?
- If the DBMS does not use a FORCE discipline, which part of the log has to processed for REDO recovery?

The first question can easily be answered: If we know that updates of incomplete transactions *can* have affected the materialized database (STEAL), we must scan the temporary log file back to the BOT entry of the *oldest* incomplete transaction to be sure that no invalid data are left in the system. The second question is not as simple. In Figure 8, REDO is started at a point that seems to be chosen arbitrarily. Why is there no REDO recovery for object A? In general, we can assume that in the case of a FORCE discipline modified pages will be written eventually because of buffer replacement. One might expect that only the contents of the most recently changed pages have to be redone—if the change was caused by a complete transaction. But look at a buffer activity record shown in Figure 9.

The situation depicted in Figure 9 is typical of many large database applications. Most of the modified pages will have been changed "recently," but there are a few hot spots like p_i, pages that are modified again and again, and, since they are *referenced* so frequently, have not been written from the buffer. After a while such pages will contain the updates of *many* complete transactions, and REDO recovery will therefore have to go back very far on the temporary log. This makes restart expensive. In general, the amount of log data to be processed for partial REDO will increase with the interval of time between two subsequent crashes. In other words, the higher the availability of the system, the more costly recovery will become. This is unacceptable for large, demanding applications.

For this reason additional measures are required for making restart costs independent of mean time between failure. Such provisions will be called *checkpoints*, and are defined as follows.

Generating a checkpoint means collecting information in a safe place, which has the effect of defining and limiting the amount of REDO recovery required after a crash.

Whether this information is stored in the log or elsewhere depends on which implementation technique is chosen; we give

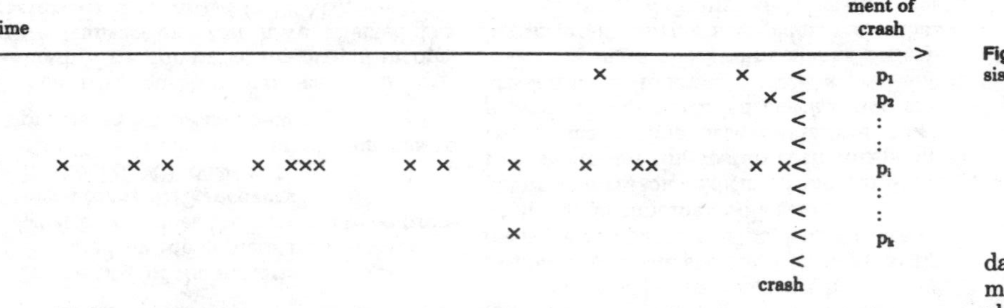

Figure 9. Age of buffer page modifications (×, page modification).

some examples in this section. Checkpoint generation involves three steps [Gray 1978]:

- Write a BEGIN_CHECKPOINT record to the temporary log file.
- Write all checkpoint data to the log file and/or the database.
- Write an END_CHECKPOINT record to the temporary log file.

During restart, the BEGIN–END bracket is a clear indication as to whether a checkpoint was generated completely or interrupted by a system crash. Sometimes checkpointing is considered to be a means for restoring the whole database to some previous state. Our view, however, focuses on transaction recovery. Therefore to us a checkpoint is a technique for optimizing crash recovery rather than a definition of a distinguished state for recovery itself. In order to effectively constrain partial REDO, checkpoints must be generated at well-defined points in time. In the following sections, we shall introduce four separate criteria for determining when to start checkpoint activities.

3.3.2 *Transaction-Oriented Checkpoints*

As previously explained, a FORCE discipline will avoid partial REDO. All modified pages are propagated before an EOT record is written to the log, which makes the transaction durable. If this record is not found in the log after a crash, the transaction will

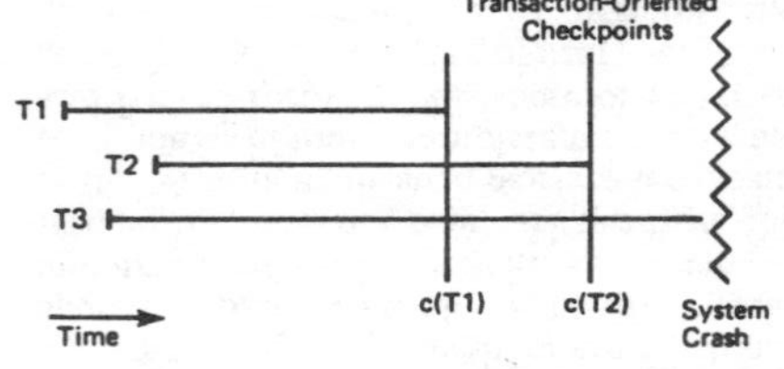

Figure 10. Scenario for transaction-oriented checkpoints.

be considered incomplete and its effects will be undone. Hence the EOT record of each transaction can be interpreted as a BEGIN_CHECKPOINT and END_CHECKPOINT, since it agrees with our definition of a checkpoint in that it limits the scope of REDO. Figure 10 illustrates transaction-oriented checkpoints (TOC).

As can be seen in Figure 10, transaction-oriented checkpoints are implied by a FORCE discipline. The major drawback to this approach can be deduced from Figure 9. Hot spot pages like p_i will be propagated each time they are modified by a transaction even though they remain in the buffer for a long time. The reduction of recovery expenses with the use of transaction-oriented checkpoints is accomplished by imposing some overhead on normal processing. This is discussed in more detail in Section 3.5. The cost factor of unnecessary write operations performed by a FORCE discipline is highly relevant for very large database buffers. The longer a page remains in the buffer, the higher is the probability of multiple updates to the same page by different transactions. Thus for DBMSs supporting large applications, transaction-oriented checkpointing is not the proper choice.

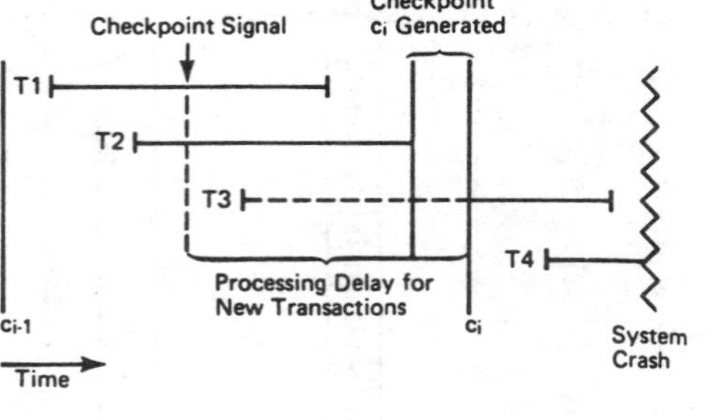

Figure 11. Scenario for transaction-consistent checkpoints.

3.3.3 *Transaction-Consistent Checkpoints*

The following transaction-consistent checkpoints (TCC) are *global* in that they save the work of all transactions that have modified the database. The first TCC, when successfully generated, creates a transaction-consistent database. It requires that all update activities on the database be quiescent. In other words, when the checkpoint generation is signaled by the recovery component, all incomplete update transactions are completed and new ones are not admitted. The checkpoint is actually generated when the last update is completed. After the END_CHECKPOINT record has been successfully written, normal operation is resumed. This is illustrated in Figure 11.

Checkpointing connotes propagating all modified buffer pages and writing a record to the log, which notifies the materialized database of a new transaction-consistent state, hence the name "transaction-consistent checkpoint" (TCC). By propagating all modified pages to the database, TCC establishes a point past which partial REDO will not operate. Since all modifications prior to the recent checkpoint are reflected in the database, REDO-log information need only be processed back to the youngest END_CHECKPOINT record found on the log. We shall see later on that the time between two subsequent checkpoints can be adjusted to minimize overall recovery costs.

In Figure 11, T3 must be redone completely, whereas T4 must be rolled back. There is nothing to be done about T1 and T2, since their updates have been propagated by generating c_i. Favorable as that may sound, the TCC approach is quite unrealistic for large multiuser DBMSs, with the exception of one special case, which is discussed in Section 3.4. There are two reasons for this:

- Putting the system into a quiescent state until no update transaction is active may cause an intolerable delay for incoming transactions.
- Checkpoint costs will be high in the case of large buffers, where many changed pages will have accumulated. With a buffer of 6 megabytes and a substantial number of updates, propagating the modified pages will take about 10 seconds.

For small applications and single-user systems, TCC certainly is useful.

3.3.4 *Action-Consistent Checkpoints*

Each transaction is considered a sequence of elementary actions affecting the database. On the record-oriented level, these actions can be seen as DML statements. Action-consistent checkpoints (ACC) can be generated when no update *action* is being processed. Therefore signaling an ACC means putting the system into quiescence on the action level, which impedes operation here much less than on the transaction level. A scenario is shown in Figure 12.

The checkpoint itself is generated in the very same way as was described for the

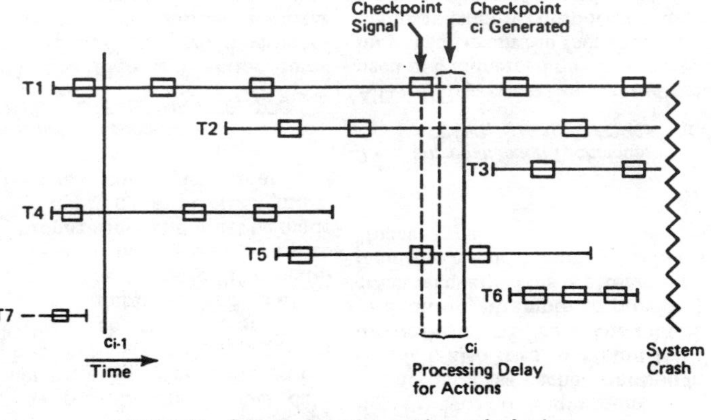

Figure 12. Scenario for action-consistent checkpoints.

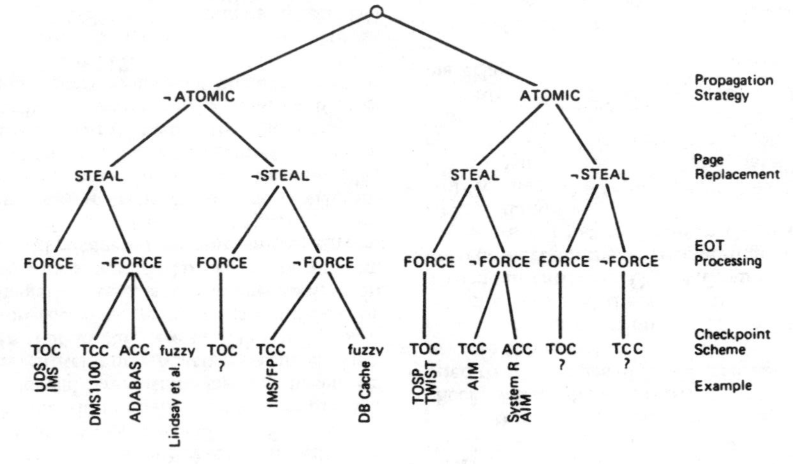

Figure 13. Classification scheme for recovery concepts.

TCC technique. In the case of ACC, however, the END_CHECKPOINT record indicates an action-consistent[4] rather than a transaction-consistent database. Obviously such a checkpoint imposes a limit on partial REDO. In contrast to TCC, it does not establish a boundary to global UNDO; however, it is not required by definition to do so. Recovery in the above scenario means global UNDO for T1, T2, and T3. REDO has to be performed for the last action of T5 and for all of T6. The changes of T4 and T7 are part of the materialized database because of checkpointing. So again, REDO-log information prior to the recent checkpoint is irrelevant for crash recovery. This scheme is much more realistic, since it does not cause long delays for incoming transactions. Costs of checkpointing, however, are still high when large buffers are used.

3.3.5 *Fuzzy Checkpoints*

In order to further reduce checkpoint costs, propagation activity at checkpoint time has to be avoided whenever possible. One way to do this is *indirect* checkpointing. Indirect checkpointing means that information about the buffer occupation is written to the log file rather than the pages themselves. This can be done with two or three write operations, even with very large buffers, and helps to determine which pages containing committed data were actually in the buffer at the moment of a crash. However, if there are hot spot pages, their REDO information will have to be traced back very far on the temporary log. So, although indirect checkpointing does reduce the costs of partial REDO, this does not in general make partial REDO independent of mean time between failure. Note also that this method is only applicable with ¬ATOMIC propagation. In the case of ATOMIC schemes, propagation always takes effect at one well-defined moment, which is a checkpoint; pages that have only been written (not propagated) are lost after a crash. Since this checkpointing method is concerned only with the temporary log, leaving the database as it is, we call it "fuzzy." A description of a particular implementation of indirect, fuzzy checkpoints is given by Gray [1978].

The best of both worlds, low checkpoint costs with fixed limits to partial REDO, is achieved by another fuzzy scheme described by Lindsay *et al.* [1979]. This scheme combines ACC with indirect checkpointing: At checkpoint time the numbers of all pages (with an update indicator) currently in buffer are written to the log file. If there are no hot spot pages, nothing else is done. If, however, a modified page is found at two subsequent checkpoints without having been propagated, it will be propagated during checkpoint generation. Hence the scope of partial REDO is limited to two checkpoint intervals. Empiric studies show that the I/O activity for checkpointing is only about 3 percent of what is required with ACC [Reuter 1981]. This scheme can be given general applicability by adjusting the number of checkpoint intervals for modified pages in buffer.

Another fuzzy checkpoint approach has been proposed by Elhardt [1982]. Since a description of this technique, called database cache, would require more details than we can present in this paper, readers are referred to the literature.

3.4 Examples of Logging and Recovery Components

The introduction of various checkpoint schemes has completed our taxonomy. Database recovery techniques can now be classified as shown in Figure 13. In order to make the classification more vivid, we have added the names of a few existing DBMSs and implementation concepts to the corresponding entries.

In this section, we attempt to illustrate the functional principles of three different approaches found in well-known database systems. We particularly want to elaborate on the cooperation between mapping, logging, and recovery facilities, using a sample database constituting four pages, A, B, C, and D, which are modified by six transactions. What the transactions do is sketched in Figure 14. The indicated checkpoint c_i is relevant only to those implementations actually applying checkpoint techniques. Prior to the beginning of Transaction 1 (T1), the DB pages were in the states A, B, C, and D, respectively.

3.4.1 *Implementation Technique: ¬ATOMIC, STEAL, FORCE, TOC*

An implementation technique involving the principles of ¬ATOMIC, STEAL, FORCE, and TOC can be found in many systems, for example, IMS [N.d.] and UDS [N.d.]. The temporary log file contains only UNDO data (owing to FORCE), whereas REDO information is written to the archive log. According to the write rules introduced in Section 3.2, we must be sure that UNDO logging has taken effect before a changed page is either replaced in the buffer or

[4] This means that the materialized database reflects a state produced by complete actions only; that is, it is consistent up to Level 3 at the moment of checkpointing.

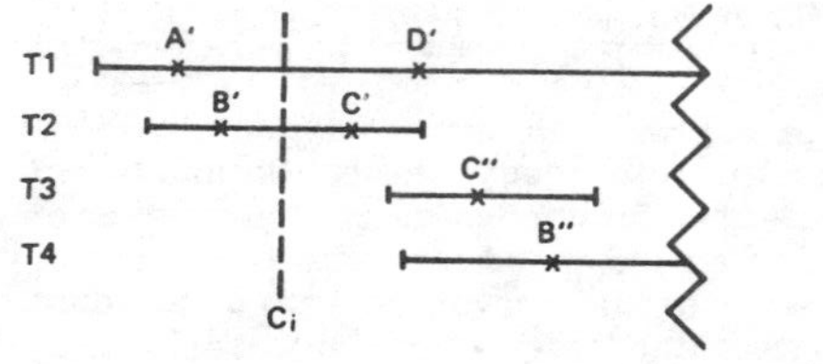

Figure 14. Transaction scenario for illustrating recovery techniques.

forced at EOT. Note that in ¬ATOMIC schemes EOT processing is interruptable by a crash.

In the scenario given in Figure 15, we need only consider T1 and T2; the rest is irrelevant to the example. According to the scenario, A′ has been replaced from the buffer, which triggered an UNDO entry to be written. Pages B′ and C′ remained in buffer as long as T2 was active. T2 reached its normal end before the crash, and so the following had to be done:

- Write UNDO information for B and C (in case the FORCE fails).
- Propagate B′ and C′.
- Write REDO information for B′ and C′ to the archive log file.
- Discard the UNDO entries for B and C.
- Write an EOT record to the log files and acknowledge EOT to the user.

Of course, there are some obvious optimizations as regards the UNDO data for pages that have not been replaced before EOT, but these are not our concern here. After the crash, the recovery component finds the database and the log files as shown in the scenario. The materialized database is inconsistent owing to ¬ATOMIC propagation, and must be made consistent by applying all UNDO information in reverse chronological order.

3.4.2 Implementation Technique: ¬ATOMIC, ¬STEAL, ¬FORCE, TCC

Applications with high transaction rates require large DB buffers to yield satisfactory performance. With sufficient buffer space, a ¬STEAL approach becomes feasible; that is, the materialized database will never contain updates of incomplete transactions. ¬FORCE is desirable for efficient EOT processing, as discussed previously (Section 3.3.2). The IMS/Fast Path in its "main storage database" version is a system designed with this implementation technique [IMS N.d.; Date 1981]. The ¬STEAL and ¬FORCE principles are generalized to the extent that there are no write operations to the database during normal processing. All updates are recorded to the log, and propagation is delayed until shutdown (or some other very infrequent checkpoint), which makes the system belong to the TCC class. Figure 16 illustrates the implications of this approach.

With ¬STEAL, there is no UNDO information on the temporary log. Accordingly, there are only committed pages in the materialized database. Each successful transaction writes REDO information during EOT processing. Assuming that the crash occurs as indicated in Figure 14, the materialized database is in the initial state, and, compared with the former current database, is old. Everything that has been done since start-up must therefore be applied to the database by processing the entire temporary log in chronological order. This, of course, can be very expensive, and hence the entire environment should be as stable as possible to minimize crashes. The benefits of this approach are extremely high transaction rates and short response times, since physical I/O during normal processing is reduced to a minimum.

The database cache, mentioned in Section 3.3, also tries to exploit the desirable properties of ¬STEAL and ¬FORCE, but, in addition, attempts to provide very fast crash recovery. This is attempted by implementing a checkpointing scheme of the "fuzzy" type.

3.4.3 Implementation Technique: ATOMIC, STEAL, ¬FORCE, ACC

ATOMIC propagation is not yet widely used in commercial database systems. This may result from the fact that indirect page mapping is more complicated and more expensive than the update-in-place technique. However, there is a well-known example of this type of implementation, based on the shadow-page mechanism in System R. This system uses action-consistent checkpointing for update propagation, and hence comes up with a consistent materialized database after a crash. More specifically, the materialized database will be consistent up to Level 4 of the mapping hierarchy and reflect the state of the most recent checkpoint; everything occurring after the most recent checkpoint will have disappeared. As discussed in Section 3.2, with an action-consistent database one can use logical transition logging based on DML statements, which System R does. Note that in the case of ATOMIC propagation the WAL principle is bound to the propagation, that is, to the checkpoints. In other words, modified pages can be written, but not propagated, without having written an UNDO log. If the modified pages pertain to incomplete transactions, the UNDO information must be on the temporary log before the pages are propagated. The same is true for STEAL: Not only can dirty pages be written; in the case of System R they can also be propagated. Consider the scenario in Figure 17.

T1 and T2 were both incomplete at checkpoint. Since their updates (A′ and B′) have been propagated, UNDO information must be written to the temporary log. In System R, this is done with logical transitions, as described in Section 3.2. EOT processing of T2 and T3 includes writing REDO information to the log, again using logical transitions. When the system crashes, the current database is in the state depicted in Figure 17; at restart the materialized database will reflect the most recent checkpoint state. Crash recovery involves the following actions:

- UNDO the modification of A′. Owing to the STEAL policy in System R, incomplete transactions can span several checkpoints. Global UNDO must be applied to all changes of failed transactions prior to the recent checkpoint.
- REDO the last action of T2 (modification of C′) and the whole transaction T3 (modification of C″). Although they are committed, the corresponding page states are not yet reflected in the materialized database.
- Nothing has to be done with D′ since this has not yet become part of the materialized database. The same is true of T4. Since it was not present when c_i was generated, it has had no effect on the materialized database.

3.5 Evaluation of Logging and Recovery Concepts

Combining all possibilities of propagating, buffer handling, and checkpointing, and

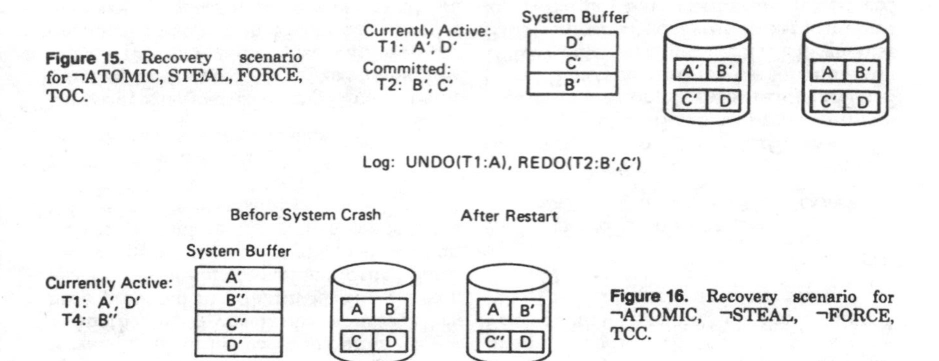

Figure 15. Recovery scenario for ¬ATOMIC, STEAL, FORCE, TOC.

Figure 16. Recovery scenario for ¬ATOMIC, ¬STEAL, ¬FORCE, TCC.

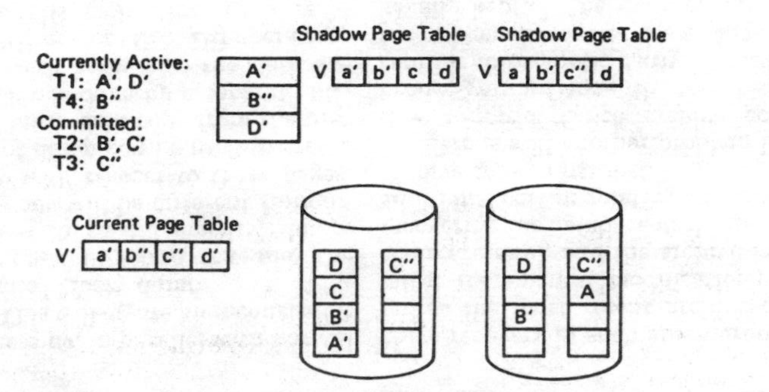

Figure 17. Recovery scenario for ATOMIC, STEAL, ¬FORCE, ACC.

Table 4. Evaluation of Logging and Recovery Techniques Based on the Introduced Taxonomy

propagation strategy	¬ATOMIC							ATOMIC				
buffer replacement	STEAL				¬STEAL			STEAL			¬STEAL	
EOT processing	FORCE	¬FORCE			FORCE	¬FORCE		FORCE	¬FORCE		FORCE	¬FORCE
checkpoint type	TOC	TCC	ACC	FUZZY	TOC	TCC	FUZZY	TOC	TCC	ACC	TOC	TCC
materialized DB state after system failure	DC	DC	DC	DC	DC	DC	DC	TC	TC	AC	TC	TC
cost of transaction UNDO	+	+	+	+	--	--	--	-	-	+	--	--
cost of partial REDO at restart	--	-	-	+	--	-	-	--	-	-	--	-
cost of global UNDO at restart	+	+	+	+	--	--	--	--	--	+	--	--
overhead during normal processing	--	--	--	--	--	--	--	+	+	+	+	+
frequency of checkpoints	+	-	-	-	+	-	-	+	-	-	+	-
checkpoint cost	+	++	++	-	+	++	+	+	++	++	+	++

Notes:
Abbreviations: DC, device consistent (chaotic); AC, action consistent; TC, Transaction consistent.
Evaluation symbols: −−, very low; −, low; +, high; ++, very high.

considering the overall properties of each scheme that we have discussed, we can derive the evaluation given in Table 4.

Table 4 can be seen as a compact summary of what we have discussed up to this point. Combinations leading to inherent contradictions have been suppressed (e.g., ¬STEAL does not allow for ACC). By referring the information in Table 4 to Figure 13; one can see how existing DBMSs are rated in this qualitative comparison.

Some criteria of our taxonomy divide the world of DB recovery into clearly distinct areas:

- ATOMIC propagation achieves an action- or transaction-consistent materialized database in the event of a crash. Physical as well as logical logging techniques are therefore applicable. The benefits of this property are offset by increased overhead during normal processing caused by the redundancy required for indirect page mapping. On the other hand, recovery can be cheap when ATOMIC propagation is combined with TOC schemes.
- ¬ATOMIC propagation generally results in a chaotic materialized database in the event of a crash, which makes physical logging mandatory. There is almost no overhead during normal processing, but without appropriate checkpoint schemes, recovery will more expensive.
- All transaction-oriented and transaction-consistent schemes cause high checkpoint costs. This problem is emphasized in transaction-oriented schemes by a relatively high checkpoint frequency.

It is, in general, important when deciding which implementation techniques to choose for database recovery to carefully consider whether optimizations of crash recovery put additional burdens on normal processing. If this is the case, it will certainly not pay off, since crash recovery, it is hoped, will be a rare event. Recovery components should be designed with minimal overhead for normal processing, provided that there is fixed limit to the costs of crash recovery.

This consideration rules out schemes of the ATOMIC, FORCE, TOC type, which can be implemented and look very appealing at first sight. According to the classification, the materialized database will always be in the most recent transaction-consistent state in implementations of these schemes. Incomplete transactions have not affected the materialized database, and successful transactions have propagated indivisibly during EOT processing. However appealing the schemes may be in terms of crash recovery, the overhead during normal processing is too high to justify their use [Haerder and Reuter 1979; Reuter 1980].

There are, of course, other factors influencing the performance of a logging and recovery component: The granule of logging (pages or entries), the frequency of checkpoints (it depends on the transaction load), etc. are important. Logging is also tied to concurrency control in that the granule of logging determined the granule of locking. If page logging is applied, DBMS must not use smaller granules of locking than pages. However, a detailed discussion of these aspects is beyond the scope of this paper; detailed analyses can be found in Chandy et al. [1975] and Reuter [1982].

4. ARCHIVE RECOVERY

Throughout this paper we have focused on crash recovery, but in general there are two types of DB recovery, as is shown in Figure 18. The first path represents the standard crash recovery, depending on the physical (and the materialized) database as well as on the temporary log. If one of these is lost or corrupted because of hardware or software failure, the second path, archive recovery, must be tried. This presupposes that the components involved have independent failure modes, for example, if temporary and archive logs are kept on different devices. The global scenario for archive recovery is shown in Figure 19; it illustrates that the component "archive copy" actually depends on some dynamically modified subcomponents. These subcomponents create new archive copies and update existing ones. The following is a brief sketch of some problems associated with this.

Creating an archive copy, that is, copying the on-line version of the database, is a very expensive process. If the copy is to be consistent, update operation on the database has to be interrupted for a long time, which is unacceptable in many applications. Archive recovery is likely to be rare, and an archive copy should not be created too frequently, both because of cost and because there is a chance that it will never be used. On the other hand, if the archive copy is very old, recovery starting from such a copy will have to redo too much work and will take too long. There are two methods to cope with this. First, the database can be copied on the fly, that is, without inter-

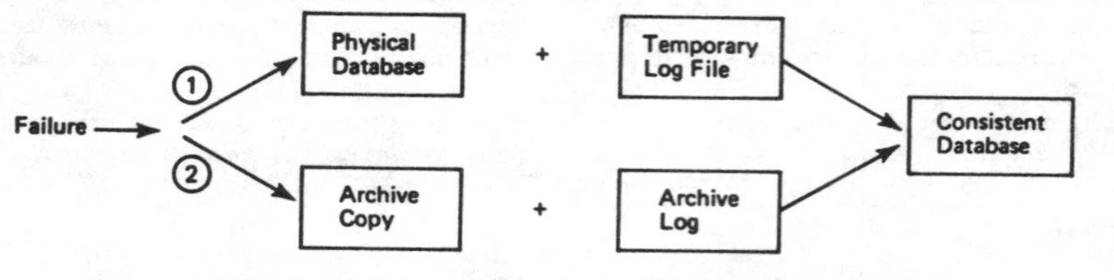

Figure 18. Two ways of DB recovery and the components involved.

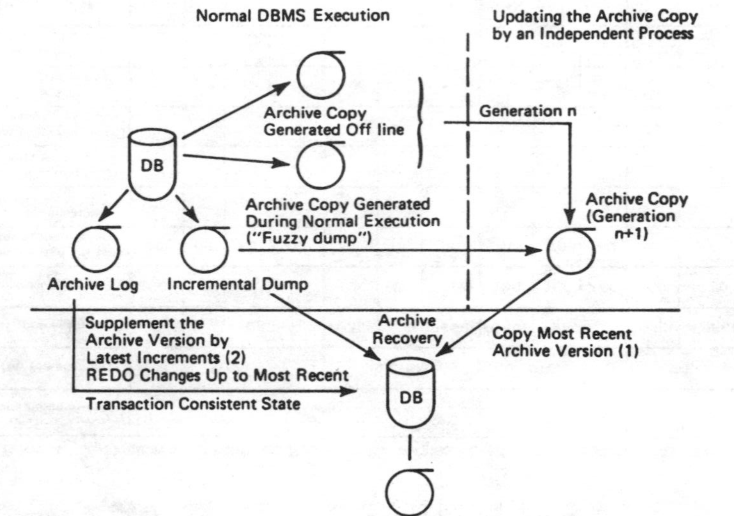

Figure 19. Scenario for archive recovery (global REDO).

rupting processing, in parallel with normal processing. This will create an inconsistent copy, a so-called "fuzzy dump."

The other possibility is to write only the changed pages to an incremental dump, since a new copy will be different from an old one only with respect to these pages. Either type of dump can be used to create a new, more up-to-date copy from the previous one. This is done by a separate off-line process with respect to the database and therefore does not affect DB operation. In the case of DB applications running 24 hours per day, this type of separate process is the only possible way to maintain archive recovery data. As shown in Figure 19, archive recovery in such an environment requires the most recent archive copy, the latest incremental modifications to it (if there are any), and the archive log. When recovering the database itself, there is little additional cost in creating an identical new archive copy in parallel.

There is still another problem hidden in this scenario: Since archive copies are needed very infrequently, they may be susceptible to magnetic decay. For this reason several generations of the archive copy are usually kept. If the most recent one does not work, its predecessor can be tried, and so on. This leads to the consequences illustrated in Figure 20.

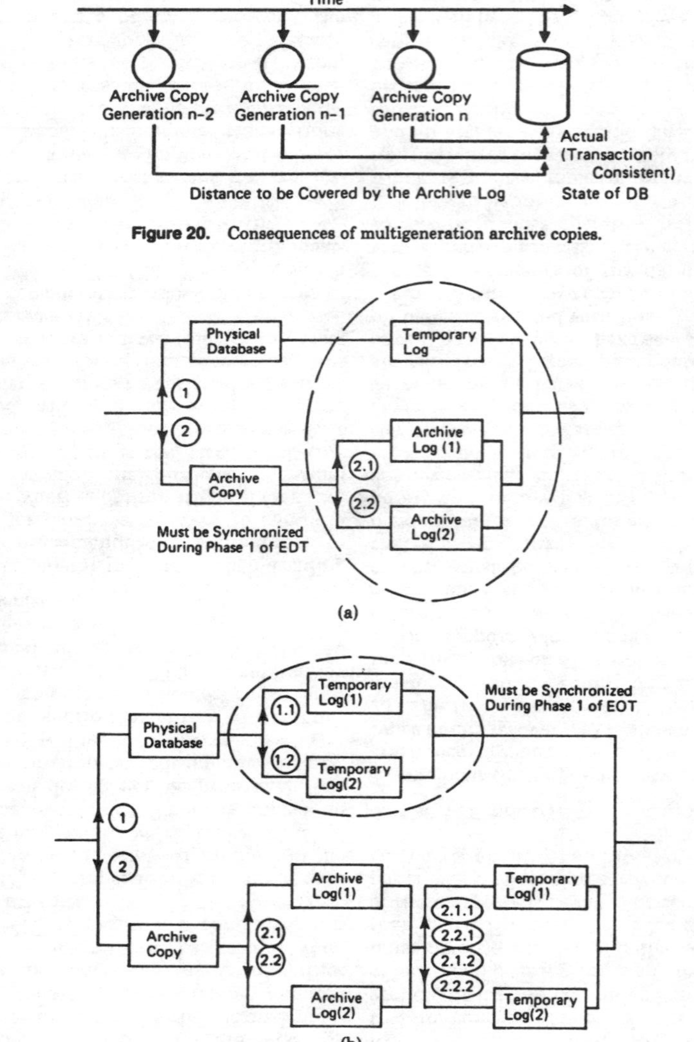

Figure 20. Consequences of multigeneration archive copies.

Figure 21. Two possibilities for duplicating the archive log.

We must anticipate the case of starting archive recovery from the *oldest* generation, and hence the archive log must span the whole distance back to this point in time. That makes the log susceptible to magnetic decay, as well, but in this case generations will not help; rather we have to duplicate the entire archive log file. Without taking storage costs into account, this has severe impact on normal DB processing, as is shown in Figure 21.

Figure 21a shows the straightforward solution: two archive log files that are kept on different devices. If this scheme is to work, all three log files must be in the same state at any point in time. In other words, writing to these files must be synchronized *at each EOT*. This adds substantial costs to normal processing and particularly affects transaction response times. The solution in Figure 21b assumes that *all log information* is written only to the temporary log during normal processing. An independent process that runs asynchronously then copies the REDO data to the archive log. Hence archive recovery finds most of the log entries in the archive log, but the temporary log is required for the most recent information. In such an environment, temporary and archive logs are no longer independent from a recovery perspective, and so we must make the temporary log very reliable by duplicating it. The resulting scenario looks much more complicated than the first one, but in fact the only additional costs are those for temporary log storage—which are usually small. The advantage here is that only two files have to be synchronized during EOT, and moreover—as numerical analysis shows—this environment is more reliable than the first one by a factor of 2.

These arguments do not, of course, exhaust the problem of archive recovery. Applications demanding very high availability and fast recovery from a media failure will use additional measures such as duplexing the whole database and all the hardware (e.g., see TANDEM [N.d.]). This aspect of database recovery does not add anything conceptually to the recovery taxonomy established in this paper.

5. CONCLUSION

We have presented a taxonomy for classifying the implementation techniques for database recovery. It is based on four criteria:

Propagation. We have shown that update propagation should be carefully distinguished from the write operation. The ATOMIC/¬ATOMIC dichotomy defines two different methods of handling low-level updates of the database, and also gives rise to different views of the database, both the materialized and the physical database. This proves to be useful in defining different crash states of a database.

Buffer Handling. We have shown that interfering with buffer replacement can support UNDO recovery. The STEAL/¬STEAL criterion deals with this concept.

EOT Processing. By distinguishing FORCE policies from ¬FORCE policies we can distinguish whether successful transactions will have to be redone after a crash. It can also be shown that this criterion heavily influences the DBMS performance during normal operation.

Checkpointing. Checkpoints have been introduced as a means for limiting the costs of partial REDO during crash recovery. They can be classified with regard to the events triggering checkpoint generation and the number of data written at a checkpoint. We have shown that each class has some particular performance characteristics.

Some existing DBMSs and implementation concepts have been classified and described according to the taxonomy. Since the criteria are relatively simple, each system can easily be assigned to the appropriate node of the classification tree. This classification is more than an ordering scheme for concepts: Once the parameters of a system are known, it is possible to draw important conclusions as to the behavior and performance of the recovery component.

ACKNOWLEDGMENTS

We would like to thank Jim Gray (TANDEM Computers, Inc.) for his detailed proposals concerning the structure and contents of this paper, and his enlightening discussions of logging and recovery. Thanks are also due to our colleagues Flaviu Cristian, Shel Finkelstein, C. Mohan, Kurt Shoens, and Irv Traiger (IBM Research Laboratory) for their encouraging comments and critical remarks.

REFERENCES

ASTRAHAN, M. M., BLASGEN, M. W., CHAMBERLIN, D. D., GRAY, J. N., KING, W. F., LINDSAY, B. G., LORIE, R., MEHL, J. W., PRICE, T. G., PUTZOLU, F., SELINGER, P. G., SCHKOLNICK, M., SLUTZ, D. R., TRAIGER, I. L., WADE, B. W., AND YOST, R. A. 1981. History and evaluation of System R. *Commun. ACM 24*, 10 (Oct.), 632–646.

BERNSTEIN, P. A., AND GOODMAN, N. 1981. Concurrency control in distributed database systems. *ACM Comput. Surv. 13*, 2 (June), 185–221.

BJORK, L. A. 1973. Recovery scenario for a DB/DC system. In *Proceedings of the ACM 73 National Conference* (Atlanta, Ga., Aug. 27–29). ACM, New York, pp. 142–146.

CHAMBERLIN, D. D. 1980. A summary of user experience with the SQL data sublanguage. In *Proceedings of the International Conference on Databases* (Aberdeen, Scotland, July), S. M. Deen and P. Hammersley, Eds. Heyden, London, pp. 181–203.

CHANDY, K. M., BROWN, J. C., DISSLEY, C. W., AND UHRIG, W. R. 1975. Analytic models for rollback and recovery strategies in data base systems. *IEEE Trans. Softw. Eng. SE-1*, 1 (Mar.), 100–110.

CHEN, T. C. 1978. Computer technology and the database user. In *Proceedings of the 4th International Conference on Very Large Database Systems* (Berlin, Oct.). IEEE, New York, pp. 72–86.

CODASYL 1973. *CODASYL DDL Journal of Development* June Report. Available from IFIP Administrative Data Processing Group, 40 Paulus Potterstraat, Amsterdam.

CODASYL 1978. CODASYL: Report of the Data Description Language Committee. *Inf. Syst. 3*, 4, 247–320.

CODD, E. F. 1982. Relational database: A practical foundation for productivity. *Commun. ACM 25*, 2 (Feb.), 109–117.

DATE, C. J. 1981. *An Introduction to Database Systems*, 3rd ed. Addison-Wesley, Reading, Mass.

DAVIES, C. T. 1973. Recovery semantics for a DB/DC System. In *Proceedings of the ACM 73 National Conference*, (Atlanta, Ga., Aug. 27–29). ACM, New York, pp. 136–141.

DAVIES, C. T. 1978. Data processing spheres of control. *IBM Syst. J. 17*, 2, 179–198.

EFFELSBERG, W., HAERDER, T., REUTER, A., AND SCHULZE-BOHL, J. 1981. Performance measurement in database systems—Modeling, interpretation and evaluation. In *Informatik Fachberichte 41*. Springer-Verlag, Berlin, pp. 279–293 (in German).

ELHARDT, K. 1982. The database cache—Principles of operation. Ph.D. dissertation, Technical University of Munich, Munich, West Germany (in German).

ESWARAN, K. P., GRAY, J. N., LORIE, R. A., AND TRAIGER, I. L. 1976. The notions of consistency and predicate locks in a database system. *Commun. ACM 19*, 11 (Nov.), 624–633.

GRAY, J. 1978. Notes on data base operating systems. In *Lecture Notes on Computer Science*, vol. 60, R. Bayer, R. N. Graham, and G. Seegmueller, Eds. Springer-Verlag, New York.

GRAY, J. 1981. The transaction concept: Virtues and limitations. In *Proceedings of the 7th International Conference on Very Large Database Systems* (Cannes, France, Sept. 9–11). ACM, New York, pp. 144–154.

GRAY, J., LORIE, R., PUTZOLU, F., AND TRAIGER, I. L. 1976. Granularity of locks and degrees of consistency in a large shared data base. In *Modeling in Data Base Management Systems*. Elsevier North-Holland, New York, pp. 365–394.

GRAY, J., MCJONES, P., BLASGEN, M., LINDSAY, B., LORIE, R., PRICE, T., PUTZOLU, F., AND TRAIGER, I. L. 1981. The recovery manager of the System R database manager. *ACM Comput. Surv. 13*, 2 (June), 223–242.

HAERDER, T., AND REUTER, A. 1979. Optimization of logging and recovery in a database system. In *Database Architecture*, G. Bracchi, Ed. Elsevier North-Holland, New York, pp. 151–168.

HAERDER, T., AND REUTER, A. 1983. Concepts for implementing a centralized database management system. In *Proceedings of the International Computing Symposium* (Invited Paper) (Nuernberg, W. Germany, Apr.), H. J. Schneider, Ed. German Chapter of ACM, B. G. Teubner, Stuttgart, pp. 28–60.

IMS/VS-DB N.d. IMS/VS-DB Primer, IBM World Trade Center, Palo Alto, July 1976.

KOHLER, W. H. 1981. A survey of techniques for synchronization and recovery in decentralized computer systems. *ACM Comput. Surv. 13*, 2 (June), 149–183.

LAMPSON, B. W., AND STURGIS, H. E. 1979. Crash recovery in a distributed data storage system. XEROX Res. Rep. Palo Alto, Calif. Submitted for publication.

LINDSAY, B. G., SELINGER, P. G., GALTIERI, C., GRAY, J. N., LORIE, R., PRICE, T. G., PUTZOLU, F., TRAIGER, I. L., AND WADE, B. W. 1979. Notes on distributed databases. IBM Res. Rep. RJ 2571, San Jose, Calif.

LORIE, R. A. 1977. Physical integrity in a large segmented database. *ACM Trans. Database Sys. 2*, 1 (Mar.), 91–104.

REUTER, A. 1980. A fast transaction-oriented logging scheme for UNDO-recovery. *IEEE Trans. Softw. Eng. SE-6* (July), 348–356.

REUTER, A. 1981. *Recovery in Database Systems*. Carl Hanser Verlag, Munich (in German).

REUTER, A. 1982. Performance Analysis of Recovery Techniques, Res. Rep., Computer Science Department, Univ. of Kaiserslautern, 1982. To be published.

SENKO, M. E., ALTMAN, E. B., ASTRAHAN, M. M., AND FEHBER, P. L. 1973. Data structures and accessing in data base systems. *IBM Syst. J. 12*, 1 (Jan.), 30–93.

SEVERANCE, D. G., AND LOHMAN, G. M. 1976. Differential files: Their application to the maintenance of large databases. *ACM Trans. Database Syst. 1*, 3 (Sept.), 256–267.

SMITH, D. D. P., AND SMITH, J. M. 1979. Relational database machines. *IEEE Comput. 12*, 3 28–38.

STONEBRAKER, M. 1980. Retrospection on a database system. *ACM Trans. Database Syst. 5*, 2 (June), 225–240.

STONEBRAKER, M., WONG, E., KREPS, P., AND HELD, G. 1976. The design and implementation of INGRES. *ACM Trans. Database Syst. 1*, 3 (Sept.), 189–222.

STURGIS, H., MITCHELL, J., AND ISRAEL, J. 1980. Issues in the design and use of a distributed file system. *ACM Oper. Syst. Rev. 14*, 3 (July), 55–69.

TANDEM. N.d. TANDEM 16, ENSCRIBE Data Base Record Manager, Programming Manual, TANDEM Computer Inc., Cupertino.

UDS, N.d. UDS, Universal Data Base Management System, UDS-V2 Reference Manual Package, Siemens AG, Munich, West Germany.

VERHOFSTADT, J. M. 1978. Recovery techniques for database systems. *ACM Comput. Surv. 10*, 2 (June), 167–195.

Operating System Support for Database Management

Michael Stonebraker
University of California, Berkeley

SUMMARY: Several operating system services are examined with a view toward their applicability to support of database management functions. These services include buffer pool management; the file system; scheduling, process management, and interprocess communication; and consistency control.

1. Introduction

Database management systems (DBMS) provide higher level user support than conventional operating systems. The DBMS designer must work in the context of the OS he/she is faced with. Different operating systems are designed for different use. In this paper we examine several popular operating system services and indicate whether they are appropriate for support of database management functions. Often we will see that the wrong service is provided or that severe performance problems exist. When possible, we offer some suggestions concerning improvements. In the next several sections we look at the services provided by buffer pool management; the file system; scheduling, process management, and interprocess communication; and consistency control. We then conclude with a discussion of the merits of including all files in a paged virtual memory.

The examples in this paper are drawn primarily from the UNIX operating system [17] and the INGRES relational database system [19, 20] which was designed for use with UNIX. Most of the points made for this environment have general applicability to other operating systems and data managers.

This research was sponsored by U.S. Air Force Office of Scientific Research Grant 78-3596, U.S. Army Research Office Grant DAAG29-76-G-0245, Naval Electronics Systems Command Contract N00039-78-G-0013, and National Science Foundation Grant MCS75-03839-A01.
Key words and phrases: database management, operating systems, buffer management, file systems, scheduling, interprocess communication
CR Categories: 3.50, 3.70, 4.22, 4.33, 4.34, 4.35
Author's address: M. Stonebraker, Dept. of Electrical Engineering and Computer Sciences, University of California, Berkeley, CA 94720.

2. Buffer Pool Management

Many modern operating systems provide a main memory cache for the file system. Figure 1 illustrates this service. In brief, UNIX provides a buffer pool whose size is set when the operating system is compiled. Then, all file I/O is handled through this cache. A file read (e.g., read X in Figure 1) returns data directly from a block in the cache, if possible; otherwise, it causes a block to be "pushed" to disk and replaced by the desired block. In Figure 1 we show block Y being pushed to make room for block X. A file write simply moves data into the cache; at some later time the buffer manager writes the block to the disk. The UNIX buffer manager used the popular LRU [15] replacement strategy. Finally, when UNIX detects sequential access to a file, it prefetches blocks before they are requested.

Conceptually, this service is desirable because blocks for which there is so-called *locality of reference* [15, 18] will remain in the cache over repeated reads and writes. However, the problems enumerated in the following subsections arise in using this service for database management.

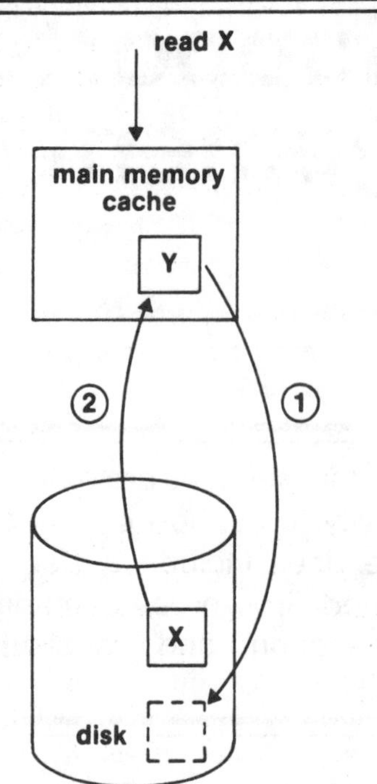

Fig. 1. Structure of a Cache.

2.1 Performance

The overhead to fetch a block from the buffer pool manager usually includes that of a system call and a core-to-core move. For UNIX on a PDP-11/70 the cost to fetch 512 bytes exceeds 5,000 instructions. To fetch 1 byte from the buffer pool requires about 1,800 instructions. It appears that these numbers are somewhat higher for UNIX than other contemporary operating systems. Moreover, they can be cut somewhat for VAX 11/780 hardware [10]. It is hoped that this trend toward lower overhead access will continue.

However, many DBMSs including INGRES [20] and System R [4] choose to put a DBMS managed buffer pool in user space to reduce overhead. Hence, each of these systems has gone to the trouble of constructing its own buffer pool manager to enhance performance.

In order for an operating system (OS) provided buffer pool manager to be attractive, the access overhead must be cut to a few hundred instructions. The trend toward providing the file system as a part of shared virtual memory (e.g., Pilot [16]) may provide a solution to this problem. This topic is examined in detail in Section 6.

2.2 LRU Replacement

Although the folklore indicates that LRU is a generally good tactic for buffer management, it appears to perform only marginally in a database environment. Database access in INGRES is a combination of:

(1) sequential access to blocks which will not be rereferenced;
(2) sequential access to blocks which will be cyclically rereferenced;
(3) random access to blocks which will not be referenced again;
(4) random access to blocks for which there is a nonzero probability of rereference.

Although LRU works well for case 4, it is a bad strategy for other situations. Since a DBMS knows which blocks are in each category, it can use a composite strategy. For case 4 it should use LRU while for 1 and 3 it should use *toss immediately.* For blocks in class 3 the reference pattern is 1, 2, 3, . . . , *n*, 1, 2, 3, ... Clearly, LRU is the worst possible replacement algorithm for this situation. Unless all *n* pages can be kept in the cache, the strategy should be to toss immediately. Initial studies [9] suggest that the miss ratio can be cut 10–15% by a DBMS specific algorithm.

In order for an OS to provide buffer management, some means must be found to allow it to accept "advice" from an application program (e.g., a DBMS) concerning the replacement strategy. Designing a clean buffer management interface with this feature would be an interesting problem.

2.3 Prefetch

Although UNIX correctly prefetches pages when sequential access is detected, there are important instances in which it fails.

Except in rare cases INGRES at (or very shortly after) the beginning of its examination of a block knows exactly which block it will access next. Unfortunately, this block is not necessarily the next one in logical file order. Hence, there is no way for an OS to implement the correct prefetch strategy.

2.4 Crash Recovery

An important DBMS service is to provide recovery from hard and soft crashes. The desired effect is for a unit of work (a transaction) which may be quite large and span multiple files to be either completely done or look like it had never started.

The way many DBMSs provide this service is to maintain an *intentions list.* When the intentions list is complete, a *commit flag* is set. The last step of a transaction is to process the intentions list making the actual updates. The DBMS makes the last operation idempotent (i.e., it generates the same final outcome no matter how many times the intentions list is processed) by careful programming. The general procedure is described in [6, 13]. An alternate process is to do updates as they are found and maintain a log of *before images* so that backout is possible.

During recovery from a crash the commit flag is examined. If it is set, the DBMS recovery utility processes the intentions list to correctly install the changes made by updates in progress at the time of the crash. If the flag is not set, the utility removes the intentions list, thereby backing out the transaction. The impact of crash recovery on the buffer pool manager is the following.

The page on which the commit flag exists must be forced to disk after all pages in the intentions list. Moreover, the transaction is not reliably committed until the commit flag is forced out to the disk, and no response can be given to the person submitting the transaction until this time.

The service required from an OS buffer manager is a *selected force out* which would push the intentions list and the commit flag to disk in the proper order. Such a service is not present in any buffer manager known to us.

2.5 Summary

Although it is possible to provide an OS buffer manager with the required features, none currently exists, at least to our knowledge. Designing such a facility with prefetch advice, block management advice, and selected force out would be an interesting exercise. It would be of interest in the context of both a paged virtual memory and an ordinary file system.

The strategy used by most DBMSs (for example, System R [4] and IMS [8]) is to maintain a separate cache in user space. This buffer pool is managed by a DBMS specific algorithm to circumvent the problems mentioned in this section. The result is a "not quite right" service provided by the OS going unused and a comparable application specific service being provided by the DBMS. Throughout this paper we will see variations on this theme in several service delivery areas.

3. The File System

The file system provided by UNIX supports objects (files) which are character arrays of dynamically varying size. On top of this abstraction, a DBMS can provide whatever higher level objects it wishes.

This is one of two popular approaches to file systems; the second is to provide a record management system inside the OS (e.g., RMS-11 for DEC machines or Enscribe for Tandem machines). In this approach structured files are provided (with or without variable length records). Moreover, efficient access is often supported for fetching records corresponding to a user supplied value (or key) for a designated field or fields. Multilevel directories, hashing, and secondary indexes are often used to provide this service.

The point to be made in this section is that the second service, which is what a DBMS wants, is not always efficient when constructed on top of a character array object. The following subsections explain why.

3.1 Physical Contiguity

The character array object can usually be expanded one block at a time. Often the result is blocks of a given file scattered over a disk volume. Hence, the next logical block in a file is not necessarily physically close to the previous one. Since a DBMS does considerable sequential access, the result is considerable disk arm movement.

The desired service is for blocks to be stored physically contiguous and a whole collection to be read when sequential access is desired. This naturally leads a DBMS to prefer a so-called extent based file system (e.g., VSAM [11]) to one which scatters blocks. Of course, such files must grow an extent at a time rather than a block at a time.

3.2 Tree Structured File Systems

UNIX implements two services by means of data structures which are trees. The blocks in a given file are kept track of in a tree (of indirect blocks) pointed to by a file control block (*i*-node). Second, the files in a given mounted file system have a user visible hierarchical structure composed of directories, subdirectories, etc. This is implemented by a second tree. A DBMS such as INGRES then adds a third tree structure to support keyed access via a multilevel directory structure (e.g., ISAM [7], B-trees [1, 12], VSAM [11], etc.).

Clearly, one tree with all three kinds of information is more efficient than three separately managed trees. The extra overhead for three separate trees is probably substantial.

3.3 Summary

It is clear that a character array is not a useful object to a DBMS. Rather, it is the abstraction presumably desired by language processors, editors, etc. Instead of providing records management on top of character arrays, it is possible to do the converse; the only issue is one of efficiency. Moreover, editors can possibly use records management structures as efficiently as those they create themselves [2]. It is our feeling that OS designers should contemplate providing DBMS facilities as lower level objects and character arrays as higher level ones. This philosophy has already been presented [5].

4. Scheduling, Process Management, and Interprocess Communication

Often, the simplest way to organize a multiuser database system is to have one OS process per user; i.e., each concurrent database user runs in a separate process. It is hoped that all users will share the same copy of the code segment of the database system and perhaps one or more data segments. In particular, a DBMS buffer pool and lock table should be handled as a shared segment. The above structure is followed by System R and, in part, by INGRES. Since UNIX has no shared data segments, INGRES must put the lock table inside the operating system and provide buffering private to each user.

The alternative organization is to allocate one run-time database process which acts as a *server*. All concurrent users send messages to this server with work requests. The one run-time server schedules requests through its own mechanisms and may support its own multitasking system. This organization is followed by Enscribe [21]. Figure 2 shows both possibilities.

Although Lauer [14] points out that the two methods are equally viable in a conceptual sense, the design of most operating systems strongly favors the first approach. For example, UNIX contains a message system (pipes) which is incompatible with the notion of a server process. Hence, it forces the use of the first alternative. There are at least two problems with the process-per-user approach.

4.1 Performance

Every time a run-time database process issues an I/O request that cannot be satisfied by data in the buffer pool, a task switch is inevita-

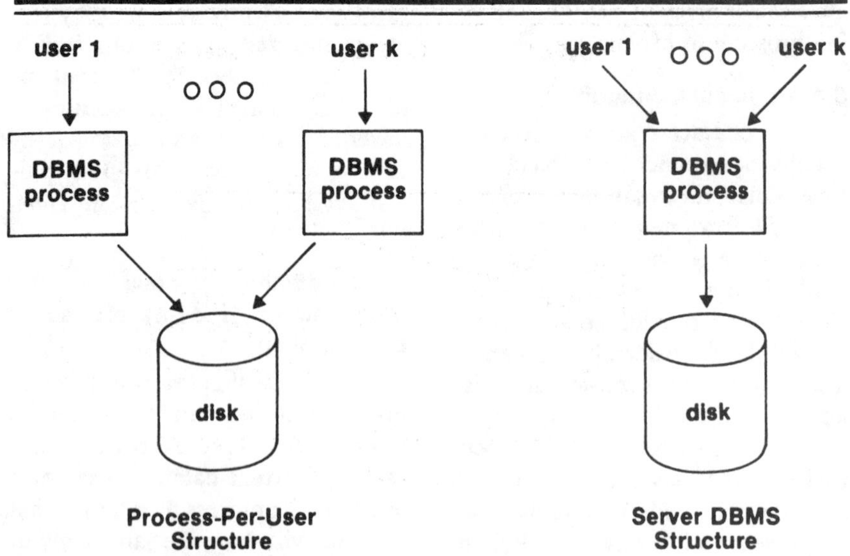

Fig. 2. Two Approaches to Organizing a Multiuser Database System.

ble. The DBMS suspends while waiting for required data and another process is run. It is possible to make task switches very efficiently, and some operating systems can perform a task switch in a few hundred instructions. However, many operating systems have "large" processes, i.e., ones with a great deal of state information (e.g., accounting) and a sophisticated scheduler. This tends to cause task switches costing a thousand instructions or more. This is a high price to pay for a buffer pool miss.

4.2 Critical Sections

Blasgen [3] has pointed out that some DBMS processes have critical sections. If the buffer pool is a shared data segment, then portions of the buffer pool manager are necessarily critical sections. System R handles critical sections by setting and releasing short-term locks which basically simulate semaphores. A problem arises if the operating system scheduler deschedules a database process while it is holding such a lock. All other database processes cannot execute very long without accessing the buffer pool. Hence, they quickly queue up behind the locked resource. Although the probability of this occurring is low, the resulting convoy [3] has a devastating effect on performance.

As a result of these two problems with the process-per-user model, one might expect the server model to be especially attractive. The following subsection explores this point of view.

4.3 The Server Model

A server model becomes viable if the operating system provides a message facility which allows *n* processes to originate messages to a single destination process. However, such a server must do its own scheduling and multitasking. This involves a painful duplication of operating system facilities. In order to avoid such duplication, one must resort to the following tactics.

One can avoid multitasking and a scheduler by a first-come-first-served server with no internal parallelism. A work request would be read from the message system and executed to completion before the next one was started. This approach makes little sense if there is more than one physical disk. Each work request will tend to have one disk read outstanding at any instant. Hence, at most one disk will be active with a non-multitasking server. Even with a single disk, a long work request will be processed to completion while shorter requests must wait. The penalty on average response time may be considerable [18].

To achieve internal parallelism yet avoid multitasking, one could have user processes send work requests to one of perhaps several common servers as noted in Figure 3. However, such servers would have to share a lock table and are only slightly different from the shared code process-per-user model. Alternately, one could have a collection of servers, each of which would send low-level requests to a group of disk processes which actually peform the I/O and handle locking as suggested in Figure 4. A disk process would process requests in first-in-first-out order. Although this organization appears potentially desirable, it still may have the response time penalty mentioned above. Moreover, it results in one message per I/O request. In reality one has traded a task switch per I/O for a message per I/O; the latter may turn out to be more expensive than the former. In the next subsection, we discuss message costs in more detail.

4.4 Performance of Message Systems

Although we have never been offered a good explanation of why messages are so expensive, the fact remains that in most operating systems the cost for a round-trip message is several thousand instructions. For example, in PDP-11/70 UNIX the number is about 5,000. As a result, care must be exercised in a DBMS to avoid overuse of a facility that is not cheap. Consequently, viable DBMS organizations will sometimes be rejected because of excessive message overhead.

4.5 Summary

There appears to be no way out of the scheduling dilemma; both the server model and the individual process model seem unattractive. The basic problem is at least, in part, the overhead in some operating systems of task switches and messages. Either operating system designers must make these facilities cheaper or provide special *fast path* functions for DBMS consumers. If this does not happen, DBMS designers will presumably continue the present prac-

COMPUTING PRACTICES

tice: implementing their own multitasking, scheduling, and message systems entirely in user space. The result is a "mini" operating system running in user space in addition to a DBMS.

One ultimate solution to task-switch overhead might be for an operating system to create a special scheduling class for the DBMS and other "favored" users. Processes in this class would never be forcibly descheduled but might voluntarily relinquish the CPU at appropriate intervals. This would solve the convoy problem mentioned in Section 4.2. Moreover, such special processes might also be provided with a fast path through the task switch/scheduler loop to pass control to one of their sibling processes. Hence, a DBMS process could pass control to another DBMS process at low overhead.

5. Consistency Control

The services provided by an operating system in this area include the ability to lock objects for shared or exclusive access and support for crash recovery. Although most operating systems provide locking for files, there are fewer which support finer granularity locks, such as those on pages or records. Such smaller locks are deemed essential in some database environments.

Moreover, many operating systems provide some cleanup after crashes. If they do not offer support for database transactions as discussed in Section 2.4, then a DBMS must provide transaction crash recovery on top of whatever is supplied.

It has sometimes been suggested that both concurrency control and crash recovery for transactions be provided entirely inside the operating system (e.g., [13]). Conceptually, they should be at least as efficient as if provided in user space. The only problem with this approach is buffer management. If a DBMS provides buffer management in addition to whatever is supplied by the operating system, then transaction management by the operating system is impacted as discussed in the following subsections.

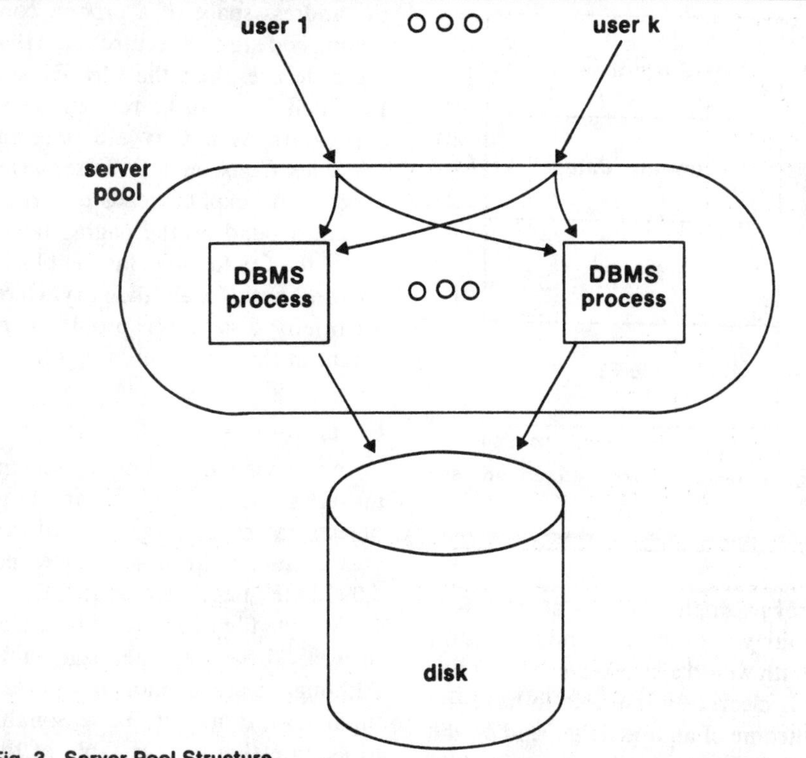

Fig. 3. Server Pool Structure.

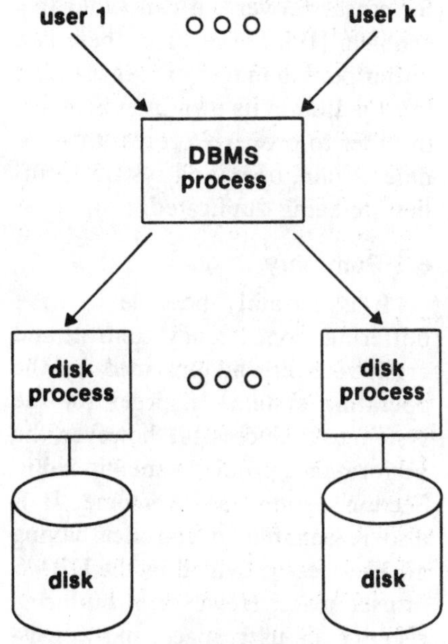

Fig. 4. Disk Server Structure.

5.1 Commit Point

When a database transaction commits, a user space buffer manager must ensure that all appropriate blocks are flushed and a commit delivered to the operating system. Hence, the buffer manager cannot be immune from knowledge of transactions, and operating system functions are duplicated.

5.2 Ordering Dependencies

Consider the following employee data:

Empname	*Salary*	*Manager*
Smith	10,000	Brown
Jones	9,000	None
Brown	11,000	Jones

and the update which gives a 20% pay cut to all employees who earn more than their managers. Presumably, Brown will be the only employee to receive a decrease, although there are alternative semantic definitions.

Suppose the DBMS updates the data set as it finds "overpaid" employees, depending on the operating system to provide backout or recover-forward on crashes. If so,

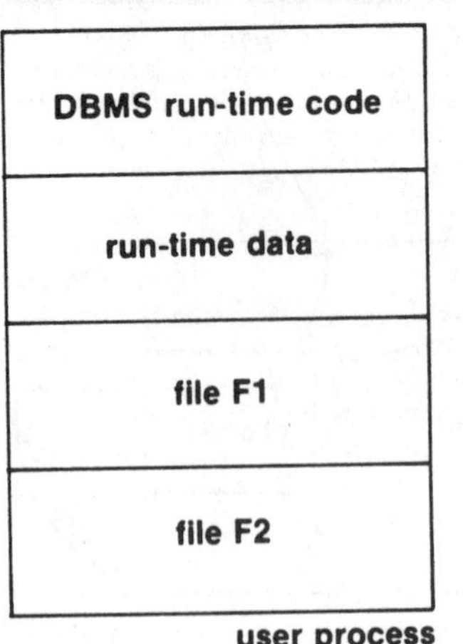

Fig. 5. Binding Files into an Address Space.

Brown might be updated before Smith was examined, and as a result, Smith would also receive the pay cut. It is clearly undesirable to have the outcome of an update depend on the order of execution.

If the operating system maintains the buffer pool and an intentions list for crash recovery, it can avoid this problem [19]. However, if there is a buffer pool manager in user space, it must maintain its own intentions list in order to properly process this update. Again, operating system facilities are being duplicated.

5.3 Summary

It is certainly possible to have buffering, concurrency control, and crash recovery all provided by the operating system. In order for the system to be successful, however, the performance problems mentioned in Section 2 must be overcome. It is also reasonable to consider having all 3 services provided by the DBMS in user space. However, if buffering remains in user space and consistency control does not, then much code duplication appears inevitable. Presumably, this will cause performance problems in addition to increased human effort.

6. Paged Virtual Memory

It is often claimed that the appropriate operating system tactic for database management support is to bind files into a user's paged virtual address space. In Figure 5 we show the address space of a process containing code to be executed, data that the code uses, and the files F1 and F2. Such files can be referenced by a program as if they are program variables. Consequently, a user never needs to do explicit reads or writes; he can depend on the paging facilities of the OS to move his file blocks into and out of main memory. Here, we briefly discuss the problems inherent in this approach.

6.1 Large Files

Any virtual memory scheme must handle files which are large objects. Popular paging hardware creates an overhead of 4 bytes per 4,096-byte page. Consequently, a 100M-byte file will have an overhead of 100K bytes for the page table. Although main memory is decreasing in cost, it may not be reasonable to assume that a page table of this size is entirely resident in primary memory. Therefore, there is the possibility that an I/O operation will induce two page faults: one for the page containing the page table for the data in question and one on the data itself. To avoid the second fault, one must *wire down* a large page table in main memory.

Conventional file systems include the information contained in the page table in a file control block. Especially in extent-based file systems, a very compact representation of this information is possible. A run of 1,000 consecutive blocks can be represented as a starting block and a length field. However, a page table for this information would store each of the 1,000 addresses even though each differs by just one from its predecessor. Consequently, a file control block is usually made main memory resident at the time the file is opened. As a result, the second I/O need never be paid.

The alternative is to bind *chunks* of a file into one's address space. Not only does this provide a multiuser DBMS with a substantial bookkeeping problem concerning whether needed data is currently addressable, but it also may require a number of bind-unbind pairs in a transaction. Since the overhead of a bind is likely to be comparable to that of a file open, this may substantially slow down performance.

It is an open question whether or not novel paging organizations can assist in solving the problems mentioned in this section.

6.2 Buffering

All of the problems discussed in Section 2 concerning buffering (e.g., prefetch, non-LRU management, and selected force out) exist in a paged virtual memory context. How they can be cleanly handled in this context is another unanswered question.

7. Conclusions

The bottom line is that operating system services in many existing systems are either too slow or inappropriate. Current DBMSs usually provide their own and make little or no use of those offered by the operating system. It is important that future operating system designers become more sensitive to DBMS needs.

A DBMS would prefer a small efficient operating system with only desired services. Of those currently available, the so-called *real-time* operating systems which efficiently provide minimal facilities come closest to this ideal. On the other hand, most general-purpose operating systems offer all things to all people at much higher overhead. It is our hope that future operating systems will be able to provide both sets of services in one environment.

References

1. Bayer, R. Organization and maintenance of large ordered indices. Proc. ACM-SIGFIDET Workshop on Data Description and Access, Houston, Texas, Nov. 1970. This paper defines a particular form of a balanced *n*-ary tree, called a B-tree. Algorithms to maintain this structure on inserts and deletes are presented. The original paper on this popular file organization tactic.

2. Birss, E. Hewlett-Packard Corp., General Syst. Div. (private communication).

3. Blasgen, M., et al. The convoy phenomenon. *Operating Systs. Rev. 13*, 2 (April 1979), 20–25. This article points out the problem with descheduling a process which has a short-term lock on an object which other processes require regularly. The impact on performance is noted and possible solutions proposed.

COMPUTING PRACTICES

4. Blasgen, M., et al. System R: An architectural update. Rep. RJ 2581, IBM Res. Ctr., San Jose, Calif., July 1979. Blasgen describes the architecture of System R, a novel full function relational database manager implemented at IBM Research. The discussion centers on the changes made since the original System R paper was published in 1976.

5. Epstein, R., and Hawthorn, P. Design decisions for the Intelligent Database Machine. Proc. Nat. Comptr. Conf., Anaheim, Calif., May 1980, pp. 237–241. An overview of the philosophy of the Intelligent Database Machine is presented. This system provides a database manager on a dedicated "back end" computer which can be attached to a variety of host machines.

6. Gray, J. Notes on operating systems. Report RJ 3120, IBM Res. Ctr., San Jose, Calif., Oct. 1978. A definitive report on locking and recovery in a database system. It pulls together most of the ideas on these subjects including two-phase protocols, write ahead log, and variable granularity locks. Should be read every six months by anyone interested in these matters.

7. IBM Corp. *OS ISAM Logic.* GY28-6618, IBM, White Plains, N.Y., June 1966.

8. IBM Corp. *IMS-VS General Information Manual.* GH20-1260, IBM, White Plains, N.Y., April 1974.

9. Kaplan, J. Buffer management policies in a database system. M.S. Th., Univ. of Calif., Berkeley, Calif., 1980. This thesis simulates various non-LRU buffer management policies on traced data obtained from the INGRES database system. It concludes that the miss rate can be cut 10–15% by a DBMS specific algorithm compared to LRU management.

10. Kashtan, D. UNIX and VMS: Some performance comparisons. SRI Internat., Menlo Park, Calif. (unpublished working paper). Kashtan's paper contains benchmark timings of operating system commands in UNIX and VMS for DEC PDP-11/780 computers. These include timings of file reads, event flags, task switches, and pipes.

11. Keehn, D., and Lacy, J. VSAM data set design parameters. *IBM Systs. J.* (Sept. 1974).

12. Knuth, D. *The Art of Computer Programming, Vol. 3: Sorting and Searching.* Addison Wesley, Reading, Mass., 1978.

13. Lampson, B., and Sturgis, H. Crash recovery in a distributed system. Xerox Res. Ctr., Palo Alto, Calif., 1976 (working paper). The first paper to present the now popular two-phase commit protocol. Also, an interesting model of computer system crashes is discussed and the notion of "safe" storage suggested.

14. Lauer, H., and Needham, R. On the duality of operating system structures. *Operating Systs. Rev. 13*, 2 (April 1979), 3–19. This article explores in detail the "process-per-user" approach to operating systems versus the "server model." It argues that they are inherently dual of each other and that either should be implementable as efficiently as the other. Very interesting reading.

15. Mattson, R., et al. Evaluation techniques for storage hierarchies. *IBM Systs. J.* (June 1970). Discusses buffer management in detail. The paper presents and analyzes serveral policies including FIFO, LRU, OPT, and RANDOM.

16. Redell, D., et al. Pilot: An operating system for a personal computer. *Comm. ACM 23*, 2 (Feb. 1980), 81–92. Redell et al. focus on Pilot, the operating system for Xerox Alto computers. It is closely coupled with Mesa and makes interesting choices in areas like protection that are appropriate for a personal computer.

17. Ritchie, D., and Thompson, K. The UNIX time-sharing system. *Comm. ACM 17*, 7 (July 1974), 365–375. The original paper describing UNIX, an operating system for PDP-11 computers. Novel points include accessing files, physical devices, and pipes in a uniform way and running the command-line interpreter as a user program. Strongly recommended reading.

18. Shaw, A. *The Logical Design of Operating Sysetms.* Prentice-Hall, Englewood Cliffs, N.J. 1974.

19. Stonebraker, M., et al. The design and implementation of INGRES. *ACM Trans. Database Systs. 1*, 3 (Sept. 1976), 189–222. The original paper describing the structure of the INGRES database management system, a relational data manager for PDP-11 computers.

20. Stonebraker, M. Retrospection on a database system. *ACM Trans. Database Systs. 5*, 2 (June 1980), 225–240. A self-critique of the INGRES system by one of its designers. The article discusses design flaws in the system and indicates the historical progression of the project.

21. Tandem Computers. *Enscribe Reference Manual.* Tandem, Cupertino, Calif., Aug. 1979.

An Evaluation of Buffer Management Strategies for Relational Database Systems

Hong-Tai Chou[†]
David J. DeWitt

Computer Sciences Department
University of Wisconsin

ABSTRACT

In this paper we present a new algorithm, DBMIN, for managing the buffer pool of a relational database management system. DBMIN is based on a new model of relational query behavior, the **query locality set model** (QLSM). Like the hot set model, the QLSM has an advantage over the stochastic models due to its ability to predict future reference behavior. However, the QLSM avoids the potential problems of the hot set model by separating the modeling of reference behavior from any particular buffer management algorithm. After introducing the QLSM and describing the DBMIN algorithm, we present a performance evaluation methodology for evaluating buffer management algorithms in a multiuser environment. This methodology employed a hybrid model that combines features of both trace driven and distribution driven simulation models. Using this model, the performance of the DBMIN algorithm in a multiuser environment is compared with that of the hot set algorithm and four more traditional buffer replacement algorithms.

1. Introduction

In this paper we present a new algorithm, DBMIN, for managing the buffer pool of a relational database management system. DBMIN is based on a new model of relational query behavior, the **query locality set model** (QLSM). Like the hot set model [Sacc82], the QLSM has an advantage over the stochastic models due to its ability to predict future reference behavior. However, the QLSM avoids the potential problems of the hot set model by separating the modeling of reference behavior from any particular buffer management algorithm. After introducing the QLSM and describing the DBMIN algorithm, the performance of the DBMIN algorithm in a multiuser environment is compared with that of the hot set algorithm and four more traditional buffer replacement algorithms.

[†]Author's current address is: Microelectronics and Computer Technology Corporation, 9430 Research Blvd., Echelon Bldg. #1, Austin, TX 78759.

A number of factors motivated this research. First, although Stonebraker [Ston81] convincingly argued that conventional virtual memory page replacement algorithms (e.g. LRU) were generally not suitable for a relational database environment, the area of buffer management has, for the most part, been ignored (contrast the activity in this area with that in the concurrency control area). Second, while the hot set results were encouraging they were, in our opinion, inconclusive. In particular, [Sacc82] [Sacc85] presented only limited simulation results of the hot set algorithm. We felt that extensive, multiuser tests of the hot set algorithm and conventional replacement policies would provide valuable insight into the effect of the buffer manager on overall system performance.

In Section 2, we review earlier work on buffer management strategies for database systems. The QLSM and DBMIN algorithm are described in Section 3. Our multiuser performance evaluation of alternative buffer replacement policies is presented in Section 4. Section 5 contains our conclusions and suggestions for future research.

2. Buffer Management for Database Systems

While many of the early studies on database buffer management focused on the double paging problem [Fern78] [Lang77] [Sher76a] [Sher76b] [Tuel76], recent research efforts have been focused on finding buffer management policies that "understand" database systems [Ston81] and know how to exploit the predictability of database reference behavior. We review some of these algorithms in this section.

2.1. Domain Separation Algorithms

Consider a query that randomly accesses records through a B-tree index. The root page of the B-tree is obviously more important than a data page, since it is accessed with every record retrieval. Based on this observation, Reiter [Reit76] proposed a buffer management algorithm, called the **domain separation** (DS) algorithm, in which pages are classified into types, each of which is separately managed in its associated domain of buffers. When a page of a certain type is needed, a buffer is allocated from the corresponding domain. If none are available for some reason, e.g. all the buffers in that domain have I/O in progress, a buffer is borrowed from another domain. Buffers inside each domain are managed by the LRU discipline. Reiter suggested a simple type assignment scheme: assign one domain to each non-leaf level of the B-tree structure, and one to the leaf level together with the data. Empirical data[1] showed that this DS algorithm provided 8-10% improvement in throughput when compared with an LRU algorithm.

The main limitation of the DS algorithm is that its concept of domain is static. The algorithm fails to reflect the dynamics of page references as the importance of a page may vary in different queries. It is obviously desirable to keep a data page resident when it is being repeatedly accessed in a nested loops join. However, it is not the case when the same page is accessed in a sequential scan. Second, the DS algorithm does not differentiate the relative importance between different types of pages. An index page will be over-written by another incoming index page under the DS algorithm, although the index page is potentially more important than a data page in another domain. Memory partitioning is another potential problem. Partitioning buffers according to domains, rather than queries, does not prevent interference among competing users. Lastly, a separate mechanism needs to be incorporated to prevent thrashing since the DS algorithm has no built-in facilities for load control.

Several extensions to the DS algorithm have been proposed. The group LRU (GLRU) algorithm, proposed by Hawthorn [Nybe84], is similar to DS, except that there exists a fixed priority ranking among different groups (domains). A search for a free buffer always starts from the group with the lowest priority. Another alternative, presented by Effelsberg and Haerder [Effe84], is to dynamically vary the size of each domain using a working-set-like [Denn68] partitioning scheme. Under this scheme, pages in domain **i** which have been referenced in the last τ_i references are exempt from replacement consideration. The "working set" of each domain may grow or shrink depending on the reference behavior of the user queries. Although empirical data indicated that dynamic domain partitioning can reduce the number of page faults (of the system) over static domain partitioning, Effelsberg and Haerder concluded that there is no convincing evidence that the page-type-oriented schemes[2] are distinctly superior to global algorithms, such as LRU and CLOCK.

2.2. "New" Algorithm

In a study to find a better buffer management algorithm for INGRES [Ston76], Kaplan [Kapl80] made two observations from the reference patterns of queries: the priority to be given to a page is not a property of the page itself but of the relation to which it belongs; each relation needs a "working set". Based on these observations, Kaplan designed an algorithm, called the "new" algorithm, in which the buffer pool is subdivided and allocated on a per-relation basis. In this "new" algorithm, each active relation is assigned a resident set which is initially empty. The resident sets of relations are linked in a priority list with a global free list on the top. When a page fault occurs, a search is initiated from the top of the priority list until a suitable buffer is found. The faulting page is then brought into the buffer and added to the resident set of the relation. The MRU discipline is employed within each relation. However, each relation is entitled to one active buffer which is exempt from replacement consideration. The ordering of relations is determined, and may be adjusted subsequently, by a set of heuristics. A relation is placed near the top if its pages are unlikely to be re-used. Otherwise, the relation is protected at the bottom. Results from Kaplan's simulation experiments suggested that the "new" algorithm performed much better than the UNIX buffer manager. However, in a trial implementation [Ston82], the "new" algorithm failed to improve the performance of an experimental version of INGRES which uses an LRU algorithm.

The "new" algorithm presented a new approach to buffer management, an approach that tracks the locality of a query through relations. However, the algorithm itself has several weak points. The use of MRU is justifiable only in limited cases. The rules suggested by Kaplan for arranging the order of relations on the priority list were based solely on intuition. Furthermore,

[1] In Reiter's simulation experiments, a shared buffer pool and a workload consisting of 8 concurrent users were assumed.

[2] The DS algorithm is called a page-type-oriented buffer allocation scheme in [Effe84].

under high memory contention, searching through a priority list for a free buffer can be expensive. Finally, extending the "new" algorithm to a multi-user environment presents additional problems as it is not clear how to establish priority among relations from different queries that are running concurrently.

2.3. Hot Set Algorithm

The hot set model proposed by Sacco and Schkolnick [Sacc82] is a query behavior model for relational database systems that integrates advance knowledge on reference patterns into the model. In this model, a set of pages over which there is a looping behavior is called a **hot set**. If a query is given a buffer large enough to hold the hot sets, its processing will be efficient as the pages referenced in a loop will stay in the buffer. On the other hand, a large number of page faults may result if the memory allocated to a query is insufficient to hold a hot set. Plotting the number of page faults as a function of buffer size, we can observe a discontinuity around the buffer size where the above scenario takes place. There may be several such discontinuities in the curve, each is called a **hot point**.

In a nested loops join in which there is a sequential scan on both relations, a hot point of the query is the number of pages in the inner relation plus one. The formula is derived by reserving enough buffers to hold the entire inner relation, which will be repeatedly scanned, plus one buffer for the outer relation, which will be scanned only once. If, instead, the scan on the outer relation is an index scan, an additional buffer is required for the leaf pages of the index. Following similar arguments, the hot points for different queries can be determined.

Applying the predictability of reference patterns in queries, the hot set model provides a more accurate reference model for relational database systems than a stochastic model. However, the derivation of the hot set model is based partially on an LRU replacement algorithm, which is inappropriate for certain looping behavior. In fact, the MRU (Most-Recently-Used) algorithm, the opposite to an LRU algorithm, is more suited for cycles of references [Thor72], because the most-recently-used page in a loop is the one that will not be re-accessed for the longest period of time. Going back to the nested loops join example, the number of page faults will not increase dramatically when the number of buffers drops below the "hot point" if the MRU algorithm is used. In this respect, the hot set model does not truly reflect the inherent behavior of some reference patterns, but rather the behavior under an LRU algorithm.

In the hot set (HOT) algorithm, each query is provided a separate list of buffers managed by an LRU discipline. The number of buffers each query is entitled to is predicted according to the hot set model. That is, a query is given a local buffer pool of size equal to its **hot set size**. A new query is allowed to enter the system if its hot set size does not exceed the available buffer space.

As discussed above, the use of LRU in the hot set model lacks a logical justification. There exist cases where LRU is the worse possible discipline under tight memory constraint. The hot set algorithm avoids this problem by always allocating enough memory to ensure that references to different data structures within a query will not interfere with one another. Thus it tends to over-allocate memory, which implies that memory may be under-utilized. Another related problem is that there are reference patterns in which LRU does perform well but is unnecessary since another discipline with a lower overhead can perform equally well.

3. The DBMIN Buffer Management Algorithm

In this section, we first introduce a new query behavior model, the **query locality set model** (QLSM), for database systems. Using a classification of page reference patterns, we show how the reference behavior of common database operations can be described as a composition of a set of simple and regular reference patterns. Like the hot set model, the QLSM has an advantage over the stochastic models due to its ability to predict future reference behavior. However, the QLSM avoids the potential problems of the hot set model by separating the modeling of reference behavior from any particular buffer management algorithm.

Next we describe a new buffer management algorithm termed DBMIN based on the QLSM. In this algorithm, buffers are allocated and managed on a **per file instance** basis. Each file instance is given a local buffer pool to hold its **locality set**, which is the set of the buffered pages associated the file instance. DBMIN can be viewed as a combination of a working set algorithm [Denn68] and Kaplan's "new" algorithm in the sense that the locality set associated with each file instance is similar to the working set associated with each process. However, the size of a locality set is determined in advance, and needs not be re-calculated as the execution of the query progresses. This predictive nature of DBMIN is close to that of the hot set algorithm. Similar to the WS and the hot set algorithm[3], DBMIN uses a dynamic partitioning scheme, in

[3] The issue of memory partitioning was not clearly addressed in [Sacc82]. However, it was later shown in [Sacc85] how dynamic memory partitioning can be achieved by decomposing a query into sub-evaluation plans, each of which is independently characterized by the hot set model.

which the total number of buffers assigned to a query may vary as files (relations) are opened and closed.

3.1. The Query Locality Set Model

The QLSM is based on the observation that relational database systems support a limited set of operations and that the pattern of page references exhibited by these operations are very regular and predictable. In addition, the reference pattern of a database operation can be decomposed into the composition of a number of simple reference patterns. Consider, for example, an index join with an index on the joining attribute of the inner relation. The QLSM will identify two locality sets for this operation: one for the sequential scan of the outer relation and a second for the index and data pages of the inner relation. In this section, we present a taxonomy for classifying the page reference patterns exhibited by common access methods and database operations[4].

Sequential References

In a sequential scan, pages are referenced and processed one after another. In many cases, a sequential scan is done only once without repetition. For example, during a selection operation on an unordered relation, each page in the file is accessed exactly once. A single page frame provides all the buffer space that is required. We shall refer to such a reference pattern as **straight sequential** (SS).

Local re-scans may be observed in the course of a sequential scan during certain database operations. That is, once in a while, a scan may back up a short distance and then start forward again. This can happen in a merge join [Blas77] in which records with the same key value in the inner relation are repeatedly scanned and matched with those in the outer relation. We shall call this pattern of reference **clustered sequential** (CS). Obviously, records in a cluster (a set of records with the same key value) should be kept in memory at the same time if possible.

In some cases, a sequential reference to a file may be repeated several times. In a nested loops join, for instance, the inner relation is repeatedly scanned until the outer relation is exhausted. We shall call this a **looping sequential** (LS) pattern. The entire file that is being repeatedly scanned should be kept in memory if possible. If the file is too large to fit in memory, an MRU replacement algorithm should be used to manage the buffer pool.

[4] A similar analysis of query reference behavior was independently derived in [Sacc85].

Random References

An **independent random** (IR) reference pattern consists a series of independent accesses. As an example, during an index scan through a non-clustered index, the data pages are accessed in a random manner. There are also cases when a locality of reference exists in a series of "random" accesses. This may happen in the evaluation of a join in which a file with a non-clustered and non-unique index is used as the inner relation, while the outer relation is a clustered file with non-unique keys. This pattern of reference is termed **clustered random** (CR). The reference behavior of a CR reference is similar to that of a CS scan. If possible, each page containing a record in a cluster should be kept in memory.

Hierarchical References

A hierarchical reference is a sequence of page accesses that form a traversal path from the root down to the leaves of an index. If the index is traversed only once (e.g. when retrieving a single tuple), one page frame is enough for buffering all the index pages. We shall call this a **straight hierarchical** (SH) reference. There are two cases in which a tree traversal is followed by a sequential scan through the leaves: **hierarchical with straight sequential** (H/SS), if the scan on the leaves is SS, or **hierarchical with clustered sequential** (H/CS), otherwise. Note that the reference patterns of an H/SS reference and an H/CS reference are similar to those of an SS reference and a CS reference, respectively.

During the evaluation of a join in which the inner relation is indexed on the join field, repeated accesses to the index structure may be observed. We shall call this pattern of reference as **looping hierarchical** (LH). In an LH reference, pages closer to the root are more likely to be accessed than those closer to the leaves. The access probability of an index page at level **i**, assuming the root is at level **0**, is inversely proportional to the ith power of the fan-out factor of an index page. Therefore, pages at an upper level (which are closer to the root) should have higher priority than those at a lower level. In many cases, the root is perhaps the only page worth keeping in memory since the fan-out of an index page is usually high.

3.2. DBMIN - A Buffer Management Algorithm Based on the QLSM

In the DBMIN algorithm, buffers are allocated and managed on a **per file instance** basis[5]. The set of

[5] Active instances of the same file are given different buffer pools, which are independently managed. However, as we will explain later, all the file instances share the same copy of a buffered page whenever possible through a global table mechanism.

buffered pages associated with a file instance is referred to as its **locality set**. Each locality set is separately managed by a discipline selected according to the intended usage of the file instance. If a buffer contains a page that does not belong to any locality set, the buffer is placed on a global free list. For simplicity of implementation, we restrict that a page in the buffer can belong to at most one locality set. A file instance is considered the owner of all the pages in its locality set. To allow for data sharing among concurrent queries, all the buffers in memory are also accessible through a global buffer table. The following notation will be used in describing the algorithm:

N - the total number of buffers (page frames) in the system;

l_{ij} - the maximum number of buffers that can be allocated to file instance **j** of query **i**;

r_{ij} - the number of buffers allocated to file instance **j** of query **i**.

Note that **l** is the desired size for a locality set while **r** is the actual size of a locality set.

At start up time, DBMIN initializes the global table and links all the buffers in the system on the global free list. When a file is opened, its associated locality set size and replacement policy are given to the buffer manager. An empty locality set is then initialized for the file instance. The two control variables **r** and **l** associated with the file instance are initialized to 0 and the given locality set size, respectively.

When a page is requested by a query, a search is made to the global table, followed by an adjustment to the associated locality set. There are three possible cases:

(1) **The page is found in both the global table and the locality set:** In this case, only the usage statistics need to be updated if necessary as determined by the local replacement policy.

(2) **The page is found in memory but not in the locality set:** If the page already has an owner, the page is simply given to the requesting query and no further actions are required. Otherwise, the page is added to the locality set of the file instance, and **r** is incremented by one. Now if **r > l**, a page is chosen and released back to the global free list according to the local replacement policy, and **r** is set to **l**. Usage statistics are updated as required by the local replacement policy.

(3) **The page is not in memory:** A disk read is scheduled to bring the page from disk into a buffer allocated from the global free list. After the page is brought into memory, proceed as in case 2.

Note that the local replacement policies associated with file instances do not cause actual swapping of pages. Their real purpose is to maintain the image of a query's "working set". Disk reads and writes are issued by the mechanism that maintains the global table and the global free list.

The load controller is activated when a file is opened or closed. Immediately after a file is opened, the load controller checks whether $\sum_i \sum_j l_{ij} < N$ for all active queries **i** and their file instances **j**. If so, the query is allowed to proceed; otherwise, it is suspended and placed at the front of a waiting queue. When a file is closed, buffers associated with its locality set are released back to the global free list. The load controller then activates the first query on the waiting queue if this will not cause the above condition to be violated.

What remains to be described is how the QLSM is used to select local replacement policies and estimate sizes for the locality sets of each file instance.

Straight Sequential (SS) References

For SS references the locality set size is obviously 1. When a requested page is not found in the buffer, the page is fetched from disk and overwrites whatever is in the buffer.

Clustered Sequential (CS) References

For CS references, if possible, all members of a cluster (i.e. records with the same key) should be kept in memory. Thus, the locality set size equals the number of records in the largest cluster divided by the blocking factor (i.e. the number of records per page). Provided that enough space is allocated, FIFO and LRU both yield the minimum number of page faults.

Looping Sequential (LS) References

When a file is being repeatedly scanned in an LS reference pattern, MRU is the best replacement algorithm. It is beneficial to give the file as many buffers as possible, up to the point where the entire file can fit in memory. Hence, the locality set size corresponds to the total number of pages in the file.

Independent Random (IR) References

When the records of a file are being randomly accessed, say through a hash table, the choice of a replacement algorithm is immaterial since all the algorithms perform equally well [King71]. Yao's formula [Yao77], which estimates the total number of pages referenced **b** in a series of **k** random record accesses, provides an (approximate) upper bound on the locality set size. In those cases where page references are sparse, there is no need to keep a page in memory after its initial reference. Thus, there are two reasonable sizes for the locality set, **1** and **b**, depending on the likelihood that each page is re-referenced. For example, we can define $r = \frac{k-b}{b}$ as the **residual value** of a page. The locality set size is 1 if $r \leq \beta$, and b otherwise; where β is the threshold above which a page is considered to have a high probability to be re-referenced.

Clustered Random (CR) References

A CR reference is similar to that of a CS reference. The only difference is, in a CR reference, records in a "cluster" are not physically adjacent, but randomly distributed over the file. The locality set size in this case can be approximated by the number of records in the largest cluster[6].

Straight Hierarchical (SH), H/SS, and H/CS References

For both SH and H/SS references each index page is traversed only once. Thus the locality set size of each is 1 and a single buffer page is all that is needed. The discussion on CS references is applicable to H/CS references, except that each member in a cluster is now a key-pointer pair rather than a data record.

Looping Hierarchical (LH) References

In an LH reference, an index is repeatedly traversed from the root to the leaf level. In such a reference, pages near the root are more likely to be accessed than those at the bottom [Reit76]. Consider a tree of height **h** and with a fan-out factor **f**. Without loss of generality, assume the tree is complete, i.e. each non-leaf node has f sons. During each traversal from the root at level 0 to a leaf at level **h**, one out of the f^i pages at level i is referenced. Therefore pages at an upper level (which are closer to the root) are more important than those at a lower level. Consequently, an ideal replacement algorithm should keep the active pages of the upper levels of a tree resident and multiplex the rest of the pages in a scratch buffer. The concept of "residual value" (defined for the IR reference pattern) can be used to estimate how many levels should be kept in memory. Let b_i be the number of pages accessed at level i as estimated by Yao's formula. The size of the locality set can be approximated by $(1+\sum_{i=1}^{j} b_i)+1$, where j is the largest i such that $\frac{k-b_i}{b_i} > \beta$. In many cases, the root is perhaps the only page worth keeping in memory, since the fan-out of an index page is usually high. If this is true, the LIFO algorithm and 3-4 buffers may deliver a reasonable level of performance as the root is always kept in memory.

[6] A more accurate estimate can be derived by applying Yao's formula to calculate the number of distinct pages referenced in a cluster.

4. Evaluation of Buffer Management Algorithms

In this section, we compare the performance of the DBMIN algorithm with the hot set algorithm and four other buffer management strategies in a multiuser environment. The section begins by describing the methodology used for the evaluation. Next, implementation details of the six buffer management algorithms tested are presented. Finally, the results of some of our experiments are presented. For a more complete presentation of our results, the interested reader should examine [Chou85].

4.1. Performance Evaluation Methodology

There were three choices for evaluating the different buffer management algorithms: direct measurement, analytical modeling, and simulation. Direct measurement, although feasible, was eliminated as too computationally expensive. Analytic modeling, while quite cost-effective, simply could not model the different algorithms in sufficient detail while keeping the solutions to the equations tractable. Consequently, we choose simulation as the basis for our evaluation.

Two types of simulations are widely used [Sher73]: **trace driven simulations** which are driven by traces recorded from a real system, and **distribution driven simulations** in which events are generated by a random process with certain stochastic structure. A trace driven model has several advantages, including creditability and fine workload characterization which enables subtle correlations of events to be preserved. However, selecting a "representative" workload is difficult in many cases. Furthermore, it is hard to characterize the interference and correlation between concurrent activities in a multiuser environment so that the trace data can be properly treated in an altered model with a different configuration. To avoid these problems, we designed a **hybrid simulation model** that combines features of both trace driven and distribution driven models. In this hybrid model, the behavior of each individual query is described by a trace string, and the system workload is dynamically synthesized by merging the trace strings of the concurrently executing queries.

Another component of our simulation model is a simulator for database systems which manages three important resources: CPU, an I/O device, and memory. When a new query arrives, a load controller (if it exists) decides, depending on the availability of the resources at the time, whether to activate or delay the query. After a query is activated, it circulates in a loop between the CPU and an I/O device to compete for resources until it finishes. After a query terminates, another new query is generated by the workload model. An active query, however, may be temporarily suspended by the load controller when the condition of over-loading is detected.

Although the page fault rate is frequently used to measure the performance of a memory management policy, minimizing the number of page faults in a multi-programmed environment does not guarantee optimal system behavior. Thus, throughput, measured as the average number of queries completed per second, was chosen as our performance metric. In the following sections, we shall describe three key aspects of the simulation model (Figure 1): workload characterization, configuration model, and performance measurement.

4.1.1. Workload Synthesis

The first step in developing a workload was to obtain single-query trace strings by running queries on the Wisconsin Storage System[7] (WiSS) [Chou83]. While WiSS supports a number of storage structures and their related scanning operations, WiSS does not directly support a high-level query interface; hence, the test queries were "hand coded". A synthetic database [Bitt83] with a well-defined distribution structure, was used in the experiments. Several types of events were recorded (with accurate timing information) during the execution of each query, including page accesses, disk I/O's, and file operations (i.e. opening and closing of files).

A trace string can be viewed as an array of event records, each of which has a tag field that identifies the type of the event. There are six important event types:

Workload Model - Trace Strings
↓
Configuration Model - Database System Simulator
↓
Performance Measurement - Throughput

A Simulation Model for Database Systems
Figure 1

page read, page write, disk read, disk write, file open, and file close. Disk read and write events come in pairs bracketing the time interval of a disk operation[8]. The corresponding record formats in the trace string are:

Page read and write

page read / write	file ID	page ID	time stamp

Disk read and write

disk read / write	file ID	page ID	time stamp

File open

file open	file ID	locality set size	replacement policy

File close

file close	file ID

The time stamps originally recorded were real (elapsed) times of the system. For reasons to be explained later, **disk read** and **write** events were removed from the trace strings, and the time stamps of other events were adjusted accordingly. In essence, the time stamps in a modified trace string reflect the virtual (or CPU) times of a query.

Since accurate timing, on the order of 100 microseconds, is required to record the events at such detailed level, the tracing were done on a dedicated VAX-11/750 under a very simple operating kernel, which is designed for the CRYSTAL multicomputer system [DeWi84]. To reduce the overhead of obtaining the trace strings, events were recorded in main memory and written to a file (provided by WiSS) after tracing had ended.

In the multiuser benchmarking methodology described in [Bora84], three factors that affect throughput in a multiuser environment were identified: the number of concurrent queries[9], the degree of data sharing, and the query mix.

The number of concurrent queries (NCQ) in each of our simulation runs was varied from 1 to 32. To study the effects of data sharing, 32 copies of the test database were replicated. Each copy was stored in a separate portion of the disk. Three levels of data sharing were defined according to the average number of concurrent queries accessing a copy of the database:

(1) full sharing, all queries access the same database;

(2) half sharing, every two queries share a copy of the database; and

(3) no sharing, every query has its own copy.

---

[7] WiSS provides RSS-like [Astr76] capabilities in the UNIX environment.

[8] The version of WiSS used for gathering the trace strings does not overlap CPU and I/O execution.

[9] The term, multiprogramming level (MPL), was used in [Bora84]. However, since it is desirable to distinguish the external workload condition from the internal degree of multiprogramming, "number of concurrent queries" (NCQ) is used here instead. Using our definitions, MPL $\leq$ NCQ under a buffer manager with load control.

The approach to query mix selection used in [Bora84] is based on a dichotomy on the consumption of two system resources, CPU cycles and disk bandwidth. For this study, this classification scheme was extended to incorporate the amount of main memory utilized by the query (Table 1). After some initial testing, six queries were chosen as the base queries for synthesizing the multiuser workload (Table 2). The CPU and disk consumptions of the queries were calculated from the single-query trace strings, and the corresponding memory requirements were estimated by the hot set model (which are almost identical to those from the query locality set model). Table 3 contains a summary description of the queries.

At simulation time, a multiuser workload is constructed by dynamically merging the single-query trace strings according to a given probability vector, which describes the relative frequency of each query type. The trace string of an active query is read and processed, one event at a time, by the CPU simulator when the query is being served by the CPU. For a page read or write event, the CPU simulator advances the query's CPU time (according to the time stamp in the event record), and forwards the page request to the buffer manager. If the requested page is not found in the buffer, the query is blocked while the page is being fetched from the disk. The exact ordering of the events from the concurrent queries are determined by the behavior of the simulated system and the time stamps recorded in the trace strings.

Query Number	CPU Usage (seconds)	Number of Disk IO's	Hot Set Size (4K-pages)
I	.53	17	3
II	.67	99	3
III	2.95	53	5
IV	3.09	120	5
V	3.47	55	17
VI	3.50	138	24

Representative Queries
Table 2

4.1.2. Configuration Model

Three hardware components are simulated in the model: a CPU, a disk, and a pool of buffers. A round-robin scheduler is used for allocating CPU cycles to competing queries. The CPU usage of each query is determined from the associated trace string, in which detailed timing information has been recorded. In this respect, the simulator's CPU has the characteristics of a VAX-11/750 CPU. The simulator's kernel schedules disk requests on a first-come-first-serve basis. In addition, an auxiliary disk queue is maintained for implementing delayed asynchronous writes, which are initiated only when the disk is about to become idle.

The disk times recorded in the trace strings tend to be smaller than what they would be in a "real" environment for two reasons: (1) the database used in the tracing is relatively small; and (2) disk arm movements are

Query Type	CPU Demand	Disk Demand	Memory Demand
I	Low	Low	Low
II	Low	High	Low
III	High	Low	Low
IV	High	High	Low
V	High	Low	High
VI	High	High	High

Query Classification
Table 1

Query #	Query Operators	Selectivity	Access Path of Selection	Join Method	Access Path of Join
I	select(A)	1%	clustered index	-	-
II	select(B)	1%	non-clustered index	-	-
III	select(A) join B	2%	clustered index	index join	clustered index on B
IV	select(A') join B	10%	sequential scan	index join	non-clustered index on B
V	select(A) join B'	3%	clustered index	nested loops	sequential scan over B'
VI	select(A) join A'	4%	clustered index	hash join	hash on result of select(A)

A,B:10K tuples; A':1K tuples; B':300 tuples; 182 bytes per tuple.

Description of Base Queries
Table 3

usually less frequent on a single user system than in a multiuser environment. Furthermore, requests for disk operations are affected by the operating conditions and the buffer management algorithm used. Therefore, the disk times recorded were replaced by a stochastic disk model, in which a random process on disk head positions is assumed. In the disk simulator, the access time of a disk operation is calculated from the timing specifications of a Fujitsu Eagle disk drive [Fuji82]. On the average, it takes about 27.6 ms to access a 4K page.

The buffer pool is under the control of the buffer manager using one of the buffer management algorithms. However, the operating system can fix a buffer in memory when an I/O operation is in progress. The size of the buffer pool for each simulation run is determined by the formula:

$$8 \cdot \frac{\sum_i p_i t_i h_i}{\sum_i p_i t_i}$$

where $\mathbf{p_i}$ is the ith element of the query mix probability vector and $\mathbf{t_i}$ and $\mathbf{h_i}$ are the CPU usage and the hot set size of query **i**, respectively. The intent was to saturate the memory at a load of eight concurrent queries so that the effect of overloading on performance under different buffer management algorithms could be observed.

4.1.3. Statistical Validity of Performance Measurements

Batch means [Sarg76] was selected as the method for estimating confidence intervals. The number of batches in each simulation run was set to 20. Analysis of the throughput measurements indicates that many of the confidence intervals fell within 1% of the mean. For those experiments in which thrashing occurred, the length of a batch was extended to ensure that all confidence intervals were within 5% of the mean.

4.2. Buffer Management Algorithms

Six buffer management algorithms, divided into two groups, were included in the experiments. The first group consisted of three simple algorithms: RAND, FIFO, and CLOCK. They were chosen because they are typical replacement algorithms and are easy to implement. It is interesting to compare their performance with that of the more sophisticated algorithms to see if the added complexity of these algorithms is warranted. Beside DBMIN, WS (the working set algorithm), and HOT (the hot set algorithm) were included in the second group. WS is one of the most efficient memory policies for virtual memory systems [Denn78]. It is intriguing to know how well it performs when applied to database systems. The hot set algorithm was chosen to represent the algorithms that have previously been proposed for database systems.

All the algorithms in the first group are global algorithms in the sense that the replacement discipline is applied globally to all the buffers in the system. Common to all three algorithms is a global table that contains, for each buffer, the identity of the residing page, and a flag indicating whether the buffer has an I/O operation in progress. Additional data structures or flags may be needed depending on the individual algorithm. Implementations of RAND and FIFO are typical, and need no further explanation. The CLOCK algorithm used in the experiments gives preferential treatment to dirty pages, i.e. pages that have been modified. During the first scan, an unreferenced dirty page is scheduled for writing, whereas an unreferenced clean page is immediately chosen for replacement. If no suitable buffer is found in the first complete scan, dirty and clean pages are treated equally during the second scan. None of the three algorithms has a built-in facility for load control. However, we will investigate later how a load controller may be incorporated and what its effects are on the performance of these algorithms.

The algorithms in the second group are all local policies, in which replacement decisions are made locally. There is a local table associated with each query or file instance for maintaining its resident set. Buffers that do not belong to any resident set are placed in a global LRU list. To allow for data sharing among concurrent queries, a global table, similar to the one for the global algorithms, is also maintained by each of the local algorithms in the second group. When a page is requested, the global table is searched first, and then the appropriate local table is adjusted if necessary. As an optimization, an asynchronous write operation is scheduled whenever a dirty page is released back to the global free list. All three algorithms in the second group base their load control on the (estimated) memory demands of the submitted queries. A new query is activated if there is sufficient free space left in the system. On the other hand, an active query is suspended when over-commitment of main memory has been detected. We adopted the deactivation rule implemented in the VMOS operating system [Foge74] in which the faulting process (i.e. the process that was asking for more memory) is chosen for suspension[10]. In the following section, we discuss implementation decisions that are pertinent to each individual algorithm in the second group.

---

[10] We also implemented the deactivation rule suggested by Opderbeck and Chu [Opde74] which deactivates the process with the least accumulated CPU time. However, no noticeable differences in performance were observed.

Working Set Algorithm

To make WS more competitive, a two-parameter WS algorithm was implemented. That is, each process is given one of the two window sizes depending on which is more advantageous to it. The two window sizes, τ_1 = **10**ms and τ_2 = **15**ms, were determined from an analysis of working set functions on the single-query trace strings. Instead of computing the working set of a query after each page access, the algorithm re-calculates the working set only when the query encounters a page fault or has used up its current time quantum.

Hot Set Algorithm

The hot set algorithm was implemented according to the outline described in [Sacc82]. The hot set sizes associated with the base queries were hand-calculated according to the hot set model (see Table 2 above). They were then stored in a table, which is accessible to the buffer manager at simulation time.

DBMIN Algorithm

The locality set size and the replacement policy for each file instance were manually determined. They were then passed (by the program that implemented the query) to the trace string recorder at the appropriate points when the single-query trace strings were recorded. At simulation time, the DBMIN algorithm uses the information recorded in the trace strings to determine the proper resident set size and replacement discipline for a file instance at the time the file is opened.

4.3. Simulation Results

Although comparing the performance of the algorithms for different query types provides insight into the efficiency of each individual algorithm, it is more interesting to compare their performance under a workload consisting of a mixture of query types[11]. Three query mixes were defined to cover a wide range of workloads:

M1 - in which all six query types are equally likely to be requested;

M2 - in which one of the two simple queries (I and II) is chosen half the time;

M3 - in which the two simple queries have a combined probability of 75%.

The specific probability distributions for the three query mixes is shown in Table 4.

[11] The performance of the single query type tests are contained in [Chou85]. In general, the behavior of the algorithms for these tests are similar to the three mixes.

Query Mix	Type I	Type II	Type III	Type IV	Type V	Type VI
M1	16.67	16.67	16.67	16.67	16.66	16.66
M2	25.00	25.00	12.50	12.50	12.50	12.50
M3	37.50	37.50	6.25	6.25	6.25	6.25

(in %)

Composition of Query Mixes
Table 4

The first set of tests were conducted without any data sharing between concurrently executing queries. In Figure 2, the throughput for the six buffer management algorithms is presented for each mix of queries. In each graph, the x axis is the number of concurrent queries (NCQ) and the y axis is the throughput of the system measured in queries per second. The presence of thrashing for the three simple algorithms is evident[12]. A relatively sharp degradation in performance can be observed in most cases. RAND and FIFO yielded the worst performance, although RAND is perhaps more stable than FIFO in the sense than its curve is slightly smoother than that of FIFO. Before severe thrashing occurred, CLOCK was generally better than both RAND and FIFO.

WS did not perform well because it failed to capture the main loops of the joins in queries V and VI. Its performance improved as the frequency of queries V and VI decreased. The efficiency of the hot set algorithm was close to that of DBMIN. When the system was lightly loaded, DBMIN was only marginally better than the rest of the algorithms. However, as the number of concurrent queries increased to 8 or more, DBMIN provided more throughput than the hot set algorithm by 7 to 13%[13] and the WS algorithm by 25 to 45%.

Effect of Data Sharing

To study the effects of data sharing on the performance of the algorithms, two more sets of experiments, each with a different degree of data sharing, were conducted. The results are plotted in Figures 3 and 4. It can be observed that, for each of the algorithms, the throughput increases as the degree of data sharing increases. This reinforces the view that allowing for data sharing among concurrent queries is important in a multi-programmed database system [Reit76] [Bora84].

[12] Data points for the three simple algorithms were gathered only up to 16 concurrent queries as it is very time-consuming to gather throughput measurements with a ±5% confidence interval when the simulated system is trapped in a thrashing state.

[13] The percentages of performance difference were calculated relative to the better algorithm.

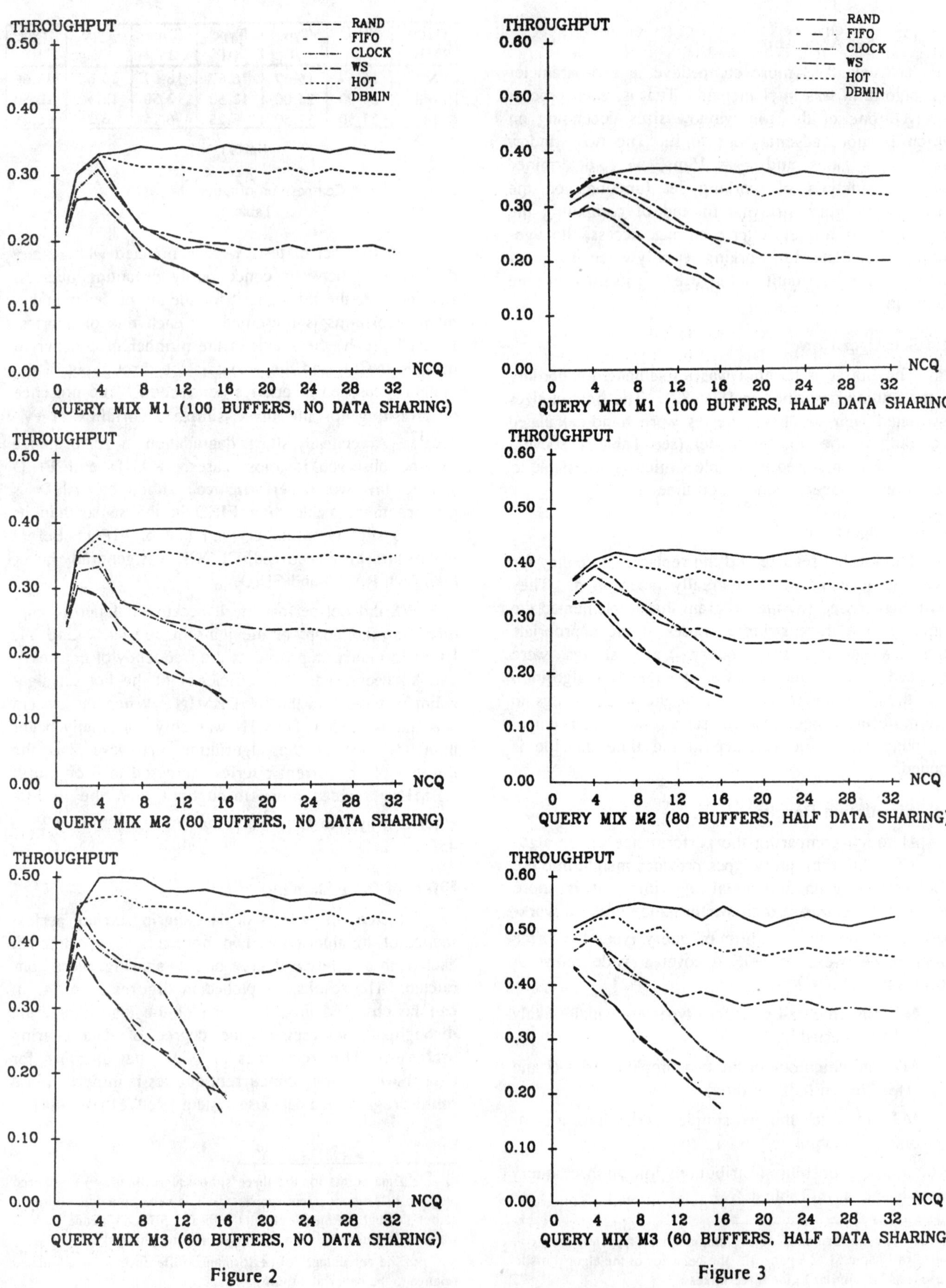

THROUGHPUT
RAND
FIFO
CLOCK
WS
HOT
DBMIN
NCQ
QUERY MIX M1 (100 BUFFERS, NO DATA SHARING)
QUERY MIX M1 (100 BUFFERS, HALF DATA SHARING)
QUERY MIX M2 (80 BUFFERS, NO DATA SHARING)
QUERY MIX M2 (80 BUFFERS, HALF DATA SHARING)
QUERY MIX M3 (60 BUFFERS, NO DATA SHARING)
QUERY MIX M3 (60 BUFFERS, HALF DATA SHARING)

Figure 2

Figure 3

The relative performance of the algorithms for half data sharing is similar to that for no data sharing. However, it is not the case for full data sharing. For query mixes M1 and M2, the efficiencies of the different algorithms were close. Because every query accessed the same copy of the database, it was easy for any algorithm to keep the important portion of the database in memory. With no surprises, RAND and FIFO performed slightly worse than other algorithms due to their inherent deficiency in capturing locality of reference. For query mix M3, however, the performance of the different algorithms again diverged. This may be attributed to the fact that small queries dominated the performance for query mix M3. The "working" portion of the database becomes less distinct as many small queries are entering and leaving the system. (In contrast, the larger queries, which intensively access a limited set of pages over a relatively long period of time, played a more important role for query mixes M1 and M2.) Therefore, algorithms that made an effort to identify the localities performed better than those that did not.

Effect of Load Control

As was observed in the previous experiments, the lack of load control in the simple algorithms had led to thrashing under high workloads. It is interesting to find out how effective those algorithms will be when a load controller is incorporated. The "50% rule" [Lero76], in which the utilization of the paging device is kept busy about half the time, was chosen partly for its simplicity of implementation and partly because it is supported by empirical evidence [Denn76].

A load controller which is based on the "50% rule" usually consists of three major components:

(1) an **estimator** that measures the utilization of the device,

(2) an **optimizer** that analyzes the measurements provided by the estimator and decides what load adjustment is appropriate, and

(3) a **control switch** that activates or deactivates processes according to the decisions made by the optimizer.

In Figure 5, the effects of a load control mechanism on the three simple buffer management algorithms is shown. A set of initial experiments established that throughput was maximized with a disk utilization of 87%. With load control, every simple algorithm in the experiments out-performed the WS algorithm. The performance of the CLOCK algorithm with load control came very close to that of the hot set algorithm. However, the results should not be interpreted literally. There are several potential problems with such a load

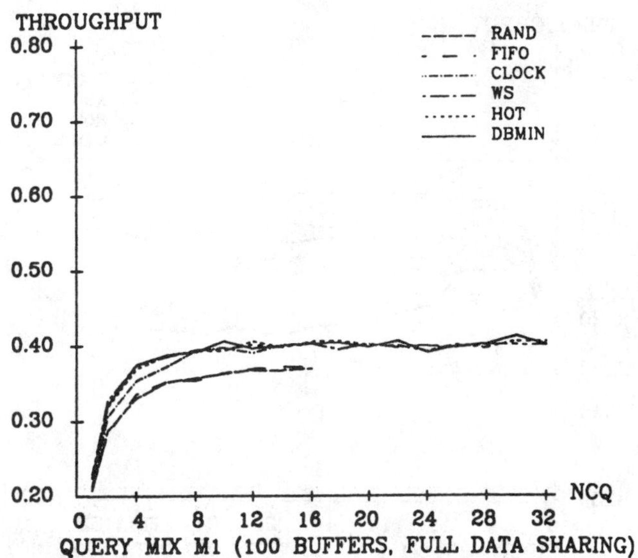

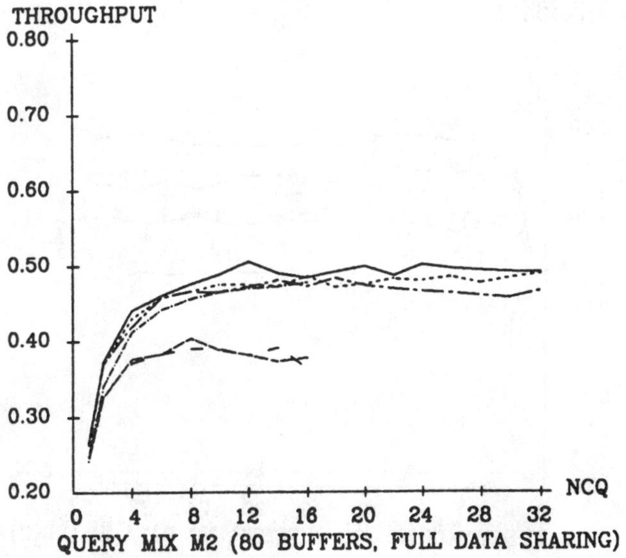

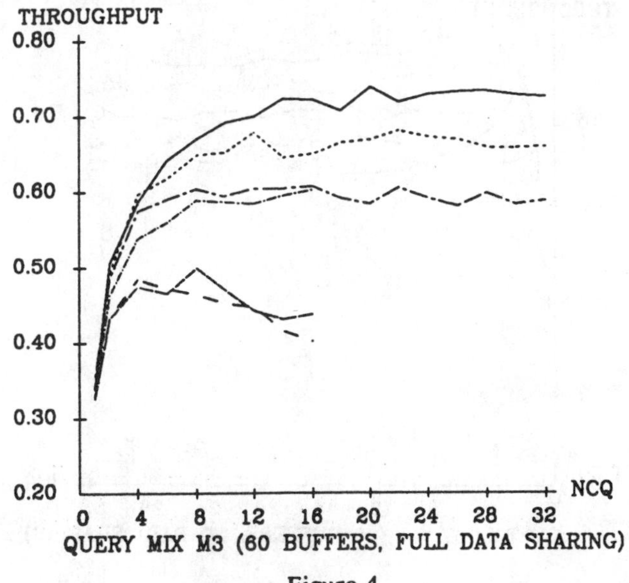

Figure 4

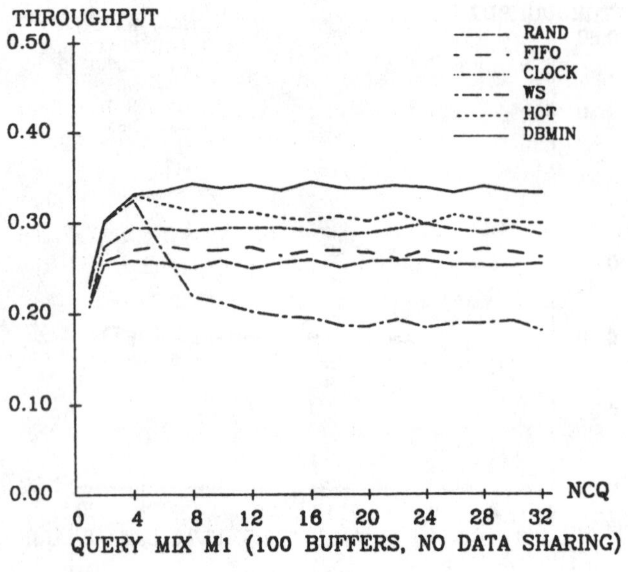

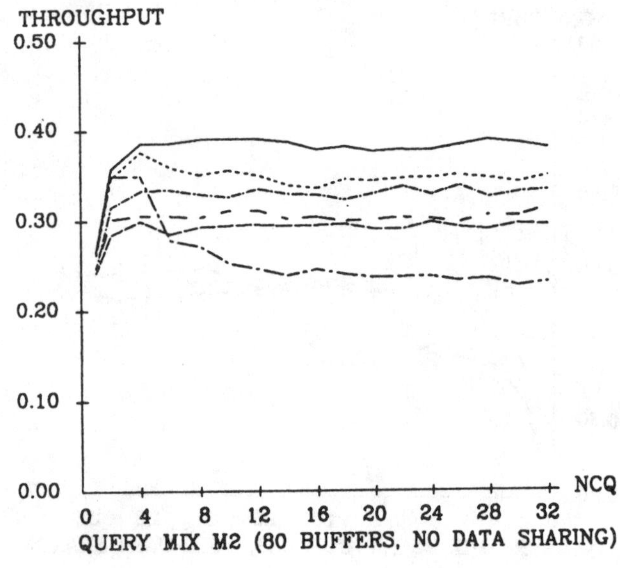

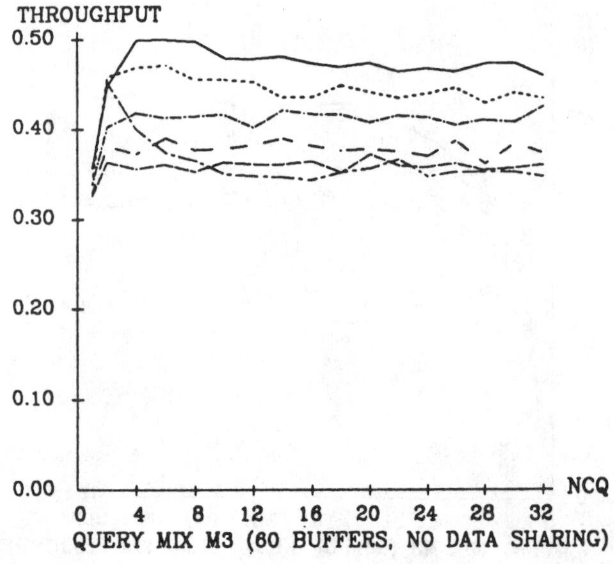

Figure 5

control mechanism which arise from the feedback nature of the load controller:

(1) Run-time overhead can be expensive if sampling is done too frequently. On the other hand, the optimizer may not respond fast enough to adjust the load effectively if analyses of the measurements are not done frequently enough.

(2) Unlike the predictive load controllers, a feedback controller can only respond after an undesirable condition has been detected. This may result in unnecessary process activations and deactivations that might otherwise be avoided by a predictive load control mechanism.

(3) A feedback load controller does not work well in an environments with a large number of small transactions which enter and leave the system before their effects can be assessed. This effect can be seen in Figure 5 as the percentage of small queries increases. Note that the so-called "small queries" (i.e. queries I and II) in our experiments still retrieve 100 tuples from the source relation. The disadvantages of a feedback load controller are likely to become even more apparent in a system with a large number of single-tuple queries.

5. Conclusions

In this paper we presented a new algorithm, **DBMIN**, for managing the buffer pool of a relational database management system. DBMIN is based on a new model of relational query behavior, the **query locality set model** (QLSM). Like the hot set model, the QLSM allows a buffer manager to predict future reference behavior. However, unlike the hot set model, the QLSM separates the modeling of referencing behavior from any particular buffer management algorithm. The DBMIN algorithm manages the buffer pool on a per file basis. The number of buffers allocated to each file instance is based on the locality set size of the file instance and will varies depending on how the file is being accessed. In addition, the buffer pool associated with each file instance is managed by a replacement policy that is tuned to how the file is being accessed.

We also presented a performance evaluation methodology for evaluating buffer management algorithms in a multiuser environment. This methodology employed a hybrid model that combines features of both trace driven and distribution driven simulation models. Using this model, we compared the performance of six buffer management algorithms. Severe thrashing was observed for the three simple algorithms: RAND, FIFO, and CLOCK. Although the introduction of a feedback load controller alleviated the problem, it created new potential problems. As expected, the three more sophisticated algorithms - WS, HOT, and

DBMIN - performed better than the simple algorithms. However, the WS algorithm did not perform as well as "advertised" for virtual memory systems [Denn78]. The last two algorithms, HOT and DBMIN, were successful in demonstrating their efficiency. In comparison, DBMIN provided 7 to 13% more throughput than HOT over a wide range of operating conditions for the tests conducted.

In [Chou85] we also examined the overhead associated with each of the WS, HOT, and DBMIN algorithms. Based on our analysis, the cost of the WS algorithm is higher than that of HOT unless the page fault rate is kept very low. In comparison, DBMIN is less expensive than both WS and HOT as less usage statistics need to be maintained.

Acknowledgements

This research was partially supported by the Department of Energy under contract #DE-AC02-81ER10920 and the National Science Foundation under grant MCS82-01870.

6. References

[Astr76] Astrahan, M. M., et. al. System R: A Relational Approach to Database Management, ACM Transactions on Database Systems, vol. 1, no. 2, June 1976.

[Bitt83] Bitton, Dina, David J. DeWitt, and Carolyn Turbyfill, Benchmarking Database Systems: A Systematic Approach, Proceedings of the Ninth International Conference on Very Large Data Bases, November 1983.

[Blas77] Blasgen, M. W. and K. P. Eswaran, Storage and Access in Relational Data Base, IBM System Journals, no. 4, pp. 363-377, 1977.

[Bora84] Boral, Haran and David J. DeWitt, A Methodology For Database System Performance Evaluation, Proceedings of the International Conference on Management of Data, pp. 176-185, ACM, Boston, June 1984.

[Chou83] Chou, Hong-Tai, David J. DeWitt, Randy H. Katz, and Anthony C. Klug, Design and Implementation of the Wisconsin Storage System, Computer Sciences Technical Report #524, Department of Computer Sciences, University of Wisconsin, Madison, November 1983.

[Chou85] Chou, Hong-Tai, Buffer Management in Database Systems, Ph.D. Thesis, University of Wisconsin, Madison, 1985.

[DeWi84] DeWitt, David J., Raphael Finkel, and Marvin Solomon, The CRYSTAL Multicomputer: Design and Implementation Experience, Computer Sciences Technical Report #553, Department of Computer Sciences, University of Wisconsin, Madison, September 1984.

[Denn68] Denning, Peter J., The Working Set Model for Program Behavior, Communications of the ACM, vol. 11, no. 5, pp. 323-333, May 1968.

[Denn76] Denning, Peter J., Kevin C. Kahn, Jacques Leroudier, Dominique Potier, and Rajan Suri, Optimal Multiprogramming, Acta Informatica, vol. 7, no. 2, pp. 197-216, 1976.

[Denn78] Denning, Peter J., Optimal Multiprogrammed Memory Management, in Current Trends in Programming Methodology, Vol.III Software Modeling, ed. Raymond T. Yeh, pp. 298-322, Prentice-Hall, Englewood Cliffs, 1978.

[Effe84] Effelsberg, Wolfgang and Theo Haerder, Principles of Database Buffer Management, ACM Transactions on Database Systems, vol. 9, no. 4, pp. 560-595, December 1984.

[Fern78] Fernandez, E.B., T. Lang, and C. Wood, Effect of Replacement Algorithms on a Paged Buffer Database System, IBM Journal of Research and Development, vol. 22, no. 2, pp. 185-196, March 1978.

[Foge74] Fogel, Marc H., The VMOS Paging Algorithm, a Practical Implementation of the Working Set Model, ACM Operating System Review, vol. 8, January 1974.

[Fuji82] Fujitsu, Limited, M2351A/AF Mini-Disk Drive CE manual, 1982.

[Kapl80] Kaplan, Julio A., Buffer Management Policies in a Database Environment, Master Report, UC Berkeley, 1980.

[King71] King, W. F. III, Analysis of Demand Paging Algorithms, in Proceedings of IFIP Congress (Information Processing 71), pp. 485-490, North Holland Publishing Company, Amsterdam, August 1971.

[Lang77] Lang, Tomas, Christopher Wood, and Icduardo B. Fernandez, Database Buffer Paging in Virtual Storage Systems, ACM Transactions on Database Systems, vol. 2, no. 4, December, 1977.

[Lero76] Leroudier, J. and D. Potier, Principles of Optimality for Multi-Programming, Proceedings of the international Symposium on Computer Performance Modeling, Measurement, and Evaluation, ACM SIGMETRICS (IFIP WG. 7.3), pp. 211-218, Cambridge, March 1976.

[Nybe84] Nyberg, Chris, Disk Scheduling and Cache Replacement for a Database Machine, Master Report, UC Berkeley, July, 1984.

[Opde74] Opderbeck, Holger and Wesley W. Chu, Performance of the Page Fault Frequency Replacement Algorithm in a Multiprogramming Environment, in Proceedings of IFIP Congress, Information Processing 74, pp. 235-241, North Holland Publishing Company, Amsterdam, August 1974.

[Reit76] Reiter, Allen, A Study of Buffer Management Policies For Data Management Systems, Technical Summary Report # 1619, Mathematics Research Center, University of Wisconsin-Madison, March, 1976.

[Sacc82] Sacco, Giovanni Maria and Mario Schkolnick, A Mechanism For Managing the Buffer Pool In A Relational Database System Using the Hot Set Model, Proceedings of the 8th International Conference on Very Large Data Bases, pp. 257-262, Mexico City, September 1982.

[Sacc85] Sacco, Giovanni Maria and Mario Schkolnick, Buffer Management in Relational Database Systems, To appear in ACM Transactions on Database Systems.

[Sarg76] Sargent, Robert G., Statistical Analysis of Simulation Output Data, Proceedings of ACM Symposium on Simulation of Computer Systems, August 1976.

[Sher73] Sherman, Stephen W. and J.C. Browne, Trace Driven Modeling: Review and Overview, Proceedings of ACM Symposium on Simulation of Computer Systems, pp. 201-207, June 1973.

[Sher76a] Sherman, Stephen W. and Richard S. Brice, I/O Buffer Performance in a Virtual Memory System, Proceedings of ACM Symposium on Simulation of Computer Systems, pp. 25-35, August, 1976.

[Sher76b] Sherman, Stephen W. and Richard S. Brice, Performance of a Database Manager in a Virtual Memory System, ACM Transactions on Database Systems, vol. 1, no. 4, December 1976.

[Ston76] Stonebraker, Michael, Eugene Wong, and Peter Kreps, The Design and Implementation of INGRES, ACM Transactions on Database Systems, vol. 1, no. 3, pp. 189-222, September 1976.

[Ston81] Stonebraker, Michael, Operating System Support for Database Management, Communications of the ACM, vol. 24, no. 7, pp. 412-418, July 1981.

[Ston82] Stonebraker, Michael, John Woodfill, Jeff Ranstrom, Marguerite Murphy, Marc Meyer, and Eric Allman, Performance Enhancements to a Relational Database System, Initial draft of a paper which appeared in TODS, vol. 8, no. 2, June, 1983.

[Thor72] Thorington, John M. Jr. and David J. IRWIN, An Adaptive Replacement Algorithm for Paged Memory Computer Systems, IEEE Transactions on Computers, vol. C-21, no. 10, pp. 1053-1061, October 1972.

[Tuel76] Tuel, W. G. Jr., An Analysis of Buffer Paging in Virtual Storage Systems, IBM Journal of Research and Development, pp. 518- 520, September, 1976.

[Yao77] Yao, S.B, Approximating Block Accesses in Database Organizations, Communications of the ACM, vol. 20, no. 4, pp. 260-261, April 1977.

Chapter 3

Distributed Database Systems

3.1 Introduction

In my opinion distributed database systems will have a **profound** impact on DBMS clients over the next decade. In short, I expect everybody will be using a distributed DBMS and single site DBMSs will be an antique curiosity within ten years. There are several reasons why I am convinced that this will occur.

First, companies are fundamentally distributed. Every company of any size has offices in many places, and there is every incentive for each location to have its own computer. If for no other reason, the cost of communication is prohibitive. One simply does not want to have a terminal in Hong Kong that accesses a computer in New York; one will quickly have a gigantic communications bill. All companies I know of end up having many computer systems, typically spread around the world. Of course, there are databases on each of these machines, and most organizations must run applications that access data in multiple databases on multiple computer systems. A simple example of such geographically distributed data can be found at Relational Technology, Inc. They maintain a customer database for U.S.A. customers at their headquarters in California. British customers are on the machine in London, German customers are on the machine in Frankfurt, and French customers are on the machine in Paris. Soon there will be additional machines at other locations. In general there is high locality of reference to the customer database. Hence, the French customers are usually accessed by the French Relational Technology personnel. However, there are also cross-database accesses. For example, sometimes a salesman wants to know all the Relational Technology customers in the world that are part of some multinational corporation, e.g., Citibank. This requires access to individual customer databases at all RTI locations. Obviously, a distributed database system that provides so-called **location transparency** will expedite such multidatabase queries.

However geographic distribution is not the only reason to have a distributed database system. It is obvious that dumb terminals will be replaced on most people's desks by workstations. This process will happen soon for knowledge workers and sooner or later for data workers, as explained in [STON88]. Moreover, most workstations will have local disks to achieve better performance. The current popularity of diskless workstations simply reflects the fact that 5 1/4 inch and 3 1/2 inch drives are not yet cheap enough. At low prices every workstation will get a disk to garner the factor of 3 in performance that can be obtained [LAZO86]. Moreover, a DBMS will run on each workstation and manage local databases. Such databases will at least contain personal data such as telephone directories and appointment calendars. In such an environment, one would clearly like to run a program that would schedule a meeting by intersecting the available times for all the participants. Obviously, this is a distributed database application. Hence the imminent presence of large numbers of workstations with disks will create the need for a distributed database system.

A further use of distributed database systems is to off-load database cycles from large, shared mainframes. Since computing on a mainframe costs more than $100,000 per MIPS (million of instructions per second), it makes perfect sense to off-load database services onto a back-end machine. Because machines based on single chip CPUs (e.g., the Sun 4) cost almost nothing compared to mainframes, it makes sense to couple multiple single-chip back-end systems into a coordinated, more powerful computing complex. Clearly one requires a distributed database system to manage data spread over multiple back-end machines. An example of a commercial product based on exactly this strategy is the Teradata DBC/1012 [TERA83].

However, probably the most important use of distributed database systems is to provide a tool to deal with the "sins of the past." Most companies already have major databases in place, often on "tired technology" systems such as IMS or IDMS. In addition, they are increasingly required to write cross-database applications. In such cases, an application must obtain data from (say) an IMS system, a DB2 system, and an INGRES system. Programmer writing such an application have a daunting job; they must understand how to access three different computer systems, often with three different operating systems, and then obtain data from three different data managers. A distributed database system that supports heterogenous local DBMSs, i.e., one that has an **open architecture** can help with this situation. Such a system can allow programmers simply to write relational queries for a composite schema containing the data in all three systems. Then the distributed DBMS worries about accessing each of the local databases to obtain desired information. To construct an open architecture distributed DBMS, one must simply support the concept of a **gateway**, which is a module specific to each local DBMS that performs the mapping from the distributed DBMS query language to the one supported by the local DBMS. Any client who requires access to two or more existing databases will be dramatically assisted by an open architecture distributed DBMS.

For the above reasons, all commercial DBMS vendors that I know of (including IBM) are hard at work on a distributed DBMS. Some (e.g., Tandem, Relational Technology, and Oracle) have products already and others will soon follow. Some vendors (e.g., INGRES and Oracle) are committed to open architecture. Others (most notably IBM) will be unlikely to offer an open architecture product.

The desired function of a distributed DBMS is straightforward and can be explained by a collection of transparencies:

1. Location transparency has already been discussed. It means that a user can submit a query that accesses distributed objects without having to know where the objects are.

2. Performance transparency means that a **distributed query optimizer** has been constructed to find a heuristically optimized plan to execute any distributed command. Obviously, if one has 1,000,000 objects in New York and 10 objects in Berkeley, one wants to perform the join by moving the 10 objects to New York and not vice-versa. Performance transparency loosely means that a query can be submitted from any node in a distributed DBMS and will run with comparable performance.

3. Copy transparency means that the system supports the optional existence of multiple copies of database objects. Hence, if a site is down, users can still access database objects by obtaining one of the other copies from another site.

4. Transaction transparency means that a user can run an arbitrary transaction that updates data at any number of sites, and the transaction behaves exactly like a local one, i.e., the ultimate effect is that the transaction either commits or aborts, and no intermediate states are possible.

5. Fragment transparency means that the distributed DBMS allows a user to cut up a relation into multiple pieces and place these pieces at multiple sites according to **distribution criteria**. For example, the following distribution criteria might control the placement of tuples from the EMP relation:

   ```
   EMP where dept = "shoe"    at Berkeley
   EMP where dept != "shoe"   at New York
   ```

In this way the tuples of a relation can be distributed and a user can access the EMP relation unaware of this distribution.

6. Schema change transparency means that a user who adds or deletes a database object from a distributed database need make the change only once (to the distributed dictionary) and does not need to change the catalogs at all sites that participate in the distributed database.
7. Local DBMS transparency requires that the distributed database system be able to provide its services without regard for what local database systems are actually managing local data.

To the best of my knowledge no system has ever been built with all these features. Three prototype distributed DBMSs with some of these characteristics were constructed in the late 1970s and early 1980s. Under DARPA contract Computer Corporation of America built SDD-1 from about 1976 to 1980. The design of SDD-1 is detailed in a collection of papers that appeared in TODS, namely [ROTH80, BERN80, BERN80b, HAMM80, BERN81]. From about 1977 to about 1981 we built Distributed INGRES at the University of California, and this system is described in [EPST78, STON79, STON86]. Lastly, a collection of researchers at IBM in San Jose built R* from about 1981 to 1985. R* is described in a collection of papers [WILL81, DANI82, WILM83, LIND84]. I have included an overview paper on R* as the first selection in this section (3.2). It states some of the above points about transparency in different terms and sketches a complete system description. This overview was written in advance of most of the implementation and represents the goals that they hoped to achieve. Many of the features, however, were never implemented, most notably fragments and copies. For a retrospection on R* consult [LIND85].

My own experience with these prototypes is the following. First, the SDD-1 system was so overconstrained by DARPA (e.g., they had to implement on top of the Datacomputer on PDP-10s and use the Arpanet) that they were probably doomed from the beginning. Even so, they managed to get a slow (but runable) prototype working.

Distributed INGRES was doomed by the nonexistence of networking software. To get anywhere on a distributed DBMS one requires the existence of TCP/IP (or equivalent) between the target machines. Since that didn't exist in 1977 when we started, we had to "grow our own." This constrained us to being in both the networking and the database business. Unfortunately the networking project failed, and we were left "hanging out to dry" until Bill Joy wrote the 4BSD networking software. During the intervening two years, the project lost momentum and decayed. The code worked well enough to do performance studies, and some numbers appear in [STON83]. However, Distributed INGRES never worked well enough for public distribution. In retrospect, we should have begun the project only after a reasonable network was in place.

On the other hand, R* had the benefit of a large team, the existance of VTAM software for communication, and insight into the mistakes of the other two systems. Hence, they managed to get their prototype working fairly reliably, and are happy to perform unscripted demonstrations. However, they consistently do demos on one machine simulating two or three, are reticent about networking performance, and privately complain about VTAM performance. Hence, I wonder how competitive R* is with existing commercial systems.

I have chosen to include four other papers in this section. As noted above, a distributed DBMS must support a distributed query optimizer and must supervise the appropriate disposition of distributed transactions and the correct updating of multiple copies of objects. Hence I have included one paper each on query processing (3.3), concurrency control (3.4), crash recovery (3.5), and copies (3.6). In the rest of this introduction I will make a couple of comments on each of these areas.

With regard to query optimization, the traditional tactic is to extend a local optimizer in two ways. First, the cost function includes an additional term dealing with network communication. Second, the search space of possible tactics is much bigger because the site where joins are constructed is now a variable and there are additional ways to perform a join. This strategy was employed by all three prototypes, and I have included an R* paper by Mackert and Lohman (3.3) as a representative example.

Second, current distributed optimizers tend to fall into two groups: those that employ so-called semijoin techniques [BERN81, YU84] and those that don't. The SDD-1 approach was to count only the cost of communication, arguing that it was the dominant cost. In such an environment, semijoins are usually attractive. On the other hand, [SELI80] argued that communication costs were rarely dominant and more typically coequal with I/O and CPU costs. With a more comprehensive cost function, semijoins are rarely attractive, and neither R* nor Distributed INGRES implemented them. Recent results (e.g., simulation results in the Mackert and Lohman paper and results in [DEWI86]) indicate that variations on hash joins may be the most cost-effective overall strategy.

A third comment is that the distributed optimizers that have been constructed so far have not contained code to deal with the following problems:

1. Load balance
2. Machine speed differences
3. Network nonuniformity
4. Administrative constraints
5. Cost constraints
6. Space constraints

A distributed optimizer allocates work to local sites, and often equally balancing the load is an important consideration. Initial work on load balancing is reported in [CARE86]. Moreover, not all machines in a distributed database system will have the same speed CPU, nor will they be connected by networking hardware of equal band width. In addition, production systems are often fully allocated from 8 am to 5 pm, and no additional work should be scheduled to them. Such administrative constraints are typical of real world systems. Furthermore, the charging algorithm is often different on different machines; hence a user would wish a join performed on the machine with the cheapest charging algorithm even if it was not the optimal location. Lastly, it is unrealistic to schedule a join between two gigabyte objects on a personal computer because the machine will clearly not have sufficient disk space for the operands, let alone the result.

As a result real-world commercial optimizer will be much more complex than the prototypes implemented in the past. Moreover, in an open architecture system, a distributed optimizer must be prepared to interface to foreign local data managers at the various sites. In my opinion the main problem with distributed optimizers is how to deal with this excessive complexity and the resulting enormous search space. While it is feasible to do exhaustive search of all possibilities in a local DBMS, this gets quickly out of hand in a distributed DBMS. Techniques to cut down the search space are clearly needed, and initial work is reported in [LAFO86].

To deal with concurrency control I have chosen the survey paper by Phil Bernstein and Nat Goodman who explain a large collection of the options (3.4). As I will explain presently, I feel that distributed concurrency control is really quite simple and that most of the techniques presented by Bernstein and Goodman are not realistic. I have included their paper because I feel that serious DBMS researchers should be aware of the various options.

As an example, I will illustrate the problems with one of the algorithms presented—the SDD-1 concurrency control scheme, which was based on timestamps and conflict graphs. This scheme unfortunately does not allow a transaction to abort, assumes that transactions within a single class are sequenced outside the model, and allows a transaction to send only one message to each site. All these assumptions are unrealistic, and timestamp techniques have not enjoyed any measure of success. Moreover, it is clearly difficult to design conflict graphs, as transactions can be arbitrarily assigned to classes. Even CCA, who invented the SDD-1 algorithms, gave up on them in their next prototype, ADAPLEX [CHAN83]. The reader is advised to evaluate carefully the reasonableness of the assumptions required in many of Bernstein's and Goodman's other options.

In my opinion, distributed concurrency control is quite simple. In an open architecture system, as noted above, distributed concurrency control must be built on top of local facilities provided by each underlying data manager. At the moment, all commercial products use some variation on dynamic locking as noted in the Introduction to Section 2. Moreover, unless there is some sort of global standard that requires a local data manager to send its local "waits-for" graph to somebody else, it will be impossible to do any sort of global deadlock detection because the prerequisite information cannot be assembled from the local data managers. Hence, timeout is the only deadlock detection scheme that will work in this environment. As a result, setting locks at the local sites within the local data manager and using timeout for deadlock detection will be the solution used.

Crash recovery, on the other hand, is a much more complex subject. A distributed transaction must be committed everywhere or aborted everywhere. Since there is a local data manager at each site, it can successfully perform a local commit or abort. The only challenge is for a transaction coordinator to ensure that all local data managers commit or all abort. The main idea is very simple, and has come to be called a two-phase commit. When the coordinator is ready to commit a global transaction he cannot simply send out a commit message to each site. The problem is that site A must flush all its log pages for the local portion of the transaction and then write a commit record. This could take one or more I/Os for a substantial transaction and consume perhaps hundreds of milliseconds on a busy system. Add perhaps a second of message delay and operating system overhead, and there is perhaps a two-second period from the time the coordinator sends out the commit message during which disaster is possible. Specifically, if site A crashes, it will not have committed the transaction, and, moreover, it will not be able to commit later because the prerequisite log pages were still in main memory at the time of the crash and therefore were lost in the crash. On the other hand, the other sites remained up and successfully committed the transaction as directed. In this scenario all sites except A have committed the transaction, and site A cannot commit. Hence we have failed to achieve the objective of every site committing. As a result, there is a **window of uncertainty** in the commit process during which a failure will be catastrophic. Such windows of uncertainty have been studied in [COOP82].

The basic solution to this problem is for the coordinator to send out a "prepare" message prior to the commit. This will instruct each local site to force all the log pages for a transaction, so that the transaction can be successfully committed even if there is a site crash.

The basic algorithm is described in the paper by Skeen (3.5), who calls it a three-phase commit. However, the idea seems to have been thought of simultaneously by several researchers. With a two-phase commit, a distributed DBMS can successfully recover from all single site failures, all multiple site failures, and certain cases of network partitions. It is expected that all commercial distributed database systems will implement a two-phase commit if they have not done so already.

The only drawback of a two-phase commit is that it requires another round of messages in the protocol. Hence, this resiliency to crashes does not come for free, and there is a definite "level of service" versus cost tradeoff. On the other hand, if all sites implement so-called stable main memory, a two-phase commit is less necessary. Basically, by using an uninterruptable power supply a computer system can ensure that main memory is readable after a failure. This will allow a distributed transaction to be committed after the machine recovers. The only additional protection that a two-phase commit would offer is protection from corrupting the buffer pool during a crash.

The final paper in this section concerns multiple copies of objects (3.6). Again a **large** number of algorithms have been proposed [THOM79, GIFF79, STON79, HERL84]. Unfortunately virtually all the algorithms are of limited utility because they fail to deal with constraints imposed by the reality of the commercial marketplace. The first constraint is that a multiple copy algorithm must be optimized for the case that the number of copies is exactly two. There are few DBMS clients interested more than two copies of a gigabyte database. In general they want two copies to ensure that they can stay up in the presence of a single failure. The second constraint is that a read request must be satisfied by performing a single physical read to exactly one copy. Any scheme that slows down reads is not likely to win much real-world acceptance.

Consequently, schemes that require a transaction to lock a quorum of the copies will fail this litmus test. They will require read locks to be set on both copies in a two-copy system in order to satisfy a read request. Such an algorithm will lose to a scheme that locks both copies only on writes and one copy on reads. Such a read-one-write-all algorithm is described in the last paper in this section (3.6), and is the only algorithm I know of that passes my litmus test. An interesting survey of other algorithms can be found in [BERN87, DAVI85].

In my opinion copies present a very hard problem that has not yet been solved. The basic problem can be illustrated by an example. Suppose I am in New York and want to cash a check. For reliability reasons there is a second copy of my checking account information in Hong Kong. Without the second copy, my transaction is local and response time will be a few seconds. However, **every** multiple copy scheme that I know of will require at least two round-trip messages to Hong Kong to commit the transaction in the presence of copies. This will ensure both that I get bad response time to my transaction and that the responsible copy algorithm is not used. The bottom line is that all copies algorithms turn local transactions into distributed transactions and thereby generate much poorer response time. A solution to this problem must be found either by assuming application-specific semantics or through some other means. A start in this direction is presented in [KUMA88].

References

[BERN80] Bernstein, P. et al., "Concurrency Control in a System for Distributed Data Bases (SDD-1)," ACM-TODS, Mar. 1980.

[BERN80b] Bernstein, P. and Shipman, D., "The Correctness of Concurrency Control Mechanisms in a System for Distributed Databases (SDD-1)," ACM-TODS, Mar. 1980.

[BERN81] Bernstein, P. et al., "Query Processing in a System for Distributed Databases (SDD-1)," ACM-TODS, Dec. 1981.

[BERN87] Bernstein, P. et al., "Concurrency Control and Recovery in Database Systems," Addison-Wesley, Reading, Mass., 1987.

[CARE86] Carey, M., and Lu, H., "Load Balancing in a Locally Distributed DB System," Proc. 1986 ACM-SIGMOD Conference on Management of Data, Washington, D. C., May 1986.

[CHAN83] Chan, A. et al., "Overview of an ADA Compatible Distributed Database Manager," Proc. 1983 ACM-SIGMOD Conference on Management of Data, San Jose, Calif., May 1983.

[COOP82] Cooper, E., "Analysis of Distributed Commit Protocols," Proc. 1982 ACM-SIGMOD Conference on Management of Data, Orlando, Fla., June 1982.

[DANI82] Daniels, D. et al., "An Introduction to Distributed Query Compilation in R*," Proc. 2nd International Conference on Distributed Databases, Berlin, Sept. 1982.

[DAVI85] Davidson, S. et al., "Consistency in Partitioned Networks," ACM Computing Surveys, Sept. 1985.

[DEWI86] Dewitt, D., "GAMMA: A High Performance Dataflow Database Machine," Proc. 1986 VLDB Conference, Kyoto, Japan, Oct. 1986.

[EPST78] Epstein, R. et al., "Distributed Query Processing in a Relational Data Base System," Proc. 1978 ACM-SIGMOD Conference on Management of Data, May 1978.

[GIFF79] Gifford, D., "Weighted Voting for Replicated Data," Proc. 7th Symposium on Operating System Principles, Dec. 1979.

[HAMM80] Hammer, M., and Shipman, D., "Reliability Mechanisms for SDD-1: A System for Distributed Databases," ACM-TODS, Dec. 1980.

[HERL84] Herlihy, M., "General Quorum Consensus: A Replication Method for Abstract Data Types," Dept. of Computer Science, CMU, Pittsburgh, Pa., CMU-CS-84-164, Dec. 1984.

[KUMA88] Kumar, A., and Stonebraker, M., "Semantics Based Transaction Management Techniques for Replicated Data," Proc. 1988 ACM-SIGMOD Conference on Management of Data, Chicago, Ill., June 1988.

[LAFO86] Lafortune, S., and Wong, E., "A State Transition Model for Distributed Query Processing," ACM-TODS, Sept. 1986.

[LAZO86] Lazowska, E. et al., "File Access Performance of Diskless Workstations," ACM TOCS, Aug. 1986.

[LIND84] Lindsay, B. et al., "Computation and Communication in R*: A Distributed Database Manager," ACM-TOCS, Feb. 1984.

[LIND85] Lindsay, B., "A Retrospection on R*: A Distributed Database Management System," IBM Research, San Jose, Calif., RJ4859, Sept. 1985.

[ROTH80] Rothnie, J. et al., "Introduction to a System for Distributed Data Bases (SDD-1)," ACM-TODS, Mar. 1980.

[SELI80] Selinger, P., and Adiba, M., "Access Path Selection in a Distributed

Database System," Proc. International Conference on Databases, Aberdeen, Scotland, July 1980.

[STON79] Stonebraker, M., "Concurrency Control and Consistency of Multiple Copies in Distributed INGRES," IEEE-TSE, Mar. 1979.

[STON83] Stonebraker, M. et al., "Performance Analysis of Distributed Data Base Systems," Proc. Third Symposium on Reliability in Distributed Software and Database Systems," Clearwater, Fla., Oct. 1983.

[STON86] Stonebraker, M., "The Design and Implementation of Distributed INGRES," in "The INGRES Papers," M Stonebraker (ed), Addison-Wesley, Reading, Mass., 1986.

[STON88] Stonebraker, M., "Future Trends in Data Base Systems," Proc. 1988 IEEE Data Engineering Conference, Los Angeles, Calif., Feb. 1988.

[TERA83] Teradata Corp., "DBC/1012 Data Base Computer Concepts and Facilities," Teradata Corp, Los Angeles, Calif., C02-0001-00, 1983.

[THOM79] Thomas, R., "A Majority Consensus Approach to Concurrency Control for Multiple Copy Distributed Database Systems," ACM-TODS, June 1979.

[WILL81] Williams, R. et al., R*: An Overview of the Architecture," IBM Research, San Jose, Calif., RJ3325, Dec. 1981.

[WILM83] Wilms, P. et al., "I Wish I were Over There: Distributed Execution Protocols for Data Definition," Proc. 1983 ACM-SIGMOD Conference on Management of Data, San Jose, Calif., May 1983.

[YU84] Yu. C. and Chang, C., "Distributed Query Processing," ACM Computing Surveys, Dec. 1984.

R*: AN OVERVIEW OF THE ARCHITECTURE

R. Williams, D. Daniels, L. Haas, G. Lapis, B. Lindsay, P. Ng, R. Obermarck, P. Selinger, A. Walker, P. Wilms and R. Yost

IBM Research, Almaden Research Center, Ca. USA.

Abstract

R* is an experimental distributed database system being developed at IBM Research to study the issues and problems of distributed data management. R* consists of a confederation of voluntarily co-operating sites, each supporting the relational model of data and communicating via IBM's CICS. A key feature of the architecture is to maintain the autonomy of each site. To achieve maximum site autonomy SQL statements are compiled, data objects are named and catalogued, and deadlock detection and recovery are all handled in a distributed manner. The R* architecture, including transaction management, commit processing, deadlock detection, system recovery, object naming, catalog management, and authorization checking is described. Some examples of the additions and changes to the SQL language needed to support distributed function are given.

1. TRENDS IN DATABASE AND DISTRIBUTED PROCESSING SYSTEMS

There are several factors leading to the development of distributed database management systems. People and organizations share data because of its intrinsic value; indeed corporations regard their data as a major asset. The number of computer installations is increasing due to declining costs of hardware. Users of these installations need to share data to do their work, and now that computers can easily be interconnected by electronic networks, distributed systems are evolving for data exchange. Database systems provide consistent views of data, concurrency control for multiple users and recovery in case of failures by using the notion of transaction processing. A database management system can therefore be expanded into a distributed database management system, DDBMS, to supply the same application features to a network of users potentially able to share all the data at all the sites.

Each site should retain local privacy and control of its own data. It is also very desirable to present data to programs and users at a site in the network as if that site were the only one. Furtermore to achieve best performance programs should run locally if all the data for the program is local to the site. Specifically there should be no central dependencies in the network; no central catalog, no central scheduler, no central deadlock detector or breaker, etc. We call this concept of maximum independence "site autonomy"[(21)].

With these goals in mind, we have designed a DDBMS, called R*, using the relational database technology. It is a follow-on project from System R [(4)], [(5)]. The SQL language[(6)] has been extended where necessary to allow for new functions but existing SQL programs that ran in System R should also run in R*.

The paper describes the environment in which R* runs and the data forms to be supported by R*. The skeletal architecture of R* is described by following the processing of a query entered at one site; query processing in R* is similar to the query processing in System R. The major issues and processes are:

- Environment and Data Definitions
- Object Naming
- Distributed Catalogs
- Transaction Management and Commit Protocols
  - Transaction Number
- Query Preparation
  - Name Resolution
  - Authorization Checking
  - Access Path Selection and Optimization
  - Views
- Query Execution
  - Concurrency
  - Deadlock Detection and Resolution
  - Logging and Recovery
- SQL Additions and Changes

R* is partially implemented (see Status section 9).

2. ENVIRONMENT & DATA DEFINITIONS FOR R*

R* consists of several database sites that communicate via CICS, an IBM software product[7], as shown in Figure 1. CICS was chosen as the communication medium to minimize our prototyping efforts so that we could concentrate on distributed database, DDB, issues. Any network configuration and interconnection topology allowed by CICS can be used in R*; CICS communications is used merely as a transport medium. R* also considers the communications medium to be unreliable, i.e., message delivery is not guaranteed, however when messages are delivered to the database software they are assumed to be delivered intact in order and without duplication. R* runs in a CICS address space, and CICS handles terminal I/O, program and task management. Note that sites in R* would typically be physically separate computer systems, but sites need to be only logically distinct, not physically distinct, especially for initial development purposes (there are already enough problems using one machine for debugging complex software)!

Data in R* is stored in tables (relations) that may be dispersed, replicated or partitioned. Combinations of these distributions are supported also; for example partitioned data may be replicated. Dispersed data means that tables T1,....Tn are uniquely stored at the various sites S1,......Sk; e.g., T1,T2 at S1; T3 at S2 etc. Replicated data means that copies of a table exist and are guaranteed to be identical at all times. All copies are updated synchronously, using a two-phase commit protocol. Partitioned data is logically one table, part of which is stored at one site, and another part(s) at another site(s). In horizontal partitioning some rows (tuples) are stored at one site, some at another site according to some disjoint separation criteria based on column values (e.g. store values 1 to 100 in site 1 and all the rest in site 2). In vertical partitioning, some columns are stored at one site, some at another, according to some column separation criteria. The vertical fragmentation must be lossless so that the original relation can be created from the vertical partitions[3] and therefore all partitions must have a set of common columns that determine the values of all columns in the complete relation, or a virtual column created artificially by the DDBMS to enable a one-to-one match of the fragmented tuples during reconstruction. Partitioned data can also be replicated. The end-user of the database need not be aware of the data distribution for query execution or for application programming. Data consistency, reassembly of partitions and access of remote data is performed by the DDBMS itself and is transparent to the end-user.

The SIRIUS/DELTA DDBMS also allows partitioned and replicated data forms[19]. The Polypheme prototype went further and allowed for heterogeneous database systems in its design. The technique was for all systems to employ a standard relational form for communications to other sites, and a mapping to the internal form at each site [1] CICS supports distributed data processing through function shipping using the Inter-Systems Communications feature[7]. Also using function shipping, TANDEM systems support distributed data, with an emphasis on availability, but few technical papers exist on their systems[34].

In R*, some tables can be snapshots of other tables[2]. Snapshot data is a copy of a relation(s) in which the data is consistent but not necessarily up-to-date. Snapshots are read-only and are intended to provide a static copy of a database (e.g. Friday's sales figures). They are not updated when the base relation is updated. They may however be periodically refreshed by recopying the data from the base relations (e.g. every Friday at 6 p.m.). Programs that only need snapshot data might run more efficiently from snapshots than from current relations. For example relations that are locally stored snapshots derived from a remote operational database would allow local programs to run much faster from the snapshots than from the operational data. Availability is increased also for transactions that use snapshot data.

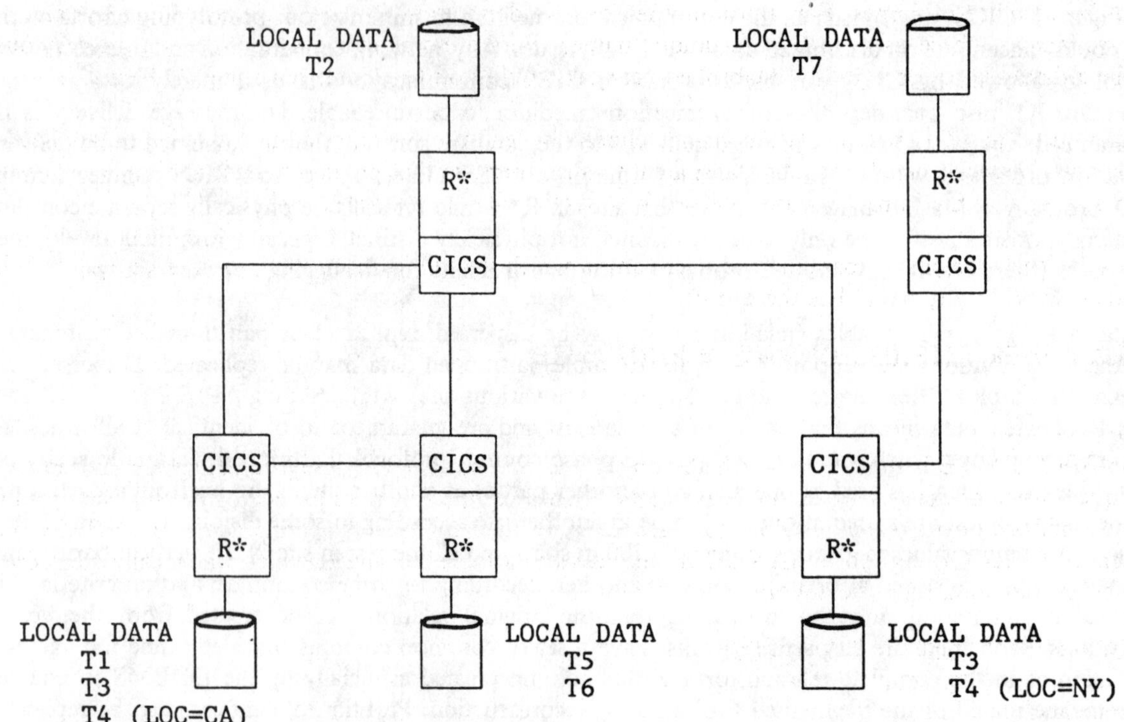

T1, T2, T5, T6, T7 : Dispersed Data
T3 : Replicated Data
T4 : Partitioned Data (by tuples with LOC=CA or LOC=NY)

Figure 1. R* Distributed Database Configuration.

3. OBJECT NAMING

The naming problem in distributed systems is to allow data sharing but without undue restrictions on an end-user's choice of names. For autonomy reasons we don't want to have a global naming system, nor do we want to force users to choose unique names. Furthermore adding a new site with a previously defined database to a previously established network would lead to terrible renaming problems.

Names used in SQL statements are names chosen by end-users writing ad-hoc queries or application programs. Network details must be transparent to such users, so that programming is as simple as possible and also so that the same programs will work correctly when entered at any site.

We solve the problem by mapping end-user names, which we call "print names", to internal System Wide Names, "SWN". An SWN has the form:

```
USER @ USER_SITE.OBJECT_NAME @ BIRTH_SITE
```

The BIRTH_SITE is the site in which the object was first created. Because site names are chosen to be unique outside of the system, an SWN is unique. Name completion rules for adding default parts to print names and synonym mapping tables for each user are used to convert a print name to an SWN. For example if BRUCE logs on in SAN_JOSE and accesses a table he calls T, which was locally created and stored in San Jose, then the SWN:

```
BRUCE @ SAN_JOSE.T @ SAN_JOSE
```

is generated.

This mapping mechanism allows different end-users to reference either the same object with different print names or different objects with the same print names. Objects may be stored and moved without impacting user code (see catalogs in section 4) and this location transparency mechanism permits site autonomy. A more complete discussion can be found in[22].

4. DISTRIBUTED CATALOGS

In the SDD-1 system[28],[28], the catalog is logically a single table, which can be fragmented and replicated. This allows catalog entries to be replicated and distributed among the data module sites. However, this also implies that local objects may have their catalog entries at a remote site and that data definition operations may not be totally local. SDD-1 does cache catalog entries to aid performance but this also adds overhead for updating purposes. A distributed version of INGRES[33] distinguishes between local relations (accessible from a single site) and global relations (accessible from all sites). The name of every global relation is stored at every site. Creation of a global relation involves broadcasting its name (and location) to all sites of the network, but cached catalog entries are supported. Thus both SDD-1 and INGRES implement a global catalog and therefore restrict site autonomy and complicate system growth. For a large network any operation requiring unanimous participation will create difficulties, and may require complex recovery mechanisms.

R* uses a distributed catalog architecture. Catalogs at each site keep and maintain information about objects in the database, including replicas or fragments, stored at that site. In addition the catalog at the birth site of an object keeps information indicating where the object is currently stored and this entry is updated if an object is moved. Cataloging of objects is done in this totally distributed manner to preserve site autonomy. An object can be located by the system from its SWN and no centralization is necessary.

For performance reasons, a catalog entry can be cached at another site so that a reference to it can be as efficient as a local reference e.g., for compiling (see section 6). A cached entry may become out-of-date if another transaction has changed the structure of or the access paths to the object after the cached entry is made; this fact is discovered during a later processing step and then the cached entry is updated from the correct catalog entry and the initial processing must be restarted. This discovery is made because entries have version numbers which are checked during subsequent processing against version numbers store in the real catalog entries to determine if the cached entry used at an earlier stage was valid. Restarting in this way is not expected to occur very often because catalog entries are relatively static.

The catalog entry for an object includes the object SWN, type and format, the access paths available, a mapping in the case of a view to lower level objects, and various statistics that assist query optimization. Each entry is identified by the SWN of an object. To find an object's catalog entry, first the local catalog, (plus the local cache), then the birth-site catalog and then the site indicated by the birth-site catalog are checked in that order, stopping when the catalog entry is found. This gives the best efficiency together with site autonomy.

5. TRANSACTION MANAGEMENT AND COMMIT PROTOCOL

5.1. Transaction Number

The DDBMS must support the notion of a **transaction**. A transaction is a recoverable sequence of database actions that either commits or aborts. If the transaction commits, all of its changes to the database take effect, but if the transaction aborts, none of its actions have any effect upon the database state. In SDD-1 and in INGRES each statement is a transaction whereas in System R one can define a transaction to be any number of SQL statements.

A transaction starts at the site where it is entered. Subsequently agents may be created at other sites to do work on behalf of the transaction. Both synchronous and asynchronous execution can be performed to take advantage of parallelism or pipelining during the compilation and execution of the transaction.

Any request to the DDBMS is given a transaction number that is made up from the site name and a sequence number (local time of day may be better) Each site is unique and the sequence is increased for each new transaction. Therefore the transaction number is both unique and ordered in the R* network. Uniqueness is necessary for identification purposes, for acquiring resources, breaking deadlocks etc. For example if a transaction starts at site A, sends work to site B, which in turn sends work to site A then it is necessary for A to know that both pieces of work are on behalf of the same transaction so that locks on data objects can be shared.If such locks could not be shared a deadlock would occur and make processing the query impossible. Ordering is used to provide a means of knowing which transaction to abort in the case of a deadlock between different transactions. R* aborts the youngest, largest numbered, transaction.

5.2. Transaction Commit Protocol

Whenever a transaction's actions involve more that one database site, the DDBMS must take special care in order to insure that the transaction termination is **uniform:** either all of the sites commit or all sites abort the effects of the transaction.

The so called "two phase" commit protocol[7],[13],[20], [24] is used in order to insure uniform transaction commitment or abortion. The two phase commit protocol allows multiple sites to coordinate transaction commit in such a way that all participating sites come to the same conclusion despite site and communication failures. There are many variations of the two phase commit protocol. In all variations there is one site, called the **coordinator**, which makes the commit or abort decision **after** all the other sites involved in the transaction are known to be recoverably **prepared** to commit or abort, and all the other sites are **awaiting** the coordinator's decision.

When the non-coordinator sites are prepared to commit and awaiting the coordinator's decision, they are not allowed to unilaterally abandon or commit the transaction. This has the effect of **sequestering** the transaction's resources, making them unavailable until the coordinator's decision is received. Before entering the prepared state, however, any site can unilaterally abort its portion of a transaction. The rest of the sites will also abort eventually. While a site is prepared to commit, local control (autonomy) over the resources held by the transaction is surrendered to the commit coordinator.

Some variations of the two phase commit protocol sequester resources longer than other variations. Rosenkrantz, Stearns, and Lewis[30] require all sites other than the single active site of the transaction to be prepared at all times. The linear commit protocols described in[13] and[20] have a commit phase with duration proportional to the number of sites involved.

R* actually uses a presumed-to-commit protocol. The number of messages required in the usual two phase commit protocol is 4(N-1), where N is the number of sites involved in the transaction, but by assuming the commit succeeds the number of messages can be reduced to 3(N-1). If a failure requiring transaction abort occurs, then all 4(N-1) messages are needed. The improvement is obtained by removing the need for acknowledging the commit message. The coordinator logs the start of the transaction commit processing and then sends messages to the other sites (called apprentices) involved in the transaction. An apprentice is a site that does work at the request of another site, which then is called the master. Each apprentice still has to log its decision and reply to the coordinator who logs the resulting decision. Therefore the apprentice has to await commit/abort instructions from the coordinator, during which time its resources are tied up. Lost commit messages are detected by a time-out, but to avoid the very long outages that could occur if a network breaks down, operator intervention must be permitted.

This presumed-to-commit protocol minimizes the duration of the commit protocol. Other variations, notably those proposed for SDD-1[15], provide mechanisms for circumventing the delay caused by coordinator failure, by sending extra messages (to nominate a backup coordinator) which prolong the commit phase in the normal case. It does not appear possible to completely eliminate the temporary loss of site autonomy during the commit procedure[18].

6. QUERY PREPARATION

6.1. Name Resolution

When an SQL statement is first seen by R*, it is parsed and then undergoes name resolution in which all SQL print names are resolved into SWNs. Then it is possible to determine if catalog entries for each database object are available locally. If any entries are missing because they are stored at remote sites and not in the local cache then a message has to be sent to the remote site to fetch catalog information for the remote objects from the birth site as described in section 4.

6.2. Authorization Checking

After name resolution the authorization of the user to perform operations indicated by the SQL statement on **local** data is checked. Because all sites are cooperating in R* voluntarily, no site wishes to trust other sites with respect to authorization. Therefore authorization checking for a remote access request must be done at the site that stores the data and all controls for accessing data must be stored at the same site as the data being controlled. It is possible to control all access to local data locally without the need to contact another site, thus preserving site autonomy. Each site is responsible for maintaining its own site authorization using passwords etc. Authorization for data access is checked for each user, but remote sites authenticate on a site-to-site basis when responding to a request for data. A remote site is trusted to have validated its own users. If this breaks down the damage is limited to the aggregate of privileges held by the users at that site.

Thus the authorization entity in R* is a user at a site, and user level authorization semantics are enforced using site level authentication[35]. For example, PAT @ SAN_JOSE is different from PAT @ YORKTOWN. An object owner, initially the creator, can grant access rights to any other user, local or remote, and that person can pass on access rights to other users if the original grant permitted subsequent grants (included the grant option). This is the same as in System R [14]. For site to site authentication in networks see encryption techniques[25],[16].

6.3. Compilation and Plan Generation

Just as with programming languages, it is possible to compile rather than interpret the database language. Compilation offloads from execution time to compile time much of the overhead of operations needed to set up the data request and thus improves the performance of repetitively executed data access requests.

For conventional programming languages, compilation is a binding process in which high level constructs are mapped to a low level instruction set, which is fixed by the machine on which the compiled code is to be run. Analogously, in a database system access requests expressed in a very high-level database language, such as SQL, can also be compiled into an access program which uses low level objects [6]. This compilation includes a binding process in which the requests are bound to required authorizations, data objects, and the paths to access them. However, one of the primary differences between the compilation of programs written in conventional programming languages and the compilation of programs written in database languages lies in the fact that the latter depends on objects that are subject to change. Between compile time and execution time, a relation may be deleted or moved, an access path may be dropped, or a required privilege may be revoked. Recompilation or invalidation is necessary when such items change.

In a DDBMS data objects accessed and access paths used may reside at a remote site and the question as to where binding should be done arises.

The approaches can be grouped into three classes:

- All binding for every request can be done at a chosen site;
- All binding can be done at the site where the request originates;
- Binding can be done in a distributed way,

at the sites where data objects are accessed.

The first approach would not function well because it is a centralized approach and suffers from poor efficiency and lack of resiliency to failure. It would require a centralized catalog and therefore an excessive amount of communications in the network. The advantages offered by a DDBMS would be mostly lost if a centralized compiler had to be used for all compilations; it would become a system bottleneck. Site autonomy would be lost in this approach of course.

The second approach is not good either. First, to preserve each site's autonomy, it should not be necessary to get agreement from all sites at which requests have been compiled before another site can change an access path for its locally stored relation. Secondly, the compiling site should not need to remember and record the physical details of data access paths at other sites since individual databases may be changed, for example by adding a new access path. Thus if a program depends on a relation that has been changed at a remote site we do not want to do a global recompilation for the whole program if we can avoid it by doing a local recompilation at the remote site for part of the program. Also, to protect data in a high level DDBMS, a user at a certain site may choose only to grant access to a view which is an abstraction of underlying physical data objects, rather than granting access to the objects themselves, which means that the entire compilation and binding cannot be done at the originating site.

The third approach overcomes the drawbacks mentioned above and offers additional advantages. The master site can decide inter-site issues and perform high-level binding and the local sites can decide local issues and do a lower-level binding (e.g. for access path selection). When compilation is distributed and the portion of program to access and manipulate a site's data objects is generated at the same site, it follows naturally that if recompilation has to be done due to changes of local objects, it can be done on a local basis. Thus distributed compilation allows for local control in apprentice sites, which preserves site autonomy. However, global optimality becomes more difficult to obtain after local changes have occurred and it is desirable to be able to do a complete global recompilation, optionally, to improve execution efficiency in some cases. Other advantages of distributed compilation are that failure resiliency is also improved by limiting the scope of actions to a local site when possible. Also different versions or releases of system code could exist at different sites and it would still work correctly.

The INGRES DDBMS [33] seems to be moving towards a compilation approach of preparing queries for execution but most distributed systems still use interpretive methods. R*, using the third approach above, performs distributed compilation [9],[26]. In R* the site where the SQL query enters becomes the master site and to compile a request for data at mutiple sites, the overall global plan for executing the program has to be created at the master and then communicated to the apprentices. The difficulty in the design of distributed compilation arises because we want to compile programs to achieve global optimality for execution but retain local site autonomy. The master site may not have complete and up-to-date knowledge of the data objects and access paths available at the apprentice sites, therefore it may make poor decisions and generate very inefficient code if it did the complete compilation. Incorrect decisions can be detected by an apprentice site by checking the version number of the information on which the decision was based, but the extra overhead of correct but distributed compilation is the cost incurred for site autonomy and data protection. The overhead in this case is to redo the entire compilation. The solution is that the master chooses the execution plan, join order, which sites do work etc. and apprentices choose how to access local data.

The global plan is a structural skeleton of the **access strategies** and is generated at the master site using the information available at the master site. If the master has insufficient catalog information about data objects at other sites, it can request the necessary information and cache it for later use. The global plan specifies the invocation sequence of the participating sites and the order of parameters. If the SQL statement requires a join, the global plan would also specify the join order and join methods.

The global plan is a high level representation of the decisions made by the master site with regard to the execution of the SQL statement. The optimal choice of access paths is discussed later in section 6.4. A global plan should be globally optimal if the information used in access path selection is correct. In addition to the global plan, the compiler at the master site also generates a set of local execution strategies for the local data objects accessed. This includes, for example, which index to use and whether sorting is done. The selection of the global plan and the local execution strategies is termed the "path selection" phase.

The global plan together with the SQL statement is sent to those remote databases that contain the data needed for this SQL statement. This processing phase is termed the "plan distribution" phase. In the global plan, references to data objects are made in terms of their relative positions in the SQL statement. The use of the SQL statement for the expression of the action needed, together with the fact that the global plan is a high level representation, solves the problem of version incompatibility of system code among DBMS's at different sites.

At the remote apprentice sites the first task performed is to check the validity of the catalog information that the master used. If an out-dated version was used, an error message is returned to the master site and the global plan is re-generated by the master using updated information. Compilation in an apprentice site follows the same pattern as at a master site except that no name resolution is needed. The decisions made by the master site concerning the interfaces among sites to execute this SQL statement will be followed. However, the apprentice is free to change the sequence of the local operations. For example, if the SQL statement requires a join, then the apprentice site can change join orders and join methods for local relations as long as the result tuples are presented in the order prescribed, if any, in the global plan. The apprentice may also use access paths unknown to the master. The access path selector in the apprentice site also generates a set of local execution strategies, which, in turn, undergo the code generation phase to produce local subsections. Figure 2 shows the compilation process.

Just as in a programming language compiler, there is a code generation step. Code is generated at the master site and at each apprentice site involved in the distributed compilation; each piece is called a subsection. Each subsection contains code both for calling its local Research Storage System,RSS, which performs local data management, and for passing data and control to other sites according to the overall plan.

The whole compilation for a SQL program or query is processed itself as a transaction. After all the subsections have been generated in the involved sites for every SQL statement in the program being prepared and no errors are detected, the master commits the compilation transaction using the two phase commit protocol. Upon receiving the "prepare" command, each apprentice stores the subsections into an access module. Besides the access module, the SQL statements and the global plans are also stored for recompilation purposes. During execution, subsections call one another as subroutines or coroutines, or they may be executed in parallel.

6.4. Access Path Selection and Optimization

To execute a query efficiently it is necessary to select access paths to data that minimize the total processing time of the query. Epstein studied this problem for distributed INGRES[7] and Selinger for SYSTEM R [31]. The SYSTEM R work has been extended for R*.

During compilation the access paths to data objects are selected and the access path selector in R* tries to minimize total predicted execution time of a SQL statement by exploring a search tree of alternatives and estimating the cost of each[32]. Three components are included to model the execution costs of SQL statements for different access paths in R*: I/O cost , CPU cost and message cost. The cost formulae have the form:

```
TOTAL_COST = I/O_COST + CPU_COST + MESSAGE_COST

I/O_COST =  I/O_WEIGHT * NUMBER_OF_PAGES_FETCHED

CPU_COST =  CPU_WEIGHT * NUMBER_OF_CALLS_TO_RSS

MESSAGE_COST = MESSAGE_COST * NUMBER_OF_MESSAGES_SENT +

          BYTE_COST * NUMBER_OF_BYTES_SENT
```

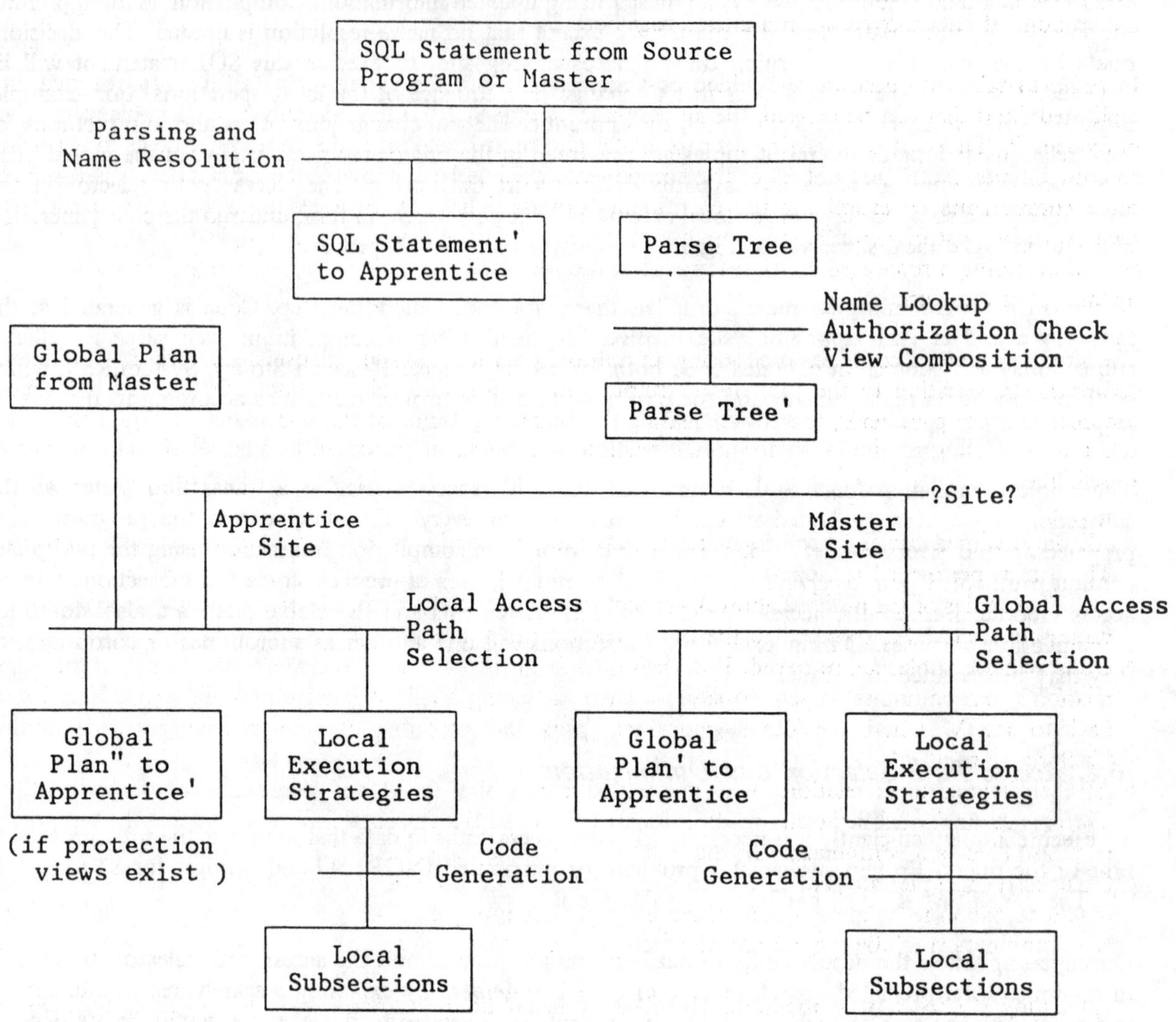

Figure 2. Skeleton of Distributed Compilation.

As in System R, the cost of an access plan is calculated as the weighted sum of the components. NUMBER_OF_CALLS_TO_RSS represents the estimated number of tuples retrieved; and MESSAGE_COST consists of a per message cost and a per byte cost. Both the number of messages and the amount of data moved are minimized together.

In order to take into account the added cost component and the variety of data forms (partitoned and replicated data) that can be created, the access path selector in R* is considerably more complex than that in System R. The cost of accessing a horizontally partitioned relation is the sum of the costs of accessing its components. Note that not all of the components need to be accessed if the path selector can exclude some components by examining the partitioning criteria. The cost of accessing a vertically partitioned relation is the cost of joining the components. Again, the partitioning criteria may reduce the cost. The cost of accessing a replicated relation for read is the minimum of the costs of accessing the replicas. For updates, it is the sum [32].

The situation is more complex in choosing an optimal path for a join of relations which reside at different databases. In addition to the join order, output tuple order, and join method, the join result location becomes another parameter, thereby increasing the branching factor of the search tree. To join the inner relation B residing at site N to the outer relation A residing or produced at site M, R* considers five possibilities:

- All the qualified tuples of the inner relation B are sent to site M and stored in a temporary relation. The join is performed at site M.
- Qualified tuples of the outer relation A are sent to site N.one at a time. Matching qualified inner relation tuples are retrieved and joined to the outer relation tuple, at site N.
- Outer relation tuples are retrieved. For each qualified tuple, a request containing the values of the outer relation's join column(s) is sent to site N. Then matching qualified inner tuples are retrieved and sent back to site M, where the join is performed. This way of obtaining inner relation tuples is termed "fetching as needed."
- All the qualified inner relation tuples are sent to a third site, site P, and stored in a temporary relation. Then (matching) qualified outer relation tuples are sent to site P to perform the join using the temporary relation. This is a combination of the first and second approaches above.
- Outer relation tuples are sent to a third site, site P, and for each of these outer relation tuples, a request is sent to the inner relation site to retrieve the matching tuples. The join is performed at site P. This is a combination of the second and third approaches above.

In executing a chosen join method, advantage is taken of the parallelism and pipelining available in processing an SQL statement. For example, fetching tuples from site A and other tuples from site B can be done in parallel. As another example while inner tuples from site A that match an outer tuple from site B are joined at site A, the next outer tuple can be fetched from site B.

6.5. Views

A view in R*, as in System R, is a non-materialized virtual relation defined by an SQL statement. It is defined in terms of one or more tables or previously defined views and during processing a view is materialized from its component objects. Views can be used as shorthand notation for reducing the amount of typing required when frequently executing complex queries, or they can be used as a protection mechanism for hiding rows or columns in underlying tables from the user of the view.

Unlike in System R, in R* view component objects may be at different sites. Therefore to provide data protection between sites a protection view is materialized only at the site owning the view. This scheme prevents sending sensitive data to a node where no user is authorized to see it. Therefore during compilation the master site generates a plan for processing the view as if it were a physical table and sends the plan and SQL statement to the apprentices where the view will be processed (and where view records will eventually materialize.) An apprentice site may itself decompose a view component in terms of other views on tables at yet other sites. In that case the apprentice acts as a master to other apprentices and must generate a plan and send subplans to its apprentice sites. The plan distribution progresses in this way until all views are resolved and may even loop back to a site that has already participated in the compilation.

7. QUERY EXECUTION

Queries are executed by running the compiled code generated during query preparation. The local subsection is loaded and executed and it calls remote subsections as needed. Messages are sent to execute remote-procedure-like calls. Local and remote sections of code call the Research Storage System RSS, which is the same as in System R. The RSS returns one record at a time when it is called; joins and other multiple record handling operations are carried out at a level above the RSS. Therefore the only new features required in the RSS are begin and end transaction functions associated with each unique transaction number. Transaction management and commit protocols to synchronize database changes at the end of a transaction were covered in section 5.

7.1. Concurrency

Distributed transaction processing requires database concurrency control mechanisms[(12),(13)] in order to avoid interference among concurrently executing transactions. The concurrency control mechanism should not require centralized services for resource allocation or deadlock detection. Distributed concurrency control algorithms, including distributed deadlock detection, which do not impact site autonomy have been developed,[(27)] and[(23,7)]. The R* techniques used for deadlock detection and resolution are different from those in System R (section 7.2), but the concurrency control mechanisms used in R* are the same as those used in System R.

7.2. Deadlock Detection and Resolution

The SDD-1 system has an interesting technique for reducing deadlock occurrences. It attempts to analyze the read and write sets of queries and group them into classes that require disjoint sets of resources. Then one query in each class can be run without interference and so no deadlock should occur. However, for unpredictable data references during query execution this technique would not work.

The distributed deadlock detection algorithm in R* attempts to maximize site autonomy, minimize messages and minimize unnecessary processing or other bottlenecks [(27)]. The basic idea is that each site does periodic deadlock detection using transaction wait-for information gathered locally or received from other sites. Real deadlock cycles are resolved and potential cycles are converted to transaction wait-for 'strings'.

Each 'string' is sent to the next site along the path of the (potential) multi-site deadlock cycle only if the first transaction number in the string is less than the last transaction number in the string. This is an optimization to reduce the number of messages sent. Note also that other orderings could be chosen. This process continues until a cycle is found. The cycle will be found at one site only (due to the transaction ordering) and only sites involved in the transaction will be involved in finding it. This is usually 2 or 3 sites only in what is potentially a very large network. When a deadlock cycle is discovered a standard deadlock cycle breaker program is run and the deadlock is broken by aborting one of the transactions (such as the one that has done the least work so far). The other sites involved in the chosen transaction will be told subsequently to abort the transaction.

An example distributed deadlock is shown in Figure 3. There are three sites 1,2,3 and three transactions X,Y,Z each of which has an agent waiting for resources at a remote site. The algorithm for breaking the deadlock can be understood by following the messages sent from site to site until the cycle is found at site 3.

7.3. Logging and Recovery

The mechanisms used for logging are the same as in System R. As previously discussed each site involved in a transaction has to log data changes and commit decisions during two phase commit. If a site or communications link fails during query execution **before** two phase commit, time-outs will occur at the calling site and the called sites and the transaction will be aborted at all sites. No resources will be sequestered after time-outs have occurred. If a failure occurs **after** a site has entered phase one of the two phase commit then its resources are held by that transaction until communications are re-established and the in-doubt transaction status is resolved and the database made consistent.

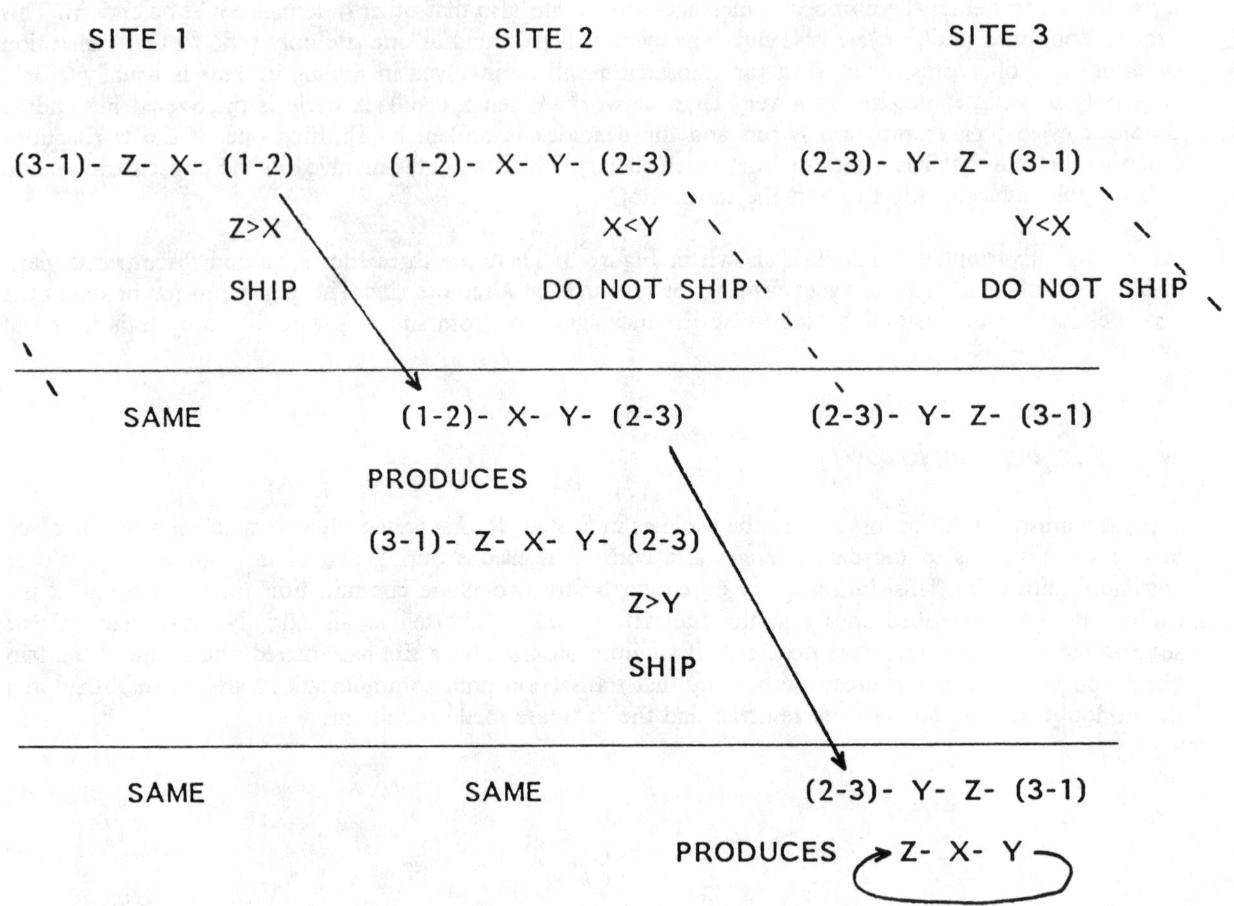

Fig. 3. Global Deadlock Detection.

8. SQL Additions and Changes

The SQL database language [6] developed for System R has been extended for R* and some example extensions are given below. These extensions are not the only ones needed, nor because of space limitations, can each be fully explained. However it is hoped that they give the reader an idea of the kind of high-level non-procedural language statements needed in a distributed database system like R*.

```
DEFINE SYNONYM <relation-name> AS <System-Wide-Name>

DISTRIBUTE TABLE <table-name> HORIZONTALLY INTO
   <name> WHERE <predicate> IN SEGMENT <segment-name@site>
   .
   .
   <name> WHERE <predicate> IN SEGMENT <segment-name@site>

DISTRIBUTE TABLE <table-name> VERTICALLY INTO
   <name> <column-name-list> IN SEGMENT <segment-name@site>
   .
   .
   <name> <column-name-list> IN SEGMENT <segment-name@site>

DISTRIBUTE TABLE <table-name> REPLICATED INTO
   <name> IN SEGMENT <segment-name@site>
   .
   .
   <name> IN SEGMENT <segment-name@site>

DEFINE SNAPSHOT <snapshot-name> (<attribute-list>)
       AS <query>
       REFRESHED EVERY <period>;

REFRESH SNAPSHOT <snapshot-name>

CREATE INDEX <name> ON <table-name>
DROP INDEX <name> FOR <table-name>

MIGRATE TABLE <table-name> TO <segment-name@site>
```

9. STATUS OF R* AND FUTURE PLANS

As of November 1981, when this paper was written, large sections of R* have been coded and tested as an experimental prototype system. The transaction management, communications environment and system interfaces for CICS running under VM or MVS have been coded and run in a single processor. The compiler, optimizer and access path selector have also been written. Code generation from the R* compiler is just beginning. R* has just started sending the first messages for remote catalog look-up and for distributed compilation. The RSS data management, deadlock detection, commit/abort processing, logging and recovery have been tested.

Future work includes linking the coded subsystems together once they are all written, the generation of code from the compiler and the execution and testing of "distributed queries" running, at first, in a single machine environment. Then we will bring up physically separate machines and test actual distributed processing with real message traffic using the CICS/ISC (Inter-Systems-Communications) facility. Next different kinds of data distributions will be examined. By that time we should be able to examine the overall behaviour of R* and to make improvements to the optimizer and to the system code to improve the performance and possibly the design too. R* is a large experimental project and we are under no illusions that we have got it all just right!

10. CONCLUSIONS

We have presented the overall architecture of R*, emphasizing those issues that affect the autonomy of the sites participating in the distributed database. A key ingredient of site autonomy is careful distribution of function and transaction management responsibility among the participating sites. Avoiding global and centralized data and control structures is required, not only to enhance local autonomy, but also to facilitate graceful system growth, data protection and failure resiliency.

Data access authorization is managed by the site holding the data and remote access requests are authenticated. Local control and stand alone processing capabilities require that all relevant catalog structures be locally stored and managed. Distributed query compilation was developed to support local site autonomy. Local representation of compiled query fragments allows local invalidation of the query if local objects or authorizations are modified. Although local control must be surrendered to the coordinator site during the transaction commit protocol, careful selection of a distributed commit protocol can minimize the duration of the loss of local control.

The R* architecture supports several kinds of data distribution. Attention has been given to efficient execution of programs by the compilation and optimization of users queries and SQL programs.

Unlike other DDBMS (e.g. INGRES [33] and SDD-1[29]), R*'s emphasis on site autonomy has led us away from shared control and globally managed or centralized catalog and name resolution structures. At the same time, R* provides transparent remote data definition and manipulation facilities, distributed transaction management, and distributed concurrency control which should simplify data sharing for both ad hoc query users and application programmers. Existing single site SQL programs and queries can be run against distributed data without modification in an R* environment and programmers can continue to develop programs without having to worry about network issues.

11. ACKNOWLEDGMENTS

The following people have contributed to the R* work also, and we would like to acknowledge their main contributions: M. Adiba who developed snapshots, J. Gray who worked on the architecture, recovery and commit, F. Putzolu who developed the RSS data management, and I. Traiger who worked on several distributed systems issues and the RSS data management.

Bibliography

1. M.Adiba, J.M.Andrade, P.Decitre, F.Fernandez and Nguyen Gia Toan, *Polypheme: An Experience in Distributed Database System Design and Implementation,* Proc. of the International Symposium on Distributed Databases, Distributed Databases, North Holland Publishing Company, Paris, March 1980.

2. M.E.Adiba and B.G.Lindsay, *Database Snapshots,* IBM Research Report RJ2772, San Jose, CA. March 1980.

3. A.V.Aho, C.Beeri and J.D.Ullman, *The Theory of Joins in Relational Databases,* ACM Transactions on Database Systems, Vol.4, No.3, September 1979, p.297.

4. M.M.Astrahan, M.W.Blasgen, D.D.Chamberlin, K.P.Eswaran, J.N.Gray, P.P.Griffiths, W.F.King, R.A.Lorie, P.R.McJones, J.W.Mehl, G.R.Putzolu, I.L.Traiger, B.Wade, and V.Watson, *System R: A Relational Approach to Database Management,* ACM Transactions on Database Systems, Vol.1, No.2, June 1976, p.97.

5. Blasgen 79′ M.W.Blasgen, M.M.Astrahan, D.D.Chamberlin, J.N.Gray, W.F.King, B.G.Lindsay, R.A.Lorie, J.W.Mehl, T.G.Price, G.R.Putzolu, M.Schkolnick, P.G.Selinger, D.R.Slutz, I.L.Traiger, B.W.Wade, and R.A.Yost, *System R: An Architectural Update,* IBM Research Report RJ2581, San Jose, CA, July 1979.

6. Chamberlin 76′ D.D.Chamberlin, M.M.Astrahan, K.P.Eswaran, P.P.Griffiths, R.A.Lorie, J.W.Mehl, P.Reisner, and B.W.Wade, *SEQUEL 2: A Unified Approach to Data Definition, Manipulation and Control,* IBM Journal of Research and Development, November 1976, p. 560. (Also, see errata in January 1979 issue).

7. CICS 78′ CICS Inter System Communication, *CICS,*VS System/Application Design Guide/ Chapter 13, Version1, Release 4, IBM Form Number SC33-0068-1, June 1978, pp.379-412.

8. *CICS,*VS Introduction to Program Logic/ Chapter 1.6, Version 1, Release 4, IBM Form Number SC33-0067-1, June 1978, pp.83-110.

9. D.Daniels, *Query Compilation in a Distributed Database System,* Masters Thesis in preparation, Department of EECS, MIT, Cambridge, Mass. For January 1982.

10. R.S.Epstein, M.Stonebraker and E.Wong, *Distributed Query Processing in Relational Database Systems,* Proc. 78 ACM SIGMOD Conference on Management of Data, Austin, Texas, May 1978.

11. R.Epstein and M.Stonebraker, *Analysis of Distributed Database Processing Strategies,* International Conference on Very Large Data Bases, Montreal , October 1980.

12. K.P.Eswaran, J.N.Gray, R.A.Lorie, and I.L.Traiger, *The Notions of Consistency and Predicate Locks in a Database System,* Communications of the ACM, Vol.19, No.11, November 1976, pp. 624-633.

13. J.N.Gray, *Notes on Data Base Operating Systems,* Operating Systems An Advanced Course, Lecture Notes in Computer Science 60, (ed. Goos and Hartmanis), Springer-Verlag, 1978, pp. 393-481.

14. P.Griffiths and B.Wade, *An Authorization Mechanism for a Relational Database System,* ACM Transactions on Database Systems, Vol.1, No.3, September, 1976, pp. 242-255.

15. M.Hammer and D.Shipman, *Reliability Mechanisms for SDD-1: A System for Distributed Databases,* Computer Corporation of America Technical Report, July 1979.

16. S.T.Kent, *Encryption-Based Protocols for Interactive User-Computer Communication,* Masters Thesis, Laboratory for Computer Science TR-162, Massachusetts Institute of Technology, Cambridge, Mass., May 1976.

17. B.W.Lampson and H.E.Sturgis, *Crash Recovery in a Distributed Data Storage System,* Communications of the ACM, to appear.

18. B.W.Lampson,, *Replicated Commit,* Workshop on Fundamental Issues in Distributed Systems, Pala Mesa, CA. Dec. (paper dated November 24), 1980.

19. J.Le Bihan, C.Esculier, G.Le Lann, L.Treille, *SIRIUS-DELTA: Un Prototype de systeme de gestion de bases de donnees reparties,* Proceedings of the International Symposium on Distributed Databases, Paris, March 1980.

20. B.G.Lindsay, P.G.Selinger, C.Galtieri, J.N.Gray, R.A.Lorie, F.Putzolu, I.L.Traiger and B.W.Wade, *Single and Multi-site Recovery Facilities,* Distributed Data Bases, Edited by I.W.Draffan and F.Poole, Cambridge University Press, 1980, Chapter 10. Also available as **Notes on Distributed Databases**, IBM Research Laboratory RJ2571, San Jose, CA., July 1979.

21. B.G.Lindsay and P.Selinger, *Site Autonomy Issues in R*: a Distributed Database Management System,* IBM Research Report RJ 2927, San Jose, CA., 1980.

22. B.G.Lindsay, *Object Naming and Catalog Management for a Distributed Database Manager,* Proceedings 2nd International Conference on Distributed Computing Systems, Paris, France, April 1981. Also: IBM Research Report RJ2914, San Jose, CA., August 1980.

23. D.A.Menasce and R.R.Muntz, *Locking and Deadlock Detection in Distributed Databases,* Proc. 3rd Berkeley Workshop on Distributed Data Management and Computer Networks, August 1978, pp. 215-232.

24. J.E.B.Moss, *Nested Transactions: An Approach to Reliable Distributed Computing,* Ph.D. Thesis, Report MIT.LCS/TR-260, Department of EECS, MIT, Cambridge, April 81/

25. R.M.Needham and M.D.Schroeder, *Using Encryption for Authentication in Large Networks of Computers,* Communications of the ACM, Vol.21, No.12, December 1978, pp. 993-999.

26. P.Ng, *Distributed Compilation and Recompilation of Database Queries,* Masters Thesis in preparation, Department of EECS, MIT, Cambridge, Mass., for January 1982.

27. R.Obermarck, *Global Deadlock Detection Algorithm,* IBM Research Laboratory RJ2845, San Jose, CA., June 1980.

28. J. B. Rothnie and N. Goodman, *An Overview of the Preliminary Design of SDD-1: A System for Distributed Databases,* Proc. 2nd Berkeley Workshop on Distributed Data Management and Computer Networks, Lawrence Berkeley Laboratory, University of California, Berkeley, CA, May 1977, pp. 39-57.

29. J.B.Rothnie, Jr., P.A.Bernstein, S.Fox, N.Goodman, M.Hammer, T.A.Landers, C.Reeve, D.Shipman, and E.Wong, *Introduction to System for Distributed Databases (SDD-1),* ACM Transaction on Database Systems, Vol.5, No.1, March 1980, p. 1.

30. D.J.Rosenkrantz, R.E.Stearns, and R.M.Lewis, *System Level Concurrency Control for Distributed Database Systems,* ACM Transaction on Database Systems, Vol.3, No.2, June 1978, pp. 178-198.

31. P.G.Selinger, M.M.Astrahan, D.D.Chamberlin, R.A.Lorie and T.G.Price, *Access Path Selection in a Relational Database Management System,* Proceedings of the ACM SIGMOD Conference, June 1979.

32. P.G.Selinger and M.Adiba, *Access Path Selection in Distributed Database Management Systems,* Proceedings of International Conference on Databases, University of Aberdeen, Scotland. July 1980. pp.204-215.

33. M.Stonebraker and E.Neuhold, *A Distributed Data Base Version of INGRES,* Proc. 2nd Berkeley Workshop on Distributed Data Management and Computer Networks, Lawrence Berkeley Lab, Univ. of California, Berkeley, CA., May 1977, pp. 19-36.

34. See sales literature. Tandem Corp., Cupertino, CA,

35. P.F.Wilms and B.G.Lindsay, *A Database Authorization Mechanism Supporting Individual and Group Authorization,* Second Seminar on Distributed Data Sharing Systems June 1981, to be published by North Holland Publishing Company, April 1982.

R* Optimizer Validation and Performance Evaluation for Distributed Queries

Lothar F. Mackert [1]
Guy M. Lohman

IBM Almaden Research Center
K55-801, 650 Harry Road, San Jose, CA 95120-6099

Abstract

Few database query optimizer models have been validated against actual performance. This paper extends an earlier optimizer validation and performance evaluation of R* to *distributed* queries, i.e. single SQL statements having tables at multiple sites. Actual R* message, I/O, and CPU resources consumed — and the corresponding costs estimated by the optimizer — were written to database tables using new SQL commands, permitting automated control from application programs for collecting, reducing, and comparing test data. A number of tests were run over a wide variety of dynamically-created test databases, SQL queries, and system parameters. Both high-speed networks (comparable to a local area network) and medium-speed long-haul networks (for linking geographically dispersed hosts) were evaluated. The tests confirmed the accuracy of R*'s message cost model and the significant contribution of local (CPU and I/O) costs, even for a medium-speed network. Although distributed queries consume more resources overall, the response time for some execution strategies improves disproportionately by exploiting both concurrency and reduced contention for buffers. For distributed joins in which a copy of the inner table must be transferred to the join site, shipping the whole inner table dominated the strategy of fetching only those inner tuples that matched each outer-table value, even though the former strategy may require additional I/O. Bloomjoins (hashed semijoins) consistently performed better than semijoins and the best R* strategies.

1. Introduction

One of the most appealing properties of relational data bases is their nonprocedural user interface. Users specify only *what* data is desired, leaving the system optimizer to choose *how* to access that data. The built-in decision capabilities of the optimizer therefore play a central role regarding system performance. Automated selection of optimal access plans is a rather difficult task, because even for simple queries there are many alternatives and factors affecting the performance of each of them.

Optimizers model system performance for some subset of these alternatives, taking into consideration a subset of the relevant factors. As with any other mathematical model, these simplifications — made for modeling and computational efficiency — introduce the potential for errors. The goal of our study was to investigate the performance and to thoroughly validate the optimizer against actual performance of a working experimental database system, R* [LOHM 85], which inherited and extended to a distributed environment [SELI 80, DANI 82] the optimization algorithms of System R [SELI 79]. This paper extends our earlier validation and performance evaluation of local queries [MACK 86] to distributed queries over either (1) a high-speed network having speeds comparable to a local-area network (LAN) or (2) over a medium-speed, long-haul network linking geographically dispersed host machines. For brevity, we assume that the reader is familiar with System R [CHAM 81] and R* [LOHM 85], and with the issues, methodology, and results of that earlier study [MACK 86].

Few of the distributed optimizer models proposed over the last decade [APER 83, BERN 81B, CHAN 82, CHU 82, EPST 78, HEVN 79, KERS 82, ONUE 83, PERR 84, WONG 83, YAO 79, YU 83] have been validated by comparison with actual performance. The only known validations, for Distributed INGRES [STON 82] and the Crystal multicomputer [LU 85], have assumed only a high-speed local-area network linking the distributed systems. Also, the Distributed INGRES study focused primarily on reducing response time by exploiting parallelism using table partitioning and broadcast messages. In contrast, R* seeks to minimize total resources consumed, has not implemented table partitioning[2], and does not presume a network broadcast capability.

There are many important questions that a thorough validation should answer:

- Under what circumstances (regions of the parameter space) does the optimizer choose a suboptimal plan, or, worse, a particularly bad plan?
- To which parameters is the actual performance most sensitive?
- Are these parameters being modeled accurately by the optimizer?
- What is the impact of variations from the optimizer's simplifying assumptions?
- Is it possible to simplify the optimizer's model (by using heuristics, for example) to speed up optimization?
- What are the best database statistics to support optimization?

Performance questions related to optimization include:

- Are there possible improvements in the implementation of distributed join techniques?
- Are there alternative distributed join techniques that are not implemented but look promising?

The next section gives an overview of distributed compilation and optimization in R*. Section 3 discusses how R* was instrumented to collect optimizer estimates and actual performance data at multiple sites in an automated way. Section 4 presents some prerequisite measurements of the cost component weights and the measurement overhead. The results for distributed joins are given in Section 5, and suggestions for improving their performance are discussed in Section 6. Section 7 contains our conclusions.

2. Distributed Compilation and Optimization

The unit of distribution in R* is a table and each table is stored at one and only one site. A ***distributed query*** is any SQL data manipulation statement that references tables at sites other than the ***query site***, the site to which an application program is submitted for compilation. This site serves as the ***master site*** which coordinates the optimization of all SQL statements embedded in that program. For each query, sites other than the master site that store a table referenced in the query are called ***apprentice sites***.

In addition to the parameters chosen for the local case:

---

1 Current address: University of Erlangen-Nürnberg, IMMD-IV, Martensstrasse 3, D-8520 Erlangen, West Germany

2 Published ideas for horizontal and vertical partitioning of tables have not been implemented in R*.

(1) the order in which tables must be joined
(2) the join method (nested-loop or merge-scan), and
(3) the access path for each table (e.g., whether to use an index or not)

optimization of a *distributed* query must also choose for each join[3]:

(4) ***the join site***, i.e. the site at which each join takes place, and,
(5) if the inner table is not stored at the join site chosen in (4), the method for transferring a copy of the inner table to the join site:
(5a) ***ship whole***: ship a copy of the entire table once to the join site, and store it there in a temporary table; or
(5b) ***fetch matches*** (see Figure 1): scan the outer table and sequentially execute the following procedure for each outer tuple:
1. Project the outer table tuple to the join column(s) and ship this value to the site of the inner table.
2. Find those tuples in the inner table that match the value sent and project them to the columns needed.
3. Ship a copy of the projected matching inner tuples back to the join site.
4. Join the matches to the outer table tuple.

Note that this strategy could be characterized as a semijoin for each outer tuple. We will compare it to semijoins in Section 6.

If a copy of an outer (possibly composite) table of a join has to be moved to another site, it is always shipped in its entirety as a blocked pipeline of tuples [LOHM 85].

Compilation, and hence optimization, is truly distributed in R*. The master's optimizer makes all *inter-site* decisions, such as the site at which inter-site joins take place, the method and order for transferring tuples between sites, etc. *Intra-site* decisions (e.g. order and method of join for tables contiguously within a single site) are only *suggested* by the master planner; it delegates to each apprentice the final decision on these choices as well as the generation of an access module to encode the work to be done at that site [DANI 82].

Optimization in R* seeks to minimize a cost function that is a linear combination of four components: CPU, I/O, and two message costs: the number of messages and the total number of bytes transmitted in all messages. I/O cost is measured in number of transfers to or from disk, and CPU cost is measured in terms of number of instructions:

$$\begin{aligned} R^{*}\_total\_cost \;=\; & W_{CPU} * (\#\_instrs) + W_{I/O} * (\#\_I/Os) \\ & + W_{MSG} * (\#\_msgs) + W_{BYT} * (\#\_bytes) \end{aligned}$$

Unlike System R, R* maintains the four cost components separately, as well as the total cost as a weighted sum of the components [LOHM 85], enabling validation of each of the cost components independently. By assigning (at database generation time) appropriate weights for a given hardware configuration, different optimization criteria can be met. Two of the most common are time (delay) and money cost [SELI 80]. For our study we set these weights so that the R* total cost estimates the total time consumed by all resources, in milliseconds. Since all the sites in our tests had equivalent hardware and software configurations, identical weights were used for each site.

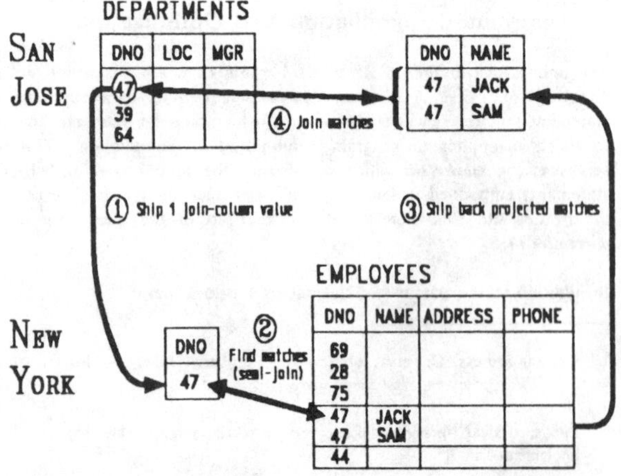

Figure 1: "Fetch-matches" transfer strategy for joining at site San Jose outer table DEPARTMENTS to inner table EMPLOYEES.

3. Instrumentation

An earlier performance study for System R [ASTR 80] demonstrated that extracting performance data using the standard database trace and debugging facilities required substantial manual interaction, severely limiting the number of test cases that could be run. Since we wanted to measure performance under a wide variety of circumstances, we added instrumentation that would automate measurements to a very high degree. The general design of this instrumentation and its application for the evaluation of local queries is described in [MACK 86], so that in this paper we recall only the main ideas and confine our discussion to its distributed aspects. Principals of our design were:

1. Add to the SQL language three statements for test control and performance monitoring which can be executed from an application program as well as interactively.
2. Develop pre-compiled application programs for automatically (a) testing queries using the SQL statements of (1) above, and (b) analyzing the data collected by step (a).
3. Store the output of the SQL statements of (1) and the application programs of (2) in database tables in order to establish a flexible, powerful interface between (1), (2a), and (2b).

We concentrate here on the first item — the SQL-level measurement tools — whose implementation was most complicated by the distribution of tables at different sites.

3.1. Distributed EXPLAIN

The EXPLAIN command writes to user-owned PLAN_TABLEs information describing the access plan chosen by the optimizer for a given SQL statement, and its estimated cost [RDT 84]. For a given distributed query, no single site has the complete access plan: the master site has the inter-site decisions and each apprentice has its local intra-site decisions. Hence the R* EXPLAIN command was augmented to store each apprentice site's plan in a local PLAN_TABLE, and the test application program was altered to retrieve that information from each apprentice's PLAN_TABLE.

3.2. Distributed COLLECT COUNTERS

This new SQL statement collects and stores in a user-owned table the current values of some 40 internal counters in the RSS* component (e.g., counts of disk reads and writes, lookups in the buffer, etc.), which R* inherited from System R, and some newly implemented counters of the communications component DC*. COLLECT COUNTERS automatically collects a (pre-defined) subset of these counters at all sites with which the user currently has open communication sessions, returns those counters to the master site, and inserts into a special user-owned table (COUNTER_TABLE) one tuple for each distinct counter at each site. Each counter value is tagged with its name, the component (RSS* or DC*) and site that maintains the counter, a timestamp, the invoking application program name, and an optional user-supplied sequence number.

The implementation of the COLLECT COUNTERS statement is dependent upon the mechanism for distributed query execution in R* [LIND 83]. The master site establishes communication sessions with all sites with which it has to have direct communication, and spawns children processes at these sites. The children may in turn establish additional sessions and spawn other children processes, creating a tree of processes that may endure through multiple transactions in an application program. Since descendant processes may spawn processes at any site, the tree may contain multiple descendant processes at a single site on behalf of the same master process (***loopback***). For collecting the counters from all sites that are involved in the current computation, we traverse the user's process tree. For each process, counters are collected at that process' site and are

3 The site at which any nested query (***subquery***) is applied must also be determined [LOHM 84], but consideration of subqueries is omitted from this paper to simplify the presentation.

returned to the master site. At the master site, each counter value is handled in the following way:

- If we have not yet inserted a tuple into the COUNTER__TABLE for the given counter from the given site (while executing the COLLECT COUNTERS statement of interest), the counter is inserted into the COUNTER__TABLE.

- RSS* counters from the given site that have already been inserted into the user's COUNTER__TABLE are discarded (loopbacks will cause redundant delivery of certain counters), because RSS* counters are database-site-specific.

- DC* counters are process-specific. If there is already a row in the COUNTER__TABLE for the given DC* counter at the given site, the counter value is added to the counter value in that row.

To be sure that sessions had been established with all sites relevant to a particular test, the test application program was altered to run the test sequence once before the first COLLECT COUNTERS statement.

3.3. FORCE OPTIMIZER

As in the local validation study, we had to be able to overrule the optimizer's choice of plan, to measure the performance of plans that the optimizer thought were suboptimal. This was done with the FORCE OPTIMIZER statement, which was implemented in a special test version of R* only. The FORCE OPTIMIZER statement chooses the plan for the *next* SQL data manipulation (optimizable) statement *only*. The user specifies the desired plan number, a unique positive integer assigned by the master site's optimizer to each candidate plan, by first using the EXPLAIN statement (discussed above) to discover the number of the desired plan. Apprentice optimization can be forced by simply telling each apprentice to utilize the optimization decisions recommended by the master's optimizer in its global plan.

3.4. Conduct of Experiments

Our distributed query tests were conducted in the same way and in the same environment as the local query tests [MACK 86], only with multiple database sites. All measurements were run at night on two totally unloaded IBM 4381's connected via a high-speed channel. Each site was initialized to provide 40 buffer pages of 4K bytes each, which were available exclusively to our test applications. This is approximately equivalent, for example, to a system with each site running 5 simultaneous transactions that are competing for 800K bytes of buffer space. The same effects of buffer size limitations that were investigated in [MACK 86] also apply to distributed queries, and thus are not discussed further in this paper. In order to vary database parameters systematically, synthetic test tables were generated dynamically, inserting tuples whose column values were drawn randomly from separate uniform distributions. For example, the join-columns' values were drawn randomly from a domain of 3000 integer values when generating the tables. All tables had the same schema: four integer and five (fixed) character fields. The tuples were 66 bytes long, and the system stored 50 of them on one page.

Each test was run several times to ensure reproduceability of the results, and to reduce the variance of the average response times. However, the reader is cautioned that these measurements are highly dependent upon numerous factors peculiar to our test environment, including hardware and software configuration, database design, etc. We made no attempt to "tune" these factors to advantage. For example, each test table was assigned to a separate DBSPACE, which tends to favor DBSPACE scans.

What follows is a sample of our results illustrating major trends for distributed queries; space considerations preclude showing all combinations of all parameters that we examined. For example, for joins we tested a matrix of table sizes for the inner and outer tables ranging from 100 to 6000 tuples (3 times the buffer size), varying the projection factor on the joined tables (50% or 100% of both tables) and the availability of totally unclustered indexes on the join columns of the outer and/or inner tables. Since unclustered index scans become very expensive when the buffer is not big enough to hold all the data and index pages of a table, the ratio between the total number of data and index pages of a table to the number of pages in the buffer is more important for the local processing cost than the absolute table size [MACK 85]. Although these tests confirmed the accuracy of the overwhelming majority of the optimizer's predictions, we will concentrate here on those aspects of the R* optimizer that were changed or exhibited anomalous behavior.

4. General Measurements

Several measurements pertaining to the optimizer as a whole were prerequisite to more specific studies. These are discussed briefly below.

4.1. Cost of Measurements

The COLLECT COUNTERS statement, the means by which we measured performance, itself consumes system resources that are tabulated by the R* internal counters. For example, collecting the counters from remote sites itself uses messages whose cost would be reflected in the counters for number of messages and number of bytes transmitted. The resources consumed by the COLLECT COUNTERS instrumentation was determined by running two COLLECT COUNTERS statements with no SQL statements in between, and reducing all other observations by those resources.

4.2. Component Weights

The R* cost component weights for any given cost objective and hardware configuration can be estimated using "back of the envelope" calculations. For example, for converting all components to milliseconds, the weight for CPU is the number of milliseconds per CPU instruction, which can be estimated as just the inverse of the MIP rate, divided by 1000 MIPS/msec. The I/O weight can be estimated as the sum of the average seek, latency, and transfer times for one 4K-byte page of data. The per-message weight can be estimated by dividing the approximate number of instructions to initiate and receive a message by the MIP rate. And the per-byte weight estimate is simply the time to send 8 bits at the *effective* transmission speed of the network, which had been measured as 4M bits/sec for our nominally 24M bit/sec (3M Byte/sec) channel-to-channel connection. These estimates, and the corresponding actual weights for our test configuration, are shown in Figure 2.

$$R^*\_total\_cost = W_{CPU} * (\#\_insts) + W_{I/O} * (\#\_I/O) + W_{MSG} * (\#\_msgs) + W_{BYT} * (\#\_bytes)$$

WEIGHT	UNITS	HARDWARE/SOFTWARE	ESTIMATE	ACTUAL
W_{CPU}	msec/inst.	IBM 4381 CPU	0.0004	0.0004
$W_{I/O}$	msec/I/O	IBM 3380 disk	23.48	17.00[4]
W_{MSG}	msec/msg.	CICS/VTAM	11.54	16.5
W_{BYTE}	msec/byte	24Mbit/sec (nom.), 4Mbit/sec (eff.)	0.002	0.002

Figure 2: Estimated and actual cost component weights.

The actual per-message and per-byte weights were measured by moving to a remote site one table of a two-table query for which the executed plan and the local (I/O and CPU) costs were well known. We chose a query that nested-loop joined a 500-tuple outer table, A, and a 100-tuple inner table, B, having an index on the join column. The plan for the distributed execution of this query had to be one that was executed sequentially (i.e., with no parallelism between sites), so that the response time (which we could measure) equalled the total resource time. By SELECTing all the columns of B, we could require that the large (3500-byte) tuples of B had to be shipped without projection, thereby ensuring that both the number (1000) and size of messages sent was high and that the local processing time was a small part (less than 30%) of the total resource time. We could control the message traffic by varying the number of tuples in B matching values in A: when none matched, only very small messages were transferred (carrying fixed-size R* control information); when each tuple in A matched exactly one tuple in B, 500 small and 500 very large messages were transferred. For a given number

4 The observed per-I/O rate is better than the estimate because the seek time was almost always less than the nominal average seek time, since R* databases are stored by VSAM in clumps of contiguous cylinders called extents.

of matching inner tuples, the query was run 10 times to get the average response (= total resource) time. The message cost was derived by subtracting from the total time the local cost, which was measured by averaging the cost of 10 executions of the same query when both A and B were at the *same* site. Knowing the number and size of the messages (using COLLECT COUNTERS) for that number of matching inner tuples allowed us to compute the per-message and per-byte weights for our test environment: 16.5 msecs. minimal transfer time, and an effective transfer rate of 4M bit/sec. Note that these figures include the instruction and envelope overheads, respectively, of R*, CICS, and VTAM [LIND 83, VTAM 85].

By varying the above per-message and per-byte weights, we could also use the observed number of messages and bytes transmitted on the high-speed channel-to-channel connection to simulate the performance for a medium-speed long-haul network linking geographically dispersed hosts: 50 msecs. minimum transfer time and effective transfer rate of 40K bit/sec (nominal rate of 56K bit/sec, less 30% overhead). The per-message weight differs because of the increased delay due to the speed of light for longer transmissions, routing through relays, etc. Unavailability of resources at remote sites unfortunately precluded validating on a real long-haul network these estimated weights.

5. Distributed Join Results

Having validated the weights used in the R* cost function, and having removed the cost of measuring performance, we were ready to validate the R* optimizer's decisions for distributed queries.

The simplest distributed query accesses a single table at a remote site. However, since partitioning and replication of tables is not supported in R*, accessing a remote table is relatively simple: a process at the remote site accesses the table locally and ships the query result back to the query site as if it were an outer table to a join (i.e., as a blocked pipeline of tuples). Since all of the *distributed* optimization decisions discussed earlier pertain to *joins* of tables at different sites, picking the optimal global plan is solely a local matter: only the access path to the table need be chosen. For this reason, we will not consider single-table distributed queries further, but focus instead entirely upon distributed join methods.

In R*, n-table joins are executed as a sequence of n-1 two-table joins. Hence thorough understanding and correct modeling of distributed two-table joins is a prerequisite to validating n-table distributed joins. Intermediate results of joins are called ***composite*** tables, and may either be returned as a pipeline of tuples or else materialized completely before the succeeding two-table join (e.g., if sorting is required for a merge-scan join). We will therefore limit our discussion in this section to that fundamental operation, the two-table join.

Our discussion will use a simple notation for expressing distributed access plans for joins. There are two different join methods: merge scan joins, denoted by the infix operator "-M-", and nested loop joins, denoted by "-N-". The operand to the left of the join operator specifies the outer table access, the right operand the inner table access. A table access consists of the table name, optionally suffixed with an "I" if we use the index on the join column of this table and/or a "W" or"F" if we ship the table whole or fetch only matching tuples, respectively. For example, AIW-M-B denotes a plan that merge-scan joins tables A and B at B's site, shipping A whole after scanning it with the index on the join column. Since the merge-scan join requires both tables to be in join-column order, this plan implies B has to be sorted to accomplish the join.

5.1. Inner Table Transfer Strategy

The choice of transfer strategy for the inner table involves some interesting trade-offs. Shipping (a copy of) the table whole ("W") transfers the most inner tuples for the least message overhead, but needlessly sends inner tuples that have no matching outer tuples and necessitates additional I/O and CPU for reading the inner at its home site and then storing it in a temporary table at the join site. Any indexes on the inner that might aid a join cannot be shipped with the table, since indexes contain physical addresses that change when tuples are inserted in the temporary table, and R* does not permit dynamic creation of temporary indexes (we will re-visit that design decision in Section 6). However, since the inner is projected and any single-table predicates are applied before it is shipped, the temporary table is potentially much smaller than its permanent version, which might make multiple accesses to it (particularly in a nested-loop join) more cost-effective.

The high-speed channel we were using for communication in our tests imposed a relatively high per-message overhead, thereby emphatically favoring the "W" strategy. Figure 3 compares the actual performance of the best plan for each transfer strategy for both the high-speed channel and the long-haul medium-speed network, when merge-scan joining[5] two indexed 500-tuple tables, C and D, shipping the inner table D and returning the result to C's site. Both tables are projected to 50% of their tuple length, the join column domain has 100 different values, and the ***join cardinality*** — the cardinality of the result of the join — was 2477. If we ship the inner table D as a whole, the best plan is CI-M-DIW, and if we fetch the matching inner tuples ("F"), CI-M-DIF is best.

For the W strategy, the message costs are only 2.9% of the total resource cost, partly due to the relatively high local cost because of the large join cardinality. For the F strategy, we spend 80.9% of the costs for communications, since for each outer tuple we have to send one message containing the outer tuple's value and at least one message containing the matching inner tuples, if any. The total of 1000 messages cannot be reduced, even if there are no matching tuples, since the join site waits for some reply from the inner's site. Note that the number of bytes transmitted as well as the number of messages is much higher for the F strategy, because each message contains relatively little data in proportion to the required R* control information. Another source for the higher number of bytes transmitted is the frequent retransmission of inner table tuples for the large join cardinality of this query. The penalty for this overhead and the discrepancy between the two transfer strategies is exaggerated by slower network speeds. For the medium-speed network in Figure 3, the per-message overhead is 49% of the cost, and the discrepancy between the two strategies increases from a factor of 4.4 to a factor of 11.6.

The importance of per-message costs dictate two sufficient (but not necessary) conditions for the F strategy to be preferred:

1. the cardinality of the outer table must be less than half the number of messages required to ship the inner as a whole, and
2. the join cardinality must be less than the inner cardinality,

after any local (non-join) predicates have been applied and the referenced columns have been projected out. The second condition assures that fewer inner tuples are transferred to the outer's site for F than for W. Since the join cardinality is estimated as the product of the inner cardinality, outer cardinality, and join-predicate selectivity, these two conditions are

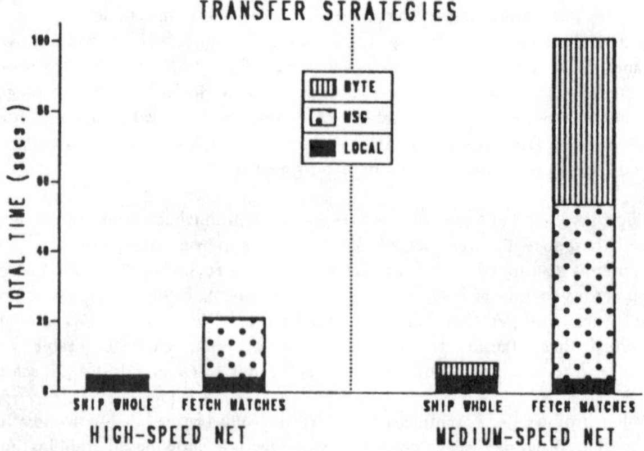

Figure 3: Comparison of the best R* plans, when using the ship-whole ("W") vs. the fetch-matches ("F") strategies for shipping the inner table, when merge-scan joining two indexed 500-tuple tables.

---

5 Nested loop joins perform very poorly for the "W" strategy, because we can not ship an index on the join column. For a fair comparison, we therefore only consider merge-scan joins.

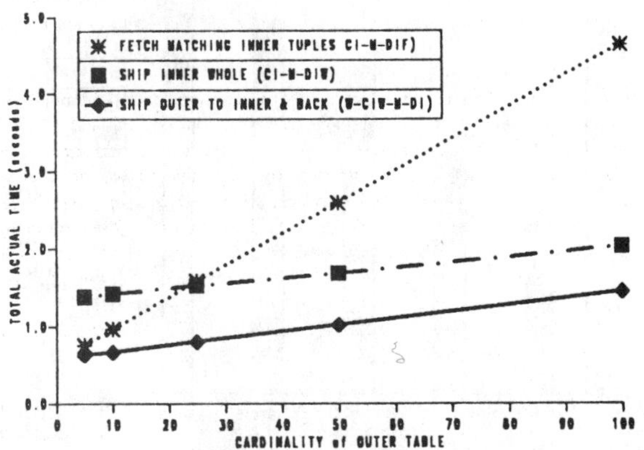

Figure 4: Shipping the outer table (C) to the inner's (D's) site and returning the result dominates both strategies for transferring the inner to the outer's site, even for small outer cardinalities (inner cardinality = 500 tuples).

equivalent to requiring that the outer cardinality be less than the minimum of (a) the inner's size (in bytes) divided by 8K bytes (the size of two messages) and (b) the inverse of the join-predicate's filter factor. Clearly these conditions are sufficiently strict that the F strategy will rarely be optimal.

Even when these conditions hold, it is likely that shipping the outer table to the inner's site and returning the result to the outer's site will be a better plan: by condition (1) the outer will be small, by condition (2) the result returned will be small, and performing the join at the inner's site permits the use of indexes on the inner. This observation is confirmed by Figure 4. The tests of Lu and Carey [LU 85] satisfied condition (2) by having a semijoin selectivity of 10% and condition (1) by cleverly altering the R* F strategy to send the outer-tuple values in one-page batches. Hence they concluded that the F strategy was preferred. Time constraints prevented us from implementing and testing this variation.

We feel that the conditions for the R* fetch-matches strategy to be preferred are so restrictive for both kinds of networks that its implementation without batching the outer-tuple values is not recommended for any future distributed database system. Therefore, henceforth we will consider only joins employing the ship-whole strategy.

5.2. Distributed vs. Local Join

Does distribution of tables improve or diminish performance of a particular query? In terms of total resources consumed, most distributed queries are more expensive than their single-site counterparts. Besides the obvious added communications cost, distributed queries also consume extra CPU processing to insert and retrieve the shipped tuples from communications buffers. In terms of response time, however, distributed queries may outperform equivalent local queries by bringing more resources to bear on a given query and by processing portions of that query in parallel on multiple processing units and I/O channels. Exploiting this parallelism is in fact a major justification for many distributed database systems [EPST 80, APER 83, WONG 83], especially multiprocessor database machines [BABB 79, DEWI 79, VALD 84, MENO 85].

The degree of simultaneity that can be achieved depends on the plan we are executing. Figure 5 compares the total resource time and the response time for some of the better R* access plans for a distributed query that joins two indexed (unclustered) 1000-tuple tables, A and B, at different sites, where the query site is A's site, the join column domain has 3000 different values, and each table is projected by 50%. For the plans shown, the ordering with respect to the total resource time is the same as the response time ordering, although this is not generally true. Plans shipping the outer table enjoy greater simultaneity because the join on the first buffer-full of outer tuples can proceed in parallel with the shipment of the next buffer-full. Plans shipping the inner table (whole) are more sequential: they must wait for the entire table to be received at the join site and inserted into a temporary table (incurring additional local cost) before proceeding with the join. For example, in Figure 5, note the difference between total resource time and response time for BIW-M-AI, as compared to the same difference for AI-M-BIW. Other plans not shown in Figure 5 that ship the inner table exhibit similar relationships to the corresponding plans that ship the outer (e.g., A-M-BW vs. BW-M-A, A-M-BIW vs. BIW-M-A, and AI-M-BW vs. BW-M-AI.). This assymmetry is unknown for local queries.

For merge joins not using indexes to achieve join-column order (e.g., A-M-BW, BW-M-A), R* sorts the two tables sequentially. Although sorting the two tables concurrently would not decrease the total resource time, it would lower the response time for those plans considerably (it should be close to the response time of BIW-M-A).

Comparing the response times for the above set of plans when the query is distributed vs. when it is local (see Figure 6), we notice that the distributed joins are faster. The dramatic differences between distributed and local for BIW-M-AI and AI-M-BIW stem from both simultaneity and the availability of two database buffers in the distributed case. However, by noting that for local joins the response time equals the resource time (since all systems were unloaded) and comparing these to the total resource times for the distributed query in Figure 5, we find that even the total resource costs for BIW-M-AI and AI-M-BIW are less than those for the local joins BI-M-AI and AI-M-BI, so parallelism alone cannot explain the improvement. The other reason is reduced contention: this particular plan is accessing both tables using unclustered indexes, which benefit greatly from larger buffers, and the distributed query enjoys twice as much buffer space as does the local query. However, not all distributed plans have

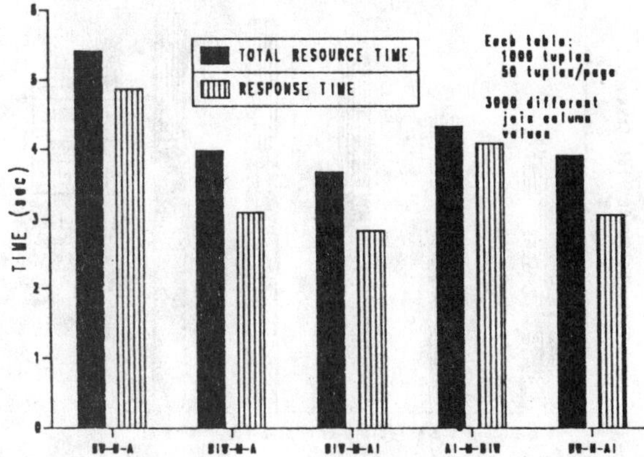

Figure 5: Resource consumption time vs. response time for various access plans, when joining 2 tables (1000 tuples each) distributed across a high-speed network.

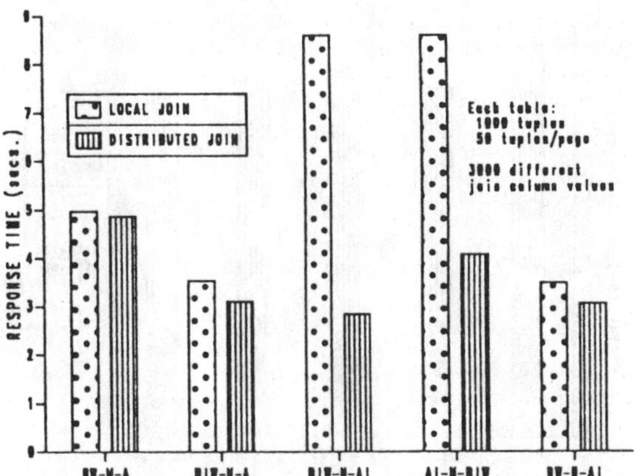

Figure 6: Response times for distributed (across a high-speed network) vs. local execution for various access plans, when joining 2 tables (1000 tuples each).

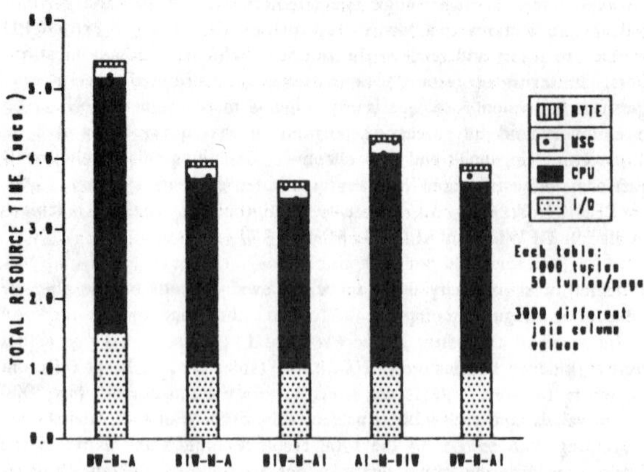

Figure 7: Relative importance of cost components for various access plans when joining 2 tables (of 1000 tuples each) distributed across a high-speed network.

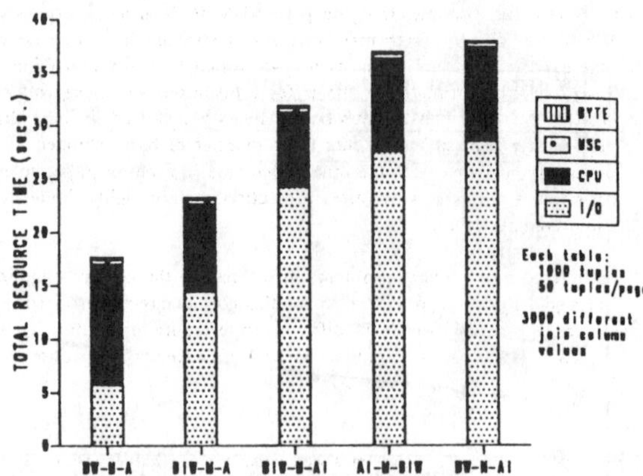

Figure 8: Relative importance of cost components for various access plans when joining 2 tables (of 2500 tuples each) distributed across a high-speed network.

better response times than the corresponding local plan; the increased buffer space doesn't much help the plans that don't access both tables using an index, and most of the distributed plans that ship the inner table to the join site (except for AI-M-BIW) are 15%-30% more expensive than their local counterpart because they exhibit a more sequential execution pattern.

For larger tables (e.g., 2500 tuples each), these effects are even more exaggerated by the greater demands they place upon the local processing resources of the two sites. However, for slower network speeds, the reverse is true; increased communications overhead results in response times for distributed plans being almost twice those of local plans. For a comparison of the resource times see Section 6.

5.3. Relative Importance of Cost Components

Many distributed query optimization algorithms proposed in the literature ignore the *intra*-site costs of CPU and I/O, arguing that those costs get dwarfed by the communication costs for the majority of queries. We have investigated the relative importance of the four cost components when joining two tables at different sites, varying the sizes of the tables and the speeds of the communication lines. Our results confirmed the analysis of Selinger and Adiba [SELI 80], which concluded that local processing costs are relevant and possibly even dominant in modelling the costs of distributed queries.

In a high-speed network such as a local-area network, message costs are of secondary importance, as shown by Figure 7 for the distributed join of two 1000-tuple tables. For our test configuration, message costs usually accounted for less (very often much less) than 10% of the total resource cost. This remained true for joins of larger tables, as shown in Figure 8 for two 2500-tuple tables. Similarly, message costs account for only 9% of the total cost for the optimal plan joining a 1000-tuple table to a 6000-tuple table, delivering the result to the site of the first table. This agrees with the measurements of Lu and Carey [LU 85].

When we altered the weights to simulate a medium-speed long-haul network, local processing costs were still significant, as shown in Figure 9 and Figure 10. In most of the plans, message costs and local processing costs were equally important, neither ever dropping under 30% of the total cost. Hence ignoring local costs might well result in a bad choice of the local parameters whose cost exceeds that of the messages. Also, the relative importance of per-message and per-byte costs reverses for the medium-speed network, because the time spent sending and receiving each message, and the "envelope" bytes appended to each message, are small compared to the much higher cost of getting the same information through a "narrower pipeline" than that of the high-speed network.

5.4. Optimizer Evaluation

How well does the R* optimizer model the costs added by distributed data? For the ship-whole table transfer strategy, for both outer and inner tables, our tests detected only minor differences (<2%) between actual costs and optimizer estimates of the number of messages and the number of bytes transmitted. The additional local cost for storing the inner table shipped whole is also correctly modelled by the optimizer, so that the

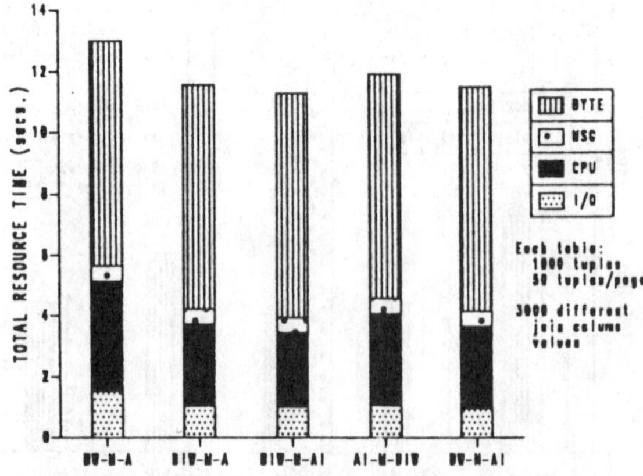

Figure 9: Relative importance of cost components for various access plans when joining 2 tables (of 1000 tuples each) distributed across a (simulated) medium-speed network.

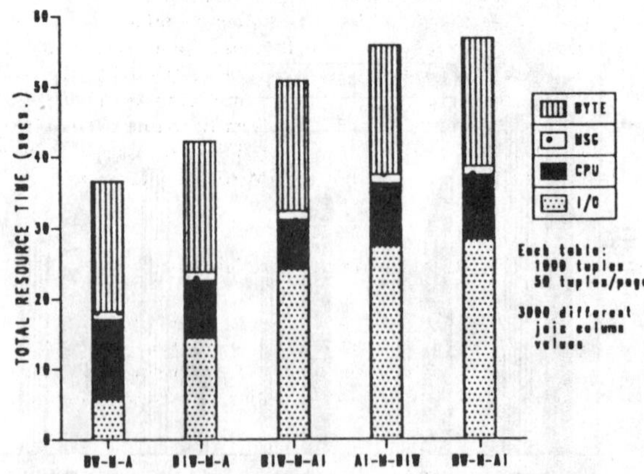

Figure 10: Relative importance of cost components for various access plans when joining 2 tables (of 2500 tuples each) distributed across a (simulated) medium-speed network.

system realizes, for example, that the plan AI-M-BIW is more expensive than BIW-M-AI. For the fetch-matches transfer strategy (for inner tables only), the expected number of messages was equal to the actual number in all cases, and the estimate for the bytes transmitted was never off by more than 25%. Although the number of bytes transferred is somewhat dependent on the join cardinality, the fixed number of bytes shipped with each message typically exceeds the inner-table data in each message, unless the inner's tuples are very wide (after projection) or are highly duplicated on the join-column value.

We encountered more severe problems in estimating the cost of shipping results of a join to the query site, because this cost is directly proportional to the join cardinality, which is difficult to estimate accurately. This problem is a special case of shipping a composite table to any site, so that these errors may be compounded as the number of tables to be joined at different sites increases.

In a high-speed network, where message costs are a small fraction of the total cost and the optimizer's decisions are based more on local processing costs, these errors (assuming that they are less than 50%) are not very crucial. For a given join ordering of tables, the choice of a site at which a particular composite table will be joined with the next inner table will depend mainly upon the indexes available on the inner, the sizes of the two tables, and possibly on the order of the composite's tuples (for a merge-scan join). However, in a medium-speed long-haul communication network, where the communications costs range from 30 to 70% of the total cost, the error in estimating the join cardinality is magnified in the overall cost estimate. In [MACK 86], we have already suggested replacing the current estimates of join cardinality with statistics collected while performing the same join for an earlier SQL statement.

Can we simplify the optimizer for high-speed local-area networks, under the assumption that message costs usually are less than 10% of the total cost? More precisely, can we, starting from the best ***hypothetical local plan*** (assuming all tables are available at the query site) for a given join, construct a distributed plan that is less than 10% more expensive than the optimum? This would considerably facilitate the optimization of distributed queries! Unfortunately the answer is no, because there may be distributed access plans that have a lower local cost than any hypothetical local plan. For example, the plan BIW-M-AI in Figure 5 has a lower local cost than any plan joining the two 1000-tuple tables locally. The corresponding hypothetical local plan BI-M-AI performs very poorly (cf. Figure 6), because the two tables do not fit into one database buffer together.

Estimates of the local processing costs for distributed queries suffered many of the same problems discovered for local queries by our earlier study. In particular, a better model is needed of the re-use of pages in the buffer when performing nested-loop joins using an unclustered index on the inner table [MACK 86]. However, the more distributed the tables participating in a join are, the better the R* optimizer estimates are. The reason for this is that join costs are estimated from the costs for producing the composite table and accessing the inner table, assuming these component costs are independent of each other. This assumption is most likely to be valid when the composite and inner tables are at different sites; tables joined locally compete for the same buffer space. For example, the estimated local costs (CPU and I/O) for joining two 1000-tuple tables locally (BI-M-AI) are the same as the estimated local costs for executing the distributed plan BIW-M-AI, but the first estimate considerably underestimates the actual local cost of BI-M-AI (see Figure 6), whereas it is very accurate for the actual local cost of BIW-M-AI (cf. Figure 5).

6. Alternative Distributed Join Methods

The R* prototype provides an opportunity to compare empirically the actual performance of the distributed join methods that were implemented in R* against some other proposed join methods for equi-joins that were not implemented in R*, but might be interesting candidates for an extension or for future systems:

1. joins using dynamically-created indexes
2. semijoins
3. joins using hashing (Bloom) filters (***Bloomjoins***)

None of these methods are new [BERN 79, DEWI 85, BRAT 85]. Our contribution is the use of performance data on a real system to compare these methods with more traditional methods. We will describe the join algorithms in detail and evaluate their performance using measured R* costs for executing sub-actions such as scans, local joins, sorting of partial results, creating indexes, etc. These costs were adjusted appropriately when necessary: for example, a page does not have to be fetched by a certain sub-action if it already resides in the buffer as a result of a previous sub-action. The alternative methods are presented both in the order in which they were proposed historically and in the order of increasingly more compact data transmission between sites. Although several hash-based join algorithms look promising based upon cost-equation analyses [DEWI 85, BRAT 85], we could not evaluate them adequately using this empirical methodology, simply because we did not have any R* performance figures for the necessary primitives.

Before comparing the methods, we will first analyze the cost for each one for a distributed equi-join of two tables S and T, residing at two different sites 1 and 2, respectively, with site 1 as the query site. Let the equi-predicate be of the form S.a = T.b, where a is a column of S and b is a column of T. For simplicity, we will consider only the two cases where both or neither S and T have an (unclustered) index on their join column(s). To eliminate interference from secondary effects, we further assume that: (1) S and T do not have any indexes on columns other than the join columns, (2) all the columns of S and T are to be returned to the user (no projection), (3) the join predicate is the only predicate specified in the query (no selection), and (4) S and T are in separate DBSPACES that contain no other tables. The extension of the algorithms to the cases excluded by these assumptions is straightforward.

6.1. Dynamically-Created Temporary Index on Inner

R* does not permit the shipment of any access structures such as indexes, since these contain physical addresses (TIDs, which contain page numbers) that are not meaningful outside their home database. Yet earlier studies of local joins have shown how important indexes can be for improving the database performance, and how in some situations creating a temporary index before executing a nested-loop join can be cheaper than executing a merge-scan join without the index [MACK 86]. This is because creating an index requires sorting only key-TID pairs, plus creation of the index structure, whereas a merge-scan join without any indexes on the tables requires sorting the projected tuples of the outer as well as the inner table. The question remains whether dynamically-created temporary indexes are beneficial in a distributed environment. The cost of each step for performing a distributed join using a dynamically-created temporary index is as follows:

1. **Scan table T and ship the whole table to site 1.** The cost for this step is equivalent to our measured cost for a remote access of a single table, subtracting the CPU cost to extract tuples from the message buffers.
2. **Store T and create a temporary index on it at site 1.** Since reading T from a message buffer does not involve any I/O cost, and either reading or writing a page costs one disk I/O, the I/O cost of writing T to a temporary table and creating an index on it will be the same as for reading it from a permanent table via a sequential scan and creating an index on that, except the temporary index is not catalogued. This cost was measured in R* by executing a CREATE INDEX statement, and then adding CPU time for the insert while subtracting the known and fixed number of I/Os to catalog pages.
3. **Execute the best plan for a local join at site 1.** Again, this cost is known from the measurements obtained by our earlier study for local joins. The I/O cost must be reduced by the number of index and data pages of T that remain in the buffer from prior steps.

6.2. Semijoin

Semijoins [BERN 79, BERN 81A, BERN 81B] reduce the tuples of T that are transferred from site 2 to site 1, when only a subset of T matches tuples in S on the join column (i.e., when the ***semijoin selectivity*** < 1), but at the expense of sending all of S.a from site 1 to site 2. The cost of each step for performing a distributed join using a semijoin when neither S.a nor T.b are indexed is as follows:

1. **Sort both S and T on the join column, producing S' and T'.** The costs measured by R* for sorting any table include reading the table initially, sorting it, and writing the sorted result to a temporary table, but not the cost of any succeeding read of the sorted temporary table.

2. **Read S'.a (at site 1), eliminating duplicates, and send the result to site 2.** This cost (and for the sort of S in the previous step) could be measured in R* for a remote "SELECT DISTINCT S.a" query, subtracting the CPU cost to extract tuples from the message buffers. If S' fits into the buffer, the previous step saves us the I/O cost; otherwise all cost components are included.
3. **At site 2, select the tuples of T' that match S'.a, yielding T", and ship them to site 1.** This cost is composed of the costs for scanning S', scanning T', handling matches, and shipping the matching tuples. Reading S'.a from the message buffer incurs no I/O cost, and scanning T' also costs only CPU instructions if T' fits into the buffer. Also, the pages of the matching tuples of T' can be transmitted to site 1 as they are found, and need not be stored, because we are using these tuples as the outer table in later steps. The cost for finding the matching tuples involves only a CPU cost that is roughly proportional to the number of matches found. The cost assessed here was derived from actual R* measurements for local queries, interpolating when the table sizes, projection factors, selection factors, etc. fell between values of those parameters used in the R* experiments.
4. **At site 1, merge-join the (sorted) temporary tables S' and T" and return the resulting tuples to the user.** This cost was measured in the same way as the previous step, less the communications cost. Note that T" inherits the join-column ordering from T'.

If there are indexes on S.a and T.b, we can either use the above algorithm or we can alter each step as follows:

1. This step and its cost can be eliminated.
2. Replace this step with a scan of S.a's index pages only (not touching any data pages) and their transmission to site 2. The cost was measured as in Step (2) above, but with an index existing on S.a; R* can detect that data pages need not be accessed.
3. Using the index on T.b, perform a local merge-scan or a nested-loop join, whichever is faster, at site 2, yielding T". Again, the cost for various local joins was measured in the earlier study; they were reduced by the cost of scanning S that was saved by taking it from the message buffer as pages arrived. Some interpolation between actual experiments was required to save re-running those experiments with the exact join cardinality that resulted here.
4. Join T" with S, using the index on S.a, again choosing between the merge-scan or nested-loop join plans whose costs were measured on R*. A known amount of I/O was subtracted for the index leaf pages that remain in the buffer from step (2).

6.3. Bloomjoin

Hashing techniques are known to be efficient ways of finding matching values, and have recently been applied to database join algorithms [BABB 79, BRAT 84, VALD 84, DEWI 85]. Bloomjoins use Bloom filters [BLOO 70] as a "hashed semijoin" to filter out tuples that have no matching tuples in a join [BABB 79, BRAT 84]. Thus, as with semijoins, Bloomjoins reduce the size of the tables that have to be transferred, sorted, merged, etc. However, the bit tables used in Bloomjoins will typically be smaller than the join-column values transmitted for semijoins. By reducing the size of the inner table at an early stage, Bloomjoins also save local costs. Whereas a semijoin requires executing an extra join for reducing the inner table, Bloomjoins only need an additional scan in no particular order. For simplicity, we use only a single hashing function; further optimization is possible by allowing multiple hashing functions [SEVE 76]. The cost of each step for performing a distributed join using a Bloomjoin when neither S.a nor T.b are indexed is as follows:

1. **Generate a Bloom filter, BfS, from table S.** The Bloom filter, a large vector of bits that are initially all set to "0", is generated by scanning S and hashing each value of column S.a to a particular bit in the vector and setting that bit to "1". As before, the cost of accessing S was measured on R*. We added 200 (machine-level) instructions per tuple (a conservative upper bound for any implementation) for hashing one value and setting the appropriate bit in the vector.
2. **Send BfS to site 2.** We assume that sending a Bloom filter causes the same R* message overhead as if sets of tuples are sent, and the number of bytes is obvious from the size of the Bloom filter.
3. **Scan table T at site 2, hashing the values of T.b using the same hash function as in Step (1). If the bit hashed to is "1", then send that tuple to site 1 as tuple stream T'.** This cost is calculated as in Step (1), but the number of tuples is reduced by the Bloom filtering. We need to estimate the reduced ***Bloomjoin cardinality*** of T, i.e. the cardinality of T'. We know it must be at least the ***semijoin cardinality of T***, SC_T, i.e. the number of tuples in T whose join-column values match a tuple in S. We must add an estimate of the number of non-matching tuples in T that erroneously survive filtration due to collisions. Let F be the size (in bits) of BfS, D_S the number of distinct values of S.a, D_T the number of distinct values of T.b, and C_T the cardinality of T. Then the number of bits set to "1" in BfS is approximated for large D_S by [SEVE 76]:

$$bits_S = F(1 - e^{-(\frac{D_S}{F})})$$

So the expected number of tuples in T', the Bloomjoin cardinality BC_T of table T, is given by

$$BC_T = SC_T + bits_S(1 - e^{-(\frac{\alpha D_T}{F})})$$

where

$$\alpha = (1 - \frac{SC_T}{C_T})$$

is the fraction of non-matching tuples in T.
4. **At site 1, join T' to S and return the result to the user.** This cost was derived as for semijoins, again using the Bloomjoin cardinality estimate for T'.

If there are indexes on S.a and T.b, we can either use the above algorithm or, as with semijoins, use the index on S.a to generate BfS -- thus saving accesses to the data pages in Step (1) — and use the index on both T.b and S.a to perform the join in Step (4).

As with semijoins, filtration can also proceed in the opposite direction: S can also be reduced before the join by sending to site 1 another Bloom filter BfT based upon the values in T. This is usually advantageous if S needs to be sorted for a merge-scan join, because a smaller S will be cheaper to sort. Filtration is maximized by constructing the more selective Bloom filter first, i.e. on the table having the fewer distinct join column values[6], and altering the Bloomjoin procedure accordingly:

- If we first produce BfS, then add step (3.5): while scanning T in step (3), generate BfT, send it to site 1, and use it to reduce S.
- If we first produce BfT, then add step (0.5): generate BfT, send it to site 1, and use it to reduce S while scanning S in step (1).

6.4. Comparison of Alternative Join Methods

Using the actual costs measured by R* as described above, we were able to compare the alternative join methods empirically with the best R* plan, for both the distributed and local join, for a two-table join with no projections and no predicates other than the equi-join on an integer column. The measured cost was total resource time, since response time will vary too much depending upon other applications executing concurrently.

Our experimental parameters for this analysis were identical to those in the previous section. We fixed the size of table A at site 1 at 1000 tuples, and varied the size of table B at site 2 from 100 to 6000 tuples. For the Bloomjoin we chose a filter size (F) of 2K bytes (16384 bits) to ensure that it would fit in one 4K byte page. Again, we assumed the availability of (unclustered) indexes on the join columns. We will discuss the impact of relaxing this and other assumed parameters where appropriate in the following, and at the end of this section.

As in the previous section, we compared the performance of the join methods under two classes of networks:

- a high-speed network (16.5 msecs. minimum transfer time, 4M bit/sec. effective transfer rate); and
- a medium-speed long-haul network (50 msecs. minimum transfer time, 40K bit/sec. effective transfer rate)

by appropriately adjusting the per-message and per-byte weights by which observed numbers of messages and bytes transmitted were multiplied. For each of these classes, we varied the query site between site 1 and site 2.

6 If this cannot be determined, simply choose the smaller table [BRAT 84].

6.4.1. High-speed Network

For a high-speed network (Figure 11), the cost of transmission is dominated by local processing costs, as shown by the following table of the average percentage of the total costs for the different join algorithms that are due to local processing costs:

Query Site	*R**	*R* + temp. index*	*Semijoin*	*Bloomjoin*
1 = site of A	88.9%	89.2%	96.5%	93.0%
2 = site of B	86.5%	91.4%	94.7%	90.1%

Temporary indexes generally provided little improvement over R* performance, because the inexpensive shipping costs permit the optimal R* plan to ship B to site 1, there to use the already-existent index on A to perform a very efficient nested-loop join. When there was no index on A, the ability to build temporary indexes improved upon the R* plan by up to 30%: A was shipped to site 2, where a temporary index was dynamically built on it and the join performed. Such a situation would be common in *multi-table* joins having a small composite table that is to be joined with a large inner, so temporary indexes would still be a desirable extension for R*.

Semijoins were advantageous only in the limited case where both the data and index pages of B fit into the buffer ($cardinality(B) \leq 1500$), so that efficient use of the indexes on A and B kept the semijoin's local processing cost only slightly higher than that of the optimal R* plan. Once B no longer fits in the buffer ($cardinality(B) \geq 2000$), the high cost of accessing B with the unclustered index precluded its use, and the added cost of sorting B was not offset by sufficient savings in the transfer cost.

Bloomjoins dominated all other join alternatives, even R* joining local tables! This should not be too surprising, because local Bloomjoins outperform local R* by 20-40%, as already shown in [MACK 86], and transmission costs represent less than 10% of the total costs. The performance gains depend upon the ratios, r_A and r_B, between the Bloomjoin cardinality and the table cardinality of A and B, respectively: r_B is relatively constant (0.31), whereas r_A is varying (e.g., 0.53 for $cardinality(B) = 2000$ and 1.0 for $cardinality(B) = 6000$). But even if those ratios are close to 1, Bloomjoins are still better than R*. For example, when $r_A=1.0$, $r_B=0.8$, and $cardinality(B) = 6000$, a Bloomjoin would still be almost two seconds faster than R*. Note that due to a much higher join cardinality in this case, the R* optimum would be more expensive than the plotted one.

Why are Bloomjoins — essentially "hashed semijoins" — so much better than semijoins? The message costs were comparable, because the Bloom filter was relatively large (1 message) compared to the number of distinct join column values, and the number of non-matching tuples not filtered by the Bloom filter was less than 10% of the semijoin cardinality. The answer is that the semijoin incurs higher local processing costs to essentially perform a second join at B's site, compared to a simple scan of B in no particular order to do the hash filtering.

The above results were almost identical when B's site (2) was the query site, because the fast network makes it cheap to ship the results back after performing the join at site 1 (desirable because table A fits in the buffer). The only exception was that temporary indexes have increased advantage over R* when A could be moved to the query site and still have an (dynamically-created temporary) index with which a fast nested-loop join could be done.

We also experimented with combining a temporary index with semijoins and Bloomjoins. Such combinations improved performance only when there were no indexes, and even then by less than 10%.

6.4.2. Medium-speed Network

In a medium-speed network, local processing costs represent a much smaller (but still very significant!) proportion of the cost for each join method:

Query Site	*R**	*R* + temp. index*	*Semijoin*	*Bloomjoin*
1 = site of A	38.5%	22.6%	46.3%	32.3%
2 = site of B	38.5%	36.0%	53.0%	41.6%

Regardless of the choice of query site, Bloomjoins dominated all other distributed join methods by 15-40% for $cardinality(B) > 100$ (compare Figure 12 and Figure 13). The main reason was smaller transmissions: the communications costs for Bloomjoins were 20-40% less than R*'s, and for $cardinality(B) \geq 1500$ shipping the Bloom filter and some non-matching tuples not filtered by the Bloom filter was cheaper than shipping B's join column for semijoins. Because of their compactness, Bloom filters can be shipped equally easily in either direction, whereas R* and R* with temporary indexes always try to perform the join at A's site to avoid shipping table B (which would cost approximately 93.2 seconds when $cardinality(B) = 6000$!).

Also independent of the choice of query site was the fact that temporary indexes improved the R* performance somewhat for bigger tables.

Only R* and semijoins change relative positions depending upon the query site. When the query site is the site of the non-varying 1000-tuple table A, semijoins are clearly better than R* (see Figure 12). When the query

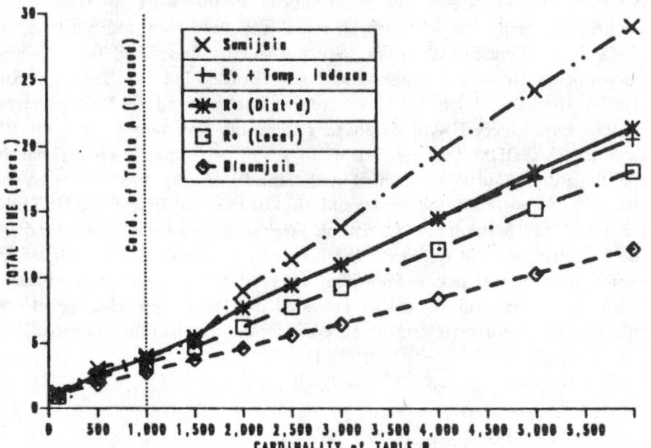

Figure 11: High-speed network; Query Site = 1 (A's site)

R*'s best distributed and local plan (measured) vs. performance of other join strategies (simulated) for a high-speed network, joining an indexed 1000-tuple table A at site 1 with an indexed table B (of increasing size) at site 2, returning the result at site 1.

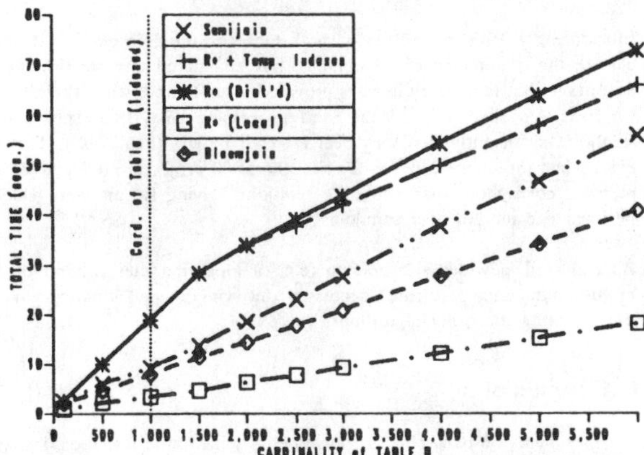

Figure 12: Medium-speed network; Query Site = 1 (A's site)

R*'s best distributed and local plan (measured) vs. performance of other join strategies (simulated) for a medium-speed network, joining an indexed 1000-tuple table A at site 1 with an indexed table B (of increasing size) at site 2, returning the result at site 1.

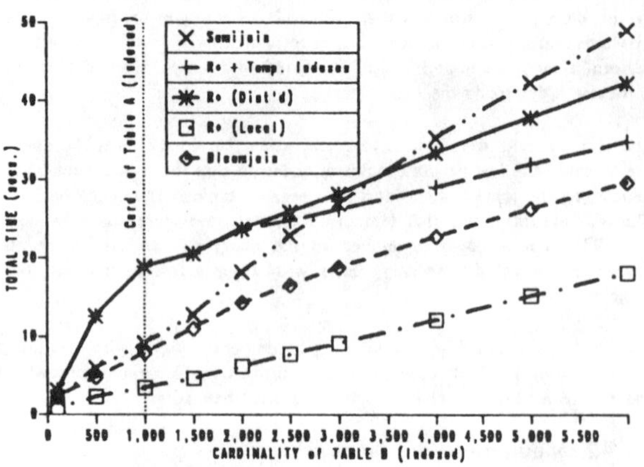

Figure 13: Medium-speed network; Query Site = 2 (B's site)

R*'s best distributed and local plan (measured) vs. performance of other join strategies (simulated) for a medium-speed network, joining an indexed 1000-tuple table A at site 1 with an indexed table B (of increasing size) at site 2, returning the result at site 2.

site is B's site, however, R* still beats semijoins when B is sufficiently large (cf. Figure 13). The reason is straightforward but important for performance on large queries. Since the join columns had a domain of 3000 different values, most of these values had matches in B when *cardinality*(*B*) ≥ 3000. Thus, the semijoin cardinality of A was close to its table cardinality, meaning that most of the tuples of A survived the semijoin and were shipped to site 2 anyway (as in the R* plan). With the additional overhead of sending the join column of B to site 1 and the higher local processing cost, semijoins could not compete.

Note that both the R* and the semijoin curves jumped when the index and data pages of table B no longer fit in the buffer (between 1500 and 2000 tuples), because they switched to sorting the tables.

6.4.3. Variation of the Experimental Parameters

Space constraints prevent us from presenting the results of numerous other experiments for different values of our experimental parameters:

- When indexes were clustered (rather than unclustered), semijoins beat R* by at most 10% (except when the query site = B's site and B is very large), but Bloomjoins still dominated all other distributed join techniques.

- Introducing a 50% projection on both tables in our join query did not change the dominance of Bloomjoins, but eliminated any performance advantage that temporary indexes provided over R* and, when the query site was A's site, reduced the local processing cost disadvantage of semijoins sufficiently that they beat R* (but by less than 10%). However, when the query site was B's site, the 50% projection reduced R*'s message costs more than those for semijoins, giving R* an even wider performance margin over semijoins.

- As expected, a wider join column (e.g., a long character column or a multi-column join predicate) decreased the semijoin performance while not affecting the other algorithms.

7. Conclusions

Our experiments on two-table distributed equi-joins found that the strategy of shipping the entire inner table to the join site and storing it there dominates the fetch-matches strategy, which incurs prohibitive per-message costs for each outer tuple even in high-speed networks.

The R* optimizer's modelling of message costs was very accurate, a necessary condition for picking the correct join site. Estimated message costs were within 2% of actual message costs when the cardinality of the table to be shipped was well known. Errors in estimating message costs originated from poor estimates of join cardinalities. This problem is not introduced by distribution, and suggestions for alleviating it by collecting join-cardinality statistics have already been advanced [MACK 86].

The modelling of local costs actually *improves* with greater distribution of the tables involved, because the optimizer's assumption of independence of access is closer to being true when tables do not interfere with each other by competing for the same resource (especially buffer space) within a given site. While more resources are consumed overall by distributed queries, in a high-speed network this results in response times that are actually less than for local queries for certain plans that can benefit from:

- concurrent execution due to pipelining, and/or
- the availability of more key resources — such as buffer space — to reduce contention.

Even for medium-speed, long-haul networks linking geographically dispersed hosts, local costs for CPU and I/O are significant enough to affect the choice of plans. Their relative contribution increases rather than decreases as the tables grow in size, and varies considerably depending upon the access path and join method. Hence no distributed query optimizer can afford to ignore their contribution.

Furthermore, the significance of local costs cannot be ignored when considering alternative distributed join techniques such as semijoins. They are advantageous only when message costs are high (e.g., for a medium-speed network) and any table remote from the join site is quite large. However, we have shown that a Bloomjoin — using Bloom filters to do "hashed semijoins" — dominates the other distributed join methods *in all cases investigated*, except when the semijoin selectivities of the outer and the inner tables are very close to 1. This agrees with the analysis of [BRAT 84].

There remain many open questions which time did not allow us to pursue. We did not test joins for very large tables (e.g., 100,000 tuples), for more than 2 tables, for varying buffer sizes, or for varying tables per DBSPACE. Experimenting with n-table joins, in particular, is crucial to validating the optimizer's selection of join order. We hope to actually test rather than simulate semijoins, Bloomjoins, and medium-speed long-haul networks.

Finally, R* employs a homogeneous model of reality, assuming that all sites have the same processing capabilities and are connected by a uniform network with equal link characteristics. In a real environment, it is very likely that these assumptions are not valid. Adapting the optimizer to this kind of environment is likely to be difficult but important to correctly choosing optimal plans for real configurations.

8. Acknowledgements

We wish to acknowledge the contributions to this work by several colleagues, especially the R* research team, and Lo Hsieh and his group at IBM's Santa Teresa Laboratory. We particularly benefitted from lengthy discussions with — and suggestions by — Bruce Lindsay. Toby Lehman (visiting from the University of Wisconsin) implemented the DC* counters. George Lapis helped with database generation and implemented the R* interface to GDDM that enabled us to graph performance results quickly and elegantly. Paul Wilms contributed some PL/I programs that aided our testing, and assisted in the implementation of the COLLECT COUNTERS and EXPLAIN statements. Christoph Freytag, Laura Haas, Bruce Lindsay, John McPherson, Pat Selinger, and Irv Traiger constructively critiqued an earlier draft of this paper, improving its readability significantly. Finally, Tzu-Fang Chang and Alice Kay provided invaluable systems support and patience while our tests consumed considerable computing resources.

Bibliography

[APER 83] P.M.G. Apers, A.R. Hevner, and S.B. Yao, Optimizing Algorithms for Distributed Queries, *IEEE Trans. on Software Engineering* **SE-9** (January 1983) pp. 57-68.

[ASTR 80] M.M. Astrahan, M. Schkolnick, and W. Kim, Performance of the System R Access Path Selection Mechanism, *Information Processing* **80** (1980) pp. 487-491.

[BABB 79] E. Babb, Implementing a Relational Database by Means of Specialized Hardware, *ACM Trans. on Database Systems* **4,1** (1979) pp. 1-29.

[BERN 79] P.A. Bernstein and N. Goodman, Full reducers for relational queries using multi-attribute semi-joins, *Proc. 1979 NBS Symp. on Comp. Network.* (December 1979).

[BERN 81A] P.A. Bernstein and D.W. Chiu, Using semijoins to solve relational queries, *Journal of the ACM* **28,1** (January 1981) pp. 25-40.

[BERN 81B] P.A. Bernstein, N. Goodman, E. Wong, C.L. Reeve, J. Rothnie, Query Processing in a System for Distributed Databases (SDD-1), *ACM Trans. on Database Systems* **6,4** (December 1981) pp. 602-625.

[BLOO 70] B.H. Bloom, Space/Time Trade-offs in Hash Coding with Allowable Errors, *Communications of the ACM* **13,7** (July 1970) pp. 422-426.

[BRAT 84] K. Bratbergsengen, Hashing Methods and Relational Algebra Operations, *Procs. of the Tenth International Conf. on Very Large Data Bases* (Singapore, 1984) pp. 323-333. Morgan Kaufmann Publishers, Los Altos, CA.

[CHAM 81] D.D. Chamberlin, M.M. Astrahan, W.F. King, R.A. Lorie, J.W. Mehl, T.G. Price, M. Schkolnick, P. Griffiths Selinger, D.R. Slutz, B.W. Wade, and R.A. Yost, Support for Repetitive Transactions and Ad Hoc Queries in System R, *ACM Trans. on Database Systems* **6,1** (March 1981) pp. 70-94.

[CHAN 82] J-M. Chang, A Heuristic Approach to Distributed Query Processing, *Procs. of the Eighth International Conf. on Very Large Data Bases* (Mexico City, September 1982) pp. 54-61. Morgan Kaufmann Publishers, Los Altos, CA.

[CHU 82] W.W. Chu and P. Hurley, Optimal Query Processing for Distributed Database Systems, *IEEE Trans. on Computers* **C-31** (September 1982) pp. 835-850.

[DANI 82] D. Daniels, P.G. Selinger, L.M. Haas, B.G. Lindsay, C. Mohan, A. Walker, and P. Wilms, An Introduction to Distributed Query Compilation in R*, *Procs. Second International Conf. on Distributed Databases* (Berlin, September 1982). Also available as IBM Research Report RJ3497, San Jose, CA, June 1982.

[DEWI 79] D.J. DeWitt, Query Execution in DIRECT, *Procs. of ACM-SIGMOD* (May 1979).

[DEWI 85] D.J. DeWitt and R. Gerber, Multiprocessor Hash-Based Join Algorithms, *Procs. of the Eleventh International Conf. on Very Large Data Bases* (Stockholm, Sweden, September 1985) pp. 151-164. Morgan Kaufmann Publishers, Los Altos, CA.

[EPST 78] R. Epstein, M. Stonebraker, and E. Wong, Distributed Query Processing in a Relational Data Base System, *Procs. of ACM-SIGMOD* (Austin,TX, May 1978) pp. 169-180.

[EPST 80] R. Epstein and M. Stonebraker, Analysis of Distributed Data Base Processing Strategies, *Procs. of the Sixth International Conf. on Very Large Data Bases* (Montreal,IEEE, October 1980) pp. 92-101.

[HEVN 79] A.R. Hevner and S.B. Yao, Query Processing in Distributed Database Systems, *IEEE Trans. on Software Engineering* **SE-5** (May 1979) pp. 177-187.

[KERS 82] L. Kerschberg, P.D. Ting, and S.B. Yao, Query Optimization in Star Computer Networks, *ACM Trans. on Database Systems* **7,4** (December 1982) pp. 678-711.

[LIND 83] B.G. Lindsay, L.M. Haas, C. Mohan, P.F. Wilms, and R.A. Yost, Computation and Communication in R*: A Distributed Database Manager, Proc. 9th ACM Symposium on Principles of Operating Systems (Bretton Woods, October 1983). Also in *ACM Transactions on Computer Systems 2*, 1 (Feb. 1984), pp. 24-38.

[LOHM 84] G.M. Lohman, D. Daniels, L.M. Haas, R. Kistler, P.G. Selinger, Optimization of Nested Queries in a Distributed Relational Database, *Procs. of the Tenth International Conf. on Very Large Data Bases* (Singapore, 1984) pp. 403-415. Morgan Kaufmann Publishers, Los Altos, CA. Also available as IBM Research Report RJ4260, San Jose, CA, April 1984.

[LOHM 85] G.M. Lohman, C. Mohan, L.M. Haas, B.G. Lindsay, P.G. Selinger, P.F. Wilms, and D. Daniels, Query Processing in R*, *Query Processing in Database Systems* (Kim, Batory, & Reiner (eds.), 1985) pp. 31-47. Springer-Verlag, Heidelberg. Also available as IBM Research Report RJ4272, San Jose, CA, April 1984.

[LU 85] H. Lu and M.J. Carey, Some Experimental Results on Distributed Join Algorithms in a Local Network, *Procs. of the Eleventh International Conf. on Very Large Data Bases* (Stockholm, Sweden, August 1985) pp. 292-304. Morgan Kaufmann Publishers, Los Altos, CA.

[MACK 85] L.F. Mackert and G.M. Lohman, Index Scans using a Finite LRU Buffer: A Validated I/O Model, IBM Research Report RJ4836 (San Jose, CA, September 1985).

[MACK 86] L.F. Mackert and G.M. Lohman, R* Optimizer Validation and Performance Evaluation for Local Queries, *Procs. of ACM-SIGMOD* (Washington, DC, May 1986 (to appear)). Also available as IBM Research Report RJ4989, San Jose, CA, January 1986.

[MENO 85] M.J. Menon, Sorting and Join Algorithms for Multiprocessor Database Machines, *NATO-ASI on Relational Database Machine Architecture* (Les Arcs, France, July 1985).

[ONUE 83] E. Onuegbe, S. Rahimi, and A.R. Hevner, Local Query Translation and Optimization in a Distributed System, *Procs. NCC 1983* (July 1983) pp. 229-239.

[PERR 84] W. Perrizo, A Method for Processing Distributed Database Queries, *IEEE Trans. on Software Engineering* **SE-10,4** (July 1984) pp. 466-471.

[RDT 84] *RDT: Relational Design Tool*, IBM Reference Manual SH20-6415. (IBM Corp., June 1984).

[SELI 79] P.G. Selinger, M.M. Astrahan, D.D. Chamberlin, R.A. Lorie, and T.G. Price, Access Path Selection in a Relational Database Management System, *Procs. of ACM-SIGMOD* (1979) pp. 23-34.

[SELI 80] P.G. Selinger and M. Adiba, Access Path Selection in Distributed Database Management Systems, *Procs. International Conf. on Data Bases* (Univ. of Aberdeen, Scotland, July 1980 pp. 204-215. Deen and Hammersly, ed.

[SEVE 76] D.G. Severance and G.M. Lohman, Differential Files: Their Application to the Maintenance of Large Databases, *ACM Trans. on Database Systems* **1,3** (September 1976) pp. 256-267.

[STON 82] M. Stonebraker, J. Woodfill, J. Ranstrom, M. Murphy, J. Kalash, M. Carey, K. Arnold, Performance Analysis of Distributed Data Base Systems, *Database Engineering* **5** (IEEE Computer Society, December 1982) pp. 58-65.

[VALD 84] P. Valduriez and G. Gardarin, Join and Semi-Join Algorithms for a Multiprocessor Database Machine, *ACM Trans. on Database Systems* **9,1** (March 1984) pp. 133-161.

[VTAM 85] *Network Program Products Planning (MVS, VSE, and VM)*, IBM Reference Manual SC23-0110-1 (IBM Corp., April 1985).

[WONG 83] E. Wong, Dynamic Rematerialization: Processing Distributed Queries using Redundant Data, *IEEE Trans. on Software Engineering* **SE-9,3** (May 1983) pp. 228-232.

[YAO 79] S.B. Yao, Optimization of Query Algorithms, *ACM Trans. on Database Systems* **4,2** (June 1979) pp. 133-155.

[YU 83] C.T. Yu, and C.C. Chang, On the Design of a Query Processing Strategy in a Distributed Database Environment, *Proc. SIGMOD 83* (San Jose, CA, May 1983) pp. 30-39.

Concurrency Control in Distributed Database Systems

PHILIP A. BERNSTEIN AND NATHAN GOODMAN

Computer Corporation of America, Cambridge, Massachusetts 02139

In this paper we survey, consolidate, and present the state of the art in distributed database concurrency control. The heart of our analysis is a decomposition of the concurrency control problem into two major subproblems: read-write and write-write synchronization. We describe a series of synchronization techniques for solving each subproblem and show how to combine these techniques into algorithms for solving the entire concurrency control problem. Such algorithms are called "concurrency control methods." We describe 48 principal methods, including all practical algorithms that have appeared in the literature plus several new ones. We concentrate on the structure and correctness of concurrency control algorithms. Issues of performance are given only secondary treatment.

Keywords and Phrases: concurrency control, deadlock, distributed database management systems, locking, serializability, synchronization, timestamp ordering, timestamps, two-phase commit, two-phase locking

CR Categories: 4.33, 4.35

CONTENTS

INTRODUCTION

The Concurrency Control Problem

Concurrency control is the activity of coordinating concurrent accesses to a database in a multiuser database management system (DBMS). Concurrency control permits users to access a database in a multiprogrammed fashion while preserving the illusion that each user is executing alone on a dedicated system. The main technical difficulty in attaining this goal is to prevent database updates performed by one user from interfering with database retrievals and updates performed by another. The concurrency control problem is exacerbated in a distributed DBMS (DDBMS) because (1) users may access data stored in many different computers in a distributed system, and (2) a concurrency control mechanism at one computer cannot instantaneously know about interactions at other computers.

Concurrency control has been actively investigated for the past several years, and the problem for nondistributed DBMSs is well understood. A broad mathematical theory has been developed to analyze the problem, and one approach, called *two-phase locking*, has been accepted as a standard solution. Current research on nondistributed concurrency control is focused on evolutionary improvements to two-phase locking, detailed performance analysis and optimization, and extensions to the mathematical theory.

Distributed concurrency control, by contrast, is in a state of extreme turbulence. More than 20 concurrency control algorithms have been proposed for DDBMSs, and several have been, or are being, implemented. These algorithms are usually complex, hard to understand, and difficult to prove correct (indeed, many are incorrect). Because they are described in different terminologies and make different assumptions about the underlying DDBMS environment, it is difficult to compare the many proposed algorithms, even in qualitative terms. Naturally each author proclaims his or her approach as best, but there is little compelling evidence to support the claims.

To survey the state of the art, we introduce a standard terminology for describing DDBMS concurrency control algorithms and a standard model for the DDBMS environment. For analysis purposes we decompose the concurrency control problem into two major subproblems, called read-write and write-write synchronization. Every concurrency control algorithm must include a subalgorithm to solve each subproblem. The first step toward understanding a concurrency control algorithm is to isolate the subalgorithm employed for each subproblem.

After studying the large number of proposed algorithms, we find that they are compositions of only a few subalgorithms. In fact, the subalgorithms used by all practical DDBMS concurrency control algorithms are variations of just two basic techniques: two-phase locking and timestamp ordering; thus the state of the art is far more coherent than a review of the literature would seem to indicate.

Examples of Concurrency Control Anomalies

The goal of concurrency control is to prevent interference among users who are simultaneously accessing a database. Let us illustrate the problem by presenting two "canonical" examples of interuser interference. Both are examples of an on-line electronic funds transfer system accessed via remote *automated teller machines* (*ATMs*). In response to customer requests, ATMs retrieve data from a database, perform computations, and store results back into the database.

Anomaly 1: Lost Updates. Suppose two customers simultaneously try to deposit money into the same account. In the absence of concurrency control, these two activities could interfere (see Figure 1). The two ATMs handling the two customers could read the account balance at approximately the same time, compute new balances in parallel, and then store the new balances back into the database. The net effect is incorrect: although two customers deposited money, the database only reflects one activity; the other deposit is lost by the system.

Anomaly 2: Inconsistent Retrievals. Suppose two customers simultaneously execute the following transactions.

Customer 1: Move $1,000,000 from Acme Corporation's savings account to its checking account.

Customer 2: Print Acme Corporation's total balance in savings and checking.

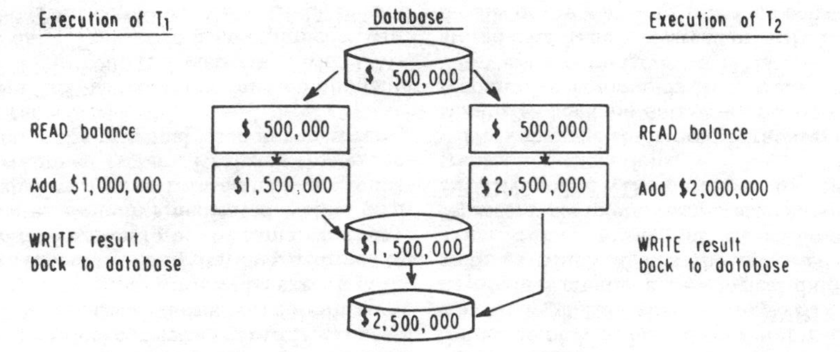

Figure 1. Lost update anomaly.

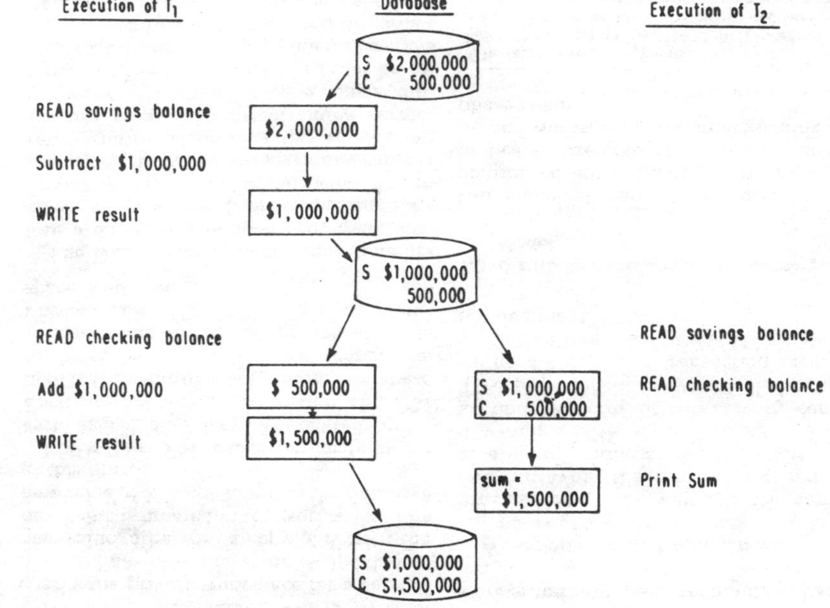

Figure 2. Inconsistent retrieval anomaly.

In the absence of concurrency control these two transactions could interfere (see Figure 2). The first transaction might read the savings account balance, subtract $1,000,000, and store the result back in the database. Then the second transaction might read the savings and checking account balances and print the total. Then the first transaction might finish the funds transfer by reading the checking account balance, adding $1,000,000, and finally storing the result in the database. Unlike Anomaly 1, the final values placed into the database by this execution are correct. Still, the execution is incorrect because the balance printed by Customer 2 is $1,000,000 short.

These two examples do not exhaust all possible ways in which concurrent users can interfere. However, these examples are typical of the concurrency control problems that arise in DBMSs.

Comparison to Mutual Exclusion Problems

The problem of database concurrency control is similar in some respects to that of mutual exclusion in operating systems. The latter problem is concerned with coordinating access by concurrent processes to system resources such as memory, I/O devices, and CPU. Many solution techniques have been developed, including locks, semaphores, monitors, and serializers [BRIN73, DIJK71, HEWI74, HOAR74].

The concurrency control and mutual exclusion problems are similar in that both are concerned with controlling concurrent access to shared resources. However, control schemes that work for one do not necessarily work for the other, as illustrated by the following example. Suppose processes P_1 and P_2 require access to resources R_1 and R_2 at different points in their execution. In an operating system, the following interleaved execution of these processes is perfectly acceptable: P_1 uses R_1, P_2 uses R_1, P_2 uses R_2, P_1 uses R_2. In a database, however, this execution is not always acceptable. Assume, for example, that P_2 transfers funds by debiting one account (R_1), then crediting another (R_2). If P_2 checks both balances, it will see R_1 after it has been debited, but see R_2 *before* it has been credited. Other differences between concurrency control and mutual exclusion are discussed in CHAM74.

1. TRANSACTION-PROCESSING MODEL

To understand how a concurrency control algorithm operates, one must understand how the algorithm fits into an overall DDBMS. In this section we present a simple model of a DDBMS, emphasizing how the DDBMS processes user interactions. Later we explain how concurrency control algorithms operate in the context of this model.

1.1 Preliminary Definitions and DDBMS Architecture

A distributed database management system (DDBMS) is a collection of sites interconnected by a network [DEPP76, ROTH77]. Each *site* is a computer running one or both of the following software modules: a transaction manager (TM) or a data manager (DM). *TMs* supervise interactions between users and the DDBMS while *DMs* manage the actual database. A *network* is a computer-to-computer communication system. The network is assumed to be perfectly reliable: if site A sends a message to site B, site B is guaranteed to receive the message without error. In addition, we assume that between any pair of sites the network delivers messages in the order they were sent.

From a user's perspective, a *database* consists of a collection of *logical data items*, denoted *X*, *Y*, *Z*. We leave the granularity of logical data items unspecified; in practice, they may be files, records, etc. A *logical database state* is an assignment of values to the logical data items composing a database. Each logical data item may be stored at any DM in the system or redundantly at several DMs. A stored copy of a logical data item is called a *stored data item*. (When no confusion is possible, we use the term *data item* for stored data item.) The stored copies of logical data item *X* are denoted $x_1, \ldots, x_m$. We typically use x to denote an arbitrary stored data item. A *stored database state* is an assignment of values to the stored data items in a database.

Users interact with the DDBMS by executing *transactions*. Transactions may be on-line queries expressed in a self-contained query language, or application programs written in a general-purpose programming language. The concurrency control algorithms we study pay no attention to the computations performed by transactions. Instead, these algorithms make all of their decisions on the basis of the data items a transaction reads and writes, and so details of the form of transactions are unimportant in our analysis. However we do assume that transactions represent complete and correct computations; each transaction, if ex-

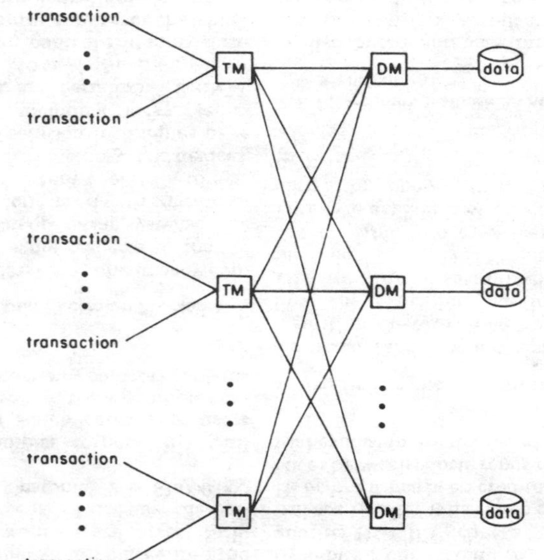

Figure 3. DDBMS system architecture.

ecuted alone on an initially consistent database, would terminate, produce correct results, and leave the database consistent. The *logical readset* (correspondingly, *writeset*) of a transaction is the set of logical data items the transaction reads (or writes). Similarly, *stored readsets* and *stored writesets* are the stored data items that a transaction reads and writes.

The correctness of a concurrency control algorithm is defined relative to users' expectations regarding transaction execution. There are two correctness criteria: (1) users expect that each transaction submitted to the system will eventually be executed; (2) users expect the computation performed by each transaction to be the same whether it executes alone in a dedicated system or in parallel with other transactions in a multiprogrammed system. Realizing this expectation is the principal issue in concurrency control.

A DDBMS contains four components (see Figure 3): transactions, TMs, DMs, and data. Transactions communicate with TMs, TMs communicate with DMs, and DMs manage the data. (TMs do not communicate with other TMs, nor do DMs communicate with other DMs.)

TMs supervise transactions. Each transaction executed in the DDBMS is supervised by a *single* TM, meaning that the transaction issues all of its database operations to that TM. Any distributed computation that is needed to execute the transaction is managed by the TM.

Four operations are defined at the transaction–TM interface. READ(X) returns the value of X (a logical data item) in the current logical database state. WRITE(X, new-value) creates a new logical database state in which X has the specified new value. Since transactions are assumed to represent complete computations, we use BEGIN and END operations to bracket transaction executions.

DMs manage the stored database, functioning as backend database processors. In response to commands from transactions, TMs issue commands to DMs specifying stored data items to be read or written. The details of the TM–DM interface constitute the core of our transaction-processing model and are discussed in Sections 1.2 and 1.3. Section 1.2 describes the TM-DM interaction in a centralized database environment, and Section 1.3 extends the discussion to a distributed database setting.

1.2 Centralized Transaction-Processing Model

A centralized DBMS consists of one TM and one DM executing at one site. A transaction T accesses the DBMS by issuing BEGIN, READ, WRITE, and END operations, which are processed as follows.

BEGIN: The TM initializes for T a *private workspace* that functions as a temporary buffer for values read from and written into the database.

READ(X): The TM looks for a copy of X in T's private workspace. If the copy exists, its value is returned to T. Otherwise the TM issues *dm-read*(x) to the DM to retrieve a copy of X from the database, gives the retrieved value to T, and puts it into T's private workspace.

WRITE(X, new-value): The TM again checks the private workspace for a copy of X. If it finds one, the value is updated to new-value; otherwise a copy of X with the new value is created in the workspace. The new value of X is *not* stored in the database at this time.

END: The TM issues *dm-write*(x) for each logical data item X updated by T. Each dm-write(x) requests that the DM update the value of X in the stored database to the value of X in T's local workspace. When all dm-writes are processed, T is finished executing, and its private workspace is discarded.

The DBMS may *restart* T any time before a dm-write has been processed. The effect of restarting T is to obliterate its private workspace and to reexecute T from the beginning. As we will see, many concurrency control algorithms use transaction restarts as a tactic for attaining correct executions. However, once a single dm-write has been processed, T cannot be restarted; each dm-write permanently installs an update into the database, and we cannot permit the database to reflect partial effects of transactions.

A DBMS can avoid such partial results by having the property of *atomic commitment*, which requires that either all of a transaction's dm-writes are processed or none are. The "standard" implementation of atomic commitment is a procedure called *two-phase commit* [LAMP76, GRAY78].[1] Suppose T is updating data items X and Y. When T issues its END, the *first phase* of two-phase commit begins, during which the DM issues *prewrite* commands for X and Y. These commands instruct the DM to copy the values of X and Y from T's private workspace onto secure storage. If the DBMS fails during the first phase, no harm is done, since none of T's updates have yet been applied to the stored database. During the *second phase*, the TM issues *dm-write* commands for X and Y which instruct the DM to copy the values of X and Y into the stored database. If the DBMS fails during the second phase, the database may contain incorrect information, but since the values of X and Y are stored on secure storage, this inconsistency can be rectified when the system recovers: the recovery procedure reads the values of X and Y from secure storage and resumes the commitment activity.

We emphasize that this is a *mathematical model* of transaction processing, an approximation to the way DBMSs actually function. While the implementation details of atomic commitment are important in designing a DBMS, they are not central to an understanding of concurrency control. To explain concurrency control algorithms we need a model of transaction execution in which atomic commitment is visible, but not dominant.

1.3 Distributed Transaction-Processing Model

Our model of transaction processing in a distributed environment differs from that in a centralized one in two areas: handling private workspaces and implementing two-phase commit.

[1] The term "two-phase commit" is commonly used to denote the distributed version of this procedure. However, since the centralized and distributed versions are identical in structure, we use "two-phase commit" to describe both.

In a centralized DBMS we assumed that (1) private workspaces were part of the TM, and (2) data could freely move between a transaction and its workspace, and between a workspace and the DM. These assumptions are not appropriate in a DDBMS because TMs and DMs may run at different sites and the movement of data between a TM and a DM can be expensive. To reduce this cost, many DDBMSs employ *query optimization procedures* which regulate (and, it is hoped, reduce) the flow of data between sites. For example, in SDD-1 the private workspace for transaction T is distributed across all sites at which T accesses data [BERN81]. The details of how T reads and writes data in these workspaces is a query optimization problem and has no direct effect on concurrency control.

The problem of atomic commitment is aggravated in a DDBMS by the possibility of one site failing while the rest of the system continues to operate. Suppose T is updating x, y, z stored at DM_x, DM_y, DM_z, and suppose T's TM fails after issuing dm-write(x), but before issuing the dm-writes for y and z. At this point the database is incorrect. In a centralized DBMS this phenomenon is not harmful because no transaction can access the database until the TM recovers from the failure. However, in a DDBMS, other TMs remain operational and can access the incorrect database.

To avoid this problem, prewrite commands must be modified slightly. In addition to specifying data items to be copied onto secure storage, prewrites also specify which other DMs are involved in the commitment activity. Then if the TM fails during the second phase of two-phase commit, the DMs whose dm-writes were not issued can recognize the situation and consult the other DMs involved in the commitment. If any DM received a dm-write, the remaining ones act as if they had also received the command. The details of this procedure are complex and appear in HAMM80.

As in a centralized DBMS, a transaction T accesses the system by issuing BEGIN, READ, WRITE, and END operations. In a DDBMS these are processed as follows.

BEGIN: The TM creates a private workspace for T. We leave the location and organization of this workspace unspecified.

READ(X): The TM checks T's private workspace to see if a copy of X is present. If so, that copy's value is made available to T. Otherwise the TM selects some stored copy of X, say x_i, and issues dm-read(x_i) to the DM at which x_i is stored. The DM responds by retrieving the stored value of x_i from the database, placing it in the private workspace. The TM returns this value to T.

WRITE(X, new-value): The value of X in T's private workspace is updated to new-value, assuming the workspace contains a copy of X. Otherwise, a copy of X with the new value is created in the workspace.

END: Two-phase commit begins. For each X updated by T, and for each stored copy x_i of X, the TM issues a prewrite (x_i) to the DM that stores x_i. The DM responds by copying the value of X from T's private workspace onto secure storage internal to the DM. After all prewrites are processed, the TM issues dm-writes for all copies of all logical data items updated by T. A DM responds to dm-write(x_i) by copying the value of x_i from secure storage into the stored database. After all dm-writes are installed, T's execution is finished.

2. DECOMPOSITION OF THE CONCURRENCY CONTROL PROBLEM

In this section we review concurrency control theory with two objectives: to define "correct executions" in precise terms, and to decompose the concurrency control problem into more tractable subproblems.

2.1 Serializability

Let E denote an execution of transactions $T_1, \ldots, T_n$. E is a *serial execution* if no transactions execute concurrently in E; that is, each transaction is executed to completion before the next one begins. Every serial execution is defined to be *correct*, because the properties of transactions (see Section 1.1) imply that a serial execution terminates properly and preserves database consistency. An execution is *serializable* if it is computationally equivalent to a serial execution, that is, if it produces the same output and has the same effect on the database as some serial execution. Since serial executions are correct and every serializable execution is equivalent to a serial one, every serializable execution is also correct. The goal of database concurrency control is to ensure that all executions are serializable.

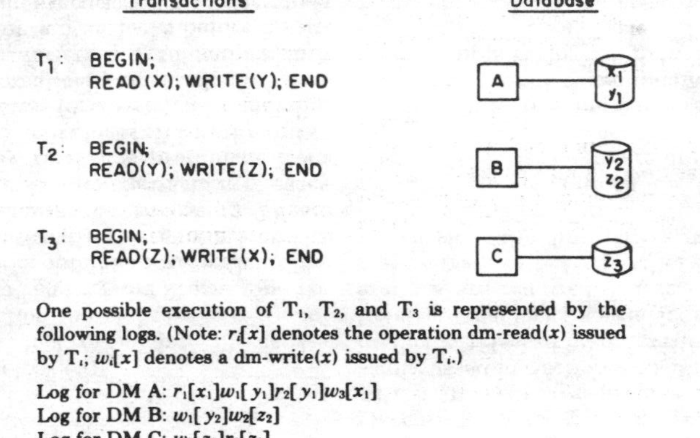

One possible execution of T_1, T_2, and T_3 is represented by the following logs. (Note: $r_i[x]$ denotes the operation dm-read(x) issued by T_i; $w_i[x]$ denotes a dm-write(x) issued by T_i.)

Log for DM A: $r_1[x_1]w_1[y_1]r_2[y_1]w_3[x_1]$
Log for DM B: $w_1[y_2]w_2[z_2]$
Log for DM C: $w_2[z_3]r_3[z_3]$

Figure 4. Modeling executions as logs.

- The execution modeled in Figure 4 is serial. Each log is itself serial; that is, there is no interleaving of operations from different transactions. At DM A, T_1 precedes T_2 precedes T_3; at DM B, T_1 precedes T_2; and at DM C, T_2 precedes T_3. Therefore, T_1, T_2, T_3 is a total order satisfying the definition of serial.
- The following execution is not serial. The logs themselves are not serial.

DM A: $r_1[x_1]r_2[y_1]w_3[x_1]w_1[y_1]$
DM B: $w_2[z_2]w_1[y_2]$
DM C: $w_2[z_3]r_3[z_3]$

- The following execution is also not serial. Although each log is serial, there is no total order consistent with all logs.

DM A: $r_1[x_1]w_1[y_1]r_2[y_1]w_3[x_1]$
DM B: $w_2[z_2]w_1[y_2]$
DM C: $w_2[z_3]r_3[z_3]$

Figure 5. Serial and nonserial loops.

The only operations that access the stored database are dm-read and dm-write. Hence it is sufficient to model an execution of transactions by the execution of dm-reads and dm-writes at the various DMs of the DDBMS. In this spirit we formally model an execution of transactions by a set of *logs*, each of which indicates the order in which dm-reads and dm-writes are processed at one DM (see Figure 4). An execution is *serial* if there is a total order of transactions such that if T_i precedes T_j in the total order, then all of T_i's operations precede all of T_j's operations in every log where both appear (see Figure 5). Intuitively, this says that transactions execute serially and in the same order at all DMs.

Two operations *conflict* if they operate on the same data item and one of the operations is a dm-write. The order in which operations execute is computationally significant if and only if the operations conflict. To illustrate the notion of conflict, consider a data item x and transactions T_i and T_j. If T_i issues dm-read (x) and T_j issues dm-write(x), the value read by T_i will (in general) differ depending on whether the dm-read precedes or follows the dm-write. Similarly, if both transactions issue dm-write(x) operations, the final value of x depends on which dm-write happens last. Those conflict situations are called *read-write* (*rw*) *conflicts* and *write-write* (*ww*) *conflicts*, respectively.

The notion of conflict helps characterize the equivalence of executions. Two executions are *computationally equivalent* if (1) each dm-read operation reads data item values that were produced by the same dm-writes in both executions; and (2) the final dm-write on each data item is the same in both executions [PAPA77, PAPA79]. Condition (1) ensures that each transaction reads the same input in both executions (and therefore performs the same computation).

Combined with (2), it ensures that both executions leave the database in the same final state.

From this we can characterize serializable executions precisely.

Theorem 1 [PAPA77, PAPA79, STEA76]

Let $T = \{T_1, \ldots, T_m\}$ *be a set of transactions and let E be an execution of these transactions modeled by logs* $\{L_1, \ldots, L_m\}$. *E is serializable if there exists a total ordering of T such that for each pair of conflicting operations* O_i *and* O_j *from distinct transactions* T_i *and* T_j *(respectively),* O_i *precedes* O_j *in any log* $L_1, \ldots, L_m$ *if and only if* T_i *precedes* T_j *in the total ordering.*

The total order hypothesized in Theorem 1 is called a *serialization order*. If the transactions had executed serially in the serialization order, the computation performed by the transactions would have been identical to the computation represented by E.

To attain serializability, the DDBMS must guarantee that all executions satisfy the condition of Theorem 1, namely, that conflicting dm-reads and dm-writes be processed in certain relative orders. *Concurrency control* is the activity of controlling the relative order of conflicting operations; an algorithm to perform such control is called a *synchronization technique*. To be correct, a DDBMS must incorporate synchronization techniques that guarantee the conditions of Theorem 1.

2.2 A Paradigm for Concurrency Control

In Theorem 1, rw and ww conflicts are treated together under the general notion of conflict. However, we can decompose the concept of serializability by distinguishing these two types of conflict. Let E be an execution modeled by a set of logs. We define several binary relations on transactions in E, denoted by $\rightarrow$ with various subscripts. For each pair of transactions, T_i and T_j

(1) $T_i \rightarrow_{rw} T_j$ if in some log of E, T_i reads some data item into which T_j subsequently writes;
(2) $T_i \rightarrow_{wr} T_j$ if in some log of E, T_i writes into some data item that T_j subsequently reads;
(3) $T_i \rightarrow_{ww} T_j$ if in some log of E, T_i writes into some data item into which T_j subsequently writes;
(4) $T_i \rightarrow_{rwr} T_j$ if $T_i \rightarrow_{rw} T_j$ or $T_i \rightarrow_{wr} T_j$;
(5) $T_i \rightarrow T_j$ if $T_j \rightarrow_{rwr} T_j$ or $T_i \rightarrow_{ww} T_j$.

Intuitively, $\rightarrow$ (with any subscript) means "in any serialization must precede." For example, $T_i \rightarrow_{rw} T_j$ means "T_i in any serialization must precede T_j." This interpretation follows from Theorem 1: If T_i reads x before T_j writes into x, then the hypothetical serialization in Theorem 1 must have T_i preceding T_j.

Every conflict between operations in E is represented by an $\rightarrow$ relationship. Therefore, we can restate Theorem 1 in terms of $\rightarrow$. According to Theorem 1, E is serializable if there is a total order of transactions that is consistent with $\rightarrow$. This latter condition holds if and only if $\rightarrow$ is acyclic. (A relation, $\rightarrow$, is *acyclic* if there is no sequence $T_1 \rightarrow T_2, T_2 \rightarrow T_3, \ldots, T_n\text{-}1 \rightarrow T_n$ such that $T_1 = T_n$.) Let us decompose $\rightarrow$ into its components, $\rightarrow_{rwr}$ and $\rightarrow_{ww}$, and restate the theorem using them.

Theorem 2 [BERN80a]

Let $\rightarrow_{rwr}$ *and* $\rightarrow_{ww}$ *be associated with execution E. E is serializable if (a)* $\rightarrow_{rwr}$ *and* $\rightarrow_{ww}$ *are acyclic, and (b) there is a total ordering of the transactions consistent with all* $\rightarrow_{rwr}$ *and all* $\rightarrow_{ww}$ *relationships.*

Theorem 2 is an immediate consequence of Theorem 1. (Indeed, part (b) of Theorem 2 is essentially a restatement of the earlier theorem.) However, this way of characterizing serializability suggests a way of decomposing the problem into simpler parts. Theorem 2 implies that rw and ww conflicts can be synchronized independently except insofar as there must be a total ordering of the transactions consistent with both types of conflicts. This suggests that we can use one technique to guarantee an acyclic $\rightarrow_{rwr}$ relation (which amounts to *read-write synchronization*) and a different technique to guarantee an acyclic $\rightarrow_{ww}$ relation (*write-write synchronization*). However, in addition to both $\rightarrow_{rwr}$ and $\rightarrow_{ww}$ being acyclic, there must also be *one* serial order consistent with *all* $\rightarrow$ relations. This serial order is the cement that binds together the rw and ww synchronization techniques.

Decomposing serializability into rw and ww synchronization is the cornerstone of our paradigm for concurrency control. It will be important hereafter to distinguish algorithms that attain either rw or ww synchronization from algorithms that solve the entire distributed concurrency control problem. We use the term *synchronization technique* for the former type of algorithm, and *concurrency control method* for the latter.

3. SYNCHRONIZATION TECHNIQUES BASED ON TWO-PHASE LOCKING

Two-phase locking (2PL) synchronizes reads and writes by explicitly detecting and preventing conflicts between concurrent operations. Before reading data item x, a transaction must "own" a *readlock on* x. Before writing into x, it must "own" a *writelock on* x. The ownership of locks is governed by two rules: (1) different transactions cannot simultaneously own *conflicting locks*; and (2) once a transaction surrenders ownership of a lock, it may never obtain additional locks.

The definition of *conflicting lock* depends on the type of synchronization being performed: for rw synchronization two locks *conflict* if (a) both are locks on the same data item, and (b) one is a readlock and the other is a writelock; for ww synchronization two locks *conflict* if (a) both are locks on the same data item, and (b) both are writelocks.

The second lock ownership rule causes every transaction to obtain locks in a *two-phase* manner. During the *growing phase* the transaction obtains locks without releasing any locks. By releasing a lock the transaction enters the *shrinking phase*. During this phase the transaction releases locks, and, by rule 2, is prohibited from obtaining additional locks. When the transaction terminates (or aborts), all remaining locks are automatically released.

A common variation is to require that transactions obtain all locks before beginning their main execution. This variation is called *predeclaration*. Some systems also require that transactions hold all locks until termination

Two-phase locking is a correct synchronization technique, meaning that 2PL attains an acyclic $\rightarrow_{rwr}$ ($\rightarrow_{ww}$) relation when used for rw (ww) synchronization [BERN79b, ESWA76, PAPA79]. The serialization order attained by 2PL is determined by the order in which transactions obtain locks. The point at the end of the growing phase, when a transaction owns all the locks it ever will own, is called the *locked point* of the transaction [BERN79b]. Let E be an execution in which 2PL is used for rw (ww) synchronization. The $\rightarrow_{rwr}$ ($\rightarrow_{ww}$) relation induced by E is identical to the relation induced by a *serial* execution E′ in which every transaction executes at its locked point. Thus the locked points of E determine a serialization order for E.

3.1 Basic 2PL Implementation

An implementation of 2PL amounts to building a *2PL scheduler*, a software module that receives lock requests and lock releases and processes them according to the 2PL specification.

The basic way to implement 2PL in a distributed database is to distribute the schedulers along with the database, placing the scheduler for data item x at the DM were x is stored. In this implementation readlocks may be implicitly requested by dm-reads and writelocks may be implicitly requested by prewrites. If the requested lock cannot be granted, the operation is placed on a waiting queue for the desired data item. (This can produce a *deadlock*, as discussed in Section 3.5.) Writelocks are implicitly released by dm-writes. However, to release readlocks, special lock-release operations are required. These lock releases may be transmitted in parallel with the dm-writes, since the dm-writes signal the start of the shrinking phase. When a lock is released, the operations on the waiting queue of that data item are processed first-in/first-out (FIFO) order.

Notice that this implementation "automatically" handles redundant data correctly. Suppose logical data item X has copies $x_1, \ldots, x_m$. If basic 2PL is used for rw synchronization, a transaction may read any copy and need only obtain a readlock on the copy of X it actually reads. However, if a transaction updates X, then it must update all copies of X, and so must obtain writelocks on all copies of X (whether basic 2PL is used for rw or ww synchronization).

3.2 Primary Copy 2PL

Primary copy 2PL is a 2PL technique that pays attention to data redundancy [STON79]. One copy of each logical data item is designated the *primary copy*; before accessing any copy of the logical data item, the appropriate lock must be obtained on the primary copy.

For readlocks this technique requires more communication than basic 2PL. Suppose x_1 is the primary copy of logical data item X, and suppose transaction T wishes to read some other copy, x_i, of X. To read x_i, T must communicate with two DMs, the DM where x_1 is stored (so T can lock x_1) and the DM where x_i is stored. By contrast, under basic 2PL, T would only communicate with x_i's DM. For writelocks, however, primary copy 2PL does not incur extra communication. Suppose T wishes to update X. Under basic 2PL, T would issue prewrites to all copies of X (thereby requesting writelocks on these data items) and then issue dm-writes to all copies. Under primary copy 2PL the same operations would be required, but only the prewrite (x_1) would request a writelock. That is, prewrites would be sent for $x_1, \ldots, x_m$, but the prewrites for $x_2, \ldots, x_m$ would not implicitly request writelocks.

3.3 Voting 2PL

Voting 2PL (or *majority consensus 2PL*) is another 2PL implementation that exploits data redundancy. Voting 2PL is derived from the majority consensus technique of Thomas [THOM79] and is only suitable for ww synchronization.

To understand voting, we must examine it in the context of two-phase commit. Suppose transaction T wants to write into X. Its TM sends prewrites to each DM holding a copy of X. For the voting protocol, the DM always responds immediately. It acknowledges receipt of the prewrite and says "lock set" or "lock blocked." (In the basic implementation it would not acknowledge at all until the lock is set.) After the TM receives acknowledgments from the DMs, it counts the number of "lockset" responses: if the number constitutes a majority, then the TM behaves as if all locks were set. Otherwise, it waits for "lockset" operations from DMs that originally said "lock blocked." Deadlocks aside (see Section 3.5), it will eventually receive enough "lockset" operations to proceed.

Since only one transaction can hold a majority of locks on X at a time, only one transaction writing into X can be in its second commit phase at any time. All copies of X thereby have the same sequence of writes applied to them. A transaction's locked point occurs when it has obtained a majority of its writelocks on each data item in its writeset. When updating many data items, a transaction must obtain a majority of locks on every data item before it issues any dm-writes.

In principle, voting 2PL could be adapted for rw synchronization. Before reading any copy of X a transaction requests readlocks on all copies of X; when a majority of locks are set, the transaction may read any copy. This technique works but is overly strong: Correctness only requires that a single copy of X be locked—namely, the copy that is read—yet this technique requests locks on all copies. For this reason we deem voting 2PL to be inappropriate for rw synchronization.

3.4 Centralized 2PL

Instead of distributing the 2PL schedulers, one can centralize the scheduler at a single site [ALSB76a, GARC79a]. Before accessing data at any site, appropriate locks must be obtained from the central 2PL scheduler. So, for example, to perform dm-read(x) where x is not stored at the central site, the TM must first request a readlock on x from the central site, wait for the central site to acknowledge that the lock has been set, then send dm-read(x) to the DM that holds x. (To save some communication, one can have the TM send both the lock request and dm-read (x) to the central site and let the central site directly forward dm-read(x) to x's DM; the DM then responds to the TM when dm-read (x) has been processed.) Like primary copy 2PL, this approach tends to require more communication than basic 2PL, since dm-reads and prewrites usually cannot implicitly request locks.

Transactions

T_1: BEGIN;
READ(X); WRITE(Y); END

T_2: BEGIN;
READ(Y); WRITE(Z); END

T_3: BEGIN;
READ(Z); WRITE(X); END

Database

A — x_1, y_1
B — y_2, z_2
C — z_3

- Suppose transactions execute concurrently, with each transaction issuing its READ before any transaction issues its END.
- This partial execution could be represented by the following logs.

DM A: $r_1[x_1]$
DM B: $r_2[y_2]$
DM C: $r_3[z_3]$

- At this point, T_1 has readlock on x_1
  T_2 has readlock on y_2
  T_3 has readlock on z_3
- Before proceeding, all transactions must obtain writelocks.
  T_1 requires writelocks on y_1 and y_2
  T_2 requires writelocks on z_2 and z_3
  T_3 requires writelock on x_1
- But
  T_1 cannot get writelock on y_2, until T_2 releases readlock
  T_2 cannot get writelock on z_3, until T_3 releases readlock
  T_3 cannot get writelock on x_1, until T_1 releases readlock
  This is a deadlock.

Figure 6. Deadlock.

3.5 Deadlock Detection and Prevention

The preceding implementations of 2PL force transactions to wait for unavailable locks. If this waiting is uncontrolled, deadlocks can arise (see Figure 6).

Deadlock situations can be characterized by *waits-for graphs* [HOLT72, KING74], directed graphs that indicate which transactions are waiting for which other transactions. Nodes of the graph represent transactions, and edges represent the "waiting-for" relationship: an edge is drawn from transaction T_i to transaction T_j if T_i is waiting for a lock currently owned by T_j. There is a deadlock in the system if and only if the waits-for graph contains a *cycle* (see Figure 7).

Two general techniques are available for deadlock resolution: *deadlock prevention* and *deadlock detection*.

3.5.1 Deadlock Prevention

Deadlock prevention is a "cautious" scheme in which a transaction is restarted when the system is "afraid" that deadlock might occur. To implement deadlock prevention, 2PL schedulers are modified as follows. When a lock request is denied, the scheduler tests the requesting transaction (say T_i) and the transaction that currently owns the lock (say T_j). If T_i and T_j pass the test, T_i is permitted to wait for T_j as usual. Otherwise, one of the two is aborted. If T_i is restarted, the deadlock prevention algorithm is called *nonpreemptive*; if T_j is restarted, the algorithm is called *preemptive*.

The test applied by the scheduler must

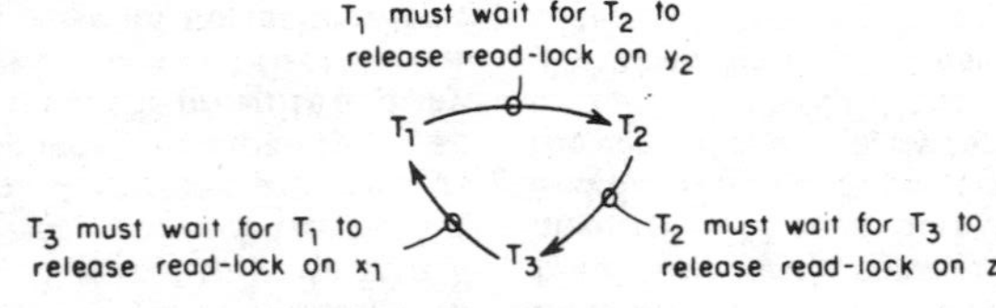

Figure 7. Waits-for graph for Figure 6.

guarantee that if T_i waits for T_j, then deadlock cannot result. One simple approach is never to let T_i wait for T_j. This trivially prevents deadlock but forces many restarts.

A better approach is to assign *priorities* to transactions and to test priorities to decide whether T_i can wait for T_j. For example, we could let T_i wait for T_j if T_i has lower priority than T_j (if T_i and T_j have *equal* priorities, T_i cannot wait for T_j, or vice versa). This test prevents deadlock because, for every edge $\langle T_i, T_j \rangle$ in the waits-for graph, T_i has lower priority than T_j. Since a cycle is a path from a node to itself and since T_i cannot have lower priority than itself, no cycle can exist.

One problem with the preceding approach is that *cyclic restart* is possible—some unfortunate transaction could be continually restarted without ever finishing. To avoid this problem, Rosenkrantz et al. [ROSE78] propose using "timestamps" as priorities. Intuitively, a transaction's timestamp is the time at which it begins executing, so old transactions have higher priority than young ones.

The technique of ROSE78 requires that each transaction be assigned a *unique* timestamp by its TM. When a transaction begins, the TM reads the local clock time and appends a unique TM identifier to the low-order bits [THOM79]. The resulting number is the desired timestamp. The TM also agrees not to assign another timestamp until the next clock tick. Thus timestamps assigned by different TMs differ in their low-order bits (since different TMs have different identifiers), while timestamps assigned by the same TM differ in their high-order bits (since the TM does not use the same clock time twice). Hence timestamps are unique throughout the system. Note that this algorithm does not require clocks at different sites to be precisely synchronized.

Two timestamp-based deadlock prevention schemes are proposed in ROSE78. *Wait-Die* is the nonpreemptive technique. Suppose transaction T_i tries to wait for T_j. If T_i has lower priority than T_j (i.e., T_i is younger than T_j), then T_i is permitted to wait. Otherwise, it is aborted ("dies") and forced to restart. It is important that T_i not be assigned a new timestamp when it restarts. *Wound-Wait* is the preemptive counterpart to *Wait-Die*. If T_i has higher priority than T_j, then T_i waits; otherwise T_j is aborted.

Both Wait-Die and Wound-Wait avoid cyclic restart. However, in Wound-Wait an old transaction may be restarted many times, while in Wait-Die old transactions never restart. It is suggested in ROSE78 that Wound-Wait induces fewer restarts in total.

Care must be exercised in using preemptive deadlock prevention with two-phase commit: a transaction must not be aborted once the second phase of two-phase commit has begun. If a preemptive technique wishes to abort T_j, it checks with T_j's TM and cancels the abort if T_j has entered the second phase. No deadlock can result because if T_j is in the second phase, it cannot be waiting for any transactions.

Preordering of resources is a deadlock avoidance technique that avoids restarts altogether. This technique requires predeclaration of locks (each transaction obtains all its locks before execution). Data items are numbered and each transaction requests locks one at a time in numeric order. The priority of a transaction is the number of the highest numbered lock it owns. Since a transaction can only wait for transactions with higher priority, no deadlocks can occur. In addition to requiring predeclaration, a principal disadvantage of this technique is that it forces locks to be obtained sequentially, which tends to increase response time.

- Consider the execution illustrated in Figures 6 and 7.
- Locks are requested at DMs in the following order:

DM A	DM B	DM C
readlock x_1 for T_1	readlock y_2 for T_2	readlock z_3 for T_3
writelock y_1 for T_1	writelock z_2 for T_2	
*writelock x_1 for T_3	*writelock y_2 for T_1	*writelock z_3 for T_2

- None of the "starred" locks can be granted and the system is in deadlock. However, the waits-for graphs at each DM are acyclic.

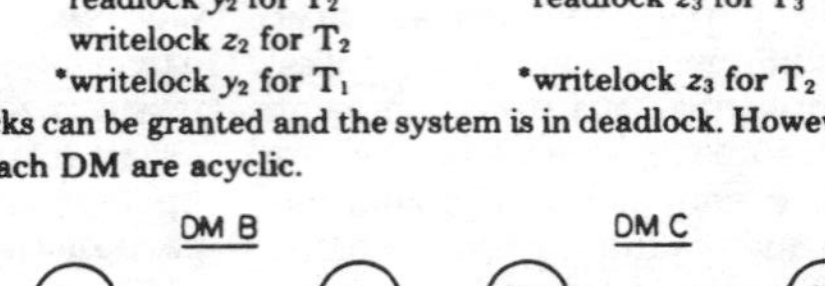

Figure 8. Multisite deadlock.

3.5.2 Deadlock Detection

In *deadlock detection*, transactions wait for each other in an uncontrolled manner and are only aborted if a deadlock actually occurs. Deadlocks are detected by explicitly constructing the waits-for graph and searching it for cycles. (Cycles in a graph can be found efficiently using, for example, Algorithm 5.2 in AHO75.) If a cycle is found, one transaction on the cycle, called the *victim*, is aborted, thereby breaking the deadlock. To minimize the cost of restarting the victim, victim selection is usually based on the amount of resources used by each transaction on the cycle.

The principal difficulty in implementing deadlock detection in a distributed database is constructing the waits-for graph efficiently. Each 2PL scheduler can easily construct the waits-for graph based on the waits-for relationships local to that scheduler. However, these local waits-for graphs are not sufficient to characterize all deadlocks in the distributed system (see Figure 8). Instead, local waits-for graphs must be combined into a more "global" waits-for graph. (Centralized 2PL does not have this problem, since there is only one scheduler.) We describe two techniques for constructing global waits-for graphs: centralized and hierarchical deadlock detection.

In the *centralized* approach, one site is designated the deadlock detector for the distributed system [GRAY78, STON79]. Periodically (e.g., every few minutes) each scheduler sends its local waits-for graph to the deadlock detector. The deadlock detector combines the local graphs into a system-wide waits-for graph by constructing the union of the local graphs.

In the *hierarchical* approach, the database sites are organized into a hierarchy (or tree), with a deadlock detector at each node of the hierarchy [MENA79]. For example, one might group sites by *region*, then by *country*, then by *continent*. Deadlocks that are local to a single site are detected at that site; deadlocks involving two or more sites of the same region are detected by the regional deadlock detector; and so on.

Although centralized and hierarchical deadlock detection differ in detail, both involve periodic transmission of local waits-for information to one or more deadlock detector sites. The periodic nature of the process introduces two problems. First, a deadlock may exist for several minutes without being detected, causing response-time degradation. The solution, executing the deadlock detector more frequently, increases the cost of deadlock detection. Second, a transaction T may be restarted for reasons other than concurrency control (e.g., its site crashed). Until T's restart propagates to the deadlock detector, the deadlock detector can find a cycle in the waits-for graph that includes T. Such a cycle is called a *phantom deadlock*. When the deadlock detector discovers a phantom deadlock, it may unnecessarily restart a transaction other than T. Special precautions are also needed to avoid unnecessary restarts for deadlocks in voting 2PL.[2]

[2] Suppose logical data item X has copies x_1, x_2, and x_3, and suppose using voting 2PL T_i owns write-locks on x_1 and x_2 but T_j's lock request for x_3 is blocked by T_j.

A major cost of deadlock detection is the restarting of partially executed transactions. Predeclaration can be used to reduce this cost. By obtaining a transaction's locks before it executes, the system will only restart transactions that have not yet executed. Thus little work is wasted by the restart.

4. SYNCHRONIZATION TECHNIQUES BASED ON TIMESTAMP ORDERING

Timestamp ordering (T/O) is a technique whereby a serialization order is selected a priori and transaction execution is forced to obey this order. Each transaction is assigned a unique timestamp by its TM. The TM attaches the timestamp to all dm-reads and dm-writes issued on behalf of the transaction, and DMs are required to process *conflicting operations* in timestamp order. The timestamp of operation O is denoted ts(O).

The definition of conflicting operations depends on the type of synchronization being performed and is analogous to conflicting locks. For rw synchronization, two operations *conflict* if (a) both operate on the same data item, and (b) one is a dm-read and the other is a dm-write. For ww synchronization, two operations *conflict* if (a) both operate on the same data item, and (b) both are dm-writes.

It is easy to prove that T/O attains an acyclic $\rightarrow_{rwr}$ ($\rightarrow_{ww}$) relation when used for rw (ww) synchronization. Since each DM processes conflicting operations in timestamp order, each edge of the $\rightarrow_{rwr}$ ($\rightarrow_{ww}$) relation is in timestamp order. Consequently, all paths in the relation are in timestamp order and, since all transactions have unique timestamps, no cycles are possible. In addition, the timestamp order is a valid serialization order.

4.1 Basic T/O Implementation

An implementation of T/O amounts to building a *T/O scheduler*, a software module that receives dm-reads and dm-writes and outputs these operations according to the T/O specification [SHAP77a, SHAP77b]. In practice, prewrites must also be processed through the T/O scheduler for two-phase commit to operate properly. As was the case with 2PL, the basic T/O implementation distributes the schedulers along with the database [BERN80a].

If we ignore two-phase commit, the basic T/O scheduler is quite simple. At each DM, and for each data item x stored at the DM, the scheduler records the largest timestamp of any dm-read(x) or dm-write(x) that has been processed. These are denoted R-ts(x) and W-ts(x), respectively. For rw synchronization, scheduler S operates as follows. Consider a dm-read(x) with timestamp TS. If TS < W-ts(x), S *rejects* the dm-read and aborts the issuing transaction. Otherwise S outputs the dm-read and sets R-ts(x) to max(R-ts(x),TS). For a dm-write(x) with timestamp TS, S rejects the dm-write if TS < R-ts(x); otherwise it outputs the dm-write and sets W-ts(x) to max(W-ts(x),TS). For ww synchronization, S rejects a dm-write(x) with timestamp TS if TS < W-ts(x); otherwise it outputs the dm-write and sets W-ts(x) to TS.

When a transaction is aborted, it is assigned a new and larger timestamp by its TM and is restarted. Restart issues are discussed further below.

Two-phase commit is incorporated by timestamping prewrites and accepting or rejecting prewrites instead of dm-writes. Once a scheduler accepts a prewrite, it must guarantee to accept the corresponding dm-write no matter when the dm-write arrives. For rw (or ww) synchronization, once S accepts a prewrite(x) with timestamp TS it must not output any dm-read(x) (or dm-write(x)) with timestamp greater than TS until the dm-write(x) is output. The effect is similar to setting a writelock on x for the duration of two-phase commit.

To implement the above rules, S *buffers* dm-reads, dm-writes, and prewrites. Let min-R-ts(x) be the minimum timestamp of any buffered dm-read(x), and define min-W-ts(x) and min-P-ts(x) analogously. Rw synchronization is accomplished as follows:

1. Let R be a dm-read(x). If ts(R) < W-ts(x), R is rejected. Else if ts(R) > min-P-ts(x), R is buffered. Else R is output.
2. Let P be a prewrite(x). If ts(P) < R-ts(x), P is rejected. Else P is buffered.
3. Let W be a dm-write(x). W is never rejected. If ts(W) > min-R-ts(x), W is buffered. (If W were output it would cause a buffered dm-read(x) to be rejected.) Else W is output.
4. When W is output, the corresponding prewrite is debuffered. If this causes min-P-ts(x) to increase, the buffered dm-reads are retested to see if any of them can be output. If this causes min-R-ts(x) to be increased, the buffered dm-writes are also retested, and so forth. This process is diagrammed in Figure 9.

Let R = dm-read (x).
Let W = dm-write (x).
R is *ready* if it precedes the earliest prewrite request:
if ts(R) < min-P-ts(x).
W is *ready* if it precedes the earliest dm-read request:
if ts (W) < min-R-ts(x).
When a dm-write(x) arrives, do the following:

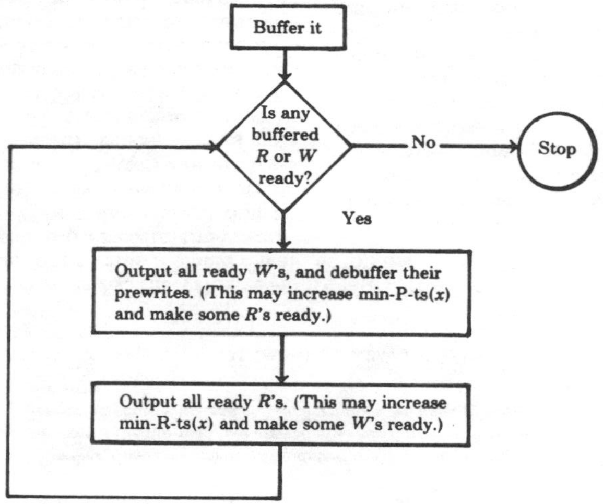

Buffer it

Is any buffered R or W ready?

No

Stop

Yes

Output all ready W's, and debuffer their prewrites. (This may increase min-P-ts(x) and make some R's ready.)

Output all ready R's. (This may increase min-R-ts(x) and make some W's ready.)

Figure 9. Buffer emptying for basic T/O rw synchronization.

Ww synchronization is accomplished as follows:

1. Let P be a prewrite(x). If ts(P) < W-ts(x), P is rejected; else P is buffered.
2. Let W be a dm-write(x). W is never rejected. If ts(W) > min-P-ts(x), W is buffered; else W is output.
3. When W is output, the corresponding prewrite is debuffered. If this causes min-P-ts(x) to be increased, the buffered dm-writes are retested to see if any can now be output. See Figure 10.

As with 2PL, a common variation is to require that transactions *predeclare* their readsets and writesets, issuing all dm-reads and prewrites before beginning their main execution.[3] If all operations are accepted,

Insofar as x_3's scheduler is concerned, T_i is waiting for T_j. However, since T_i has a *majority* of the copies locked, T_i can proceed without waiting for T_j. This fact should be incorporated into the deadlock resolution scheme to avoid unnecessary restarts.

[3] These prewrites are nonstandard relative to the definition in Section 1.4. Since new values for the data items in the writeset are not yet known, these prewrites do *not* instruct DMs to store values on secure storage; instead, prewrite (x) merely "warns" the DM to expect a dm-write (x) in the near future. However, these prewrites are processed by synchronization algorithms exactly as "standard" ones are.

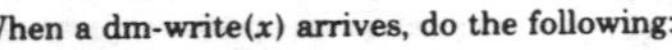
When a dm-write(x) arrives, do the following:

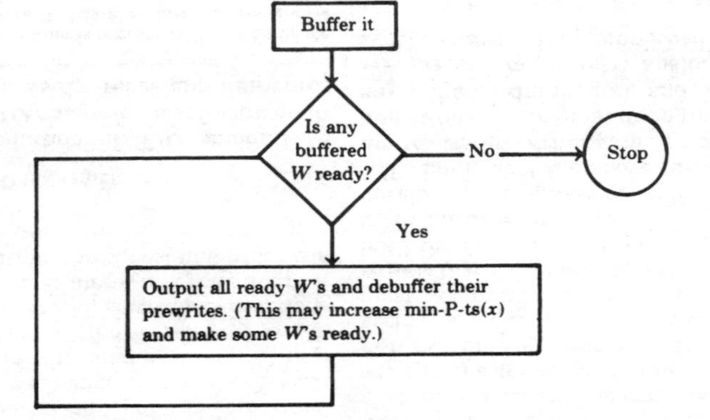
Buffer it
Is any buffered W ready?
No
Stop
Yes
Output all ready W's and debuffer their prewrites. (This may increase min-P-ts(x) and make some W's ready.)

Figure 10. Buffer emptying for basic T/O ww synchronization.

the transaction is guaranteed to execute without danger of restart. Another variation is to *delay* the processing of operations to wait for operations with smaller timestamps. The extreme version of this heuristic is *conservative T/O*, described in Section 4.4.

4.2 The Thomas Write Rule

For ww synchronization the basic T/O scheduler can be optimized using an observation of THOM79. Let W be a dm-write(x), and suppose ts(W) < W-ts(x). Instead of rejecting *W we can simply ignore it*. We call this the *Thomas Write Rule* (*TWR*). Intuitively, TWR applies to a dm-write that tries to place obsolete information into the database. The rule guarantees that the effect of applying a set of dm-writes to x is identical to what would have happened had the dm-writes been applied in timestamp order.

If TWR is used, there is no need to incorporate two-phase commit into the ww synchronization algorithm; the ww scheduler always accepts prewrites and never buffers dm-writes.

4.3 Multiversion T/O

For rw synchronization the basic T/O scheduler can be improved using *multiversion data items* [REED78]. For each data item x there is a *set* of R-ts's and a set of ⟨W-ts, value⟩ pairs, called *versions*. The R-ts's of x record the timestamps of all executed dm-read(x) operations, and the versions record the timestamps and values of all executed dm-write(x) operations. (In practice one cannot store R-ts's and versions forever; techniques for deleting old versions and timestamps are described in Sections 4.5 and 5.2.2.)

Multiversion T/O accomplishes rw synchronization as follows (ignoring two-phase commit). Let R be a dm-read(x). R is processed by reading the version of x with largest timestamp less than ts(R) and adding ts(R) to x's set of R-ts's; see Figure 11a. R is never rejected. Let W be a dm-write(x), and let *interval*(W) be the interval from ts(W) to the smallest W-ts(x) > ts(W);[4] see Figure 11b. If any R-ts(x) lies in interval(W), W is rejected; otherwise W is output and creates a new version of x with timestamp ts(W).

To prove the correctness of multiversion T/O, we must show that every execution is equivalent to a serial execution in timestamp order [BERN80b]. Let R be a dm-read(x) that is processed "out of order"; that is, suppose R is executed after a dm-write(x) whose timestamp exceeds ts(R). Since R ignores all versions with timestamps greater than ts(R), the value read by R is identical to the value it would have read had it been processed in timestamp order. Now let W be a dm-write(x) that is processed "out of order"; that is, suppose it is executed after a dm-read(x) whose timestamp exceeds ts(W). Since W was not rejected, there exists a version of x with timestamp TS such that ts(W) < TS < ts(dm-read). Again the effect is identical to a timestamp-ordered execution.

For ww synchronization, multiversion T/O is essentially an embellished version of TWR. A dm-write(x) always creates a new version of x with timestamp ts(dm-write) and is never rejected.

Integrating two-phase commit requires that dm-reads and prewrites (but not dm-writes) be buffered as in basic T/O. Let P be a buffered prewrite(x): *interval*(P) is the interval from ts(P) to the smallest W-ts(x) > ts(P). Rw synchronization is performed as follows:

1. Let R be a dm-read(x). R is never rejected. If ts(R) lies in interval(prewrite(x)) for some buffered prewrite(x), then R is buffered. Else R is output.
2. Let P be a prewrite(x). If some R-ts(x) lies in interval(P), P is rejected. Else P is buffered.
3. Let W be a dm-write(x). W is always output immediately.
4. When W is output, its prewrite is debuffered, and the buffered dm-reads are retested to see if they can now be output. See Figure 12.

Two-phase commit is not an issue for ww synchronization, since dm-writes are never rejected for ww synchronization.

(a) Let us represent the versions of a data item x on a "time line":

Values: V_1 V_2 V_3 ··· V_{n-1} V_n

W-timestamps: 5 10 20 ··· 92 100

To process a dm-read(x) with timestamp 95, find the biggest *W*-timestamp less than 95; in this case 92. That is the version you read. So in this case, the value read by the dm-read is V_{n-1}.

(b) Let us represent the *R*-timestamps of x similarly:

R-timestamps: 5 7 15 ··· 92 95

Values: V_1 V_2 V_3 ··· V_{n-1} V_n

W-timestamps: 5 10 20 92 100

Let W be dm-write(x) with timestamp 93. Interval(W) = (93,100).

To process W we create a new version of x with that timestamp.

R-timestamps: 5 7 15 92 95

Values: V_1 V_2 V_3 ··· V_{n-1} V V_n

W-timestamps: 5 10 20 ··· 92 93 100

However, this new version "invalidates" the dm-read of part (a), because if the dm-read had arrived after the dm-write, it would have read value V instead of V_{n-1}. Therefore, we must reject the dm-write.

Figure 11. Multiversion reading and writing.

[4] Interval(W) = (ts(W),∞) if no W-ts(x) > ts (W) exists.

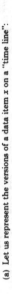

Let R = dm-read(x). R is *ready* if ts(R) $\notin$ interval (P), where P is any buffered prewrite(x).
When a dm-write arrives do the following:

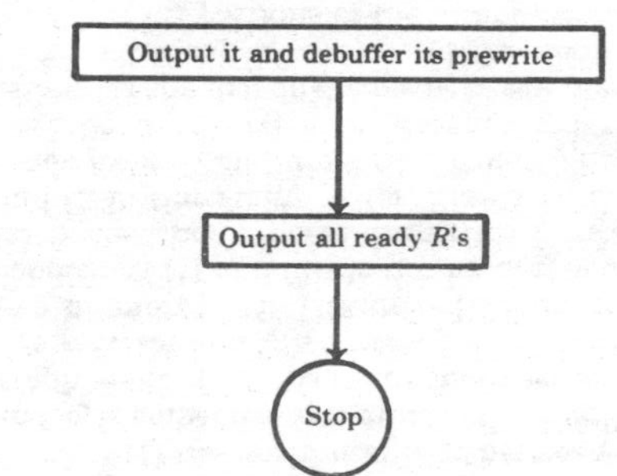

Figure 12. Buffer emptying for multiversion T/O.

4.4 Conservative T/O

Conservative timestamp ordering is a technique for eliminating restarts during T/O scheduling [BERN80a]. When a scheduler receives an operation O that might cause a future restart, the scheduler *delays* O until it is sure that no future restarts are possible.

Conservative T/O requires that each scheduler receive dm-reads (or dm-writes) from each TM in timestamp order. For example, if scheduler S_j receives dm-read(x) followed by dm-read(y) from TM_i, then ts(dm-read(x)) $\leq$ ts(dm-read(y)). Since the network is assumed to be a FIFO channel, this timestamp ordering is accomplished by requiring that TM_i *send* dm-reads (or dm-writes) to S_j in timestamp order.[5]

Conservative T/O buffers dm-reads and dm-writes as part of its normal operation. When a scheduler buffers an operation, it remembers the TM that sent it. Let min-R-ts(TM_i) be the minimum timestamp of any buffered dm-read from TM_i, with min-R-ts(TM_i) = $-\infty$ if no such dm-read is buffered. Define min-W-ts(TM_i) analogously.

Conservative T/O performs rw synchronization as follows:

1. Let R be a dm-read(x). If ts(R) > min-W-ts(TM) for any TM in the system, R is buffered. Else R is output.
2. Let W be a dm-write(x). If ts(W) > min-R-ts(TM) for any TM, W is buffered. Else W is output.
3. When R or W is output or buffered, this may increase min-R-ts(TM) or min-W-ts(TM); buffered operations are retested to see if they can now be output.

The effect is that R is output if and only if (a) the scheduler has a buffered dm-write from every TM, and (b) ts(R) < minimum timestamp of any buffered dm-write. Similarly, W is output if and only if (a) there is a buffered dm-read from every TM, and (b) ts(W) < minimum timestamp of any buffered dm-read. Thus R (or W) is output if and only if the scheduler has received every dm-write (or dm-read) with smaller timestamp that it will ever receive.

Ww synchronization is accomplished as follows:

1. Let W be a dm-write(x). If ts(W) > min-W-ts(TM) for any TM in the system, W is buffered; else it is output.
2. When W is buffered or output, this may increase min-W-ts(TM); buffered dm-writes are retested accordingly.

The effect is that the scheduler waits until it has a buffered dm-write from every TM and then outputs the dm-write with smallest timestamp.

Two-phase commit need not be tightly integrated into conservative T/O because dm-writes are never rejected. Although prewrites must be issued for all data items updated, these operations are not processed by the conservative T/O schedulers.

The above implementation of conservative T/O suffers three major problems: (1) If some TM never sends an operation to some scheduler, the scheduler will "get stuck" and stop outputting. (2) To avoid the first problem, every TM must communicate regularly with every scheduler; this is infeasible in large networks. (3) The implementation is overly conservative; the ww algorithm, for instance, processes *all* dm-writes in timestamp order, not merely conflicting ones. These problems are addressed below.

Null Operations. To solve the first problem, TMs are required to periodically send timestamped *null operations* to each scheduler in the absence of "real" traffic. A null operation is a dm-read or dm-write whose sole purpose is to convey timestamp information and thereby unblock "real" dm-reads and prewrites. An impatient scheduler can prompt a TM for a null operation by sending a "request message." For example, for rw synchronization suppose scheduler S wants to process a dm-read with timestamp TS, but does not have a buffered dm-write from TM_i. S can send a message to TM_i requesting a null-dm-write with timestamp greater than TS.

A variation is to use null operations with *very large* (perhaps infinite) timestamps. For example, if TM_i rarely needs to issue dm-reads to S, TM_i can send S a null-dm-read with infinite timestamp signifying that TM_i does not intend to communicate with S until further notice.

Transaction Classes. Transaction classes [BERN78a, BERN80d] is a technique for reducing communication in conservative T/O and for supporting a less conservative scheduling policy. As in predeclaration, assume that every transaction's readset and writeset are known in advance. A *class* is defined by a readset and a writeset (see Figure 13). Transaction T is a *member* of class C if readset(T) is a subset of readset(C) and writeset(T) is a subset of writeset(C). (Classes need not be disjoint.)

- A *class* is defined by a readset and a writeset. For example,

  C_1: readset = $\{x_1\}$, writeset = $\{y_1, y_2\}$
  C_2: readset = $\{x_1, y_2\}$, writeset = $\{y_1, y_2, z_2, z_3\}$
  C_3: readset = $\{y_2, z_3\}$, writeset = $\{x_1, z_2, z_3\}$
- A transaction is a member of a class if its readset is a subset of the class readset and its writeset is a subset of the class writeset. For example,

  T_1: readset = $\{x_1\}$, writeset = $\{y_1, y_2\}$
  T_2: readset = $\{y_2\}$, writeset = $\{z_2, z_3\}$
  T_3: readset = $\{z_3\}$, writeset = $\{x_1\}$
- T_1 is a member of C_1 and C_2
- T_2 is a member of C_2 and C_3
- T_3 is a member of C_3

Figure 13. Transaction classes.

Class definitions are not expected to change frequently during normal operation of the system. Changing a class definition is akin to changing the database schema and requires mechanisms beyond the scope of this paper. We assume that class definitions are stored in static tables that are available to any site requiring them.

Classes are associated with TMs. Every transaction that executes at a TM must be a member of a class associated with the TM. If a transaction is submitted to a TM that has no class containing it, the transaction is forwarded to another TM that does. We assume that every class is associated with exactly one TM, and vice versa. The class associated with TM_i is denoted C_i. To execute transactions that are members of class C at two TMs, we define another class C′ with the same definition as C and associate C with one TM and C′ with the other. To execute transactions that are members of two classes at one site, we multiprogram two TMs at that site.

Classes are exploited by conservative T/O schedulers as follows. Consider rw synchronization and suppose scheduler S wants to output a dm-read(x). Instead of waiting for dm-writes with smaller timestamps from all TMs, S need only wait for dm-writes *from those TMs whose class writeset contains x*. Similarly, to process a dm-write (x), S need only wait for dm-reads with smaller timestamp from those TMs whose class readset contains x. Thus communication requirements are decreased, and the level of concurrency in the system is increased. Ww synchronization proceeds similarly.

Conflict Graph Analysis. Conflict graph analysis is a technique for further improving the performance of conservative T/O with classes. A *conflict graph* is an undirected graph that summarizes potential conflicts between transactions in different classes. For each class C_i the graph contains two nodes, denoted r_i and w_i, which represent the readset and writeset of C_i. The edges of the graph are defined as follows (see Figure 14): (1) For each class

[5] This can be implemented by requiring that TMs process transactions serially. Alternatively, we can require that transactions issue all dm-reads before beginning their main execution, and all dm-writes after terminating their main execution. Then transactions can execute concurrently, although they must terminate in timestamp order.

Define C_1, C_2, C_3 as in Figure 13.

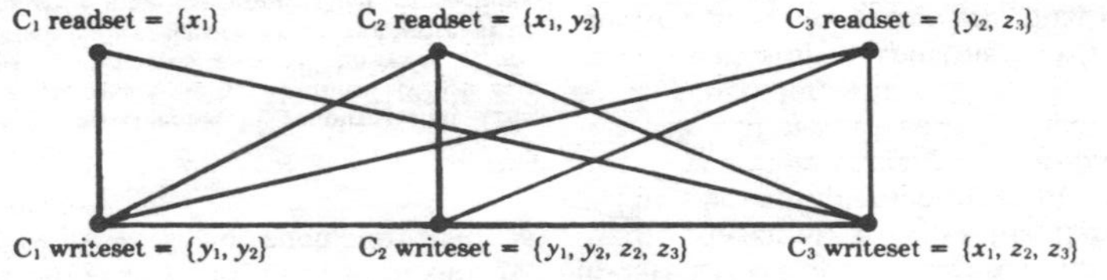

Figure 14. Conflict graph.

C_i there is a *vertical edge* between r_i and w_i; (2) for each pair of classes C_i and C_j (with $i \neq j$) there is a *horizontal edge* between w_i and w_j if and only if writeset(C_i) intersects writeset(C_j); (3) for each pair of classes C_i and C_j (with $i \neq j$) there is a *diagonal edge* between r_i and w_j if and only if readset(C_i) intersects writeset(C_j).

Intuitively, a horizontal edge indicates that a scheduler S may be forced to delay dm-writes for purposes of ww synchronization. Suppose classes C_i and C_j are connected by a horizontal edge (w_i, w_j), indicating that their class writesets intersect. If S receives a dm-write from C_i, it must delay the dm-write until it receives all dm-writes with smaller timestamps from C_j. Similarly, a diagonal edge indicates that S may need to delay operations for rw synchronization.

Conflict graph analysis improves the situation by identifying interclass conflicts that cannot cause nonserializable behavior. This corresponds to identifying horizontal and diagonal edges that do not require synchronization. In particular, schedulers need only synchronize dm-writes from C_i and C_j if either (1) the horizontal edge between w_i and w_j is embedded in a *cycle* of the conflict graph; or (2) portions of the intersection of C_i's writeset and C_j's writeset are stored at two or more DMs [BERN80c]. That is, if conditions (1) and (2) do not hold, scheduler S need not process dm-writes from C_i and C_j in timestamp order. Similarly, dm-reads from C_i and dm-writes from C_j need only be processed in timestamp order if either (1) the diagonal edge between r_i and w_j is embedded in a cycle of the conflict graph; or (2) portions of the intersection of C_i's readset and C_j's writeset are stored at two or more DMs.

Since classes are defined statically, conflict graph analysis is also performed statically. The analysis produces a table indicating which horizontal and vertical edges require synchronization and which do not. This table, like class definitions, is distributed in advance to all schedulers that need it.

4.5 Timestamp Management

A common criticism of T/O schedulers is that too much memory is needed to store timestamps. This problem can be overcome by "forgetting" old timestamps.

Timestamps are used in basic T/O to reject operations that "arrive late," for example, to reject a dm-read(x) with timestamp TS_1 that arrives after a dm-write(x) with timestamp TS_2, where $TS_1 < TS_2$. In principle, TS_1 and TS_2 can differ by an arbitrary amount. However, in practice it is unlikely that these timestamps will differ by more than a few minutes. Consequently, timestamps can be stored in small tables which are periodically purged.

R-ts's are stored in the *R-table* with entries of the form $\langle x, \text{R-ts} \rangle$; for any data item x, there is at most one entry. In addition, a variable, *R-min*, tells the maximum value of any timestamp that has been purged from the table. To find R-ts(x), a scheduler searches the R-table for an $\langle x, \text{TS} \rangle$ entry. If such an entry is found, R-ts(x) = TS; otherwise, R-ts(x) ≤ R-min. To err on the side of safety, the scheduler assumes R-ts(x) = R-min. To update R-ts(x), the scheduler modifies the $\langle x, \text{TS} \rangle$ entry, if one exists. Otherwise, a new entry is created and added to the table. When the R-table is full, the scheduler selects an appropriate value for R-min and deletes all entries from the table with smaller timestamp. W-ts's are managed similarly, and analogous techniques can be devised for multiversion databases.

Maintaining timestamps for conservative T/O is even cheaper, since conservative T/O requires only timestamped operations, not timestamped data. If conservative T/O is used for rw synchronization, the R-ts's of data items may be discarded. If conservative T/O is used for both rw and ww synchronization, W-ts's can be eliminated also.

5. INTEGRATED CONCURRENCY CONTROL METHODS

An integrated concurrency control method consists of two components—an rw and a ww synchronization technique—plus an interface between the components that attains condition (b) of Theorem 2: a total ordering of the transactions consistent with all $\longrightarrow_{rwr}$ and $\longrightarrow_{ww}$ relationships. In this section we list 48 concurrency control methods that can be constructed using the techniques of Sections 3 and 4.

Approximately 20 concurrency control methods have been described in the literature. Virtually all of them use a *single* synchronization technique (either 2PL or T/O) for both rw and ww synchronization. Indeed, most methods use the same *variation* of a single technique for both kinds of synchronization. However, such homogeneity is neither necessary nor especially desirable.

For example, the analysis of Section 3.2 suggests that using basic 2PL for rw synchronization and primary copy 2PL for ww synchronization might be superior to using basic 2PL (or primary copy 2PL) for both. More outlandish combinations may be even better. For example, one can combine basic 2PL with TWR. In this method ww conflicts never cause transactions to be delayed or restarted; multiple transactions can write into the same data items concurrently (see Section 5.3).

In Sections 5.1 and 5.2 we describe methods that use 2PL and T/O techniques for both rw and ww synchronization. The concurrency control methods in these sections are easy to describe given the material of Sections 3 and 4; the description of each method is little more than a description of each component technique. In Section 5.3 we list 24 concurrency control methods that combine 2PL and T/O techniques. As we show in Section 5.3, methods of this type have useful properties that cannot be attained by pure 2PL or T/O methods.

5.1 Pure 2PL Methods

The 2PL synchronization techniques of Section 3 can be integrated to form 12 *principal 2PL methods*:

Method	rw technique	ww technique
1	Basic 2PL	Basic 2PL
2	Basic 2PL	Primary copy 2PL
3	Basic 2PL	Voting 2PL
4	Basic 2PL	Centralized 2PL
5	Primary copy 2PL	Basic 2PL
6	Primary copy 2PL	Primary copy 2PL
7	Primary copy 2PL	Voting 2PL
8	Primary copy 2PL	Centralized 2PL
9	Centralized 2PL	Basic 2PL
10	Centralized 2PL	Primary copy 2PL
11	Centralized 2PL	Voting 2PL
12	Centralized 2PL	Centralized 2PL

Each method can be further refined by the choice of deadlock resolution technique (see Section 3.5).

The interface between each 2PL rw technique and each 2PL ww technique is straightforward. It need only guarantee that "two-phasedness" is preserved, meaning that *all* locks needed for both the rw and ww technique must be obtained before any lock is released by *either* technique.

5.1.1 *Methods Using Basic 2PL for rw Synchronization*

Methods 1–4 use basic 2PL for rw synchronization. Consider a logical data item X with copies $x_1, \ldots, x_m$. To read X, a transaction sends a dm-read to *any* DM that stores a copy of X. This dm-read implicitly requests a readlock on the copy of X at that DM. To write X, a transaction sends prewrites to *every* DM that stores a copy of X. These prewrites implicitly request writelocks on the corresponding copies of X. For all four methods, these writelocks conflict with *readlocks* on the same copy, and may also conflict with other *writelocks* on the same copy, depending on the specific ww synchronization technique used by the method.

Since locking conflict rules for writelocks will vary from copy to copy, we distinguish three types. An *rw writelock* only conflicts with readlocks on the same data item. A *ww writelock* only conflicts with ww writelocks on the same data item. And an *rww writelock* conflicts with readlocks, ww writelocks, and rww writelocks. Thus, using basic 2PL for rw synchronization, every prewrite sets rw writelocks, and may set stronger locks depending on the ww technique.

Method 1: *Basic 2PL for ww synchronization.* All writelocks are rww writelocks; that is, for $i = 1, \ldots, m$, a writelock on x_i conflicts with either a readlock or a writelock on x_i. This is the "standard" distributed implementation of 2PL.

Method 2: *Primary copy 2PL for ww synchronization.* Writelocks only conflict on the primary copy. An rww writelock is used on the primary copy, while rw writelocks are used on the others.

Method 3: *Voting 2PL for ww synchronization.* A DM responds to a prewrite(x_i) by ***attempting*** to set an rww writelock on x_i. However, if another transaction already owns an rww writelock on x_i, the DM only sets an rw writelock and leaves a request for an rww writelock pending. A transaction can write into any copy of X after it obtains rww writelocks on a majority of copies. This is similar to the method proposed in GIFF79.

Method 4: *Centralized 2PL for ww synchronization.* To write into X, a transaction must first explicitly request a ww writelock on X from a centralized 2PL scheduler. The rw writelocks set by prewrites *never* conflict with each other.

In all four methods, readlocks are explicitly released by lock releases while writelocks are implicitly released by dm-writes. Lock releases may be transmitted in parallel with dm-writes. In Method 4, *after all* dm-writes have been executed, additional lock releases must be sent to the centralized scheduler to release writelocks held there.

5.1.2 Methods Using Primary Copy 2PL for rw Synchronization

Methods 5–8 use primary copy 2PL for rw synchronization. Consider a logical data item X with copies $x_1, \ldots, x_m$, and assume x_1 is the primary copy. To read X, a transaction must obtain a readlock on x_1. It may obtain this lock by issuing a dm-read(x_1). Alternatively, the transaction can send an explicit lock request to x_1's DM; when the lock is granted the transaction can read *any* copy of X.

To write into X, a transaction sends prewrites to *every* DM that stores a copy of X. A prewrite(x_1) implicitly requests an rw writelock. Prewrites on other copies of X may also request writelocks depending on the ww technique.

Method 5: *Basic 2PL for ww synchronization.* For $i = 2, \ldots, m$, prewrite(x_i) requests a ww writelock. Since the writelock on x_1 must also conflict with readlocks on x_1, prewrite(x_1) requests an rww writelock.

Method 6: *Primary copy 2PL for ww synchronization.* Prewrite(x_1) requests an rww writelock on x_1. Prewrites on other copies do not request any locks. This method was originally proposed by STON79 and is used in Distributed INGRES [STON77].

Method 7: *Voting 2PL for ww synchronization.* When a scheduler receives a prewrite(x_i) for $i \neq 1$, it tries to set a ww writelock on x_i. When it receives a prewrite(x_1), it tries to set an rww writelock on x_1; if it cannot, then it sets an rw writelock on x_1 (if possible) before waiting for the rww writelock. A transaction can write into every copy of X after it obtains a ww (or rww) writelock on a majority of copies of X.

Method 8: *Centralized 2PL for ww synchronization.* Transactions obtain ww writelocks from a centralized 2PL scheduler. Thus a prewrite(x_1) requests an rw writelock on x_1; for $i = 2, \ldots, m$, prewrite(x_i) does not request any lock.

Lock releases for Methods 5–8 are handled as in Section 5.1.1.

5.1.3 Methods Using Centralized 2PL for rw Synchronization

The remaining 2PL methods use centralized 2PL for rw synchronization. Before reading (or writing) any copy of logical data item X, a transaction must obtain a readlock (or rw writelock) on X from a centralized 2PL scheduler. Before writing X, the transaction must also send prewrites to every DM that stores a copy of X. Some of these prewrites implicitly request ww writelocks on copies of X, depending on the specific method.

Method 9: *Basic 2PL for ww synchronization.* Every prewrite requests a ww writelock.

Method 10: *Primary copy 2PL for ww synchronization.* If x_1 is the primary copy of X, a prewrite(x_1) requests a ww writelock. Prewrites on other copies do not request any writelocks.

Method 11: *Voting 2PL for ww synchronization.* Every prewrite *attempts* to set a ww writelock. A transaction can write into every copy of X after it obtains ww writelocks on a majority of copies of X.

Method 12: *Centralized 2PL for ww synchronization.* All locks are obtained at the centralized 2PL scheduler. Before writing into any copy of X, an rww writelock on X is obtained from the centralized scheduler. Prewrites set no locks at all. Method 12 is the "standard" implementation of centralized 2PL (called *primary site* in ALSB76a).

Lock releases for Methods 9–12 are handled as in Section 5.1.1.

5.2 Pure T/O Methods

The T/O synchronization techniques of Section 5 can also be integrated to form 12 *principal T/O methods*:

Method	rw technique	ww technique
1	Basic T/O	Basic T/O
2	Basic T/O	Thomas Write Rule (TWR)
3	Basic T/O	Multiversion T/O
4	Basic T/O	Conservative T/O
5	Multiversion T/O	Basic T/O
6	Multiversion T/O	TWR
7	Multiversion T/O	Multiversion T/O
8	Multiversion T/O	Conservative T/O
9	Conservative T/O	Basic T/O
10	Conservative T/O	TWR
11	Conservative T/O	Multiversion T/O
12	Conservative T/O	Conservative T/O

(That there are also 12 2PL methods is coincidental.)

Each T/O method that incorporates a conservative component can be refined by including classes and conflict graph analysis (see Sections 4.4.2 and 4.4.3).

The interface between rw and ww synchronization techniques is even simpler for T/O methods than for 2PL. The only requirement is that both techniques use the *same* timestamp for any given transaction.

5.2.1 Methods Using Basic T/O for rw Synchronization

Methods 1–4 use basic T/O for rw synchronization. All four methods require R-ts's for each data item. Methods 1, 2, and 4 require W-ts's, while in Method 3 each data item has a set of timestamped versions; for Method 3, let W-ts(x) denote x's largest timestamp. Each method buffers dm-reads and prewrites for two-phase commitment purposes; let min-R-ts(x) and min-P-ts(x) be the minimum timestamps of any buffered dm-read(x) and prewrite(x), respectively.

These methods can be described by the following steps. Let R be a dm-read(x), P a prewrite(x), and W a dm-write(x).

1. If ts(R) < W-ts(x), R is rejected. Else if ts(R) > min-P-ts(x), R is buffered. Else R is output and R-ts(x) is set to max(R-ts(x), ts(R)).
2. If ts(P) < R-ts(x) or *condition (A)*[6] holds, P is rejected. Else P is buffered.
3. If ts(W) > min-R-ts(x) or *condition (B)*[6] holds, W is buffered. Else W is output and W-ts(x) is set to max(W-ts(x), ts(W)). For Method 3, a new version of x is created with timestamp ts(W).
4. When W is output, its prewrite is debuffered and the buffered dm-reads and dm-writes are retested to see if any can now be output.

Method 1: *Basic T/O for ww synchronization.* Condition (A) is ts(P) < W-ts(x) and condition (B) is ts(W) > min-P-ts(x). Note that min-R-ts(x) > min-P-ts(x), since R is buffered only if ts(R) > min-P-ts(x). Also, when W is output, ts(W) > W-ts(x), since condition (B) forces dm-writes on a given x to be output in timestamp order. Thus step 3 simplifies to

3. If ts(W) > min-P-ts(x), W is buffered. Else W is output and W-ts(x) is set to ts(W).

Method 2: *TWR for ww synchronization.* Conditions (A) and (B) are null. However,

[6] Conditions (A) and (B) are determined by the new technique. See the following.

if ts(W) < W-ts(x), W has no effect on the database.

Method 3: *Multiversion T/O for ww synchronization.* Like Method 2 except that W always creates a new version of x.

Method 4: *Conservative T/O for ww synchronization.* Condition (A) is null. For each TM, let min-W-ts(TM) be the minimum timestamp of any buffered dm-write from that TM. Condition (B) is ts(W) > min-W-ts(TM) for some TM. As in Method 1, this causes dm-writes on a given x to be output in timestamp order, and step 3 simplifies to

3. If ts(W) > min-R-ts(x) or ts(W) > min-W-ts(TM) for some TM, W is buffered. Else W is output and W-ts(x) is set to ts(W).

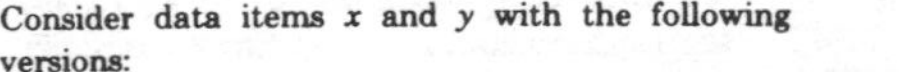

5.2.2 Methods Using Multiversion T/O for rw Synchronization

Methods 5–8 use multiversion T/O for rw synchronization and require a set of R-ts's and a set of versions for each data item. These methods can be described by the following steps. Define R, P, W, min-R-ts, min-W-ts, and min-P-ts as above; let interval(P) be the interval from ts(P) to the smallest W-ts(x) > ts(P).

1. R is never rejected. If ts(R) lies in interval(prewrite(x)) for some buffered prewrite(x), then R is buffered. Else R is output and ts(R) is added to x's set of R-ts's.
2. If some R-ts(x) lies in interval(P) or *condition (A)* holds, then P is rejected. Else P is buffered.
3. If *condition (B)* holds, W is buffered. Else W is output and creates a new version of x with timestamp ts(W).
4. When W is output, its prewrite is debuffered, and buffered dm-reads and dm-writes are retested.

Method 5: *Basic T/O for ww synchronization.* Condition (A) is ts(P) < max-W-ts(x) and condition (B) is ts(W) > min-P-ts(x). Condition (A) implies that interval(P) = (ts(P), ∞); some R-ts(x) lies in that interval if and only if ts(P) < maximum R-ts(x). Thus step 2 simplifies to

2. If ts(P) < max W-ts(x) or ts(P) < max R-ts(x), then P is rejected. Else it is buffered.

Because of this simplification, the method only requires that the maximum R-ts(x) be stored.

Condition (B) forces dm-writes on a given data item to be output in timestamp order. This supports a systematic technique for "forgetting" old versions. Let max-W-ts(x) be the maximum W-ts(x) and let min-ts be the minimum of max-W-ts(x) over all data items in the database. No dm-write with timestamp less than min-ts can be output in the future. Therefore, insofar as update transactions are concerned, we can safely forget all versions timestamped less than min-ts. TMs should be kept informed of the current value of min-ts and queries (read-only transactions) should be assigned timestamps greater than min-ts. Also, after a new min-ts is selected, older versions should not be forgotten immediately, so that active queries with smaller timestamps have an opportunity to finish.

Method 6: *TWR for ww synchronization.* This method is *incorrect.* TWR requires that W be ignored if ts(W) < max W-ts(x). This may cause later dm-reads to be read incorrect data. See Figure 15. (Method 6 is the only incorrect method we will encounter.)

Method 7: *Multiversion T/O for ww synchronization.* Conditions (A) and (B) are null. Note that this method, unlike all previous ones, never buffers dm-writes.

Method 8: *Conservative T/O for ww synchronization.* Condition (A) is null. Condition (B) is ts(W) > min-W-ts(TM) for some TM. Condition (B) forces dm-writes to be output in timestamp order, implying interval(P) = (ts(P), ∞). As in Method 5, this simplifies step 2:

2. If ts(P) < max R-ts(x), P is rejected; else it is buffered.

Like Method 5, this method only requires that the maximum R-ts(x) be stored, and it supports systematic "forgetting" of old versions described above.

5.2.3 Methods Using Conservative T/O for rw Synchronization

The remaining T/O methods use conservative T/O for rw synchronization. Methods 9 and 10 require W-ts's for each data item, and Method 11 requires a set of versions for each data item. Method 12 needs no data item timestamps at all. Define R, P, W and min-P-ts as in Section 5.2.1; let min-R-ts(TM) (or min-W-ts(TM)) be the minimum timestamp of any buffered dm-read (or dm-write) from TM.

1. If ts(R) > min-W-ts(TM) for any TM, R is buffered; else it is output.
2. If *condition (A)* holds, P is rejected. Else P is buffered.
3. If ts(W) > min-R-ts(TM) for any TM or *condition (B)* holds, W is buffered. Else W is output.
4. When W is output, its prewrite is debuffered. When R or W is output or buffered, buffered dm-reads and dm-writes are retested to see if any can now be output.

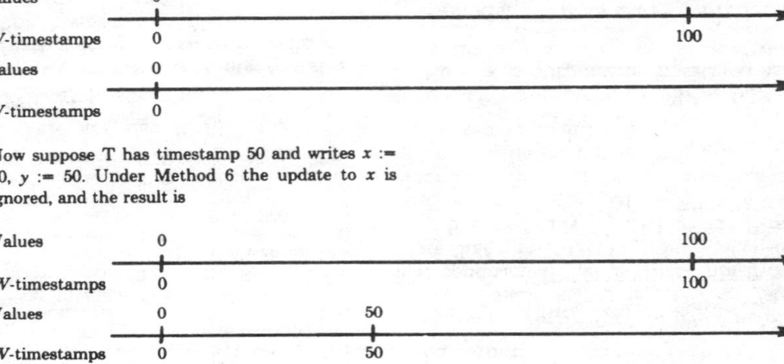

• Consider data items x and y with the following versions:
Values 0 100
x
W-timestamps 0 100
Values 0
y
W-timestamps 0
• Now suppose T has timestamp 50 and writes x := 50, y := 50. Under Method 6 the update to x is ignored, and the result is
Values 0 100
x
W-timestamps 0 100
Values 0 50
y
W-timestamps 0 50
• Finally, suppose T' has timestamp 75 and reads x and y. The values it will read are x = 0, y = 50, which is incorrect. T' *should* read x = 50, y = 50.

Figure 15. Inconsistent retrievals in Method 6.

Method 9: *Basic T/O for ww synchronization.* Condition (A) is ts(P) < W-ts(x), and condition (B) is ts(W) > min-P-ts(x).

Method 10: *TWR for ww synchronization.* Conditions (A) and (B) are null. However, if ts(W) < W-ts(x), W has no effect on the database.

This method is essentially the SDD-1 concurrency control [BERN80d], although in SDD-1 the method is refined in several ways. SDD-1 uses classes and conflict graph analysis to reduce communication and increase the level of concurrency. Also, SDD-1 requires predeclaration of read-sets and only enforces the conservative scheduling on dm-reads. By doing so, it forces dm-reads to wait for dm-writes, but does not insist that dm-writes wait for all dm-reads with smaller timestamps. Hence dm-reads can be rejected in SDD-1.

Method 11: *Multiversion T/O for ww synchronization.* Conditions (A) and (B) are null. When W is output, it creates a new version of x with timestamp ts(W). When R is output it reads the version with largest timestamp less than ts(R).

This method can be optimized by noting the multiversion T/O "automatically" prevents dm-reads from being rejected, and makes it unnecessary to buffer dm-writes. Thus step 3 can be simplified to

3. W is output immediately.

Method 12: *Conservative T/O for ww synchronization.* Condition (A) is null; condition (B) is ts(W) > min-W-ts(TM) for some TM. The effect is to output W if the scheduler has received *all* operations with timestamps less than ts(W) that it will ever receive. Method 12 has been proposed in CHEN80, KANE79, and SHAP77a.

5.3 Mixed 2PL and T/O Methods

The major difficulty in constructing methods that combine 2PL and T/O lies in developing the interface between the two techniques. Each technique guarantees an acyclic $\rightarrow_{rw}$ (or $\rightarrow_{ww}$) relation when used for rw (or ww) synchronization. The interface between a 2PL and a T/O technique must guarantee that the combined $\rightarrow$ relation (i.e., $\rightarrow_{rw} \cup \rightarrow_{ww}$) remains acyclic. That is, the interface must ensure that the serialization order induced by the rw technique is consistent with that induced by the ww technique. In Section 5.3.1 we describe an interface that makes this guarantee. Given such an interface, *any* 2PL technique can be integrated with *any* T/O technique. Sections 5.3.2 and 5.3.3 describe such methods.

5.3.1 The Interface

The serialization order induced by any 2PL technique is determined by the locked points of the transactions that have been synchronized (see Section 3). The serialization order induced by any T/O technique is determined by the timestamps of the synchronized transactions. So to interface 2PL and T/O we *use locked points to induce timestamps* [BERN80b].

Associated with each data item is a *lock timestamp*, L-ts(x). When a transaction T sets a lock of x, it simultaneously retrieves L-ts(x). When T reaches its locked point it is assigned a timestamp, ts(T), greater than any L-ts it retrieved. When T releases its lock on x, it updates L-ts(x) to be max(L-ts(x), ts(T)).

Timestamps generated in this way are consistent with the serialization order induced by 2PL. That is, ts(T_j) < ts(T_k) if T_j must precede T_k in any serialization induced by 2PL. To see this, let T_1 and T_n be a pair of transactions such that T_1 must precede T_n in any serialization. Thus there exist transactions $T_1, T_2, \ldots, T_{n-1}, T_n$ such that for $i = 1, \ldots, n-1$ (a) T_i's locked point precedes T_{i+1}'s locked point, and (b) T_i released a lock on some data item x before T_{i+1} obtained a lock on x. Let L be the L-ts(x) retrieved by T_{i+1}. Then ts(T_i) < L < ts(T_{i+1}), and by induction ts(T_1) < ts(T_n).

5.3.2 Mixed Methods Using 2PL for rw Synchronization

There are 12 principal methods in which 2PL is used for rw synchronization and T/O is used for ww synchronization:

Method	rw technique	ww technique
1	Basic 2PL	Basic T/O
2	Basic 2PL	TWR
3	Basic 2PL	Multiversion T/O
4	Basic 2PL	Conservative T/O
5	Primary copy 2PL	Basic T/O
6	Primary copy 2PL	TWR
7	Primary copy 2PL	Multiversion T/O
8	Primary copy 2PL	Conservative T/O
9	Centralized 2PL	Basic T/O
10	Centralized 2PL	TWR
11	Centralized 2PL	Multiversion T/O
12	Centralized 2PL	Conservative T/O

Method 2 best exemplifies this class of methods, and it is the only one we describe in detail. Method 2 requires that every stored data item have an L-ts and a W-ts. (One timestamp can serve both roles, but we do not consider this optimization here.)

Let X be a logical data item with copies $x_1, \ldots, x_m$. To read X, transaction T issues a dm-read on any copy of X, say x_i. This dm-read implicitly requests a readlock on x_i, and when the readlock is granted, L-ts(x_i) is returned to T. To write into X, T issues prewrites on every copy of X. These prewrites implicitly request rw writelocks on the corresponding copies, and as each writelock is granted, the corresponding L-ts is returned to T. When T has obtained all of its locks, ts(T) is calculated as in Section 5.3.1. T attaches ts(T) to its dm-writes, which are then sent.

Dm-writes are processed using TWR. Let W be dm-write(x_j). If ts(W) > W-ts(x_j), the dm-write is processed as usual (x_j is updated). If, however, ts(W) < W-ts(x_j), W is *ignored*.

The interesting property of this method is that *writelocks never conflict with writelocks*. The writelocks obtained by prewrites are only used for rw synchronization, and only conflict with readlocks. This permits transactions to execute concurrently to completion even if their writesets intersect. Such concurrency is never possible in a pure 2PL method.

5.3.3 Mixed Methods Using T/O for rw Synchronization

There are also 12 principal methods that use T/O for rw synchronization and 2PL for ww synchronization:

Method	rw technique	ww technique
13	Basic T/O	Basic 2PL
14	Basic T/O	Primary copy 2PL
15	Basic T/O	Voting 2PL
16	Basic T/O	Centralized 2PL
17	Multiversion T/O	Basic 2PL
18	Multiversion T/O	Primary copy 2PL
19	Multiversion T/O	Voting 2PL
20	Multiversion T/O	Centralized 2PL
21	Conservative T/O	Basic 2PL
22	Conservative T/O	Primary copy 2PL
23	Conservative T/O	Voting 2PL
24	Conservative T/O	Centralized 2PL

These methods all require *predeclaration of writelocks*. Since T/O is used for rw synchronization, transactions must be assigned timestamps before they issue dm-reads. However, the timestamp generation technique of Section 5.3.1 requires that a transaction be at its locked point before it is assigned its timestamp. Hence every transaction must be at its locked point before it issues any dm-reads; in other words, every transaction must obtain all of its writelocks before it begins its main execution.

To illustrate these methods, we describe Method 17. This method requires that each stored data item have a set of R-ts's and a set of ⟨W-ts, value⟩ pairs (i.e., versions). The L-ts of any data item is the maximum of its R-ts's and W-ts's.

Before beginning its main execution, transaction T issues prewrites on every copy of every data item in its writeset.[7] These prewrites play a role in ww synchronization, rw synchronization, and the interface between these techniques.

Let P be a prewrite(x). The ww role of P is to request a ww writelock on x. When the lock is granted, L-ts(x) is returned to T; this is the interface role of P. Also when the lock is granted, P is buffered and the rw synchronization mechanism is informed that a dm-write with timestamp greater than L-ts(x) is pending. This is its rw role.

When T has obtained all of its writelocks, ts(T) is calculated as in Section 5.3.1 and T begins its main execution. T attaches ts(T) to its dm-reads and dm-writes and rw synchronization is performed by multiversion T/O, as follows:

1. Let R be a dm-read(x). If there is a buffered prewrite(x) (other than one issued by T), and if L-ts(x) < ts(T), then R is buffered. Else R is output and reads the version of x with largest timestamp less than ts(T).
2. Let W be a dm-write(x). W is output immediately and creates a new version of x with timestamp ts(T).
3. When W is output, its prewrite is debuffered, and its writelock on x is released. This causes L-ts(x) to be updated to max(L-ts(x), ts(T)) = ts(T).

One interesting property of this method is that restarts are needed only to prevent or break deadlocks caused by ww synchronization; rw conflicts never cause restarts. This property cannot be attained by a pure 2PL method. It can be attained by pure T/O methods, but only if conservative T/O is used for rw synchronization; in many cases conservative T/O introduces excessive delay or is otherwise infeasible.

The behavior of this method for queries is also interesting. Since queries set no writelocks, the timestamp generation rule does not apply to them. Hence *the system is free to assign any timestamp it wishes to a query*. It may assign a small timestamp, in which case the query will read old data but is unlikely to be delayed by buffered prewrites; or it may assign a large timestamp, in which case the query will read current data but is more likely to be delayed. No matter which timestamp is selected, however, *a query can never cause an update to be rejected*. This property cannot be easily attained by any pure 2PL or T/O method.

We also observe that this method creates versions in timestamp order, and so sys-

[7] Since new values for the data items in the writeset are not yet known, these prewrites do not instruct DMs to store values on secure storage; they merely "warn" DMs to "expect" the corresponding dm-writes. See footnote 3.

tematic forgetting of old versions is possible (see Section 5.2.2). In addition, the method requires only *maximum* R-ts's; smaller ones may be instantly forgotten.

CONCLUSION

We have presented a framework for the design and analysis of distributed database concurrency control algorithms. The framework has two main components: (1) a system model that provides common terminology and concepts for describing a variety of concurrency control algorithms, and (2) a problem decomposition that decomposes concurrency control algorithms into read-write and write-write synchronization subalgorithms.

We have considered synchronization subalgorithms outside the context of specific concurrency control algorithms. Virtually all known database synchronization algorithms are variations of two basic techniques—two-phase locking (2PL) and timestamp ordering (T/O). We have described the principal variations of each technique, though we do not claim to have exhausted all possible variations. In addition, we have described ancillary problems (e.g., deadlock resolution) that must be solved to make each variation effective.

We have shown how to integrate the described techniques to form complete concurrency control algorithms. We have listed 47 concurrency control algorithms, describing 25 in detail. This list includes almost all concurrency control algorithms described previously in the literature, plus several new ones. This extreme consolidation of the state of the art is possible in large part because of our framework set up earlier.

The focus of this paper has primarily been the *structure* and *correctness* of synchronization techniques and concurrency control algorithms. We have left open a very important issue, namely, performance.

The main performance metrics for concurrency control algorithms are system throughput and transaction response time. Four cost factors influence these metrics: intersite communication, local processing, transaction restarts, and transaction blocking. The impact of each cost factor on system throughput and response time varies from algorithm to algorithm, system to system, and application to application. This impact is not understood in detail, and a comprehensive quantitative analysis of performance is beyond the state of the art. Recent theses by Garcia-Molina [GARC79a] and Reis [REIS79a] have taken first steps toward such an analysis but there clearly remains much to be done.

We hope, and indeed recommend, that future work on distributed concurrency control will concentrate on the performance of algorithms. There are, as we have seen, many known methods; the question now is to determine which are best.

APPENDIX. OTHER CONCURRENCY CONTROL METHODS

In this appendix we describe three concurrency control methods that do not fit the framework of Sections 3–5: the certifier methods of Badal [BADA79], Bayer et al. [BAYE80], and Casanova [CASA79], the majority consensus algorithm of Thomas [THOM79], and the ring algorithm of Ellis [ELLI77]. We argue that these methods are not practical in DDBMSs. The certifier methods look promising for *centralized* DBMSs, but severe technical problems must be overcome before these methods can be extended correctly to distributed systems. The Thomas and Ellis algorithms, by contrast, are among the earliest algorithms proposed for DDBMS concurrency control. These algorithms introduced several important techniques into the field but, as we will see, have been surpassed by recent developments.

A1. Certifiers

A1.1 The Certification Approach

In the certification approach, dm-reads and prewrites are processed by DMs first-come/first-served, with no synchronization whatsoever. DMs do maintain summary information about rw and ww conflicts, which they update every time an operation is processed. However, dm-reads and prewrites are never blocked or rejected on the basis of the discovery of such a conflict.

Synchronization occurs when a transaction attempts to terminate. When a transaction T issues its END, the DBMS decides whether or not to *certify*, and thereby commit, T.

To understand how this decision is made, we must distinguish between "total" and "committed" executions. A *total execution* of transactions includes the execution of all operations processed by the system up to a particular moment. The *committed execution* is the portion of the total execution that only includes dm-reads and dm-writes processed on behalf of committed transactions. That is, the committed execution is the total execution that would result from aborting all active transactions (and not restarting them).

When T issues its END, the system tests whether the committed execution augmented by T's execution is serializable, that is, whether after committing T the resulting committed execution would still be serializable. If so, T is committed; otherwise T is restarted.

There are two properties of certification that distinguish it from other approaches. First, synchronization is accomplished entirely by restarts, never by blocking. And second, the decision to restart or not is made *after* the transaction has finished executing. No concurrency control method discussed in Sections 3–5 satisifies both these properties.

The rationale for certification is based on an optimistic assumption regarding run-time conflicts: if very few run-time conflicts are expected, assume that most executions are serializable. By processing dm-reads and prewrites without synchronization, the concurrency control method never delays a transaction while it is being processed. Only a (fast, it is hoped) certification test when the transaction terminates is required. Given optimistic transaction behavior, the test will usually result in committing the transaction, so there are very few restarts. Therefore certification simultaneously avoids blocking and restarts in optimistic situations.

A certification concurrency control method must include a *summarization algorithm* for storing information about dm-reads and prewrites when they are processed and a *certification algorithm* for using that information to certify transactions when they terminate. The main problem in the summarization algorithm is avoiding the need to store information about already-certified transactions. The main problem in the certification algorithm is obtaining a *consistent* copy of the summary information. To do so the certification algorithm often must perform some synchronization of its own, the cost of which must be included in the cost of the entire method.

A1.2 Certification Using the → Relation

One certification method is to construct the → relation as dm-reads and prewrites are processed. To certify a transaction, the system checks that → is acyclic [BADA79, BAYE80, CASA79].[8]

To construct →, each site remembers the most recent transaction that read or wrote each data item. Suppose transactions T_i and T_j were the last transactions to (respectively) read and write data item x. If transaction T_k now issues a dm-read(x), $T_j \rightarrow T_k$ is added to the summary information for the site and T_k replaces T_i as the last transaction to have read x. Thus pieces of → are distributed among the sites, reflecting run-time conflicts at each site.

To certify a transaction, the system must check that the transaction does not lie on a cycle in → (see Theorem 2, Section 2). Guaranteeing acyclicity is sufficient to guarantee serializability.

There are two problems with this approach. First, it is in general not correct to delete a certified transaction from →, even if all of its updates have been committed. For example, if $T_i \rightarrow T_j$ and T_i is active but T_j is committed, it is still possible for $T_j \rightarrow T_i$ to develop; deleting T_j would then cause the cycle $T_i \rightarrow T_j \rightarrow T_i$ to go unnoticed when T_i is certified. However, it is obviously not feasible to allow → to grow indefinitely. This problem is solved by Casanova [CASA79] by a method of encoding information about committed transactions in space proportional to the number of active transactions.

A second problem is that *all* sites must be checked to certify *any* transaction. Even

[8] In BAYE80 certification is only used for rw synchronization whereas 2PL is used for ww synchronization.

sites at which the transaction never accessed data must participate in the cycle checking of $\rightarrow$. For example, suppose we want to certify transaction T. T might be involved in a cycle $T \rightarrow T_1 \rightarrow T_2 \rightarrow \cdots \rightarrow T_{n-1} \rightarrow T_n \rightarrow T$, where each conflict $T_k \rightarrow T_{k+1}$ occurred at a different site. Possibly T only accessed data at one site; yet the $\rightarrow$ relation must be examined at n sites to certify T. This problem is currently unsolved, as far as we know. That is, any *correct* certifier based on this approach of checking cycles in $\rightarrow$ must access the $\rightarrow$ relation at *all* sites to certify each and every transaction. Until this problem is solved, we judge the certification approach to be impractical in a distributed environment.

A2. Thomas' Majority Consensus Algorithm

A2.1 The Algorithm

One of the first published algorithms for distributed concurrency control is a certification method described in THOM79. Thomas introduced several important synchronization techniques in that algorithm, including the Thomas Write Rule (Section 3.2.3), majority voting (Section 3.1.1), and certification (Appendix A1). Although these techniques are valuable when considered in isolation, we argue that the overall Thomas algorithm is not suitable for distributed databases. We first describe the algorithm and then comment on its application to distributed databases.

Thomas' algorithm assumes a fully redundant database, with every logical data item stored at every site. Each copy carries the timestamp of the last transaction that wrote into it.

Transactions execute in two phases. In the first phase each transaction executes locally at one site called the transaction's *home site*. Since the database is fully redundant, any site can serve as the home site for any transaction. The transaction is assigned a unique timestamp when it begins executing. During execution it keeps a record of the timestamp of each data item it reads and, when its executes a write on a data item, processes the write by recording the new value in an *update list*. Note that each transaction must read a copy of a data item before it writes into it. When the transaction terminates, the system augments the update list with the list of data items read and their timestamps at the time they were read. In addition, the timestamp of the transaction itself is added to the update list. This completes the first phase of execution.

In the second phase the update list is sent to every site. Each site (including the site that produced the update list) *votes* on the update list. Intuitively speaking, a site votes yes on an update list if it can certify the transaction that produced it. After a site votes yes, the update list is said to be *pending* at that site. To cast the vote, the site sends a message to the transaction's home site, which, when it receives a majority of yes or no votes, informs all sites of the outcome. If a majority voted yes, then all sites are required to commit the update, which is then installed using TWR. If a majority voted no, all sites are told to discard the update, and the transaction is restarted.

The rule that determines when a site may vote "yes" on a transaction is pivotal to the correctness of the algorithm. To vote on an update list U, a site compares the timestamp of each data item in the readset of U with the timestamp of that same data item in the site's local database. If any data item has a timestamp in the database different from that in U, the site votes *no*. Otherwise, the site compares the readset and writeset of U with the readset and writeset of each pending update list at that site, and if there is no rw conflict between U and any of the pending update lists, it votes *yes*. If there is an rw conflict between U and one of those pending requests, the site votes *pass* (abstain) if U's timestamp is larger than that of all pending update lists with which it conflicts. If there is an rw conflict but U's timestamp is smaller than that of the conflicting pending update list, then it sets U aside on a *wait queue* and tries again when the conflicting request has either been committed or aborted at that site.

The voting rule is essentially a certification procedure. By making the timestamp comparison, a site is checking that the readset was not written into since the transaction read it. If the comparisons are satisfied, the situation is as if the transaction had locked its readset at that site and held the locks until it voted. The voting rule is thereby guaranteeing rw synchronization with a certification rule approximating rw 2PL. (This fact is proved precisely in BERN79b.)

The second part of the voting rule, in which U is checked for rw conflicts against pending update lists, guarantees that conflicting requests are not certified concurrently. An example illustrates the problem. Suppose T_1 reads X and Y, and writes Y, while T_2 reads X and Y, and writes X. Suppose T_1 and T_2 execute at sites A and B, respectively, and X and Y have timestamps of 0 at both sites. Assume that T_1 and T_2 execute concurrently and produce update lists ready for voting at about the same time. Either T_1 or T_2 must be restarted, since neither read the other's output; if they were both committed, the result would be nonserializable. However both T_1's and T_2's update lists will (concurrently) satisfy the timestamp comparison at both A and B. What stops them from both obtaining unanimous yes votes is the second part of the voting rule. After a site votes on one of the transactions, it is prevented from voting on the other transaction until the first is no longer pending. Thus it is not possible to certify conflicting transactions concurrently. (We note that this problem of concurrent certification exists in the algorithms of Section A1.2, too. This is yet another technical difficulty with the certification approach in a distributed environment.)

With the second part of the voting rule, the algorithm behaves as if the certification step were atomically executed at a primary site. If certification were centralized at a primary site, the certification step at the primary site would serve the same role as the majority decision in the voting case.

A2.2 Correctness

No simple proof of the serializability of Thomas' algorithm has ever been demonstrated, although Thomas provided a detailed "plausibility" argument in THOM79. The first part of the voting rule can correctly be used in a centralized concurrency control method since it implies 2PL [BERN79b], and a centralized method based on this approach was proposed in KUNG81. The second part of the voting rule guarantees that for every pair of conflicting transactions that received a majority of yes votes, all sites that voted yes on both transactions voted on the two transactions in the same order. This makes the certification step behave just as it would if it were centralized, thereby avoiding the problem exemplified in the previous paragraph.

A2.3 Partially Redundant Databases

For the majority consensus algorithm to be useful in a distributed database environment, it must be generalized to operate correctly when the database is only partially redundant. There is reason to doubt that such a generalization can be accomplished without either serious degradation of performance or a complete change in the set of techniques that are used.

First, the majority consensus decision rule apparently must be dropped, since the voting algorithm depends on the fact that all sites perform exactly the same certification test. In a partially redundant database, each site would only be comparing the timestamps of the data items stored at that site, and the significance of the majority vote would vanish.

If majority voting cannot be used to synchronize concurrent certification tests, apparently some kind of mutual exclusion mechanism must be used instead. Its purpose would be to prevent the concurrent, and therefore potentially incorrect, certification of two conflicting transactions, and would amount to locking. The use of locks for synchronizing the certification step is not in the spirit of Thomas' algorithm, since a main goal of the algorithm was to avoid locking. However, it is worth examining such a locking mechanism to see how certification can be correctly accomplished in a partially redundant database.

To process a transaction T, a site produces an update list as usual. However, since the database is partially redundant, it may be necessary to read portions of T's readset from other sites. After T terminates, its update list is sent to every site that contains part of T's readset or writeset. To certify an update list, a site first sets local locks on the readset and writeset, and then (as in the fully redundant case) it compares the update list's timestamps with the database's timestamps. If they are identical, it votes yes; otherwise it votes no. A unanimous vote of yes is needed to commit the updates. Local locks cannot be released until the voting decision is completed.

While this version of Thomas' algorithm for partially redundant data works correctly, its performance is inferior to standard 2PL. This algorithm requires that the same locks be set as in 2PL, and the same deadlocks can arise. Yet the probability of restart is higher than in 2PL, because even after all locks are obtained the certification step can still vote no (which cannot happen in 2PL).

One can improve this algorithm by designating a primary copy of each data item and only performing the timestamp comparison against the primary copy, making it analogous to primary copy 2PL. However, for the same reasons as above, we would expect primary copy 2PL to outperform this version of Thomas' algorithm too.

We therefore must leave open the problem of producing an efficient version of Thomas' algorithm for a partially redundant database.

A2.4 Performance

Even in the fully redundant case, the performance of the majority consensus algorithm is not very good. First, repeating the certification and conflict detection at each site is more than is needed to obtain serializability: a centralized certifier would work just as well and would only require that certification be performed at one site. Second, the algorithm is quite prone to restarts when there are run-time conflicts, since restarts are the only tactic available for synchronizing transactions, and so will only perform well under the most optimistic circumstances. Finally, even in optimistic situations, the analysis in GARC79a indicates that centralized 2PL outperforms the majority consensus algorithm.

A2.5 Reliability

Despite the performance problems of the majority consensus algorithm, one can try to justify the algorithms on reliability grounds. As long as a majority of sites are correctly running, the algorithm runs smoothly. Thus, handling a site failure is free, insofar as the voting procedure is concerned.

However, from current knowledge, this justification is not compelling for several reasons. First, although there is no cost when a site fails, substantial effort may be required when a site recovers. A centralized algorithm using backup sites, as in ALSB76a, lacks the symmetry of Thomas' algorithm, but may well be more efficient due to the simplicity of site recovery. In addition, the majority consensus algorithm does not consider the problem of atomic commitment and it is unclear how one would integrate two-phase commit into the algorithm.

Overall, the reliability threats that are handled by the majority consensus algorithm have not been explicitly listed, and alternative solutions have not been analyzed. While voting is certainly a possible technique for obtaining a measure of reliability, the circumstances under which it is cost-effective are unknown.

A3. Ellis' Ring Algorithm

Another early solution to the problem of distributed database concurrency control is the ring algorithm [ELLI77]. Ellis was principally interested in a proof technique, called *L systems*, for proving the correctness of concurrent algorithms. He developed his concurrency control method primarily as an example to illustrate L-system proofs, and never made claims about its performance. Because the algorithm was only intended to illustrate mathematical techniques, Ellis imposed a number of restrictions on the algorithm for mathematical convenience, which make it infeasible in practice. Nonetheless, the algorithm has received considerable attention in the literature, and in the interest of completeness, we briefly discuss it.

Ellis' algorithm solves the distributed concurrency control problem with the following restrictions:

(1) The database must be fully redundant.
(2) The communication medium must be a ring, so each site can only communicate with its successor on the ring.
(3) Each site-to-site communication link is pipelined.
(4) Each site can supervise no more than one active update transaction at a time.
(5) To update any copy of the database, a transaction must first obtain a lock on the entire database at all sites.

The effect of restriction 5 is to force all transactions to execute *serially*; no concurrent processing is ever possible. For this reason alone, the algorithm is fundamentally impractical.

To execute, an update transaction migrates around the ring, (essentially) obtaining a lock *on the entire database at each site*. However, the lock conflict rules are nonstandard. A lock request from a transaction that originated at site A conflicts at site C with a lock held by a transaction that originated from site B if B = C and either A = B or A's priority < B's priority. The daisy-chain communication induced by the ring combined with this locking rule produces a deadlock-free algorithm that does not require deadlock detection and never induces restarts. A detailed description of the algorithm appears in GARC79a.

There are several problems with this algorithm in a distributed database environment. First, as mentioned above, it forces transactions to execute serially. Second, it only applies to a fully redundant database. And third, the daily-chain communication requires that each transaction obtain its lock at one site at a time, which causes communication delay to be (at least) linearly proportional to the number of sites in the system.

A modified version of Ellis' algorithm that mitigates the first problem is proposed in GARC79a. Even with this improvement, performance analysis indicates that the ring algorithm is inferior to centralized 2PL. And, of course, the modified algorithm still suffers from the last two problems.

ACKNOWLEDGMENT

This work was supported by Rome Air Development Center under contract F30602-79-C-0191.

REFERENCES

AHO75 AHO, A. V., HOPCROFT, E., AND ULLMAN, J. D. *The design and analysis of computer algorithms*, Addison-Wesley, Reading, Mass., 1975.

ALSB76a ALSBERG, P. A., AND DAY, J. D. "A principle for resilient sharing of distributed resources," in *Proc. 2nd Int. Conf. Software Eng.*, Oct. 1976, pp. 562–570.

ALSB76b ALSBERG, P. A., BELFORD, G.C., DAY, J. D., AND GRAPLA, E. "Multi-copy resiliency techniques," Center for Advanced Computation, AC Document No. 202, Univ. Illinois at Urbana-Champaign, May 1976.

BADA78 BADAL, D. Z., AND POPEK, G. J. "A proposal for distributed concurrency control for partially redundant distributed data base system," in *Proc. 3rd Berkeley Workshop Distributed Data Management and Computer Networks*, 1978, pp. 273–288.

BADA79 BADAL, D. Z. "Correctness of concurrency control and implications in distributed databases," in *Proc. COMPSAC 79 Conf.*, Chicago, Ill., Nov. 1979.

BADA80 BADAL, D. Z. "On the degree of concurrency provided by concurrency control mechanisms for distributed databases," in *Proc. Int. Symp. Distributed Databases*, Versailles, France, March 1980.

BAYE80 BAYER, R., HELLER, H., AND REISER, A. "Parallelism and recovery in database systems," *ACM Trans. Database Syst.* **5**, 2 (June 1980), 139–156.

BELF76 BELFORD, G. C., SCHWARTZ, P. M., AND SLUIZER, S. "The effect of back-up strategy on database availability," CAC Document No. 181, CCTCWAD Document No. 5515, Center for Advanced Computation, Univ. Illinois at Urbana-Champaign, Urbana, Feb. 1976.

BERN78a BERNSTEIN, P. A., GOODMAN, N., ROTHNIE, J. B., AND PAPADIMITRIOU, C. A. "The concurrency control mechanism of SDD-1: A system for distributed databases (the fully redundant case)," *IEEE Trans. Softw. Eng.* **SE-4**, 3 (May 1978), 154–168.

BERN79a BERNSTEIN, P. A., AND GOODMAN, N. "Approaches to concurrency control in distributed databases," in *Proc. 1979 Natl. Computer Conf.*, AFIPS Press, Arlington, Va., June 1979.

BERN79b BERNSTEIN, P. A., SHIPMAN, D. W., AND WONG, W. S. "Formal Aspects of Serializability in Database Concurrency Control," *IEEE Trans. Softw. Eng.* **SE-5**, 3 (May 1979), 203–215.

BERN80a BERNSTEIN, P. A., AND GOODMAN, N. "Timestamp based algorithms for concurrency control in distributed database systems," *Proc. 6th Int. Conf. Very Large Data Bases*, Oct. 1980.

BERN80b BERNSTEIN, P. A., GOODMAN, N., AND LAI, M. Y. "Two Part Proof Schema for Database Concurrency Control," in *Proc. 5th Berkeley Workshop Distributed Data Management and Computer Networks*, Feb. 1980.

BERN80c BERNSTEIN, P. A., AND SHIPMAN, D. W. "The correctness of concurrency control mechanisms in a system for distributed databases (SDD-1)," in *ACM Trans. Database Syst.* **5**, 1 (March 1980), 52–68.

BERN80d BERNSTEIN, P., SHIPMAN, D. W., AND ROTHNIE, J. B. "Concurrency control in a system for distributed databases (SDD-1)," in *ACM Trans. Database Syst.* **5**, 1 (March 1980), 18–51.

BERN81 BERNSTEIN, P. A., GOODMAN, N., WONG, E., REEVE, C. L., AND ROTHNIE, J. B. "Query processing in SDD-1," *ACM Trans. Database Syst.* **6**, 2, to appear.

BREI79 BREITWIESER, H., AND KERSTEN, U. "Transaction and catalog management of the distributed file management system DISCO," in *Proc. Very Large Data Bases*, Rio de Janerio, 1979.

BRIN73 BRINCH-HANSEN, P. *Operating system principles*, Prentice-Hall, Englewood Cliffs, N. J., 1973.

CASA79 CASANOVA, M. A. "The concurrency control problem for database systems," Ph.D. dissertation, Harvard Univ.; Tech. Rep. TR-17-79, Center for Research in Computing Technology, 1979.

CHAM74 CHAMBERLIN, D. D., BOYCE, R. F., AND TRAIGER, I. L. "A deadlock-free scheme for resource allocation in a database environment," *Info. Proc.* **74**, North-Holland, Amsterdam, 1974.

CHEN80 CHENG, W. K., AND BELFORD, G. C. "Update Synchronization in Distributed Databases," in *Proc. 6th Int. Conf. Very Large Data Bases*, Oct. 1980.

DEPP76 DEPPE, M. E., AND FRY, J. P. "Distributed databases: A summary of research," in *Computer networks*, vol. 1, no. 2, North-Holland, Amsterdam, Sept. 1976.

DIJK71 DIJKSTRA, E. W. "Hierarchical ordering of sequential processes," *Acta Inf.* **1**, 2 (1971), 115–138.

ELLI77 ELLIS, C. A. "A robust algorithm for updating duplicate databases," in *Proc. 2nd Berkeley Workshop Distributed Databases and Computer Networks*, May 1977.

ESWA76 ESWARAN, K. P., GRAY, J. N., LORIE, R. A., AND TRAIGER, I. L. "The notions of consistency and predicate locks in a database system." *Commun. ACM* **19**, 11 (Nov. 1976), 624–633.

GARC78 GARCIA-MOLINA, H. "Performance comparisons of two update algorithms for distributed databases," in *Proc. 3rd Berkeley Workshop Distributed Databases and Computer Networks*, Aug. 1978.

GARC79a GARCIA-MOLINA, H. "Performance of update algorithms for replicated data in a distributed database," Ph.D. dissertation, Computer Science Dept., Stanford Univ., Stanford, Calif., June 1979.

GARC79b GARCIA-MOLINA, H. "A concurrency control mechanism for distributed data bases which use centralized locking controllers," in *Proc. 4th Berkeley Workshop Distributed Databases and Computer Networks*, Aug. 1979.

GARC79c GARCIA-MOLINA, H. "Centralized control update algorithms for fully redundant distributed databases," in *Proc. 1st Int. Conf. Distributed Computing Systems* (IEEE), New York, Oct. 1979, pp. 699–705.

GARD77 GARDARIN, G., AND LEBAUX, P. "Scheduling algorithms for avoiding inconsistency in large databases," in *Proc. 1977 Int. Conf. Very Large Data Bases* (IEEE), New York, pp. 501–516.

GELE78 GELEMBE, E., AND SEVCIK, K. "Analysis of update synchronization for multiple copy databases," in *Proc. 3rd Berkeley Workshop Distributed Databases and Computer Networks*, Aug. 1978.

GIFF79 GIFFORD, D. K. "Weighted voting for replicated data," in *Proc. 7th Symp. Operating Systems Principles*, Dec. 1979.

GRAY75 GRAY, J. N., LORIE, R. A., PUTZULO, G. R., AND TRAIGER, I. L. "Granularity of locks and degrees of consistency in a shared database," IBM Res. Rep. RJ1654, Sept. 1975.

GRAY78 GRAY, J. N. "Notes on database operating systems," in *Operating Systems: An Advanced Course*, vol. 60, *Lecture Notes in Computer Science*, Springer-Verlag, New York, 1978, pp. 393–481.

HAMM80 HAMMER, M. M., AND SHIPMAN, D. W. "Reliability mechanisms for SDD-1: A system for distributed databases," *ACM Trans. Database Syst.* **5**, 4 (Dec. 1980), 431–466.

HEWI74 HEWITT, C. E. "Protection and synchronization in actor systems," Working Paper No. 83, M.I.T. Artificial Intelligence Lab., Cambridge, Mass., Nov. 1974.

HOAR74 HOARE, C. A. R. "Monitors. An operating system structuring concept," *Commun. ACM* **17**, 10 (Oct. 1974), 549–557.

HOLT72 HOLT, R. C. "Some deadlock properties of computer systems," *Comput. Surv.* **4**, 3 (Dec. 1972) 179–195.

KANE79 KANEKO, A., NISHIHARA, Y., TSURUOKA, K., AND HATTORI, M. "Logical clock synchronization method for duplicated database control," in *Proc. 1st Int. Conf. Distributed Computing Systems* (IEEE), New York, Oct. 1979, pp. 601–611.

KAWA79 KAWAZU, S., MINAMI, ITOH, S., AND TERANAKA, K. "Two-phase deadlock detection algorithm in distributed databases," in *Proc. 1979 Int. Conf. Very Large Data Bases* (IEEE), New York.

KING74 KING, P. F., AND COLLMEYER, A. J. "Database sharing—an efficient method for supporting concurrent processes," in *Proc. 1974 Nat. Computer Conf.*, vol. 42, AFIPS Press, Arlington, Va., 1974.

KUNG79 KUNG, H. T., AND PAPADIMITRIOU, C. H. "An optimality theory of concurrency control for databases," in *Proc. 1979 ACM-SIGMOD Int. Conf. Management of Data*, June 1979.

KUNG81 KUNG, H. T., AND ROBINSON, J. T. "On optimistic methods for concurrency control," *ACM Trans. Database Syst.* **6**, 2, (June 81), 213–226.

LAMP76 LAMPSON, B., AND STURGIS, H. "Crash recovery in a distributed data storage system," Tech. Rep., Computer Science Lab., Xerox Palo Alto Research Center, Palo Alto, Calif., 1976.

LAMP78 LAMPORT, L. "Time, clocks and ordering of events in a distributed system," *Commun. ACM* **21**, 7 (July 1978), 558–565.

LELA78 LELANN, G. "Algorithms for distributed data-sharing sytems which use tickets," in *Proc. 3rd Berkeley Workshop Distributed Databases and Computer Networks*, Aug. 1978.

LIN79 LIN, W. K. "Concurrency control in multiple copy distributed data base system," in *Proc. 4th Berkeley Workshop Distributed Data Management and Computer Networks*, Aug. 1979.

MENA79 MENASCE, D. A., AND MUNTZ, R. R. "Locking and deadlock detection in distributed databases," *IEEE Trans. Softw. Eng.* **SE-5**, 3 (May 1979), 195–202.

MENA80 MENASCE, D. A., POPEK, G. J., AND MUNTZ, R. R. "A locking protocol for resource coordination in distributed databases," *ACM Trans. Database Syst.* **5**, 2 (June 1980), 103–138.

MINO78 MINOURA, T. "Maximally concurrent transaction processing," in *Proc. 3rd Berkeley Workshop Distributed Databases and Computer Networks*, Aug. 1978.

MINO79 MINOURA, T. "A new concurrency control algorithm for distributed data base systems," in *Proc. 4th Berkeley Workshop Distributed Data Management and Computer Networks*, Aug. 1979.

MONT78 MONTGOMERY, W. A. "Robust concurrency control for a distributed information system," Ph.D. dissertation, Lab. for Computer Science, M.I.T., Cambridge, Mass., Dec. 1978.

PAPA77 PAPADIMITRIOU, C. H., BERNSTEIN, P. A., AND ROTHNIE, J. B. "Some computational problems related to database concurrency control," in *Proc. Conf. Theoretical Computer Science*, Waterloo, Ont., Canada, Aug. 1977.

PAPA79 PAPADIMITRIOU, C. H. "Serializability of concurrent updates," *J. ACM* **26**, 4 (Oct. 1979), 631–653.

RAHI79 RAHIMI, S. K., AND FRANTS, W. R. "A posted update approach to concurrency control in distributed database systems," in *Proc. 1st Int. Conf. Distributed Computing Systems* (IEEE), New York, Oct. 1979, pp. 632–641.

RAMI79 RAMIREZ, R. J., AND SANTORO, N. "Distributed control of updates in multiple-copy data bases: A time optimal algorithm," in *Proc. 4th Berkeley Workshop Distributed Data Management and Computer Networks*, Aug. 1979.

REED78 REED, D. P. "Naming and synchronization in a decentralized computer system, Ph.D. dissertation, Dept. of Electrical Engineering, M.I.T., Cambridge, Mass., Sept., 1978.

REIS79a REIS, D. "The effect of concurrency control on database management system performance," Ph.D. dissertation, Computer Science Dept., Univ. California, Berkeley, April 1979.

REIS79b REIS, D. "The effects of concurrency control on the performance of a distributed database management system," in *Proc. 4th Berkeley Workshop Distributed Data Management and Computer Networks*, Aug. 1979.

ROSE79 ROSEN, E. C. "The updating protocol of the ARPANET's new routing algorithm: A case study in maintaining identical copies of a changing distributed data base," in *Proc. 4th Berkeley Workshop Distributed Data Management and Computer Networks*, Aug. 1979.

ROSE78 ROSENKRANTZ, D. J., STEARNS, R. E., AND LEWIS, P. M. "System level concurrency control for distributed database systems," *ACM Trans. Database Syst.* **3**, 2 (June 1978), 178–198.

ROTH77 ROTHNIE, J. B., AND GOODMAN, N. "A survey of research and development in distributed databases systems," in *Proc. 3rd Int. Conf. Very Large Data Bases* (IEEE), Tokyo, Japan, Oct. 1977.

SCHL78 SCHLAGETER, G. "Process synchronization in database systems." *ACM Trans. Database Syst.* **3**, 3 (Sept. 1978), 248–271.

SEQU79 SEQUIN, J., SARGEANT, G., AND WILNES, P. "A majority consensus algorithm for the consistency of duplicated and distributed information," in *Proc. 1st Int. Conf. Distributed Computing Systems* (IEEE), New York, Oct. 1979, pp. 617–624.

SHAP77a SHAPIRO, R. M., AND MILLSTEIN, R. E. "Reliability and fault recovery in distributed processing," in *Oceans '77 Conf. Record*, vol. II, Los Angeles, 1977.

SHAP77b SHAPIRO, R. M., AND MILLSTEIN, R. E. "NSW reliability plan," Massachusetts Tech. Rep. 7701-1411, Computer Associates, Wakefield, Mass., June 1977.

SILB80 SILBERSCHATZ, A., AND KEDEM, Z. "Consistency in hierarchical database systems," *J. ACM* **27**, 1 (Jan. 1980), 72–80.

STEA76 STEARNS, R. E., LEWIS, P. M. II, AND ROSENKRANTZ, D. J. "Concurrency controls for database systems," in *Proc. 17th Symp. Foundations Computer Science* (IEEE), 1976, pp. 19–32.

STEA81 STEARNS, R. E., AND ROSENKRANTZ, J. "Distributed database concurrency controls using fore-values," in *Proc. 1981 SIGMOD Conf.* (ACM).

STON77 STONEBRAKER, M., AND NEUHOLD, E. "A distributed database version of INGRES," in *Proc. 2nd Berkeley Workshop Distributed Data Management and Computer Networks*, May 1977.

STON79 STONEBRAKER, M. "Concurrency control and consistency of multiple copies of data in distributed INGRES, *IEEE Trans. Softw. Eng.* **SE-5,** 3 (May 1979), 188–194.

THOM79 THOMAS, R. H. "A solution to the concurrency control problem for multiple copy databases," in *Proc. 1978 COMPCON Conf.* (IEEE), New York.

VERH78 VERHOFSTAD, J. S. M. "Recovery and crash resistance in a filing system," in *Proc. SIGMOD Int. Conf. Management of Data* (ACM), New York, 1977, pp. 158–167.

A Partial Index of References

1. *Certifiers*: BADA79, BAYE80, CASA79, KUNG81, PAPA79, THOM79
2. *Concurrency control theory*: BERN79b, BERN80c, CASA79, ESWA76, KUNG79, MINO78, PAPA77, PAPA79, SCHL78, SILB80, STEA76
3. *Performance*: BADA80, GARC78, GARC79a, GARC79b, GELE78, REIS79a, REIS79b, ROTH77
4. *Reliability*
   General: ALSB76a, ALSB76b, BELF76, BERN79a, HAMM80, LAMP76
   Two-phase commit: HAMM80, LAMP76
5. *Timestamp-ordered scheduling (T/O)*
   General: BADA78, BERN78a, BERN80a, BERN80b, BERN80d, LELA78, LIN79, RAMI79
   Thomas' Write Rule: THOM79
   Multiversion timestamp ordering: MONT78, REED78
   Timestamp and clock management: LAMP78, THOM79
6. *Two-phase locking (2PL)*
   General: BERN79b, BREI79, ESWA76, GARD77, GRAY75, GRAY78, PAPA79, SCHL78, SILB80, STEA81
   Distributed 2PL: MENA80, MINO79, ROSE78, STON79
   Primary copy 2PL: STON77, STON79
   Centralized 2PL: ALSB76a, ALSB76b, GARC79b, GARC79c
   Voting 2PL: GIFF79, SEQU79, THOM79
   Deadlock detection/prevention: GRAY78, KING74, KAWA79, ROSE78, STON79

NONBLOCKING COMMIT PROTOCOLS*

Dale Skeen

Computer Science Division
EECS Department
University of California
Berkeley, California

"From a certain point onward there is no longer any turning back. That is the point that must be reached."
- Kafka

ABSTRACT

Protocols that allow operational sites to continue transaction processing even though site failures have occurred are called nonblocking. Many applications require nonblocking protocols. This paper investigates the properties of nonblocking protocols. Necessary and sufficient conditions for a protocol to be nonblocking are presented and from these conditions a method for designing them is derived. Both a central site nonblocking protocol and a decentralized nonblocking protocol are presented.

1. Introduction

Recently, considerable research interest has been focused on distributed data base systems [LORI77, ROTH77, SCHA78, SVOB79]. Several systems have been proposed and are in various stages of implementation, including SDD-1 [HAMM79], SYSTEM-R [LIND79], and Ingres [STON79]. It is widely recognized that distributed crash recovery is vital to the usefulness of these systems. However, resilient protocols are hard to design and they are expensive. Crash recovery algorithms are based on the notion that certain basic operations on the data are logically indivisible. These operations are called transactions.

*This research was sponsored by the U.S. Air Force Office of Scientific Research Grant 78-3596, the U.S. Army Research Office Grant DAAG29-76-G-0245, and the Naval Electronics Systems Command Contract N00039-78-G-0013.

Transaction Management

By definition, a transaction on a distributed data base system is an atomic operation: either it executes to completion or it appears never to have executed at all. However, a transaction is rarely a physically atomic operation, rather, during execution it must be decomposed into a sequence of physical operations. This discrepancy between logical atomicity (as seen by the application) and physical atomicity poses a significant problem in the implementation of distributed systems. This problem is amplified when transaction atomicity must be preserved across multiple failures. Nonetheless, most applications require that a notion of transaction atomicity (above the level of physical atomicity) be supported and made resilient to failures.

Preserving transaction atomicity in the single site case is a well understood problem [LIND79, GRAY79]. The processing of a single transaction is viewed as follows. At some time during its execution, a commit point is reached where the site decides to commit or to abort the transaction. A commit is an unconditional guarantee to execute the transaction to completion, even in the event of multiple failures. Similarly, an abort is an unconditional guarantee to "back out" the transaction so that none of its results persist. If a failure occurs before the commit point is reached, then immediately upon recovering the site will abort the transaction. Commit and abort are irreversible. See [LIND79] for a discussion on implementing this abstraction of transaction management.

The problem of guaranteeing transaction atomicity is compounded when more than one site is involved. Given that each site has a local recovery strategy that provides atomicity at the local level, the problem becomes one of insuring that the sites either unanimously abort or unanimously commit. A mixed decision results in an inconsistent data base.

Protocols for preserving transaction atomicity are called commit protocols. Several commit protocols have been proposed [ALSB76, HAMM79, LAMP76, LIND79, STON79] The simplest commit protocol that allows unilateral abort is the two phase commit protocol illustrated in figure 1 [GRAY79, LAMP76]. This protocol uses a designated site (site 1 in the figure) to coordinate the execution of the transaction at the other sites. In the first phase of the protocol the coordinator distributes the transaction to all sites, and then each site individually votes on whether to commit (yes) or abort (no) it. In the second phase, the coordinator collects all the votes and informs each site of the outcome. In the absence of failures, this protocol preserves atomicity.

Nonblocking Commit Protocols

Consider what happens in the two phase protocol if both the coordinator and the second site crash after the third site has voted on the transaction, but before the third has received a commit message. There are several possible execution states of the transaction; two are of interest.

First, either of the failed sites may have aborted the transaction. Secondly, all sites may have decided to commit the protocol. In the latter situation, if the coordinator failed between sending commit messages and if the second site failed after receiving a commit message, then the transaction has been committed at the second site. Since site three has no way of determining the status of the transaction at the second site, it can not safely proceed. Instead, execution of the transaction must be blocked at site three until one of the failed sites has recovered.

The two phase commit protocol is an example of a blocking protocol: operational sites sometimes wait on the recovery of a failed sites. Locks must be held on the database while the transaction is blocked.

A protocol that never requires operational sites to block until a failed site has recovered is called a nonblocking protocol.

Termination and Recovery Protocols

When the occurrence of site failures render the continued execution of the commit protocol impossible, then a termination protocol is invoked. The purpose of a termination protocol is to terminate transaction execution as quickly as possible at the operational sites. The protocol, of course, must guarantee transaction atomicity. Clearly, a termination

---

SITE 1	SITE 2
(1) Transaction is received. "Start Xact" is sent.	
	"Start Xact" is received. Site 2 votes: "yes" to commit, "no" to abort. The vote is sent to site 1.
(2) The vote is received. If vote="yes" and site 1 agrees, then "commit" is sent; else, "abort" is sent.	
	Either "commit" or "abort" is received and processed.

Figure 2. The two-phase commit protocol (2 sites).

protocol can accomplish its task only if a nonblocking commit protocol is used. In section 6, we derive a centralized termination protocol.

The final class of protocols required to handle site failures are called recovery protocols. These protocols are invoked by failed sites to resume transaction processing. Recovery protocols are not discussed in this paper, interested readers are referred to [LIND79, HAMM79, SKEE81a].

In the next section we present the formalisms required in the remainder of the paper. Commit protocols are modelled by finite state automata. The local state and the global state of a transaction are defined.

In the third section two prevalent commit paradigms are presented: the central site model and the decentralized model. It is shown that protocols in both models have synchronization points. This property will be used in designing nonblocking protocols.

In section fourth the major results of the paper are presented. First, necessary and sufficient conditions for a protocol to be nonblocking are derived. Next, we demonstrate that "buffer states" can be added to a protocol to make it nonblocking. For most practical protocols, a single buffer state is sufficient.

In the fifth section we present a protocol invoked to terminate the transaction at the operational sites after the occurrence of (multiple) site failures.

Throughout the paper two assumptions about the underlying communications network are made:

(1) point-to-point communication is possible between two operational sites (i.e. the network never fails),

(2) the network can detect the failure of a site (e.g. by a "timeout") and can reliably report this to an operational site.

2. Formal Model Summarized

In this section, we use a generalization of the formal model introduced in [SKEE81a] to describe commit protocols. Transaction execution at each site is modelled as a finite state automaton (FSA), with the network serving as a common input/output tape to all sites. The states of the FSA for site i are called the local states of site i.

A state transition involves the site reading a (nonempty) string of messages addressed to it, writing a string of messages, and moving to the next local state. The change of local state is an instantaneous event, marking the end of the transition (and all associated activity). In the absence of a site failure, a state transition is an atomic event. State transitions at one site are asynchronous with respect to transitions at other sites.

In figure 2, this model is illustrated for the two phase commit protocol of figure 1. One FSA describes the protocol executed by the coordinator, while the other describes the protocol executed by each slave. Each FSA has four (local) states: an initial state (q_i), a wait state (w_i), an abort state (a_i), and a commit state (c_i). Abort and commit are final states, indicating that the transaction has been either aborted or committed,

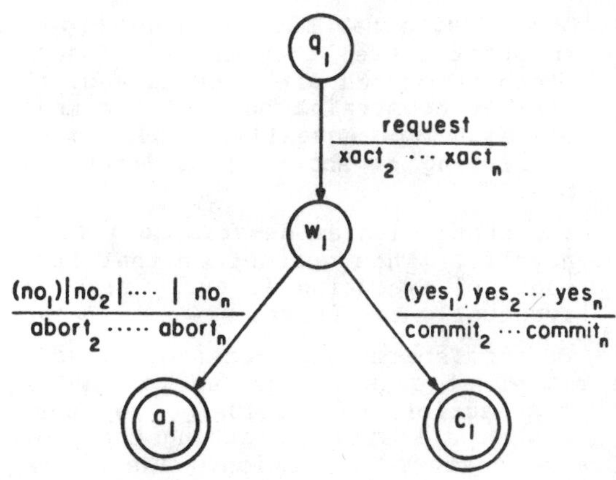

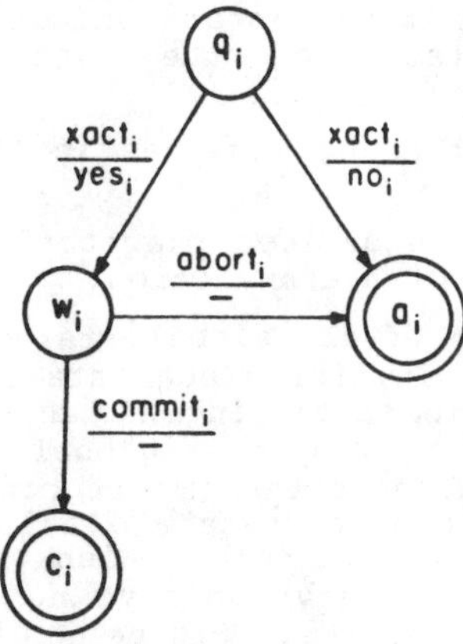

Figure 2. The FSA's for the two phase commit (n sites).

respectively.

Figure 2 also illustrates the conventions used in the remainder of the paper. Local states for site i are subscripted with i. Messages sent or received by a slave are subscripted with that slave's site number.

The finite state automata describing a commit protocol exhibit the following four properties:

(1) The FSA's are nondeterministic. The behavior of each FSA is not known apriori because of the possibility of deadlocks, failures, and user aborts. Moreover, when multiple messages are addressed to a site, the order of receiving the messages is arbitrary.

(2) The final states of the FSA's are partitioned into two sets: the abort states, and the commit states.

(3) Once a site has made a transition to an abort state, then transitions to nonabort states are not allowed. A similar constraint holds for commit states. Consequently, the act of committing or aborting is irreversible.

(4) The state diagram describing a FSA is acyclic. This guarantees that the protocol executing at every site will eventually terminate.

Protocols are often characterized by the number of phases required to commit the transaction. Intuitively, a phase occurs when all sites executing the protocol make a state transition. The number of phases in a protocol is a rough measure of its complexity and cost (in messages). Distributed protocols generally require at least two phases.

Global Transaction State

The global state of a distributed transaction is defined to consist of:

(1) a global state vector containing the local states of the participating FSA's and

(2) the outstanding messages in the network.

The global state defines the complete processing state of a transaction.

The graph of all global states reachable from the initial global state is instrumental in specifying and analyzing protocols. For example, a global state is said to be inconsistent if it contains both a local commit state and a local abort state. Protocols which maintain transaction atomicity can have no inconsistent global states. Figure 3 gives the reachable state graph for the two phase protocol discussed earlier.

A global state is said to be a final state if all local states contained in the state vector are final states. A global state is a terminal state if from it there are no immediately reachable successors. A terminal state that is not a final state is a deadlocked state: the transaction will never be successfully completed.

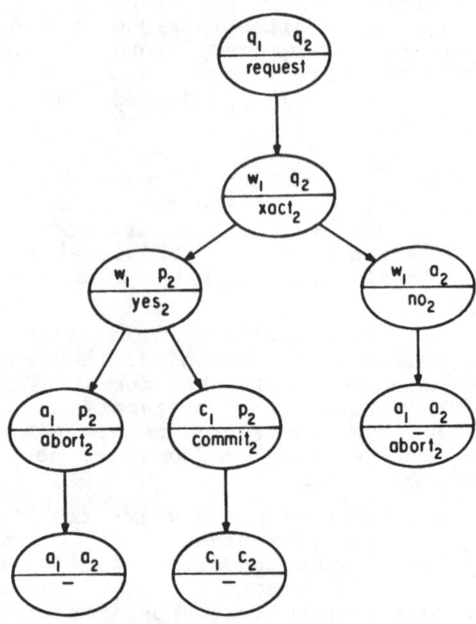

Figure 3. Reachable state graph for the two phase commit protocol.

Given that the state of site i is known to be s_i, then it is possible to derive from the global state graph the local states that may be concurrently occupied by other sites. This set of states is called the concurrency set for state s_i[1]

Although the reachable global state graph grows exponentially with the number of sites, in practice we seldom need to actually construct the graph. In subsequent sections, we will be able to infer most properties of the graph by examining properties of the local states.

Committable States

A local state is called committable if occupancy of that state by any site

[1]Formally, the concurrency set of state s_i is the set of all local states s_j, where $i \neq j$, such that s_i and s_j are contained in the same (reachable) global state.

implies that all sites have voted yes on committing the transaction. A site that is not committable is called noncommittable[2]. Intuitively, a site in a noncommittable state does not know whether all the other sites have voted to commit.

In the two phase protocol of figure 2, the only committable state is the commit state (c_i); all other states are noncommittable. Recall, that this protocol is a blocking protocol, and it is common for blocking protocols to have only one committable state. We will assert (without proof) that nonblocking protocols always have more than one committable state.

Site Failures

Since the sending of more than one message is not a physically atomic operation, it can not be assumed that local state transitions are atomic under site failures. A site may only partially complete a transition before failing. In particular, only part of the messages that were to be sent during a transition may, in fact, be transmitted.

Failures cause an exponential growth in the number of reachable global states. Fortunately, it will never be necessary to construct the (reachable) global state graph with failures. In the subsequent sections, any reference to global state graphs will be to graphs in the absence of failures.

3. The Two Paradigms for Commit Protocols

Almost every commit protocol can be classified into either one of two generic classes of commit protocols: the central site class or the (completely) decentralized class. These classes represent two very distinct philosophies in commit protocols. In this section, we characterize and give an example of each class. The examples were chosen because they are the simplest and most renowned protocols in these classes. However, neither example is a nonblocking protocol. In the next section we will show how to extend both of them to become nonblocking protocols.

The Central Site Model

This model uses one site, the coordinator to direct transaction processing at all the participating sites, which we will denote as slaves.

[2] To call "noncommittable" states "abortable" would be misleading, since a transaction that is not in a final commit state at any site can still be aborted. In fact, sometimes transactions in committable (but not commit) states will be aborted because of failures.

The properties of protocols in this class are:

(1) There is a single coordinator, executing the coordinator protocol.

(2) All other participants (slaves) execute the slave protocol.

(3) A slave can communicate only with the coordinator.

(4) During each phase of the protocol the coordinator sends the same message to each slave and waits for a response from each one.

The two phase protocol presented in figures 1 and 2 is the simplest example of a central site protocol. Other examples can be found in [LAMP76, HAMM79, SKEE81a]. Central site protocols are popular in literature because they are relatively cheap, conceptually simple, and robust to most single site failures. Their major weakness is their vulnerability to a coordinator failure.

Property (4) assures that the sites progress through the protocol at approximately the same rate. Let us define this property as follows:

> Definition. A protocol is said to be synchronous within one state transition if one site never leads another site by more than one state transition during the execution of the protocol.

The central site protocol (including both the coordinator protocol and the slave protocol) is "synchronous within one state transition". This property will be used in constructing nonblocking central site commit protocols.

The Decentralized Model

In a fully decentralized approach, each site participates as an equal in the protocol and executes the same protocol. Every site communicates with every other site.

Decentralized protocols are characterized by successive rounds of message interchanges. We are interested in a rather stylized approach to decentralized protocols: during a round of message interchange, each site will send the identical message to every other site. A site then waits until it has received messages from all its cohorts before beginning the next round of message interchange. To simplify the subsequent discussion, during a message interchange we will speak as if sites send messages to themselves.

The simplest decentralized commit protocol is the decentralized two phase commit illustrated in figure 4. All participating sites run this protocol.

(Messages are doubly subscripted: the first subscript refers to the sending site, the second refers to the receiving site.)

In the first phase each site receives the "start xact" message[3], decides whether to unilaterally abort, and sends that decision to each of its cohorts. In the second phase, each site accumulates all the abort decisions and moves to a final state.

Like the central site two phase protocol, the decentralized two phase protocol is synchronous within one state transition. Sites progress through the protocol at approximately the same rate.

4. Nonblocking Commit Protocols

In this section we present the major result of this paper: necessary and sufficient conditions for a protocol to be nonblocking. We then augment the protocols presented in the last section to construct nonblocking protocols.

The Fundamental Nonblocking Theorem

When a site failure occurs, the operational sites must reach a consensus on committing the transaction by examining their local states.

Site i (i = 1, 2, ⋯ n)

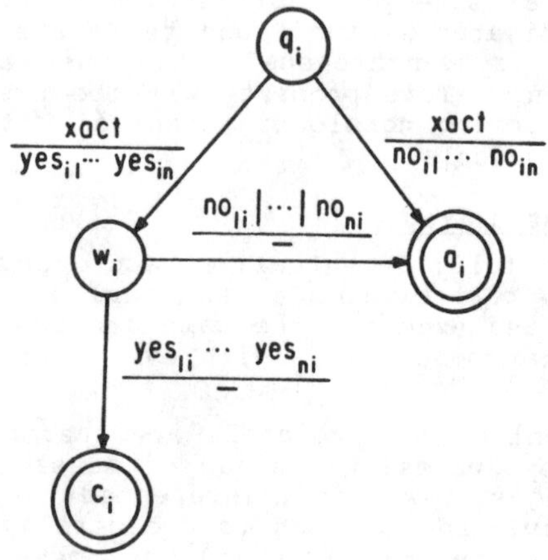

Figure 4. The decentralized two phase commit protocol (n sites).

[3] We do not model the mechanism by which the transaction is distributed to the sites. This is most likely performed by the site receiving the transaction request from the application.

Let us consider the simplest case, where only a single site remains operational. This site must be able to infer the progress of the other sites solely from its local state. Clearly, the site will be able to safely abort the transaction if and only if the concurrency set for its local state does not contain a commit state. On the other hand, for the site to be able to safely commit, its local state must be "committable" and the concurrency set for its state must not contain an abort state.

A blocking situation arises whenever the concurrency set for the local state contains both a commit and an abort state. A blocking situation also arises whenever the site is in a "noncommittable" state and the concurrency set for that state contains a commit state -- the site can not commit because it can not infer that all sites have voted yes on committing, and it can not abort because another site may have committed the transaction before crashing. Notice that both two phase commit protocols can block for either reason.

These observations imply the following simple but powerful result.

> Theorem 1 (the fundamental nonblocking theorem). A protocol is nonblocking if and only if it satisfies both of the following conditions (for every participating site):
>
> (1) there exists no local state such that its concurrency set contains both an abort and a commit state,
>
> (2) there exist no noncommittable state whose concurrency set contains a commit state.

Again, the single operational site case demonstrated the necessity of the conditions stated in the theorem. To prove sufficiency, we must shown that it is always possible to terminate the protocol, in a consistent state, at all operational sites In section 5 we present a termination protocol that will successfully terminate the transaction executed by any commit protocol obeying both conditions of the fundamental nonblocking theorem.

A useful implication of this theorem is the following corollary.

> Corollary. A commit protocol is nonblocking with respect to k-1 site failures (2 < k <= the number of participating sites) if and only if there is a subset of k sites that obeys both conditions of the fundamental nonblocking theorem.

It is obvious that a protocol with k sites obeying the fundamental theorem will be nonblocking as long as one of those k sites remains operational. (The case where k=2 is a special case that has been examined in [SKEE81b].)

The fundamental nonblocking theorem provides a way to check whether a protocol is nonblocking; however, it does not provide a methodology for constructing nonblocking protocols. In the next section we develop a set of design rules that yield nonblocking protocols. These rules take the form of structural constraints.

Buffer States

The two phase central site (slave) protocol and the two phase decentralized protocol are very similar: they are structurally equivalent, and they are both synchronous within one state transition. These similarities, especially the latter, suggests that a common solution to the blocking problem may exist. Their common structure, which is illustrated in figure 5 for reference, constitutes the canonical two phase commit protocol.

Consider a protocol that is synchronous within one state transition. The concurrency set for a given state in the protocol can contain only the states that are adjacent to the given state and the given state, because the states of the participating sites never differ by more than a single state transition. In the canonical two phase commit protocol, the concurrency set of state q contains q, w and a. The concurrency set for state w contains all of the local states of the protocol.

This observation together with the fundamental nonblocking theorem yields:

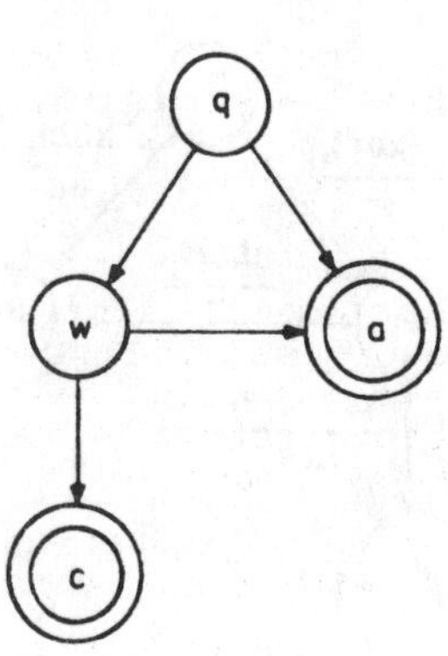

Figure 5. The canonical two phase commit protocol.

Lemma. A protocol that is synchronous within one state transition is nonblocking if and only if:

(1) it contains no local state adjacent to both a commit and an abort state, and

(2) it contains no noncommittable state that is adjacent to a commit state.

State w violates both constraints of the lemma. To satisfy the lemma we can introduce a buffer state between the wait state (w) and the commit state (c). This new protocol is illustrated in figure 6. Since the new state is a committable state, both conditions of the lemma are satisfied. The buffer state can be thought of a "prepare to commit" state, and therefore, is labelled p in the illustration.

We will refer to this protocol as the canonical nonblocking protocol. It is a three phase protocol.

The above lemma is a very strong result. Since all proposed commit protocols are synchronous within one state transition, the lemma can be applied directly. In [SKEE81b] the lemma is generalized to apply to less "synchronous" protocols.

The lemma imposes constraints on the local structure of a protocol. This is convenient since it is much easier to design protocols using local constraints than using global constraints. As an example, the canonical three phase protocol was designed using the constraints

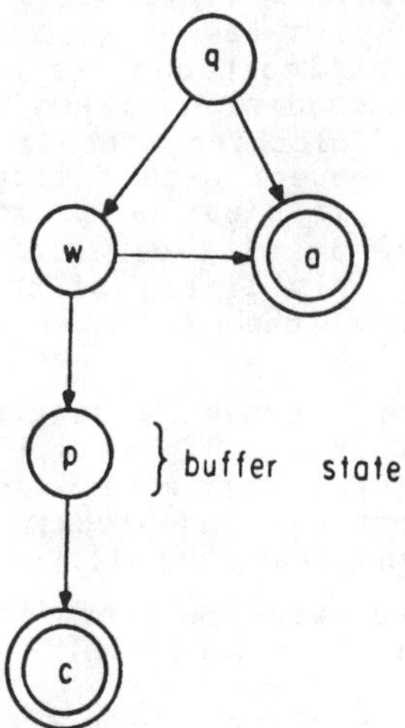

Figure 6. The canonical nonblocking commit protocol.

given in the lemma.

The significance of the canonical three phase commit protocol is that it can be specialized to yield practical nonblocking protocols. In the next sections, two nonblocking protocols are presented -- a central site protocol and a decentralized protocol. Both protocols were derived directly from the canonical three phase protocol.

A Nonblocking Central Site Protocol

A nonblocking central site protocol is illustrated in figure 7. The slave protocol is the canonical three phase protocol (with appropriate messages added). The coordinator protocol is also a three phase protocol that is a straightforward extension of the two phase coordinator protocol. The "prepare" (p) state in the coordinator directs the slaves into their corresponding "prepare" state.

A Nonblocking Decentralized Protocol

A nonblocking decentralized protocol is illustrated in figure 8. Again, the protocol is the canonical nonblocking protocol. The addition of the "prepare" state translates to another round of messages in the decentralized class.

5. Termination Protocols

Termination protocols are invoked when the occurrence of site failures render the continued execution of the commit protocol impossible. This occurs when the coordinator fails in a central site protocol, or when any site fails during a decentralized protocol. The purpose of the termination protocol is to terminate the transaction at all operational sites in a consistent manner.

Clearly, a termination protocol can accomplish its task only if the current state of at least one operational site obeys the conditions given in the fundamental nonblocking theorem. However, since subsequent site failures may occur during the termination protocol, in the worst case it will be able to terminate correctly only if all of the operational sites obey the fundamental nonblocking theorem.

We now present a central site termination protocol. It will successfully terminate the transaction as long as one site executing a nonblocking commit protocol remains operational.

A decentralized termination protocol is presented in [SKEE81b].

Central Site Termination Protocol

The basic idea of this scheme is to choose a coordinator, which we will call a backup coordinator, from the set of operational sites. The backup coordinator will complete the transaction by directing all the remaining sites toward a commit or an

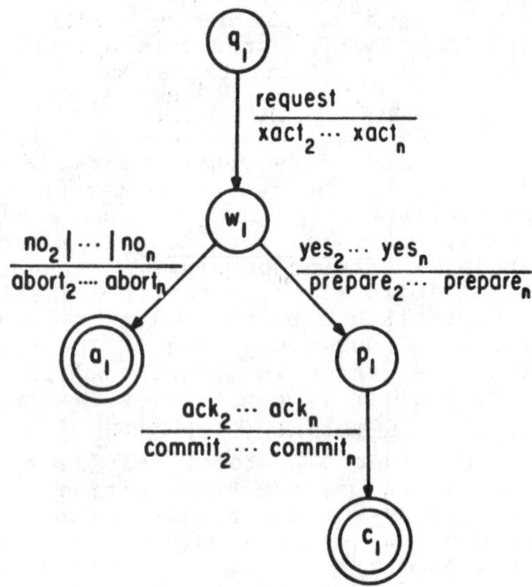

Site i (i = 2, 3 ··· n)

(slave)

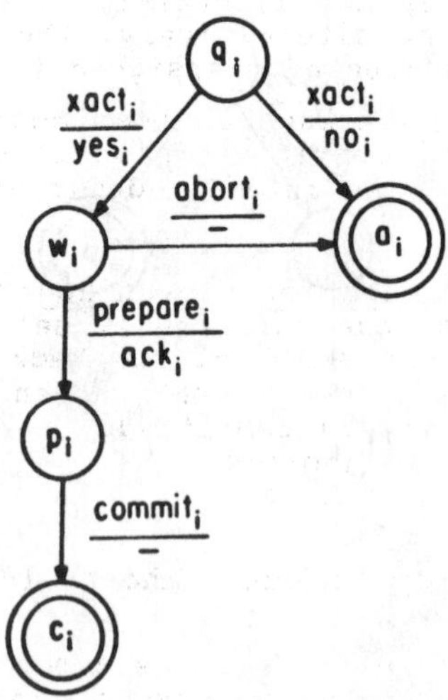

Figure 7. A (three phase) nonblocking central site commit protocol.

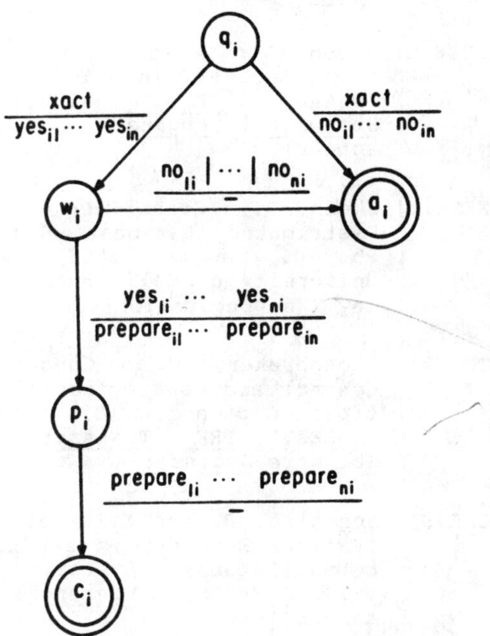

Figure 8. A (three phase) nonblocking decentralized commit protocol.

abort. Since the backup can fail before terminating the transaction, the protocol must be reentrant.

Backup coordinators were introduced in SDD-1 [HAMM79]. The scheme presented is a modification of that scheme.

When the termination protocol is invoked, a backup must be chosen. The method used is not important. The sites could vote, or alternatively, the choice could be based on a preassigned ranking.

Once the backup has been chosen, it will base the commit decision only on its local state. The rule for deciding is:

> Decision Rule For Backup Coordinators. If the concurrency set for the current state of the backup contains a commit state, then the transaction is committed. Otherwise, it is aborted.

The backup executes the following two phase protocol:

Phase 1: The backup issues a message to all sites to make a transition to its local state. The backup then waits for an acknowledgment from each site.

Phase 2: The backup issues a commit or abort message to each site. (By applying the decision rule given above.)

If the backup is initially in a commit or an abort state, then the first phase can be omitted.

Phase 1 of the backup protocol is necessary because the backup may fail. By insuring that all sites are in the same state before committing (aborting), the backup insures that subsequent backup coordinators will make the same commit decision. A proof of correctness for this protocol can be found in [SKEE81b].

Let us consider an invocation of the protocol by the canonical three phase commit protocol. The backup will chose to abort on states q, w, and a, and to commit on states p and c. If the chosen backup was in state p initially, then the messages sent to all sites are:

(1) "move to state p", and

(2) "commit".

6. Conclusion

In this paper we formally introduced the nonblocking problem and the associated terminology. Although this problem is widely recognized by practitioners in distributed crash recovery, it is the author's belief that this is the first time that the problem has been treated formally in the literature.

Also, the two most popular commit classes -- central site and decentralized -- were characterized. Every published commit protocol is a member of one of the classes. These classes are likely to prevail in the future.

We illustrated each commit class with a two phase protocol. Two phase protocols are popular because they are the simplest and the cheapest (in the number of messages) protocols that allow unilateral abort by an arbitrary site. Unfortunately, two phase protocols can block on site failures.

The major contributions of this paper are the fundamental nonblocking theorem and, from it, necessary and sufficient conditions for designing both central site and distributed nonblocking protocols.

We presented two such nonblocking protocols: the three phase central site and the three phase distributed commit protocols. The three phase protocols were derived from the two phase protocols by adding a "prepare to commit" state. This addition is the least modification that can be made to a two phase protocol in order for it to satisfy the fundamental nonblocking theorem. Therefore, such three phase protocols are the simplest (and cheapest) nonblocking protocols.

Nonetheless, an additional phase imposes a substantial overhead (in the number of messages). This overhead can be reduced by having only a few sites execute the three phase protocol; the remaining can execute the cheaper two phase protocol. The transaction will not block as long as one of the sites executing the three phase protocol remains operational. Since two site failures are always necessary to block a transaction ([SKEE81b]), the number of sites executing the three phase protocol should be greater than two.

Lastly, we presented a termination protocol to be invoked when a coordinator fails in a central site commit protocol or when any site fails in a decentralized commit protocol.

It is not necessary that the commit protocol and the termination protocol belong to the same class. In some environments, it maybe reasonable to run a central site commit protocol and a distributed termination protocol.

REFERENCES

[ALSB76] Alsberg, P. and Day, J., "A Principle for Resilient Sharing of Distributed Resources," Proc. 2nd International Conference on Software Engineering, San Francisco, Ca., October 1976.

[GRAY79] Gray, J. N., "Notes on Database Operating Systems," in Operating Systems: An Advanced Course, Springer-Verlag, 1979.

[HAMM79] Hammer, M. and Shipman, D., "Reliability Mechanisms for SDD-1: A System for Distributed Databases," Computer Corporation of America, Cambridge, Mass., July 1979.

[LAMP76] Lampson, B. and Sturgis, H., "Crash Recovery in a Distributed Storage System," Tech. Report, Computer Science Laboratory, Xerox Parc, Palo Alto, California, 1976.

[LIND79] Lindsay, B.G. et al., "Notes on Distributed Databases", IBM Research Report, no. RJ2571 (July 1979).

[LORI77] Lorie, R., "Physical Integrity in a Large Segmented Data Base," ACM Transactions on Data Base Systems, Vol. 2, No. 1, March 1977.

[ROTH77] Rothnie, J. B., Jr. and Goodman, N., "A Survey of Research and Development in Distributed Database Management," Proc. Third Int. Conf. on Very Large Databases, IEEE, 1977.

[SKEE81a] Skeen, D., "A Formal Model of Crash Recovery in a Distributed System", IEEE Transactions on Software Engineering, (to appear).

[SKEE81b] Skeen, D., "Crash Recovery in a Distributed Database System," Ph. D. Thesis, EECS Dept., University of California, Berkeley (in preparation).

[STON79] Stonebraker, M., "Concurrency Control and Consistency of Multiple Copies in Distributed INGRES," IEEE Transactions on Software Engineering, May 1979.

[SCHA78] Schapiro, R. and Millstein, R., "Failure Recovery in a Distributed Database System," Proc. 1978 COMPCON Conference, September 1978.

[SVOB79] Svobodova, L., "Reliability Issues in Distributed Information Processing Systems," Proc. 9th IEEE Fault Tolerant Computing Conference, Madison, Wisc., June 1979.

AN EFFICIENT, FAULT-TOLERANT PROTOCOL FOR REPLICATED DATA MANAGEMENT

Amr El Abbadi[*]
Computer Science Department
Cornell University

Dale Skeen
IBM Research Laboratory
San Jose

Flaviu Cristian
IBM Research Laboratory
San Jose

ABSTRACT

The objective of data replication is to increase data availability in the presence of processor and link failures and to decrease data retrieval costs by reading local or close copies of data. Moreover, concurrent execution of transactions on replicated data bases must be equivalent to the serial execution of the same transactions on non-replicated databases.

We present a pedagogical derivation of a replicated data management protocol which meets the above requirements. The protocol tolerates any number of component omission and performance failures (even when these lead to network partitioning), and handles any number of (possibly simultaneous) processor and link recoveries. It implements the reading of a logical object efficiently--by reading the nearest, available copy. When reads outnumber writes and failures are rare, the protocol performs better than other known protocols.

1. INTRODUCTION

The objective of data replication in a distributed database system is to increase data availability and decrease data access time. By data replication, we mean maintaining several *physical* copies, usually at distinct locations, of a single *logical* data base object. A *replica control* protocol is responsible for coordinating physical accesses to the copies of a logical data object so that they behave like a *single* copy insofar as users can tell [BGb]. Such a protocol translates a logical write of a data object x into a set of physical writes on copies of x, and translates a logical read of x into a set of reads on one or more physical copies of x. To really increase data availability, a replica control protocol must be *tolerant* of commonly occurring system component *failures*. To minimize the overhead caused by replication, the protocol should minimize the number of physical accesses required for implementing one logical access.

This paper presents a replica control protocol tolerant of a large class of failures, including: processor and communication link crashes, partitioning of the communications network, lost messages, and slow responding processors and communication links. Any number of (possibly simultaneous) processor and link recoveries is also handled. The major strength of the protocol is that it implements the reading of a logical object very *efficiently*: a read of a logical object, when permitted, is accomplished by accessing only the nearest, available physical copy of the object. Since reads outnumber writes in most applications, this strategy is expected to reduce the total cost of accessing replicated data objects.

Our protocol belongs to a class of protocols that *adapt* to detected failures and recoveries. An integral part of the protocol is a subprotocol that maintains at each processor in the system an approximate view of the current communication topology. This view can be used to optimize the transla-

----

[*]This author's work was partially supported by a grant from the Sperry Corporation.

tion of logical data accesses performed by transactions into physical data accesses.

The protocol compares favorably with other proposed replica control protocols. It tolerates the same fault classes as majority voting [T] and quorum consensus [G], and does so with fewer accesses to copies, assuming that read requests outnumber write requests and that fault occurrences are rare events. It also tolerates the same fault classes as the "missing write" protocol [ES], but, unlike that protocol, uses a "read-one" rule for reading logical data objects even in the presence of failures. Our protocol is also simpler than the "missing write" protocol. In particular, it does not require the extra logging of transaction information that is required by that protocol when failures occur.

2. FAILURE ASSUMPTIONS

System components (processors, links) can fail in many ways, from occasional processor crashes and lost messages to Byzantine failures, where components may act in arbitrary, even malicious, ways. We wish to consider those component failures that have a reasonable chance of occurring in practical systems and that can be handled by algorithms of moderate complexity and cost. The most general failure classes satisfying this criteria are *omission failures* and *performance failures* [CASD].

An *omission failure* occurs when a component never responds to a service request. Typical examples of such failures include processor crashes, occasional message losses due to transmission errors or overflowing buffers, and communication link crashes. A *performance failure* occurs when a system component fails to respond to a service request within the time limit specified for the delivery of that service. Occasional message delays caused by overloaded processors and network congestion are examples of performance faults. An important subclass of omission and performance failures is the class of *partition failures*. A partition failure divides a system into two or more disjoint sets of processors, where no member of one set can communicate in a timely manner with a member of another set. Our objective is to design a replica control protocol that is tolerant of *any number* of omission and performance failures.

3. SYSTEM MODEL

A distributed system consists of a finite set of processors, $P=\{1,2,...,n\}$, connected by a communication network. In the absence of failures the network provides the service of routing messages between any two processors. Processors or links may fail, leading to an inability to communicate within reasonable delays. Failed processors and links can recover spontaneously or because of system maintenance. Thus, the system of processors that can communicate with each other is a *dynamically evolving system*.

In the following discussion, we will not be concerned with the details of the physical interconnection of the processors (e.g. a point-to-point versus a bus-oriented interconnection) or with the detailed behavior of the message routing algorithm. Instead, we need only consider whether two processors are capable of communicating through messages. We model the current *can-communicate* relation between processors by a *communication graph*. The nodes of the graph represent processors, and a undirected edge between two nodes $a,b \in P$ indicates that if a and b send messages to each other, these are received within a specified time limit. We call a connected component of a communication graph a *communication cluster*. A *communication clique* is a communication cluster which is *totally connected*, that is, there is an edge in the communication graph between every pair of processors in the cluster. In the absence of failures, a communication graph is a single clique. The crash of a processor p results in a graph that contains a trivial cluster consisting of the single node p. A partition failure results in a graph containing two or more clusters.

We do not assume that the can-communicate relation is transitive. Thus, it is possible that a and b can communicate, and b and c can communicate, but a and c can*not* communicate. (Note that if the can-communicate relation is transitive, then all communications clusters are cliques.) In a system in which failure occurrences lead quickly to the establishment of new communication routes, which avoid the failed system components, communication clusters can be expected to be cliques most of the time.

For the purpose of adapting to changes in the communication topology, each processor maintains a local "view" of the can-communicate relation. Each processor's *view* is that processor's current *estimate* of the set of processors with which it believes that communication is possible. The function

$$\text{view}: P \rightarrow \mathcal{P}(P)$$

(where $\mathcal{P}(P)$ denotes the powerset of P) gives the current view of each processor $p \in P$.

A replicated database consists of a set of *logical data objects* L. Each logical object $l \in L$ is implemented by a nonempty set of physical data objects (the *copies* of l) that are stored at different processors. The copy of l stored at processor p is denoted by l_p. The function

$$\text{copies}: L \rightarrow \mathcal{P}(P)$$

gives for each logical object l the set of processors that possess physical copies of l.

Transactions issue read and write operations on logical objects. A *replicated data management protocol* is responsible for implementing logical operations (as they occur in transactions) in terms of physical operations on copies. For a protocol to be correct, the database system must exhibit the same externally observable behavior as a system executing transactions serially in a nonreplicated database system [TGGL]. This property is known as *one-copy serializability* [BGb].

One popular approach for designing a replicated data management protocol is to decompose the algorithm into two parts: a *replica control* protocol that translates each logical operation into one or more physical operations, and a *concurrency control* protocol that synchronizes the execution of physical operations [BGb]. The concurrency control protocol ensures that an execution of the translated transactions (in which logical access operations are replaced by physical operations) is serializable, that is, equivalent to some serial execution. But the concurrency control protocol does not ensure one-copy serializability, since it knows nothing about logical objects. (It may, for example, permit two distinct transactions to update in parallel different copies of the same logical object.) Given this, the replica control protocol ensures that transaction execution is one-copy serializable.

The term *event* is used to denote a primitive atomic action in the system. Among other things, we consider the reading and writing of physical objects and the sending and receiving of messages to be events. An *execution* of a set of transactions is finite set of events partially ordered by the *happens-before* relation studied in [L]. We assume that the set of events restricted to a given processor is totally ordered by the happens-before relation. That is to say, if e and f are events occurring at the same processor, then either e happens-before f or f happens-before e. Consequently, the operations executed on a given physical object are totally ordered. An execution is *serial* if its set of events is totally ordered by the happens-before relation, and if, for every pair of transactions T_1 and T_2, either all physical data operations of T_1 happen-before all physical operations of T_2, or vice versa.

4. REPLICA CONTROL

Following the decomposition outlined above, we now derive a protocol for correctly managing replicated data in the presence of any number of omission and performance failures. In this section, the emphasis is on giving the properties a replica control protocol should possess and on showing that any implementation exhibiting these properties satisfies our correctness criteria. In the next section, we describe in some detail one protocol and show that it exhibits the desired properties.

Ideally, we would like to design a replica control protocol that can be combined with any correct concurrency control protocol. However, this seems to be difficult to achieve given our performance objectives. Consequently, we will restrict the class of allowable concurrency control protocols to those ensuring a stronger property known as conflict-preserving serializability [H]. Two physical operations *conflict* if they operate on the same physical object and at least one of them is a write. An execution E of a set of transactions T is *conflict-preserving (CP) serializable* if there exists an equivalent serial execution E_S of T that preserves the order of execution of conflicting operations (i.e. if op_1 and op_2 are conflicting physical operations and op_1 happens-before op_2 in E, then op_1 happens-before op_2 in E_S) [H]. Henceforth in our discussion, we will assume the existence of a concurrency control protocol ensuring that

(A1) The execution of any set of transactions (viewed as a set of physical operations) is conflict-preserving serializable.

Practically speaking, restricting the class of concurrency control protocols to those enforcing CP-serializability is inconsequential, since all published, general-purpose concurrency control protocols are members of this class. This includes two-phase locking [EGLT], optimistic concurrency control [KR], timestamp ordering [BSR], and all distributed protocols surveyed by Bernstein and Goodman [BGa].

Our performance objective is to provide cheap read access while offering a high level of data availability. In order to understand better what is attainable, let us first consider a "clean" failure environment in which two simplifying assumptions hold. The first assumption is that the can-communicate relation is transitive:

(A2) All communication clusters are cliques.

The second assumption (unrealistically) posits that changes in the communication topology (resulting from failures and recoveries) are instantly detected by all affected processors.

(A3) The view of each processor contains only itself and processors adjacent to it in the current communication graph.

Thus, from A2 and A3 we can conclude that the views of processors in the same communication cluster are *equal* and the views of processors in different clusters are *disjoint*.

Given the above assumptions, the following rules can be used to control access to logical objects. When processor p executes an operation (either a read or a write) on a logical object l, it first checks whether a (possibly weighted) majority of the copies of l reside on processors in its local view. If not, it aborts the operation. Otherwise, for a read, it reads the nearest copy which resides on a processor in its view; and for a write, it writes all copies on processors in its view.

When integrated with an appropriate cluster initialization protocol, which ensures that all copies of a logical object accessible in a newly established cluster have the most up-to-date value assigned to that object, the above rules can form the basis of a correct replica control protocol. The "majority rule" ensures that only one cluster can access a logical object at a time, and the "read-one/write-all rule" ensures that the copies of an object in a cluster act as a single copy. Together, these rules ensure that all executions are one-copy serializable.

The above rules are simple, intuitive, and ensure a high level of data availability, provided the communication information maintained by the processors is *accurate*. Unfortunately, the correctness of the rules depends heavily on assumptions A2 and A3. If either is relaxed, non-one-copy-serializable executions can result.

Example 1. Figure 1 gives a possible communication graph for three processors when assumption (A2) is relaxed. The graph indicates that processors A and B are no longer able to communicate due to, for example, failures that have occurred during a run of the algorithm that establishes the routing between A and B. Both processors however are able to communicate with C, and C with them.

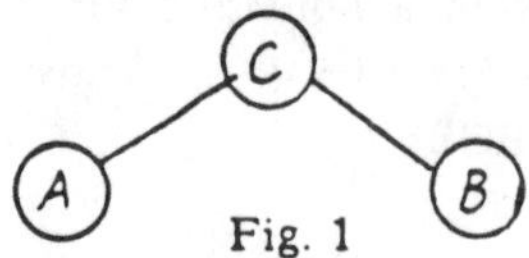

Fig. 1

We thus have: view(A)={A,C}, view(B)={B,C} and view(C)={A,B,C}. Let each processor contain a copy of a logical data object x initialized to 0. Assuming that all copies are weighted equally, each processor will consider x to be accessible, since each has a majority of the copies in its view. Now, let A and then B execute a transaction that increments x by 1. Based on its own view, processor A reads its local copy of x and updates both C's copy and its own. Similarly, B reads its local copy of x (which still contains 0) and updates both C's copy and its own. Observe that after two successive increments, all copies of x contain 1. Clearly, the execution of these transactions is not one-copy serializable. □

Example 2. Consider an initially partitioned system that undergoes re-partitioning as shown in Figure 2.

Two processors (B and D) detect the occurrence of the new partition immediately and update their

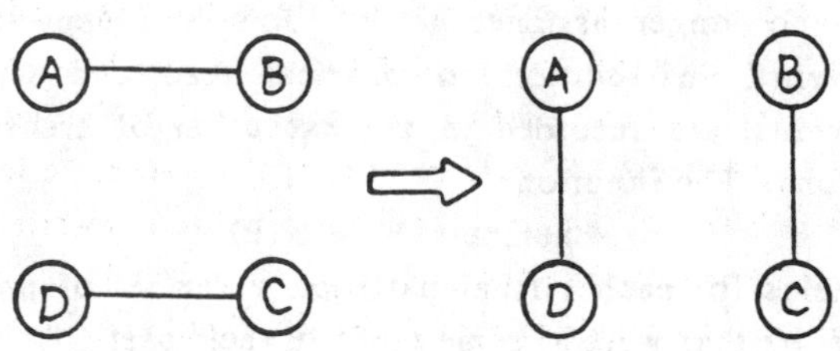

Figure 2.

views. The other two processors (A and C) do not detect it until later. Table 1 shows the intermediate system state after the view updates in B and D and before the updates in A and C.

	old view	new view
A	A,B	A,B
B	A,B	B,C
C	C,D	C,D
D	C,D	A,D

TABLE 1

Assume that, while the views are inconsistent, each processor p executes a transaction T_p. Table 2 gives the transaction executed at each processor, and also the data objects stored there. The superscripts on the objects denote "weights".

	copies	transactions
A	a^2,b	T_A: read(b),write(a)
B	b^2,c	T_B: read(c),write(b)
C	c^2,d	T_C: read(d),write(c)
D	d^2,a	T_D: read(a),write(d)

TABLE 2

Consider the execution of T_A at processor A. Since $B \in view(A)$, A can read its local copy of b. Since A's copy of a has weight 2, A can update it, and, furthermore, A will not attempt to update D's copy since $D \notin view(A)$. Hence, in the execution of the transaction, A accesses its local copies only. The execution of transactions T_B, T_C, and T_D proceed similarly, with each process modifying only its local copies. The result is serializable but not one-copy serializable. □

As example 1 illustrates, the correctness of the simple replica control protocol critically depends on the property that no two processors with different views be able to access a common set of copies. Example 2 illustrates that even in a well-behaved communication network, where transitivity of the can-communicate relation is assured, processors can not independently and asynchronously update their views.

The principal idea in our replica control protocol is to use the majority and the read/write rules mentioned above, but to circumvent the anomalies illustrated in examples 1 and 2 by placing appropriate restrictions on *when* and *how* processors may update their views. Toward this goal, we introduce the notion of a virtual partition. Roughly speaking, a *virtual partition* is a set of communicating processors that have agreed on a common view and on a common way to test for membership in the partition. For the purposes of transaction processing, only processors that are assigned to the same virtual partition may communicate. Hence, a virtual partition can be considered a type of "abstract" communication cluster where processors join and depart in a disciplined manner and communication is limited by mutual consent. In contrast, in a real communication cluster processors join and depart abruptly (and often inopportunely) because of failures and recoveries. It is desirable, of course, for virtual partitions to approximate the real communication capabilities of a system.

The common view of the members in a virtual partition represents a shared estimation of the set of processors with which communication is believed possible. When a processor detects an inconsistency between its view and the can-communicate relation (by not receiving an expected message or by receiving a message from a processor not in its view), it can unilaterally depart from its current virtual partition. (Since the departing processor may no longer be able to communicate with the other members of its virtual partition, it should be able to depart autonomously, without communicating with any other processor.) After departing, the processor can invoke a protocol to establish a new virtual partition. This protocol, which is part of the replica control protocol, creates a new virtual partition, assigns a set of processors to the partition, and updates those processors' views. An objective of the protocol is for the new virtual partition to correspond to a maximal set of communicating processors. However, since failures and recoveries can occur during the execution of the view update protocol, it is possible that a virtual partition resulting from a protocol execution only partially achieves this objective.

We identify virtual partitions by unique identifiers, and we denote the set of virtual partition identifiers by V. At any time, a processor is assigned to at most one virtual partition. The instantaneous assignment of processors to virtual partitions is given by the partial function

$$vp: P \rightarrow V,$$

where vp is not defined for a processor p if p is not assigned to any virtual partition. We use the total function

$$defview: P \rightarrow \{true,false\}$$

to characterize the domain of vp. That is, defview(p) is true if p is currently assigned to some virtual partition, and is false otherwise.

In order to ensure that the simple "read-one/write-all" rules achieve one-copy serializability, we require the following properties from any protocol managing processor's views and their assignment to virtual partitions. Letting p and q denote arbitrary processors, the first two properties are

(S1) View consistency: If defview(p)&defview(q) and vp(p)=vp(q), then view(p)=view(q).

(S2) Reflexivity: If defview(p) then p $\in$ view(p)

Property S1 states the requirement that processors assigned to the same virtual partition have the same view. With a slight abuse of notation, we let view(v) denote the view common to all members of virtual partition v. Property S2 enforces the requirement that every processor should be able to communicate with itself. From S1 and S2, one can infer that the view of a processor (when defined) is a superset of the processors in its virtual partition, and thereby, a superset of the processors with which it *may* communicate in order to process transactions.

The final property restricts the way a processor may join a new virtual partition. Let p denote any processor and let v and w denote arbitrary virtual partitions. Let *join(p,v)* denote the event where p changes its local state to indicate that it is currently assigned to v. Similarly, let *depart(p,v)* denote the event of p changing its local state to indicate that it is no longer assigned to v. Join and departure events, in addition to physical read and write events, are recorded in the execution of transactions. The function

$$members: V \rightarrow \mathcal{P}(P)$$

yields for each virtual partition v the set of processors that were at some point in their past (but not necessarily contemporaneously) assigned to v. The third property is

(S3) Serializability of virtual partitions: For any execution E produced by the replicated data management protocol, the set of virtual partition identifiers occurring in E can be totally ordered by a relation << which satisfies the condition:

if $v << w$ *and* $p \in (members(v) \cap view(w))$, *then* *depart(p,v) happens-before join(q,w) for any* $q \in members(w)$.

Loosely speaking, this property says that before any processor may join a new partition w, every processor p in view(w) must first depart from its current virtual partition. Note that the property does not require p to eventually join w. S3 prevents anomalies of the type illustrated in Example 2, where a processor (B) detects changes in the can-communicate relation, adopts a new view, and begins processing transactions before another processor (C) in the same communication cluster detects the changes. Any ordering over the virtual partitions occurring in a given execution that satisfies condition S3 is called a legal *creation order* for the virtual partitions. In general, there will be many legal creation orders for a given execution.

Comparing requirements S1-S3 to requirements A2-A3, we find that the former ones are considerably weaker than the latter. A3 requires that processors' views reflect the current can-communicate relation. S1-S3, on the other hand, do not imply any relationship between the processors' views and the can-communicate relation. A3 implies that a processor will always know the members of its communication cluster. In general, a processor will never know the set of processors in its virtual partition (but it will know a superset--the processors in its view). Under S1-S3, the views of processors in different virtual partitions may overlap; whereas, under A2, the views of processors in different clusters must be disjoint. Finally and most significantly, requirements S1-S3 are attainable under realistic failure assumptions (see §5). Requirements A2-A3 are not.

The intuitive replica control rules mentioned previously for the "clean" failure environment can now be reformulated in terms of the weaker notion of a *virtual partition*. The first four rules are

(R1) Majority rule. A logical object l is *accessible* from a processor p assigned to a virtual partition only if a (possibly weighted) majority of copies of l reside on processors in view(p).

(R2) Read rule. Processor p implements the logical read of l by checking if l is accessible from it and, if so, sending a physical read request to any processor $q \in view(p) \cap copy(l)$. (If q does not respond, then the physical read can be retried at another processor or the logical read can be aborted.)

(R3) Write rule. Processor p implements the logical write of l by checking if l is accessible from it and, if so, sending physical write requests to all processors $q \in view(p) \cap copies(l)$ which are accessible and have copies of l. (If any physical write request can not be honored, the logical write is aborted).

(R4) All physical operations carried out on account of a transaction t must be executed by processors of the same virtual partition v. In this case we say that t *executes in* v.

Rules R1-R3 are straightforward interpretations of the simple replica control rules. Rule R4 expresses the communication restriction that is placed on virtual partitions. In particular, a processor p accepts a physical access request from processor q only if p and q are assigned to the same virtual partition (that is, if defview(p) and vp(p) = vp(q)). Observe that R4 requires a transaction to be aborted if any of the processors executing it joins a new partition. (In §6, we will discuss an optimization that avoids this most of the time.)

The final rule concerns propagating the up-to-date values of logical objects to copies on processors that were previously in different partitions.

(R5) Partition initialization rule. Let p be a processor that has joined a new virtual partition v, and let l_p be a copy of a logical object l that is accessible in v. The first operation on l_p must be either a write of l_p performed on behalf of a transaction executing in v, or a *recover(l_p)* operation that writes into l_p the *most recent* value of l written by a transaction executing in some virtual partition u such that $u << v$ for any legal creation order $<<$.

Stated less formally, R5 says that before copy l_p can be read in partition v, it must contain the most recent value assigned to l in the current partition or in a previous partition. Note that the desired value of l can be found at one of the processors in view(v) because a majority of l's copies must reside at processors in view(v) for l to be accessible in v (by R1), and a majority of l's copies is written by each logical write of l (by R3).

The above properties can be used to design a correct replica control protocol.

Theorem 1. Let R be a replica control protocol obeying properties S1-S3 and R1-R5 and let C be a concurrency control protocols that ensures CP-serializability of physical operations. Any execution of transactions produced by R and C is one-copy serializability.

The proof of this theorem, which uses notions introduced in [BGb], is given in [ESC]. The proof actually proves a stronger result.

Theorem 1'. Let R and C be protocols as above. For every execution E produced by R and C, and every legal creation order $<<$ over the virtual partitions in E, there exists a serial execution E_S, equivalent to E, with the property: *if $v << w$, then all transactions executing in v occur in E_S before any transaction executing in w.*

Hence, with regard to serializability, we can consider transactions to execute in an order consistent with a creation order of virtual partitions. That is to say, for an execution with a creation order $<<$, if transaction t_1 executes in v and transaction t_2 executes in w and $v << w$, then we can consider t_1 to "execute before" t_2.

Although a replica control protocol satisfying S1-S3 and R1-R5 produces only one-copy serializable executions, the executions may exhibit a curious and, for some applications, undesirable property. Specifically, transactions may not read the most up-to-date (in real time) copies of logical objects. This can occur because views of different virtual partitions that exist simultaneously can overlap. Consequently, the same logical object can be simultaneously accessible in these partitions. Note that only one of these partitions will be able to write the object, since a logical write requires a majority of the copies to reside on processors actually in the same partition; however, the other partitions will be able to read the object and, therefore, will be able to read out of date values. This phenomena is not detectable by applications executing transactions since, by design, applications can not send messages across partition boundaries. However, this could be detected by a user that moves from a processor in one partition to a processor in another.

The capability of a processor to read stale data indicates that the processor's view no longer accurately reflects the can-communicate relation. This situation arises most often when a processor is slow to detect the occurrence of a failure. For most systems, such situations can be expected to be short-lived. If desired, a distributed systems can periodically send probe messages in order to bound the staleness of the data (the next section discusses probing in more detail). Nonetheless, there appears to be no practical way to completely eliminate the reading of stale data when using the majority and read/write rules.

5. THE REPLICA CONTROL PROTOCOL

We now describe a replica control protocol satisfying the properties presented in the previous section. In the design of the protocol we have assumed that the can-communicate relation will be transitive most of the time, although the correctness of the protocol does not depend on this. We have also chosen to emphasize clarity over performance. Consequently, for any real implementation, a number of significant optimizations are possible. We discuss some of these in the next section.

The replica control protocol consists of two simpler protocols:

1) the *virtual partition management* protocol, which assigns processors to virtual partitions and ensures that all copies of a logical object which are accessible in a newly formed partition have the most up-to-date values,

2) the *logical read/write* protocol that controls logical object accessibility and translates the logical operations issued by transactions into physical read/write operations.

Requirements S1-S3, which constrain the behavior of a virtual partition management protocol, and rules R1-R5 are sufficient for ensuring one-copy serializability. Nevertheless S1-S3 is not by itself a satisfactory specification for a useful virtual partition management protocol, since it does not require that the assignment of processors to virtual partitions mirror the current communication capabilities of a system. In fact, a trivial protocol that never assigns any processor to a virtual partition, or that constantly assigns each processor to its own virtual partition satisfies the specification S1-S3. Clearly, the availability of logical objects is influenced by how closely the views of the processors of a virtual partition mirror the current can-communicate relation. If a processor excludes from its view a processor with which it can communicate, then some logical objects will unnecessarily be deemed inaccessible by rule R1. If, on the hand, a processor p includes in its view a processor q with which it can not communicate, then p will not be be able to write logical objects with copies on q (because of the write-all rule).

To ensure high logical data availability, we introduce a supplementary *liveness* constraint on the discrepancy between processor views and reality. Let us say that a failure or recovery *affects* a processor if it causes in the communication graph the deletion or addition of an edge that is incident to the processor. A failure or recovery affects a set of processors if it affects any processor in the set. The liveness constraint is

(L1) Let C be a nontrivial clique in the communication graph existing at time t. There exists a constant Δ such that, if no failures or recoveries affecting C occur during the time interval $[t,t+\Delta]$, then at $t+\Delta$ the view of each processor in C contains all processors in C.

The replica control protocol is implemented at each processor by several concurrent *tasks* that communicate through shared variables. Figure 3 gives the main task, which declares the shared variables and schedules the tasks of the virtual partition management protocol and the read/write protocol, in that order.

```
1  main task Replica-Control-Protocol;

2  type vp-id = record  n: integer;  p: P;  end;

3  shared var  cur-id, max-id: vp-id init (0,myid);
4      assigned: Boolean init true;
5      lview: set of P init {myid};
6      locked: set of L  init {};
7      local: set of L;

8  schedule(Monitor-VP-Creations);
9  schedule(Send-Probes,Monitor-Probes);
10 schedule(Physical-Access);
11 schedule(Logical-Read,Logical-Write);
```

Figure 3.

A virtual partition identifier (a "vp-id"; see line 2) consists of a sequence number and a processor identifier. Virtual partition identifiers are totally ordered by the relation "$\prec$":

$$id_1 \prec id_2 \equiv (id_1.n < id_2.n) \vee (id_1.n = id_2.n) \& (id_1.p < id_2.p).$$

The shared variable "assigned" is true on a processor p if p is currently assigned to a virtual partition, and is false otherwise. (In what follows, "$assigned_p$" denotes the "assigned" variable on processor p.) The variable "$cur\text{-}id_p$" stores the identifier of the virtual partition to which p was last assigned. Thus, when "$assigned_p$" is true, "$cur\text{-}id_p$" contains the identifier of the virtual partition to which p *is* assigned. The "$max\text{-}id_p$" variable records the largest partition identifier seen so far by processor p, and "$lview_p$" records the local view of p. The variable "locked" contains the set of logical objects whose physical copies must be assigned the same (most up-to-date) values after a new virtual partition is created. If a logical object $l \in L$ is in $locked_p$, l cannot be accessed on processor p. The variable "$local_p$" contains the set of objects that have copies at p. The relation between the concrete variables "assigned," "lview," and "cur-id" and the abstract functions "defview", "view" and "vp" introduced in §4 is:

$$defview(p) = assigned_p$$
$$assigned_p \Rightarrow (vp(p) = cur\text{-}id_p) \; \& \; (view(p) = lview_p).$$

The meaning of the "schedule($T_1,...,T_k$)" primitive is "for every $T \in \{T_1,...,T_k\}$, if task T is currently inactive start an execution of T, otherwise do nothing."

The virtual partition management protocol, the first of the two major components of the replica control protocol, enforces the liveness constraint (L1), the restrictions S1 through S3, and the partition initialization rule (R5). The timely detection of changes in communication capability, needed to enforce the liveness constraint, is accomplished through periodic probe messages. When a change in communication capability is detected, the creation of a new virtual partition is attempted.

The process of virtual partition creation requires three phases. In the first phase, a processor that detects the change in communication capabilities, say s, computes an identifier v for a new virtual partition that it will attempt to establish. The identifier v is greater than all sequence numbers seen so far by s, and is guaranteed to be globally unique. Processor s then sends an invitation to join the new virtual partition identified v to all processors in P. A processor q accepts the invitation only if it has not already received another invitation to join a higher numbered partition. After accepting or initiating an invitation and before committing itself to a virtual partition, a processor is not assigned to any virtual partition.

In the second phase, the initiator s defines the view of the new partition v as being the set A of all accepting processors from which it has heard, and it sends the new view to all processors in A. Upon receiving the new view A, an accepting processor q assigns itself to the virtual partition v (and updates its view to A) only if it has not, in the meantime, accepted an invitation to join a higher numbered virtual partition. Hence, at the end of the second phase, only a subset of the processors in A might actually be assigned to the virtual partition v they have accepted to join at an earlier moment.

The third phase starts after a processor is assigned to a new virtual partition. The purpose of this phase is to ensure that all physical copies of a logical object accessible in a newly formed virtual partition have the most up-to-date value before they are made accessible to transactions.

Observe that the above process handles the case where several processors in the same cluster simultaneously attempt to establish new partitions. In the absence of additional failures, only the processor generating the highest numbered partition identifier will succeed.

Let us now examine in some detail the tasks implementing virtual partition creation. The process is initiated by calling a procedure "Create-new-VP" (Figure 4). This procedure first checks to see if the processor knows of an ongoing virtual partition creation (line 2). If so (i.e., "assigned" equals false), then partition creation is not attempted. Otherwise, the procedure departs from the current virtual partition (line 3), computes a new virtual partition identifier, composed from the successor of the largest sequence number seen so far and the local processor name obtained by invoking the predefined function "myid" (line 4), and then schedules the task "Create-VP" (line 5), which actually controls the execution of the first two phases of the virtual partition management protocol. The symbols "<" and ">" are used to delimit critical sections, which provide mutual exclusion on accesses to shared variables.

```
1  procedure Create-new-VP;

2  <if assigned
3  then assigned←false;
4       max-id←(max-id.n+1,myid);
5       schedule(Create-VP(max-id))
6  fi;>
```

Figure 4.

The "Create-VP" task (Figure 5) sends an invitation to join the partition identified "new-id" to all processors (line 3) and records in "A" the identity of all processors that accept to join the new virtual partition (lines 4-13). The δ parameter in line 5 is an upper bound on the message transmission delay between any two processors. After waiting long enough to receive all responses, and after verifying that no invitation to join a higher numbered virtual partition has been received in the meantime (line 14), a commit message is sent to all accepting processors (lines 15-17), the variable "locked" is initialized to the set of all logical objects accessible in view "A" and which have local copies, the task "Update-Copies-in-View" is scheduled, and "Create-VP" ends. The Boolean function (line 18)

$$\text{accessible}: L \times \mathcal{P}(P) \rightarrow \{\text{true}, \text{false}\},$$

is true for some logical object $l \in L$ and subset $A \subseteq P$ if a (weighted) majority of copies of l reside on processors in A.

```
1  task Create-VP(in new-id: vp-id);

2  var A: set of P; S: Timer; r: P; v: vp-id;

3  for each p∈P-{myid} do
4     send(p,"newvp",new-id);
5  S.set(2δ); A←{myid};
6  cycle
7   select from
8    receive("OK",v,r) → if v=new-id
9                          then A←A∪{r} fi;
10   □
11   S.timeout          → exit loop;
12  end select
13 endcycle;
14 <if new-id=max-id
15  then cur-id←max-id; lview←A; assigned←true;
16     for each p∈P-{myid} do
17          send(p,"commit",cur-id,A);
18     locked←{l | l∈L&accessible(l,lview)&l∈local};
19     schedule(Update-Copies-in-View);
20 fi;>
```

Figure 5.

The task responsible for generating responses to invitations to join new virtual partitions is "Monitor-VP-Creations" (Figure 6). This task accepts invitations to join new virtual partitions which are higher numbered than the greatest virtual partition identifier ever seen (lines 5-10). In order to avoid an indefinite waiting for a commit message, a timer "T" is set for a duration of 3δ, sufficient for the initiator to compute a view (2δ) and send it to all accepting processors (δ). After accepting an invitation to join a new virtual partition "v", if no other higher numbered invitations are received and a timely commit message for the virtual partition "v" is received, a processor commits itself to "v" (lines 12-20). If no timely commit message is received

```
1  task Monitor-VP-Creations;

2  var A: set of P; T: Timer; v: vp-id;

3  cycle
4   select from
5    receive("newvp",v)  →
6              <if max-id<v
7               then max-id←v; assigned←false;
8                 send(v.p,ack,v,myid);
9                 T.set(3δ);
10              fi>
11   □
12   receive("commit",v,A) →
13             <if v=max-id
14              then cur-id←max-id; lview←A;
15                assigned←true;
16                locked←{l | l∈L& ∈local&
17                            accessible(l,lview)};
18                schedule(Update-Copies-in-View);
19                T.reset;
20              fi>
21   □
22   T.timeout                  →
23             <max-id←(max-id.n+1,myid);
24              schedule(Create-VP(max-id))>
25  end select
26 endcycle;
```

Figure 6.

(either because the message notifying the acceptance to join was lost, or the initiator has failed, or the commit message was lost) an attempt to form a new virtual partition is started (lines 22-24).

The periodic probing process is implemented in two tasks. During each probe period (of length π), the "Send-probes" task (Figure 7) of a processor p sends message probes to all other processors. Processor p then waits to receive acknowledgements from all processors in its partition (lines 13-20). After the maximum roundtrip message time (2δ) has elapsed, p compares the set of acknowledging processors to its current view (line 21). Any discrepancy detection triggers the creation of a new virtual partition.

The "Monitor-Probes" task (see Figure 8) for processor p, processes the probe messages received from other processors. A probe message with a partition identifier equal to p's current identifier is acknowledged; one with an identifier less than p's is ignored, because the message may be an old message that was delayed in transmission; and one with an identifier greater than p's identifier triggers the creation of a new virtual partition, because the receipt of such a message unambiguously demonstrates the capability of communication between processors in different virtual partitions.

```
1  task Send-Probes;

2  const π: time; %period of probing%

3  var  T: timer;  R: set of P;
5     n: integer init 0;  %probe sequence no.%
6     m: integer;  q: P;

7  cycle
8    <if assigned
9     then for each p∈P-{myid}
10             do send("probe",myid,cur-id,n)>;
11       T.set(2δ);
12       R← {myid};
13       cycle
14          select from
15            receive("ack",q,m) →
16                       if m=n then R ← R∪{q}
17            □
18            T.timeout  → exit loop;
19          endselect
20       endcycle
21       <if (assigned) & (R≠lview)
22        then Create-New-VP  fi>;
23       n ← n+1;
24       wait(π-2δ);
25    else  wait(π) >
26    fi;
27 endcycle;
```

Figure 7.

```
1  task Monitor-Probes;

2  cycle receive("probe",q,v,m);
3    <if assigned
4     then if v=cur-id → send(q,"ack",myid,m);
5            □
6            v<cur-id → skip;
7            □
8            cur-id<v →  Create-New-VP;
9          fi
10     fi>;
11 endcycle;
```

Figure 8.

The implementation given for the tasks Send-Probes, Monitor-Probes, Create-VP, and Monitor-VP-Creations satisfies the requirements S1 through S3. Satisfaction of requirement S1 is ensured from the use of a single processor, the initiator, to determine the view of a virtual partition. Satisfaction of requirement S2 is easy to verify. Satisfaction of requirement S3 follows from the fact that the relation $\prec$ defined over virtual partition identifiers is indeed a legal creation order.

The implementation also satisfies the liveness condition (L1) when the parameter Δ is set to $\pi+8\delta$. This value is computed as follows. After a clique C forms, it may take 3δ time units for all ongoing instances of "Create-VP" to finish. It may take another π time units for the processors in C to send probes, and an additional 2δ to receive the acknowledgements. The results of probing may cause additional invocations of "Create-VP", and these will take 3δ to complete. Now if no failures or recoveries affecting C occur during any of this, then within $\pi+8\delta$ time units all processors in C have committed to the invocation of "Create-VP" generating the highest virtual partition identifier.

After a processor is assigned to a new virtual partition, it has to make sure that all physical copies accessible in the new virtual partition possess the most recent value assigned to the logical object they represent (rule R5). To determine the most recent value of a logical object, we will make use of the fact that the relation $\prec$ is a legal creation order. From this and Theorem 1', it follows that the most recent write operation on a logical object l is executed in the highest numbered virtual partition among those partitions containing logical writes to l.

For the purpose of identifying the value produced by the most recent write of l, each processor stores with its local copy of l the virtual partition identifier associated with the latest logical write of l. On each processor p, the partial functions (suitably initialized)

value: L → Value,

date: L → V,

yield the value and the most recent assignment date for the logical objects stored on p. Thus, value(l) denotes the value of the local copy of the logical object l and date(l) denotes the virtual partition identifier (or logical date) current when the local copy of l was last updated.

```
1  task Update-Copies-in-View;
2  var old-id: vp-id;
3  old-id←cur-id;
4  for each l∈locked
5  cobegin
6      var R: set of P; val: Value; d: vp-id init (0,0);
7      <R←copies(l)∩lview>;
8      for each p∈R
9      cobegin
10         var d_p: vp-id;  v_p: Value;
11         send(p,"read",l,cur-id);
12         receive(p,l,v_p,d_p)
             [no-response: Create-new-VP; exit task];
13         if d<d_p then d←d_p; val←v_p fi;
14     coend;
15     <if assigned & old-id=cur-id
16      then value(l)←val; date(l)←d fi;
17     locked←locked-{l};>
18 coend;
```

Figure 9.

The task "Update-Copies-in-View" for processor p (see Figure 9) brings all accessible copies up-to-date (see requirement R5). Recall that the local copies of accessible logical objects are locked by the virtual partition creation process prior to invoking this task. For each locked logical object l that has a copy on p (line 7) the most recent value "val" assigned to some physical copy of l is retrieved (lines 8-14). This value is assigned to the local copy of l and the copy is unlocked, assuming that p has not joined a new partition since this task was initiated (lines 15-17). The assignment of the most update value to p's copies of logical objects is done in parallel (this is the meaning intended for the construct "for each p∈P cobegin ... coend"). The exception handling notation of [C] is used in line 12 to specify the action to be executed when expected messages fail to be received.

The tasks responsible for enforcing rules R1-R3 are given in Figures 10-12. The tasks Logical-Read and Logical-Write signal an "abort" exception when a logical object l, which has to be read or written by a transaction, is inaccessible on the processor on which the transaction runs. In such a case the transaction has to be aborted.

```
task Logical-Read(in l: L, out val: Value)[abort];

<if assigned & accessible(l,lview)
then p←nearest(copies(l)∩lview);
     send(p,"read",l,cur-id);
     receive(p,l,val,d)
        [no-response: Create-new-VP; signal abort];
else signal abort;>
```

Figure 10.

```
task Logical-Write(in l: L,val: Value)[abort];

var A: set of P;

<if assigned & accessible(l,lview)
then P←copies(l)∩lview;
   for each p∈P
   cobegin
     send(p,"write",l,val,cur-id);
     receive(p,l,ack)
        [no-response: Create-new-VP; signal abort];
   coend
else signal abort;>
```

Figure 11.

```
task Physical-Access;

cycle
 select from
   receive(p,"read",l,v)    →
            wait until (l∉locked);
            <if assigned & v=cur-id
             then send(p,l,value(l),date(l)) fi>;
   □
   receive(p,"write",l,val,v) →
            wait until (l∉locked);
            <if assigned & v=cur-id
             then value(l)←val; date(l)←cur-id;
                  send(p,l,ack);
             fi>;
 endselect
endcycle;
```

Figure 12.

6. OPTIMIZATIONS

The partition initialization protocol sketched in the previous section can be improved in several ways. This section suggests ways of improving its efficiency in an environment containing a large number of processors and large data objects. We also discuss a modification to rule R4 that reduces the number of aborted transactions when two-phase locking is used as the underlying concurrency control protocol.

Rule R5 requires that a processor p upon joining virtual partition v bring its copy of an accessible object l "up-to-date" by reading a copy of l with the largest *date* less than v. In the simple implementation given, p finds this copy by reading all copies on processors in its view. However, p can optimize its search for an up-to-date copy by making use of the recent partition assignment history of each processor in view(p). Let *previous*$_v$*(q)* denote the largest virtual partition less than v that q was a member of. The optimized search strategy is for p to consider the processors in view(p) in decreasing order of their previous$_v$ values. The desired up-to-date value of l is found at a processor q such that:

(1) $\text{previous}_v(q) = \max\{\text{previous}_v(r) \mid r \in \text{view}(p)$ & l was accessible in $\text{previous}_v(r)\}$

Now, if processor p satisfies the role of q in the above condition, then p holds an up-to-date copy of l and no initialization for l_p is necessary.

The values of previous$_v$(q) for all $q \in \text{view}(v)$ can be collected by the initiator in the first phase of the protocol creating v, and this set of values can be distributed to all members of v in the second phase of the protocol at no extra cost in messages or time.

The scenario where a subset of the members of a virtual partition, say v, splits off and forms a new virtual partition w is of practical importance because it occurs frequently. (It occurs, for example, when some members of v detect the failure of another member of v.) In such a scenario, all members of w contain the up-to-date copies of all accessible objects. Consequently, no initialization is required. This special case can be detected using the values of previous$_w$, specifically, in this case previous$_w$(p)=v for every p that is a member of w.

In the partition initialization protocol of §5, a copy is brought up-to-date by reading another copy, *in its entirety*. If the object is large, a more economical approach is to apply to the out-of-date copy all of the writes that it missed. This, however, requires an efficient procedure for specifying and extracting the values of the missed writes.

Specification of the missing writes is made easy by applying Theorem 1'. Consider a copy of l with date v and on a processor currently assigned to partition w. Roughly speaking, Theorem 1' tells us that the copy missed the writes of transactions executing in virtual partitions with identifiers greater than v and less than or equal to w. Thus, this out-of-date copy can be brought up-to-date efficiently if the system can support a query on an arbitrary copy of the form: *retrieve (the values of) all physical writes on copy c by any transaction executing in u such that* $v<u\leq w$. Such queries can be supported by labelling the records of objects with "dates" in the same way that copies are currently labelled with dates, or by keeping a database log [GMBLLPPT] of all writes and their associated "dates."

One unfortunate consequence of rule R4 is that whenever a processor p joins a new partition, all ongoing transactions that have accessed a copy on p must be aborted. This can be very costly and should be avoided, if possible. It is not easy, though, to find a weaker version of R4--one requiring fewer abortions--without restricting the concurrency control protocol. On the other hand, if a particular concurrency control protocol is assumed, a weaker version of R4 can often be found.

Consider, for example, an implementation using a distributed version of two-phase locking [EGLT]. Assume that copies (rather than objects) are locked and that locks are held until the end of a transaction. In such a system, a transaction can be allowed to execute in a *set* of virtual partitions V_T, without compromising one-copy serializability, if the following conditions hold:

(1) The set of logical objects referenced by T is accessible in every virtual partition in V_T.

(2) The set of processors holding copies that were physically read or written by T are contained in the view of every virtual partition in V_T.

(3) The recover operation (see R5) does not read a copy that is locked for writing.

7. DISCUSSION

We have presented a replica control protocol based on the intuitive ideas that (1) a communication cluster can access a logical object if it contains a (weighted) majority of the object's copies and (2) logical operations are translated into physical operations on the copies *within a cluster* using the "read-one/write-all" rule. Although the basic ideas of the protocol are simple conceptually, its correct implementation is quite subtle because we did not assume that failures are "clean." In addition to providing high fault-tolerance, the proposed protocol implements logical reads very efficiently.

The novelty of our protocol lies in the fact that the virtual partition management subprotocol makes a large class of failures (namely omission and performance failures) look like "clean" communication failures that partition the network. As a result, protocols that have been designed for partition failures can be used in conjunction with our virtual partition management protocol in a more general and realistic processing environment. For example, many proposed data management schemes (e.g. [BGRCK, D, SW]) for partitioned systems require partition detection and, furthermore, assume A2 and A3. Generally, these schemes require nothing stronger than properties S1 through S3. Therefore, these schemes can use the virtual partition management protocol to "detect" virtual partitions and operate on them as if they were real partitions.

ACKNOWLEDGMENTS

We would like to thank Shel Finkelstein, Jim Gray, Bruce Lindsay, and Irv Traiger for a number of useful comments.

REFERENCES

[BGa] Bernstein, P., and Goodman, N., "Concurrency Control in Distributed Database Systems," *ACM Computing Surveys 13*, 2, (June 1981) 185-222.

[BGb] Bernstein, P., and Goodman, N., "The Failure and Recovery Problem for Replicated Databases," *Proc. 2nd ACM Symp. on Princ. of Distributed Computing*, Montreal, Quebec, August 1983, 114-122.

[BGRCK] Blaustein, B.T., Garcia-Molina, H., Ries, D.R., Chilenskas, R.M., and Kaufman, C.W., "Maintaining Replicated Databases Even in the Presence of Network Partitions," *EASCON*, 1983.

[BSR] Bernstein, P., Shipman, D., and Rothnie, Jr., J., "Concurrency Control in a System for Distributed Databases (SDD-1)," *ACM Transactions on Database Systems 5*, 1 (March 1980), 18-51.

[C] Cristian, F., "Correct and Robust Programs," *IEEE Trans. on Software Engineering SE-10*, 2 (March 1984), 163-174.

[CASD] Cristian F., Aghili H., Strong R., and Dolev D. "Fault-Tolerant Atomic Broadcasts: from Simple Message Diffusion to Byzantine Agreement," Tech. Report, IBM Research San Jose, 1984.

[D] Davidson, S., "Optimism and Consistency in Partitioned Distributed Database Systems," *ACM Transactions on Database Systems 9*, 3 (September 1984), 456-482.

[ES] Eager, D., and Sevcik, K., "Achieving Robustness in Distributed Data Base Systems," *Transactions on Database Systems 8*, 3 (September 83), 354-381.

[EGLT] Eswaran, K., Gray, J., Lorie, R., and Traiger, I., "The Notions of Consistency and Predicate Locks in a Database System," *Comm. of the ACM 19*, 11 (November 1976), 624-633.

[ESC] El Abbadi, A., Skeen, D., and Cristian, F., "An Efficient, Fault-Tolerant Protocol for Replicated Data Management," Tech. Report, IBM Research San Jose, 1985.

[G] Gifford, D., "Weighted Voting for Replicated Data," *Proc. of the 7th Symposium on Operating Systems Principles* Dec. 1979.

[GMBLLPPT] Gray, J., McJones, P., Blasgen, M., Lindsay, B., Lorie, R., Price, T., Putzulo, F., and Traiger, I., "The Recovery Manager of the System R Database Manager," *ACM Computing Surveys 13*, 2 (June 1981), 223-242.

[H] Hadzilacos, V., "Issues of Fault Tolerance in Concurrent Computations," Tech. Report 11-84, Harvard University, Center for Research in Computing Technology, Cambridge, Massachusetts (June 1984).

[KR] Kung, H., and Robinson, J., "On Optimistic Methods for Concurrency Control," *ACM Transactions on Database Systems 6*, 2 (June 1982), 213-226.

[L] Lamport, L., "Time, Clocks, and the Ordering of Events in a Distributed System," *Comm. of the ACM 21*, 7, (July 1978) 558-565.

[SW] Skeen, D., and Wright, D., "Increasing Availabilty in Partitioned Database Systems". *Proc. 3nd ACM Symp. on Princ. of Database Systems*, Waterloo, Canada, April 1984, 290-299. TR 83-581 Dept. of Computer Science, Cornell University, Ithaca NY 14853.

[TGGL] Traiger, I.L., Gray, J.N., Galtieri, C.A., and Lindsay, B.G., "Transactions and Consistency in Distributed Database Systems," *Transactions on Database Systems Vol. 7*, 3 (September 1982), 323-342.

[T] Thomas, R.H., "A Majority Consensus Approach to Concurrency Control for Multiple Copy Data Bases," *ACM Transactions on Database Systems 4*, 2 (June 1979) 180-209.

Chapter 4

Performance And Database Machines

4.1 Introduction

I begin this section on high-performance database machines by discussing the standard benchmarking experience of typical DBMS users. They refine the list of candidate systems to those that seem appropriate and get a "short list" of systems to benchmark. Three seems a typical number. They then take a small application and code it using each of the three systems. Along the way they are pressured by each of the vendors to change the benchmark to give advantage to that vendor's system. Ultimately the application is coded, and there is one winner and two losers. Each loser, of course, asks to see the benchmark and the user solution. Each will then suggest ways to tune up the benchmark to run faster on their systems. Such hints will include things like rearranging the qualification so the optimizer gets the right plan instead of the wrong plan (a favorite tactic of systems that have a weak optimizer). A second tactic is to change the storage structure so the set of commands goes faster, while a third tactic is to separate single composite commands into separate ones that run faster. In general any user-implemented benchmark can be tuned up substantially by the vendor specialists. Hence, after the vendor specialists have processed the user benchmark, there may be a new winner and two new losers. The next step is for the two losers to request to run the benchmark on their beta-test system that will be out in production "soon." All vendors have a runable "next system" most of the time. After each vendor has run the application on its beta system, there may be a new winner and two new losers.

At the end of this process a user who has not had experience in DBMSs will probably be more confused than before. To avoid this kind of experience, standard benchmarks should be able to provide a "level playing field," though which users can get a sense of DBMS performance on a standard collection of commands.

Two standard benchmarks that have enjoyed widespread use are included in this section. The earlier one was the so-called Wisconsin benchmark [BITT83], and I have included in this book a retrospection on the benchmark written by some of the original authors in 1987 (4.2). In it, they present some of the limitations of the benchmark. I would like to stress a couple of points they mention. First, any person who designs a benchmark is in a "no win" situation, i.e., he can only be criticized. External observers will find fault with the benchmark as artificial or incomplete in one way or another. Vendors who do poorly on the benchmark will criticize it unmercifully. On the other hand, vendors who do well will likely say the benchmark is poor but that one should use it anyway. The Wisconsin benchmark is no exception to this situation, and the authors are a bit overly defensive about the benchmark in their retrospection.

However, I want to give just one example on why designing a good benchmark is very hard. One of my consulting clients was having a terrible problem with a commercial DBMS. It was capable of loading records into a database at a rate of about ten per second. This dismal performance (about a factor of 50 off the competitive norm) nearly caused the client's application to fail. This shortcoming would probably have altered the client's purchasing decision, had he been aware of it during the period of vendor evaluation. The Wisconsin benchmark has no load commands; consequently, if this client had run that benchmark on the target system he would not have been made aware of the problem.

Another comment on the Wisconsin benchmark is that it is fairly easy for a vendor to make his system look good on the Wisconsin benchmark. Since it contains no queries harder than three-way joins, vendors can easily patch their optimizers to choose the right plan on the Wisconsin queries. Such a patched optimizer will do no better than before on a six-way join. Consequently, the benchmark is too easy for vendors to circumvent by patching their systems.

Because the Wisconsin benchmark is a single-user test, it does not expose flaws that might be present in any vendor's transaction management system. Moreover, because production applications tend to stress this component of a system, Jim Gray decided to formalize a second benchmark. Even though the paper (4.3) is authored anonomously, Jim was largely responsible for its content. Although it contains three multiuser tests, only the TP1 benchmark has achieved popularity, and it has become the near universal "litmus test" of performance in commercial data-processing shops. Primarily it stresses the transaction management component of a system, the ability of a system to avoid "hot spots," and the overhead of the system on simple transactions. As such, it tests completely different functions from the Wisconsin benchmark. As with any benchmark, it is very easy to criticize, but I want to make only three critical comments about TP1.

First, the benchmark is best done using non-standard SQL features. In particular, it is four SQL commands together with a begin XACT and an END XACT statement. If a vendor has implemented procedures as database objects in his DBMS, he can cross the boundary to the data manager exactly once, execute the procedure, and then return. This will lower the number of boundary crossings from 12 to 2 and result in a 2030 percent performance improvement. A standard benchmark should not be constructed whose best solution uses features that are not in ANSI/SQL.

Second, TP1 is basically a benchmark of cashing a check. In the benchmark it is assumed that the DBMS is dynamically maintaining the amount of money in the drawer of each teller, as well as the total amount of cash in the branch. I am at a loss to explain why TP1 dynamically maintains the latter item, because it is rarely accessed and could easily be computed on demand. Moreover, every banker I have ever met alleges that he does not do so. Hence, TP1 is not very representative of real debit/credit applications.

The last comment that I want to make is that it is easy to cheat on TP1. One standard tactic used by vendors with weak locking systems is to cut the TP1 database into a substantial number of physical data bases. The number of databases can be adjusted so each one can be processing commands one at a time and locking problems will not be exposed.

Although the constructor of a benchmark is widely criticized, I feel that standard benchmarks are of value to the user community. Moreover, I feel that somebody should construct a third standard benchmark. It appears that business transactions are getting "heavier" over time. For example, one airline reservation system added a query that allowed clients to ask:

> Find me the cheapest fare from X to Y. I don't care how often I stop or how long the wait is.

This is basically a transitive closure of the route map and now constitutes 15 percent of the load on that airline's system. This example illustrates that the size of transactions is tending to increase dramatically as business becomes more complex. Hence, it would be a service to the user community for someone to construct a transaction processing benchmark with more complex commands than TP1.

This section then turns to the possibility of hardware database machines. There have been any number of proposals that attempt to perform database services faster or more reliably. We have one paper in each area in the remainder of this section. The issue of high reliability has been largely ignored by the research community, and tactics in this area have largely come from commercial vendors, most notably Tandem and recent startups that that are trying to compete with Tandem. Jim Gray has classified errors into:

- Hardware errors (i.e., disk crashes)
- Software errors (i.e., DBMS crashes)
- Operator errors (i.e., accidental file erasure)
- Environment errors (i.e., power outage)

In current Tandem systems, the relative frequency of reported errors for these classifications respectively is about 1, 3, 2, 15. Since a Tandem system requires a double hardware error to fail, it is clear that this class of errors has been largely eliminated. Moreover, over time hardware is getting more reliable and its mean time to failure is rising. Hence hardware errors will decrease in significance in the future. Operator errors are also declining as system administrators learn the obvious technique:

To get rid of operator errors, get rid of operators

To the extent possible, systems should be designed to avoid the presence of a human at the master console. Lastly, environment errors are 70 percent power outages, and my opinion is that an uninterruptable power supply represents a cheap, cost-effective means to deal with this problem. The remaining 30 percent are failures of communication lines, about which there is little that the DBMS can do. Although they receive widespread press coverage, floods and earthquakes constitute a negligible percentage of environment problems. Hence, in my opinion it is likely that software errors will become the dominant cause of failures in future systems.

The literature in this area largely presents techniques for dealing with hardware errors, and I have included a survey paper by Won Kim in this collection (4.4). It should be clearly stressed that the mechanisms discussed by Kim deal with a small minority of the total problem. Moreover, recovering from software errors presents a much more difficult technical challenge. It is trite to say, "Let's design DBMS code that doesn't contain errors." All current DBMSs are very complex programs that are never totally bug free, in spite of extensive testing by vendors. Moreover, program verification techniques are a long way from being able to run on the 100,00 lines of code in a typical DBMS. Hence, nobody has a good idea on how to avoid software errors. The only other alternative is to realize that large software systems are going to fail and then design them to recover from errors instantaneously. Hence, when a software failure is observed in the OS or DBMS, the appropriate system software simply crashes and recovers. If recovery is fast enough, the perception of high availability will be achieved. A storage manager with reduced recovery time is discussed in [STON87], and this is a fertile area for new research ideas. The design of operating systems with fast recovery time is an equally fertile area that has been totally overlooked by the research community.

There have been innumerable proposals to construct hardware database machines to provide high-performance operations. In general these have been proposed by hardware types with a clever solution in search of a problem on which it might work. The oldest proposals were based on building associative disks, e.g., RAP [OZKA75], CASSM [SU75] and RARES [LIN76]. The basic idea was to put a microprocessor on each read head of a moving head disk drive. In this way, a cylinder could be searched in parallel and higher performance perhaps achieved. These proposals did not find widespread acceptance because software indexing can beat hardware brute force on most applications. For example, to find Mike Stonebraker's salary, one can associatively search a disk a cylinder at a time or one can hash to the correct bucket and get the record in one seek and one read. For most commands, software techniques will win. In addition, updating the database tended to receive scant attention from the associative disk proposals. The only commercially available associative disk hardware that I know of is the CAFS system from ICL [BABB79].

Next there were a collection of proposals based on associate CCD devices or magnetic bubbles, e.g., DIRECT [DEWI79] and RAP-2 [SCHU79]. These came at a time when it looked like one of these technologies might be able to replace magnetic disks as a storage medium. Hence, they should be thought of as "zero-rpm" associative disks. These systems did not achieve acceptance for the same reason as associative disks; software indexing beats hardware brute force. In addition, one must build an ultra-high-speed controller for a zero-rpm associative disk. Hence the bottleneck in an associate system is often the controller, that must issue instructions to worker processors at a high rate.

More recently there have been other more exotic proposals that combine the above techniques with sort engines [KITS83] or other processors [BANE79]). In fact [HSIA83] presents a wide collection of such suggestions. I do not see anyway to build cost-effective controllers for machines of this complexity. In short, it seems that most proposals come from hardware types who don't really understand the DBMS application area very well. Suffice it to say that none of these proposals has seen a commercial implementation.

There have also been a collection of so-called back-end machine proposals. The earliest was by [CANA74] who discussed off-loading IDMS onto a back-end machine. The problem with off-loading a record-at-a-time language is excessive message traffic. This point is clearly made by [HAGM86], who shows that access method function cannot be off-loaded successfully onto a back-end machine. The clear result is that only relational systems can be successfully off-loaded, and the Britton-Lee IDM 500 [EPST80] is a commercial example of this architecture.

The IDM uses a single specialized processor to perform high-speed database functions (the database accelerator). In my opinion, however, the rapidly declining price of general-purpose, single-chip CPUs makes custom hardware unattractive. Moreover, one would prefer an architecture where multiple processors could be used to provide any needed degree of performance on a user application. Hence, in my opinion the best approach to high-performance database systems should be based on conventional multiprocessor techniques.

One option is to connect a collection of cheap processors onto a local area network and then run a distributed database system on the configuration. Such architectures are "software database machines" and the Teradata DBC/1012 [TERA83] is a commercial example of something close to this architecture that uses Intel 82386 processors. The only custom hardware in the Teradata machine is the so-called Y-net, which provides data communication and hardware sorting. If the Teradata machine used conventional Ethernet technology for communication and software sorting, as some have suggested, then it would be a pure software database machine. Another example of this architecture is the BUBBA machine from MCC [COPE88]. I have included the GAMMA paper in this collection (4.5) as a representative example of this approach because it is an easily accessible and comprehensive system.

Another approach to providing a software database machine would be to connect a collection of cheap processors in a shared memory configuration and then run a modified single-site data manager on this computing complex. Such shared memory machines are exemplified by the SEQUENT Symmetry machine and the ENCORE Multimax, and one example description of the database software for this environment is contained in [STON88]. The relative advantages of the shared nothing (e.g., GAMMA) approach compared to the shared memory approach has been hotly debated [GAWL87]. It will be interesting to see how both architectures fare in the future.

References

[BABB79] Babb, E., "Implementing a Relational Data Base by Means of Specialized Hardware," ACM-TODS, Mar. 1979.

[BANE79] Banerjee. J. et al., "DBC—A Database Computer Computer for Very Large Data Bases," IEEE Transactions on Computers, June 1979.

[BITT83] Bitton, D. et al., "Benchmarking Database Systems: A Systematic Approach," Proc. 1983 VLDB Conference, Florence, Italy, Nov. 1983.

[CANA74] Canaday, R. et al., "A Backend Computer for Database Management," CACM, Oct. 1974.

[COPE88] Copeland, G. et al., "Data Placement in BUBBA," MCC Technical Report, MCC, Austin Tex., Feb. 1988.

[DEWI79] Dewitt, D., "DIRECT—A Multiprocessor Organization for Supporting Relational Database Management Systems," IEEE Transactions on Computers, June 1979.

[EPST80] Epstein, R., and Hawthorn, P., "Design Decisions for the Intelligent Data Base Machine," Proc. 1980 National Computer Conference, Anaheim, Calif., May 1980.

[GAWL87] Gawlich, D. (ed.), Proceedings of the 2nd High Performance Transaction Processing Systems Workshop, Asilomar, Calif., Sept. 1987.

[HAGM86] Hagmann, R., and Ferrari, D., "Performance Analysis of Several Backend Database Architectures," ACM-TODS, Mar. 1986.

[HSIA83] Hsiao, D. (ed.), "Advanced Database Machine Architecture," Prentice-Hall, Englewood Cliffs, N.J., 1983.

[KITS83] Kitsuregawa, M. et al., "GRACE: Relational Algebra Machine Based on Hash and Sort—Its Design Concepts," Journal of Information Processing, Nov. 1983.

[LIN76] Lin, C. et al., "The Design of a Rotating Associative Memory for Relational Database Management Applications," ACM-TODS, Mar. 1976.

[OZKA75] Ozkaharan, E. et al., "RAP—An Associative Processor for Data Base Management," Proc. 1975 National Computer Conference, Anaheim, Calif., June 1975.

[SCHU79] Schuster, S. et al., "RAP.2—An Associative Processor for Databases and Its Applications," IEEE Transactions on Computers, June 1979.

[STON87] Stonebraker, M., "The POSTGRES Storage System," Proc. 1987 VLDB Conference, Brighton, Eng., Sept. 1987.

[STON88] Stonebraker, M. et al., "The Design of XPRS," Electronics Research Laboratory, University of California, Report M88/07, Feb. 1988.

[SU75] Su S. et al., "CASSM: A Cellular System for Very Large Data Bases," Proc. 1st Very Large Data Base Conference, Framingham, Mass., Sept. 1975.

[TERA83] Teradata Corp., "DBC/1012 Data Base Computer: Concepts and Facilities," Teradata Corp., Los Angeles, Calif., 1983.

A RETROSPECTIVE ON THE WISCONSIN BENCHMARK

Dina Bitton
University of Illinois at Chicago

Carolyn Turbyfill
Tandem Computers - Cupertino, California

ABSTRACT

The Wisconsin benchmark was one of the first attempts at formalizing experimental performance evaluation of relational database systems. Timeliness, simplicity, and portability made this benchmark widely used in industry and research environments. As a result, measurements for a large number of systems and configurations have become available, creating a useful source for performance comparisons.

However, the benchmark is limited in scope and should not be used as a reliable comparison tool between systems. This paper is a critical retrospective on the design and usage of the Wisconsin benchmark. The most common criticisms of the benchmark include the structure and size of the synthetic test database, the difficulty in scaling, the restricted set of test queries, and, above all, the fact that it is only a single user benchmark. We address these criticisms and delimit the range of information that the benchmark can reliably provide.

1. INTRODUCTION

Although there exist widely accepted performance metrics for measuring the computation power of different computer architectures on numeric applications, the reliable measurement of database management systems is an area of controversy. Vendors of relational database systems quote *transaction rates* that are hard to interpret since transaction profiles and workloads can vary. Several attempts have been made at defining standard performance metrics for relational database systems. Two benchmarks are currently used by many vendors and researchers: the *Debit-Credit benchmark* [Ano85] and the *Wisconsin benchmark* [BDT83]. The two benchmarks both use synthetically generated data and controlled workloads. However, they differ in their targets. The Debit-Credit benchmark focuses on measuring the transaction throughput power, including network and presentation services of a system designed to support large volumes of short update transactions. The Wisconsin benchmark focuses on measuring the performance of access methods and query optimization in a relational database system.

In this paper, we describe the Wisconsin benchmark and present a critical retrospective of its design and usage. The benchmark was orginally conceived as an experiment in benchmarking methodology. It was one of the first attempts at formalizing experimental performance evaluation of relational database systems. As first described in [BDT83], the Wisconsin benchmark uses a synthetically generated database that occupies approximately 5 megabytes of storage, and a set of simple relational queries with predetermined selectivities and output size. It measures performance in terms of stand alone elapsed time of these test queries. The benchmark's simplicity makes it easy to implement on any relational database system, and its results are straightforward to interpret. Timeliness, simplicity, and portability make the benchmark widely used in industry and research environments. The availability of measurements for a large number of systems and configurations provides a useful source for performance comparisons.

As described in [BDT83] and in this paper, the Wisconsin benchmark is primarily a *single user* benchmark. However, two studies have been published that extend it to *multiuser* benchmarks [BT84, BD85].

System designers and users of database systems who implemented the benchmark have criticized the original design on numerous points. Among the most common criticisms are those about the structure and size of the database, the difficulty in scaling the benchmark to high-end or low-end systems, the restricted and unrealistic set of test queries, and above all the fact that the single user mode is not representative of a system's performance on a real application.

As we describe the benchmark and the motivation behind certain design decisions, we will address these criticisms (and concede many of them). We will also show how certain queries can be modified to correctly test the originally targeted system parameter.

The rest of this paper is organized as follows. Section 2 describes the test database and address some of the criticisms that were made about its limitations. Section 3 motivates and describes the design of the test queries. Section 4 describes the test environment for the benchmark. Section 5 explains why the stand alone query response time was chosen as the performance metric in the Wisconsin benchmark, and identifies other relevant metrics. Section 6 addresses problems that arise in analyzing the benchmark measurements. Section 7 concludes by summarizing the limitations of the benchmark and delimiting the range of information that it can reliably provide.

2. THE TEST DATABASE

The test database consists of 5 synthetic relations, with identical attributes but different cardinalities. Each relation has 16 attributes, 13 integer attributes and 3 string attributes. The integers are 2 bytes and the strings are 52 bytes. Assuming no storage overhead, this results in tuple widths of 182 bytes. The test database in the original Wisconsin benchmark contained 3 relations: *OneK* (1,000 tuples) and 2 copies of *TenK* (10,000 tuples). The attributes for a 10,000 tuple relation are described in Table 1 and an SQL schema specification for the database is given in Appendix A.

The attribute values in each relation are uniformly distributed so that they facilitate controlling selectivities, partitioning aggregates and varying the number of duplicates in a projection. It is also straightforward to build a primary or secondary index on some of the attributes. The range of the integer attribute is implied by its name (Table 1). For instance, the attribute "thousand" has one thousand distinct values between 0 and 999 inclusive. For test queries requiring indices, 3 indices were built, a clustered index on unique2, and nonclustered indices on unique1 and on hundred. Each of the 3 string attributes is 52 characters long, with 3 distinguishing characters occurring in positions 1, 27 and 52. These distinguishing characters allow for 26^3 unique strings, thus enough for the 10,000 tuple relation. The remainder of the positions contain the same padding character. With the unique string attributes (stringu1 and stringu2), the leftmost significant character is varied most frequently, followed by the middle and the last significant characters.

TABLE 1. Description of the Attributes in Relation TenK

Name	Type	Range	Order	Comment
unique1	int	0 - 9999	random	candidate key
unique2	int	0 - 9999	random	declared key
two	int	0-1	rotating	0,1,0,1,...
four	int	0-3	rotating	0,1,2,3,0,1...
ten	int	0-9	rotating	0,1,...,9,0,...
twenty	int	0-19	rotating	0,1,...,19,0,...
hundred	int	0-99	rotating	0,1,...,99,0,...
thousand	int	0-999	random	
twothous	int	0-1999	random	
fivethous	int	0-4999	random	
tenthous	int	0-9999	random	candidate key
odd100	int	50	rotating	1,3,5,...,99,1,...
even100	int	50	rotating	2,4,6,...,100,2,...
stringu1	char	A...A...A-V...V...T	random	candidate key
stringu2	char	A...A...A-V...V...T	rotating	candidate key
string4	char	A...A...A-V...V...V	rotating	

The smaller relation *OneK* has the same attributes as the relation *TenK*, with identical ranges and cardinalities except where the number of tuples in a relation precludes an attribute from having all of the integer values within the specified range. For example, in OneK, unique1 and unique2 contain values in the range of 0 to 999.

The Wisconsin test database has been criticized on numerous points: tuple length, data types, structure of the strings and distributions of attribute values. We will explain why certain decisions were made in the original design, but concede many of these criticisms.

2.1 Attribute Types

Only 2-byte integers and fixed length strings are represented in the benchmark. Although it would be hard to justify 2-byte integers today, during the benchmark's design development there were two reasons for that decision. One was to allow many attributes in a relatively small tuple width. The other was that DIRECT, the database machine measured in the original benchmark, was implemented using 16 bit (PDP 11/23) processors and supported only 2 byte integers.

The strings have been rightfully criticized for being too long (52 bytes), of fixed length, and unrealistically structured. The string length, 52 characters, was arbitrarily chosen to be twice as long as the number of letters in the alphabet. According to expert opinion and an ad-hoc survey of common applications, fixed and variable length strings of 20 or 30 characters are more common.[1] Furthermore, most strings can be differentiated by the first few characters in the string. Thus having 2 out of the 3 distinguishing characters at the middle and the end of the strings makes string comparisons longer than they should be.

All values of the attributes in the test database are uniformly distributed. To model more realistic distributions, at least a few nonuniformly distributed attributes should have been included. Uniform distributions make the job of the benchmarker easier, but they also make the job of the query optimizer more straightforward than it would be in a real environment.

Finally, the attribute ranges used in the test database are too small. In particular, every value in the range of the candidate keys is used to obtain the required number of unique values. This restricts the type of insertion tests that can be constructed (see Section 3.5).

In retrospect, a standard data definition language and portable data types should have been used [Tur87]. In particular, data types more representative of those used in actual applications should have been modelled, such as 4 byte integers, 20-byte strings, decimals, alphanumerics, and floating point numbers. Furthermore, it would be preferable to leave some attributes unspecified, so that users could customize the test database to the needs of their application.

2.2 Database Structure

Like the length of strings, the tuple width (182 bytes for a standard storage organization of the relations) is an unwieldy number for computations. This arbitrary length was intended to avoid giving any system an advantage through some fortuitous alignment of tuples in pages. However, it makes measurements harder to interpret and the database size harder to scale.

The structure and size of the relations also make scaling difficult. For instance, the 2 byte signed integer key restricts the maximum size of the database to 32,768 tuples. The Wisconsin test database is frequently too small, or too large, for the DBMS being tested.[2] A benchmark database should be designed to allow for systematic scaling of attribute ranges and values [Tur87]. In particular, it should be possible to model the same fixed selectivities (e.g., 100 tuples) and relative selectivities (e.g., 1% relation cardinality) for different database sizes.

---

1. Clearly, certain applications do not conform to this model. In particular, databases storing documents often contain text fields with hundreds or thousands of characters. Other engineering applications may have very large records.
2. In benchmarks of the Teradata and Gamma database machine, the *TenK* relation was scaled to 100,000 and 1,000,000 tuples [DGS88].

3. THE TEST QUERIES

The structure of the test database facilitates constructing relational queries with systematic control of selectivity and output size. For instance, the following SQL query retrieves 10% of the TenK relation:

*SELECT * FROM tenk*
WHERE unique2 < 1000 ;

Using the same ten thousand tuple relation, we can project a single attribute where 99% of the values are duplicates:

SELECT DISTINCT hundred FROM tenk ;

In order to isolate and explain the effect of different query parameters on response time we chose to vary only one parameter at a time with each test query, while setting other parameters to the following default values when possible:

1. 1,000 tuples in result.
2. All 16 attributes in the result.
3. Result output mode - result tuples inserted into a relation.
4. Integer attributes in selection predicates.
5. One relation queried - *TenK*.

In retrospect, the default result size should have been smaller than 1,000 tuples, and not all 16 attributes should have been included in the result tuples. Analyzing the results, these defaults sometimes confound the interpretation of the benchmark results (see Section 5). Furthermore, query predicates were always very simple, which made query optimization straightforward. In particular, selection predicates always used literals. Query optimization is more difficult when a predicate uses a program variable whose value is undefined when the access plan is chosen.

In the design of the test queries, three basic performance factors are varied: storage structure of the relation, indexing, and selectivity. To measure the effect of indexing, most test queries have three versions: one that uses no index, one that can take advantage of a primary index and one that can only use a secondary index. Typically, the two index variations are obtained by using the key, unique2, with the primary index, and the candidate key, unique1, with the secondary index. In retrospect, testing only single field indices was not sufficient and at least one multiattribute index should have been included.

In order to test the query processing algorithms, a *relational instruction set* including all types of relational queries and updates is composed:

1. Selections with different selectivities.
2. Projections with different percentages of duplicate attributes.
3. 2-way and 3-way joins.
4. Simple aggregates and aggregate functions.
5. Updates: insert, delete, update.

In total there are 32 test queries. The queries were originally phrased in Quel [BDT83]. Appendix B contains the literal translation of these queries into standard SQL [Dat87]. The performance factors that we intended to model with each test, and guidelines for analyzing the test results are described in detail below.

3.1 Selections

The speed at which a database system or machine can process a selection operation depends on a number of different factors including:

1. Hardware speed, architecture and quality of software.
2. Storage organization of the relation and indices.
3. Impact of the selectivity factor.
4. Query output mode.

The benchmark investigates the impact of these four factors. An important factor we missed was attribute type, particularly in testing the impact of specialized hardware. For instance, specialized hardware can speed up comparisons of variable length strings, an attribute type we omitted.

The storage organizations evaluated in the benchmark are representative of most DBMS's:

1. Sequential (heap) organization.
2. Primary clustered index. (Relation is sorted on key unique2.)
3. Clustered hashed index. (Tuple placement by hashing on key unique2. Used only for Query 7.)
4. Secondary, dense, non-clustered index (on unique1 and hundred).

In order to isolate the cost of formatting and displaying tuples to a user's terminal, the tests include selection queries that insert their result tuples into a relation (Queries 1 to 6, in Appendix B), and selections with output to the screen (Queries 7 and 8). The 6 selections into a relation model two levels of selectivity (1% and 10%) and three storage structures (no index, primary index, secondary index). The selections to the screen select 1 and 100 tuples.

In evaluating the performance of a system on these test selections, the following criteria should be applied. Selections into a relation clearly separate the impact of indexing from the effect of communication lines and display of tuples on a terminal screen. Thus the stand alone elapsed time of these queries should be close to the disk I/O time plus the CPU overhead required to read the source tuples and write the target tuples. The selections without indices would usually be ad-hoc queries, thus not necessarily fast. However, their response time should be close to the time it would take to read the TenK relation from the disk. In extent-based file systems, this time should be much lower that 500 random page accesses (assuming that the TenK relation is stored on 500, 4 K-byte pages). For selections with clustered indices, the response time should be that acceptable for a very short interactive query. In general, acceptable bounds for the response time of the selections with a non-clustered index should be close to the time required for one random disk access per tuple retrieved (that is less than 3 seconds per 100 tuples).

In order to obtain a measure of the time required for formatting and displaying tuples to a user terminal, selection queries are rephrased so that the result is displayed to a screen rather than inserted into a result relation. Comparison of the selections of 100 tuples with two different output modes (Query 3 and Query 8) provides an estimate for the time to format and display 100 result tuples. Retrieving the result to the screen can result in the response time being dominated by the time required to format data and transmit it to the screen. It is estimated that this takes about 15 msec per tuple with a high speed communication line to the terminal [Eps87].

3.2 Joins

In testing join queries two factors are of interest:

1. The basic join algorithms utilized by the query optimizer (e.g. nested-loops, sort-merge, or hashed join), and whether it takes advantage of a primary or secondary index when it is available.

2. The optimization of complex joins.

There are 3 test join queries, each with 3 versions corresponding to no index, a clustered index and a nonclustered index on the join attribute (Queries 9 to 17). In these joins, two source relations are always ten thousand tuple relations. When a selection is performed before the join, the size of the operand relation is reduced by a factor of ten. With a 1 megabyte buffer pool, ten thousand tuples of length 182 bytes in each source relation are enough to cause substantial I/O activity, and make visible the effect of varying input parameters (such as query complexity and join selectivity factors).

The join tests fail to adequately model important types of queries that a query optimizer would normally have to deal with. The 3 join queries are 1:1 joins, preceded by 0, 1, or 2 selections. The tests do not include outer joins, or sparse joins where techniques such as bit filtering can be used effectively.

Only one aspect of query optimization is modelled, by performing zero, one or two selection operations before the join:

1. JoinABprime (Query 9) joins A and Bprime.

2. JoinAselB (Query 10) selects on relation B and joins the selected relation with A.

3. JoinCselAselB (Query 11) involves two selections, followed by two joins.

Our objective was to systematically build a more complex query by adding joins and selections, and then to test the optimizer by executing the queries two ways: as one query and then as 2 queries executed in optimal order. If the query optimizer executed the queries correctly, the elapsed time required to execute a given join as one query should have been less than the time required to execute it as several queries. Unfortunately, as designed and reported in [BDT83], the query complexity was not built up systematically for several reasons [Tur87]:

1. The result composition differed from the default of 16 attributes. The 2- and 3-way joins retrieved 32 attributes, all of the attributes from two relations. This means that one join in the 3-way join was actually a semi-join. The result should have been composed 16 attributes from all three relations.

2. In the 2-way join (JoinAselB), two 10,000 tuple relations were used. In the 3-way join two 10,000 tuple relations and one 1,000 tuple relation were joined. To systematically build up join complexity, three 10,000 tuple relations should be used, and the result should have been composed from every relation in the join.

3. The time for compiling the queries was included in the elapsed time. This meant that when joinAselB, a select-join query, was broken into two queries; a selection (MakeBprime) followed by a join (JoinABprime), the elapsed time consisted of the time required to compile two queries instead of one. Hence, query compilation time was a confounding variable in these experiments [BT86, BHT87].

In measuring join queries on a number of systems, we found that, for joins more than for any other type of queries, each system's performance varies widely with the kind of assumptions that are made (e.g., indices versus no indices, special hardware versus no special hardware, complex versus simple join, etc.). For joins without indices, the performance of a system will be unacceptable (i.e., several hours) unless an appropriate algorithm, such as a sort-merge or hash join is used, or a join index is built on-the-fly. One curious anomaly that we observed on a number of systems is the fact that joinAselB (a selection followed by a join) may run faster than joinABprime (the same join without selection).

3.3 Projections

Tests for projections should evaluate the access method used by the query optimizer to eliminate duplicate tuples. Implementation of the projection operation is normally done in two phases. First a pass is made through the source relation to discard unwanted attributes. A second phase is necessary in order to eliminate any duplicate tuples that may have been introduced as a side effect of the first phase (i.e. elimination of an attribute which is the key or some part of the key). The first phase requires a complete scan of the relation. The second phase is usually performed by sorting or hashing. Secondary storage structures such as indices are not useful in performing this operation.

Although a comprehensive benchmark should include queries projecting on different types and subsets of attributes, we reported only the following two queries. The first query (Query 18, Appendix B) projects the 10,000 tuple relation with a projectivity factor of 1%. Thus, it eliminates 99% duplicate records and produces 100 tuples:

SELECT DISTINCT hundred FROM Tenk;

The second query (Query 19, Appendix B) is a projection of the 1,000 tuple relation, with a 100% projectivity factor:

*SELECT * FROM onek;*

The second query was included because the default result: 1,000 tuples, 16 attributes, 182,000 bytes, is identical to the relation *OneK*. Without duplicate elimination, projecting the 1,000 tuple relation allows us to isolate the cost of retrieving the default result from disk and outputting it; other than reading the data in and formatting it, no other query processing takes place. With duplicate elimination, this particular query provides us with an estimate for the cost of duplicate elimination involved in any retrieval "into" a result relation. In order to make this estimate as accurate as possible, it is desirable to minimize the time of getting the relation off the disk. This effect is partially achieved by actually running 10 copies of the same query in sequence, and dividing the total run time by 10. In retrospect, duplicate elimination should have been tested with a relation large enough to cause substantial I/O activity.

3.4 Aggregates

In testing aggregate queries, both simple aggregate operations (e.g., minimum value of an attribute) and complex aggregate functions should be considered. In an aggregate function, the tuples of a relation are first partitioned into non-overlapping subsets. After partitioning, an aggregate operation such as MIN is computed for each partition. The test queries for aggregates should test:

1. The algorithms used for aggregation.
2. Whether an index is effectively used, when it is available.

The tests include 3 aggregate queries, with 2 versions (no index, secondary index) for each query:

1. MIN Scalar Aggregate (Queries 20 and 24)
2. MIN Aggregate Function, 100 partitions (Queries 21 and 25)
3. SUM Aggregate Function, 100 partitions (Queries 22 and 26)

In retrospect, it would have been sufficient to include only one of the aggregate functions (either the MIN or SUM). The indexed scalar aggregate provides a straightforward test of whether the query optimizer attempts to use an available index in order to reduce the execution time of the queries. To compute the minimum on the key, a smart query optimizer would recognize that the query could be executed by using the index alone. For the two aggregate function queries, one should anticipate that any attempt to use the secondary, non-clustered index on the partitioning attribute would actually slow the query down as a scan of the complete relation through such an index will generally result in each data page being accessed several times. One alternative algorithm is to ignore the index, sort on the partitioning attribute and then make a final pass collecting the results. Another algorithm which works very well if the number of partitions is not too large is to make a single pass through the relation hashing on the partitioning attribute.

3.5 Updates

Test queries for updates should provide measures for:

1. the cost of updating a relation and the indices that exist on it
2. the overhead of concurrency control and recovery.

These costs are only partially measured by our update tests. Only four simple update queries are included in the benchmark:

1. Insert 1 tuple
2. Update key of 1 tuple
3. Update non key attribute of 1 tuple
4. Delete 1 tuple

The queries are run first with no index available, then with indices built on the relation TenK. In order to account for the cost of updating indices in a significant way, three indices are built, one primary index and two secondary indices,

The response time for these update queries in their 2 versions (without and with indices) should give some indication of whether the advantage of having an index to help locate the tuple being modified outweighs the cost of updating the index. However, these simple update tests fail to adequately evaluate a system's ability to deal with a number of important problems:

1. Updating different indices, in simple and bulk updates.
2. The *Halloween Problem* [Tan87].
3. Validity checking.
4. Concurrency control and recovery.

With only four single tuple updates, not enough updates are performed to cause a significant reorganization of the index pages. In particular, insertions are only performed at the end of a column's range. To allow insertions in other positions would require changing the range of at least one candidate key, so that some values within the range are missing (in the Wisconsin test database, the range is from 0 to 9,999 and all values are present in the relation).

Bulk updates, e.g., insertions and deletions of a set of 1,000 tuples should also have been included. In a benchmark of the main memory database system *OBE* [BT86], bulk insertions and deletions quantified the long delays required to update a fully inverted structure of relations. For *OBE* running on an IBM 3081, it took 140 seconds to delete 1,000 tuples from the TenK relation, compared to .24 seconds to delete 1 tuple.

In order to isolate differences in the cost of updating different indices, it is desirable to have the selection predicate on an attribute other than the attribute updated. Otherwise, the cost of updating a particular index is confounded with the cost of selecting the tuple to be updated.

The updates with indices have been criticized for impersonating the *Halloween Problem* [Tan87], which applies to queries of the form:

UPDATE payroll
SET salary = salary + 1;

If this query uses an index ascending on salary, then it will try to give all employees an infinite raise. A simplistic approach to avoid this problem is to refuse to use an index on a field that is mentioned in an update clause. This fix may impose an unnecessary performance penalty. In particular, the following query in the Wisconsin benchmark is not an instance of the Halloween Problem, although it has been treated as such by some systems:

```
/* Update key of 1 tuple, clustered index available on key */
UPDATE TenK1
SET unique2 = 10002
    WHERE unique2 = 10001;
```

An interesting observation in some systems can be the low cost of the insert compared to the cost of the delete. The explanation for this discrepancy is that new tuples are often inserted without checking if they are not already present in the relation. Thus, inserting a tuple only involves writing a new tuple, while deleting a tuple requires scanning the entire relation first. Clearly, in this case, the gain in performance is at the expense of validity checking. Additional test queries should have been included to explicitly account for validity checking, and measure its cost.

Finally, a more realistic evaluation of update queries would require running these tests in a multiprogramming environment, so that the effects of concurrency control could be measured.

4. THE TEST ENVIRONMENT

The benchmark was originally designed to compare the performance of one of the first commercially available database machines, the Britton Lee IDM500, with software database systems running on general purpose computers. To make the comparison as fair as possible, we placed the following restrictions on the hardware and system configuration in the test environment:

1. A 1 to 2 MIPS CPU such as the Vax 780 or IBM 4341.
2. A 1 megabyte main memory buffer pool.
3. 2 disks comparable to the Fujitsu Eagle: one for the database relations and one for the system including database software.
4. No concurrency control or logging.

The size of the test database (5 megabytes, with 1.8 megabytes for the default relation) was specified for a 1-megabyte buffer pool. The buffer pool was cleared between tests by scanning a large relation unrelated to the subsequent test. When normalizing disk configurations, our criterion was that the 1.8 megabyte relation should be read from disk in 8 to 10 seconds. The tests were run without concurrency control enabled; no logging occurred. If we had enable concurrency control, an additional disk for logging would have been required.

In retrospect, we should have had an additional disk to store the results of queries when the output was inserted into a relation. By storing large results on the same disk as the queried relations, sequential scans of relations were interrupted by writes to the result relation. In addition, we should have included queries with the concurrency control and recovery manager enabled, in order to measure the overhead associated with these functions. This would have required an additional disk for logging. An important factor to be considered in comparing systems and interpreting the results is the granularity of locking (record, page, or relation locks).

5. PERFORMANCE METRICS

The only metric considered in the Wisconsin benchmark is the elapsed time of each of the 32 test queries. Clearly other metrics, measuring database setup time and memory requirements, should be of interest.

5.1 Query Response Time

We ran multiple instances of a single query in each test and computed the average response time. The test queries are run in single user stand alone mode. In this mode, query response time is given by the elapsed time on the host machine. In single user, stand alone mode, the response time for a query is a reliable and valid measure of the minimum response time for a query, with one qualification. The true minimum response time for a query occurs when all of the necessary data for a query is already in main memory. This situation should be avoided by insuring that useful data from previous queries was not left in database buffers. We did this by alternately referencing two different copies of the TenK relation in successive queries in each test. (See Appendix B.)

5.2 Other Metrics

Other metrics of interest are the database setup time, and the time for building indices. The Wisconsin benchmark did not consider these metrics. Measures for the time to load or unload relations could have been obtained with tests of bulk updates. For example, the Teradata machine, which distributes relations to multiple processes and disks, redistributed and inserted tuples at a rate of 100 tuples per second [DGS88].

5.3 Confounding Variables

In initial tests, we found that our experiments were confounded; that is, unanticipated factors interfered with our analysis of the results. We will briefly discuss three of these confounding factors: DBMS overhead, query output mode, and duplicate elimination.

5.3.1 DBMS Overhead

For a particular test the impact of system overhead, such as the open database command, is diminished by running 10 versions of the same query in sequence and then taking the average time. For instance, to select 1 tuple on the key of the relation TenK, 10 different predicates are chosen using a table of random numbers. A more systematic way to isolate this overhead would be by running a *null query* on a table T that contains only 1 tuple [Tur87]:

SELECT x from T where x = 0 ;

5.3.2 Query Output Mode and Duplicate Elimination

There are three alternative ways of measuring the time required for a query: writing them into a relation on disk, writing them into a system file or sending them to the user's screen. Defaults for DBMS's vary as to whether duplicate elimination is performed with different output modes. Using the ANSI Standard SQL, this problem can be avoided by specifying DISTINCT or ALL in the retrieval predicate.

6. BENCHMARK RESULTS AND ANALYSIS

Since the Wisconsin benchmark was originally run, in 1983, both hardware and DBMS software have changed significantly. Hence, the performance numbers that were reported in [BDT83] are no longer representative of current releases of the same systems and of other commercial systems not included in the original benchmark. To provide a new baseline for comparison of benchmark measurements, more current numbers from three commercial systems are presented in Appendix C of this paper. Unlike in the original benchmark, we have made no attempt at normalizing the hardware and system configurations. For instance, two of the systems are software database systems running on a single CPU general purpose machine; the third is a parallel backend database machine configured with 24 processors [DGS88]. Furthermore, all three systems were tested with concurrency control and logging enabled.

In Appendix C, as in the original benchmark, the only measurement reported is the elapsed time for a query. This limits the conclusions that can be drawn from the data. On the basis of elapsed time only, and without additional information, such as the amount of paging, CPU and disk utilization, it is not possible to isolate the cause of unexpectedly high elapsed times for even simple queries, such as selections involving a relation scan. Other related work [Eps87, Rub87] suggests that current implementations of disk database systems are CPU intensive.

In analyzing the elapsed time for queries, it is important (but not always possible) to know the query execution plan chosen by the query optimizer. In the absence of this information, one number that serves as a fundamental indication of system performance is the time to scan a relation. The easiest way to measure this is to force a relation scan by selecting 1 tuple on a relation with no relevant indices available. While this test was included in the original suite of benchmark tests, it was unfortunately not reported in [BDT83]. The closest number reported is for Query 1, a selection retrieving 100 tuples, with no index available (see Appendix C).

In Table 2, we present computed and measured time bounds for scanning the 10,000 tuple test relation TenK. The first four rows consider I/O time for reading the relation from disk. We consider both sequential and random I/O. The next 3 rows consider the CPU time required to process 10,000 tuples. Table 2 contains both computed and measured numbers. The measurements are of the *OBE* system [BT86, BHT87] which is a prototype of a main memory database system (MMDBS). In benchmarking OBE, we were able to isolate both the elapsed time to sequentially read the TenK relation in from disk and the pure CPU time required to scan the same relation when it was entirely resident in main memory. The computed sequential I/O time in row 1 is the time to transfer 1.82 megabytes at 3 megabytes per second (the raw data rate of the IBM 3380 disk). The measured sequential I/O time in row 2 is the elapsed time for OBE, under the VM operating system on an IBM 3081, to read 1.82 megabytes from a 3380 disk. The computed random I/O times in rows 3 and 4 correspond to reading the relation with 1 random disk access per 4096 byte block. In rows 5 and 6, we show the CPU time required to scan the memory resident relation TenK on an IBM 3081 and an IBM 4341. The 4341 is a 1.4 MIPS machine that is comparable to the processors on which the original benchmark was run. In row 7, the computed CPU time is based on a crude estimate of 1 millisecond (1,000 instructions on a 1 MIPS machine) per tuple processed. In a conventional database system, as opposed to an MMDBS, this time includes DBMS and operating system overhead for disk I/O.

The computed and measured times in Table 2 for scanning the relation TenK range from .6 to 13.65 seconds. In our experience, on single CPU conventional database systems, the fastest the relation 10K was scanned was 8 seconds (see Appendix C, Query 1).

TABLE 2. I/O and CPU Time for Scanning TenK Relation

	Source	Parameters	Seconds
1.	Computed Sequential I/O	3 Mbyte/sec	0.60
2.	Measured Sequential I/O	IBM 3380	1.28
3.	Computed Random I/O	15ms/access	6.60
4.	Computed Random I/O	30ms/access	13.65
5.	Measured CPU Time	IBM 3081	0.59
6.	Measured CPU Time	IBM 4341	3.10
7.	Computed CPU Time	1 ms/tuple	10.00

7. SUMMARY

We have described and motivated the design of the test database and queries in a widely used benchmark, the Wisconsin benchmark. Pointing out a number of design flaws, we have indicated limitations in the levels of the following performance factors that the benchmark considers:

1. Attribute types and distributions: Only 2-byte integers and fixed length character strings, all uniformly distributed, are included.

2. Relation size and structure: The test database is 5 megabytes and is not properly structured for scaling.

3. Query set: Important query types, in particular certain types of joins and updates, are missing.

The popularity of the benchmark is based on the availability of performance measurements from other systems, which allows for quick comparisons between systems. However, the benchmark should be seen mainly as a tool for debugging systems. The workload represented by the benchmark is not representative of real world workloads. Parameters chosen for the database and test queries were deliberately limited in order to focus on benchmarking methodology. Furthermore, a number of factors that confound the analysis of the benchmark were inadvertently introduced in the design of the tests: query-parsing time, large result size (1,000 tuples in most queries), and inappropriate selection predicates.

The only metric considered is the stand alone query-elapsed time. Measurements obtained in single user mode can provide useful information to the system designer when they isolate the performance of access methods, query-processing algorithms, effect of special hardware, or special operating system features. However, they only provide a best case estimate for query response time in an underutilized resource environment. As such, these measurements only constitute a baseline and cannot be considered as realistic approximations of what query response time will be in a real environment.

The Wisconsin benchmark should be viewed as an experiment in benchmarking methodology. It has been useful as one point of reference for debugging and comparing database systems. However, it is not a comprehensive tool for making fair and precise comparisons between systems.

ACKNOWLEDGEMENTS

We would like to thank Jim Gray for his thorough and insightful comments on multiple versions of this paper.

REFERENCES

[Ano85] Anon et al., "A Measure of Transaction Processing Power," *Datamation*, 1985.

[BDT83] Bitton D., DeWitt D.J., and Turbyfill C., "Benchmarking Database Systems, a Systematic Approach," *Proc. Ninth International Conf. on Very Large Data Bases*, November 1983. (Also University of Wisconsin Technical Report CS-TR 526, December 1983.)

[BT84] Bitton D. and Turbyfill C., "Design and Analysis of Multiuser Benchmarks for Database Systems," *Technical Report 84-589*, Cornell University, 1984. (also appeared in *Proc. HICSS-18*, January 1985).

[BD85] Boral H. and DeWitt D.J., "A Methodology for Benchmarking Database Systems," *Proc. ACM Sigmod*, June 1984.

[BT86] Bitton D. and Turbyfill C., "Performance Evaluation of Main Memory Database Systems," *Technical Report 86-731*, Cornell University, 1986.

[BHT87] Bitton D., Hanrahan M., and C. Turbyfill, "Performance of Complex Queries in Main Memory Database Systems," *Proc. Third International Conf. on Data Engineering*, Los Angeles, February 1987.

[Dat87] Date, C.J., *A Guide to the SQL Standard*, Addison-Wesley, Menlo Park, Ca., 1987.

[DGS88] DeWitt D.J, Ghandeharizadeh S., and Schneider D., "A Performance Analysis of the Gamma Database Machine," *Technical Report CS-TR 742*, University of Wisconsin, January 1988.

[Eps87] Epstein R., "Today's Technology is producing High-Performance Relational Database Systems," *Sybase Newsletter*, 1987.

[Rub87] Rubenstein et al., "Benchmarking Simple Database Operations," *Proc. ACM Sigmod*, June 1987.

[Tan87] Tandem Database Group, "Non Stop SQL," Tandem Technical Report 87.4, 1987.

[Tur87] Turbyfill C., "Comparative Benchmarking of Relational Database Systems," *Ph.D. Dissertation*, Technical Report 87-871, Cornell University, September 1987.

APPENDIX A

SQL SCHEMA FOR THE WISCONSIN BENCHMARK

Notes:

1. Block size and extent size are system dependent.
2. Wisconsin benchmark used a scratch disk to load test database.
3. The original benchmark used SMALLINT (2 bytes) instead of INTEGER for all numeric data types.
4. Tables must also be created for queries that retrieve into relations, (e.g., Bprime is declared like OneK).
5. For queries without indices, organization for each table is heap. For queries with indices, organization is a primary clustered index on unique2, a nonclustered index on unique1 and a nonclustered index on hundred.

```
CREATE TABLE onek
  (unique1        INTEGER NOT NULL,
   unique2        INTEGER NOT NULL PRIMARY KEY,
   two            INTEGER NOT NULL,
   four           INTEGER NOT NULL,
   ten            INTEGER NOT NULL,
   twenty         INTEGER NOT NULL,
   hundred        INTEGER NOT NULL,
   thousand       INTEGER NOT NULL,
   twothousand    INTEGER NOT NULL,
   fivethous      INTEGER NOT NULL,
   tenthous       INTEGER NOT NULL,
   odd            INTEGER NOT NULL,
   even           INTEGER NOT NULL,
   stringu1       CHARACTER(52) NOT NULL,
   stringu2       CHARACTER(52) NOT NULL,
   string4        CHARACTER(52) NOT NULL)
CREATE TABLE tenk1
  (unique1        INTEGER NOT NULL,
   unique2        INTEGER NOT NULL PRIMARY KEY,
   two            INTEGER NOT NULL,
   four           INTEGER NOT NULL,
   ten            INTEGER NOT NULL,
   twenty         INTEGER NOT NULL,
   hundred        INTEGER NOT NULL,
   thousand       INTEGER NOT NULL,
   twothousand    INTEGER NOT NULL,
   fivethous      INTEGER NOT NULL,
   tenthous       INTEGER NOT NULL,
   odd            INTEGER NOT NULL,
   even           INTEGER NOT NULL,
   stringu1       CHARACTER(52) NOT NULL,
   stringu2       CHARACTER(52) NOT NULL,
   string4        CHARACTER(52) NOT NULL)

CREATE TABLE tenk2
                  /* same structure as tenk1 */
```

```
--QUERY 8 (clustered index)
--Selection with 1% selectivity factor
--Retrieve to screen
select * from tenk1
where (tenk1.unique2 > 301) and (tenk1.unique2 < 402)

--QUERIES 9 (no index) and 12 (clustered index)
--JoinAselB
insert into temp
select * from tenk1, tenk2
where (tenk1.unique2 = tenk2.unique2)
and (tenk2.unique2 < 1000)

--QUERY MakeBprime
insert into Bprime
select * from tenk1
where tenk1.unique2 < 1000

--QUERIES 10 (no index) and 13 (clustered index)
--JoinABprime
insert into temp
select * from tenk1, Bprime
where tenk1.unique2 = Bprime.unique2

--QUERIES 11 (no index) and 14 (clustered index)
--JoinCselAselB
insert into temp
select * from onek, tenk1
where (onek.unique2 = tenk1.unique2)
and (tenk1.unique2 = tenk2.unique2)
and (tenk1.unique2 < 1000) and (tenk2.unique2 < 1000)

--QUERY 15 (nonclustered index)
--sJoinAselB: "s" = secondary index
insert into temp
select * from tenk1, tenk2
where (tenk1.unique1 = tenk2.unique1)
and (tenk2.unique1 < 1000)

--QUERY 16 (nonclustered index)
--sJoinABprime: "s" = secondary index
insert into temp
select * from tenk1, Bprime
where tenk1.unique1 = Bprime.unique1

--QUERY 17 (nonclustered index)
--sJoinCselAselB: "s" = secondary index
insert into temp
select * from onek, tenk1
where (onek.unique1 = tenk1.unique1)
and (tenk1.unique1 = tenk2.unique1)
and (tenk1.unique1 < 1000) and (tenk2.unique1 < 1000)
```

APPENDIX B

THE 32 TEST QUERIES

Notes:

1. 10 variants of all selection, insert, update, and delete queries used (see Section 5.1). For instance, for query1 the first four variants used the selection predicates:

   "... where tenk1.unique2 < 100"
   "... where tenk2.unique2 > 9899"
   "... where (tenk1.unique2 > 301) and (tenk1.unique2 < 402)"
   "... where (tenk2.unique2 > 675) and (tenk2.unique2 < 776)"

   Only one variant of each query shown below.

2. Available indices indicated: clustered index on unique2, nonclustered index on unique1, and nonclustered index on hundred.

3. "temp" is used as generic name for result relation when result is retrieved into relation.

4. Queries 1, 2, 3, 4, 5, 6, and 8 are range selections. The "between" predicate in SQL could be used to express conjunctions of 2 range predicates as 1 predicate in these queries.

```
--QUERIES 1 (no index) and 3 (clustered index)
--Selection with 1% selectivity factor
insert into temp
select * from tenk1
where (tenk1.unique2 > 301) and (tenk1.unique2 < 402)

--QUERIES 2 (no index) and 4 (clustered index)
--Selection with 10% selectivity factor
insert into temp
select * from tenk1
where (tenk1.unique2 > 647) and (tenk1.unique2 < 1648)

--QUERY 5 (nonclustered index)
--Selection with 1% selectivity
insert into temp
select * from tenk1
where (tenk1.unique1 > 301) and (tenk1.unique1 < 402)

--QUERY 6 (nonclustered index)
--Selection with 10% selectivity factor
insert into temp
select * from tenk1
where (tenk1.unique1 > 647) and (tenk1.unique1 < 1648)

--QUERY 7 (clustered index)
--can use clustered hashed index if available
--Select 1 tuple to screen
select * from tenk1 where tenk1.unique2 = 2001
```

```
--QUERY 18
--Projection with 1% selectivity factor
insert into temp
select distinct two, four, ten, twenty, hundred, string4
from tenk1
--QUERY 19
--Project all of onek
insert into temp
select * from onek
--QUERIES 20 (no indices) and 23 (with indices)
--Minimum scalar aggregate
insert into temp
select min(tenk1.unique2)
from tenk1
--QUERIES 21 (no indices) and 24 (with indices)
--Minimum aggregate function
insert into temp
select min(tenk1.twothous)
from tenk1
group by tenk1.hundred
--QUERIES 22 (no indices) and 25 (with indices)
--Sum aggregate function
insert into temp
select sum(tenk1.twothous)
from tenk1
group by tenk1.hundred
--QUERIES 27 (no indices) and 30 (with indices)
--Delete 1 tuple
delete from tenk1
where tenk1.unique2 = 10001
--QUERIES 28 (no indices) and 31 (with indices)
--Update key
update tenk1
set unique2 = 10001
where tenk1.unique2 = 1491
--QUERY 32
--Update indexed nonkey attribute
update tenk1
set unique1 = 10001
where tenk1.unique1 = 1491
--QUERIES 26 (no indices) and 29 (with indices)
--Insert 1 tuple
Insert into tenk1
values (10001,74,0,2,0,10,50,688,1950,4950,9950,1,100,
MxxxxxxxxxxxxxxxxxxxxxxxxxGxxxxxxxxxxxxxxxxxxxxxxxxC,
GxxxxxxxxxxxxxxxxxxxxxxxxxCxxxxxxxxxxxxxxxxxxxxxxxxA,
OxxxxxxxxxxxxxxxxxxxxxxxxxOxxxxxxxxxxxxxxxxxxxxxxxxO)
```

APPENDIX C

RECENT NUMBERS FOR WISCONSIN BENCHMARK QUERIES

Elapsed time in seconds on:
Software System "X" on IBM 4341
Software System "Y" on IBM 4381
Teradata Database Machine

Query	IBM 4341	IBM 4381	Teradata
1	15	8.8	6.7
2	37	20	15.1
3	3.2	1.3	6.7
4	28	7.7	16
5	12	2.7	7.8
6	39	15	17
7	0.8	0.2	-
8	4	0.9	-
9	132	185	35
10	132	1000	36
11	126	1000	28
12	55	15	22
13	65	16	25
14	80	22	24
15	97	31	35
16	84	32	38
17	160	39	27
18	29	110	-
19	29	18	-
20	20	14	6
21	22	98	8.7
22	24	98	8.9
23	8.5	10	4.2
24	23	105	-
25	24	102	-
26	0.6	0.2	0.9
27	12	10	-
28	12	5.8	-
29	0.7	0.2	0.9
30	0.6	0.1	0.7
31	13	6	2.6
32	13	6	0.5

A Measure of Transaction Processing Power

Anon Et Al

February 1985

ABSTRACT

Three benchmarks are defined: Sort, Scan and DebitCredit. The first two benchmarks measure a system's input/output performance. DebitCredit is a simple transaction processing application used to define a throughput measure -- Transactions Per Second (TPS). These benchmarks measure the performance of diverse transaction processing systems. A standard system cost measure is stated and used to define price/performance metrics.

TABLE OF CONTENTS

Who Needs Performance Metrics?

A measure of transaction processing power is needed -- a standard which can measure and compare the throughput and price/performance of various transaction processing systems.

Vendors of transaction processing systems quote Transaction Per Second (TPS) rates for their systems. But there isn't a standard transaction, so it is difficult to verify or compare these TPS claims. In addition, there is no accepted way to price a system supporting a desired TPS rate. This makes it impossible to compare the price/performance of different systems.

The performance of a transaction processing system depends heavily on the system input/output architecture, data communications architecture and even more importantly on the efficiency of the system software. Traditional computer performance metrics, Whetstones, MIPS, MegaFLOPS and GigaLIPS, focus on CPU speed. These measures do not capture the features that make one transaction processing system faster or cheaper than another.

This is Tandem Technical Report TR85.2. A condensed version of this paper appears in Datamation, April 1, 1985

This paper is an attempt by two dozen people active in transaction processing to write down the folklore we use to measure system performance. The authors include academics, vendors, and users. A condensation of this paper appears in Datamation (April 1, 1985).

We rate a transaction processing system's performance and price/performance by:

* Performance is quantified by measuring the elapsed time for two standard batch transactions and throughput for an interactive transaction.

* Price is quantified as the five-year capital cost of the system equipment exclusive of communications lines, terminals, development and operations.

* Price/Performance is the ratio Price over Performance.

These measures also gauge the peak performance and performance trends of a system as new hardware and software is introduced. This is a valuable aid to system pricing, sales and purchase.

We rate a transaction processing system by its performance on three generic operations:

* A simple interactive transaction.
* A minibatch transaction which updates a small batch of records.
* A utility which does bulk data movement.

This simplistic position is similar to Gibson's observation that if you can load and store quickly, you have a fast machine [Gibson].

We believe this simple benchmark is adequate because:

* The interactive transaction forms the basis for the TPS rating. It is also a litmus test for transaction processing systems -- it requires the system have at least minimal presentation services, transaction recovery, and data management.

* The minibatch transaction tells the IO performance available to the Cobol programmer. It tells us how fast the end-user IO software is.

* The utility program is included to show what a really tricky programmer can squeeze out of the system. It tells us how fast the real IO architecture is. On most systems, the utilities trick the IO software into giving the raw IO device performance with almost no software overhead.

In other words, we believe these three benchmarks indicate the performance of a transaction processing system because the utility benchmark gauges the IO hardware, the minibatch benchmark gauges the IO software and the interactive transaction gauges the performance of the online transaction processing system.

The particular programs chosen here have become part of the folklore of computing. Increasingly, they are being used to compare system performance from release to release and in some cases, to compare the price/performance of different vendor's transaction processing systems.

The basic benchmarks are:

DebitCredit: A banking transaction interacts with a block-mode terminal connected via X.25. The system does presentation services to map the input for a Cobol program which in turn uses a database system to debit a bank account, do the standard double entry book-keeping and then reply to the terminal. 95% of the transactions must provide one second response time. Relevant measures are throughput and cost.

Scan: A minibatch Cobol transaction sequentially scans and updates one thousand records. A duplexed transaction log is automatically maintained for transaction recovery. Relevant measures are elapsed time, and cost.

Sort: A disc sort of one million records. The source and target files are sequential. Relevant measures are elapsed time, and cost.

A word of caution: these are performance metrics, not function metrics. They make minimal demands on the network (only x.25 and very minimal presentation services), transaction processing (no distributed data), data management (no complex data structures), and recovery management (no duplexed or distributed data).

Most of us have spent our careers making high-function systems. It is painful to see a metric which rewards simplicity -- simple systems are faster than fancy ones. We really wish this were a function benchmark. It isn't.

Surprisingly, these minimal requirements disqualify many purported transaction processing systems, but there is a very wide spectrum of function and useability among the systems that have these minimal functions.

Our Performance and Price Metrics

What is meant by the terms: elapsed time, cost and throughput? Before getting into any discussion of these issues, you must get the right attitude. These measures are very rough. As the Environmental Protection Agency says about its milage ratings, "Your actual performance may vary depending on driving habits, road conditions and queue lengths -- use them for comparison purposes only". This cavalier attitude is required for the rest of this paper and for performance metrics in general -- if you don't believe this, reconsider EPA milage ratings for cars.

So, what is meant by the terms: elapsed time, cost and throughput?

ELAPSED TIME

Elapsed Time is the wall-clock time required to do the operation on an otherwise empty system. It is a very crude performance measure but it is both intuitive and indicative. It gives an optimistic performance measure. In a real system, things never go that fast, but someone got it to go that fast once.

COST

Cost is a much more complex measure. Anyone involved with an accounting system appreciates this. What should be included? Should it include the cost of communications lines, terminals, application development, personnel, facilities, maintenance, etc.? Ideally, cost would capture the entire "cost-of-ownership". It is very hard to measure cost-of-ownership. We take a myopic vendor's view: cost is the 5-year capital cost of vendor supplied hardware and software in the machine room. It does not include terminal cost, communications costs, application development costs or operations costs. It does include hardware and software purchase, installation and maintenance charges.

This cost measure is typically one fifth of the total cost-of-ownership. We take this narrow view of cost because it is simple. One can count the hardware boxes and software packages. Each has a price in the price book. Computing this cost is a matter of inventory and arithmetic.

A benchmark is charged for the resources it uses rather than the entire system cost. For example, if the benchmark runs for an hour, we charge it for an hour. This in turn requires a way to measure system cost/hour rather than just system cost. Rather than get into discussions of the cost of money, we normalize the discussion by ignoring interest and imagine that the system is straight-line depreciated over 5 years. Hence an hour costs about 2E-5 of the five year cost and a second costs about 5E-9 of the five year cost.

Utilization is another tough issue. Who pays for overhead? The answer we adopt is a simple one: the benchmark is charged for all operating system activity. Similarly, the disc is charged for all disc activity, either direct (e.g. application input/output) or indirect (e.g. paging).

To make this specific, lets compute the cost of a sort benchmark which runs for an hour, uses 2 megabytes of memory and two discs and their controllers.

Package	Package cost	Per hour cost	Benchmark cost
Processor	80K$	1.8$	1.8$
Memory	15K$	.3$	.3$
Disc	50K$	1.1$	1.1$
Software	50K$	1.1$	1.1$

			4.3$

So the cost is 4.3$ per sort.

The people who run the benchmark are free to configure it for minimum cost or minimum time. They may pick a fast processor, add or drop memory, channels or other accelerators. In general the minimum-elapsed-time system is not the minimum-cost system. For example, the minimum cost Tandem system for Sort is a one processor two disc system. Sort takes about 30 minutes at a cost of 1.5$. On the other hand, we believe a 16 processor two disc Tandem system with 8Mbytes per processor could do Sort within ten minutes for about 15$ -- six times faster and 10 times as expensive. In the IBM world, minimum cost generally comes with model 4300 processors, minimum time generally comes with 308x processors.

The macho performance measure is throughput -- how much work the system can do per second. MIPS, GigaLIPS and MegaFLOPS are all throughput measures. For transaction processing, transactions per second (TPS) is the throughput measure.

A standard definition of the unit transaction is required to make the TPS metric concrete. We use the DebitCredit transaction as such a unit transaction.

To normalize the TPS measure, most of the transactions must have less than a specified response time. To eliminate the issue of communication line speed and delay, response time is defined as the time interval between the arrival of the last bit from the communications line and the sending of the first bit to the communications line. This is the metric used by most teleprocessing stress testers.

Hence the Transactions Per Second (TPS) unit is defined as:

TPS: Peak DebitCredit transactions per second with 95% of the transactions having less than one second response time.

Having defined the terms: elapsed time, cost and throughput, we can now define the various benchmarks.

The Sort Benchmark

The sort benchmark measures the performance possible with the best programmers using all the mean tricks in the system. It is an excellent test of the input-output architecture of a computer and its operating system.

The definition of the sort benchmark is simple. The input is one-million hundred-byte records stored in a sequential disc file. The first ten bytes of each record are the key. The keys of the input file are in random order. The sort program creates an output file and fills it with the input file sorted in key order. The sort may use as many scratch discs and as much memory as it likes.

Implementors of sort care about seeks, disc io, compares, and such. Users only care how long it takes and how much it costs. From the user's viewpoint, relevant metrics are:

Elapsed time: the time from the start to the end of the sort program.

Cost: the time weighted cost of the sort software, the software and hardware packages it uses.

In theory, a fast machine with 100mb memory could do the job in a minute at a cost of 20$. In practice, elapsed times range from 10 minutes to 10 hours and costs between 1$ and 100$. A one hour 10$ sort is typical of good commercial systems.

The Scan Benchmark

The Sort benchmark indicates what sequential performance a wizard can get out of the system. The Scan benchmark indicates the comparable performance available to end-users: Cobol programmers. The difference is frequently a factor of five or ten.

The Scan benchmark is based on a Cobol program which sequentially scans a sequential file, reading and updating each record. Such scans are typical of end-of-day processing in online transaction processing systems. The total scan is broken into minibatch transactions each of which scans one thousand records. Each minibatch transaction is a Scan transaction.

The input is a sequential file of 100 byte records stored on one disc. Because the data is online, Scan cannot get exclusive access to the file and cannot use old-master new-master recovery techniques. Scan must use fine granularity locking so that concurrent access to other parts of the file is possible while Scan is running. Updates to the file must be protected by a system maintained duplexed log which can be used to reconstruct the file in case of failure.

Scan must be written in Cobol, PLI or some other end-user application interface. It must use the standard IO library of the system and otherwise behave as a good citizen with portable and maintainable code. Scan cannot use features not directly supported by the language.

The transaction flow is:

```
    OPEN file SHARED, RECORD LOCKING
    PERFORM SCAN 1000 TIMES
                BEGIN -- Start of Scan Transaction
                BEGIN-TRANSACTION
                PERFORM 1000 TIMES
                  READ file NEXT RECORD record WITH LOCK
                  REWRITE record
                COMMIT-TRANSACTION
                END  -- End of Scan Transaction
   CLOSE FILE
```

The relevant measures of Scan are:

Elapsed time: The average time between successive BeginTransaction steps. If the data is buffered in main memory, the flush to disc must be included.

Cost: the time weighted system cost of Scan.

In theory, a fast machine with a conventional disc and flawless software could do Scan in .1 second. In practice elapsed times range from 1 second to 100 seconds while costs range from .001$ to .1$. Commercial systems execute scan for a penny with ten second elapsed time.

The DebitCredit Benchmark

The Sort and Scan benchmarks have the virtue of simplicity. They can be ported to a system in a few hours if it has a reasonable software base -- a sort utility, Cobol compiler and a transactional file system. Without this base, there is not much sense considering the system for transaction processing.

The DebitCredit transaction is a more difficult benchmark to describe or port -- it can take a day or several months to install depending on the available tools. On the other hand, it is the simplest application we can imagine.

A little history explains how DebitCredit became a de facto standard. In 1973 a large retail bank wanted to put its 1,000 branches, 10,000 tellers and 10,000,000 accounts online. They wanted to run a peak load of 100 transactions per second against the system. They also wanted high availability (central system availability of 99.5%) with two data centers.

The bank got two bids, one for 5M$ from a minicomputer vendor and another for 25M$ from a major-computer vendor. The mini solution was picked and built [Good]. It had a 50K$/TPS cost whereas the other system had a 250K$/TPS cost. This event crystalized the concept of cost/TPS. A generalization (and elaboration) of the bread-and-butter transaction to support those 10,000 tellers has come to be variously known as the TP1, ET1 or DebitCredit transaction [Gray].

In order to make the transaction definition portable and explicit, we define some extra details, namely the communication protocol (x.25) and presentation services.

The DebitCredit application has a database consisting of four record types. History records are 50 bytes, others are 100 bytes.

```
* 1,000 branches        ( .1 Mb,   random access )
* 10,000 tellers        ( 1  Mb    random access)
* 10,000,000 accounts   ( 1  Gb    random access)
* a 90 day history      ( 10 Gb    sequential   ).
```

The transaction has the flow:

```
DebitCredit:
  BEGIN-TRANSACTION
  READ     MESSAGE FROM TERMINAL (100 bytes)
  REWRITE ACCOUNT    (random)
  WRITE    HISTORY   (sequential)
  REWRITE TELLER     (random)
  REWRITE BRANCH     (random)
  WRITE    MESSAGE TO  TERMINAL (200 bytes)
  COMMIT-TRANSACTION
```

A few more things need to be said about the transaction. Branch keys are generated randomly. Then a teller within the branch is picked at random. Then a random account at the branch is picked 85% of the time and a random account at a different branch is picked 15% of the time. Account keys are 10 bytes, the other keys can be short. All data files must be protected by fine granularity locking and logging. The log file for transaction recovery must be duplexed to tolerate single failures, data files need not be duplexed. 95% of the transactions must give at least one second response time. Message handling should deal with a block-mode terminal (eg IBM 3270) with a base screen of 20 fields. Ten of these fields are read, mapped by presentation services and then remapped and written as part of the reply. The line protocol is x.25.

The benchmark scales as follows. Tellers have 100 second think times on average. So at 10TPS, store only a tenth of the database. At 1TPS store one hundredth of the database. At one teller, store only one ten thousandth of the database and run .01 TPS.

Typical costs for DebitCredit appear below. These numbers come from real systems, hence the anomaly that the lean-and-mean system does too many disc ios. Identifying these systems makes an interesting parlor game.

	K-inst	IO	TPS	K$/TPS	¢/T	Packets
Lean and Mean	20	6	400	40	.02	2
Fast	50	4	100	60	.03	2
Good	100	10	50	80	.04	2
Common	300	20	15	150	.75	4
Funny	1000	20	1	400	2.0	8

The units in the table are:

K-inst: The number of thousands of instructions to run the transaction. You might think that adding 10$ to your bank account is a single instruction (add). Not so, one system needs a million instructions to do that add. Instructions are expressed in 370 instructions or their equivalent and are fuzzy numbers for non-370 systems.

DiscIO: The number of disc io required to run the transaction. The fast system does two database IO and two log writes.

TPS: Maximum Transactions Per Second you can run before the largest system saturates (response time exceeds one second). This is a throughput measure. The good system peaks at 50 transactions per second.

K$/TPS: Cost per transaction per second. This is just system cost divided by TPS. It is a simple measure to compute. The funny system costs 400K$ per transaction per second. That is, it costs 400K$ over 5 years and can barely run one transaction per second with one second response time. The cost/transaction for these systems is .5E-8 times the K$/TPS.

¢/T: Cost per transaction (measured in pennies per transaction). This may be computed by multiplying the system $/TPS by 5E-9.

Packets: The number of X.25 packets exchanged per transaction. This charges for network traffic. A good system will send two X.25 packets per transaction. A bad one will send four times that many. This translates into larger demands for communications bandwidth, longer response times at the terminals and much higher costs. X.25 was chosen both because it is a standard and because it allows one to count packets.

Observations On The DebitCredit Benchmark

The numbers in the table above are ones achieved by vendors benchmarking their own systems. Strangely, customers rarely achieve these numbers -- typical customers report three to five times these costs and small fractions of the TPS rating. We suspect this is because vendor benchmarks are perfectly tuned while customers focus more on getting it to work at all and dealing with constant change and growth. If this explanation is correct, real systems are seriously out of tune and automatic system tuning will reap enormous cost savings.

The relatively small variation in costs is surprising -- the TPS range is 400 but the K$/TPS range is 10. In part the narrow cost range stems from the small systems being priced on the minicomputer curve and hence being much cheaper than the mainframe systems. Another factor is that disc capacity and access are a major part of the system cost. The disc storage scales with TPS and disc accesses only vary by a factor of 5. Perhaps the real determinant is that few people will pay 400 times more for one system over a competing system.

There are definite economies of scale in transaction processing -- high performance systems have very good price/performance.

It is also surprising to note that a personal computer with appropriate hardware and data management software supports one teller, scales to .01 TPS, and costs 8K$ -- about 800K$/TPS! Yes, that's an unfair comparison. Performance comparisons are unfair.

There are many pitfalls for the data management system running DebitCredit. These pitfalls are typical of other applications. For example, the branch database is a high-traffic small database, the end of the history file is a hotspot, the log may grow rapidly at 100TPS unless it is compressed, the account file is large but it must be spread across many discs because of the high disc traffic to it, and so on. Most data management systems bottleneck on software performance bugs long before hardware limits are reached [Gawlick], [Gray2].

The system must be able to run the periodic reporting -- sort merge the history file with the other account activity to produce 1/20 of the monthly statements. This can be done as a collection of background batch jobs that run after the end-of-day processing and must complete before the next end-of-day. This accounts for the interest in the scan and sort benchmarks.

Criticism

Twenty four people wrote this paper. Each feels it fails to capture the performance bugs in his system. Each knows that systems have already evolved to make some of the assumptions irrelevant (e.g. intelligent terminals now do distributed presentation services). But these benchmarks have been with us for a long time and provide a static yardstick for our systems.

There is particular concern that we ignore the performance of system startup (after a crash or installation of new software), and transaction startup (the first time it is called). These are serious performance bugs in some systems. A system should restart in a minute, and should NEVER lose a 10,000 terminal network because restart would be unacceptably long. With the advent of the 64kbit memory chip (not to mention the 1mbit memory chip), program loading should be instantaneous.

The second major concern is that this is a performance benchmark. Most of us have spent our careers making high-function systems. It is painful to see a metric which rewards simplicity -- simple systems are faster than fancy ones. We really wish this were a function benchmark. It isn't.

In focusing on DebitCredit, we have ignored system features which pay off in more complex applications: e.g. clustering of detail records on the same page with the master record, sophisticated use of alternate access paths, support for distributed data and distributed execution, and so on. Each of these features has major performance benefits. However, benchmarks to demonstrate them are too complex to be portable.

Lastly, we have grave reservations about our cost model.

First, our "cost" ignores communications costs and terminal costs. An ATM costs 50K$ over 5 years, the machine room hardware to support it costs 5K$. The communications costs are somewhere in between. Typically, the machine room cost is 10% of the system cost. But we can find no reasonable way to capture this "other 90%" of the cost. In defense of our cost metric, the other costs are fixed, while the central system cost does vary by an order of magnitude

Second, our "cost" ignores the cost of development and maintenance. One can implement the DebitCredit transaction in a day or two on some systems. On others it takes months to get started. There are huge differences in productivity between different systems. Implementing these benchmarks is a good test of a system's productivity tools. We have brought it up (from scratch) in a week, complete with test database and scripts for the network driver. We estimate the leanest-meanest system would require six months of expert time to get DebitCredit operational. What's more, it has no Sort utility or transaction logging.

Third, our "cost" ignores the cost of outages. People comprise 60% of most DP budgets. People costs do not enter into our calculations at all. We can argue that a system with 10,000 active users and a 30 minute outage each week costs 100K$/TPS just in lost labor over five years. Needless to say, this calculation is very controversial.

In defense of our myopic cost model, it is the vendor's model and the customer's model when money changes hands. Systems are sold (or not sold) based on the vendor's bid which is our cost number.

Summary

Computer performance is difficult to quantify. Different measures are appropriate to different application areas. None of the benchmarks described here use any floating point operations or logical inferences. Hence MegaFLOPS and GigaLIPS are not helpful on these applications. Even the MIPS measure is a poor metric -- one software system may use ten times the resources of another on the same hardware.

Cpu power measures miss an important trend in computer architecture: the emergence of parallel processing systems built out of modest processors which deliver impressive performance by using a large number of them. Cost and throughput are the only reasonable metrics for such computer architectures.

In addition, input-output architecture largely dominates the performance of most applications. Conventional measures ignore input-output completely.

We defined three benchmarks, Sort, Scan and DebitCredit. The first two benchmarks measure the system's input/output performance. DebitCredit is a very simple transaction processing application.

Based on the definition of DebitCredit we defined the Transactions Per Second (TPS) measure:

TPS: Peak DebitCredit transactions per second with 95% of the transactions having less than one second response time.

TPS is a good metric because it measures software and hardware performance including input-output.

These three benchmarks combined allow performance and price/performance comparisons of systems.

In closing, we restate our cavalier attitude about all this: "Actual performance may vary depending on driving habits, road conditions and queue lengths -- use these numbers for comparison purposes only". Put more bluntly, there are lies, damn lies and then there are performance measures.

References

[Gibson] Gibson, J.C., "The Gibson Mix", IBM TR00.2043, June 1970.

[Gawlick] Gawlick, D., "Processing of Hot Spots in Database Systems", Proceedings of IEEE COMPCON, San Francisco, IEEE Press, Feb. 1985.

[Gray] Gray, J., "Notes on Database Operating Systems", pp. 395-396, In Lecture Notes in Computer Science, Vol. 60, Bayer-Seegmuller eds., Springer Verlag, 1978.

[Gray2] Gray, J., Gawlick, D., Good, J.R., Homan, P., Sammer, H.R. "One Thousand Transactions Per Second", Proceedings of IEEE COMPCON, San Francisco, IEEE Press, Feb. 1985. Also, Tandem TR 85.1.

[Good] Good, J. R., "Experience With a Large Distributed Banking System", IEEE Computer Society on Database Engineering, Vol. 6, No. 2, June 1983.

[Anon Et Al] Dina Bitton of Cornell, Mark Brown of DEC, Rick Catell of Sun, Stefano Ceri of Milan, Tim Chou of Tandem, Dave DeWitt of Wisconsin, Dieter Gawlick of Amdahl, Hector Garcia-Molina of Princton, Bob Good of BofA, Jim Gray of Tandem, Pete Homan of

Tandem, Bob Jolls of Tandem, Tony Lukes of HP, Ed Lawoska of U. Washington, John Nauman of 3Com, Mike Pong of Tandem, Alfred Spector of CMU, Kent Trieber of IBM, Harald Sammer of Tandem, Omri Serlin of FT News, Mike Stonebraker of Berkeley, Andras Reuter of U. Kaiserslutern, Peter Weinberger of ATT.

Highly Available Systems for Database Applications

WON KIM

IBM Research Laboratory, San Jose, California 95193

As users entrust more and more of their applications to computer systems, the need for systems that are continuously operational (24 hours per day) has become even greater. This paper presents a survey and analysis of representative architectures and techniques that have been developed for constructing highly available systems for database applications. It then proposes a design of a distributed software subsystem that can serve as a unified framework for constructing database application systems that meet various requirements for high availability.

Categories and Subject Descriptors: A.1 **[General Literature]**: Introductory and Survey; C.1.2 **[Processor Architectures]**: Multiple Data Stream Architectures (Multiprocessors)—*interconnection architectures*; C.4 **[Computer Systems Organization]**: Performance of Systems—*reliability, availability, and serviceability*; H.2.4 **[Database Management]**: Systems—*distributed systems, transaction processing*

General Terms: Reliability

Additional Key Words and Phrases: Database concurrency control and recovery, relational database

CONTENTS

INTRODUCTION

In this paper we examine major hardware and software aspects of highly available systems. Its scope is limited to those systems designed for database applications. Database applications require multiple paths from the processor to the disks, which gives rise to some difficult issues of system architecture and engineering. Further, they involve the software issues of concurrency control, recovery from crashes, and transaction management.

In a typical business data processing environment, a user message from a terminal invokes an application program. The application program interacts with a transaction manager to initiate and terminate (commit or abort) a transaction. Once a transaction has been initiated, the application program repeatedly interacts with a database manager to retrieve and update records in the database.

A transaction is a collection of reads and writes against a database that is treated as a unit [Gray 1978]. If a transaction completes, its effect becomes permanently recorded in the database; otherwise, no trace of its effect remains in the database. To support the notion of a transaction, undo log of data before updates and redo log of data after updates are used to allow a transaction to be undone or redone after crashes. The Write Ahead Log protocol often is used to ensure that the log is flushed to the disk before the updated database records are written to the disk.

The most fundamental requirement in constructing a highly available system for database applications is that each major hardware and software component must at least be duplicated. At minimum, the system requires two processors. There may have to be two paths connecting the processors, and it is desirable to have at least two paths from the processors to the database, that is, two I/O subsystems consisting of a channel (I/O processor), controller, and disk drives. The disk controllers must be multiported, so that they may be connected to more than one processor.

On the software side, the system needs five essential ingredients: (1) a network communication subsystem, (2) a data communication subsystem, (3) a database manager (or a file system), (4) a transaction manager, and (5) the operating system.

The network communication subsystem must support interprocess(or) communication within a cluster of locally distributed processors. If the highly available system is a node on a geographically distributed system, the communication subsystem must also support internode communication.

The data communication subsystem is the terminal handler that receives user requests, invokes application programs, and delivers the results that it receives from the database/transaction manager.

The database manager must support the two fundamental capabilities of concurrency control and recovery. That is, it must guarantee that the database remains consistent despite interleaved reads and writes to the database by multiple concurrent transactions. Techniques such as locking and time stamping have been developed and extensively studied for this purpose [Bernstein and Goodman 1981; Kohler 1981].

The transaction/database manager must ensure that the database consistency is not compromised by system failures or transaction failures caused by software errors or deadlocks. In particular, it must be able to recover from transaction failures and soft crashes, which corrupt only the contents of the main memory, as well as from hard crashes, which destroy the contents of the disks. For recovery from soft crashes, the undo and redo logs of transactions are used [Gray et al. 1981; Haerder and Reuter 1983]. To recover from hard crashes, systems rely on periodic dumping of the database into archival storage.

The operating system is needed not only to run the other software components, but also to detect most of the common, low-level software/hardware errors that occur. Most computer systems rely on program checks (interrupts) and machine checks to detect such errors. Program checks are used to detect exceptions and events that occur during execution of the program [IBM 1980]. Exceptions include the improper specification or use of instructions and data, for example, arithmetic overflow or underflow, and addressing or protection violation. Machine checks are used to report machine malfunctions, such as memory parity errors, I/O errors, and missing interrupts. The hardware provides information that assists the operating system in determining the location of the malfunction and extent of the damage caused by it.

Most systems have been designed to survive the failure of a single software/hard-

Author's current address: Microelectronics and Computer Technology Corporation, 9430 Research Boulevard, Austin, Texas 78759.

ware component. If a system is to be truly continuously operational, however, it must guarantee availability during multiple concurrent failures of software/hardware components, during on-line changes of such components, and during on-line physical reconfiguration of the database itself. To support the full range of high-availability requirements, the operating system must be supplemented with a software subsystem that can manage all software and hardware components of a system. Such a software subsystem will receive failure reports from the system components and reconfiguration requests from the system operator. It will analyze the status of all the resources it manages, and compute the optimal configuration of the system both in response to multiple concurrent failures of components and requests for load balancing. Further, it will initiate and monitor system reconfiguration, effecting mid-course correction of a reconfiguration that does not succeed. Finally, it will diagnose a class of failures that other components fail to recognize.

The systems introduced in the following paragraphs are often considered highly available, and are used as examples of various architectures and stratagems throughout the remainder of this paper, particularly in Sections 3 through 6. A certain number of these systems do not, in my opinion, meet the criteria for classification as highly available; these are discussed in Section 2.

Tandem Computers has been successful for several years in marketing fault-tolerant computer systems, which shield the users from various types of failures of the software and hardware components. Other companies have entered this market, including August Systems, Auragen Systems, Computer Consoles, Stratus Computer, Synapse Computer, Syntrex, Sequoia, Tolerant Systems, and others [Electronic Business 1981; IEEE 1983]. Of these, Auragen, Computer Consoles, Stratus, and Synapse have focused on transaction processing; August Systems aims at industrial and commercial process control.

A number of other systems address the issue of reliability and availability: Syntrex is marketing a local network file server called GEMINI; the MARK III Cluster File System, developed by General Electric, provides time-sharing services for its telephone-switching network users; and the Distributive Computing Facility developed by Bank of America automates the teller functions for accounts.

In addition, the late 1970s SRI SIFT project for aircraft control evoked the August Systems' products; Bolt Beranek and Newman (BBN) developed the PLURIBUS system for use as a highly reliable communications processor on ARPANET; and during the 1960s AT&T developed No. 1 ESS and No. 2 ESS (Electronic Switching System) for telephone switching services.

System D, a distributed transaction-processing system, was created as a prototype at IBM Research in San Jose with availability and modular growth as its major objectives, and there are other research projects currently under way at IBM Research to investigate availability and performance issues under various software/hardware structures.

The remainder of this paper is organized as follows. In Section 1, a taxonomy of system structures that has been used to construct highly available systems is developed, and a discussion is provided of the advantages and disadvantages of four possible structures. An intuitive set of criteria for highly available systems is given in Section 2. Systems belonging to each of the four system structures are surveyed and critiqued, where possible, in Sections 3 through 6. The discussions in these sections focus on various philosophies of system structure and transaction processing. In Section 7 the functions and structure of a software subsystem that provides a framework for high availability are described.

In view of the fact that such issues as concurrency control, recovery, transaction model, and network communications have been extensively addressed elsewhere, these aspects of highly available systems will not be given detailed treatment. Further, it is generally recognized that such mundane sources as downed telephone lines, careless computer operators, lack of defensive coding, and the way in which the operating system reacts to failures that it detects can seriously limit the availability of a system. Although important, such aspects are not within the scope of this paper.

1. MACHINE AND STORAGE ORGANIZATION TAXONOMY

Two fundamental decisions in constructing a multiple-processor system are the choice of machine organization and physical storage organization. The discussion in this section of the advantages and disadvantages of typical machine and storage organizations significantly benefits from Traiger [1983]. Two conventional techniques for organizing multiple processors are loosely coupled and tightly coupled multiprocessor organizations. In tightly coupled systems, two or more processors share main memory and disks, typically through an interconnection switch, and execute one copy of the operating system residing in the shared main memory. A local cache memory is usually associated with each processor to enhance access speed. In loosely coupled systems, each processor has not only a local cache memory but also its own main memory, and may or may not share disks with other processors. Each processor executes its own copy of the operating system from its own main memory. There are various ways to loosely couple the processors, including shared bus structures, cross-point switches, point-to-point links such as channel-to-channel adapters, and globally shared memories, as in Cm* [Swan et al. 1977].

Tightly coupled multiprocessor systems, such as the Synapse N+1 System, and BBN's PLURIBUS, offer important potential advantages. First, they naturally present a single-system image, since multiple processors execute one copy of the operating system and a common job queue. Second, the processors do not need to communicate via interprocessor messages, with their inherent overhead. However, this performance advantage may be offset by certain problems imposed by this architecture. First, there is contention among processors for the use of shared memory and other shared resources. This must somehow be reduced, especially if the cost/performance of the system is to keep up with its expansion as extra processors are added. Second, potentially complex techniques must be supported to ensure that the contents of each processor's cache memory are up-to-date.

In addition to these performance concerns, there is a potential availability problem with tightly coupled multiprocessors. All processors run the same operating system from shared main memory, and thus, when the operating system is corrupted or the shared memory system fails, the entire system must be restarted. Therefore application systems designed to run on a tightly coupled multiprocessor system must be able to restart very quickly in order to guarantee high overall availability.

Just as there are two techniques for organizing multiple processors, there are two ways to organize disks, and thus the database. One is to assign a set of disks to one processor and allow access to it only through that processor; the other is to have all of the processors share all the disks. The two techniques of organizing multiple processors and the two techniques of organizing disks are combined to give rise to four distinct system structures. The tightly coupled multiprocessor organization and the shared database organization results in a system structure that is called a tightly coupled system with a shared database. The loosely coupled multiprocessor organization gives rise to three other system structures. When a database is split into N partitions and each partition is stored in one set of disks assigned to one of N processors, the resulting system structure is called a loosely coupled multiprocessor with a partitioned database. When each of N processors can directly access the entire database, stored in one set of disks, the system structure is called a loosely coupled multiprocessor with a shared database. When an entire database is replicated in each set of disk volumes attached to each of N processors, and each processor computes the same user request in parallel, the resulting structure is called a loosely coupled multiprocessor with redundant computation.

The Tandem NonStop System, the Auragen System 4000, the Stratus Continuous Processing System, IBM's System D prototype (and its sequel, the Highly Available Systems project), Bank of America's Distributive Computing Facility, and AT&T's Stored Program Controlled Network are loosely coupled multiprocessors with partitioned databases. In this architecture, a database manager residing in each processor owns and manages the partition of the database assigned to that processor. Any user request (transaction) that requires access to more than one database partition is satisfied by message communication among the database managers that own the necessary partitions. Communication overhead is the single most significant disadvantage of the loosely coupled system with a partitioned database. There are two aspects to this interprocess(or) communication overhead: One is the messages sending requests to servers and receiving results from servers; another aspect is the messages and processing involved in the distributed commit protocol that ensures that the database, which is distributed across processors, is left in a globally consistent state when the transaction completes or aborts.

Some variation of the two-phase commit protocol described by Gray is used in committing or aborting a distributed transaction [Gray 1978]. One of the participating transaction managers is designated as the commit coordinator. During phase 1, the commit coordinator sends a "prepare to commit" message to all other participants. The participants reply with "yes" or "no" messages to the coordinator and enter phase 2. If the coordinator receives "yes" votes from all participants, it sends a "commit" message to all participants. If any participant replied with a "no" vote, the coordinator sends an "abort" message to all the participants. During phase 1 all participants retain the right to unilaterally abort the transaction. However, once they enter phase 2, they no longer can unilaterally abort the transaction; they must obey the decision of the commit coordinator.

Loosely coupled multiprocessor systems with shared database architecture, such as GE's MARK III Cluster File System, Computer Consoles' Power System, and IBM's AMOEBA research project [Traiger 1983], offer a potentially enhanced availability over a tightly coupled multiprocessor system, since the operating system is not shared among the processors. One disadvantage, however, is the lack of a single-system image; that is, system operators and system programmers must contend with multiple copies of the operating system. One important advantage of this architecture over a loosely coupled multiprocessor system with a partitioned database is that it avoids the difficult problem of deciding which partition of the database should be stored in which processors' disks. Processors may be added to the system without having to repartition the database, and new disk drives may be added without having to worry about which processors should own them.

However, contention on the shared disks is a potential problem, with each processor moving the disk arms to random positions. Further, algorithms for coordinating the global locking and logging of database updates must be carefully designed. A global locking technique in which all database managers must acquire and release locks through a single global lock manager will cause excessive communication overhead and create a bottleneck for performance and availability.

Loosely coupled multiprocessor systems with redundant computation, such as Syntrex's GEMINI file server, and SRI's SIFT (as well as its offspring, the Basic Controller of August Systems, Inc.), achieve fault tolerance by having more than one task perform the same computation and then comparing the results of the computation. In such applications as spacecraft control and process control in a nuclear power plant, correct results of computations are more critical than is the case in typical database applications. Further, the computations are well defined, and the results are often known in advance. For such applications, it makes sense to have multiple processors perform the same computations in order to detect and (even correct) conflicting results. But for office word-processing or transaction-processing applications, this approach may not be desirable.

For applications that require time-consuming computations and/or disk accesses, there tend to be ample opportunities for program checks and machine checks to detect low-level failures, and for time-outs or defensive coding to detect high-level failures. Unless the need for error detection and correction is highly critical, the redundant-computation approach appears to waste the processing power of the system. Further, the exchange of data and status information among the replicated tasks for each input and output is a considerable performance overhead.

2. INTUITIVE CRITERIA FOR HIGH AVAILABILITY

Now we must address the problem of what is meant by availability. The overall availability of a system may intuitively be defined as the ratio between the time when the end user and applications actually have access to all the database and the time when the end user and applications require access to the database. For example, if users require the system to be up for 8 hours a day and the system is actually up for 6 hours during the 8 hours, the availability of the system is 6/8 = .75 during the 8-hour period.

It is more difficult to precisely define a single measure of availability. In the first place, it is not clear how to define the "mission duration" for the system. In spacecraft control applications, the mission duration is clearly defined: While the spacecraft is in orbit, the system must be available 24 hours per day. In business data processing applications, however, the mission duration can be several years. At what point in the life of a system, and for how long, should we measure availability? During one arbitrary month, a year after the installation of the system?

In the second place, should the entire database be available for access by authorized users during the entire duration? For example, when a single database partition becomes inaccessible in a loosely coupled multiprocessor architecture with a partitioned database, one may take the view that the system is no longer available. In fact, this is my view for the purposes of this paper. However, one may equally well take the more charitable view that the system is still largely available, since users may access other database partitions and perform useful work [Good 1983].

Similarly, in a geographically distributed environment, it is not entirely clear where to draw the line on availability, for example, when a node of the system cannot communicate with another node and consequently cannot access data owned and managed by the other node.

Very few vendors of the systems that we are considering have provided availability figures for public review. Suffice it to say here that, however one may define it, often a highly available system is expected to provide higher than 99 percent overall availability.

We use the following criteria to classify a system for database applications as highly available. The first three are hard criteria and provide the rationale for including and excluding detailed discussion of various systems in this paper. The last two are soft criteria, satisfied by very few existing systems and mainly included for future considerations.

(1) The system must support transaction-processing or file server capabilities, specifically concurrency control and recovery techniques, to maintain database consistency. A distributed database system must support a distributed commit protocol to ensure global consistency of the database.

BBN's PLURIBUS [Katsuki et al. 1978], SRI's SIFT design [Wensley et al. 1978], the Basic Controller system now being marketed by August Systems Inc. [Kinnucan 1981], and AT&T's No. 1 ESS and No. 2 ESS [Spencer and Vigilante 1969] do not satisfy this criterion, and will not be discussed in detail in the system survey portion of this paper.

(2) The system must support automatic takeover of full workload by a backup process when a primary process fails. This criterion excludes systems that rely on manual replacement of failed processors to survive a single failure.

The problem with the manual replacement approach is that (1) the responsibility of detecting failure often falls on users or the operators, and (2) the new processor is aware of either the database or the terminals and hence applications, and the system must be cold-started.

Japan National Railways' MARS train seat reservation system, a loosely coupled multiprocessor system with a partitioned database, does not support the concept of backup processes at the present time [Tsukigi and Hasegawa 1983]. Hence, when the processor that manages one partition of the database crashes, no user can access the database partition until the database manager that owns it can be restarted. This system is not given detailed treatment here.

IBM's Information Management System (IMS) with the data-sharing feature [Strickland et al. 1982] is a loosely coupled multiprocessor system with a shared database, with an IMS/VS system in two different processors, each able to access the database in shared disks. When one IMS/VS crashes, its terminals lose access to the database until it can be restarted, and the surviving IMS/VS is not aware of the transactions in process on the system that failed, and hence cannot abort or complete them. We do not consider this system highly available.

The Stratus system does not currently support the concept of primary–backup processes; however, in view of the great extent to which the system incorporates hardware fault tolerance and capabilities for on-line system reconfiguration, it is classified as a highly available system.

(3) The system must survive at least a single failure of such major components as processor, I/O channel, I/O controller, disk drives, and interprocessor communication medium. In particular, a single failure should not make any part of the database inaccessible to the users for beyond a reasonable recovery duration. A reasonable recovery duration may be 1 minute for a mini- and microprocessor system and perhaps 10 minutes for a mainframe, because of the larger number of terminals and applications dealt with by a mainframe system.

This criterion does not imply that a single point of failure is unacceptable, rather that when a single point of failure exists, it must not cause overall availability to suffer.

For example, the Synapse N+1 System has a single point of failure in its shared main memory, but is designed to recover quickly and provides high overall availability. System D has a single point of failure in the electronic switch that connects a pair of processors with the shared disks and terminals, but the probability of failure of such a switch is very low and hence does not severely compromise overall availability.

(4) The system should support on-line integration of repaired or new hardware/software components. Further, in the case of a partitioned database, the system should support on-line migration of the database from one disk system to another.

(5) Additional features aimed at making the component failures transparent to the users may be useful. One is the ability to automatically restart transactions in progress when system crash occurs, which may require the data communication subsystem to log the transaction request on the disk. Another is for the interprocessor communication subsystem to reroute messages originally targeted to a failed process to its backup. In view of the fact that transactions in typical business data processing are short-lived, that is, they complete within a few seconds, it does not appear that important to burden a system with these additional capabilities.

3. LOOSELY COUPLED SYSTEMS WITH A PARTITIONED DATABASE

This section provides overviews of architectures and transaction-processing strategies as employed in the Tandem NonStop System, Auragen System 4000, Stratus/32 Continuous Processing System, AT&T's Stored Program Controlled Network, Bank of America's Distributive Computing Facility, and System D.

It is noted that the Auragen, Stratus, AT&T, and Bank of America systems are actually loosely coupled clusters of processors, in which each cluster consists of two or more processors and manages one partition of the database. The cluster itself is not necessarily a loosely coupled multiprocessor architecture. Further, the Auragen, AT&T, and Bank of America systems currently do not support distributed on-line transaction processing: User requests are completely processed within one cluster, without requiring the participation of other clusters.

Figure 1. Tandem NonStop system architecture.

3.1 Tandem NonStop System

The NonStop System, developed by Tandem Computers about 1976, has made important contributions to the area of high availability [Bartlett 1978; Katzman 1977, 1978]. As shown in Figure 1, each processor module consists of a central processing unit (CPU), memory, interface to an interprocessor bus system called Dynabus, and an I/O channel. Each of the I/O controllers is connected to two processors via its dual-port arrangement, and each processor is connected to all other processors via a dual Dynabus. Further, as shown in Figure 2, each processor is connected to a pair of disk controllers, which in turn maintain a string of up to four pairs of (optionally) mirrored disk drives. Mirroring is supported in the I/O supervisor, which issues two disk writes for each page of data to be written to the disk. Thus it is clear that the system provides many paths to data, and hence the data are available to the user regardless of any single failure of a disk drive, disk controller, I/O channel, or processor.

The Tandem system was designed to continue operation through any single component failure, and also to allow the failure to be repaired without affecting the availability of the rest of the system. Each processor module has a separate power supply, which can be shut off to replace the failed module without affecting the rest of the system. Similarly, each I/O controller is powered by two power supplies associated with the two processors to which it is attached, and can be powered down by a corresponding switch, without affecting the rest of the system. Thus the I/O controllers survive a single power failure, and each I/O controller and processor module can be repaired without shutting down the rest of the system.

In order to detect a processor failure in the Tandem system, each processor broadcasts an "I-AM-ALIVE" message every 1 second and checks for an "I-AM-ALIVE" message from every other processor every 2 seconds [Bartlett 1978]. If a processor decides that another processor has failed to send the "I-AM-ALIVE" message, it initiates recovery actions, as described later. Although there is a possibility that different processors may reach different decisions as to which processor has crashed, the single-failure assumption precludes consideration (and prevention) of such a possibility.

This "active" failure-detection approach of the Tandem system helps to detect a processor failure soon after it occurs. However, it is not very useful to say that a

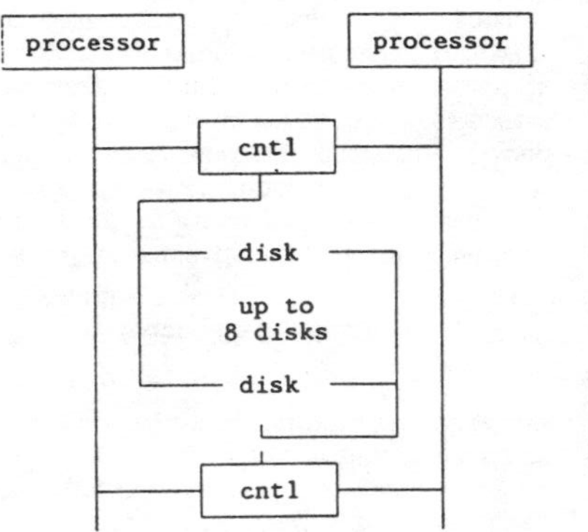

Figure 2. Tandem NonStop disk subsystem organization.

processor is "alive" simply because it can send the "I-AM-ALIVE" message, when tasks running in it may have crashed. Software failures must be detected by message time-outs.

The operating system that runs on the Tandem NonStop System is called Guardian. It is constructed of processes that communicate by using messages. Guardian provides high availability of processes by maintaining a primary–backup pair of processes, each in a different processor. The primary process periodically sends checkpoint information to its paired backup process, so that the backup will stand ready to take over as soon as the primary process fails. The checkpoint data from a primary I/O process contain information about the files that are opened and closed. The backup I/O process opens and closes the checkpointed files while the primary is still active, so that in the event of failure of the primary, the backup recovers and proceeds with normal processing without the time overhead of opening the files.

An "ownership" bit is associated with each of the two ports of an I/O controller, which indicates to each port whether it is the primary or backup. Only one port is active for the primary I/O process; the other is used only in the event of a path failure to the primary port, and any attempt to access data through the backup port is rejected. Upon detecting or being notified of the failure of the primary process, the backup process instructs Guardian to issue a TAKE OWNERSHIP command to the backup port. This command causes the I/O controller to swap its two ownership bits and do a controller reset.

The database/transaction manager that runs on the Tandem system is called ENCOMPASS [Borr 1981]. ENCOMPASS consists of four functional components: a database manager, a terminal manager, a transaction manager, and a distributed transaction manager. The ENCOMPASS database manager is implemented as a primary/backup I/O process (called the DISCPROCESS) pair per disk volume. In other words, a primary database manager in one processor and its backup in another processor own the partition of the database stored in the disk volume to which the two processors are connected. The primary database manager checkpoints to the backup, so that if the primary fails before completing a transaction, the backup may take over the disk volume and redo committed transactions and abort incomplete ones.

To run transactions against the database, the user provides two sets of programs: the Screen COBOL program and application server programs. The Screen COBOL program performs screen formatting and sequencing, data mapping, and field validation, and sends transaction requests to application server programs. The application server programs perform application functions against the database by invoking the database manager, the DISCPROCESS.

The Screen COBOL program is interpreted by the terminal management component of ENCOMPASS, called Terminal Control Process (TCP). TCP is also configured as a process pair; the primary TCP checkpoints the backup TCP with data extracted by the Screen COBOL program from input screens.

The transaction management component of ENCOMPASS, which implements the conventional model of transactions, is called Transaction Monitoring Facility (TMF). TMF consists of a lock manager, a log manager (called the AUDITPROCESS), and a recovery manager (called the BACKOUTPROCESS) to provide concurrency control and recovery of interleaved execution of concurrent transactions. The user's Screen COBOL program interfaces with TMF to indicate the beginning and end of a transaction. The Screen COBOL program receives a transaction identification from TMF at the beginning of a transaction, and attaches the transaction identification to all transaction request messages that it sends to the application server programs. When the Screen COBOL program notifies end of transaction, TMF initiates a transaction commit protocol to complete the transaction and make the effect of the transaction permanent. TMF does not support a global deadlock detection mechanism; deadlocks are detected by time-out, where the time limit is specified as part of lock requests.

3.2 AT&T's Stored Program Controlled Network

AT&T's Stored Program Controlled (SPC) Network [Cohen et al. 1983] consists of two key components: the Network Control Point (NCP) and the Action Point (ACP), as shown in Figure 3. The NCP is a database system which manages a database of customer records that is geographically distributed over a network of computers interconnected by the Common Channel Interoffice Signaling (CCIS) network. The ACP is a telephone call processing system, and is a highly reliable No. 4 ESS.

When a call is made to a customer of the expanded 800 services or Direct Services Dialing Capability (DSDC) services, the call is routed to an ACP. The ACP transmits the request to an NCP, which maintains the customer record. The NCP returns the response to the ACP, which in turn routes the call according to the response from the NCP. An administrative system called the User Support System (USS) is used to insert new customer records and update existing ones. The USS sends records to be inserted or updated through the Operations Support Network (OSN).

This system may require several NCPs, according to NCP capacity, performance requirements and market forecasts. The database is partitioned and each partition is assigned to two NCPs, one primary and one backup, for call processing. A database partition is replicated in an NCP and its backup. One NCP may be a backup to another NCP with respect to one database partition, and a primary to that NCP with respect to another partition of the database. When a primary NCP fails and there are insufficient data at the site to restore its operation, its backup takes over while continuing to function as the primary for another database partition.

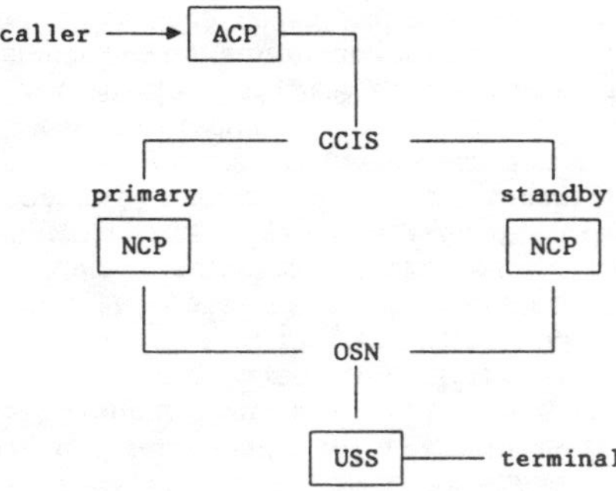

Figure 3. AT&T's Stored Program Controlled Network.

Each NCP is constructed using a 3B-20D processor [Mitze et al. 1983]. A 3B-20D consists of two identical processors: One component processor is active and the other is a standby at any given time. Each has its own main memory and control unit. Further, both processors share all the disks, and each processor has indirect access to the main memory of the other.

During normal operation, the active processor updates the main memory of the standby processor, which is ready at all times to take over if the primary should fail. At each NCP, the I/O channel, disk controller, and links to its standby NCP are duplicated. Further, the database partition managed by an NCP is quadruplicated, and stored in four separate sets of disk drives connected to the 3B-20D. The standby NCP in turn keeps four copies of the database partition.

For a customer record to be updated under normal conditions, a transaction is sent to the primary NCP with which the record is associated. The primary NCP checks the

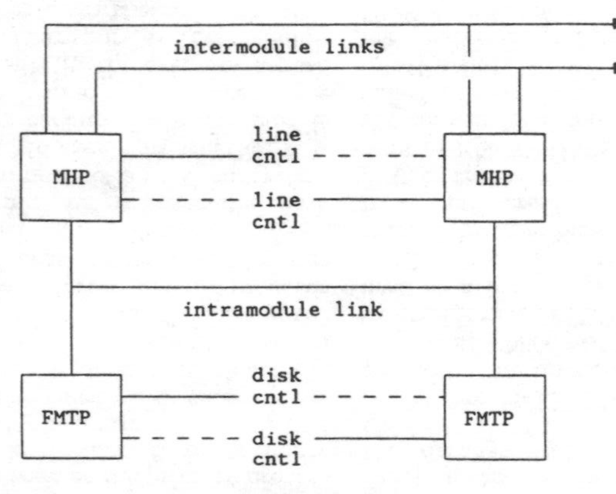

Figure 4. A module of Bank of America's DCF.

transaction for consistency and authorization; if it is valid, the primary NCP logs the transaction on the disk and sends an acknowledgment to the user. The primary NCP makes changes to its database and sends the update to its backup. The backup NCP applies the update to its database and acknowledges the primary, at which point the primary inserts a record in the transaction log and finishes the transaction. In the event of a network partition, when a primary NCP is disconnected from its backup NCP due to failure of the communication line, the primary updates its database without requiring agreement from its backup, but maintains a special history log of database changes, which it sends to its backup when communication is restored.

3.3 Bank of America's Distributive Computing Facility

Bank of America developed the Distributive Computing Facility (DCF) around 1978 to automate teller functions for customer checking and savings accounts [Good 1983]. By leased lines, branch offices access a customer accounts database in two data centers in Los Angeles and San Francisco. Each data center houses a DCF cluster, which consists of eight DCF modules interconnected by a local-area network. Each DCF module is a local-area network of four GA16/440 minicomputers, which manages one partition of the customer accounts database. Two of the four processors in a DCF module are communications front ends called Message Handling Processors (MHP). The other two are database back ends called File Management Transaction Processors (FMTP). The four processors communicate via a bus called the intramodule link.

As shown in Figure 4, each module is configured such that, under normal operation, each MHP is paired with one FMTP to operate on half the module's lines and database. When one MHP fails, the other takes control of all the lines. When one FMTP fails, the other takes control of the entire database of the module.

The DCF uses a simple scheme for detecting processor failures. Each processor has a watchdog timer, which it periodically resets. If the timer is not reset on schedule, the DCF module shuts the processor down and notifies the peer processor to assume full work load. When an MHP times out on a transaction request to an FMTP, it assumes that the FMTP is dead and starts sending subsequent transactions to the other FMTP. The transaction messages are not logged, and so any transaction in progress on a failed MHP or FMTP is lost.

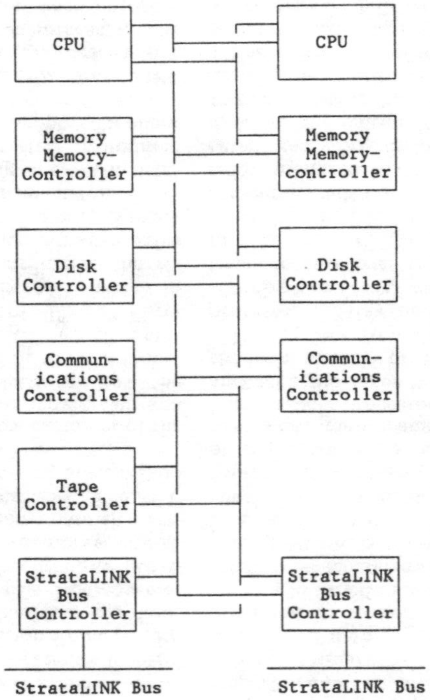

Figure 5. A Processing Module of Stratus/32.

3.4 Stratus/32 Continuous Processing System

The Stratus/32 Continuous Processing System [Kastner 1983; Stratus 1982] consists of 1–32 Processing Modules, where each Processing Module consists of duplicated CPU, memory, controller, and I/O as shown in Figure 5. The memory may be configured to be redundant or nonredundant, as the two memory subsystems are not paired with the two CPUs. In a redundant configuration, the CPUs read from and write to both memory subsystems simultaneously; in a nonredundant configuration, each memory subsystem becomes an independent unit and the memory capacity is doubled. Each Processing Module has duplicated power supplies. The Processing Modules are connected through a dual-bus system called the StrataLINK.

The duplicated components (CPU and controllers) of a Processing Module each perform the same computation in parallel. Each component (board), in turn, consists of two identical sets of hardware components on the same board. As shown in Figure 6 for a disk controller, a hardware logic compares the results of the computation by the duplicated boards. If the results are identical, they are sent to the bus or device. Otherwise, the results are not sent, the board is automatically disabled, and an interrupt signal is sent to the Stratus VOS operating system. However, processing continues with the duplexed board of the Processing Module.

All detected hardware malfunctions are reported to a maintenance software, which determines the cause and nature of the malfunction. The board is automatically restarted if the malfunction was caused by

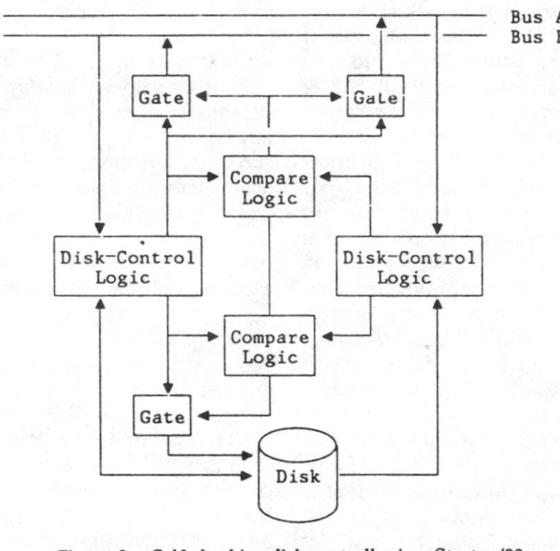

Figure 6. Self-checking disk controller in a Stratus/32.

a transient error, whereas permanent errors result in the board remaining out of service and a report being sent to an operator terminal.

The Stratus system supports optional mirroring of disk volumes. It also allows on-line removal and replacement of all duplexed boards and associated peripheral devices; in particular, it allows on-line integration of a new Processing Module. When a duplexed component is replaced, the new component is automatically brought to the same state as its partner. For example, the second disk in a dual-disk system is brought up-to-date while the first disk is used for normal processing. The VOS operating system accomplishes this by writing new blocks of pages to both disks and copying blocks from the first disk to the second concurrently with normal processing.

Further, the Stratus system allows the memory subsystems to be dynamically reconfigured to redundant or nonredundant mode, without taking the Processing Module off line.

The Stratus system supports transaction processing by providing a Transaction Processing Facility (TPF), VOS File System, the StrataNET network communications subsystem, and a Forms Management Facility. The system does not currently support a database management system; TPF invokes the File System to manipulate the database. TPF supports a two-phase commit protocol for on-line distributed transaction processing.

The Stratus system's continuous comparison of the results of computation from duplicated hardware components on the same board significantly reduces the probability of a hardware-induced error from propagating and corrupting the system and data integrity, provided that the hardware that compares the results does not malfunction. Further, the Stratus hardware and operating system provide protection against some system crashes induced by software errors, such as attempts by one user's program to cross another user's address space, to read or write into the operating system, to write into executable code, or to execute data.

The Stratus system does not currently support the concept of a backup subsystem, and hence applications running on Stratus may not survive software-induced crashes. The Stratus fault-tolerance philosophy is based on the view that the hardware can detect errors and automatically shut down a malfunctioning component while an identical component operating in parallel continues to function, thus ensuring database integrity and providing continuous processing of user requests. In my opinion, this approach does not safeguard the system against crashes induced by a class of errors that even the most sophisticated operating systems cannot cope with. For instance, IBM's System/370 and its Multiple Virtual System (MVS) operating system [IBM 1979] provide extensive measures to detect hardware and software failures and to repair and recover from them. Yet, applications running on MVS, and MVS itself, do occasionally crash, usually as a result of software failures.

3.5 Auragen System 4000

The Auragen System 4000, developed at Auragen Systems Corp., New Jersey, consists of 2–32 clusters of tightly coupled multimicroprocessors interconnected by a dual-bus system [Gostanian 1983]. Each cluster consists of three MC68000s, its own local memory, several types of I/O controllers, power supply, and battery backup. One of the 68000s is used exclusively to execute the operating system, whereas the other two are used to execute user tasks. Each cluster periodically broadcasts an "I-AM-ALIVE" message to detect failure of other clusters; the time-out mechanism is used to detect process failures. All peripheral devices are dual ported and are attached to two different clusters. The Auragen system allows disks to be configured in mirrored pairs, and mirroring may be specified on a file basis.

The Auragen database system, called AURELATE, is based on the ORACLE relational database system [Weiss 1980]. As in the Tandem system, Auragen 4000 supports a primary–backup pair of processes, implemented within the AUROS operating system, which is an enhanced version of UNIX III. To reduce the number of checkpoint messages, the AUROS operating system sends a collection of transaction messages to both the primary and the backup. After the primary has processed a predetermined number of these transaction messages, the backup is notified to process the checkpoint message. Once the backup finishes processing the checkpoint message, it is removed from the message queue.

The Auragen system's current recovery technique is based on the roll-forward approach. When the backup takes over for the primary, it begins execution at the last point of synchronization with the primary. That is, it begins with the last checkpoint message in its message queue. A technique has been proposed that does not allow the backup to redo work that already may have been done by the primary before the crash [Gostanian 1983].

The recovery technique requires an undo log to allow transaction abort. However, a redo log is optional and is used for recovery from a single disk crash, when disk mirroring is not used. Since a backup process will redo in-progress transactions, Auragen's proposal for commit processing does not call for the Write-Ahead Log protocol. However, this leaves the system unprotected from simultaneous failures of both the primary and backup processes.

3.6 System D Prototype

System D is a distributed transaction-processing system designed and prototyped at IBM Research, San Jose, as a vehicle for research into availability and incremental growth of a locally distributed network of computers [Andler et al. 1982]. The system was implemented on a network of Series/1 minicomputers interconnected with an insertion ring, and was the predecessor to the Highly Available Systems project currently under way at IBM Research, San Jose [Aghili et al. 1983; Kim 1982]. Although System D is not itself a highly available system, its rather novel transaction-processing and failure-diagnosis strategies warrant discussion here.

The System D transaction-processing software consists of three distinct types of modules: application, data manager, and storage manager modules. A module is a function that exists in a node and may consist of one or more processes called agents. The application module, called A, provides user interfaces for interactive users or application programmers. The data manager module, called D, transforms the record-level requests from the A module to

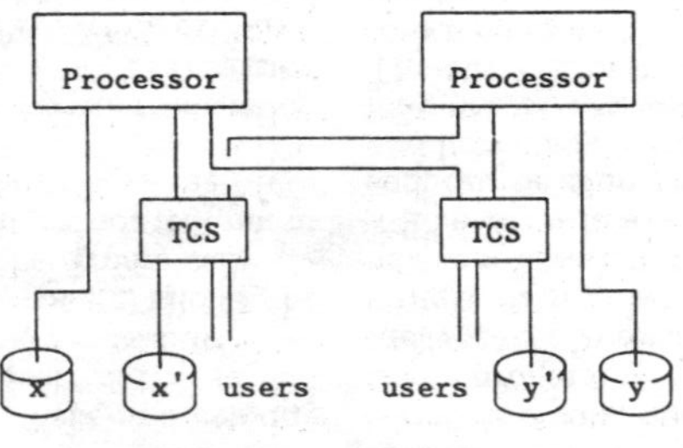

Figure 7. Processor pair in System D.

page-level requests for the storage module. All the changes made by an application are kept locally in the data manager module, which sends them to the storage manager only when the application commits the data changes to stable storage. The storage manager module, called S, supports multiple concurrent transactions against the physical database and database recovery from failures.

As shown in Figure 7, terminals and shared disks are connected to a pair of processors through an electronic switch, called a Two-Channel Switch (TCS). Only one of the processors has access to the shared disks and terminals at any given time. The processor periodically resets the timer in the TCS; if this does not occur on schedule, the TCS switches the shared disks and terminals over to the other processor. Thus, rather than requiring the processors to communicate with each other, System D gives the TCS the task of detecting the failure of a processor. Moreover, the TCS prevents a processor that is declared dead from writing to the disk.

System D provides a software subsystem called the Resource Manager (RM), which is responsible for diagnosing and taking appropriate actions to recover from the failures of modules and agents. The basic premise of its design is that the time-out mechanism detects all failures, including deadlock, agent or module crash, communication medium failure, or processor failure. Failures are detected only when service requests are sent.

Rather than the Tandem-like notion of primary and backup processes, System D supports multiple agents of a module running in the same processor. The Resource Manager attempts to bring down and restart failed agents, while normal service requests are handled by other agents. In the event of a processor failure, agents are brought up in the backup processor and all transactions in progress are aborted. The initial program load (IPL) of a low-end processor normally takes under 1 minute, which was considered a reasonable recovery duration, and System D was designed to avoid the overhead of maintaining synchronized pairs of primary and backup processes.

The failure-diagnosis logic described below was necessary because of the inadequate failure-detection capabilities of the operating system on which System D ran. The RM attempts to diagnose the problem by first attempting to establish communication with the node in which the agent is running. If the response is positive, the RM issues an "ABORT_TRANSACTION" command to the agent. The rationale here is that the service-request message may have experienced a data- or timing-dependent error that may not recur if the transaction is aborted and resubmitted. Successful processing of the "ABORT_TRANSACTION" command also indicates that the agent involved probably has not crashed.

If the transaction cannot be aborted, the RM attempts to bring down and restart the agent, since the code or the control structure of the agent may have been destroyed. If the agent cannot be brought down, the RM attempts to shut down and restart the module itself, since the control structures shared by the agents of the module may have crashed. If the RM fails to shut down and restart the module, probably the remote RM or the operating system has crashed, in which case an IPL must be executed remotely for the node in question.

Now, if the RM fails to establish communication with the node in which the resource resides or if the remote IPL was not successful, it will try to communicate with the RM in the backup node of the resource, since the TCS has probably switched. If the TCS has not switched over, the RM attempts to remotely execute an IPL for the node in which the resource resides. The reason is that initially it may have failed to communicate with the RM in that node because the RM, the CSS, or the operating system in that node may have crashed.

The standard two-phase commit protocol allows each node to unilaterally abort the transaction as long as the commit protocol has not entered the second phase. The design of System D recognizes that this privilege, often called site autonomy, is not so important in a locally distributed environment, and implements a different commit protocol [Andler et al. 1982]. In a sense, the System D protocol requires just a single phase and as soon as the commit coordinator decides to commit; no other node may abort the transaction.

In System D, actual updates to the database are not made until the transaction commits. At transaction commit, the transaction's log, maintained by the D module, is sent to the S module that is designated the commit coordinator, the first S module that receives page request from the D module. The commit coordinator writes the log to the disk and acknowledges the D module. The D module then sends "commit" messages to the other participating S modules. Each participant writes its log to the disk and then makes database changes.

The recovery procedure for this commit protocol is as follows. Upon restart, an S module re-DOes the changes in its local transaction log. The module then requests complete logs from any commit coordinators for transactions that are known to them but unknown to the recovering module, and runs these transactions serially in any order.

4. TIGHTLY COUPLED SYSTEMS WITH A SHARED DATABASE

The Synapse N+1 Computer System is an on-line transaction-processing system, developed by Synapse Computer Corporation [Jones 1983], which provides a dual path from a processor to the database stored in secondary storage devices. As Figure 8 shows, Synapse N+1 is a tightly coupled multiprocessor system with shared memory, in which processing is divided between general-purpose processors (GPP) and I/O processors (IOP), each of which is based on the Motorola 68000. Currently, up to 28 processors may be attached to a dual-bus system called the Synapse Expansion Bus.

GPPs execute user programs and most of the Synapse's Synthesis operating system from the shared memory. IOPs each manage up to 16 I/O controllers or communications subsystems. IOPs have direct memory access (DMA) capability to the shared main memory, but execute part of Synthesis from their own local memory. The Advanced Communications Subsystem (ACS) is a 68000-based communications controller, and the Multiple-Purpose Controller (MPC) is a controller for various devices. Whereas the Tandem NonStop system powers each processor with a separate power supply, the entire Synapse N+1 is powered by one set of duplicated power supplies.

Synapse enhances availability simply by having one additional processor, disk controller, and disk drive than what is necessary for satisfactory performance. This extra component is not an idle backup; it is used for normal transaction processing. When a component fails, the system sometimes has to restart, and reconfigure itself without the failed component.

The Synapse system also supports mirroring of disks. Mirroring is supported in the IOP, where two disk writes are issued for each page of data to be written to the disk. It is interesting that the Synapse system allows mirroring of disks on a logical volume basis, rather than physical volume.

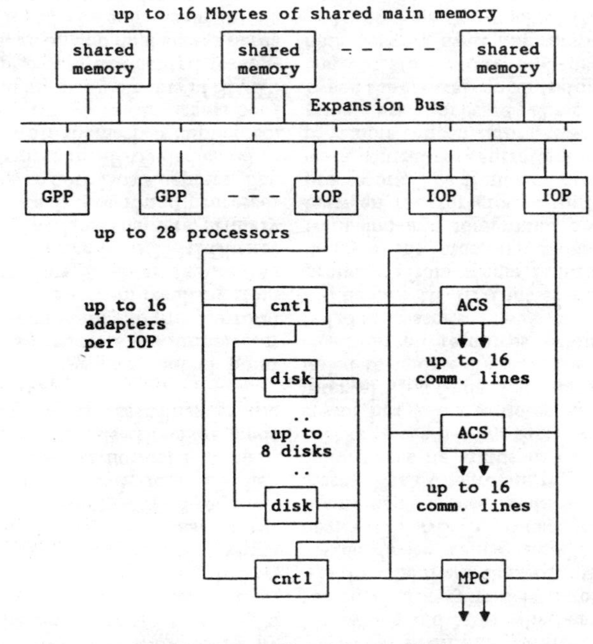

Figure 8. Synapse N+1 System architecture.

A logical volume may be all or part of a physical volume. Mirroring a logical volume is more flexible than mirroring a physical volume; for example, it allows storage on the same physical volume of a separate database that does not require high availability (and its associated overhead).

Synapse N+1 supports recoverable transactions using the Write-Ahead Log protocol. The Synapse database manager is a relational system. Further, the database may be migrated from one physical disk volume to another and may undergo structural changes without taking the applications off line.

The Synthesis operating system incorporates various techniques to optimize the performance of production transaction-processing systems. One is the placement of its database system directly above the kernel of Synthesis, rather than on top of the file system as has been the case with most database systems. The reason for this decision was to reduce the overhead associated with I/O requests from the database system to the operating system, both to retrieve data from disk, and to store the log of database changes after transaction processing.

An interesting side benefit of this approach is that higher levels of the Synthesis operating system can use the capabilities of the database system to query and manipulate data about operating system objects, such as files and devices. In particular, a higher level of the Synthesis operating system, called the transaction-processing domain, records the state of currently active applications in the database. An application consists of a number of programs; each program takes as input a screenful of information, processes it, and outputs a screen. The state information of an active application consists of a user identification, the identification of the current screen, the contents of its variable fields, and the next program to execute. During restart following a crash, the transaction-processing domain creates and dispatches a task for each terminal using this state information.

Another performance optimization in Synthesis is the elimination of task-switch overhead by replacing task switches with cross-domain (address space) calls. In other words, each of the domains (layers) of Synthesis has direct addressability to a partition of the segmented virtual address space, and a request from a task for an operating system service is implemented as a jump to the address space of the server's domain.

In order to reduce contention on the shared memory, Synapse adopted a caching scheme in which modifications to the cache in each GPP are not written through (to the shared memory), and fetch requests for the portion of the shared memory read and modified by another GPP in its cache are resolved between the processors.

The Synapse system has implemented failure detection, reconfiguration, and restart procedures in a read-only memory (ROM). Its failure detection distinguishes two classes of failures: process-fatal failure and system-fatal failure. A process-fatal failure causes the process and its associated transaction to be aborted and restarted, whereas a system-fatal failure results in a restart of the entire system.

The kernel of the operating system is capable of recognizing any failures caused by internal machine checks and is responsible for initiating the reconfiguration and restart of the system. In particular, it activates self-test code to verify whether each major hardware component is operational. After any failed components are configured out of the system, each domain (layer) of the operating system is reinitialized. Since the database system is a layer directly above the kernal operating system, transaction restart and recovery take place at this time.

Since the processing is divided between the GPPs and IOPs, and the IOPs run part of the operating system from their own local memories, the risk of total system failure due to corruption of the operating system is somewhat reduced. However, as long as the GPPs execute most of the operating system out of shared main memory, this risk is still present. This problem cannot be resolved even if shared memory is made redundant. Synapse N+1 does not support a redundant shared memory.

5. LOOSELY COUPLED MULTIPROCESSOR SYSTEM WITH A SHARED DATABASE

General Electric's MARK III Cluster File System and Computer Consoles' Power System use the loosely coupled multiprocessor architecture, in which each processor may access any of the disks. The AMOEBA project [Traiger 1983] at IBM Research, San Jose, also uses the same architecture, but is still in the research stage.

5.1 GE MARK III

MARK III is a time-sharing system developed by the Information Services Business Division of General Electric to provide its customers with local-call access to MARK III computing capabilities [Weston 1978]. The primary objectives of the system were high availability, reliability, and maintainability. Three supercenters (computing centers), located in Ohio, Maryland, and Amsterdam, provide computing power to the users. The computing facilities at a supercenter typically consist of front-end processors, MARK III foreground processors, and MARK III background processors, as shown in Figure 9.

The front-end processors are network front-end processors (central concentrators). The foreground processors support interactive users, whereas the background processors provide batch-processing capabilities. The foreground and background processors are interconnected via a Bus Adapter, which allows job and file movement between the foreground and background systems.

The Bus Adapter consists of a microprocessor, programmable read-only memory (PROM) control memory, and channel interfaces to the background systems. The microprocessor polls each of the channel interfaces for data transfer requests; each request is fully processed before the next request is serviced.

In 1975 GE developed new software to allow a single foreground processor of the

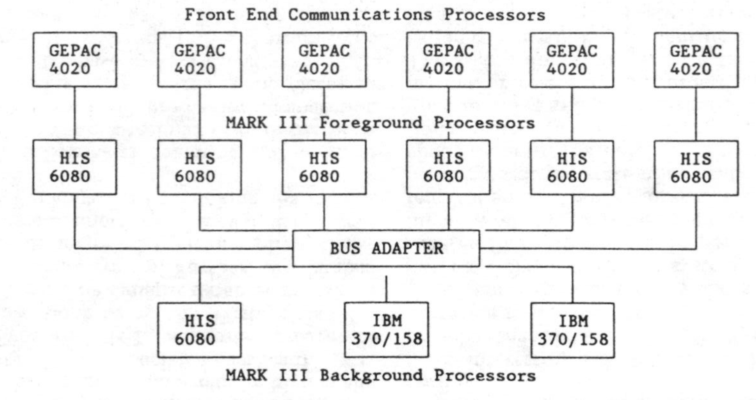

Figure 9. GE's MARK III Cluster File System architecture.

MARK III system to access more than one disk system at a time. This new system, called the Cluster File System, controls concurrent access to multiple-disk systems from multiple foreground processors by maintaining the access-conflict tables in one stable memory device accessible to all foreground processors. The Scratch Pad (SPAD) was developed to provide the high reliability, nonvolatility, and fast access time that such a memory device requires. All data transfers to and from the disk systems take place over normal I/O channels, but access-control decisions are made through use of the access tables in the SPAD.

Since the SPAD is the central point through which all requests are funneled, it was built with redundancy to prevent total failure of the cluster system resulting from the SPAD and Bus Adapter failure. As shown in Figure 10, the MARK III Cluster File System has two Bus Adapters, primary and secondary. Each foreground processor has access paths to both Bus Adapters. The memory and devices in SPAD dedicated to each disk system are themselves duplicated. Each of the Bus Adapters can access both the primary and backup elements of SPAD. The Bus Adapter was augmented to support the functions of, and dual access paths to, the SPAD, and the microcode in the Bus Adapter does dual read and write to the SPAD memory.

The SPAD contains 16 memory and logic devices (8 primary and 8 backup), each for a separate disk system. The Maryland supercenter supports seven disk systems. Each device contains the access-conflict table, which indicates whether a particular file in a disk system is in use and if so whether the file is sharable by other users.

One device, called the Cluster Control device (CLUSCON), is used for such global functions as processor status and recovery status. Each foreground processor periodically places its status in CLUSCON and checks to see if any other foreground processor has failed to do so in the previous interval. If it finds that another processor failed to update its status, it proceeds to clean up all resources belonging to the failed processor.

The MARK III Cluster File System is protected from single failures by redundancy in the interconnections between the front-end and foreground processors and between the foreground and background processors. The front-end processors (network central concentrators) are connected to remote concentrators, to which user terminals are connected. The connection between the central concentrators and remote concentrators is accomplished via redundant network-switching computers.

An obvious drawback of the MARK III Cluster File System is that the SPAD may become a performance bottleneck, especially with an expanded system, since each front-end processor must access it before accessing a shared file.

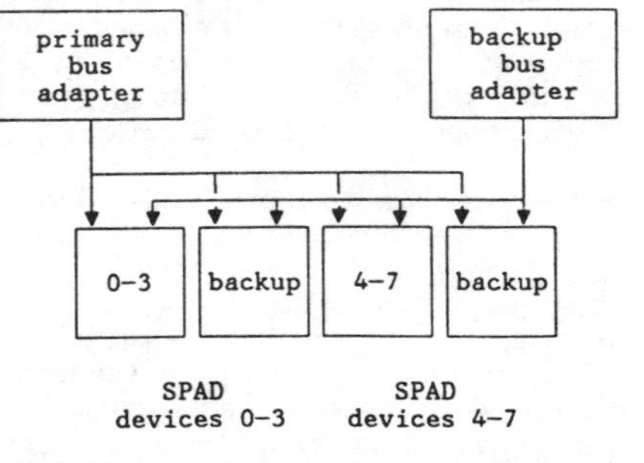

Figure 10. Redundancy in the Bus Adapter and SPAD.

5.2 Computer Consoles' Power System

The Power Series systems have been developed at Computer Consoles, Inc., Rochester, New York [West et al. 1983]. The system is based on Motorola 68000s, and consists of a number of application processors and two coordination processors with front-end processors. The processors communicate via a dual-bus system called the Data Highway, as shown in Figure 11.

Each application processor (AP) is directly connected to all disks, and independently executes different user applications in parallel. The interprocessor coordination controllers (ICC) synchronize global operations among the APs, which consist mostly of lock requests to gain access to the shared database and system status changes due to reconfiguration. At any given time, one ICC is active and the other is a standby. The standby ICC is the only idle component of the system. The front-end processors (FEP) perform screen formatting, distribute transactions to APs, receive replies from APs, and assist in recovery from some system failures. Further, FEPs attempt to balance the load on the APs by distributing the transactions to the APs on the basis of application configuration and flow control information.

Unlike many systems that implement transaction management on top of a general-purpose operating system, the Power System combines process management and transaction management into its PERPOS operating system. The PERPOS operating system supports a number of features to enhance performance of critical applications. To allow concurrent execution of transactions with different response requirements, it provides facilities to fix critical applications in memory and run them before other applications.

Since the database manager in each AP can access the entire database, the Power System only needs the standard concurrency control and recovery techniques used for a central database. In particular, it does not need the coordinated commit protocol required by loosely coupled multiprocessors with partitioned databases.

Transaction recovery is done in a straightforward manner. The AP that receives the transaction from the FEP logs the transaction on the disk. When the FEP detects that the AP crashed, it requests another AP to abort the transaction and restart it from the log of the failed AP.

As in other systems, interprocessor message time-outs are used to detect processor failures. In addition, the primary ICC periodically polls the APs and FEPs to detect failures of processors that do not happen to be in communication with other processors. The ICC supports on-line system reconfiguration after a disk crash and on-line integration of new or repaired disks.

The primary ICC does not keep the standby up-to-date on the global lock table and the system configuration information. Rather, when the primary ICC fails, the standby requests status and lock information from all the APs and reconstructs the global lock table.

In order to reduce the communication overhead resulting from lock requests to the ICC, the system distinguishes shared files and nonshared files. When an AP opens a file for the first time, it considers the file nonshared, and does not make a lock request to the global lock manager in the ICC. When an AP opens a file currently owned by another AP, that file becomes a

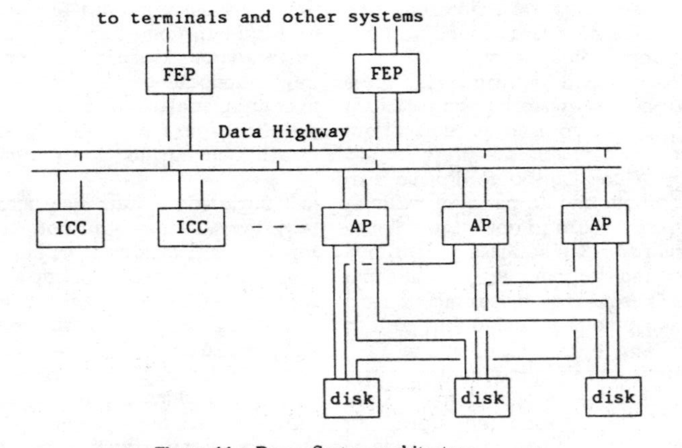

Figure 11. Power System architecture.

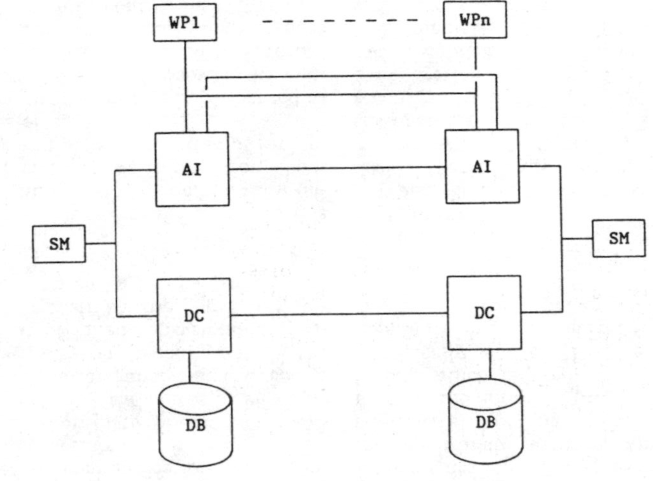

Figure 12. Syntrex's GEMINI file server architecture.

shared file under the jurisdiction of the global lock manager.

One potential drawback of the Power System architecture is that, as the number of APs increases, the ICCs may become a performance bottleneck. Further, the Power System's performance may be enhanced by generalizing its locking technique to the lock hierarchy technique similar to that found in IMS/VS [Strickland et al. 1982]. In this scheme, the database is logically partitioned, with each partition assigned to a different data manager that can acquire and release locks on data objects within its partition. The data manager consults the global lock manager only when it must lock and unlock objects outside its partition. This strategy potentially allows transfer of updated data pages from the buffer pool of one partition's data manager to another data manager. Traiger [1983] speculates on this in more detail.

6. REDUNDANT COMPUTATION SYSTEMS: SYNTREX'S GEMINI FILE SERVER

GEMINI is a file server developed by Syntrex, Inc., with the objective of uninterrupted operation, without backup, in the event of a single failure of any hardware or software component [Cohen et al. 1982]. Up to 14 workstations (word-processing terminals) connected to a GEMINI file server on a local-area network can share files and printers. A GEMINI system may be connected to other GEMINI systems through an Ethernet-like network.

As shown in Figure 12, GEMINI consists of two identical halves. Each half has the Aquarius interface (AI), a disk controller (DC), and a shared memory (SM), as well as a secondary storage system. The AI is a communications subsystem, implemented on an Intel 8088 microprocessor, that operates between GEMINI and the workstations, and between the AIs in each half. The DC, implemented on an Intel 8086, provides file storage and management for the workstations. Communication between an AI and a DC takes place through the shared memory (SM).

The two halves of GEMINI perform identical computations. Each half receives the same request from the workstations and retrieves and updates files in its secondary storage. When both halves are operational, one is designated the master and the other the slave. The only difference between them is that only the results from the master are returned to the workstations.

Each half continuously monitors the well-being of the other half. When one half crashes, it is powered off and the other half continues as the master. While one half is down, its secondary storage system becomes out of date; when it is repaired, a utility is run to bring its secondary storage system up-to-date. The active system is suspended until copying is completed. Thus GEMINI does not support on-line reintegration of repaired components.

A time-out mechanism is used in the communication between the AIs of GEMINI and the workstations. If the workstation times out on its request, it retransmits the request; if GEMINI times out, it goes to receive mode and waits for the workstation to time out and retransmit the request. This means that the workstation time-out value is longer than the GEMINI time-out.

Another aspect of the reliability measures incorporated in the AI is the periodic self-checks, including auditing of input buffers, checking of the clock, memory tests, and testing of the DC and the communication link between the AIs. If any test fails, the AI logs the failure and, if possible, informs the other AI.

The heart of mutual checking in GEMINI is embedded in the AI–AI communications procedures. The availability and reliability of GEMINI critically depends on the assumption that the disk controllers (DC) of both halves receive and perform the same computation, and therefore that the two secondary storage systems are left with the same data at the end of computation. Since it is possible for one AI to receive a correctly transmitted request while the other receives the request with a transmission error, the two AIs are required to exchange status information about the requests that they received. The request is processed only when both AIs agree that they received the same request [without a character redundancy check (CRC) error].

Similarly, the AIs exchange information about the results of the computation to verify their correctness. It is possible for one AI to have completed a computation before the other is done. In such a situation, the slow half sends a notice that it is "working on the request," to prevent the other half from concluding that it is down. GEMINI takes precautions against an infinite sequence of "I am done" and "I am working on it" messages between the AIs. Since the results of computations may be too long, sometimes only the types of results are exchanged between the AIs. Therefore it appears that sometimes GEMINI may not detect conflicting results generated by the two AIs. Further, when GEMINI does detect conflicting results, it arbitrarily assumes that the master is correct. A meaningful vote really cannot be taken with less than three processors.

7. A FRAMEWORK FOR THE MANAGEMENT OF SYSTEM CONFIGURATION

It is clear from the preceding discussions that the design of existing systems has been guided by the single-failure assumption; that is, these systems can become unavailable if a software or hardware component fails while another related component has failed. Despite the general success of some of these systems, notably the Tandem system, the single-failure assumption may not be valid. Future systems may be required to tolerate multiple concurrent failures.

Most existing systems and those that are currently being developed are constructed with mini- and microcomputers. If relatively expensive medium- to high-end processors were to be used, it might not be economically feasible to keep spares around for use as replacements for malfunctioning processors. In that case, the mean time to repair such processors could be relatively long, increasing the probability that other subsystems or processors might go down before the failed processors are repaired.

In addition, the software in most existing systems was developed from scratch to run on minicomputers and to support only prospective new customers. Existing database and operating systems required by medium- to high-end processors tend to be complex, and the mean time between failures for these systems due to software-induced failures is expected to be shorter than that for simple transaction-processing systems that run under relatively simple operating systems.

If a system is to be continuously operational, it must guarantee availability not only during multiple concurrent failures of software and hardware components, but also during on-line changes of software and hardware components and on-line physical reconfiguration of the database and database backups. The latter problems do not appear to be properly addressed by most systems. Syntrex GEMINI, for example, requires system shutdown when a repaired processor is reintegrated into the system, and in general most systems force applications off line when the database is physically reorganized.

An architecture of a distributed software subsystem that can serve as a framework for constructing database application systems to meet most availability requirements is outlined in the remainder of this section. This software subsystem is called an *auditor*. The description of the functions and architecture of the auditor given here is based largely on my own research. A design based on this is currently being implemented for the Highly Available Systems project at IBM Research, San Jose [Aghili et al. 1983].

An auditor is a framework for total coherent management of software and hardware components of a highly available distributed system. It will serve as the repository of failure reports from various components of the system and reconfiguration requests from the system operator (for on-line changes). It will analyze the status of all resources it manages, and compute the optimal configuration of the system in response to multiple concurrent failures of components and requests for load balancing. Further, it will initiate system reconfiguration and monitor its progress in order to effect mid-course correction of a reconfiguration that does not succeed, and finally, it will diagnose a class of failures that other components fail to recognize.

From the discussions of the survey portion of this paper, it should have become clear to the reader that most systems provide many of the functions outlined for the auditor. All systems discussed support automatic detection of process and processor failures, followed by automatic switchover to a backup or notification to the service center. Many systems also support on-line integration of new or repaired software (process) and hardware components (processor, I/O controller, disk drives).

However, the implementation of the auditor functions in many systems suffers from two shortcomings. First, these functions have often been implemented as a loose collection of specialized routines, rather than as a single coherent subsystem. Second, the functions often are implemented to tolerate only a single failure of the system resources; as a result, the systems cannot cope with multiple failures, even when they have sufficient hardware redundancy.

Within this framework, one auditor will reside in each processor, but only one of the auditors may be designated as the audit coordinator. As pointed out by Garcia-Molina [1982], to allow each auditor to initiate reconfiguration may cause confusion or result in a less than optimal system configuration, and the notion of the audit coordinator is therefore central to the operation of the audit mechanism. If the coordinator crashes, a new coordinator must first be established, either by an election, as suggested by Garcia-Molina [1982], or by means of a dynamic succession list to which all the auditors have previously agreed [Kim 1982]. A succession list contains the system-wide unique rank for each auditor to indicate which subordinate auditor will take over the responsibilities of the audit coordinator once the current coordinator crashes. The authenticated version of the Byzantine consensus protocol proposed by Dolev and Strong [1982] and the version-number method discussed by Kim [1982] are possible techniques to ensure agreement on the succession list in the presence of failures of communication lines, processes, and processors.

The audit coordinator should be responsible for analyzing the states of all other subordinate auditors, analyzing the reports and initiating system reconfiguration, the replacement of failed subsystems or processors with their backups, and (re)integration of repaired (or new) subsystems or processors. The audit coordinator will also serve as the arbitrator of conflicting reports from different auditors, and is responsible for maintaining a stable configuration database which contains information about the status and physical location of each of the subsystems.

Such an auditor may be implemented as a collection of six asynchronous tasks: configuration-database task, audit task, reconfiguration task, state-report task, diagnose task, and operator-control task. The task structure of an auditor and the flow of control among the auditor tasks are illustrated in Figure 13.

The configuration-database task maintains a consistent and up-to-date configuration database. All queries and updates to the configuration database by other auditor tasks are directed to this task. Changes to the configuration database are exclusively handled by the configuration-database task of the audit coordinator. After each change, the configuration-database tasks of the subordinate auditors are given the most up-to-date copy of the configuration database. Although the configuration database viewed by a subordinate auditor may be temporarily out of date, consistency of the system configuration is not compromised since critical decisions can only be made by the audit coordinator.

The audit task is primarily responsible for coordinated surveillance of process and processor failures. The audit task of a subordinate auditor collects the local state reports from the state-report task, and delivers them to the audit task of the coordinator. The audit task of the coordinator receives these state reports from subordinate auditors, and analyzes them to determine whether any process or processor has failed.

One way for the audit coordinator to receive state reports is to periodically poll the subordinate auditors. An interesting alternative to polling by the audit coordinator is the approach proposed by Walter [1982], which requires each "auditor" to periodically send an "I-AM-ALIVE" message to its immediate neighbor on a virtual ring of "auditors." When an auditor does not receive the "I-AM-ALIVE" message within a certain time interval, it may request the audit coordinator to initiate reconfiguration.

When the audit task of the coordinator decides that a failure has occurred, or when it receives a reconfiguration request from the operator control task, it activates the reconfiguration task. Changes to system configuration are reflected in the configuration database after the reconfiguration task completes. The audit task of the coordinator is also responsible for preparing the succession list and securing its trans-

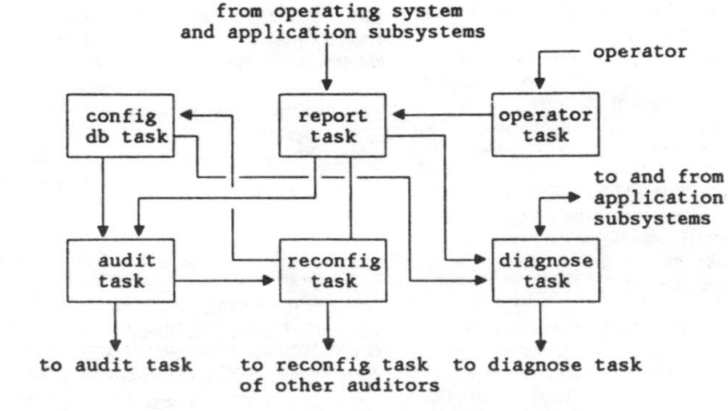

Figure 13. The task structure of an auditor.

mission to the audit tasks of subordinate auditors.

The reconfiguration task is responsible for processing the reconfiguration requests received from the audit task of the audit coordinator. Upon receiving a request, it initiates reconfiguration and monitors its successful completion. If the audit coordinator fails during a reconfiguration process, then the new coordinator completes the reconfiguration. Any change to the system configuration is stored in the configuration database. A report is sent back to the audit task of the coordinator upon completion of a reconfiguration request.

The state-report task receives state reports from the local database subsystems, interprocessor communication subsystem, and the operating system, as well as reconfiguration requests from the system operator. It manages this collection of state reports and makes it available to the local audit task and other auditor tasks.

The diagnose task is responsible for exposing process failures that may have gone undetected by the operating system or the process itself. It may also collect complaints from database subsystems about possible misbehavior of other subsystems (e.g., time-outs and lost messages). To establish availability or misbehavior of subsystems, it may resort to functional tests, such as checking if messages pass through queues, tracking down the messages exchanged by subsystems, and executing simple transactions whose results are known. This sometimes will require collaboration among the diagnose tasks of several auditors. Its findings are packaged into a state report and sent to a database subsystem (e.g., to report the loss of a message and the need for its retransmission) or to the state-report task (e.g., to report a subsystem crash that has remained undetected by the operating system).

The complexity of the diagnose task depends on the extent to which other software subsystems assist in identifying failures. If the operating system is capable of serving as a repository of hardware and program failures, and application software contains a reasonable amount of defensive code to detect impossible software states, the diagnose task can be quite simple. If this is not the case, the diagnose task may have to be designed in a manner similar to the Resource Manager of System D to expose the nature of failures.

The operator-control task is the auditor's interface to the system operator. By using this interface, the operator may query the system configuration or request a system reconfiguration.

8. CONCLUDING REMARKS

This paper has provided a survey and analysis of the architectures and availability techniques used in database application systems designed with availability as a primary objective. We found that all existing systems have been designed under the single-failure assumption, but that some of the systems contain single points of failure and cannot survive failures of some single components. Rather, these systems are designed to restart quickly to provide high overall availability.

All of the systems may be classified into four distinct architectures: loosely coupled multiprocessor systems with a partitioned database, tightly coupled multiprocessor systems with a shared database, loosely coupled multiprocessor systems with a shared database, and multiprocessor systems that perform redundant computations and compare the results. Of these, the loosely coupled multiprocessor with either a partitioned or shared database appears to offer the best framework for building a highly available system. Either architecture is conducive to incremental expansion and offers a natural boundary between data managers, which makes it difficult for a malfunctioning data manager to corrupt other data managers. Of course, both architectures require a low-overhead communications subsystem to process user requests that require access to more than one database partition. A difficult problem posed by the partitioned database, however, is that of deciding which database partition should be owned by which processor, so as to minimize the volume of processing requiring collaboration among more than one data manager. Potential drawbacks of the shared database approach are contention on shared disks and the difficulty of coordinating the global locking and the logging of database changes.

The tightly coupled multiprocessor architecture with a shared database compromises availability in favor of a potential performance advantage over the loosely coupled system with a partitioned database. However, before this potential advantage in performance can be realized, the problems of contention among processors for the use of shared memory and other shared resources, especially as more processors are added, must be resolved.

Although the redundant-computation approach may make sense for applications such as spacecraft and industrial process control, it does not appear particularly suitable for typical database applications. The exchange of status information among the replicated tasks to verify correctness of each input and output could seriously impede the performance of a production system.

A continuously operational database application systems must guarantee availability not only during multiple concurrent failures of software and hardware components but also during on-line changes of software and hardware components, on-line physical reconfiguration of the database, and generation of backup databases. An architecture was outlined in Section 7 of a distributed software subsystem called an auditor, which can serve as a framework for constructing database application systems to meet these requirements.

ACKNOWLEDGMENTS

Irv Traiger (IBM Research, San Jose) read an initial version of this paper and made numerous valuable suggestions that helped to significantly improve the technical contents and presentation of the paper. John West of Computer Consoles, Richard Gostanian of Auragen Systems, Bob Good of Bank of America, Steve Jones of Synapse Computer, and Dave Cohen of AT&T Bell Labs kindly provided answers to various technical questions I had about their systems. The referees and Randy Katz made various constructive comments on an earlier version of this paper. Finally, a technical editor did a superb job of shaping the paper into publishable form.

REFERENCES

AGHILI, H., ASTRAHAN, M., FINKELSTEIN, S., KIM, W., MCPHERSON, K., SCHKOLNICK, M., AND STRONG, M. 1983. A prototype for a highly available database system. IBM Res. Rep. RJ3755, IBM Research, San Jose, Calif., Jan. 17.

ANDLER, S., DING, I., ESWARAN, K., HAUSER, C., KIM, W., MEHL, J., AND WILLIAMS, R. 1982. System D: A distributed system for availability. In *Proceedings of the 8th International Conference on Very Large Data Bases* (Mexico City, Mexico D.F., Sept.), pp. 33–44.

BARTLETT, J. 1978. A nonstop operating system. In *Proceedings of the 1978 International Conference on System Sciences* (Honolulu, Hawaii, Jan.).

BERNSTEIN, P., AND GOODMAN, N. 1981. Concurrency control in distributed database systems. *ACM Comput. Surv. 13*, 2 (June), 185–221.

BORR, A. 1981. Transaction monitoring in ENCOMPASS (TM): Reliable distributed transaction processing. In *Proceedings of the 7th International Conference on Very Large Databases* (Cannes, France, Sept. 9–11). IEEE, New York, pp. 155–165. ACM, New York.

COHEN, D., HOLCOMB, J. E., AND SURY, M. B. 1983. Database management strategies to support network services. *IEEE Q. Bull. Database Eng. 6*, 2 (June), special issue on Highly Available Systems.

COHEN, N. B., HALEY, C. B., HENDERSON, S. E., AND WON, C. L. 1982. GEMINI: A reliable local network. In *Proceedings of the 6th Workshop on Distributed Data Management and Computer Networks* (Berkeley, Calif., Feb.), pp. 1–22.

DOLEV, D., AND STRONG, H. R. 1982. Polynomial algorithms for multiple processor agreement. In *Proceeding of the 14th ACM Symposium on Theory of Computing* (San Francisco, May 5–7). ACM, New York, pp. 401–407.

ELECTRONIC BUSINESS 1981. October issue.

GARCIA-MOLINA, H. 1982. Elections in a distributed computing system. *IEEE Trans. Comput. C-31*, 1 (Jan.), pp. 48–59.

GOOD, B. 1983. Experience with Bank of America's distributive computing System. In *Proceedings of the IEEE CompCon* (Mar.). IEEE Computer Society, Los Angeles.

GOSTANIAN, R. 1983. The Auragen System 4000. *IEEE Q. Bull. Database Eng. 6*, 2 (June), special issue on Highly Available Systems.

GRAY, J. N. 1978. Notes on data base operating systems. IBM Res. Rep. RJ2188, IBM Research, San Jose, Calif., Feb.

GRAY, J. N., MCJONES, P., BLASGEN, M., LINDSAY, B., LORIE, R., PRICE, T., PUTZOLU, F., AND TRAIGER, I. 1981. Recovery manager of a data management system. *ACM Comput. Surv. 13*, 2 (June), 223–242.

HAERDER, T., AND REUTER, A. Principles of transaction-oriented database recovery. *ACM Comput. Surv. 15*, 4 (Dec.), 287–317.

IBM 1979. OS/VS2 MVS multiprocessing: An introduction and guide to writing, operating, and recovery procedures. Form No. GC28-0952-1, File No. S370-34, International Business Machines.

IBM 1980. IBM System/370 principles of operation. Form No. GA22-7000-6, File No. S370-01, International Business Machines.

IEEE 1983. *IEEE Q. Bull. Database Eng. 6*, 2, (June), special issue on Highly Available Systems.

JONES, S. 1983. Synapse's approach to high application availability. In *Proceedings of the IEEE Spring CompCon* (Mar.). IEEE Computer Society, Los Angeles.

KASTNER, P. C. 1983. A fault-tolerant transaction processing environment. *IEEE Q. Bull. Database Eng. 6*, 2 (June), special issue on Highly Available Systems.

KATSUKI, D., ELSAM, E. S., MANN, W. F., ROBERTS, E. S., ROBINSON, J. G., SKOWRONSKI, F. S., AND WOLF, E. W. 1978. Pluribus—An operational fault-tolerant multiprocessor. *Proc. IEEE 66*, 10 (Oct.) 1146–1159.

KATZMAN, J. A. 1977. System architecture for NonStop computing. In *Proceedings of the CompCon* (Feb). IEEE Computer Society, Los Angeles. pp. 77–80.

KATZMAN, J. A. 1978. A fault tolerant computer system. In *Proceedings of the 1978 International Conference on System Sciences* (Honolulu, Hawaii, Jan.).

KIM, W. 1982. Auditor: A framework for highly available DB/DC systems. In *Proceedings of the 2nd Symposium on Reliability in Distributed Software and Database Systems* (Pittsburgh, Pa., July). *IEEE* Computer Society, Silver Spring, Md., pp. 76–84.

KINNUCAN, P. 1981. An industrial computer that 'can't fail.' *Mini-Micro Syst.* (Mar.), 29–34.

KOHLER, W. 1981. A survey of techniques for synchronization and recovery in decentralized computer systems. *ACM Comput. Surv. 13*, 2 (June), 149–183.

MITZE, R. W., ET. AL. 1983. The 3B-20D processor and DMERT as a base for telecommunications applications. *Bell Syst. Tech. J. Comput. Sci. Syst. 62*, 1 (Jan.), 171–180.

SPENCER, A. C., AND VIGILANTE, F. S. 1969. System organization and objectives, *Bell Syst. Tech. J.* (Oct.), 2607–2618, special issue on No. 2 ESS.

STRATUS 1982 *Stratus/32 System Overview.* Stratus Computers, Natick, Mass.

STRICKLAND, J. P., UHROWCZIK, P. P., AND WATTS, V. L. 1982. IMS/VS: An evolving system. *IBM Syst. J. 21*, 4, 490–510.

SWAN, R., FULLER, S. H., AND SIEWIOREB, D. P. 1977. Cm*—A modular, multi-microprocessor. In *Proceedings of the National Computer Conference* (Dallas, Tex., June 13–16), vol. 45. AFIPS Press, Reston, Va., pp. 637–644.

TRAIGER, I. 1983. Trends in systems aspects of database management. In *Proceedings of the British Computer Society 2nd International Conference on Databases* (Cambridge, England, Aug. 30–Sept. 2).

TSUKIGI, K., AND HASEGAWA, Y. 1983. The travel reservation on-line network system. *IEEE Q. Bull. Database Eng. 6*, 1 (Mar.), special issue on Database Systems in Japan.

WALTER, B. 1982. A robust and efficient protocol for checking the availability of remote sites. In *Proceedings of the 6th Workshop on Distributed Data Management and Computer Networks* (Berkeley, Calif., Feb.), pp. 45–68.

WEISS, H. M. 1980. The ORACLE data base management system. *Mini-Micro Syst.* (Aug.), 111–114.

WENSLEY, J. H., LAMPORT, L., GOLDBERG, J., GREEN, M., LEVITT, K., MELLIAR-SMITH, P. M., SHOSTAK, R., AND WEINSTOCK, C. 1978. SIFT: Design and analysis of fault-tolerant computer for aircraft control. *Proc. IEEE 66*, 10 (Oct.), 1240–1255.

WEST, J. C., ISMAN, M. A., AND HANNAFORD, S. G. 1983. Transaction processing in the PERPOS operating system. *IEEE Q. Bull. Database Eng. 6*, 2 (June), special issue on Highly Available Systems.

WESTON, J. 1978. General Electric's MARK III Cluster System. Presented to the American Institute of Industrial Engineers, Jan. 31.

GAMMA - A High Performance Dataflow Database Machine

David J. DeWitt Robert H. Gerber
Goetz Graefe Michael L. Heytens
Krishna B. Kumar M. Muralikrishna

Computer Sciences Department
University of Wisconsin

Abstract

In this paper, we present the design, implementation techniques, and initial performance evaluation of Gamma. Gamma is a new relational database machine that exploits dataflow query processing techniques. Gamma is an operational prototype consisting of 20 VAX 11/750 computers. In addition to demonstrating that parallelism can really be made to work in a database machine context, the Gamma prototype shows how parallelism can be controlled with minimal control overhead through a combination of the use of algorithms based on hashing and the pipelining of data between processes.

1. Introduction

While the database machine field has been a very active area of research for the last 10 years, only a handful of research prototypes [OZKA75, LEIL78, DEWI79, STON79, HELL81, SU82, GARD83, FISH84, KAKU85, DEMU86] and three commercial products [TERA83, UBEL85, IDM85] have ever been built. None have demonstrated that a highly parallel relational database machine can actually be constructed.

In this paper, we present the design of Gamma, a new relational database machine that exploits dataflow query processing techniques. Gamma is a fully operational prototype whose design is based on what we learned from building our earlier multiprocessor database machine prototype (DIRECT) and several years of subsequent research on the problems raised by the DIRECT prototype. Our evaluation of DIRECT [BITT83] showed a number of major flaws in its design. First, for certain types of queries, DIRECT's performance was severely constrained by its limited I/O bandwidth. This problem was exaggerated by the fact that DIRECT attempted to use parallelism as a substitute for indexing. When one looks at indices from the viewpoint of I/O bandwidth and CPU resources, what an index provides is a mechanism to avoid searching a large piece of the database to answer certain types of queries. With I/O bandwidth a critical resource in any database machine [BORA83], the approach used by DIRECT, while conceptually appealing, leads to disastrous performance [BITT83]. The other major problem with DIRECT was that the number of control actions (messages) required to control the execution of the parallel algorithms used for complex relational operations (e.g. join) was proportional to the product of the sizes of the two input relations. Even with message passing implemented via shared memory, the time spent passing and handling messages dominated the processing and I/O time for this type of query.

The remainder of this paper is organized as follows. The architecture of Gamma and the rationale behind this design is presented in Section 2. In Section 3, we describe the process structure of the Gamma software and discuss how these processes cooperate to execute queries. In Section 4 we describe the algorithms and techniques used to implement each of the relational algebra operations. In Section 5, we present the results of our preliminary performance evaluation of Gamma. Our conclusions and future research directions are described in Section 6.

2. Hardware Architecture of GAMMA

2.1. Solutions to the I/O Bottleneck Problem

Soon after conducting our evaluation of the DIRECT prototype, we realized that limited I/O bandwidth was not just a problem with DIRECT. As discussed in [BORA83], changes in processor and mass storage technology have affected all database machine designs. During the past decade, while the CPU performance of single chip microprocessors has improved by at least two orders of magnitude (e.g. Intel 4040 to the Motorola 68020), there has been only a factor of three improvement in I/O bandwidth from commercially available disk drives (e.g. IBM 3330 to IBM 3380). These changes in technology have rendered a number of database machine designs useless and have made it much more difficult to exploit massive amounts of parallelism in any database machine design.

In [BORA83], we suggested two strategies for improving I/O bandwidth. One idea was to use a very large main memory as a disk cache [DEWI84a]. The second was the use of a number of small disk drives in novel configurations as a replacement for large disk drives and to mimic the characteristics of parallel read-out disk drives. A number of researchers have already begun to look at these ideas [SALE84, KIM85, BROW85, LIVN85] and Tandem has a product based on this concept [TAND85].

Although this concept looks interesting, we feel that it suffers from the following drawback. Assume that the approach can indeed be used to construct a mass storage subsystem with an effective bandwidth of, for example, 100 megabytes/second. As illustrated by Figure 1, before the data can be processed it must be routed through an interconnection network (e.g. banyan switch, cross-bar) which must have a bandwidth of at least[1] 100 megabytes/second. If one believes the fabled "90-10" rule, most of the data moved is not needed in the first place.

Figure 2 illustrates one alternative design. In this design, conventional disk drives are used and associated with each disk drive is a processor. With enough disk drives (50 drives at 2 megabytes/second

[1] 100 megabytes/second are needed to handle the disk traffic. Additional bandwidth would be needed to handle processor to processor communications.

each) the I/O bandwidth of the two alternatives will be equivalent. However, the second design has a number of what we consider to be significant advantages. First, the design reduces the bandwidth that must be provided by the interconnection network by 100 megabytes/second. By associating a processor with each disk drive and employing algorithms that maximize the amount of processing done locally, the results in [DEWI85] demonstrate that one can significantly cut the communications overhead. A second advantage is that the design permits the I/O bandwidth to be expanded incrementally. Finally, the design may simplify exploiting improvements in disk technology.

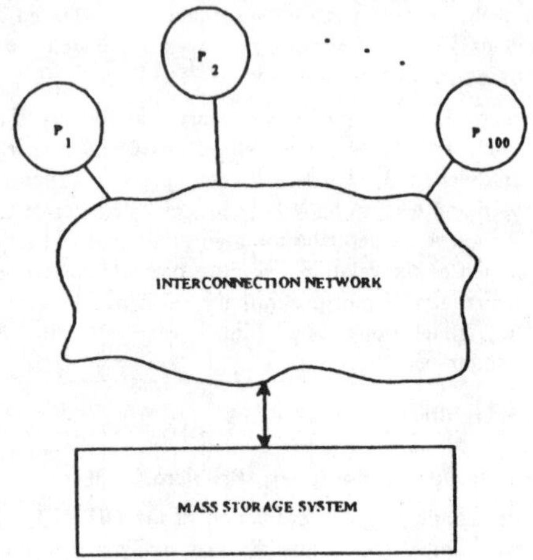

Figure 1

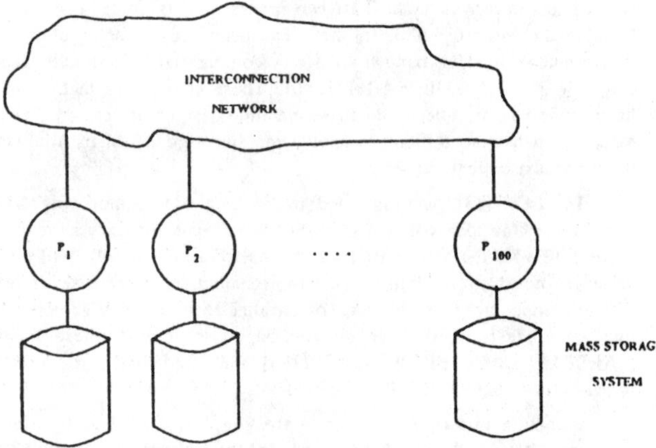

Figure 2

This alternative, on which Gamma is based, seems to have been pioneered by Goodman [GOOD81] in his thesis work on the use of the X-tree multiprocessor for database applications. It is also the basis of several other active database machine projects. In the case of the MBDS database machine [DEMU86], the interconnection network is a 10 megabit/second Ethernet. In the SM3 project [BARU84], the interconnection network is implemented as a bus with switchable shared memory modules. In the Teradata product [TERA83], a tree structured interconnection network termed the Y-net is employed.

2.2. Gamma Hardware

The architecture of the current prototype of the Gamma database machine is shown in Figure 3. Presently, Gamma consists of 20 VAX 11/750 processors, each with two megabytes of memory. An 80 megabit/second token ring developed for us [DEWI84b] by Proteon Associates is used to connect the processors to each other and to another VAX running Berkeley UNIX. This processor acts as the host machine for Gamma. Attached to eight of the processors are 160 megabyte Fujitsu disk drives (8") which are used for database storage.

2.3. Discussion

One may wonder how Gamma (or MBDS [DEMU86]) is different from a distributed database system running on a local area network. As will become obvious in the next section, Gamma has no notion of site autonomy, has a centralized schema, and a single point for initiating the execution of all queries. Furthermore, the operating system used by Gamma has no capability to dynamically load new programs, has lightweight processes with shared memory, and does not provide demand paging.

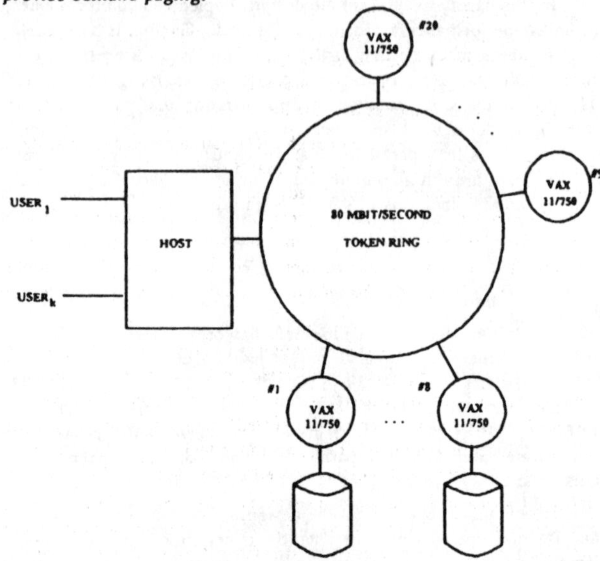

Gamma Hardware Configuration
Figure 3

3. Design of the Gamma System Software

3.1. Storage Organization

All relations in Gamma are **horizontally partitioned** [RIES78] across all disk drives in the system. The Gamma query language (gdl - a extension of QUEL [STON76]) provides the user with four alternative ways of distributing the tuples of a relation:

- round robin
- hashed
- range partitioned with user-specified placement by key value
- range partitioned with uniform distribution

As implied by its name, in the first strategy when tuples are loaded into a relation, they are distributed in a round-robin fashion among all disk drives. This is the strategy employed in MBDS [DEMU86] and is the default strategy in Gamma for relations created as the result of a query. If the hashed strategy is selected, a randomizing function is applied to the key attribute of each tuple (as specified in the partition command of gdl) to select a storage unit. This technique is used by the Terradata database machine [TERA83]. In the third strategy the user specifies a range of key values for each site. For example, with a 4 disk system, the command **partition employee on emp_id (100, 300, 1000)** would result in the following distribution of tuples:

Distribution Condition	Processor #
emp_id ≤ 100	1
100 < emp_id ≤ 300	2
300 < emp_id ≤ 1000	3
emp_id > 1000	4

At first glance, this distribution is similar to the partitioning mechanism supported by VSAM [WAGN73] and the TANDEM file system [ENSC85]. There is, however, a significant difference. In VSAM and in the Tandem file system, if a file is partitioned on a key, then at each site the file must be kept in sorted order on that key. This is not the case in Gamma. In Gamma, there is no relationship between the partitioning attribute of a file and the order of the tuples at a site. To understand the motivation for this capability consider the following banking example. Each tuple contains three attributes: account_#, balance, and branch_#. 90% of the queries fetch a single tuple using account_#. The other 10% of the queries find the current balance for each branch. To maximize throughput, the file would be partitioned on account_#. However, rather than building a clustered index on account_# as would be required with VSAM and the Tandem file system, in Gamma, a clustered index would be built on branch_# and a non-clustered index would be built on account_#. This physical design will provide the same response time for the single tuple queries and a much lower response time for the other queries.

If a user does not have enough information about his data file to select key ranges, he may elect the final distribution strategy. In this strategy, if the relation is not already loaded, it is initially loaded in a round robin fashion. Next, the relation is sorted (using a parallel merge sort) on the partitioning attribute and the sorted relation is redistributed in a fashion that attempts to equalize the number of tuples at each site. Finally, the maximum key value at each site is returned to the host processor.

Once a relation has been partitioned, Gamma provides the normal mechanisms for creating clustered (primary) and non-clustered (secondary) indices on each fragment of the relation. However, a special multiprocessor index is constructed when a relation is horizontally partitioned using either of the two range techniques. As shown in Figure 4, the disks, and their associated processors, can be viewed as nodes in a primary, clustered index.[2] The root page of the index is maintained as part of the schema information associated with the index on the host machine. As will be described below, this root page is used by the query optimizer to direct selection queries on the key attribute to the appropriate sites for execution.

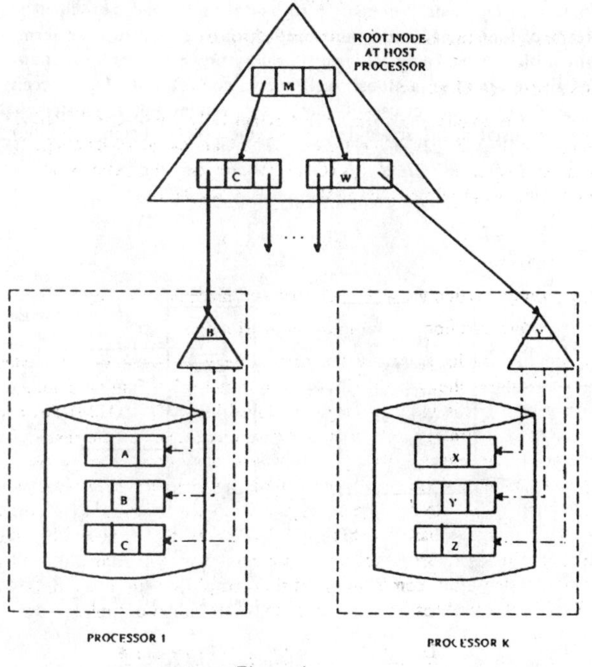

Figure 4

[2] A multiprocessor index may consist of only 1 level if indices have not been created at the disks.

3.2. Gamma Process Structure

In Figure 5, the structure of the various processes that form the software of Gamma is specified. Along with indicating the relationships among the processes, Figure 5 specifies one possible mapping of processes to processors. In discussing the role each process plays in Gamma, we will indicate other alternative ways of mapping Gamma processes to machines. The role of each process is described briefly below. Their interaction is described in more detail in the following section.

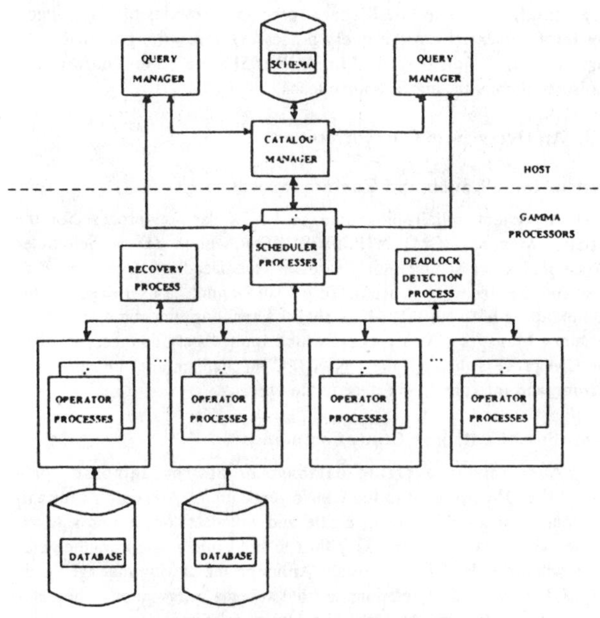

Gamma Process Structure
Figure 5

Catalog Manager — The function of the Catalog Manager is to act as a central repository of all conceptual and internal schema information for each database. The schema information is permanently stored in a set of UNIX files on the host and is loaded into memory when a database is first opened. Since multiple users may have the same database open at once and since each user may reside on a machine other than the one on which the Catalog Manager is executing, the Catalog Manager is responsible for insuring consistency among the copies cached by each user.

Query Manager — There is one query manager process associated with each active Gamma user. The query manager is responsible for caching schema information locally, providing an interface for ad-hoc queries using gdl, query parsing, optimization, and compilation.

Scheduler Processes — While executing, each "complex" (i.e. multisite) query is controlled by a scheduler process. This process is responsible for activating the Operator Processes used to execute the nodes of a compiled query tree. Since a message between two query processors is twice as fast as a message between a query processor and the host machine (due to the cost of getting a packet through the UNIX operating system), we elected to run the scheduler processes in the database machine instead of the host. At the present time, all are run on a single processor. Distributing the scheduler processes on multiple machines would be relatively straightforward as the only information shared among them is a summary of available memory for each query processor. This information is centralized to facilitate load balancing. If the schedulers were distributed, access would be accomplished via remote procedure calls.

Operator Process — For each operator in a query tree, at least one Operator Process is employed at each processor participating in the execution of the operator. The structure of an operator process and the mapping of relational operators to operator processes is discussed in more detail below.

Deadlock Detection Process — Gamma employs a centralized deadlock detection mechanism. This process is responsible for collecting fragments of the "wait-for" graph from each lock manager, for locating cycles, and selecting a victim to abort.

Log Manager — The Log Manager process is responsible for collecting log fragments from the query processors and writing them on the log. The algorithms described in [AGRA85] are used for coordinating transaction commit, abort, and rollback.

3.3. An Overview of Query Execution

System Initialization and Gamma Invocation

At system initialization time, a UNIX daemon process for the Catalog Manager (CM) is initiated along with a set of Scheduler Processes, a set of Operator Processes, the Deadlock Detection Process and the Recovery Process. To invoke Gamma, a user executes the command "gdl" from the UNIX shell. Executing this command starts a Query Manager (QM) process which immediately connects itself to the CM process through the UNIX IPC mechanism and then presents a command interpreter interface to the user.

Execution of Database Utility Commands

After parsing a **create database** or **destroy database** command, the QM passes it to the CM for execution. A **create database** command causes the CM to create and initialize the proper schema entries and create the necessary files to hold information on the relations when the database is closed. Although the catalog manager uses UNIX files instead of relations to hold schema information, the catalog structure it employs is that of a typical relational database system. When a **destroy database** command is executed, its actual execution is delayed until all current users of the database have exited. The first step in executing an **open database** command is for the QM to request the schema from the CM. If no other user currently has the requested database open, the CM first reads the schema into memory from disk and then returns a copy of the schema to the requesting QM. The QM caches its copy of the schema locally until the database is closed.

When a user attempts to execute any command that changes the schema of a database (e.g create/destroy relation, build/drop index, partition, etc), the QM first asks the CM for permission. If permission is granted, the QM executes the command, and then informs the CM of the outcome. If the command was executed successfully, the CM records the changes in its copy of the schema and then propagates them to all query managers with the same database open [HEYT85]. A lock manager within the CM ensures catalog consistency.

Query Execution

Gamma uses traditional relational techniques for query parsing, optimization [SELI79, JARK84], and code generation. The optimization process is somewhat simplified as Gamma only employs hash-based algorithms for joins and other complex operations [DEWI85]. Queries are compiled into a tree of operators. At execution time, each operator is executed by one or more operator processes at each participating site.

In the process of optimizing a query, the query optimizer recognizes that certain queries can be executed at a single site. For example, consider a query containing only a selection operation on the relation shown in Figure 4 (assume that q is the name of the attribute on which the relation has been partitioned). If, for example, the selection condition is "q > A and q ≤ C" then the optimizer can use the root page of the multiprocessor index on q to determine that the query only has to be sent to Processor #1.

In the case of a single site query, the query is sent directly by the QM to the appropriate processor for execution. In the case of a multiple site query, the optimizer establishes a connection to an idle scheduler process through a dispatcher process. The dispatcher process, by controlling the number of active schedulers, implements a simple load control mechanism based on information about the degree of CPU and memory utilization at each processor. Once it has established a connection with a scheduler process, the QM sends the compiled query to the scheduler process and waits for the query to complete execution. The scheduler process, in turn, activates operator processes at each query processor selected to execute the operator. Finally, the QM reads the results of the query and returns them through the ad-hoc query interface to the user or through the embedded query interface to the program from which the query was initiated.

In the case of a multisite query, the task of assigning operators to processors is performed in part by the optimizer and in part by the scheduler assigned to control the execution of the query. For example, the operators at the leaves of a query tree reference only permanent relations. Using the query and schema information, the optimizer is able to determine the best way of assigning these operators to processors. The root node of a query tree is either a **store** operator in the case of a "retrieve into" query or a **spool** operator in the case of a retrieve query (ie. results are returned to the host). In the case of a **Store** operator, the optimizer will assign a copy of the query tree node to a process at each processor with a disk. Using the techniques described below, the **store** operator at each site receives result tuples from the processes executing the node which is its child in the query tree and stores them in its fragment of the result relation (recall that **all** permanent relations are horizontally partitioned). In the case of a **spool** node at the root of a query tree, the optimizer assigns it to a single process; generally, on a diskless[3] processor.

3.4. Operator and Process Structure

In Gamma, the algorithms for all operators are written as if they were to be run on a single processor. As shown in Figure 6, the input to an Operator Process is a stream of tuples and the output is a stream of tuples that is demultiplexed through a structure we term a **split table**. After being initiated, a query process waits for a control message to arrive on a global, well-known control port. Upon receiving an operator control packet, the process replies with a message that identifies itself to the scheduler. Once the process begins execution,

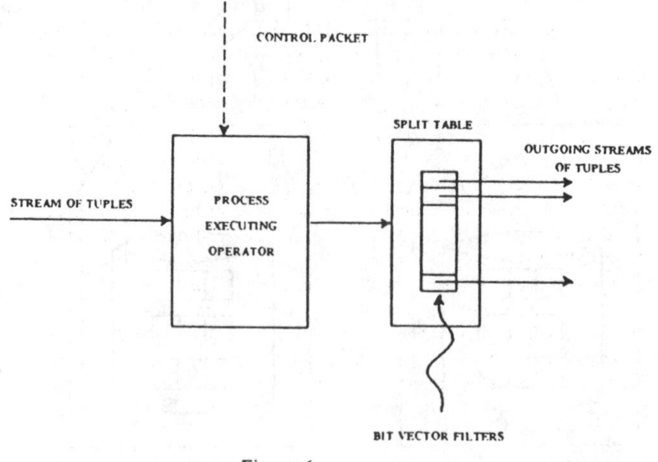

Figure 6

[3] The communications software provides a back-pressure mechanism so that the host can slow the rate at which tuples are being produced if it cannot keep up.

it continuously reads tuples from its input stream, operates on each tuple, and uses a split table to route the resulting tuple to the process indicated in the split table. When the process detects the end of its input stream, it first closes the output streams and then sends a control message to its scheduler indicating that it has completed execution. Closing the output streams has the side effect of sending "end of stream" messages to each of the destination processes. With the exception of these three control messages, execution of an operator is completely self-scheduling. Data flows among the processes executing a query tree in a dataflow fashion.

The split table defines a mapping of values to a set of destination processes. Gamma uses three different types of split tables depending on the type of operation being performed. For example, consider the use of a split table shown in Figure 7 in conjunction with the execution of a join operation using 4 processors. Each process producing source tuples for the join will apply a hash function to the join attribute of each output tuple to produce a value between 0 and 3. This value is then used as an index into the split table to obtain the address of the destination process that should receive the tuple.

Value	Destination Process
0	(Processor #3, Port #5)
1	(Processor #2, Port #13)
2	(Processor #7, Port #6)
3	(Processor #9, Port #15)

An Example Split Table
Figure 7

The second type of split table used by Gamma produces tuple streams that are partitioned on discrete ranges of non-hashed attribute values. In this case, the upper bound of each partition range serves as a key value for each entry in the split table. These range partitioned split tables are used when permanent relations are fragmented using either of the range partitioning strategies described in Section 3.1. These split tables are also applicable when the split attribute targeted by an operation at the leaf of a query tree is the horizontal partitioning attribute (HPA) for a relation. In this case, the split table is initialized with the boundary values defined for the source relation's HPA with the effect that each fragment of the source relation is processed locally. For join operations, if the outer relation is horizontally partitioned on the join attribute, then the relation will generally not be transmitted across the network. In this case, the inner relation of the join would be partitioned and distributed according to the HPA ranges of the fragments of the outer relation at each site.

Gamma uses a third form of split tables when tuples are distributed in a round robin fashion among destination processes. For this distribution strategy, tuples are routed to destination processes represented in the split table, independently of the table's key values.

To enhance the performance of certain operations, an array of bit vector filters [BABB79, VALD84] is inserted into the split table as shown in Figure 6. In the case of a join operation, each join process builds a bit vector filter by hashing the join attribute values while building its hash table using the outer relation [BRAT84, DEWI85, DEWI84a, VALD84]. When the hash table for the outer relation has been completed, the process sends its filter to its scheduler. After the scheduler has received all the filters, it sends them to the processes responsible for producing the inner relation of the join. Each of these processes uses the set of filters to eliminate those tuples that will not produce any tuples in the join operation.

3.5. Operating and Storage System

Gamma is built on top of an operating system developed specifically for supporting database management systems. NOSE provides multiple, lightweight processes with shared memory. A non-preemptive scheduling policy is used to help prevent convoys [BLAS79] from occurring. NOSE provides reliable communications between NOSE processes on Gamma processors and to UNIX processes on the host machine. The reliable communications mechanism is a timer-based, one bit stop-and-wait, positive acknowledgement protocol [TANE81]. A delta-T mechanism is used to re-establish sequence numbers [WATS81]. File, record, index, and scan services in NOSE are based on the Wisconsin Storage System (WiSS) [CHOU85]. Critical sections of WiSS are protected using the semaphore mechanism provided by NOSE. To enhance performance, the page format used by WiSS includes the message format required for interprocessor communications by NOSE. Thus, a page can be read from disk and sent to another processor without requiring that tuples be copied from the page in the buffer pool into an outgoing message template.

4. Query Processing Algorithms

4.1. Selection Operator

The performance of the selection operator is a critical element of the overall performance of any query plan. If a selection operator provides insufficient throughput, then the amount of parallelism that can be effectively applied by subsequent operators is limited. Gamma's use of horizontally partitioned relations and closely coupled processor/disk pairs addresses the I/O bottleneck from a macro-system perspective. However, the efficiency of individual selection operator processes on distinct processors is still important. For a given set of resources, a well-tuned selection operator should provide the necessary throughput to ensure that the rest of the system is effectively utilized.

To achieve the maximum possible throughput, Gamma uses three complementary techniques. First, indices are used whenever possible. Second, selection predicates are compiled into machine language procedures to minimize their execution time. Finally, a limited form of read-ahead is used in order to overlap the processing of one page with the I/O to get the "next" page of the relation from disk.

4.2. Join

The multiprocessor hash-join algorithm used by Gamma is based on a partitioning of source relations into disjoint subsets called **buckets** [GOOD81, KITS83a,b, BRAT84, DEWI84a, VALD84, DEWI85]. The partitioned buckets represent disjoint subsets of the original relations. These partitions have the important characteristic that all tuples with the same join attribute value share the same bucket. The potential power of this partitioning lies in the fact that a join of two large relations can be reduced to the separate joins of many smaller relation buckets [KITS83a,b].

Gamma's Hash Join Algorithm

In Gamma, the tuple streams that are consumed by a hash-join operation are produced by operators using hash-based split tables. These tuple streams partition the tuples based on their join attribute values. As identical split tables are applied to both source relations of a join, a join of two large relations is reduced to the separate joins of many smaller relation buckets. In Gamma, these separate, independent joins provide a natural basis for parallelism. The following discussion considers the details of how this parallelism is achieved and exploited.

Hash-join operators are activated in a manner that is uniform with all other operators. There is an additional control interaction, however, that is unique to the hash-join operator. This control message is required because there are two distinct phases to the hash-partitioned join algorithm. In the first phase, termed the **building phase**, the join operator accepts tuples from the first source relation and uses the tuples to build in-memory hash tables and bit vector filters. At the end of this building phase, a hash-join operator sends a message to the scheduler indicating that the building phase has been completed. Once the scheduler determines that all hash-join operators have finished the building phase, the scheduler sends a message to each join operator directing the operators to begin the second phase of the operation, the **probing phase**. In this phase, individual join operator processes accept tuples from the second source relation. These tuples are used to probe the previously built hash-tables for tuples with matching join attribute values. At the end of the probing phase, each of the join operators sends a message to the scheduler indicating that the join operation has been completed.

An important characteristic of this algorithm is the simplicity of the interactions between the scheduler and participating operator processes. The net cost of activating and controlling a hash-join operator is five messages per site. (In effect, the building and probing phases of a join operation are considered separate operators for purposes of control.) All other data transfers can proceed without further control intervention by the scheduler.

In addition to controlling individual join operators, the scheduler must also synchronize the join with the operators of adjacent nodes in the query tree. In particular, the scheduler must initiate the operators which will be producing the input tuple streams for the join. The production of these tuple streams must coincide with the activation of the building and probing phases of the hash-join operator.

Hash Table Overflow

During the building phase of the multiprocessor hash-join algorithm, if buckets grow unacceptably large, the in-memory hash tables may overflow. The choice of an appropriate hash function will tend to randomize the distribution of tuples across buckets and, as such, will minimize the occurrence of hash table overflow. Additionally, in order to decrease the likelihood of hash table overflow, the optimizer attempts to build query trees that minimize the size of the relations that are accessed during the building phase of the hash-join algorithm. For joins in the interior of a query tree, this is a difficult task.

When hash-table overflow occurs, a local join operator narrows the dimensions of the tuple partition that is used for the construction of the hash table, in effect creating two subpartitions. One subpartition is used for hash table construction and the other is dumped to an overflow file on disk (possibly remote). Tuples that have already been added to the hash table, but now belong to the overflow subpartition, are removed from the table. As subsequent tuples are read from the input stream, they are either added to the hash table or appended to the overflow file.

When the local join operator notifies the scheduler of the completion of the building phase, it identifies the repartitioning scheme that was used for the handling of any overflow condition. With this knowledge the scheduler can alter the split tables of the second, probing source relation in such a manner that the overflow subpartitions are directly spooled to disk, bypassing the join operators. After the initial non-overflow subpartitions have been joined, the scheduler recursively applies the join operation to the spooled, overflow subpartitions. This method will fail in the case that the combined sizes of tuples having identical join attribute values exceeds the size of available memory. In such a case, a hash-based variation of the nested loops join algorithm is applied [BRAT84, DEWI85].

4.3. Update Operators

For the most part, the update operators (replace, delete, and append) are implemented using standard techniques. The only exception is a replace operation that modifies the partitioning attribute. In this case, rather than writing the modified tuple back into the local fragment of the relation, the modified tuple is passed through a split table to determine where the modified tuple should reside.

5. Performance Evaluation

In this section, we present the results of our preliminary performance evaluation of Gamma. This evaluation is neither extensive nor exhaustive. For example, we have not yet conducted any multiuser tests. Rather, these tests only serve to demonstrate the feasibility of the hardware architecture and software design of Gamma. Concerns of correctness rather than absolute speed have necessarily dominated the current phase of development.

All our tests were run with the host in single user mode. Elapsed time at the host was the principal performance metric. This value was measured as the time between the points at which the query was entered by the user and the point at which it completed execution.

5.1. Test Database Design and Results

The database used for these tests is based on the synthetic relations described in [BITT83]. Each relation consists of ten thousand tuples of 208 bytes. Each tuple contains thirteen, four byte integer attributes followed by three, 52 byte character string attributes.

All permanent relations used in the following tests have been horizontally partitioned on attribute Unique1 which is a candidate key with values in the range 0 through 9,999. Range partitioning was used to equally distribute tuples among all sites. For example, in a configuration with four disks, all tuples with Unique1 values less than 2500*i reside on disk i. All result relations are distributed among all sites using round-robin partitioning. The presented response times represent an average for a set of queries designed to ensure that each query i leaves nothing in a buffer pool of use to query i+1.

5.2. Selection Queries

In evaluating the performance of selection queries in a database machine that supports the concept of horizontal partitioning and multiprocessor indices, one must consider a number of factors: the selectivity factor of the query, the number of participating sites, whether or not the qualified attribute is also the horizontal partitioning attribute, which partitioning strategy has been utilized, whether or not an appropriate index exists, and the type of the index (clustered or non-clustered). If the qualified attribute is the horizontal partitioning attribute (HPA) and the relation has been partitioned using one of the range partitioning commands, then the partitioning information can be used to direct selection queries on the HPA to the appropriate sites. If the hashed partitioning strategy has been chosen, then exact match queries (e.g. HPA = value) can be selectively routed to the proper machine. Finally, if the round-robin partitioning strategy has been selected, the query must be sent to all sites. If the qualified attribute is not the HPA, then the query must also go to all sites.

To reduce the number of cases considered in this preliminary evaluation, we restricted our attention to the following four classes of selection queries:

	selection clause on	clustered index on
S1	Unique1 (HPA)	no index
S2	Unique1 (HPA)	Unique1
S3	Unique2 (non-HPA)	no index
S4	Unique2 (non-HPA)	Unique2

We restricted classes S1 and S2 further by designing the test queries such that the operation is always executed on a single site. This was accomplished by having the horizontal partitioning ranges cover the qualifications of the selection queries. Since queries in both classes S3 and S4 reference a non-HPA attribute, they must be sent to every site for execution. Each of the selection tests retrieved 1,000 tuples out of 10,000 (10% selectivity). The result relation of each query was partitioned in a round-robin fashion across all sites (regardless of how many sites participated in the actual execution of the query). Thus, each selection benefits equally from the fact that increasing the number of disks decreases the time required for storing the result relation.

The results from these selection tests are displayed in Figure 8. For each class of queries, the average response time is plotted as a function of the number of processors (with disks) used to execute the query. Figure 8 contains a number of interesting results. First, as

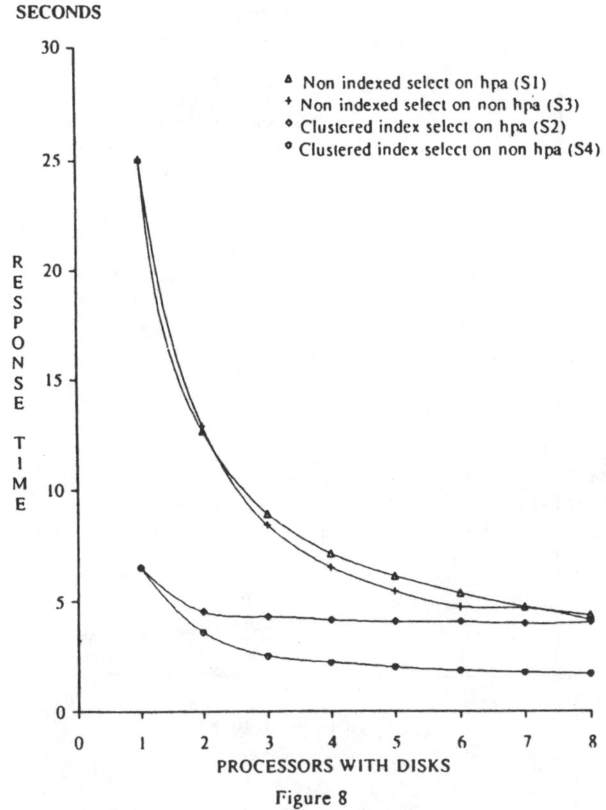

Figure 8

the number of processors is increased, the execution time of S1 and S3 queries drops. This decrease is due to the fact that as the number of processors is increased, each processor scans proportionally less data. Since the entire relation is always scanned in the S3 case, the results for S3 indicate that parallel, non-indexed access can provide acceptable performance for large multiprocessor configurations when there is sufficient I/O bandwidth available.

It is important to understand the difference between the S1 and S3 queries in Figure 8. While both have approximately the same response time, S1 would have a higher throughput rate in a multiuser test since only a single processor is involved in executing the query (assuming, of course, that the queries were uniformly distributed across all processors).

At first, we were puzzled by the fact that S3 was slightly faster than S1. In fact, one might have expected exactly the opposite result due to the overhead (in S3) of initiating the query at multiple sites. In both cases, each processor scans the same number of source tuples. In addition, since the result relation (which has the same size in both cases) is partitioned across all sites, the cost of storing the result relation is the same. The difference seems to be the number of processors used to distribute the tuples in the result relation. In case S1, one processor produces all the result tuples which must be distributed to the other sites. In case S3, all processors produce approximately the same number of result tuples (since Unique2 attribute values are randomly ordered when the file is horizontally partitioned on Unique1). Thus, the cost of distributing the result tuples is spread among all the processors. This explains why the gap between the S1 and S3 curves widens slightly as the number of processors is increased. The anomaly in the curves that occurs when 7 or 8 processors are used is discussed in Section 5.4.

Cases S2 and S4 illustrate different effects of horizontal partitioning and physical database design on response time. In the case of single site, indexed selections on the partitioning attribute (such as S2), increasing the number of disks (and, hence, decreasing the size of the relation fragment at each site) only decreases the cost of the index traversal (by reducing the number of levels in the index) and not the number of leaf (data) pages retrieved from disk. While this effect might be noticeable for single tuple retrievals, the number of levels in the index does not change across the range of sites evaluated. Instead, we attribute the drop in response time as the number of processors is increased from 1 to 2 as a consequence of increasing the number of disks used to store the result relation. Thus, scanning the source relation on site 1 can be partially overlapped with storing half the result relation on site 2. As the number of processors is increased from 2 to 3 one sees a very slight improvement. After three processors, little or no improvement is noticed as the single processor producing the result relation becomes the bottleneck.

In the case of S4 (an indexed selection on a non-partitioning attribute), the query is executed at every site. Since Unique2 attribute values are randomly distributed across all sites, each processor produces approximately the same number of result tuples. Thus, as the number of sites is increased, the response time decreases. The performance of case S4 relative to S3 illustrates how parallelism and indices can be used to complement each other.

An observant reader might have noticed that while the speedup factors for S1 and S3 are fairly close to linear, there is very little improvement in response time for S4 when the number of processors is doubled from 4 to 8. Given the way queries in class S4 are executed, it would be reasonable to expect a linear speedup in performance as the number of processors is increased. The reason this does not occur, while a little difficult to describe, is quite interesting. First, it is not a problem of communications bandwidth. Consider a 4 processor system. Each site produces produces approximately 1/4 of the result relation. Of these 250 tuples, each site will send 63 to each of the other three sites as result tuples are always distributed in a round-robin fashion. Thus, a total of 750 tuples will be sent across the network. At 208 bytes/tuple, this is a total of 1.2 million bits. At 80 million bits/second, approximately 2/100s of a second is required to redistribute the result relation.

The problem, it seems, is one of congestion at the network interfaces. Currently, the round-robin distribution policy is implemented by distributing tuples among the output buffers on a tuple-by-tuple basis. At each site in an 8 processor system, 8 qualifying tuples can change the state of the 8 output buffers from *non-empty* to *full*. Since the selection is through a clustered index, these 8 tuples may very well come from a single disk page or at most two pages. Thus, with 8 processors, 64 output buffers will become full at almost exactly the same time. Since the network interface being used at the current time has buffer space for only two incoming packets, five packets to each site have to be retransmitted (the communications software short-circuits a transmission by a processor to itself). The situation is complicated further by the fact that the acknowledgments for the 2 messages that do make it through, have to compete with retransmitted packets to their originating site (remember, everybody is sending to everybody). Since it is likely that some of the acknowledgements will fail to be received before the transmission timer goes off, the original packets may be retransmitted even though they arrived safely.

One way of at least alleviating this problem is to use a page-by-page round-robin policy. By page-by-page, we mean that the first output buffer is filled before any tuples are added to the second buffer. This strategy, combined with a policy of randomizing to whom a processor sends its first output page, should improve performance significantly as the production of output pages will be more uniformly distributed across the execution of the operation.

Rather than fixing the problem and rerunning the tests, we choose to leave this rather negative result in the paper for a couple of reasons. First, it illustrates how critical communication's issues can be. One of the main objectives in constructing the Gamma prototype is to enable us to study and measure interprocessor communications so that we can develop a better understanding of the problems involved in scaling the design to larger configurations. By sweeping the problem under the rug, Gamma would have looked better but an important result would have been lost (except to us). Second, the problem illustrates the importance of single user benchmarks. The same problem might not have showed up in a multiuser benchmark as the individual processors would be much less likely to be so tightly synchronized.

As a point of reference, the IDM500 database machine (10 MHz CPU with a database accelerator and an equivalent disk) takes 22.3 seconds for S1 selections. The IDM500 time for S2 selections is 5.2 seconds. Finally, the time in Gamma to retrieve a single tuple using a multiprocessor index such as that used for S2 is 0.14 seconds.

5.3. Join Queries

As with selection queries, there are a variety of factors to consider in evaluating the performance of join operations in Gamma. For the purposes of this preliminary evaluation, we were particularly interested in the relative performance of executing joins on processors with and without disks. We used the following query as the basis for our tests:

```
range of X is tenKtupA
range of Y is tenKtupB
retrieve into temp (X.all, Y.all)
where (X.Unique2A = Y.Unique2B) and (Y.Unique2B < 1000)
```

Each relation was horizontally partitioned on its Unique1 attribute. Execution of this query proceeds in two steps. First, the building phase of the join (see Section 4.2) is initiated. This phase constructs a hash table using the tenKtupA relation on each processor participating in the execution of the join operator. Ordinarily, the optimizer chooses the smallest source relation (measured in bytes) for processing during the building phase. In this query, the source relations can be predicted to be of equal size as the qualification on the tenKtupB relation can be propagated to the tenKtupA relation.

Once the hash tables have been constructed and the bit vector filters have been collected and distributed by the scheduler, the second phase begins. During this phase, the selection on tenKtupB is executed concurrently with the probing phase of the join operation.

Since Unique2 is not the HPA for either source relation, all sites participate in the execution of the selection operations. The relations resulting from the selection and join operations contain 1,000 tuples.

To reduce the number of cases considered, joins were either performed solely on processors with disks attached or solely at processors without disks. For convenience, we refer to these joins, respectively, as local joins and remote joins. We performed four sets of joins with the following characteristics:

	clustered indices on	join performed at processors
J1	no index	without disks (remote)
J2	no index	with disks (local)
J3	Unique2B	without disks (remote)
J4	Unique2B	with disks (local)

The results of these join tests are displayed in Figure 9. For each class of queries the average response time is plotted as a function of the number of processors with disks that are used. For the remote joins, an equal number of processors without disks are also used. Figure 9 demonstrates that there is not a performance penalty for joining tuples on sites remote from the source of the data. In fact, joins on processors without disks are actually slightly faster than those performed on processors with disks. The following discussion addresses this somewhat counterintuitive, but intriguing result.

Two factors contribute to making remote joins slightly faster than local joins (with respect, at least, to a response time metric). First, when joins are performed locally, the join and select operators compete with each other for CPU cycles from the same processor. Second, since Gamma can transfer sequential streams of tuples between processes on two different processors at almost the same rate

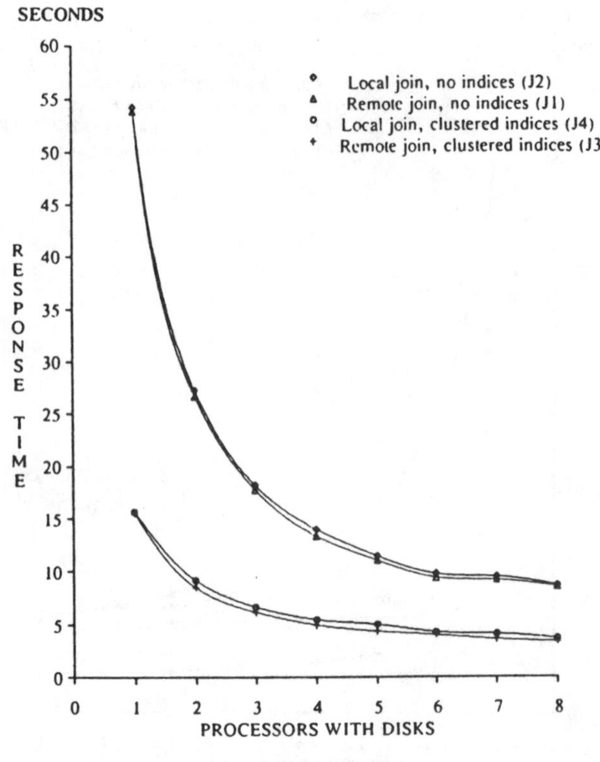

Figure 9

as between processes on the same machine, there is only a very minor response time penalty for executing operations remotely. Additional CPU cycles are, however, consumed while executing the communications protocol. Thus, there is likely to be a loss in throughput in a multiuser environment. We intend to explore the significance of this loss in future benchmark tests.

Since twice as many processors are used by the remote join design, one might wonder why the response times for remote joins were not half those of the corresponding local joins. Since the building and probing phases of the join operator are not overlapped, the response time of the join is bounded by the sum of the elapsed times for the two phases. For the cases tested, it turns out that the execution time for the building and probing phases is dominated by the selections on the source relations. There is, however, another benefit that accrues from offloading the join operator that is not reflected in a response time metric. When the join operation is offloaded, the processors with disks can effectively support a larger number of concurrent selection and store operations.

While remote joins only marginally outperform local joins, we consider the implications significant. Having demonstrated that a complex operation such as a join can be successfully offloaded from processors with disks provides a basis for expanding the design spectrum for multiprocessor database machines.

As a point of reference for the join times of Figure 9, the IDM500 took 84.3 seconds for J2 joins and 14.3 seconds for joins of type J4.

5.4. Speedup of Join Elapsed Times

In Figure 10, response-time speedup curves are presented for the join tests described in the previous section. These results confirm our hopes that multiprocessor, partitioned hash-join algorithms can effectively provide a basis for a highly parallel database machine. The anomalous shape of the speedup curves for systems with 7 or 8 disks can be attributed to two factors. First, the seventh and eighth disks

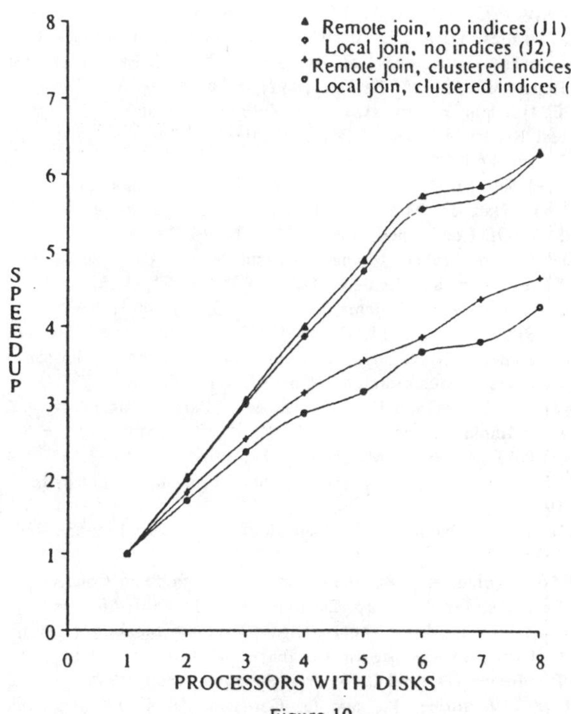

Figure 10

that were added to the system have only 82%[4] the performance of each of the other six disks. With evenly partitioned source relations, these slower disks increased the time required for scanning each of the source relations. All of this additional time is directly reflected in increased response times for join operations because the building and probing phases of the join operation are not overlapped.

A second factor also contributes to the shape of the speedup curve for systems with large numbers of processors. The ratio of control messages to data messages per processor increases as processors are added to the system. This factor only becomes significant once the volume of tuples processed by each processor becomes small. In the join tests presented, this effect may become noticeable when as few as eight disks are used because the Gamma query optimizer recognizes that the qualification on the first source relation (tenKtupB) can be propagated to tenKtupA. Therefore, only 1000 tuples are produced by the selections on each source relation. When join operators are active on eight processors, this means that each join operator will process approximately fourteen data pages from each relation and five control messages.

The reduced (and less impressive) speedup factors for joins J3 and J4 appear to be a consequence of the reduced speedup obtained for selection S4 which is executed as part of join queries J3 and J4 (see Section 5.2). As discussed above, for the join tests conducted, the execution time for the building and probing phases of the join is dominated by the selections on the source relations.

As Gamma enters a more mature stage of development, further speedup results will be obtained from queries that generate more massive amounts of data. For the current time, we present the speedup data for purposes of illustrating the potential that the system promises.

6. Conclusions

In this paper we have presented the design of a new relational database machine, Gamma. Gamma's hardware design is quite simple. Associated with each disk drive is a processor and the processors are interconnected via an interconnection network. The initial prototype consists of 20 VAX 11/750 processors interconnected with an 80 megabit/second token ring. Eight of the processors have a 160 megabyte disk drive. This design, while quite simple, provides high disk bandwidth without requiring the use of unconventional mass storage systems such as parallel read-out disk drives. A second advantage is that the design permits the I/O bandwidth to be expanded incrementally. To utilize the I/O bandwidth available in such a design, all relations in Gamma are horizontally partitioned across all disk drives.

In order to minimize the overhead associated with controlling intraquery parallelism, Gamma exploits dataflow query processing techniques. Each operator in a relational query tree is executed by one or more processes. These processes are placed by the scheduler on a combination of processors with and without disk drives. Except for 3 control messages, 2 at the beginning of the operator and 1 when the operator terminates execution, data flows between between the processes executing the query without any centralized control.

The preliminary performance evaluation of Gamma is very encouraging. The design provides almost linear speedup for both selection and join operations as the number of processors used to execute an operation is increased. Furthermore, the results obtained for a single processor configuration were demonstrated to be very competitive with a commercially available database machine. Once we have completed the prototype, we plan on conducting a thorough evaluation of the single and multiuser performance of the system. This evaluation will include both more complex queries and non-uniform distributions of attribute values.

[4] This value was determined by measuring the elapsed time of scanning a 10,000 tuple relation on the two sets of disk drives. While all the drives are 160 megabyte Fujitsu drives, six are newer 8" drives while the other two are older 14" drives.

Acknowledgements

This research was partially supported by the Department of Energy under contract #DE-AC02-81ER10920, by the National Science Foundation under grants, DCR-8512862, MCS82-01870 and MCS81-05904, and by a Digital Equipment Corporation External Research Grant.

7. References

[AGRA85] Agrawal, R., and D.J. DeWitt, "Recovery Architectures for Multiprocessor Database Machines," Proceedings of the 1985 SIGMOD Conference, Austin, TX, May, 1985.

[BABB79] Babb, E., "Implementing a Relational Database by Means of Specialized Hardware", ACM Transactions on Database Systems, Vol. 4, No. 1, March, 1979.

[BARU84] Baru, C. K. and S.W. Su, "Performance Evaluation of the Statistical Aggregation by Categorization in the SM3 System," Proceedings of the 1984 SIGMOD Conference, Boston, MA, June, 1984.

[BITT83] Bitton D., D.J. DeWitt, and C. Turbyfill, "Benchmarking Database Systems - A Systematic Approach," Proceedings of the 1983 Very Large Database Conference, October, 1983.

[BLAS79] Blasgen, M. W., Gray, J., Mitoma, M., and T. Price, "The Convoy Phenomenon," Operating System Review, Vol. 13, No. 2, April, 1979.

[BORA83] Boral H. and D. J. DeWitt, "Database Machines: An Idea Whose Time has Passed," in **Database Machines**, edited by H. Leilich and M. Missikoff, Springer-Verlag, Proceedings of the 1983 International Workshop on Database Machines, Munich, 1983.

[BRAT84] Bratbergsengen, Kjell, "Hashing Methods and Relational Algebra Operations", Proceedings of the 1984 Very Large Database Conference, August, 1984.

[BROW85] Browne, J. C., Dale, A. G., Leung, C. and R. Jenevein, "A Parallel Multi-Stage I/O Architecture with Self-Managing Disk Cache for Database Management Applications," in **Database Machines: Proceedings of the 4th International Workshop**, Springer Verlag, edited by D. J. DeWitt and H. Boral, March, 1985.

[CHOU85] Chou, H-T, DeWitt, D. J., Katz, R., and T. Klug, "Design and Implementation of the Wisconsin Storage System (WiSS)", Software Practices and Experience, Vol. 15, No. 10, October, 1985.

[DEMU86] Demurjian, S. A., Hsiao, D. K., and J. Menon, "A Multi-Backend Database System for Performance Gains, Capacity Growth, and Hardware Upgrade," Proceedings of Second International Conference on Data Engineering, Feb. 1986.

[DEWI79] DeWitt, D.J., "DIRECT - A Multiprocessor Organization for Supporting Relational Database Management Systems," IEEE Transactions on Computers, June, 1979.

[DEWI84a] DeWitt, D. J., Katz, R., Olken, F., Shapiro, D., Stonebraker, M. and D. Wood, "Implementation Techniques for Main Memory Database Systems", Proceedings of the 1984 SIGMOD Conference, Boston, MA, June, 1984.

[DEWI84b] DeWitt, D. J., Finkel, R., and Solomon, M., "The Crystal Multicomputer: Design and Implementation Experience," to appear, IEEE Transactions on Software Engineering. Also University of Wisconsin–Madison Computer Sciences Department Technical Report, September, 1984.

[DEWI85] DeWitt, D., and R. Gerber, "Multiprocessor Hash-Based Join Algorithms," Proceedings of the 1985 VLDB Conference, Stockholm, Sweden, August, 1985.

[ENSC85] "Enscribe Programming Manual," Tandem Part# 82583-A00, Tandem Computers Inc., March 1985.

[FISH84] Fishman, D.H., Lai, M.Y., and K. Wilkinson, "Overview of the Jasmin Database Machine," Proceedings of the 1984 SIGMOD Conference, Boston, MA, June, 1984.

[GARD83] Gardarin, G., et. al., "Design of a Multiprocessor Relational Database System," Proceedings of the 1983 IFIP Conference, Paris, 1983.

[GOOD81] Goodman, J. R., "An Investigation of Multiprocessor Structures and Algorithms for Database Management", University of California at Berkeley, Technical Report UCB/ERL, M81/33, May, 1981.

[HELL81] Hell, W. "RDBM - A Relational Database Machine," Proceedings of the 6th Workshop on Computer Architecture for Non-Numeric Processing, June, 1981.

[HEYT85a] Heytens, M., "The Gamma Query and Catalog Managers," Gamma internal design documentation, December, 1985.

[IDM85] The IDM 310 Database Server, Britton-Lee Inc., 1985.

[JARK84] Jarke, M. and J. Koch, "Query Optimization in Database System," ACM Computing Surveys, Vol. 16, No. 2, June, 1984.

[KAKU85] Kakuta, T., Miyazaki, N., Shibayama, S., Yokota, H., and K. Murakami, "The Design and Implementation of the Relational Database Machine Delta," in **Database Machines: Proceedings of the 4th International Workshop**, Springer Verlag, edited by D. DeWitt and H. Boral, March, 1985.

[KIM85] Kim, M. Y, "Parallel Operation of Magnetic Disk Storage Devices," in **Database Machines: Proceedings of the 4th International Workshop**, Springer Verlag, edited by D. DeWitt and H. Boral, March, 1985.

[KITS83a] Kitsuregawa, M., Tanaka, H., and T. Moto-oka, "Application of Hash to Data Base Machine and Its Architecture", New Generation Computing, Vol. 1, No. 1, 1983.

[KITS83b] Kitsuregawa, M., Tanaka, H., and T. Moto-oka, "Architecture and Performance of Relational Algebra Machine Grace", University of Tokyo, Technical Report, 1983.

[LEIL78] Leilich, H.O., G. Stiege, and H.Ch. Zeidler, "A Search Processor for Database Management Systems," Proceedings of the 4th VLDB International Conference, 1978.

[LIVN85] Livny, M., Khoshafian, S., and H. Boral, "Multi-Disk Management Algorithms," Proceedings of the International Workshop on High Performance Transaction Systems, Pacific Grove, CA, September 1985.

[OZKA75] Ozkarahan E.A., S.A. Schuster, and K.C. Smith, "RAP - An Associative Processor for Data Base Management," Proc. 1975 NCC, Vol. 45, AFIPS Press, Montvale N.J.

[RIES78] Ries, D. and R. Epstein, "Evaluation of Distribution Criteria for Distributed Database Systems," UCB/ERL Technical Report M78/22, UC Berkeley, May, 1978.

[SALE84] Salem, K., and H. Garcia-Molina, "Disk Striping", Technical Report No. 332, EECS Department, Princeton University, December 1984.

[SELI79] Selinger,P. G., et. al., "Access Path Selection in a Relational Database Management System," Proceedings of the 1979 SIGMOD Conference, Boston, MA., May 1979.

[STON76] Stonebraker, Michael, Eugene Wong, and Peter Kreps, "The Design and Implementation of INGRES", ACM Transactions on Database Systems, Vol. 1, No. 3, September, 1976.

[STON79] Stonebraker, M. R., "MUFFIN: A Distributed Database Machine," University of California, Electronics Research Laboratory, Memorandum UCB/ERL M79/28, May 1979.

[SU82] Su, S.Y.W and K.P. Mikkilineni, "Parallel Algorithms and their Implementation in MICRONET", Proceedings of the 8th VLDB Conference, Mexico City, September, 1982.

[TAND85] 4120-V8 Disk Storage Facility, Tandem Computers Inc., 1985.

[TANE81] Tanenbaum, A. S., **Computer Networks**, Prentice-Hall, 1981.

[TERA83] Teradata: DBC/1012 Data Base Computer Concepts & Facilities, Teradata Corp. Document No. C02-0001-00, 1983.

[UBEL85] Ubell, M., "The Intelligent Database Machine (IDM)," in **Query Processing in Database Systems**, edited by Kim, W., Reiner, D., and D. Batory, Springer-Verlag, 1985.

[VALD84] Valduriez, P., and G. Gardarin, "Join and Semi-Join Algorithms for a Multiprocessor Database Machine", ACM Transactions on Database Systems, Vol. 9, No. 1, March, 1984.

[WAGN73] Wagner, R.E., "Indexing Design Considerations," IBM System Journal, Vol. 12, No. 4, Dec. 1973, pp. 351-367.

[WATS81] Watson, R. W., "Timer-based mechanisms in reliable transport protocol connection management", *Computer Networks* 5, pp. 47-56, 1981.

Chapter 5

User Interfaces

5.1 Introduction

I would like to start off this introduction with the complaint often voiced by Professor Larry Rowe of the University of California, Berkeley, "Why aren't researchers more interested in user interfaces?" There simply aren't a lot of good papers that deal with this important area. There are at least two good reasons for paying attention to user interfaces:

1. The needs of user interface programs drives requirements for function in database systems.

2. The "value added" that a database system provides will increasingly be in the front-end tools that go with it because a high-performance SQL engine will increasingly be a commodity product.

In addition, I would like to complain loudly about the community of programming language (PL) researchers. Many of the issues that are taken up by the papers in this section would benefit immensely by a contribution from this community. However, researchers skilled in programming languages and environments have nearly universally avoided dealing with I/O in general and data base applications in particular. Larry Rowe of Berkeley and Malcolm Atkinson of the University of Edinburgh are notable (and lonely) exceptions to this statement.

I would like to extend an open invitation to PL researchers to become involved in databases. Moreover, it seems inevitable that the community will have to accept, because future programming environments are going to be database oriented. Specifically, computer programs, functions, statements, specifications, etc. are all going to be database objects, and editors, compilers, linkers, etc. are going to be database application programs. The current round of CASE (computer-assisted software engineering) products clearly point the way in this area.

There are three important types of user interface programs:

- Host language embeddings
- Application generators
- End-user interfaces

and we have a paper on each topic in this section. To provide database access from within a general purpose language, there are exactly three options:

1. A subroutine call package
2. A preprocessor
3. A new general purpose language

Using the first option, one would provide a subroutine call library that programmers can call from their favorite programming language. Programs written for such interfaces tend to be difficult to read and quite ugly. On the other hand, it is straightforward to implement a subroutine call interface for multiple programming languages quickly. Example systems that support this level of interface include Sybase and IMS.

The second available option is to write a preprocessor for some specific programming language. DBMS statements embedded in this programming language would be extracted by the preprocessor and replaced by appropriate function calls that would be processed by the normal compiler. This preprocessor approach is the one used by both System R and INGRES, and it is an interesting exercise to contrast the two interfaces presented in [ALLM76] and [CHAM81].

The problem with preprocessors is that they are rather like "glueing an apple onto a pancake." One is trying to interface a set-at-a-time query language to a record-at-a-time programming environment. Moreover, the type systems of the two languages are different, because the programming language has no notion of the type "relation." Lastly, iteration over sets of qualifying records is tedious to deal with in the preprocessor. It is clear that these problems are easy to solve if one can integrate database access into the programming language. The only reason that this has not been followed in the commercial marketplace is that the compiler people and the database people usually are not on speaking terms with each other.

The first paper in this section (5.2) presents the design of one programming language for database access. The paper by Joachim Schmidt was chosen because Pascal R was the first proposal for a combined language. Other languages with the same goals include RIGEL [ROWE79], UDL [DATE76], and Galileo [ALBA85]. This class of papers is an elegant exposition of the right way to do things. Unfortunately, this approach is doomed to irrelevance by the standardization of the preprocessor approach for SQL.

A second reason that this approach is doomed is that this level of programming language is inappropriate to writing data-intensive applications. For example, the standard application does something like the following:

1. Put an input form up on the screen.
2. Have an end-user enter data into the form.
3. Do one or more database accesses.
4. Put a result form up on the screen.

If one programs such an application in Cobol extended by a database preprocessor, it is several pages of code, most of it in presentation services (code to deal with the screen). One is much better off programming in a high-level language that has forms as a data type and an automatic run-time library to position the cursor in forms, accept input, and do validity checking. Such a language should also support moving values directly from forms to database queries and the output of queries directly back into forms. In other words, one wants to be able to write the above program in half a page of code. Only so-called fourth generation languages allow one to do this. The second paper in this section (5.3) presents a sketch of one of the cleanest fourth generation languages, namely FADS. Other languages available commercially include Natural (from Software AG), Ideal (from ADR), Focus (from Information Builders), ABF (from Relational Technology), and Powerhouse (from Cognos). Such interfaces have been shown to provide a programmer productivity factor of three to ten times over coding in a normal programming language with embedded SQL calls. As a result, the reader should keep in mind that virtually all future database intensive applications will be written in a fourth-generation language. Hence a serious database scholar should be familiar with this class of interfaces.

It has been evident for years that SQL and QUEL are not end-user languages. Although it has been proved that truck drivers and secretaries can learn query languages in a couple of hours [THOM75, REIS75], it is equally true that they won't do so in practice. To verify the above observation, simply ask any substantial user of a relational database system what fraction of his end-user interactions are expressed in SQL. Hence there is a need for easier-to-use end-user query interfaces than simply writing query language statements, and there has been some work in this area. The languages QBE [ZLOO75] and Cupid [MCDO75] were early attempts to use graphics to advantage. In my opinion these systems are simply not "idiot proof," i.e., they are not easy enough to use. A second approach would be to use natural language, and over the years there have been many attempts, e.g., [CODD74, HEND78]. In fact, commercial natural language offerings are available from Artificial Intelligence Corp, BBN, and Natural Language Products. In my opinion natural language systems are very big and very slow and do not correctly solve a high enough fraction of human utterances to be useful. When the interface responds "huh -- please rephrase," I am ready to put my fist through the terminal screen. My feeling is that natural language systems will not find widespread acceptance until voice recognition systems become practical. At that time I will be more willing to repeat my query using different words. In the meantime, end-user interfaces are likely to be

specialized
and
graphically-oriented.

Put differently, they will not attempt to implement the full power of SQL but will make simple things really easy. Moreover, "a picture is worth 1000 words," and Macintosh-style graphics can be used to great advantage. The third paper written by Rick Catell is an example of this sort of facility (5.4).

I wish to make one comment about browsing-style end-user interfaces. In general they wish to identify a set of records and then browse forward or backward through this collection. The notion of cursors present in ANSI/SQL is not general enough to support the needs of this class of programs, and ANSI/SQL will have to move to more general mechanisms such as those in [STON84].

I should close this section with a mention of new user interface paradigms. Spreadsheets and, more recently, Hypercard contain easy-to-understand concepts accessible to nonprogrammers. End users are seemingly willing to learn 1-2-3 and similar products. Therefore, users would obviously like to get 1-2-3 objects out of a database. Over time, popular PC products will get database interfaces, and it is entirely possible that these products will become "fifth-generation languages" and drive future DBMS requirements.

References

[ALBA85] Albano. A. et al., "Galileo: A Strongly Typed, Interactive Conceptual Language," ACM-TODS, June 1985.

[CODD74] Codd, E., "Seven Steps to Rendezvous With the Casual User," in "Data Base Management," Klimbie, J., and Koffeman, K. (eds), North Holland, Amsterdam, 1974.

[CHAM81] Chamberlin, D., "Support for Repetitive Transactions and Ad-hoc Queries in System R," ACM-TODS, Mar. 1981.

[DATE76] Date, C., "An Architecture for High Level Language Database Extensions," Proc. 1976 ACM-SIGMOD Conference on Management of Data, San Jose, Calif., June 1976.

[HEND78] Hendrix, G. et al., "Developing a Natural Language Interface to Complex Data," ACM-TODS, June 1978.

[MCDO75] McDonald, N. and Stonebraker, M., "CUPID: The Friendly Query Language," Proc. 1975 ACM-Pacific, San Francisco, Calif., Apr. 1975.

[REIS75] Reisner, P. et al., "Human Factors Evaluation of Two Data Base Query Languages: SQUARE and SEQUEL," Proc. 1975 National Computer Conference, Anaheim, Calif., June 1975.

[ROWE79] Rowe, L., and Shoens, K., "Data Abstraction, Views, and Updates in RIGEL," Proc. 1979 ACM-SIGMOD Conference on Management of Data, Boston, Mass., June 1979.

[STON84] Stonebraker, M., and Rowe, L., "Data Base Portals: A New Application Program Interface," Proc. 1984 VLDB Conference, Singapore, Sept. 1984.

[THOM75] Thomas, J., and Gould, J., "A Psychological Study of Query by Example," Proc. 1975 National Computer Conference, Anaheim, Calif., June 1975.

[ZLOO75] Zloof, M., "Query by Example," Proc. 1975 National Computer Conference, Anaheim, Calif., June 1975.

Some High Level Language Constructs for Data of Type Relation

JOACHIM W. SCHMIDT
Universität Hamburg, West Germany

For the extension of high level languages by data types of mode relation, three language constructs are proposed and discussed: a repetition statement controlled by relations, predicates as a generalization of Boolean expressions, and a constructor for relations using predicates. The language constructs are developed step by step starting with a set of elementary operations on relations. They are designed to fit into PASCAL without introducing too many additional concepts.

Key Words and Phrases: database, relational model, relational calculus, data type, high level language, nonprocedural language, language extension
CR Categories: 4.22, 4.33, 4.34

1. INTRODUCTION

A certain class of programming problems involves the processing of data with the following properties: there is a large amount of data, the data has internal connections, and the data must be made available to many users.

Since Codd's original paper [5], relations have been increasingly used in the solution of such database programming problems.

The "classical" language constructs for the processing of data organized around relations are by now accepted to be essentially: (a) primitive instructions for altering relations at the level of individual tuples: insertion, deletion, and modification; and (b) powerful retrieval facilities operating on relations at the level of sets of tuples: relational calculus- and algebra-oriented query languages.

In recent years numerous data sublanguages have been proposed, and some implemented, which contain these constructs to a greater or lesser extent. They differ from one another mainly in the conceptions of what user friendliness means [2, 4, 17].

A version of this paper was presented at the International Conference on the Management of Data, 1977, in Toronto, Canada—an annual conference of ACM SIGMOD.
Author's permanent address: Universität Hamburg, Institut für Informatik, Schlüterstrasse 70, D-2000 Hamburg 13, West Germany. Present address: University of Toronto, Computer Systems Research Group, Toronto M5S 1A4, Canada.

Traditionally a database with its associated data language is seen as an independent system; data is interchanged with users or with programmed systems through fixed interfaces in the form of I/O areas. Problems which arise from the integration of database language constructs, such as a data structure relation, in high level languages have up to now seldom been investigated [7, 1, 14]. Such investigations are of interest from at least two points of view: first for the extension of existing high level languages, and second for the further development of database concepts themselves, in particular the relation concept.

The currently prevalent high level programming languages have no constructs for the processing of large amounts of interrelated data. The file concept does not offer a general solution to this problem; files may be able to hold large quantities of data but the connections between data elements are inadequately handled, both at the level of high level language operations and at the level of access paths. As demonstrated by the example of the programming language SAIL [8] which contains ALGOL 60 and LEAP [12] data structures, there exists quite clearly a need for an algorithmic language with efficient constructs for handling intricately connected data.

Such investigations can also serve as a vehicle for the further development of the relation concept itself. The necessity for such development shows up, for example, in the previously mentioned difference in power between altering instructions and retrieval facilities. Whereas for a single retrieval command, all connections between relation tuples which are necessary for the answer to a query are evaluated, only a single tuple in a single relation can be inserted, deleted, or updated by an altering instruction. The user must therefore, in general, code a consistent database alteration transaction as a sequence of such altering instructions, each affecting a single relation. The user thereby bears most of the responsibility for the central problem of the integrity of the database.

A similar problem situation in general purpose programming languages led to the development of the concept of abstract data types [10]. A stack variable, for example, could be implemented in a high level programming language by means of an array variable, a Boolean variable, and an integer variable. These variables must be altered consistently when the value of the stack variable is changed (e.g. by push or pop). We could analogously define alterations in a database as operations on abstract data types and implement them as procedures on relations. In more recent work, Schmid and Swenson [13] for example, the beginnings of such a development can be discerned. The further development of database language constructs, however, cannot be discussed in the limited context of data sublanguages. On the contrary, this assumes to a great extent the concepts of high level programming languages.

These tendencies will not be further discussed in this paper (see e.g. [15]). In Section 2 the definition of types of mode relation and the declaration of relation variables are briefly described, together with the elementary read and write operations for relations. Section 3 introduces a repetition statement controlled by a relation variable. The generalization of Boolean expressions to predicates is handled in Section 4. In Section 5 the concept of a generalized relation constructor is discussed. Finally Section 6 outlines the state of the implementation and some further development. It should be noted that the language constructs have been designed to fit into PASCAL [16] without the introduction of too many additional concepts.

2. ELEMENTARY OPERATIONS ON RELATIONS

The definition of data types of mode relation is based upon data types of mode record. The value of a variable of a particular relation type is a set of tuples, each of which is in turn of the record type laid down in the definition of the relation type. The fields of these records will be taken to be of scalar type or of type string ("flat" records). Furthermore these types are presumed to be ordered types.

A second component of the definition of a relation type is the designation of certain fields of the relation tuples as a key. A key list characterizes a particular part of the tuple by enumerating the corresponding field identifiers. For these fields it holds that among the tuples of the relation a particular value assignation occurs at most once. The values of the key fields therefore uniquely determine a tuple in the relation. An ordering of the key values is defined by the presumed ordering on the values of the individual key fields and by the order of the key field identifiers in the key list.

Example 1. If employees are characterized by the attributes employee number (unique), employee status, and employee name, then we can define relation variable *employees* as follows:

```
.
.
type erectype = record enr, estatus:integer; ename:string end;
     ereltype = relation ⟨enr⟩ of erectype;
var  employees:ereltype;
.
.
```

Along with data types of mode relation, operations are defined which allow values of relation variables to be altered and to be read tuple by tuple.

2.1 Elementary Altering Operations

A value change of a relation variable can occur through insertion, deletion, or modification of tuples. These operations are not in fact "elementary" insofar as through them not single tuples, but whole sets of tuples (i.e. again a relation variable), can be inserted, deleted, or modified. However, these operations alter at any given time the value of only one relation variable.

The *insertion operator* :+ brings about the insertion of tuples into the target operand to its left, dependent on the source operand to its right:

```
rel1 :+ rel2;
```

Source and target operands are relation variables of the same type. Into *rel*1 are inserted copies of those tuples of *rel*2 whose key values do not already occur in any tuple of *rel*1. The source operand *rel*2 remains unchanged.

The *deletion operator* :— brings about the deletion of tuples in the target operand dependent on the source operand:

```
rel1 :— rel2;
```

Source and target operands are relation variables of the same type. From *rel*1 are deleted those tuples also contained in *rel*2. The source operand *rel*2 remains unchanged.

The *replacement operator* :& brings about the replacement of tuples in the target operand dependent on the source operand:

```
rel1 :& rel2;
```

Source and target operands are relation variables of the same type. Each tuple of *rel*1 whose key value occurs in a tuple of *rel*2 is replaced by a copy of the corresponding tuple in *rel*2. The source operand remains unchanged. Note that key values cannot be changed with the aid of the replacement operator.

The *assignment operator* := assigns relation values between relation variables of the same type:

```
rel1 := rel2;
```

A generalization of admissable source operands towards relational expressions will be treated in Section 5.

2.2 An Elementary Relation Constructor

An anonymous 1-tuple relation can be constructed from a record variable with the aid of the elementary relation constructor [..]. Of course any combination of fields fulfills for this relation the requirements for a key; these relations are therefore type-compatible with every relation variable whose type definition is based on the type of the record variable, e.g.

```
rel := [rec];
```

The empty relation is denoted correspondingly by [ ].

Example 2. A tuple with employee number 2, employee name Nessie, and employee status 1 is to be inserted in the relation *employees*.

```
.
.
type  erectype = record enr, estatus:integer; ename:string end;
      ereltype = relation ⟨enr⟩ of erectype;
var   erec:erectype;
      employees:ereltype;
begin .
      .
      .
      erec.enr := 2;
      erec.estatus := 1;
      erec.ename := 'nessie';
      employees :+ [erec]
end.
```

2.3 Elementary Retrieval Operations

Two standard procedures low(*rel*) and next(*rel*) are defined for the tuple-wise reading of relation variables. Furthermore the Boolean function aor(*rel*) (all of relation) and for each relation an implicitly declared buffer variable *rel*↑ are available.

The tuple of the relation *rel* with the lowest key value is assigned to the buffer *rel*↑ by the procedure call low(*rel*). The tuple with the next highest key value is assigned to *rel*↑ by the procedure call next(*rel*). If such a tuple does not exist then aor(*rel*) becomes true and *rel*↑ becomes undefined.

Example 3. Find those employees with the status of an assistant professor (employee status 2).

Solution 3.1.

```
.
.
type  erectype = record enr, estatus:integer; ename:string end;
      ereltype = relation ⟨enr⟩ of erectype;
var   employees, result:ereltype;
begin .
      :
      result := [ ];
      low(employees);
      while not aor(employees) do
      begin if employees↑.estatus = 2 then result :+ [employees↑];
               next(employees)
      end
end.
```

The solution method underlying this example program accesses relations tuplewise and in order, in the main controlled by the user. It is not generally satisfying for several reasons:

The ordering of tuple access by increasing key value is unnecessary from the point of view of program logic.

With respect to problem orientation the language constructs available for relations up to now are inadequate; this rapidly becomes evident with more complex examples. The above program is a solution in terms of the file concept and not in terms of relational databases.

For particular problems these elementary constructs are insufficient, e.g. nested loops accessing the same relation cannot be programmed.

The notation could be more concise.

There is little possibility for automatic optimization of accesses, for example by free choice of ordering or by processing of sets of tuples.

In the following sections we will develop step-by-step language constructs which should to a great extent overcome such objections.

3. THE REPETITION STATEMENT foreach

The foreach statement has the general form:

```
⟨foreach statement⟩ ::= foreach ⟨control record variable⟩
                        in ⟨range relation variable⟩
                        do ⟨statement⟩
```

The execution of a statement may be repeated with the aid of the foreach statement. For each repetition the control variable is assigned an arbitrary new tuple from the range relation until all tuples of the relation have been used. The control variable is declared implicitly to have the same record type that the range relation is based on. The scope of the control variable definition is the statement following **do**; within this scope the key values of the control variable and the range relation must not be altered. By using the foreach statement the solution for Example 3 becomes:

Solution 3.2.

```
.
.
{type definitions and variable declarations as in 3.1.}
.
.
begin .
      :
      result := [ ];
      foreach erec in employees do
         if erec.status = 2 then result :+ [erec]
end.
```

For a further example we introduce the relation *timetable* listing lectures held by employees and described by attributes employee number and course number, together with day, time, and place of each lecture.

Example 4. Find all those employees who lecture on Fridays.

Solution 4.1.

```
.
.
type  erectype = record enr, estatus:integer; ename:string end;
      ereltype = relation ⟨enr⟩ of erectype;
      trectype = record tenr, tcnr, ttime:integer;
                        tday, troom:string end;
      treltype = relation ⟨tenr, tcnr, tday⟩ of trectype;
var   employees, result:ereltype;
      timetable:treltype;
begin .
      :
      result := [ ];
      foreach erec in employees do
        foreach trec in timetable do
          if (erec.enr = trec.tenr) and (trec.tday = 'friday')
          then result :+ [erec]
end.
```

If we look at the example and its solution more closely we notice that:

The inner loop with range relation *timetable* is in general traversed too often; that is, whenever an entry for a particular employee's lecture held on Friday has been found, the remainder of the relation *timetable* is nevertheless processed.

If an employee lectures several times on a Friday, the corresponding employee record is inserted several times into the result. By virtue of the definition of the insertion operator this does not, however, affect the value of the target operand.

It would also be possible to avoid repeated insertions quite easily by programming an extra exit from the loop. In view of the developments in the following section, and for didactic reasons, we shall not bother to do this here.

The inner loop is only necessary to test a condition; in this particular case a condition on the value of the control variable *trec*. The control variable *erec* on the other hand is also needed for the construction of the result relation.

This state of affairs is more evident in the following solution for Example 4:

Solution 4.2.

```
.
.
{type definitions as in 4.1.}
.
.
var     employees, result:ereltype;
        timetable:treltype;
        some_trec_in_timetable:boolean;
begin .
        .
        .
        result := [ ];
        foreach erec in employees do
        begin some_trec_in_timetable := false;
          foreach trec in timetable do
            some_trec_in_timetable := some_trec_in_timetable or
            (erec.enr = trec.tenr) and (trec.tday = 'friday');
          if some_trec_in_timetable then result :+ [erec]
        end
end.
```

The additional exit from the inner loop is again omitted for didactic reasons.

Example 5. Find all employees who give no lectures.

This example contains a universal condition.

Solution 5.1.

```
.
.
{type definitions as in 4.1.}
.
.
var     employees, result:ereltype;
        timetable:treltype;
        all_trec_in_timetable:boolean;
begin .
        .
        .
        result := [ ];
        foreach erec in employees do
        begin all_trec_in_timetable := true;
          foreach trec in timetable do
            all_trec_in_timetable := all_trec_in_timetable and (erec.enr ≠ trec.tenr);
          if all_trec_in_timetable then result :+ [erec]
        end
end.
```

It seems natural for such problems, in which relations are used in testing one or all of their tuples against a certain condition, not to use repetition constructs but to introduce a special construct more related to this problem.

4. PREDICATES OVER RELATIONS

Examples 4 and 5 each require two nested loops. However, in both cases the outer loop and the inner loop have quite different significances in the logic of the program.

The outer loop over the range relation *employees* uses a logical condition evaluated by means of the inner loop—this is especially clear in Solutions 4.2 and 5.1. In both examples the condition governs the insertion of the value of the outer control variable into the result relation. Consequences will be discussed in Section 5.

The inner loop over the range relation *timetable* evaluates this condition. The condition itself is respectively an **or** connection (Example 4) or an **and** connection (Example 5) of Boolean terms involving tuples of the relation *timetable*, and is implemented by the foreach statement.

In the context of predicate logic these conditions are first-order predicates. This is more evident if one introduces range coupled quantifiers, i.e. quantifiers for which, together with the control variable (bound variable), the scope over which its value ranges must also be given (analogous to the foreach statement).

Predicates over relations will therefore be defined thus:

```
⟨predicate⟩ ::= ⟨quantifier⟩ ⟨control record variable⟩
                    in ⟨range relation variable⟩
                       (⟨logical expression⟩)
⟨logical expression⟩ ::= ⟨term⟩ | ⟨term⟩ ⟨logical operator⟩ ⟨logical expression⟩
⟨quantifier⟩ ::= some | all
⟨logical operator⟩ ::= and | or
```

Terms consist of components of the control variable, program variables, or constants, connected by the relational operators $=, <, >, \neq, \leq, \geq$; terms may also be predicates.

The implicitly declared control variable of the predicate is again of that record type in the range relation declaration.

4.1 The Existential Quantifier some

The predicate

```
some rec in rel (⟨logical expression⟩)
```

is true iff at least one value of the control variable *rec* makes the logical expression true. The values of the control variable are defined by the tuples of the range relation *rel*. In general the logical expression will contain apart from bound variables further program variables and constants.

The solution for Example 4 using the **some** quantifier now looks like this:

Solution 4.3.

```
.
.
{definitions and declarations as in 4.1.}
.
.
begin .
      .
      .
      result := [ ];
      foreach erec in employees do
        if some trec in timetable ((erec.enr = trec.tenr) and (trec.tday = 'friday'))
        then result :+ [erec]
end.
```

The tiresome problem of an additional exit from the loop has now disappeared for the user, and has been shifted on to the implementor responsible for the efficient implementation of predicates. An efficient implementation can above all exploit the fact that inside a predicate individual tuples of the range relation are not used as statement variables. The sequential processing of individual tuples can therefore be replaced by processing tuple sets in parallel. Comparing the three solutions developed for Example 4, we see that:

Solution 4.1, "**while not** aor(*timetable*) **do**," describes a sequential tuple-wise processing ordered by key values.

Solution 4.2, "**foreach** *trec* **in** *timetable* **do**," proceeds sequentially and tuple-wise but with no specific ordering.

Solution 4.3, "**some** *trec* **in** *timetable*," can be implemented by processing tuple sets in parallel.

If one considers that these tuple sets are so large in practice that they must be kept on secondary storage, these differences are highly significant.

4.2 The Universal Quantifier all

The predicate

all *rec* **in** *rel* (⟨*logical expression*⟩)

is true iff all values of the control variable *rec* make the logical expression true. The values of the control variable are defined by the tuples of the range relation *rel*.

Using the **all** quantifier, the solution to Example 5 can be written thus:
Solution 5.2.

```
.
.
{definitions and declarations as in 5.1.}
.
.
begin .
      :
      result := [ ];
      foreach erec in employees do
        if all trec in timetable (erec.enr ≠ trec.tenr)
        then result :+ [erec]
end.
```

4.3 Nested Quantifiers

Predicates may contain several quantifiers. For an appropriate example we introduce a third relation that describes courses by their attributes course number (unique), course level, and course title.

Now an extension to Example 5:

Example 6. Find those employees who give no lectures above the first year (course level 1).

This example requires both a universal and existential condition.

Solution 6.1.

```
.
.
type  erectype  = record enr, estatus:integer; ename:string end;
      ereltype  = relation ⟨enr⟩ of erectype;
      trectype  = record tenr, tcnr, ttime:integer;
                         tday, troom:string end;
      treltype  = relation ⟨tenr, tcnr, tday⟩ of trectype;
      crectype  = record cnr, clevel:integer; cname:string end;
      creltype  = relation ⟨cnr⟩ of crectype;
var   employees, result:ereltype;
      timetable:treltype;
      courses:creltype;
begin .
      .
      .
      result := [ ];
      foreach erec in employees do
        if all trec in timetable ((erec.enr ≠ trec.tenr) or
           some crec in courses ((trec.tcnr = crec.cnr) and (crec.clevel = 1)))
        then result :+ [erec]
end.
```

It becomes evident with examples like this that data elements in a database are typically not processed in isolation but together with their mutual logical connections: A particular tuple of the relation *employees* is only further processed when it stands in a particular relation to the tuples of *timetable* and furthermore there is a particular tuple in the relation *courses* such that ... .

The actual processing of the tuples is so far identical in all examples: Dependent upon a predicate they are inserted into the result relation or not. The solutions to a large class of problems in retrieving data from databases can be programmed in this way.

We are now ready to go one step further and develop a specific language construct for this standard programming problem based on the constructs introduced so far.

5. GENERALIZING THE RELATION CONSTRUCTOR

With the concepts developed so far the value of a relation variable can be altered by deleting, inserting, or modifying tuples and by assigning a relation-valued expression. These expressions are, however, up to now limited to single relation variables and to the elementary relation constructor introduced in Section 2.2. The elementary constructor is only capable of making a 1-tuple relation $[x]$ from a record variable x. This restriction has led, in all the examples handled so far, to the construction of new relations according to the following schema: tuple-wise access to the source relation, sequential processing of these tuples as records, and tuple-wise construction of the result relation. On the other hand, in the quantifiers and the logical expressions we already have the necessary prerequisites for a generalization of the relation constructor along the lines

$[x \textbf{ in } X: P(x, r, s, \ldots)]$

where x is the free variable which describes the result tuple, X is a range relation which holds the possible value tuples for x, and P is some logical expression which depends on the free variable, and possibly on further bound variables r, s, etc., and on constants.

5.1 Construction of Subrelations

A first step in generalizing the relation constructor leads to the definition

```
⟨general relation constructor⟩ ::= [each ⟨control record variable⟩
                                     in ⟨range relation variable⟩:
                                        ⟨logical expression⟩]
```

The implicitly declared control variable is again of the same record type as that of the range relation. The logical expression has the usual logical and relational operators, and it may also contain quantifiers. As operands, the logical expression may contain components of the free control variable of the constructor and possibly of the bound variables of predicates, as well as program variables and constants.

With the aid of the general relation constructor, the solutions of the previous examples may be further simplified:

Solutions 3.3, 4.4, 5.3, 6.2.

```
.
.
.
type  erectype  = record enr, estatus:integer; ename:string end;
      ereltype  = relation ⟨enr⟩ of erectype;
      trectype  = record tenr, tcnr, ttime:integer;
                         tday, troom:string end;
      treltype  = relation ⟨tenr, tcnr, tday⟩ of trectype;
      crectype  = record cnr, clevel:integer; cname:string end;
      creltype  = relation ⟨cnr⟩ of crectype;
var   employees, result3, result4, result5, result6:ereltype;
      timetable:treltype;
      courses:creltype;
begin .
      .
      .
      result3 := [each erec in employees:erec.estatus = 2];
      result4 := [each erec in employees:some trec in timetable ((erec.enr = trec.tenr) and
                       (trec.tday = 'friday'))];
      result5 := [each erec in employees:all trec in timetable (erec.enr ≠ trec.tenr)];
      result6 := [each erec in employees:all trec in timetable ((erec.enr ≠ trec.tenr) or
                       some crec in courses ((trec.tcnr = crec.cnr) and (crec.clevel = 1)))]
end.
```

In the proposed form the relation constructor can only create subrelations from one relation variable. The general case of the construction of relations with the aid of several free variables and arbitrary result tuples made up of their components will be treated in the next section.

5.2 The General Relation Constructor

In its most general form a relation constructor can be defined using several free variables. Its value is a relation defined by tuples whose components come from components of the free variables of the constructor, and maybe program variables and constants:

```
⟨general relation constructor⟩ ::= [each (⟨target component list⟩)
                                     for   ⟨control record variable list⟩
                                     in    ⟨range relation variable list⟩:
                                           ⟨logical expression⟩]
⟨target component list⟩ ::= ⟨target component⟩ | ⟨target component⟩; ⟨target component list⟩
⟨target component⟩ ::= ⟨control record component variable⟩ | ⟨variable⟩ | ⟨constant⟩ | empty
```

The correspondence between the control variables and the range variables is implied by their position in the respective lists. The previously defined relation constructor of Section 5.1 is a special case of this more general constructor.

A fourth relation will be introduced for the last example; this relation contains the publications of the employees, described by the title, the year of publication, and, to identify the associated employee, an employee number.

Example 7. For those employees who give lectures, find the names and the title and year of their publications.

Solution 7.1.

```
.
.
type  erectype  = record enr, estatus:integer; ename:string end;
      ereltype  = relation ⟨enr⟩ of erectype;
      prectype  = record ptitle:string; pyear, penr:integer end;
      preltype  = relation ⟨ptitle, penr⟩ of prectype;
      trectype  = record tenr, tcnr, ttime:integer;
                         tday, troom:string end;
      treltype  = relation ⟨tenr, tcnr, tday⟩ of trectype;
var   employees:ereltype;
      papers:preltype;
```

```
        timetable:treltype;
        result:relation ⟨rname, rtitle⟩ of
                record rname, rtitle:string; ryear:integer end;
   begin .
        .
        .
        result := [each (erec.ename; prec.ptitle; prec.pyear)
                  for erec, prec in employees, papers:
                  (prec.penr = erec.enr) and
                  some trec in timetable (erec.enr = trec.tenr)]
   end.
```

Specific problems with constructed relations, such as the definition of their keys and the possibility of checking keys at compilation time, will be treated elsewhere.

The relational constructor has certain advantages over the previous methods of solution:

It is a nonprocedural (very high level) language construct, in the sense that the user does not program a procedure which produces the result, but gives merely a declaration of certain properties of the result.

The notation is concise and keeps the important information textually together. This increases the readability for the user and facilitates a more efficient implementation.

The relation constructor may be given well-defined semantics in a similar way to predicate calculus.

The set of meaning preserving transformations of constructors is, in the context of predicate calculus, comprehensible. The freedom in the execution of the constructor thus obtained is very desirable for optimization.

At this point similarities to Codd's data sublanguage ALPHA [6] should be stressed. In particular the representation of queries in this calculus oriented language is closely akin to the relational constructor presented here. However, Codd considers relational calculus as an application of predicate calculus, whereas the relational constructor has been developed from, and integrated in, the concepts of a programming language.

6. SYSTEM IMPLEMENTATION AND FURTHER DEVELOPMENT

The various language constructs treated here are being incorporated into the PASCAL compiler for the DECsystem-10 [9] of the Institute for Informatics at Hamburg University. Apart from the necessary modifications to the compiler, a run-time system is being produced for the execution of the relational constructor and the predicates. This basically consists of an algorithm derived from that of Palermo [11] with additional optimization and supported by some advanced access methods. A first version of the system is expected to be available during the summer of 1977.

For the user, a relational database counts as an external variable and can—in analogy to external PASCAL files—be connected to a user program through a formal parameter in the program header. For the examples in this paper the program would appear thus:

```
program dbuser (informatics77);
type  .
      .
      .
      ereltype = ... ;
      preltype = ... ;
      creltype = ... ;
      treltype = ... ;
var   informatics77:database employees:ereltype; papers:preltype;
                             courses:creltype; timetable:treltype end;
      result1, result2, ...:ereltype;
      result7:relation ⟨rname, rtitle⟩ of record ... end;
begin with informatics77 do
      ⋮
end.
```

In parallel to the implementation of the constructs so far developed, we are evaluating various further developments starting from standard PASCAL with respect to their applicability to database problems. With the aid of the **class** concept in [3], objects in a database can be declared in a form which hides the details of the database realization from the user, while improving data integrity and data security (see [15]). Problems of simultaneous access can be investigated using the **monitor** concept in [3].

7. SUMMARY

We have proposed three language constructs for use with data types of mode relation as extensions to a high level language, in particular to PASCAL. These constructs are: a repetition statement controlled by a relation; predicates, as extensions of Boolean expressions; and a general relation constructor, dependent on predicates. The language constructs have been developed stepwise from the most elementary operations on relations.

For the purpose of information retrieval from a relational database the relation constructor provides a solution which, in the context of a general purpose programming language, seems satisfactory.

For other questions, such as the problem of altering data consistently, or simultaneous processing of a database by several users, the proposals can serve as a framework for further investigations.

ACKNOWLEDGMENTS

I would like to thank H. Fischer, M. Jarke, D. Meyer, H.-H. Nagel, and W. Ullmer for their encouragement and the many critical and constructive comments.

REFERENCES

1. ALLMAN, E., STONEBRAKER, M., AND HELD, G. Embedding a relational data sublanguage in a general purpose programming language. SIGPLAN Notices (ACM) *8*, 2 (Feb. 1976), 25–35.

2. Boyce, R.F., Chamberlin, D.D., King III, F.W., and Hammer, M.M. Specifying queries as relational expressions: The SQUARE data sublanguage. *Comm. ACM 18*, 11 (Nov. 1975), 621–628.
3. Brinch Hansen, P. The programming language Concurrent Pascal. *IEEE Trans. Software Eng. SE-1*, 2 (June 1975), 199–207.
4. Chamberlin, D.D., and Boyce, R.F. SEQUEL: A structural English query language. Proc. ACM SIGMOD Workshop, Ann Arbor, Mich., May 1974, pp. 249–264.
5. Codd, E.F. A relational model of data for large shared data banks. *Comm. ACM 13*, 6 (June 1970), 377–387.
6. Codd, E.F. A data base sublanguage founded on the relational calculus. Proc. ACM SIGFIDET Workshop, San Diego, Calif., Nov. 1971, pp. 35–68.
7. Earley, J. Relational level data structures for programming languages. *Acta Informatica 2*, 4 (Dec. 1973), 293–309.
8. Feldman, J.A., Low, J.R., Swineheart, D.C., and Taylor, R.H. Recent developments in SAIL—an ALGOL-based language for artificial intelligence. Proc. AFIPS 1972 FJCC, Vol. 41, AFIPS Press, Montvale, N.J., pp. 1193–1202.
9. Friesland, G., Grosse-Lindemann, C.-O., Lorenz, F.H., Nagel, H.-H., and Stirl, P.-J. A PASCAL compiler bootstrapped on a DEC-system-10. 3. GI-Fachtagung über Programmiersprachen, *Lecture Notes in Computer Science, Vol. 7*, B. Schlender and W. Frielinghaus, Eds., Springer-Verlag, Berlin, 1974, pp. 101–113.
10. Liskov, B., and Zilles, S. Programming with abstract data types. SIGPLAN Notices (ACM) *9*, 4 (April 1974), 50–59.
11. Palermo, F.P. A data base search problem. Proc. 4th Comptr. and Inform. Sci. Symp., J.T. Tou, Ed., Plenum Press, New York, pp. 67–101.
12. Rovner, P.D., and Feldman, J.A. The LEAP language and data structure. Information Processing 68, North-Holland Pub. Co., Amsterdam, 1969, pp. 579–585.
13. Schmid, H.A., and Swenson, J.R. On the semantics of the relational data model. Proc. ACM SIGMOD Conf., San Jose, Calif., May 1975, pp. 211–223.
14. Schmidt, J.W. Untersuchung einer Erweiterung von Pascal zu einer Datenbanksprache. Mitteilung Nr. 28, Inst. für Informatik., U. Hamburg, Hamburg, Germany, March 1976.
15. Schmidt, J.W. Type concepts for database definition: An investigation based on extensions to Pascal. Bericht Nr. 34, Inst. für Informatik., U. Hamburg, Hamburg, Germany, May 1977.
16. Wirth, N. The programming language PASCAL. *Acta Informatica 1*, 1 (May 1971), 35–63.
17. Zloof, M.M. Query by example. Proc. AFIPS 1975 NCC, AFIPS Press, Montvale, N.J., pp. 431–438.

Received March 1977; revised May 1977

"Fill-in-the-Form" Programming†

Lawrence A. Rowe

Computer Science Division, EECS Department
University of California
Berkeley, CA 94720

ABSTRACT

This paper describes a new style of programming, called "fill-in-the-form" programming, for the development of interactive database applications. The applications being developed and the application development environment use the same form and menu interface. High level tools are provided to define interfaces for database query/update and for generating reports or graphs. Our experiences with two systems that are based on this programming paradigm are described.

1. Introduction

A wide variety of computer applications fall into the category of *Interactive Information Systems* (IIS). These applications allow several people to access and update data stored in a database. The applications do not involve much computation but they do involve significant user interaction with the application. The typical interface is a form displayed on a video display through which data can be entered or displayed. Example applications are a software bug report system, a journal submission tracking system, or a personnel management system.

For the past several years we have been developing application development environments (ADE) for writing these applications that use a style of programming we call "fill-in-the-form" programming. An application is composed of a collection of *frames* that contain a *form* where data is entered or displayed and a menu of *operations* the user can execute. The user moves between different frames executing operations to perform whatever action is required. An example frame in a software bug report system is shown in figure 1. The frame has operations that allow a user to retrieve (**Query**) or enter (**Append**) bug reports. To enter a bug report, the user fills in the form and executes the **Append** operation. The system provides built-in commands using a keyboard and/or a pointing device such as a mouse to move to different fields in the form, enter and edit data, and to invoke an operation.

The ADE uses the same "fill-in-the-form" interface as the applications being developed. In other words, the ADE is a collection of frames with operations to define frames, forms, and database relations. The ADE provides frame-types that a programmer can use to construct an application:

1. menu frames for specifying menu interfaces,
2 query/update frames for specifying data browsers,
3. report frames for specifying interfaces to generate reports,

Bug Report

Name:________ Priority: ________

Reported:________ Status:________

Module:________

Description

Response

Help **Append** **Query** **End**

Figure 1. A sample bug report frame.

† This research was supported by the Air Force Office of Scientific Research under Contract 83-0254.

4. graph frames for specifying interfaces to generate graphs, and
5. user-defined frames for specifying interfaces with application specific operations.

Applications are defined by filling in forms that describe how a generic frame should be customized for the specific usage (e.g., for a query/update frame, the form and the mapping between the form and the database). In addition, the ADE allows frames to be tested while they are being defined without requiring that the entire application be compiled and linked.

Two systems have been implemented that are based on the idea of "fill-in-the-form" programming. The Forms Application Development System (FADS) was a prototype system implemented at the University of California, Berkeley to test whether this approach to developing IIS's was viable [RoS82, Sho82]. The prototype was built as a front-end to the INGRES relational database management system [Sta76]. FADS provided only one type of frame (user-defined) but it was readily apparent that applications could be developed quickly and that they were easy to modify. As a result, a local company developed a commercial product, called Application-By-Forms (ABF) [RTI84b], that was based on and extended the ideas in FADS. ABF introduced the notion of other higher level frames (e.g., query/update, report, and graph).

This "fill-in-the-form" approach to developing IIS's can be contrasted with other approaches that are based on extending conventional programming languages or report writer languages. The first approach extends a conventional programming language with constructs to access a database and do screen I/O [HoK84, RoS83, TAN80, RTI84a]. We call such a language a *database/screen programming language*. This approach has several problems. First, programs are much too long because the programmer is forced to specify too much detail. As a result, too much time is required to develop an application and the applications are expensive to maintain and extend. Second, conventional programming languages do not provide support for high-level tools such as reportwriters and database browsers [Cat80, Her80, StK82, RTI84c, Zlo75]. Either these high-level tools must be interfaced to the application program or recoded for each application. Lastly, a database/screen language cannot be used by end-users because too much programming expertise is required.

The second approach to developing IIS's is to extend a report writer language with screen I/O constructs [IBI82, NCS83, Cul83, Cin83, ADR83]. These extended languages are called *Fourth Generation Languages* (4GL). Because a 4GL has an integrated report writer language, they make writing some parts of an application easier. However, the screen I/O constructs are similar to the low-level I/O commands found in the database/screen languages. These systems do not provide high-level commands for specifying operation menus, selecting the code to be executed when a user invokes an operation, specifying help screens, or for specifying other elements of a user dialogue. The user-interface must be coded in the low-level constructs. Consequently, a programmer must write a significant amount of code just to define a simple interface. A second problem with 4GL's is that they are large, monolithic languages which over time have had more and more constructs added to them. The facilities found in high-level tools are typically added to the system by adding constructs to the language. The resulting languages are large and complex and they require considerable training in order to learn how to use them. Another problem is that since these languages evolved rather than being designed, the syntax and semantics are often confusing and inconsistent.

A "fill-in-the-form" ADE is a better approach than these alternatives for several reasons. First, the system has a standard interface. All user-interfaces are defined by frames which standardize how operations are displayed and executed and how data is displayed and entered into the system.

The second advantage of the forms-based approach is that the system supports a collection of high-level tools. For example, tools can be provided for developing data browsers and for defining reports and graphs. These high-level tools make specifying an application easier because the tool has been designed to solve a particular problem (e.g., report writing or graph design). The frame concept is used to integrate these high-level tools into the ADE. In contrast to monolithic languages, a "fill-in-the-form" ADE has several different languages, each customized to a particular usage. Systems composed of several languages typically have two problems: 1) learning the system is difficult and 2) data incompatibility between subsystems. The forms-based interface and online help facilities makes the problem of learning multiple languages less critical. And, the data incompatibility problem does not arise because all data is stored in the database and accessed through a standard query language.

Third, a "fill-in-the-form" ADE allows applications to be developed interactively. The programmer can easily switch between defining an application and running it and he can test partially completed applications. The system also supports a source level debugger that makes it easier to identify and correct bugs.

Another feature of a "fill-in-the-form" ADE is that numerous defaults are provided to simplify the specification of an application. For example, given the definition of a relation, the system will automatically define a form that can be used to query and update data in the relation. Another example is that a default report or graph definition will be generated for a relation or view. By using defaults, applications can be developed very quickly. Moreover, well-designed defaults allow naive users to generate reasonable applications without requiring them to learn the entire system.

The reasons given thus far have focused primarily on prototype applications in which the objective is to get the application running as soon as possible. To achieve this goal, reliability and performance are sacrificed. This trade-off makes sense unless the application will be used in a production environment. For production applications the user-interface must be "bullet-proofed" for naive users and the reports and forms must be fine-tuned to display the data in the best way possible. Moreover, the performance of the application is more critical because it will be run many times or used simultaneously by many users. The ADE's described here have capabilities that allow the programmer to turn a prototype application into a production application. For example, as mentioned above the system allows the programmer to customize a default form or report. Or, if the programmer is willing to bind features of the application, it can be compiled to run more efficiently (e.g., the forms used in an application can be compiled into an executable program rather than being loaded from the database at run-time). Consequently, if the programmer is willing to specify more detail or invest more time compiling the application, he can improve its reliability, performance, and user-interface.

This paper describes the principles behind a "fill-in-the-form" application development environment and presents examples that show how an application is defined. The paper is organized as follows. The second section describes a simple bug report system that will be used to illustrate this style of program development. Section 3 describes the application development environment and shows how different types of frames are defined. Section 4 discusses the productivity improvements possible with a "fill-in-the-form" system. The last section summarizes the paper.

2. A Sample Application

This section describes a sample application. The application is a simple bug report system. The data for this example is stored in one relation with the following schema:

```
BUG( name = text(15),
     priority = (A, B, C),
     reported = date,
     status = (ENTERED, ASSIGNED, FIXED),
     module = text(15),
     description = text(512),
     response = text(512)
   )
```

The *name* attribute is a short name for the bug. The *priority*, *reported*, and *status* attributes describe the relative importance of the bug, the date on which the bug was reported, and the current status of the bug. The *module* attribute identifies to which system component the bug belongs (i.e., an indication of what component has a bug in it). The *description* attribute is a long text description of the bug provided by the person who submits the bug report. The *response* attribute is a long text description filled in by the maintenance programmer after the bug is fixed to indicate how the problem was resolved.

A bug report application is used by many people, including technical support personnel, maintenance programmers, and managers, who are responsible for tracking bugs that are reported and insuring that they are fixed. Figure 2 shows a directed graph that presents an overview of the application. Each node in the graph is a frame and an edge between two nodes indicates that an operation in the frame at which the edge originates calls the frame at which the edge points.

Figure 3 shows the top-level menu frame that is displayed when the application is run. If the user selects the **BrowseBugs** operation, the query/update frame shown in figure 1 is called. The user can browse 'A' priority bugs entered since 1 November 1984 by filling in the form as shown in figure 4 and executing the **Query** operation. Figure 5 shows the screen after the first qualifying bug report has been displayed. Notice that the same form is used to display the data but that a new operation menu is supplied that allows the user to modify or delete the currently displayed bug report or to move to the previous or next bug report. After browsing the bug reports of interest, the user can return to the frame shown in figure 4 by executing the **End** operation. Executing the **End** operation in this frame returns the user to the top-level menu frame.

Figure 6 shows the frame for producing a report that lists bugs in a selected system module that were reported during some time period. This frame is called when the user executes the **BugReport** operation in the menu frame. To generate the report, the user fills in the report parameters and executes the **RunReport** operation. The

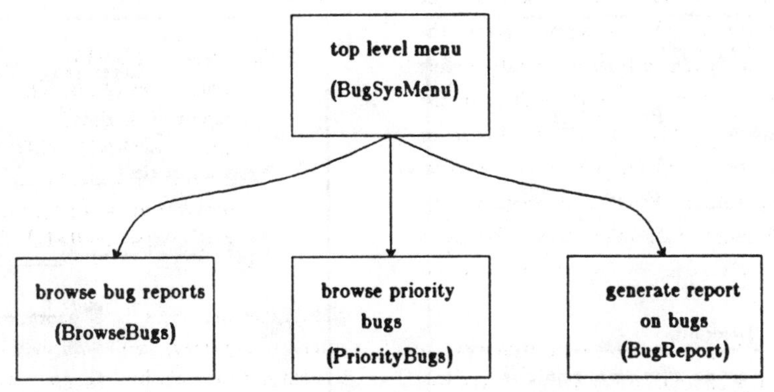

Figure 2. Bug report application overview.

Bug Report System

Help	enter help system
BrowseBugs	browse bug reports
PriorityBugs	summarize priority bugs
BugReport	run report listing bugs
End	exit application

Help BrowseBugs PriorityBugs BugReport End

Figure 3. Top level menu.

Bug Report

Name:__________ Priority: *A*

Reported: $\geq$ *1 Nov 1984* Status:__________

Module:__________

Description

Response

Help Append Query End

Figure 4. Query specification to browse bug reports.

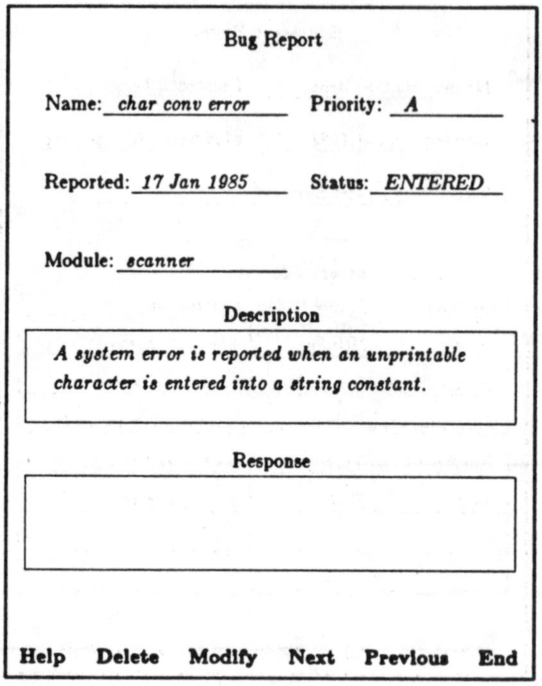

Bug Report	
Name: *char conv error*	Priority: *A*
Reported: *17 Jan 1985*	Status: *ENTERED*
Module: *scanner*	

Description

A system error is reported when an unprintable character is entered into a string constant.

Response

Help Delete Modify Next Previous End

Figure 5. Query/update frame after query is executed.

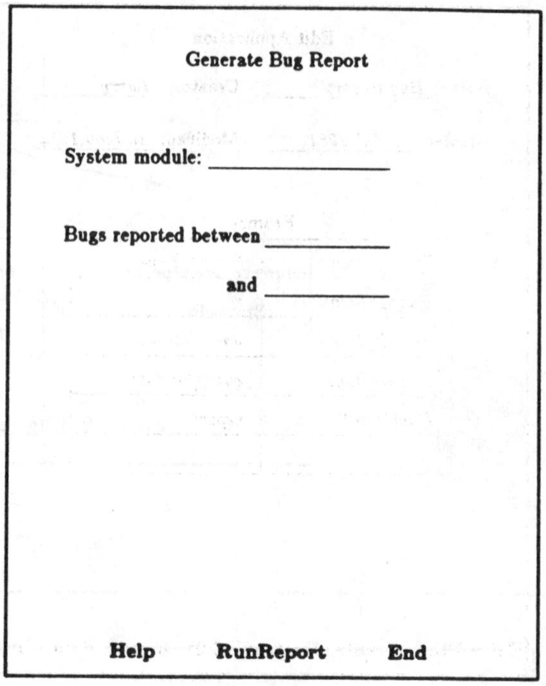

Generate Bug Report

System module: ____

Bugs reported between ____

and ____

Help RunReport End

Figure 6. A report frame.

report would be displayed on the user's terminal or spooled to a printer depending on how the application was defined. This frame is an example of a report frame.

This section has described a simple application. The next section shows how this application is defined.

3. The Application Development Environment

This section describes the application development environment and illustrates how frames are defined. Three frame types are discussed: menu, query/update, and user-defined.

The ADE is composed of a collection of frames that the programmer moves between to define the relations, forms, frames, reports, and graphs that make up the application. Figure 7 shows the edit application frame as it would appear after the four frames in the simple bug report application have been defined.

The field labeled *Name* gives the name of the application and is filled in by the programmer when the application is created. The *Creator* field identifies who created the application. This field is automatically filled in by the system when the application is created. The *Created* and *Modified* fields show the dates when the application was created and when it was last modified. These fields are also updated automatically by the system. As will be seen below, this information is kept for every object defined in an application (e.g., frames, forms, reports, etc.). The table in the middle of the frame lists the frames that have been defined for this application. The name and type of each frame is given. A table such as this one is called a *table field* and is actually a window on a larger data set. The user has commands that allow him to scroll forwards and backwards through the table looking at the various entries.

The edit application frame has operations to compile the application for production use (**Bind**), to create and destroy applications (**Create** and **Destroy**), to edit the definition of a frame (**Edit**), to invoke an ad hoc query interface (**Ingres**), and to run the application (**Run**). In addition, the frame includes operations to enter the help system (**Help**) or to exit the current frame (**End**).

The programmer can examine the definition of a frame by selecting the desired frame in the table field and

Edit Application

Name: *Bug Report* Creator: *Larry*

Created: *5 Jul 1984* Modified: *10 Nov 1984*

Frames

Frame Name	Frame Type
BugSysMenu	*menu*
PriorityBugs	*user-defined*
BrowseBugs	*query/update*
BugReport	*report*

Help Bind Create Destroy Edit Ingres Run End

Figure 7. Application definition frame.

Edit Menu Frame

Name: *BugSysMenu* Creator: *Larry*

Created: *5 Jul 1984* Modified: *10 Sep 1984*

Title: *Bug Report System*

Menu Operations

Op Name	Frame	Description
Help	*HelpSys*	*enter help system*
BrowseBugs	*BrowseBugs*	*browse bug reports*
PriorityBugs	*PriorityBugs*	*summarize priority bugs*
BugReport	*BugReport*	*run report listing bugs*
End	*Exit*	*exit application*

Help Call Edit Ingres End

Figure 8. Definition of menu frame.

executing the **Edit** operation. Suppose the programmer selected the top-level menu frame, named *BugSysMenu*, that was shown in figure 3. The definition of this frame is shown in figure 8. Notice that the object information (i.e., frame name, creator, creation date, and modification date) is similar to the information displayed in the edit application frame. Because a menu frame has a predefined structure and operations are limited to calling other frames, the programmer has to specify very little to define the frame. The programmer specifies the title that will be displayed across the top of the frame and, for each operation, he gives the operation name, the frame to call when the operation is executed, and a brief description of the operation. In the menu frame being defined, the operation names are listed across the bottom of the frame and in the middle of the frame along with the descriptions to show the user what each operation does (see figure 3).

The operations provided in this frame allow the programmer to call the frame being defined (**Call**), to edit another object (**Edit**), or to invoke the ad hoc query interface (**Ingres**). The programmer can change the definition of an operation or he can add or delete an operation by modifying the information displayed in the table field that lists the operations.

The structure of a menu frame is fixed by the system. If the programmer does not like this particular structure, he can define a menu as a user-defined frame which allows him to specify the form and to write arbitrary code for the operations. However, the programmer will have to specify more detail to define it.

Query/update frames, like the frames shown in figures 1, 4, and 5, are common interfaces in IIS's. To define a query/update frame, the programmer must specify the form through which the data will be displayed and entered and the mapping between the form and the relations in the database. Figure 9 shows the definition of the *BrowseBugs* frame shown above. The form used in the *BrowseBugs* frame is named *BugForm*. A form is defined or modified by invoking the form editor with the **FormEdit** operation. The form editor is a "what-you-see-is-what-you-get" editor for forms. The programmer can control the definition and placement of fields and descriptive text (e.g., titles, field labels, and other explanatory text) in the form. The form editor also allows the programmer to specify field display enhancements (e.g., inverse video and blinking), edit checks on data entered into a field, and other attributes that control the user interaction (e.g., manadatory fields). If the programmer had not specified a

Edit Query/Update Frame

Name: *BrowseBugs* Creator: *Larry*

Created: *15 Jul 1984* Modified: *8 Dec 1984*

Form: *BugForm* Interface: *record*

Relations

Relation Names
BUG

Help Call DBMap Edit FormEdit Ingres End

Figure 9. Definition of query/update frame.

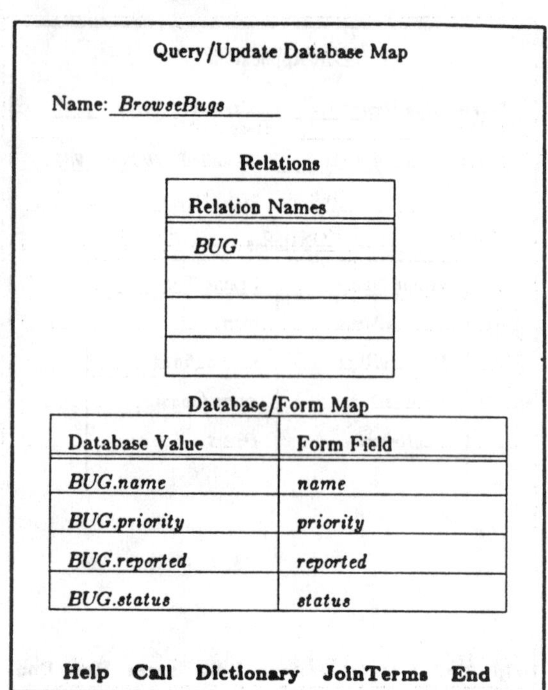

Query/Update Database Map

Name: *BrowseBugs*

Relations

Relation Names
BUG

Database/Form Map

Database Value	Form Field
BUG.name	*name*
BUG.priority	*priority*
BUG.reported	*reported*
BUG.status	*status*

Help Call Dictionary JoinTerms End

Figure 10. Definition of the database/form map.

form for the query/update frame, the system would automatically generate one for the relations identified in the database mapping.

The *Interface* field defines the style of interface for the frame. In this case, a "record" interface is used which means that only one record in the relation is displayed at a time. And, the mapping between the form and the database is very simple because the data is taken from only one relation, the *BUG* relation.

The mapping is specified in a different frame that is called by executing the **DBMap** operation. The database mapping frame is shown in figure 10. In this simple example, the database values do not involve computation and the relation attribute names and the form field names are the same. By filling in the mapping table field differently, both constraints can be changed. If a more complex mapping between the database and the form is required such as a join between one or more relations, the programmer can execute the **JoinTerms** operation which calls a frame that allows him to specify the mapping.

The system supports two other query/update interfaces: "table" and "master/detail." A "table" interface displays several records through a table field. A "master/detail" interface simultaneously displays one record from one relation through a record interface and several records from a second relation through a table field. For example, suppose there was a second relation that maintained information about the modules in the system with the following definition

```
MODULE(   module=text(15),
          responsible=text(20)
      )
```

Figure 11 shows a "master/detail" interface where the *MODULE* relation is the master and the *BUG* relation is the detail. The mapping between this form and the database must specify that the relations *MODULE* and *BUG* are joined on the *module* attribute and that only the *name*, *reported*, and *priority* attributes in *BUG* are to be displayed. In addition, the programmer must specify whether the "master" record should be deleted when the last "detail" record is deleted.

The problem of specifying complex mappings such as this one is equivalent to the view update problem [Cha75, Day76, Sto75]. ABF solved this problem by constraining what mappings can be specified and allowing the programmer to choose a semantic interpretation. An alter-

Module Bug Summary

Module: ____________ Responsible: ____________

Outstanding Bugs

Name	Reported	Priority

Help **Append** **Query** **End**

Figure 11. Example of a master/detail interface.

Outstanding Bugs By Module

Bug Summary

Module Name	Number Bugs
parser	*10*
query optimizer	*8*
access methods	*5*
unload utility	*4*

Help **BugDetail** **End**

Figure 12. Example of a user-defined frame.

native approach would be to extend the database model so that the correct semantics could be inferred from the database schema.

Query/update frames have proven to be very useful building blocks for IIS's. By providing several choices for these interfaces, query/update frames can be used in more places. The alternative is to force the programmer to specify the interface as a user-defined frame. If a user-defined frame was used, the programmer would have to specify more detail or provide less function at the interface (e.g., the user might not be able to query on arbitrary fields). The "fill-in-the-form" programming environment simplifies the specification of query/update frames and provides the "glue" for integrating them into an application.

The last frame type that will be discussed is a user-defined frame. A user-defined frame gives the programmer complete control over the frame. He specifies the form using the form editor and codes the operations in a high-level programming language, called the *Operation Specification Language* (OSL). Figure 12 shows an example of a user-defined frame. It lists the modules in a software system and a count of the outstanding bugs in each module. The frame has three operations: **Help**, **BugDetail**, and **End**. The **Help** and **End** operations are the standard ones found in most frames.[1] The **BugDetail** operation calls another frame that lists the outstanding bugs in the selected module. Since this frame does not correspond to any generic frame type supported by the ADE, it must be defined by the programmer as a user-defined frame.

The definition frame for a user-defined frame is shown in figure 13. The structure of this frame is similar to the other frames for defining frames. The object name, creator, creation date, and modification date are shown at the top. The frame also shows the name of the form used in the frame and lists the names of the operations that have been defined for the frame. The operation list is displayed through a table field, labeled *Op Names*. Below that field is a text field, labeled *Operation Definition*, that displays

[1] Neither FADS nor ABF made these operations mandatory in every frame. However, they have been included in almost all application frames. An obvious extension would be to include them in the frame model support by the ADE so the programmer would not have to specify them. Frames could be defined that would make it easier to specify help frames and the help text could be stored in the database which would make it easier to manage and allow it to be used in several different contexts (e.g., as on-line help or in manuals).

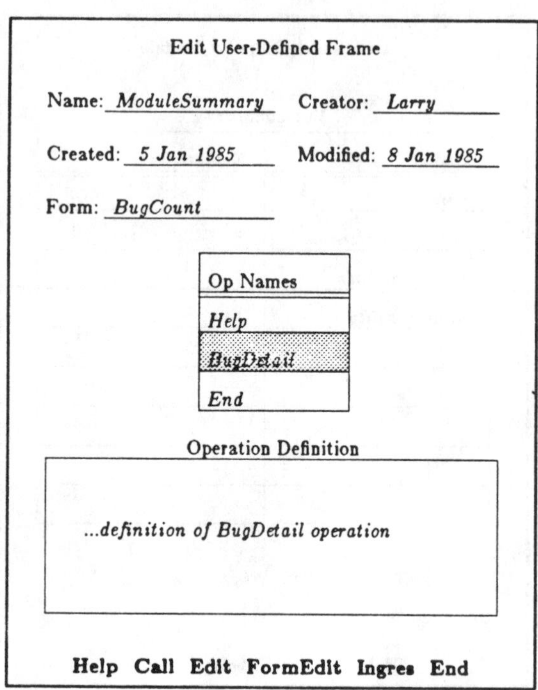

Figure 13. Definition frame for user-defined frames.

the specification for one of the operations. The programmer can edit the specification or select another operation name which causes the definition of that operation to be displayed in the text field. Commands are also provided that allow the programmer to add or delete operations or to change the name of an operation.

Operations are coded in OSL. OSL has constructs for accessing the data in a form or in the database, for calling other frames similar to the way procedures are called in a programming language, and for specifying control-flow for the application. In addition, procedures coded in a conventional programming language can be called so that there is a way to escape if OSL does not provide a required construct. A more detailed description of the features of OSL is given elsewhere [RTI84b].

As powerful as user-defined frames are, the goal of a forms-based programming environment is to use them for only a small percentage of the frames in an application. The reason for this goal is that high-level frames require less specification when they are defined and they allow the programmer to develop his applications in larger "chunks." Consequently, applications can be developed quicker and, to the extent the programmer does not have to wade through code, they can be modified more easily.

This section has shown how menu, query/update, and user-defined frames are defined in a "fill-in-the-form" ADE.

4. Discussion

This section describes the savings that can be achieved when using a "fill-in-the-form" ADE. Following that, future research directions are discussed.

Our experience with FADS and ABF indicates that an application would require 10 to 20 times more lines of code if it had been coded in a database/screen language or a 4GL. This code compaction is due to several factors. First, the frame model for specifying an application subsumes many lines of code that would have to be specified for each frame in an application if it were coded in one of the other languages.

Second, the high-level tools substantially reduce the amount of code the programmer must specify to define part of the application. The high-level tool acts as a program generator that the programmer can parameterize to meet the needs of his specific application. The frame model simplifies the integration of this generated code into the application.

A third reason fewer lines of code are required is that database/screen languages and 4GL's typically have three names for a data value: 1) a name for the field in the form, 2) a name for the attribute in the relation, and 3) a name for a variable that the program manipulates. Many lines of code are used to copy these values between the database, the program, and the form. For example, to display a database value in a form field, two statements are required: one to copy the value from the database to the program variable and one to copy it from the variable to the form field. In contrast, in OSL each field in a form has an implicitly defined variable with the same name as the field. Each time a value is assigned to this variable, the value is automatically displayed to the user through the form. To display a database value in a form field, the attribute is assigned to the form field (i.e., the implicit variable with the same name). Consequently, only one statement is required rather than two. This saving may not seem like much, but if you examine sample applications you will find that is saves many lines of code.

Another way to measure the productivity improvement achieved by a new programming language or system is to quantify the time required to create an application. Using ABF, the simple bug report application described above can be defined in less than 30 minutes. It would take a very sophisticated and experienced programmer to produce this application in the same time with a database/screen language or 4GL.

As we have gotten more experience with these systems it has become clear that there are many different frame types the ADE might support. We are currently working on a new system that will allow programmers to define their own frame types (i.e., user-defined frame types). With this facility, an organization could customize the frame types for their environment or application. They would get the productivity gains made possible by a "fill-in-the-form" programming environment without having to give up the flexibility found in a general purpose programming language.

Other directions we are pursuing are to define high-level tools for other application domains, such as office automation [Pro85], and to take advantage of new user-interface technologies such as bit-mapped display and mouse interfaces to improve the ADE.

5. Summary

This paper has described a new paradigm for developing interactive database applications. The paradigm is based on the idea of filling in forms to define an application. Two systems have been implemented and experience with them shows this approach to application development to improve programmer productivity and to produce applications that are easier to maintain and extend.

Acknowledgements

I want to thank Joe Cortopassi, Arthur Hochberg, and Kurt Shoens who worked on the development of the ideas presented here and reviewed earlier drafts of this paper.

References

[ADR83] *ADR/IDEAL - Application Development Reference Manual*, S12G-01-00, Applied Data Research, Inc., Aug. 1983.

[Cat80] R. R. G. Cattell, "An Entity-Based User Interface", *Proc. 1980 ACM-SIGMOD Conference on Management of Data*, May 1980.

[Cha75] D. Chamberlin and al, "Views Authorization and Locking in a Relational Database System", *Proc. NCC*, 1975, 425-430.

[Cin83] *Series 80 MANTIS User's Guide*, Release 3.5, Pub. No. P19-0001, Cincom Systems, Inc., 1983.

[Cul83] *Application Development System/Online - Reference Guide*, Release 1.1, Cullinet Software, Aug. 1983.

[Day76] U. Dayal, "On the Updatability of Relational Views", *Proc. 4th VLDB*, 1976, 368-377.

[Her80] C. Herot, "SDMS: A Spatial Data Base System", *Trans. Database Systems*, Dec. 1980.

[HoK84] E. Horowitz and A. Kemper, High-Level Input/Output Facilities in a Database Programming Language, Unpublished manuscript, Univ. South. Calif., June 1984.

[IBI82] *Focus Users Manual*, Information Builders, Inc., New York, NY, 1982.

[NCS83] *NOMAD2 Reference Manual*, National CSS, Wilton, CT, Jan. 1983.

[Pro85] R. Probst, *BOISE: An INGRES-based Office Information System*, MS Report, U.C. Berkeley, May 1985.

[RoS82] L. A. Rowe and K. A. Shoens, "FADS - A Forms Application Development System", *ACM SIGMOD 1982 Int. Conf. on Mgt of Data*, June 1982.

[RoS83] L. A. Rowe and K. A. Shoens, "Programming Language Constructs for Screen Definition", *IEEE Trans. on Software Eng. TSE-9*, 1 (Jan. 1983).

[RTI84a] *EQUEL/C User's Guide*, Version 3.0, VAX/VMS, Relational Technology, Inc., Berkeley, CA, May 1984.

[RTI84b] *INGRES ABF (Applications By Forms) User's Guide*, Version 3.0, VAX/VMS, Relational Technology, Inc., Berkeley, CA, May 1984.

[RTI84c] *INGRES QBF (Query By Forms) User's Guide*, Version 3.0, VAX/VMS, Relational Technology, Inc., Berkeley, CA, May 1984.

[Sho82] K. A. Shoens, *A Form Application Development System*, PhD Thesis, U.C. Berkeley, Nov. 1982.

[Sto75] M. R. Stonebraker, "Implementation of Integrity Constraints and Views by Query Modification", *Proc. SIGMOD*, 1975, 65-78..

[Sta76] M. R. Stonebraker and al, "The Design and Implementation of INGRES", *ACM Trans. Database Systems*, Sep. 1976, 189-222.

[StK82] M. Stonebraker and J. Kalash, "TIMBER: A Sophisticated Relation Browser", *Proc. 8th Very Large Data Base Conference*, Sep. 1982.

[TAN80] "Tandem 16 Pathway Reference Manual", 82041, Tandem Computers Inc., Feb. 1980.

[Zlo75] M. M. Zloof, "Query by Example", *Proc. NCC 44* (1975).

Entity-Relationship Database User Interfaces

T. R. Rogers, R. G. G. Cattell

Information Management Group
Sun Microsystems, Incorporated
Mountain View, California

Abstract

We report on experience with database user interfaces that are entity-relationship oriented, rather than relation-oriented, and provide a new level of ease-of-use for information management. Our goal is to allow technical workers with little or no knowledge of database systems, query languages, or relational terminology to use databases to solve simple information management problems. Our tools also provide new capabilities for expert users, such as database browsing using a mouse and database display using bitmap graphics.

Keywords: Entity-Relationship, Ease-of-Use

1. Introduction

Relation-oriented user interfaces allow the definition and manipulation of tables. The default interfaces deal with a single table at a time; the relationship between the data in different tables is in the mind of the user instead of being supported by further semantics and primitives in the database system or its user interface. By contrast, an entity-relationship user interface supports the definition and manipulation of entities, which may be instantiated as many records from many tables, and relationships, which are instantiated as one or many records from one table. Our model supports entities and relationships similar to those defined in the entity-relationship data model [Chen 76].

In this paper, we briefly discuss features of the underlying database system that is required to support entity-relationship interfaces. We then describe the architecture and operation of two new tools that were made possible by the underlying entity-relationship platform.

2. Database System

We feel that a database system must provide *at least* four classes of features in order to support entity-relationship capabilities in a production engineering environment. First, an entity-relationship database system must support data model independent capabilities such as concurrency control, report generation, forms-based data entry and data modification, large amounts of persistent data, and transactions for recovery. Next, the system has to support all relational capabilities since these provide the necessary simplicity and power for many types of database activity. We do not want to lose or trade such important capabilites for entity-relationship features. In addition, we require the DBMS be extended to support entity definition primitives, such that an entity consists of a record from an entity table plus records from all of the other tables in the database that reference the entity record. The last feature class for entity-relationship operations involves capabilities for entity manipulation with acceptable interactive response time. Many relational systems support embedded query languages, but almost no relational systems support the performance we require for entity-relationship user interfaces [Rubenstein 87] [Learmont 87].

We now discuss the architecture and operation of two new entity-relationship user interfaces. The first tool is schemadesign, used to define the database schema. The other tool is databrowse, used for editing and browsing data in the database.

3. Schemadesign

Schemadesign is a window-based tool with which users can graphically create and display the database schema by using an entity-relationship diagram. Schemadesign's graphical representation is much easier to understand than the linear listing of tables in conventional relational systems. It is most commonly used by database administrators to define databases; however, it is also a very useful tool for viewing the schema for an existing database. The tool contains a message window for messages and a command subwindow for typing in information or clicking commands with the mouse. The editing subwindow is used for mouse and keyboard entry operations.

In Figure 1, two types of boxes are shown in the editor subwindow: entity (square) boxes and oblong (relationship) boxes. Entity boxes are used to represent tables with keys, and relationship boxes denote tables that have no key. Typically, relationship tables reference at least two entities, although this is not a requirement. Relationship tables can be transformed into entity tables by defining a key for them.

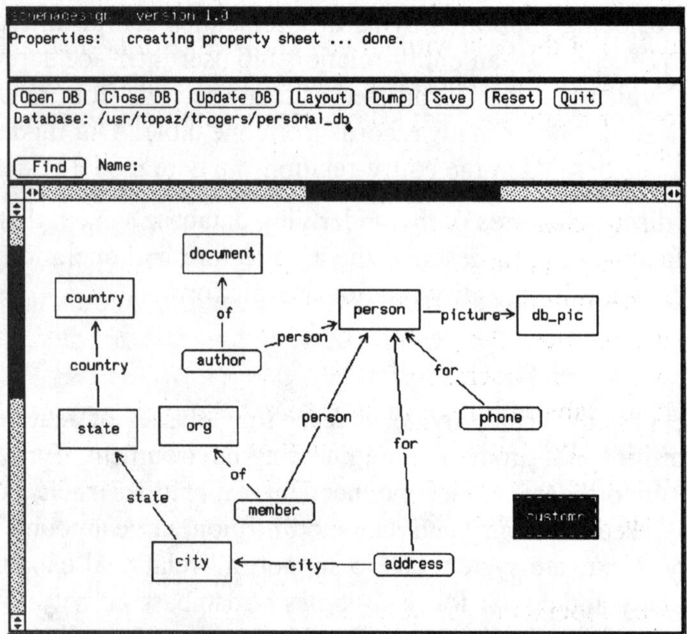

Figure 1: schemadesign with customr table selected

Constraint-checking through the use of a built-in referential integrity [Codd 81] feature provides a level of data integrity checking not found in most database management systems. The constraint checking is provided by the database system itself; it is not provided as an add-on by schemadesign. The arrows drawn between the boxes represent graphically what would be referred to as foreign keys in the relational model, although most relational database management systems do not implement them. The ability to perform integrity checks when records are inserted, deleted, or modified is recognized as a key entity-relationship enhancement to a database system [Schwarz 86]. In fact, such extensions are being considered for for inclusion in the ANSI SQL2 standard [ANSI 87]. As an example, the referential integrity facility would prevent the deletion of an organization referenced by its members. Likewise, it would not be possible to directly add a person as a member of an organization if the organization did not exist in the database.

There are three main steps to using schemadesign:

Identify 'entities'

The user identifies entities (objects) in the real world that he wants to model in the database system. Examples are people, cities, and documents.

Make entity tables for them

An entity table is created for each real-world object. Creating a table using schemadesign is a simple process of menu/mouse selection and table naming. A "property sheet" provides field name entry and field type selection and definition, as shown in Figure 2. Data types for fields are defined either by selecting the type with the mouse by clicking on the circle made from arrows icon or by selecting the type from a pull-down menu. For example, in Figure 2 we illustrate using a menu to select the string data type for the logon_name field.

Identify features

A feature can be thought of as more information about an entity. Examples would be the age of a person or a list of the organizations to which the person belongs. There are a few simple rules to follow when identifying features of entities. Following these guidelines encourages normalization ([Date 85] [Codd 72]) of the data without any knowledge of normalization theory on the part of the user. The user makes either fields or relationship tables for the features depending on whether they are 1-to-1 or many-to-1 with the corresponding entity, respectively. For example, since a person has only one date of birth, date of birth is said to be "1-to-1" with the person entity. Therefore, we model this relationship in our schema by making the date of birth feature a field in the entity table for person. Similarly, since an employee can have many phones (such as one at work, one in the car, and one at home), i.e. phone numbers share a "many-to-1" relationship with a person, we capture this information in the schema with the relationship table phone. It has a field in it that references the people entity. In this manner, we can add as many phones for the same person as we like. Schemadesign lets the user create many-to-1 relationships simply by selecting the reference table with the mouse, selecting connect from a menu, and drawing a line to the referenced (entity) table. The required reference field in the referencing table is automatically generated. It is also very simple to model many-to-many relationships by composing them out of 1-to-many connections: drawing two or more connections from a reference table to entity tables.

Schemadesign helps the user understand the structure of the schema by not allowing the creation of a database from an incorrectly defined schema. Although it is possible to automatically generate reference fields, the tables do not become fully defined until the entity tables have key fields defined for them. In Figure 1, we notice that the customr table is surrounded by a dotted box. This indicates that the customr table is not completely defined. In this particular case, it is not defined because no key field has been specified.

In addition to schema definition, schemadesign allows easy schema modification. Users delete or rename tables and fields by selecting commands from a pop-up menu, and they can customize the graphical layout of lines and icons. Scrollbars can be used to move about in large schemas, and a find facility is available to locate tables with particular names. B-tree and password properties can also be changed using schemadesign. After modification, schemadesign automatically reconfigures the existing database as necessary to fit the new design.

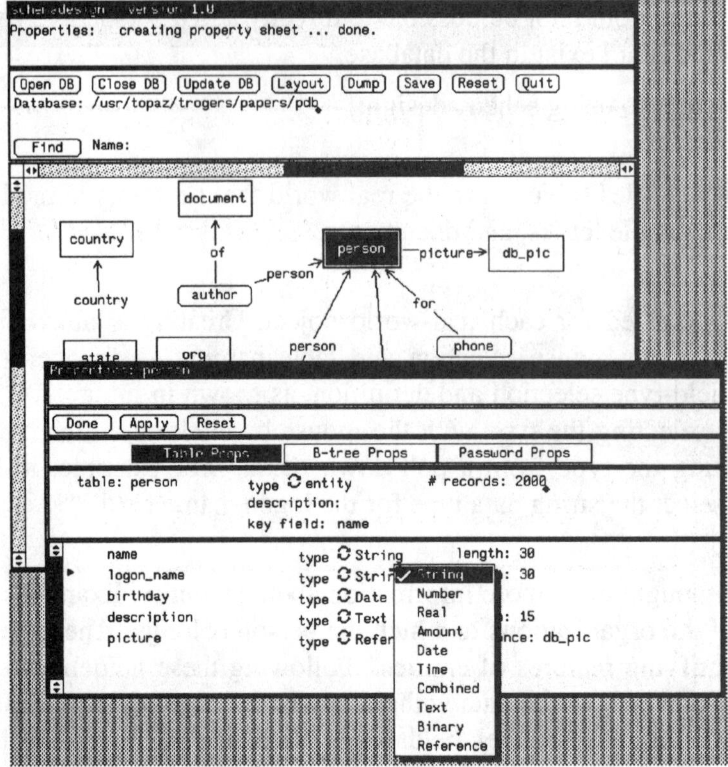

Figure 2: schemadesign with property sheet and menu

We have found that a graphical display is a useful and powerful tool for both the neophyte and expert users. We are implementing further extensions for the tool such as a "verbose mode" to allow seeing all fields for a table at once, and a group move facility to allowing moving a number of tables and references as one unit.

4. Databrowse

Databrowse is a window-based program that allows viewing and editing of logical entities instead of the single records found in conventional relational databases. It is built upon the standard SunView window system [Sun 86d] and the ERIC SunUNIFY programmatic interface [Sun 86b]. It can also be used to browse and edit information in the schema, but not change the schema itself.

Databrowse has a number of subwindows. From top to bottom they are a message subwindow for messages; a command subwindow for selecting entities and relationships, changing between databases anywhere in the computer network, and other operations; an editor-browser subwindow for viewing and editing data; a text subwindow for displaying and editing text fields; and a picture display subwindow with a picture editing subwindow. The text subwindow is only present if the database contains text fields, and the picture subwindows are only present if the database contains picture fields.

Data can be displayed in the familiar tabular format as shown in Figure 3. The person table was selected simply by using the mouse and a menu which are also displayed in the figure. Table names and entity names appear in **bold** face. Each field name (label) has a colon appended to it. Most data appears as ASCII text, but picture fields appear as camera icons. The user can scroll back and forth through the table using the scrollbars. Not shown is a property sheet that allows the user to tailor data display characteristics.

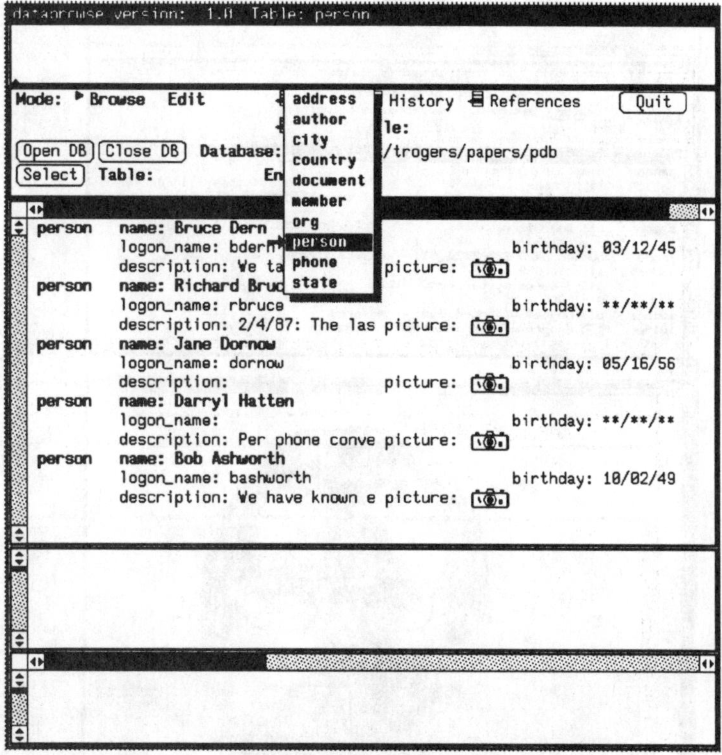

Figure 3: databrowse in table mode displaying person records

In addition to looking at single tables, databrowse lets the user view entities. The data in an entity consists of information from a number of records in potentially many different tables in the database. The user can click on any bold face data, with the exception of table names, to display an entity. For instance, if the user clicks on either "Bob Ashworth" or the field label "name:" for Bob Ashworth in Figure 3, the editor-browser subwindow is erased and the new entity information is displayed as shown in Figure 4. The entity record itself is above the dotted line, and the reference records are listed below the dotted line. The entity name which is a field in each referencing record is not shown, to reduce the display of redundant data. There are several ways to scroll to the other reference records for this person that are not shown in the figure.

Databrowse can be used to store pictures either in the database itself, or pictures can be stored in files, with simply the file name in the database. The underlying database system supports the binary data type, but it is only used by databrowse to store pictures. User-written programs can do whatever they want with the binary fields, however, including using them for storing binary program files, images, or other types of unformatted data. In Figure 3 the person's picture is displayed by clicking the camera icon or the "picture:" field label. The selected camera remains in reverse video.

Note that the instantiated entity is *not* one record, and it is *not* possible to get the necessary display information using a relational view. It would be difficult to get the same display information using a purely relational system. First, a simple relational view would be cumbersome because the targetlist of the view would have to be needlessly complicated. Second, a join would not work in any case where there was no matching record in any one of the join tables, unless the outer join syntax were supported [Date 83]. Third, retrieving the information would probably have to be done as a series of two-table queries which would take too long. Using the underlying capabilities of ERIC, the new display of an entity is obtained directly from the database in a fraction of a second, without read-ahead or caching in the program.

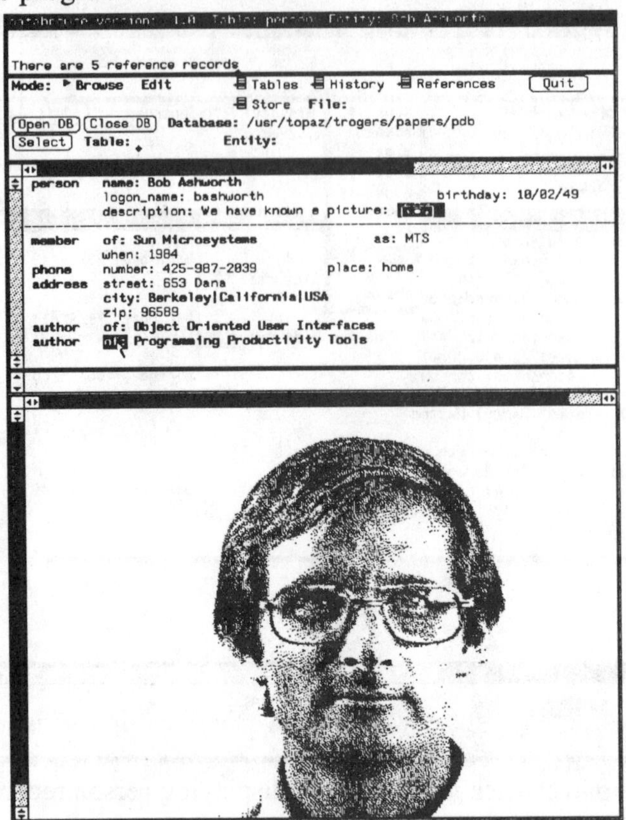

Figure 4: databrowse with picture selected

After viewing the person entity, the user may want to see more information about one of the papers that the person authored. This is done simply by clicking on the name of the paper or the field label for the particular paper. In Figure 4, we show the user selecting the "of:" field label. Figure 5 shows the new entity (the paper) being displayed. There are several new features shown in this figure. Foremost is the fact that the user is now in edit mode, and can edit any data on the screen. In this mode, labels are used for browsing and data, when clicked, can be edited. Delete, "D", and insert, "I", boxes are shown. It is possible to use these to delete reference records and add reference records. These operations, of course, are subject to the referential integrity constraints applied by the underlying database system.

Note that no forms design is necessary for accessing an entity. Databrowse essentially creates a default form. In editing mode, an empty record is shown for each reference record type that has no actual records which reference the current entity. Included is a reference menu item which shows a menu of referencing from which a specific reference set can be chosen. The default form has most of the desired information about an entity, which is what the user wants most of the time.

Databrowse can also be used for text manipulation. Text fields are edited by the user in the text subwindow which has the full power of the normal Sun View text editor. It is possible to scan in entire pages of data using scanners, or an ASCII text file can be created outside of databrowse with the user's favorite text editor. The file can then be read into the text subwindow for editing. When the editing is completed, the text can be saved to the database or a file. In Figure 5 we show the contents of the description field for the document. We could just as easily have stored the entire document in the database. As with picture fields, the selected field is highlighted using reverse video.

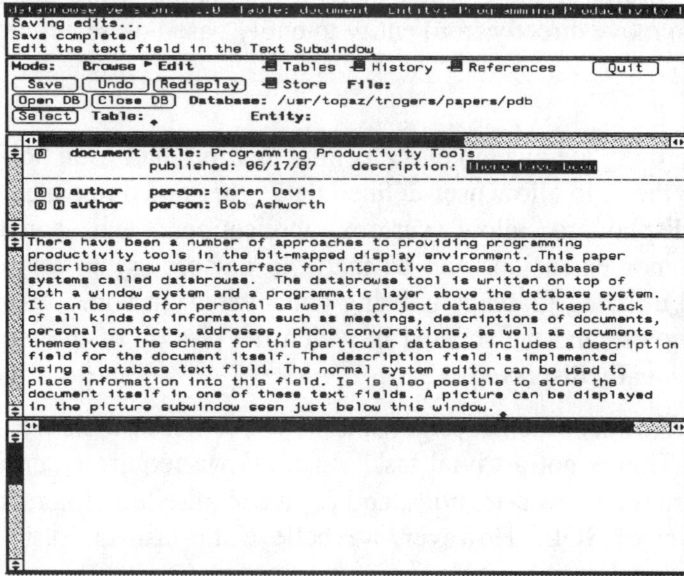

Figure 5: databrowse with text selected for editing

5. Related Work

The idea of an entity-relationship diagram editor such as schemadesign is not new -- almost anyone who read the original [Chen 76] probably thought of it. Surprisingly, there have been few actual commercial implementations until recently [Chen 87] [CCA 87] [ETH 87]. There have also been some research prototypes in this direction [Chan 80] [Gold 85].

We have presented experience with the implementation and use of such a tool, and demonstrate that such a tool can easily be built on a relational system. In our experience, our users have always tended to draw entity-relationship diagrams on paper; now this task has been automated.

The databrowse tool is unique in both the research and development worlds, to our knowledge, except for the author's previous work [Cattell 83]. The two features that make databrowse unique are its entity-centric orientation, possible only through custom form design in other systems, and its browsing capability to move between database entities. The closest comparable work is probably [Motro 86], who reports on navigating entity-relationship connections by typing natural-language-like commands.

Other work on so-called database "browsers" has actually consisted of *scrolling* through records in a single table [Stonebraker 82] or of typing queries that allow a "fuzzier" specification of data [Motro 87]. Larson [Lars 86] also reports on some early similar approaches for browsing.

There is some work analogous to databrowse in the user's mode of interaction. Recently, [Delisle 86] reports work on such a system for hypertext. However, hypertext lacks the underlying database structure provided by the relational system, and thus (1) the same database of entities and relationships cannot be queried through other means, and (2) there is less uniformity of structure, so users are more likely to get confused [Mantei 82].

Unlike databrowse, some systems allow query specification and thus "browsing" from a graphical schema representation [Wong 82] [King 84] [Fogg 84] [Gold 85] [Lars 86] or from combinations of menus and type-in areas [Grap 87]. This is generally a multi-step process of moving between specification and query results or incremental query construction using the schema whereas databrowse allows the user to move directly from entity to entity based on selection of actual data values.

6. Future Work

Schemadesign and databrowse are available as a commercial product [Sun 86b]. We are looking at a number of extensions to them, to allow user-defined data types and associated procedures, control of databrowse's record display to allow custom applications, and convenience features for schemadesign. Some minor extensions can be made to databrowse to allow queries, and a more sophisticated query tool utilizing graphics is being constructed. In addition, we have built a tighter coupling between databrowse and the schema in which the portion of the schema corresponding to the current entity is graphically displayed.

We are also porting databrowse, schemadesign, and the collection of tools we build to other commercial database products. This is not a trivial task, since (1) we require extensions to the underlying relational model to incorporate new semantics, and (2) we require high interactive performance often not available at the level of SQL. However, we believe the task is feasible with most DBMSs, including some non-relational ones.

7. Summary

We have built entity-relationship user interfaces to a DBMS oriented towards ease-of-use. Schemadesign focuses on a difficult problem in DBMS ease-of-use: designing a database. It provides a simple several-step process not requiring knowledge of relational design and normalization theory. Databrowse provides a default form for database entities spanning many tables. In our experience this is the database "form" that is required for most applications, and thus provides a user interface with no further action on the part of the user after schema design. Furthermore, the browsing provides an easy-to-use alternative to a more complex query language for casual users. We use databrowse in our every-day work. Both databrowse and schemadesign are also interesting to "experts". Databrowse browsing provides a fast way to get to simple pieces of data, and schemadesign diagrams are an efficient way to view database designs. Together, they implement zooming, panning, and rudimentary filtering functionality in Larson's browsing taxonomy [Lars 86].

Acknowledgements

Mike Freedman and Bob Marti implemented schemadesign. Tom Rogers implemented databrowse. Tim Learmont, Mike Freedman, Bob Marti, Richard Berger, and Liz Chambers worked on the underlying ERIC implementation.

References

[ANSI 87]

ANSI SQL2 base document. ANSI X3H2-87-144, July 1987.

[Astrahan 80]

Astrahan, et. al: *A History and Evaluation of System R*. IBM Technical Report RJ2843, June 12, 1980.

[CCA 87]
CCA: *DB Designer - Product literature.* Cambridge, MA.

[Cattell 83]
Cattell, R. G. G.: *Design and Implementation of a Relationship-Entity-Datum Data Model.* Xerox PARC Technical Report CSL-83-4, April 1983, see Section 7.

[Chan 80]
Chan, E. and Lochovsky, F.: *A Graphical Database Design Aid Using the Entity-Relationship Model.* In Entity-Relationship Approach to Systems Analysis and Design, North-Holland, 1980, pp 295-310.

[Chen 76]
Chen, P.: *An Entity-Relationship Model -- Towards a Unifyed View of Data.* ACM Transactions on Database Systems, 1, 1. January 1976.

[Chen 87]
Chen & Associates, Inc.: *ER designer - Product literature.* Baton Rouge, LA.

[Codd 72]
Codd, E.: *Further Normalization of the Data Base Relational Model.* Data Base Systems, Courant Computer Science Symposia Series, Vol. 6. Prentice-Hall. 1972.

[Codd 81]
Codd, E.: *Referential Integrity.* Proceedings of the Seventh International Conference on Very Large Data Bases, Cannes, France, September, 1981.

[Date 81]
Date, C.J.: *Referential Integrity.* Proc. 7th Int. Conf. on Very Large Databases, 1981, pp. 2-12.

[Date 83]
Date, C.J.: *The Outer Join.* IBM Technical Report TR 03.181. January 1982.

[Date 85]
Date, C.: An Introduction to Database Systems. Volume 1. Fourth Edition. Addison-Wesley. September 1985.

[Delisle 86]
Delisle, N. and Schwartz, M.: *Neptune: a Hypertext System for CAD Applications.* ACM SIGMOD Proceedings, 1986.

[ETH 87]
Institut fur Informatik, ETH: *Gambit - Product literature*, Zurich, Switzerland.

[Fogg 84]
Fogg, D.: *Lessons from a "Living In a Database" Graphical Query Interface.* Proceedings ACM SIGMOD 84, pp 100-106.

[Gold 85]
Goldman, K.J., Goldman, S.A., Kanellakis, P.C., Zdonik, S.B.,: *ISIS: Interface for a Semantic Information System.* Proceedings ACM SIGMOD 85, pp. 328-342.

[Grap 87]
Soretas-Graphael: *G-BASE - Product literature.* Waltham, MA.

[King 84]
King, R.: *Sembase: a Semantic DBMS.* Proceedings 1st International Workshop on Expert Database Systems, Kiawah Island, South Carolina, October 24-27, 1984, pp. 151-171.

[Lars 86]
Larson, J.A.: *A Visual Approach to Browsing in a Database Environment.* IEEE Computer, June 86, pp. 62-71.

[Learmont 87]
Learmont, T., and Cattell, R. G. G.: *Object-Oriented Database Systems.* To appear in Springer's *Topics in Information Systems* Series.

[Mantei 82] Mantei, M.: *Disorientation Behavior in Person-Computer Interaction.* PhD dissertation, University of Southern California, 1982.

[Motro 86]
Motro, A.: *BAROQUE: A Browser for Relational Databases.* ACM TOOIS 4, 2, April 1986, pp 164-181.

[Motro 87]
Motro, A.: *VAGUE: A User Interface to Relational Databases that Permits Vague Queries.* CS Dept, University of Southern California.

[Rubenstein 87]
Rubenstein, W. R., Cattell, R. G. G.: *Benchmarking Simple Database Operations.* Proceedings ACM SIGMOD 1987, pp 387-394.

[Schwarz 86]
Schwarz, P, et. al.: *Extensibility in the Starburst Database System.* Proceedings of the 1986 International Workshop on Object-Oriented Database Systems, September 23-26 1986, pp. 85-92.

[Stonebraker 82]
Stonebraker, M. and Kalash, J.: *TIMBER: A Sophisticated Relation Browser.* Proceedings of the Eighth International Conference on Very Large Databases, September 1982, pp 1-10.

[Sun 86b]
Sun Microsystems, Inc.: *SunSimplify Programmer's Manual.* Sun Microsystems, Mountain View, California, 1986.

[Sun 86d]
Sun Microsystems, Inc.: *Sun View Programmer's Guide.* Sun Microsystems, Mountain View, California, 1986.

[Tuori 86]
Tuori, Martin: *A Framework for Browsing in the Relational Data Model.* PhD thesis, University of Toronto CSRG, 1986.

[Wong 82]
Wong, H.K.T., Kuo, I.: *GUIDE: Graphical User Interface for Database Exploration.* Proceedings of the Eighth International Conference on Very Large Databases, September 1982, pp 22-32.

Chapter 6

New Data Models

6.1 Introduction

The relational model was popularized in the early 1970s and has largely replaced the older hierarchical and network data models since that time. Moreover, there have been many attempts to construct "postrelational" models. So far, attempts have not borne much fruit. In this introduction I go through my taxonomy of the various attempts. Before starting, I must advise the reader that data models have much in common with religion. People usually hold strong beliefs in each area; often these beliefs are not based on rational principles; and people are typically attached to the the first system they ever used. Hence there was heated controversy among the reviewers of this book about which papers were worth including. Additionally, many researchers will probably disagree with my comments that follow.

The earliest alternate data model was the **entity-relationship** model, and we have included Chen's original paper as our first selection (6.2). The advocates of the E-R model suggest that the relational model is "semantically impoverished" and that it be extended with the concepts of:

- Entities
- Attributes
- Relationships

The E-R model attracted a following and Peter Chen has been organizing an annual conference as a focus for its development. In my opinion the E-R model has an obvious utility for some tasks, in particular for performing logical database design for relational systems. See [WONG80] for one use of the E-R model for this task. In fact, virtually all commercial relational database design tools require the database administrator to express data using the E-R model. They all contain capabilities for adding, deleting, and modifying the resulting E-R diagrams and for transforming them into "semantically good" relational schemas. Most will additionally output the necessary commands to create the schema for specific commercial relational systems. The technically advanced systems also store their E-R information in the relational system for which they are producing designs.

To the best of my knowledge, there are no commercial database products that use the entity-relationship model as their underlying data model. The failure of the E-R model to achieve wider utility is somewhat puzzling, but there are a variety of possible explanations. First, the timing was bad. The database field was going through the "great wars" between the CODASYL and relational camps. Hence, launching another data model on the scene did not receive a receptive audience. Also the major research groups had already started relational prototypes; they were not about to retrofit something else in midstream. However, the biggest problem was probably that the relational model offered an obvious and dramatic advantage over older hierarchical and network approaches. The E-R model, on the other hand, was not seen to be dramatically better than the relational model. Although it did capture more semantics than the relational model, there were several things it didn't do well at all. First, nonbinary relationships are not natural to express in the E-R model. For example, a marriage ceremony is a relationship between a man, a woman, and a person empowered to perform such ceremonies. Also, the E-R model tended to support query languages that only allowed connection between entities that participated in relationships. For example, to find all the employees older than Smith, one could write in QUEL:

```
range of e is emp
retrieve (emp.name) where emp.age > e.age and e.name = "Smith"
```

Clearly one would never think to add an m to n relationship between employees representing "older than." Such ad hoc ways of relating entities were natural in the relational model but difficult or unnatural in the CODASYL, hierarchical, and E-R models,

In summary the E-R model is a "niche model," useful in certain special circumstances but not in the mainstream of database management.

Historically the next attempt at a new data model was the **functional** model. It is obvious that one can think of an E-R model in the following manner. Suppose each entity has a unique identifier, say employee i.d. for employees. Then, all attributes of an employee can be thought of as functions of the employee id. Moreover, any 1 to 1 or 1 to n relationships can also be considered as a function from one entity identifier to another entity identifier. This prompted researchers to think of a database as a collection of functions, and the best known proposal along these lines is DAPLEX, which we have included as our second paper in this section (6.3).

The functional model has an obvious appeal but also a collection of problems. First m to n relationships are not natural to express as functions, and DAPLEX had to resort to some bizarre constructs to model this situation. Moreover, ad hoc relationships, like the one on ages above, are hard to represent. Finally, the functional model is somewhat simpler than the E-R model because there are fewer building blocks, but it seems to suffer from the same drawbacks that plague the E-R model, i.e., it is not enough better than the relational model to attract attention. Hence, the functional model has achieved no commercial acceptance. Ideas from this model have been incorporated into later research prototypes, most notably IRIS [FISH87], but the model has had little additional impact.

The next model to appear on the scene was the **semantic** data model. Researchers continued complaining about the "semantic poverty" of the relational model. It was common to bandy about one's favorite hard data modelling problem and to indicate how difficult it was to do in a relational context. The solution was to construct a data model with more semantic content by including other constructs such as:

- Classes [HAMM81]
- Roles [BACH77]
- Objects with no fixed type or composition [COPE84]
- Set valued attributes (repeating groups) [ZANI83]
- Unnormalized relations [LUM85]
- Class variables (aggregation) [SMIT77]
- Category attributes and summary tables [OZSO85]
- Molecular objects [BATO85]
- Is-a hierarchies [SMIT77, GOLD83]
- Part-of hierarchies [KATZ85]
- Convoys [CODD79, HAMM81]
- Referential integrity (inclusion dependencies) [DATE81]
- Grouping connections [HAMM81]
- Equivalence relationships [KATZ86]
- Ordered relations [STON83]
- Long fields [LORI83]
- Hierarchical objects [LORI83]
- Multiple kinds of time [SNOD85]
- Snapshots [ADIB80]
- Synonyms [LOHM83]
- Table names as a data value [LOHM83]
- Automatic sampling [ROWE83]
- Recursion or at least transitive closure [ULLM85]

- Semantic attributes [SPOO84]
- Unique identifiers [CODD79, POWE83]

Obviously a database system would never have all these constructs. Hence the challenge is to pick a collection of extension primitives that yield large leverage. Our next two papers indicate two of the more widely known semantic data models, namely SDM (6.4) and GEM (6.5), which added semantic constructs to the relational model.

In my opinion SDM is too complex to be useful as the data model of an actual database system. I expect it might find some utility as a data description language that could be mapped into some other data model. As such, it might be considered as a replacement for the E-R model. However, I feel that it has strayed way too far in the direction of adding complexity to the data model. In addition, there is no data manipulation language presented in the proposal, so the interested implementer must invent one.

On the other hand, GEM represents a much leaner attempt. Basically it is a relational model with the addition of sets as a data type, generalization, and a new data type called instance of a tuple in another relation. I feel that the major contribution of GEM may well be the clean definition of the "nested dot" notation, that has been picked up and generalized by others, notably [STON84].

Semantic data models are now "passé," and the research community has now embraced the **object-oriented** data model. It is very difficult to give a coherent description of what an object-oriented data model actually is. In fact, every conference schedules a panel discussion with a collection of researchers trying to define the term. I agree with Peter Buneman who categorized *object-oriented* as a semantically overloaded term, i.e., it means anything to anybody. Unfortunately, the object-oriented subcommunity lacks a persuasive, articulate spokesperson to present their point of view. Hence I had great difficulty picking a paper that coherently expresses their point of view. After much reflection I decided to include the original Gemstone paper (6.6) and the recent Orion paper (6.7).

Object-oriented data models are either a regenerative throwback to the early 1970s or a revolutionary new concept, depending on who you talk to. Moreover, in an environment where the exact meaning of the word *object-oriented* is unknown, it is a little difficult to have a rational discussion on the subject. Moreover, the first thing that any object-oriented researcher usually says is "everything is an object," a phrase that conveys no information at all.

I will make an attempt to explain what proponents tend to mean by *object-oriented*, what is good about it, and also why some people think it is a throwback to the 1970s. The object-oriented researchers usually really mean a specific collection of techniques when they use the word *object-oriented*, namely:

- A database system with a rich type system
- Inheritance
- Union types
- Unique identifiers

Traditional DBMSs have great trouble representing nonbusiness data-processing objects such as complex numbers, text, spatial objects, vectors, etc. Clearly a DBMS with a powerful type system is a good idea, and I have devoted Section 7 of this book to that subject. Secondly, is-a hierarchies or inheritance is a semantic construct that is either thought to be fantastic or useless depending on who you talk to. Suffice it to say that it is an easy-to-implement technique that has a significant following. An easy-to-read introduction to this subject appears on [STEF86].

Union types are another nice idea. Basically, one might have an application that dealt with employees. Moreover, an employee might be on loan to another department in the same company or on loan to a customer of the company. Clearly the attribute "on-loan-to" is either a customer i.d. or a department name. A DBMS that can support such types would clearly be a nice thing. However, there are substantial technical difficulties with supporting union types, including indexing and query optimization issues. Hence, whether union types will find widespread acceptance remains to be seen. Lastly, having unique identifiers for records is clearly a good idea. The notion of keys in the relational model expresses this concept, and it would be nice to have a system that automatically gave each record a unique identifier to handle cases in which the user has no attribute in mind for the job.

In summary, the object-oriented researchers are exploiting a collection of ideas that have considerable appeal and can easily be added to any data model.

Some object-oriented researchers are trying to build persistent Smalltalk [GOLD83]. The gist of their point of view is that Smalltalk is wonderful;

its only problem is that it lacks persistent objects. Hence, why not generalize it to work on persistent data. The problem with this approach is that Smalltalk is a system characterized by

- Record-at-a-time access
- Physical pointers

One must "navigate" through a "spaghetti" data structure from some "entry point" to desired data. This reminds many of the CODASYL systems which were resoundingly criticized for exactly these characteristics. Hence this approach is considered a throwback to the CODASYL era by many DBMS researchers. A similar point was made in [ULLM87].

As the object-oriented researchers mature their ideas, they will clearly propose set-at-a-time languages and replace their spaghetti with other structures. At some future time it may be possible to give an accurate characterization of their exact contribution, but that would be premature now.

Finally there is a camp of people who are partial to the relational model. After all, it has been very successful in business data-processing applications. It seems premature to abandon it because it does not do particular things in its current form. In my opinion the big drawbacks of the current model are:

- Anemic type systems
- No support for complex objects
- No rules

Both Starburst [LIND87] and POSTGRES [STON86] could be classified as extended relational systems that attempt to rectify the situation without discarding the relational model completely. These extensions are in the same vein as the proposal for RM/T by Ted Codd, which I have included as the final paper in this section (6.8).

In my opinion the commercial vendors will largely follow the relational model and will generalize it to solve some of the current drawbacks of DB2 and the ANSI standard. Hence one should expect various supersets of SQL with added capabilities in the area of object management from the commercial vendors. On the other hand, there will also be vendors of object managers that do not generalize SQL, such as Gemstone [COPE84] and Vbase from Ontologic. It will be interesting to see how these two classes of systems fare in the marketplace. My personal opinion is that the SQL extensions have an obvious commercial appeal that will be difficult to counter.

Lastly, I feel that the ultimate impact of ANSI standardization may well be low because of the desire by vendors to superset SQL. If all vendors have their own (incompatible) superset of SQL, an application builder will have the unfortunate choice of using enticing but nonstandard features or remaining within standard SQL and having a difficult time with object management. I expect clients to opt for the first choice, thereby rendering their applications nonstandard. This point is further discussed in [STON88].

References

[ADIB80] Adiba, M.E., and Lindsay, B.G., "Database Snapshots," IBM San Jose Res. Tech. Rep. RJ-2772, Mar. 1980.

[BACH77] Bachman, C., and Daya, M., "The Role Concept in Database Models," Proc. 1977 VLDB Conference, Tokyo, Japan, Oct. 1977.

[BATO85] Batory, D., and Kim, W., "Modeling Concepts for VLSI CAD Objects," ACM-TODS, Sept. 1985.

[CODD79] Codd, E., "Extending Database Relations to Capture More Meaning," ACM-TODS, Dec 1979.

[COPE84] Copeland, G., and Maier, D., "Making Smalltalk a Database System," Proc. 1984 ACM-SIGMOD Conference on Management of Data, Boston, Mass., June 1984.

[DATE81] Date, C., "Referential Integrity," Proc. Seventh International VLDB Conference, Cannes, France, Sept. 1981.

[FISH87] Fishman, D. et al., "IRIS: An Object-oriented Database System," ACM-TOOIS, Jan. 1987.

[GOLD83] Goldberg, A., and Robson, D., "Smalltalk-80: The Language and Its Implementation," Addison-Wesley, Reading, Mass., 1983.

[HAMM81] Hammer, M., and McLeod, D., "Database Description with SDM: A Semantic Database Model," ACM-TODS, Sept. 1981.

[KATZ85] Katz, R.H., Information Management for Engineering Design, Springer-Verlag, 1985.

[KATZ86] Katz, R. et al., "Version Modeling Concepts for Computer-Aided Design Databases," Proc. 1986 ACM-SIGMOD International Conference on Management of Data, Washington, D.C., May 1986.

[LIND87] Lindsay, B. et al., "A Data Management Extension Architecture," Proc. 1987 ACM-SIGMOD Conference on Management of Data, San Francisco, Calif., May 1987.

[LOHM83] Lohman, G. et al., Remotely Senses Geophysical Databases: Experience and Implications for Generalized DBMS, Proc. 1983 ACM-SIGMOD International Conference on Management of Data, San Jose, Calif., May 1983.

[LORI83] Lorie, R., and Plouffe, W., "Complex Objects and Their Use in Design Transactions," Proc. Eng. Design Applications of ACM-IEEE Data Base Week, San Jose, Ca, May 1983.

[LUM85] Lum, V., et al., "Design of an Integrated DBMS to Support Advanced Applications," Proc. Int. Conf. on Foundations of Data Org., Kyoto Univ., Japan, May 1985.

[OZSO85] Ozsoyoglu, G. et al., "A Language and a Physical Organization Technique for Summary Tables," Proc. 1985 ACM-SIGMOD International Conference on Management of Data, Austin, Tex., June 1985.

[POWE83] Powell, M., "Database Support for Programming Environments," Proc. Eng. Design Applications of ACM-IEEE Data Base Week, San Jose, Calif., May 1983.

[ROWE83] Rowe, N., "Top-Down Statistical Estimation on a Database," Proc. 1983 ACM-SIGMOD International Conference on Management of Data, San Jose, Calif., May 1983.

[SMIT77] Smith, J., and Smith D., "Database Abstractions: Aggregation and Generalization," ACM-TODS, July 1977.

[SNOD85] Snodgrass, R., and Ahn, I., "A Taxonomy of Time in Databases," Proc. 1985 ACM-SIGMOD International Conference on Management of Data, Austin, Tex., June 1985.

[SPON84] Spooner, D., "Database Support for Interactive Computer Graphics," Proc. 1984 ACM-SIGMOD International Conference on Management of Data, Boston, Mass., June 1984.

[STEF86] Stefik, M., and Bobrow, D., "Object-oriented Programming: Themes and Variations," The AI Magazine, Jan. 1986.

[STON83] Stonebraker, M., "Document Processing in a Relational Database System," ACM TOOIS, Apr. 1983.

[STON84] Stonebraker, M., "QUEL as a Data Type," Proc. 1984 ACM-SIGMOD Conference on Management of Data, Boston, Mass., June 1984.

[STON86] Stonebraker, M., and Rowe, L., "The Design of POSTGRES," Proc. 1986 ACM-SIGMOD Conference on Management of Data, Washington, D.C., May 1986.

[STON88] Stonebraker, M., "Future Trends in Data Base Systems," Proc. IEEE Data Engineering Conference, Los Angeles, Calif., Feb. 1988.

[ULLM85] Ullman, J., "Implementation of Logical Query Languages for Databases," ACM-TODS, Sept. 1985.

[ULLM87] Ullman, J., "Database Theory: Past and Future," Proc. 1987 ACM Symposium on Principles of Database Systems.

[WONG80] Wong, E., and Katz, R., "Logical Design and Schema Conversion for Relational and DBTG Databases," Proc. 1980 E-R Conference, Los Angeles, Calif.

[ZANI83] Zaniolo, C., "The Database Language GEM," Proc. 1983 ACM-SIGMOD Conference on Management of Data, San Jose, Calif., May 1983.

The Entity-Relationship Model—Toward a Unified View of Data

PETER PIN-SHAN CHEN
Massachusetts Institute of Technology

A data model, called the entity-relationship model, is proposed. This model incorporates some of the important semantic information about the real world. A special diagrammatic technique is introduced as a tool for database design. An example of database design and description using the model and the diagrammatic technique is given. Some implications for data integrity, information retrieval, and data manipulation are discussed.

The entity-relationship model can be used as a basis for unification of different views of data: the network model, the relational model, and the entity set model. Semantic ambiguities in these models are analyzed. Possible ways to derive their views of data from the entity-relationship model are presented.

Key Words and Phrases: database design, logical view of data, semantics of data, data models, entity-relationship model, relational model, Data Base Task Group, network model, entity set model, data definition and manipulation, data integrity and consistency
CR Categories: 3.50, 3.70, 4.33, 4.34

1. INTRODUCTION

The logical view of data has been an important issue in recent years. Three major data models have been proposed: the network model [2, 3, 7], the relational model [8], and the entity set model [25]. These models have their own strengths and weaknesses. The network model provides a more natural view of data by separating entities and relationships (to a certain extent), but its capability to achieve data independence has been challenged [8]. The relational model is based on relational theory and can achieve a high degree of data independence, but it may lose some important semantic information about the real world [12, 15, 23]. The entity set model, which is based on set theory, also achieves a high degree of data independence, but its viewing of values such as "3" or "red" may not be natural to some people [25].

This paper presents the entity-relationship model, which has most of the advantages of the above three models. The entity-relationship model adopts the more natural view that the real world consists of entities and relationships. It incorporates some of the important semantic information about the real world (other work in database semantics can be found in [1, 12, 15, 21, 23, and 29]). The model can achieve a high degree of data independence and is based on set theory and relation theory.

The entity-relationship model can be used as a basis for a unified view of data. Most work in the past has emphasized the difference between the network model and the relational model [22]. Recently, several attempts have been made to reduce the differences of the three data models [4, 19, 26, 30, 31]. This paper uses the entity-relationship model as a framework from which the three existing data models may be derived. The reader may view the entity-relationship model as a generalization or extension of existing models.

This paper is organized into three parts (Sections 2–4). Section 2 introduces the entity-relationship model using a framework of multilevel views of data. Section 3 describes the semantic information in the model and its implications for data description and data manipulation. A special diagrammatic technique, the entity-relationship diagram, is introduced as a tool for database design. Section 4 analyzes the network model, the relational model, and the entity set model, and describes how they may be derived from the entity-relationship model.

2. THE ENTITY-RELATIONSHIP MODEL

2.1 Multilevel Views of Data

In the study of a data model, we should identify the levels of logical views of data with which the model is concerned. Extending the framework developed in [18, 25], we can identify four levels of views of data (Figure 1):

(1) Information concerning entities and relationships which exist in our minds.

(2) Information structure—organization of information in which entities and relationships are represented by data.

(3) Access-path-independent data structure—the data structures which are not involved with search schemes, indexing schemes, etc.

(4) Access-path-dependent data structure.

In the following sections, we shall develop the entity-relationship model step by step for the first two levels. As we shall see later in the paper, the network model, as currently implemented, is mainly concerned with level 4; the relational model is mainly concerned with levels 3 and 2; the entity set model is mainly concerned with levels 1 and 2.

2.2 Information Concerning Entities and Relationships (Level 1)

At this level we consider entities and relationships. An *entity* is a "thing" which can be distinctly identified. A specific person, company, or event is an example of an entity. A *relationship* is an association among entities. For instance, "father-son" is a relationship between two "person" entities.[1]

[1] It is possible that some people may view something (e.g. marriage) as an entity while other people may view it as a relationship. We think that this is a decision which has to be made by the enterprise administrator [27]. He should define what are entities and what are relationships so that the distinction is suitable for his environment.

A version of this paper was presented at the International Conference on Very Large Data Bases, Framingham, Mass., Sept. 22–24, 1975.
Author's address: Center for Information System Research, Alfred P. Sloan School of Management, Massachusetts Institute of Technology, Cambridge, MA 02139.

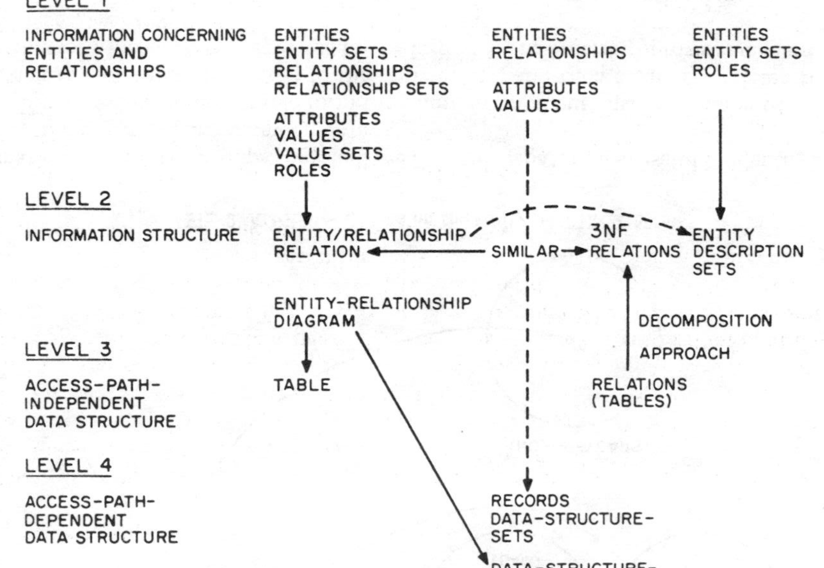

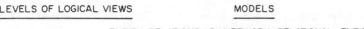

Fig. 1. Analysis of data models using multiple levels of logical views

The database of an enterprise contains relevant information concerning entities and relationships in which the enterprise is interested. A complete description of an entity or relationship may not be recorded in the database of an enterprise. It is impossible (and, perhaps, unnecessary) to record every potentially available piece of information about entities and relationships. From now on, we shall consider only the entities and relationships (and the information concerning them) which are to enter into the design of a database.

2.2.1 Entity and Entity Set. Let e denote an entity which exists in our minds. Entities are classified into different *entity sets* such as EMPLOYEE, PROJECT, and DEPARTMENT. There is a predicate associated with each entity set to test whether an entity belongs to it. For example, if we know an entity is in the entity set EMPLOYEE, then we know that it has the properties common to the other entities in the entity set EMPLOYEE. Among these properties is the aforementioned test predicate. Let E_i denote entity sets. Note that entity sets may not be mutually disjoint. For example, an entity which belongs to the entity set MALE-PERSON also belongs to the entity set PERSON. In this case, MALE-PERSON is a subset of PERSON.

2.2.2 Relationship, Role, and Relationship Set. Consider associations among entities. A *relationship set*, R_i, is a mathematical relation [5] among n entities, each taken from an entity set:

$$\{[e_1, e_2, \ldots, e_n] \mid e_1 \in E_1, e_2 \in E_2, \ldots, e_n \in E_n\},$$

and each tuple of entities, $[e_1, e_2, \ldots, e_n]$, is a *relationship*. Note that the E_i in the above definition may not be distinct. For example, a "marriage" is a relationship between two entities in the entity set PERSON.

The *role* of an entity in a relationship is the function that it performs in the relationship. "Husband" and "wife" are roles. The ordering of entities in the definition of relationship (note that square brackets were used) can be dropped if roles of entities in the relationship are explicitly stated as follows: $(r_1/e_1, r_2/e_2, \ldots, r_n/e_n)$, where r_i is the role of e_i in the relationship.

2.2.3 Attribute, Value, and Value Set. The information about an entity or a relationship is obtained by observation or measurement, and is expressed by a set of attribute-value pairs. "3", "red", "Peter", and "Johnson" are values. Values are classified into different *value sets*, such as FEET, COLOR, FIRST-NAME, and LAST-NAME. There is a predicate associated with each value set to test whether a value belongs to it. A value in a value set may be equivalent to another value in a different value set. For example, "12" in value set INCH is equivalent to "1" in value set FEET.

An *attribute* can be formally defined as a function which maps from an entity set or a relationship set into a value set or a Cartesian product of value sets:

$$f: E_i \text{ or } R_i \rightarrow V_i \text{ or } V_{i_1} \times V_{i_2} \times \cdots \times V_{i_n}.$$

Figure 2 illustrates some attributes defined on entity set PERSON. The attribute AGE maps into value set NO-OF-YEARS. An attribute can map into a Cartesian product of value sets. For example, the attribute NAME maps into value sets FIRST-NAME, and LAST-NAME. Note that more than one attribute may map from the same entity set into the same value set (or same group of value sets). For example, NAME and ALTERNATIVE-NAME map from the entity set EMPLOYEE into value sets FIRST-NAME and LAST-NAME. Therefore, attribute and value set are different concepts although they may have the same name in some cases (for example, EMPLOYEE-NO maps from EMPLOYEE to value set EMPLOYEE-NO). This distinction is not clear in the network model and in many existing data management systems. Also note that an attribute is defined as a function. Therefore, it maps a given entity to a single value (or a single tuple of values in the case of a Cartesian product of value sets).

Note that relationships also have attributes. Consider the relationship set PROJECT-WORKER (Figure 3). The attribute PERCENTAGE-OF-TIME, which is the portion of time a particular employee is committed to a particular project, is an attribute defined on the relationship set PROJECT-WORKER. It is neither an attribute of EMPLOYEE nor an attribute of PROJECT, since its meaning depends on both the employee and project involved. The concept of attribute of relationship is important in understanding the semantics of data and in determining the functional dependencies among data.

2.2.4 Conceptual Information Structure. We are now concerned with how to organize the information associated with entities and relationships. The method proposed in this paper is to separate the information about entities from the infor-

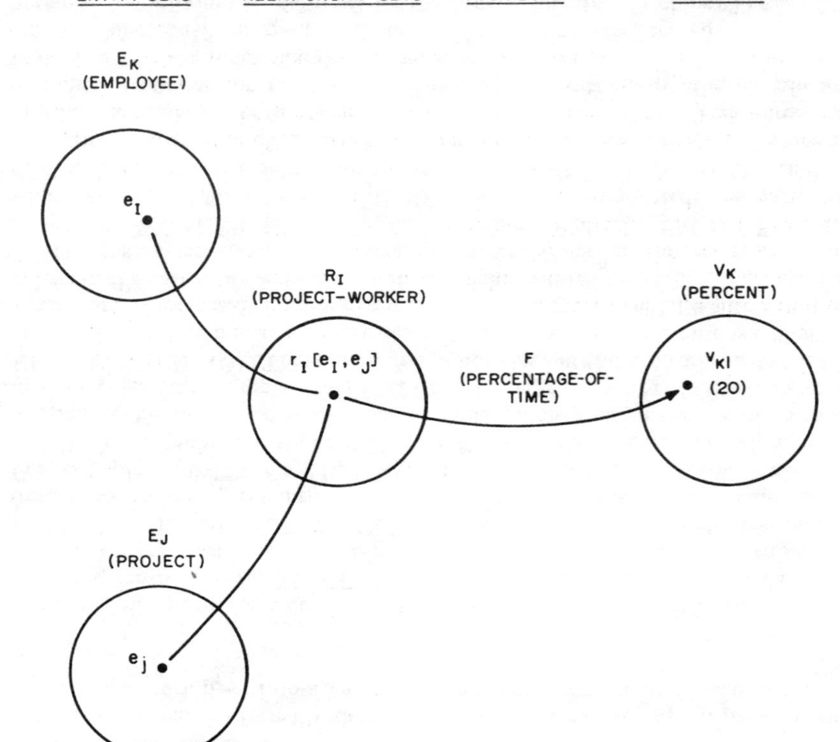

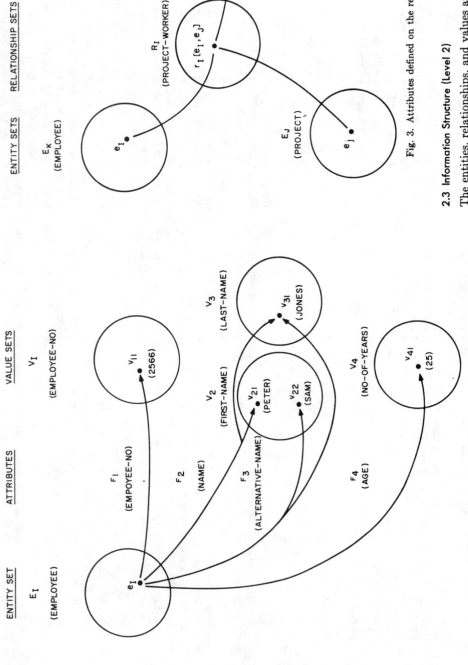

Fig. 2. Attributes defined on the entity set PERSON

mation about relationships. We shall see that this separation is useful in identifying functional dependencies among data.

Figure 4 illustrates in table form the information about entities in an entity set. Each row of values is related to the same entity, and each column is related to a value set which, in turn, is related to an attribute. The ordering of rows and columns is insignificant.

Figure 5 illustrates information about relationships in a relationship set. Note that each row of values is related to a relationship which is indicated by a group of entities, each having a specific role and belonging to a specific entity set.

Note that Figures 4 and 2 (and also Figures 5 and 3) are different forms of the same information. The table form is used for easily relating to the relational model.

Fig. 3. Attributes defined on the relationship set PROJECT-WORKER

2.3 Information Structure (Level 2)

The entities, relationships, and values at level 1 (see Figures 2–5) are conceptual objects in our minds (i.e. we were in the conceptual realm [18, 27]). At level 2, we consider representations of conceptual objects. We assume that there exist direct representations of values. In the following, we shall describe how to represent entities and relationships.

2.3.1 Primary Key. In Figure 2 the values of attribute EMPLOYEE-NO can be used to identify entities in entity set EMPLOYEE if each employee has a different employee number. It is possible that more than one attribute is needed to identify the entities in an entity set. It is also possible that several groups of attributes may be used to identify entities. Basically, an *entity key* is a group of attributes such that the mapping from the entity set to the corresponding group of value sets is one-to-one. If we cannot find such one-to-one mapping on available data, or if simplicity in identifying entities is desired, we may define an artificial attribute and a value set so that such mapping is possible. In the case where

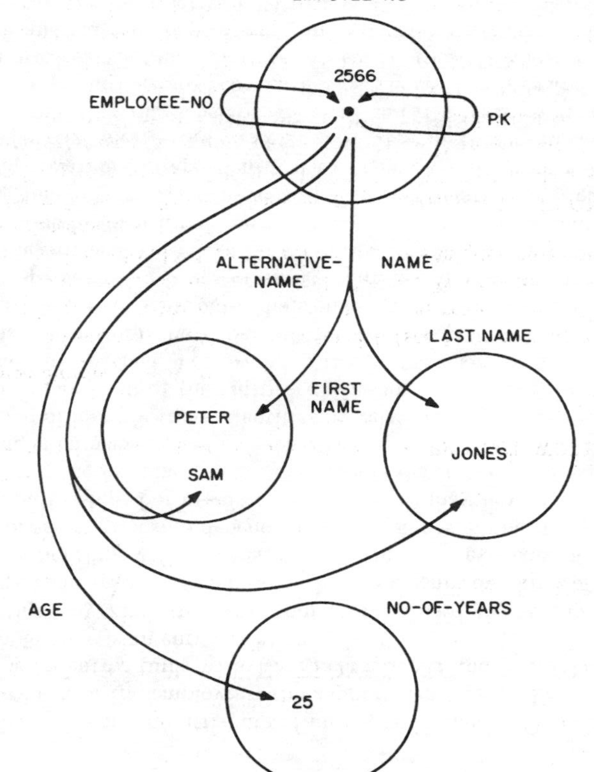

Fig. 4. Information about entities in an entity set (table form)

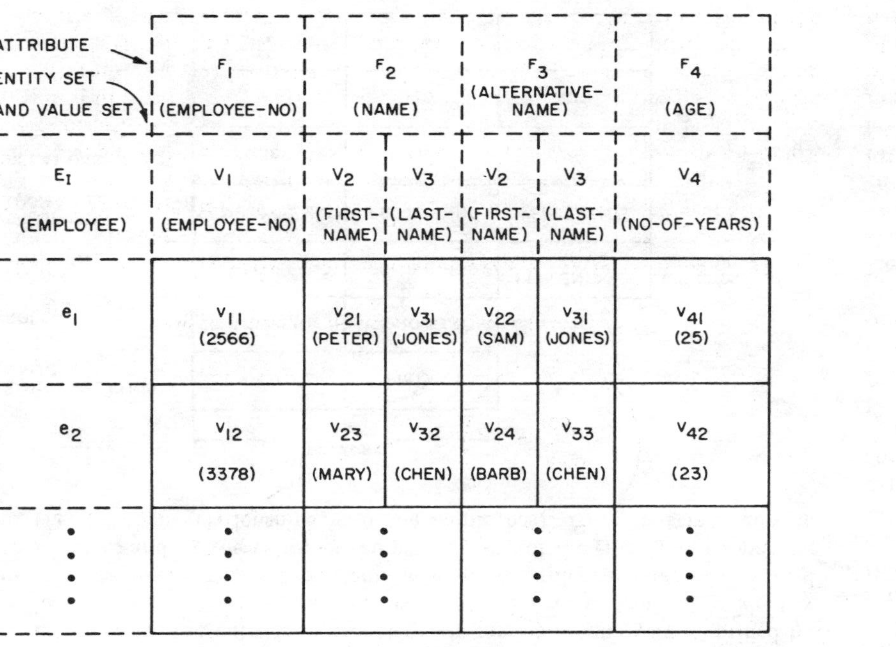

Fig. 5. Information about relationships in a relationship set (table form)

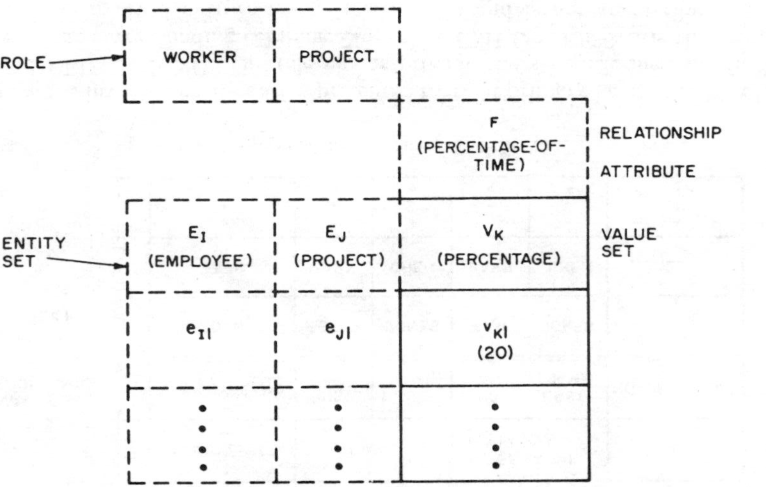

Fig. 6. Representing entities by values (employee numbers)

several keys exist, we usually choose a semantically meaningful key as the *entity primary key* (PK).

Figure 6 is obtained by merging the entity set EMPLOYEE with value set EMPLOYEE–NO in Figure 2. We should notice some semantic implications of Figure 6. Each value in the value set EMPLOYEE–NO represents an entity (employee). Attributes map from the value set EMPLOYEE–NO to other value sets. Also note that the attribute EMPLOYEE–NO maps from the value set EMPLOYEE–NO to itself.

2.3.2 Entity/Relationship Relations. Information about entities in an entity set can now be organized in a form shown in Figure 7. Note that Figure 7 is similar to Figure 4 except that entities are represented by the values of their primary keys. The whole table in Figure 7 is an *entity relation*, and each row is an *entity tuple*.

Since a relationship is identified by the involved entities, the *primary key of a relationship* can be represented by the primary keys of the involved entities. In

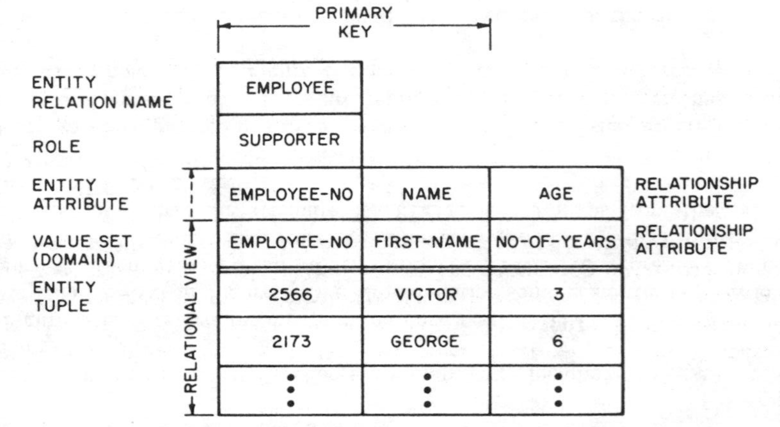

	EMPLOYEE-NO (PRIMARY KEY)	NAME		ALTERNATIVE-NAME		AGE
ATTRIBUTE	EMPLOYEE-NO	NAME		ALTERNATIVE-NAME		AGE
VALUE SET (DOMAIN)	EMPLOYEE-NO	FIRST-NAME	LAST-NAME	FIRST-NAME	LAST-NAME	NO-OF-YEARS
ENTITY (TUPLE)	2566	PETER	JONES	SAM	JONES	25
	3378	MARY	CHEN	BARB	CHEN	23
	⋮	⋮	⋮	⋮	⋮	⋮

Fig. 7. Regular entity relation EMPLOYEE

Figure 8, the involved entities are represented by their primary keys EMPLOYEE-NO and PROJECT-NO. The role names provide the semantic meaning for the values in the corresponding columns. Note that EMPLOYEE-NO is the primary key for the involved entities in the relationship and is not an attribute of the relationship. PERCENTAGE-OF-TIME is an attribute of the relationship. The table in Figure 8 is a *relationship relation*, and each row of values is a *relationship tuple*.

In certain cases, the entities in an entity set cannot be uniquely identified by the values of their own attributes; thus we must use a relationship(s) to identify them. For example, consider dependents of employees: dependents are identified by their names and by the values of the primary key of the employees supporting them (i.e. by their relationships with the employees). Note that in Figure 9,

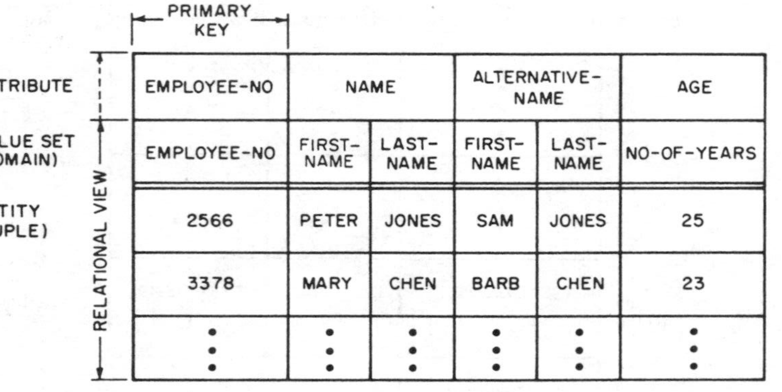

ENTITY RELATION NAME	EMPLOYEE	PROJECT	
ROLE	WORKER	PROJECT	
ENTITY ATTRIBUTE	EMPLOYEE-NO	PROJECT-NO	PERCENTAGE-OF-TIME (RELATIONSHIP ATTRIBUTE)
VALUE SET (DOMAIN)	EMPLOYEE-NO	PROJECT-NO	PERCENTAGE
RELATIONSHIP TUPLE	2566	31	20
	2173	25	100
	⋮	⋮	⋮

Fig. 8. Regular relationship relation PROJECT-WORKER

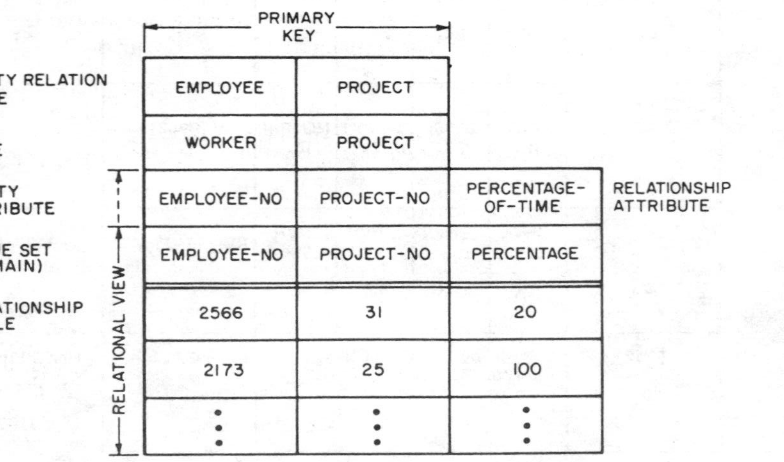

ENTITY RELATION NAME	EMPLOYEE		
ROLE	SUPPORTER		
ENTITY ATTRIBUTE	EMPLOYEE-NO	NAME	AGE
VALUE SET (DOMAIN)	EMPLOYEE-NO	FIRST-NAME	NO-OF-YEARS
ENTITY TUPLE	2566	VICTOR	3
	2173	GEORGE	6
	⋮	⋮	⋮

Fig. 9. A weak entity relation DEPENDENT

EMPLOYEE-NO is not an attribute of an entity in the set DEPENDENT but is the primary key of the employees who support dependents. Each row of values in Figure 9 is an entity tuple with EMPLOYEE-NO and NAME as its primary key. The whole table is an entity relation.

Theoretically, any kind of relationship may be used to identify entities. For simplicity, we shall restrict ourselves to the use of only one kind of relationship: the binary relationships with $1{:}n$ mapping in which the existence of the n entities on one side of the relationship depends on the existence of one entity on the other side of the relationship. For example, one employee may have n ($= 0, 1, 2, \ldots$) dependents, and the existence of the dependents depends on the existence of the corresponding employee.

This method of identification of entities by relationships with other entities can be applied recursively until the entities which can be identified by their own attribute values are reached. For example, the primary key of a department in a company may consist of the department number and the primary key of the division, which in turn consists of the division number and the name of the company.

Therefore, we have two forms of entity relations. If relationships are used for identifying the entities, we shall call it a *weak entity relation* (Figure 9). If relationships are not used for identifying the entities, we shall call it a *regular entity relation* (Figure 7). Similarly, we also have two forms of relationship relations. If all entities in the relationship are identified by their own attribute values, we shall call it a *regular relationship relation* (Figure 8). If some entities in the relationship are identified by other relationships, we shall call it a *weak relationship relation*. For example, any relationships between DEPENDENT entities and other entities will result in weak relationship relations, since a DEPENDENT entity is identified by its name and its relationship with an EMPLOYEE entity. The distinction between regular (entity/relationship) relations and weak (entity/relationship) relations will be useful in maintaining data integrity.

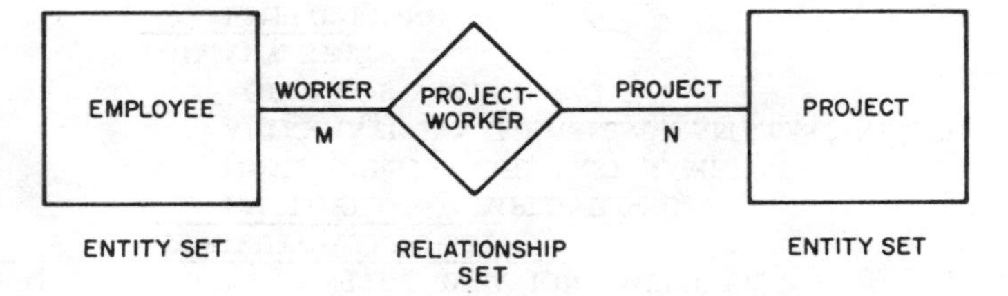

Fig. 10. A simple entity-relationship diagram

3. ENTITY-RELATIONSHIP DIAGRAM AND INCLUSION OF SEMANTICS IN DATA DESCRIPTION AND MANIPULATION

3.1 System Analysis Using the Entity-Relationship Diagram

In this section we introduce a diagrammatic technique for exhibiting entities and relationships: the entity-relationship diagram.

Figure 10 illustrates the relationship set PROJECT–WORKER and the entity sets EMPLOYEE and PROJECT using this diagrammatic technique. Each entity set is represented by a rectangular box, and each relationship set is represented by a diamond-shaped box. The fact that the relationship set PROJECT–WORKER is defined on the entity sets EMPLOYEE and PROJECT is represented by the lines connecting the rectangular boxes. The roles of the entities in the relationship are stated.

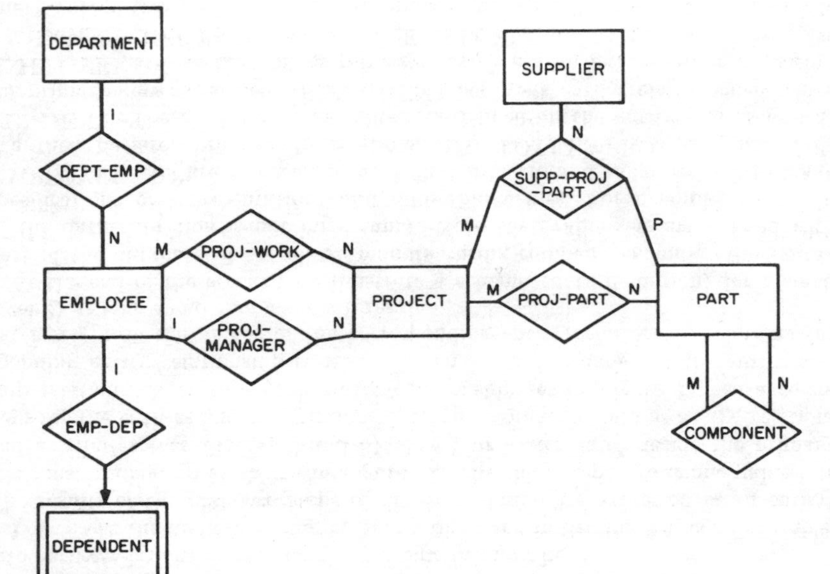

Fig. 11. An entity-relationship diagram for analysis of information in a manufacturing firm

Figure 11 illustrates a more complete diagram of some entity sets and relationship sets which might be of interest to a manufacturing company. DEPARTMENT, EMPLOYEE, DEPENDENT, PROJECT, SUPPLIER, and PART are entity sets. DEPARTMENT–EMPLOYEE, EMPLOYEE–DEPENDENT, PROJECT–WORKER, PROJECT–MANAGER, SUPPLIER–PROJECT–PART, PROJECT–PART, and COMPONENT are relationship sets. The COMPONENT relationship describes what subparts (and quantities) are needed in making superparts. The meaning of the other relationship sets need not be explained.

Several important characteristics about relationships in general can be found in Figure 11:

(1) A relationship set may be defined on more than two entity sets. For example, the SUPPLIER–PROJECT–PART relationship set is defined on three entity sets: SUPPLIER, PROJECT, and PART.

(2) A relationship set may be defined on only one entity set. For example, the relationship set COMPONENT is defined on one entity set, PART.

(3) There may be more than one relationship set defined on given entity sets. For example, the relationship sets PROJECT–WORKER and PROJECT–MANAGER are defined on the entity sets PROJECT and EMPLOYEE.

(4) The diagram can distinguish between $1{:}n$, $m{:}n$, and 1:1 mappings. The relationship set DEPARTMENT–EMPLOYEE is a $1{:}n$ mapping, that is, one department may have n ($n = 0, 1, 2, \ldots$) employees and each employee works for only one department. The relationship set PROJECT–WORKER is an $m{:}n$ mapping, that is, each project may have zero, one, or more employees assigned to it and each employee may be assigned to zero, one, or more projects. It is also possible to express 1:1 mappings such as the relationship set MARRIAGE. Information about the number of entities in each entity set which is allowed in a relationship set is indicated by specifying "1", "m", "n" in the diagram. The relational model and the entity set model[2] do not include this type of information; the network model cannot express a 1:1 mapping easily.

(5) The diagram can express the *existence dependency* of one entity type on another. For example, the arrow in the relationship set EMPLOYEE–DEPENDENT indicates that existence of an entity in the entity set DEPENDENT depends on the corresponding entity in the entity set EMPLOYEE. That is, if an employee leaves the company, his dependents may no longer be of interest.

Note that the entity set DEPENDENT is shown as a special rectangular box. This indicates that at level 2 the information about entities in this set is organized as a weak entity relation (using the primary key of EMPLOYEE as a part of its primary key).

3.2 An Example of a Database Design and Description

There are four steps in designing a database using the entity-relationship model: (1) identify the entity sets and the relationship sets of interest; (2) identify semantic information in the relationship sets such as whether a certain relationship

[2] This mapping information is included in DIAM II [24].

set is an $1{:}n$ mapping; (3) define the value sets and attributes; (4) organize data into entity/relationship relations and decide primary keys.

Let us use the manufacturing company discussed in Section 3.1 as an example. The results of the first two steps of database design are expressed in an entity-relationship diagram as shown in Figure 11. The third step is to define value sets and attributes (see Figures 2 and 3). The fourth step is to decide the primary keys for the entities and the relationships and to organize data as entity/relationship relations. Note that each entity/relationship set in Figure 11 has a corresponding entity/relationship relation. We shall use the names of the entity sets (at level 1) as the names of the corresponding entity/relationship relations (at level 2) as long as no confusion will result.

At the end of the section, we illustrate a schema (data definition) for a small part of the database in the above manufacturing company example (the syntax of the data definition is not important). Note that value sets are defined with specifications of representations and allowable values. For example, values in EMPLOYEE-NO are represented as 4-digit integers and range from 0 to 2000. We then declare three entity relations: EMPLOYEE, PROJECT, and DEPENDENT. The attributes and value sets defined on the entity sets as well as the primary keys are stated. DEPENDENT is a weak entity relation since it uses EMPLOYEE.PK as part of its primary key. We also declare two relationship relations: PROJECT-WORKER and EMPLOYEE-DEPENDENT. The roles and involved entities in the relationships are specified. We use EMPLOYEE.PK to indicate the name of the entity relation (EMPLOYEE) and whatever attribute-value-set pairs are used as the primary keys in that entity relation. The maximum number of entities from an entity set in a relation is stated. For example, PROJECT-WORKER is an $m{:}n$ mapping. We may specify the values of m and n. We may also specify the minimum number of entities in addition to the maximum number. EMPLOYEE-DEPENDENT is a weak relationship relation since one of the related entity relations, DEPENDENT, is a weak entity relation. Note that the existence dependence of the dependents on the supporter is also stated.

DECLARE	VALUE-SETS	REPRESENTATION	ALLOWABLE-VALUES
	EMPLOYEE-NO	INTEGER (4)	(0,2000)
	FIRST-NAME	CHARACTER (8)	ALL
	LAST-NAME	CHARACTER (10)	ALL
	NO-OF-YEARS	INTEGER (3)	(0,100)
	PROJECT-NO	INTEGER (3)	(1,500)
	PERCENTAGE	FIXED (5.2)	(0,100.00)

```
DECLARE   REGULAR ENTITY RELATION EMPLOYEE
          ATTRIBUTE/VALUE-SET:
              EMPLOYEE-NO/EMPLOYEE-NO
              NAME/(FIRST-NAME, LAST-NAME)
              ALTERNATIVE-NAME/(FIRST-NAME,LAST-NAME)
              AGE/NO-OF-YEARS
          PRIMARY KEY:
              EMPLOYEE-NO

DECLARE   REGULAR ENTITY RELATION PROJECT
          ATTRIBUTE/VALUE-SET:
              PROJECT-NO/PROJECT-NO
          PRIMARY KEY:
              PROJECT-NO

DECLARE   REGULAR RELATIONSHIP RELATION PROJECT-WORKER
          ROLE/ENTITY-RELATION.PK/MAX-NO-OF-ENTITIES
              WORKER/EMPLOYEE.PK/m
              PROJECT/PROJECT.PK/n      (m:n mapping)
          ATTRIBUTE/VALUE-SET:
              PERCENTAGE-OF-TIME/PERCENTAGE

DECLARE   WEAK RELATIONSHIP RELATION EMPLOYEE-DEPENDENT
          ROLE/ENTITY-RELATION.PK/MAX-NO-OF-ENTITIES
              SUPPORTER/EMPLOYEE.PK/1
              DEPENDENT/DEPENDENT.PK/n
          EXISTENCE OF DEPENDENT DEPENDS ON
          EXISTENCE OF SUPPORTER

DECLARE   WEAK ENTITY RELATION DEPENDENT
          ATTRIBUTE/VALUE-SET:
              NAME/FIRST-NAME
              AGE/NO-OF-YEARS
          PRIMARY KEY:
              NAME
              EMPLOYEE.PK THROUGH EMPLOYEE-DEPENDENT
```

3.3 Implications on Data Integrity

Some work has been done on data integrity for other models [8, 14, 16, 28]. With explicit concepts of entity and relationship, the entity-relationship model will be useful in understanding and specifying constraints for maintaining data integrity. For example, there are three major kinds of constraints on values:

(1) Constraints on *allowable values* for a value set. This point was discussed in defining the schema in Section 3.2.

(2) Constraints on *permitted* values for a certain attribute. In some cases, not all allowable values in a value set are permitted for some attributes. For example, we may have a restriction of ages of employees to between 20 and 65. That is,

$$\text{AGE}(e) \in (20{,}65), \text{ where } e \in \text{EMPLOYEE}.$$

Note that we use the level 1 notations to clarify the semantics. Since each entity/relationship set has a corresponding entity/relationship relation, the above expression can be easily translated into level 2 notations.

(3) Constraints on *existing values* in the database. There are two types of constraints:

(i) Constraints between sets of existing values. For example,

$$\{\text{NAME}(e) \mid e \in \text{MALE-PERSON}\} \subseteq \{\text{NAME}(e) \mid e \in \text{PERSON}\}.$$

(ii) Constraints between particular values. For example,

$$\text{TAX}(e) \leq \text{SALARY}(e),\ e \in \text{EMPLOYEE}$$

or

$$\text{BUDGET}(e_i) = \sum \text{BUDGET}(e_j),\ \text{where } e_i \in \text{COMPANY},\ e_j \in \text{DEPARTMENT} \text{ and } [e_i,e_j] \in \text{COMPANY-DEPARTMENT}.$$

3.4 Semantics and Set Operations of Information Retrieval Requests

The semantics of information retrieval requests become very clear if the requests are based on the entity-relationship model of data. For clarity, we first discuss the situation at level 1. Conceptually, the information elements are organized as in Figures 4 and 5 (on Figures 2 and 3). Many information retrieval requests can be considered as a combination of the following basic types of operations:

(1) Selection of a subset of values from a value set.

(2) Selection of a subset of entities from an entity set (i.e. selection of certain rows in Figure 4). Entities are selected by stating the values of certain attributes (i.e. subsets of value sets) and/or their relationships with other entities.

(3) Selection of a subset of relationships from a relationship set (i.e. selection of certain rows in Figure 5). Relationships are selected by stating the values of certain attribute(s) and/or by identifying certain entities in the relationship.

(4) Selection of a subset of attributes (i.e. selection of columns in Figures 4 and 5).

An information retrieval request like "What are the ages of the employees whose weights are greater than 170 and who are assigned to the project with PROJECT-NO 254?" can be expressed as:

$\{\text{AGE}(e) \mid e \in \text{EMPLOYEE}, \text{WEIGHT}(e) > 170,$
$[e, e_j] \in \text{PROJECT-WORKER}, e_j \in \text{PROJECT},$
$\text{PROJECT-NO}(e_j) = 254\};$

or

{AGE(EMPLOYEE) | WEIGHT(EMPLOYEE) > 170,
[EMPLOYEE,PROJECT] ∈ PROJECT-WORKER,
PROJECT-NO(EMPLOYEE) = 254}.

To retrieve information as organized in Figure 6 at level 2, "entities" and "relationships" in (2) and (3) should be replaced by "entity PK" and "relationship PK." The above information retrieval request can be expressed as:

{AGE(EMPLOYEE.PK) | WEIGHT(EMPLOYEE.PK) > 170
(WORKER/EMPLOYEE.PK,PROJECT/PROJECT.PK) ∈ {PROJECT-WORKER.PK},
PROJECT-NO (PROJECT.PK) = 254}.

To retrieve information as organized in entity/relationship relations (Figures 7, 8, and 9), we can express it in a SEQUEL-like language [6]:

```
SELECT   AGE
FROM     EMPLOYEE
WHERE    WEIGHT > 170
AND      EMPLOYEE.PK =
         SELECT   WORKER/EMPLOYEE.PK
         FROM     PROJECT-WORKER
         WHERE    PROJECT-NO = 254.
```

It is possible to retrieve information about entities in two different entity sets without specifying a relationship between them. For example, an information retrieval request like "List the names of employees and ships which have the same

Table I. Insertion

level 1	level 2
operation: insert an entity to an entity set	*operation:* create an entity tuple with a certain entity-PK *check:* whether PK already exists or is acceptable
operation: insert a relationship in a relationship set *check:* whether the entities exist	*operation:* create a relationship tuple with given entity PKs *check:* whether the entity PKs exist
operation: insert properties of an entity or a relationship *check:* whether the value is acceptable	*operation:* insert values in an entity tuple or a relationship tuple *check:* whether the values are acceptable

Table II. Updating

level 1	level 2
operation: • change the value of an entity attribute	*operation:* • update a value *consequence:* • if it is not part of an entity PK, no consequence • if it is part of an entity PK, •• change the entity PKs in all related relationship relations •• change PKs of other entities which use this value as part of their PKs (for example, DEPENDENTS' PKs use EMPLOYEE'S PK)
operation: • change the value of a relationship attribute	*operation:* • update a value (note that a relationship attribute will not be a relationship PK)

Table III. Deletion

level 1	level 2
operation: • delete an entity *consequences:* • delete any entity whose existence depends on this entity • delete relationships involving this entity • delete all related properties	*operation:* • delete an entity tuple *consequences* (applied recursively): • delete any entity tuple whose existence depends on this entity tuple • delete relationship tuples associated with this entity
operation: • delete a relationship *consequences:* • delete all related properties	*operation:* • delete a relationship tuple

age" can be expressed in the level 1 notation as:

$$\{(\text{NAME}(e_i),\text{NAME}(e_j)) \mid e_i \in \text{EMPLOYEE}, e_j \in \text{SHIP}, \text{AGE}(e_i) = \text{AGE}(e_j)\}.$$

We do not further discuss the language syntax here. What we wish to stress is that information requests may be expressed using set notions and set operations [17], and the request semantics are very clear in adopting this point of view.

3.5 Semantics and Rules for Insertion, Deletion, and Updating

It is always a difficult problem to maintain data consistency following insertion, deletion, and updating of data in the database. One of the major reasons is that the semantics and consequences of insertion, deletion, and updating operations usually are not clearly defined; thus it is difficult to find a set of rules which can enforce data consistency. We shall see that this data consistency problem becomes simpler using the entity-relationship model.

In Tables I–III, we discuss the semantics and rules[3] for insertion, deletion, and updating at both level 1 and level 2. Level 1 is used to clarify the semantics.

4. ANALYSIS OF OTHER DATA MODELS AND THEIR DERIVATION FROM THE ENTITY-RELATIONSHIP MODEL

4.1 The Relational Model

4.1.1 The Relational View of Data and Ambiguity in Semantics. In the relational model, *relation*, R, is a mathematical relation defined on sets $X_1, X_2, \ldots, X_n$:

$$R = \{(x_1, x_2, \ldots, x_n) \mid x_1 \in X_1, x_2 \in X_2, \ldots, x_n \in X_n\}.$$

The sets $X_1, X_2, \ldots, X_n$ are called *domains*, and $(x_1, x_2, \ldots, x_n)$ is called a *tuple*. Figure 12 illustrates a relation called EMPLOYEE. The domains in the relation are EMPLOYEE-NO, FIRST-NAME, LAST-NAME, FIRST-NAME, LAST-NAME, NO-OF-YEAR. The ordering of rows and columns in the relation has no significance. To avoid ambiguity of columns with the same domain in a relation, domain names are qualified by *roles* (to distinguish the role of the domain in the relation). For example, in relation EMPLOYEE, domains FIRST-NAME and LAST-NAME may be qualified by roles LEGAL or ALTERNATIVE. An *attribute name* in the relational model is a domain name concatenated with a role name [10]. Comparing Figure 12 with Figure 7, we can see that "domains" are basically equivalent to value sets. Although "role" or "attribute" in the relational model seems to serve the same purpose as "attribute" in the entity-relationship model, the semantics of these terms are different. The "role" or "attribute" in the relational model is mainly used to distinguish domains with the same name in the same relation, while "attribute" in the entity-relationship model is a function which maps from an entity (or relationship) set into value set(s).

Using relational operators in the relational model may cause semantic ambiguities. For example, the join of the relation EMPLOYEE with the relation EMPLOYEE-PROJECT (Figure 13) on domain EMPLOYEE-NO produces the

ROLE		LEGAL	LEGAL	ALTERNATIVE	ALTERNATIVE	
DOMAIN	EMPLOYEE-NO	FIRST-NAME	LAST-NAME	FIRST-NAME	LAST-NAME	NO-OF-YEARS
TUPLE	2566	PETER	JONES	SAM	JONES	25
	3378	MARY	CHEN	BARB	CHEN	23

Fig. 12. Relation EMPLOYEE

PROJECT-NO	EMPLOYEE-NO
7	2566
3	2566
7	3378

Fig. 13. Relation EMPLOYEE-PROJECT

[3] Our main purpose is to illustrate the semantics of data manipulation operations. Therefore, these rules may not be complete. Note that the consequence of operations stated in the tables can be performed by the system instead of by the users.

		LEGAL	LEGAL	ALTERNATIVE	ALTERNATIVE	
PROJECT-NO	EMPLOYEE-NO	FIRST-NAME	LAST-NAME	FIRST-NAME	LAST-NAME	NO-OF-YEARS
7	2566	PETER	JONES	SAM	JONES	25
3	2566	PETER	JONES	SAM	JONES	25
7	3378	MARY	CHEN	BARB	CHEN	23

Fig. 14. Relation EMPLOYEE-PROJECT' as a "join" of relations EMPLOYEE and EMPLOYEE-PROJECT

relation EMPLOYEE-PROJECT' (Figure 14). But what is the meaning of a join between the relation EMPLOYEE with the relation SHIP on the domain NO-OF-YEARS (Figure 15)? The problem is that the same domain name may have different semantics in different relations (note that a role is intended to distinguish domains in a given relation, not in all relations). If the domain NO-OF-YEAR of the relation EMPLOYEE is not allowed to be compared with the domain NO-OF-YEAR of the relation SHIP, different domain names have to be declared. But if such a comparison is acceptable, can the database system warn the user?

In the entity-relationship model, the semantics of data are much more apparent. For example, one column in the example stated above contains the values of AGE of EMPLOYEE and the other column contains the values of AGE of SHIP. If this semantic information is exposed to the user, he may operate more cautiously (refer to the sample information retrieval requests stated in Section 3.4). Since the database system contains the semantic information, it should be able to warn the user of the potential problems for a proposed "join-like" operation.

4.1.2 Semantics of Functional Dependencies Among Data. In the relational model, "attribute" B of a relation is *functionally dependent* on "attribute" A of the same relation if each value of A has no more than one value of B associated with it in the relation. Semantics of functional dependencies among data become clear

SHIP-NO	NAME	NO-OF-YEARS
037	MISSOURI	25
056	VIRGINIA	10

Fig. 15. Relation SHIP

in the entity-relationship model. Basically, there are two major types of functional dependencies:

(1) Functional dependencies related to description of entities or relationships. Since an attribute is defined as a function, it maps an entity in an entity set to a single value in a value set (see Figure 2). At level 2, the values of the primary key are used to represent entities. Therefore, nonkey value sets (domains) are functionally dependent on primary-key value sets (for example, in Figures 6 and 7, NO-OF-YEARS is functionally dependent on EMPLOYEE-NO). Since a relation may have several keys, the nonkey value sets will functionally depend on any key value set. The key value sets will be mutually functionally dependent on each other. Similarly, in a relationship relation the nonkey value sets will be functionally dependent on the prime-key value sets (for example, in Figure 8, PERCENTAGE is functionally dependent on EMPLOYEE-NO and PROJECT-NO).

(2) Functional dependencies related to entities in a relationship. Note that in Figure 11 we identify the types of mappings ($1{:}n$, $m{:}n$, etc.) for relationship sets. For example, PROJECT-MANAGER is a $1{:}n$ mapping. Let us assume that PROJECT-NO is the primary key in the entity relation PROJECT. In the relationship relation PROJECT-MANAGER, the value set EMPLOYEE-NO will be functionally dependent on the value set PROJECT-NO (i.e. each project has only one manager).

The distinction between level 1 (Figure 2) and level 2 (Figures 6 and 7) and the separation of entity relation (Figure 7) from relationship relation (Figure 8) clarifies the semantics of functional dependencies among data.

4.1.3 3NF Relations Versus Entity-Relationship Relations. From the definition of "relation," any grouping of domains can be considered to be a relation. To avoid undesirable properties in maintaining relations, a normalization process is proposed to transform arbitrary relations into the first normal form, then into the second normal form, and finally into the third normal form (3NF) [9, 11]. We shall show that the entity and relationship relations in the entity-relationship model are similar to 3NF relations but with clearer semantics and without using the transformation operation.

Let us use a simplified version of an example of normalization described in [9]. The following three relations are in first normal form (that is, there is no domain whose elements are themselves relations):

EMPLOYEE (EMPLOYEE-NO)
PART (PART-NO, PART-DESCRIPTION, QUANTITY-ON-HAND)
PART-PROJECT (PART-NO, PROJECT-NO, PROJECT-DESCRIPTION,
PROJECT-MANAGER-NO, QUANTITY-COMMITTED).

Note that the domain PROJECT-MANAGER-NO actually contains the EMPLOYEE-NO of the project manager. In the relations above, primary keys are underlined.

Certain rules are applied to transform the relations above into third normal form:

EMPLOYEE' (EMPLOYEE-NO)
PART' (PART-NO, PART-DESCRIPTION, QUANTITY-ON-HAND)

PROJECT' (<u>PROJECT-NO</u>, PROJECT-DESCRIPTION, PROJECT-MANAGER-NO)
PART-PROJECT' (<u>PART-NO</u>, <u>PROJECT-NO</u>, QUANTITY-COMMITTED).

Using the entity-relationship diagram in Figure 11, the following entity and relationship relations can be easily derived:

entity relations	PART'' (PART-NO, PART-DESCRIPTION, QUANTITY-ON-HAND) PROJECT'' (PROJECT-NO, PROJECT-DESCRIPTION) EMPLOYEE'' (EMPLOYEE-NO)
relationship relations	PART-PROJECT'' (PART/PART-NO, PROJECT/PROJECT-NO, QUANTITY-COMMITTED) PROJECT-MANAGER'' (PROJECT/PROJECT-NO, MANAGER/EMPLOYEE-NO).

The role names of the entities in relationships (such as MANAGER) are indicated. The entity relation names associated with the PKs of entities in relationships and the value set names have been omitted.

Note that in the example above, entity/relationship relations are similar to the 3NF relations. In the 3NF approach, PROJECT-MANAGER-NO is included in the relation PROJECT' since PROJECT-MANAGER-NO is assumed to be functionally dependent on PROJECT-NO. In the entity-relationship model, PROJECT-MANAGER-NO (i.e. EMPLOYEE-NO of a project manager) is included in a relationship relation PROJECT-MANAGER since EMPLOYEE-NO is considered as an entity PK in this case.

Also note that in the 3NF approach, changes in functional dependencies of data may cause some relations not to be in 3NF. For example, if we make a new assumption that one project may have more than one manager, the relation PROJECT' is no longer a 3NF relation and has to be split into two relations as PROJECT'' and PROJECT-MANAGER''. Using the entity-relationship model, no such change is necessary. Therefore, we may say that by using the entity-relationship model we can arrange data in a form similar to 3NF relations but with clear semantic meaning.

It is interesting to note that the decomposition (or transformation) approach described above for normalization of relations may be viewed as a bottom-up approach in database design.[4] It starts with arbitrary relations (level 3 in Figure 1) and then uses some semantic information (functional dependencies of data) to transform them into 3NF relations (level 2 in Figure 1). The entity-relationship model adopts a top-down approach, utilizing the semantic information to organize data in entity/relationship relations.

4.2 The Network Model

4.2.1 Semantics of the Data-Structure Diagram. One of the best ways to explain the network model is by use of the *data-structure diagram* [3]. Figure 16(a) illustrates a data-structure diagram. Each rectangular box represents a record type.

[4] Although the decomposition approach was emphasized in the relational model literature, it is a procedure to obtain 3NF and may not be an intrinsic property of 3NF.

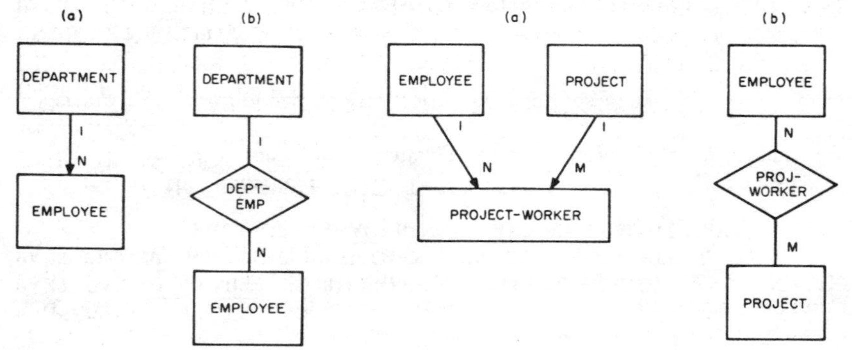

Fig. 16. Relationship DEPARTMENT-EMPLOYEE
(a) data structure diagram
(b) entity-relationship diagram

Fig. 17. Relationship PROJECT-WORKER
(a) data structure diagram
(b) entity-relationship diagram

The arrow represents a data-structure-set in which the DEPARTMENT record is the *owner-record*, and one owner-record may own n ($n = 0, 1, 2, \ldots$) *member-records*. Figure 16(b) illustrates the corresponding entity-relationship diagram. One might conclude that the arrow in the data-structure diagram represents a relationship between entities in two entity sets. This is not always true. Figures 17(a) and 17(b) are the data-structure diagram and the entity-relationship diagram expressing the relationship PROJECT-WORKER between two entity types EMPLOYEE and PROJECT. We can see in Figure 17(a) that the relationship PROJECT-WORKER becomes another record type and that the arrows no longer represent relationships between entities. What are the real meanings of the arrows in data-structure diagrams? The answer is that an arrow represents an $1{:}n$ relationship between two *record* (not entity) types and also implies the existence of an access path from the owner record to the member records. The data-structure diagram is a representation of the organization of records (level 4 in Figure 1) and is not an exact representation of entities and relationships.

4.2.2 Deriving the Data-Structure Diagram. Under what conditions does an arrow in a data-structure diagram correspond to a relationship of entities? A close comparison of the data-structure diagrams with the corresponding entity-relationship diagrams reveals the following rules:

1. For $1{:}n$ binary relationships an arrow is used to represent the relationship (see Figure 16(a)).

2. For $m{:}n$ binary relationships a "relationship record" type is created to represent the relationship and arrows are drawn from the "entity record" type to the "relationship record" type (see Figure 17(a)).

3. For k-ary ($k \geq 3$) relationships, the same rule as (2) applies (i.e. creating a "relationship record" type).

Since DBTG [7] does not allow a data-structure-set to be defined on a single record type (i.e. Figure 18 is not allowed although it has been implemented in [13]), a "relationship record" is needed to implement such relationships (see

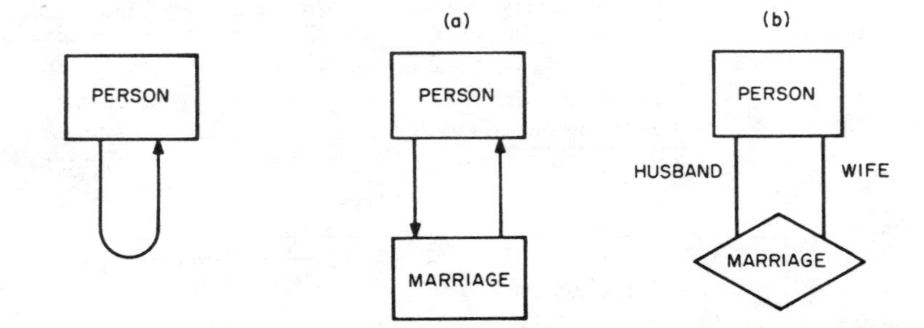

Fig. 18. Data-structure-set defined on the same record type

Fig. 19. Relationship MARRIAGE (a) data structure diagram (b) entity-relationship diagram

Figure 19(a)) [20]. The corresponding entity-relationship diagram is shown in Figure 19(b).

It is clear now that arrows in a data-structure diagram do not always represent relationships of entities. Even in the case that an arrow represents a $1:n$ relationship, the arrow only represents a unidirectional relationship [20] (although it is possible to find the owner-record from a member-record). In the entity-relationship model, both directions of the relationship are represented (the roles of both entities are specified). Besides the semantic ambiguity in its arrows, the network model is awkward in handling changes in semantics. For example, if the relationship between DEPARTMENT and EMPLOYEE changes from a $1:n$ mapping to an $m:n$ mapping (i.e. one employee may belong to several departments), we must create a relationship record DEPARTMENT-EMPLOYEE in the network model.

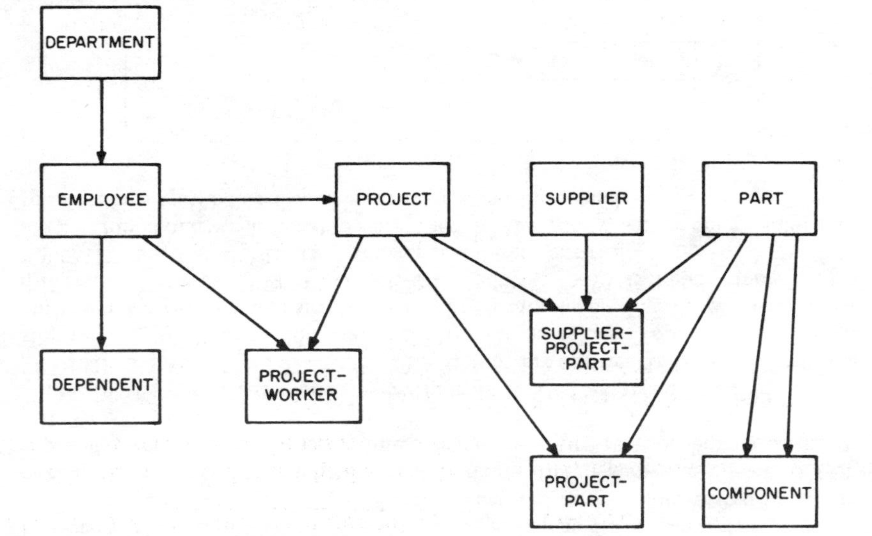

Fig. 20. The data structure diagram derived from the entity-relationship diagram in Fig. 11

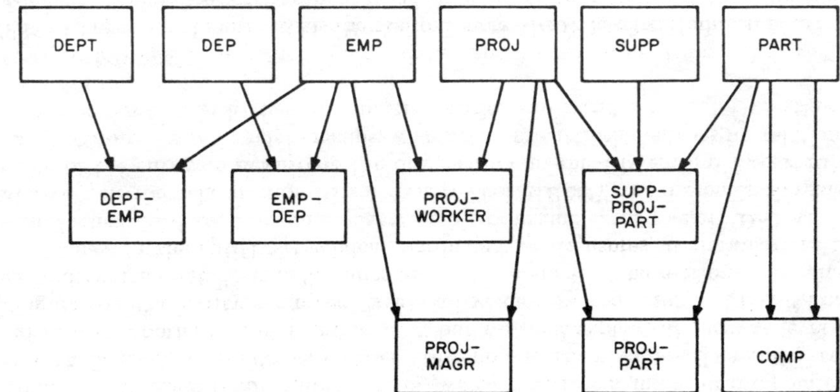

Fig. 21. The "disciplined" data structure diagram derived from the entity-relationship diagram in Fig. 11

In the entity-relationship model, all kinds of mappings in relationships are handled uniformly.

The entity-relationship model can be used as a tool in the structured design of databases using the network model. The user first draws an entity-relationship diagram (Figure 11). He may simply translate it into a data-structure diagram (Figure 20). using the rules specified above. He may also follow a discipline that every entity or relationship must be mapped onto a record (that is, "relationship records" are created for all types of relationships no matter that they are $1:n$ or $m:n$ mappings). Thus, in Figure 11, all one needs to do is to change the diamonds to boxes and to add arrowheads on the appropriate lines. Using this approach three more boxes—DEPARTMENT-EMPLOYEE, EMPLOYEE-DEPENDENT, and PROJECT-MANAGER—will be added to Figure 20 (see Figure 21). The validity constraints discussed in Sections 3.3–3.5 will also be useful.

4.3 The Entity Set Model

4.3.1 The Entity Set View. The basic element of the entity set model is the entity. Entities have names (*entity names*) such as "Peter Jones", "blue", or "22". Entity names having some properties in common are collected into an *entity-name-set*, which is referenced by the *entity-name-set-name* such as "NAME", "COLOR", and "QUANTITY".

An entity is represented by the entity-name-set-name/entity-name pair such as NAME/Peter Jones, EMPLOYEE-NO/2566, and NO-OF-YEARS/20. An entity is described by its association with other entities. Figure 22 illustrates the entity set view of data. The "DEPARTMENT" of entity EMPLOYEE-NO/2566 is the entity DEPARTMENT-NO/405. In other words, "DEPARTMENT" is the role that the entity DEPARTMENT-NO/405 plays to describe the entity EMPLOYEE-NO/2566. Similarly, the "NAME", "ALTERNATIVE-NAME", or "AGE" of EMPLOYEE-NO/2566 is "NAME/Peter Jones", "NAME/Sam Jones", or "NO-OF-YEARS/20", respectively. The description of the entity EMPLOYEE-

NO/2566 is a collection of the related entities and their roles (the entities and roles circled by the dotted line). An example of the *entity description* of "EMPLOYEE-NO/2566" (in its full-blown, unfactored form) is illustrated by the set of role-name/entity-name-set-name/entity-name triplets shown in Figure 23. Conceptually, the entity set model differs from the entity-relationship model in the following ways:

(1) In the entity set model, everything is treated as an entity. For example, "COLOR/BLACK" and "NO–OF–YEARS/45" are entities. In the entity-relationship model, "blue" and "36" are usually treated as values. Note treating values as entities may cause semantic problems. For example, in Figure 22, what is the difference between "EMPLOYEE-NO/2566", "NAME/Peter Jones", and "NAME/Sam Jones"? Do they represent different entities?

(2) Only binary relationships are used in the entity set model,[5] while n-ary relationships may be used in the entity-relationship model.

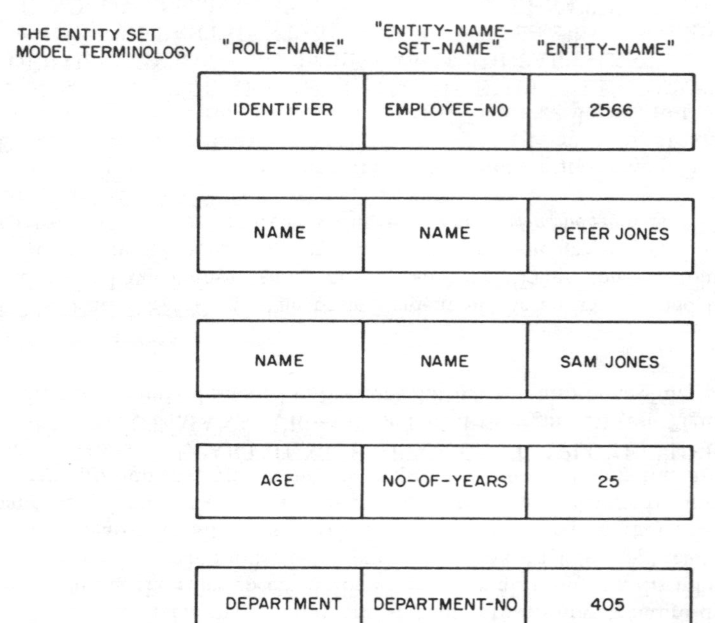

Fig. 22. The entity-set view

THE ENTITY-RELATIONSHIP MODEL TERMINOLOGY	ATTRIBUTE OR ROLE	VALUE SET	VALUE
THE ENTITY SET MODEL TERMINOLOGY	"ROLE-NAME"	"ENTITY-NAME-SET-NAME"	"ENTITY-NAME"
	IDENTIFIER	EMPLOYEE-NO	2566
	NAME	NAME	PETER JONES
	NAME	NAME	SAM JONES
	AGE	NO-OF-YEARS	25
	DEPARTMENT	DEPARTMENT-NO	405

Fig. 23. An "entity description" in the entity-set model

4.3.2 Deriving the Entity Set View. One of the main difficulties in understanding the entity set model is due to its world view (i.e. identifying values with entities). The entity-relationship model proposed in this paper is useful in understanding and deriving the entity set view of data. Consider Figures 2 and 6. In Figure 2, entities are represented by e_i's (which exist in our minds or are pointed at with fingers). In Figure 6, entities are represented by values. The entity set model works both at level 1 and level 2, but we shall explain its view at level 2 (Figure 6). The entity set model treats all value sets such as NO–OF–YEARS as "entity-name-sets" and all values as "entity-names." The attributes become role names in the entity set model. For binary relationships, the translation is simple: the role of an entity in a relationship (for example, the role of "DEPARTMENT" in the relationship DEPARTMENT–EMPLOYEE) becomes the role name of the entity in describing the other entity in the relationship (see Figure 22). For n-ary ($n > 2$) relationships, we must create artificial entities for relationships in order to handle them in a binary relationship world.

ACKNOWLEDGMENTS

The author wishes to express his thanks to George Mealy, Stuart Madnick, Murray Edelberg, Susan Brewer, Stephen Todd, and the referees for their valuable sug-

[5] In DIAM II [24], n-ary relationships may be treated as special cases of identifiers.

gestions (Figure 21 was suggested by one of the referees). This paper was motivated by a series of discussions with Charles Bachman. The author is also indebted to E.F. Codd and M.E. Senko for their valuable comments and discussions in revising this paper.

REFERENCES

1. Abrial, J.R. Data semantics. In *Data Base Management*, J.W. Klimbie and K.L. Koffeman, Eds., North-Holland Pub. Co., Amsterdam, 1974, pp. 1–60.
2. Bachman, C.W. Software for random access processing. *Datamation 11* (April 1965), 36–41.
3. Bachman, C.W. Data structure diagrams. *Data Base 1*, 2 (Summer 1969), 4–10.
4. Bachman, C.W. Trends in database management—1975. Proc., AFIPS 1975 NCC, Vol. 44, AFIPS Press, Montvale, N.J., pp. 569–576.
5. Birkhoff, G., and Bartee, T.C. *Modern Applied Algebra*. McGraw-Hill, New York, 1970.
6. Chamberlin, D.D., and Raymond, F.B. SEQUEL: A structured English query language. Proc. ACM-SIGMOD 1974, Workshop, Ann Arbor, Michigan, May, 1974.
7. CODASYL. Data base task group report. ACM, New York, 1971.
8. Codd, E.F. A relational model of data for large shared data banks. *Comm. ACM 13*, 6 (June 1970), 377–387.
9. Codd, E.F. Normalized data base structure: A brief tutorial. Proc. ACM-SIGFIDET 1971, Workshop, San Diego, Calif., Nov. 1971, pp. 1–18.
10. Codd, E.F. A data base sublanguage founded on the relational calculus. Proc. ACM-SIGFIDET 1971, Workshop, San Diego, Calif., Nov. 1971, pp. 35–68.
11. Codd, E.F. Recent investigations in relational data base systems. Proc. IFIP Congress 1974, North-Holland Pub. Co., Amsterdam, pp. 1017–1021.
12. Deheneffe, C., Hennebert, H., and Paulus, W. Relational model for data base. Proc. IFIP Congress 1974, North-Holland Pub. Co., Amsterdam, pp. 1022–1025.
13. Dodd, G.G. APL—a language for associate data handling in PL/I. Proc. AFIPS 1966 FJCC, Vol. 29, Spartan Books, New York, pp. 677–684.
14. Eswaran, K.P., and Chamberlin, D.D. Functional specifications of a subsystem for data base integrity. Proc. Very Large Data Base Conf., Framingham, Mass., Sept. 1975, pp. 48–68.
15. Hainaut, J.L., and Lecharlier, B. An extensible semantic model of data base and its data language. Proc. IFIP Congress 1974, North-Holland Pub. Co., Amsterdam, pp. 1026–1030.
16. Hammer, M.M., and McLeod, D.J. Semantic integrity in a relation data base system. Proc. Very Large Data Base Conf., Framingham, Mass., Sept. 1975, pp. 25–47.
17. Lindgreen, P. Basic operations on information as a basis for data base design. Proc. IFIP Congress 1974, North-Holland Pub. Co., Amsterdam, pp. 993–997.
18. Mealy, G.H. Another look at data base. Proc. AFIPS 1967 FJCC, Vol. 31, AFIPS Press, Montvale, N.J., pp. 525–534.
19. Nijssen, G.M. Data structuring in the DDL and the relational model. In *Data Base Management*, J.W. Klimbie and K.L. Koffeman, Eds., North-Holland Pub. Co., Amsterdam, 1974, pp. 363–379.
20. Olle, T.W. Current and future trends in data base management systems. Proc. IFIP Congress 1974, North-Holland Pub. Co., Amsterdam, pp. 998–1006.
21. Roussopoulos, N., and Mylopoulos, J. Using semantic networks for data base management. Proc. Very Large Data Base Conf., Framingham, Mass., Sept. 1975, pp. 144–172.
22. Rustin, R. (Ed.). Proc. ACM-SOGMOD 1974—debate on data models. Ann Arbor, Mich., May 1974.
23. Schmid, H.A., and Swenson, J.R. On the semantics of the relational model. Proc. ACM-SIGMOD 1975, Conference, San Jose, Calif., May 1975, pp. 211–233.
24. Senko, M.E. Data description language in the concept of multilevel structured description: DIAM II with FORAL. In *Data Base Description*, B.C.M. Dougue, and G.M. Nijssen, Eds., North-Holland Pub. Co., Amsterdam, pp. 239–258.
25. Senko, M.E., Altman, E.B., Astrahan, M.M., and Fehder, P.L. Data structures and accessing in data-base systems. *IBM Syst. J. 12*, 1 (1973), 30–93.
26. Sibley, E.H. On the equivalence of data base systems. Proc. ACM-SIGMOD 1974 debate on data models, Ann Arbor, Mich., May 1974, pp. 43–76.
27. Steel, T.B. Data base standardization—a status report. Proc. ACM-SIGMOD 1975, Conference, San Jose, Calif., May 1975, pp. 65–78.
28. Stonebraker, M. Implementation of integrity constraints and views by query modification. Proc. ACM-SIGMOD 1975, Conference, San Jose, Calif., May 1975, pp. 65–78.
29. Sundgren, B. Conceptual foundation of the infological approach to data bases. In *Data Base Management*, J.W. Klimbie and K.L. Koffeman, Eds., North-Holland Pub. Co., Amsterdam, 1974, pp. 61–95.
30. Taylor, R.W. Observations on the attributes of database sets. In *Data Base Description*, B.C.M. Dougue and G.M. Nijssen, Eds., North-Holland Pub. Co., Amsterdam, pp. 73–84.
31. Tsichritzis, D. A network framework for relation implementation. In *Data Base Description*, B.C.M. Douge and G.M. Nijssen, Eds., North-Holland Pub. Co., Amsterdam, pp. 269–282.

The Functional Data Model and the Data Language DAPLEX

DAVID W. SHIPMAN
Computer Corporation of America

DAPLEX is a database language which incorporates:

(1) a formulation of data in terms of entities;
(2) a functional representation for both actual and virtual data relationships;
(3) a rich collection of language constructs for expressing entity selection criteria;
(4) a notion of subtype/supertype relationships among entity types.

This paper presents and motivates the DAPLEX language and the underlying data model on which it is based.

Key Words and Phrases: database, language, functional data model
CR Categories: 4.22, 4.33

1. INTRODUCTION

1.1 The Goals of the Language

DAPLEX is a data definition and manipulation language for database systems, grounded in a concept of data representation called the functional data model. DAPLEX may be considered to be a syntactic embodiment of the functional data model and throughout this paper the two terms will be used interchangeably.

A fundamental goal of DAPLEX is to provide a "conceptually natural" database interface language. That is, the DAPLEX constructs used to model real-world situations are intended to closely match the conceptual constructs a human being might employ when thinking about those situations. Such conceptual naturalness, to the extent it has been achieved, presumably simplifies the process of writing and understanding DAPLEX requests, since the translation between the user's mental representation and its formal expression in DAPLEX is more direct.[1]

[1] To some extent this "naturalness" has been a goal of other data models. For example, the "simplicity" which is often cited as an objective of the relational data model [7] is similar to naturalness in some respects, but it also includes the notions of minimality (i.e., a small number of data constructs) and nonredundancy (i.e., representation of a single "fact" only once in the database). These latter attributes of the relational model are almost certainly not characteristic of the way humans model the world. DAPLEX is prepared to sacrifice these goals in favor of a more natural representation.

Author's present address: Massachusetts Institute of Technology, Research Laboratory of Electronics, Room 36-597, Cambridge, MA 02139.

The basic constructs of DAPLEX are the *entity* and the *function*. These are intended to model conceptual objects and their properties. We may, for example, model a particular student and the courses he is taking as entities, with the function "course of" defined to map one to the other. (A DAPLEX function, in general, maps a given entity into a *set* of target entities.)

Often some properties of an object are derived from properties of other objects to which it is related. For example, assume that courses have an "instructor of" property. We may then consider an "instructors of" property which relates students to their instructors. Such a property would be based on the "instructor of" property of those courses in which the student is enrolled. The principle of conceptual naturalness dictates that it be possible for users to treat such derived properties as if they were primitive. This follows, for example, from the observation that properties which are "derived" in one database formulation may be "primitive" in another, even though the same real-world situation is being modeled. Such alternative representations of the same facts are modeled in DAPLEX by the notion of *derived function*.

The problem of database representation is complicated by the fact that no single model of reality may be appropriate for all users and problem domains. The properties which are considered relevant and the mechanisms by which they are most naturally referenced vary across differing world views. Even the decision as to what constitutes an object depends on the world view assumed. Some users might prefer, for example, to view the enrollment of a student in a course as an entity having its own properties, while for others, dealing with enrollments as objects would be unnatural and awkward. To cope with these issues, DAPLEX provides for the construction of separate *user views* of the database. Because user views are specified in terms of derived functions, complex interrelationships among views may be accommodated.

In short, the DAPLEX language is an attempt to provide a databae system interface which allows the user to more directly model the way he thinks about the problems he is trying to solve.

1.2 A Quick Look at DAPLEX

Consider the query,

> "What are the names of all students taking EE courses from assistant professors?"

In DAPLEX this is expressed as

```
FOR EACH Student
  SUCH THAT FOR SOME Course(Student)
    Name(Dept(Course)) = "EE" AND
    Rank(Instructor(Course)) = "ASSISTANT PROFESSOR"
  PRINT Name(Student)
```

(DAPLEX requests can be read in an English-like manner: "For each student such that, for some course of the student, the name of the department of the course is EE and the rank of the instructor of the course is assistant professor, print the name of the student.")

Figure 1 is a graphic representation of the data description for the database against which this query is issued. The rounded enclosures indicate entity types

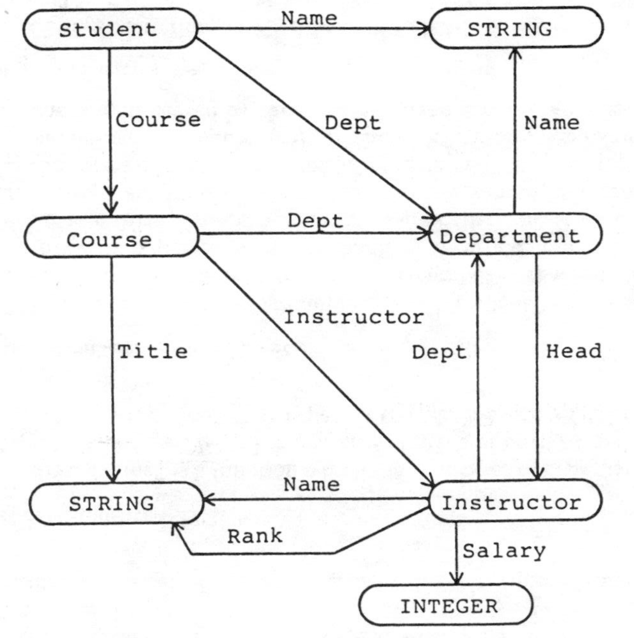

Fig. 1. The university database.

and the arrows depict functions mapping their argument types into their result types.[2]

In this example the FOR EACH statement iterates over a set of entities of type "Student", executing its for-body, the PRINT statement, for each member of the set. Here, the set of entities under consideration has been qualified by a SUCH THAT clause. SUCH THAT will consider all "Student" entities, testing them against a qualifying predicate. The qualification here further involves quantification as indicated by the phrase "FOR SOME Course(Student)". Within this phrase, the variable "Student" refers to the particular student under consideration by SUCH THAT. "Course" is a function defined over students that returns a set of course entities. If the following Boolean predicate is true for at least one of the courses, then the student entity will pass the SUCH THAT qualification. This Boolean predicate consists of two comparisons joined by the Boolean operator AND. Notice the nested functional notation here. In the expression "Name(Dept(Course))", "Course" refers to the particular "Course" entity under consideration by the FOR SOME phrase. When the "Dept" function is applied to this entity, the result is a "Department" entity indicating the department under which the course is offered. "Name" is a function which may be applied to "Department" entities to return the STRING entity which indicates the name of the department. This STRING entity is compared to the string "EE".

1.3 Relation to Previous Work

Data modeling has been one of the major themes of database research over the past ten years. DAPLEX is an outgrowth of this work. As extensive summaries of the field appear elsewhere [1, 10, 12], only particularly relevant research will be discussed here.

The notion of a functional data model was first introduced by Sibley and Kershberg [15]. This work explored the use of the functional approach as a tool for modeling the data structures representable under the three dominant data models (hierarchical, relational, and network). However, the payoff resulting from the concept of derived functions was not recognized.

The semantic data model of McLeod and Hammer [9, 12] does recognize the potential inherent in the notion of derived data. In addition, this work includes a great deal of pioneering research into the descriptive capabilities needed to represent, in the database, useful semantic properties of the real world being modeled. This work, however, has not concentrated on extracting the underlying primitives of the proposed model or on expressing its ideas within a concise notational framework. To a large extent, DAPLEX is an attempt to provide such a framework for many of the ideas in this model.

In a concurrent effort, Buneman [5] has developed a functional notation for data which incorporates many of the concepts underlying the functional data model proposed here. His notation is based on the functional programming (FP) notation advocated by Backus [4]. While Buneman's notation is not entirely suitable as a user interface language, it may well be useful as an internal representation for portions of the DAPLEX syntax.

In addition, some reference should be made to the work of Smith and Smith [16], whose explorations of the issues of generalization and aggregation lead directly or indirectly to many of the concepts embodied in DAPLEX; to the work of Bachman [3], whose role model bears many similarities to the use of types in DAPLEX; and to the work of Kent [11], who argues persuasively of the disadvantages of record-based data modeling. Rowe and Shoens [14] introduced the notion of procedural encapsulation of view updates. System R [2] and INGRES [17] both employ data dictionaries defined in terms of the native data model.

Many, if not most, of the ideas incorporated in DAPLEX have been adapted from previous work in database management. What is significant about DAPLEX is the fact that these ideas have been integrated into a single framework, the functional data model, and expressed in a syntax which tends to avoid unnecessary awkwardness.

The remainder of this paper includes sections describing data definition, data manipulation, derived data, metadata, and applications examples. It should be pointed out that the study of the DAPLEX language and its implications is a continuing effort and that details of the design should be considered preliminary. No implementation currently exists. The appendix presents the complete specification of the language as it stands.

[2] The formal DAPLEX description of this database is given in the following section. Readers familiar with the AI literature will recognize that we are essentially dealing with a form of *semantic net* [13]. It should also be pointed out that the simple graphical notation indicated here is not adequate to represent the full power of the data description capability.

```
DECLARE Student ( ) =>> ENTITY
DECLARE Name (Student) => STRING
DECLARE Dept (Student) => Department
DECLARE Course (Student) =>> Course

DECLARE Course ( ) =>> ENTITY
DECLARE Title (Course) => STRING
DECLARE Dept (Course) => Department
DECLARE Instructor (Course) => Instructor

DECLARE Instructor ( ) =>> ENTITY
DECLARE Name (Instructor) => STRING
DECLARE Rank (Instructor) => STRING
DECLARE Dept (Instructor) => Department
DECLARE Salary (Instructor) => INTEGER

DECLARE Department ( ) =>> ENTITY
DECLARE Name (Department) => STRING
DECLARE Head (Department) => Instructor
```

Fig. 2. Data description.

2. DATA DEFINITION

2.1 The DECLARE Statement

Figure 2 illustrates the data definition statements needed to express the data structure which is graphically presented in Figure 1. All of the statements shown here are DECLARE statements. They establish functions in the system. Functions are used to express both entity types and what we have been calling the "properties" of an entity.

Let us consider a number of the statements in this description. First, we look at

DECLARE Name(Student) ⇒ STRING

This states that "Name" is a function which maps entities of type "Student" to entities of type STRING. STRING is one of a number of entity types provided by the system along with such other types as INTEGER and BOOLEAN. The statement

DECLARE Dept(Student) ⇒ Department

states that "Dept" is a function which applied to a "Student" entity returns an entity of type "Department". It is important to remember that when the "Dept" function is applied, a department entity itself is returned, not a department number or other identifier. These two functions are called *single-valued* as they always return a single entity. (Strictly speaking, single-valued functions return a set of entities consisting of a single element.) Single-valued functions are indicated by use of a single-headed arrow (⇒) in their definition. An example of a *multivalued* function, indicated by the double-headed arrow (⇒»), is

DECLARE Course(Student) ⇒» Course

Here the "Course" function, applied to a "Student" entity, returns a set of entities of type "Course". A multivalued function may return the empty set.

All function applications evaluate to sets of entities in the mathematical sense; that is, the sets are considered unordered and do not contain duplicates.[3]

The functions we have examined so far take a single argument. It is also possible for functions to take no arguments. For example,

DECLARE Student ( ) ⇒» ENTITY

Here the function "Student" evaluates to a set of entities. ENTITY is the system-provided type of all entities. By convention, zero-argument functions define entity types. Thus the statement above has a dual purpose; it declares the function "Student" and it defines the entity type "Student". All and only those entities returned by the "Student" function are of type "Student".

Multivalued functions are initialized to return the empty set. Single-valued functions must be explicitly initialized by the user.[4] Further instantiation of functions takes place through update statements, discussed in Section 3.4.

2.2 Multiple Argument Functions

We have just considered functions of zero and one argument. However, functions taking any number of arguments may be declared. For example, we could augment the data description of Figure 2 with the statement

DECLARE Grade(Student, Course) ⇒ INTEGER

The "Grade" function might return the grade which "Student" obtained in "Course".

Other data modeling mechanisms often force the creation of new entity types in such a situation, for example, [6]. In these systems it is necesssary to view, for example, the enrollment of a student in a course as a conceptual object, and then to assign a "grade of" property to that "object." With DAPLEX, the mandatory creation of such potentially unnatural entity types is avoided.

A difficulty with the function declaration above is that it specifies the function "Grade" as well defined for every "Student"–"Course" pair, while in fact the function should only exist for those courses in which the student is enrolled. The more sophisticated declaration that follows circumvents this problem:

DECLARE Grade(Student, Course(Student)) ⇒ INTEGER

2.3 Function Inversion

The reader may be concerned that DAPLEX functions map in only one direction. Thus, given a "Course" entity, we may apply the function "Instructor" to obtain the instructor of the course. But, given an "Instructor" entity, how do we determine the courses he teaches? This problem is solved through the use of function inversion, as illustrated by

```
DEFINE Course(Instructor) =>>
  INVERSE OF Instructor(Course)
```

[3] As we see later, however, the language does include facilities which allow the user to associate orders with certain sets of entities.

[4] Formally, single-valued functions are initialized to a particular entity which is only of type ENTITY. Because the value of the function is of the wrong type, any reference to the function will cause a run-time error. Further, the transaction (i.e., top-level DAPLEX statement) will abort if the function has not been properly initialized by the end of the transaction (see Appendix, Section A2.2.2).

```
DECLARE Person ( ) =>> ENTITY
DECLARE Name (Person) => STRING

DECLARE Student ( ) =>> Person
DECLARE Dept (Student) => Department
DECLARE Course (Student) =>> Course

DECLARE Employee ( ) =>> Person
DECLARE Salary (Employee) => INTEGER
DECLARE Manager (Employee) => Employee

DECLARE Instructor ( ) =>> Employee
DECLARE Rank (Instructor) => STRING
DECLARE Dept (Instructor) => Department
```

Fig. 3. Subtypes.

We now have a function "Course" which can be applied to "Instructor" entities. In so doing, we have entered the domain of derived functions (notice the keyword DEFINE has replaced DECLARE). Section 4 is devoted to the definition and use of derived data, and in that section the subject of function inversions is taken up again.

2.4 Subtypes and Supertypes

Rather than declare "Student" and "Instructor" entities, as is done in Figure 2, the more general specification given in Figure 3 might be used. Here, by defining students as persons and instructors as employees, who in turn are persons, we have implied a number of *subtype* and *supertype* relationships.

In Figure 3 the "Student" function is defined to return a set of "Person" entities. That is, the set of "Student" entities is a subset of the set of "Person" entities. This implies that any "Student" entity also has the "Name" function defined over it since it is necessarily a "Person" entity as well.

Similar comments apply to the specification of the "Employee" type, as well as to the "Instructor" type, a subtype of the type "Employee". An "Instructor" entity has "Name", "Salary" and "Manager" functions specified over it as well as "Rank" and "Dept".

The mechanisms discussed above organize types into a hierarchy. However, use of the INTERSECTION OF or UNION OF operators, described in Section 4, results in a lattice of entity types.

2.5 Function Names

A single entity may be a member of several types. A particular "Student" entity, for example, may be an "Instructor" entity as well. This can give rise to potential ambiguities in function invocation. Earlier, the "Course" function was defined over "Instructor" entities to return the courses the instructor teaches. But the "Course" function was also declared above to map a "Student" entity into the courses the student is taking. When we apply the function "Course" to an entity which is both a "Student" and an "Instructor", which courses do we get?

The resolution of this dilemma lies in the fact that the two "Course" functions *are different functions.* Consequently they are given different *internal names* even though their *external names* are the same. Such a situation is generally referred to as "function name overloading." The internal name of a function is generated by enclosing in square brackets the external function name and the argument types over which it was originally specified. Thus the internal names of our two functions are [Course(Instructor)] and [Course(Student)].

Which function is chosen depends on the role the argument entity plays in the user's request. If the entity is currently being viewed as a student, then [Course(Student)] is applied. If it is being viewed as an instructor, then [Course(Instructor)] is applied instead.

The formal notion of *role*, discussed in Section 3.6, is used to achieve these results. Briefly, role associates an entity type with every expression in the language. External function names are disambiguated by determining the role of their argument expressions.

2.6 Ordered Data

Order forms a natural part of a user's conception of reality and consequently has been incorporated into the design of DAPLEX. An explicit ordering facility eliminates the need for the artificial "ordering attributes" sometimes required with other data models.

Any multivalued function may have an order associated with the members of the set it returns. In particular, types may be ordered by associating an order with the zero-argument function which defines the type.

Orders may be system maintained or user maintained. A system-maintained ordering is based on the evaluation of expressions defined over the elements of the set to be ordered. An example would be the ordering of instructors by rank and salary, or the ordering of students by the number of courses which they are taking. User-maintained orders are defined explicitly via update statements in the language. Examples might include the ordering of the musical notes in a melody, the ordering of the stops on a subway line, or the ordering of statements in a computer program.

The syntax relevant to orders is rather conventional. The reader is directed to the appendix for further details.

3. DATA MANIPULATION

3.1 Expressions and Statements

The basic elements of the DAPLEX syntax are statements and expressions. Statements direct the system to perform some action and include the data definition statements and FOR loops. Expressions, which always appear within statements, evaluate to a set of entities. As seen in the example query of Section 1, expressions may involve qualification, quantification, Boolean operators, and comparisons. Figure 4 presents a decomposition and labeling of the syntactic units of this query according to the syntax specification of the appendix.

3.2 Some Syntactic Tricks

This section discusses two syntactic devices, namely, nested function calls and implicit looping variables, which are designed to increase the "conceptual conciseness" of DAPLEX. A conceptually concise language is one which reduces the need for introducing artificial elements when formally specifying a query.

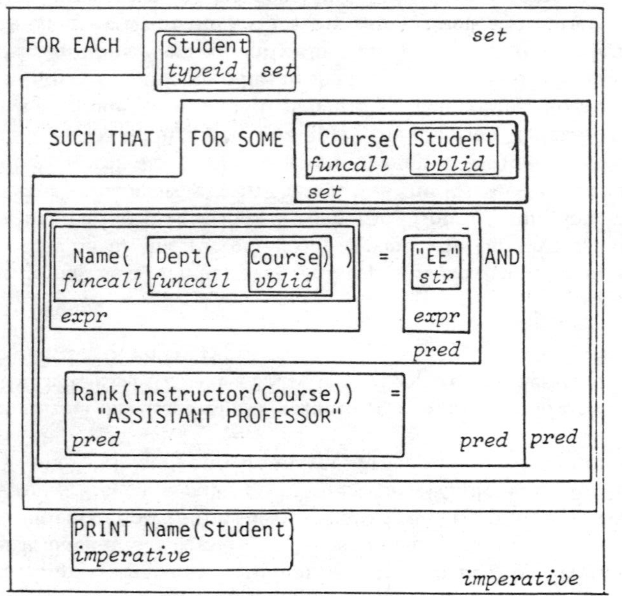

Fig. 4. Anatomy of a request.

The functional notation readily lends itself to functional nesting. Consider the following predicate from Figure 4:

Rank(Instructor(Course)) = "ASSISTANT PROFESSOR"

The advantage of such a construct is that it is not necessary to introduce the additional instructor variable which would be required if function nesting were not permitted. In languages without function nesting, the above predicate would have to be expressed as something analogous to the following:

```
FOR SOME Instructor
  Instructor(Course) = Instructor AND
  Rank(Instructor) = "ASSISTANT PROFESSOR"
```

Another way the language is made conceptually concise is through the use of implicitly declared looping variables. Consider the query, "Which employees earn more than their managers?" This could be expressed in DAPLEX as

```
FOR EACH X IN Employee ( )
  SUCH THAT Salary (X) >
    Salary(Manager (X))
  PRINT Name(X)
```

However, the following semantically equivalent rendition is preferred, since it avoids the introduction of the explicit looping variable "X":

```
FOR EACH Employee
  SUCH THAT Salary(Employee) >
    Salary(Manager(Employee))
  PRINT Name(Employee)
```

In the later query, the symbol "Employee" is used in two distinct senses. In the first line, it refers to the entity type "Employee" and references the entire set of "Employee" entities.[5] In succeeding lines the symbol "Employee" is a looping variable. It is bound successively to the members of the iteration set, as is the symbol "X" in the former query.

Each set expression in DAPLEX has associated with it a reference variable. Operators which iterate over the set, such as FOR EACH and SUCH THAT in the preceding example, successively bind this variable to the entities in the iteration set. The reference variable typically appears in the body of the iterating operator and references the particular entity being considered in the current iteration. By using the IN operator, the user is able to explicitly specify the reference variable associated with a set. Otherwise the reference variable is implicitly declared, usually to be the same symbol as the first identifier in the set expression.[6]

Although the implicit variable declaration results in more readable requests, the explicit form is provided in DAPLEX for two reasons. The first is that this syntax is expected to be easier for a database front end (such as a natural language front end) to generate. The second is that there are circumstances in which two or more variables must range over the same set of entities and in which implicit variable declarations would assign both variables the same name. Such usage is illustrated in the following (exceedingly) awkward rendition of the preceding query.

```
FOR EACH X IN Employee
  SUCH THAT FOR SOME Y IN Employee
    Y = Manager (X) AND
    Salary (X) > Salary (Y)
  PRINT Name (X)
```

It is important to note, however, that it is almost never necessary to use explicit reference variables. Through such techniques as nested functional notation, DAPLEX eliminates the need for multiple variables ranging over the same set in nearly all cases. In fact, a good rule of thumb is that whenever explicit ranging variables must be specified, the query is probably poorly formulated.

3.3 Aggregation

Aggregation functions include AVERAGE, TOTAL, COUNT, MAXIMUM, and MINIMUM. Consider the request, "How many instructors are in the EE department?"

```
PRINT COUNT (Instructor
  SUCH THAT Name (Dept(Instructor)) = "EE")
```

The argument to the COUNT function is a set of "Instructor" entities, and COUNT simply returns the cardinality of that set.

[5] "Employee" here is equivalent to "Employee( )." In general, a symbol which is a type name evaluates to the set of entities of that type, *unless* the symbol has been already bound in the local context to a particular entity. Such binding of symbols occurs, for example, with formal parameters (see Section 4.1) and with the explicit and implicit looping variables discussed in this section.

[6] The precise rules for implicit declaration of reference variables are given in the appendix. Note that although this symbol is often a type name, it need not be.

The set orientation of DAPLEX presents a problem for aggregation in general. Assume we wish to know the average salary of instructors in the EE department. We cannot take the average of the *set* of such salaries because the set notion does not allow duplicates. (The average of $15,000, $25,000, and $15,000 would be $20,000 if we simply took the average of the set of salaries.) The following notation resolves this problem. "What is the average salary of instructors in the EE department?"

```
PRINT AVERAGE (Salary(Instructor) OVER Instructor
  SUCH THAT Name (Dept(Instructor)) = "EE")
```

The semantics of this query are as follows. The OVER operator takes a set specification and an expression defined over members of that set. Here the set involved is a particular set of "Instructor" entities. This set does not contain duplicates. For each member of this set, the given expression is evaluated. (Note that "Instructor" in this expression is an implicit looping variable.) Each resulting value is included in the average independent of whether or not duplicate values are present. Strictly speaking, the OVER expression evaluates not to a set but to a bag.[7] The cardinality of the bag is the same as the cardinality of OVER's set operand.

3.4 Updating

Update statements are used to specify the value returned by a function when applied to particular entities. Some examples illustrate the syntax involved. "Add a new student named Bill to the EE department and enroll him in 'Systems Analysis' and 'Semiconductor Physics',"

```
FOR A NEW Student
  BEGIN
  LET Name (Student) = "Bill"
  LET Dept (Student) = THE Department SUCH THAT
      Name (Department) = "EE"
  LET Course (Student) =
      {THE Course SUCH THAT Name (Course) =
           "Systems Analysis",
       THE Course SUCH THAT Name (Course) =
           "Semiconductor Physics"}
  END
```

The following illustrates the incremental updating of multivalued functions. "Drop 'Introductory Physics' from John's courses and add 'Organic Chemistry',"[8]

```
FOR THE Student SUCH THAT Name (Student) = "John"
  BEGIN
  EXCLUDE Course (Student) =
    THE Course SUCH THAT Name (Course) =
      "Introductory Physics"
  INCLUDE Course (Student) =
    THE Course SUCH THAT Name (Course) =
      "Organic Chemistry"
  END
```

[7] A *bag*, sometimes called a *multiset*, is a set which may contain duplicate elements.

[8] A less awkward version of this request is presented in Section 4.1.

3.5 Function Evaluation

Update statements set the value a function is to return when it is applied to particular arguments. In the context of a DAPLEX expression, however, a function's arguments are not always individual entities but rather sets of entities. This is simply a result of the fact that the argument to a function is an expression, and expressions, in general, evaluate to a set. When a function is evaluated, the result is the union of all entities returned by the function applied to all members of its argument set. Thus, "List all courses taken by EE students,"

```
FOR EACH
    Course (Student SUCH THAT Dept (Student) = "EE")
  PRINT Title (Course)
```

The argument to the "Course" function here is a set of "Student" entities. The evaluation of the function returns the set of all courses taken by any of these students. Note that each course is listed only once.[9]

A corollary to the function evaluation convention is that functions with null set arguments evaluate to the null set.

3.6 Value, Role, and Order

We are now ready to consider some of the more subtle aspects of expression evaluation in DAPLEX. Three components are associated with every expression evaluation. These are the expression *value*, the expression *role*, and the expression *order*. The expression value is the set of entities returned by evaluating the expression. The expression role is the entity type under which these entities are to be interpreted when resolving external function name ambiguities. The expression order is the ordering associated with these entities.

So far in our discussions we have been almost exclusively concerned with expression value. Clearly, it is the most important aspect of expression evaluation.

An expression's role is used only in determining internal function names (see Section 2.5). The role of an expression can always be determined by a static analysis of the request and the data description; accessing of the actual database is not required.

An expression's order is only relevant when the expression is used with the operator FOR EACH . . . IN ORDER, with expressions involving the keywords PRECEDING and FOLLOWING and with predicates which compare two entities based on their order. Otherwise the order is ignored.

The value, role, and order of an expression are calculated from the value, role, and order, respectively, of its subexpressions. The appendix gives complete rules for obtaining value, role, and order for each of the expression types in DAPLEX.

The following example illustrates the use of expression role. "Among the students who are also instructors, list those who are taking a course which

[9] Had we, for some reason, desired duplicate courses to be listed, the query would have been expressed as

```
FOR EACH Student SUCH THAT Dept (Student) = "EE"
  FOR EACH Course (Student)
    PRINT Title (Course)
```

they teach,"

```
FOR EACH Student SUCH THAT
  SOME Course (Student) =
    SOME Course (Student AS Instructor)
  PRINT Name (Student)
```

The operator AS converts the role of an expression without affecting its value or order. In the first use of the function name "Course", the argument to the function has the role "Student". Therefore, the internal function name for this invocation is [Course (Student)]. In the second use of the function name "Course", the argument to the function has been converted to have the role "Instructor". Consequently, the internal function name for this invocation is [Course (Instructor)]. It should also be noted that the AS expression evaluates to the null set (and consequently the qualifying predicate evaluates to FALSE) when the current "Student" is not of type "Instructor".

3.7 General-Purpose Operators and Control Structures

It is intended that DAPLEX be embedded in a general-purpose high-level language. Consequently, syntax for general-purpose operators and control structures are not specified here, as this would be supplied by the high-level language. Nonetheless, the examples here have made use of such constructs (e.g., PRINT, AND, BEGIN . . . END are all assumed to be supplied by the high-level language). The semantics in these cases should be cl.

4. DERIVED DATA

4.1 The DEFINE Statement

The use of derived data dramatically extends the naturalness and usability of a database system. In the context of the functional data model, "derived data" is interpreted to mean "derived function definitions." Essentially we are defining new properties of objects based on the values of other properties. Derived functions are specified by means of DEFINE statements.[10]

To define a function "Instructor" over "Student" entities which returns the instructors of courses the student is taking, use

```
DEFINE Instructor(Student) ⟹
  Instructor(Course(Student))
```

The function "Instructor" may now be used in queries exactly as if it had been a primitive function. The user need not be aware that it is derived data.

As another example, assume we wish to define a "grade point average" property of students:

```
DEFINE GradePointAverage(Student) ⟹
  AVERAGE(Grade(Student, Course)
    OVER Course(Student))
```

[10] Derived functions behave as if their values were recomputed on each access. This does not imply, however, that they actually need be. An implementation strategy which stored the derived function values would be perfectly acceptable so long as it produced the same values as a recompute-on-each-access strategy. This would involve updating a stored value when the values on which it is based have changed.

"Student" is being used as a formal parameter within the body of the DEFINE statements above. When the derived function is evaluated, this variable is bound to the actual argument supplied. In cases where a function takes more than one argument of the same type, the IN operator can be used.[11] Thus, to define a Boolean function which compares two students on the basis of their respective grade point averages, use

```
DEFINE Brighter(S1 IN Student, S2 IN Student) ⟹
  GradePointAverage(S1) > GradePointAverage(S2)
```

Derived functions mayalso be defined over the system-supplied entity types. For example,

```
DEFINE Student(STRING) ⟹ INVERSE OF Name(Student)
DEFINE Course(STRING) ⟹ INVERSE OF Title(Course)
```

These functions map a STRING into a set of "Students" or "Courses", respectively. The update request presented earlier in Section 3.4 can now be written more straightforwardly as follows: "Drop 'Introductory Physics' from John's courses and add 'Organic Chemistry',"[12]

```
FOR THE Student("John")
  BEGIN
  EXCLUDE Course(Student) =
    THE Course("Introductory Physics")
  INCLUDE Course(Student) =
    THE Course("Organic Chemistry")
  END
```

4.2 Conceptual Abstractions

Consider the query, "Which instructors earn over twice the average salary for instructors in their departments?" In the DAPLEX rendition that follows, the query is broken into three parts. First, a function mapping departments to their instructors is defined. Next, a property of "instructors' average salary" is defined for departments. Finally, this property is used to find the desired instructors.

```
DEFINE Instructor(Department) ⟹
  INVERSE of Department(Instructor)

DEFINE InstAvgSal(Department) ⟹
  AVERAGE (Salary(Instructor)
    OVER Instructor(Department))

FOR EACH Instructor
  SUCH THAT
    Salary(Instructor) >
      2*InstAvgSal(Dept(Instructor))
  PRINT Name(Instructor)
```

This request illustrates a profound capability of derived functions: the ability to specify and name conceptual abstractions. This ability is the essence of structured programming, abstract data types, and subroutines. It lies at the core

[11] This is not a special case but follows from the fact that the function arguments specified in DECLARE and DEFINE statements may be arbitrary DAPLEX expressions (see the appendix).

[12] Yet another version of this request appears in Section 4.4.

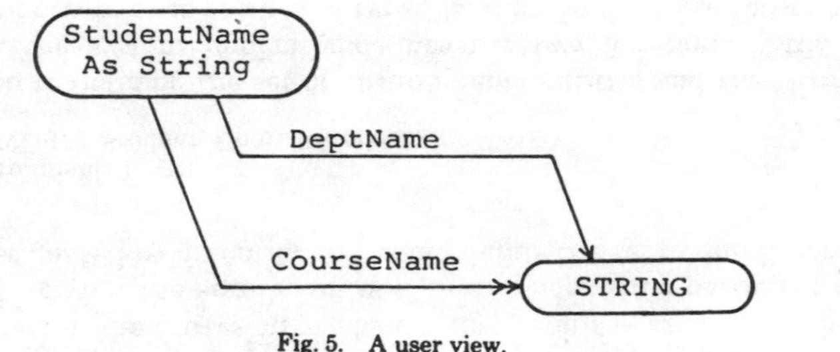

Fig. 5. A user view.

of good software engineering practice. Derived data provides this capability in DAPLEX.

4.3 User Views

For reasons of convenience a user may not wish to see the database as depicted in Figures 1 and 2, but rather as it is depicted in Figure 5. Here, the only user-defined entity type is "StudentName", a subtype of STRING, and all of the functions over "StudentName" return STRING entities. The derived function definitions that follow convert the original database to this new view:

```
DEFINE StudentName( ) ⟹ Name(Student( ))

DEFINE DeptName(StudentName AS STRING) ⟹
  Name(Dept(THE Student (StudentName)))

DEFINE CourseName(StudentName AS STRING) ⟹
  Title(Course(THE Student(StudentName)))
```

These definitions provide the user with access to the functions he desires. For example, "What department is Mary in?" can be expressed as[13]

```
PRINT DeptName("Mary")
```

User views are often for purposes of security as well as convenience. That is, not only may it be desirable for the user to have access to the new definitions but also for him to be prevented from directly invoking the underlying functions. To accomplish this, the new user view is defined in a different name space (i.e., different "module" or "package") from the old view.[14] A secure system, then, would only allow the user to access the name space in which the new view is defined. In addition to this security consideration, the name space distinction is needed when certain function renamings take place. For example, if the new view were to reference the course titles of a student with a function called "Course" rather than one called "CourseName," separate name spaces would be needed to distinguish this new "Course" function from the original one.

[13] Some discussion of the use of the AS STRING phrase in the preceding definitions is in order. As the example illustrates, these functions are not defined over entities of type "StudentName" but rather over entities of type STRING (but only those STRING entities which also happen to be names of students). That is, the internal names of these functions are [DeptName(STRING)] and [CourseName(STRING)]. Had we instead used

```
DEFINE DeptName(StudentName) ⟹
  Name(Dept(THE Student(StudentName)))
```

a function with internal name [DeptName(StudentName)] would have been defined and then we would have had to express "What department is Mary in?" as

```
PRINT DeptName("Mary" AS StudentName)
```

Since an AS phrase must be used somewhere, it is preferable to include it once in the definition of the function rather than require it every time the function appears in a request.

[14] The "package" or "module" facility is assumed to be provided by the high-level language (see Section 3.7).

4.4 Updating Derived Data

Suppose we have the following update request expressed over the view constructed in the preceding section, "Change Jack's department to Biology",

```
LET DeptName("Jack") = "Biology"
```

There are several cnceivable interpretations of this request in terms of the underlying primitive functions. The first, and most plausible, is that Jack is to be registered in the Biology department; that is,[15]

```
LET Dept(THE Student("Jack")) = THE Department("Biology")
```

The second, somewhat less plausible, is that the name of Jack's current department, say the Mathematics department, is to be changed to "Biology"; that is,

```
LET Name(Dept(THE Student("Jack"))) = "Biology"
```

Yet a third alternative, similar to the proposal of Dayal [8] for updating views in the relational data model, would be to create a new department which is given the name "Biology" and to which Jack is assigned; that is,

```
FOR A NEW Department
  BEGIN
  LET Name(Department) = "Biology"
  LET Dept(THE Student("Jack")) = Department
  END
```

It is not possible for the system to intuit which of these three meanings is desired.

In DAPLEX, the semantics for updating derived data are explicitly provided by the user. This is accomplished with the PERFORM . . . USING construct. For example, updates to the derived function "CourseName" might reasonably be defined as follows:

```
PERFORM
  INCLUDE CourseName(StudentName AS STRING) = Title
USING
  INCLUDE Course(THE Student(StudentName)) =
    THE Course(Title)

PERFORM
  EXCLUDE CourseName(StudentName AS STRING) = Title
USING
  EXCLUDE Course(THE Student(StudentName)) =
    THE Course(Title)
```

With these update specifications, the request presented earlier in Sections 3.4

[15] We are assuming for these examples a previous definition,

```
DEFINE Department(STRING) ⟹ INVERSE of Name(Department)
```

and 4.1 may be expressed even more succinctly, "Drop 'Introductory Physics' from John's courses and add 'Organic Chemistry',"

```
EXCLUDE CourseName("John") = "Introductory Physics"
INCLUDE CourseName("John") = "Organic Chemistry"
```

The PERFORM . . . USING statement directs the system to execute the body of the statement whenever the indicated update operation is performed. It is important to point out that this facility merely allows users to provide the *illusion* of derived data updating. The system does not, for example, validate the PERFORM . . . USING statement to ensure that it results in the intended derived data update. Finally, it should be noted that a derived data update is illegal unless an appropriate PERFORM . . . USING directive has been declared.

4.5 Some Special Operators for Defining Functions

In this section we examine the operators INVERSE OF, TRANSITIVE OF, INTERSECTION OF, UNION OF, DIFFERENCE OF, and COMPOUND OF. These operators are used only in function definitions.

To invert the function [Instructor(Course)], we could use

```
DEFINE Course(Instructor) ⇒> Course SUCH THAT
  Instructor = Instructor(Course)
```

It is more convenient, however, to define this function as

```
DEFINE Course(Instructor) ⇒>
  INVERSE OF Instructor(Course)
```

A simple modification of this syntax allows us to define transitive closures. For example,

```
DEFINE Superior(Employee) ⇒>
  TRANSITIVE OF Manager(Employee)
```

The function [Superior(Employee)] returns the set containing the manager of the employee, the manager's manager, the manager's manager, etc.

The INTERSECTION OF, UNION OF, and DIFFERENCE OF operators may be used to form set intersections, unions, and differences. They are most useful in creating new types. For example,

```
DEFINE StudentTeacher( ) ⇒>
  INTERSECTION OF Student, Instructor
```

The COMPOUND OF operator is used to create derived entities corresponding to the elements of the Cartesian product of its operands. As an example, assume that we wish to view the enrollment of a given student in a particular course as a "thing" designated by an entity. We could define the set of enrollment entities by

```
DEFINE Enrollment( ) ⇒>
  COMPOUND OF Student, Course(Student)
```

In addition to defining the set of "Enrollment" entities and the "Enrollment" entity type, the system implicitly defines the two functions "Student" and "Course" to operate over entities of type "Enrollment". These return the "Student" and "Course" entities upon which the compound entity was based. The entity is fully specified by the values of these system-defined functions. That is, no two "Enrollment" entities correspond to the same "Student"–"Course" entity pair. If the set of students or their courses are altered, the set of enrollments automatically reflects this change.

4.6 Constraints

Assume we wish to enforce the constraint that a department's head must come from within the department. We could define the following function over "Department" entities:

```
DEFINE NativeHead(Department) ⇒
  Dept(Head(Department)) = Department
```

This function will evaluate to TRUE for those departments which satisfy the desired constraint and to FALSE for those which do not. By inserting the keyword CONSTRAINT, we define a *constraint* which instructs the system to abort any update transactions which leave the function value FALSE for any department. Thus

```
DEFINE CONSTRAINT NativeHead(Department) ⇒
  Dept(Head(Department)) = Department
```

Constraints may also be specified over the database as a whole. For example, to ensure that the number of managers is always less than the number of nonmanagement employees, use

```
DEFINE Manager( ) ⇒> Manager(Employee( ))
DEFINE NonManager( ) ⇒> DIFFERENCE OF Employee, Manager
DEFINE CONSTRAINT TooManyChiefs( ) ⇒
  COUNT(Manager( )) < COUNT(NonManager( ))
```

The *trigger* capability is related to that for constraints. When a trigger has been installed over a function definition, a specified imperative is executed whenever the function changes from FALSE to TRUE. To inform the department head whenever more than 45 students are enrolled in a class, we might use[16]

```
DEFINE Student(Class) ⇒ INVERSE OF Class(Student)
DEFINE TRIGGER Overbooked(Class) ⇒
    COUNT(Student(Class)) > 45
  SendMessage(Head(Dept(Class)), "Overbooked:",
      Title(Class))
```

5. DATABASE SYSTEM CONSIDERATIONS

5.1 Data Description as Data

The data description is itself data. In a DAPLEX system implementation, the data description can be queried as ordinary data. The design of the data description for the data description, that is, the metadescription, is not specified here and depends, to some extent, on the details of system implementation. In any

[16] In this request "SendMessage" is a procedure defined in the high-level language.

case, of course, it is possible for individual users to define their own view of the data description.

The metadescription includes entities of type FUNCTION. A special system function APPLY is also provided. APPLY takes one or more arguments, the first of which is a function entity, and returns the value of that function applied to the remaining arguments.

Access to metadata is especially useful in building sophisticated interfaces (e.g., natural language front ends) for the naive user, who is often unfamiliar with the structure of the database he is using.

5.2 Updating Metadata

Metadata is normally updated using DECLARE and DEFINE statements. It is also possible for users to update the data description using update statements operating over entities of type FUNCTION. Such updates do not directly update the metadata but instead manipulate a system-provided metadata user view. PERFORM . . . USING statements trap updates to the metadata user view and perform whatever system-internal measures are necessary (such as allocating storage or establishing indices) to effect the desired metadata update.

5.3 Storage Attributes

Storage attributes are associated with each function as metadata. The storage attributes direct the system as to how the data are to be physically organized on the storage medium. Like other metadata, storage attributes may be updated via the metadata user view. These storage attributes indicate how functions are to be internally represented, which data items are to be located near each other, and whether indexed access via function values is to be provided. For derived functions, the storage statements can indicate whether the function values are to be physically stored or recomputed each time they are referenced. A general discussion of storage considerations is beyond the scope of this paper.

6. EXAMPLE APPLICATIONS

6.1 DAPLEX Front Ends

The data modeling capabilities of DAPLEX incorporate those of the hierarchical, relational, and network models, the principal database models in use today. This suggests the possibility of DAPLEX front ends for existing databases and database systems.

As an example, consider a relational version of the database of Figures 1 and 2. This is illustrated in Figure 6. Figure 7 shows the isomorphic DAPLEX description. It is clear that the relational model is a subset of the functional model since the isomorphic DAPLEX description of any relational database will be subject to the following limitations:

(1) No multivalued functions are allowed.
(2) Functions cannot return user-defined entities.
(3) Multiple-argument functions are not allowed.
(4) There are no subtypes.

Having specified the isomorphic description, and assuming the existence of a suitable data manipulation translator, DAPLEX requests can be written against the relational database. However, the full benefits of the DAPLEX approach will not be available because of the limitations in the underlying data model. What is needed is to define derived functions which provide a more convenient view of the database. The additional definitions in Figure 8 transform the description of Figure 7 to conform to that of the original DAPLEX example of Figure 2. Having specified these functions, we may now write DAPLEX queries as if we were working with the DAPLEX database.

The derived functions of Figure 8 can be thought of as adding semantic information which is not expressible in the relational data model. Figure 9 shows the steps for transforming a DAPLEX request into a relational request in the data language QUEL [8]. Figure 9a shows the original request. After the substitutions indicated by derived function definitions are performed, the query will

STUDENT

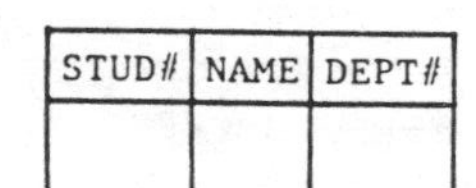

STUD#	NAME	DEPT#

COURSE

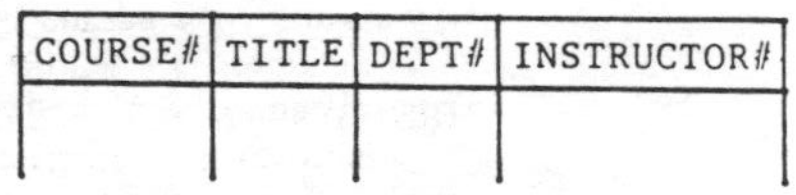

COURSE#	TITLE	DEPT#	INSTRUCTOR#

ENROLLMENT

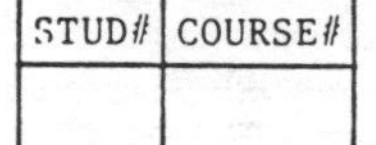

STUD#	COURSE#

INSTRUCTOR

INSTRUCTOR#	NAME	RANK	DEPT#	SALARY

DEPARTMENT

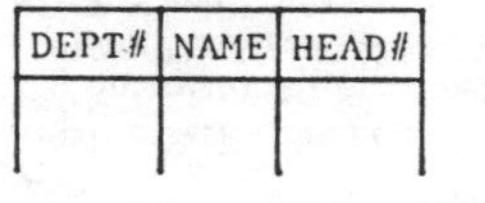

DEPT#	NAME	HEAD#

Fig. 6. Relational data description.

```
DECLARE Student( ) ⇒ ENTITY
DECLARE Stud#(Student) → INTEGER
DECLARE Name(Student) → STRING
DECLARE Dept#(Student) → INTEGER

DECLARE Course( ) ⇒ ENTITY
DECLARE Course#(Course) → INTEGER
DECLARE Title(Course) → STRING
DECLARE Dept#(Course) → INTEGER
DECLARE Instructor#(Course) → INTEGER

DECLARE Enrollment( ) ⇒ ENTITY
DECLARE Stud#(Enrollment) → INTEGER
DECLARE Course#(Enrollment) → INTEGER

DECLARE Instructor( ) ⇒ ENTITY
DECLARE Instructor#(Instructor) → INTEGER
DECLARE Name(Instructor) → STRING
DECLARE Rank(Instructor) → STRING
DECLARE Dept#(Instructor) → INTEGER
DECLARE Salary(Instructor) → INTEGER

DECLARE Department( ) ⇒ ENTITY
DECLARE Dept#(Department) → INTEGER
DECLARE Name(Department) → STRING
DECLARE Head#(Department) → INTEGER
```

Fig. 7. The relational description in DAPLEX.

```
DEFINE Dept(Student) → Department SUCH THAT
  Dept#(Department) = Dept#(Student)

DEFINE Course(Student) → Course SUCH THAT
  FOR SOME Enrollment
    Stud#(Student) = Stud#(Enrollment) AND
    Course#(Enrollment) = Course#(Course)

DEFINE Dept(Course) → Department SUCH THAT
  Dept#(Course) = Dept#(Department)

DEFINE Instructor(Course) → Instructor SUCH THAT
  Instructor#(Instructor) = Instructor#(Course)

DEFINE Dept(Instructor) → Department SUCH THAT
  Dept#(Instructor) = Dept#(Department)

DEFINE Head(Department) → Instructor SUCH THAT
  Instructor#(Instructor) = Head#(Department)
```

Fig. 8. Definitions for the functional view.

```
     FOR EACH Student SUCH THAT
       FOR SOME Course(Student)
(a)      Name(Dept(Course)) = "EE" AND
         Rank(Instructor(Course)) = "ASSISTANT PROFESSOR"
       PRINT Name (Student)

     FOR EACH Student SUCH THAT
       FOR SOME (Course SUCH THAT
         FOR SOME Enrollment
           Stud#(Student) = Stud#(Enrollment) AND
           Course#(Enrollment) = Course#(Course))
         (FOR SOME (Department SUCH THAT
(b)            Dept#(Department) = Dept#(Course))
           Name(Department) = "EE")
         AND
         (FOR SOME (Instructor SUCH THAT
             Instructor#(Instructor) = Instructor#(Course))
           Rank(Instructor) = "ASSISTANT PROFESSOR")
       PRINT Name(Student)

     FOR EACH Student SUCH THAT
       FOR SOME Course
       FOR SOME Enrollment
       FOR SOME Department
       FOR SOME Instructor
         Stud#(Student) = Stud#(Enrollment) AND
(c)      Course#(Enrollment) = Course#(Course) AND
         Dept#(Department) = Dept#(Course) AND
         Name(Department) = "EE" AND
         Instructor#(Instructor) = Instructor#(Course) AND
         Rank(Instructor) = "ASSISTANT PROFESSOR"
       PRINT Name(Student)

     RANGE OF S IS Student
     RANGE OF C IS Course
     RANGE OF E IS Enrollment
     RANGE OF D IS Department
     RANGE OF I IS Instructor
(d)  RETRIEVE S. Name WHERE
       S.Stud# = E.Stud# AND
       E.Course# = C.Course# AND
       D.Dept# = C. Dept# AND
       D.Name = "EE" AND
       I.Instructor# = C.Instructor# AND
       I.Rank = "ASSISTANT PROFESSOR"
```

Fig. 9. Steps in request translation.

appear as shown in Figure 9b. This query can be reorganized using simple syntactic transformations to arrive at the representation in Figure 9c. The corresponding QUEL query is shown in Figure 9d.

6.2 Database Networks

The notion of DAPLEX front ends can be adapted to provide an interface to a network of dissimilar database management systems, as illustrated in Figure 10. An isomorphic DAPLEX description is written for each of the local databases in

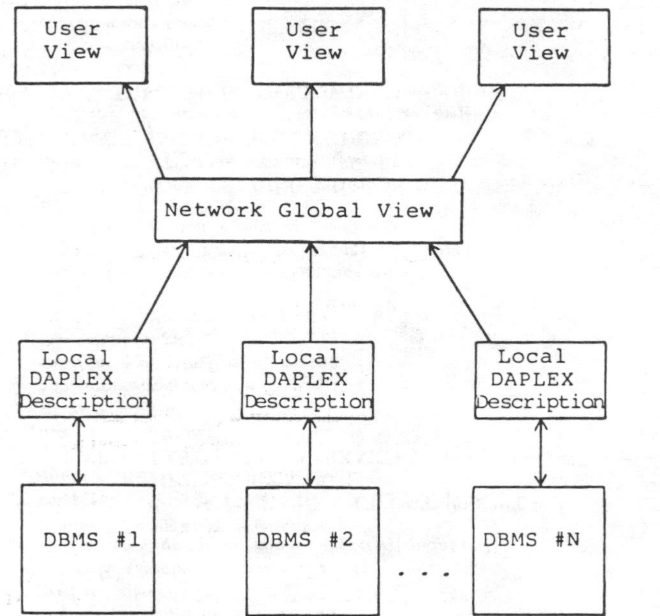

Fig. 10. Networked databases.

the network. These are then converted, via view mechanisms, into a common unified view of the entire network database. DAPLEX provides the global language by which this database is accessed. Individual user views may be defined over the global database as necessary.

7. CONCLUSION

The principal characteristics of DAPLEX can be summarized as follows:

(1) Data is modeled in terms of entities. Database entities are meant to bear a one-to-one correspondence to the "real-world" entities in the user's mental conception of reality.

(2) Relationships between data are expressed as functions, exploiting an established programming metaphor. Identical functional notation is used to reference both "primitive" and "derived" relationships. Conceptual conciseness is enhanced through the use of nested function reference. Functions may be multivalued, returning sets of entities.

(3) The request language is based on the notion of looping through entity sets. Expressions in the language are, in general, set valued. Sets are specified using the functional notation with special operators for qualification and quantification. A simple aggregation semantics, also based on looping, is incorporated. Looping variables are typically declared implicity.

(4) Computational power is provided through the general-purpose operators of a high-level language. While not emphasized in this paper, this capability is crucial to the development of realistic applications systems.

(5) Derived functions allow users to represent arbitrary entity relationships directly by defining them in terms of existing relationships. We have seen one example request (in Sections 3.4, 4.1, and 4.4) become progressively simpler through the introduction of appropriate derived functions. In effect, the derived function capability allows application semantics to be encoded into the data description, thereby allowing requests to be expressed directly in terms of those semantics. Updating of derived relationships is supported through procedures explicitly supplied by the user.

(6) Entity types are defined as functions taking no arguments. Notions of subtype and supertype follow naturally from this formulation.

(7) User views are implemented in terms of derived functions. It was shown how DAPLEX views may be constructed over existing databases represented in terms of traditional models, thus lending support to the use of DAPLEX as a "universal" database language for heterogeneous networked databases.

APPENDIX. SPECIFICATION OF DAPLEX

A1. Syntax

The DAPLEX syntax is described in terms of the syntax specification language proposed by Wirth [18]. To quote the original proposal describing the specification language:

> This meta language can therefore conveniently be used to define its own syntax, which may serve here as an example of its use. The word *identifier* is used to denote *nonterminal symbol*, and *literal* stands for *terminal symbol*. For brevity, *identifier* and *character cf1are not defined in further detail.*
>
> *syntax* = {*production*}.
> *production* = *identifier* "=" *expression* ".".
> *expression* = *term* {"|" *term*}.
> *term* = *factor* {*factor*}.
> *factor* = *identifier* | *literal* | "(" *expression* ")" | "[" *expression* "]" | "{" *expression* "}".
> *literal* = """" *character* {*character*} """".
>
> Repetition is denoted by curly brackets, i.e. {*a*} stands for $\epsilon|a|aa|aaa|\ldots$. Optionality is expressed by square brackets, i.e. [*a*] stands for $a|\epsilon$. Parentheses merely serve for grouping, e.g. $(a|b)c$ stands for $ac|bc$. Terminal symbols, i.e. literals, are enclosed in quote marks (and, if a quote mark appears as a literal itself, it is written twice), which is consistent with common practice in programming languages.

In Figure 11 we define the DAPLEX syntax itself.

A2. Semantics

A2.1 *Expressions*

***expr* = *set* | *singleton*.**

Expressions evaluate to either singletons or sets.

A2.1.1 *Sets.* The properties of a *set* are its value, role, order, and reference variable. Value, role, and order are discussed in Section 3.6. The reference variable

```
program = {statement}.
statement = declarative | imperative.
declarative = "DECLARE" funcspec ("⇒"|"⇛") expr [order]|
  "DEFINE" funcspec ("⇒"|"⇛")
    (expr|
    "INVERSE" "OF" funcspec) |
    "TRANSITIVE" "OF" expr |
    "COMPOUND" "OF" tuple |
    ("INTERSECTION"|"UNION") "OF" expr {"," expr} |
    "DIFFERENCE" "OF" expr "," expr |
    )[order].
  "DEFINE" "CONSTRAINT" funcspec "⇒" boolean|
  "DEFINE" "TRIGGER" funcspec "⇒" boolean imperative|
  "PERFORM" update "USING" imperative.
funcspec = funcid "(" [tuple] ")".
tuple = expr {"," expr}.
expr = set | singleton.
set = mvfuncall | typeid |
    "{" [singleton {"," singleton}] "}"|
    set "SUCH" "THAT" pred |
    set comp (singleton | quant set)|
    identifier IN set | expr AS typeid |
    "(" set ")" | gpset.
singleton = constant | vblid | svfuncall | aggcall | pred |
    "THE" set | "A" "NEW" typeid |
    "THE" set ("PRECEDING"|"FOLLOWING") singleton |
    "(" singleton ")" | gpsingleton.
svfuncall = funcall.
mvfuncall = funcall.
funcall = funcid "(" [tuple] ")".
aggcall = aggid "(" bag ")".
bag = expr | singleton "OVER" tuple.
pred = boolean |
    "FOR" (singleton | quant set) pred |
    (singleton | quant set) comp (singleton | quant set)|
    quant set ("EXIST"|"EXISTS").
comp = ">"|"<"|"="|"EQ"|"NE"|"LT"|"GT"|"LE"|"GE".
quant = "SOME"|"EVERY"|"NO"|
    ("AT" ("LEAST"|"MOST")|"EXACTLY") integer.
integer = singleton.
string = singleton.
boolean = singleton.
constant = int | str | bool.
int = digit {digit}.
str = """" character {character} """".
bool = "TRUE"|"FALSE".
imperative = forloop | update | gpimperative
forloop = "FOR" "EACH" set [order] imperative |
    "FOR" singleton imperative.
order = "IN" "ORDER"
      {"BY" [("ASCENDING"|"DESCENDING")] singleton}.
update = "LET" svfuncall "=" singleton |
    ("LET"|"INCLUDE"|"EXCLUDE") mvfuncall "=" expr |
    "INSERT" mvfuncall "=" (singleton | set [order])
        ("PRECEDING"|"FOLLOWING") singleton |
vblid = identifier.
typeid = identifier.
funcid = identifier.
aggid = identifier.
```

Fig. 11. DAPLEX syntactic specification.

is used as the formal parameter or looping variable corresponding to the *set*. In the syntactic specifications that follow, digit suffixes may be appended to symbols for purposes of reference.

set = mvfuncall.

Value: the *set* returned by the multivalued function application
Role: that of *mvfuncall*
Order: that of *mvfuncall*
Reference Variable: the *funcid* in the *mvfuncall*

set = typeid.

Value: the set of entities of this type (this usage is vald only when the *typeid* identifier is not currently bound as a reference variable)
Role: *typeid*
Order: that of the type
Reference Variable: *typeid*

set = "{" *singleton* { "," *singleton* } "}".

Value: a *set* consisting of the listed *singletons* (All *singletons* must have the same type)
Role: the type of the *singletons*
Order: the listed order
Reference Variable: none (if a reference variable is desired it must be explicitly declared using the IN operator)

set = set1 "SUCH" "THAT" *pred.*

Value: those members of *set1* for which *pred* is true (in evaluating *pred*, the reference variable is bound to the member of *set1* being tested)
Role, order, reference variable: that of *set1*

set = set1 comp singleton.

Value: those members of *set1* bearing the *comp* relationship to the *singleton*
Role, order, reference variable: that of *set1*

set = set1 comp quant set2.

Value: those members of *set1* bearing the *comp* relationship to the specified quantity of members of *set2* (in evaluating *set2*, the reference variable of *set1* is bound to the member under consideration)
Role, order, reference variable: that of *set1*

set = identifier "IN" *set1.*

Value, role, order: that of *set1*
Reference Variable: identifier

set = expr "AS" *typeid.*

Value: those members of *expr* which are of the specified type
Role: *typeid*
Order, reference variable: that of *expr*

set = "(" ***set1*** ")".

Value, role, order, reference variable: that of *set1* (this construct is used only for syntactic grouping)

set = ***gpset***.

gpset is a *set*-valued expression in the general-purpose syntax. Value, role, order, and reference variable are not specified here.

A2.1.2 *Singletons*. Only value, role, and reference variable need be specified for *singletons*, as the order is trivial.

singleton = ***constant***.

Value: that of the *constant*
Role: the type of the *constant*
Reference Variable: none

singleton = ***vblid***.

Value: *vblid* must be bound to a particular entity
Role: that of the *expr* for which this is the reference variable
Reference Variable: *vblid*

singleton = ***sufuncall*** | ***aggcall***.

Value: the entity returned by the single-valued function or aggregation application
Role: that of *sufuncall* or *aggcall*
Reference Variable: the *funcid* in the *sufuncall* or *aggid* in *aggcall*

singleton = ***pred***.

Value, role, reference variable: that of *pred*

singleton = "THE" ***set***.

Value: The single member of *set* (if *set* evaluates to more than one member an error is flagged)
Role, reference variable: that of *set*

singleton = "A" "NEW" ***typeid***.

Value: a new entity of the specified type
Role: *typeid*
Reference Variable: *typeid*

singleton = "THE" ***set*** ("PRECEDING" | "FOLLOWING") ***singleton***.

Value: the member of *set* preceding or following *singleton* according to the order of *set* (*singleton* must be a member of *set*)
Role, reference variable: that of *set*

singleton = "(" ***singleton*** ")".

Value, role, reference variable: that of *singleton*

singleton = ***gpsingleton***.

gpsingleton is an entity valued expression in the general-purpose syntax. Value, role, order, and reference variable are not specified here.

A2.1.3 *Predicates*. The role of all predicates is BOOLEAN, and there is no reference variable, thus only value needs to be specified.

pred = ***boolean***.

Value: that of the *boolean* constant or expression

pred = "FOR" ***singleton pred1***.

Value: that of *pred1* evaluated with *singleton*'s reference variable bound to the value of *singleton*

pred = "FOR" ***quant set pred1***.

Value: TRUE if *pred1* evaluates to true for the specified quantity of members of *set*, FALSE otherwise

pred = ***singleton1 comp singleton2***.

Value: TRUE if *singleton1* bears the *comp* relation to *singleton2*, FALSE otherwise (the reference variable of *singleton1* is bound to the value of *singleton1* during evaluation of *singleton2*)

pred = ***singleton comp quant set***.

Value: TRUE if *singleton* bears the *comp* relation to the specified quantity of members of *set*, FALSE otherwise (the reference variable of *singleton* is bound to the value of *singleton* during evaluation of *set*)

pred = ***quant set comp singleton***.

Value: TRUE if the specified quantity of members of *set* bear the relation *comp* to *singleton*, FALSE otherwise (the reference variable of *set* is bound to the member under consideration during the evaluation of *singleton*)

pred = ***quant set1 comp quant set2***.

Value: TRUE if the specified quantity of members of *set1* bears relation *comp* to the specified quantity of members of *set2*, FALSE otherwise (the reference variable of *set1* is bound to the member under consideration during the evaluation of *set2*, the scope of the first quantifier extends over that of the second)

pred = ***quant set*** ("EXIST" | "EXISTS").

Value: TRUE if the specified quantity of members of *set* exist, FALSE otherwise (note that this predicate is vacuously TRUE for the quantifier EVERY)

comp = ">"|"<"|"="|"EQ"|"NE"|"LT"|"GT"|"LE"|"GE".

The comparators >, <, LT, GT, LE, and GE require that their operands have the same role. In such cases the comparisons are with respect to that role's order. The operators =, EQ, and NE do not require their operands to have the same role. In such cases, the comparison is based solely on the values of the operands.

quant = "SOME"|"EVERY"|"NO"|
("AT" ("LEAST"|"MOST")|"EXACTLY") *integer*.

The quantifier semantics should be self-evident.

A2.1.4 *Miscellaneous Expressions*

svfuncall = *funcall*.
mvfuncall = *funcall*.
funcall = *funcid* "(" [*tuple*] ")".
tuple = *expr* {"," *expr*}.

svfuncalls are those invoking single-valued functions, *mvfuncalls* those invoking multivalued functions. The value returned by the *funcall* is the union of the results obtained by applying the function to each element of *tuple*. The elements of *tuple* are constructed in the following way. This method allows *exprs* in *tuple* to contain the reference variables of preceding *exprs*. First, the first *expr* is evaluated to return a set of entities. Then, for each member of the set, the reference variable for the first *expr* is bound to the member of the set and the second *expr* is evaluated. This continues until all of the constituent *exprs* have been processed. Note that when reference variables of preceding *exprs* are not present, *tuple* simply evaluates to the cross product of the *expr* sets. Example: The tuple "Student ( ),Course(Student)" refers to those student-course pairs for which the course is a course of the student.

The *funcid* and the roles of the argument *exprs* specify a particular internal function name. It is this function which is applied to the argument values. The internal function name is determined in the following manner in order to avoid ambiguous reference. First, the set is constructed consisting of all internal names which have the specified *funcid* and proper number of arguments and which are defined over the types or the supertypes of the types which are the roles of the argument *expr*. If this set is empty, the *funcall* is illegal (undefined). The designated internal name is that member, *M*, of this set such that, for every argument position, there exists no other member defined over some subtype of the type over which *M* is defined at that argument position. If there is no such *M*, then the function reference is illegal (ambiguous). Example: If "expr1" has role "type1," "expr2" has role "type2," "super1" is a supertype of "type1" but not of "type2," "super2" is a supertype of "type2" but not of "type1," and the only internal names are "[*F*(type1,super2)]" and "[*F*(super1,type2)]", then the reference "*F*(expr2,expr1)" is illegal (undefined) and the reference "*F*(expr1,expr2)" is illegal (ambiguous).

aggcall = *aggid* "(" *bag* ")".
bag = *expr* | *singleton* "OVER" *tuple*.

In the case of *expr*, each element of the *set* is passed to the aggregator specified by *aggid*. In the case of an OVER phrase, *singleton* is evaluated for each element of *tuple* and the result is passed to the aggregator. During evaluation of *singleton*, the reference variables for each constituent expression of *tuple* are bound to the corresponding element of the expression value.

A2.1.5 *Typed Expressions and Constants*

integer = *singleton1*.
string = *singleton2*.
boolean = *singleton3*.
constant = *int* | *str* | *bool*.
int = *digit* {*digit*}.
str = """" *character* {*character*} """".
bool = "TRUE" | "FALSE".

singleton1 must be of type INTEGER. *singleton2* must be of type STRING. *singleton3* must be of type BOOLEAN. *ints* have type INTEGER, *strs* STRING and *bools* BOOLEAN.

A2.2 *Statements*

program = {*statement*}.
statement = *declarative* | *imperative*.

programs consist of *statements* which are either *declaratives* or *imperatives*.

A2.2.1 *Declaratives*

declarative =
"DECLARE" *funcspec* ("⇒" | "⇒>") *expr* [*order*].
funcspec = *funcid* "(" [*tuple*] ")".

This declares primitive functions, which are directly updatable. If "⇒" is used, the function is single-valued; if "⇒>", it is multivalued. If the function takes arguments, the type of the function is the role of *expr*. If there are no arguments, the *funcid* is implicitly declared to be a *typeid* and the function has type *funcid*, which is considered a subtype of the role of *expr*. The order of the function is determined by *order*. The internal name of the function is constructed from the *funcid* and the roles of the *exprs* in *tuple*.

declarative =
"DEFINE" *funcspec* ("⇒" | "⇒>") *expr* [*order*].

This declares a derived function. The value of a derived function is computed on each invocation by evaluating *expr*. This evaluation is done with the reference variables of the *exprs* in *funcspec* bound to the corresponding actual arguments. Type, order and internal function name are determined as for actual primitive functions. It is not possible to directly update a derived function, however the PERFORM . . . USING construct allows such updates to be simulated.

declarative = "DEFINE" *funcspec1* ("⇒" | "⇒>")
"INVERSE" "OF" *funcspec2* [*order*].

funcspec1 and *funcspec2* must specify one-argument functions. The role of the argument *expr* in *funcspec1* must be the same as the type of *funcspec2*. The value of a *funcall* on the new function will be those entities which, when supplied as arguments to the function specified by *funcspec2*, return the actual argument in the *funcall*. The type of *funcspec1* is the role of the *expr* argument in *funcspec2*, and the default order is the order of that type.

declarative = "DEFINE" *funcspec* ("⇒" | "⇒>")
"TRANSITIVE" "OF" *expr* [*order*].

funcspec must involve exactly one argument which must have the same role as *expr*. *expr* must contain the reference variable for the formal argument in *funcspec*. The value of the defined function is the union of the values of *expr* evaluated with the reference variable bound to the actual function argument and to all other values which the function returns.

declarative = "DEFINE" *funcspec* ("⇒"|"⇒>")
"COMPOUND" "OF" *tuple* [*order*].

funcspec must specify a zero-argument function. The new type being defined will be a subtype of ENTITY and will include one entity for each element of *tuple*. For each *expr* component of *tuple*, the system will implicitly define an access function. The access function will map entities of the new type into the corresponding component of the tuple associated with the entity. The *funcid* of the access function is the reference variable of the corresponding *expr* in *tuple*.

declarative = "DEFINE" *funcspec* ("⇒"|"⇒>")
("INTERSECTION"|"UNION") "OF" *expr* {"," *expr*} [*order*].
declarative = "DEFINE" *funcspec* ("⇒"|"⇒>")
"DIFFERENCE" "OF" *expr* "," *expr* [*order*].

A derived function is declared. If the function takes arguments, then each of the *exprs* must be of the same type which becomes the type of the function. If the function takes no arguments, a new type is being defined. The function is of that type, which is considered to be a subtype of each of the roles of the *exprs*. The value of the function is the intersection, union or difference of the sets obtained by evaluating the *exprs*. In the case of functions which take arguments, this evaluation takes place with the reference variables of the *funcspec* arguments bound to the corresponding actual values.

declarative =
"DEFINE" "CONSTRAINT" *funcspec* "⇒" *boolean*.

The function is defined as if the keyword CONSTRAINT were not present. In addition, if any top-level statement (i.e., a program statement) completes with the function having the value FALSE for any arguments, the statement is aborted; that is, any updates it had performed are undone.

declarative =
"DEFINE" "TRIGGER" *funcspec* "⇒" *boolean imperative*.

The function is defined as if the keyword TRIGGER and the *imperative* were not present. In addition, whenever the function becomes TRUE for any arguments, *imperative* is executed. This execution is performed with the reference variables of the *funcspec* arguments bound to the entities for which the function has become true. When multiple triggers are activated, the order of execution of the corresponding *imperatives* is arbitrary.

declarative = "PERFORM" *update* "USING" *imperative*.

update specifies a statement which updates a derived function. *update* will contain a *funcspec* and a *vblid* which formally represents the value to which the derived function is to be set. *imperative* typically contains this *vblid* as well as the reference variable for the formal arguments of the *funcspec*. When an update statement is executed which corresponds to the format of update, then these variables are bound to the actual parameters appearing in the update statement and *imperative* is executed. The *imperative* would presumably effect the desired update to the derived function but this is not guaranteed nor is it checked for. Use of the A NEW operator against a derived type will have the effect of INCLUDEing the new entity in that type and all its supertypes. These implicit INCLUDEs also trigger a matching PERFORM . . . USING imperative.

A2.2.2 *Imperatives*

imperative = *forloop* | *update* | *gpimperative*.

The *gpimperatives* are imperative statements in the general-purpose language and are not further specified here.

forloop = "FOR" "EACH" *set* [*order*] *imperative*.

The *imperative* is executed for each member of *set* with the reference variable for *set* bound to that member. If *order* is supplied without any BY-phrases then the members of *set* are processed according to the order associated with *set*. If *order* is supplied with BY-phrases then the members of *set* are processed in the order specified by the BY-phrases. Otherwise, the order of processing is arbitrary.

forloop = "FOR" *singleton imperative*.

imperative is executed with the reference variable of *singleton* bound to the value of *singleton*.

update = "LET" *svfuncall* "=" *singleton*.

The value returned by the function referenced by *svfuncall* when applied to the actual arguments in *svfuncall* is changed to the value of *singleton*. The role of *singleton* and that of *svfuncall* must be the same.

update = ("LET"|"INCLUDE"|"EXCLUDE") *mvfuncall* "=" *expr*.

The value returned by the function referenced by *mvfuncall* when applied to the actual arguments in *mvfuncall* is changed. For LET, it becomes the value of *expr*. For INCLUDE, it becomes the union of the current value of *mvfuncall* and that of *expr*. For EXCLUDE, it becomes the difference of the current value of *mvfuncall* and that of *expr*. The role of *expr* and that of *mvfuncall* must be the same. If an update statement has the effect that some *funcall* returns an incorrect type, that *funcall* is illegal, and the situation must be corrected before the *program statement* is exited. No update statement for explicitly deleting entities from the database is provided, since entities are effectively deleted when they can no longer be referenced. This is typically done by excluding the entity from all of the types in which it participates.

update = "INSERT" *mvfuncall* "=" (*singleton1* | *set* [*order*])
("PRECEDING"|"FOLLOWING") *singleton2*.

mvfuncall must refer to an explicitly ordered function. The value of the *mvfuncall* becomes the union of its previous value and the value of *singleton1* or *set*. If a *set* is specified, the elements are partially ordered with respect to *singleton2* (which must be a current value of *mvfuncall*) as indicated by the

PRECEDING/FOLLOWING keyword. If *order* is supplied, then it specifies their new relative order within *mvfuncall*, otherwise they are mutually unordered. If any inserted elements are already being returned by *mvfuncall*, then they are reordered. The roles of *expr*, *singleton* and *mvfuncall* must be the same.

A2.2.3 *Orders*

order = "IN" "ORDER" {"BY" [("ASCENDING"|"DESCENDING")] *singleton*}.

The order syntax is used to specify a partial order for a *set*. When used in a function declaration or definition, the absence of a BY-phrase indicates that an explicitly ordered function is being defined. When used in a FOR EACH or INSERT statement, the absence of a BY-phrase indicates that the existing order associated with the *set* is to be used. When multiple BY-phrases are included, the first is the primary ordering, the second the secondary ordering, the third the tertiary ordering, etc. The partial order for each BY-phrase is determined by evaluating *singleton* for each member of the *set* with the reference variable for the *set* bound to that member. The relative order of the members of *set* is that of the relative order of the corresponding values of *singleton* relative to the order associated with *singleton*'s role. While *order* may specify a total order, it in general specifies a partial order. In the case of the FOR EACH statement and expressions involving PRECEDING/FOLLOWING or the *comp* operators, however, a total order is required. In these cases, the system supplies an arbitrary total order which conforms to the partial order. However, this total order is guaranteed not to change during the execution of any single statement.

ACKNOWLEDGMENTS

The author wishes to thank the many members of the Cambridge area database community for their helpful discussions and criticisms of the DAPLEX design. Special thanks are due Jim Rothnie for helping the author develop an understanding of the significance of the proposed approach and for his long-standing personal encouragement.

REFERENCES

1. Special Issue on Data-Base Management Systems. *ACM Comput. Surv. 8*, 1 (March 1976), 1–151.
2. Astrahan, M.M., et al. System R: Relational approach to database management. *ACM Trans. Database Syst. 1*, 2 (June 1976), 97–137.
3. Bachman, C.W., and Daya, M. The role concept in database models. *Proc. Int. Conf. Very Large Databases*, Tokyo, Japan, Oct. 1977, pp. 464–476.
4. Backus, J. Can programming be liberated from the von Neumann style? A functional style and its algebra of programs. *Commun. ACM 21*, 8 (Aug. 1978), 613–641.
5. Buneman, P., and Frankel, R.E. FQL—A functional query langauge. *Proc. ACM SIGMOD Conf.*, Boston, Mass., May–June 1979, pp. 52–58.
6. Chen, P.P.S. The entity-relationship model: Toward a unified view of data. *ACM Trans. Database Syst. 1*, 1 (March 1976), 9–36.
7. Codd, E.F. A relational model of data for large shared data banks. *Commun. ACM 13*, 6 (June 1970), 377–387.
8. Dayal, U., and Bernstein, P.A. On the updatability of relational views. *Proc. 4th Int. Conf. Very Large Databases*, Berlin, West Germany, Sept. 1978, pp. 368–377.
9. Hammer, M., and McLeod, D. The semantic data model: A modelling mechanism for database applications. *Proc. 1978 SIGMOD Conf.*, Austin, Tex., May 1978, pp. 26–35.
10. Kent, W. *Data and Reality*. North-Holland, Amsterdam, 1978.
11. Kent, W. Limitations of record-based information models. *ACM Trans. Database Syst. 4*, 1 (March 1979), 107–131.
12. McLeod, D. A semantic data base model and its associated structured user interface. Ph.D. Dissertation, Dep. Electrical Engineering and Computer Science, M.I.T., Cambridge, Mass., 1978.
13. Quillian, H.R. Semantic memory. In *Semantic Information Processing*, M. Minsky, Ed. M.I.T. Press, Cambridge, Mass., 1968.
14. Rowe, L., and Shoens, K. Data abstraction views and updates in RIGEL. *Proc. ACM SIGMOD Conf.*, Boston, Mass., May–June 1979, pp. 71–81.
15. Sibley, E.H., and Kershberg, L. Data architecture and data model considerations. *Proc. AFIPS Nat. Computer Conf.*, Dallas, Tex., June 1977, pp. 85–96.
16. Smith, J.M., and Smith, D.C.P. Database abstractions: Aggregation and generalization. *ACM Trans. Database Syst. 2*, 2 (June 1977), 105–133.
17. Stonebraker, M., Wong, E., Kreps, B., and Held, G. The design and implementation of INGRES. *ACM Trans. Database Syst. 1*, 3 (Sept. 1976), 189–222.
18. Wirth, N. What can we do about the unnecessary diversity of notation for syntactic definitions? *Commun. ACM 20*, 11 (Nov. 1977), 822–823.

Received March 1979; revised November 1979; accepted August 1980

Database Description with SDM: A Semantic Database Model

MICHAEL HAMMER
Massachusetts Institute of Technology
and
DENNIS McLEOD
University of Southern California

SDM is a high-level semantics-based database description and structuring formalism (database model) **for databases. This database model is designed to capture more of the meaning of an** application **environment than is possible with contemporary database models. An** SDM specification describes a **database in terms of the kinds of entities that exist in the application environment,** the classifications **and groupings of those entities, and the structural interconnections among them.** SDM provides a **collection of high-level modeling primitives to capture the semantics of an** application environment. **By accommodating derived information in a database structural specification,** SDM allows the same **information to be viewed in several ways; this makes it possible to directly** accommodate the variety **of needs and processing requirements typically present in database applications.** The design of the **present SDM is based on our experience in using a preliminary version of it.**

SDM is designed to enhance the effectiveness and usability of database systems. An SDM database **description can serve as a formal specification and documentation tool for a database;** it can provide **a basis for supporting a variety of powerful user interface facilities, it can serve as a conceptual database model in the database design process; and, it can be used as the database** model **for a new kind of database management system.**

Key Words and Phrases: database management, database models, database semantics, database definition, database modeling, logical database design
CR Categories: 3.73, 3.74, 4.33

1. INTRODUCTION

Every database is a *model* of some real world system. At all times, the contents of a database are intended to represent a snapshot of the state of an *application environment*, and each change to the database should reflect an event (or sequence of events) occurring in that environment. Therefore, it is appropriate that the structure of a database mirror the structure of the system that it models. A database whose organization is based on naturally occurring structures will be easier for a database designer to construct and modify than one that forces him to translate the primitives of his problem domain into artificial specification constructs. Similarly, a database user should find it easier to understand and employ a database if it can be described to him using concepts with which he is already familiar.

The global user view of a database, as specified by the database designer, is known as its (*logical*) *schema*. A schema is specified in terms of a database description and structuring formalism and associated operations, called a *database model*. We believe that the data structures provided by contemporary database models do not adequately support the design, evolution, and use of complex databases. These database models have significantly limited capabilities for expressing the meaning of a database and to relate a database to its corresponding application environment. The *semantics* of a database defined in terms of these mechanisms are not readily apparent from the schema; instead, the semantics must be separately specified by the database designer and consciously applied by the user.

Our goal is the design of a higher-level database model that will enable the database designer to naturally and directly incorporate more of the semantics of a database into its schema. Such a semantics-based database description and structuring formalism is intended to serve as a natural application modeling mechanism to capture and express the structure of the application environment in the structure of the database.

1.1 The Design of SDM

This paper describes *SDM*, a database description and structuring formalism that is intended to allow a database schema to capture much more of the meaning of a database than is possible with contemporary database models. SDM is designed to provide features for the natural modeling of database application environments. In designing SDM, we analyzed many database applications, in order to determine the structures that occur and recur in them, assessed the shortcomings of contemporary database models in capturing the semantics of these applications, and developed strategies to address the problems uncovered. This design process was iterative, in that features were removed, added, and modified during various stages of design. A preliminary version of SDM was discussed in [21]; however, this initial database model has further revised and restructured based on experience with its use. This paper presents a detailed specification of SDM, examines its applications, and discusses its underlying principles.

SDM has been designed with a number of specific kinds of uses in mind. First, SDM is meant to serve as a formal specification mechanism for describing the meaning of a database; an SDM schema provides a precise documentation and communication medium for database users. In particular, a new user of a large and complex database should find its SDM schema of use in determining what information is contained in the database. Second, SDM provides the basis for a variety of high-level semantics-based user interfaces to a database; these interface facilities can be constructed as front-ends to existing database management systems, or as the query language of a new database management system. Such

This research was supported in part by the Joint Services Electronics Program through the Air Force Office of Scientific Research (AFSC) under Contract F44620-76-C-0061, and, in part by the Advanced Research Projects Agency of the Department of Defense through the Office of Naval Research under Contract N00014-76-C-0944. The alphabetical listing of the authors indicates indistinguishably equal contributions and associated funding support.

Authors' addresses: M. Hammer, Laboratory for Computer Science, Massachusetts Institute of Technology, Cambridge, MA 02139; D. McLeod, Computer Science Department, University of Southern California, University Park, Los Angeles, CA 90007.

interfaces improve the process of identifying and retrieving relevant information from the database. For example, SDM has been used to construct a user interface facility for nonprogrammers [28]. Finally, SDM provides a foundation for supporting the effective and structured design of databases and database-intensive application systems.

SDM has been designed to satisfy a number of criteria that are not met by contemporary database models, but which we believe to be essential in an effective database description and structuring formalism [22]. They are as follows.

(1) The constructs of the database model should provide for the explicit specification of a large portion of the *meaning* of a database. Many contemporary database models (such as the CODASYL DBTG network model [11, 47] and the hierarchical model [48]) exhibit compromises between the desire to provide a user-oriented database organization and the need to support efficient database storage and manipulation facilities. By contrast, the relational database model [12, 13] stresses the separation of user-level database specifications and underlying implementation detail (data independence). Moreover, the relational database model emphasizes the importance of understandable modeling constructs (specifically, the nonhierarchic relation), and user-oriented database system interfaces [7, 8].

However, the *semantic expressiveness* of the hierarchical, network, and relational models is limited; they do not provide sufficient mechanism to allow a database schema to describe the meaning of a database. Such models employ overly simple data structures to model an application environment. In so doing, they inevitably lose information about the database; they provide for the expression of only a limited range of a designer's knowledge of the application environment [4, 36, 49]. This is a consequence of the fact that their structures are essentially all record-oriented constructs; the appropriateness and adequacy of the record construct for expressing database semantics is highly limited [17, 22–24, 27]. We believe that it is necessary to break with the tradition of record-based modeling, and to base a database model on structural constructs that are highly user oriented and expressive of the application environment. To this end, it is essential that the database model provide a rich set of features to allow the direct modeling of application environment semantics.

(2) A database model must support a *relativist* view of the meaning of a database, and allow the structure of a database to support alternative ways of looking at the same information. In order to accommodate multiple views of the same data and to enable the evolution of new perspectives on the data, a database model must support schemata that are flexible, potentially logically redundant, and integrated. *Flexibility* is essential in order to allow for multiple and coequal views of the data. In a *logically redundant* database schema, the values of some database components can be algorithmically derived from others. Incorporating such derived information into a schema can simplify the user's manipulation of a database by statically embedding in the schema data values that would otherwise have to be dynamically and repeatedly computed. Furthermore, the use of derived data can ease the development of new applications of the database, since new data required by these applications can often be readily adjoined to the existing schema. Finally, an *integrated* schema explicitly describes the relationships and similarities between multiple ways of viewing the same information. Without a degree of this critical integration, it is difficult to control the redundancy and to specify that the various alternative interpretations of the database are equivalent.

Contemporary, record-oriented database models do not adequately support relativism. In these models, it is generally necessary to impose a single structural organization of the data, one which inevitably carries along with it a particular interpretation of the data's meaning. This meaning may not be appropriate for all users of the database and may furthermore become entirely obsolete over time. For example, an association between two entities can legitimately be viewed as an attribute of the first entity, as an attribute of the second entity, or as an entity itself; thus, the fact that an officer is currently assigned as the captain of a ship could be expressed as an attribute of the ship (its current captain), as an attribute of the officer (his current ship), or as an independent (assignment) entity. A schema should make all three of these interpretations equally natural and direct. Therefore, the conceptual database model must provide a specification mechanism that simultaneously accommodates and integrates these three ways of looking at an assignment. Conventional database models fail to adequately achieve these goals.

Similarly, another consequence of the primacy of the principle of relativism is that, in general, the database model should not make rigid distinctions between such concepts as entity, association, and attribute. Higher-level database models that do require the database schema designer to sharply distinguish among these concepts (such as [9, 33]) are thus considered somewhat lacking in their support of relativism.

(3) A database model must support the definition of schemata that are *based on abstract entities*. Specifically, this means that a database model must facilitate the description of relevant *entities* in the application environment, *collections* of such entities, *relationships* (associations) among entities, and *structural interconnections* among the collections. Moreover, the entities themselves must be distinguished from their syntactic identifiers (*names*); the user-level view of a database should be based on actual entities rather than on artificial entity names.

Allowing entities to represent themselves makes it possible to directly reference an entity from a related one. In record-oriented database models, it is necessary to cross reference between related entities by means of their identifiers. While it is of course necessary to eventually represent "abstract" entities as symbols inside a computer, the point is that users (and application programs) should be able to reference and manipulate abstractions as well as symbols; internal representations to facilitate computer processing should be hidden from users.

Suppose, for example, that the schema should allow a user to obtain the entity that models a ship's current captain from the ship entity. To accomplish this, it would be desirable to define an attribute "Captain" that applies to every ship, and whose value is an officer. To model this information using a record-oriented database model, it is necessary to select some identifier of an officer record (e.g., last name or identification number) to stand as the value of the "Captain" attribute of a ship. For example, using the relational database model, we might have a relation SHIPS, one of whose attributes is Officer__name, and a relation

OFFICERS, which has Officer__name as a logical key. Then, in order to find the information about the captain of a given ship, it would be necessary to join relations SHIPS and OFFICERS on Officer__name; an explicit cross reference via identifiers is required. This forces the user to deal with an extra level of indirection and to consciously apply a join to retrieve a simple item of information.

In consequence of the fact that contemporary database models require such surrogates to be used in connections among entities, important types of semantic integrity constraints on a database are not directly captured in its schema. If these semantic constraints are to be expressed and enforced, additional mechanisms must be provided to supplement contemporary database models [6, 16, 19, 20, 45]. The problem with this approach is that these supplemental constraints are at best ad hoc, and do not integrate all available information into a simple structure. For example, it is desirable to require that only captains who are known in the database be assigned as officers of ships. To accomplish this in the relational database model, it is necessary to impose the supplemental constraint that each value of attribute Captain__name of SHIPS must be present in the Captain__name column of relation OFFICERS. If it were possible to simply state that each ship has a captain attribute whose value is an officer, this supplemental constraint would not be necessary.

The design of SDM has been based on the principles outlined above which are discussed at greater length in [22].

2. A SPECIFICATION OF SDM

The following general principles of database organization underlie the design of SDM.

(1) A database is to be viewed as a collection of *entities* that correspond to the actual objects in the application environment.
(2) The entities in a database are organized into *classes* that are meaningful collections of entities.
(3) The classes of a database are not in general independent, but rather are logically related by means of *interclass connections*.
(4) Database entities and classes have *attributes* that describe their characteristics and relate them to other database entities. An attribute value may be derived from other values in the database.
(5) There are several primitive ways of defining interclass connections and derived attributes, corresponding to the most common types of information redundancy appearing in database applications. These facilities integrate multiple ways of viewing the same basic information, and provide building blocks for describing complex attributes and interclass relationships.

2.1 Classes

An *SDM database* is a collection of entities that are organized into classes. The structure and organization of an SDM database is specified by an *SDM schema*, which identifies the classes in the database. Appendix A contains an example SDM schema for a portion of the "tanker monitoring application environment"; a specific syntax (detailed in Appendix B) is used for expressing this schema. Examples in this paper are based on this application domain, which is concerned with monitoring and controlling ships with potentially hazardous cargoes (such as oil tankers), as they enter U.S. coastal waters and ports. A database supporting this application would contain information on ships and their positions, oil tankers and their inspections, oil spills, ships that are banned from U.S. waters, and so forth.

Each class in an SDM schema has the following features.

(1) A *class name* identifies the class. Multiple synonymous names are also permitted. Each class name must be unique with respect to all class names used in a schema. For notational convenience in this paper, class names are strings of uppercase letters and special characters (e.g., OIL__TANKERS), as shown in Appendix A.

(2) The class has a collection of *members*: the entities that constitute it. The phrases "the members of a class" and "the entities in a class" are thus synonymous. Each class in an SDM schema is a homogeneous collection of one type of entity, at an appropriate level of abstraction.

The entities in a class may correspond to various kinds of objects in the application environment. These include objects that may be viewed by users as:

(a) concrete objects, such as ships, oil tankers, and ports (in Appendix A, these are classes SHIPS, OIL__TANKERS, and PORTS, respectively);
(b) events, such as ship accidents (INCIDENTS) and assignments of captains to ships (ASSIGNMENTS);
(c) higher-level entities such as categorizations (e.g., SHIP__TYPES) and aggregations (e.g., CONVOYS) of entities;
(d) names, which are syntactic identifiers (strings), such as the class of all possible ship names (SHIP__NAMES) and the class of all possible calendar dates (DATES).

Although it is useful in certain circumstances to label a class as containing "concrete objects" or "events" [21], in general the principle of relativism requires that no such fixed specification be included in the schema; for example, inspections of ships (INSPECTIONS) could be considered to be either an event or an object, depending upon the user's point of view. In consequence, such distinctions are not directly supported in SDM. Only name classes (classes whose members are names) contain data items that can be transmitted into and out of a database, for example, names are the values that may be entered by, or displayed to, a user. Nonname classes represent abstract entities from the application environment.

(3) An (optional) textual *class description* describes the meaning and contents of the class. A class description should be used to describe the specific nature of the entities that constitute a class and to indicate their significance and role in the application environment. For example, in Appendix A, class SHIPS has a description indicating that the class contains ships with potentially hazardous cargoes that may enter U.S. coastal waters. Tying this documentation directly to schema entries makes it accessible and consequently more valuable.

(4) The class has a collection of attributes that describe the members of that class or the class as a whole. There are two types of attributes, classified according to *applicability*.

(a) A *member attribute* describes an aspect of each member of a class by logically connecting the member to one or more related entities in the same or another class. Thus a member attribute is used to describe each member of some class. For example, each member of class SHIPS has attributes Name, Captain, and Engines, which identify the ship's name, its current captain, and its engines (respectively).

(b) A *class attribute* describes a property of a class taken as a whole. For example, the class INSPECTIONS has the attribute Number, which identifies the number of inspections currently in the class; the class OIL__TANKERS has the attribute Absolute__legal__top__speed which indicates the absolute maximum speed any tanker is allowed to sail.

(5) The class is either a *base class* or a *nonbase class.* A base class is one that is defined independently of all other classes in the database; it can be thought of as modeling a primitive entity in the application environment, for example, SHIPS. Base classes are mutually disjoint in that every entity is a member of exactly one base class. Of course, at some level of abstraction all entities are members of class "THINGS"; SDM provides the notion of base class to explicitly support cutting off the abstraction below that most general level. (If it is desired that all entities in a database be members of some class, then a single base class would be defined in the schema.)

A nonbase class is one that does not have independent existence; rather, it is defined in terms of one or more other classes. In SDM, classes are structurally related by means of *interclass connections.* Each nonbase class has associated with it one interclass connection. In the schema definition syntax shown in Appendix A, the existence of an interclass connection for a class means that it is nonbase; if no interclass connection is present, the class is a base class. In Appendix A, OIL__TANKERS is an example of a nonbase class; it is defined to be a subclass of SHIPS which means that its membership is always a subset of the members of SHIPS.

(6) If the class is a base class, it has an associated list of groups of member attributes; each of these groups serves as a logical key to uniquely identify the members of a class (*identifiers*). That is, there is a one-to-one correspondence between the values of each identifying attribute or attribute group and the entities in a class. For example, class SHIPS has the unique identifier Name, as well as the (alternative) unique identifier Hull__number.

(7) If the class is a base class, it is specified as either *containing duplicates* or *not containing duplicates.* (The default is that duplicates are allowed; in the schema syntax used in Appendix A, "duplicates not allowed" is explicitly stated to indicate that a class may not contain duplicate members.) Stating that duplicates are not allowed amounts to requiring the members of the class to have some difference in their attribute values; "duplicates not allowed" is explicit shorthand for requiring all of the member attributes of a class taken together to constitute a unique identifier.

2.2 Interclass Connections

As specified above, a nonbase class has an associated interclass connection that defines it. There are two main types of interclass connections in SDM: the first allows subclasses to be defined and the second supports grouping classes. These interclass connection types are detailed as follows.

2.2.1 *The Subclass Connection.* The first type of interclass connection specifies that the members of a nonbase class (S) are of the same basic entity type as those in the class to which S is related (via the interclass connection). This type of interclass connection is used to define a subclass of a given class. A *subclass* S of a class C (called the *parent class*) is a class that contains some, but not necessarily all, of the members of C. The very same entity can thus be a member of many classes, for example, a given entity may simultaneously be a member of the classes SHIPS, OIL__TANKERS, and MERCHANT__SHIPS. (However, only one of these may be a base class.) This is the concept of "subtype" [21, 25, 31, 32, 41] which is missing from most database models (in which a record belongs to exactly one file).

In SDM, a subclass S is defined by specifying a class C and a predicate P on the members of C; S consists of just those members of C that satisfy P. Several types of predicates are permissible.

(1) A predicate on the member attributes of C can be used to indicate which members of C are also members of S. A subclass defined by this technique is called an *attribute-defined subclass.* For example, the class MERCHANT__SHIPS is defined (in Appendix A) as a subclass of SHIPS by the member attribute predicate "where Type = 'merchant'"; that is, a member of SHIPS is a member of MERCHANT__SHIPS if the value of its attribute Type is "merchant." (A detailed discussion of member attribute predicates is provided in what follows. The usual comparison operators and Boolean connectives are allowed.)

(2) The predicate "where specified" can be used to define S as a *user-controllable subclass* of C. This means that S contains at all times only entities that are members of C. However, unlike an attribute-defined subclass, the definition of S does not identify which members of C are in S; rather, database users "manually" add to (and delete from) S, so long as the subclass limitation is observed. For example, BANNED__SHIPS is defined as a "where specified" subclass of "SHIPS"; this allows some authority to ban a ship from U.S. waters (and possibly later rescind that ban).

An essential difference between attribute-defined subclasses and user-controllable subclasses is that the membership of the former type of subclass is determined by other information in the database, while the membership of the latter type of subclass is directly and explicitly controlled by users. It would be possible to simulate the effect of a user-controllable subclass by an attribute-defined subclass, through the introduction of a dummy member attribute of the parent class whose sole purpose is to specify whether or not the entity is in the subclass. Subclass membership could then be predicated on the value of this attribute. However, this would be a confusing and indirect method of capturing the semantics of the application environment; in particular, there are cases in which the method of determining subclass membership is beyond the scope of the database schema (e.g., by virtue of being complex).

(3) A subclass definition predicate can specify that the members of subclass S are just those members of C that also belong to two other specified data-

base classes (C_1 and C_2); this provides a class *intersection* capability. To insure a type-compatible intersection, C_1 and C_2 must both be subclasses of C, either directly or through a series of subclass relationships. For example, the class BANNED__OIL__TANKERS is defined as the subclass of SHIPS that contains those members common to the classes OIL__TANKERS and BANNED__SHIPS.

In addition to an intersection capability, a subclass can be defined by class *union* and *difference*. A union subclass contains those members of C in either C_1 or C_2. For example, class SHIPS__TO__BE__MONITORED is defined as a subclass of SHIPS with the predicate "where is in BANNED__SHIPS or is in OIL__TANKERS__REQUIRING__INSPECTION." A difference subclass contains those members of C that are not in C_1. For example, class SAFE__SHIPS is defined as the subclass of SHIPS with the predicate "where is not in BANNED__SHIPS."

The intersection, union, and difference subclass definition primitives allow *set-operator-defined subclasses* to be specified; these primitives are provided because they often represent the most natural means of defining a subclass. Moreover, these operations are needed to effectively define subclasses of user-controllable subclasses. For example, class intersection (rather than a member attribute predicate) must be used to define class SHIPS__TO__BE__MONITORED; since BANNED__SHIPS and OIL__TANKERS__REQUIRING__INSPECTION are both user-controllable subclasses, no natural member attributes of either of these classes could be used to state an appropriate defining member attribute predicate for SHIPS__TO__BE__MONITORED.

(4) The final type of subclass definition allows a subclass S to be defined as consisting of all of the members of C that are currently values of some attribute A of another class C_1. That is, class S contains all of the members of C that are a value of A. This type of class is called an *existence subclass*. For example, class DANGEROUS__CAPTAINS is defined as the subclass of OFFICERS satisfying the predicate "where is a value of Involved__captain of INCIDENTS"; this specifies that DANGEROUS__CAPTAINS contains all officers who have been involved in an incident.

2.2.2 *The Grouping Connection.* The other type of interclass connection allows for the definition of a nonbase class, called a *grouping class* (G), whose members are of a higher-order entity type than those in the underlying class (U). A grouping class is *second order*, in the sense that its members can themselves be viewed as classes; in particular, they are classes whose members are taken from U.

The following options are available for defining a grouping class.

(1) The grouping class G can be defined as consisting of all classes formed by collecting the members of U into classes based on having a common value for one or more designated member attributes of U (an *expression-defined grouping class*). A *grouping expression* specifies how the members of U are to be placed into these groups. The groups formed in this way become the members of G, and the members of a member of G are called its *contents*. For example, class SHIP__TYPES in Appendix A is defined as a grouping class of SHIPS with the grouping expression "on common value of Type". The members of SHIP__TYPES are not ships, but rather are groups of ships. In particular, the intended interpretation of SHIP__TYPES is as a collection of types of ships, whose instances are the contents (members) of the groups that constitute SHIP__TYPES. This kind of grouping class represents an abstraction of the underlying class. That is, the elements of the grouping class correspond in a sense to the shared property of the entities that are its contents, rather than to the collection of entities itself.

If the grouping expression used to define a grouping class involves only a single-valued attribute, then the groups partition the underlying class; this is the case for SHIP__TYPES. However, if a multivalued attribute is involved, then the groups may have overlapping contents. For example, the class CARGO__TYPE__GROUPS can be defined as a grouping class on SHIPS with the grouping expression "on common value of Cargo__types"; since Cargo__types is multivalued, a given ship may be in more than one cargo type category. Although the grouping mechanism is limited to single grouping expressions (namely, on common value of one or more member attributes), complex grouping criteria are possible via derived attributes (as discussed in what follows).

It should be clear that the contents of a group are a subclass of the class underlying the grouping. The grouping expression used to define a grouping class thus corresponds to a collection of attribute-defined subclass definitions. For example, for SHIP__TYPES, the grouping expression "on common value of Type" corresponds to the collection of subclass member attribute predicates (on SHIPS) "Type = 'merchant'," "Type = 'fishing'," and "Type = 'military'." Some or all of these subclasses may be independently and explicitly defined in the schema. In Appendix A, the class MERCHANT__SHIPS is defined as a subclass of SHIPS, and it is also listed in the definition of SHIP__TYPES as a class that is explicitly defined in the database ("groups defined as classes are MERCHANT__SHIPS"). In general, when a grouping class is defined, a list of the names of the groups that are explicitly defined in the schema is to be included in the specification of the interclass connection; the purpose of this list is to relate the groups to their corresponding subclasses in the schema.

(2) A second way to define a grouping class G is by providing a list of classes ($C_1, C_2, \ldots, C_n$) that are defined in the schema; these classes are the members of the grouping class (an *enumerated grouping class*). Each of the classes ($C_1, C_2, \ldots, C_n$) must be explicitly defined in the schema as an (eventual) subclass of the class U that is specified as the class underlying the grouping. This grouping class definition capability is useful when no appropriate attribute is available for defining the grouping and when all of the groups are themselves defined as classes in the schema. For example, a class TYPES__OF__HAZARDOUS__SHIPS can be defined as "grouping of SHIPS consisting of classes BANNED__SHIPS, BANNED__OIL__TANKERS, and SHIPS__TO__BE__MONITORED."

(3) A grouping class G can be defined to consist of user-controllable subclasses of some underlying class (a *user-controllable grouping class*). In effect, a user-controllable grouping class consists of a collection of user-controllable subclasses. For example, class CONVOYS is defined as a grouping of SHIPS "as specified." In this case, no attribute exists to allow the grouping of ships into convoys and individual convoys are not themselves defined as classes in the schema; rather, each member of CONVOYS is a user-controllable group of ships that users may

add to or delete from. This kind of grouping class models simple "aggregates" over a base class: arbitrary collections of entities manipulated by users.

2.2.3 *Multiple Interclass Connections.* As specifed above, each nonbase class in an SDM schema has a single interclass connection associated with it. While it is meaningful and reasonable in some cases to associate more than one interclass connection with a nonbase class, the uncontrolled use of such multiple interclass connections could introduce undesirable complexity into a schema. In consequence, only a single interclass connection (the most natural one) should be used to define a nonbase class.

To illustrate this point, consider for example the class RURITANIAN__OIL__TANKERS. Clearly, this class could be specified as an attribute-defined subclass of OIL__TANKERS (by the interclass connection "subclass of OIL__TANKERS where Country.Name = 'Ruritania'"), or as a subclass of RURITANIAN__SHIPS (by the interclass connection "subclass of RURITANIAN__SHIPS where Cargo__types contains 'oil'"); these definitions are, in a sense, semantically equivalent. The possibility of allowing multiple (semantically equivalent) interclass connections to be specified for a nonbase class was considered, but it was determined that such a feature could introduce considerable complexity: The mechanism could be used to force two class definitions that are not semantically equivalent to define classes with the same members. For example, one could associate interclass connections that define the class of all Ruritanian ships and the class of all dangerous ships with a single class, intending to force the sets of members of these two possibly independent collections to be the same. In sum, without a carefully formulated and powerful notion of semantic equivalence [30], it was determined that multiple interclass connections for a nonbase class should not be allowed in SDM. Of course, multiple class names and judiciously selected class descriptions can be used to convey additional definitions, for example, naming a class BANNED__SHIPS and RURITANIAN__OIL__TANKERS to indicate that the two sets of ships are intended to be one and the same.

2.3 Name Classes

Entities are application constructs that are directly modeled in an SDM schema. In the real world, entities can be denoted in a number of ways; for example, a particular ship can be identified by giving its name or its hull number, by exhibiting a picture of it, or by pointing one's finger at the ship itself. Operating entirely within SDM, the typical way of referencing an entity is by means of an entity-valued attribute that gives access to the entity itself. However, there must also be some mechanism that allows for the outside world (i.e., users) to communicate with an SDM database. This will typically be accomplished by data being entered or displayed on a computer terminal. However, one cannot enter or display a real entity on such a terminal; it is necessary to employ representations of them for that purpose. These representations are called SDM *names*. A name is any string of symbols that denotes an actual value encountered in the application environment; the strings "red," "128," "8/21/78," and "321-004" are all names. A name class in SDM is a collection of strings, namely, a subclass of the built-in class STRINGS (which consists of all strings over the basic set of alphanumeric characters).

Every SDM name class is defined by means of the interclass connection "subclass." The following methods of defining a class S of names are available.

(1) The class S can be defined as the intersection, union, or difference of two other name classes.
(2) The class S can be defined as a subclass of some other name class C with the predicate "where specified," which means that the members of S belong to C, but must be explicitly enumerated. In Appendix A class COUNTRY__NAMES is defined in this way.
(3) A predicate can be used to define S as a subclass of C. The predicate specifies the subset of C that constitutes S by indicating constraints on the format of the acceptable data values. In Appendix A, classes ENGINE__SERIAL__NUMBERS, DATES, and CARGO__TYPE__NAMES are defined in this way. CARGO__TYPE__NAMES has no format constraints, indicating that all strings are valid cargo type names. ENGINE__SERIAL__NUMBERS and DATES do have constraints that indicate the patterns defining legal members of these classes. Note that for convenience, the particular name classes NUMBERS, INTEGERS, REALS, and YES/NO (Booleans) are also built into SDM; these classes have obvious definitions. (Further details of the format specification language used here are presented in [26].)

2.4 Attributes

As stated above, each class has an associated collection of attributes. Each attribute has the following features.

(1) An *attribute name* identifies the attribute. An attribute name must be unique with respect to the set of all attribute names used in the class, the class's underlying base class, and all eventual subclasses of that base class. (As decribed in [30], this means that attribute names must be unique within a "family" of classes; this is necessary to support the attribute inheritance rules described in what follows.) As with class names, multiple synonymous attribute names are permitted. For notational convenience in this paper, attribute names are written as one uppercase letter followed by a sequence of lowercase letters and special characters (e.g., the attribute Cargo__types of class SHIPS), as shown in Appendix A.
(2) The attribute has a *value* which is either an entity in the database (a member of some class) or a collection of such entities. The value of an attribute is selected from its underlying *value class*, which contains the permissible values of the attribute. Any class in the schema may be specified to be the value class of an attribute. For example, the value class of member attribute Captain of SHIPS is the class OFFICERS. The value of an attribute may also be the special value *null* (i.e., no value).
(3) The *applicability* of the attribute is specified by indicating that the attribute is either:

    (a) a member attribute, which applies to each member of the class, and so has a value for each member (e.g., Name of SHIPS); or
    (b) a class attribute, which applies to a class as a whole, and has only one value for the class (e.g., Number of INSPECTIONS).

(4) An (optional) *attribute description* is text that describes the meaning and purpose of the attribute. For example, in Appendix A, the description of Captain of SHIPS indicates that the value of the attribute is the current captain of the ship. (This serves as an integrated form of database documentation.)

(5) The attribute is specified as either *single valued* or *multivalued.* The value of a single-valued attribute is a member of the value class of the attribute, while the value of a multivalued attribute is a subclass of the value class. Thus, a multivalued attribute itself defines a class, that is, a collection of entities. In Appendix A, the class OIL_TANKERS has the single-valued member attribute Hull_type and the multivalued member attribute Inspections. (In the schema definition syntax used in Appendix A, the default is single valued.) It is possible to place a constraint on the size of a multivalued attribute, by specifying "multivalued with size between X and Y," where X and Y are integers; this means that the attribute must have between X and Y values. For example, attribute Engines of SHIPS is specified as "multivalued with size between 0 and 10"; this means that a SHIP has between 0 and 10 engines.

(6) An attribute can be specified as *mandatory*, which means that a null value is not allowed for it. For example, attribute Hull_number of SHIPS is specified as "may not be null"; this models the fact that every SHIP has a Hull_number.

(7) An attribute can be specified as *not changeable*, which means that once set to a nonnull value, this value cannot be altered except to correct an error. For example, attribute Hull_number of SHIPS is specified as "not changeable."

(8) A member attribute can be required to be *exhaustive* of its value class. This means that every member of the value class of the attribute (call it A) must be the A value of some entity. For example, attribute Engines of SHIPS "exhausts value class," which means that every engine entity must be an engine of some ship.

(9) A multivalued member attribute can be specified as *nonoverlapping* which means that the values of the attribute for two different entities have no entities in common; that is, each member of the value class of the attribute is used at most once. For example, Engines of SHIPS is specified as having "no overlap in values," which means that any engine can be in only one ship.

(10) The attribute may be related to other attributes, and/or defined in terms of other information in the schema. The possible types of such relationships are different for member and class attributes, and are detailed in what follows.

2.4.1 *Member Attribute Interrelationships.* The first way in which a pair of member attributes can be related is by means of inversion. Member attribute A_1 of class C_1 can be specified as the *inverse* of member attribute A_2 of C_2 which means that the value of A_1 for a member M_1 of C_1 consists of those members of C_2 whose value of A_2 is M_1. The inversion interattribute relationship is specified symmetrically in that both an attribute and its inverse contain a description of the inversion relationship. A pair of inverse attributes in effect establish a binary association between the members of the classes that the attributes modify. (Although all attribute inverses could theoretically be specified, if only one of a pair of such attributes is relevant, then it is the only one that is defined in the schema, that is to say, no inverse specification is provided.) For example, attribute Ships_registered_here of COUNTRIES is specified in Appendix A as the inverse of attribute Country_of_registry of SHIPS; this establishes the fact that both are ways of expressing in what country a ship is registered. This is accomplished by

(1) specifying that the value class of attribute Country_of_registry of SHIPS is COUNTRIES, and that its inverse is Ships_registered_here (of COUNTRIES);

(2) specifying that the value class of attribute Ships_registered_here of COUNTRIES is SHIPS, and that its inverse is Country_of_registry (of SHIPS).

The second way in which a member attribute can be related to other information in the database is by *matching* the value of the attribute with some member(s) of a specified class. In particular, the value of the match attribute A_1 for the member M_1 of class C_1 is determined as follows.

(1) A member M_2 of some (specified) class C_2 is found that has M_1 as its value of (specified) member attribute A_2.

(2) The value of (specified) member attribute A_3 for M_2 is used as the value of A_1 for M_1.

If A_1 is a multivalued attribute, then it is permissible for each member of C_1 to match to several members of C_2; in this case, the collection of A_3 values is the value of attribute A_1. For example, a matching specification indicates that the value of the attribute Captain for a member S of class SHIPS is equal to the value of attribute Officer of the member A of class ASSIGNMENTS whose Ship value is S.

Inversion and matching provide multiple ways of viewing n-ary associations among entities. Inversion permits the specification of binary associations, while matching is capable of supporting binary and higher degree associations. For example, suppose it is necessary to establish a ternary association among oil tankers, countries, and dates, to indicate that a given tanker was inspected in a specified country on a particular date. To accomplish this, a class could be defined (say, COUNTRY_INSPECTIONS) with three attributes: Tanker_inspected, Country, and Date_inspected. Matching would then be used to relate these to appropriate attributes of OIL_TANKERS, COUNTRIES, and DATES that also express this information. Inversions could also be specified to relate the relevant member attributes of OIL_TANKERS (e.g., Countries_in_which_inspected), COUNTRIES (e.g., Tankers_inspected_here), DATES, and COUNTRY_INSPECTIONS (see Figure 1).

The combined use of inversion and matching allows an SDM schema to accommodate relative viewpoints of an association. For instance, one may view the ternary relationship in the above example as an inspection entity (a member of class COUNTRY_INSPECTIONS), or as a collection of attributes of the entities that participate in the association. Similarly, a binary relationship defined as a pair of inverse attributes could also be viewed as an association entity, with matching used to relate that entity to the relevant attributes of the associated entities [30].

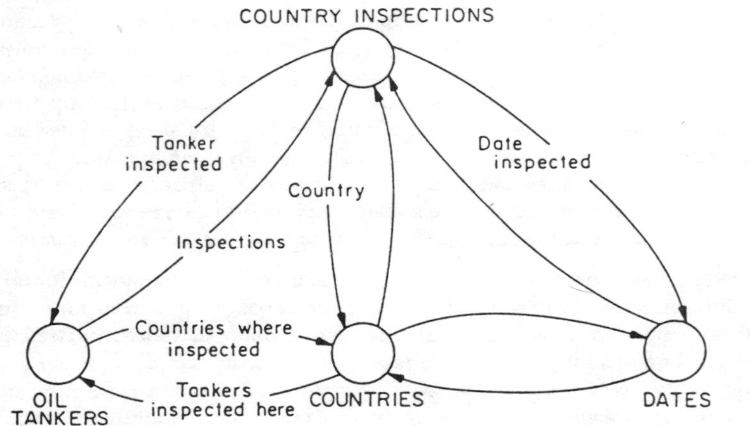

Fig. 1. Multiple perspectives on the "Country Inspections" association. Circles denote classes and are labeled with class names. Arrows denote member attributes, labeled by name, with the arrowhead pointing to the attribute's value class. For brevity, only some of the possible attributes are named (as would be the case in many real SDM schemata).

2.4.1.1 *Member Attribute Derivations.* As described above, inversion and matching are mechanisms for establishing the equivalence of different ways of viewing the same essential relationships among entities. SDM also provides the ability to define an attribute whose value is calculated from other information in the database. Such an attribute is called *derived*, and the specification of its computation is its associated *derivation*.

The approach we take to defining derived attributes is to provide a small vocabulary of high-level attribute derivation primitives that directly model the most common types of derived information. Each of these primitives provides a way of specifying one method of computing a derived attribute. More general facilities are available for describing attributes that do not match any of these cases: A complex derived attribute is defined by first describing other attributes that are used as building blocks in its definition and then applying one of the primitives to these building blocks. For example, attribute Superiors of OFFICERS is defined by a derivation primitive applied to attribute Commander, and in turn, attribute Contacts is defined by a derivation primitive applied to Superiors and Subordinates. This procedure can be repeated for the building block attributes themselves, so that arbitrarily complex attribute derivations can be developed.

2.4.1.2 *Mappings.* Before discussing the member attribute derivation primitives, it is important to present the concept of *mapping*. A mapping is a concatenation of attribute names that allows a user to directly reference the value of an attribute of an attribute. A mapping is written, in general, as a sequence of attribute names separated by quotation marks. For example, consider the mapping "Captain.Name" for class SHIPS. The value of this mapping, for each member S of SHIPS, is the value of attribute Name of that member O of OFFICERS that is the value of Captain for S. In this case, the attributes Captain of SHIPS and Name of OFFICERS are single valued; in general, this need not be the case. For example, consider the mapping for SHIPS "Engines. Serial__number." Attribute Engines is multivalued which means that "Engines. Serial__number" may also be multivalued. This mapping evaluates to the serial numbers of the engines of a ship. Similarly, the mapping for SHIPS "Captain.Superiors.Name" evaluates to the names of all of the superiors of the captain of a ship. This mapping is multivalued since at least one of the steps in the mapping involves a multivalued attribute. The value of a mapping "$X.Y.Z$," where X, Y, and Z are multivalued attributes, is the class containing each value of Z that corresponds to a value of Y for some value of X.

2.4.1.3 *Member Derivation Primitives.* The following primitives are provided to express the derivation of the value of a member attribute; here, attribute A_1 of member M_1 of class C_1 is being defined in terms of the relationship of M_1 to other information in the database.

(1) A_1 can be defined as an *ordering* attribute. In this case, the value of A_1 denotes the sequential position of M_1 in C_1 when C_1 is ordered by one or more other specified (single-valued) member attributes (or mappings) of C_1. Ordering is by increasing or decreasing value (the default is increasing). For example, the attribute Seniority of OFFICERS has the derivation "order by Date__commissioned." The OFFICER with the earliest date commissioned will then have Seniority value of 1. Ordering within groups is also possible: "order by A_2 within A_3" specifies that the value of A_1 is the sequential position of M_1 within the group of entities that have the same value of A_3 as M_1, as ordered by the value of A_2. (A_2 and A_3 may be mappings as well as attributes.) For example, attribute Order__for__tanker of INSPECTIONS has the derivation "order by decreasing Date within Tanker," which orders the inspections for each tanker. The value class of an ordering attribute is INTEGERS.

(2) The value of attribute A_1 can be declared to be a Boolean value that is "yes" (true) if M_1 is a member of some other specified class C_2, and "no" (false) otherwise. Thus, the value class of this *existence* attribute is YES/NO. For example, attribute Is__tanker__banned? of class OIL__TANKERS has the derivation "if in BANNED__SHIPS."

(3) The value of attribute A_1 can be defined as the result of combining all the entities obtained by recursively tracing the values of some attribute A_2. For instance, attribute Superiors of OFFICERS has the derivation "all levels of values of Commander"; the value of the attribute includes the immediate commander of the officer, his commander's superiors, and so on. Note that the value class of Commander is OFFICERS; this must be true for this kind of recursive attribute derivation to be meaningful. It is also possible to specify a maximum number of levels over which to repeat the recursion, namely, "up to N levels" where N is an integer constant; this would be useful, for example, to relate an officer to his subordinates and their subordinates.

(4) When a grouping class is defined, the derived multivalued member attribute *Contents* is automatically established. The value of this attribute is the

collection of members (of the class underlying the grouping) that form the contents of that member. For example, each member of the grouping class SHIP__TYPES has as the value of its Contents attribute the class of all ships of the type in question.

(5) The value of a member attribute can be specified to be derived from and equal to the value of some other attribute or mapping. For instance, attribute Date__last__examined of OIL__TANKERS has the derivation "same as Last__inspection.Date." (Note that this, in effect, introduces a member attribute as shorthand for a mapping.)

(6) Attribute A_1 can be defined as a *subvalue* attribute of some other (multivalued) member attribute or mapping (A_2). The value of A_2 is specified as consisting of a subclass of the value of A_1 that satisfies some specified predicate. For example, attribute Last__two__inspections of class OIL__TANKERS is defined as "subvalue of Inspections where Order__for__tanker ≤ 2."

(7) The value of a member attribute can be specified as the intersection, union, or difference of two other (multivalued) member attributes or mappings. For example, attribute Contacts of OFFICERS has the definition "where is in Superiors or is in Subordinates," indicating that its value consists of an officer's superiors and subordinates.

(8) A member attribute derivation can specify that the value of the attribute is given by an arithmetic expression that involves the values of other member attributes or mappings. The involved attributes/mappings must have numeric values, that is, they must have value classes that are (eventual) subclasses of NUMBERS. The arithmetic operators allowed are addition ("+"), subtraction ("−"), multiplication ("*"), division ("/"), and exponentiation ("!"). For example, attribute Top__speed__in__miles__per__hour of OIL__TANKERS has the derivation "= Absolute__top__speed/1.1" (to convert from knots).

(9) The operators "maximum," "minimum," "average," and "sum" can be applied to a member attribute or mapping that is multivalued; the value class of the attributes involved must be an (eventual) subclass of NUMBERS. The maximum, minimum, average, or sum is taken over the collection of entities that comprise the current value of the attribute or mapping.

(10) A member attribute can be defined to have its value equal to the number of members in a multivalued attribute or mapping. For example, attribute Number__of__instances of SHIP__TYPES has the derivation "number of members in Contents." "Number of unique members" is used similarly. "Number of members" and "number of unique members" differ only when duplicates are present in the multivalued attribute involved.

2.4.1.4 *The Definition of Member Attributes.* We now specify how these derivation mechanisms for derived attributes may be applied. The following rules are formulated in order to allow the use of derivations while avoiding the danger of inconsistent attribute specifications.

(1) Every attribute may or may not have an inverse; if it does, the inverse must be defined consistently with the attribute.
(2) Every member attribute A_1 satisfies one of the following cases.
   (a) A_1 has exactly one derivation. In this case, the value A_1 is completely specified by the derivation. The inverse of A_1 (call it A_2), if it exists, may not have a derivation or a matching specification.
   (b) A_1 has exactly one matching specification. In this case, the value of A_1 is completely specified by its relationships with an entity (or entities) to which it is matched (namely, member(s) of some class C). The inverse of A_1 (call it A_2), if it exists, may not have a derivation. It can have a matching specification, but this must match A_2 to C in a manner consistent with the matching specification of A_1.
   (c) A_1 has neither a matching specification nor a derivation. In this case, it may be the case that the inverse of A_1 (call it A_2) has a matching specification or a derivation; if so, then one of the above two cases ((a) or (b)) applies. Otherwise, A_1 and A_2 form a pair of primitive values that are defined in terms of one another, but which are independent of all other information in the database.

With regard to updating the database, we note that in case (c), a user can explicitly provide a value for A_1 or for A_2 (and thereby establish values for both of them). In cases (a) and (b), neither A_1 nor A_2 can be directly modified; their values are changed by modifying other parts of the database.

2.4.2 *Class Attribute Interrelationships.* Attribute derivation primitives analogous to primitives (5)–(10) for member attributes can be used to define derived class attributes, as these primitives derive attribute values from those of other attributes. Of course, instead of deriving the value of a member attribute from the value of other member attributes, the class attribute primitives will derive the value of a class attribute from the value of other class attributes. In addition, there are two other primitives that can be used in the definition of derived class attributes.

(1) An attribute can be defined so that its value equals the number of members in the class it modifies. For example, attribute Number of INSPECTIONS has the derivation "number of members in this class."
(2) An attribute can be defined whose value is a function of a numeric member attribute of a class; the functions supported are "maximum," "minimum," "average," and "sum" taken over a member attribute. The computation of the function is made over the members of the class. For example, the class attribute Total__spilled of OIL__SPILLS has the derivation "sum of Amount__spilled over members of this class."

2.4.3 *Attribute Predicates for Subclass Definition.* As stated earlier, a subclass can be defined by means of a predicate on the member attributes of its parent class. Having described the specifics of attributes, it is now possible to detail the permissible types of attribute predicates. In particular, an attribute predicate is a simple predicate or a Boolean combination of simple predicates; the operators used to form such a Boolean combination are "and," "or," and "not." A simple predicate has one of the following forms:

(1) MAPPING SCALAR__COMPARATOR CONSTANT;
(2) MAPPING SCALAR__COMPARATOR MAPPING;
(3) MAPPING SET__COMPARATOR CONSTANT;

(4) MAPPING SET__COMPARATOR CLASS__NAME;
(5) MAPPING SET__COMPARATOR MAPPING.

Here, MAPPING is any mapping (including an attribute name as a special case); SCALAR__COMPARATOR is one of "=," "≠," ">," "≥," "<," and "≤"; CONSTANT is a string or number constant; SET__COMPARATOR is one of: "is contained in," "is properly contained in," "contains," and "properly contains"; CLASS__NAME is the name of some class defined in the schema. For illustration, an example of each of these five forms is provided below along with an indication of its meaning; the first two predicates define subclasses of class OFFICERS, while the third, fourth, and fifth apply to class SHIPS:

(1) Country__of__license = 'Panama' (officers licensed in Panama);
(2) Commander.Date__commissioned > Date__commissioned (officers commissioned before their commander);
(3) Cargo__types contains 'oil' (ships that can carry oil);
(4) Captain is contained in DANGEROUS__CAPTAINS (ships whose captain in the class containing officers that are bad risks);
(5) Captain.Country__of__license is contained in Captain.Superior.Country__of__license (ships commanded by an officer who has a superior licensed in the same country as he).

2.4.4 *Attribute Inheritance.* As noted earlier, it may often be the case that an entity in an SDM database belongs to more than one class. SDM classes can and frequently do share members, for example, a member of OIL__TANKERS is also a member of SHIPS; a member of OIL__SPILLS is also in INCIDENTS. As a member of a class C, a given entity E has values for each member attribute associated with C. But in addition, when viewed as a member C, E may have additional attributes that are not directly associated with C, but rather are *inherited* from other classes. For example, since all oil tankers are ships, each member T of the class OIL__TANKERS inherits the member attributes of SHIPS. In addition to the attributes Hull__type, Is__tanker__banned, Inspections, Number__of__times__inspected, Last__inspection, Last__two__inspections, Date__last__examined, and Oil__spills__involved__in, which are explicitly associated with OIL__TANKERS, T also has the attributes Name, Hull__number, Type, etc.; these are not mentioned in the definition of OIL__TANKERS but are inherited from SHIPS (a superclass of OIL__TANKERS). The value of each inherited attribute of tanker T is simply the value of that attribute of T when it is viewed as a member of SHIPS; the very same ship entity that belongs to OIL__TANKERS belongs also to SHIPS, so that the value of each such inherited attribute is well defined.

The following specific rules of attribute inheritance are applied in SDM.

(1) A class S that is an attribute-defined subclass of a class U, or a user-controllable subclass of U, inherits all of the member attributes of U. For example, since RURITANIAN__OIL__TANKERS is an attribute-defined subclass of OIL__TANKERS, RURITANIAN__OIL__TANKERS inherits all of the member attributes of OIL__TANKERS; in turn, members of OIL__TANKERS inherit all of the member attributes of SHIPS.
Class attributes describe properties of a class taken as a whole and so are not inherited by an attribute-defined or user-controllable subclass. In order for an attribute to be inherited from class U by class S, both its meaning and its value must be the same for U and S. This is not true in general for class attributes. Although a subclass may have a similar class attribute to one defined for its parent class, for example, Number__of__members, their values will in general not be equal.
(2) A class S defined as an intersection subclass of classes U_1 and U_2 inherits all of the member attributes of U_1 and all of the member attributes of U_2. For example, the class BANNED__OIL__TANKERS, defined as containing all members of SHIP that are in both BANNED__SHIPS and OIL__TANKERS, inherits all attributes of BANNED__SHIPS as well as all of the attributes of OIL__TANKERS. This follows since each member of BANNED__OIL__TANKERS is both an oil tanker and a banned ship and so must have the attributes of both. Note that since BANNED__SHIPS and OIL__TANKERS are themselves defined as subclasses, they may inherit attributes from their parent classes which are in turn inherited by BANNED__OIL__TANKERS.
(3) A class S defined as the union of classes U_1 and U_2 inherits all of the member attributes shared by U_1 and U_2. For example, the class SHIPS__TO__BE__MONITORED inherits the member attributes shared by BANNED__SHIPS and OIL__TANKERS__REQUIRING__INSPECTION (which turn out to be all of the member attributes of SHIPS).
(4) A subclass S defined as the difference of classes, namely, consisting of all of the members in a class U that are not in class U_1, inherits all of the member attributes of U. This case is similar to (1), since S is a subclass of U.

These inheritance rules determine the attributes associated with classes that are defined in terms of interclass connections. These rules need not be explicitly applied by the SDM user; they are an integral part of SDM and are automatically applied wherever appropriate.

2.4.4.1 *Further Constraining an Inherited Member Attribute.* An important constraint may be placed on inherited attributes in an SDM schema. This constraint requires that the value of an attribute A inherited from class C_1 by class C_2 be a member of a class C_3 (C_3 is a subclass of the value class of A). To specify such a constraint, the name of the inherited attribute is repeated in the definition of the member attributes of the subclass, and its constrained value class is specified. For example, attribute Cargo__types is inherited by MERCHANT__SHIPS from SHIPS; its repetition in the definition of MERCHANT__SHIPS indicates that the value class of Cargo__types for MERCHANT__SHIPS is restricted to MERCHANT__CARGO__TYPE__NAMES. Values of attribute Cargo__types of SHIPS must satisfy this constraint. If the value being inherited does not satisfy this constraint, then the attribute's value is null.

2.5 Duplicates and Null Values

As specified above, an SDM class is either a set or a multiset: It may or may not contain duplicates. If a class has unique identifiers, then it obviously cannot have duplicates. If unique identifiers are not present, then the default is that duplicates are allowed. However, a class can be explicitly defined with "duplicates not allowed." Duplicates may also be present in attribute values, since attribute derivation specifications and mappings can yield duplicates.

In point of fact, the existence or nonexistence of duplicates is only of importance when considering the number of members in a class or the size of a multivalued attribute.On most occasions, the user need not be concerned with whether or not duplicates are present. Consequently, the only SDM primitives that are affected by duplicates are those that concern the number of members in a class and the size of an attribute. The SDM interclass connections and attribute derivation primitives are defined so as to propagate duplicates in an intuitive manner. For example, attribute-defined and user-controllable subclasses contain duplicates if and only if their parent class contains duplicates; and, if the class underlying a grouping has duplicates, the contents of the groups will similarly contain duplicates. Further details of this approach to handling duplicates are provided in [27].

As stated above, any attribute not defined as "mandatory" may have "null" as its value. While the treatment of null values is not a simple issue, we state that for the purposes here null is treated just like any other data value. A detailed discussion of null value handling is beyond the scope of this paper (see [14] for such a discussion).

2.6 SDM Data Definition Language

As noted above, this paper provides a specific *database definition language* (*DDL*) for SDM. The foregoing description of SDM did not rely on a specific DDL syntax although the discussion proceeded through numerous examples expressed in a particular sample DDL syntax. Many forms of DDL syntax could be used to describe SDM schemas, and we have selected one of them in order to make the specification of SDM precise.

The syntax of SDM DDL is presented in Appendix B, expressed in Backus–Naur Form style. The particular conventions used are described at the beginning of Appendix B. For the most part, the syntax description is self-explanatory; however, the following points are worthy of note.

(1) Syntactic categories are capitalized (with no interspersed spaces, but possibly including "__"s). All lowercase strings are in the language itself, except those enclosed in "*"s; the latter are descriptions of syntactic categories whose details are obvious.

(2) Indentation is an essential part of the SDM DDL syntax. In Appendix B, the first level of indentation is used for presentation, while all others indicate indentation in the syntax itself. For example, MEMBER__ATTRIBUTES is defined as consisting of "member attributes," followed by a group of one or more member attribute items (placed vertically below "member attributes").

(3) Many rules that constrain the set of legal SDM schemata are not included in the syntax shown in the figure. For example, in SDM, the rule that attributes of different applicability (member attributes and class attributes) must not be mixed is not included in the syntax, as its incorporation therein would be too cumbersome. A similar statement can be made for the rules that arithmetic expressions must be computed on attributes whose values are numbers, that a common underlying class must exist for classes defined by multiset operator interclass connections, and so forth.

2.7 Operations on an SDM Database

An important part of any database model is the set of operations that can be performed on it. The operations defined for SDM allow a user to derive information from a database, to update a database (adding new information to it or correcting information in it), and to include new structural information in it (change an SDM schema) [27]. Note that operations to derive information from an SDM schema are closely related to SDM primitives for describing derived information (e.g., nonbase classes and derived attributes). There is a vocabulary of basic SDM operations that are application environment independent and predefined. The set of permissible operations is designed to permit only semantically meaningful manipulations of an SDM database. User-defined operations can be constructed using the primitives. A detailed specification of the SDM operations is beyond the scope of this paper.

3. DISCUSSION

In this paper, we have presented the major features of SDM, a high-level data modeling mechanism. The goal of SDM is to provide the designer and user of a database with a formalism whereby a substantial portion of the semantic structure of the application environment can be clearly and precisely expressed. Contemporary database models do not support such direct conceptual modeling, for a number of reasons that are summarized above and explored in greater detail in [22]. In brief, these conventional database models are too oriented toward computer data structures to allow for the natural expression of application semantics. SDM, on the other hand, is based on the high-level concepts of entities, attributes, and classes.

In several ways, SDM is analogous to a number of recent proposals in database modeling, including [1, 3, 5, 9, 14, 31, 33, 34, 39–41, 43, 46]. Where SDM principally differs from these is in the extent of the structure of the application domain that it can capture and in its emphasis on relativism, flexibility, and redundancy. An SDM schema does more than just describe the kinds of objects that are captured in the database; it allows for substantial amounts of structural information that specifies how the entities and their classes are related to one another. Furthermore, it is a fundamental premise of SDM that a semantic schema for a database should directly support multiple ways of viewing the same information, since different users inevitably will have differing slants on the database and even a single user's perspective will evolve over time. Consequently, redundant information (in the form of nonbase classes and derived attributes) plays an important role in an SDM schema, and provides the principal mechanism for expressing multiple versions of the same information.

3.1 The Design of SDM

In the design of SDM, we have sought to provide a higher level and richer modeling language than that of conventional database models, without developing a large and complex facility containing a great many features (as exemplified by some of the knowledge representation and world modeling systems developed by the artificial intelligence community, e.g., [35, 51]). We have sought neither absolute minimality, with a small number of mutually orthogonal constructs, nor a profusion of special case facilities to precisely model each slightly different type of application. There is a significant trade-off between the complexity of a modeling facility and its power, naturalness, and precision. If a database model contains a large number of features, then it will likely be difficult to learn and to apply; however, it will have the potential of realizing schemata that are very sharp and precise models of their application domains. On the other hand, a model with a fairly minimal set of features will be easier to learn and employ, but a schema constructed with it will capture less of the particular characteristics of its application.

We have sought a middle road between these two extremes, with a relatively small number of basic features, augmented by a set of special features that are particularly useful in a large number of instances. We adhere to the principle of the well-known "80–20" rule; in this context, this rule would suggest that 80 percent of the modeling cases can be handled with 20 percent of the total number of special features that would be required by a fully detailed modeling formalism. Thus, a user of SDM should find that the application constructs that he most frequently encounters are directly provided by SDM, while he will have to represent the less common ones by means of more generic features. To this end, we have included such special facilities as the inverse and matching mechanisms for attribute derivation, but have not, for example, sought to taxonomize entity types more fully (since to do so in a meaningful and useful way would greatly expand the size and complexity of SDM). We have also avoided the introduction of a huge number of attribute derivation primitives, limiting ourselves to the ones that should be of most critical importance. For example, there does not exist a derivation primitive for class attributes to determine what percentage the members of the class constitute of another class. Such special cases would be most usefully handled by means of a general-purpose computational mechanism.

SDM as presented in this paper is neither complete nor final. SDM as a whole is open to any number of extensions. The most significant omission in this paper is that of the operations that can be applied to an SDM database: the database manipulation facility associated with the database definition facility presented here. Such a presentation would be too lengthy for this paper and can be found in [27]. In brief, however, the design of SDM is strongly based on the duality principle between schema and procedure, as developed in [21]. From this perspective, any query against the database can be seen as a reference to a particular virtual data item; whether that item can easily be accessed in the database, or whether it can only be located by means of the application of a number of database manipulation operations, depends on what information has been included in the schema by the database designer. Frequently retrieved data items would most likely be present in the schema, often as derived data, while less commonly requested information would have to be dynamically computed. In both cases, however, the same sets of primitives should be employed to describe the data item(s) in question, since dynamic data retrieval and static definitions of derived data are fundamentally equivalent, differing only in the occasions of their binding. Thus the SDM database manipulation facility strongly resembles the facilities described above for computing nonbase classes and derived attributes. Among other beneficial consequences, this duality allows for a natural evolution of the semantic schema to reflect changing patterns of use and access: As certain kinds of requests become more common, they can be incorporated as derived data into the schema and thereby greatly simplify their retrieval.

3.2 Extensions

Numerous extensions can be made to SDM as presented here. These include extending SDM by means of additional general facilities, as well as tailoring special versions of it (by adding application environment specific facilities). For example, as it currently is defined, derived data is continuously updated so as always to be consistent with the primitive data from which it is computed. Alternative, less dynamic modes of computation could be provided, so that in some cases derived data might represent a snapshot of some other aspect of the database at a certain time. Similarly, a richer set of attribute inheritance rules, possibly under user control, might be provided to enable more complex relationships between classes and their subclasses. In the other direction, a current investigation is being conducted with the goal of simplifying SDM and accommodating more relativism [30]. Further, an attempt is currently under way to construct a version of SDM that contains primitives especially relevant to the office environment (such as documents, events, and organization hierarchies), to facilitate the natural modeling and description of office structures and procedures.

3.3 Applications

We envision a variety of potential uses and applications for SDM. As described in this paper, SDM is simply an abstract database modeling mechanism and language that is not dependent on any supporting computer system. One set of applications uses SDM in precisely this mode to support the process of defining and designing a database as well as in facilitating its subsequent evolution. It is well known that the process of logical database design, wherein the database administrator (DBA) must construct a schema using the database model of the database management system (DBMS) to be employed, is a difficult and error-prone procedure [10, 30, 31, 37, 38, 42, 44, 50]. A primary reason for this difficulty is the distance between the semantic level of the application and the data structures of the database model; the DBA must bridge this gap in a single step, simultaneously conducting an information requirements analysis and expressing the results of his analysis in terms of the database model. What is lacking is a formalism in which to express the information content of the database in a way that is independent of the details of the database model associated with the underlying DBMS. SDM can be used as a higher-level database model in which the DBA describes the database prior to designing a logical schema for it. There are a number of advantages to using the SDM in this way.

(1) An SDM schema will serve as a specification of the information that the database will contain. All too often, only the most vague and amorphous English language descriptions of a database exist prior to the database design process. A formal specification can more accurately, completely, and consistently communicate to the actual designer the prescribed contents of the database. SDM provides some structure for the logical database design process. The DBA can first seek to describe the database in high-level semantic terms, and then reduce that schema to a more conventional logical

design. By decomposing the design problem in this way, its difficulty as a whole can be reduced.

(2) SDM supports a basic methodology that can guide the DBA in the design process by providing him with a set of natural design templates. That is, the DBA can approach the application in question with the intent of identifying its classes, subclasses, and so on. Having done so, he can select representations for these constructs in a routine, if not algorithmic, fashion.

(3) SDM provides an effective base for accommodating the evolution of the content structure, and use of a database. Relativism, logical redundancy, and derived information support this natural evolution of schemata.

A related use of SDM is as a medium for documenting a database. One of the more serious problems facing a novice user of a large database is determining the information content of the database and locating in the schema the information of use to him. An SDM schema for a database can serve as a readable description of its contents, organized in terms that a user is likely to be able to comprehend and identify. A cross-index of the schema would amount to a semantic data dictionary, identifying the principal features of the application environment and cataloging their relationships. Such specifications and documentation would also be independent of the DBMS being employed to actually manage the data, and so could be of particular use in the context of DBMS selection or of a conversion from one DBMS to another. An example of the use of SDM for specification and documentation is [15].

On another plane are a number of applications that require that SDM schema for a database be processed and utilized by a computer system. One such application would be to employ SDM as the conceptual schema database model for a DBMS within the three-schema architecture of the ANSI/SPARC proposal [2]. In such a system, the conceptual schema is a representation of the fundamental semantics of the database. The external views of the data (those employed by programmers and end-users) are defined in terms of it, while a mapping from it to physical file structures establishes the database's internal schema (storage and representation). Because of its high level and support for multiple views, SDM could be effectively employed in this role. Once occupying such a central position in the DBMS, the SDM schema could also be used to support any number of "intelligent" database applications that depend on a rich understanding of the semantics of the data in question. For example, an SDM schema could drive an automatic semantic integrity checker, which would examine incoming data and test its plausibility and likelihood of error in the context of a semantic model of the database. A number of such systems have been proposed [16, 19, 20, 45], but they are generally based on the use of expressions in the first-order predicate calculus that are added to a relational schema. This approach introduces a number of problems, ranging from the efficiency of the checking to the modularity and reliability of the resulting model. By directly capturing the semantics in the schema rather than in some external mechanism, SDM might more directly support such data checking. Another "semantics-based" application to which SDM has been applied is an interactive system that assists a naive user, unfamiliar with the information content of the database, in formulating a query against it [28].

It might even be desirable to employ SDM as the database model in terms of which all database users see the database. This would entail building an SDM DBMS. Of course, a high-level database model raises serious problems of efficiency of representation and processing. However, it can also result in easier and more effective use of the data which may in the aggregate dominate the performance issues. Furthermore, SDM can be additionally extended to be more than just a database model; it can serve as the foundation for a total integrated database programming language in which both the facilities for accessing a database and those for computing with the data so accessed are combined in a coherent and consistent fashion [18]. And, SDM can provide a basis for describing and structuring logically decentralized and physically distributed database systems [22, 29].

APPENDIX A. AN SDM SCHEMA FOR THE TANKER MONITORING APPLICATION ENVIRONMENT

```
SHIPS
 description: all ships with potentially hazardous cargoes that
   may enter U.S. coastal waters
 member attributes:
   Name
     value class: SHIP__NAMES
   Hull__number
     value class: HULL__NUMBERS
     may not be null
     not changeable
   Type
     description: the kind of ship, for example, merchant or fishing
     value class: SHIP__TYPE__NAMES
   Country__of__registry
     value class: COUNTRIES
     inverse: Ships__registered__here
   Name__of__home__port
     value class: PORT__NAMES
   Cargo__types
     description: the type(s) of cargo the ship can carry
     value class: CARGO__TYPE__NAMES
     multivalued
   Captain
     description: the current captain of the ship
     value class: OFFICERS
     match: Officer of ASSIGNMENTS on Ship
   Engines
     value class: ENGINES
     multivalued with size between 0 and 10
     exhausts value class
     no overlap in values
   Incidents__involved__in
     value class: INCIDENTS
     inverse: Involved__ship
     multivalued
 identifiers:
   Name
   Hull__number
```

```
INSPECTIONS
  description: inspections of oil tankers
  member attributes:
    Tanker
      description: the tanker inspected
      value class: OIL__TANKERS
      inverse: Inspections
    Date
      value class: DATES
    Order__for__tanker
      description: the ordering of the inspections for a tanker
        with the most recent inspection having value 1
      value class: INTEGERS
      derivation: order by decreasing Date within Tanker
  class attributes:
    Number
      description: the number of inspections in the database
      value class: INTEGERS
      derivation: number of members in this class
  identifiers:
    Tanker + Date
COUNTRIES
  description: countries of registry for ships
  member attributes:
    Name
      value class: COUNTRY__NAMES
    Ships__registered__here
      value class: SHIPS
      inverse: Country__of__registry
      multivalued
  identifiers:
    Name
OFFICERS
  description: all certified officers of ships
  member attributes:
    Name
      value class: PERSON__NAMES
    Country__of__license
      value class: COUNTRIES
    Date__commissioned
      value class: DATES
    Seniority
      value class: INTEGERS
      derivation: order by Date__commissioned
    Commander
      description: the officer in direct command of this officer
      value class: OFFICERS
    Superiors
      value class: OFFICERS
      derivation: all levels of values of Commander
      inverse: Subordinates
      multivalued
    Subordinates
      value class: OFFICERS
      inverse: Superiors
      multivalued
    Contacts
      value class: OFFICERS
      derivation: where is in Superiors or is in Subordinates
  identifiers:
    Name
ENGINES
  description: ship engines
  member attributes:
    Serial__number
      value class: ENGINE__SERIAL__NUMBERS
    Kind__of__engine
      value class: ENGINE__TYPE__NAMES
  identifiers:
    Serial__number
INCIDENTS
  description: accidents involving ships
  member attributes:
    Involved__ship
      value class: SHIPS
      inverse: Incidents__involved__in
    Date
      value class: DATES
    Description
      description: textual explanation of the accident
      value class: INCIDENT__DESCRIPTIONS
    Involved__captain
      value class: OFFICERS
  identifiers:
    Involved__ship + Date + Description
ASSIGNMENTS
  description: assignments of captains to ships
  member attributes:
    Officer
      value class: OFFICERS
    Ship
      value class: SHIPS
  identifiers:
    Officer + Ship
OIL__TANKERS
  description: oil-carrying ships
  interclass connection: subclass of SHIPS where Cargo__types
    contains 'oil'
  member attributes:
    Hull__type
      description: specification of single or double hull
      value class: HULL__TYPE__NAMES
    Is__tanker__banned?
      value class: YES/NO
      derivation: if in BANNED__SHIPS
    Inspections
      value class: INSPECTIONS
      inverse: Tanker
      multivalued
    Number__of__times__inspected
      value class: INTEGERS
```

```
        derivation: number of unique members in Inspections
      Last__inspection
        value class: MOST__RECENT__INSPECTIONS
        inverse: Tanker
      Last__two__inspections
        value class: INSPECTIONS
        derivation: subvalue of inspections where
          Order__for__tanker ≤ 2
        multivalued
    Date__last__examined
      value class: DATES
      derivation: same as Last__inspection.Date
    Oil__spills__involved__in
      value class: INCIDENTS
      derivation: subvalue of Incidents__involved__in
        where is in OIL__SPILLS
      multivalued
  class attributes:
    Absolute__top__legal__speed
      value class: KNOTS
    Top__legal__speed__in__miles__per__hour
      value class: MILES__PER__HOUR
      derivation: = Absolute__top__legal__speed/1.1
RURITANIAN__SHIPS
  interclass connection: subclass of SHIPS where
    Country.Name = 'Ruritania'
RURITANIAN__OIL__TANKERS
  interclass connection: subclass of OIL__TANKERS where
    Country.Name = 'Ruritania'
MERCHANT__SHIPS
  interclass connection: subclass of SHIPS where Type = 'merchant'
  member attributes:
    Cargo__types
      value class: MERCHANT__CARGO__TYPE__NAMES
OIL__SPILLS
  interclass connection: subclass of INCIDENTS where
    Description = 'oil spill'
  member attributes:
    Amount__spilled
      value class: GALLONS
    Severity
      derivation: = Amount__spilled/100,000
  class attributes:
    Total__spilled
      value class: GALLONS
      derivation: sum of Amount__spilled over members of this class
MOST__RECENT__INSPECTIONS
  interclass connection: subclass of INSPECTIONS where
    Order__for__tanker = 1
DANGEROUS__CAPTAINS
  description: captains who have been involved in an accident
  interclass connection: subclass of OFFICERS where is a value of Involved__captain of
    INCIDENTS
BANNED__SHIPS
  description: ships banned from U.S. coastal waters
  interclass connection: subclass of SHIPS where specified
  member attributes:
    Date__banned
      value class: DATES
OIL__TANKERS__REQUIRING__INSPECTION
  interclass connection: subclass of OIL__TANKERS where specified
BANNED__OIL__TANKERS
  interclass connection: subclass of SHIPS where
    is in BANNED__SHIPS and is in OIL__TANKERS
SAFE__SHIPS
  description: ships that are considered good risks
  interclass connection: subclass of SHIPS where is not in BANNED__SHIPS
SHIPS__TO__BE__MONITORED
  description: ships that are considered bad risks
  interclass connection: subclass of SHIPS where is in BANNED__SHIPS
    or is in OIL__TANKERS__REQUIRING__INSPECTION
SHIP__TYPES
  description: types of ships
  interclass connection: grouping of SHIPS on common value of Type
    groups defined as classes are MERCHANT__SHIPS
  member attributes:
    Instances
      description: the instances of the type of ship
      value class: SHIPS
      derivation: same as Contents
      multivalued
    Number__of__ships__of__this__type
      value class: INTEGERS
      derivation: number of members in Contents
CARGO__TYPE__GROUPS
  interclass connection: grouping of SHIPS on common value of
    Cargo__types
TYPES__OF__HAZARDOUS__SHIPS
  interclass connection: grouping of SHIPS consisting of classes
    BANNED__SHIPS, BANNED__OIL__TANKERS,
    SHIPS__TO__BE__MONITORED
CONVOYS
  interclass connection: grouping of SHIPS as specified
  member attributes:
    Oil__tanker__constituents
      description: the oil tankers that are in the convoy (if any)
      value class: SHIPS
      derivation: subvalue of Contents where is in OIL__TANKERS
      multivalued
CARGO__TYPE__NAMES
  description: the types of cargo
  interclass connection: subclass of STRINGS
MERCHANT__CARGO__TYPE__NAMES
  interclass connection: subclass of CARGO__TYPE__NAMES
    where specified
COUNTRY__NAMES
  interclass connection: subclass of STRINGS where specified
ENGINE__SERIAL__NUMBERS
  interclass connection: subclass of STRINGS where format is
```

```
    "H"
    number where integer and ≥1 and ≤999
    "—"
    number where integer and ≥0 and ≤999999
DATES
  description: calendar dates in the range "1/1/75" to "12/31/79"
  interclass connection: subclass of STRINGS where format is
    month: number where ≥1 and ≤12
    "/"
    day: number where integer and ≥1 and ≤31
    "/"
    year: number where integer and ≥1970 and ≤2000
    where (if (month = 4 or = 5 or = 9 or = 11) then day ≤30)
      and (if month = 2 then day ≤29)
    ordering by year, month, day
ENGINE_TYPE_NAMES
  interclass connection: subclass of STRINGS where specified
GALLONS
  interclass connection: subclass of STRINGS where format is
    number where integer
HULL_NUMBERS
  interclass connection: subclass of STRINGS where format is
    number where integer
HULL_TYPE_NAMES
  description: single or double
  interclass connection: subclass of STRINGS where specified
INCIDENT_DESCRIPTIONS
  description: textual description of an accident
  interclass connection: subclass of STRINGS
KNOTS
  interclass connection: subclass of STRINGS where format is
    number where integer
MILES_PER_HOUR
  interclass connection: subclass of STRINGS where format is
    number where integer
PORT_NAMES
  interclass connection: subclass of STRINGS
PERSON_NAMES
  interclass connection: subclass of STRINGS
SHIP_NAMES
  interclass connection: subclass of STRINGS
SHIP_TYPE_NAMES
  description: the names of the ship types, for example, merchant
  interclass connection: subclass of STRINGS where specified
```

APPENDIX B. SYNTAX OF THE SDM DATA DEFINITION LANGUAGE

The following list is given to clarify and define some of the items and terms used in this appendix.

(1) The left side of a production is separated from the right by a "←."
(2) The first level of indentation in the syntax description is used to help separate the left and right sides of a production; all other indentation is in the SDM data definition language.
(3) Syntactic categories are capitalized while all literals are in lowercase.
(4) { } means optional.
(5) [ ] means one of the enclosed choices must appear; choices are separated by a ";" (when used with "{ }" one of the choices may optionally appear).
(6) ⟨ ⟩ means one or more of the enclosed can appear, separated by spaces with optional commas and an optional "and" at the end.
(7) ⟨⟨ ⟩⟩ means one or more of the enclosed can appear, vertically appended.
(8) • • encloses a "meta"-description of a syntactic category (to informally explain it).

```
SCHEMA ←
  ⟨⟨CLASS⟩⟩
CLASS ←
  ⟨CLASS_NAME⟩
    {description: CLASS_DESCRIPTION}
    {[BASE_CLASS_FEATURES; INTERCLASS_CONNECTION]}
    {MEMBER_ATTRIBUTES}
    {CLASS_ATTRIBUTES}
CLASS_NAME ←
  •string of capitals possibly including special characters•
CLASS_DESCRIPTION ←
  •string•
BASE_CLASS_FEATURES←
  {[duplicates allowed; duplicates not allowed]}
  {⟨⟨IDENTIFIERS⟩⟩}
IDENTIFIERS ←
  [ATTRIBUTE_NAME; ATTRIBUTE_NAME + IDENTIFIERS]
MEMBER_ATTRIBUTES ←
  member attributes:
    ⟨⟨MEMBER_ATTRIBUTE⟩⟩
CLASS_ATTRIBUTES ←
  class attributes:
    ⟨⟨CLASS_ATTRIBUTE⟩⟩
INTERCLASS CONNECTION ←
  [SUBCLASS; GROUPING_CLASS]
SUBCLASS ←
  subclass of CLASS_NAME where SUBCLASS_PREDICATE
GROUPING ←
  [grouping of CLASS_NAME on common value of ⟨ATTRIBUTE_NAME⟩
    {groups defined as classes are ⟨CLASS_NAME⟩};
  grouping of CLASS_NAME consisting of classes ⟨CLASS_NAME⟩;
  grouping of CLASS_NAME as specified]
SUBCLASS_PREDICATE ←
  [ATTRIBUTE_PREDICATE;
  specified;
  is in CLASS_NAME and is in CLASS_NAME;
  is not in CLASS_NAME;
  is in CLASS_NAME or is in CLASS_NAME;
  is a value of ATTRIBUTE_NAME of CLASS_NAME;
  format is FORMAT]
ATTRIBUTE_PREDICATE ←
  [SIMPLE_PREDICATE; (ATTRIBUTE_PREDICATE);
  not ATTRIBUTE_PREDICATE;
```

```
    ATTRIBUTE_PREDICATE and ATTRIBUTE_PREDICATE;
    ATTRIBUTE_PREDICATE or ATTRIBUTE_PREDICATE]
  SIMPLE_PREDICATE ←
    [MAPPING SCALAR_COMPARATOR [CONSTANT; MAPPING];
    MAPPING SET_COMPARATOR [CONSTANT; CLASS_NAME; MAPPING]]
  MAPPING ←
    [ATTRIBUTE_NAME; MAPPING.ATTRIBUTE_NAME]
  SCALAR_COMPARATOR ←
    [EQUAL_COMPARATOR; >; ≥; <; ≤]
  EQUAL COMPARATOR ←
    [=; ≠]
  SET_COMPARATOR ←
    [is {properly} contained in; {properly} contains]
  CONSTANT ←
    •a string or number constant•
  FORMAT ←
    •a name class definition pattern•
    (see [26])
  MEMBER_ATTRIBUTE ←
    (ATTRIBUTE_NAME)
      {ATTRIBUTE_DESCRIPTION}
      value class:CLASS_NAME
      {inverse:ATTRIBUTE_NAME}
      {[match:ATTRIBUTE_NAME of CLASS_NAME on ATTRIBUTE_NAME];
      derivation:MEMBER_ATTRIBUTE_DERIVATION]}
      {single valued; multivalued {with size between CONSTANT and CONSTANT}}
      {may not be null}
      {not changeable}
      {exhausts value class}
      {no overlap in values}
  CLASS ATTRIBUTE ←
    (ATTRIBUTE_NAME)
      {ATTRIBUTE_DESCRIPTION}
      value class:CLASS_NAME
      derivation:CLASS_ATTRIBUTE_DERIVATION]}
      {single valued; multivalued {with size between CONSTANT and CONSTANT}}
      {may not be null}
      {not changeable}
  ATTRIBUTE_NAME ←
    •string of lowercase letters beginning with a capital and possibly
    including special characters•
  ATTRIBUTE DESCRIPTION ←
    "•string•"
  MEMBER_ATTRIBUTE_DERIVATION ←
    [INTERATTRIBUTE_DERIVATION;
    MEMBER-SPECIFIC_DERIVATION]
  CLASS_ATTRIBUTE_DERIVATION ←
    [INTERATTRIBUTE_DERIVATION;
    CLASS-SPECIFIC_DERIVATION]
  INTERATTRIBUTE_DERIVATION ←
    [same as MAPPING;
    subvalue of MAPPING where [is in CLASS_NAME; ATTRIBUTE_PREDICATE];
    where [is in MAPPING and is in MAPPING; is in MAPPING or is in MAPPING;
    is in MAPPING and is not in MAPPING];
    = MAPPING_EXPRESSION;
    [maximum; minimum; average; sum] of MAPPING;
    number of {unique} members in MAPPING]
  MEMBER-SPECIFIC_DERIVATION ←
    [order by [increasing; decreasing] (MAPPING)
    {within (MAPPING)};
    if in CLASS_NAME;
    [up to CONSTANT; all] levels of values of ATTRIBUTE_NAME;
    contents]
  CLASS-SPECIFIC_DERIVATION ←
    [number of {unique} members in this class;
    [maximum; minimum; average; sum] of ATTRIBUTE_NAME over
      members of this class]
  MAPPING EXPRESSION ←
    [MAPPING; (MAPPING); MAPPING NUMBER_OPERATOR MAPPING]
  NUMBER OPERATOR ←
    [+; −; •; /; !]
```

ACKNOWLEDGMENTS

The authors wish to thank the following persons for their comments on the current or earlier versions of this paper, SDM, and related work: Antonio Albano, Arvola Chan, Peter Chen, Ted Codd, Dennis Heimbigner, Roger King, Peter Kreps, Frank Manola, Paula Newman, Diane and John Smith. In particular, Diane and John Smith helped the authors realize some of the weaknesses of an earlier version of SDM vis-a-vis relativism. Ted Codd's RM/T model has also provided many ideas concerning the specifics of SDM. DAPLEX (of Dave Shipman) and FQL (of Peter Buneman and Robert Frankel) have aided us in formulating various SDM constructs (e.g., mapping). Work performed at the Computer Corporation of America (under Frank Manola) and at the Lockheed California Company (under Don Kawamoto) has provided valuable input regarding the practical use of SDM. Finally, the referees provided many helpful comments concerning both the substance and presentation of this paper; their observations and suggestions are gratefully acknowledged.

Note: Because of the lack of neuter personal pronouns in English, the terms "he," "his," etc., are used throughout this paper to refer to an individual who may be either male or female.

REFERENCES

1. ABRIAL, J.R. Data semantics. In *Database Management*. J. Klimbie and K. Koffeman. Eds. North-Holland, Amsterdam, 1974.
2. ANSI/X3/SPARC (STANDARDS PLANNING AND REQUIREMENTS COMMITTEE). Interim report from the study group on database management systems. *FDT* (*Bulletin of ACM SIGMOD*) 7, 2 (1975).
3. BACHMAN, C.W. The role concept in data models. In *Proc. Int. Conf. Very Large Databases*. Tokyo, Japan, Oct. 1977.
4. BILLER, H., AND NEUHOLD, E.J. Semantics of databases: The semantics of data models. *Inf. Syst. 3* (1978), 11–30.
5. BUNEMAN, P., AND FRANKEL, R.E. FQL—A functional query language. In *Proc. ACM SIGMOD Int. Conf. Management of Data*, Boston, Mass., 1979.

6. Buneman, P., and Morgan, H.L. Implementing alerting techniques in database systems. In *Proc. COMPSAC'77*, Chicago, Ill., Nov. 1977.
7. Chamberlin, D.D. Relational database management systems. *Comput. Surv. 8*, 1 (March 1976), 43–66.
8. Chang, C.L. A hyper-relational model of databases. IBM Res. Rep. RJ1634, IBM, San Jose, Calif., Aug. 1975.
9. Chen, P.P.S. The entity-relationship model: Toward a unified view of data. *ACM Trans. Database Syst. 1*, 1 (March 1976), 9–36.
10. Chen, P.P.S. The entity-relationship approach to logical database design. Mono. 6, QED Information Sciences, Wellesley, Mass., 1978.
11. Codasyl Committee on Data System Languages. Codasyl database task group report. ACM, New York, 1971.
12. Codd, E.F. A relational model of data for large shared data banks. *Commun. ACM 13*, 6 (June 1970), 377–387.
13. Codd, E.F. Further normalization of the database relational model. In *Database Systems*, Courant Computer Science Symposia 6, R. Rustin, Ed. Prentice-Hall, Englewood Cliffs, N.J., 1971, pp. 65–98.
14. Codd, E.F. Extending the database relational model to capture more meaning. *ACM Trans. Database Syst. 4*, 4 (Dec. 1979), 397–434.
15. Computer Corporation of America. DBMS—Independent CICIS specifications. Tech. Rep. CCA, Cambridge, Mass., 1979.
16. Eswaran, K.P., and Chamberlin, D.D. Functional specifications of a subsystem for database integrity. In *Proc. Int. Conf. Very Large Databases*, Framingham, Mass., Sept. 1975.
17. Hammer, M. Research directions in database management. In *Research Directions in Software Technology*, P. Wegner, Ed. The M.I.T. Press, Cambridge, Mass., 1979.
18. Hammer, M., and Berkowitz, B. DIAL: A programming language for data-intensive applications. Working Paper, M.I.T. Lab. Computer Science, Cambridge, Mass., 1980.
19. Hammer, M., and McLeod, D. Semantic integrity in a relational database system. In *Proc. Int. Conf. Very Large Databases*, Framingham, Mass., Sept. 1975.
20. Hammer, M., and McLeod, D. A framework for database semantic integrity. In *Proc. 2nd Int. Conf. Software Engineering*, San Francisco, Calif., Oct. 1976.
21. Hammer, M., and McLeod, D. The semantic data model: A modelling mechanism for database applications. In *Proc. ACM SIGMOD Int. Conf. Management of Data*, Austin, Tex., 1978.
22. Hammer, M., and McLeod, D. On the architecture of database management systems. In *Infotech State-of-the-Art Report on Data Design*. Pergamon Infotech Ltd., Berkshire, England, 1980.
23. Kent, W. *Data and Reality*. North-Holland, Amsterdam, 1978.
24. Kent, W. Limitations of record-based information models. *ACM Trans. Database Syst. 4*, 1 (March 1979), 107–131.
25. Lee, R.M., and Gerritsen, R. Extended semantics for generalization hierarchies. In *Proc. ACM SIGMOD Int. Conf. Management of Data*, Austin, Tex., 1978.
26. McLeod, D. High level definition of abstract domains in a relational database system. *J. Comput. Languages 2*, 3 (1977).
27. McLeod, D. A semantic database model and its associatetd structured user interface. Tech. Rep., M.I.T. Lab. Computer Science, Cambridge, Mass., 1978.
28. McLeod, D. A database transaction specification methodology for end-users. Tech. Rep., Computer Science Dep., Univ. Southern California, Los, Angeles, Calif., 1980.
29. McLeod, D., and Heimbigner, D. A federated architecture for database systems. In *Proc. Nat. Computer Conf.*, Anaheim, Calif., 1980.
30. McLeod, D., and King, R. Applying a semantic database model. In *Proc. Int. Conf. Entity-Relationship Approach to Systems Analysis and Design*, Los Angeles, Calif., Dec. 1979.
31. Mylopoulos, J., Bernstein, P.A., and Wong, H. K. T. A language facility for designing interactive database-intensive applications. In *Proc. ACM SIGMOD Int. Conf. Management of Data*, Austin, Tex., 1978.
32. Palmer, I. Record subtype facilities in database systems. In *Proc. 4th Int. Conf. Very Large Databases*, Berlin, West Germany, Sept. 1978.
33. Pirotte, A. The entity-property-association model: An information-oriented database model. Tech. Rep., M.B.L.E. Res. Lab., Brussels, Belgium, 1977.
34. Roussopoulos, N. Algebraic data definition. In *Proc. 6th Texas Conf. Computing Systems*, Austin, Tex., Nov. 1977.
35. Schank, R.C. Identification of conceptualizations underlying natural language. In *Computer Models of Thought and Language*, R.C. Schank and K.M. Colby, Eds. W.H. Freeman, San Francisco, Calif., 1973.
36. Schmid, H.A., and Swenson, J.R. On the semantics of the relational data model. In *Proc. ACM SIGMOD Int. Conf. Management of Data*, San Jose, Calif., 1975.
37. Senko, M.E. Information systems: Records, relations, sets, entities, and things. *Inf. Syst. 1*, 1 (1975), 3–14.
38. Senko, M.E. Conceptual schemas, abstract data structures, enterprise descriptions. In *Proc. ACM Int. Computing Symp.*, Belgium, April 1977.
39. Shipman, D. W. The functional data model and the data language DAPLEX. *ACM Trans. Database Syst. 6*, 1 (March 1981), 140–173.
40. Smith, J.M., and Smith, D.C.P. Database abstractions: Aggregation. *Commun. ACM 20*, 6 (June 1977), 405–413.
41. Smith, J.M., and Smith, D.C.P. Database abstractions: Aggregation and generalization. *ACM Trans. Database Syst. 2*, 2 (June 1977), 105–133.
42. Smith, J.M., and Smith, D.C.P. Principles of conceptual database design. In *Proc. NYU Symp. Database Design*, New York, May 1978.
43. Smith, J.M., and Smith, D.C.P. A database approach to software specification. Tech. Rep. CCA-79-17, Computer Corporation of America, Cambridge, Mass., April 1979.
44. Solvberg, A. A contribution to the definition of concepts for expressing users' information system requirements. In *Proc. Int. Conf. Entity-Relationship Approach to Systems Analysis and Design*, Los Angeles, Calif., Dec. 1979.
45. Stonebraker, M.R. High level integrity assurance in relational database management systems. Electronics Res. Lab. Rep. ERL-M473, Univ. California, Berkeley, Calif., Aug. 1974.
46. Su, S.Y.W., and Lo, D.H. A semantic association model for conceptual database design. In *Proc. Int. Conf. Entity-Relationship Approach to Systems Analysis and Design*, Los Angeles, Calif., Dec. 1979.
47. Taylor, R.W., and Frank, R.L. CODASYL database management systems. *Comput. Surv. 8*, 1 (March 1976), 67–104.
48. Tsichritzis, D.C., and Lochovsky, F.H. Hierarchical database management: A survey. *Comput. Surv. 8*, 1 (March 1976), 105–124.
49. Wiederhold, G. *Database Design*. McGraw-Hill, New York, 1977.
50. Wiederhold, G., and El-Masri, R. Structural model for database design. In *Proc. Int. Conf. Entity-Relationship Approach to Systems Analysis and Design*, Los Angeles, Calif., Dec. 1979.
51. Wong, H.K.T., and Mylopoulos, J. Two views of data semantics: A survey of data models in artificial intelligence and database management. *INFOR 15*, 3 (Oct. 1977), 344–382.

The Database Language GEM

Carlo Zaniolo

Bell Laboratories
Holmdel, New Jersey 07733

ABSTRACT

GEM (an acronym for General Entity Manipulator) is a general-purpose query and update language for the DSIS data model, which is a semantic data model of the Entity-Relationship type. GEM is designed as an easy-to-use extension of the relational language QUEL, providing support for the notions of entities with surrogates, aggregation, generalization, null values, and set-valued attributes.

1. INTRODUCTION

A main thrust of computer technology is towards simplicity and ease of use. Database management systems have come a long way in this respect, particularly after the introduction of the relational approach [Ullm], which provides users with a simple tabular view of data and powerful and convenient query languages for interrogating and manipulating the database. These features were shown to be the key to reducing the cost of database-intensive application programming [Codd1] and to providing a sound environment for back-end support and distributed databases.

The main limitation of the relational model is its semantic scantiness, that often prevents relational schemas from modeling completely and expressively the natural relationships and mutual constraints between entities. This shortcoming, acknowledged by most supporters of the relational approach [Codd2], has motivated the introduction of new *semantic data models*, such as that described in [Chen] where reality is modeled in terms of entities and relationships among entities, and that presented in [SmSm] where relationships are characterized along the orthogonal coordinates of *aggregation* and *generalization*. The possibility of extending the relational model to capture more meaning — as opposed to introducing a new model — was investigated in [Codd2], where *surrogates* and *null values* were found necessary for the task.

Most previous work with semantic data models has concentrated on the problem of modeling reality and on schema design; also the problem of integrating the database into a programming environment supporting abstract data types has received considerable attention [Brod, KiMc]. However, the problem of providing easy to use queries and friendly user-interfaces for semantic data models has received comparatively little attention[1]. Thus the question not yet answered is whether semantic data models can retain the advantages of the relational model with respect to ease of use, friendly query languages and user interfaces, back-end support and distributed databases.

This work continues the DSIS effort [DSIS] to enhance the UNIX* environment with a DBMS combining the advantages of the relational approach with those of semantic data models. Thus, we begin by extending the relational model to a rich semantic model supporting the notions of entities with surrogates, generalization and aggregation, null values and set-valued attributes. Then we show that simple extensions to the relational language QUEL are sufficient to provide an easy-to-use and general-purpose user interface for the specification of both queries and updates on this semantic model.

1. To the extent that the functional data model [SiKe] can be viewed as a semantic data model, DAPLEX [Ship] supplies a remarkable exception to this trend.

* UNIX is a trademark of Bell Laboratories.

```
ITEM( Name: c, Type: c, Colors: {c}) key(Name);
DEPT (Dname: c, Floor: i2) key(Dname) ;
SUPPLIER (Company: c, Address: c) key(Company);
SALES ( Dept: DEPT, Item: ITEM, Vol: i2) key(Dept, Item) ;
SUPPLY (Comp: SUPPLIER, Dept: DEPT, Item: ITEM, Vol: i2) ;
EMP (Name: c, Spv: EXMPT null allowed, Dept: DEPT,
    [EXMPT(Sal: i4), NEXMPT(Hrlwg: i4, Ovrt: i4)],
    [EMARRIED (Spouse#: i4), others]) key (Name), key (Spouse#) ;
```

Figure 1. A GEM schema describing the following database:

ITEM:	*for each item, its name, its type, and a set of colors*
DEPT:	*for each department its name and the floor where it is located.*
SUPPLIER:	*the names and addresses of supplier companies.*
SALES:	*for each department and item the volume of sales.*
SUPPLY:	*what company supplies what item to what department in what volume (of current stock).*
EMP:	*the name, the supervisor, and the department of each employee;*
EXMPT:	*employees can either be exempt (all supervisors are) or*
NEXMPT:	*non-exempt; the former earn a monthly salary while the latter have an hourly wage with an overtime rate.*
EMARRIED:	*Employees can either be married or not; the spouse's social security number is of interest for the married ones.*

2. THE DATA MODEL

Figure 1 gives a GEM schema for an example adapted from that used in [LaPi]. The attributes Dept and Item in SALES illustrate how an aggregation is specified by declaring these two to be of type DEPT and ITEM, respectively. Therefore, Dept and Item have occurrences of the entities DEPT and ITEM as their respective values. The entity EMP supplies an example of generalization hierarchy consisting of EMP and two generalization sublists shown in brackets. The attributes Name, Spv and Dept are common to EMP and its subentities in brackets. The first generalization sublist captures the employment status of an employee and consists of the two mutually exclusive subentities EXMPT and NEXMPT (an employee cannot be at the same time exempt and nonexempt). The second generalization sublist describes the marital status of an employees who can either be EMARRIED or belong to the **others** category. Although not shown in this example, each subentity can be further subclassified in the same way as shown here, and so on.

The Colors attribute of entity ITEM is of the set type, meaning that a set of (zero of more) colors may be associated with each ITEM instance; each member of that set is of type c (character string).

Name and Spouse# are the two keys for this family. However, since the uniqueness constraint is waived for keys that are partially or totally null Spouse# is in effect a key for the subentity EMARRIED only.

We will next define GEM's Data Definition Language, using the same meta-notation as in [IDM] to define its syntax. Thus {...} denote a set of zero or more occurrences, while [...] denotes one or zero occurrences. Symbols enclosed in semiquotes denote themselves.

A GEM *schema* consists of a set of uniquely named entities.

1. <Schema>: { <Entity> ; }

An *entity* consists of a set of one or more attributes and the specification of zero or more keys.

2. <Entity>: <EntName> (<AttrSpec>
 { , <AttrSpec> }) { Key }

Attributes can either be single-valued, or be a reference (alias a link) attribute, or be set-valued or represent a generalization sublist.

3. <AttrSpec>: <SimpleAttr> | <RefAttr>
 | <SetAttr> | <Generalization sublist>

4. <SimpleAttr>: <DataAttr> [<null spec>]

5. <DataAttr>: <AttrName> ':' <DataType>

GEM's data types include 1-, 2- and 4-byte integers (respectively denoted by i1, i2 and i4), character strings (denoted by c) and all the remaining IDM's types [IDM].

The user can allow the value of a data attribute to be null either by supplying a regular value to serve in this role, or by asking the system to supply a special value for this purpose (additional storage may be associated with this solution).

6. <null spec>: **null**':' <datavalue> | **null**':' **system**

The option **null allowed** must be entered to allow a null link in a reference attribute.

7. <RefAttr>:
 <AttrName>':' <EntName> [**null allowed**]

Set-valued attributes are denoted by enclosing the type definition in braces.

8. <SetAttr>: <AttrName>':' '{' <DataType>'}'

A generalization sublist defines a choice between two or more disjoint alternatives enclosed in brackets. The keyword **others** is used to denote that the entity need not belong to one the subentities in the list.

9. <Generalization sublist>:
 '[' <Entity> {, <Entity>} , <Entity> ']'
 | '[' <Entity> {, <Entity> } , **others** ']'

Repeated applications of this rule produce a hierarchy of entities called an *entity family*. We have the following conventions regarding the names of a schema.

Names: All entity names must be unique within a schema. Attribute names must be unique within an entity-family (i.e., a top level entity and its subentities). Attributes and entities can be identically named.

Any subset of the attributes from the various entities in a family can be specified to be a key; no two occurrences of entities in the family can have the same non-null key value.

The DDL above illustrates the difference between the relational model and the GEM model. Productions 1 and 2 basically apply to GEM as well as to the relational model, with relations corresponding to entities. In the declaration of attributes, however, a relational system would be limited to the pattern:

<AttrSpec>: <SimpleAttr>

<SimpleAttr>: <DataAttr>

Instead GEM's data model is significantly richer than the relational one. However, we will show that it is possible to deal with this richer semantics via simple extensions to the QUEL language and also to retain the simple tabular view of data on which the congeniality of relational interfaces is built.

3. A GRAPHICAL VIEW of GEM SCHEMAS

DBMS users' prevailing view of schemas is graphical, rather than syntactic. IMS users, for instance, perceive their schemas as hierarchies; Codasyl users view them as networks. Relational users view their database schema and content as row-column tables; this view is always present in a user's mind, and often drawn on a piece of paper as an aid in query formulation. Moreover, relational systems also use the tabular format to present query answers to users. For analogous reasons, it would be very useful to have a graphical — preferably tabular — representation for GEM schemas. A simple solution to this problem is shown in Figure 2.

There is an obvious correspondence between the in-line schema in Figure 1 and its pictorial representation in Figure 2; all entity names appear in the top line, where the nesting of brackets defines the generalization hierarchy. A blank entry represents the option "others". Under each entity-name we find the various attributes applicable to this entity. For reasons of simplicity we have omitted type declarations for all but reference attributes. However, it should be clear that these can be added, along with various graphical devices to represent keys and the option "null allowed" to ensure a complete correspondence between the graphical representation and the in-line definition such as that of Figure 1. Such a representation is all a user needs to realize which queries are meaningful and which updates are correct, and which are not[2].

2. A network-like representation can be derived from this by displaying the reference attributes as arrows pointing from one entity to another. The result is a graph similar to a DBTG data structure diagram with the direction of the arrows reversed. More alluring representations (e.g., using double arrows and lozenges) may be useful for further visualizing the logical structure of data (e.g., to represent the generalization hierarchies); but they do not help a user in formulating GEM queries.

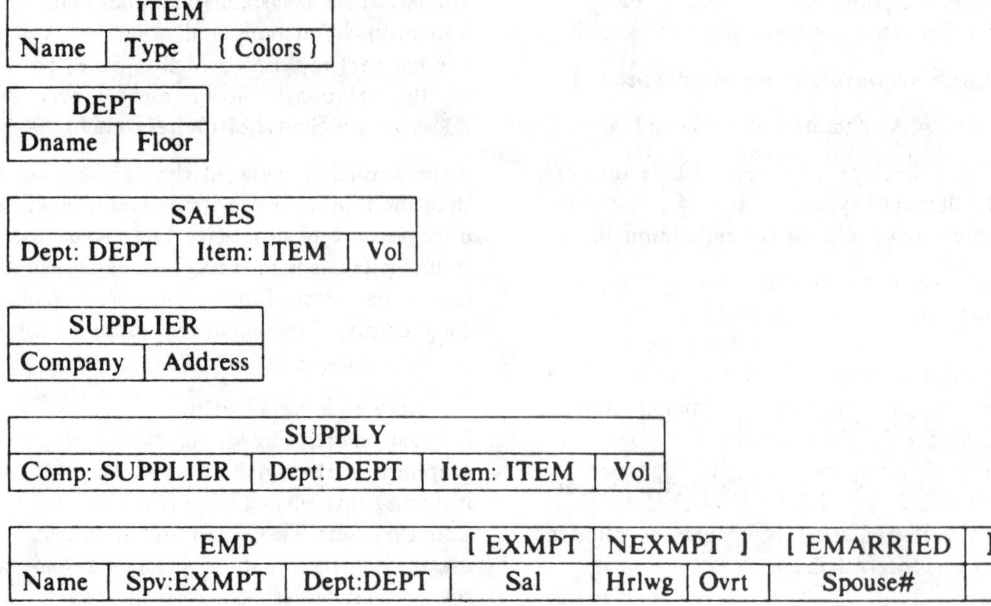

Figure 2. A graphical representation of the GEM schema of Figure 1.

Query results of GEM are also presented in output as row-column tables derived from these tables.

4. THE QUERY LANGUAGE

GEM is designed to be a generalization of QUEL [INGR]; both QUEL and IDM's IDL are upward-compatible with GEM. Whenever the underlying schema is strictly relational (i.e., entities only have data attributes):

<AttrSpec> → <SimpleAttr> → <DataAttr>,

GEM is basically identical to QUEL, with which we expect our readers to be already familiar. However, GEM allows entity names to be used as range variables without an explicit declaration. Thus the query, "Find the names of the departments located on the third floor," that in QUEL can be expressed as

range of dep **is** DEPT
retrieve (dep.Dname)
where dep.Floor=3

Example 1. List each department on the 3rd floor.

in GEM can also be expressed as:

retrieve (DEPT.Dname) **where** DEPT.Floor = 3

Example 2. Same as Example 1.

The option of omitting range declarations improves the conciseness and expressivity of many queries, particularly the simple ones; nor does any loss of generality occur since range declarations can always be included when needed.

The query of Example 2 is therefore interpreted by GEM as if it were as follows:

range of DEPT **is** DEPT
retrieve (DEPT.Dname)
where DEPT.Floor=3

Example 3. Same as examples 1 and 2.

Thus in the syntactic context of the **retrieve** and **where** clauses, DEPT is interpreted as a range variable (ranging over the entity DEPT).

Besides this syntactic sweetening, GEM contains new constructs introduced to handle the richer semantics of its data model; these are discussed in the next sections.

5. AGGREGATION and GENERALIZATION

A *reference* (alias *link*) attribute in GEM has as value an entity occurrence. For instance in the entity SALES, the attribute Dept has an entity of type DEPT as value, and Item an entity of type ITEM, much in the same way as the attribute Vol has an integer as value. Thus, while SALES.Vol is an integer, SALES.Dept is an entity of type DEPT and SALES.Item is an entity of type ITEM. An entity occurrence cannot be printed as such. Thus, the statement,

```
range of S is SALES
retrieve (S)
```

Example 4. A syntactically incorrect query.

is incorrect in GEM (as it would be in QUEL). Therefore, these statements are also incorrect:

```
range of S is SALES
retrieve (S.Dept)
```

Example 5. An incorrect query.

and

```
retrieve (SALES.Item)
```

Example 6. A second incorrect query.

Thus, reference attributes cannot be printed. However both single-valued and set-valued attributes can be obtained by using QUEL's usual dot-notation; thus

```
retrieve (SALES.Vol)
```

Example 7. Find the volumes of all SALES.

will get us the volumes of all SALES. Moreover, since SALES.Dept denotes an entity of type DEPT, we can obtain the value of Floor by simply applying the notation ".Floor" to it. Thus,

```
retrieve (SALES.Dept.Floor)
where SALES.Item.Name="SPORT"
```

Example 8. Floors where departments selling items of type SPORT are located.

will print all the floors where departments that sell sport items are located. The importance of this natural extension of the dot notation cannot be overemphasized; as illustrated by the sixty-six queries in Appendix II of [Zani3], it supplies a very convenient and natural construct that eliminates the need for complex join statements in most queries. For instance, the previous query implicitly specifies two joins: one of SALES with DEPT, the other of SALES with ITEM. To express the same query, QUEL would require three range variables and two join conditions in the **where** clause.

A comparison to functional query languages may be useful here. Reference attributes can be viewed as functions from an entity to another, and GEM's dot-notation can be interpreted as the usual dot-notation of functional composition. Thus GEM has a functional flavor; in particular it shares with languages such as DAPLEX [Ship] the convenience of providing a functional composition notation to relieve users of the burden of explicitly specifying joins. Yet the functions used by GEM are strictly single-valued non-redundant functions; multivalued and inverse functions and other involved constructs are not part of GEM, which is based on the bedrock of the relational theory and largely retains the "Spartan simplicity" of the relational model.

Joins implicitly specified through the use of the dot notation will be called *functional joins*. An alternative way to specify joins is by using *explicit entity joins*, where entity occurrences are directly compared, to verify that they are the same, using the *identity test operator*, **is**[3]. For instance the previous query can also be expressed as follows:[4]

```
range of S is SALES
range of I is ITEM
range of D is DEPT
retrieve (D.Floor)
where D is S.Dept and S.Item is I
                          and I.Type="SPORT"
```

Example 9. Same query as in example 8.

Comparison operators such as =, !=, >, >=, <, and <= are not applicable to entity occurrences.

The names of entities and their subentities — all in the top row of our templates — are unique and can be used in two basic ways. Their first use is in defining range variables. Thus, to request the name and the salary of each married employee one can write:

```
range of e is EMARRIED
retrieve (e.Name, e.Sal)
```

Example 10. Find the name and salary of each married employee.

or simply,

```
retrieve (EMARRIED.Name, EMARRIED.Sal)
```

Example 11. Same as in example 10.

Thus all attributes within an entity can be applied to any of its subtypes (without ambiguity since their names are unique within the family).

---

3. The operator **isnot** is used to test that two objects are not identical.

4. queries in Examples 8 and 9 are equivalent only under the assumption that the Dept attribute in SALES cannot be null. If some SALES occurrences have a null Dept link, then the results of the two queries are not the same, as discussed in detail in the section on null values.

Subentity names can also be used in the qualification conditions of a **where** clause. For instance, an equivalent restatement of the last query is

retrieve (EMP.Name, EMP.Sal)
where EMP **is** EMARRIED

Example 12. Same as example 11.

(Retrieve the name and salary of each employee who is an employee-married.) For all those employees who are married but non-exempt this query returns their names and a null salary. Thus, it is different from

retrieve (EXMPT.Name, EXMPT.Sal)
where EXMPT **is** EMARRIED

Example 13. Find all exempt employees that are married.

that excludes all non-exempt employees at once. The query,

retrieve (EMP.Name) **where**
EMP **is** EXMPT **or** EMP **is** EMARRIED

Example 14. Find all employees that are exempt or married.

will retrieve the names of all employees that are exempt or married.

In conformity to QUEL, GEM also allows the use of the keyword **all** in the role of a target attribute. Thus to print the whole table ITEM one need only specify,

retrieve (ITEM.**all**)

Example 15. Use of **all**.

In the presence of generalization and aggregation the **all** construct can be extended as follows. Say that t ranges over an entity or a subentity E. Then "t.**all**" specifies *all simple and set-valued attributes in E and its subentities.* Thus,

retrieve (EMP.**all**)
where EMP.Sal > EMP.Spv.Sal

Example 16. Extended use of **all**.

returns the name, the salary, the hourly wage and overtime rate, and the spouse's social security number of every employee earning more than his or her supervisor (the values of some of these attributes being null, of course); while

retrieve (EXMPT.**all**)
where EXMPT.Sal > EXMPT.Spv.Sal

Example 17. Use of **all** *with subentities.*

returns only the salaries of those employees.

The following query gives another example of the use of entity joins and the use of subentity names as default range variables (EMP and EMARRIED are the two variables of our query).

retrieve (EMARRIED.Name)
where EMP.Name="J.Black"
and EMP.Dept **is** EMARRIED.Dept

Example 18. Find all married employees in the same department as J.Black.

6. NULL VALUES

A important advantage of GEM over other DBMSs is that it provides for a complete and consistent treatment of null values. The theory underlying our approach was developed in [Zani1, Zani2], where a rigorous justification is given for the practical conclusions summarized next.

GEM conveniently provides several representations of null values in storage and in output tables; at the logical level, however, all occurrences of nulls are treated according to the no-information interpretation discussed in [Zani1].

A three-valued logic is required to handle qualification expressions involving negation. Thus, a condition such as,

ITEM.Type= "SPORT"

evaluates to **null** for an ITEM occurrence where the Type attribute is null. Boolean expressions of such terms are evaluated according to the three-valued logic tables of Figure 3. Qualified tuples are only those that yield a TRUE value; tuples that yield FALSE or the logical **null** are discarded.

It was suggested in [Codd2] that a **null** version of a query should also be provided to retrieve those tuples where the qualification, although not yielding TRUE, does not yield FALSE either. By contrast it was shown in [Zani2] that the TRUE version suffices once the expression "t.A **is null**" and its negation "t.B **isnot null**" are allowed in the qualification expression. Therefore, we have included these clauses in GEM. Thus, rather than requesting a null version answer for the query in Example 2, a user will instead enter this query:

OR	T	F	**null**
T	T	T	T
F	T	F	**null**
null	T	**null**	**null**

AND	T	F	**null**
T	T	F	**null**
F	F	F	F
null	**null**	F	**null**

NOT	
T	F
F	T
null	**null**

Figure 3. Three-valued logic tables.

range of dep **is** DEPT
retrieve (dep.Name)
where dep.Floor **is null**

Example 19. Find the departments whose floors are unspecified.

Indeed, this query returns the names of those departments that neither meet nor fail the qualification of Example 2 (dep.Floor =3).

In [Zani2] it is shown that a query language featuring the three-valued logic with the extension described above is complete — relational calculus and relational algebra are equivalent in power, as query languages. GEM, which is also complete, consists of a mixture of relational calculus and algebra, just like QUEL. In particular, both languages draw from the relational algebra inasmuch as they use set-theoretic notions to eliminate the need for universal quantifiers in queries. The treatment of set and aggregate operations in the presence of null values will be discussed in the next section.

R	
#	A
1	a1
2	a2
3	a3

S			
#	B	Ref1:R	Ref2:R
6	b1	1	2
7	b2	2	**null**

Figure 4. A database.

Null values make possible a precise definition of the notion of implicit join defined by the dot-notation. For concreteness consider the database of Figure 4. On this database, the query

retrieve (S.B, S.Ref1.A)

Example 21. Implicit join without nulls.

produces the following table. (For clarity we show the reference columns although they are never included in the output presented to a user.)

#	B	Ref1	A
6	b1	1	a1
7	b2	2	a2

Figure 5. The result of example 21.

However, the query

retrieve (S.B, S.Ref2.A)

Example 22. Implicit join with nulls.

generates the table,

#	B	Ref2	A
1	b1	2	a2
2	b2	**null**	**null**

Figure 6. Result of example 22.

We can compare these queries with the explicit-join queries:

retrieve (S.B, R.A) **where** S.Ref1 **is** R

Example 23. Explicit join without nulls.

and

retrieve (S.B, R.A) **where** S.Ref2 **is** R

Example 24. Explicit join with null.

Since two entities are identical if and only if their surrogate values are equal, these queries are equivalent (in a system that, unlike GEM, allows direct access to surrogate values) to:

retrieve (S.B, R.A) **where** S.Ref1=R.#

Example 25. Implementing Example 23 by joining on surrogates.

and,

retrieve (S.B, R.A) **where** S.Ref2=R.#

Example 26. Implementing Example 24 by joining on surrogates.

Applying the three-valued logic described above, one concludes that the queries of Examples 21 and 25 return the same result; however, the query of Example 22 produces the table of Figure 6, while that of Example 26 produces the same table but without the last row.

It can be proved that an implicit functional join, such as the one of Figure 6, corresponds to a semi-union join [Zani1], alias a semi-outer join [Codd2], which is in turn defined as the union of S with the entity join, S ⋈ R. Therefore, implicit functional joins are equivalent to explicit entity joins whenever the reference attributes are not null. Therefore, queries of Examples 8 and 9 are equivalent only under the assumption that SALES.Dept is not allowed to be null. However, nulls in SALES.Item would have no effect, since such tuples are discarded anyway because of the qualification, I.Type="SPORT".

7. SET-VALUED ATTRIBUTES and OPERATORS

The availability of set-valued attributes adds to the conciseness and expressivity of GEM schemas and queries. For instance, in the schema of Figure 2, we find a set of colors for each item:

ITEM (Name, Type, {Colors})

This information could also be modeled without set-valued attributes, as follows,

NewITEM (Name, Type, Color)

However, Name is a key in ITEM, but not in NewITEM, where the key is the pair (Name, Color). Thus the functional dependency of Type (that denotes the general category in which a merchandise ITEM lies) on Name is lost with this second schema.

A better solution, from the modeling viewpoint, is to normalize NewITEM to two relations: an ITEM relation without colors, and a COLOR relation containing item identifiers and colors. But this would produce a more complex schema and also more complex queries.

Thus inclusion of set-valued attributes is desirable also in view of the set and aggregate functions already provided by QUEL. In QUEL, and therefore in GEM, the set-valued primitives are provided through the (grouped) **by** construct. For example, a query such as, "for each item print its name, its type and the number of colors in which it comes" can be formulated as follows:

range of I **is** NewITEM
retrieve (I.Name, I.Type,
Tot=**count**(I.Color **by** I.Name, I.Type))

Example 27. Use of **by**.

(Since Type is functionally dependent on Name, I.Type can actually be excluded from the **by** variables without changing the result of the query above.)

Using the set-valued Colors in ITEM, the same query can be formulated as follows:

range of I **is** ITEM
retrieve (I.Name, I.Type, Tot=count(I.Colors))

Example 28. Example 27 with a set-valued attribute.

Thus, ITEM basically corresponds to NewITEM grouped by Name, Type. Therefore, we claim that we now have a more complete and consistent user interface, since GEM explicitly supports as data types those aggregate and set functions that QUEL requires and supports as query constructs.

In order to provide users with the convenience of manipulating aggregates GEM supports the set-comparison primitives included in the original QUEL [HeSW]. Thus, in addition to the set-membership test operator, **in**, GEM supports the following operators:

=	(set) equals
!=	(set) does not equal
>	properly contains
>=	contains
<	is properly contained in
<=	is contained in

These constructs were omitted in recent commercial releases of QUEL [QUEL]. This is unfortunate, since many useful queries cannot be formulated easily without them — as demonstrated by the sixty-six queries in Appendix II of [Zani3].

Unfortunately, set operators are also very expensive to support in standard relational systems. Our approach to this problem is two-fold. First we plan to map subset relationships into equivalent aggregate expressions that are more efficient to support. Then we plan to exploit the fact that set-valued attributes can only be used in this capacity, so that substantial improvements in performance can be achieved by specialized storage organizations. Performance improvements obtained by declaring set-valued attributes may alone justify their addition to the relational interface.

In the more germane domain of user convenience, set-valued attributes entail a more succinct and expressive formulation of powerful queries. For instance, the query "Find all items for which there exist items of the same type with a better selection of colors," can be expressed as follows:

range of I1 for ITEM
range of I2 for ITEM
retrieve (I1.**all**) **where**
I1.Type = I2.Type **and** I1.Colors < I2.Colors

Example 29. Items offering an inadequate selection of colors (for their types).

Thus, set-valued attributes can only be operands of set-valued operators and aggregate functions. The latter, however, can also apply to sets of values from single-valued attributes and reference attributes. Thus, to find all the items supplied to all departments one can use the following query:

retrieve (SUPPLY.Item.Name) **where**
{SUPPLY.Dept **by** SUPPLY.Item} >= {DEPT}

Example 30. Items supplied to all departments.

Observe that sets are denoted by enclosing them in braces. Also, GEM enforces the basic integrity tests on set and aggregate functions (sets must consist of elements of compatible type).

In the presence of null values, the set operators must be properly extended. A comprehensive solution of this complex problem is presented in [Zani1]; for the specific case at hand (sets of values rather than sets of tuples), that reduces to the following simple rule: Null values are excluded from the computation of all aggregate functions or expressions; moreover, they must also be disregarded in the computation of the subset relationship.

8. UPDATES

GEM supports QUEL's standard style of updates, via the three commands *insert*, *delete* and *replace*. Thus,

append to DEPT (Dname="SHOES", Floor= 2)

Example 31. Add the shoe department, 2nd floor.

adds the shoe department to the database.

To insert a soap-dish that comes in brass and bronze finishes, one can write:

append to ITEM (Name="Soap-dis",
Type="Bath", Colors={brass, bronze})

Example 32. Inserting a new item.

Attributes that do not appear in the target list are set to **null** if single-valued; if set-valued, they are assigned the empty set.

The statement,

append to ITEM (Name= "towel-bar",
Type= ITEM.Type, Colors= ITEM.Colors)
where ITEM.Name = "Soap-dish"

Example 33. Completing our bathroom set.

allows us to add a towel-bar of the same type and colors as our soap-dish. (According to the syntax of the **append to** statement, the first occurrence of "ITEM" is interpreted as an entity name, while the others are interpreted as range variables declared by default.)

Hiring T. Green, a new single employee in the shoe department under J. Black, with hourly wage of $ 5.40 and overtime multiple of 2.2, can be specified by the statement,

append to EMP (Name="T.Green", Spv=
EXMPT, Dept = DEPT, Hrlwg=5.40, Ovrt=2.2)
where EXMPT.Name="J.Black"
and DEPT.Dname= "SHOE"

Example 34. Adding a new single non-exempt employee.

In this statement, we can replace EMP by NEXMPT without any change in meaning since the fact that Hrlwg and Ovrt are not null already implies that the employee is non-exempt. Moreover, since no attribute of EMARRIED is mentioned in the target list, the system will set the new EMP to **others**, rather than EMARRIED. (If no attribute of either EXMPT or NEXMPT were in the target list an error message would result, since **others** is not allowed for this generalization sublist.)

If after a while T. Green becomes an exempt employee with a salary of $12000 and a supervisor yet to be assigned, the following update statement can be used:

replace EMP (Spv = **null**, Sal= 12000)
where EMP.Name = "T.Green"

Example 35. Tom Green becomes exempt and loses his supervisor.

Note that the identifier following a **replace** is a range variable, unlike the identifier following a **append to**. The fact that salary is assigned a new value forces an automatic change of type from NEXMPT to EXMPT. Finally, note the assignment of **null** to a reference attribute.

GEM also allows explicit reassignment of entity subtypes. Thus the previous query could, more explicitly, be formulated as follows:

replace NEXMPT
with EXMPT (Spv=**null**, Sal= 12000)
where NEXMPT.Name= "T.Green"

Example 36. Same as Example 35.

Say now that after being married for some time, T. Green divorces; then the following update can be used:

replace EMARRIED **with** EMP
where EMP.Name= "T.Green"

Example 37. T. Green leaves wedlock.

This example illustrates the rule that, when an entity e1 is replaced with an ancestor entity e2, all the entities leading from e1 to e2 are set to **others**. Thus the EMP T. Green will be set to **others** than EMARRIED.

The deletion of an entity occurrence will set to **null** all references pointing to it. Thus the resignation of T. Green's supervisor,

delete EMP.Spv
where EMP.Name = "T.Green"

Example 38. T. Green's supervisor quits.

causes the Spv field in T. Green's record, and in the records of those under the same supervisor, to be set to **null** (if null were not allowed for Spv, then the update would abort and an error message be generated), and then the supervisor record is deleted[5].

5. Of course, according to standard management practices T. Green's people may instead be reassigned to another supervisor, e.g. Green's boss; this policy can be implemented by preceding the deletion of Green's record with an update reassigning his people.

A request such as,

delete EXMPT
where EXMPT.Name="T.Green"

Example 39. T. Green goes too.

is evaluated as the following:

delete EMP
where EMP.Name="T.Green"
and EMP **is** EXMPT

Example 40. Same as above.

Thus, since T. Green is exempt, his record is eliminated; otherwise it would not be.

9. CONCLUSION

A main conclusion of this work is that relational query languages and interfaces are very robust. We have shown that with suitable extensions the relational model provides a degree of modeling power that matches or surpasses those of the various conceptual and semantic models proposed in the literature. Furthermore, with simple extensions, the relational language QUEL supplies a congenial query language for such a model. The result is a friendly and powerful semantic user interface that retains, and in many ways surpasses, the ease of use and power of a strictly relational one. Because of these qualities, GEM provides an attractive interface for end-users; moreover, as shown in [Andr], it supplies a good basis on which to build database interfaces for programming languages.

The approach of extending the relational model is preferable to adopting a new semantic model for many reasons. These include compatibility and graceful evolution, since users that do not want the extra semantic features need not learn nor use them; for these users GEM reduces to QUEL. Other advantages concern definition and ease of implementation. As indicated in this paper and shown in [Tsur, TsZa], all GEM queries can be mapped into equivalent QUEL expressions. In this way a precise semantic definition and also a notion of query completeness for GEM can be derived from those of QUEL, which in turn maps into the relational calculus [Ullm]. This is a noticeable improvement with respect to many semantic data models that lack formal, precise definitions. Finally, the mapping of GEM into standard QUEL supplies an expeditious and, for most queries, efficient means of implementation; such an implementation, planned for the commercial database machine IDM 500, is described in [Tsur, TsZa].

Acknowledgments

The author is grateful to J. Andrade and S. Tsur for helpful discussions and recommendations on the design of GEM. Thanks are due to D. Fishman, M. S. Hecht, E. Y. Lien, E. Wolman and the referees for their comments and suggested improvements.

References

[Andr] Andrade J. M. "Genus: a programming language for the design of database applications," Internal Memorandum, Bell Laboratories, 1982.

[Brod] Brodie, M.L., "On Modelling Behavioural Semantics of Databases," *7th Int. Conf. Very Large Data Bases*, pp. 32-42, 1981.

[Codd1] Codd, E.F., "Relational Database: A Practical Foundation for Productivity" *Comm. ACM*, 25,2, pp. 109-118, 1982.

[Codd2] Codd, E.F., "Extending Database Relations to Capture More Meaning," *ACM Trans. Data Base Syst.*, 4,4, pp. 397-434, 1979.

[Chen] Chen, P.P., "The Entity-Relationship Model – Toward an Unified View of Data," *ACM Trans. Database Syst.*, 1, 1, pp. 9-36, 1976.

[DSIS] Lien, Y.E., J.E. Shopiro and S. Tsur. "DSIS – A Database System with Interrelational Semantics," *7th Int. Conf. Very Large Data Bases*, pp. 465-477, 1981.

[HeSW] Held, G.D, M.R. Stonebraker and E. Wong, "INGRES: a Relational Data Base System," *AFIPS Nat. Computer Conf.*, Vol. 44, pp. 409-416, 1975.

[KiMc] King, R. and D. McLeod, "The Event Database Specification Model," *2nd Int. Conf. Databases – Improving Usability and Responsiveness*, Jerusalem, June 22-24, 1982.

[IDM] IDM 500 Software Reference Manual. Ver. 1.3, Sept 1981. Britton-Lee Inc., 90 Albright Way, Los Gatos, CA, 95030.

[INGR] Stonebraker, M., E. Wong, P. Kreps and G. Held. "The Design and Implementation of INGRES", *ACM Trans on Database Syst.* 1:3, pp. 189-222, 1976.

[LaPi] Lacroix, M. and A. Pirotte, "Example queries in relational languages," MBLE Tech. note 107, 1976 (MBLE, Rue Des Deux Gares 80, 1070 Brussels).

[QUEL] Woodfill, J. et al., "INGRES Version 6.2 Reference Manual," Electronic Research Laboratory, Memo UCB/ERL-M78/43, 1979.

[Ship] Shipman, D.W., "The Functional Model and the Lata Language DAPLEX," *ACM Trans. Data Base Syst.*, 6,1, pp. 140-173, 1982.

[SiKe] Sibley, E.H. and L. Kershberg, "Data Architecture and Data Model Considerations," *AFIPS Nat. Computer Conf.*, pp. 85-96,1977.

[SmSm] Smith, J.M. and C.P. Smith, "Database Abstractions: Aggregation and Generalization," *ACM Trans. Database Syst.*, 2, 2, pp. 105-133, 1977.

[Tsur] Tsur, S., "Mapping of GEM into IDL," internal memorandum, Bell Laboratories, 1982.

[TsZa] Tsur, S. and C. Zaniolo, "The Implementation of GEM – Supporting a Semantic Data Model on a Relational Backend", submitted for publication.

[Ullm] Ullman, J., "Principles of Database Systems," Computer Science Press, 1980.

[Zani1] Zaniolo, C., "Database Relations with Null Values," *ACM SIGACT-SIGMOD Symposium on Principles of Database Systems*, Los Angeles, California, March 1982.

[Zani2] Zaniolo, C., "A Formal Treatment of Nonexistent Values in Database Relations," Internal Memorandum, Bell Laboratories, 1983.

[Zani3] Zaniolo, C., "The Database language GEM," Internal Memorandum, Bell Laboratories, 1982.

Appendix I: GEM SYNTAX

This syntax is an extension of, and use the same metanotation as, that of [IDM]. Thus {...} denote a set of zero or more occurrences, while [..] denotes one or zero occurrences. Symbols enclosed in semiquotes denote themselves.

```
retrieve [ unique ] ( <query target list> ) [where <qualification> ]

<query target list>     : <query target element> '{' , <query target element> '}'
<query target element>  : <attribute> /* a simple or set-valued attribute*/
                        | <name> = <expression>
                        | <name> = <set>
<attribute>             : <variable> . <name>
<variable>              : <variable> { . <name> } /* every <name> must denote a reference attribute/*
                        | <range variable>  /* declared in the range statement/*
                        | <entity name>     /* range variable by default/*
<expression>            : <aggregate>  /* count(), average(), etc. /*
                        | <attribute>  /* a simple attribute/*
                        | <constant>
                        | - <expression>
                        | ( <expression> )
                        | <function> /* see [IDM] for a definition of functions /*
<set>                   : <attribute> /* a set-valued attribute/*
                        | '{' <extended expr> [ by <extended expr> { , <extended expr> } ]
                            [ where <qualification> ] '}'
                        | <constants set>
<extended expr>         : <expression> | <variable>
<constants set>         : '{' '}' | '{' <constant> {, <constant>} '}'
<qualification>         : ( <qualification> )
                        | not <qualification>
                        | <qualification> and <qualification>
                        | <qualification> or <qualification>
                        | <clause>
<clause>                : <expression> <relop> <expression>
                        | < extended expr> in <set>
                        | <set> <relop> <set>
                        | <attribute> <identity test> null
                        | <variable> <identity test> <variable>
<relop>                 : = | != | < | <= | > | >=
<identity test>         : is | isnot

append [ to] <entity name> ( < update target list>)

delete <variable> [ where <qualification> ]

replace <variable> [with <entity name>] (<update target list>)

<update target list> : <update target element> '{' , <update target element> '}'

<update target element>     : <name> = <expression> /* <name> of a simple attribute */
                            | <name> = <variable> /* <name> of a reference attribute*/
                            | <name> = <set> /* <name> of a set attribute */
                            | <name> = null /* <name> of a simple or reference attribute/*
```

Making Smalltalk a Database System

George Copeland
Servio Logic Corporation

David Maier
Oregon Graduate Center
and
Servio Logic Corporation

Abstract

To overcome limitations in the modeling power of existing database systems and provide a better tool for database application programming, Servio Logic Corporation is developing a computer system to support a set-theoretic data model in an object-oriented programming environment. We recount the problems with existing models and database systems. We then show how features of Smalltalk, such such as operational semantics, its type hierarchy, entity identity and the merging of programming and data language, solve many of those problems. Nest we consider what Smalltalk lacks as a database system: secondary storage management, a declarative semantics, concurrency, past states. To address these shortcomings, we needed a formal data model. We introduce the GemStone data model, and show how it helps to define path expressions, a declarative semantics and object history in the OPAL language. We summarize similar approaches, and give a brief overview of the GemStone system implementation.

1. Introduction

The areas of database systems, programming languages and artificial intelligence already have large overlaps in some areas [PP]. Designing a state-of-the-art system in one field means employing ideas from the other two fields. Databases require better integrated application programming interfaces, expert systems must deal with large collections of base facts, and programming languages need richer ways to model their data. Current database systems are primarily an effort to implement an abstract data type over the memory of a machine, rather than to support easy and natural modeling of real-world enterprises. They hide the complexities of file systems and indexing techniques, and provide a degree of physical data independence. The next generation of database systems will be knowledge management systems, with more support for data semantics, inferencing and general purpose programming [DE].

Servio Logic Corporation is designing a programming system for database applications, presently called GemStone, that avoids the restrictions and problems of current commercial database systems. The GemStone language, OPAL, incorporates ideas from knowledge representation, abstract data types, and object-oriented programming, as well as semantic data languages, set-theoretic data models, nonprocedural query languages and temporal semantics. It provides rich data modeling facilities with a natural interface to a high-level programming language. This paper considers the choice of Smalltalk-80* [GR] as a basis for the OPAL language, and outlines the enhancements we made to Smalltalk to derive the OPAL language and GemStone system.

2. Shortcomings of Commercial Database Systems

We outline, in this section, the limitations of existing database systems in the areas of data modeling and programming interfaces. We also set forth the GemStone design goals that address each limitation.

A. Type Definition Facilities: Most database systems supply a fixed set of simple types—integer, real and character string—and perhaps a few specialized types, such as date or money. However, they lack the ability to define new simple types and to add operations to the existing types. We can't create a new "employee number" type with a non-standard ordering, or a new operator "nearest payday" on dates, without going outside the database system to an application programming language. The constructors for higher-level types are also limited. The relational model supports "tuple" and "set of homogeneous tuples" (relation). The hierarchical model supports "segment" and "tree of segments". The network model has "record" and "owned list of record" (CODASYL set). A value in a record itself cannot be a structured data item, except for limited support of repeating fields. The operations for higher-level types are induced by the type constructors and cannot be extended. The operations are similar in the three models: access or set a field in a tuple, segment or record; traverse a relation, tree or list in some order; select a record from a structured data item based on a Boolean condition. In addition, the relational model supports operations on entire relations, such as project and join. Even so, the set of operators can't be augmented within the database system.

A final point: Database systems don't separate

cleanly type definition from data declaration. For example, in relational systems, it is seldom possible to define a relation type (scheme) independently of declaring a relation to be of that type. Thus, redundant specification is necessary to declare several relations as instances of that type.

Some design goals of GemStone are to support arbitrary levels of data structuring, to allow definitions of operations on types, and to uniformly separate type definition from type instantiation.

B. Artificial Restrictions: Database systems abound with restrictions on legal database schemes and databases. The limitations often arise from implementation artifacts creeping into the data model. Examples are limits on field lengths, the number of fields in a record, number of files, number of relations in a query, number of indexable fields, number of records in a file and depth of repeating groups.

A design goal of GemStone is to avoid arbitrary limits on the sizes of schemes and data items. Only the size of secondary storage should impose size limits on data items.

C. Structural Limitations: The data structuring capabilities of current database systems do not adequately support the complexities and variations that occur in real data. Records (segments, tuples) of a given type must be identical in structure. Every record of a given type must have the same fields and a field must draw its values from the same type in each record. At best there is an allowance for null values or missing fields. Databases are less accommodating of an extra middle name or the possibility that a company car may be assigned to a department or to an individual employee. Current systems also have restrictions on how the data structuring operations may be applied. Tuples in relations are flat records of atomic values, with no repetition of fields. A set in the network model can't have owner and member records of the same type. In the hierarchical model, databases must be strict trees; segment instances can't share subsegments (except through logical pointers).

Dynamic modification of schemes is supported only in a few extant systems. Modifying a type, such as a relation scheme, requires reformatting an entire file.

GemStone design goals are to allow for variations in structured objects, to allow arbitrary data items as values, and to support modification of database schemes without database restructuring.

D. Modeling Power: Whenever data structures in a database system won't support the actual structure of information in the real world, then the form of the real-world information gets over-simplified in the database scheme, or it must be encoded into available data structures. If the structure of the real world is over-simplified, the utility and reliability of the data is compromised. For example, if a database scheme only allows for a single middle name, two people who are distinguishable by name might become indistinguishable in the database. When information is encoded, such as flattening a set-valued field into several tuples, application programs must deal with the encoding. Encoding information also means that a database needs extra integrity constraints to ensure that only legitimate encodings appear.

A data model provides ***entity identity*** if the data representing any entity can be referenced directly as a unit, and the entity may explicitly appear multiple places in a database without any pointer or other indirection mechanism visible to users. Lack of entity identity leads to inconvenience in modeling and proliferation of constraints. In the relational model, to reflect that two people have the same set of children requires either a relation representing named sets of children, or a rather complicated data dependency. In the first case, the indirect reference to the set is visible to users. In the second case, the set of children cannot be referenced as a unit. Entity identity also allows easier sharing of data between data items. In the relational model, two tuples for employees assigned to the same department must represent that commonality through logical pointers to the same department tuple. Logical pointing requires that the database designer find or create a key in the departments relation. Some update anomalies come about because names of entities are used for logical pointers. Consider the previous case when employee tuples use department name to indicate the link to a department. What happens when we want to change the department name? Object-based data models provide entity identity, but other data models can be adapted for entity identity. The trend in extending the relational model is adding surrogates for tuples [Cd]. The network model supports some degree of object identity, but not in an arbitrary manner. A record may belong to more than one set, but not to two instances of the same set type.

Commercial databases to date haven't supported a hierarchy of types. We can't exploit the similarities between, say, employees and managers. so as to define common operations. Type hierarchies are common in AI systems, have been suggested for data modeling by Smith and Smith [SS] and others, and provide the organizational framework in the TAXIS data model [MBW].

Another problem with current systems is that update commands are machine-oriented. Commands insert, delete and modify parts of data items. Such updates do not necessarily correspond to any possible change in the real world, such as changing an employee's birthdate. Changes in the state of the real world typically involve updates to several database objects. Hiring an employee could involve insertions in several relations. Furthermore, the database updates for a real-world change needn't be of the same sort. Changing the times a course meets could entail both insertions and deletions in a database. Being able to model real-world changes is a powerful capability for a database system. It can help in choosing implementations for data structures, and reduce the overhead in integrity checking, since updates can be made to preserve constraints. Applications are easier to write, because common operations on the database can be expressed succinctly. In those cases where some encoding of information is needed, say for time or space efficiency, the encoding and decoding can be hidden in the update operations.

A GemStone design goal is to provide powerful data modeling capabilities through both flexible data structuring and the ability to model real-world changes.

E. Access to Past States of a Database: A temporal extension to a data model provides historical access for users and an error recovery mechanism [Cp]. Although historical access is common in manual systems, it is usually not provided in automated database systems.

People are not only interested in the current state of systems. They are also interested in the events and trends that led to a particular state, to help decide what to do next. For example, accounting, legal, financial, manufacturing and engineering applications keep and use history for auditing, trend analysis, patent applications and management tracking. For databases to be useful as models for these systems, they must capture and provide access to history as well as current state. Temporal extensions of data models are a hot research topic of late, but the results of that research haven't reached commercial systems yet, except in the form of time series packages.

Deletion was invented as a means of reusing expensive on-line computer storage. However, the cost of on-line mass storage has been rapidly decreasing. Furthermore, several emerging technologies, such as write-once optical disk [Mi], vertical recording magnetic disks [El1] and rewritable magneto-optical disks [El2] promise a significant reduction in cost per bit of on-line storage. A temporal data model replaces deletion by maintaining object history, thereby exploiting this cost trend by offering historical access for users.

Most database systems do keep a history in the form of checkpoints and recovery logs, usually stored on removable media for error recovery. However, they provide no convenient or efficient way for users to access history. A temporal data model provides both historical access and error recovery.

A GemStone design goal is to explicitly capture the history of database states as part of the data model, and to support queries that access past states.

F. Separation of Languages: In the past, computer systems have placed more emphasis on programs than data. That focus manifests itself in the design of traditional programming languages, where data that exists for the life of the program (variables) is treated differently from data that persists after execution (files). Files generally provide for much less data structure than program variables, requiring user-generated encodings for structured values written to files. In the database world, data manipulation languages do not support arbitrary computations on database objects, necessitating an interface to a general-purpose programming language. One language must be embedded in the other, either the programming language in the database language, as in PRTV [To], or the more frequent situation of calls to the database system from the programming language.

The problem with having two languages is "impedance mismatch." One mismatch is conceptual--the data language and the programming languages might support widely different programming paradigms. One could be a declarative language while the other is strictly procedural. Sometimes even a third language is involved, the operating system command language, which further complicates database interaction. The other mismatch is structural--the languages don't support the same data types, so some structure is reflected back at the interface. For example, we can access a relational database using SQL from COBOL, but when the time comes to do some computation, COBOL can only operate at the tuple level. The relational structure is lost. The reflection problem is particularly severe for entity-based data models, where identity can be lost if an entity must be mapped to a character string, a record or whatever to be passed to an application program.

A GemStone design goal is to have a single language for data manipulation, general computation and system commands.

3. Our Strategy

Our task at Servio Logic was to design a database system that overcomes the limitations listed above. We wanted a more flexible data model, embedded in a general-purpose programming language. We began with a set-theoretic data model, designed a calculus and algebra for it, and developed an algorithm to translate queries from algebra to calculus. We chose Pascal as the point of departure for the OPAL programming language. That choice proved unsatisfactory. Pascal data type definitions do not support adding operations to a type, nor hierarchies of types. Also, the Pascal type definition paradigm is rigid about typing of subparts of structures, and does not support entity identity well. Multiple use of a data item only takes place through logical references, as in the relational model, or through explicit pointers, which clashed with GemStone design goals. In addition, we saw no clean way to add system commands to Pascal.

We wanted types to have a more operational semantics, and to support entity identity better. In trying to modify Pascal to accommodate our goals, we ended up with something resembling an object-oriented programming language. The resulting data language didn't look much like Pascal at all. We knew there would be user reluctance to switch to a database system that required learning a language dissimilar to any common programming language. We scrapped the Pascal-based version of OPAL, and to begin anew with an object-oriented language, Smalltalk-80 (ST80), as a basis. While ST80 does not have a wide following of users yet, we felt it was the direction of data languages of the future, and there was enough existing literature to acquaint potential users with the concepts of the language.

4. Smalltalk-80

4.1. A Short Description

ST80 is based on three concepts: *object*, *message*, and *class*. An object is essentially private memory with a public interface. The private memory is structured as a list of named or numbered *instance variables*. An object accepts messages that ask it to access, modify or return a portion of its private memory. So that each object does not have to carry around a list of messages it handles, objects are organized into classes. A class is a group of structurally similar objects that respond to the same set of messages. The class definition contains the procedures (*methods*) that its objects use to respond to messages. Classes are organized in a (strict) hierarchy, so that they can share common structure and methods in a superclass.

For example, an object of class **ArrayedCollection** has messages to put a value at a certain index, return the value at a certain index, create a textual display of its entire value, and "grow" itself to accommodate more values. We can define a class

Employee, with each instance having a name, a set of departments and a salary. Instances might accept messages to return the employee's name, change the employee's salary, or assign the employee to different departments. A subclass **Manager** of class **Employee** could define additional structure, such as the department managed, and additional messages, such as one to return a list of subordinate employees.

4.2. What it Brings

ST80 has a simple and elegant paradigm for general-purpose programming that meshed well with our data model. ST80 objects gave us entity identity; a single object can be a component of several other objects. ST80 also provides a clear distinction between identity and structural equivalence of entities. Two entities are identical if they are represented by the same object. Two entities can have equivalent structures (have all component values the same), but not be the same object. Thus, we can distinguish, say, two gates in a circuit that have all the same characteristics, but are not physically the same gate. While this identity-equivalence distinction is not present explicitly in other commercially used models, users should recognize it when modeling their enterprises. The distinction is most obvious during update, where if two objects share a component, updates to that component through one object are visible in the other object.

The class mechanism of ST80 handled our requirements for type definition. Messages and methods give us a means to define types with operations, and to hide encodings. The class mechanism provides a hierarchy of types, albeit a strict hierarchy, so that similar types an share operations. Classes give a means of controlling the updates that can be performed on a data object, through a class's message protocol. Also, classes make database schemes easy to modify, and new variants can be constructed easily with the subclass mechanism.

Finally, we note that ST80 treats system components as full-fledged objects, giving a natural and uniform way to issue system commands from within the ST80 language.

4.3. What it Lacks

The ST80 language met our needs for type definition and general computation within a data language. Why couldn't we take the ST80 system as is and use it as the basis of a database system? The first problem is that ST80 does not handle large numbers of data items or large data items. Only 32K objects are allowed in most implementations, and the maximum size for an object is 64K bytes. We need to handle more and larger data items for the databases we want to support, such as long documents and graphical images. There are also several arbitrary size limits in the ST80 system, such as the number of variables in a method, which could be exceeded in applications we anticipate. Being a single-user system, ST80 lacks the amenities of a production database system: concurrent access of data by multiple users, recovery mechanisms, and database administrator control over replication, authorization and auxiliary structures. Because ST80 is a strictly procedural language, it does not have any declarative constructs for data manipulation. We feel that associative access to subparts of an object is a necessary aid to application program design. Also, a declarative semantics allows more flexibility in evaluating queries, and that flexibility is needed to support reasonable optimization on queries involving large amounts of data.

The ST80 model of data, while meeting many of our requirements, does not have everything we want. It does not support object histories--past values of instance variables are not retained. We want optional instance variables, without a storage penalty in instances not containing the optional variables, and the ability to add new variables to existing instances, which ST80 does not provide. We also want a path syntax for navigating through objects, and to allow assignments to path expressions. That feature allows a user to circumvent the class protocol for updating objects, but sometimes it is the most natural way to define methods.

5. Enhancing Smalltalk as a Database Language

Our first concern in designing the GemStone system is to provide a database system with more modeling power and flexibility than is available currently in commercial systems. We actually developed a data model for GemStone before beginning the design of the OPAL language. We will first introduce the Set Theoretic Data Model (STDM), and discuss its advantages over previous models. STDM turned out to be a reasonable approximation of the object structure of ST80. The structure of all the classes provided with ST80 is too complex to provide the basis for a useful data model. STDM takes a more uniform view of objects, treating most as labeled sets, and that treatment allows a fairly simple path syntax and set calculus.

We then turn to a temporal extension of STDM, and indicate how histories of object states are structured and accessed. Finally in this section, we consider the merger of ST80 and the STDM, resulting in the OPAL language and a slightly modified model, the GemStone Data Model.

5.1. A Short Description of STDM STDM is based on labeled sets of heterogeneous values, which themselves can be sets or simple values. The model builds on the work of Childs [Chi], but is not identical to his model. A piece of an STDM database might look like

```
Acme: {Departments: {A12: {Name: 'Sales', Managers: {'Nathen', 'Roberts'},
                           Budget: 142,000},
                     {A16: {Name: 'Research', Managers: {'Carter'},
                           Budget: 256,500},
                     ...},
       Employees: {E62: {Name: {First: 'Ellen', Last: 'Burns'}
                           Salary: 24,650, Depts: {'Marketing'}},
                   E83: {Name: {First: 'Robert', Last: 'Peters'},
                           Salary: 24,000, Depts: {'Sales','Planning'},
                           Phones:{3949, 3882}},
                   ...}}
```

(Examples in this section are not necessarily expressed in OPAL syntax.) STDM has *simple types*, generally subsets of number or character types, and *sets*. A set (denoted with {...}) has *elements*, each of which has an *element name* that labels the element and a *value*, which can be from a simple type or a set. In the sixth line of the database segment above, Name: {First: 'Ellen', Last: 'Burns'} is an element with element name **Name** and {First: 'Ellen', Last: 'Burns'} as the value. Essentially, elements function as identifier-value pairs. No two elements in a set may have the same element name.

For sets without labels, arbitrary aliases are used as element names. Presumably, the database system can generate unique aliases upon demand. In the database fragment above, the labels for department and employee sets (A12, A16,..., E62, E83,...) are aliases. In the example, we have elided element names for sets of simple values, such as {'Nathen', 'Roberts'}.

STDM uses a path syntax for accessing subparts of a set. If X is a variable whose value is the set above, then sample path expressions are X!Departments!A16!Managers and X!Employees!E62!Name.

We have developed a set-calculus query system for the STDM. As an example query, suppose we want to know employees and managers such that the employee is in the manager's department, and the employee's salary is more than 10% of the department's budget. The set-calculus expression for this query is

```
{{Emp: e, Mgr: m} where
  (e ∈ X!Employees) and
  (∃ d ∈ X!Departments) [(m ∈ d!Managers) and
     (d!Name ∈ e!Depts) and (e!Salary > 0.10 * d!Budget)]}
```

Note that a declarative syntax is needed for easy navigation through sets with aliases as element names, such as Employees. We have developed a set algebra, and an algorithm to translate a set-calculus expression to a set-algebra expression.

5.2. Advantages of STDM

STDM is a more powerful modeling mechanism than data models supported in other commercial systems. Any place a simple value can occur, we can have a set of values, or a structured value. There is unlimited nesting of sets, so a single value can have arbitrarily detailed internal structure. STDM is also flexible: optional element names in a set are handled, and elements with new element names can be added to a set. The value associated with a particular element name is not restricted to a single type. For sets representing company cars, the element name AssignedTo could have a value that is an employee, a department or a set of departments.

The power and the flexibility of STDM allows closer and more direct modeling of real-world domains. Many standard data structures can be represented straightforwardly with STDM sets. Arrays may be represented by sets with numbers as element names:

{1: {'Anders', 'Roberts'},
2: {'Roberts', 'Ching'},
3: {'Albrecht', 'Ching'}}

The index set for an array need not be positive integers—with a little more set structure it could be an arbitrary type. Record structures, with arbitrary levels and types of subrecords, are represented naturally in STDM. A relation is represented as a set of tuples, where each tuple is a set with element names corresponding to attributes of the relation. For example, the relation

A	B	C
1	3	4
1	5	4

is represented by the set

{T1: {A: 1, B: 3, C: 4},
T2: {A: 1, B: 5, C: 4}}.

Data structured as in the hierarchical model have a direct representation in STDM, by modeling a segment as a set, with elements that are field values or sets of child segments. STDM can model arbitrary combinations of arrays, sets and records.

Some structures, handled readily in STDM, would require significant encoding to fit in the relational or hierarchical models. A set-valued attribute, such as children of an employee, has to be "flattened" into several tuples in the relational model, one per child. For example, the set structure

{Name: {First: 'Robert', Last: 'Peters'},
Children: {'Olivia', 'Dale', 'Paul'}}

comes out as a three-tuple relation:

FirstName	LastName	Child
Robert	Peters	Olivia
Robert	Peters	Dale
Robert	Peters	Paul

However, under such a representation, the set of children does not exist anywhere as a single object. An alternative would be to form an additional relation to represent sets of children. This alternative requires names for the sets of children, and introduces an artifact at the user level, requiring extra joins to bring the description of an employee together. There is unavoidable redundancy in either approach: Some value is going to be repeated three times. Operations on the set, other than insertions and deletions, are awkward to express. For example, stipulating one set is the subset of another set requires two quantifiers in relational calculus. STDM, while requiring some encoding for certain data items, at least preserves the integrity of entities. A set of children can be represented and manipulated as a single data item at some level. Reducing the amount of encoding to model real-world entities, and being able to preserve the integrity of those entities, makes data easier to understand and applications simpler to write.

The declarative syntax for STDM simplifies many application programs. It also allows much more access planning by the database system than with an equivalent query specified procedurally. The set calculus provides the basis for a declarative query syntax. A distinguishing feature of our calculus, as compared to relational calculus, is that variables can be bound to functions of other variables, rather than only to fixed database objects. Because a variable may assume a value that is a structured object, a condition such as

m ∈ d!Managers,

makes sense.

5.3. Adding History to Objects

5.3.1. Transaction Time vs. Event Time

The first question to face when adding time to a data model is What kind of time to incorporate? *Transaction time* is the time when an event is recorded in the database. *Event time* is the time when an event occurs in the real world GemStone uses transaction time to record history, rather than event time. We discuss that choice.

In many databases, transaction time and event time are either the same or close enough to be considered equivalent. Furthermore, as computer systems are used to more completely automate our real-world systems, databases are increasingly becoming more real-time, in which the official time of an event is the moment when the event is recorded in the database. Even though a database is a model of a real-world system, the database itself is a real-world system. Thus, the recording process itself is a significant real-world event whose event time is its transaction time.

Transaction time has a simple semantics that is application independent. Thus, transaction time is easily automated by a database system. In contrast, the semantics of event time is application dependent, so that event time is difficult for a database system to automate on behalf of users. Note that the use of transaction time to record history in GemStone does not imply that event time cannot be captured as user-defined data. In fact, the extendibility of classes that OPAL provides allows any semantics for time to easily be added by users. Since transaction time is system-generated, and cannot be modified by users, it provides high integrity. In contrast, event time must be modifiable by users when a discrepancy is discovered between the real world and its database model.

When we venture to extend the scope of computer science, we often have no empirical basis within our young field upon which to base our decisions. In the case of extending a data model to manage history, we do have some empirical basis in the fields of accounting and other recordkeeping disciplines. Accountants have dealt with the issue of transaction time vs. event time for many years, if not centuries. They have seen as fundamental the consideration of the recording process itself as a significant real-world event. Reed [Re1, Re2] argues that storing transaction time is useful for synchronizing concurrent transactions. This observation offers the possibility of sharing the overhead of generating and storing the transaction time over both functions.

5.3.2. The Temporal Extension

In the data model presented so far, we represent each element of an object as an element name-value pair. We represent history in STDM by replacing an element's single value with a set of values. The element name is associated with each value via a transaction time. The binding between an element name and its associated value is indexed by time. For example, if E is a set representing an employee, then E!Salary is actually a mapping from transaction times to values giving the salaries of the employee in past and present states of the database. If T represents a point in time, then E!Salary@T gives the value of E's salary at time T. That is, E!Salary@T is the value that E!Salary had in the state of the database that existed at time T. The relationship between an element name and a particular value

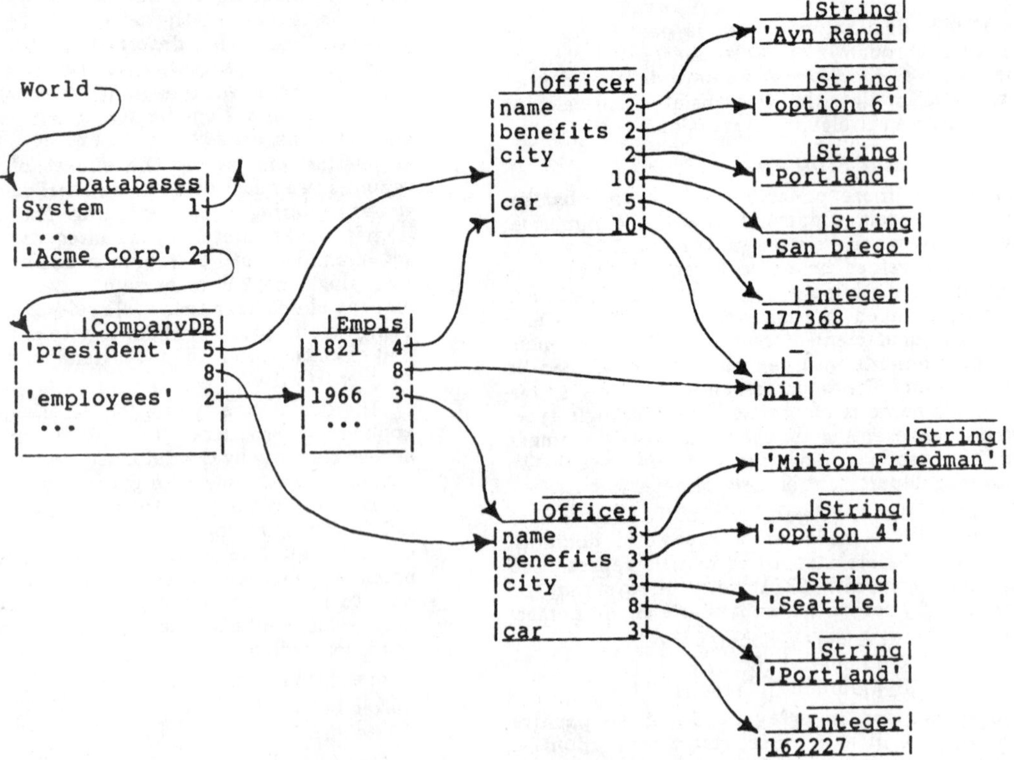

Figure 1: A Database with History

begins at the transaction time for the value, and ends when a new value is associated with the same element and a later transaction time. Objects themselves do not have time. Only their relationships with their elements are indexed by time.

The example in Figure 1 illustrates the temporal extension. The numbers at the right side of each box represent the transaction times of relationships. The example shows that at time 8, the company president was changed from 'Ayn Rand' to 'Milton Friedman'. The example represents a history of two presidents. Ayn was president from time 5 to 8. Milton was president from time 8 to the current time. Prior to this change, Milton had worked for the company in Seattle. His new appointment required a move to Portland. The example represents a history of Ayn as an employee from 2 to 8. The fact that Ayn left as an employee is indicated by the relationship in the employees object with her employee number 1821 as an element name and with time 8, whose value is the object nil. Shortly after leaving the company, Ayn moved to San Diego. She was allowed to continue to use her company car until her move at time 10.

A current transaction can access the new company president by the path expression

World!'Acme Corp'!'president'

or at a time in the recent past with the path expression

World!'Acme Corp'!'president'@10.

If the argument of @ were 7, then the previous president would be accessed. As another example, the previous president's current city, San Diego, can be accessed by the path

World!'Acme Corp'!'president'@7!city.

5.4. Merging ST80 and STDM

As we said, STDM was conceived before ST80 was chosen as the basis for OPAL. STDM provides the basis to add path syntax, set calculus and object history to ST80 to get OPAL. Conversely, there some deficiencies in STDM that ST80 helped overcome. While STDM is powerful and flexible, it did not provide all the modeling power we wanted. STDM does not support entity identity, except for simple, non-changeable values. STDM sets are unlike mathematical sets, in that any set instance can be an element in at most one other set. In mathematical sets, of course, an element may be a member of several sets. If two sets represent two employees in the same department, they could have logical pointer to the same department set, or they could duplicate the department set as an element. Neither alternative is entirely satisfactory. The first requires navigating across data objects at the logical level; the second entails added complexity when updating a department description. Furthermore, without entity identity, STDM cannot capture network schemes directly, where a single record may be an element of several sets. STDM does not have a good type definition mechanism. We had a hard time deciding whether types should be associated with sets or elements, or both; how to describe types; how to specify operations on instances of a type; and how to factor element names from instances of a type. Also, we had no structure on types--there was no type hierarchy.

Definition of operations for a type was especially important to us, as certain real-world structures still required encoding. Thus, we needed a mechanism for information hiding, to make database objects appear and behave as their real-world counterparts. For example, to make a relation behave as a relation, we needed a tuple to appear as a mapping rather than a set. We also wanted to define subclasses of simple types with operators and orderings different from the parent type.

STDM does not provide a general programming interface. Set calculus is its only vehicle for describing set access and update. We needed a procedural language to support the set algebra. Further, we found many examples where procedural updates would be clearer and more succinct than the calculus equivalents. We also wanted to include general computations in the conditions of calculus expressions.

Merging STDM with ST80 to overcome these deficiencies is straightforward. We can identify sets and simple values in STDM with objects in ST80 and elements with instance variable-value pairs. Just as STDM induced changes in ST80 to get OPAL, ST80 dictated changes in STDM. We call the revised model the GemStone Data Model (GSDM). In STDM we had concentrated on names--path names and element names--in trying to assign types. In GSDM the focus became values (objects), and that is where typing went on. We still feel that some typing of element names could give us big performance advantages, such as more flexibility on access paths when processing declarative queries. and we are looking at this extension to OPAL, as are others [Bl, Ha].

The switch from Pascal to ST80 as a basis for OPAL was propitious. We have a single language for general programming, data manipulation and system commands, with excellent support for data and operation definition. There is no impedance mismatch between application language and database language, which we noted is particularly troublesome for a database that tries to support entity identity. GSDM has true entity identity, not just entity integrity. GSDM retains the time dimension, path expressions and set calculus from STDM. We have been able to incorporate declarative statements in OPAL without departing from Smalltalk syntax. Thus, our realization of set calculus is particularly powerful, as it can *include* procedural parts, and can be *included in* procedural methods.

We have been careful to preserve entity identity in GSDM as regards time. Although entity identity is important in databases that do not model history, it is even more important when object history is modeled. Identity is a property of an object that spans time. When an object is instantiated, it is given a globally unique identity. It lives forever with that identity, although the value of its elements may change, and it may not be accessible from other objects in some states of the database. In OPAL, we have eschewed the !-@ notation for navigating through object histories in favor of a *time dial*. We feel that almost all navigation through history would be within a single past state of the database. Setting the time dial to time T is the same as appending @T to each component in a path expression. A useful feature of the time dial is the system variable SafeTime. A read-only transaction can set its time dial to SafeTime to get the most recent state for which no currently running transaction can make changes.

Support for views drops out almost for free. We can construct an object that provides a view, and that object can employ other objects, procedural statements and calculus expressions to define the extension of the view. Furthermore, since the view object can retain connections to the objects that contributed to the view, and since it can support its own methods for messages, view updates are more manageable than in other data models.

6. Enhancing Smalltalk as a Database System

The language extensions covered in the last section do not make ST80 into a database system. The problems of supporting concurrent access to large amounts of data, along with replication and recovery, remained to be solved. We have added classes and primitive methods to OPAL to provide transaction control, storage hints and requests for replication of data. Of course, the biggest requirement of the GemStone system is that it manage objects with all these database features efficiently. In this section we briefly cover the current implementation of GemStone.

The GemStone system is currently being implemented on special-purpose hardware, although we anticipate purely software versions to run on other vendors' hardware. We expect to obtain efficiency by having the database system control secondary storage directly, without an intervening operating system. A separate operating system would be somewhat oblivious to the storage needs and access patterns of the database system. Also, an independent operating system can play havoc with requirements on database consistency, security and recoverability. Disk access will always be by entire tracks, as a track is the natural unit of physical access for a disk. Also, by having a declarative query language, we have the latitude in processing queries to exploit fully secondary storage layout, directories, and special hardware.

Communication with GemStone is done in blocks of OPAL source code. Compilation and execution of those blocks is done entirely in the GemStone system.

The system structure of GemStone is similar to that of ST80, minus display and file system classes, but with additions for set calculus, path syntax, time, concurrency, authorization, recovery, replication and directories. The display part of ST80 is not currently needed, as our present implementation has GemStone running on its own hardware and communicating to user interface programs on host machines through a network link. We do envisage a stand-alone GemStone system eventually, which would support display control. All file system duties are assumed by the database system.

The GemStone system has two main parts, the *Executor* and the *Object Manager*. The Executor is responsible for controlling sessions in the GemStone system on behalf of users on host machines. The Executor handles communications between GemStone and host software: receiving blocks of code, returning results and error messages. It maintains a *Compiler* and *Interpreter* for each active user. The Interpreter is an abstract stack machine that executes *compiledMethods* consisting of sequences of *bytecodes*, much the same as the ST80 interpreter. It dispatches bytecodes, performs stack manipulations and some primitive methods, and makes calls to the Object Manager. The Compiler requires some modifications from the ST80 compiler. Most are small changes in syntax or for slightly different bytecodes, but a large addition is needed translate calculus expressions into procedural form.

The Object Manager performs the same operations as the ST80 object memory, but is quite different in structure. The Object Manager also handles operations related to concurrency and secondary storage management: transaction control, authorization, data replication, recovery and directory management. In addition, the Object Manager responds to messages to conduct its fetches in some previous state of the database. Each user session in the GemStone system has its own invocation of the Interpreter, and its own Object Manager with a private object space. Sessions have shared access to the permanent database through transactions.

In the standard implementation of the ST80 object memory, objects are represented as blocks of contiguous words of memory, with *object-oriented pointers* (OOPs) to the values of instance variables. Since GemStone objects retain history, they grow with time, and a fixed block of memory is not a feasible representation. In the GemStone Object Manager, the implementation of objects is based upon *associations*. An element is represented as an element name and a table of associations. The associations are pairs of transaction times and object pointers, each representing that the element acquired the object as its value at the time given by the transaction time. The mapping from arbitrary times to value for an element can easily be realized from this table. Objects are broken into elements and associations, which are organized into a linked list under a header for the object. A directory may be interposed between the object header and the participating elements. Such a directory is useful when an object has a long history, or it represents a set without labels, whose elements will likely be accessed associatively, rather than through element names. Between objects, pointers to elements are usually physical pointers, as we expect most of the data to be strict tree structures. Thus, physical access paths parallel logical access where objects aren't shared. Where an object is an element of more than one set, one logical path is chosen as the basis for the physical access path, and other references to the object use a *global object-oriented pointer* (GOOP). The GOOP is resolved through a *global object table* to get the primary logical path to the object, from which its physical access path can be deduced.

The Object Manager has several major subcomponents. The *Transaction Manager* is shared by all invocations of the Object Manager, and handles concurrent use of the permanent database in an optimistic manner. It records accesses to the database for each session, and validates them for consistency when a transaction commits. The *Directory Manager* creates and maintains directories. Directories use standard techniques modified to handle object histories. One headache has been that hints given in OPAL for structuring directories must be translated for use by the Object Manager. Another problem is using a nested element as a discriminator. Since that element may be different in different states of the database, its object may need to appear along two branches of the directory.

The *Linker* incorporates updates made by a transaction in the permanent database at commit time, calling for restructuring of directories as needed. The Linker is called by the *Boxer*, whose job it is to fit objects into tracks after database changes. The *Track Manager* schedules reads and writes of tracks. The *Commit Manager* provides ***safe writing*** for groups of tracks. Safe writing guarantees that all the tracks in the group get written, or none get written, and that the tracks in the group replace their old versions atomically.

The time dimension of GSDM leads to one simplification in the GemStone Object Manager over ST80 object memory. Database objects in the past never go away, as references exist to them in some state of the database, and, theoretically, all past states of a database are preserved. Thus, no garbage collection need be done on database objects. Temporary objects created by user sessions may have to be garbage collected. However, again the task is eased, as an entire session workspace can be discarded at the end of a session. A database administrator can explicitly move objects to other media, such as tape or write-only memory. Hence, while conceptually the entire history of the database exists, some objects in it may become temporarily or permanently inaccessible.

7. Similar Approaches

Others have attempted to make ST80 a better vehicle for database applications. Most of those efforts concentrate on supporting data in secondary storage. Probably the best-known extension to secondary storage is the Large Object-Oriented Memory (LOOM) [KK]. LOOM maintains a two-level object space in main memory and on disk. Objects are moved to main memory from disk as needed. LOOM does not meet our needs for four reasons. First, it is intended for a single user system. Second, while it allows many more objects than standard Smalltalk implementations, it retains the same maximum size for objects. Third, it uses the standard Smalltalk representation of objects. That representation is not suitable for us, as we have objects with a time dimension. For objects with a large history, we may want to bring only a fragment of the object into memory. Fourth, LOOM hasn't completely dealt with the problems of clustering and indexing in secondary storage.

Several recent data models undertake to solve many of the same problems that GSDM does. The Cypres database system [Ca] supports an entity-relationship-datum data model with a strong notion of object identity. However, Cypres does not provide general-purpose programming, nor operations definition for types. Morgenstern [Mo] describes the data model for the IM project at ISI. That model is also entity-based, and it provides a hierarchy of data types, but again, it doesn't provide operation definition. IM does address integrity constraints in greater depth than we have yet.

Programming language-data language integration has been tried in combinations other than a set-theoretic data model with an object-oriented language. Some of the first attempts were adding relations to highly-typed languages such as Pascal. Two examples are Pascal/R [Sch] and PLAIN [W+]. IBM has at least two efforts in the area. One is the EAS-E system [MMP], which provides a network data model in a structured-English programming language. The other is the IDE project at the Los Angeles Scientific Center [Ne], which uses an object-based data model. ADAplex [C+] combines the Daplex functional data model with the object-based language Ada. Beech [Be] describes IDL, which has an object-based data model, with a Formula type for defining operations on classes of objects. Finally, the combination of a relational database system with a logic programming language, such as Prolog, has gathered many adherents [Da, Pa1, Pa2, Wa].

8. Acknowledgements

Fred Boals did the initial work on the set calculus to set algebra translation algorithm, and Bob Johnson brought it to its current form. The adaptation of OPAL from ST80 was done for the most part by Alan Purdy and Jason Penney. The design of the Object Manager is due to Dave Schrader, Bob Bretl, Allen Otis, Walt Gorman, Pat Timlick and Lynn Nelson. Most of these people read earlier versions of this paper, and while the authors should accept responsibility for remaining errors themselves, they prefer to ascribe blame to the others.

9. Bibliography

[Be] D. Beech Introducing the integrated data model. Hewlett-Packard Computer Science Laboratory technical note CSL-15, January 1983. 2.

[Bl] A.H. Borning, D.H.H. Ingalls. A type declaration and inference system for Smalltalk. Univ. of Washington Computer Science TR 81-08-02a, November 1981.

[Ca] R.G.G. Cattell. Design and implementation of a relationship-entity-datum data model. Xerox PARC report CSL-83-4, May 1983.

[C+] A. Chan, et al. DDM: An Ada-compatible distributed database manager. Digest of Papers, COMPCON '83, February-March 1983, 422-425.

[Chi] D.L. Childs. Feasibility of a set-theoretic data structure based on a reconstituted definition of relation. IFIP '68, North-Holland, 1969, 162-172.

[Cd] E.F. Codd. Extending the database relational model to capture more meaning. *ACM TODS 4*, 4, December 1978, 397-434.

[Cp] G. Copeland. What if mass storage were free? *IEEE Computer 15*, 7, July 1982.

[Da] V. Dahl. On database systems development through logic. *ACM TODS 7* 1, March 1982, 102-123.

[DE] *Database Engineering 6*, 4, December 1983: issue on expert systems and database systems.

[El1] *Electronics 56*, 8. Perpendicular bits up density of prototype disk drives. April 1983.

[El2] *Electronics 56*, 14. Erasable optical disk system could be available by 1985. July 1983.

[GR] A. Goldberg, D. Robson. *Smalltalk-80: The Language and its Implementation*. Addison-Wesley, 1983.

[Ha] R. Hagmann. Preferred classes: a proposal for faster Smalltalk-80 execution. In *Smalltalk-80: Bits of History, Words of Advice*, G. Krasner, Ed., Addison-Wesley, 1983, 323-330.

[KK] T. Kaehler, T. Krasner. LOOM--Large object-oriented memory for Smalltalk-80 systems. In *Smalltalk-80: Bits of History, Words of Advice*, G. Krasner, Ed., Addison-Wesley, 1983, 251-272.

[MMP] A. Malhotra, H.M. Markowitz, D.P. Pazel. EAS-E: An integrated approach to application development. *ACM TODS 8*, 4, December 1983, 515-542.

[Mi] S.W. Miller, editor. Special issue on mass storage systems. *IEEE Computer 15*, 7, July 1982.

[Mo] M. Morgenstern. Active databases as a paradigm for enhanced computing environments. VLDB IX, Florence, Italy, October 1983.

[MBW] J. Mylopoulos, P.A. Bernstein, H.K.T. Wong. A language facility for designing database-intensive applications. *ACM TODS 5*, 2, June 1980, 185-207.

[Ne] P. Newman. Techniques for environment integration. Computer Science colloquium, Oregon Graduate Center, October 1983.

[Pa1] K. Parsaye. Database management, knowledge base management and expert system development in Prolog. ACM SIGMOD Database Week, Databases for Business and Office Applications, San Jose, May 1983, 159-178.

[Pa2] K. Parsaye. Logic programming in relational databases. In [DE], 20-29.

[PP] Proceedings of the Workshop on Data Abstraction, Databases and Conceptual Modeling, Pingree Park, Colorado. SIGMOD Record 11, 2, February 1981.

[Sch] J.W. Schmidt. Some high level constructs of data type relation. *ACM TODS 2*, 3, September 1977, 247-261.

[SS] J.M. Smith and D.C.P. Smith. Database Abstractions: Aggregation and Generalization. *ACM TODS 2*, 2, June 1977, 105-133.

[To] S.P.J. Todd. The Peterlee Relational Test Vehicle—a system overview. *IBM Systems Journal 15*, 4, December 1976, 285-308.

[Wa] D.H.D. Warren. Efficient processing of interactive relational queries expressed in logic. VLDB VII, Cannes, France, September 1981, 272-281.

[W+] A.I. Wasserman, et al. The data management facility of PLAIN. ACM SIGPLAN Notices 16, 5, May 1981, 59-80.

Data Model Issues for Object-Oriented Applications

JAY BANERJEE, HONG-TAI CHOU, JORGE F. GARZA, WON KIM, DARRELL WOELK, and NAT BALLOU
MCC
and
HYOUNG-JOO KIM
University of Texas

Presented in this paper is the data model for ORION, a prototype database system that adds persistence and sharability to objects created and manipulated in object-oriented applications. The ORION data model consolidates and modifies a number of major concepts found in many object-oriented systems, such as objects, classes, class lattice, methods, and inheritance. These concepts are reviewed and three major enhancements to the conventional object-oriented data model, namely, schema evolution, composite objects, and versions, are elaborated upon. Schema evolution is the ability to dynamically make changes to the class definitions and the structure of the class lattice. Composite objects are recursive collections of exclusive components that are treated as units of storage, retrieval, and integrity enforcement. Versions are variations of the same object that are related by the history of their derivation. These enhancements are strongly motivated by the data management requirements of the ORION applications from the domains of artificial intelligence, computer-aided design and manufacturing, and office information systems with multimedia documents.

Categories and Subject Descriptors: H.1.2 [**Models and Principles**]: User/Machine Systems—*human information processing*; H.2.1 [**Database Management**]: Logical Design—*data models*; H.4.1 [**Information Systems Applications**]: Office Automation

General Terms: Design, Theory

Additional Key Words and Phrases: Composite object, object-oriented database, schema evolution, version management

1. INTRODUCTION

In recent years, object-oriented programming has gained a tremendous popularity in the design and implementation of emerging data-intensive application systems. These include artificial intelligence (AI), computer-aided design and manufacturing (CAD/CAM), and office information systems (OIS) with multimedia documents [2, 8, 15]. Object-oriented programming offers a number of important advantages for these applications over traditional control-oriented programming. One is the modeling of all conceptual entities with a single concept, namely, objects. An *object* represents anything from a simple number, say, the number 25, to a complex entity, such as an automobile or an insurance agency. The state of an object is captured in the *instance variables*. The behavior of an object is captured in *messages* to which an object responds. The messages completely define the semantics of an object.

Another advantage of object-oriented programming is the notion of a *class hierarchy* and *inheritance* of properties (instance variables and messages) along the class hierarchy. The class hierarchy captures the IS-A relationship between a class and its *subclass* (equivalently, a class and its *superclass*). All subclasses of a class inherit all properties defined for the class and can have additional properties local to them. The notion of property inheritance along the hierarchy facilitates top-down design of the database, as well as applications.

We are presently prototyping an object-oriented database system, called ORION, to support the data management needs of object-oriented applications from the CAD/CAM, AI, and OIS domains. The intended applications for ORION impose two types of requirements: advanced functionality and high performance. The ORION architecture has been designed to satisfy these requirements. ORION will provide a number of advanced features that conventional commercial database systems do not, including version control and change notification [7], storage and presentation of unstructured multimedia data [31], and dynamic changes to the database schema [4]. For high performance, ORION will support appropriate access paths and techniques for query processing, buffer management, and concurrency control.

To derive an object-oriented application interface to ORION, our initial plan was simply to use a data model from some of the existing object-oriented systems [28] or object-oriented data models [1, 3, 24]. However, two major problems rendered this approach impossible. One was that there is no consensus about the object-oriented model; different object-oriented systems support different notions of objects. We had to extract and consolidate a number of major concepts found in many object-oriented systems and use them as the basis for our data model.

Another problem was that most existing object-oriented systems are programming language systems [6, 13, 20, 21, 22, 29]. As such, their data models completely ignore many important database issues, such as deletions of persistent objects, dynamic changes to the database schema, and predicate-based query capabilities. They also lack concepts that are important to applications, such as *composite objects* and *aggregate objects* for defining and manipulating complex collections of related objects. Further, they do not include version control, which most application systems in the CAD/CAM and OIS domains require. We had to augment the basic set of object concepts with these additional concepts and capabilities.

In Section 2, we provide a review of the fundamental object-oriented concepts, including approaches to the problem of conflict resolution, which arises when a class inherits properties from one or more superclasses, and our own approach to supporting predicate-based queries against the database. In Section 3 we

Authors' addresses: J. Banerjee, H.-T. Chou, J. F. Garza, W. Kim, and D. Woelk, Database Program, MCC, 3500 West Balcones Center Drive, Austin, TX 78759. N. Ballou, AI/KBS Program, MCC, 3500 West Balcones Center Drive, Austin, TX 78759; H.-J. Kim, Department of Computer Sciences, University of Texas, Austin, TX 78712.

introduce a formal framework for understanding the taxonomy and semantics of schema change operations that we allow, including changes to the class definitions and the class lattice structure. In Section 4 we define the semantics of composite objects and show their integration into the object-oriented data model. Section 5 shows the integration of our model of versions into the object-oriented data model.

2. OBJECT-ORIENTED CONCEPTS

Existing object-oriented systems exhibit significant differences in their support of the object-oriented paradigm; Stefik and Bobrow [28] provide an excellent account of different variations of the object concepts. In this section we review the basic object concepts, and, where appropriate, show how we have refined them to suit the requirements of our applications in a database environment.

2.1 Basic Concepts

In object-oriented systems, all conceptual entities are modeled as objects. An ordinary integer or string is as much an object as is a complex assembly of parts, such as an aircraft or a submarine. An object consists of some private memory that holds its state. The private memory is made up of the values for a collection of instance variables. The value of an instance variable is itself an object and therefore has its own private memory for its state (i.e., its instance variables). A primitive object, such as an integer or a string, has no instance variables. It only has a value, which itself is an object. More complex objects contain instance variables, which, in turn, contain other instance variables. Further, two objects may have instance variables that refer to a common object. For example, the value of the Manufacturer instance variable of a vehicle may be an object that represents a certain auto company, and that same auto company may also be the value of the Employer instance variable of a person.

The behavior of an object is encapsulated in *methods*. Methods consist of code that manipulates or returns the state of an object. Methods are a part of the definition of the object. Methods, as well as instance variables, however, are not visible from outside of the object. Objects can communicate with one another through messages. Messages, together with any arguments that may be passed with the messages, constitute the public interface of an object. For each message understood by an object, there is a corresponding method that executes the message. An object reacts to a message by executing the corresponding method and returning an object in response.

A program may create and reference a large number of objects. A database may contain an even larger collection of objects. If every object is to carry its own instance variable names and its own methods, the amount of information to be specified and stored can become unmanageably large. For this reason, as well as for conceptual simplicity, "similar" objects are grouped together into a *class*. All objects belonging to the same class are described by the same instance variables and the same methods. They all respond to the same messages. Objects that belong to a class are called *instances* of that class. A class describes the form (instance variables) of its instances and the operations (methods) applicable to its instances. Thus, when a message is sent to an instance, the method that implements that message is found in the definition of the class.

ORION supports two features to further reduce redundant storage and specification of objects: shared-value and default-value instance variables. For such variables, a value must be specified. For a *shared-value variable* of a class, all instances of the class take on the specified value. This is similar to the class variable concept in Smalltalk [13]. For a *default-value variable*, those instances of a class whose value for the instance variable is not specified take on the specified default value. It is certainly possible for the user to implement the concept of default values through the use of a special-purpose instance creation method for each class. However, for ORION applications that use default values extensively, the provision of the default value concept as a modeling feature makes the creation of classes considerably simpler.

For example, we may define instance variables Medium and TakeoffDistance for the class Aircraft. The instance variable Medium may be shared valued and take on the same value for every aircraft. The instance variable TakeoffDistance, on the other hand, may have a default value of 300. In case a new aircraft is created and its takeoff distance is not specified, the value of that variable is 300.

In ORION, as in most object-oriented systems, both classes and instances are viewed as objects. This is necessary mainly for uniformity in the handling of messages. Messages are sent to objects. In most cases messages are sent to instance objects. However, how can one, for example, create an instance object in the first place? Since the instance does not exist, it cannot be sent a message to create itself. This problem is solved by treating a class as a (class) object. To create an instance of a class, a message is sent to the corresponding class object. There are also many other situations in which it is necessary to send messages to class objects, including inquiry of the definition of a class, changing the definition of a class, and so on.

Grouping objects into classes helps avoid the specification and storage of much redundant information. The concept of a *class hierarchy* extends this *information hiding* capability one step further. A class hierarchy is a hierarchy of classes in which an edge between a node and a child node represents the IS-A relationship; that is, the child node is a specialization of the parent node (and conversely, the parent node is a generalization of the child node [27]). For a parent–child pair of nodes on a class hierarchy the parent is called the superclass of the child, and the child is called the subclass of the parent. The instance variables and methods (collectively called properties) specified for a class are shared (inherited) by all its subclasses. Additional properties also may be specified for each of the subclasses. A class needs to inherit properties only from its immediate superclass. Since the latter inherits properties from its own superclass, it follows by induction that a class inherits properties from every class in its *superclass chain*.

Smalltalk [12] originally restricted a class to only a single superclass. In other words, the class hierarchy was limited to being a tree. Most other object-oriented systems, as well as the recent version of Smalltalk, have relaxed this restriction. In these systems (and in ORION) a class can have more than one superclass. Thus the class hierarchy is generalized to a lattice. (We borrow the term *lattice* from the literature on object-oriented systems to mean a directed acyclic graph structure.)

We emphasize, however, that ORION still requires instance objects to belong to only one class. Sometimes, it is useful to allow an instance object to belong to more than one class. That is, an instance object, such as "my-car," may belong to two different classes, say, LandVehicle and PetroleumFueledMotorizedVehicle. We have concluded that the consequences of this generality are lower performance and a large increase in system complexity. This results from the fact that the structure of an instance object is completely variable; since it can belong to any number of classes, its instance variables cannot be determined a priori, and the identifiers of all classes to which an instance belongs must be stored with each and every instance. Only by examining the content of an instance object and determining the classes to which it belongs will it be possible to determine its instance variables and methods. To model "my-car" in the above example, the ORION user must create a new class called Automobile with two superclasses LandVehicle and PetroleumFueledMotorizedVehicle. All instances of cars, including "my-car," then belong to the Automobile class, rather than to two different classes.

It is often desirable not to require the value of an instance variable to belong to a particular class, that is, not to bind the possible values of the instance variable to any single class. This means that two different instances of the same class may reference objects from two different classes, through the same instance variable. For example, the VehicleId of one aircraft may be an integer object, and that of another aircraft may be a string object. In other words, the class definition for Aircraft does not bind the possible values of VehicleId to either the integer class or the string class.

However, for the purposes of integrity control, it is also desirable to bind the domain (called *data type* in conventional programming languages, such as Pascal and C) of an instance variable to a specific class (and therefore implicitly to all subclasses of the class). For example, the Manufacturer instance variable of the Aircraft class may be bound to the class Company. Thus a manufacturer is a company. Further, if the Company class has subclasses, the instance variable Manufacturer may also take on as its value an instance of any subclass of Company. Thus ORION supports both typing and no typing.

2.2 Class Lattice and Conflict Resolution

The class lattice simplifies data modeling and often requires fewer classes to be specified than are required with a class hierarchy. In a class lattice, however, a class has multiple superclasses and thus inherits properties from each of the superclasses. This feature is often referred to as *multiple inheritance* [21, 28]. In a class lattice, two types of conflicts may arise in the names of instance variables and methods. One is the conflict between a class and its superclass (this type of problem also arises in a class hierarchy). Another is between the superclasses of a class; this is the consequence of multiple inheritance. In this section we discuss approaches to resolving these two types of inheritance conflicts.

In all systems we are aware of, name conflicts between a class and its superclasses are resolved by giving precedence to the definition within the class over that in its superclasses. For example, if the class definition for a class Aircraft specifies an instance variable VehicleId, it is the definition used for every Aircraft instance. This definition overrides any definition that may be inherited from any superclass.

The approach used in many systems to resolve name conflicts among superclasses of a given class is as follows. If an instance variable or a method with the same name appears in more than one superclass of a class C, the one chosen by default is that of the first superclass in the list of (immediate) superclasses for C. For example, as shown in Figure 1, the class Submarine has to inherit an instance variable Size either from the superclass WaterVehicle (which defines Size) or from NuclearPoweredVehicle (which inherits Size from its superclass MotorizedVehicle). If, in the definition of the class Submarine, NuclearPoweredVehicle is specified as the first superclass, Size will be inherited from NuclearPoweredVehicle.

Since this default conflict resolution scheme hinges on the permutation of the superclasses of a class, unlike most other systems, ORION allows the user to explicitly change this permutation at any time. Further, ORION provides two ways in which a user can override the default conflict resolution.

(1) The user may explicitly inherit one instance variable or method from among several conflicting ones. For example, in Figure 1, the user who defines the class Submarine may choose to inherit the instance variable Size from WaterVehicle rather than from NuclearPoweredVehicle, even if NuclearPoweredVehicle is the first superclass in the list of superclasses of Submarine.

(2) The user may explicitly inherit one or more instance variable or method that have the same name and rename them within the new class definition. For example, the definer of the class Submarine may specify that the instance variable Size be inherited from WaterVehicle with the new name CrewSize, and also from NuclearPoweredVehicle with the name Size (ORION ensures that all names inherited or defined within a class are distinct).

2.3 ORION Class Lattice and the Set Class

We mentioned earlier that the capability of issuing predicate-based queries against a large database of persistent objects is an important requirement in a database environment. A few operational object-oriented database systems support associative queries [3, 24]. However, most existing object-oriented systems are programming language systems, and as such they do not support associative queries. In this section we provide our simple extension to the existing notion of a class lattice as a formal basis for allowing queries against unnamed instances of classes.

As in any object-oriented system, ORION defines a class called OBJECT as the root of the class lattice. The class lattice includes not only all user-defined classes, but also all system-defined classes. Figure 2 shows all ORION-defined classes as subclasses of the OBJECT class. The class PType provides the basis for defining all classes that can be used as primitive domains of instance variables. The class Collection consists of objects that are collections of other objects. A subclass of Collection is the class Set, each of whose instances is a set (a collection of objects with no duplicates) [9, 13]. Whereas the class Collection supplies messages for iterating over the elements in a collection object, the class Set supplies further messages for searching the elements of a set, adding an element

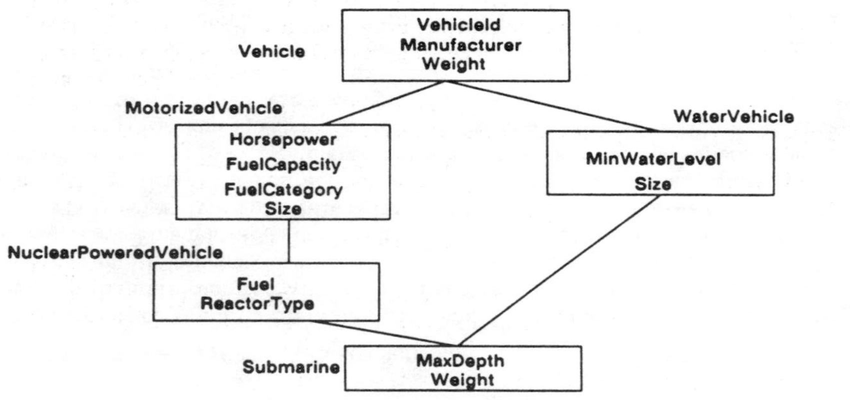

Fig. 1. Resolution of name conflicts among instance variables.

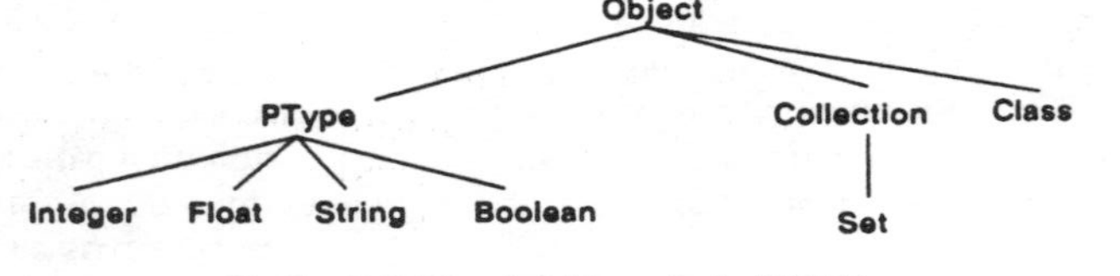

Fig. 2. Primitive class hierarchy in ORION.

to a set, etc. We may define subclasses of the Collection class later in order to add additional capabilities on lists of objects, such as doubly linked lists, stacks, and queues. Each class object belongs to a class, the system-defined class Class. All class objects are instances of this class. To create a new class, a message needs to be sent to the Class class.

For each user-defined class and for the class PType and its subclasses, ORION implicitly defines a corresponding class, a Set-Of class, as a subclass (immediate or indirect) of the Set class. These Set-Of classes form a lattice parallel to the lattice of user-defined classes. For example, the class lattice of Figure 3a is implicitly expanded to the lattice of Figure 3b.

One special instance of the Set-Of class of a user-defined class C is the set of all instances of the class C. Another special instance of the Set-Of class of a user-defined class C is the set of all instances of C or its subclasses. The notion of a set object is particularly important for a database of persistent objects, which outlive programs that created them. While a program is in execution, objects created by a program can be referenced through symbols that point to them. A program's symbol table provides handles into objects. However, a newly started program has direct reference to instances of classes through its symbol table. Instead, the program can refer to the two special set objects in the Set-of class of a class C, thereby referring either to all instances of C, or to all instances of C and its subclasses. A simple naming convention may be used to refer to these

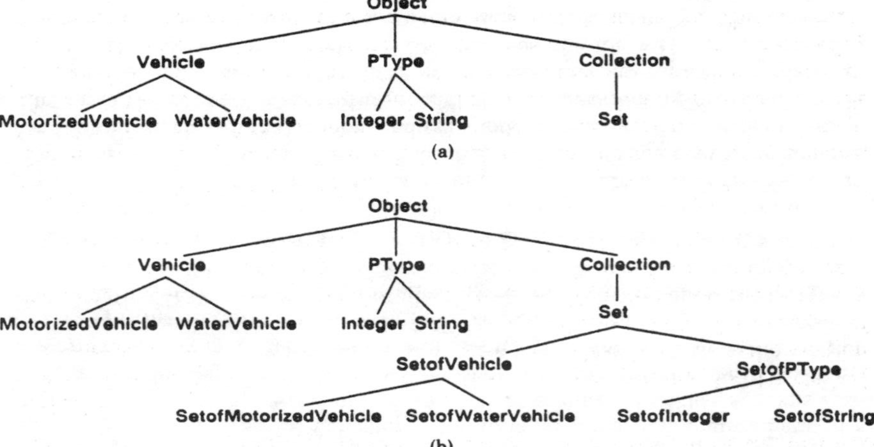

Fig. 3. Expansion of a class hierarchy (a) with set classes (b). (a) Primitive class hierarchy. (b) Class hierarchy expanded with set classes.

objects, for example, the name C to refer to the set object that contains all instances of the class C, and the name C* to refer to the set object that contains all instances of C and its subclasses. Predicate-based queries are messages to these set objects and return subsets of these sets.

For example, for the class MotorizedVehicle, the system defines a class SetofMotorizedVehicle, which has at least one instance, the set object containing all instances of the class MotorizedVehicle. This special set object provides a handle into the instances of the class MotorizedVehicle. Individual instances of MotorizedVehicle may be referenced as elements of this set.

Another motivation for the automatic generation of the Set-Of classes corresponding to user-defined classes is that instance variables often require values that are sets of objects. Just as any other object, set objects must belong to some class. Without the notion of implicitly defined Set-Of classes to which such objects can belong, the user will either have to create a class explicitly to capture the structure and semantics of these objects or treat them as instances of the class OBJECT, thereby losing their semantics.

3. SCHEMA EVOLUTION

ORION applications require considerable flexibility in dynamically defining and modifying the database schema, that is, the class definitions and the inheritance structure of the class lattice [19, 31]. Existing object-oriented systems support only a few types of changes to the schema, without requiring system shutdown. This is the consequence of the fact that existing object-oriented systems are programming language systems. We note that even existing conventional database systems allow only a few types of schema changes: For example, SQL/DS only allows the dynamic creation and deletion of relations (classes) and the addition of new columns (instance variables) in a relation [14]. This is because the applications they support (conventional record-oriented business applications) do not require more than a few types of schema changes; also the data models they support are not as rich as object-oriented data models.

In this section we first provide a taxonomy of schema change operations supported in ORION. We then present a framework for understanding and enforcing the semantics of each of the schema change operations. The framework consists of the set of properties, which we call *invariants of the class lattice*, and a set of rules for resolving ambiguities in enforcing the invariants. Finally, we describe the semantics of some of the schema change operations to illustrate the application of the schema evolution framework. We refer the reader to our earlier work [4] for more detailed discussions of the contents of this section. A graphics-based schema editor has been implemented to validate the semantics of schema evolution. A detailed presentation of the schema editor will be given in a forthcoming paper.

3.1 Taxonomy of Schema Evolution

Changes to the class lattice can be broadly categorized as (1) changes to the contents of a node, (2) changes to an edge, and (3) changes to a node. ORION allows all three types of changes. These changes can be classified further. In particular, changing the contents of a node implies adding or dropping instance variables or methods, or changing the properties of existing instance variables or methods. The schema change taxonomy is as follows:

- (1) Changes to the contents of a node (a class)
  - (1.1) Changes to an instance variable
    - (1.1.1) Add a new instance variable to a class
    - (1.1.2) Drop an existing instance variable from a class
    - (1.1.3) Change the Name of an instance variable of a class
    - (1.1.4) Change the Domain of an instance variable of a class
    - (1.1.5) Change the inheritance (Parent) of an instance variable (inherit another instance variable with the same name)
    - (1.1.6) Change the Default value of an instance variable
    - (1.1.7) Manipulate the Shared value of an instance variable
      - (1.1.7.1) Add a Shared value
      - (1.1.7.2) Change the Shared value
      - (1.1.7.3) Drop the Shared value
  - (1.2) Changes to a method
    - (1.2.1) Add a new method to a class
    - (1.2.2) Drop an existing method from a class
    - (1.2.3) Change the Name of a method of a class
    - (1.2.4) Change the Code of a method in a class
    - (1.2.5) Change the inheritance (Parent) of a method (inherit another method with the same name)
- (2) Changes to an edge
  - (2.1) Make a class S a superclass of a class C
  - (2.2) Remove a class S from the superclass list of a class C
  - (2.3) Change the order of superclasses of a class C
- (3) Changes to a node
  - (3.1) Add a new class
  - (3.2) Drop an existing class
  - (3.3) Change the name of a class

3.2 Invariants of Schema Evolution

In this section we summarize the properties of the class lattice that we can extract from our data model. We call these properties *invariants* of the class lattice. Any changes to the class definitions and to the structure of the class lattice must preserve these properties.

3.2.1 *Class Lattice Invariant.* The class lattice is a *rooted* and *connected directed acyclic graph* with labeled edges. The directed acyclic graph (DAG) has exactly one root, the class OBJECT. The DAG is connected; that is, there are no isolated nodes. Edges are labeled such that all edges directed to any given node have distinct labels (the edges are used to aid conflict resolution, as we show in Section 3.3).

3.2.2 *Distinct Name Invariant.* All instance variables and methods of a class, whether locally defined or inherited, must have distinct names.

3.2.3 *Distinct Identity Invariant.* All instance variables and methods of a class have distinct origin. For example, referring back to Figure 1, the class Submarine can inherit the instance variable Weight from either the class WaterVehicle or the class NuclearPoweredVehicle. In both these superclasses, however, Weight has the same origin, namely, the instance variable Weight of the class Vehicle, where Weight was originally defined. Therefore, the class Submarine must have only one occurrence of the instance variable Weight.

3.2.4 *Full Inheritance Invariant.* A class must inherit all instance variables and methods from each of its superclasses. There is no selective inheritance, unless the full inheritance invariant should lead to a violation of the distinct name and distinct identity invariants.

3.2.5 *Domain Compatibility Invariant.* If an instance variable V_2 of a class C is inherited from an instance variable V_1 of a superclass of C, then the domain of V_2 must either be the same as that of V_1, or a subclass of V_1. For example, if the domain of instance variable Manufacturer in the Vehicle class is the Company class, then the Manufacturer of a MotorizedVehicle can be a Company or a subclass of Company, for example, a MotorizedVehicleCompany.

3.3 Rules of Schema Evolution

The invariants of the class lattice hold at every quiescent state of the schema, that is, before and after a schema change operation. They guide the definition of the semantics of every meaningful schema change operation by ensuring that the change does not leave the schema in an *inconsistent* state (one that violates an invariant). Occasionally, however, several meaningful ways of interpreting a schema change will result in a consistent schema. To select one that is semantically the most meaningful, we need *rules* that govern our schema change semantics. The rules fall into three categories: default conflict resolution rules, property propagation rules, and DAG manipulation rules.

3.3.1 *Default Conflict Resolution Rules.* The following three rules select a single inheritance option whenever there is a name or identity conflict. They ensure that the distinct name and distinct identity invariants are satisfied in a deterministic way. The user may override the default conflict resolution rules by explicit requests to resolve conflicts differently.

Rule 1. If an instance variable is defined within a class C, and its name is the same as that of an instance variable of one of its superclasses, the newly defined instance variable is selected over the conflicting instance variable of the superclass.

Rule 2. If two or more superclasses of a class C have instance variables with the same name, but distinct origin, the instance variable selected for inheritance is that from the first superclass (corresponding to the node with the lowest labeled edge coming into C) among conflicting superclasses.

Rule 3. If two or more superclasses of a class C have instance variables with the same origin, the instance variable with the most specialized (restricted) domain is selected for inheritance. However, if the domains are the same, or if one domain is not a superclass of the other, the instance variable inherited is that of the first superclass among conflicting superclasses.

For example, in Figure 1, if the domain of Manufacturer of NuclearPoweredVehicle is Company, and the domain of Manufacturer of WaterVehicle is WaterVehicleCompany, which is a subclass of Company, the instance variable inherited into the class Submarine is the Manufacturer instance variable from the class WaterVehicle.

3.3.2 *Property Propagation Rules.* The properties of an instance variable, once defined or inherited into a class, can be modified in a number of ways. In particular, its name, domain, default value, or shared value may be changed. Also, an instance variable that is not presently a shared value can be made one, or vice versa. Further, the properties of a method belonging to a class may be modified by changing its name or code. The following rule provides guidelines for supporting all changes to the properties of instance variables and methods.

Rule 4. When the properties of an instance variable or method in a class C are changed, the changes are propagated to all subclasses of C that had inherited them, unless these properties were previously redefined within the subclasses.

For example, if the instance variable Weight of the class Vehicle has its default value changed to 2000, then the same must be done to Weight in all subclasses of Vehicle. However, if Weight had earlier been explicitly assigned a default value of 1000 in the class MotorizedVehicle (which is a subclass of Vehicle), then MotorizedVehicle will not accept the change. Consequently, the change will also not be propagated to the subclasses of MotorizedVehicle that had inherited Weight from MotorizedVehicle.

Rule 4 requires that changes to names of instance variables and methods also be propagated. However, the propagation of name changes or of newly added instance variables or methods of a class may introduce new conflicts in the subclasses. We take the position that name changes are made primarily to resolve conflicts and as such should not introduce new conflicts. By a similar reasoning, we take the view that new instance variables and methods that give rise to new conflicts should not be propagated. Hence we have the following rule, which modifies Rule 4.

Rule 5. A name change or a newly added instance variable or method is propagated to only those subclasses that encounter no new name conflicts as a consequence of this schema modification. A subclass that does not inherit this modification does not propagate it to its own subclasses. For the purposes of propagation of changes to subclasses, Rule 5 overrides Rule 2.

3.3.3 *DAG Manipulation Rules.* We need a set of rules that govern the addition and deletion of nodes and edges from the class lattice. The following rule ensures that drastic changes are avoided when a new edge is added to a class lattice.

Rule 6. (*Edge Addition Rule*). If a class A is made a superclass of a class B, then A becomes the last superclass of B. Thus any name conflicts that may be triggered by the addition of this superclass will not require any default resolution; that is, name conflicts can be ignored. If a newly inherited instance variable causes an identity conflict, Rule 3 must be applied to resolve the conflict.

The deletion of an edge from node A to node B may cause node B to become isolated in the case in which class A is the only superclass of class B. The following rule is necessary to prevent such a violation of the class lattice invariant, which requires that the DAG be connected.

Rule 7 (*Edge Removal Rule*). If class A is the only superclass of class B, and A is removed from the superclass list of B, then B is made an immediate subclass of each of A's superclasses. The ordering of these new superclasses of B is the same as the ordering of superclasses of A (clearly, A and B will now have the same collection of superclasses).

The addition of a new node should not violate the class lattice invariant. If the new node has no superclasses, it becomes an isolated node, violating the class lattice invariant. Hence we have the following rule.

Rule 8 (*Node Addition Rule*). If no superclasses are specified for a newly added class, the root class OBJECT is the default superclass of the new class.

The deletion of a node A is a three-step operation: first the deletion of all edges from A to its subclasses, then the deletion of all edges directed into A from its superclasses, and finally the deletion of node A itself. We need the following rule to ensure the preservation of the class lattice invariant when deleting a node.

Rule 9 (*Node Removal Rule*). For the deletion of edges from A to its subclasses, Rule 7 is applied if any of the edges is the only edge to a subclass of A. Further, no system-defined classes can be deleted.

3.4 Semantics of Schema Evolution

In this section we provide a description of the semantics of some of the schema change operations, to illustrate the application of the invariants of the class lattice and the schema change rules. We note that there is one very important aspect of schema evolution that the discussions of this section do not properly address. It concerns methods of a class containing references to inherited instance variables. For example, when an instance variable V is dropped from a class S, a method defined in a class C, a subclass of S, that references V will no longer be operable. It is possible to efficiently detect methods that may become inoperable as a result of schema change operations. However, we defer to a forthcoming paper detailed discussions of how we address this and other problems with methods in the context of schema evolution.

(1) *Define a new class C.* The new class C may be created as a specialization of an existing class or classes. The latter classes can be specified as the superclasses of the new class. As discussed earlier, the instance variables specified for C will override any conflicting instance variables inherited from the superclasses (by rule 1). If there is a name conflict involving the instance variables that C inherits from its superclasses, default conflict resolution rules 2 and 3 are used, unless the user explicitly overrides the default rules.

The class C may also be defined without any superclasses. In this case, C is made a subclass of Object (rule 8). The user may, at a later time, add superclasses for C, in which case Object will no longer be an immediate superclass of C.

(2) *Add a new instance variable to a class C.* The new instance variable, in case of a conflict with an already inherited instance variable, will override the inherited variable (rule 1). In that case, the inherited instance variable must be dropped from C and replaced with the new instance variable, and existing instances of C will take on the value nil or user-specified default for the new instance variable.

If C has subclasses, they will inherit the new instance variable of C. If there is a conflict with an instance variable that they have already defined or inherited, the new variable is ignored (rule 5). If there is no conflict, the subclasses inherit the new instance variable, together with a default value, if any.

(3) *Drop a class C.* Whenever a class definition is dropped, all its instances are deleted automatically, since instances cannot exist outside of a class. However, subclasses of C, if any, are not dropped; subclasses of C will lose C as their superclass. However, if C was their only superclass, they will gain C's superclasses as their immediate superclasses (rule 9).

Further, when a class C is dropped, its subclasses will lose the instance variables (and methods) that they had previously inherited from C. If, in the process, a subclass of C loses an instance variable V that was selected over a conflicting instance variable in another superclass of that subclass, it will now inherit the alternate definition of V (to maintain the full inheritance invariant). Consequently, the instances of any such subclass will lose their present values for V and inherit the default value (or nil) under the new definition of V.

When an instance of the class C is dropped, all objects that reference it will now be referencing a nonexistent object. The user will need to modify those references when they are encountered. ORION will not automatically identify references to nonexistent objects because of the performance overhead.

If the class C being dropped is presently the domain of an instance variable V_1 of some other class, V_1's domain becomes the first superclass of the class C. Of course, the user has the choice of specifying a new domain for V_1.

(4) *Drop an instance variable V from a class C.* The instance variable V is dropped from the definition (and from the instances) of the class C. To maintain the full inheritance invariant, C will inherit V from another superclass if there has been a name conflict involving V. All subclasses of C will also be affected if they have inherited V. If C or a subclass of C has methods that refer to V, such methods will now become invalid. The user can either delete these methods or redefine them to make all references consistent with the new definition of C and its subclasses.

(5) *Change the domain of an instance variable V of a class C.* The domain of an instance variable is itself a class. The domain, class D, of an instance variable V of a class C may only be changed to a superclass of D. The values of existing instances of the class C are not affected in any way. If the domain of an instance variable V must be changed in any other way, V must be dropped, and a new instance variable must be added in its place.

4. COMPOSITE OBJECTS

Many applications require the ability to define and manipulate a set of objects as a single logical entity [3, 9, 15, 19, 23, 28, 31]. For example, a vehicle is an object that contains a body object, which has a set of door objects, and each door has a position object and a color object. In other words, a body object exclusively belongs to (is a part of) a vehicle instance, and a set of doors, in turn, belongs to a body, and so on. In general, a complex object, such as a vehicle, forms a hierarchical structure of exclusive component objects. We define a *composite object* as an object with a hierarchy of exclusive component objects, and refer to the hierarchy of classes to which the objects belong as a *composite object hierarchy*.

The object-oriented data model, in its conventional form, is sufficient to represent a collection of related objects. However, it does not capture the IS-PART-OF relationship between objects; one object simply *references*, but does not own, other objects. A composite object hierarchy captures the IS-PART-OF relationship between a parent class and its component classes, whereas a class hierarchy represents the IS-A relationship between a superclass and its subclasses.

Composite objects add to the integrity features of an object-oriented data model through the notion of dependent objects. A *dependent object* is one whose existence depends on the existence of other objects and that is owned by exactly one object. For example, the body of a vehicle is owned by one specific vehicle and cannot exit without the vehicle that contains it. As such, a dependent object cannot be created if its owner does not already exist. This means that a composite object hierarchy must be instantiated in a top-down fashion; the root object of a composite object hierarchy must be created first, then the objects at the next level, and so on. When a constituent object of a composite object is deleted, all its dependent objects must also be deleted.

We note that an object may contain references to both dependent objects and independent objects, or to only dependent or independent objects. We use the term *aggregate object* to refer to such a general collection of objects. A composite object is a special case of an aggregate object.

The definition of a set of objects as a composite object also offers an opportunity for performance improvement. ORION considers a composite object as a unit for clustering related objects on disk. This is because, if an application accesses the root object, it is often likely to access all (or most) dependent objects as well. Thus it is advantageous to store all constituents of a composite object as close to one another as possible on secondary storage.

The notion of composite objects has been investigated by various researchers. It has been called a complex object in IBM's experimental extension to SQL/DS [14] and a composite object in LOOPS [5]. Our contribution in this paper is in showing the integration of the data modeling concept of composite objects into an object-oriented data model. In particular, after a formal definition of composite objects, we specify our semantics of composite objects and relate them to object-oriented concepts. We then illustrate the composite object semantics in terms of schema definition, and creation and deletion of composite objects. We also indicate our approach to implementing composite objects, including enforcement of the semantics of composite objects, and physical clustering.

4.1 Definitions

A composite object can be defined in BNF as follows:

⟨Composite Object⟩ ::= ⟨Composite Object Root⟩ (⟨Linked Dependent⟩*),
⟨Linked Dependent⟩ ::= ⟨Instance Variable⟩ ⟨Dependent Object⟩,
⟨Dependent Object⟩ ::= ⟨Leaf Object⟩
| ⟨Dependent Object Root⟩ (⟨Linked Dependent⟩*)
| {⟨Dependent Object⟩*}.

In the above definition, the * is a metasymbol that denotes an indefinite number of occurrences. A composite object has a special instance object, called the *root object*. The root of the composite object is connected to multiple *dependent objects*, each through an instance variable in the root object. Each dependent object can be a simple object (with no dependent objects), or it can itself be the root of a hierarchical structure. A dependent object can also be a set of objects. In a composite object, the same instance object cannot be referenced more than once. Thus the definition of a composite object is a hierarchy of instance objects (and not a general digraph). However, all instance objects within a composite object can be referenced by instance objects that do not belong to the composite object, and these references can have the complete generality of a digraph, including digraphs with cycles.

The instance objects that constitute a composite object belong to classes that are also organized in a hierarchy. This hierarchical collection of classes is called a *composite object schema*. A nonroot class on a composite object schema is called a *component class*. Each nonleaf class on a composite object schema has one or more instance variables that serve as links, called *composite links*. We call instance variables that serve as composite links *composite instance variables*.

In Figure 4, we illustrate a composite object schema for vehicles. The classes that are connected by bold lines form the composite object schema. The *root class* is the class Vehicle. Through instance variables Body, Drivetrain, and Color, vehicle instances are linked to their dependent objects, which belong to classes AutoBody, AutoDrivetrain, and String. (An instance variable with a primitive domain, such as Integer or String, can always be considered a composite link. A value from a primitive domain can be freely copied; hence every reference to such an object can be exclusive. Thus two vehicles can have the color red because each vehicle refers to a separate string object "red.") The Vehicle class has another instance variable called Manufacturer, but it is not a link to dependent objects. The instances of AutoBody and AutoDrivetrain, in turn, are connected to other dependent objects. A vehicle composite object then is an instance of the class Vehicle, together with an instance of each of the classes AutoBody, AutoDrivetrain, and String (for Color). The brace in the figure indicates a set object. The instance variable Doors of the class AutoBody represents a set of Door instances, each of which has a Position and Color.

4.2 Semantics of Composite Objects

In this section we define the semantics of composite objects within an object-oriented framework. First, the semantics of a composite link are as follows: If there is a composite link from a class A to a class B through an instance variable V_a of A, an instance of B can be referenced through V_a by only one instance of A. There can be other instance objects that can also reference this instance of B, but any such reference cannot be through another composite link. In other words, if an instance object is referenced through a composite link, it must be the only composite link to the object. For example, an instance of the class Vehicle can have a composite link to an instance of the class AutoBody through the instance variable Body. No other instance of Vehicle can refer to this instance of AutoBody through the instance variable Body. Further, if an instance of some other class, say Inventory, has a reference to this instance of AutoBody, the reference must be through an instance variable that is not a composite link.

The composite link property of an instance variable of a class is inherited by subclasses of that class. For example, if the class Automobile is a subclass of Vehicle, it inherits the instance variable Body from Vehicle. Further, because Body is a composite link in the Vehicle class, it will also be a composite link in the Automobile class.

A composite instance variable may later be changed to a noncomposite instance variable, that is, it may lose the composite link property. If a class A has a composite link to a class B through an instance variable V and V becomes a noncomposite instance variable, then the class B may become the root class of a composite object schema through its composite links to other classes.

However, we do not allow a noncomposite instance variable to acquire the composite link property later. An instance object may be referenced by any number of instances of a class through a noncomposite instance variable. However, a dependent object of a composite object may be referenced by only one

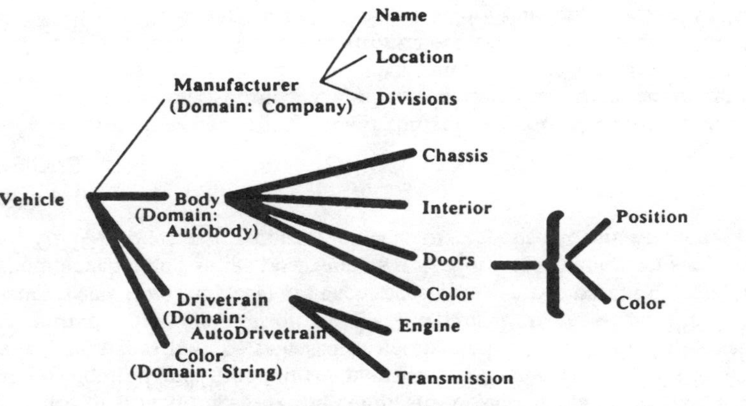

Fig. 4. Vehicle composite hierarchy.

instance of a class through a composite instance variable of the class. Therefore, to change a noncomposite instance variable to a composite instance variable makes it necessary to verify that existing instances are not referenced by more than one instance through the instance variable. This, in turn, makes it necessary to maintain a list of reference counts for each instance object, one reference count for each instance variable through which the instance object may be referenced.

Next, composite objects can further enhance information hiding through the notion of *value propagation* [5]. Default values can be propagated from an instance object to all its dependent objects, thereby simplifying the definition of dependent objects. For example, the color of the body of a vehicle is, by default, the color of the vehicle. We note that value propagation refers to the sharing of the value of an instance variable between instance objects, whereas inheritance is the sharing of the name of an instance variable (and method) between classes.

Values can be propagated only if an object has an instance variable that has the same name as some instance variable of a higher level object. Propagation of a value to a lower level object takes place from the lowest level containing object that has an appropriate value. Further, if the default value of a higher level object is changed, the new value is propagated as the default value of the dependent objects. As an example, in Figure 4 the default color of the doors can be the same as that of the vehicle's body or of the vehicle. If a vehicle's body did not have an instance variable named Color, or (if it did have such an instance variable, but) if the instance variable had no value assigned to it, then every door can assume its default color from the vehicle (bypassing the vehicle's body).

Value propagation is not automatic; it must be specified in the definition of the composite object schema. For example, unless indicated in the definition, the body of a vehicle does not assume the color of the vehicle. Once value propagation is specified, it takes precedence over inheritance from superclasses. For example, let us assume in Figure 4 that the domain of the instance variable Body of the class Vehicle is the class AutoBody, and that AutoBody inherits the instance variable Color from its superclass SolidMatter. This class hierarchy is shown in Figure 5. Let us also assume that the default value of Color in SolidMatter is "blue." The color of a vehicle's body will not be blue; instead, it will assume the color of its containing vehicle.

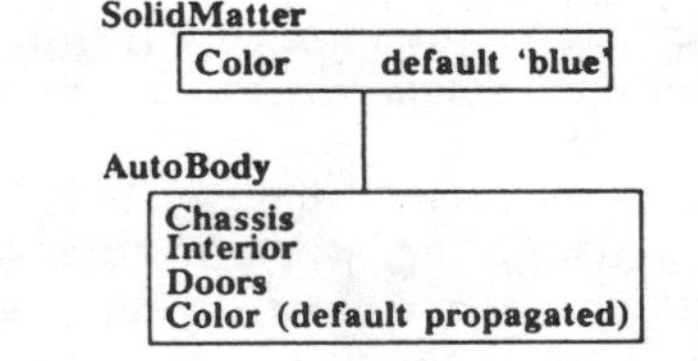

Fig. 5. The class hierarchy of AutoBody.

4.3 Schema Definition, Creation, and Deletion of Composite Objects

A composite object schema is created through composite instance variables. These instance variables have component classes as their domains. For example, the class Vehicle in Figure 4 has a composite link to the class AutoBody through the instance variable Body. The instance variable Body has as domain the class Autobody, and it has the composite link property. The Vehicle class has another instance variable Drivertrain, whose domain is the class AutoDrivetrain, and which is also a composite link. The classes AutoBody and AutoDrivetrain similarly have composite instance variables.

Although Autobody is the domain of the composite instance variable Body of the class Vehicle, it may be used as the domain of other instance variables, including other composite instance variables. In fact, if Vehicle has two subclasses Car and Truck, they both inherit the instance variable Body, along with its domain (AutoBody) and the composite link property. However, an instance of AutoBody can be referenced by only one instance object through a composite instance variable. A particular instance of AutoBody cannot simultaneously be a part of both a Car and a Truck.

An instance object can be made a part of a composite object only at the time of creation of that instance object. The integrity requirement for composite objects is that any instance object within a composite object cannot be referenced through more than one composite link. This integrity requirement is easily enforced. The only way in which a nonnull value can be assigned to a composite instance variable is by simultaneously creating that value (a dependent instance object). Any attempt to assign a nonnull value to a composite instance variable separately is rejected, because in our implementation instance objects within a composite object do not carry the identifier of the composite object to which they belong. Thus, for example, if an existing Body instance were to be separately assigned to a Vehicle instance, it would be prohibitively expensive to determine whether that body is already a part of some other vehicle. If that body were indeed a part of another vehicle, it would then have two parents, violating the integrity constraint on vehicle composite objects.

An instance object, once it is created as a dependent object, cannot have independent existence. Therefore, if any instance object within a composite object is deleted, it causes a recursive deletion of instances that depend on the object. The parent of this instance object now has a dangling reference. On a subsequent attempt to access an object through such a dangling reference, the application may choose to replace it with a null value.

A dependent object remains a dependent object throughout its existence, unless a composite link is redefined in the schema as a noncomposite link. The only way in which a composite link between instance objects can be severed is by either deleting the dependent object or making it a part of some other composite object through an ExchangePart message.

4.4 Clustering of Composite Objects

In ORION all instances of the same class are placed in the same storage segment. Thus a class is associated with a single segment, and all its instances reside in that segment. The user does not have to be aware of segments; ORION automatically allocates a separate segment for each class. For clustering composite objects, however, it is often advantageous to store instances of multiple classes in the same segment. User assistance is required to determine which classes should share the same segment.

The user may issue a message, a Cluster message, as a hint for ORION to cluster instances of a class with instances of other classes. A Cluster message specifies a list of class names, ListofClassNames. Instances of classes listed in the ListofClassNames are to be placed in a single segment. The initial size of the segment and any later increments to that size may be specified optionally. The user may sometimes need to cluster a new class C with some existing classes that have already been allocated a segment. In such case the user needs to issue a Cluster message, in which the ListofClassNames is a pair, namely, the class C and any of the existing clases with which C should share a segment. C will then share the same segment with the existing classes.

As we have seen already, a dependent object is linked to its parent when it is created; as such, a dependent object can be stored close to its parent. Ideally, the constituents of a composite object should be stored clustered at all times. In general, this requirement is not a difficult one. A composite object can be stored in a sequence of linked pages. If the composite object increases in size, a new page can be acquired and linked in the manner of a B-tree. If a composite object shrinks in size, pages may be released or compacted. The only difficulty seems to arise with the implementation of the ExchangePart message. When two dependent objects (two subtrees) are exchanged between two parent objects, they really should exchange storage positions as well. For implementation simplicity, however, ORION does not recluster objects in response to an ExchangePart message.

5. VERSIONS

There is a general consensus that version control is one of the most important functions in various data-intensive application domains, such as integrated CAD/CAM systems and OISs dealing with compound documents [3, 10, 11, 16–18, 25, 26, 30]. Users in such environments often need to generate and experiment with multiple versions of an object before selecting one that satisfies their requirements.

In this section, we show our approach to integrating version concepts into an object-oriented data model, including some of the salient implementation issues. A full description of our model of versions, along with a preliminary consideration of its implementation, is given in Chou [7]. The model is appropriate for a federated system of a central server and a number of autonomous workstations sharing objects through the server.

5.1 Version Semantics

In our current prototype we distinguish two types of versions on the basis of the types of operations that may be allowed on them. They are transient versions and working versions.

A *transient version* has the following properties:

(1) It can be updated by the user who created it.
(2) It can be deleted by the user who created it.
(3) A new transient version may be derived from an existing transient version. The existing transient version then is "promoted" to a working version.

A *working version* has the following properties:

(1) It is considered stable and cannot be updated.
(2) It can be deleted by its owner.
(3) A transient version can be derived from a working version.
(4) A transient version can be "promoted" to a working version. Promotion may be explicit (user specified) or implicit (system determined).

We impose the update restriction on the working version because it is considered stable, and thus transient versions can be derived from it. If a working version is to be directly updated after one or more transient versions have been derived from it, we need a set of careful update algorithms (for insert, delete, update) that will ensure that the derived versions will not see the updates in the working version.

5.2 Version Name Binding

There are two ways to *bind* an object with another versioned object: static and dynamic. In *static binding*, the reference to an object includes the full name of the object, the object identifier, and the version number. In *dynamic binding* [3, 11, 18], the reference needs to specify only the object identifier and may leave the version number unspecified. The system selects the default version number. Clearly, dynamic binding is useful, since transient or working versions that are referenced may be deleted and new versions created.

We need to examine the issue of selecting default versions for dynamic binding. In other proposals, the default selected is often the "most recent" version. This simple defaulting scheme is not appropriate in our model. One difficulty is that in our model version history is represented in a hierarchy, the *version-derivation hierarchy*. In particular, we allow more than one transient version to be derived from a working version. In a linear-derivation scheme, where only one version may be derived from any version [10], the most recent version has the implicit meaning that it is the "most correct" or "most complete." However, a version-derivation hierarchy, in which any number of new versions may be derived from any node on the hierarchy any time, potentially has any number of "most recent" versions in this sense. Therefore, we need to allow the user to specify a particular version on the version-derivation hierarchy as the default version. In the absence of a user-specified default, the system selects the version with the "most recent" timestamp as the default.

5.3 Implementation

Because of the performance overhead in supporting versions, we require the application to indicate whether a class is *versionable*. When an instance of a versionable class is created, a *generic object* for that instance is created, along with the first version of that instance. A generic object is essentially a data structure for the version-derivation hierarchy of an instance of a versionable class. It is deleted when the version-derivation hierarchy for its instance contains no versioned object. A generic object consists of the following system-defined instance variables:

(1) an object identifier,
(2) a default version number,
(3) a next-version number,
(4) a version count, and
(5) a set of version descriptors, one for each existing version on the version-derivation hierarchy of the object.

The default version number determines which existing version on the version-derivation hierarchy should be chosen when a partially specified reference is dynamically bound. The next-version number is the version number to be assigned to the next version of the object that will be created. It is incremented after being assigned to the new version.

A version descriptor contains control information for each version on a version-derivation hierarchy. It includes

(1) the version number of the version,
(2) the version number of the parent version,
(3) the identifier of the versioned object, and
(4) the schema version number associated with the version

The version of schema used for version V_i of an object may be different from that used for version V_j derived from V_i. For example, after a transient version is derived, the user may modify the schema for the transient version. Then the original version and the transient version will use different schemas. This is the reason for including the schema version number for each versioned object. We note, however, that a version of schema for an object X is in general shared by multiple versions of X. For example, if a transient version is derived from a working version, both versions may use the same version of schema. A detailed discussion of our proposal for supporting versions of schemas will be given in a forthcoming paper.

A generic object is also an object and as such has an object identifier. Each version of an instance object of a versionable class contains three system-defined instance variables. One is the identifier of the generic object. The others are the version number of the version and the version status (transient or working). The generic object identifier is required, so that, given a version of an instance object, any other versions of the instance object may be efficiently found. The version number is needed simply to distinguish a version of an instance object from other versions of the instance object. The version status is necessary so that the system may easily reject an update on working versions.

A versioned object is created initially by the *create* command, which creates the generic-object data structure for the object. The *derive* command is used to derive a new transient version and allocate a new version number for it. If the parent was a transient version, it is automatically promoted to a working version. The *replace* operation causes the contents of a transient version to be replaced by a work-space copy the user specifies. A transient version is explicitly promoted to a working version, making the version nonupdatable, through the *promote* command. The user may delete a version or an entire version-derivation hierarchy using the *delete* command. If the delete is against a generic object, all versions of the instance for which the generic object was created are deleted. If a working version is deleted from which other versions have been derived, the version is deleted, but the fact that the version existed is not deleted from the generic object. The user uses the *set_default* command to specify the default version on a version-derivation hierarchy of an object. A specific version number or the keyword "most-recent" may be specified as the default.

6. CONCLUDING REMARKS

In this paper we first provided a brief review of the basic object-oriented concepts that we extracted from existing object-oriented systems to form the basis of an object-oriented data model. Then we elaborated on three major enhancements to the conventional object-oriented data model. First was schema evolution, or the capability of making a wide variety of changes to the database schema, including class definitions and the structure of the class lattice, without requiring a database reorganization or system shutdown. We provided a taxonomy for schema changes that an object-oriented database system should allow and introduced a framework for understanding the semantics of the schema changes. Second was the concept of composite objects. A composite object is a collection of objects that recursively captures the IS-PART-OF relationship between pairs of objects. Composite objects should be used for enforcing this IS-PART-OF relationship and, as units of storage clustering and retrieval for improving system performance. We elaborated on the semantics of composite objects and showed their integration into an object-oriented data model in terms of schema definition and creation and clustering of composite objects. Third was version control. We discussed the semantics of versions and showed how they are integrated into the object-oriented data model.

The basic object-oriented concepts and the three enhancements we discussed in this paper, as well as a number of other important features, are presently being incorporated into ORION. ORION is a prototype object-oriented database system under implementation in the Database Program at MCC as a research vehicle for developing a database technology for object-oriented applications from the

CAD/CAM, AI, and OIS domains. The system is intended to directly support some of the applications under development in the AI/KBS (knowledge base system) Program at MCC and to receive feedback about the performance and functionality of the system from them. Because the AI/KBS applications are being implemented in Common LISP, in order to be closely coupled with them, we are implementing ORION in Common LISP to execute on the Symbolics LISP machines. The application interface to ORION then is an object-oriented extension to LISP, much as Flavors [29] and ObjectLISP [22] are, and includes message passing protocol, class lattice, and property inheritance along the class lattice. We are integrating ORION message-passing protocol with LISP function calls so that, to the extent possible, ORION applications can view both ORION objects and LISP structures without having to move from one programming environment to another.

ACKNOWLEDGMENTS

We thank Fred Lochovsky, editor of this issue, and the reviewers for their constructive comments on an earlier draft of this paper. They helped us to correct some technical inaccuracies and improve the overall presentation of the paper.

REFERENCES

1. AFSARMANESH, H., KNAPP, D., MCLEOD, D., AND PARKER, A. An object-oriented approach to VLSI/CAD. In *Proceedings of the 11th International Conference on Very Large Data Bases* (Stockholm, Sweden, Aug.). VLDB Endowment, Saratoga, Calif., 1985.
2. AHLSEN, M., BJORNERSTEDT, A., BRITTS, S., HULTEN, C., AND SODERLUND, L. An architecture for object management in OIS. *ACM Trans. Office Inf. Syst. 2*, 3 (July 1984), 173–196.
3. ATWOOD, T. M. An object-oriented DBMS for design support applications. In *Proceedings of IEEE First International Conference on Computer-Aided Technologies 85* (Montreal, Canada, Sept.). IEEE, New York, 1985, pp. 299–307.
4. BANERJEE, J., KIM, H. J., KIM, W., AND KORTH, H. F. Schema evolution in object-oriented persistent databases. In *Proceedings of the 6th Advanced Database Symposium* (Tokyo, Japan, Aug.). Information Processing Society of Japan's Special Interest Group on Database Systems, 1986, pp. 23–31.
5. BOBROW, D. G., AND STEFIK, M. *The LOOPS Manual.* Xerox PARC, Palo Alto, Calif., 1983.
6. BOBROW, D. G., KAHN, K., KICZALES, G., MASINTER, L., STEFIK, M., AND ZDYBEL, F. *CommonLoops: Merging Common Lisp and Object-Oriented Programming*, Intelligent Systems Laboratory Series ISL-85-8. Xerox PARC, Palo Alto, Calif., 1985.
7. CHOU, H. T., AND KIM, W. A unifying framework for version control in a CAD environment. In *Proceedings of the 12th International Conference on Very Large Data Bases* (Kyoto, Japan). VLDB Endowment, Saratoga, Calif., 1986, pp. 336–344.
8. CHRISTODOULAKIS, S., VANDERBROEK, J., LI, J., WAN, S., WANG, Y., PAPA, M., AND BERTINO, E. Development of a multimedia information system for an office environment. In *Proceedings of the 10th International Conference on Very Large Data Bases* (Singapore, 1984). VLDB Endowment, Saratoga, Calif., Calif. pp. 261–271.
9. COPELAND, G., AND MAIER, D. Making Smalltalk a database system. In *Proceedings of the ACM SIGMOD International Conference on the Management of Data* (June 18–21, Boston, Mass.). ACM, New York, 1984, pp. 316–325.
10. DADAM, P., LUM, V., AND WERNER, H. Integration of time versions into a relational database system. In *Proceedings of the 10th International Conference on Very Large Data Bases* (Singapore, Aug. 1984). VLDB Endowment, Saratoga, Calif., pp. 509–522.
11. DITTRICH, K., AND LORIE, R. Version support for engineering database systems. IBM Research Rep. RJ4769, IBM Research, San Jose, Calif., July 1985.
12. GOLDBERG, A. Introducing the Smalltalk-80 system. *BYTE 6*, 8 (Aug. 1981), 14–26.
13. GOLDBERG, A., AND ROBSON, D. *Smalltalk-80: The Language and Its Implementation.* Addison-Wesley, Reading, Mass., 1983.
14. IBM CORPORATION. SQL/Data System: Concepts and Facilities. GH24-5013-0, File No. S370-50, IBM Corporation, San Jose, Jan. 1981.
15. IEEE. *Database Eng. 8*, 4 (Dec. 1985), Special Issue on Object-Oriented Systems, F. Lochovsky, Ed. IEEE, New York.
16. KAISER, G., AND HABERMANN, A. An environment for system version control. Tech. Rep., Dept. of Computer Science, Carnegie-Mellon University, Pittsburgh, Pa., Nov. 1982.
17. KATZ, R., AND LEHMAN, T. Database support for versions and alternatives of large design files. *IEEE Trans. Softw. Eng. SE-10*, 2 (Mar. 1984), 191–200.
18. KATZ, R., CHANG, E., AND BHATEJA, R. Version modeling concepts for computer-aided design databases. In *Proceedings of the ACM SIGMOD International Conference on Management of Data* (Washington, D.C., May 28–30). ACM, New York, 1986.
19. KIM, W. CAD database requirements. Tech. Rep., MCC, Austin, Tex., July 1985.
20. KRASNER, G., Ed. *Smalltalk-80: Bits of History, Words of Advice.* Addison-Wesley, Reading, Mass., 1983.
21. LMI, INC. *Lisp Machine Manual.* LMI, Cambridge, Mass., 1983.
22. LMI, INC. *ObjectLISP User Manual.* LMI, Cambridge, Mass., 1985.
23. LORIE, R., AND PLOUFFE, W. Complex objects and their use in design transactions. In *Proc. ACM Database Week: Eng. Design Appl.* (May 1983), 115–121.
24. MAIER, D., STEIN, J., OTIS, A., AND PURDY, A. Development of an object-oriented DBMS. Tech. Rep. CS/E-86-005, Oregon Graduate Center, Beaverton, Oreg., Apr. 1986.
25. MCLEOD, D., NARAYANASWAMY, K., AND BAPA RAO, K. An Approach to Information Management for CAD/VLSI Applications. In *Proceedings of the Conference on Databases for Engineering Applications, Database Week 1983 (ACM*, May). ACM, New York, 1983, pp. 39–50.
26. ROCHKIND, M. The source code control system. *IEEE Trans. Softw. Eng. SE-1*, 4 (Dec. 1975), 364–370.
27. SMITH, J., AND SMITH, D. Database abstractions: Aggregation and generalization. *ACM Trans. Database Syst. 2*, 2 (June 1977), 105–133.
28. STEFIK, M., AND BOBROW, D. G. Object-oriented programming: Themes and variations. *AI Magazine* (Jan. 1986), 40–62.
29. SYMBOLICS, INC. *FLAV Objects, Message Passing, and Flavors.* Symbolics, Cambridge, Mass., 1984.
30. TICHY, W. Design implementation, and evaluation of a revision control system. In *Proceedings of the 6th IEEE International Conference on Software Engineering* (Sept.). IEEE, New York, 1982.
31. WOELK, D., KIM, W., AND LUTHER, W. An object-oriented approach to multimedia databases. In *Proceedings of ACM SIGMOD Conference on the Mangement of Data* (Washington, D.C., May 28–30). ACM, New York, 1986.

Received August 1986; revised November 1986; accepted December 1986

Extending the Database Relational Model to Capture More Meaning

E. F. CODD
IBM Research Laboratory

During the last three or four years several investigators have been exploring "semantic models" for formatted databases. The intent is to capture (in a more or less formal way) more of the meaning of the data so that database design can become more systematic and the database system itself can behave more intelligently. Two major thrusts are clear:

(1) the search for meaningful units that are as small as possible—*atomic semantics*;
(2) the search for meaningful units that are larger than the usual *n*-ary relation—*molecular semantics*.

In this paper we propose extensions to the relational model to support certain atomic and molecular semantics. These extensions represent a synthesis of many ideas from the published work in semantic modeling plus the introduction of new rules for insertion, update, and deletion, as well as new algebraic operators.

Key Words and Phrases: relation, relational database, relational model, relational schema, database, data model, database schema, data semantics, semantic model, knowledge representation, knowledge base, conceptual model, conceptual schema, entity model
CR Categories: 3.70, 3.73, 4.22, 4.29, 4.33, 4.34, 4.39

1. INTRODUCTION

The relational model for formatted databases [5] was conceived ten years ago, primarily as a tool to free users from the frustrations of having to deal with the clutter of storage representation details. This implementation independence coupled with the power of the algebraic operators on *n*-ary relations and the open questions concerning dependencies (functional, multivalued, and join) within and between relations have stimulated research in database management (see [30]). The relational model has also provided an architectural focus for the design of databases and some general-purpose database management systems such as MACAIMS [13], PRTV [38], RDMS(GM) [41], MAGNUM [19], INGRES [37], QBE [46], and System R [2].

During the last few years numerous investigations have been aimed at capturing (in a reasonably formal way) more of the meaning of the data, while preserving independence of implementation. This activity is sometimes called *semantic data modeling*. Actually, the task of capturing the meaning of data is a never-ending one. So the label "semantic" must not be interpreted in any absolute sense. Moreover, database models developed earlier (and sometimes attacked as "syntactic") were not devoid of semantic features (take domains, keys, and functional dependence, for example). The goal is nevertheless an extremely important one because even small successes can bring understanding and order into the field of database design. In addition, a meaning-oriented data model stored in a computer should enable it to respond to queries and other transactions in a more intelligent manner. Such a model could also be a more effective mediator between the multiple external views employed by application programs and end users on the one hand and the multiple internally stored representations on the other.

In recent papers on semantic data modeling there is a strong emphasis on structural aspects, sometimes to the detriment of manipulative aspects. Structure without corresponding operators or inferencing techniques is rather like anatomy without physiology. Some investigations have retained clear links with the relational model and have therefore benefited from inheriting the operators of this model—just as the relational model retained clear links with predicate logic and can therefore inherit its inferencing techniques.

With regard to meaning, two complementary quests are evident:

(1) What constitutes an atomic fact (atomic semantics)?
(2) What larger clusters of information constitute meaningful units (molecular semantics)?

After a review of the relational model, we introduce a classification scheme for entities, properties, and associations. We then discuss extensions to the relational model to reflect this classification and to support such aspects of molecular semantics as abstraction by generalization and by Cartesian aggregation. The extended model is intended primarily for database designers and sophisticated users.

2. THE RELATIONAL MODEL

We shall now give a brief definition of the relational model, in which we emphasize that the algebraic operators are just as much a part of the model as are the structures. The operators permit, among other things, precise discussion of alternative schemata (both base and view) for particular applications of the relational model. We shall also point out the close relationship that exists between the relational model and first-order predicate logic (although it is incorrect to equate the two as in [43]).

To help distinguish relational systems from nonrelational ones, we suggest the following definitions. A database system is *fully relational* if it supports:

(1) the structural aspects of the relational model;
(2) the insert-update-delete rules;
(3) a data sublanguage at least as powerful as the relational algebra, even if all facilities the language may have for iterative loops and recursion were deleted from that language.

A version of this work was presented at the 1979 International Conference on Management of Data (SIGMOD), Boston, Mass., May 30–June 1, 1979.
Author's address: IBM Research Laboratory K01/282, 5600 Cottle Road, San Jose, CA 95193.

A database system that supports (1) and (2), but not (3) is *semirelational.* Note that a fully relational system need not support the relational algebra in a literal sense, but must support its power. Besides being a yardstick of power, the algebra is intended to be a precise intellectual tool for treating such issues as model design, view definition, and restructuring.

2.1 Structures

A *domain* is a set of values of similar type: for example, all possible part serial numbers for a given inventory or all possible dates for the class of events being recorded. A domain is *simple* if all of its values are atomic (nondecomposable by the database management system).

Let $D_1, D_2, \ldots, D_n$ be n ($n > 0$) domains (not necessarily distinct). The *Cartesian product* $\times\{D_i: i = 1, 2, \ldots, n\}$ is the set of all n-tuples $\langle t_1, t_2, \ldots, t_n \rangle$ such that $t_i \in D_i$ for all i. A relation R is defined on these n domains if it is a subset of this Cartesian product. Such a relation is said to be of degree n.

In place of the index set $(1, 2, \ldots, n)$ we may use any unordered set, provided we associate with each tuple component not only its domain, but also its distinct index, which we shall henceforth call its *attribute*. Accordingly, the n distinct attributes of a relation of degree n distinguish the n different uses of the domains upon which that relation is defined (remember that the number of distinct domains may be less than n). A *tuple* then becomes a set of pairs $(A:v)$, where A is an attribute and v is a value drawn from the domain of A, instead of a sequence $\langle v_1, v_2, \ldots, v_n \rangle$.

A *relation* then consists of a set of tuples, each tuple having the same set of attributes. If the domains are all simple, such a relation has a tabular representation with the following properties.

(1) There is no duplication of rows (tuples).
(2) Row order is insignificant.
(3) Column (attribute) order is insignificant.
(4) All table entries are atomic values.

The notation $R(A:a, B:b, C:c, \ldots)$ is used to represent a time-varying relation R having an attribute A taking values from a domain a, an attribute B taking values from a domain b, etc. When, for expository reasons, the domains can be ignored, such a relation will be represented as $R(A, B, C, \ldots)$ or even as R. However, for correct interpretation of an expression (and especially an assignment statement), the order in which attributes are cited may be crucial (see THETA-JOIN below).

A *relational database* is a time-varying collection of data, all of which can be accessed and updated as if they were organized as a collection of time-varying tabular (nonhierarchic) relations of assorted degrees defined on a given set of simple domains. *Base relations* are those which are defined independently of other relations in the database in the sense that no base relation is completely derivable (independently of time) from any other base relation(s). *Derived relations* are those which can be completely derived from the base relations. It is this kind of relation which is normally employed to provide users or application programs with their own *views* of the database. The declared relations may include derived relations as well as all of the base relations. Later, when we have introduced certain additional concepts, we shall define *semiderived relations*, a class which subsumes the derived relations.

If U is a collection of attributes of a relation, the *U-component* of a tuple t of that relation is the set of $(A:v)$ pairs obtained by deleting from t those pairs having an attribute not in U.

Between tabular relations there are no structural links such as pointers. Associations between relations are represented solely by values. These associations are exploited by high-level operators.

With each relation is associated a set of candidate keys. K is a *candidate key* of relation R if it is a collection of attributes of R with the following time-independent properties.

(1) No two rows of R have the same K-component.
(2) If any attribute is dropped from K, the uniqueness property (1) is lost.

For each base relation one candidate key is selected as the *primary key*. For a given database, those domains upon which the simple (i.e., single-attribute) primary keys are defined are called the *primary domains* of that database. Note that not all component attributes of a compound (i.e., multiattribute) primary key need be defined on primary domains. Primary domains are important for the support of transactions such as "remove supplier 3 from the database," in which we wish to remove 3 wherever it occurs as a supplier serial number, but not in any of its other uses.

All insertions into, updates of, and deletions from base relations are constrained by the following two rules.

Rule 1 (entity integrity): No primary key value of a base relation is allowed to be null or to have a null component.

Rule 2 (referential integrity): Suppose an attribute A of a compound (i.e., multiattribute) primary key of a relation R is defined on a primary domain D. Then, at all times, for each value v of A in R there must exist a base relation (say S) with a simple primary key (say B) such that v occurs as a value of B in S.

The *relational model* consists of

(1) a collection of time-varying tabular relations (with the properties cited above—note especially the keys and domains);
(2) the insert-update-delete rules (Rules 1 and 2 cited above);
(3) the relational algebra described in Sections 2.2 and 2.3 below.

Closely associated with the relational model are various decomposition concepts which are semantic in nature (being time-invariant properties of time-varying relations). Examples of such concepts are nonloss (natural) joins and functional dependencies [6], multivalued dependencies [10, 44], and normal forms. For details see [3] which provides a tutorial on the subject; see also [39].

2.2 Relational Algebra (Excluding Null Values)

Since relations are sets, the usual set operators such as UNION, INTERSECTION, and SET DIFFERENCE are applicable. However, they are constrained to apply only to pairs of *union-compatible* relations, i.e., relations whose attributes are in a one-to-one correspondence such that corresponding attributes are defined on the same domain. This constraint guarantees that the result is a relation. CARTESIAN PRODUCT is applicable without constraint.

We now define operators specifically for the manipulation of n-ary relations. In what follows R, S denote relations; A, B_1, B_2, C denote collections of attributes; c is a tuple of appropriate degree, and with appropriate domains.

THETA-SELECT (sometimes called RESTRICT)

Let θ be one of the binary relations $<, \leq, =, \geq, >, \neq$ that is applicable to attribute(s) A and tuple c. Then $R[A\ \theta\ c]$ is the set of tuples of R, each of whose A-components bears relation θ to tuple c. Instead of tuple c, other attribute(s) B of R may be cited, provided that A, B are defined on common domains. Then $R[A\ \theta\ B]$ is the set of tuples of R, each of which satisfies the condition that its A-component bear relation θ to its B-component. When θ is equality (a very common case), the THETA-SELECT operator is simply called SELECT.

Examples of THETA-SELECT

R

A	B	C
p	1	2
p	2	1
q	1	2
r	2	5
r	2	3

$R[A \neq r]$

A	B	C
p	1	2
p	2	1
q	1	2

$R[A = r]$

A	B	C
r	2	5
r	2	3

$R[B > C]$

A	B	C
p	2	1

PROJECTION

$R[A_1, A_2, \ldots, A_n]$ is the relation obtained by dropping all columns of R except those specified by $A_1, A_2, \ldots, A_n$ and then dropping redundant duplicate rows.

Examples of PROJECTION

R

A	B	C
p	1	2
p	2	1
q	1	2
r	2	5
r	2	3

$R[A, B]$

A	B
p	1
p	2
q	1
r	2

$R[B, C]$

B	C
1	2
2	1
2	5
2	3

$R[B]$

B
1
2

We can now define the third class of relations. *Semiderived relations* are those which have a projection (with at least one attribute) that is a derived relation (see weak redundancy in [5]). For example, if $R(A, B)$ is a base relation and $S(A, C)$ is a relation such that

$$S[A] = (R[B = b])[A]$$

and attribute C is defined on a domain not used in any of the base relations (hence S is not derivable), then S is semiderived. As we shall see, there are many uses for semiderived relations. Note that there is no stipulation that a relational database will be designed to have minimal redundancy, although this is an option that may be chosen. Thus, the declared relations may include semiderived and even derived relations as well as the base relations.

THETA-JOIN

Given relations $R(A, B_1)$ and $S(B_2, C)$ with B_1, B_2 defined on a common domain, let θ be one of the binary relations $=, <, \leq, \geq, >, \neq$ that is applicable to the domain of attributes B_1, B_2. The theta-join of R on B_1 with S on B_2 is denoted by $R[B_1\ \theta\ B_2]S$. It is the concatenation of rows of R with rows of S whenever the B_1-component of the R-row bears relation θ to the B_2-component of the S-row. When θ is equality, the operator is called EQUI-JOIN. Of all the THETA-JOINS, only EQUI-JOIN yields a result that *necessarily* contains two identical columns (one derived from B_1, the other from B_2). More generally, θ may be permitted to be any binary relation that is applicable to the domain of B_1 and B_2.

Examples of THETA-JOIN

R

A	B	C
p	1	2
p	2	1
q	1	2
r	2	5
r	3	3

S

D	E
2	u
3	v
4	u

$R[C = D]S$

A	B	C	D	E
p	1	2	2	u
q	1	2	2	u
r	3	3	3	v

$R[C > D]S$

A	B	C	D	E
r	3	3	2	u
r	2	5	2	u
r	2	5	3	v
r	2	5	4	u

If the relations being theta-joined have some attribute names in common, the names for the attributes of the resulting relation must be specified. For example, if each of the relations R, S has attributes A, B, and all four attributes are defined on a common domain, we may define several possible theta-joins of R with S. One such definition is:

$$T(D, E, F, G) = R(A, B)[B > B]S(A, B)$$

and, using an order-of-citation convention, this means that the source of values for attribute D in T is attribute A in R. Similarly, for attributes E, F, G in T, the respective sources are attributes B in R, A in S, and B in S.

NATURAL JOIN

This join is the same as EQUI-JOIN except that redundant columns generated by the join are removed. Natural join is the one used in normalizing a collection of relations.

Example of NATURAL JOIN. Relations R, S are those tabulated above.

$R[C*D]S$ (A	B	C	E)
p	1	2	u
q	1	2	u
r	3	3	v

DIVIDE

Given relations $R(A, B_1)$ and $S(B_2)$ with B_1 and B_2 defined on the same domain(s), then, $R[B_1 \div B_2]S$ is the maximal subset of $R[A]$ such that its Cartesian product with $S[B_2]$ is included in R. This operator is the algebraic counterpart of the universal quantifier.

Example of DIVIDE

R (A	B)
p	1
p	2
p	3
q	1
r	1
r	3

S (C)
1
3

$R[B \div C]S$ (A)
p
r

2.3 Extensions of the Algebra for Null Values

The two most important types of null value have the meanings "value at present unknown" and "property inapplicable." An approach that handles both types of nulls is described in [40]. A rather general attack on the problem of dealing with partial information is described in [22]. Here, we shall concern ourselves with only the "value at present unknown" type of null and denote it by ω (see [5] for more details). The following treatment should be regarded as preliminary and in need of further research.

In the basic relational model nulls are excluded from every component of a primary key of a base relation. Apart from this constraint, any occurrence of the value-unknown type of null can be replaced in an updating operation by a nonnull value, and vice versa, unless there is an explicit integrity constraint disallowing this.

The first question which arises is: what is the truth value of $x = y$ if x or y or both are null? An appropriate result in each of these cases is the unknown truth value, rather than true or false. Accordingly, we adopt a three-valued logic for use in extracting data from databases that may contain null values. We use the same symbol "ω" to denote the unknown truth value, because truth values can be stored in databases and we want the treatment of all unknown or null values to be uniform. The three-valued logic is based upon the following truth tables:

AND	F	ω	T
F	F	F	F
ω	F	ω	ω
T	F	ω	T

OR	F	ω	T
F	F	ω	T
ω	ω	ω	T
T	T	T	T

NOT(F) = T; NOT(ω) = ω; NOT(T) = F

The existential and universal quantifiers behave like iterated OR and AND, respectively.

With regard to set membership $\in$ and set inclusion $\subseteq$, we assign the truth value ω to the expressions: $\omega \in S$ and $\{\omega\} \subseteq S$, whenever S is a nonempty unary relation (even if S does contain a null value). This may seem a bit counterintuitive at first, but one way to make it seem more acceptable is to think of each occurrence of ω as a placeholder for a possibly distinct value. To be more precise, a truth-valued expression has the value ω if and only if (after replacing any defined variables by their defining expressions in terms of individual variables) both of the following conditions hold.

(1) Each occurrence of ω in the expression can be replaced by a nonnull value (possibly a distinct one for every occurrence) so as to yield the value T for the expression.

(2) Each occurrence of ω in the expression can be replaced by a nonnull value (possibly a distinct one for every occurrence) so as to yield the value F for the expression.

We shall call this the *null substitution principle*. The three-valued logic described above is consistent with this principle. The following examples illustrate the application of this principle to set membership and set inclusion. Let $\varnothing$ denote the empty set and R, S, T, U, V denote the following relations:

R
ω
1

S
ω
1
2

T	
ω	1
y	ω

U	
x	ω
ω	3

V	
x	ω
y	3
z	1

The following expressions have the truth value F:

$$\omega \in \varnothing \qquad T \subseteq S \qquad V \subseteq U \qquad U \subseteq R.$$

The following expressions have the truth value ω:

$$R \subseteq S \qquad S \subseteq R \qquad T \subseteq U \qquad U \subseteq T.$$
$$T \subseteq V \qquad U \subseteq V$$

In passing, we note that this scheme for nulls has certain properties which may appear paradoxical at first. For example, take the relation EMP with attributes NAME and AGE. The expression

$$(\text{EMP}[\text{AGE} \leq 50] \cup \text{EMP}[\text{AGE} > 50])[\text{NAME}]$$

does not necessarily yield the set of all employee names. If, however, we interpret the term EMP[AGE ≤ 50] as the set of tuples in EMP whose AGE-component is known in the database to be less than or equal to 50, and EMP[AGE > 50] as the set whose AGE-component is known to be greater than 50, the paradoxical aspect disappears. This kind of interpretation does not require that all of the tautologies of two-valued logic be preserved by the three-valued logic (contrast with [40]).

By applying the null substitution principle to inequality testing, we can avoid the arbitrary step of giving ω any place in a numerical or lexicographic ordering. In accordance with this principle, we assign the truth value ω to the expressions $x\ \theta\ y$, where θ is any one of $<, \leq, \geq, >$ whenever x or y is null.

For every positive integer n, the n-tuple consisting of n null values (each of course accompanied by its attribute) is a legal tuple, but a nonbase n-ary relation may contain at most one such tuple, and a base relation cannot contain such a tuple at all. As usual, no relation may contain duplicate tuples. In applying this nonduplication rule, a null value in one tuple is regarded as the same as a null value in another. This identification of one null value with another may appear to be in contradiction with our assignment of truth value to the test $\omega = \omega$. However, tuple identification for duplicate removal is an operation at a lower level of detail than equality testing in the evaluation of retrieval conditions. Hence, it is possible to adopt a different rule. The consequences for UNION, INTERSECTION, and DIFFERENCE are illustrated below.

R		S		R ∪ S		R ∩ S		R − S	
ω	ω	ω	ω	ω	ω	ω	ω		
u	ω	u	ω	u	ω	u	ω		
u	1	u	1	u	1	u	1		
ω	1			ω	1			ω	1

Now, let us look at the effect of this type of null upon the remaining operators of the relational algebra. CARTESIAN PRODUCT remains unaffected. PROJECTION behaves as expected, provided that one remembers how the nonduplication rule is applied to tuples with null-valued components. The following examples illustrate projection.

R

A	B	C
u	ω	ω
v	1	ω
w	ω	1
x	1	ω
y	ω	1

R[B, C]

B	C
ω	ω
1	ω
ω	1

R[C]

C
ω
1

The THETA-JOIN operator entails concatenation of pairs of tuples subject to some specified condition θ holding between certain components of these tuples. The evaluation of the condition for any candidate pair of tuples yields the truth value F or ω or T. We retain the join operator that concatenates only those pairs of tuples for which the condition evaluates to T and call it a TRUE THETA JOIN. In addition, we introduce a MAYBE THETA JOIN that concatenates only those pairs of tuples for which the specified condition evaluates to ω.

The MAYBE version of an operator is denoted by placing the symbol ω after the theta symbol (e.g., $=\omega$) or operator symbol (e.g., $\div\omega$). The following examples illustrate the TRUE and MAYBE EQUI-JOINs and the TRUE and MAYBE LESS-THAN JOINs.

R

A	B
u	ω
ω	2
w	1

S

C
ω
2

R[B = C]S

A	B	C
ω	2	2

R[B = ωC]S

A	B	C
u	ω	ω
u	ω	2
ω	2	ω
w	1	ω

R[B < C]S

A	B	C
w	1	2

R[B < ωC]S

A	B	C
same as R[B = ωC]S		

If we wish to select only those rows of R that have ω as their B-component, we may form the MAYBE EQUI-JOIN of R with a relation T whose only element is a single nonnull value (any such value will do, provided it is drawn from the same underlying domain that attribute B is defined on) and then PROJECT the result on A, B. In the case above, the reader can verify that the final result is a relation whose only element is the pair $(A{:}u,\ B{:}\omega)$. Treatment of null values by the THETA-SELECT operator (TRUE and MAYBE versions) follows the same pattern as the THETA-JOIN operators.

DIVISION is treated in a similar manner. The original operator based upon true inclusion (inclusion testing that yields T) is retained and called TRUE DIVISION. A new division operator $\div\omega$ is introduced which entails only maybe inclusion (inclusion testing that yields ω), and this is called MAYBE DIVISION. The following examples illustrate the two kinds of division.

R

A	B
u	1
u	2
u	3
w	2
w	ω
z	3

S

C
2
3

T

C
2
ω

R[B ÷ C]S

A
u

R[B ÷ C]T

A
empty

R[B ÷ ωC]S

A
w

R[B ÷ ωC]T

A
u
w

The following operator permits two relations to be subjected to union, even if they are not union-compatible. Nevertheless, the result is always a relation.

OUTER UNION

Let R, S be relations which have attribute(s) B in common and no others. Let the remaining attribute(s) of R be A, and those of S be C. Let

$$R_1(A, B, C) = R \times (C{:}\omega)$$

$$S_1(A, B, C) = (A{:}\omega) \times S$$

where × denotes Cartesian product. The outer union of R and S is given by

$$R \textcircled{\cup} S = R_1 \cup S_1.$$

Note that in the special case that R and S are union-compatible,

$$R \textcircled{\cup} S = R \cup S.$$

Example of OUTER UNION

R (A	B	C)
p	1	2
p	2	1
q	1	2

S (B	D)
2	u
3	v

$R \textcircled{\cup} S$ (A	B	C	D)
p	1	2	ω
p	2	1	ω
q	1	2	ω
ω	2	ω	u
ω	3	ω	v

In a similar manner, we could define OUTER versions of INTERSECTION and DIFFERENCE also.

Both the NATURAL and EQUI-JOINs lose information when the relations being joined do not have equal projections on the join attributes. To preserve information regardless of the equality of these projections, we need joins that can generate null values whenever necessary. Such joins were proposed independently in [16, 20, 23, 44].

OUTER THETA-JOIN

Given relations $R = R(A, B_1)$ and $S = S(B_2, C)$ with B_1, B_2 defined on a common domain, let

$$T = R[B_1 \ \theta \ B_2]S$$

$$R_1 = R - T[A, B_1]$$

$$S_1 = S - T[B_2, C].$$

Then the outer theta-join is defined by

$$R[B_1 \textcircled{\theta} B_2]S = T \cup (R_1 \times (B_2{:}\omega, C{:}\omega)) \cup ((A{:}\omega, B_1{:}\omega) \times S_1)$$

where ∪ denotes union and × denotes Cartesian product.

Example of OUTER EQUI-JOIN

S (S#	SCITY)
s1	c4
s2	c2
s4	c1
s6	c1
s7	c3

J (J#	JCITY)
j1	c1
j2	c2
j3	c2
j4	c5

Define $SJ = S[SCITY \textcircled{=} JCITY]J$

SJ (S#	SCITY	JCITY	J#)
s1	c4	ω	ω
s2	c2	c2	j2
s2	c2	c2	j3
s4	c1	c1	j1
s6	c1	c1	j1
s7	c3	ω	ω
ω	ω	c5	j4

OUTER NATURAL JOIN

Given relations $R(A, B_1)$ and $S(B_2, C)$ as before, and relations T, R_1, S_1 defined as above with = replacing theta, then the outer natural join of R on B_1 with S on B_2 is defined by

$$R[B_1 \textcircled{*} B_2]S = T[A, B_1, C] \cup (R_1 \times (C{:}\omega)) \cup ((A{:}\omega) \times S_1).$$

Example of OUTER NATURAL JOIN. Define $T(S\#, CITY, J\#) = S[SCITY \textcircled{*} JCITY]J$ where relations S, J are as tabulated above.

T (S#	CITY	J#)
s1	c4	ω
s2	c2	j2
s2	c2	j3
s4	c1	j1
s6	c1	j1
s7	c3	ω
ω	c5	j4

In this treatment, if an operator generates one or more nulls, these nulls are always of the type "value at present unknown," which is consistent with the open world interpretation (see Section 3). If we were dealing with relations having a closed world interpretation, the "property inapplicable" type would be more appropriate.

3. RELATIONSHIP TO PREDICATE LOGIC

We now describe two distinct ways in which the relational model can be related to predicate logic. Suppose we think of a database initially as a set of formulas in first-order predicate logic. Further, each formula has no free variables and is in as atomic a form as possible (e.g, A & B would be replaced by the component formulas A, B). Now suppose that most of the formulas are simple assertions of the form $Pab \cdots z$ (where P is a predicate and $a, b, \ldots, z$ are constants), and that the number of distinct predicates in the database is few compared with the number of simple assertions. Such a database is usually called *formatted*, because the major part of it lends itself to rather regular structuring. One obvious way is to factor out the predicate common to a set of simple assertions and then treat the set as an instance of an n-ary relation and the predicate as the name of the relation. A database so structured will then consist of two parts: a regular part consisting of a collection of time-varying relations of assorted degree (this is sometimes called the *extension*) and an irregular part consisting of predicate logic formulas that are relatively stable over time (this is sometimes called the *intension*, although it may not be what the logicians Russell and Whitehead originally intended by this word). One may also view the intension as a set of integrity constraints (i.e., conditions that define all of the allowable extensions) and thus decouple these notions from variability with time.

One may choose to interpret the absence of an admissible tuple from a base relation as a statement that the truth value of the corresponding atomic formula is (1) unknown; (2) false. If (1) is adopted, we have the *open world interpretation*. If (2) is adopted, we have the *closed world interpretation* (see [28]). Although the closed world interpretation is usually the one adopted for commercial databases, there is a case for permitting some relations (e.g., P-relations of Section 7) to have the open world interpretation, while others (e.g., E-relations for kernel entity types to be discussed in Sections 5 and 6) have the closed world interpretation.

Whether the open or closed interpretation is adopted, the relational model is closely related to predicate logic. It is this closeness which accounts for the plethora of relational data sublanguages that are based on predicate logic. For a probing and thorough comparison of such languages, see [20, 27].

Undisciplined application of predicate logic in designing a database could yield an incomprehensible and unmanageable set of assertions. Some issues which arise when attempting to introduce discipline are the following.

(1) Can we be more precise about what constitutes a simple assertion?
(2) What other regularities can be exploited in a formatted database?
(3) To what extent can these additional regularities be represented in readily analyzable data structures as opposed to procedures?

In attempting to provide an answer to these questions, we shall employ popular informal terms like "entity," "property," and "association" to motivate extensions to the relational model. Eventually, we arrive at a formal system called RM/T (T for Tasmania, where these ideas were first presented [9]). This system can be interpreted in many different ways. Certain interpretations should satisfy the so-called 2-concept school in semantic modeling, while others should satisfy the 3-concept school (see [25, p. 27]).

4. DESIGNATION OF ENTITIES

The need for unique and permanent identifiers for database entities such as employees, suppliers, parts, etc., is clear. User-defined and user-controlled primary keys in the relational model were originally intended for this purpose. There are three difficulites in employing user-controlled keys as *permanent surrogates* for entities.

(1) The actual values of user-controlled keys are determined by users and must therefore be subject to change by them (e.g., if two companies merge, the two employee databases might be combined with the result that some or all of the serial numbers might be changed).
(2) Two relations may have user-controlled keys defined on distinct domains (e.g., one uses social security, while the other uses employee serial number) and yet the entities denoted are the same.
(3) It may be necessary to carry information about an entity either before it has been assigned a user-controlled key value or after it has ceased to have one (e.g., an applicant for a job and a retiree).

These difficulties have the important consequence that an equi-join on common key values may not yield the same result as a join on common entities. A solution—proposed in part in [4] and more fully in [14]—is to introduce entity domains which contain system-assigned surrogates. Database users may cause the system to generate or delete a surrogate, but they have no control over its value, nor is its value ever displayed to them.

Surrogates behave as if each entity (regardless of type) has its own permanent surrogate, unique within the entire database. Actually, under the covers, such surrogates may have to be changed (e.g., when two previously independent databases are combined into one), but the following property is preserved at all times: Two surrogates are equal in the relational model if and only if they denote the same entity in the perceived world of entities. Note that the system would create distinct surrogates for two entities as a result of user input that, in effect, asserts the distinctness of these entities. A special *coalescing command* enables a user to tell the system that two objects that were previously asserted to be distinct, are, in fact, one and the same.

In any RM/T database one of the underlying domains serves as the source of all surrogates; this is called the *E-domain*. Any attribute defined on the E-domain is called an *E-attribute*. For easy recognition of such attributes, we adopt the convention that they are given names ending in the special character "ɇ."

Introduction of the E-domain, E-attributes, and surrogates does not make user-controlled keys obsolete. Users will often need entity identifiers (such as part serial numbers) that are totally under their control, although they are no longer compelled to invent a user-controlled key if they do not wish to.

They will have to remember, however, that it is now the surrogate that is the primary key and provides truly permanent identification of each entity. The capability of making equi-joins on surrogates implies that users see the headings of such columns but not the specific values in those columns.

5. ENTITY TYPES

Entities may, of course, have several types (e.g., a supplier may also be a customer). When information regarding an entity is first entered into a database, the input must specify at least one type for that entity—it need not specify anything more unless it is of a type used to describe some other entity (in which case the entity whose description is being augmented must also be specified). In subsequent sections we shall deal with automatic inference of other applicable types when these are inferable from the given one(s).

In any RM/T database there is a unary relation (called an *E-relation*) for each entity type. As a matter of convention, the relation is given the same name as the entity type which the relation represents, while its sole attribute is named by appending the character "ɇ" at the end of the relation name. Such an attribute is also given additional names (aliases) if the corresponding entity type is a subtype of other entity types. In such a case, there is one alias for each superentity type, and this alias consists of the relname of the supertype followed by the character "ε."

The main purpose of an E-relation is to list all the surrogates of entities that have that type and are currently recorded in the database. One reason for establishing these E-relations explicitly is that an entity may change type dynamically. A firm that was both a supplier and a customer may become just a supplier. We shall see other reasons below.

The possibility that an entity may change its type or types means that we must distinguish two purposes for removal of an entity surrogate from an E-relation:

(1) complete removal of the entity from the database, which means deleting tuples wherever its surrogate appears in a unique tuple identifier role and replacing all other occurrences by a special surrogate E-null that means "entity unknown" [26];

(2) dynamic loss of one type for an entity accompanied by the survival of some other type for that same entity, which means removal of its surrogate from the E-relation for that type and from E-relations for certain other types implied by the type being lost but not implied by the types being retained—this will become clearer later—plus corresponding tuple deletions and surrogate replacements as in (1), but excluding those that are associated with the entity in its remaining types.

Rule 3 (entity integrity in RM/T): In conformity with the ground rules for surrogates, E-relations accept insertions and deletions, but not updates. In conformity with Rule 1 for the basic relational model, E-relations do not accept null values.

6. CLASSIFICATION OF ENTITIES AND ASSOCIATIONS

Entities and their types can be classified by whether they

(1) fill a subordinate role in describing entities of some other type, in which case they are called *characteristic*;

(2) fill a superordinate role in interrelating entities of other types, in which case they are called *associative*;

(3) fill neither of the above roles, in which case they are called *kernel*.

Entities and their types may be related to one another by criteria other than description and association used above. Entity type e_1 is said to be a *subtype* of entity type e_2 if all entities of type e_1 are necessarily entities of type e_2. For example, in a database dealing with employees in general and salesmen employees in particular, the entity type salesman would be a subtype of the entity type employee. Any entity type (characteristic, kernel, or associative) may have one or more subtypes, which in turn may also have subtypes. A subtype of a characteristic entity type is also characteristic; a subtype of a kernel entity type is also kernel; and a subtype of an associative entity type is also associative.

Those kernel entity types that are not subtypes of any other entity type are called *inner kernel*. Each inner kernel entity type is defined independently of all other entity types. Barring any integrity constraints that are specialized to a particular database (as opposed to integrity constraints that are inherent in and

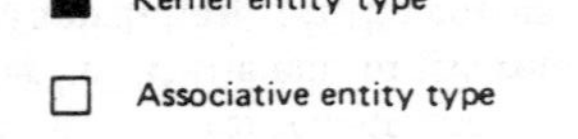

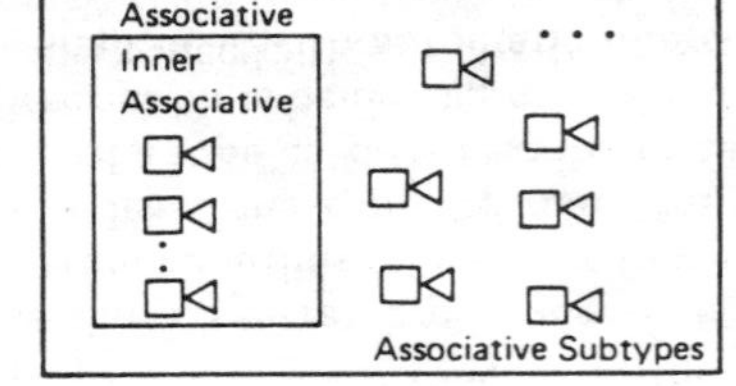

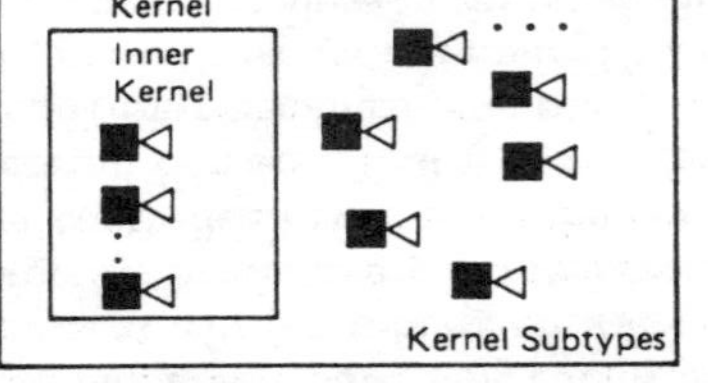

Fig. 1. Classification of entity types

a fundamental part of the data model itself), an inner kernel entity is not existence dependent on any other entity of any type.

Objects which interrelate entities but do not themselves have the status of entities will be called *nonentity associations*. The main distinction between associative entities and nonentity associations is this: Associative entities, like kernel entities, are allowed to have characteristic entities as well as immediate properties, whereas nonentity associations are allowed to have immediate properties only. These and other differences discussed below stem from the difficulty of specifying a cross reference to a particular association when it has no surrogate identifying it uniquely. The prime reason for including nonentity associations in RM/T is an expository one: to show how weak these associations are in contrast to associative entities.

Figure 1 represents the classification of entity types in a simplified way (it does not show that characteristic entity types may themselves have subtypes). Note that the term *inner associative entity type* is applied to an associative entity type that is not the subtype of any other entity type.

This classification scheme is similar in some respects, but certainly not identical, to classifications introduced in [32, 42]. Schmid and Swenson included nonentity associations in their scheme, but not associative entities—in RM/T the former are dispensable, while the latter are indispensable.

7. ENTITIES AND THEIR IMMEDIATE PROPERTIES

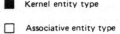

We have seen that the E-relation for a given entity type asserts the existence of those entities having that type. The immediate (single-valued) properties of an entity type are represented as distinctly named attributes of one or more property-defining relations, called P-relations. Each P-relation has as its primary key an E-attribute whose main function is to tie the properties of each entity to the assertion of its existence in the E-relation. Each surrogate appearing in this E-attribute uniquely identifies the entity being described. Furthermore, it uniquely identifies the tuple of which it is part because the properties are single valued. The naming of attributes of P-relations conforms to the following convention: For any entity type *e* and any pair of P-relations for *e*, the only attributes these relations have in common are their primary keys.

The role of this E-attribute is that of a unique identifier for the relation in which it appears. We shall call this role the *K-role*. Accordingly, each P-relation has exactly one E-attribute that has the K-role. Such a relation may have one or more other E-attributes, but their roles are purely *referential*, i.e., that of a foreign key rather than a primary key.

Insertions into P-relations and deletions from E-relations are governed by the following rule.

Rule 4 (property integrity): A tuple *t* may not appear in a P-relation unless the corresponding E-relation asserts the existence of the entity which *t* describes. In other words, the surrogate primary key component of *t* must occur in the corresponding E-relation.

There has been much debate about whether the immediate properties of an entity should be represented together in one property-defining relation (one extreme) or split into as many binary relations as there are properties to be recorded (the other extreme). The first is in accord with the PJ/NF [11] discipline, while the second conforms to the *irreducible relation* approach [12, 29]. The normal forms (other than 1NF) are not mandatory—they are merely guidelines for database design. Both the original relational model and RM/T leave this decision to the model user. RM/T (and to a lesser extent RM) provides operators to convert from one form to the other.

In database definition one advantage of binary P-relations is that each corresponding property has a relation name, an attribute name, and a domain name, all of which can be exploited to mnemonic advantage. A second *claimed* advantage for binary P-relations is that the addition of a new property type to the database can be effected by mere addition of one more P-relation. However, in RM/T this advantage is applicable no matter whether the properties are presently organized into binary relations exclusively or *n*-ary relations of assorted degrees.

The reader is cautioned to avoid jumping to the conclusion that binary relations are somehow superior to *n*-ary relations as a representational primitive. Even with immediate properties, there are questionable decompositions. Figure 2 shows one organization for the immediate properties of employees. In this and similar examples we may wish to decompose property relations no further than *minimal meaningful units*. Should, for example, the day, month, and year components of a date be represented in separate binary P-relations? Should the street number, street name, city, and state components of an address be so separated? Besides using the notion of minimal meaningful unit, we may wish to adopt the criterion of avoiding occurrences of the "property inapplicable" null value; this objective can often be reached without binary atomization.

Employee

Emp ¢
α

(E-Relation)

Employee_Number

Emp ¢	ID
α	7777

(P-Relation)

Employee_Name

Emp ¢	First	Middle	Last
α	John	James	Buck

(P-Relation)

Employee_Address

Emp ¢	No	Street	City	State
α	765	Joy	Fun	Tas

(P-Relation)

Employee_Birthdate

Emp ¢	Yr	Mo	Da
α	1945	1	30

(P-Relation)

Fig. 2. Entity and property relations

Even if the principal schema were based exclusively on binary relations (and we shall return to this topic in a later section), there would still be a need to apply *n*-ary joins to obtain higher degree relations in order to define views, study view integration, and represent a broad class of queries. With RM/T we take the position that one man's minimal meaningful unit is not necessarily another's.

Note that the appropriate join for defining a view that encapsulates some or all of the immediate properties of an entity type in a single *n*-ary relation is the OUTER NATURAL JOIN of all P-relations for this type on the E-attributes with the K-role (see Example A in Section 15.4). This join is appropriate no matter how fine or coarse the property decomposition is.

To explain how the P-relations for a given entity type are tied to the E-relation for that type, we shall make use of the following RM/T objects and properties. The *relname* of a relation is the character string representation of the name of that relation. The relname of a (presumably transient) relation, to which an assignment has not been made, is null. Every base relation has a nonnull relname. Further, every derived relation which is cited on the left-hand side of an assignment statement has a nonnull relname. The *relname domain* (abbreviated RN-domain) is the domain of all relnames in the database.

Now we introduce the *property graph relation* (PG-relation) that indicates which P-relations represent property types associated with which E-relation.

Both of the attributes of PG are defined on the RN-domain. One attribute is named SUB to indicate its subordinate role, while the other is named SUP to indicate its superior role. If m, n are, respectively, the names of a P-relation and an E-relation, let the expressions $p(m)$, $e(n)$ denote the property type represented by that P-relation and the entity type denoted by that E-relation, respectively. The pair (SUB:m, SUP:n) belongs to PG iff $p(m)$ is a property type for entity type $e(n)$.

One may think of the collection of P-relations for a given E-relation as constituting a *property molecule type*, which is bound together by tuples in the PG-relation.

8. MULTIVALUED AND INDIRECT PROPERTIES OF ENTITIES

Entity types are so defined that each multivalued property of an entity p is cast in the form of a characteristic entity q together with immediate properties for q.

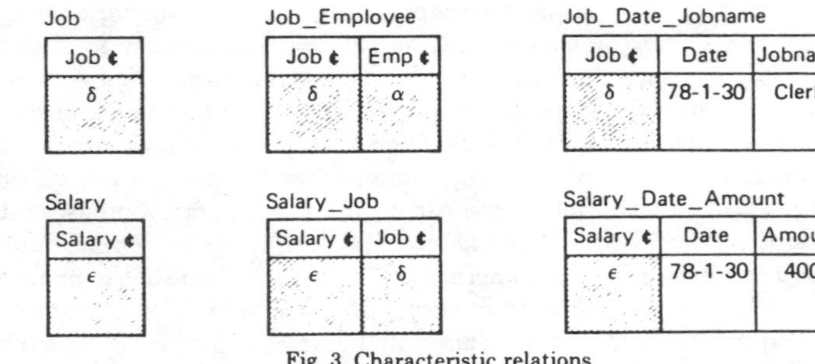

Job

Job ¢
δ

Job_Employee

Job ¢	Emp ¢
δ	α

Job_Date_Jobname

Job ¢	Date	Jobname
δ	78-1-30	Clerk

Salary

Salary ¢
ε

Salary_Job

Salary ¢	Job ¢
ε	δ

Salary_Date_Amount

Salary ¢	Date	Amount
ε	78-1-30	400

Fig. 3. Characteristic relations

A characteristic entity may itself have one or more characteristic entities subordinate to it. A familiar example is that of employees (a kernel entity type), each of whom has a job history (characteristic entity type subordinate to employees) whose immediate properties are date attained position and name of position. This information is augmented by salary history (characteristic entity type subordinate to job history) whose immediate properties are date of salary change and new salary (see Figure 3).

The need for a characteristic entity type described above arises from a strictly multivalued dependence (i.e., one that is not a functional dependence). Another way in which a characteristic entity type may arise is from a transitive functional dependence [6]. In this case an entity type e has an immediate property p, which in turn has an immediate property q (e.g., a highway segment has one of several types of surface material, which in turn has a porosity). An entity type that is characteristic with respect to highway segments can be introduced to represent the types of surface material on these segments. Porosity then becomes an immediate property of this entity type.

The characteristic entity types that provide description of a given kernel entity type form a strict hierarchy, which we call the *characteristic tree.* In this tree, entity type p is the parent of entity type q if q is an immediate characteristic of p (i.e., not a characteristic of a characteristic of p). A kernel entity type may, of course, have no characteristic entity types describing it. In this case its characteristic tree is a single node, the kernel entity type itself.

To represent the collection of characteristic trees, we introduce the *characteristic graph relation* (CG-relation), a binary relation whose two attributes are defined on the RN-domain, one with the SUB role, the other with the SUP role (as with the PG-relation). Its interpretation is as follows: The pair (SUB:m, SUP:n) belongs to CG if entity type $e(m)$ is immediately subordinate to entity type $e(n)$ in one of the characteristic hierarchies.

Insertion and deletion of characteristic entities are governed by the following rule.

Rule 5 (characteristic integrity): A characteristic entity cannot exist in the database unless the entity it describes most immediately is also in the database.

One may think of the collection of characteristic relations for a given E-relation as constituting a *characteristic molecule type*, which is bound together by tuples in the CG-relation.

9. ASSOCIATIONS

9.1 Associative Entities

The representation of associative entities in RM/T is the same as that of kernel entities. Thus, there is an E-relation for each associative entity type and zero or more P-relations. Figure 4 shows an example of an assignment association between employees and projects, where each assignment is treated as an entity and P-relations are used to record the employee and project surrogates plus the start date of the assignment.

If a given associative entity type has subordinate characteristic entity types, there will be corresponding tuples in the CG-relation to define the tree of these types and there will be characteristic relations to support each of the characteristic entity types involved.

Insertion, update, and deletion of associative entities are governed by the following rule.

Rule 6 (association integrity): Unless there is an explicit integrity constraint to the contrary, an associative entity can exist in the database (i.e., there is a corresponding surrogate in the appropriate E-relation), even though one or more entities participating in that association are unknown. In such a case the surrogate E-null is used to indicate that a participating entity is unknown.

To force automatic deletion of an association when an entity participating in that association is deleted, one may easily add the explicit constraint that the corresponding attribute of an appropriate P-relation cannot accept a null value. Such a constraint is part of the application of RM/T, rather than an integral part of RM/T itself.

An associative entity type interrelates entities of other types (kernel or associative or both). Let us refer to these other types as *immediate participants* in the given associative entity type. To support the specification of which entity types participate in which associative entity types, we introduce the *association graph relation* (AG-relation), a binary relation just like the CG-relation except for its interpretation: (SUB:m, SUP:n) belongs to AG, if the entity type $e(m)$ participates immediately in the definition of associative entity type $e(n)$. Note that the transitive closure of AG is a partial order, but not necessarily a tree or collection of trees.

It is important to observe that when one association type has another association type as a participant, proper use of surrogates in the higher level association for referencing specific lower level participants can remove a potential source of ambiguity (in the same way that proper use of user-controlled keys in the basic relational model can remove such an ambiguity). To illustrate this ambiguity, suppose we have two RM/T relations *IS* and *CAN* each having attributes *S¢*

Assign

Assign ¢
λ

Assign_Emp_Project

Assign ¢	Emp ¢	Project ¢
λ	α	μ

Assign_Date

Assign ¢	Start_Date
λ	78-1-1

Fig. 4. Associative entity

(supplier surrogates), *P¢* (part surrogates), and *C¢* (city surrogates):

$$IS\ (\ S¢{:}e\quad P¢{:}e\quad C¢{:}e\ )$$
$$CAN\ (\ S¢{:}e\quad P¢{:}e\quad C¢{:}e\ )$$

where $(s{:}e, p{:}e, c{:}e)$ belongs to *IS* if supplier *s is* supplying part *p* from city *c*; and $(s{:}e, p{:}e, c{:}e)$ belongs to *CAN* if supplier *s can* supply part *p* from city *c*.

Suppose also there is a need to represent a higher level association that relates each *IS* pair (s, p) to the project(s) receiving parts with serial number *p*. Suppose one were to establish an RM/T relation *TO*(*S¢*:*e*, *P¢*:*e*, *J¢*:*e*), where the attribute *J¢* is defined on project surrogates. It is not clear from this declaration whether the pairs (s, p) in *TO* are pairs from *IS* or pairs from *CAN* or just any arbitrary pairs of supplier and part surrogates. A separate integrity constraint of the form

$$TO[S¢, P¢] \subseteq IS[S¢, P¢]$$

helps to resolve this ambiguity at the type level, but not at the instance level. This is because there may be two or more occurrences of the pair (s, p) in the *IS* relation—say $(s, p, c1)$ and $(s, p, c2)$—and it is then not clear whether an occurrence of (s, p) in the *TO* relation is referring to $(s, p, c1)$ or $(s, p, c2)$.

By use of associative entities in RM/T the ambiguity can be resolved both at the type and instance level. We would have RM/T relations as follows:

$$IS\ (\ IS¢{:}e\quad S¢{:}e\quad P¢{:}e\quad C¢{:}c¢ \cdots\ )$$
$$CAN\ (\ CAN¢{:}e\quad S¢{:}e\quad P¢{:}e\quad C¢{:}c¢ \cdots\ )$$
$$TO\ (\ TO¢{:}e\quad IS¢{:}e\quad \cdots\ )$$

where the attribute *IS¢* in the relation *TO* refers to specific entities and hence specific tuples in the *IS* relation.

One may think of the collection of entity types participating (immediately or otherwise) in a given associative entity type as constituting an *associative molecule type*, which is bound together by tuples in the AG-relation.

9.2 Nonentity Associations

A nonentity association type has no E-relation. There is no surrogate associated with an association of this type. Hence, there is no dependable way (i.e., system-controlled way) to refer to it in either the PG-relation or the AG-relation. For the same reason, it cannot participate as a component in another association.

A nonentity association type is represented by a single *n*-ary relation whose attributes include the E-attributes identifying the entity types participating in the association together with the immediate properties (if any) of this association. Figure 5 shows how the assignment of employees to projects might be treated as a nonentity association type.

The insertion, update, and deletion behavior is governed by Rule 2 of the basic relational model. Thus, a nonentity association may not exist in the database unless the entities it interrelates are present therein.

Assignment

Emp ¢	Project ¢	Start_Date
α	μ	78-1-1

Fig. 5. Nonentity association

9.3 Decomposition of Associations

Thoughts, including those that pertain to description of a database, do not arise neatly decomposed into minimal meaningful units.

Given an association involving n ($n > 2$) participating entity types, a database designer who has only binary relational tools to work with would very likely immediately decompose such an association into *n anchored* binary relations (each relating one participant to the entity domain for the association itself). Suppose that, had he cast the association in *n*-ary form and studied its possible nonloss decompositions, he could have found that the association is decomposable into two or more relatively independent associations of lower degree, each of which could then be separately decomposed (if desired) into binary relations. We would then say that his immediate decomposition into binaries was premature. We call this the *premature binary decomposition trap*. This trap is complementary to the connection trap in [5].

In attempting to arrive at minimal meaningful units, the designer would be well advised to make use of all the theory of *n*-ary relations that has been built up over the past decade. There are now such concepts as PJ/NF (otherwise known as 5NF) [11], irreducible relations, atomic decomposition [45], well-defined relations [33], independent relations [29], and primitive relations [26], all of which can be used as guidelines for decomposition. While all these concepts deal primarily with projections that are invertible by nonloss natural joins, the last two also take into account new interrelation integrity constraints that might be needed if decomposition is taken too far or poor choices are made when two or more decomposition options are available.

Note that, in general, a nonentity association cannot be split up (without information loss) into anchored binary projections in the same way associative entities can because there is no entity domain to rejoin the projections together. For this and other reasons, RM/T may be applied to database design completely avoiding the nonentity association concept altogether.

10. CARTESIAN AGGREGATION

An important dimension for forming larger meaningful units is that of *Cartesian aggregation*. Smith and Smith [33] call it simply aggregation, but we wish to distinguish it from other forms of aggregation such as statistical aggregation and cover aggregation (discussed below). According to Smith and Smith, Cartesian aggregation is an abstraction in which a relationship between objects is regarded as a higher level object.

Cartesian aggregation in RM/T is broken down into three types:

(1) aggregation of simple properties yields an entity type (characteristic or kernel or associative);

(2) aggregation of characteristic entities yields an entity type (characteristic or kernel or associative);

(3) aggregation of any combination of kernel and associative entity types yields either an associative entity type or a nonentity association type.

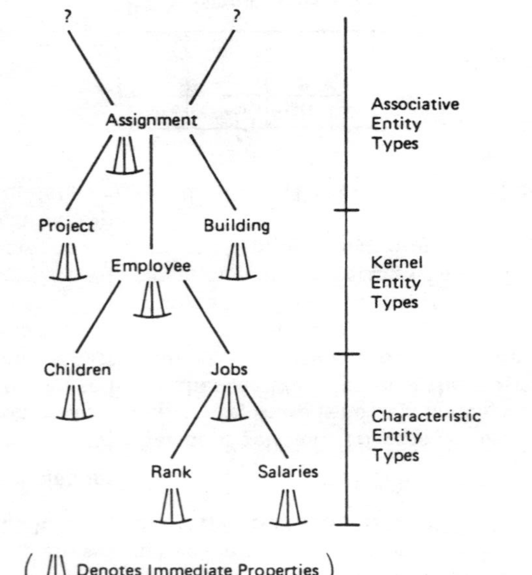

Fig. 6. Cartesian aggregation

The first kind of Cartesian aggregation is supported in RM/T by the P-relations together with the PG-relation; the second type by the characteristic relations together with the CG-relation; and the third type by the kernel relations, associative relations, and the AG-relation. Figure 6 provides an example of Cartesian aggregation.

While RM/T can be applied with the Smith and Smith constraint that abstraction by Cartesian aggregation must yield a concept namable by a simple English noun, the model itself is not constrained in this way, since this constraint is too imprecise.

11. GENERALIZATION

11.1 Unconditional Generalization

Another important dimension for forming larger meaningful units is that of generalization. It has received a good deal of attention in the context of semantic nets [18, 31, 35]. Here we are concerned with it in the context of n-ary relations. Smith and Smith [34] define *generalization* as an abstraction in which a set of similar objects is regarded as a generic object. There are two aspects to this notion: instantiation and subtype. Both are forms of *specialization*, and their inverses are forms of generalization. The extensional counterpart of instantiation is set membership, while that of subtype is set inclusion. As shown in Figure 7, to obtain particular engineers from the generic object (or type) engineer, instantiation must be applied. The types engineer, secretary, and trucker are each subtypes of the type employee. An entity type e together with its immediate subtypes,

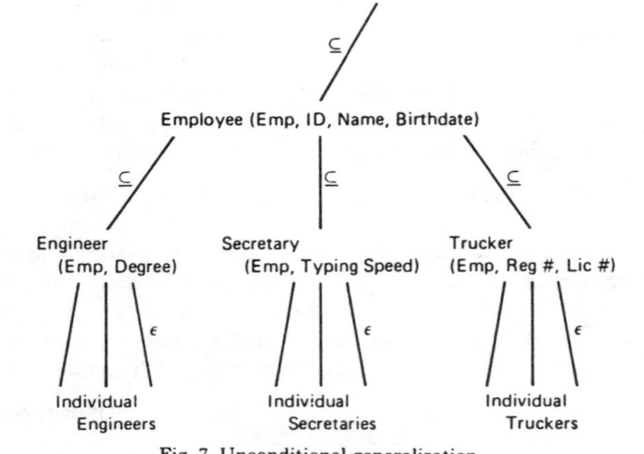

Fig. 7. Unconditional generalization

their subtypes, and so on constitute the *generalization hierarchy* of e. This hierarchy is yet another molecule type.

Why should we separate the members of a generalization hierarchy into different entity types? We do this only if different kinds of facts are to be recorded about different members of the hierarchy. If these types were not represented separately, we would have a single large relation with many occurrences of the special null value which means "value inapplicable." Associated with a generalization hierarchy is the *property inheritance rule*: Given any subtype e, all of the properties of its parent type(s) are applicable to e. For example, all of the properties of employees in general are applicable to salesmen employees in particular.

The E-relations introduced above take care of generalization by membership. To handle generalization by inclusion, we introduce the *unconditional gen inclusion relation* (UGI-relation), a ternary relation representing a labeled graph. Two attributes of UGI are defined on the RN-domain (one with the SUB role, the other with the SUP role), while the third attribute is defined on the category label domain called *PER*. The triple (SUB:m, SUP:n, PER:p) belongs to UGI if entity type $e(m)$ is an immediate subtype of entity type $e(n)$ per category p. In other words, the E-relation whose name is represented by character string m is constrained to be included (by reason of generalization per category p) in the E-relation whose name is represented by the character string n. Note that UGI contains only the immediate unconditional inclusion constraints that are associated with the semantic notion of generalization. Thus, if (SUB:m, SUP:n, PER:p) and (SUB:n, SUP:k, PER:p) belong to UGI, (SUB:m, SUP:k, PER:p) does not.

The transitive closure of the UGI-relation represents a partial order of the entity types, but not necessarily a collection of trees, since an entity type may be generalized by inclusion into two or more entity types. For example, female engineers might be generalized into engineers on the one hand and female employees on the other.

Consider the family of entity types in some generalization hierarchy. Normally, *it* would be good database design to represent common properties and characteristics of these entity types as high up in that hierarchy as possible, taking full advantage of the property inheritance rule. However, RM/T itself does not place such a constaint upon generalization hierarchies—this is considered to be a design discipline that the user of RM/T may choose to adopt or reject.

The following rule governs insertions and deletions of surrogates.

Rule 7 (subtype integrity): Whenever a surrogate (say *s*) belongs to the E-relation for an entity of type *e*, *s* must also belong to the E-relation for each entity type of which *e* is a subtype.

11.2 Alternative Generalization

We may augment the usual notion of generalization hierarchy by noting that an entity type may be generalized into two or more *alternative* types. For example, in a database concerning customers (see Figure 8), suppose that a customer may be a company, partnership, or individual person and each of these is a legal unit. Suppose also that different attributes are to be recorded for each of these five entity types. Then, in addition to recording in UGI the unconditional inclusion of customers, companies, partnerships, and individuals in legal units, we should also record elsewhere the alternative or conditional inclusion of customers in companies, partnerships, and individuals. To support this, we introduce the *alternative gen inclusion relation* (AGI-relation), a ternary relation just like the UGI-relation, except for its interpretation: (SUB:*m*, SUP:*n*, PER:*p*) belongs to AGI if the E-relation with name *m* is constrained to be conditionally included in E-relation *n* by reason of generalization per category *p*.

Suppose information about a new entity is being inserted and just one of its several types is specified. Then the system can (and, according to Rule 7, must) automatically insert the surrogate generated for this entity not only in the E-relation directly representing the declared type, but also in the E-relation for every entity that, according to UGI and AGI, is superordinate to the declared entity. Both graph relations must be consulted, because *A* may be alternatively subordinate to *B* and *C*, which in turn are unconditionally subordinate to *D*; hence *A* is unconditionally, but not immediately, subordinate to *D*.

To illustrate the operational distinction between UGI and AGI, consider the introduction of a new customer into a database that conforms to Figure 8. By consulting UGI the system ascertains that the surrogate for this customer must be entered into the E-relation for legal units as well as that for customers. By consulting AGI it ascertains that more extensional information is needed to determine whether to enter the surrogate into the E-relation for companies, partnerships, or individuals. Until this information is forthcoming, the system cannot determine whether the customer in question inherits properties from a company, partnership, or individual. Accordingly, AGI (in contrast to UGI) alerts the system to the need to obtain, if necessary, and consult extensional information for guidance.

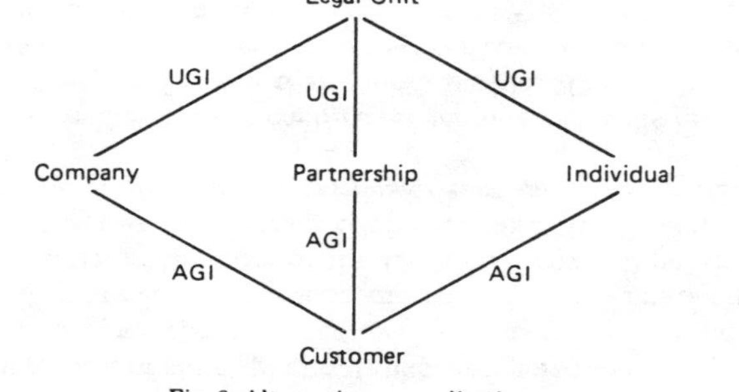

Fig. 8. Alternative generalization

12. COVER AGGREGATION

A convoy of ships is certainly an aggregation of some kind. However, it is not an abstraction by Cartesian aggregation, nor is it an abstraction by generalization (after all, ships are neither instantiations nor subtypes of convoys). Hammer and McLeod [15] include this kind of aggregation in their model, and we shall use their example.

Consider a database that keeps track of properties of individual ships and convoys. When information about a new ship is inserted, it is normally not known in what convoys (if any) this ship will participate. Figure 9 should make the distinctive aspects of this kind of aggregation clear. The *cover type* CONVOY means that the database is keeping track of convoys in general. CONVOY ALPHA is a particular convoy, one of several in existence at this time. SAUCY SUE designates a ship that happens to be in CONVOY ALPHA. There is a subconvoy of ALPHA to which SAUCY SUE also belongs. Note that the inclusion of SUBCONVOY in CONVOY ALPHA is not an inclusion-based generalization (SUBCONVOY is an extensionally, rather than intensionally, defined subset of ALPHA). Moreover, the membership of SAUCY SUE in CONVOY ALPHA is not a membership-based generalization (SAUCY SUE is not a particular convoy or kind of convoy).

It happens in the convoy example that a ship cannot normally be a member of two convoys at once. If we regard lone ships as singleton convoys, then the CONVOY concept partitions the class of ships. The disjointness of convoys does not carry over into all other examples of cover aggregation. Consider people and clubs in place of ships and convoys: People can belong to many different clubs simultaneously. So, in general, this type of aggregation constitutes a cover rather than a partition—hence its name.

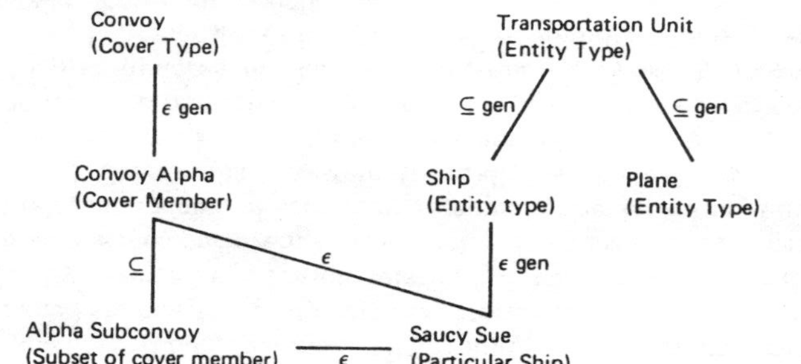

Fig. 9. Cover aggregation and generalization

A typical cover member may or may not be homogeneous in type. For example, a task force may consist of ships, planes, tanks, and personnel.

Each cover aggregation type is treated by RM/T as an entity type, having the usual E-relation plus possible P-relations and possible subordinate characteristic relations. For example, in the case of the CONVOY cover type, the E-relation would list the surrogates for existing convoys, while the P-relations and any characteristic relations would list properties of each convoy regarded as a single generic object.

Although it is possible to treat each cover member as a distinct entity type, this would normally be neither necessary nor desirable. Membership of individual entities (ships) in a cover member (particular convoy) is represented by a graph relation defined on the E-domain in the obvious way.

To enable the system to control the input of members of cover members, we introduce the *cover membership relation* (KG-relation), a graph relation on the RN-domain which specifies for every cover aggregation type what are the allowable types that may become members of cover members (e.g., are just ships allowed as members of convoys or are planes allowed too?).

13. EVENT PRECEDENCE

Entities of event type are those which have as part of their description a time of occurrence or a start time and/or a stop time. Note that not all entities with time attributes are events. For example, an associative entity which indicates that supplier x can supply item y with a delivery time of three months is not itself an event.

Ordering of events in time plays a major role in certain databases. Provision for recording this ordering at the type level represents a step toward supporting scripts (see [17]).

Event e_1 succeeds event e_2 if the time of occurrence/start of e_1 is strictly later than the time of occurrence/completion of e_2 (according to whether these events are perceived as instantaneous or not). Some types of events are unconditionally followed by one or more other event types. Such succession is normally a partial order. It is represented in RM/T by the *unconditional successor relation* (US-relation), a graph relation on the RN-domain. (SUB:m, SUP:n) belongs to this relation if an event of type $e(m)$ must be succeeded by an event of type $e(n)$, and there is no intermediate event type e such that e is an unconditional successor of $e(m)$ and $e(n)$ is an unconditional successor of e.

Similarly, some types of events are alternative successors to others, and this alternative succession is represented by the *alternative successor relation* (AS-relation) in a similar manner to the unconditional succession.

When an event e_2 succeeds an event e_1, this obviously means that e_1 is a predecessor of e_2, but it does not mean that e_1 is necessarily the *only* predecessor of e_2—even if e_2 is the only successor of e_1. Hence, we need two more graph relations to describe precedence between event types: UP for unconditional precedence and AP for alternative precedence.

To illustrate the use of these graph relations, suppose we have a database that includes records of orders placed with suppliers and records of shipments that have been accepted as input to the inventory (the corresponding event entity types will be called orders and shipments). Suppose that we prohibit acceptance of shipments into the inventory unless there is an unfilled order covering the items in question. Then, relation UP would have a tuple (SUB:orders, SUP:shipments) that asserts that every acceptance of a shipment is unconditionally preceded by an order. In addition, relation AS would have a tuple that asserts that one possible successor event to the placing of an order is the acceptance of a shipment (shipments can, of course, be rejected). This intensional information can be used by the database system to challenge the validity of particular acceptances not covered by corresponding orders.

More generally, the relations US, AS, UP, AP provide a means of constraining insertions to and updates of the event relations supporting an event type. Otherwise, their behavior under insertion, update, and deletion is determined by whether they are kernel or associative.

14. RM/T CATALOG

RM/T contains its own extensible catalog to facilitate transformations between different organizations of common information as may be encountered in the process of view integration. The following relations constitute the catalog structure:

CATR (R¢ RELNAME RELTYPE)
CATRA (RA¢ R¢ A¢)
CATA (A¢ ATTNAME USERKEY)
CATAD (AD¢ A¢ D¢)
CATD (D¢ DOMNAME VTYPE ORDERING)
CATC (C¢ PERNAME)
CATRC (RC¢ R¢ C¢)

where CATR, CATA, and CATD describe the relations, attributes, and domains, respectively; CATRA interrelates relations and their attributes; CATAD interrelates attributes and their domains; CATRC interrelates relations and categories (see below for details). In addition, attributes R¢, A¢, D¢, C¢ are defined on the E-domain and contain surrogates for entities of type relation, attribute, domain, and category label, respectively; attributes RA¢, AD¢, RC¢ are also defined on the E-domain and contain surrogates for associative entities of type relation–attribute, attribute–domain, and relation–category–label, respectively. The remaining attributes are listed below with a brief explanation:

RELNAME	relname of relation (defined on RN-domain);
ATTNAME	attname of attribute;
DOMNAME	domname of domain;
PERNAME	category label (defined on PER-domain);
RELTYPE	type of object represented by relation;
USERKEY	indicates whether attribute participates in a user-defined key for corresponding relation;
VTYPE	syntactic type of value;
ORDERING	indicates whether > is applicable between values in corresponding domain.

Given a category c, an entity type is called *top per c* if it has at least one subordinate entity type per *c*, but no superordinate per *c*. Relation CATRC contains at least one tuple for every category. For each category in the database, it lists the relations which represent top entity types per that category. The meaning of the other relations in the catalog should be obvious.

Appropriate reltypes are specified for a relation by concatenating appropriate letters from the following list:

A associative entity type relation;
C characteristic entity type relation;
E E-relation;
G graph relation;
I inner kernel entity type relation;
K kernel entity type relation;
L edge-labeled;
N nonentity association relation;
P property relation;
T event entity type relation.

For example, a relation representing a kernel event entity type would have reltype TK; one that represents an edge-labeled digraph would have the reltype LG.

15. OPERATORS FOR RM/T

The following operators are intended to permit both the schema information and the database extension to be manipulated in a uniform way.

15.1 Name Operators

NOTE

Let R be a relation. NOTE(R) is the relname of R (i.e., the character string representation of the name of R) provided R has been assigned such a name by a user; else NOTE(R) is null. For our present purposes we do not need to extend this operator to objects other than relations. Many relations generated as intermediate results will not have relnames. Every base relation must, however, be given a relname.

TAG

Let R be a relation. Then

$$\text{TAG}(R) = R \times \{\text{NOTE}(R)\}$$

where × denotes Cartesian product.

DENOTE

Let r be the relname of a relation. Then DENOTE(r) is the relation denoted by r. When applied to relations that have relnames, the operators NOTE and DENOTE are inverses of one another.

DENOTE may also be applied to a unary relation that is a set of relnames. Let R be such a relation. Then DENOTE(R) is the set of all those relations whose relname is in R.

15.2 Set Operators

COMPRESS

Let f be an associative and commutative operator that maps a pair of relations into a relation (for example, a join). Let Z be a set of relations such that f can be validly applied to every pair of relations in Z. Then COMPRESS(f, Z) is the relation obtained by repeated pairwise application of f to the relations in Z. An alternative notation for COMPRESS(f, Z) is f/Z.

APPLY

Let f be a unary operator that maps relations into relations, and Z a set of relations (not necessarily union compatible). Then APPLY(f, Z) yields the set of all relations $f(z)$ where z is a member of Z. For convenience, we adopt the convention that if a set of relations is cited in an algebraic expression in one or more places where a relation name would be syntactically valid, then the expression is evaluated for every member of the set. However, (1) the expression must be enclosed in parentheses and preceded by the word APPLY, and (2) no more than one *set of relations* may be cited within the scope of a single APPLY (any number of individual relations may be cited).

PARTITION BY ATTRIBUTE: PATT

Let R be a relation with attribute A (possibly compound). R may have attributes other than A. Then PATT(R, A) is the set of relations obtained by partitioning R per all the distinct values of A. For all relations R having an attribute A:

$$R = \text{UNION/PATT}(R, A).$$

PARTITION BY TUPLE: PTUPLE

Let R be a relation. PTUPLE(R) is the set of relations obtained by promoting each tuple of R into a single-tuple relation. Note that R = UNION/PTUPLE(R).

PARTITION BY RELATION: PREL

Let R be a relation. PREL(R) is the set of relations whose only member is the relation R. Note that R = UNION/PREL(R).

SETREL

This operator takes as arguments any number of explicitly named relations and yields a set of relations. An appropriate expression is:

$$\text{SETREL}(R_1, R_2, \ldots, R_n).$$

15.3 Graph Operators

The following operators are included for convenient manipulation of the directed graph relations (PG, CG, AG, UGI, AGI, US, AS, UP, AP, KG). Relation R is a *digraph relation* if it is of degree at least two and has the following properties: (1) two of its attributes are defined on a common domain; (2) one of these has the SUB role, the other has the SUP role; (3) no other attributes have the SUB or SUP role. Relation R is an *edge-labeled digraph relation* if (1) it is a digraph relation of degree at least three; (2) exactly one of its attributes has the PER (labeling) role; and (3) for every m, n, p no two tuples of R have (SUB:m,

SUP:n, PER:p) in common. A digraph relation that is not edge-labeled is called *unlabeled.*

OPEN

Case 1. Let R be an *unlabeled* digraph relation (i.e., no attribute has the PER role). Then OPEN(R) yields a copy of R with all nonimmediate subordinations removed; i.e., it is the maximal subset R_1 of R having the property that if (SUB:m, SUP:n) belongs to R_1, then *either* there does not exist any k for which both (SUB:m, SUP:k) and (SUB:k, SUP:n) belong to R_1, *or else* the existence of such a k implies that $k = m$ or $k = n$.

Case 2. Let R be an *edge-labeled* digraph relation. OPEN(R) yields the maximal subset R_1 of R with the property that if (SUB:m, SUP:n, PER:p) belongs to R_1, then *either* there does not exist any k for which both (SUB:m, SUP:k, PER:p) and (SUB:k, SUP:n, PER:p) belong to R_1, *or else* the existence of such a k implies that $k = m$ or $k = n$.

CLOSE

Case 1. Let R be an *unlabeled* digraph relation. CLOSE(R) is the transitive closure of R; i.e., it is the minimal superset of R such that if both (SUB:m, SUP:k) and (SUB:k, SUP:n) belong to R, then (SUB:m, SUP:n) belongs to CLOSE(R). Tuples in CLOSE(R) that do not also belong to R have null values for those attributes other than the SUB and SUP attributes.

Case 2. Let R be an *edge-labeled* diagraph relation. CLOSE(R) yields the minimal superset of R such that if both (SUB:m, SUP:k, PER:p) and (SUB:k, SUP:n, PER:p) belong to R, then (SUB:m, SUP:n, PER:p) belongs to CLOSE(R). Tuples in CLOSE(R) that do not also belong to R have null values for those attributes other than the SUB, SUP, and PER attributes.

Note that for all digraph relations R:

$$\begin{aligned} \text{OPEN(OPEN}(R)) &= \text{OPEN}(R), \\ \text{OPEN(CLOSE}(R)) &= \text{OPEN}(R), \\ \text{CLOSE(CLOSE}(R)) &= \text{CLOSE}(R), \end{aligned}$$

while for all unlabeled digraph relations R of degree 2 and all edge-labeled digraph relations R of degree 3:

$$\text{CLOSE(OPEN}(R)) = \text{CLOSE}(R).$$

With higher degree digraph relations, OPEN may lose information (contained in attributes other than SUB, SUP, and PER) which CLOSE cannot regenerate.

STEP

Case 1. Let R be an *unlabeled* digraph relation that does not have an attribute SEP (which stands for separation). Let Z be the set of all attributes of R other than SUB and SUP. STEP(R) is the set of all tuples of the form

$$(\text{SUB}{:}x,\ \text{SUP}{:}y,\ Z{:}z,\ \text{SEP}{:}n)$$

where (SUB:x, SUP:y, Z:z) belongs to R and n is the least number of edges of the graph which separate node x from node y.

Case 2. Let R be an *edge-labeled* digraph relation that does not have an attribute SEP. Let Z be the set of all attributes of R other than SUB, SUP, and PER. STEP(R) is the set of all tuples of the form

$$(\text{SUB}{:}x,\ \text{SUP}{:}y,\ \text{PER}{:}p,\ Z{:}z,\ \text{SEP}{:}n)$$

where (SUB:x, SUP:y, PER:p, Z:z) belongs to R and n is the least number of edges with the label p separating node x from node y.

15.4 Examples

Example A. Combine all of the P-relations for the entity type employee into a single comprehensive P-relation, without losing information and without assuming any knowledge of the number of such relations.

First we obtain the names of all P-relations for the entity type employee.

$$R_1 \leftarrow \text{PG[SUP = emp] [SUB]}.$$

Remember that PG is the property graph relation. Then we obtain the corresponding set of relations:

$$R_2 \leftarrow \text{DENOTE}(R_1).$$

Finally, we repeatedly apply the outer natural join $\circledast$ on the attribute EMP¢ (common to all relations in the set):

$$R_3 \leftarrow (\circledast\ \text{EMP¢})/R_2,$$

where $\circledast$ followed by an attribute or collection of attributes indicates that the outer natural join is to be performed with respect to these attributes as join attributes.

Suppose we combine the expressions for R_1, R_2, R_3 into a single expression and replace emp by r, where r is the relname of any entity type. Let us denote the result by:

$$\text{PROPERTY}(r) = (\circledast\ r, \text{'¢'})/\text{DENOTE(PG[SUP} = r\text{] [SUB])}.$$

PROPERTY accordingly maps a relname of an entity type into the corresponding comprehensive P-relation.

Example B. Obtain the employee name and jobtype for all employees with an excellent rating, assuming that:

(1) There are distinct entity types for each jobtype (e.g., secretary, trucker, engineer, etc.) and the jobtype category partitions the set of employees.
(2) The immediate generalization of these types is to the entity type employee.
(3) Employee name and jobtype are recorded in one or more of the P-relations associated with employee.
(4) Rating is recorded separately in a P-relation for each jobtype.

$$R_1 \leftarrow \text{UGI[SUP = emp, PER = jobtype] [SUB]}.$$

Remember that UGI is the unconditional gen inclusion relation. R_1 is therefore a unary relation that lists all the names of all the E-relations that are unconditionally immediately subordinate to the employee relation.

$$R_2 \leftarrow \text{APPLY(PROPERTY}, R_1).$$

ACKNOWLEDGMENT

The author has drawn heavily on the published ideas of Smith and Smith; LaCroix and Pirotte; Hall, Owlett, and Todd; Schmid and Swenson; Hammer and McLeod. The stimulus to write this paper came from the many provocative utterances contained in the Proceedings of the IFIP TC-2 of 1976 and 1977 [24, 25]. The author is grateful to William Armstrong, Donald Cameron, Christopher Date, Ronald Fagin, John Sowa, Stephen Todd, and the referees for helpful comments on a draft of this paper.

REFERENCES

(Note. References [1, 7, 21, 36] are not cited in the text.)

1. Aho, A. H., Beeri, C., and Ullman, J. The theory of joins in relational databases. Proc. 19th IEEE Symp. on Foundations of Comptr. Sci., 1977.
2. Astrahan, M. M., et al. System R: Relational approach to database management. *ACM Trans. Database Syst. 1*, 2 (June 1976), 97–137.
3. Beeri, C., Bernstein, P., and Goodman, N. A sophisticate's introduction to database normalization theory. Proc. Int. Conf. on Very Large Data Bases, Berlin, Sept. 1978, pp. 113–124.
4. Cadiou, J. M. On semantic issues in the relational model of data. Proc. 5th Symp. on Math. Foundations of Comptr. Sci., 1976, Gdansk, Poland, *Lecture Notes in Computer Science 45*, Springer-Verlag, pp. 23–38.
5. Codd, E. F. A relational model of data for large shared data banks. *Comm. ACM 13*, 6 (June 1970), 377–387.
6. Codd, E. F. Further normalization of the database relational model. In *Database Systems*, Courant Computer Science Symposia 6, R. Rustin, Ed., Prentice-Hall, Englewood Cliffs, N.J., 1971, pp. 65–98.
7. Codd, E. F. Recent investigations in relational database systems. Information Processing 74, North-Holland Pub. Co., Amsterdam, 1974, pp. 1017–1021.
8. Codd, E. F. Understanding relations (Installment No. 7). FDT (Bulletin of ACM SIGMOD) *7*, 3–4 (Dec. 1975), 23–28.
9. Codd, E. F. Extending the database relational model. Invited talk presented at the Australian Comptr. Sci. Conf., Hobart, Tasmania, Feb. 1–2, 1979.
10. Fagin, R. Multivalued dependencies and a new normal form for relational databases. *ACM Trans. Database Syst. 2*, 3 (Sept. 1977), 262–278.
11. Fagin, R. Normal forms and relational database operators. Proc. ACM SIGMOD Conf., Boston, Mass., May 30–June 1, 1979.
12. Falkenberg, E. Concepts for modelling information. In *Modelling in Data Base Management Systems*, G. M. Nijssen, Ed., North-Holland Pub. Co., Amsterdam, 1976.
13. Goldstein, R. C., and Strnad, A. L. The MACAIMS data management system. Proc. 1970 ACM SICFIDET Workshop on Data Description and Access, Houston, Tex., Nov. 15–16, 1970.
14. Hall, P., Owlett, J., and Todd, S. Relations and entities. In *Modelling in Data Base Management Systems*, G. M. Nijssen, Ed., North-Holland Pub. Co., Amsterdam, 1976.
15. Hammer, M. M., and McLeod, D. J. The semantic data model: A modelling mechanism for database applications. Proc. ACM SIGMOD Conf., Austin, Tex., May 31–June 2, 1978.
16. Heath, I. J. Private communication, April 1971.
17. Hemphill, L. G., and Rhyne, J. R. A model for knowledge representation in natural language query systems. IBM Res. Rep. RJ2304, IBM Res. Lab., San Jose, Calif., Sept. 1978.
18. Hendrix, G. G. Encoding knowledge in partitioned networks. Tech. Note 164, SRI International, Menlo Park, Calif., June 1978.
19. Jordan, D. E. Implementing production systems with relational data bases. Proc. ACM Pacific Conf., San Francisco, Calif., April 1975.
20. LaCroix, M., and Pirotte, A. Generalized joins. SIGMOD Record (ACM) *8*, 3 (Sept. 1976), 14–15.
21. LaCroix, M., and Pirotte, A. Example queries in relational languages. Tech. Note N107, Manufacture Belge de Lampes et de Materiel Electronique, Brussels, Belgium, Jan. 1976; revised Sept. 1977.
22. Lipski, Jr., W. On semantic issues connected with incomplete information databases. *ACM Trans. Database Syst. 4*, 3 (Sept. 1979), 262–296.
23. Merrett, T. H. Relations as programming language elements. *Inform. Processing Lett. 6*, 1 (Feb. 1977), 29–33.
24. Nijssen, G. M., Ed. *Modelling in Database Management Systems.* North-Holland Pub. Co., Amsterdam, 1976.
25. Nijssen, G. M., Ed. *Architecture and Models in Database Management Systems.* North-Holland Pub. Co., Amsterdam, 1977.
26. Pirotte, A. The entity-property-association model: An information-oriented database model. Rep. R343, Manufacture Belge de Lampes et de Materiel Electronique, Brussels, Belgium, March 1977.
27. Pirotte, A. Linguistic aspects of high-level relational languages. Rep. R367, Manufacture Belge de Lampes et de Materiel Electronique, Brussels, Belgium, Jan. 1978.
28. Reiter, R. On closed world data bases. In *Logic and Data Bases*, H. Gallaire and J. Minker, Eds., Plenum Press, New York, 1978.
29. Rissanen, J. Independent components of relations. *ACM Trans. Database Syst. 2*, 4 (Dec. 1977), 317–325.
30. Rissanen, J. Theory of relations for databases—a tutorial survey. Proc. Symp. on Math. Foundations of Comptr. Sci., 1978, Zakopane, Poland, *Lecture Notes in Computer Science*, Springer-Verlag, pp. 536–551.
31. Roussopoulos, N., and Mylopoulos, J. Using semantic networks for database management. Proc. Int. Conf. on Very Large Databases, Sept. 1975.
32. Schmid, H. A., and Swenson, J. R. On the semantics of the relational data model. Proc. ACM SIGMOD Conf. on Manage. of Data, San Jose, Calif., May 1975, pp. 211–223.
33. Smith, J. M., and Smith, D. C. P. Database abstractions: Aggregation. *Comm. ACM 20*, 6 (June 1977), 405–413.
34. Smith, J. M., and Smith, D. C. P. Database abstractions: Aggregation and generalization. *ACM Trans. Database Syst. 2*, 2 (June 1977), 105–133.
35. Sowa, J. F. Conceptual structures for a database interface. *IBM J. Res. Develop. 20*, 4 (July 1976), 336–357.
36. Sowa, J. F. Definitional mechanisms for conceptual graphs. Proc. Int. Workshop on Graph Grammars, Bad Honnef, West Germany, Nov. 1978.
37. Stonebraker, M., Wong, E., Kreps, P., and Held, G. The design and implementation of INGRES. *ACM Trans. Database Syst. 1*, 3 (Sept. 1976), 189–222.
38. Todd, S. J. P. The Peterlee relational test vehicle. *IBM Syst. J. 15*, 4 (1976), 285–308.
39. Ullman, J. D. *Theory of Relational Databases.* To appear.
40. Vassiliou, Y. Null values in data base management: A denotational semantics approach. Proc. ACM SIGMOD 1979 Int. Conf. on Manage. of Data, Boston, Mass., May 30–June 1, 1979.
41. Whitney, V. K. M. RDMS: A relational data management system. Proc. Fourth Int. Symp. on Comptr. and Inform. Sci., Miami Beach, Fla., Dec. 14–16, 1972, Plenum Press, New York.
42. Wiederhold, G. *Database Design.* McGraw-Hill, New York, 1977.
43. Wong, H. K. T., and Mylopoulos, J. Two views of data semantics: A survey of data models in artificial intelligence and database management. *Informatics 15*, 3 (Oct. 1977), 344–383.
44. Zaniolo, C. Analysis and design of relational schemata for database systems. Tech. Rep. UCLA-ENG-7669, Ph.D. Th., U. of California at Los Angeles, Los Angeles, Calif., July 1976.
45. Zaniolo, C., and Melkanoff, M. A. A formal approach to the definition and design of conceptual schemas for database systems. To appear in *ACM Trans. Database Syst.*
46. Zloof, M. M. Query-by-example: A data base language. *IBM Syst. J. 16*, 4 (1977), 324–343.

Received March 1979; revised August 1979

order sets are UNION, INTERSECTION, and SET DIFFERENCE. Various other operators (e.g., OUTER UNION) may be applied to them. To create these sets of relations, manipulate them, and manipulate the graph relations, the operators have been added (the terms "domain object" and "range object" refer to the domain and range of the operator) where relname set means a unary relation that is a set of relnames (see Table II).

17. CONCLUSION

We have attempted to define an extended relational model that captures more of the meaning of the data. Meaningful units of information larger than the individual n-ary relation have been introduced in such a way that apparently competing semantic approaches recorded elsewhere may all be represented therein or translated thereto. The result is a model with a richer variety of objects than the original relational model, additional insert–update–delete rules, and some additional operators that make the algebra more powerful (and unfortunately more complicated). We reiterate that incorporation of larger meaningful units is a never-ending task, and therefore this model is only slightly more semantic than the previous one.

A data model that is to act as

(1) a conceptual framework for defining a wide class of formatted databases and
(2) a mediator between stored representations and user views

should probably have at least four personalities; a tabular personality (e.g., the extensions of relations in the relational model), a set-theoretic personality (e.g., the relational algebra), an inferential string-formula personality (e.g., predicate logic in modern notation), and a graph-theoretic personality (e.g., labeled, directed hypergraphs for relations). The tabular form is needed for displaying and/or modifying extensional data (especially for those users who need to be protected from the detailed organization of the knowledge supporting the extensional data). The set-theoretic personality is needed to support search without navigation. The predicate logic personality permits stringwise expression of intensional knowledge and the application of general inferencing techniques. The graphical personality permits psychologically attractive pictures to be drawn for the special class of users who are designing the database, maintaining the supporting knowledge, or developing specialized inferencing techniques.

Note that only the tabular and set-theoretic aspects of RM/T are presented here. Clearly, there are several kinds of graphs which can be associated with RM/T. In addition to representing n-ary relations by hypergraphs, each graph relation has an immediate representation as a directed graph (in certain cases edge-labeled).

Other extensions of the relational model are under consideration: for example, additional support for the time dimension and for a nonforgetting mode of operation. It is hoped that RM/T can be developed into a general-purpose restructuring algebra for databases. It should be remembered, however, that the extensions in RM/T are primarily intended for the minority consisting of database designers and sophisticated users; most users will probably prefer the simplicity of the basic relational model.

Table I

RM/T object		Purpose
surrogate		system-controlled entity representative
relname		string rep of name of database relation
reltype		string rep of relation type
E-null	*	surrogate denoting "entity unknown"
E-domain	*	domain of active surrogates
PER-domain	*	domain of category labels
RN-domain	*	domain of relnames
E-att		attribute defined on E-domain
RN-att		attribute defined on RN-domain
PER-att		label in graph relation
SEP-att		separation of one node from another
SUB-att		subordinate in graph relation
SUP-att		superior in graph relation
CATR-rel	%*	list of all relnames and their reltypes
CATRA-rel	%*	relations and their attributes
CATA-rel	%*	list of all attributes
CATAD-rel	%*	attributes and their domains
CATD-rel	%*	list of all domains
CATC-rel	%*	list of all categories
CATRC-rel	%*	categories and their top entity types
E-rel		list of surrogates for a given entity type
P-rel		immediate properties of entity type
PG-rel	*	property graph
CG-rel	*	characteristic graph
AG-rel	*	association graph
UGI-rel	*	unconditional gen inclusion graph
AGI-rel	*	alternative gen inclusion graph
US-rel	*	unconditional successor graph
AS-rel	*	alternative successor graph
UP-rel	*	unconditional predecessor graph
AP-rel	*	alternative predecessor graph
KG-rel	*	membership in cover aggregate types

Note: In any RM/T database there is only one object of each type marked with an asterisk. The relations marked % have E-relation counterparts not listed explicitly here.

Table II

RM/T operator	Domain object	Range object
NOTE	relation	relname
TAG	relation	relation
DENOTE	relname	relation
	relnameset	set of relations
COMPRESS	set of relations	relation
APPLY	set of relations	set of relations
PATT	relation	set of relations
PTUPLE	relation	set of relations
PREL	relation	set of relations
SETREL	relation(s)	set of relations
OPEN	graph relation	graph relation
CLOSE	graph relation	graph relation
STEP	graph relation	graph relation

R_2 is a set of P-relations, each of which is the comprehensive P-relation for one of the relnames in R_1.

$$R_3 \leftarrow \text{APPLY}(R_2[\text{RATING} = \text{excellent}]).$$

R_3 is a set of relations just like R_2 except that each relation in R_3 is a restriction of its counterpart in R_2.

$$R_4 \leftarrow \text{APPLY}(R_3[\text{EMP¢}]).$$

R_4 is a set of relations obtained by projecting each relation in R_3 on the attribute EMP¢.

$$R_5 \leftarrow (\text{PROPERTY(emp)})[\text{EMP¢, NAME, JOBTYPE}].$$

The comprehensive P-relation for the entity type employee is projected onto its surrogate, name, and jobtype attributes.

$$R_6 \leftarrow \text{UNION/APPLY}(R_4[\text{EMP¢} = \text{EMP¢}]R_5).$$

Each relation in the set R_4 is joined by entity employee to relation R_5. The result is compressed by repeated union to yield R_6, the required output.

The final expression is an example of a join by entity, in contrast to a join by property.

Example C. A database contains information about employees. The properties and characteristics pertinent to all employees are linked per PG and CG with the entity type employee. In addition, employees are categorized by

(1) jobtype—engineer, secretary, technician, etc.;
(2) employment status—permanent and temporary.

Distinct sets of properties and characteristics are recorded for all these different specializations. The generalization graph UGI shows the engineer, secretary, technician, etc., entity types being subordinate to the employee entity type per jobtype, and the permanent and temporary entity types subordinate to the employee entity type per status.

Obtain a ternary relation R such that (E-domain:x, RN-domain:y, PER-domain:z) belongs to R iff x is the surrogate of an employee, y is the entity type of x per category z. In effect, we are converting category information into a new attribute of a relation at the parent level.

$$R_1 \leftarrow \text{UGI}[\text{SUP} = \text{emp}]\,[\text{SUB, PER}].$$

Relation R_1 lists the names of all the relations that are immediate subordinates of employee in the generalization graph.

$$R_2 \leftarrow \text{DENOTE}(R_1[\text{SUB}]).$$

R_2 is the corresponding set of relations.

$$R_3 \leftarrow \text{APPLY}(\text{TAG}, R_2).$$

The set R_3 is obtained by taking each relation in R_2 and appending to it a column that contains as many occurrences of the relname for that relation as there are tuples in the relation.

$$R_4 \leftarrow \text{UNION/APPLY}(R_3[\text{RN}*\text{SUB}]R_1).$$

The natural join with relation R_1 is applied to each relation in R_3, using relname attributes. The resulting set of relations is compressed by repeated application of union to yield the desired relation.

Example D. Combine all of the information in the RM/T graph relations into one relation R having attributes SUB, SUP, PER, and RN, where (SUB:m, SUP:n, PER:p, RN:q) belongs to R iff

(1) q is the relname of a labeled graph relation and (SUB:m, SUP:n, PER:p) belongs to q; *or*
(2) q is the relname of an unlabeled graph relation, p is null, and (SUB:m, SUP:n) belongs to q.

Assume the reltype of graph relations is G. Make no assumption about the number of graph relations in RM/T or their names.

$$R_1 \leftarrow \text{DENOTE}(\text{CATR}\,[\text{RELTYPE} = G]\,[\text{RN}]),$$
$$R_2 \leftarrow \text{APPLY}(\text{TAG}, R_2),$$
$$R \leftarrow \textcircled{\cup}/R_2.$$

The outer union is needed in the last statement because not all graph relations in RM/T have the same degree.

16. SUMMARY OF RM/T

Systematic use of entity domains (including avoidance of nonentity associations) enables RM/T to support widely divergent viewpoints on atomic semantics, ranging from the extreme position that the minimal meaningful unit is always a binary relation to other more moderate positions. The four dimensions of molecular semantics supported by RM/T are Cartesian aggregation, generalization, cover aggregation, and event precedence (see Figure 10).

We now summarize the special objects and operators we have introduced in extending the relational model. Table I lists the objects, while Table II lists the algebraic operators. We use "att" and "rel" as abbreviations for "attribute" and "relation," respectively.

Sets of n-ary relations have been introduced as an additional type of object for algebraic manipulation. The conventional set operators applicable to these higher

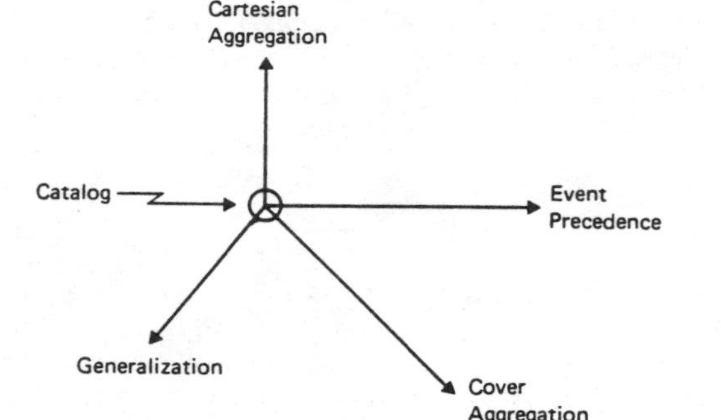

Fig. 10. Four dimensions of RM/T

Chapter 7

Extendibility

7.1 Introduction

The current wisdom is that relational systems work well for business data-processing applications. If you stray from data that looks like the SUPPLIER-PARTS-SUPPLY example popularized by Codd or the EMP-DEPT example also in widespread use, relational systems tend to run into trouble very quickly. My favorite example concerns a user of a commercial DBMS who wished to store information on financial bonds in a database. His application entailed computing the amount of interest paid on a bond, and he stored the date the bond was purchased along with the date the bond was sold. The DBMS which he was using supported DATE as a data type and allowed two dates to be subtracted to obtain their difference, or the number of days any user owned a bond. Presumably one could multiple this number by the interest rate paid by the bond to get the amount of money due to the bond holder.

Unfortunately this approach failed. It turns out that a bond holder receives the same amount of interest on a financial bond during each month regardless how long the month is. In other words, the bond calendar has 12 months, each of 30 days duration. Hence if the user subtracted February 15 from March 15, he expected to get 30 days as an answer. Of course the DBMS computed the difference as 28 days (at least in 1987). Because the user had different semantics for time than the DBMS, he was forced to retrieve both dates into an application program, compute the correct subtraction and then put the result back in the database. To a first approximation this required two query language commands, where one would have sufficed if the correct definition of subtraction on dates had been available. This omission cost the user about 50 percent in performance.

In nonbusiness application areas these problems abound. In CAD applications one wants to put two- and three-dimensional objects in a DBMS. Mail and hypertext are obvious DBMS candidate applications that require putting documents in a database. Next-generation CASE tools will obviously put specifications for computer programs in databases. The oil companies all want to put vectors of observations from seismic experiments into databases. Even the system catalogs of current relational systems contain new types of objects. For example, application development systems want to put the definitions of forms, reports, and graphs in a database. In all these areas, current relational systems tend to work poorly, in that user queries are cumbersome to express and execute with unreasonably bad performance.

One solution proposed is to allow a DBMS to be customized with user-written routines that supports the needed function. This function can be in the area of:

1. Additional data types (e.g., complex numbers)
2. Additional operators on data items (e.g., complex addition)
3. Additional aggregate operators (e.g., third largest)
4. Additional operators on relations (e.g., transitive closure)
5. Additional access methods (e.g., extendible hashing)
6. Modifications to the data model supported

In general, areas 1 - 3 require that the query optimizer and run-time system be converted to being table driven off a data structure containing the known types and operators. Area 4 requires the ability to insert complex new algorithms into the optimizer and run-time system. Area 5 requires very careful separation of transaction management from the access method code and then making this level a replaceable module. Lastly, area 6 requires the optimizer have absolutely no built-in knowledge of the data model.

In this section I have chosen two papers that represent attempts to do extensions in various of these areas. The first paper (7.2) concentrates on supporting extensions in areas 1, 2, 3, and 5. It does not attempt to deal with areas 4 and 6. On the other hand, the second paper, on EXODUS (7.3), is more ambitious and discusses the problems in the other two areas.

Extendibility is one of the few ideas that virtually everyone agrees are good ones. Hence many of the new prototypes under construction are doing something in this area, including Starburst [LIND87], Orion [BANE87], IRIS [FISH87], GENESIS [BATO86], and Probe [DAYA85]. The interested reader should consult these other systems for additional approaches to extendibility.

Other papers worth reading include [GRAE87], which contains a more complete design for an extendible optimizers, [LORI83], which discusses an early System R extension, and [OSBO86], which contains an abstract data type proposal similar to the one in POSTGRES. Lastly, the reader should consult a special issue on extendible systems in the bulletin of the IEEE Technical Committee on Data Engineering [CARE87].

A last comment concerns the relationship between so-called object-oriented data models (OODBs) and extendible systems. Most OODBs allow a user to create new classes of objects, write new methods for these classes, and then apply the method to an instance of an object class by "sending a message" to it. As near as I can deduce, the following translation table applies:

OODB Word	**Corresponding Conventional Word**
Class	Type
Object	Instance of a type
Method	Function
Message	Function call

Hence OODBs suggest supporting new types and new functions on these types. Consequently, the literature in this area could be interpreted as attempting extensions in areas 1 and 2.

It is inappropriate to criticize so obviously a good idea. Moreover, I expect to find the idea will gravitate quickly into commercial products. The only unknown element is how much skill will be required by the person implementing the extensions. It is clear that system houses will have the required sophistication; however, extensions may prove daunting for less-skilled persons.

References

[BANE87] Banerjee, J. et al., "Semantics and Implementation of Schema Evolution in Object-oriented Databases," Proc. 1987 ACM-SIGMOD Conference on Management of Data, San Francisco, Calif., May 1987.

[BATO86] Batory, D.S. et al, "GENESIS: A Reconfigurable Database Management System," University of Texas at Austin, Technical Report TR-B6-07, Austin, Tex., March 1986.

[CARE87] Carey, M. (ed.), "Special Issue on Extensible Database Systems," Database Engineering, June 1987.

[DAYA85] Dayal, U. et al., "PROBE—A Research Project in Knowledge-oriented Database Systems," Technical Report CCA-85-03, Computer Corporation of America, Cambridge, Mass., 1985.

[FISH87] Fishman, D. et al., "IRIS: An Object-oriented Database Management System," ACM-TOOIS, Jan. 1987.

[GRAE87] Graefe, G. and Dewitt, D., "The EXODUS Optimizer Generator," Proc. 1987 ACM-SIGMOD Conference on Management of Data, San Francisco, Calif., May 1987.

[LIND87] Lindsay, B., "A Data Management Extension Architecture," Proc. 1987 ACM-SIGMOD Conference on Management of Data, San Francisco, Calif., May 1987.

[LORI83] Lorie, R., and Plouffe, W., "Complex Objects and their Use in Design Transactions," Proc. Databases for Engineering Applications, Database Week 1983, May 1983.

[OSBO86] Osborne, S., and Heaven, T., "The Design of a Relational Database System with Abstract Data Types for Domains," ACM-TODS, Sept. 1986.

INCLUSION OF NEW TYPES IN RELATIONAL DATA BASE SYSTEMS

Michael Stonebraker
EECS Dept.
University of California, Berkeley

Abstract

This paper explores a mechanism to support user-defined data types for columns in a relational data base system. Previous work suggested how to support new operators and new data types. The contribution of this work is to suggest ways to allow query optimization on commands which include new data types and operators and ways to allow access methods to be used for new data types.

1. INTRODUCTION

The collection of built-in data types in a data base system (e.g. integer, floating point number, character string) and built-in operators (e.g. +, -, *, /) were motivated by the needs of business data processing applications. However, in many engineering applications this collection of types is not appropriate. For example, in a geographic application a user typically wants points, lines, line groups and polygons as basic data types and operators which include intersection, distance and containment. In scientific application, one requires complex numbers and time series with appropriate operators. In such applications one is currently required to simulate these data types and operators using the basic data types and operators provided by the DBMS at substantial inefficiency and complexity. Even in business applications, one sometimes needs user-defined data types. For example, one system [RTI84] has implemented a sophisticated date and time data type to add to its basic collection. This implementation allows subtraction of dates, and returns "correct" answers, e.g.

"April 15" - "March 15" = 31 days

This definition of subtraction is appropriate for most users; however, some applications require all months to have 30 days (e.g. programs which compute interest on bonds). Hence, they require a definition of subtraction which yields 30 days as the answer to the above computation. Only a user-defined data type facility allows such customization to occur.

Current data base systems implement hashing and B-trees as fast access paths for built-in data types. Some user-defined data types (e.g. date and time) can use existing access methods (if certain extensions are made); however other data types (e.g. polygons) require new access methods. For example R-trees [GUTM84], KDB trees [ROBI81] and Grid files are appropriate for spatial objects. In addition, the introduction of new access methods for conventional business applications (e.g. extendible hashing [FAGI79, LITW80]) would be expeditied by a facility to add new access methods.

This research was sponsored by the U.S. Air Force Office of Scientific Research Grant 83-0254 and the Naval Electronics Systems Command Contract N39-82-C-0235

A complete extended type system should allow:

1) the definition of user-defined data types
2) the definition of new operators for these data types
3) the implementation of new access methods for data types
4) optimized query processing for commands containing new data types and operators

The solution to requirements 1 and 2 was described in [STON83]; in this paper we present a complete proposal. In Section 2 we begin by presenting a motivating example of the need for new data types, and then briefly review our earlier proposal and comment on its implementation. Section 3 turns to the definition of new access methods and suggests mechanisms to allow the designer of a new data type to use access methods written for another data type and to implement his own access methods with as little work as possible. Then Section 4 concludes by showing how query optimization can be automatically performed in this extended environment.

2. ABSTRACT DATA TYPES

2.1. A Motivating Example

Consider a relation consisting of data on two dimensional boxes. If each box has an identifier, then it can be represented by the coordinates of two corner points as follows:

create box (id = i4, x1 = f8, x2 = f8, y1 = f8, y2 = f8)

Now consider a simple query to find all the boxes that overlap the unit square, ie. the box with coordinates (0, 1, 0, 1). The following is a compact representation of this request in QUEL:

```
retrieve (box.all) where not
  (box.x2 <= 0 or box.x1 >= 1
  or box.y2 <= 0 or box.y1 >= 1)
```

The problems with this representation are:

The command is too hard to understand.

The command is too slow because the query planner will not be able to optimize something this complex.

The command is too slow because there are too many clauses to check.

The solution to these difficulties is to support a box data type whereby the box relation can be defined as:

create box (id = i4, desc = box)

and the resulting user query is:

retrieve (box.all) where box.desc !! "0, 1, 0, 1"

Here "!!" is an overlaps operator with two operands of data type box which returns a boolean. One would want a substantial collection of operators for user defined types. For example, Table 1 lists a collection of useful operators for the box data type.

Fast access paths must be supported for queries with qualifications utilizing new data types and operators. Consequently, current access methods must be extended to operate in this environment. For example, a reasonable collating sequence for boxes would be on ascending area, and a B-tree storage structure could be built for boxes using this sequence. Hence, queries such as

```
retrieve (box.all) where box.desc AE "0,5,0,5"
```

Binary operator	symbol	left operand	right operand	result
overlaps	!!	box	box	boolean
contained in	<<	box	box	boolean
is to the left of	<L	box	box	boolean
is to the right of	>R	box	box	boolean
intersection	??	box	box	box
distance	"	box	box	float
area less than	AL	box	box	boolean
area equals	AE	box	box	boolean
area greater	AG	box	box	boolean

Unary operator	symbol	operand	result
area	AA	box	float
length	LL	box	float
height	HH	box	float
diagonal	DD	box	line

Operators for Boxes

Table 1

should use this index. Moreover, if a user wishes to optimize access for the !! operator, then an R-tree [GUTM84] may be a reasonable access path. Hence, it should be possible to add a user defined access method. Lastly, a user may submit a query to find all pairs of boxes which overlap, e.g:

```
range of b1 is box
range of b2 is box
retrieve (b1.all, b2.all) where b1.desc !! b2.desc
```

A query optimizer must be able to construct an access plan for solving queries which contains user defined operators.

We turn now to a review of the prototype presented in [STON83] which supports some of the above function.

2.2. DEFINITION OF NEW TYPES

To define a new type, a user must follow a registration process which indicates the existence of the new type, gives the length of its internal representation and provides input and output conversion routines, e.g:

```
define type-name length = value,
                 input  = file-name
                 output = file-name
```

The new data type must occupy a fixed amount of space, since only fixed length data is allowed by the built-in access methods in INGRES. Moreover, whenever new values are input from a program or output to a user, a conversion routine must be called. This routine must convert from character string to the new type and back. A data base system calls such routines for built-in data types (e.g. ascii-to-int, int-to-ascii) and they must be provided for user-defined data types. The input conversion routine must accept a pointer to a value of type character string and return a pointer to a value of the new data type. The output routine must perform the converse transformation.

Then, zero or more operators can be implemented for the new type. Each can be defined with the following syntax:

```
define operator token = value,
                left-operand = type-name,
                right-operand = type-name,
                result = type-name,
                precedence-level like operator-2,
                file = file-name
```

For example:

```
define operator token = !!,
                left-operand = box,
                right-operand = box,
                result = boolean,
                precedence like *,
                file = /usr/foobar
```

All fields are self explanatory except the precedence level which is required when several user defined operators are present and precedence must be established among them. The file /usr/foobar indicates the location of a procedure which can accept two operands of type box and return true if they overlap. This procedure is written in a general purpose programming language and is linked into the run-time system and called as appropriate during query processing.

2.3. Comments on the Prototype

The above constructs have been implemented in the University of California version of INGRES [STON76]. Modest changes were required to the parser and a dynamic loader was built to load the required user-defined routines on demand into the INGRES address space. The system was described in [ONG84].

Our initial experience with the system is that dynamic linking is not preferable to static linking. One problem is that initial loading of routines is slow. Also, the ADT routines must be loaded into data space to preserve sharability of the DBMS code segment. This capability requires the construction of a non-trivial loader. An "industrial strength" implementation might choose to specify the user types which an installation wants at the time the DBMS is installed. In this case, all routines could be linked into the run time system at system installation time by the linker provided by the operating system. Of course, a data base system implemented as a single server process with internal multitasking would not be subject to any code sharing difficulties, and a dynamic loading solution might be reconsidered.

An added difficulty with ADT routines is that they provide a serious safety loophole. For example, if an ADT routine has an error, it can easily crash the DBMS by overwriting DBMS data structures accidentally. More seriously, a malicious ADT routine can overwrite the entire data base with zeros. In addition, it is unclear whether such errors are due to bugs in the user routines or in the DBMS, and finger-pointing between the DBMS implementor and the ADT implementor is likely to result.

ADT routines can be run in a separate address space to solve both problems, but the performance penalty is severe. Every procedure call to an ADT operator must be turned into a round trip message to a separate address space. Alternately, the DBMS can interpret the ADT procedure and guarantee safety, but only by building a language processor into the run-time system and paying the performance penalty of interpretation. Lastly, hardware support for protected procedure calls (e.g. as in Multics) would also solve the problem.

However, on current hardware the prefered solution may be to provide two environments for ADT procedures. A protected environment would be provided for debugging purposes. When a user was confident that his routines worked correctly, he could install them in the unprotected DBMS. In this way, the DBMS implementor could refuse to be concerned unless a bug could be produced in the safe version.

We now turn to extending this environment to support new access methods.

3. NEW ACCESS METHODS

A DBMS should provide a wide variety of access methods, and it should be easy to add new ones. Hence, our goal in this section is to describe how users can add new access methods that will efficiently support user-defined data types. In the first subsection we indicate a registration process that allows implementors of new data types to use access methods written by others. Then, we turn to designing lower level DBMS interfaces so the access method designer has minimal work to perform. In this section we restrict our attention to access methods for a single key field. Support for composite keys is a straight forward extension. However, multidimensional access methods that allow efficient retrieval utilizing subsets of the collection of keys are beyond the scope of this paper.

3.1. Registration of a New Access Method

The basic idea which we exploit is that a properly implemented access method contains only a small number of procedures that define the characteristics of the access method. Such procedures can be replaced by others which operate on a different data type and allow the access method to "work" for the new type. For example, consider a B-tree and the following generic query:

retrieve (target-list) where relation.key OPR value

A B-tree supports fast access if OPR is one of the set:

{=, <, <=, >=, >}

and includes appropriate procedure calls to support these operators for a data type (s). For example, to search for the record matching a specific key value, one need only descend the B-tree at each level searching for the minimum key whose value exceeds or equals the indicated key. Only calls on the operator "<=" are required with a final call or calls to the

TEMPLATE-1	AM-name	condition
	B-tree	P1
	B-tree	P2
	B-tree	P3
	B-tree	P4
	B-tree	P5
	B-tree	P6
	B-tree	P7

TEMPLATE-2	AM-name	opr-name	opt	left	right	result
	B-tree	=	opt	fixed	type1	boolean
	B-tree	<	opt	fixed	type1	boolean
	B-tree	<=	req	fixed	type1	boolean
	B-tree	>	opt	fixed	type1	boolean
	B-tree	>=	opt	fixed	type1	boolean

Templates for Access Methods

Table 2

AM	class	AM-name	opr	generic name	opr-id opr	Ntups	Npages
	int-ops	B-tree	=	=	id1	N / Ituples	2
	int-ops	B-tree	<	<	id2	F1 * N	F1 * NUMpages
	int-ops	B-tree	<=	<=	id3	F1 * N	F1 * NUMpages
	int-ops	B-tree	>	>	id4	F2 * N	F2 * NUMpages
	int-ops	B-tree	>=	>=	id5	F2 * N	F2 * NUMpages
	area-op	B-tree	AE	=	id6	N / Ituples	3
	area-op	B-tree	AL	<	id7	F1 * N	F1 * NUMpages
	area-op	B-tree	AG	>	id8	F1 * N	F1 * NUMpages

The AM Relation

Table 3

routine supporting "=".

Moreover, this collection of operators has the following properties:

P1) key-1 < key-2 and key-2 < key-3 then key-1 < key-3
P2) key-1 < key-2 implies not key-2 < key-1
P3) key-1 < key-2 or key-2 < key-1 or key-1 = key-2
P4) key-1 <= key-2 if key-1 < key-2 or key-1 = key-2
P5) key-1 = key-2 implies key-2 = key-1
P6) key-1 > key-2 if key-2 < key-1
P7) key-1 >= key-2 if key-2 <= key-1

In theory, the procedures which implement these operators can be replaced by any collection of procedures for new operators that have these properties and the B-tree will "work" correctly. Lastly, the designer of a B-tree access method may disallow variable length keys. For example, if a binary search of index pages is performed, then only fixed length keys are possible. Information of this restriction must be available to a type designer who wishes to use the access method.

The above information must be recorded in a data structure called an access method **template**. We propose to store templates in two relations called TEMPLATE-1 and TEMPLATE-2 which would have the composition indicated in Table 2 for a B-tree access method. TEMPLATE-1 simply documents the conditions which must be true for the operators provided by the access method. It is included only to provide guidance to a human wishing to utilize the access method for a new data type and is not used internally in the system. TEMPLATE-2, on the other hand, provides necessary information on the data types of operators. The column "opt" indicates whether the operator is required or optional. A B-tree must have the operator "<=" to build the tree; however, the other operators are optional. Type1, type2 and result are possible types for the left operand, the right operand, and the result of a given operator. Values for these fields should come from the following collection;

a specific type, e.g. int, float, boolean, char
fixed, i.e. any type with fixed length
variable, i.e. any type with a
 prescribed varying length format
fix-var, i.e. fixed or variable
type1, i.e. the same type as type1
type2, i.e. the same as type2

After indicating the template for an access method, the designer can propose one or more collections of operators which satisfy the template in another relation, AM. In Table 3 we have shown an AM containing the original set of integer operators provided by the access method designer along with a collection added later by the designer of the box data type. Since operator names do not need to be unique, the field opr-id must be included to specify a unique identifier for a given operator. This field is present in a relation which contains the operator specific information discussed in Section 2. The fields, Ntups and Npages are query processing parameters which estimate the number of tuples which satisfy the qualification and the number of pages touched when running a query using the operator to compare a key field in a relation to a constant. Both are formulas which utilize the variables found in Table 4, and values reflect approximations to the computations found in [SELI79] for the case that each record set occupies an individual file. Moreover, F1 and F2 are surogates for the following quantities:

F1 = (value - low-key) / (high-key - low-key)
F2 = (high-key - value) / (high-key - low-key)

With these data structures in place, a user can simply modify relations to B-tree using any class of operators defined in the AM relation. The only addition to the modify command

Variable	Meaning
N	number of tuples in a relation
NUMpages	number of pages of storage used by the relation
Ituples	number of index keys in an index
Ipages	number of pages in the index
value	the constant appearing in: rel-name.field-name OPR value
high-key	the maximum value in the key range if known
low-key	the minimum value in the key range if known

Variables for Computing Ntups and Npages

Table 4

is a clause "using class" which specifies what operator class to use in building and accessing the relation. For example the command

modify box to B-tree on desc using area-op

will allow the DBMS to provide optimized access on data of type box using the operators {AE,AL,AG}. The same extension must be provided to the index command which constructs a secondary index on a field, e.g:

index on box is box-index (desc) using area-op

To illustrate the generality of these constructs, the AM and TEMPLATE relations are shown in Tables 5 and 6 for both a hash and an R-tree access method. The R-tree is assumed to support three operators, contained-in (<<), equals (==) and contained-in-or-equals (<<=). Moreover, a fourth operator (UU) is required during page splits and finds the box which is the union of two other boxes. UU is needed solely for maintaining the R-tree data structure, and is not useful for search purposes. Similarly, a hash access method requires a hash function, H, which accepts a key as a left operand and an integer number of buckets as a right operand to produce a hash bucket as a result. Again, H cannot be used for searching purposes. For compactness, formulas for Ntups and Npages have been omitted from Table 6.

3.2. Implementing New Access Methods

In general an access method is simply a collection of procedure calls that retrieve and update records. A generic abstraction for an access method could be the following:

open (relation-name)

This procedure returns a pointer to a structure containing all relevant information about a relation. Such a "relation control block" will be called a descriptor. The effect is to make the relation accessible.

close (descriptor)

This procedure terminates access to the relation indicated by the descriptor.

get-first (descriptor, OPR, value)

This procedure returns the first record which satisfies the qualification

..where key OPR value

get-next (descriptor, OPR, value, tuple-id)

TEMPLATE-1	AM-name	condition
	hash	Key-1 = Key-2 implies H(key1) = H(key-2)
	R-tree	Key-1 << Key-2 and Key-2 << Key-2 implies Key-1 << key-3
	R-tree	Key-1 << Key-2 implies not Key-2 << Key-1
	R-tree	Key-1 <<= Key-2 implies Key-1 << Key-2 or Key-1 == Key-2
	R-tree	Key-1 == Key-2 implies Key-2 == Key-1
	R-tree	Key-1 << Key-1 UU Key-2
	R-tree	Key-2 << Key-1 UU Key-2

TEMPLATE-2	AM-name	opr-name	opt	left	right	result
	hash	=	opt	fixed	type1	boolean
	hash	H	req	fixed	int	int
	R-tree	<<	req	fixed	type1	boolean
	R-tree	==	opt	fixed	type1	boolean
	R-tree	<<=	opt	fixed	type1	boolean
	R-tree	UU	req	fixed	type1	boolean

Templates for Access Methods

Table 5

AM	class	AM-name	opr name	generic opr	opr-id	Ntups	Npages
	box-ops	R-tree	==	==	id10		
	box-ops	R-tree	<<	<<	id11		
	box-ops	R-tree	<<=	<<=	id12		
	box-ops	R-tree	UU	UU	id13		
	hash-op	hash	=	=	id14		
	hash-op	hash	H	H	id15		

The AM Relation

Table 6

This procedure gets the next tuple following the one indicated by tuple-id which satisfies the qualification.

get-unique (descriptor, tuple-id)

This procedure gets the tuple which corresponds to the indicated tuple identifier.

insert (descriptor, tuple)

This procedure inserts a tuple into the indicated relation

delete (descriptor, tuple-id)

This procedure deletes a tuple from the indicated relation.

replace (descriptor, tuple-id, new-tuple)

This procedure replaces the indicated tuple by a new one.

build (descriptor, keyname, OPR)

Of course it is possible to build a new access method for a relation by successively inserting tuples using the insert procedure. However, higher performance can usually be obtained by a bulk loading utility. Build is this utility and accepts a descriptor for a relation along with a key and operator to use in the build process.

There are many different (more or less similar) access method interfaces; see [ASTR76, ALLC80] for other proposals. Each DBMS implementation will choose their own collection of procedures and calling conventions.

If this interface is publicly available, then it is feasible to implement these procedures using a different organizing principle. A clean design of open and close should make these routines universally usable, so an implementor need only construct the remainder. Moreover, if the designer of a new access method chooses to utilize the same physical page layout as some existing access method, then replace and delete do not require modification, and additional effort is spared.

The hard problem is to have a new access method interface correctly to the transaction management code. (One commercial system found this function to present the most difficulties when a new access method was coded.) If a DBMS (or the underlying operating system) supports transactions by physically logging pages and executing one of the popular concurrency control algorithms for page size granules, (e.g. [BROW81, POPE81, SPEC83, STON85] then the designer of a new access method need not concern himself with transaction management. Higher level software will begin and end transactions, and the access method can freely read and write pages with a guarantee of atomicity and serializability. In this case the access method designer has no problems concerning transactions, and this is a significant advantage for transparent transactions. Unfortunately, much higher performance will typically result if a different approach is taken to both crash recovery and concurrency control. We now sketch roughly what this alternate interface might be.

With regard to crash recovery, most current systems have a variety of special case code to perform logical logging of events rather than physical logging of the changes of bits. There are at least two reasons for this method of logging. First, changes to the schema (e.g. create a relation) often require additional work besides changes to the system catalogs (e.g. creating an operating system file in which to put tuples of the relation). Undoing a create command because a transaction is aborted will require deletion of the newly created file. Physical backout cannot accomplish such extra function. Second, some data base updates are extremely inefficient when physically logged. For example, if a relation is modified from B-tree to hash, then the entire relation will be written to the log (perhaps more than once depending on the implementation of the modify utility). This costly extra I/O can be avoided by simply logging the command that is being performed. In the unlikely event that this event in the log must be undone or redone, then the modify utility can be rerun to make the changes anew. Of course, this sacrifices performance at recovery time for a compression of the log by several orders of magnitude.

If such logical logging is performed, then a new access method must become involved in logging process and a clean event-oriented interface to logging services should be provided. Hence, the log should be a collection of **events**, each having an event-id, an associated **event type** and an arbitrary collection of data. Lastly, for each event type, T, two procedures, REDO(T) and UNDO(T) are required which will be called when the log manager is rolling forward redoing log events and rolling backward undoing logged events respectively. The system must also provide a procedure,

LOG (event-type, event-data)

which will actually insert events into the log. Moreover, the system will provide a collection of **built-in event types**. For each such event, UNDO and REDO are available in system libraries. Built-in events would include:

replace a tuple
insert a tuple at a specific tuple identifier address
delete a tuple
change the storage structure of a relation
create a relation
destroy a relation

A designer of a new access method could use the built-in events if they were appropriate to his needs. Alternately, he could specify new event types by writing UNDO and REDO procedures for the events and making entries in a system relation holding event information. Such an interface is similar to the one provided by CICS [IBM80].

We turn now to discussing the concurrency control subsystem. If this service is provided transparently and automatically by an underlying module, then special case concurrency control for the system catalogs and index records will be impossible. This approach will severely impact performance as noted in [STON85]. Alternately, one can follow the standard scheduler model [BERN81] in which a module is callable by code in the access methods when a concurrency control decision must be made. The necessary calls are:

read (object-identifier)
write (object-identifier)
begin
abort
commit
savepoint

and the scheduler responds with yes, no or abort. The calls to begin, abort, commit and savepoint are made by higher level software, and the access methods need not be concerned with them. The access method need only make the appropriate calls on the scheduler when it reads or writes an object. The only burden which falls on the implementor is to choose the appropriate size for objects.

The above interface is appropriate for data records which are handled by a conventional algorithm guaranteeing serializability. To provide special case parallelism on index or system catalog records, an access method requires more control over concurrency decisions. For example, most B-tree implementations do not hold write locks on index pages which are split until the end of the transaction which performed the insert. It appears easiest to provide specific lock and unlock calls for such special situations, i.e:

lock (object, mode)
unlock (object)

These can be used by the access method designer to implement special case parallelism in his data structures.

The last interface of concern to the designer of an access method is the one to the buffer manager. One requires five procedures:

get (system-page-identifier)
fix (system-page-identifier)
unfix (system-page-identifier)
put (system-page-identifier)
order (system-page-identifier,
  event-id or system-page-identifier)

The first procedure accepts a page identifier and returns a pointer to the page in the buffer pool. The second and third procedures pin and unpin pages in the buffer pool. The last call specifies that the page holding the given event should be written to disk prior to the indicated data page. This information is necessary in write-ahead log protocols. More generally, it allows two data pages to be forced out of memory in a specific order.

An access method implementor must code the necessary access method procedures utilizing the above interfaces to the log manager, the concurrency control manager and the buffer manager. Then, he simply registers his access method in the two TEMPLATE relations.

3.3. Discussion

A transparent interface to the transaction system is clearly much preferred to the complex collection of routines discussed above. Moreover, the access method designer who utilizes these routines must design his own events, specify any special purpose concurrency control in his data structures, and indicate any necessary order in forcing pages out of the buffer pool. An open research question is the design of a simpler interface to these services that will provide the required functions.

In addition, the performance of the crash recovery facility will be inferior to the recovery facilities in a conventional system. In current transaction managers, changes to indexes are typically not logged. Rather, index changes are recreated from the corresponding update to the data record. Hence, if there are n indexes for a given object, a single log entry for the data update will result in n+1 events (the data update and n index updates) being undone or redone in a conventional system. Using our proposed interface all n+1 events will appear in the log, and efficiency will be sacrificed.

The access method designer has the least work to perform if he uses the same page layout as one of the built-in access methods. Such an access method requires get-first, get-next, and insert to be coded specially. Moreover, no extra event types are required, since the built-in ones provide all the required functions. R-trees are an example of such an access method. On the other hand, access methods which do not use the same page layout will require the designer to write considerably more code.

4. QUERY PROCESSING AND ACCESS PATH SELECTION

To allow optimization of a query plan that contains new operators and types, only four additional pieces of information are required when defining an operator. First, a selectivity factor, Stups, is required which estimates the expected number of records satisfying the clause:

...where rel-name.field-name OPR value

A second selectivity factor, S, is the expected number of records which satisfy the clause

...where relname-1.field-1 OPR relname-2.field-2

Stups and S are arithmetic formulas containing the predefined variables indicated earlier in Table 4. Moreover, each variable can have a suffix of 1 or 2 to specify the left or right operand respectively.

Notice that the same selectivity appears both in the definition of an operator (Stups) and in the entry (Ntups) in AM if the operator is used in an index. In this case, Ntups from AM should be used first, and supports an if-then-else specification used for example in the [SELI79] for the operator "=" as follows:

selectivity = (1 / Ituples) ELSE 1/10

In this example selectivity is the reciprocal of the number of index tuples if an index exists else it is 1/10. The entry for Ntups in AM would be (N / Ituples) while Stups in the operator definition would be N / 10.

The third piece of necessary information is whether merge-sort is feasible for the operator being defined. More exactly, the existence of a second operator, OPR-2 is required such that OPR and OPR-2 have properties P1-P3 from Section 3 with OPR replacing "=" and OPR-2 replacing "<". If so, the relations to be joined using OPR can be sorted using OPR-2 and then merged to produce the required answer.

The last piece of needed information is whether hash-join is a feasible joining strategy for this operator. More exactly, the hash condition from Table 6 must be true with OPR replacing "=".

An example of these pieces of information for the operator, AE, would be:

```
define operator token = AE,
                left-operand = box,
                right-operand = box,
                result = boolean,
                precedence like *,
                file = /usr/foobar,
                Stups = 1,
                S = min (N1, N2),
                merge-sort with AL,
                hash-join
```

We now turn to generating the query processing plan. We assume that relations are stored keyed on one field in a single file and that secondary indexes can exist for other fields. Moreover, queries involving a single relation can be processed with a scan of the relation, a scan of a portion of the primary index, or a scan of a portion of one secondary index. Joins can be processed by iterative substitution, merge-sort or a hash-join algorithm. Modification to the following rules for different environments appears straigth-forward.

Legal query processing plans are described by the following statements.

1) Merge sort is feasible for a clause of the form:

relname-1.field-1 OPR relname-2.field-2

if field-1 and field-2 are of the same data type and OPR has the merge-sort property. Moreover, the expected size of the result is S. The cost to sort one or both relations is a built-in computation.

2) Iterative substitution is always feasible to perform the join specified by a clause of the form:

relname-1.field-1 OPR relname-2.field-2

The expected size of the result is calculated as above. The cost of this operation is the cardinality of the outer relation multiplied by the expected cost of the one-variable query on the inner relation.

3) A hash join algorithm can be used to perform a join specified by:

relname-1.field-1 OPR relname-2.field-2

if OPR has the hash-join property. The expected size of the result is as above, and the cost to hash one or both relations is another built-in computation.

4) An access method, A for relname can be used to restrict a clause of the form

relname.field-name OPR value

only if relname uses field-name as a key and OPR appears in the class used in the modify command to organize relname. The expected number of page and tuple accesses are given by the appropriate row in AM.

5) A secondary index, I for relname can be used to restrict a clause of the form:

relname.field-name OPR value

only if the index uses field-name as a key and OPR appears in the class used to build the index. The expected number of index page and tuple accesses is given by the appropriate row in AM. To these must be added 1 data page and 1 data tuple per index tuple.

6) A sequential search can always be used to restrict a relation on a clause of the form:

relname.field-name OPR value

One must read NUMpages to access the relation and the expected size of the result is given by Stups from the definition of OPR.

A query planner, such as the one discussed in [SELI79] can now be easily modified to compute a best plan using the above rules to generate legal plans and the above selectivities rather than the current hard-wired collection of rules and selectivities. Moreover, a more sophisticated optimizer which uses statistics (e.g. [KOOI82, PIAT84] can be easily built that uses the above information.

5. CONCLUSIONS

This paper has described how an abstract data type facility can be extended to support automatic generation of optimized query processing plans, utilization of existing access methods for new data types, and coding of new access methods. Only the last capability will be difficult to use, and a cleaner high performance interface to the transaction manager would be highly desirable. Moreover, additional rules in the query optimizer would probably be a useful direction for evolution. These could include when to cease investigating alternate plans, and the ability to specify one's own optimizer parameters, e.g. the constant W relating the cost of I/O to the cost of CPU activity in [SELI79].

REFERENCES

[ALLC80] Allchin, J. et. al., "FLASH: A Language Independent Portable File Access Method," Proc. 1980 ACM-SIGMOD Conference on Management of Data, Santa Monica, Ca., May 1980.

[ASTR76] Astrahan, M. et. al., "System R: A Relational Approach to Data," ACM-TODS, June 1976.

[BERN81] Bernstein, P. and Goodman, N., "Concurrency Control in Distributed Database Systems," ACM Computing Surveys, June 1981.

[BROW81] Brown, M. et. al., "The Cedar DBMS: A Preliminary Report," Proc. 1981 ACM-SIGMOD Conference on Management of Data, Ann Arbor, Mich., May 1981.

[FAGI79] Fagin, R. et. al., "Extendible Hashing: A Fast Access Method for Dynamic Files," ACM-TODS, Sept. 1979.

[GUTM84] Gutman, A., "R-trees: A Dynamic Index Structure for Spatial Searching," Proc. 1984 ACM-SIGMOD Conference on Management of Data, Boston, Mass. June 1984.

[IBM80] IBM Corp, "CICS System Programmers Guide," IBM Corp., White Plains, N.Y., June 1980.

[KOOI82] Kooi, R. and Frankfurth, D., "Query Optimization in INGRES," IEEE Database Engineering, September 1982.

[LITW80] Litwin, W., "Linear Hashing: A New Tool for File and Table Addressing," Proc. 1980 VLDB Conference, Montreal, Canada, October 1980.

[ONG84] Ong, J. et. al., "Implementation of Data Abstraction in the Relational System, INGRES," ACM SIGMOD Record, March 1984.

[PIAT84] Piatetsky-Shapiro, G. and Connell, C., "Accurate Estimation of the Number of Tuples Satisfying a Condition," Proc. 1984 ACM-SIGMOD Conference on Management of Data, Boston, Mass. June 1984.

[POPE81] Popek, G., et. al., "LOCUS: A Network Transparent, High Reliability Distributed System," Proc. Eighth Symposium on Operating System Principles, Pacific Grove, Ca., Dec. 1981.

[RTI84] Relational Technology, Inc., "INGRES Reference Manual, Version 3.0," November 1984.

[ROBI81] Robinson, J., "The K-D-B Tree: A Search Structure for Large Multidimensional Indexes," Proc. 1981 ACM-SIGMOD Conference on Management of Data, Ann Arbor, Mich., May 1981.

[SELI79] Selinger, P. et. al., "Access Path Selection in a Relational Database Management System," Proc. 1979 ACM-SIGMOD Conference on Management of Data, Boston, Mass., June 1979.

[SPEC83] Spector, A. and Schwartz, P., "Transactions: A Construct for Reliable Distributed Computing," Operating Systems Review, Vol 17, No 2, April 1983.

[STON76] Stonebraker, M. et al., "The Design and Implementation of INGRES," TODS 2, 3, September 1976.

[STON83] Stonebraker, M. et. al., "Application of Abstract Data Types and Abstract Indices to CAD Data," Proc. Engineering Applications Stream of Database Week/83, San Jose, Ca., May 1983.

[STON85] Stonebraker, M. et. al., "Interfacing a Relational Data Base System to an Operating System Transaction Manager," SIGOPS Review, January 1985.

The Architecture of the EXODUS Extensible DBMS

Michael J. Carey David J. DeWitt
Daniel Frank Goetz Graefe
M. Muralikrishna Joel E. Richardson
Eugene J. Shekita

Computer Sciences Department
University of Wisconsin

ABSTRACT

With non-traditional application areas such as engineering design, image/voice data management, scientific/statistical applications, and artificial intelligence systems all clamoring for ways to store and efficiently process larger and larger volumes of data, it is clear that traditional database technology has been pushed to its limits. It also seems clear that no single database system will be capable of simultaneously meeting the functionality and performance requirements of such a diverse set of applications. In this paper we describe the preliminary design of EXODUS, an extensible database system that will facilitate the fast development of high-performance, application-specific database systems. EXODUS provides certain kernel facilities, including a versatile storage manager and a type manager. In addition, it provides an architectural framework for building application-specific database systems, tools to partially automate the generation of such systems, and libraries of software components (e.g., access methods) that are likely to be useful for many application domains.

1. INTRODUCTION

Until recently, research and development efforts in the database management systems area have focused on supporting traditional business applications. The design of database systems capable of supporting non-traditional application areas, including engineering applications for CAD/CAM and VLSI data, scientific and statistical applications, expert database systems, and image/voice applications, has emerged as an important new research direction. These new applications differ from conventional applications such as transaction processing and from each other in a number of important ways. First, each requires a different set of data modeling tools. The types of entities and relationships that must be described for a VLSI circuit design are quite different from those of a banking application. Second, each new application area has a specialized set of operations that must be efficiently supported by the database system. It makes little sense to talk about doing joins between satellite images. Efficient support for the specialized operations of each new application area is likely to require new types of storage structures and access methods as well. For example, R-Trees [Gutt84] are a useful access method for storing and manipulating VLSI data. For managing image data, the database system needs to support large multidimensional arrays as a basic data type; storing images as tuples in a relational database system is generally either impossible or terribly inefficient. Finally, a number of new application areas require support for multiple versions of entities [Daya85, Katz86].

Recently, a number of new database system research projects have been initiated to address the needs of this emerging class of applications: EXODUS[1] at the University of Wisconsin [Care85a, Care86], PROBE at CCA [Daya85], POSTGRES [Ston86b] at Berkeley, GEMSTONE at the Oregon Graduate Center [Cope84, Maie86], and GENESIS [Bato86] at the University of Texas-Austin. Although the goals of these projects are similar, and each uses some of the same mechanisms to provide extensibility, the overall approach of each project is quite different. For example, POSTGRES will be a more "complete" database management system, with a query language (POSTQUEL), a predefined way of supporting complex objects (through the use of POSTQUEL and procedures as a data type), support for "active" databases via triggers and alerters, and inferencing. Extensibility will be provided via new data types, operators, access methods, and a simplified recovery mechanism. A stated goal is to "make as few changes as possible to the relational model". The objective of the PROBE project, on the other hand, is to develop an advanced DBMS with support for complex objects and operations on them, dimensional data (in both space and time dimensions), and a capability for intelligent query processing. Unlike POSTGRES, PROBE will provide a mechanism for directly representing complex objects. Like EXODUS, PROBE will use a rule-based approach to query optimization so that the query optimizer may be extended to handle new database operators, new methods for existing operators, and new data types. An extended version of DAPLEX [Ship81] is to be used as the query language for PROBE. GEMSTONE, with its query language OPAL, is a complete object-oriented database system that encapsulates a variety of ideas from the areas of knowledge representation, object-oriented and non-procedural programming, set-theoretic data models, and temporal data modeling.

In contrast to these efforts, and like GENESIS, EXODUS is being designed as a modular (and modifiable) system rather than as a "complete" database system intended to handle all new application areas. In some sense, EXODUS is a software engineering project — the goal is to provide a collection of kernel DBMS facilities plus software tools to facilitate the semi-automatic generation of high-performance, application-specific DBMSs for new applications. In this paper we describe the overall architecture of EXODUS. Section 2 presents an overview of the components of EXODUS. Section 3 describes the lowest level of the system, the Storage Object Manager, summarizing material from [Care86]. Sec-

[1] EXODUS: A departure, in this case, from the ways of the past. Also an EXtensible Object-oriented Database System.

tion 4 describes the EXODUS Type Manager, which provides a general schema management facility that can be extended with application-specific abstract data types. Section 5 addresses a difficult task in extending a database system: the addition of new access methods. EXODUS simplifies this task by hiding most of the storage, concurrency control, and recovery issues from the access method implementor via a new programming language, E; E is an extension of C that includes support for persistent objects via the Storage Object Manager of EXODUS. Section 6 discusses how application-specific database operations are implemented in EXODUS, and Section 7 describes the rule-based approach to query optimization employed in EXODUS. Section 8 outlines some of the user interface issues that lie ahead, and Section 9 briefly summarizes the paper and discusses our implementation plans.

2. AN OVERVIEW OF THE EXODUS ARCHITECTURE

In this section we describe the architecture of the EXODUS database system. Since one of the principal goals of the EXODUS project is to construct an **extensible** yet high-performance database system, the design reflects a careful balance between what EXODUS provides the *user*[2] and what the *user* must explicitly provide. Unlike POSTGRES and PROBE, EXODUS is not intended to be a complete system with provisions for user-added extensions. Rather, it is intended more as a toolbox that can be easily adapted to satisfy the needs of new application areas. Two basic mechanisms are employed to help achieve this goal: where feasible, we furnish a generic solution that should be applicable to any application-specific database system. As an example, EXODUS supplies at its lowest level a layer of software termed the Storage Object Manager which provides support for concurrent and recoverable operations on arbitrary size storage objects. Our feeling is that this level provides sufficient capabilities such that user-added extensions will most probably be unnecessary. However, due to both generality and efficiency considerations, a single generic solution is not possible for every component of a database system.

In cases where one generic solution is inappropriate, EXODUS instead provides either a **generator** or a **library** to aid the user in generating the appropriate software. As an example, we expect EXODUS to be used for a wide variety of applications, each with a potentially different query language. As a result, it is not possible for EXODUS to furnish a single generic query language, and it is accordingly impossible for a single query optimizer to suffice for all applications. Instead, we provide a generator for producing query optimizers for algebraic languages. The EXODUS query optimizer generator takes as input a collection of rules regarding the operators of the query language, the transformations that can be legally applied to these operators (e.g., pushing selections before joins), and a description of the methods that can be used to execute each operator (including their costs and side effects); as output, it produces an optimizer for the application's query language in the form of C source code.

In a conventional database system environment it is customary to consider the roles of two different classes of individuals: the database administrator and the user. In EXODUS, a third type of individual is required to customize EXODUS into an application-specific database system. While we referred to this individual as a "user" in the preceding paragraphs, he or she is not a user in the normal sense (i.e., an end user, such as a bank teller or a cartographer). Internally, we refer to this "user" of the EXODUS facilities as a "database implementor" or DBI. While the Jim Grays of the world would clearly make outstanding DBIs, our goal is to engineer EXODUS so that only a moderate amount of expertise is required to architect a new system using its tools. Once EXODUS has been customized into an application-specific database system, the DBI's role is completed and the role of the database administrator begins.

We present an overview of the design of EXODUS in the remainder of this section. While EXODUS is a toolkit and not a complete DBMS, we find that it is clearer to describe the system from the viewpoint of an application-specific database system that was constructed using it. In doing so, we hope to make it clear which pieces of the system are provided without modification, which must be produced using one of the EXODUS generators, and which must be directly implemented by the DBI using the E programming language.

2.1. EXODUS System Architecture

Figure 1 presents the structure of an application-specific database management system implemented using EXODUS. The following tools are provided to aid the DBI in the task of generating such a system:

(1) The Storage Object Manager.

(2) The E programming language and its compiler for writing database system software.

(3) A generalized Type Manager for defining and maintaining schema information.

(4) A library of type independent access methods which can be used to associatively access storage objects.

(5) Lock manager and recovery protocol stubs to simplify the task of writing new access methods and other database operators.

(6) A rule-based query optimizer and compiler.

(7) Tools for constructing user front ends.

At the bottom level of the system is the Storage Object Manager. The basic abstraction at this level is the storage object, an untyped, uninterpreted variable-length byte sequence of arbitrary size. The Storage Object Manager provides capabilities for reading, writing, and updating storage objects (or pieces of them) without regard for their size. To further enhance the functionality provided by this level, buffer management, concurrency control, and recovery mechanisms for operations on shared storage objects are also provided. Finally, a versioning mechanism that can be used to implement a variety of application-specific versioning schemes is supported. A more detailed description of the Storage Object Manager and its capabilities is presented in Section 3.

Although not shown in Figure 1, which depicts the runtime structure of an EXODUS-based DBMS, the next major component is the E programming language[3] and compiler. E is the implementation language for all components of the sys-

[2] Our use of the word *user* will be more carefully explained in the following paragraphs.

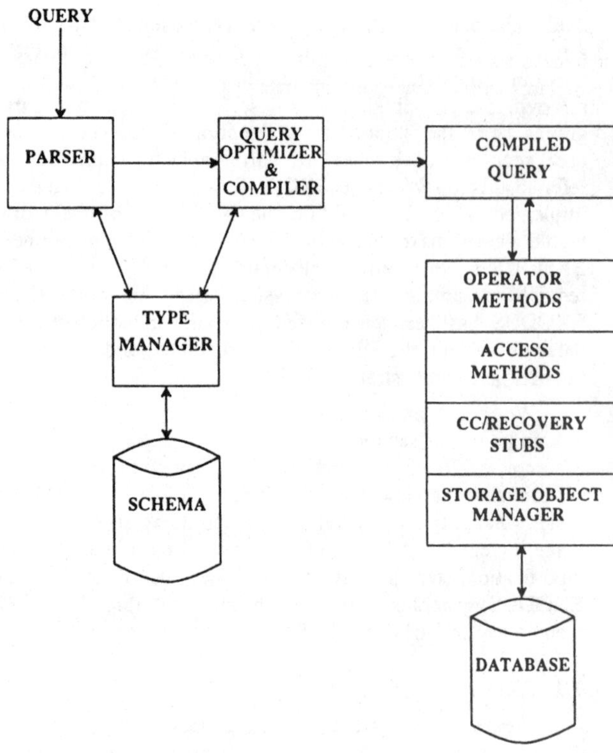

Figure 1: EXODUS System Architecture.

tem for which the DBI must provide code. E extends C by adding the notion of persistent objects to the language's type definition repertoire. References to persistent objects look just like references to other C structures; the DBI's index code can thus deal with arrays of key-pointer pairs, for example. Whenever persistent objects are referenced, the E translator is responsible for adding the appropriate calls to fix/unfix buffers, read/write the appropriate piece of the underlying storage object, lock/unlock objects, log images and events, etc. Thus, the DBI is freed from having to worry about the internal structure of persistent objects. For buffering, concurrency control and recovery, the E language includes statements for associating locking, buffering, and recovery protocols with variables that reference persistent objects. Thus, the DBI is provided with a mechanism by which he or she can exercise control (declaratively) — insuring that the appropriate mechanisms are employed. E should not be confused with either database programming languages such as RIGEL [Rowe79], Pascal/R [Schm77], Theseus [Shop79], or PLAIN [Kers81], as these languages were intended to simplify the development of database applications code through a closer integration of database and programming language constructs, or with object-oriented query languages such as OPAL [Cope84, Maie86] — the objective of E is to simplify the development of **internal** systems software for a DBMS.

Layered above the Storage Object Manager is a collection of access methods that provide associative access to files of storage objects and further support for versioning (if desired). For access methods, EXODUS will provide a library of type-independent index structures including B+ trees, Grid files [Niev84], and linear hashing [Litw80]. These access methods will be implemented using the "type parameter" capability provided by the E language (as described in Section 5). This capability enables existing access methods to be used with DBI-defined abstract data types without modification — as long as the capabilities provided by the data type satisfy the requirements of the access methods. In addition, a DBI may wish to implement new types of access methods in the process of developing an application-specific database system. EXODUS provides two mechanisms to greatly simplify this task. First, since new access methods are written in E, the DBI is shielded from having to map main memory data structures onto storage objects and from having to write code to deal with locking, buffering, and recovery protocols. EXODUS also simplifies the task of handling concurrency control and recovery for new access methods using a form of layered transactions, as discussed in Section 5.

While the capabilities provided by the Storage Object Manager and Access Methods Layer are general purpose and are intended to be utilized in each application-specific DBMS constructed using EXODUS, the third layer in the design, the Operator Methods Layer, contains a mix of DBI-supplied code and EXODUS-supplied code. As implied by its name, this layer contains a collection of methods that can be combined with one another in order to operate on (typed) storage objects. EXODUS will provide a library of methods for a number of operators that operate on a single type of storage object (e.g., selection), but it will not provide application or data model specific methods. For example, it cannot provide methods for implementing the relational join operator or for examining an object containing satellite image data for the signature of a particular crop disease. In general, the DBI will need to implement one or more methods for each operator in the query language associated with the target application. E will again serve as the implementation language for this task.

At the center of the EXODUS architecture is the Type Manager. The EXODUS Type Manager is designed to provide schema support for a wide variety of application-specific database systems. The data modeling facilities provided by the Type Manager are basically those of a generalized class hierarchy with multiple inheritance. Class definitions are based on a collection of base types (e.g., integer, real, character, and object ID) and type constructors (record, array, set, and bag); class instances (called typed objects) are mapped onto storage objects in a one-to-one manner. For example, using the class definition facilities, it is possible to declare a class of typed objects that include fields consisting of very large multidimensional real arrays. The Type Manager also provides facilities that allow the DBI to customize it for a given application by creating new base types and operations on these types using an abstract data type facility. In designing the Type Manager, our feeling was that by providing a sufficiently powerful data modeling tool that exploited the capabilities of the Storage Object Manager, the modeling needs of a very wide range of applications could be handled with no loss of efficiency. Furthermore, given a generalized

[3] The name E was selected because the language is an extension of C and because the name D would have had a number of unpleasant connotations: dumb, deficient, a poor grade, DeWitt, ...

class hierarchy, it seems that one can model most, if not all, existing data models. Section 4 presents a more detailed overview of the capabilities provided by the Type Manager.

Execution of a query in EXODUS follows a set of transformations similar to that of a relational query in System R [Astr76]. After parsing, the query is optimized, and then compiled into an executable form. The parser is responsible for transforming the query from its initial form into an initial tree of database operators. During the parsing and optimization phases, the Type Manager is invoked to extract the necessary schema information. The executable form produced by the query compiler consists of a rearranged tree of operator methods (i.e., particular instances of each operator) to which query specific information such as selection predicates (e.g., name = "Mike" and salary > $200,000) will be passed as parameters. As mentioned earlier, EXODUS provides a generator for producing the optimization portion of the query compiler. To produce an optimizer for an application-specific database system, the DBI must supply a description of the operators of the target query language, a list of the methods that can used to implement each operator, a cost formula for each operator method, and a collection of transformation rules. The optimizer generator will transform these description files into C source code for an optimizer for the target query language. At query execution time, this optimizer behaves as we have just described, taking a query expressed as a tree of operators and transforming it into an optimized execution plan expressed as a tree of methods.

Finally, the organization of the top level of a database system generated using EXODUS will depend on whether the goal is to support some sort of interactive interface, an embedded query interface such as EQUEL [Allm76], or an altogether different form of interface. We plan to provide a generator to facilitate the creation of interactive interfaces, and we are exploring the use of the Cornell Program Synthesizer Generator [Reps84] as a user interface generator for EXODUS[4]. This tool provides the facilities needed for implementing structured editors for a wide variety of programming languages, the goal of such editors being to help programmers formulate syntactically and semantically correct programs. Since the syntax and semantics of typical query languages are much simpler than that of most modern programming languages, it is clear that we will be able to apply the tool in this way; it remains to be seen whether or not it is really "too powerful" (i.e., overkill) for our needs. As for supporting queries that are embedded programs, two options exist. First, if the program simply contains calls to operator methods, bypassing the parser and optimizer, then a linker can be used to bind the program with the necessary methods (which can be viewed as a library of procedures). The second option, which will be a difficult task, is to provide a generalized tool to handle programs with embedded queries (ala EQUEL). It will be relatively easy to provide a generic preprocessor which will extract queries and replace them with calls to object modules produced by the parser, optimizer, and compiler; however, it is unclear how to make the underlying interface between the application program and database system independent of the (application-specific) data model. For example, in the relational model a tuple-at-a-time or portal [Ston84] interface is commonly used, whereas with the Codasyl data model, the database system and application program exchange currency indicators as well as record occurrences. These issues will be explored further in the future.

[4] We are presently building a QUEL interface using this tool.

3. THE STORAGE OBJECT MANAGER

In this section we summarize the key features of the design of the EXODUS Storage Object Manager. We begin by discussing the interface that the Storage Object Manager provides to higher levels of the system, and then we describe how arbitrarily large storage objects are handled efficiently. We discuss the techniques employed for versioning, concurrency control, recovery, and buffer management for storage objects, and we close with a brief discussion about files of storage objects (known as file objects). A more detailed discussion of these issues can be found in [Care86].

3.1. The Storage Object Manager Interface

The Storage Object Manager provides a procedural interface. This interface includes procedures to create and destroy file objects and to open and close file objects for file scans. For scanning purposes, the Storage Object Manager provides a call to get the object ID of the next object within a file object. It also provides procedures for creating and destroying storage objects within a file. For reading storage objects, the Storage Object Manager provides a call to get a pointer to a range of bytes within a given storage object; the desired byte range is read into the buffers, and a pointer to the bytes there are returned to the caller. Another call is provided to inform EXODUS that these bytes are no longer needed, which "unpins" them in the buffer pool. For writing storage objects, a call is provided to tell EXODUS that a subrange of the bytes that were read have been modified (information that is needed for recovery to take place). For shrinking/growing storage objects, calls to insert bytes into and delete bytes from a specified offset in a storage object are provided, as is a call to append bytes to the end of an object. Finally, for transaction management, the Storage Object Manager provides begin, commit, and abort transaction calls; additional hooks are provided to aid the access methods layer in implementing concurrent and recoverable operations for new access methods efficiently (as discussed in Section 5).

In addition to the functionality outlined above, the Storage Object Manager is designed to accept a variety of performance-related hints. For example, the object creation routine mentioned above accepts hints about where to place a new object (i.e., "place the new object near the object with id *X*") and about how large the object is expected to be (on the average, if it varies); it is also possible to hint that an object should be alone on a disk page and the same size as the page (which will be useful for the access methods level). The buffer manager accepts hints about the size and number of buffers to use and what replacement policy to employ. These hints will be supported by allowing a *scan group* to be specified with each object access, and then having the buffer manager accept these hints on a per-scan-group basis, allowing easy support of buffer management policies like DBMIN [Chou85].

3.2. Storage Objects and Operations

As described earlier, the **storage object** is the basic unit of data in the Storage Object Manager. Storage objects can be either small or large, a distinction that is hidden from higher layers of EXODUS software. Small storage objects reside on a single disk page, whereas large storage objects occupy potentially many disk pages. In either case, the object identifier (OID) of a storage object is an address of the form *(page #, slot #)*. The OID of a small storage object points to the object on disk; for a large storage object, the OID points to its *large object header*. A large object header can reside on a slotted page with other large object headers and small storage objects, and it contains pointers to other pages involved in the representation of the large object. Other pages in large storage objects are private rather than being shared with other objects (although pages are shared between versions of a storage object). When a small storage object grows to the point where it can no longer be accommodated on a single page, the Storage Object Manager will automatically convert it into a large storage object, leaving its object header in place of the original small object. We considered the alternative of using logical surrogates for OID's rather than physical addresses, as in other recent proposals [Cope84, Ston86b], but efficiency considerations led us to opt for a "physical surrogate" scheme — with logical surrogates, it would always be necessary to access objects via a dense surrogate index[5].

Figure 2 shows an example of our large object data structure; it was inspired by Stonebraker's ordered relation structure [Ston83], but there are a number of significant differences [Care86]. Conceptually, a large object is an uninterpreted byte sequence; physically, it is represented as a B+ tree like index on byte position within the object plus a collection of leaf blocks (with all data bytes residing in the leaves). The large object header contains a number of *(count, page #)* pairs, one for each child of the root. The count value associated with each child pointer gives the maximum byte number stored in the subtree rooted at that child, and the rightmost child pointer's count is therefore also the size of the object. Internal nodes are similar, being recursively defined as the root of another object contained within its parent node, so an absolute byte offset within a child translates to a relative offset within its parent node. The left child of the root in Figure 2 contains bytes 1-421, and the right child contains the rest of the object (bytes 422-786). The rightmost leaf node in the figure contains 173 bytes of data. Byte 100 within this leaf node is byte 192 + 100 = 292 within the right child of the root, and it is byte 421 + 292 = 713 within the object as a whole. Searching is accomplished by computing overall offset information while descending the tree to the desired byte position. As described in [Care86], object sizes up to 1 GB or so can be supported with only three tree levels (header and leaf levels included).

Associated with the large storage object data structure are algorithms to *search* for a range of bytes (and perhaps update them), to *insert* a sequence of bytes at a given point in the object, to *append* a sequence of bytes to the end of the object, and to *delete* a sequence of bytes from a given point in the object. The insert, append, and delete operations are novel because inserting or deleting an arbitrary number of bytes (as opposed to a single byte) into a large storage object poses some unique problems compared to inserting or deleting a single record from an ordered relation. Algorithms for these operations are described in detail in [Care86] along with results from an experimental evaluation of their storage utilization and performance characteristics. The evaluation

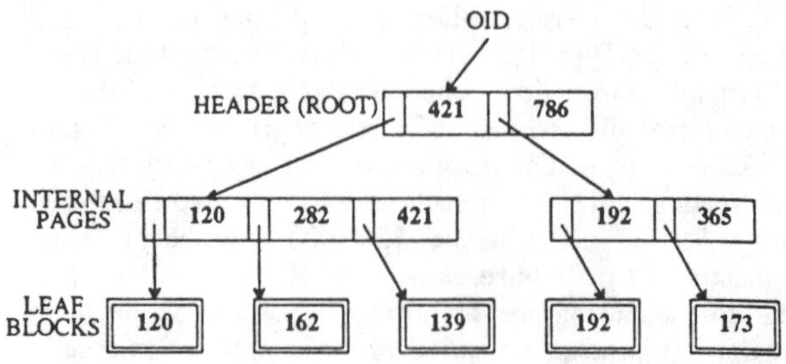

Figure 2: An example of a large storage object.

showed that the EXODUS storage object mechanism can provide operations on very large dynamic objects at relatively low cost, and at a reasonable level of storage utilization (typically 80% or higher).

3.3. Versions of Storage Objects

The Storage Object Manager provides primitive support for versions of storage objects. One version of each storage object is retained as the current version, and all of the preceding versions are simply marked (in their object headers) as being old versions. The reason for only providing a primitive level of version support is that different EXODUS applications may have widely different notions of how versions should be supported [Ston81, Dada84, Katz84, Bato85, Clif85, Klah85, Snod85, Katz86]. We do not omit version management altogether for efficiency reasons — it would be prohibitively expensive, both in terms of storage space and I/O cost, to maintain versions of large objects by maintaining entire copies of objects.

Versions of large storage objects are maintained by copying and updating the pages that differ from version to version. Figure 3 illustrates this by an example. The figure shows two versions of the large storage object of Figure 2, the original version, V_1, and a newer version, V_2. In this example, V_2 was created by deleting the last 36 bytes from V_1. Note that V_2 shares all nodes of V_1 that are unchanged, and it has its own

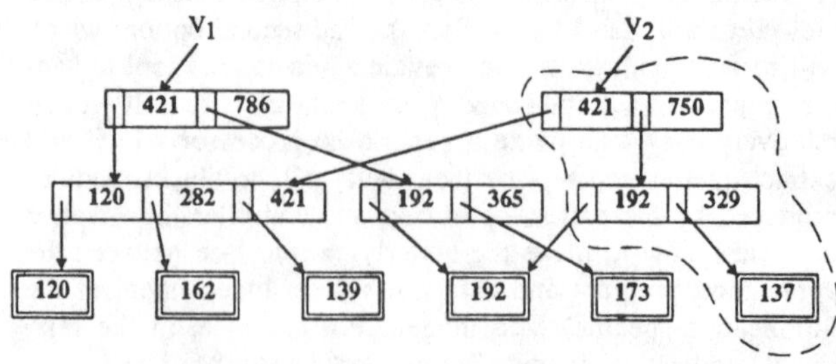

Figure 3: Two versions of a large storage object.

[5] This is true unless the objects are kept sorted on surrogate ID. In this case, a non-dense surrogate index can be used.

copies of each modified node. A new version of a large storage object will always contain a new copy of the path from the root to the new leaf (or leaves); it may also contain copies of other internal nodes if the change affects a large fraction of the object. Since the length of the path will usually be two or three, however, and the number of internal pages is small relative to the number of pages of actual data (due to high fanout for internal nodes), the overhead for versioning large objects in this scheme is small — for a given fixed tree height, it is basically proportional to the difference between adjacent versions, and not to the size of the objects.

Besides allowing for the creation of new versions of large storage objects, which is supported by allowing the insert, append, delete, and write (i.e., read and modify a byte range) operations to be invoked with versioning turned on, the Storage Object Manager also supports deletion of versions. This is necessary for efficiency as well as to maintain the clean abstraction. The problem is that when deleting a version of a large object, we must avoid discarding any of the object's pages that are shared (and thus needed) by other versions of the same object. [Care86] describes an efficient version deletion algorithm that addresses this problem, providing a way to delete one version with respect to a set of other versions that are to be retained.

3.4. Concurrency Control and Recovery

The Storage Object Manager provides concurrency control and recovery services for storage objects. Two-phase locking [Gray79] of byte ranges within storage objects is used for concurrency control, with a "lock entire object" option being provided for cases where object level locking will suffice. To ensure the integrity of the internal pages of large storage objects while insert, append, and delete operations are operating on them (e.g., changing their counts and pointers), non-two-phase B+ tree locking protocols [Baye77] are employed. For recovery, small storage objects are handled using before/after-image logging and in-place updating at the object level [Gray79]. Recovery for large storage objects is handled using a combination of shadowing and logging — updated internal pages and leaf blocks are shadowed up to the root level, with updates being installed atomically by overwriting the old object header with the new header [Verh78]. The name and parameters of the operation that caused the update are logged, and a log sequence number [Gray79] is maintained on each large object's root page; this is done to ensure that operations on large storage objects can be logically undone or redone as needed. A similar scheme is used for versioned objects, but the before-image of the updated large object header (or entire small object) is retained as an old version of the object.

3.5. Buffer Management for Storage Objects

An objective of the EXODUS Storage Object Manager design is to minimize the amount of copying from buffer space that is required. A second (related) objective is to allow sizable portions of large storage objects to be scanned directly in the buffer pool by higher levels of EXODUS software. To accommodate these needs, buffer space is allocated in variable-length *buffer blocks*, which are integral numbers of contiguous pages, rather than in single-page units. When an EXODUS client requests that a sequence of N bytes be read from an object X, the non-empty portions of the leaf blocks of X containing the desired byte range will be read into one contiguous buffer block by obtaining a buffer block of the appropriate size from the buffer space manager and then reading the pages into the buffer block in (strict) byte sequence order, placing the first data byte from a leaf page in the position immediately following the last data byte from the previous page. (Recall that leaf pages of large storage objects are usually not entirely full.) A scan descriptor will be maintained for the current region of X being scanned, including such information as the OID of X, a pointer to its buffer block, the length of the actual portion of the buffer block containing the bytes requested by the client, a pointer to the first such byte, and information about where the contents of the buffer block came from. The client will receive a pointer to the scan descriptor through which the buffer contents may be accessed[6]. Free space for the buffer pool will be managed using standard dynamic storage allocation techniques, and buffer block allocation and replacement will be guided by the Storage Object Manager's hint mechanism.

3.6. File Objects

File objects are collections of storage objects, and they are useful for grouping objects together for several purposes. First, the EXODUS Storage Object Manager provides a mechanism for sequencing through all of the objects in a file, so that related objects can be placed in a common file for sequential scanning purposes. Second, objects within a given file are placed on disk pages allocated to the file, so file objects provide support for objects that need to be co-located on disk. Like large storage objects, a file object is identified by an OID which points to its root (i.e., an object header); storage objects and file objects are distinguished by a header bit. Like large storage objects, file objects are represented by an index structure similar to a B+ tree, but the key for the index is different in this case — a file object index uses *disk page number* as its key. Each leaf page of the file object index contains a collection of page numbers for slotted pages contained in the file. (The pages themselves are managed separately using standard disk allocation techniques.) The file object index thus serves as a mechanism to gather the pages of a file together, but it also has several other nice properties — it facilitates the scanning of all of objects within a given file object *in physical order* for efficiency, and it allows fast deletion of an object with a given OID from a file object (since the OID includes a page number, which is the key for the file object index). Note that since all of the objects in a file are directly accessible via their OIDs, a file object is *not* comparable to a surrogate index — any indices on the objects within a given file will contain entries that point directly to the objects being indexed, a feature important for performance. Further discussion of file object representation, operations, concurrency control, and recovery may be found in [Care86].

4. THE TYPE MANAGER

4.1. Overview

As described earlier, the goal of the EXODUS Type Manager is to provide schema support for the needs of a wide range of application-specific database systems. The Type

[6] As is discussed in Section 5, the E language actually hides this structure from the DBI.

Manager maintains two important and interrelated categories of schema information: the *class hierarchy* and the *file catalog*. A class defines a storage object (or typed object) consisting of named fields, each of which is either of some *base type* or of a constructed type. Classes may inherit the fields of one or more other classes; a class which does so is called a subclass, and its ancestors are called superclasses. The hierarchy of subclasses and superclasses forms a lattice [Ait86], as we do not restrict a class to having one unique immediate superclass (i.e., we use the term hierarchy loosely here). If class A is a subclass of both classes B and C, then it possesses all the fields of those two classes. If B and C contain a field name in common, the definition of A must either choose one or else rename one or both fields for use in A. Ultimately, all classes are subclasses of root class *Object*. Information about the type hierarchy is stored in a set of objects of class *Class*. Class is a metaclass, in the same sense that the relation catalog of a traditional relational system is a meta-relation. The class Class is a subclass of Object, and other classes may inherit from it, but it is special in that both Object and Class, in addition to other classes, are predefined in objects of class Class.

When a file is created, it is constrained to contain objects of only one class. This is not as restrictive as it first sounds, as all objects are transitively of every class from which they inherit. Thus, a file of objects of class Object may contain objects of every subclass in the lattice. If classes Employee and Dependent are subclasses of Person, and Manager is a subclass of Employee, then a file of Person can contain objects of class Person, Employee, Dependent, and Manager. The Type Manager maintains a file catalog containing information about the class of each file and statistical information on the file (such as the cardinalities of each subclass within the file) for use during query optimization.

4.2. Type Capabilities: Default and User Defined

A typed object is basically a record constructed from instances of base and constructed types. Base types are fixed length abstract objects, accessible only through the set of operations defined on them. These correspond to the abstract data types of ADT INGRES [Ston86a] or of conventional programming languages. Constructed types are collections of base types that may vary in length. The EXODUS default base types include integer, real, character, and object ID. In addition, EXODUS provides support for the addition of base types (e.g., rectangles or complex numbers), allowing new base types to be defined and permitting operators on these new types to be declared by the DBI and implemented using the E programming language (as described in Section 5). DBI-defined base types are compiled into the Type Manager when the new application-specific DBMS is generated (as shown in Figure 4). This approach to providing abstract data types was chosen because it simplifies their implementation (see [Ston86a] for a discussion of alternative strategies for implementing ADTs); also, it helps tighten the security loophole that arises when ADTs are supported in a database system by restricting when and by whom new types can be defined. We do not view this restriction as seriously limiting, as we expect the definition of the types needed by an application to happen only when the DBI designs the application-specific DBMS.

The constructed types provided by EXODUS include variable length arrays, ordered and unordered sets and bags

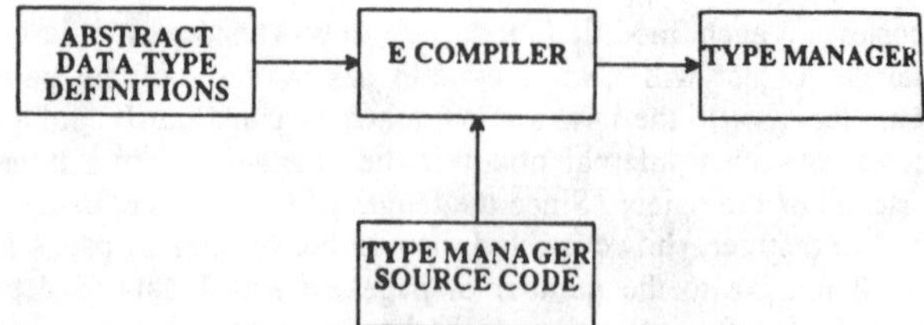

Figure 4: Adding new base types.

(multisets), and records. Constructed types differ from base types in that their subcomponents are individually accessible. In addition, constructed types may contain other constructed types (e.g. an array of records is permissible.). Whenever possible, such as for arrays of fixed length records, the query optimizer/compiler will produce code which minimizes the amount of run time interpretation incurred in accessing an instance of a constructed type. Constructed types also have certain predefined operations available on them (which depend on the type). Subscripting is universally available, but its meaning varies. For example, Array[3] always refers to the third element of Array, but Set[3] refers to the third element in an arbitrarily imposed ordering on Set (which may not survive across insertions and deletions); for Set, subscripting is simply used to enumerate its elements. Set addition, subtraction, and intersection may be applied to sets and multisets (with appropriately varying semantics). Several predefined functions are also declared on constructed types. For example, cardinality(field) gives the number of elements in type "field", and various string operations are available for arrays of characters[7] (including the ordering operators). Facilities are planned to permit the definition of additional constructed types and operations on them in a manner similar to that by which new base types and operations are declared.

As a final note, observe that the presence of object IDs as a base type plus the set of constructed types makes it possible to model more complex recursive types (e.g., typed objects within other typed objects) at a higher level of an application-specific DBMS. We expect this extensible type system to be sufficiently powerful to serve most applications satisfactorily.

5. ACCESS METHODS IN EXODUS

Application-specific database systems will undoubtedly vary from one another in the access methods that they employ. For example, while B+ trees and an index type based on some form of dynamic hashing are usually sufficient for conventional business database systems (e.g., a relational DBMS), a database system for storing and manipulating spatial data is likely to need a spatial index structure such as the KDB tree [Robi81], R tree [Gutt84], or Grid file [Niev84] structures. We plan to provide a library of available access methods in EXODUS, but we expect this library to grow — new, specialized index structures will undoubtedly continue to be developed as emerging database applications seek higher and higher performance. A complication is that a given index structure is expected to be able to handle data of a variety of types (e.g., integers, reals, character strings, and even newly-defined types) as long as the data type meets the prerequisites

[7] Note that 'string' is not a base type, but rather a variable-length array of characters.

for correct operation of the index structure (e.g., a B+ tree requires the existence of a total ordering operator for its key type) [Ston86a]; this includes operating on data types that are not defined by the DBI until after the index code has been completely written and debugged.

As described in Section 2, access methods reside on top of the Storage Object Manager of EXODUS in the architecture of application-specific database systems. In addition, type information from the Type Manager must be provided to the access methods code in order for it to properly deal with user-defined types. One of the goals of the EXODUS project is to simplify the task of adding new access methods to a new or existing application-specific database system. The major sources of complexity in adding a new access method seem to be (i) programming (and verifying) the access method algorithms, (ii) mapping the access method data structure(s) onto the primitive objects provided by the storage system, (iii) making the access method code interact properly with the buffer manager, and (iv) ensuring that concurrency control and recovery are handled correctly and efficiently. Although the access method designer is probably only interested in item (i), this can comprise as little as 30% of the actual code that he or she must write in order to add an access method to a typical commercial DBMS, with items (ii)-(iv) comprising the remaining 70% [Ston85]. To improve this situation — dramatically, we hope — EXODUS provides a programming language for the DBI to use when implementing new access methods (and other operations). This language, E, effectively shields the DBI from items (ii)-(iv) — the E translator produces code to handle these details based on the DBI's index code plus a few declarative "hints".

In the remainder of this section, we outline the way in which new access methods are added to EXODUS, including how the E database implementation language extends C, how access method implementation is simplified by E, and how buffering, concurrency control, and recovery issues are handled "under the covers" in a nearly transparent fashion.

5.1. The E Implementation Language

The E language is basically C [Kern78] with the addition of a small set of EXODUS-specific constructs[8]. Its main additions to C are a notion of *persistent object variables*, which have a one-to-one correspondence with storage objects; an *OID* data type, for storage object ID's; *parameterized types* and the addition of *type* as a legitimate data type for parameters of E procedures[9], to make access methods code capable of dealing with multiple data types[10]; and several new type constructors for defining fields of persistent objects, including variable-length arrays, sets, and bags, in addition to C's fixed length array and record constructors. By providing these facilities, E allows the DBI to define and then to manipulate the internal structure of storage objects for an access method (e.g., a B+ tree node) in a more natural way than by making direct calls to the Storage Object Manager and explicitly coding structure overlays and offset computations. In particular, E allows the DBI to ignore the fact that storage objects can be arbitrarily large; the E translator will insert appropriate calls to get the storage object byte ranges needed by the DBI. The output of the E language translator is C source code with EXODUS-specific constructs replaced by collections of appropriate lower-level C constructs, additional routine parameters, and calls to the Storage Object Manager. In other words, the Storage Object Manager is effectively the E translator's "target machine", and the resulting C source code will be linked with the Storage Object Manager.

In addition to these facilities, the E language provides the DBI with declarative access to the Storage Object Manager's hint facilities (which were described in Section 3). Associated with each persistent object variable in an E source program is a scan descriptor as described in Section 3; when such a variable is declared in the E source code, hints may be attached to its definition. In the absence of hints, E will provide reasonable default assumptions, but hints make it possible for a knowledgeable DBI to tune the performance of his or her code by recommending the appropriate lock protocol, buffer replacement strategy, object size, etc., to be associated with a persistent object (scan) variable.

5.2. Writing Access Methods in E

To demonstrate the usefulness of the E implementation language and to further explain its features, let us consider how the DBI might go about defining a B+ tree node and a pointer to such a node. To describe the internal structure of a B+ tree node, the DBI would define a C-like structure to represent its contents. The *BTnode* defined in Figure 5 is an example of such a definition; note that it relies on a parameter *keyType* which must be specified when the type is used to define a variable. To define a pointer variable *n* for B+ tree nodes, a standard C pointer definition is preceded by the keyword *persistent* to inform the E translator that the pointer will reference a persistent object. In addition to defining a persistent pointer variable (with which E will associate a scan descriptor), *n*'s definition also hints to the E translator that new B+ tree nodes should be one page in size, that hierarchical locking should be used for this scan (as explained in the next subsection), and that a LIFO buffer management policy with three buffer blocks should be used for the scan.

Given these definitions, the DBI can proceed to access and manipulate storage objects as though they were standard in-memory C structures. Figure 5 also gives an example code fragment from a B+ tree search routine. In this code fragment, the pointer variable *n* contains the OID of a B+ tree node, and *LessThan* is a function parameter that was passed to *BTsearch* (i.e., it is the ordering operator used to build the index to be searched). Each time the E translator encounters a statement in which *n* is dereferenced, it will translate this reference into a sequence of several C statements — at runtime this sequence will check to see if the appropriate bytes of the object are already in the buffer pool by inspecting *n*'s scan descriptor, calling the Storage Object Manager to read the

[8] The constructs described here will comprise the first version of E. A second version is planned which will include the same class-based type system with multiple inheritance as the Type Manager uses. It should also be noted that the exact syntax and semantics described here are only preliminary.

[9] We allow parameters of type *type*, but we disallow variables and other entities of type *type*.

[10] We are currently studying the best way to provide the type-related power needed to solve this problem. We are in the process of searching the programming languages literature for insight, so the mechanism that we finally adopt may differ somewhat from that described here.

```
typedef struct {
  int count;
  struct {
    keyType key;
    OID *ptr;
  } kp[];
} BTnode ( keyType );
...


OID BTsearch( treePtr, keyType, searchKey, LessThan, ... )
OID treePtr;
TYPE keyType;
keyType searchKey;
INT ( *LessThan )();
...
{
  INT i, limit;

  persistent BTnode( keyType ) *n   # obj-size = PAGE;
    locking = HIER;   bfrmgt = (LIFO, 3) #;
  ...
    ...
    i = 0;
    limit = n->count;
    while (i++ < limit && LessThan(n->kp[i].key, searchKey));
    ...
  ...
}
```

Figure 5: Excerpts from E code for searching a B+ tree.

desired bytes (and perhaps subsequent bytes) into the buffer pool if not, and then the actual reference will take place in memory. Since *keyType* is unknown when this code is compiled, the E translator will rely on the query compiler to generate and pass in (under the covers) a machine language code fragment that performs the necessary offset computation; the code for *BTsearch* will simply use this code fragment. (Note that the schema information needed to produce code for the offset computation will be available from the Type Manager at query compilation time.) Finally, since *n* is defined within the scope of the routine *BTsearch*, it (but not the objects that it is used to reference) will cease to exist when the routine terminates.

Other operations on persistent object types will be provided as well. For example, to create a storage object, the DBI will call *new(FileName, n)* to create a new object in file *FileName* and set *n* to point at it. To dispose of an object, a *dispose(FileName, n)* call will be used. Other routines will also be provided, including routines to open, scan, and close file objects. The E translator will recognize these calls and replace them with appropriate lower-level Storage Object Manager calls.

5.3. Transparent Transaction Management

We have described how the E language simplifies the DBI's job by allowing access method structures and algorithms to be expressed in a natural way, and we have indicated how the E translator adds Storage Object Manager calls when producing C code. In this section we describe how concurrency control and recovery fit into the picture; the problem is complicated by the fact that access methods often require non-two-phase locking protocols and have specialized recovery requirements for performance reasons [Ston86a]. These functions are handled by the E translator through a combination of *layered transactions* and *protocol stubs.*

5.3.1. Layered Transactions

Transaction management for access methods in EXODUS is loosely based on the layered transaction model proposed by Weikum [Weik84]. Weikum's model is based on the notion of architectural layers of a database system, with each layer presenting a set of objects and associated operations to its client layers. Each operation is a "mini-transaction" (or nested transaction) in its own right, and thus a transaction in a client layer can be realized as a series of mini-transactions in one or more of its servant layers. Concurrency control is enforced using two-phase locking on objects within a given layer of the system. Objects in a servant layer are locked on behalf of the transaction in its client layer, and these locks are held until the client transaction completes. Recovery is layered in a similar manner. As a mini-transaction executes, it writes level-specific recovery information to the log; when it completes, its log information is removed and replaced by a simpler client-level representation of the entire operation. To undo the effects of an incomplete layered transaction at a given level, the effects of a number of completed mini-transactions plus one in-progress mini-transaction must be undone; we must first undo the incomplete mini-transaction (recursively, in general) using its log information, then run the inverse of each completed mini-transaction. Weikum proposes what amounts to a per-transaction stack-based log for recovery.

While we draw much inspiration from Weikum, our access method transaction management facilities differ in some respects. First, EXODUS is not strictly hierarchical in nature, instead being a collection of interacting modules. (This does not invalidate the notion of a layered transaction, however.) Also, we provide more general locking than the strict two-phase model in Weikum's proposal, allowing locks set by a servant to be either explicitly released or passed to its client. This is particularly important for access methods, as two-phase locking (even within a single index operation) is often considered to be unacceptable [Baye77]. Lock passing is also needed to prevent phantoms when a new key-pointer pair is inserted into an index — unless the client retains a lock on the index leaf page, other transactions may run into consistency problems due to incorrect existence information. Lastly, efficient log management is essential to overall performance, and we view Weikum's per-transaction stack-based log as too unwieldy. Instead, we employ standard circular log management techniques, ignoring entries for completed mini-transactions during recovery processing.

Returning to our discussion of access methods, note that the access methods layer presents objects (e.g., indices) and operations (e.g., insert, delete, search, etc.) to its clients. If a client transaction executes a series of inserts, its effects can be undone via a series of corresponding deletes. The access methods layer, in turn, is a client of the Storage Object Manager, which presents storage objects and such operations as create object, insert bytes, append bytes, etc.

5.3.2. Protocol Stubs

Layered transactions will simplify the task of writing access methods because calls to other layers can be viewed as primitive, atomic operations. However, this is just a transaction model; the task of actually implementing the model still remains. For example, someone must still write the code to handle B+ tree locking and recovery, and getting this correct can be quite difficult. EXODUS provides a collection of protocol stubs, managed by the E translator, to shield the DBI from the details of this problem as much as possible. Briefly, a protocol stub is an abstraction of a particular locking protocol, implemented as a collection of code fragments (which the E translator inserts at appropriate points during the compilation of an E program) plus related data structures. The code fragments consist of locking/logging calls to the EXODUS transaction manager (a component of the Storage Object Manager). The data structures describe information on lock modes (and their compatibility) which is passed to and used by the lock manager. We currently expect that the generation of new protocol stubs will be a complicated task, and that stubs will be considered by the average DBI as being a non-extensible part of the basic EXODUS system. The *use* of existing stubs will be easy, on the other hand, and EXODUS will provide a collection of stubs for two-phase locking and for the hierarchical locking (or lock chaining) protocol of [Baye77]. A DBI writing a new access method will only need to (1) select the desired protocol at compile time via E's declarative hints, as mentioned earlier; (2) bracket each access method operation with begin and end transaction keywords in E; and then maybe (3) include one or two stub-specific routine calls in the access method operation code (an example of which is given below).

As a concrete example, we briefly sketch a protocol suitable for concurrent and recoverable access to most sorts of hierarchical index structures. The basic idea is to use the B+ tree lock-chaining protocol of [Baye77] for concurrency control, and to use shadowing for operation-atomicity [Verh78]. Consider a B+ tree insert operation: Using lock chaining as we descend the tree, we can release locks on all ancestors of a safe node once we have locked that node. To realize this protocol, the hierarchical locking protocol stub will implicitly set locks on nodes as they are referenced, keeping track of the path of locked nodes. When the DBI's code determines that a "safe" node has been reached, it can call a lock stub routine called *top-of-scope* to announce that previously accessed nodes (excluding the current one) are no longer in the tree scope of interest to the insert operation. The appropriate lock release operations can then be transparently handled by the lock stub routine. As for recovery, the insert operation will cause node splitting to occur up to the last *top-of-scope*. If changed nodes below this level are automatically shadowed, then the insert can be atomically installed at end-of-operation by overwriting the *top-of-scope* node after its descendent pages have been safely written to disk [Care85b]. (While the Storage Object Manager does not directly support shadow-based recovery, the E translator can generate C code which uses the versioning mechanism of the Storage Object Manager to accomplish this task.)

5.4. Other Uses of E

We have described in some detail how the E language provides the DBI with a facility for writing access method operations without worrying about such issues as the size of objects, making calls to the Storage Object Manager, or access method specific concerns of concurrency control and recovery. E is actually more than just an implementation language for access methods — the facilities that it provides can and will be used for writing other operations that need to access pieces of storage objects while preferably ignoring the details of the Storage Object Manager's interface. For example, E will be used to define new base types using its enhanced C type system, and it can then be used to implement any operators that the DBI wishes to provide for operating on application-specific base types. Since such operations may need to deal with arbitrarily large portions of objects — for example, the DBI might wish to add an ADT called "matrix" and then provide a matrix multiplication operator — the DBI's job will be significantly simpler if he or she can write the desired code without regard for the size of the underlying storage objects. As another example, multiple versions of objects can be supported in the access methods layer through the use of version indices [Katz84]. For applications requiring version management, it is likely that the DBI will implement the desired facilities at this level of the EXODUS system and in the E language. As with access methods, we anticipate providing some level of version support via a library of routines, and we again expect that the library will grow in time.

6. OPERATOR METHODS

The Operator Methods Layer contains the E procedures used to implement the operators provided to the user of the database system. For each operator, one or more procedures (or methods) may exist. For example, in a relational DBMS this layer might contain both nested-loops and sort-merge implementations of the relational join operation. In general, the operators associated with a data model are *schema independent*. That is, the operators (and their corresponding implementations) are defined independently of any conceptual schema information — the join operator, for example, will join any two relations as long as the corresponding join attributes are compatible with one another (even if the result happens to be semantically meaningless).

There are two strategies for implementing such generic operators. First, the procedures implementing the operators could request the necessary schema information at run-time from the Type Manager. The second strategy is to have the query optimizer and compiler compile the necessary schema information into code fragments that the compiled query can pass to the operator method at run-time. For example, in the case of the join, the optimizer would produce four code fragments: two to extract the source relation join attributes (with one procedure for each source relation), one to compare the two join attributes, and one to compose a result tuple from the two source tuples. Since this latter approach is the approach used to pass comparison information to the access methods, we have also adopted it for use in this layer.

Instead of providing generic (and, hence, semantics-free) operators to the database users, a number of researchers [Webe78, Rowe79, Derr86, Lyng86] have proposed to provide only "schema dependent" operations to the users. For example, in a database of employees and departments, the type of operations supported would be of the form hire-employee, change-job, etc. When the hire-employee operation is invoked, the necessary base entities are updated in such a fashion as to insure that the database remains consistent. Given the capabilities of EXODUS, implementing this style of operators is quite obviously feasible. The DBI could implement the operators directly using the functionality provided by the Access Methods and Storage Object Manager. Alternatively, they could be implemented using more generic operators. It appears that the database administrator of an IRIS database [Derr86, Lyng86] is expected to implement the schema-specific operators using an underlying relational database system.

As is the case for access methods, we anticipate providing some level of operator support via a library of methods. For example, most data models are likely to want methods for performing associative accesses (i.e. selection) and for scanning through all of the objects contained in a particular file object.

7. RULE BASED QUERY OPTIMIZATION AND COMPILATION

Given the unforeseeably wide variety of data models we hope to support with EXODUS, each with its own operators (and corresponding methods), EXODUS includes an optimizer *generator* that produces an application-specific query optimizer from an input specification. The generated optimizer repeatedly applies algebraic transformations to a query and selects access paths for each operation in the transformed query. This transformational approach is outlined by Ullman for relational DBMSs [Ullm82], and it has been used in the Microbe database project [Nyug82] with rules coded as Pascal procedures. We initially considered using a rule-based AI language to implement a general-purpose optimizer, and then to augment it with data model specific rules. Prolog [Warr77, Cloc81], OPS5 [Forg81], and LOOPS [Bobr83] seemed like interesting candidates, as each provides a built-in "inference engine" or search mechanism. However, this convenience also limits their use, as their search algorithms are rather fixed and hard to augment with search heuristics (which are very important for query optimization). Based on this limitation, and also on further considerations such as call compatibility with other EXODUS components and optimizer execution speed, we decided instead to provide an optimizer generator which produces an optimization procedure in the programming language C [Kern78].

The generated optimization procedure takes a query as its input, producing an access plan as its output. A query in this context is a tree-like expression with logical operators as internal nodes (e.g., a join in a relational DBMS) and sets of objects (e.g., relations) as leaves. We do not regard it as part of the optimizer's task to produce an initial algebraic query tree from a non-procedural expression; this will be done by the user interface and parser. An access plan is a tree with operator methods as internal nodes (e.g., a hash join method) and with files or indices as leaves. Once an access plan is obtained, it will then be transformed into an iterative program using techniques due to Freytag [Frey85, Frey86].

There are four key elements which must be given to the optimizer generator (in a description file) in order for it to generate an optimizer: (1) the operators, (2) the methods, (3) the transformation rules, and (4) the implementation rules. Operators and their methods are characterized by their name and arity. Transformation rules specify legal (equivalence-preserving) transformations of query trees, and consist of two expressions and an optional condition. The expressions contain place holders for lower parts of the query which will not be affected by the transformation, and the condition is a C code fragment which is inserted into the optimizer at the appropriate place. Finally, an implementation rule consists of a method, an expression that the method implements, and an optional condition. As an example, here is an excerpt from the description file for a relational DBMS:

```
%operator 2 join
%method 2 hash-join merge-join
join (R, S) <-> join (S, R);
join (R, S) by hash-join (R, S);
```

Both the operator and method declarations specify the number of inputs. The symbol "<->" denotes equivalence, and "by" is a keyword for implementation rules. If merge-join is only useful for joining sorted relations, then a rule for merge-join would have to include a condition to test whether each input relation is sorted.

In addition to this declarative description of the data model, the optimizer requires the DBI to supply a collection of procedures. First, for each method, a cost function must be supplied that calculates the method's cost given the characteristics of the method's input. The cost of an access plan is defined as the sum of the costs of the methods involved. Second, a property function is needed for each operator and each method. Operator property functions determine logical properties of intermediate results, such as their cardinalities and record widths. Method property functions determine physical properties (ie. side effects), such as sort order in the example above.

The generated optimization procedure operates by maintaining two principal data structures, MESH and OPEN. MESH is a directed acyclic graph containing all the alternative operator trees and access plans that have been explored so far. A rather complex pointer structure is employed to ensure that equal subexpressions are stored and optimized only once, and also that accesses and transformations can be performed quickly. OPEN is a priority queue containing the set of applicable transformations; these are ordered by the cost decrease which would be expected from applying the transformations.

MESH is initialized to contain a tree with the same structure as the original query. The method with the lowest cost estimate is selected for each node using the implementation rules, and then possible transformations are determined and inserted into OPEN using the transformation rules. The optimizer then repeats the following transformation cycle until OPEN is empty: The most promising transformation is selected from OPEN and applied to MESH. For all nodes generated by the transformation, the optimizer tries to find an equal node in MESH to avoid optimizing the same expression twice. (Two nodes are equal if they have the same operator, the same argument, and the same inputs.) If an equal node is found, it is used to replace the new node. The remaining new nodes are matched against the transformation rules and analyzed, and methods with lowest cost estimates are selected.

This algorithm has several parameters which serve to improve its efficiency. First, the *promise* of each transformation is calculated as the product of the top node's total cost and the *expected cost factor* associated with the transformation rule. A matching transformation with a low expected cost factor will be applied first. Expected cost factors provide an easy way to ensure that restrictive operators are moved down in the tree as quickly as possible; it is a general heuristic that the cost is lower if constructive operators such as join and transitive closure have less input data. Second, while it seems to be wasted effort to perform an equivalence transformation if it does not yield a cheaper solution, sometimes such a transformation is necessary as an intermediate step to an even less expensive access plan. Such transformations represent hill climbing, and we limit their application through the use of a *hill climbing factor*. Third, when a transformation results in a lower cost, the parent nodes of the old expression must be reanalyzed to propagate cost advantages. It appears to be a difficult problem to select values for each of these parameters which will guarantee both optimal access plans and good optimizer performance. Thus, it is would be nice if they could be determined and adjusted automatically. Our current prototype initializes all expected cost factors to 1, the neutral value, and then adjusts them using sliding geometric averages. This has turned out to be very effective in our preliminary experiments. We are currently experimenting with the hill climbing and reanalyzing factors to determine the best method of adjustment.

8. EXODUS USER INTERFACES

As discussed in Section 2, a database system must provide facilities for both ad hoc and embedded queries. While tuple-at-a-time and portal [Ston84] interfaces look appropriate for record-oriented database systems, we have only just begun thinking about how to provide a more general technique for handling embedded queries in programs. Certainly, given the goals of the EXODUS project, we will need to develop data model independent techniques to interface programs to application specific database systems, but this may prove to be quite difficult. For example, it is hard to envision a generic interface tool that could satisfactorily interface a VLSI layout tool to a VLSI database system; in such an environment, it may be that the only sensible approach is to in the database system, thus enabling the program to directly access typed objects in the buffer pool. Alternatively, it may be possible to provide a library of interface tools: portals for browsing sets of objects, graphical interfaces for other applications, etc. We intend to explore alternative solutions to this problem in the future.

For ad hoc query interfaces, tools based on attribute grammars appear promising. Unlike the grammars used by generators like YACC, which can be used for little besides parsing the syntax of an input query, grammars which allow complex sets of attributes and attribution functions may capture the semantics of a query, incorporating knowledge of schema information to guide query construction, detect errors, and generate appropriate structures for transmission to the optimizer. To test these ideas we are constructing a QUEL interface using the Cornell Program Synthesizer Generator [Reps84]. The Generator takes a formal input specification, producing as its output an interactive, syntax- and semantics-driven editor similar in flavor to Emacs. For a query language, the editor will guide the user step-by-step in creating properly formed queries and will transform this calculus representation of the query into a syntax tree in the operator language recognized by the optimizer. During the process of producing this syntax tree, the editor will be responsible for translating from a calculus representation to an initial algebraic representation of the query. The editor will call on the Type Manager to provide access to schema information, as schema information determines a large part of the underlying semantics of the query. Since the concrete syntax of the query language, its abstract syntax, and the translation between the abstract syntax and the database operator language are all generated automatically from a formal specification, it should be a straightforward process to change or enhance the language recognized by the user interface.

9. SUMMARY AND CURRENT STATUS

In this paper we described the preliminary design of EXODUS, an extensible database system intended to simplify the development of high-performance, application-specific database systems. As we explained, the EXODUS model of the world includes three classes of database experts — ourselves, the designers and implementors of EXODUS; the database implementors, or DBIs, who are responsible for using EXODUS to produce various application-specific DBMSs; and the database administrators, or DBAs, who are the managers of the systems produced by the DBIs. In addition, of course, there must be users of application-specific DBMSs, namely the engineers, scientists, office workers, computer-aided designers, and other groups that the resulting systems will support. The focus of this paper has been the overall architecture of EXODUS and the tools available to aid the DBI in his or her task.

As we described, EXODUS includes two components that require little or no change from application to application — the Storage Object Manager, a flexible storage manager that provides concurrent and recoverable access to storage objects of arbitrary size, and the Type Manager, a class-based schema management subsystem whose repertoire of base types can be extended by the DBI. In addition, EXODUS provides libraries of database system components that are likely to be widely applicable, including components for access methods, version management, and simple operations. The corresponding system layers are constructed by the DBI through a combination of borrowing components from the libraries and writing new components. To make writing new components as painless as possible, EXODUS provides the E database implementation language to largely shield the DBI from the details of internal object formats, buffer management, concurrency control, and recovery protocols. At the upper level of the system, EXODUS provides a generator that produces a query optimizer and compiler from a description of the available operations and methods, and tools for generating application-specific front-end software are also planned.

The preliminary design of EXODUS is now nearing completion, including all of the components that have been described here. Our plans call for the design to be completed by July 1986, at which point implementation will begin for the

Storage Object Manager, the Type Manager, and the E programming language. Some preliminary prototyping work has already been done in order to validate the Storage Object Manager's algorithms for operating on large storage objects [Care86], and a first implementation of the rule-based query optimizer generator is partially operational as well. Our hope is that we will have initial implementations of most of the key components of EXODUS by the beginning of 1987. We hope to bring a relational DBMS up on top of EXODUS soon thereafter as a demonstration of the EXODUS approach.

10. ACKNOWLEDGEMENTS

This research was partially supported by the Defense Advanced Research Projects Agency under contract N00014-85-K-0788, by the Department of Energy under contract #DE-AC02-81ER10920, by the National Science Foundation under grants MCS82-01870 and DCR-8402818, and by an IBM Faculty Development Award.

REFERENCES

[Ait86] Ait-Kaci, H. and R. Nasr, "Logic and Inheritance," Proceedings of the 1986 POPL Conference, St. Petersburg, FA, January 1986.

[Allm76] Allman, E., Held, G. and M. Stonebraker, "Embedding a Data Manipulation Language in a General Purpose Programming Language," *Proceedings of the 1976 SIGPLAN-SIGMOD Conference on Data Abstraction*, Salt Lake City, Utah, March 1976.

[Astr76] Astrahan, M., et. al., "System R: Relational Approach to Database Management", *ACM Transactions on Data Systems* 1, 2, June 1976.

[Bato85] Batory, D., and W. Kim, *Support for Versions of VLSI CAD Objects*, M.C.C. Working Paper, March 1985.

[Bato86] Batory, D., Barnett, J., Garza, J., Smith, K., Tsukuda, K., Twichell, C., and T. Wise, "GENESIS: A Reconfigurable Database Management System," Technical Report, TR-86-07, Department of Computer Sciences, University of Texas at Austin, March 1986.

[Baye77] Bayer, R., and Schkolnick, M., "Concurrency of Operations on B-trees", *Acta Informatica* 9, 1977.

[Bobr83] Bobrow, D.G. and M. Stefik, "The LOOPS Manual," in LOOPS Release Notes, XEROX, Palo Alto, CA., 1983.

[Care85a] Carey, M. and D. DeWitt, "Extensible Database Systems", *Proceedings of the Islamorada Workshop on Large Scale Knowledge Base and Reasoning Systems*, February 1985.

[Care85b] Carey, M., DeWitt, D., and M. Stonebraker, personal communication, July 1985.

[Care86] Carey, M. J., DeWitt, D. J., Richardson, J. E., and E. Shekita, "Object and File Management in the EXODUS Extensible Database System," *Proceedings of the 1986 VLDB Conference*, Kyoto, Japan, August 1986, to appear.

[Chou85] Chou, H-T., and D. DeWitt, "An Evaluation of Buffer Management Strategies for Relational Database Systems", *Proceedings of the 1985 VLDB Conference*, Stockholm, Sweden, August 1985.

[Clif85] Clifford, J., and A. Tansel, "On An Algebra for Historical Relational Databases: Two Views", *Proceedings of the 1985 SIGMOD Conference*, Austin, Texas, May 1985.

[Cloc81] Clocksin, W. and C. Mellish, Programming in Prolog, Springer-Verlag, New York, 1981.

[Cope84] Copeland, G. and D. Maier, "Making Smalltalk a Database System", *Proceedings of the 1984 SIGMOD Conference*, Boston, MA, May 1984.

[Dada84] Dadam, P., V. Lum, and H-D. Werner, "Integration of Time Versions into a Relational Database System", *Proceedings of the 1984 VLDB Conference*, Singapore, August 1984.

[Daya85] Dayal, U. and J. Smith, "PROBE: A Knowledge-Oriented Database Management System", *Proceedings of the Islamorada Workshop on Large Scale Knowledge Base and Reasoning Systems*, February 1985.

[Derr86] Derrett, N., Fishman, D., Kent, W., Lyngaek, P., and T. Ryan, "An Object-Oriented Approach to Data Management," *Proceedings of the 1986 COMPCON Conference*, San Francisco, CA., February 1986.

[Forg81] Forgy, C.L. "OPS5 Reference Manual," Computer Science Technical Report 135, Carnegie-Mellon University, 1981.

[Frey85] Freytag, C.F. "Translating Relational Queries into Iterative Programs," Ph.D. Thesis, Harvard University, September 1985.

[Frey86] Freytag, C.F. and N. Goodman, "Translating Relational Queries into Iterative Programs Using a Program Transformation Approach," *Proceedings of the 1986 ACM SIGMOD Conference*, May 1986, to appear.

[Gray79] Gray, J., "Notes On Database Operating Systems", in *Operating Systems: An Advanced Course*, R. Bayer, R. Graham, and G. Seegmuller, eds., Springer-Verlag, 1979.

[Gutt84] Guttman, T., "R-Trees: A Dynamic Index Structure for Spatial Searching", *Proceedings of the 1984 SIGMOD Conference*, Boston, MA, May 1984.

[Katz84] Katz, R. and T. Lehman, "Database Support for Versions and Alternatives of Large Design Files", *IEEE Transactions on Software Engineering* SE-10, 2, March 1984.

[Katz86] Katz, R., E. Chang, and R. Bhateja, "Version Modeling Concepts for Computer-Aided Design Databases", *Proceedings of the 1986 SIGMOD Conference*, Washington, DC, May 1986, to appear.

[Kern78] Kernighan, B.W. and D.N. Ritchie, *The C Programming Language*, Prentice-Hall, Englewood Cliffs, N.J., 1978.

[Kers81] Kersten, M. L. and A. I. Wasserman, "The Architecture of the PLAIN Data Base Handler." *Software — Practice and Experience*, V 11, 1981, pp. 175- 186.

[Klah85] Klahold, P., G. Schlageter, R. Unland, and W. Wilkes, "A Transaction Model Supporting Complex Applications in Integrated Information Systems", *Proceedings of the 1985 SIGMOD Conference*, Austin, TX, May 1985.

[Litw80] Litwin, W. "Linear Hashing: A New Tool for File and Table Addressing," Proceedings of the 1980 VLDB Conference, Montreal, Canada, October 1980.

[Lyng86] Lyngbaek, P. and W. Kent, "A Data Modeling Methodology for the Design and Implementation of Information Systems", *Proceedings of the 1986 SIGMOD Conference*, Washington, DC, May 1986, to appear.

[Nguy82] Nguyen, G.T., Ferrat, L., and H. Galy, "A High-Level User Interface for a Local Network Database System," *Proceedings of the IEEE Infocom*, pp. 96-105, 1982.

[Maie86] Maier, D., Stein, J., Otis, A., and A. Purdy, "Development of an Object Oriented DBMS," Technical Report CS/E-86-005, Oregon Graduate Center, April 1986.

[Niev84] Nievergelt, J., H. Hintenberger, H., and Sevcik, K.C., "The Grid File: An Adaptable, Symmetric Multikey File Structure,", *ACM Transactions on Database Systems*, Vol. 9, No. 1, March 1984.

[Reps84] Reps, T. and T. Teitelbaum, "The Synthesizer Generator," *Proceedings of the ACM SIGSOFT/SIGPLAN Software Engineering Symposium on Practical Software Development Environments*, Pittsburgh, Penn., Apr. 23-25, 1984. Appeared as joint issue: *SIGPLAN Notices* (ACM) *19*, 5, May 1984, and *Soft. Eng. Notes* (ACM) 9, 3, May 1984, 42-48.

[Robi81] Robinson, J.T., "The k-d-B-tree: A Search Structure for Large Multidimentional Dynamic Indexes," *Proceedings of the 1981 SIGMOD Conference*, June, 1981.

[Rowe79] Rowe, L. and K. Schoens, "Data Abstraction, Views, and Updates in RIGEL, Proceedings of the 1979 SIGMOD Conference, Boston, MA., 1979.

[Schm77] Schmidt, J., "Some High Level Constructs for Data of Type Relations," *ACM Transactions on Database Systems*, 2, 3, September 1977.

[Ship81] Shipman, D., "The Functional Data Model and the Data Language DAPLEX", *ACM Transactions on Database Systems* 6, 1, March 1981.

[Shop79] Shopiro, J., "Theseus — A Programming Language for Relational Databases," *ACM Transactions on Database Systems* 4, 4, December 1979.

[Snod85] Snodgrass, R., and I. Ahn, "A Taxonomy of Time in Databases", *Proceedings of the 1985 SIGMOD Conference*, Austin, TX, May 1985.

[Ston81] Stonebraker, M., "Hypothetical Data Bases as Views", *Proceedings of the 1981 SIGMOD Conference*, Boston, MA, May 1981.

[Ston83] Stonebraker, M., H. Stettner, N. Lynn, J. Kalash, and A. Guttman, "Document Processing in a Relational Database System", *ACM Transactions on Office Information Systems* 1, 2, April 1983.

[Ston84] Stonebraker, M., and L. Rowe, "Database Portals - A New Application Program Interface," *Proceedings of the 1984 VLDB Conference*, Singapore, August 1984.

[Ston85] Stonebraker, M., personal communication, July 1985.

[Ston86a] Stonebraker, M., "Inclusion of New Types in Relational Data Base Systems," *Proceedings of the 2nd Data Engineering Conference*, Los Angeles, CA., February, 1986.

[Ston86b] Stonebraker, M., and L. Rowe, "The Design of POSTGRES", *Proceedings of the 1986 SIGMOD Conference*, Washington, DC, May 1986, to appear.

[Ullm82] Ullman, J.D., *Principles of Database Systems*, Computer Science Press, Rockville, MD., 1982.

[Verh78] Verhofstad, J., "Recovery Techniques for Database Systems", *ACM Computing Surveys* 10, 2, June 1978.

[Warr77] Warren, D.H., Pereira, L.M., and F. Pereira, "PROLOG - The language and its implementation compared with Lisp," *Proceedings of ACM SIGART-SIGPLAN Symp. on AI and Pro- gramming Languages*, 1977.

[Webe78] Weber, H. "A Software Engineering View of Database Systems," *Proceedings of the 1978 VLDB Conference*, pp. 36-51, 1978.

[Weik84] Weikum, G., and H-J. Schek, "Architectural Issues of Transaction Management in Multi-Layered Systems," *Proceedings of the 1984 VLDB Conference*, Singapore, August 1984.

Chapter 8

Integration Of Knowledge And Data Management

8.1 Introduction

It is fairly clear to most researchers that knowledge and data management should be tightly integrated in future systems. The overriding reason can be illustrated by a simple example. Every company processes purchase orders for goods and services that they buy. In addition, all enforce many rules on how the processing of purchase orders must be done. For example:

- All purchase orders over $100 must be signed by a manager.
- All purchase orders over $2000 must be signed by a department head.
- All purchase orders over $10,000 must be signed by the President.
- All purchase orders for computer equipment must be signed by the MIS director.
- All purchase orders for consulting services are disallowed.
- All purchase orders for goods within California must have sales tax added.

Such rules are currently either in people's heads (where they are vulnerable to employee turnover) or in application programs (where they are difficult to change or understand). In either case rules are difficult to enforce because any new program that updates the purchase order database must be extended with code to enforce them. The rules are also difficult to change because appropriate programs must be modified when particular rules change.

Companies have a multitude of rules that control business practices, especially as these practices relate to large shared databases. A cleaner approach than hard code in application programs will find instant widespread acceptance.

A better technology would be to store the rules in a **knowledge base**, which will allow them to be shared, updated, and automatically applied. There are two approaches to such a knowledge base. It can be managed by a **knowledge manager** separate from the DBMS or it can be integrated into the DBMS. In the first case, one would store rules in a system such as OPS5 [FORG81], S1 [TEKN86], Kee [INTE85], or Prolog [CLOC81]. Such a rule manager would then be coupled to a DBMS. Whenever data objects were required by the rule manager to decide whether to fire a rule, it would run a DBMS query to obtain appropriate information. This approach has been termed *loose coupling*, and example proposals on how to accomplish it are contained in [ABAR86, CERI86].

Loose coupling will work only if the application involved has two characteristics:

1. The data needed by the rules of the application must be **static.** If the knowledge manager retrieves a data object whose

value is changing, the knowledge manager must either lock the object for the duration of the rule session or must use out-of-date data. This latter course of action is very risky because the knowledge manager will be making inferences based on facts from the database that are no longer true.

2. The knowledge manager must be able to retrieve a small portion of the database on which to base its inferences. For example, in an air traffic control database, there might be a rule that an action must be taken if any two airplanes in the database are less than five miles apart. To enforce this rule, the entire database must be retrieved for access by the knowledge manager. For any database of significant size, this approach will be unrealistic. Applications which can retrieve a small portion of the database for use by the knowledge manager have been termed *partitionable.* Consequently, loose coupling will work only for static, partitionable problems.

Other applications require an approach that more tightly couples data and knowledge management. In my opinion virtually all problems that entail both a rule base and a database are not partitionable. Hence there is extreme interest in **tight coupling** approaches to knowledge management. In this section we present two approaches to tight coupling.

The first approach can be illustrated by a simple example. Suppose one has a genealogical database consisting in part of the PARENT relation as follows:

PARENT (name, offspring name)

Suppose further that one has a rule written in a Prolog-style notation, which defines an ancestor as:

ANCESTOR (x,y) := ANCESTOR (x,z), PARENT (z,y)

Loosely this means that x is an ancestor of y if there exists a person z such that x is the ancestor of z and z is the parent of y. After defining this rule, a user could ask questions about ancestors. For example, the user might want to know all the ancestors of a particular person, John, expressed again in a Prolog-style notation as:

ANCESTOR (x, John) :=

The brute force way to solve this request is to substitute John in the above rule to get:

ANCESTOR (x, John) := ANCESTOR (x,z), PARENT (z, John)

The right-hand side can be evaluated by first running a subquery to find the parents of John, which produces a list L of qualifying persons, and then solving the query by evaluating

ANCESTOR (x, L)

This will require iterative application of the above algorithm until the list of qualifying persons that is being built up as the answer fails to grow.

More efficient solutions to recursive queries such as this one are a very active area of research. Every database conference in the last couple of years has had several papers on the subject, and a sampling of techniques can be found in [IONA87, SACC87 ULLM85]. We have chosen the paper by Bancilhon and Ramikrishnan as our first paper (8.2) because it is not impossible to read and covers the major approaches.

There are many who argue that general recursive queries are not a very interesting research topic because few real-world applications contain them. The genealogical queries of interest as well as all parts-explosion queries I can think of are examples of **transitive closure** queries. Hence one should concentrate on solving transitive closure queries, and an approach along these lines is presented in [ROSE86].

The other objection that is leveled at recursive query optimization is that it sheds no light on a common application of rules. Consider for example, the following collection of rather facetious rules:

SALARY (Mike, 1000)
SALARY (Joe, x) := SALARY (Mike, x)
SALARY (George, x) := SALARY (Joe, x)
SALARY (Fred, x) := SALARY (George, x)
SALARY (Bob, x) := SALARY (Fred, x)

Loosely, this states that Bob makes the same salary as Fred who makes the same salary as George who makes the same salary as Joe who makes the same salary as Mike who earns 1000. If we now ask a query:

SALARY (Bob, x)

there are five rules that might be applicable. After it is determined that the salary of Fred must be found as a subgoal, there are still five rules that might be applicable. Obviously the brute force approach (and the one used by Prolog) would end up evaluating 25 rules to find the 5 that are required to determine the answer. The key performance indicator for this query is efficiently determining the rules that apply. This should be contrasted to the ancestor rule for which the key performance determinant is efficiently solving a single recursive rule. Avoiding a combinatorial explosion when many rules might apply is the key goal of the second paper in this section which describes the approach being taken in POSTGRES (8.3).

Note that the POSTGRES paper proposes extending a conventional query language with simple constructs to express rules. The approach is to make as few changes to a standard relational query language as possible. On the other hand, the first paper (8.2) suggests that rules should be expressed in a logic programming language. Clearly, a user will not interact with a DBMS by expressing queries in SQL and rules in a logic language. Hence a side effect of the first point of view is that users will also use a logic programming language for conventional data manipulation. Some would argue that experience with earlier languages such as Data Language Alpha [CODD71] showed the futility of languages of this sort.

In summary, the two approaches presented attack very different problems. Both are full of shortcomings. For example, it must be possible to deal intelligently with exceptions to rules [BORG85]. There is the classical example that "all birds fly," with the exception "penguins are birds that don't fly." In addition, protection and view support are, in theory, merely special purpose rule systems. Hence, they should be expressible using the same rules system available to end users. Put differently, a next-generation DBMS should not have special purpose code for protection or view support but should simply use the rule system for these functions. Next, some believe that rule driven query optimizers, along the lines of [GRAE87], are a good idea. It should be possible to use the same paradigm to express optimizer rules so that maximum leverage can be obtained from this construct. Lastly, the specification and implementation of rule support must be plausibly simple so that application builders and database administrators can understand and use the new function.

I want to close his section with two final observations. First, a rule has the general form:

If condition then action.

Often the action part of the rule is complex and might take several query language commands to express, for example,

If bad-review then fire-employee.

The specification of fire-employee is a **procedure** that contains query language commands, interspersed with conditional statements and perhaps the definition of local variables and resulting computations on them. Some have argued that procedures should be added to DBMSs as a normal data type [STON87]. The basic position is twofold:

1. Procedures are a powerful modelling tool for complex applications.

2. Procedures are necessary in transaction processing to save messages. If TP1 can be defined as a database procedure, the execution of TP1 will require only one round-trip between the application and the DBMS, whereas if the application must pass individual SQL commands to the DBMS, six or seven round-trips will be required.

The point to be made here is that a system that includes support for either procedures or rules can obtain the value of the other construct with modest added complexity. Hence both constructs or neither construct should probably be supported.

The second comment concerns a recent informal workshop [LAGU88] on future trends in database systems. The participants concluded that integration of rules and database was one of the most important current research areas. I expect rapid progress in this area over the next few years.

References

[ABAR86] Abarbanel, R., and Williams, M., "A Relational Representation for Knowledge Bases," Proc. 1st International Conference on Expert Database Systems, Charleston, S.C., Apr. 1986.

[BORG85] Borgida, A., "Language Features for Flexible Handling of Exceptions in Information Systems," ACM-TODS, Dec. 1985.

[CERI86] Ceri, S. et al., "Interfacing Relational Database and Prolog Efficiently," Proc. 1st International Conference on Expert Data Bases, Charleston, S.C., Apr. 1986.

[CLOC81] Clocksin, W., and Mellish, C., "Programming in Prolog," Springer-Verlag, West Berlin, Germany, 1981.

[CODD71] Codd, E., "A Data Base Sublanguage Founded on the Relational Calculus," Proc. 1971 ACM-SIGFIDET Workshop on Data Description, Access and Control, San Diego, Calif., Nov. 1971.

[FORG81] Forgy, C., "The OPS5 User's Manual," Carnegie-Mellon Univ., Technical Report, 1981.

[GRAE87] Graefe, G., and Dewitt, D., "The EXODUS Optimizer Generator," Proc. 1987 ACM-SIGMOD Conference on Management of Data, San Francisco, Calif., May 1987.

[IOAN87] Ioannidis, Y., and Wong, E., "Query Optimization by Simulated Annealing," Proc. 1987 ACM-SIGMOD International Conference on Management of Data, San Francisco, Calif., May 1987.

[INTE85] IntelliCorp, "KEE Software Development System Users Manual," IntelliCorp, Palo Alto, Calif., 1985.

[LAGU88] Laguna Beach Participants, "Future Directions in DBMS Research," International Computer Science Institute, Berkeley, Calif., Feb. 1988.

[ROSE86] Rosenthal, A. et al., "Traversal Recursion: A Practical Approach to Supporting Recursive Queries," Proc. 1986 ACM-SIGMOD International Conference on Management of Data, Washington, D.C., June 1986.

[SACC87] Sacca, D., and Zaniolo, C., "Magic Counting Methods," Proc. 1987 ACM-SIGMOD International Conference on Management of Data, San Francisco, Calif., May 1987.

[STON87] Stonebraker, M. et al., "Extending a Data Base System With Procedures," ACM-TODS, Sept. 1987.

[TEKN86] Teknowledge Inc., "S1 Reference Manual," Teknowledge, Palo Alto, Calif., 1986.

[ULLM85] Ullman, J., "Implementation of Logical Query Languages for Data Bases," ACM-TODS, Sept. 1985.

An Amateur's Introduction to Recursive Query Processing Strategies †

Francois Bancilhon (1)
Raghu Ramakrishnan (2)

(1): Altair
BP 105, 78153 Le Chesnay Cedex, France

(2): Computer Sciences Department
University of Wisconsin-Madison, Madison, 53706, USA

ABSTRACT

This paper surveys and compares various strategies for processing logic queries in relational databases. The survey and comparison is limited to the case of Horn Clauses with evaluable predicates but without function symbols. The paper is organized in three parts. In the first part, we introduce the main concepts and definitions. In the second, we describe the various strategies. For each strategy, we give its main characteristics, its application range and a detailed description. We also give an example of a query evaluation. The third part of the paper compares the strategies on performance grounds. We first present a set of sample rules and queries which are used for the performance comparisons, and then we characterize the data. Finally, we give an analytical solution for each query/rule system. Cost curves are plotted for specific configurations of the data.

1. Introduction

The database community has recently manifested a strong interest in the problem of evaluating "logic queries" against relational databases. This interest is motivated by two converging trends: (i) the desire to integrate database technology and artificial intelligence technology i.e., to extend database systems, to provide them with the functionality of expert systems thus creating "knowledge base systems" and (ii) the desire to integrate logic programming technology and database technology i.e., to extend the power of the interface to the database system to that of a general purpose language. The second goal is of a somewhat different nature and has found in its ranks proponents of object oriented, functional and imperative as well as logic based programming languages. The logic programming camp is relying on the fact that logic programming and relational calculus have the same underlying mathematical model, namely first order logic.

Of course, database researchers already know how to evaluate logic queries: the view mechanism, as offered by most relational systems, is a form of support of a restricted set of logic queries. But those logic queries are restricted to be non-recursive and the problem of efficiently supporting recursive queries is still open.

In the past five years, following the pioneering work by Chang, Shapiro and McKay, and Henschen and Naqvi, numerous strategies have been proposed to deal with recursion in logic queries. The positive side of this work is that there are a lot of algorithms offered to solve *the* problem. The negative side is that we do not know how to make a choice of an algorithm. It seems reasonable to say that all these strategies can

† This is a revised version of the paper that appeared under the same title in the proceedings of SIGMOD 86.
This work was performed while the first author was at MCC, Austin, and the second author was at the University of Texas at Austin and visiting MCC.

only be compared on three grounds: functionality (i.e., application domain), performance and ease of implementation. However, each of these algorithms is described at a different level of detail, and it is sometimes difficult to understand their differences. In fact, we shall claim later in this paper that some of them are indeed identical. Each comes with little or no performance analysis, and the application domain is not always easy to identify. We try in this paper to evaluate these algorithms with respect to these three criteria. We describe all the algorithms at the same level of detail and demonstrate their behavior on common examples. This is not always easy to do since some of them are fairly well formalized while others are merely sketched as an idea.

For each one of them, we state in simple terms the application domain. Finally, we give a first simple comparison of the performance of these algorithms. Choosing a simple set of typical queries, a simple characterization of the data and a simple cost function, we give an analytical evaluation of the cost of each strategy. The results give a first insight into the respective value of all the proposed strategies.

The rest of the paper is organized as follows: In section 2 we present our definitions and notations, and introduce the main ideas. In section 3 we present the main features of the strategies, and describe each one individually, and finally, in section 4, we present the performance evaluation methodology and results.

2. Logic Databases

2.1. An Example

Let us start by discussing informally an example. Here is what we call a "logic database":

parent(cain,adam).
parent(abel,adam).
parent(cain,eve).
parent(abel,eve).
parent(sem,abel).
ancestor(X,Y) :- ancestor(X,Z),ancestor(Z,Y).
ancestor(X,Y) :- parent(X,Y).
generation(adam,1).
generation(X,I) :- generation(Y,J), parent(X,Y),J=I-1.
generation(X,I) :- generation(Y,J), parent(Y,X),J=I+1.

Note that this is a purely syntactic object. In this database, we have a set of predicate or relation names (parent, ancestor and generation), a set of arithmetic predicates (I=J+1, I=J-1) and a set of constants (adam, eve, cain, sem and abel). Finally, we have a set of variables (X,Y and Z). The database consists of a set of sentences ending with a period. "parent(cain,adam)" is a fact, and "ancestor(X,Y) :- parent(X,Y)" is a rule.

Let us now associate a meaning with the database. We first associate with each constant an object from the real world: thus, with "adam" we associate the individual whose name is "adam". Then, we associate with each arithmetic predicate name the corresponding arithmetic operator. Then we can interpret intuitively each fact and each rule. For instance we interpret "parent(cain,adam)" by saying that the predicate parent is true for the couple (cain,adam), and we interpret the rule

ancestor(X,Y) :- ancestor(X,Z), ancestor(Z,Y).

by saying that if there are three objects X, Y and Z such that ancestor(X,Z) is true and ancestor(Z,Y) is true then ancestor(X,Y) is true.

This leads to an interpretation which associates with each predicate a set of tuples. For instance with the predicate ancestor we associate the interpretation {(cain,adam), (abel,adam), (cain,eve), (abel,eve), (sem,abel), (sem,adam), (sem,eve)}, and with the predicate generation we associate the interpretation {(adam,1), (eve,1), (cain,2), (abel,2), (sem,3)}

The problem is to answer queries, given the logic database. For instance given a query of the form generation(sem,?) or ancestor(?,adam), how do we find the answer: generation(sem,3) and {ancestor(cain,adam), ancestor(abel,adam), ancestor(sem,adam)}?

Let us now formalize all the notions encountered in this example and define a logic database. We first define it syntactically, then we attach an interpretation to this syntax.

2.2. Syntax of a Logic Database

We first define four sets of names: *variable* names, *constant* names, *predicate* or *relation* names and *evaluable predicate* names.

We adopt the Prolog convention of denoting variables by strings of characters starting with an upper case letter and constants by strings of characters starting with a lower case letter or integers. For instance X1, Father and Y are variables, while john, salary and 345 are constants.

We use identifiers starting with lower case letters for predicates names and relation names (evaluable and non-evaluable).

We use the term relation (from database terminology) and predicate (from logic terminology) indifferently to represent the same object. We shall however interpret them differently: a relation will be interpreted by a set of tuples and a predicate by a true/false function. There is a fixed arity associated with each relation/predicate.

The set of evaluable predicate names is a subset of the set of predicate names. We will not be concerned with their syntactic recognition; in the examples it will be clear from the name we use. The main examples of evaluable predicate names are arithmetic predicates. For instance, sum, difference and greater-than are examples of evaluable predicates of arity 3, 3 and 2 respectively, while parent and ancestor are non-evaluable predicates of arity 2.

A *literal* is of the form p(t1,t2,...,tn) where p is a predicate name of arity n and each ti is a constant or a variable. For instance father(john,X), ancestor(Y,Z), id(john,25,austin) and sum(X,Y,Z) are literals. An *instantiated* literal is one which does not contain any variables. For instance id(john,doe,25,austin) is an instantiated literal, while father(john,Father) is not.

We allow ourselves to write evaluable literals using functions and equality for the purpose of clarity. For instance, Z = X+Y denotes sum(X,Y,Z), I = J+1 denotes sum(J,1,I), and X > 0 denotes greater-than(X,0).

If p(t1,t2,...,tn) is a literal, we call (t1,t2,...,tn) a *tuple*.

A *rule* is a statement of the form

p :- q1,q2,...,qn.

where p and the qi's are literals such that the predicate name in p is a non-evaluable predicate. p is called the *head* of the rule, and each of the qi's is called a *goal*. The conjunction of the qi's is the *body* of the rule. We have adopted the Prolog notation of representing implication by ':-' and conjunction by ','. For instance

uncle(john,X) :- brother(X,Y), parent(john,Y).

is a rule with head "uncle(john,X)" and body "brother(X,Y), parent(john,Y)".

A *ground clause* is a rule in which the body is empty. A *fact* is a ground clause which contains no variables. For instance

loves(X,john).
loves(mary,susan).

are ground clauses, but only the second of these is a fact.

A *database* is a set of rules; note that this set is not ordered. Given a database, we can partition it into a set of facts and the set of all other rules. The set of facts is called the *extensional* database, and the set of all other rules is called the *intensional* database.

2.3. Interpretation of a Logic Database

Up to now our definitions have been purely syntactical. Let us now give an interpretation of a database. This will be done by associating with each relation name in the database a set of instantiated tuples. We first assume that with each evaluable predicate p is associated a set natural(p) of instantiated tuples which we call its *natural interpretation.* For instance, with the predicate *sum* is associated an infinite set of all the 3-tuples (x,y,z) of integers such that the sum of x and y is z. In general the natural interpretation of an evaluable predicate is infinite.

Given a database, an *interpretation* of this database is a mapping which associates with each relation name a set of instantiated tuples.

A *model* of a database is an interpretation I such that:

1. for each evaluable predicate p, I(p) = natural(p), and,
2. for any rule, p(t) :- q1(t1),q2(t2),...,qn(tn), for any instantiation σ of the variables of the rule such that σ(ti) is in the interpretation of qi for all i then σ(t) is is in the interpretation of p.

This is simply a way of saying that, in a model, if the right hand side is true then the left hand side is also true. This implies that for every fact p(x) of the database the tuple x belongs to the interpretation of p.

Of course, for a given database there are many models. The nice property of Horn Clauses is that among all these models there is a *least* one (least in the sense of set inclusion), which is the one we choose as *the* model of the database (Van Emden and Kowalski [1976]). Therefore from now on, when we talk about the model or the interpretation of a database, we mean its least model.

Notice that because of the presence of evaluable arithmetic predicates the minimal model is, in general, not finite.

Let p be an n-ary predicate. An *adornment* of p is a sequence *a* of length n of b's and f's (Ullman [1985]). For instance bbf is an adornment of a ternary predicate, and fbff is an adornment of predicate of arity 4. An adornment is to be interpreted intuitively as follows: the i-th variable of p is bound (respectively free) if the i-th element of *a* is b (respectively f). Let p(x1,x2,...,xn) be a literal, an adornment a1a2...an of that literal is an adornment of p such that :

(i) if xi is a constant then ai is b,
(ii) if xi = xj then ai = aj

We denote adornments by superscripts. A *query form* is an adorned predicate. Examples of query forms are $father^{bf}$, id^{bffb} .

A *query* is a query form and an instantiation of the bound variables. We denote it by an adorned literal where all the bound positions are filled with the corresponding constants and the free positions are filled by distinct free variables. Therefore $father^{bf}$ (john,X) and id^{bffb} (john,X,Y,25) are queries. The distinction between queries and query forms are that query forms are actually compiled, and at run-time their parameters will be instantiated. Notice that father(X,X) is not a query form in this formalism.

The *answer* to a query q(t) is the set: {q(σ(t)) | σ is an instantiation of t, and σ(t) is in the interpretation of q}.

2.4. Structuring and Representing the Database

A predicate which only appears in the intensional database is a *derived* predicate. A predicate which appears only in the extensional database or in the body of a rule is a *base* predicate.

For performance reasons, it is good to decompose the database into a set of pure base predicates (which can then be stored using a standard DBMS) and a set of pure derived predicates. Fortunately, such a decomposition is always possible, because every database can be rewritten as an "equivalent" database containing only base and derived predicates. By equivalent, we mean that all the predicate names of the original database appear in the modified database and have the same interpretation.

We obtain this equivalent database in the following way: consider any predicate p that is neither base nor derived. By definition, we have a set of facts for p, and p appears on the left of some rules. So we simply introduce a new predicate p_ext and do the following:

1. replace p by p_ext in each fact of p,
2. add a new rule of the form p(X1,X2,...,Xn) :- p_ext(X1,X2,...,Xn) where n is the arity of p.

Example:

```
father(a,b).
parent(b,c).
grandfather(b,d).
grandfather(X,Y) :- father(X,Z),parent(Z,Y).
```

becomes:

```
father(a,b).
parent(b,c).
grandfather_ext(b,d).
grandfather(X,Y) :- father(X,Z),parent(Z,Y).
grandfather(X,Y) :- grandfather_ext(X,Y).
```

Most authors have chosen to describe a set of rules through some kind of graph formalism. Predicate Connection Graphs, as presented in McKay and Shapiro [1981], represent the relationship between rules and predicates. Rule/goal graphs, as presented in Ullman [1985], carry more information because predicates and rules are adorned by their variable bindings. We have chosen here to keep the rule/goal graph terminology while using unadorned predicates.

The *rule/goal* graph has two sets of nodes: square nodes which are associated with predicates, and oval nodes which are associated with rules. If there is a rule of the form

r: p:- p1,p2,...,pn

in the intensional database, then there is an arc going from node r to node p, and for each predicate pi there is an arc from node pi to node r.

Here is an example of an intensional database. For the sake of simplicity, we have omitted the variables in the rules:

```
r1   p1 :- p3,p4
r2   p2 :- p4,p5
r3   p3 :- p6,p4,p3
r4   p4 :- p5,p3
r5   p3 :- p6
r6   p5 :- p5,p7
r7   p5 :- p6
r8   p7 :- p8,p9
```

The rule/goal graph is:

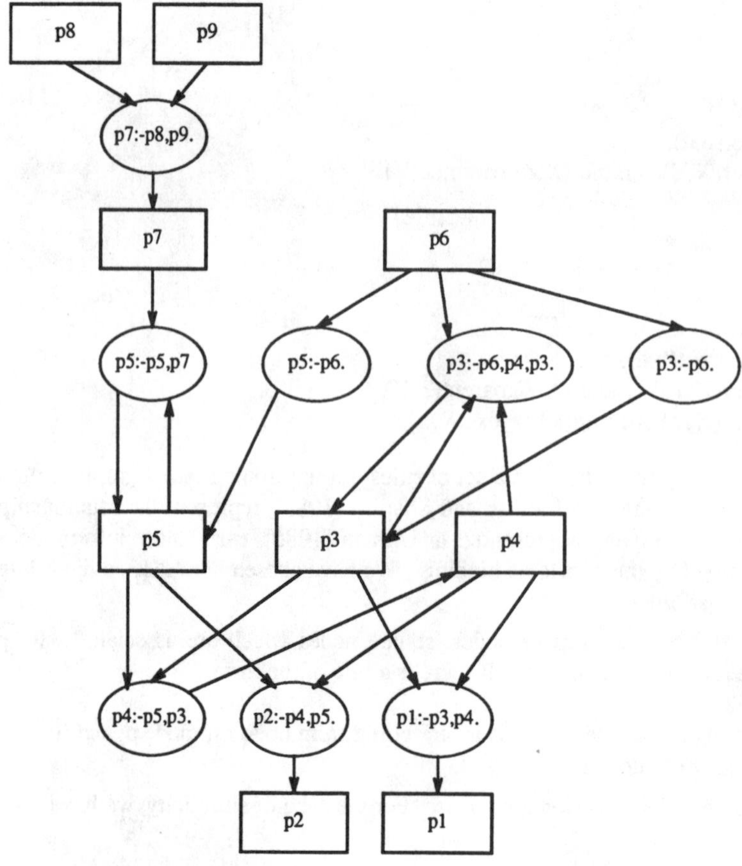

2.5. Recursion

Recursion is often discussed in the single rule context. For the purpose of clarity and simplicity, let us first give some temporary definitions in this context. We say that a rule is recursive if it is of the form

p(t) :- ...,p(t'),... .

For instance the rule

ancestor(X,Y) :- ancestor(X,Z),parent(Z,Y).

is recursive.

An interesting subcase is that of linear rules. Linear rules play an important role because (i) there is a belief that most "real life" recursive rules are indeed linear, and (ii) algorithms have been developed to handle them efficiently.

We say that a rule is linear if it is recursive, and the recursive predicate appears once and only once on the right. This property is sometime referred to as regularity (Chang [1981]). We believe the term linear to be more appropriate, and we think that regularity should be kept for another concept (which is not defined here).

For instance the rule:

sg(X,Y) :- p(X,XP),p(Y,YP),sg(XP,YP).

is linear, while the rule

ancestor(X,Y) :- ancestor(X,Z),ancestor(Z,Y).

is not.

These definitions are fairly simple in the single rule context. They are a little more involved in the context of a set of rules where properties have to be attached to predicates instead of rules. Consider the following database:

p(X,Y) :- b1(X,Z),q(Z,Y).
q(X,Y) :- p(X,Z),b2(Z,Y).

Neither of the rules are recursive according to the above definition, while clearly both predicates p and q are recursive.

We now come to the general definitions of recursion in the multirule context. Let p and q be two predicates. We say that p *derives* q (denoted p → q) if it occurs in the body of a rule whose head predicate is q. We define →+ to be the transitive closure (*not* the reflexive transitive closure) of →. A predicate p is said to be *recursive* if p →+ p. Two predicates p and q are *mutually recursive* if p →+ q and q →+ p. It can be easily shown that mutual recursion is an equivalence relation on the set of recursive predicates. Therefore the set of recursive predicates can be decomposed into disjoint blocs of mutually recursive predicates.

Given a set of rules, we say that the rule
p :- p1,p2,...,pn is *recursive* iff there exists pi in the body of the rule which is mutually recursive to p.

A recursive rule p :- p1,p2,...,pn is *linear* if there is one and only one pi in the body of the rule which is mutually recursive to p. A set of rules is *linear* if every recursive rule in it is linear. For instance, the following system is linear:

r1 p(X,Y) :- p1(X,Z),q(Z,Y).
r2 q(X,Y) :- p(X,Z),p2(Z,Y).
r3 p(X,Y) :- b3(X,Y).
r4 p1(X,Y) :- b1(X,Z),p1(Z,Y).
r5 p1(X,Y) :- b4(X,Y).
r6 p2(X,Y) :- b2(X,Z),p2(Z,Y).
r7 p2(X,Y) :- b5(X,Y).

The set of recursive predicates is {p,q,p1,p2}, the set of base predicates is {b1,b2,b3,b4,b5}. The blocks of mutually recursive predicates are {[p,q],[p1],[p2]}. The recursive rules are r1, r2, r4 and r6, and the system is linear even though rules r1 and r2 both have two recursive predicates on their right.

We say that two recursive rules are mutually recursive iff the predicates in their heads are mutually recursive. This defines an equivalence relation among the recursive rules.

Thus mutual recursion defines an equivalence class among recursive predicates and among the recursive rules, (Bancilhon [1985]). Therefore, it groups together all predicates which are mutually recursive to one another, i.e which must be evaluated as a whole. It also groups together all the rules which participate in evaluating those blocks of predicates. Let us now see how this can be represented in the rule/goal graph. We define the *reduced rule/goal graph* as follows:

Square nodes are associated with non-recursive predicates or with blocks of mutually recursive predicates and, oval nodes are associated with non-recursive rules or with blocks of mutually recursive rules. The graph essentially describes the non-recursive part of the database by grouping together all the predicates which are mutually recursive to one another and isolating the recursive parts. For every non-recursive rule of the form r: p:- p1,p2,...,pn, there is an arc going from node r to node p (if p is non-recursive), or to node [p], which is the node representing the set of predicates mutually recursive to p (if p is recursive). For each non-recursive predicate pi, there is an arc from the node pi to the node r, and for each recursive predicate pj there is an arc going from [pj] the node representing the set of predicates mutually recursive to pj.

Finally, each bloc of recursive rules [r] is uniquely associated to a set of mutually recursive predicates [p], and we draw an arc from [p] to [r] and an arc from [r] to [p]. We also draw an arc from q (if q is non-recursive) or from [q] (if q is recursive) to [r] if there is a rule in [r] which has q in its body. This grouping of recursive predicates in blocks of strongly connected components is presented in Morris et al. [1986].

Here is the representation of the previous database:

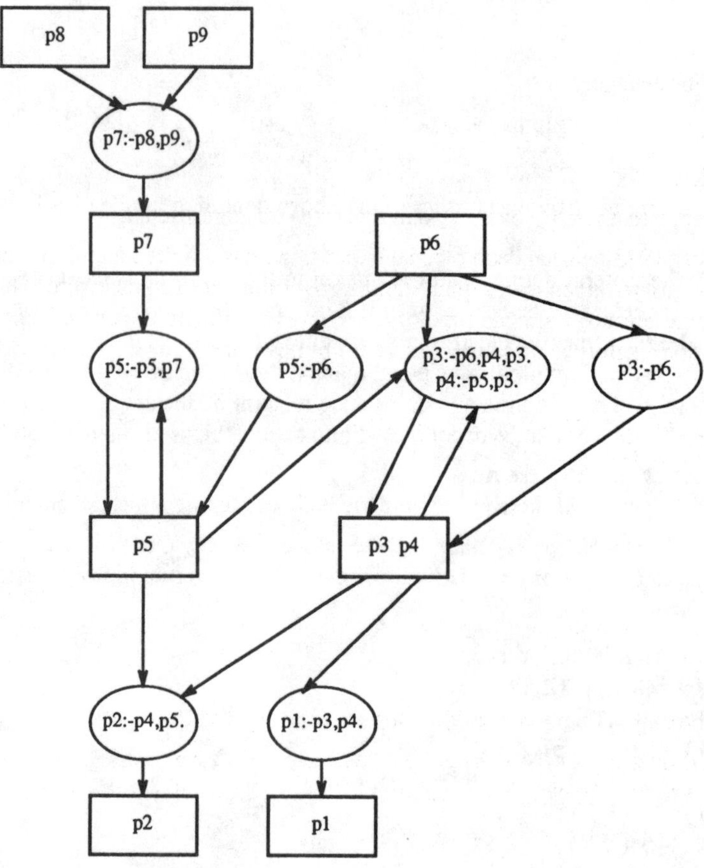

2.6. Safety of Queries

Given a query q in a database D, we say that q is *safe* in D if the answer to q is finite. Obviously unsafe queries are highly undesirable.

Sources of unsafeness are of two kinds

(i) the evaluable arithmetic predicates are interpreted by infinite tables. Therefore they are unsafe by definition. For instance the query greater-than(27,X) is unsafe.

(ii) rules with free variables in the head which do not appear in the body are a source of unsafeness in the presence of evaluable arithmetic predicates (the arithmetic predicates provide an infinite underlying domain, and the variable from the head of the rule which does not appear on the right ranges over that domain). Thus for instance, in the system

```
good-salary(X) :- X > 100000.
like(X,Y) :- nice(X).
nice(john).
```

the query like(john,X)? is unsafe because, in the minimal model of the database like(john,x) is true for every integer x. Note that if the first rule was not there, like(john,X)? would be safe and have answer like(john,john).

The problem of safety has received a lot of attention recently (Afrati et al. [1986], Kifer and Lozinskii [1987], Krishnamurthy et al. [1988], Ramakrishnan et al. [1987], Ullman [1985], Ullman and Van Gelder [1985], Van Gelder and Topor [1987], Zaniolo [1986]). We shall not survey those results here but merely present some simple sufficient syntactic conditions to guarantee safety. A rule is *range restricted* if every variable of the head appears somewhere in the body. Thus in this system:

```
r1   loves(X,Y) :- nice(X).
r2   loves(X,Y) :- nice(X),human(Y).
```

r1, which corresponds to "nice people love everything", is not range restricted while r2, which corresponds to "nice people love all humans", is. Obviously, every ground rule which is not a fact is not range restricted. For instance

loves(john,X).

is not range restricted.

A set of rules is range restricted if every rule in this set is range restricted.

It is known (Reiter [1978]) that if each evaluable predicate has a finite natural interpretation, and if the set of rules is range restricted, then every query defined over this set of rules is safe. This applies obviously to the case where there are no evaluable predicates. However, if there are evaluable predicates with infinite natural interpretations, safety is no longer assured. We now present a simple sufficient condition for safety in the presence of such predicates.

A rule is *strongly safe* iff: (1) it is range restricted, and (2) every variable in an evaluable predicate term also appears in at least one base predicate.

For example, the rule

well-paid(X) :- has-salary(X,Y), Y > 100K.

is strongly safe, whereas

great-salary(X) :- X > 100K.

is not strongly safe.

A set of rules is strongly safe if every rule in this set is strongly safe.

Any query defined over a set of strongly safe rules is safe. However, while this is a sufficient condition, it is not necessary. We can develop better conditions for testing safety, or leave it to the user to ensure that his queries are safe.

2.7. Effective Computability.

Safety, in general, does not guarantee that the query can be effectively computed. Consider for instance:

p1(1,X,Y) :- X≥Y.
p2(X,Y,2) :- X≤Y.
p(X,Y) :- p1(X,Z,Z),p2(Z,Z,Y).

The query p(X,Y) is safe (the answer is {p(1,2)}), but there is no general evaluation strategy which will compute the answer and terminate.

However, strongly safe rules are guaranteed to be safe *and* effectively computable.

In fact, while we might often be willing to let the user ensure that his queries are safe, it is desirable to ensure that the query can be computed without materializing "infinite" intermediate results. We now present a sufficient condition for ensuring this.

We first need some information about the way arithmetic predicates can propagate bindings. So we characterize each arithmetic predicate by a set of *safety dependencies* (Zaniolo [1986]). A safety dependency is a couple (X → Y) where X is a set of attributes and Y is a set of attributes. It is to be interpreted intuitively as "if the values of the X attributes are fixed then there is a finite number of values of the Y attributes associated with them". Therefore, while their semantics is different from that of functional dependencies, they behave in the same fashion (and have the same axiomatization). Of course, we assume that the natural interpretation of the evaluable predicate satisfies the set of safety dependencies.

For instance, the ternary arithmetic predicate "sum" has the safety dependencies:

{1,2} → {3}
{1,3} → {2}
{2,3} → {1}

while the arithmetic predicate "greater than" has only trivial safety dependencies.

Now consider a rule, and define each variable in the body to be *secure* if it appears in a non-evaluable predicate in the body or if it appears in position i in an evaluable predicate p and there is a subset I of the variables of p which are secure and I →{i}. Note that the definition is recursive.

A rule is *bottom-up evaluable* if

1. it is range restricted, and
2. every variable in the body is secure.

For instance:

p(X,Y) :- Y=X+1, X=Y1+Y2, p(Y1,Y2).

is bottom-up evaluable because (i) Y1 and Y2 are secure (they appear in p which is non-evaluable), (ii) in X=Y1+Y2, the safety dependency {Y1,Y2} → {X} holds, therefore X is secure, and (iii) in Y=X+1, the safety dependency {X} → {Y} holds, therefore Y is secure.

On the contrary

p(X,Y) :- X>Y1, q(Y1,Y).

is not bottom-up evaluable because X is not secure.

A set of rules is bottom-up evaluable if every rule in this set is bottom-up evaluable.

Any computation using only a set of bottom-up evaluable rules can be carried out without materializing infinite intermediate results. The computation proceeds in a strictly bottom-up manner, using values for the body variables to produce values for the head variables. The bottom-up evaluability criterion ensures that the set of values for body variables is finite at each step. However, there may be an infinite number of steps. For example, if we repeatedly apply the bottom-up evaluable rule given above, at each step we have a finite number of values (in this case, a unique value) for Y1 and Y2, and hence for X and Y. However, we can apply the rule an infinite number of times, producing new values for X and Y at each step.

3. Classification of the Strategies

In the past five years, a large number of strategies to deal with Horn rules have been presented in the literature. A strategy is defined by (i) an application domain (i.e., a class of rules for which it applies) and (ii) an algorithm for replying to queries given such a set of rules.

In studying the strategies, we found that the methods were described at different levels of detail and using different formalisms, that they were sometimes very difficult to understand (and sometimes were understood differently by subsequent authors), that the application domain was not always very clearly defined, and that no performance evaluation was given for any of the strategies, which left the choice of a given strategy completely open when the application domain was the same. Finally, we found that some of the strategies were in fact the same.

We think that the strategies should be compared according to the following criteria (i) size of the application domain, (the larger the better), (ii) performance of the strategy, (the faster the better) and (iii) ease of implementation (the simpler the better). While the last criterion is somehow subjective, the first two should be quantifiable. In this section, we give a complete description of our understanding of the strategies and of their application domains, and we demonstrate each one of them through an example. As much as possible, we have tried to use the same example, except for some ''specialized'' strategies where we have picked a specific example which exhibits its typical behavior.

3.1. Characteristics of the Strategies

3.1.1. Query Evaluation vs. Query Optimization

Let us first distinguish between two approaches: one first class of strategies consists of an actual query evaluation algorithm, i.e. a program which, given a query and a database, will produce the answer to the query. We will call these *methods*. Representatives of this class are: *Henschen-Naqvi, Query/Subquery (QSQ)* or *Extension Table, APEX, Prolog, Naive Evaluation* and *Semi-Naive Evaluation.*

The strategies in the second class assume an underlying simple strategy (which is in fact naive or semi-naive evaluation) and optimize the rules to make their evaluation more efficient. They can all be described as *term rewriting systems.* These include: *Aho-Ullman, Counting and Reverse Counting, Magic Sets,*

Generalized Magic Sets and *Kifer-Lozinskii*.

Note that this distinction is somehow arbitrary: each of the optimization strategies could be described as a method (when adding to it naive or semi-naive evaluation). However, this decomposition has two advantages: (i) it *might* make sense from an implementation point of view to realize the optimization strategies as term rewriting systems on top of an underlying simpler method such as naive evaluation, and (ii) from a pedagogical standpoint, they are much easier to understand this way, because presenting them as term rewriting systems indeed captures their essence.

The subsequent characteristics only relate to pure methods.

3.1.2. Interpretation vs. Compilation

A method can be *interpreted* or *compiled*. The notion is somehow fuzzy, and difficult to characterize formally. We say that the strategy is compiled if it consists of two phases: (i) a compilation phase, which accesses only the intensional database, and which generates an "object program" of some form, and (ii) an execution phase, which executes the object program against the facts only. A second characteristic of compiled methods is that all the database query forms (i.e., the query forms on base relations which are directly sent to the DBMS) are generated during the compilation phase. This condition is very important, because it allows the DBMS to precompile the the query forms. Otherwise the database query forms are repetitively compiled by the DBMS during the execution of the query, which is a time consuming operation. If these two conditions do not hold, we say that the strategy is interpreted. In this case, no object code is produced and there is a fixed program, the "interpreter", which runs against the query, the set of rules and the set of facts.

3.1.3. Recursion vs. Iteration

A rule processing strategy can be *recursive* or *iterative*. It is iterative if the "target program" (in case of a compiled approach) or the "interpreter" (in case of the interpreted approach) is iterative. It is recursive if this program is recursive, i.e., uses a stack as a control mechanism. Note that in the iterative methods, the data we deal with is statically determined. For instance, if we use temporary relations to store intermediate results, there are a finite number of such temporary relations. On the contrary, in recursive methods the number of temporary relations maintained by the system is unbounded.

3.1.4. Potentially Relevant Facts

Let D be a database and q be a query. A fact p(a) is *relevant* to the query iff there exists a derivation p(a) →* q(b) for some b in the answer set. The notion of relevant fact was introduced in Lozinskii [1985], we use it here with a somewhat different meaning. If we know all the relevant facts in advance, instead of using the database to reply to the query, we can use the relevant part of the database only, thus cutting down on the set of facts to be processed. A *sufficient set of relevant facts* is a set of facts such that replacing the database by this set of facts gives the same answer to the query. Unfortunately, in general there does not exist a unique minimal set of facts as the following example shows:

```
suspect(X) :- long-hair(X).
suspect(X) :- alien(X).
long-hair(antoine).
alien(antoine).
```

Minimal sets of facts with respect to the query suspect(X)? are {long-hair(antoine)} and {alien(antoine)}. The second unfortunate thing about relevant facts is that it is in general impossible to find all the relevant facts in advance without spending as much effort as in replying to the query. Thus, all methods have a way of finding a super-set of relevant facts. We call this set the *set of potentially relevant facts*. A set of potentially relevant facts is *valid* if it contains a sufficient set of relevant facts. An obvious but not very interesting valid set is the set of all facts of the database.

3.1.5. Top Down vs. Bottom Up

Consider the following set of rules and the query:

ancestor(X,Y) :- parent(X,Z), ancestor(Z,Y).
ancestor(X,Y) :- parent(X,Y).
query(X) :- ancestor(john,X).

We can view each of these rules as productions in a grammar. In this context, the database predicates (parent in this example) appear as terminal symbols, and the derived predicates (ancestor in this example) appear as the non-terminal symbols. Finally, to pursue the analogy, we shall take the distinguished symbol to be query(X). Of course, we know that the analogy does not hold totally, for two reasons: (i) the presence of variables and constants in the literals and (ii) the lack of order between the literals of a rule (for instance "parent(X,Z), ancestor(Z,Y)" and "ancestor(Z,Y), parent(X,Z)" have the same meaning). But we shall ignore these differences, and use the analogy informally.

Let us now consider the language generated by this "grammar". It consists of

{parent(john,X);
parent(john,X),parent(X,X1);
parent(john,X),parent(X,X1),parent(X1,X2);
...}

This language has two interesting properties: (i) it consists of first order sentences involving only base predicates, i.e., each word of this language can be directly evaluated against the database, and (ii) if we evaluate each word of this language against the database and take the union of all these results, we get the answer to the query.

There is a minor problem here: the language is not finite, and we would have to evaluate an infinite number of first order sentences. To get out of this difficulty, we use termination conditions which tell us when to stop. An example of such a termination condition is: if one word of the language evaluates to the empty set, then all the subsequent words will also evaluate to the empty set, so we can stop generating new words. Another example of a termination condition is: if a word evaluates to a set of tuples, and all these tuples are already in the evaluation of the words preceding it, then no new tuple will ever be produced by the evaluation of any subsequent word, thus we can stop at this point.

All query evaluation methods in fact do the following:

(i) generate the language, (ii) while the language is generated, evaluate all its sentences and (iii) at each step, check for the termination condition.

Therefore, there are essentially two classes of methods: those which generate the language bottom up, and those which generate the language top-down. The bottom-up strategies start from the terminals (i.e., the base relations) and keep assembling them to produce non-terminals (i.e derived relations) until they generate the distinguished symbol (i.e., the query). The top-down strategies start from the distinguished symbol (the query) and keep expanding it by applying the rules to the non-terminals (derived relations). As we shall see, top-down strategies are often more efficient because they "know" which query is being solved, but they are more complex. Bottom up strategies are simpler, but they compute a lot of useless results because they do not know what query they are evaluating.

4. The Methods

We shall use the same example for most of the methods. The intensional database and query are:

R1 ancestor(X,Y) :- parent(X,Z),ancestor(Z,Y).
R2 ancestor(X,Y) :- parent(X,Y).
R3 query(X) :- ancestor(aa,X).

The extensional database is:

parent(a,aa).
parent(a,ab).
parent(aa,aaa).
parent(aa,aab).
parent(aaa,aaaa).
parent(c,ca).

4.1. Naive Evaluation

Naive Evaluation is a bottom-up, compiled, iterative strategy.

Its application domain is the set of bottom-up evaluable rules.

In a first phase, the rules which derive the query are compiled into an iterative program. The compilation process uses the reduced rule/goal graph. It first selects all the rules which derive the query. A temporary relation is assigned to each derived predicate in this set of rules. A statement which computes the value of the output predicate from the value of the input predicates is associated with each rule node in the graph. With each set of mutually recursive rules, there is associated a loop which applies the rules in that set until no new tuple is generated. Each temporary relation is initialized to the empty set. Then computation proceeds from the base predicates capturing the nodes of the graph.

In this example, the rules which derive the query are {R1, R2, R3}, and there are two temporary relations: ancestor and query. The method consists in applying R2 to parent, producing a new value for ancestor, then applying R1 to ancestor until no new tuple is generated, then applying R3.

The object program is:

begin
initialize ancestor to the empty set;
evaluate (ancestor(X,Y) :- parent(X,Y));
insert the result in ancestor;
while "new tuples are generated" **do**
  begin
  evaluate (ancestor(X,Y) :- parent(X,Z), ancestor(Z,Y)) using the current value of ancestor;
  insert the result in ancestor
  end;
evaluate (query(X) :- ancestor(aa,X));
insert the result in query
end.

The execution of the program against the data goes as follows:

Step 1: Apply R2.
The resulting state is:
ancestor = {(a,aa), (a,ab), (aa,aaa), (aa,aab), (aaa,aaaa), (c,ca)}
query = {}

Step 2: Apply R1.
The following new tuples are generated:
ancestor: {(a,aaa), (a,aab), (aa,aaaa)}
And the resulting state is:
ancestor = {(a,aa), (a,ab), (aa,aaa), (aa,aab), (aaa,aaaa), (c,ca), (a,aaa), (a,aab), (aa,aaaa)}
query = {}

New tuples have been generated so we continue:

Step 3: Apply R1.
The following tuples are generated:
ancestor: {(a,aaa), (a,aab), (aa,aaaa), (a,aaaa)}
The new state is:

ancestor = {(a,aa), (a,ab), (aa,aaa), (aa,aab), (aaa,aaaa), (c,ca), (a,aaa), (a,aab), (aa,aaaa), (a,aaaa)}
query = {}

Because (a,aaaa) is new, we continue:

Step 4: Apply R1.
The following tuples are generated:
ancestor: {(a,aaa), (a,aab), (aa,aaaa), (a,aaaa)}

Because there are no new tuples, the state does not change and we move to R3.

Step 5: Apply R3.
The following tuples are produced:
query: {(aa,aaa), (aa,aaaa)}
The new state is:
ancestor = {(a,aa), (a,ab), (aa,aaa), (aa,aab), (aaa,aaaa), (c,ca), (a,aaa), (a,aab), (aa,aaaa), (a,aaaa)}
query = {(aa,aaa), (aa,aaaa), (aa,aab)}.

The algorithm terminates.

In this example, we note the following problems: (i) the entire relation is evaluated, i.e., the set of potentially relevant facts is the set of facts of the base predicates which derive the query, and (ii) step 3 completely duplicates step 2.

Naive evaluation is the most widely described method in the literature. It has been presented in a number of papers under different forms. The inference engine of SNIP, presented in McKay and Shapiro [1981], is in fact an interpreted version of naive evaluation. The method described in Chang [1981], while based on a very interesting language paradigm and restricted to linear systems, is a compiled version of naive evaluation based on relational algebra. The method in Marque-Pucheu [1983] is a compiled version of naive evaluation using a different algebra of relations. The method in Bayer [1985] is another description of naive evaluation. The framework presented in Delobel [1986] also uses naive evaluation as its inference strategy. SNIP is, to our knowledge, the only existing implementation in the general case.

4.2. Semi-Naive Evaluation

Semi-naive evaluation is a bottom-up, compiled and iterative strategy.

Its application range is the set of bottom-up evaluable rules.

This method uses the same approach as naive evaluation, but tries to cut down on the number of duplications. It behaves exactly as naive evaluation, except for the loop mechanism where it tries to be smarter.

Let us first try to give an idea of the method as an extension of naive evaluation. Let p be a recursive predicate; consider a recursive rule having p as a head predicate and let us write this rule:

$$p :- \phi(p1,p2,...,pn,q1,q2,...,qm).$$

where ϕ is a first order formula, p1,p2,...,pn are mutually recursive to p, and q1,q2,..,qm are base or derived predicates, which are not mutually recursive to p.

In the naive evaluation strategy, all the qi's are fully evaluated when we start computing p and the pi's. On the other hand p and the pi's are all evaluated inside the same loop (together with the rest of predicates mutually recursive to p).

Let pj(i) be the value of the predicate pj at the i-th iteration of the loop. At this iteration, we compute

$$\phi(p1(i),p2(i),...,pn(i),q1,q2,...,qm).$$

During that same iteration each pj receives a set of new tuples. Let us call this new set dpj(i). Thus the value of pj at the beginning of step (i+1) is pj(i) + dpj(i) (where + denotes union).

At step (i+1) we evaluate

$$\phi((p1(i)+dp1(i)),...,(pn(i)+dpn(i)),q1,...,qm),$$

which, of course, recomputes the previous expression (because ϕ is monotonic).

The ideal however, is to compute only the *new* tuples i.e the expression:

$$d\phi(p1(i),dp1(i),...,pn(i),dpn(i),q1,...,qm) = \phi((p1(i)+dp1(i)),...,(pn(i)+dpn(i)),q1,...,qm) - \phi(p1(i),...,pn(i),q1,...,qm)$$

The basic principle of the semi-naive method is the evaluation of the differential of ϕ instead of the entire ϕ at each step. The problem is to come up with a first order expression for $d\phi$, which does not contain any difference operator. Let us assume there is such an expression, and describe the algorithm. With each recursive predicate p are associated four temporary relations p.before, p.after, dp.before and dp.after. The object program for a loop is as follows:

```
while "the state changes" do
 begin
 for all mutually recursive predicates p do
   begin
   initialize dp.after to the empty set;
   initialize p.after to p.before;
   end
 for each mutually recursive rule do
   begin
   evaluate dφ(p1,dp1,...,pn,dpn,q1,...,qn) using the current values of
   pi.before for pi and of dpi.before for dpi;
   add the resulting tuples to dp.after;
   add the resulting tuples to p.after
   end
 end.
```

All we have to do now is provide a way to generate $d\phi$ from ϕ. The problem is not solved in its entirety and only a number of transformations are known. In Bancilhon [1985], some of them are given in terms of relational algebra.

It should be noted however, that for the method to work, the only property we have to guarantee is that:

$$\phi(p1+dp1,...) - \phi(p1,...) \subseteq d\phi(p1,dp1,...) \subseteq \phi(p1+dp1,...)$$

Clearly, the closer $d\phi(p1,dp1,...)$ is to $(\phi(p1+dp1,...) - \phi(p1,...))$, the better the optimization is. In the worse case, where we use ϕ for $d\phi$, semi-naive evaluation behaves as naive evaluation. Here are some simple examples of rewrite rules:

if $\phi(p,q) = p(X,Y),q(Y,Z)$, **then** $d\phi(p,dp,q) = dp(X,Y),q(Y,Z)$

More generally when ϕ is linear in p, the expression for $d\phi$ is obtained by replacing p by dp.

if $\phi(p1,p2) = p1(X,Y),p2(Y,Z)$,
then $d\phi(p,dp) = p1(X,Y),dp2(Y,Z)+dp1(X,Y),p2(Y,Z)+dp1(X,Y),dp2(Y,Z)$

Note that this is not an exact differential but a reasonable approximation.

The idea of semi-naive evaluation underlies many papers. A complete description of the method based on relational algebra is given in Bancilhon [1985]. The idea is also present in Bayer [1985].

It should also be pointed out that, in the particular case of linear rules, because the differential of $\phi(p)$ is simply $\phi(dp)$, it is sufficient to have an inference engine which only uses the new tuples. Therefore many methods which are restricted to linear rules do indeed use semi-naive evaluation. Note also that when the rules are not linear, applying naive evaluation only to the "new tuples" is an incorrect method (in the sense that it does not produce the whole answer to the query). This can be easily checked on the recursive rule:

ancestor(X,Y) :- ancestor(X,Z),ancestor(Z,Y).

In this case, if we only feed the new tuples at the next stage, the relation which we compute consists of the ancestors whose distance to one another is a power of two.

To our knowledge, outside of the special case of linear rules, the method as a whole has not been implemented.

4.3. Iterative Query/Subquery

Iterative Query/Subquery (QSQI) is an interpreted, top-down strategy.

Its application domain is the set of range restricted rules without evaluable predicates.

The method associates a temporary relation with every relation which derives the query, but the computation of the predicates deriving the query is done at run time. QSQI also stores a set of queries which are currently being evaluated. When several queries correspond to the same query form, QSQI stores and executes them as a single object. For instance, if we have the queries p(a,X) and query p(b,X), we can view this as query p({a,b},X). We call such an object a *generalized query*. The state memorized by the algorithm is a couple <Q,R>, where Q is a set of generalized queries, and R is a set of derived relations, together with their current values.

The iterative interpreter is as follows:

```
Initial state is <{query(X)},{}>
while the state changes do
 for all generalized queries in Q do
   for all rules whose head matches the generalized query do
      begin
      unify rule with the generalized query;
      (i.e propagate the constants. this generates new generalized queries for
      each derived predicate in the body by looking up the base relations.)
      generate new tuples;
      (by replacing each base predicate on the right by its value and every
      derived predicate by its current temporary value.)
      add these new tuples to R;
      add these new generalized queries to Q
      end
```

Let us now run this interpreter against our example logic database:

The initial state is: <{query(X)},{}>

Step 1

We try to solve query(X). Only rule R3 applies. The unification produces the generalized query ancestor({aa},X). This generates temporary relations for query and ancestor with empty set values. Attempts at generating tuples for this generalized query fail.

The new state vector is:

<{query(X),ancestor(aa,X)}, {ancestor={},query={}}>

Step 2

A new generalized query has been generated, so we go on. We try to evaluate each of the generalized queries: query(X) does not give anything new, so we try ancestor({aa},X).
Using rule R2, and unifying, we get parent(aa,X). This is a base relation, so we can produce a set of tuples. Thus we generate a value for ancestor which contains all the tuples of parent(aa,X) and the new state vector is:

<{query(X),ancestor(aa,X)}, {ancestor={(aa,aaa),(aa,aab)},query={}}>

We now solve ancestor(aa,X) using R1. Unification produces the expression :

parent(aa,Z),ancestor(Z,Y).

We try to generate new tuples from this expansion and the current ancestor value but get no tuples. We also generate new generalized queries by looking up parent and instantiating Z. This produces the new expression:

parent(aa,{aaa,aab}),ancestor({aaa,aab},Z).

This creates two new queries which are added to the generalized query and the new state is:

<{query(X),ancestor({aa,aaa,aab},X)}, {ancestor={(aa,aaa),(aa,aab)},query={}}>

Step 3

New generalized queries and new tuples have been generated so we continue. We first solve query(X) using R3 and get the value {(aa,aaa), (aa,aab)} for query. The resulting new state is:

<{query(X),ancestor({aa,aaa,aab},X)}, {ancestor={(aa,aaa),(aa,aab)}, query={(aa,aaa),(aa,aab)}}>

We now try to solve ancestor({aa,aaa,aab},X). Using R2, we get parent({aa,aaa,aab),X) which is a base relation and generates the following tuples in ancestor: {(aa,aaa),(aa,aab),(aaa,aaaa)}. This produces the new state:

<{query(X),ancestor({aa,aaa,aab},X)}, {ancestor={(aa,aaa),(aa,aab),(aaa,aaaa)},
query={(aa,aaa),(aa,aab)}}>

We now solve ancestor({aa,aaa,aab},X)} using R1 and we get: parent({aa,aaa,aab},Z),ancestor(Z,Y). We bind Z by going to the parent relation, and we get: parent({aa,aaa,aab},{aaa,aab,aaaa}), ancestor({aaa,aab,aaaa},Y). This generates the new generalized query ancestor({aaa,aab,aaaa},Y) and the new state:

<{query(X),ancestor({aa,aaa,aab,aaaa},X)}, {ancestor={(aa,aaa),(aa,aab),(aa,aaaa),(aaa,aaaa)},
query={(aa,aaa),(aa,aaaa),(aa,aab)}}>

Step 4

A new generalized query has been generated, so we continue. Solving the ancestor queries using R2 will not produce any new tuples, and solving it with R3 will not produce any new generalized query nor any tuples. The algorithm terminates.

Concerning the performance of the method, one can note that (i) the set of potentially relevant facts is better than for naive (in this example it is optimal), and (ii) QSQI has the same duplication problem as naive evaluation: each step entirely duplicates the previous strategy.

Iterative Query/Subquery is presented in Vieille [1986]. To our knowledge it has not been implemented.

4.4. Recursive Query/Subquery or Extension Tables

Recursive Query/Subquery (QSQR) is a top-down interpreted recursive strategy.

The application domain is the set of range restricted rules without evaluable predicates.

It is of course a recursive version of the previous strategy. As before, we maintain temporary values of derived relations and a set of generalized queries. The state memorized by the algorithm is still a couple <Q,R>, where Q is a set of generalized queries and R is a set of derived relations together with their current values. The algorithm uses a selection function which, given a rule, can choose the first and the next derived predicate in the body to be "solved".

The recursive interpreter is as follows:

```
procedure evaluate(q)  (* q is a generalized query *)
begin
while "new tuples are generated" do
  for all rules whose head matches the generalized query do
    begin
    unify the rule with the generalized query; (i.e., propagate the constants)
    until there are no more derived predicates on the right do
      begin
```

```
        choose the first/next derived predicate according to the selection function;
        generate the corresponding generalized query;
        (This is done by replacing in the rule each base predicate by its value
        and each previously solved derived predicate by its current value).
        eliminate from that generalized query the queries that are already in Q;
        this produces a new generalized query q';
        add q' to Q;
        evaluate(q')
        end;
      replace each evaluated predicate by its value and evaluate the generalized query q;
      (This can be done in some order without waiting for all predicates to be evaluated.)
      add the results in R;
      return the results
      end
end.
Initial state is <{query(X)},{}>
evaluate(query(X)).
```

It is important to note that this version of QSQ is very similar to Prolog. It solves goals in a top-down fashion using recursion, and it considers the literals ordered in the rule (the order is defined by the selection function). The important differences with Prolog are: (i) the method is set-at-a-time instead of tuple-at-a-time, through the generalized query concept, and (ii) as pointed out in Dietrich and Warren [1985], the method uses a dynamic programming approach of storing the intermediate results and re-using them when needed. This dynamic programming feature also solves the problem of cycles in the facts: while Prolog will run in an infinite loop in the presence of such cycles, QSQR will detect them and stop the computation when no new tuple is generated. Thus, QSQR is complete over its application domain whereas Prolog is not.

Here is the ancestor example:

```
evaluate(query(X))
  use rule R3
  query(X) :- ancestor(aa,X)
  this generates the query ancestor({aa},X)
  new state is: <{ancestor({aa},X), query(X)},{}>
  evaluate(ancestor({aa},X)
    Step 1 of the iteration
    use rule R1
    ancestor({aa},Y) :- parent({aa},Z), ancestor(Z,Y).
    by looking up parent we get the bindings {aaa,aab} for Z.
     this generates the query ancestor({aaa,aab},X)
    new state is: <{ancestor({aa,aaa,aab},X), query(X)},{}>
    evaluate (ancestor({aaa,aab},X))
    (this is a recursive call)
      Step 1.1
      use R1
      ancestor({aaa,aab},Y) :- parent({aaa,aab},Z),ancestor(Z,Y).
      by looking up parent we get the binding {aaaa} for Z
      new state is: <{ancestor({aa,aaa,aab,aaaa},X), query(X)},{}>
      evaluate(ancestor({aaaa},X))
      (this is a recursive call)
        Step 1.1.1
        use R1
        ancestor({aaaa},Y) :- parent({aaaa},Z),ancestor(Z,Y).
        by looking up parent we get no binding for Z
        use R2
```

```
            ancestor({aaaa},Y) :- parent({aaaa},Y)
            this fails to return any tuple
            end of evaluate(ancestor({aaaa},X))
            Step 1.1.2
            nothing new is produced
            end of evaluate(ancestor({aaaa},Y))
        use R2
        ancestor({aaa,aab},Y) :- parent({aaa,aab},Y)
        this returns the tuple ancestor(aaa,aaaa)
        new state is: <{ancestor({aa,aaa,aab,aaaa},X),
        query(X)}, {ancestor={(aaa,aaaa)}}>
        Step 1.2
        same as Step 1, nothing new produced
        end of evaluate (ancestor({aaa,aab},X))
          (popping from the recursion in rule R1, we have:)
          a new tuple generated - ancestor(aa,aaaa)
        new state is: <{ancestor({aa,aaa,aab,aaaa},X), query(X)},
                    {ancestor={(aaa,aaaa), (aa,aaaa)}}>
      use rule R2
      ancestor({aa},X) :- parent({aa},Y)
      returns the tuples ancestor(aa,aaa) and ancestor(aa,aab)
      new state is: <{ancestor({aa,aaa,aab,aaaa},X), query(X)},{ancestor={(aaa,aaaa),(aa,aaaa),(aa,aaa),(aa,aab)}}>
      Step 2
      nothing new produced
      end of evaluate({aa},X)
    generate tuples from R3
    new state is: <{ancestor({aa,aaa,aab,aaaa},X), query(X)},{ancestor={(aaa,aaaa),
              (aa,aaaa),(aa,aaa),(aa,aab)},query=(aa,aaaa), (aa,aaa),(aa,aab)}}>
    end of evaluate(query(X))
```

Recursive Query/Subquery is described in Vieille [1986]. A compiled version has been implemented on top of the INGRES relational system. In Dietrich and Warren [1985], along with a good survey of some of these strategies, a method called "extension tables" is presented. It is, up to a few details, the same method.

4.5. Henschen-Naqvi

Henschen-Naqvi is a top-down, compiled and iterative method.

The application domain is that of linear range restricted rules.

The method has a compilation phase which generates an iterative program. That iterative program is then run against the data base. The general strategy is fairly complex to understand, and we shall restrict ourselves to describing it in the "typical case" which is:

```
p(X,Y) :- up(X,XU),p(XU,YU),down(YU,Y).
p(X,Y) :- flat(X,Y).
query(X) :- p(a,X).
```

Note that the relation names *up* and *down* are not to be confused with the notions "top-down" or "bottom-up", which are characteristics of evaluation strategies. Let us introduce some simple notation, which will make reading the algorithm much simpler. Since we are only dealing with binary relations, we can view these as set-to-set mappings. Thus, the relation r associates with each set A a set B, consisting of all the elements related to A by r. We denote A.r the image of A by r, and we have:

$$A.r = \{ y \mid r(x,y) \text{ and } x \in A \}$$

If we view relations as mappings, we can compose them, and we shall denote r.s the composition of r and s. Therefore:

$$A.(r.s) = (A.r).s$$

This approach is similar to the formalism described in Gardarin and Maindreville [1986]. We shall denote the composition of relation r n times with itself r^n. Finally we shall denote set union by '+'. Once this notation is introduced, it is easy to see that the answer to the query is

$$\{a\}.flat + \{a\}.up.flat.down + \{a\}.up.up.flat.down.down + \ldots + \{a\}.up^n.flat.down^n + \ldots$$

The state memorized by the algorithm is a couple <V,E>, where V is a the value of a unary relation and E is an expression. At each step, using V and E, we compute some new tuples and compute the new values of V and E.

The iterative program is as follows:

```
V :={a};
E := λ;        /* the empty string */
while ''new tuples are generated in V'' do
  begin
  /* produce some answer tuples */
  answer := answer + V.flat.E;
  /* compute the new value */
  V := V.up ;
  /* compute the new expression */
  E := E | .down;
  end.
```

Note that E is an *expression*, and is augmented each time around the loop by concatenating ''.down'' to it through the ''cons'' operator. As can be seen from this program, at step i, the value V represents $\{a\}.up^i$ and the expression E represents $down^i$. Therefore the produced tuples are:

$$\{a\}.up^i.flat.down^i.$$

This is not meant to be a complete description of the method, but a description of its behavior in the typical case.

The Henschen-Naqvi method is described in Henschen and Naqvi [1984]. The method has been implemented in the case described here. This implementation can be found in Laskowski [1984]. An equivalent strategy is described using a different formalism in Gardarin and Maindreville [1986]. The performance of the strategy is compared to Semi-Naive evaluation and another method (not described here) in Han and Lu [1986].

4.6. Prolog

Prolog (Roussel [1975]) is a top-down, interpreted and recursive method.

The application domain of Prolog is difficult to state precisely: (i) it is data dependent in the sense that the facts have to be acyclic for the interpreter to terminate, and (ii) there is no simple syntactic characterization of a terminating Prolog program. The job of characterizing the ''good'' rules is left to the programmer.

We consider its execution model to be well known and will not describe it. In fact Prolog is a programming language and not a general strategy to evaluate Horn clauses. We essentially mention Prolog for the sake of completeness and because it is interesting to compare its performance to the other strategies.

4.7. APEX

APEX is a strategy which is difficult to categorize. It is partly compiled in the sense that a graph similar to the predicate connection graph is produced from the rules, which takes care of some of the preprocessing needed for interpretation. It is not fully compiled in the sense that the program which runs against the database is still unique (but driven by the graph). It is, however, clearly recursive, because the interpreter program is recursive. Finally, it is partly top-down and partly bottom-up as will be seen in the interpreter.

The application domain of APEX is the set of range restricted rules which contain no constants and no evaluable predicates.

The interpreter takes the form of a recursive procedure, which, given a query, produces a set of tuples for this query. It is as follows:

```
procedure solve(query,answer)
begin
answer := {};
if query q is on a base relation
then evaluate q against the date base
else
  begin
  select the relevant facts for q in the base predicates;
  put them in relevant;
  while new tuples are generated do
    begin
    for each rule do (this can be done in parallel)
      begin
      instantiate the right predicates with the relevant facts and produce tuples for the left predicate;
      add these tuples to the set of relevant facts;
      initialize the set of useful facts to the set of relevant facts;
      for each literal on the right do (this can be done in parallel)
        begin
        for each matching relevant fact do
          begin
          plug the fact in the rule and propagate the constants;
          this generates a new rule and a new set of queries;
          for all these new queries q' do
            begin
            solve(q',answer(q')) (this is the recursion step)
            add answer(q') to the useful facts
            end
          end
        instantiate the right predicates with the useful facts;
        produce tuples for the left predicate;
        add these to the relevant facts;
        extract the answer to q from the relevant facts
        end
      end
    end
  end.
end;
solve(query(X),answer).
```

Let us now run this program against our ancestor example. We cannot have a constant in the rules and we must modify our rule set and solve directly the query ancestor(aa,X):

solve (ancestor(aa,X), answer)
we first select the relevant base facts.
relevant = {parent(aa,aaa),parent(aa,aab)};
we now start the main iteration:
Step 1
rule R1
ancestor(X,Y) :- parent(X,Z), ancestor(Z,Y)

```
we cannot produce any new tuple from this rule because ancestor
does not yet have any relevant fact
useful = {parent(aa,aaa),parent(aa,aab)};
process parent(X,Z)
  use parent(aa,aaa)
    the new rule is
    parent(aa,aaa),ancestor(aaa,Y)
    solve(ancestor(aaa,Y),answer1)
    ... (this call is not described)
    this returns
    {ancestor(aaa,aaaa)}, which we add to useful
    useful = {parent(aa,aaa),parent(aa,aab),ancestor(aaa,aaaa)};
  use parent(aa,aab)
    the new rule is
    parent(aa,aab),ancestor(aab,Y)
    solve(ancestor(aab,Y),answer2)
    ... (this call is not described)
    this returns nothing
process ancestor(Z,Y)
we instantiate parent and ancestor with the useful facts.
this produces ancestor(aa,aaaa)
we add it to the relevant facts:
relevant = {parent(aa,aaa),parent(aa,aab), ancestor(aa,aaaa)};

rule R2
  ancestor(X,Y) :- parent(X,Y)
  using the relevant facts we produce {ancestor(aa,aaa),ancestor(aa,aab)}
  we add these to relevant:
  relevant = {parent(aa,aaa),parent(aa,aab), ancestor(aa,aaa), ancestor(aa,aab), ancestor(aa,aaaa)};
  this rule does not produce any subquery

Step 2
  will not produce anything new,
  and so the algorithm stops.
```

The APEX method is described in Lozinskii [1985]. The method has been implemented.

5. The Optimization Strategies

We now turn to the description of the second class of strategies: the optimization strategies.

The main drawbacks of the naive evaluation method are:

1. The potential set of relevant facts is too large (i.e., it does not make good use of the query bindings), and
2. It generates a lot of duplicate computation.

A number of optimization strategies have recently been proposed to overcome these two difficulties.

5.1. Aho-Ullman

Aho and Ullman (Aho and Ullman [1979]) present an algorithm for optimizing recursive queries by commuting selections with the least fixpoint operator (LFP). The input is an expression

$$\sigma_F(LFP(r=f(r))$$

where f(r) is a monotonic relational algebra expression (under the ordering of set inclusion) and contains at most one occurrence of r. The output is an equivalent expression where the selection has been pushed through as far as possible.

We introduce their notation and ideas through an example. Consider:

a(X,Y) :- a(X,Z), p(Z,Y).

a(X,Y) :- p(X,Y).

q(X) :- a(john,X).

Aho-Ullman write this as:

$$\sigma_{a_1=john}(LFP(a = a.p \cup p))$$

In this definition, *a* is a relation which is defined by a *fixpoint* equation in relational algebra, and *p* is a base relation. If we start with *a* empty and repeatedly compute *a* using the rule a = a.p ∪ p, at some iteration, there is no change (since the relation *p* is finite). Because the function used in the fixpoint equation is monotonic, this is the *least fixpoint* of the fixpoint equation (Tarski [1955]). It is the smallest relation *a* which satisfies the equation, i.e. contains every tuple which can be generated by using the fixpoint rule, and no tuple which cannot. The query is simply the selection a_1=john applied to this relation. Thus, the query is a selection applied to the transitive closure of p.

We now describe how the Aho-Ullman algorithm optimizes this query. We use '.' to denote composition, which is a join followed by projecting out the join attributes. We begin with the expression

$$\sigma_{a_1=john}(a)$$

and by replacing a by f(a) we generate

$$\sigma_{a_1=john}(a.p \cup p))$$

By distributing the selection across the join, we get

$$\sigma_{a_1=john}(a.p) \cup \sigma_{a_1=john}(p).$$

Since the selection in the first subexpression only involves the first attribute of a, we can rewrite it as

$$\sigma_{a_1=john}(a) \,.\, p$$

We observe that this contains the subexpression

$$\sigma_{a_1=john}(a)$$

which was the first expression in the series. If we denote this by E, the desired optimized expression is then

$$LFP(E = E.p \cup \sigma_{a_1=john}(p))$$

This is equivalent to the Horn Clause query:

a(john,Y) :- a(john,Z), p(Z,Y).
a(john,Y) :- p(john,Y).
q(X) :- a(john,X).

The essence of the strategy is to construct a series of equivalent expressions starting with the expression $\sigma_F(r)$ and repeatedly replacing the single occurrence of r by the expression f(r). Note that each of these expressions contains just one occurrence of R. In each of these expressions, we push the selection as far inside as possible. Selection distributes across union, commutes with another selection and can be pushed ahead of a projection. However, it distributes across a Cartesian product Y × Z only if the selection applies to components from just one of the two arguments Y and Z. The algorithm fails to commute the selection with the LFP operator if the (single) occurrence of r is in one of the arguments of a Cartesian product across which we cannot distribute the selection. We stop when this happens or when we find an expression of the form $h(g(\sigma_F(r)))$ and one of the previous expressions in the series is of the form $h(\sigma_F(r))$. In the latter case, the equivalent expression that we are looking for is h(LFP(s=g(s))), and we have succeeded in pushing the selection ahead of the LFP operator.

We note in conclusion that the expression f(r) must contain no more than one occurrence of *r*. For instance, the algorithm does not apply in this case:

$$\sigma_{a_1=john}(LFP(a = a.a \cup p))$$

Aho and Ullman also present a similar strategy for commuting projections with the LFP operator, but we do not discuss it here.

5.2. Static Filtering

The Static Filtering algorithm is an extension of the Aho-Ullman algorithm described above. However, rules are represented as rule/goal graphs rather than as relational algebra expressions, and the strategy is described in terms of *filters* which are applied to the arcs of the graph. It is convenient to think of the data as flowing through the graph along the arcs. A *filter* on an arc is a selection which can be applied to the tuples flowing through that arc, and is used to reduce the number of tuples that are generated. Transforming a given rule/goal graph into an equivalent graph with (additional) filters on some arcs is equivalent to rewriting the corresponding set of rules.

The execution of a query starts with the nodes corresponding to the base relations sending all their tuples through all arcs that leave them. Each axiom node that receives tuples generates tuples for its head predicate and passes them on through all its outgoing arcs. A relation node saves all new tuples that it receives and passes them on through its outgoing arcs. Computation stops (with the answer being the set of tuples in the query node) when there is no more change in the tuples stored at the various nodes at some iteration. We note that this is simply Semi-Naive evaluation.

Given filters on all the arcs leaving a node, we can 'push' them through the node as follows. If the node is a relation node, we simply place the disjunction of the filters on each incoming arc. If the node is an axiom node, we place on each incoming arc the strongest consequence of the disjunction that can be expressed purely in terms of the variables of the literal corresponding to this arc.

The objective of the optimization algorithm is to place the "strongest" possible filters on each arc. Starting with the filter which represents the constant in the query, it repeatedly pushes filters through the nodes at which the corresponding arcs are incident. Since the number of possible filters is finite, this algorithm terminates. It stops when further pushing of filters does not change the graph, and the graph at this point is equivalent to the original graph (although the graph at intermediate steps may not). Note that since the disjunction of 'true' with any predicate is 'true', if any arc in a loop is assigned the filter 'true', all arcs in the loop are subsequently assigned the filter 'true'.

Consider the transitive closure example that we optimized using the Aho-Ullman algorithm. We would represent it by the following axioms:

R1 a(X,Y) :- a(X,Z), p(Z,Y).
R2 a(X,Y) :- p(X,Y).
R3 q(X) :- a(john,X).

Given below is the corresponding system graph, before and after optimization (We have omitted the variables in the axioms for clarity):

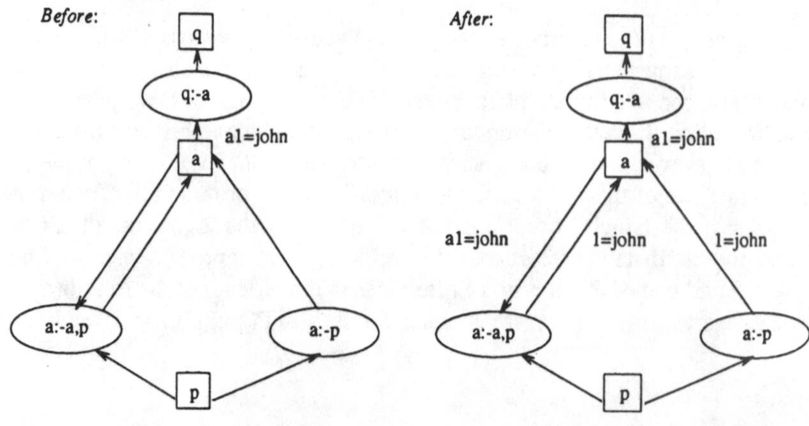

We begin the optimization by pushing the selection through the relation node a. Thus the arcs from R1 to *a* and from R2 to *a* both get the filter '1=john' (We have simplified the conventions for keeping track of variables - '1' refers to the first attribute of the corresponding head predicate). We then push these filters through the corresponding axiom nodes, R1 and R2. Pushing '1=john' through node R2 puts the filter 'p_1=john' on the arc from *p* to R2. Pushing '1=john' through node R1 puts the filter 'a_1=john' on the arc from *a* to R1. Note that it does not put anything on the arc from *p* to R1 (empty filters are equivalent to 'true'). There are no arcs entering *p*, and the filter on the arc from *a* to R1 does not change the disjunction of the filters on arcs leaving *a* (which is still 'a_1=john'). So the algorithm terminates here.

The analogy with the Aho-Ullman algorithm is easily seen when we recognize that a filter is a selection, pushing through a relation node is distribution across a $\cup$ and pushing through an axiom node is distribution across a Cartesian product. In general, the optimizations achieved by the two algorithms are identical. However, the Static Filtering algorithm is more general in that it successfully optimizes some expressions containing more than one occurrence of the defined predicate. An example is the expression

$$\sigma_{a_1=john}(LFP(a = (a.p \cup a.q \cup p)))$$

The Aho-Ullman algorithm does not apply in this case because there are two occurrences of R in f(R). The Static Filtering algorithm optimizes this to

$$LFP((\sigma_{a_1=john}(a) . p) \cup (\sigma_{a_1=john}(a) . q) \cup (\sigma_{a_1=john}(p)))$$

Essentially, it improves upon the Aho-Ullman algorithm in that it is able to distribute selection across some unions where both arguments contain r.

Further, the algorithm can work directly upon certain mutually recursive rules, for example

```
R1  r(X,Y) :- b(X), s(X,Y).
R2  s(X,Y) :- c(X), r(X,Y).
R3  q(X) :- r(X,john).
```

Before applying the Aho-Ullman algorithm, these rules must be rewritten as follows

```
R1  r(X,Y) :- b(X), c(X), r(X,Y).
R2  q(X) :- r(X,john).
```

Note that the Static Filtering algorithm fails to optimize both

$$\sigma_{a_1=john}(LFP(a = a.a \cup p)), \text{ and}$$

$$\sigma_{a_1=john}(LFP(a = a.p \cup p.a \cup p))$$

In this description, we have treated only the "static" filtering approach of Kifer and Lozinskii. Elsewhere, they have also proposed "dynamic" filters (Kifer and Lozinskii [1986b]), which are not determined at compile time but are computed at run time, and this approach is similar to Generalized Magic Sets, discussed later in this section.

5.3. Magic Sets

The idea of the Magic Sets optimization is to simulate the sideways passing of bindings a la Prolog by the introduction of new rules. This cuts down on the number of potentially relevant facts.

The application domain is the set of bottom-up evaluable rules.

We shall describe the strategy in detail, using as an example a modified version of the same-generation rule set:

```
sg(X,Y) :- p(X,XP),p(Y,YP),sg(YP,XP).
sg(X,X).
query(X) :- sg(a,X).
```

Note that in this version the two variables XP and YP have been permuted. Note also that the second rule is not range restricted. The first step of the magic set transformation is the introduction of adornments and the generation of adorned rules.

Given a system of rules, the *adorned rule system* (Ullman [1985]) is obtained as follows:
For each rule r and for each adornment *a* of the predicate on the left, generate an adorned rule: Define recursively an argument of a predicate in the rule r to be *distinguished* (Henschen and Naqvi [1984]) if either it is bound in the adornment *a*, or it is a constant, or it appears in a base predicate occurrence that has a distinguished variable. Thus, the sources of bindings are (i) the constants and (ii) the bindings in the head of the rule. These bindings are propagated through the base predicates. If we consider each distinguished argument to be bound, this defines an adornment for each derived literal on the right. The adorned rule is obtained by replacing each derived literal by its adorned version.

If we consider the rule

sg(X,Y) :- p(X,XP),p(Y,YP),sg(YP,XP).

with adornment bf on the head predicate, then X is distinguished because it is bound in sg(X,Y), XP is distinguished because X is distinguished and p(X,XP) is a base predicate; these are the only distinguished variables. Thus the new adorned rule is

sg^{bf} (X,Y) :- p(X,XP),p(Y,YP),sg^{fb} (YP,XP).

If we consider a set of rules, this process generates a set of adorned rules. The set of adorned rules has size K.R where R is the size of the original set of rules and K is a factor exponential in the number of attributes per derived predicate. So, for instance, if every predicate has three attributes, then the adorned system is eight times larger than the original system. However, we do not need the entire adorned system and we only keep the adorned rules that derive the query. In our example the reachable adorned system is:

sg^{bf} (X,Y) :- p(X,XP),p(Y,YP),sg^{fb} (YP,XP).
sg^{fb} (X,Y) :- p(X,XP),p(Y,YP),sg^{bf} (YP,XP).
sg^{bf} (X,X).
sg^{fb} (X,X).
$query^{f}$ (X) :- sg^{bf} (a,X).

Clearly, this new set of rules is equivalent to the original set in the sense that it will generate the same answer to the query.

The magic set optimization consists in generating from the given set of rules a new set of rules, which are equivalent to the original set with respect to the query, and such that their bottom-up evaluation is more efficient. This transformation is done as follows: (i) for each occurrence of a derived predicate on the right of an adorned rule, we generate a magic rule. (ii) For each adorned rule we generate a modified rule.

Here is how we generate the magic rule: (i) choose an adorned literal predicate p on the right of the adorned rule r, (ii) erase all the other derived literals on the right, (iii) in the derived predicate occurrence replace the name of the predicate by magic.p^{a} where *a* is the literal adornment, and erase the non distinguished variables, (iv) erase all the non distinguished base predicates, (v) in the left hand side, erase all the non distinguished variables and replace the name of the predicate by *magic.p* $1^{a'}$, where p1 is the predicate on the left, and a' is the adornment of the predicate p1, and finally (vi) exchange the two magic predicates.

For instance the adorned rule:

sg^{bf} (X,Y) :- p(X,XP),p(Y,YP),sg^{fb} (YP,XP).

generates the magic rule:

$magic^{fb}$ (XP) :- p(X,XP), $magic^{bf}$ (X).

Note that the magic rules simulate the passing of bound arguments through backward chaining. (We have dropped the suffix "sg" in naming the magic predicates since it is clear from the context.)

Here is how we generate the modified rule: For each rule whose head is p.a, add on the right hand side the predicate magic.p.a(X) where X is the list of distinguished variables in that occurrence of p. For instance the adorned rule:

sg^{bf} (X,Y) :- p(X,XP),p(Y,YP),sg^{fb} (YP,XP).

generates the modified rule:

sg^{bf} (X,Y) :- p(X,XP),p(Y,YP),$magic^{bf}$ (X), sg^{fb} (YP,XP).

Finally the complete modified set of rules for our example is:

$magic^{fb}$ (XP) :- p(X,XP), $magic^{bf}$ (X).
$magic^{bf}$ (YP) :- p(Y,YP),$magic^{fb}$ (Y).
$magic^{bf}$ (a).
sg^{bf} (X,Y) :- p(X,XP),p(Y,YP),$magic^{bf}$ (X),sg^{fb} (YP,XP).
sg^{fb} (X,Y) :- p(X,XP),p(Y,YP),$magic^{fb}$ (Y),sg^{bf} (YP,XP).
sg^{bf} (X,X) :- $magic^{bf}$ (X).
sg^{fb} (X,X) :- $magic^{bf}$ (X).
query.f(X) :- sg^{bf} (a,X).

The idea of the magic set strategy was presented in Bancilhon et al [1986] and the precise algorithm is described in Bancilhon et al [1986a]. To our knowledge, the strategy is not implemented.

5.4. Counting and Reverse Counting.

Counting and Reverse Counting are derived from the magic set optimization strategy.

They apply under two conditions: (i) the data is acyclic and (ii) there is at most one recursive rule for each predicate, and it is linear.

We first describe counting using the ''typical'' single linear rule system:

```
p(X,Y) :- flat(X,Y).
p(X,Y) :- up(X,XU),p(XU,YU),down(YU,Y).
query(Y) :- p(a,Y).
```

The idea consists in introducing magic sets (called *counting* sets) in which elements are numbered by their distance to the element a. Remember that the magic set essentially marks all the *up* ancestors of a and then applies the rules in a bottom-up fashion to only the marked ancestors. In the counting strategy, at the same time we mark the ancestors of john, we number them by their distance from a. Then we can ''augment'' the p predicate by numbering its tuples and generate them by levels as follows:

```
counting(a,0).
counting(X,I) :-counting(Y,J),up(Y,X),I=J+1.
p'(X,Y,I) :- counting(X,I),flat(X,Y).
p'(X,Y,I) :- counting(X,I),up(X,XU), p'(XU,YU,J),down(YU,Y),I=J-1.
query(X) :- p'(a,X,0).
```

Thus at each step, instead of using the entire magic set, we only use the tuples of the correct level, thus minimizing the set of relevant tuples. But in fact, it is useless to compute the first attribute of the p predicate. Thus the system can be further optimized into:

```
counting(a,0).
counting(X,I) :-counting(Y,J),up(Y,X),I=J+1.
p''(Y,I) :- counting(X,I),flat(X,Y).
p''(Y,I) :- p''(YU,J),down(YU,Y),I=J-1,J>0.
query(X) :- p''(Y,0).
```

It is interesting to notice that this new set of rules is in fact simulating a stack.

Reverse counting is another variation around the same idea. It works as follow: (i) first compute the magic set, then (ii) for each element b in the magic set number all its *down* descendants and its *up* descendants and add to the answer all the *down* descendants having the same number as a (because a is in the *up* descendants). This gives the following equivalent system:

```
magic(a).
magic(Y) :- magic(X),up(X,Y).
des.up(X,X,0) :- magic(X).
des.down(X',Y,0) :- magic(X'),flat(X',Y).
des.up(X',X,I) :- des.up(X',Y,J),up(X,Y),I=J+1.
des.down(X',X,I) :- des.down(X',Y,J),down(Y,X),I=J+1.
query(Y) :- des.up(X',a,Y),des.down(X',Y,I).
```

This can be slightly optimized by limiting ourselves to the b's that will join with *flat* and restricting the *down* des's to be in the magic set. This generates the following system:

```
magic(a).
magic(Y) :- magic(X),up(X,Y).
des.up(X,X,0) :- magic(X),flat(X,Y).
des.down(X',Y,0) :- magic(X'),flat(X',Y).
des.up(X',X,I) :- magic(X),des.up(X',Y,J),up(X,Y),I=J+1.
des.down(X',X,I) :- des.down(X',Y,J),down(Y,X),I=J+1.
sg(a,Y) :- des.up(X',a,Y),des.down(X',Y,I).
```

Note that we still have the problem of a "late termination" on *down* because we number *all* the descendants in *down*, even those of a lower generation than a.

The idea of counting was presented in Bancilhon et al [1986] and a formal description of counting and of an extension called "magic counting" was presented in the single rule case in Sacca and Zaniolo [1986a]. Counting was extended to progams containing function symbols in Sacca and Zaniolo [1986b]. Reverse counting is described in Bancilhon et al. [1986a]. They have not been implemented.

5.5. Generalized Magic Sets

This is a generalization of the Magic Sets method and is described in Beeri and Ramakrishnan [1987]. The intuition is that the Magic Sets method works essentially by passing bindings obtained by solving body predicates "sideways" in the rule to restrict the computation of other body predicates. The notion of *sideways information passing* is formalized in terms of labeled graphs. A sideways information passing graph is associated with each rule, and these graphs are used to define the Magic Sets transformation. (In general, many such graphs exist for each rule, each reflecting one way of solving the predicates in the body of the rule; and we may choose any one of these and associate it with the rule.)

There are examples, such as transitive closure defined using double recursion, in which the original Magic Sets transformation achieves no improvement over Semi-Naive evaluation. Intuitively, this is because the only form of sideways information passing that it implements consists of using base predicates to bind variables. Thus, in the same generation example discussed earlier, the predicate *p* is used to bind the variable XP. The method, however, fails to pass information through derived predicates, and so it fails with transitive closure expressed using double recursion (since the recursive rule contains no base predicates in the body). Consider the rule:

```
a(X,Y) :- a(X,Z), a(Z,Y).
```

Given a query a(john,Y), the Magic Sets method recognizes that X is bound (since it is bound in the adornment *bf* corresponding to the head of the rule). However, Z is considered free. So it generates the following adorned rule:

$$a^{bf}(X,Y) :- a^{bf}(X,Z), a^{ff}(Z,Y).$$

Clearly, the method computes the entire ancestor relation. To succeed in binding Z, the first occurrence of *a* in the body must be used.

The generalized version of the method succeeds in passing information through derived predicates as well.

As with the original Magic Sets strategy, a set of *adorned rules* is first obtained from the given rules, and these adorned rules are then used to produce the optimized set of rules. Both these steps are now directed, however, by the notion of *sideways information passing graphs* (sips). A sip corresponding to the above rule that binds Z is:

$$h \rightarrow_X a.1,\ h, a.1 \rightarrow_Z a.2$$

The predicate *h* denotes the bound part of the head. This graph indicates that the head binds X and this is used in solving the first occurrence of *a*, and further, this solution is used to bind Z in solving the second occurrence of *a*. This generates the adorned rule:

a^{bf} (X,Y) :- a^{bf} (X,Z), a^{bf} (Z,Y).

The magic rules corresponding to the two occurrences of *a* are:

magic(X) :- magic(X).
magic(Z) :- magic(X), a^{bf} (X,Z).

The first rule is trivial and may be discarded. In addition, we obtain the rule magic(john) from the query. The modified rules are obtained exactly as in the Magic Sets method, by adding magic predicates to the bodies of the original rules.

We do not present the details here. The reader is referred to Beeri and Ramakrishnan [1987], where Counting and variants of both Magic Sets and Counting are generalized as well. The work in [Beeri and Ramakrishnan [1987] still imposes one restriction on rules: every variable that appears in the head of a rule must also appear in the body. This ensures that every tuple produced in a bottom-up execution is ground. † On the other hand, this restriction disallows the use of certain effective logic programming techniques, such as difference lists, and makes it difficult to utilize partially bound arguments. This restriction is lifted in Ramakrishnan [1988], and thus, it is shown that the rewriting techniques (i.e., Magic Sets, Counting, etc.) can be generalized to deal with arbitrary logic programs.

The ''Alexander'' strategy described in Rohmer et al. [1986] is essentially a variant of the Generalized Magic Sets strategy.

The dynamic filtering approach of Kifer and Lozinskii is similar to the Generalized Magic Sets strategy, although it cannot implement some sideways information passing graphs. The dynamic filters essentially perform as magic sets, but this is a run-time strategy, and the overhead of computing and applying the filters falls outside our framework. We do not discuss dynamic filtering further in this paper.

6. Summary of Strategy Characteristics.

A summary of the characteristics of each strategy is presented in Table 1. We emphasize that this table contains some approximations and refer the reader to the actual descriptions for clarifications. For example, although Magic Sets and Generalized Magic Sets have the same application range, the latter succeeds in optimizing some queries in this range that the former cannot. (Magic Sets essentially reduces to Semi-Naive evaluation in these cases.) Several of these strategies have been further developed since this paper was written. We refer the reader to Beeri and Ramakrishnan [1987], Ramakrishnan [1988], Kifer and Lozinskii [1986b, 1988], Sacca and Zaniolo [1987] and Vieille [1988] for some of these further developments. (We also note that there has been significant related research that cannot be viewed as development of work discussed in this paper. It is outside the scope of this paper to review this work, and the interested reader is urged to consult the recent database literature. The collection of papers in Minker [1988] is a good starting point.)

† The reader who is familiar with logic programs should note that this restriction makes an important optimization possible - the expensive operation of ***unification*** can always be replaced by the less expensive operation of ***matching***, since one of the two arguments to the unification procedure is always ground, given that all generated tuples are ground.

Table 1: Summary of Strategy Characteristics

Method	*Application Range*	*Top down vs. Bottom Up*	*Compiled vs. Interpreted*	*Iterative vs. Recursive*
Naive Evaluation	Bottom-up Evaluable	Bottom Up	Compiled	Iterative
Semi-Naive Evaluation	Bottom-up Evaluable	Bottom Up	Compiled	Iterative
Query/Subquery	Range Restricted No Arithmetic	Top Down	Interpreted	Iterative
Query/Subquery	Range Restricted No Arithmetic	Top Down	Interpreted	Recursive
APEX	Range Restricted No Arithmetic Constant Free	Mixed	Mixed	Recursive
Prolog	User responsible	Top Down	Interpreted	Recursive
Henschen-Naqvi	Linear	Top Down	Compiled	Iterative
Aho-Ullman	Strongly Linear	Bottom Up	Compiled	Iterative
Kifer-Lozinskii	Range Restricted No Arithmetic	Bottom Up	Compiled	Iterative
Counting	Strongly Linear	Bottom Up	Compiled	Iterative
Magic Sets	Bottom-up evaluable	Bottom Up	Compiled	Iterative
Generalized M. Sets	Bottom-up evaluable	Bottom-up	Compiled	Iterative

7. Framework for Performance Evaluation

We now turn to the problem of comparing the above strategies. To perform a comparison of the strategies we must:

1. Choose a set of rules and queries which will represent our benchmark.
2. Choose some test data which will represent our extensional database.
3. Choose a cost function to measure the performance of each strategy.
4. Evaluate the performance of each query against the extensional databases.

We first describe the four queries used as ''typical'' intensional databases. Then, we present our characterization of the data. Each relation is characterized by four parameters and it is argued that a number of familiar data structures, e.g. trees, can be described in this framework. We describe our cost metric, which is the size of the intermediate results before duplicate elimination. We present analytical cost functions for each query evaluation strategy on each query. The cost functions are plotted for three sets of data - tree, inverted tree and cylinder. We discuss these results informally.

7.1. Workload: Sample Intensional Databases and Queries

Instead of generating a general mix, we have chosen four queries that have the properties of exercising various important features of the strategies. We are fully aware of the fact that this set is insufficient to provide a complete benchmark, but we view this work as a first step towards a better understanding of the performance behavior of the various strategies.

The queries are three different versions of the ancestor query and a version of the same-generation query. The first one is just a classical ancestor rule and query with the first attribute bound.

Query 1
```
a(X,Y) :- p(X,Y).
a(X,Y) :- p(X,Z),a(Z,Y).
query(X) :- a(john,X).
```

Because most strategies are representation dependent, we have studied the same example with the second attribute bound instead of the first. This will allow us to determine which strategies can solve both cases.

Query 2
```
a(X,Y) :- p(X,Y).
a(X,Y) :- p(X,Z),a(Z,Y).
query(X) :- a(X,john).
```

The third version of the ancestor example specifies ancestor using double recursion. This enables us to see how the strategies react to the non linear case. This example being fully symmetric, it is sufficient to test it with its first attribute bound.

Query 3
```
a(X,Y) :- p(X,Y).
a(X,Y) :- a(X,Z),a(Z,Y).
query(X) :- a(john,X).
```

Finally, to study something more complex than transitive closure, we have chosen a generalized version of the same generation example, bound on its first attribute.

Query 4
```
p(X,Y) :- flat(X,Y).
p(X,Y) :- up(X,XU),p(XU,YU), down(YU,Y).
query(X) :- p(john,X).
```

7.2. Characterizing Data: Sample Extensional Databases

Because we decided on an analytical approach, we had to obtain tractable formulae for the cost of each strategy against each query. Therefore, each relation must be characterized by a *small* set of parameters. Fortunately, because of the choice of our workload, we can restrict our attention to binary relations.

We represent every binary relation by a directed graph and view tuples as edges and domain elements as nodes. Nodes are arranged in layers and each edge goes from a node in one layer to a node in the next. Note that in these graphs each node has at least one in-edge or one out-edge. Nodes in the first layer have no incoming edges and nodes in the last layer have no outgoing edges. We assume that edges are randomly distributed with a uniform distribution.

This formalism does not represent cycles. Nor does it represent short cuts, where a short cut is the existence of two paths of different length going from one point to another. Clearly, they would violate our assumption that nodes were arranged in layers with edges going from nodes in one layer to the next.

Let R be a binary relation and A be a set. Recall that we denote by A.R the set:

$$A.R = \{y \mid x \in A \text{ and } R(x,y)\}$$

We characterize a binary relation R by:

(1) F_R the *fan-out* factor,
(2) D_R the *duplication* factor,
(3) h_R the *height*, and
(4) b_R the *base*.

F_R and D_R are defined as follows: given a ''random'' set A of n nodes from R, the size of A.R is n F_R before duplicate elimination. D_R is the duplication factor in A.R, i.e. the ratio of the size of A.R before and after duplicate elimination. Thus the size of A.R after duplicate elimination is n F_R/D_R.

We call $E_R = F_R/D_R$ the *expansion* factor of R.

The base b_R is the number of nodes that do not have any antecedents. The height h_R is the length of the longest chain in R.

When no confusion is possible, we shall simply use F, D, h and b instead of F_R, D_R, h_R and b_R.

The typical structure consists of a number of layers. There are (h_R+1) layers of nodes in the structure, numbered from top to bottom (as 0 to h). There are b_R nodes in level 0.

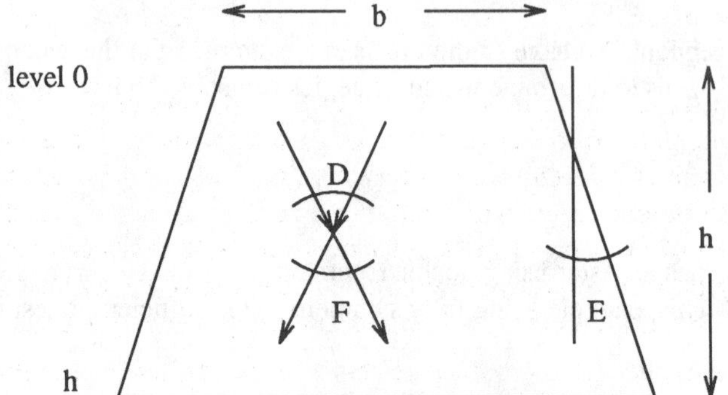

This ''parametrized structure'' is fairly general and can represent a number of typical configurations:

A binary balanced tree of height k is defined by:
F=2; D=1; h=k; b=1

The same binary tree upside down is defined by:
F=1; D=2; h=k, b=2^k

A list of length k is defined by:
F=1; D=1; h=k; b=1

A set of n lists of length k is defined by:
F=1; D=1; h=k; b=n

A parent relation, where each person has two children and each child has two parents is defined by:
F=2; D=2; h=number of generations; b=number of people of unknown parentage

We emphasize that we assume the data to be *random*, with a uniform distribution. Thus, the values F and D are average values. Our characterization of a binary tree, for instance, describes a random (but layered) data structure in which the average values of F and D are 2 and 1 respectively. An actual binary tree has a regular pattern (*each* internal node has exactly one incoming and two outgoing edges incident on it) and this is not captured by our characterization.

Our assumption that the duplication factor is independent of the size is a very crude approximation. For instance it implies that if you start from one node you still generate some duplicates. Obviously the duplication factor increases with the size of the start set. Therefore, our approximation overestimates the number of duplicates. However, it becomes reasonable as the size of the start set becomes large. It is also dependent upon our assumption that the data is random and not regular.

Let us now turn to the problem of characterizing inter-relation relationships. Let A and B be two sets. The *transfer ratio* of A with respect to B, denoted $T_{A.B}$ is the number such that given a random set of n nodes in A, the size of $A \cap B$ after duplicate elimination is n $T_{A.B}$. In other words, given a set of nodes in A, the transfer ratio is the fraction of these nodes that also appear in set B. Note that $0 \le T \le 1$.

This definition can be extended to binary relations by considering only the columns of the relations. We shall denote the i-th column of R by Ri. Thus, given two binary relations R and S, the number of tuples in the (ternary) result of the join of R and S is n $T_{R2.S1}$, where n is the number of tuples in R.

7.3. The Cost Metrics

We have chosen for our cost measure the number of *successful inferences* performed by the system.

Consider a rule:

$$p \text{ :- } q1, q2, \ldots, qn$$

A *successful inference* (or *firing*) associated with this rule is of the form (*id, t, t1, t2, ... , tn*), where *t1* through *tn* are (ground) tuples in *q1* through *qn* and *t* is a tuple in *p*. It denotes that the truth of *t1* through *tn* is used to establish that *t* is true, by applying the given rule. There is (conceptually) an identifier *id* associated with this inference because it is possible that this inference is repeatedly made, and we wish to measure this.

The simplest way to obtain this cost function is to measure the size of the intermediate results *before* duplicate elimination.

We note that this cost measure does not count *unsuccessful* inferences, i.e. uses of the rule in which the tuples *t1* through *tn* fail to establish *t* (for example, because they do not agree on the values they assign to common variables). Also, since the cost measure is independent of the number of *q*'s, in this model the measure of complexity of the join, the cartesian product, intersection and selection is the size of the result; the measure of complexity of union is the sum of the sizes of the arguments (each tuple present in both argument is going to fire twice); and the measure of complexity of projection is the size of the argument. Readers familiar with performance evaluation of relational queries might be surprised by these measures.

Our concern, however, is primarily with recursive queries. In particular, all but one of our queries (ancestor using double recursion) are *linear*, i.e., the body of each recursive rule contains exactly one occurrence of the recursive predicate. We justify our measurement of only successful inferences by the observation that the number of successful inferences (for the recursive predicate) at one step constitutes the operand at the next step. We justify the approximation in estimating the cost of a join in terms of the size of just one of the operands as follows. The join represented by the predicates in the body of a rule may be thought of as a fixed "operator" that is repeatedly applied to the relation corresponding to the recursive predicate. It is reasonable to assume that the cost of each such application is proportional to the size of this relation (the operand). By measuring the size of this intermediate relation over all steps, we obtain a cost that is proportional to the actual cost.

In essence, our cost is a measure of one important factor in the performance of a query evaluation system, the number of successful inferences, rather than a measure of the actual run-time performance. This cost model is studied further in Bancilhon [1985].

8. Notation and Preliminary Derivations

In this section, we explain the notation and terminology used in analytically deriving the cost functions. We also derive some expressions that are used in the analysis of some of the strategies. The derivations of these expressions are of some interest in their own right, since they are good examples of the techniques we use in subsequent analyses.

We denote multiplication by simply juxtaposing the operands. Where there is ambiguity, parentheses are used to clarify the expression, or we use * to denote multiplication.

We denote the number of nodes at level i in relation R by $n_R(i)$, the total number of nodes in R by N_R, and the total number of edges in R (which is the number of tuples in R) by A_R. Where no confusion is possible, we drop the subscripts.

We denote the sum of the (h+1)st elements of the geometric series of ratio E by gsum(E,h), thus:

$$\text{gsum}(E,h) = (1 + E + E^2 + E^3 + \ldots + E^h)$$

From the definition of the expansion factor E, we have n(i+1)=n(i)E. So the total number of nodes is:

$$N = b(1 + E + E^2 + E^3 + \ldots + E^h)$$
$$= (b)\text{gsum}(E,h)$$

Clearly, the number of edges entering level i is n(i-1)F, and the number of edges leaving level i is n(i)F. Thus the total number of edges is:

$$A = bF + bEF + bE^2F + ... + bE^{(h-1)}F$$
$$= bF(1 + E + E^2 + ... + E^{(h-1)})$$
$$= (bF)gsum(E,h-1)$$

We denote by h' the *average* level:

$$h' = h - \left\lfloor \frac{\sum_{i=1}^{h}(i*n(i))}{N} \right\rfloor$$

It denotes the mean level at which we pick a node, assuming nodes are uniformly distributed. We have actually defined h' as the distance of the mean level from the highest level h for notational convenience, since this is a quantity we use extensively.

We define the length of an arc (a,b) in the transitive closure of R (which we denote by R*) to be the length of the path of R that generates it. (Note that this is well-defined because there are no short-cuts.)

Since an arc is represented by its end points, the number of arcs of length k with a given first node can be computed as the number of distinct nodes reachable from the given node by a path of length k. So, starting from a given node, on the average we can reach E distinct nodes by a path of length 1, E^2 distinct nodes by a path of length 2, and so on. The number of arcs of length k going from level i to level (i+k) is thus:

$$n(i)E^k = n(i+k)$$

Of course, if D is not one, this is an approximation that depends on our assumption of random data. In particular, it breaks down for regular data, such as an actual inverted tree. The intuition is as follows. The parameters F and D are used to estimate the number of *arcs* of length k, as opposed to the number of *paths* of length k. Several paths may generate the same arc (i.e., they have the same end points). Thus, we use the parameters F and D to estimate this ''duplication'' of arcs. This approximation depends upon the randomness of data - in an inverted tree, for instance, the number of paths is exactly the number of arcs because there is a unique path between any two points. The inverted tree is one instance of a family of data structures with given values of F (=1) and D (=2), and in this particular instance, due to the regular pattern in the data, the above approximation breaks down. In general, however, for such a structure the number of paths is *not* equal to the number of arcs; and if the data is randomly (and uniformly) distributed, our approximation is accurate.

We denote by $a_{R*}(k)$ the number of arcs of length exactly k in R*. Where the context is clear, we write a(k).

a(k) is obtained by summing all the arcs of length k that enter level i for i = k to h. Thus:

$$a(k) = n(k) + n(k+1) + ... + n(h)$$
$$= n(k)\ gsum(E,h-k)$$

Finally, given a relation R(A,B), its transpose R^T(B,A) is defined to be such that R^T(B,A) holds iff R(A,B) holds, for all pairs (A,B). We have the following relationships:

$F_{R^T} = D_R$,
$D_{R^T} = F_R$,
$E_{R^T} = 1/E_R$,
$h_{R^T} = h_R$,
$h'_{R^T} = h_R - h'_R$, and
$b_{R^T} = b_R E_R^{h_R}$.

9. Cost Evaluation

For each strategy and for each query, we have analytically evaluated the cost of computing the given query using the given strategy. The cost is expressed as a function of the data parameters F, D, h and b. The formulae are listed in Appendix 1, and their derivations are contained in Bancilhon and Ramakrishnan [1987]. To compare these fairly complex formulae, we have plotted a number of curves, some of which are included in the appendix.

10. Graphical Comparison of the Costs

The curves shown in the appendix show the relative performance of the various strategies on each of the sample queries for three sets of data. They are relations in which the tuples are arranged in a tree structure, an inverted tree structure, and a "cylinder". A cylinder is a structure in which each layer has b nodes and each node has on the average two incoming and two outgoing arcs. We present below a sample relation of each type:

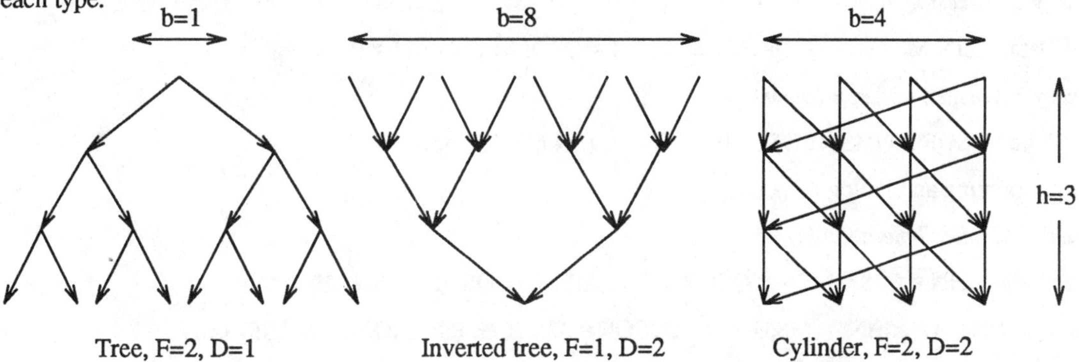

Tree, F=2, D=1 Inverted tree, F=1, D=2 Cylinder, F=2, D=2

The choice of these structures was made in order to study the effects of uneven distribution of the data and the effects of duplication. We have fixed the sizes of all relations at 100,000 tuples. For the tree structure, we vary the shape by changing the fan-out F while keeping the number of arcs (which is the number of tuples) constant. Clearly, decreasing the fan-out increases the depth of the structure and vice-versa. Similarly, the shape of the inverted tree is varied by varying the duplication factor. The shape of the cylinder is varied by varying the ratio of breadth b to height h, again keeping the number of arcs constant.

For each query and data structure, we plot the cost of each strategy against the shape of the data (measured in terms of the parameter used to vary it). Thus, for each query, we plot cost vs. F for the tree, cost vs. D for the inverted tree, and cost vs. b/h for the cylinder. We do this for each strategy. The cost is computed using the cost functions listed in the appendix. We have sometimes displayed a subset of the curves (for the same query and data structure) over a different range, to allow a better comparison.

For the ancestor queries, we plot the cost of each strategy for the cases when the parent relation has 100,000 tuples and the data in it has the shape of a tree, an inverted tree and a cylinder.

For the same generation example, we have assumed that the relations *up* and *down* are identical and that the fan-out and duplication for the relation flat are both equal to 1. We have also assumed that the transfer ratio from up to flat is equal to the transfer ratio from flat to down. We have assumed that all three relations (*up*, *flat* and *down*) have 100,000 tuples. We plot the cost of each strategy as the shape of *up* and *down* varies for a total of six cases: the cases when the structure is a tree, an inverted tree and a cylinder, with the transfer ratio equal to 1 and 0.01 (100% and 1% respectively).

10.1. Summary of the Curves

There are several important points to be seen in the curves. For a given query, there is a clear ordering of the various strategies that usually holds over the entire range of data. The difference in performance between strategies is by orders of magnitude, which emphasizes the importance of choosing the right strategy. The cost of the optimal strategy is less than 10,000 in each of the queries we have considered, over the entire range of data. The size of the data is 100,000 tuples. This indicates that recursive queries can be implemented efficiently.

We present a summary of the ordering of the strategies, as seen in the corresponding curves. We use ≪ to denote an order of magnitude or greater difference in performance, and for a given query, we list in parentheses those strategies that perform identically for all data. We refer to the various strategies using the following acronyms for brevity: HN (Henschen-Naqvi), C (Counting), MS (Magic Sets), GMS (Generalized Magic Sets), QSQR, QSQI, APEX, P (Prolog), SN (Semi-Naive), N (naive) and SF (Static Filtering).

Query 1 (Ancestor.bf)

Tree: (HN,C) ≪ (QSQR,APEX) = P ≈ (MS,GMS) ≪ QSQI ≪ (SN,SF) ≪ N

Inverted tree: (HN,C) ≪ (QSQR,APEX) ≈ (MS,GMS) ≪ P ≪ QSQI ≪ (SN,SF) ≪ N

Cylinder: (HN,C) ≪ (QSQR,APEX) ≈ (MS,GMS) ≪ QSQI ≪ (SN,SF) ≪ N ≪ P

Query 2 (Ancestor.fb)

All Data: (HN,MS,GMS,QSQR,SF) ≪ APEX ≈ QSQI ≪ SN ≪ N ≈ P

Query 3 (Ancestor.bf, non-linear)

All data: QSQR ≈ GMS ≪ QSQI ≪ APEX ≪ (SN,MS,SF) ≪ N

(HN, Counting and Prolog do not apply)

Query 4 (Same Generation.bf)

Tree: C ≪ HN ≈ (MS,GMS) ≪ QSQR = P ≪ APEX ≪ QSQI ≪ (SN,SF) ≪ N

Inverted tree: C ≪ HN ≈ (MS,GMS) ≪ QSQR ≈ APEX ≪ P ≈ QSQI ≪ (SN,SF) ≪ N

Cylinder: C ≪ HN ≈ (MS,GMS) ≪ QSQR ≪ APEX ≪ QSQI ≪ (SN,SF) ≪ N ≪ P

To summarize the ancestor results, the following order is seen to hold for the ancestor queries:

(HN, C) ≪ QSQR ≈ (MS,GMS) ≪ APEX ≈ QSQI ≪ SN ≪ N

There are some exceptions and additions to the above ordering. In the non-linear case, Henschen-Naqvi and Counting do not apply, and Magic Sets reduces to Semi-Naive. Static Filtering performs like Semi-Naive, except in the case where the second argument is bound, and in this case it performs like QSQR. APEX performs like QSQR in the case where the first argument is bound. Prolog performs poorly when it cannot propagate the constant in the query (the case where the second argument is bound), as expected. When it can propagate the constant, its performance degrades sharply with duplication, especially as the depth of the data structure increases. This is readily seen from the curves for the cylinder.

To summarize the same generation results, we have:

C ≪ HN ≈ (MS,GMS) ≪ QSQR ≪ APEX ≪ QSQI ≪ (SN, SF) ≪ (P, N)

Prolog behaves like QSQR when there is no duplication (tree). With duplication, its performance degrades so sharply with an increase in the depth of the data structure that we have classified it with Naive, although it performs better than Semi-Naive over a wide range.

10.2. Interpreting the Results

These results indicate that the following three factors greatly influence the performance:

1. The amount of *duplication* of work,
2. The size of the set of *relevant facts*, and
3. The size (number and arity) of intermediate relations.

By duplication of work, we refer to the repeated firing of a rule on the same data. This can occur due to duplication in the data (e.g. Prolog), or due to an iterative control strategy that does not remember previous firings (e.g. QSQI and Naive). Consider the second factor. A fact p(a) is *relevant* to a given query q iff there exists a derivation $p(a) \rightarrow^* q(b)$ for some b in the answer set. If we know all the relevant facts in advance, instead of using the database to reply to the query, we can use the relevant part of the database only, thus cutting down on the set of facts to be processed. It is in general impossible to find all the relevant facts in advance without spending as much effort as in replying to the query. Thus, all methods have a way of finding a super-set of relevant facts. We call this set the *set of potentially relevant facts*. As this set becomes smaller, i.e., contains fewer and fewer facts that are *not* relevant, the work done in evaluating the query clearly decreases. The third factor is hard to define precisely. Strategies that only look at sets of nodes rather than sets of arcs perform better than those that look at sets of arcs, by an order of magnitude or more. They are less generally applicable since this often involves a loss of information. This usually leads to non-termination unless the database has certain properties, such as linearity of rules and acyclicity of the extensional database. And of course, strategies that create more intermediate relations pay for it in increased costs, since the addition of a tuple to a relation (intermediate or otherwise) represents a firing.

The following discussion is intended to clarify these concepts, as well as to explain the performance of the various strategies in terms of these three factors.

10.2.1. The Ancestor Queries

We begin by looking at the ancestor queries. The effect of duplication is seen by considering Prolog and QSQI, both of which do duplicate work, for different reasons. When the first argument is bound, Prolog performs like QSQR on a tree data structure, where exactly one arc enters each node (equivalently, there is exactly one way of deriving a given answer). With duplication (i.e. on the average more than one arc enters a given node) performance degrades dramatically. Prolog's performance for the same query on a cylinder is comparable to Naive evaluation, a difference of several orders of magnitude! We note that the set of relevant facts is comparable in the two cases, being the set of nodes reachable from the node denoting the constant in the query (which will henceforth be referred to as the query node). However, in the case of the cylinder, these nodes can be reached along several paths and Prolog infers them afresh along each path. QSQI performs duplicate computation for a different reason, which is that its iterative control strategy does not remember previous firings. Essentially, there are as many steps (executions of the control loop) as the longest path from the query node, and all nodes reached by a path of length less than or equal to i are recomputed at all steps after the ith. This can be seen by comparing QSQR and QSQI and noting that QSQI is orders of magnitude worse in all cases. QSQR uses the same set of relevant facts (the reachable nodes) and differs only in that it has a recursive control strategy that avoids precisely this duplication. Naive evaluation also does a lot of duplicate work, for the same reason as QSQI, i.e., it does not remember previous firings. Semi-Naive differs from Naive only in that it remembers all previous firings and does not repeat them. Thus, the effect of duplication can also be seen in the difference between Naive and Semi-Naive.

The effect of a smaller set of relevant facts can be seen in the vast difference between Magic Sets and Semi-Naive. Magic Sets is simply Semi-Naive applied to the set of relevant facts, which is determined to be the set of reachable nodes except in the doubly recursive case. In this case, the first phase of the Magic Sets strategy, which computes the set of relevant facts, fails and the Magic Sets strategy degenerates to Semi-Naive. This effect can also be seen in the behavior of Prolog on a tree data structure (which means we eliminate the effect of duplication) when the first argument is free. Prolog's depth first strategy is unable to propagate the constant in the second argument of the query. In other words, it must consider all facts in the database, and its performance degrades by several orders of magnitude. Similarly, the Static Filtering strategy degenerates to Semi-Naive when the optimization algorithm fails to push down the constant in the query. We note that pushing the constant (i.e., the selection that it represents) is equivalent to cutting down on the number of relevant facts.

QSQR succeeds in restricting the set of relevant facts to the set of nodes reachable from the query node even in the non-linear version of ancestor. It does this at the cost of implementing the recursive control, which is a cost that we do not understand at this stage. QSQI also succeeds in restricting the set of relevant facts, but performs a great deal of duplicate computation. The Magic Sets algorithm uses the entire parent relation for the set of relevant facts and so degenerates to Semi-Naive. APEX, for reasons explained below, also uses a much larger set of relevant facts. So, although it improves upon Semi-Naive computation in this case, it is much worse than QSQR. The Generalized Magic Sets strategy, however, succeeds in restricting the set of relevant facts to those reachable from the query node, thus illustrating its wider applicability.

Henschen-Naqvi and Counting do not apply and Prolog does not terminate.

The behavior of APEX illustrates the interesting distinction between the set of relevant facts and the set of *useful* facts. The first step in the APEX strategy is to find what APEX calls the set of relevant facts (which is actually a subset of the set of relevant facts as we have defined it, since it does not include all facts than could derive an answer). In the ancestor examples, these are facts from the relation parent, and the firing of the first rule adds them to the ancestor relation. Subsequently, these facts are substituted (in turn) into both the parent and ancestor predicates in the body of the second rule. Except in the first case, this leads to subqueries whose answers are not relevant. For example, in the case where the second argument is bound to john, the set of relevant (a la APEX) facts is the set of facts p(X,john). By substituting these into the parent predicate in the second rule, we generate the query a(john,?). This computes the ancestors of john, whereas the given query a(?,john) asks for the descendants of john. This is because APEX does not make the distinction that facts of the form p(X,john) are relevant to the query a(?,john) only when substituted into the ancestor predicate in the second rule. This is a distinction that the Magic Sets strategy makes, and it thereby reduces the number of useless firings.

We now consider the third factor, the arity of the intermediate relations. The two strategies that use unary intermediate relations are the Henschen-Naqvi and Counting strategies. In essence, at step i they compute the set of relevant facts that is at a distance i from the query node. Let us denote this set by Si. At the next step, they compute the set of those nodes in parent to which there is an arc from a node in Si. Thus, they compute all nodes reachable from john, and further they compute each node at most D times where D is the duplication factor. However, the unary relations strategy fails to terminate if the query node is in a cycle. Also, neither the Henschen-Naqvi nor the Counting strategy applies when there are non-linear rules.

Magic Sets computes exactly the same set of relevant facts and does no duplicate work. However, in the second phase at step i it computes all arcs in the transitive closure of parent (restricted to the set of relevant facts) of length i. In particular, this includes all arcs of length i rooted at john. This is the answer, and this is essentially all that the more specialized methods, Henschen-Naqvi and Counting, compute. Everything else that the Magic Sets strategy does is useless computation. Thus, the cost of the Magic Sets strategy is the number of arcs in the transitive closure of the subtree rooted at john (i.e. the subtree of nodes reachable from john).

The recursive control of QSQR generates subqueries using precisely the nodes in set Si at step i, and the answer to each of these subqueries is the set of all nodes in the subtree rooted at that node. By induction, it is easy to see that the total cost involved in computing a query is the number of arcs in the transitive closure of the subgraph rooted at that query node. (The cost is thus similar to that of Magic Sets.) The intermediate relations here are the (binary) sets of answers to each subquery. This seems to indicate the power of a recursive control strategy since it succeeds in reducing both the set of relevant facts and the amount of duplicate work.

10.2.2. The Same Generation Query

We conclude this discussion by explaining the performance of the various strategies in the same generation query in terms of these three factors. Counting has the best performance since it uses the smallest set of relevant facts (the nodes of *up* that are reachable from the query node), does not do duplicate computation, and further, uses unary intermediate relations. It executes the query in two phases. In the first phase, at step i, it computes the set of all nodes in *up* that are reachable from the query node via a path of length i. In the second phase, it first computes the nodes of *down* that are reachable from this set via an arc of flat, still retaining the distance of each set from the query node. In subsequent iterations, it steps through *down* once each time, such that each node in a set that is i steps away from the query node in *up* is the root of paths of length i in *down*.

Henschen-Naqvi uses the same set of relevant facts, and is a unary strategy, but it does a lot of duplicate work. It is a single phase algorithm that does the same amount of work as the first phase of Counting in computing sets of *up* nodes along with their distances from the query node. However, it steps through *down* i times for each set at a distance i from the query node in *up*. Since it does not keep track of the work it does in step i at step i+1, it repeats a lot of the work in stepping through *down*. (Unless, of course, the data is such that there is no duplication of work. This corresponds to the data configuration in the worst case for Counting - the additional book-keeping done by Counting is unnecessary since the data ensures that there is no duplication of work in stepping through *down*.)

The set of relevant facts for Magic Set and QSQR is again the set of *up* nodes reachable from the query node. They do not perform duplicate computation. However, they work with binary relations, in effect computing all paths with equal lengths in *up* and *down* linked by a single arc in flat. Thus, their performance is inferior to that of Counting. Further, QSQR's left to right strategy forces us to create intermediate relations for up^* and $up^*.sg$, where up^* denotes the transitive closure of *up*. Since the Magic Set strategy does not impose any order of evaluation, we can do with the single intermediate relation *sg*. The cost of the additional inferences required to create the intermediate relations causes a large difference in the costs of the two strategies.

Our graphs show the performance of Magic Set to be identical to that of Henschen-Naqvi. It is to be expected that they perform similarly since the duplicate work done by Henschen-Naqvi is offset by the fact that they work with binary relations. However, their performance is not really identical. It appears to be so in our curves for two reasons. The first is our approximation of the number of arcs of length 1 to n(l)gsum(E,h-l). The second is the fact that we plot the curves for cases where *up* and *down* are identical. Under these conditions, the expressions for the performance of these methods become identical.

QSQI is similar to QSQR except that at each step, it duplicates the work of the previous steps, and so it is inferior to Magic Set and QSQR. Semi-Naive uses binary relations, and although it does not do duplicate work, this is outweighed by the fact that the set of relevant facts is all the nodes in *up*. So it performs worse than QSQI. Static Filtering degenerates to Semi-Naive since the optimization strategy fails to make any improvements to the system graph. Prolog is similar to QSQR when there is no duplication in the data, but its cost increases exponentially with the depth of the data structure when there is duplication. Naive evaluation uses the entire set of nodes in *up* as relevant facts, does duplicate work since it does not remember firings, and uses binary intermediate relations. With the exception of Prolog over a certain range, it is clearly the worst strategy.

Finally, we note that when the transfer ratio T is 0.01 (1%), the cost of computing the answer by Naive or Semi-Naive evaluation is essentially that of computing all arcs in the relation *flat*, and so the two methods perform almost identically.

11. Related Work

The performance issue was addressed informally through the discussion of a set of examples in Bancilhon et al. [1986b]. Han and Lu [1986] contains study of the performance of a set of four evaluation strategies (including Naive and Henschen-Naqvi and two others not considered here) on the same generation example, using randomly generated data. Their model is based on the selectivity of the join and select operations and the sizes of the data relations. They consider both CPU and IO cost. We have chosen to concentrate on one aspect of the problem, which is the number of successful firings (measured using the sizes of the intermediate relations), and have studied a wider range of strategies, queries and data.

12. Conclusions and Caveats

We have presented a performance comparison of ten methods. Even though the "benchmark" we have used is incomplete, the cost measure too elementary and the approximations crude, we found the results to be valuable. The robustness of the results (at least on our workload), both in terms of the order of magnitude differences between the costs of the strategies and in terms of invariance of the results to the parameters that we varied, was a surprise. We have also been able to explain most of our results through three factors: duplication, relevant facts and unary vs. binary. While the first two factors were well known, the third one came as a surprise, even though it was probably already understood in Sacca and Zaniolo [1986].

Our conclusions may be summarized as follows:

1. For a given query, there is a clear ordering of the strategies.
2. The more specialized strategies perform significantly better.
3. Recursion is a powerful control structure which reduces the number of relevant facts and eliminates duplicate work.
4. The choice of the right strategy is critical since the differences in performance are by orders of magnitude.

5. Three factors which greatly influence performance are: (i) duplication of work, (ii) the set of relevant facts, and (iii) the number and arity of the intermediate relations.

The results seem robust in that the performance of the various strategies usually differ by orders of magnitude, which allows a wide latitude for the approximations in the model and cost evaluation. Also, the curves rarely intersect, which means that the relative ordering of the strategies is maintained in most cases over the entire range of data.

However, it must be emphasized that our cost function makes some crude approximations. The cost of join is linear in the size of the result, a consequence of our using the size of intermediate relations as the cost measure. We also ignore the cost of disk accesses, and the cost of implementing a recursive control strategy. Our model suffers from the approximation that duplication is independent of the size of the start set.

Finally, our sample data and queries are limited, and the results must be extrapolated to other data and queries with caution, especially since the results show some variance in the relative performance of the strategies for different sets of data and queries. In particular, our benchmark is limited to the type of data and query where there is a *large* amount of data and the size of the answer to the query is *small*. This clearly favors the "smart" strategies and obscures, for instance, the fact that Semi-Naive performs as well as any other strategy when computing the entire transitive closure of a relation Bancilhon [1986]. Further, our data contains no cycles or shortcuts. This is an important limitation since it favors some of the specialized strategies. For instance, there are cases where Counting performs worse than Magic Sets Bancilhon et al. [1986a]. This is not shown by our results since these cases involve shortcuts in the data.

13. Acknowledgements

We wish to thank Bill Alexander, Patrick Valduriez and Ken Smith for careful proofreading of parts of the manuscript. We are extremely grateful to Paris Kanellakis, Eliezer Lozinskii, Jeff Ullman, Laurent Vieille and Carlo Zaniolo who provided enlightening comments and suggested many corrections and improvements to the paper. We thank the anonymous referees of Bancilhon and Ramakrishnan [1987] for numerous comments which improved the technical content and presentation of this paper.

14. References

1. F. Afrati, C. Papadimitriou, G. Papageorgiou, A. Roussou, Y. Sagiv and J.D. Ullman [1986], "Convergence of Sideways Query Evaluation," *Proc. 5th ACM SIGMOD-SIGACT Symposium on Principles of Database Systems, 1986.*

2. A. Aho and J. D. Ullman [1979], "Universality of Data Retrieval Languages," *Proc. 6th ACM Symposium on Principles of Programming Languages, 1979, pp 110-120.*

3. F. Bancilhon [1986], "Naive Evaluation of Recursively Defined Relations," in *On Knowledge Base Management Systems - Integrating Database and AI Systems, Brodie and Mylopoulos, Eds., Springer-Verlag, 1986, pp 165-178.*

4. F. Bancilhon [1985], "A Note on the Performance of Rule Based Systems," *MCC Technical Report DB-022-85, 1985.*

5. F. Bancilhon, D. Maier, Y. Sagiv and J.D. Ullman [1986a], "Magic Sets and Other Strange Ways to Implement Logic Programs," *Proc. 5th ACM SIGMOD-SIGACT Symposium on Principles of Database Systems, 1986, pp 1-15.*

6. F. Bancilhon, D. Maier, Y. Sagiv and J.D. Ullman [1986b], "Magic Sets: Algorithms and Examples," *Unpublished Manuscript, 1986.*

7. F. Bancilhon and R. Ramakrishnan [1987], "Performance Evaluation of Data Intensive Logic Programs", To appear in *Foundations of Deductive Databases and Logic Programming, Ed. J. Minker, Morgan Kaufman, 1987.*

8. R. Bayer [1985], "Query Evaluation and Recursion in Deductive Database Systems," *Unpublished Manuscript, 1985.*

9. C. Beeri and R. Ramakrishnan [1987], "On the Power of Magic," *Proc. 6th ACM SIGMOD-SIGACT-SIGART Symposium on Principles of Database Systems, 1987, pp 269-283.*

10. C. Chang [1981], "On the Evaluation of Queries Containing Derived Relations in Relational Databases," In *Advances in Data Base Theory, Vol.1, H.Gallaire, J. Minker and J.M. Nicolas, Plenum Press, New York, 1981, pp 235-260.*

11. U. Dayal, A. Buchmann, D. Goldhirsch, S. Heiler, F. Manola, J. Orenstein and A. Rosenthal [1986], "PROBE- a Research Project in Knowledge-Oriented Database Systems: Preliminary Analysis," *Technical Report, CCA-85-03, July 1985.*

12. C. Delobel [1986], "Bases de Donnees et Bases de Connaissances: Une Approche Systemique a l'Aide d'une Algebre Matricielle des Relations," *Journees Francophones, Grenoble, January 1986, pp 101-134.*

13. S.W. Dietrich and D.S. Warren [1985], "Dynamic Programming Strategies for the Evaluation of Recursive Queries," *Unpublished Report, 1985.*

14. H. Gallaire, J. Minker and J.-M. Nicolas [1984], "Logic and Data Bases: A Deductive Approach," *Computing Surveys, Vol. 16, No 2, June 1984, pp 153-185.*

15. G. Gardarin and Ch. de Maindreville [1986], "Evaluation of Database Recursive Logic Programs as Recurrent Function Series," *Proc. SIGMOD 86, Washington, D.C., May 1986, pp 177-186.*

16. J. Han and H. Lu [1986], "Some Performance Results on Recursive Query Processing in Relational Database Systems," *Proc. Data Engineering Conference, Los Angeles, February 1986, pp 533-539.*

17. L. Henschen and S. Naqvi [1984], "On Compiling Queries in Recursive First-Order Data Bases," *JACM, Vol 31, January 1984, pp 47-85.*

18. M. Kifer and E. Lozinskii [1986a], "Filtering Data Flow in Deductive Databases," *Proc. International Conference on Database Theory, Lecture Notes in Computer Science, No. 243, Springer-Verlag, 1986, pp 186-202.*

19. M. Kifer and E. Lozinskii [1986b], "A Framework for an Efficient Implementation of Deductive Databases," *Proc. 6th Advanced Database Symposium, 1986, pp 109-116.*

20. M. Kifer and E. Lozinskii [1988], "SYGRAF: Implementing Logic Programs in a Database Style," *To appear, IEEE Trans. on Software Engineering, 1988.*

21. R. Krishnamurthy, R. Ramakrishnan and O. Shmueli [1988], "A Framework for Testing Safety and Effective Computability of Extended Datalog," *To appear, Proc. ACM-SIGMOD Conference, 1988.*

22. K. Laskowski [1984], "Compiling Recursive Axioms in First Order Databases," *Masters Thesis, Northwestern University, 1984*

23. E. Lozinskii [1985], "Evaluating Queries in Deductive Databases by Generating," *Proc. 11th International Joint Conference on Artificial Intelligence, 1985, pp 173-177.*

24. G. Marque-Pucheu [1983], "Algebraic Structure of Answers in a Recursive Logic Database," *To appear in Acta Informatica.*

25. G. Marque-Pucheu, J. Martin-Gallausiaux and G. Jomier [1984], "Interfacing Prolog and Relational Database Management Systems," *in New Applications of Databases, Gardarin and Gelenbe Eds, Academic Press, London, 1984.*

26. D. McKay and S. Shapiro [1981], "Using Active Connection Graphs for Reasoning with Recursive Rules," *Proc. 7th International Joint Conference on Artificial Intelligence, 1981, pp 368-374.*

27. J. Minker [1988], "Foundations of Deductive Databases and Logic Programming," *Ed. J. Minker, Morgan Kaufmann, 1988.*

28. K. Morris, J. Ullman and A. Van Gelder [1986], "Design Overview of the NAIL! System," *Proceedings of the 3rd International Conference on Logic Programming, London, July 1986.*

29. R. Ramakrishnan [1988], "Magic Templates: A Spell-Binding Approach to Logic Programs," *Technical Report, Computer Sciences Department, Univ. of Wisconsin-Madison, 1988.*

30. R. Ramakrishnan, F. Bancilhon and A. Silberschatz [1987], "Safety of Horn Clauses with Infinite Relations," *Proc. 6th ACM SIGMOD-SIGACT Symposium on Principles of Database Systems, 1987.*

31. J. Rohmer, R. Lescoeur and J.M. Kerisit [1986], "The Alexander Method: A Technique for the Processing of Recursive Axioms in Deductive Databases," *New Generation Computing 4, 3, 1986, pp 273-285.*

32. A. Rosenthal, S. Heiler, U. Dayal and F. Manola [1986], "Traversal Recursion: A Practical Approach to Supporting Recursive Applications," *Proc. ACM-SIGMOD Conference, 1986.*

33. P. Roussel [1975], "PROLOG, Manuel de Reference et de Utilisation," *Groupe Intelligence Artificielle, Universite Aix-Marseille II, 1975.*

34. D. Sacca and C. Zaniolo [1986a], "On the Implementation of a Simple Class of Logic Queries for Databases," *Proc. 5th ACM SIGMOD-SIGACT Symposium on Principles of Database Systems, 1986, pp 16-23.*

35. D. Sacca and C. Zaniolo [1986b], "The Generalized Counting Method for Recursive Logic Queries," *Proc. First International Conference on Database Theory, 1986.*

36. D. Sacca and C. Zaniolo [1987], "Magic Counting Methods," *Proc. ACM-SIGMOD Conference, 1987, pp 49-59.*

37. S. Shapiro and D. McKay [1980], "Inference with Recursive Rules," *Proc. 1st Annual National Conference on Artificial Intelligence, August, 1980.*

38. S. Shapiro, J. Martins and D. McKay [1982], "Bi-Directional Inference," *Proc. 4th Annual Conference of the Cognitive Science Society, Ann Arbor, Michigan, 1982.*

39. A. Tarski [1955], "A Lattice Theoretical Fixpoint Theorem and its Applications" *Pacific Journal of Mathematics 5, 1955, pp 285-309*

40. J.D. Ullman [1985], "Implementation of Logical Query Languages for Databases," *Transactions on Database Systems, Vol. 10, No. 3, 1985, pp 289-321.*

41. J. Ullman and A. Van Gelder [1985], "Testing Applicability of Top-Down Capture Rules," *Technical Report, Stanford University, STAN-CS-85-1046, 1985.*

42. P. Valduriez and H. Boral [1986], "Evaluation of Recursive Queries Using Join Indices," *Proc. First Intl. Conference on Expert Database Systems, Charleston, 1986.*

43. M. Van Emden and R. Kowalski [1976], "The Semantics of Predicate Logic as a Programming Language," *JACM, Vol 23, No 4, October 1976, pp 733-742.*

44. A. Van Gelder and R. Topor [1987], "Safety and Correct Translation of Relational Calculus Formulas," *Proc. 6th ACM SIGMOD-SIGACT Symposium on Principles of Database Systems, 1987.*

45. L. Vieille [1986], "Recursive axioms in Deductive Databases: The Query/Subquery Approach," *Proc. First Intl. Conference on Expert Database Systems, Charleston, 1986, pp 179-194.*

46. L. Vieille [1988], "From QSQ towards QoSaQ: Global Optimization of Recursive Queries," *To appear in "Proc. 2nd Intl. Conf. on Expert Database Systems", Ed. L. Kerschberg, 1988.*

47. C. Zaniolo [1985], "The Representation and Deductive Retrieval of Complex Objects," *Proc. 11th Int. Conference on Very Large Data Bases, Stockholm, September 1985.*

48. C. Zaniolo [1986], "Safety and Compilation of Non-Recursive Horn Clauses," *Proc. First Intl. Conference on Expert Database Systems, Charleston, 1986.*

15. Appendix 1: The Cost Functions

Query 1 (Ancestor.bf)

1.1 Naive evaluation $D\sum_{i=1}^{h}(h-i+1).a(i) + E.gsum(E,h'-1).$

1.2 Semi-Naive Evaluation $D\sum_{i=1}^{h}a(i) + E.gsum(E,h'-1).$

1.3 QSQ, Iterative $E.gsum(E,h'-1) + F.\sum_{i=1}^{h'}(h'-i+1).i.E^{i-1}$

1.4 QSQ, Recursive $(F+E).gsum(E,h'-1) + D\sum_{i=1}^{h'}E^{i}.gsum(E,h'-i)$

1.5 Henschen-Naqvi $(F+E).gsum(E,h'-1)$

1.6 Prolog $gsum(F,h') + E.gsum(E,h'-1) + \sum_{i=1}^{h'}(F^{i}).gsum(F,h'-i)$

1.7 APEX $(F+E).gsum(E,h'-1) + D\sum_{i=1}^{h'}E^{i}.gsum(E,h'-i)$

1.8 Kifer-Lozinskii $D\sum_{i=1}^{h}a(i)+E.gsum(E,h'-1)$

1.9 Magic Sets $(F+E).gsum(E,h'-1) + D\sum_{i=1}^{h'}E^{i}.gsum(E,h'-i)$

1.10 Counting $(F+E).gsum(E,h'-1)$

Query 2 (Ancestor.fb)

2.1 Naive evaluation $D\sum_{i=1}^{h}(h-i+1).a(i) + (1/E).gsum(1/E,h-h'-1)$

2.2 Semi-Naive Evaluation $D\sum_{i=1}^{h}a(i) + (1/E).gsum(1/E,h-h'-1)$

2.3 QSQ, Iterative $(1/E).gsum(1/E,h-h'-1) + D.\sum_{i=1}^{h-h'}(h-h'-i+1).i.(1/E)^{i-1}$

2.4 QSQ, Recursive $1 + (1/E).gsum(1/E,h-h'-1) + F.\sum_{i=1}^{h-h'}(1/E)^{i}.gsum(1/E,h-h'-i)$

2.5 Henschen-Naqvi $(D+1/E).gsum(1/E,h-h'-1)$

2.6 Prolog $(1/E).gsum(1/E,h-h'-1) + \sum_{i=1}^{h}n(i).gsum(F,h-i)$

2.7 APEX $(1/E)^{(h-h')}.(E.gsum(E,h-1)+D\sum_{i=1}^{h}E^{i}.gsum(E,h-i))$

2.8 Kifer-Lozinskii (D+1/E).gsum(1/E, h-h'-1)

2.9 Magic Sets $1 + (1/E).gsum(1/E,h-h'-1) + F.\sum_{i=1}^{h-h'} (1/E)^i.gsum(1/E,h-h'-i)$

2.10 Counting (D+1/E).gsum(1/E,h-h'-1)

Query 3 (Ancestor.bf, Non-Linear Version)

3.1 Naive evaluation $E.gsum(E,h'-1) + D\sum_{i=1}^{h}(\log(h/i)+1).(i-1).a(i)$

3.2 Semi-Naive Evaluation $E.gsum(E,h'-1) + D\sum_{i=1}^{h}(i-1).a(i)$

3.3 QSQ, Iterative $E.gsum(E,h'-1) + F.\sum_{i=1}^{h'} (h'-i+1).i.E^{i-1}$

3.4 QSQ, Recursive $F+E.gsum(E,h'-1)+D\sum_{i=2}^{h'} (i-1).E^i$

3.5 Henschen-Naqvi Does not apply.

3.6 Prolog Does not terminate.

3.7 APEX $E.gsum(E,h'-1) + (1/E)^{h-h'}.(D\sum_{i=1}^{h}(i-1).E^i.gsum(E,h-i))$

$+ E^{h'}.(F\sum_{i=1}^{h}(i-1).(1/E)^i.gsum(1/E,h-i))$

3.8 Kifer-Lozinskii $E.gsum(E,h'-1) + D\sum_{i=1}^{h}(i-1).a(i)$

3.9 Magic Sets $E.gsum(E,h'-1) + D\sum_{i=1}^{h}(i-1).a(i)$

3.10 Counting Does not apply.

Query 4 (Same Generation.bf)

In the following expressions, $h'_{up.down} = \min(h'_{up},h'_{down})$, and $h_{up.down} = \min(h_{up},h_{down})$.

4.1 Naive evaluation

$$A_{flat} + T_{up2.flat1}.E_{flat}.T_{flat2.down1}.D_{down}.\sum_{i=1}^{h_{up.down}} (h_{up.down}-i+1).a_{up}(i).E^i_{down} +$$

$$T_{up2.flat1}.E_{flat}.T_{flat2.down1}.F_{down}.\sum_{i=1}^{h'_{up.down}} (E_{up}.E_{down})^i$$

4.2 Semi-Naive Evaluation

$$A_{flat} + T_{up2.flat1}.E_{flat}.T_{flat2.down1}.D_{down}.\sum_{i=1}^{h_{up.down}} a_{up}(i).E^i_{down} +$$

$$T_{up2.flat1}.E_{flat}.T_{flat2.down1}.F_{down}.\sum_{i=1}^{h'_{up.down}} (E_{up}.E_{down})^i$$

4.3 QSQ, Iterative

$$(h'_{up.down}+1).F_{flat}+$$

$$T_{up2.flat1}.F_{flat}\sum_{i=1}^{h'_{up.down}} (h'_{up.down}-i+1).E_{up}{}^i +$$

$$E_{flat}.T_{up2.flat1}.T_{flat2.down1}.F_{down}.\sum_{i=1}^{h'_{up.down}} (h'_{up.down}-i+1).E^i_{up}.\text{gsum}(E_{down},i-1) +$$

$$T_{up2.flat1}.E_{flat}.T_{flat2.down1}.F_{down}.\sum_{i=1}^{h'_{up.down}} (E_{up}.E_{down})^i$$

4.4 QSQ, Recursive

$$F_{up}.\text{gsum}(E_{up},h'_{up}-1) + E_{up}.\text{gsum}(E_{up},h'_{up}-1).T_{up2.flat1}.F_{flat} +$$

$$T_{up2.flat1}.E_{flat}.T_{flat2.down1}.D_{down}.\sum_{i=1}^{h'_{up.down}} E^i_{up}.\text{gsum}(E_{up},h'_{up}-i).E^i_{down} +$$

$$T_{up2.flat1}.E_{flat}.T_{flat2.down1}.F_{down}.\sum_{i=1}^{h'_{up.down}} (E_{up}.E_{down})^i$$

4.5 Henschen-Naqvi

$$F_{up}.\text{gsum}(E_{up},h'_{up}-1) +$$

$$\sum_{i=1}^{h'_{up.down}} (E^i_{up}.T_{up2.flat1}.F_{flat} + T_{up2.flat1}.E_{flat}.T_{flat2.down1}.F_{down}.E^i_{up}.\text{gsum}(E_{down},i-1)) +$$

$$T_{up2.flat1}.E_{flat}.T_{flat2.down1}.F_{down}.\sum_{i=1}^{h'_{up.down}} (E_{up}.E_{down})^i$$

4.6 Prolog

$$\text{gsum}(F_{up},h'_{up}-1) + F_{up}.\text{gsum}(F_{up},h'_{up}-1).T_{up2.flat1}.F_{flat} +$$

$$T_{up2.flat1}.F_{flat}.T_{flat2.down1}.\sum_{i=1}^{h'_{up.down}} F^i_{up}.\text{gsum}(F_{up},h'_{up}-i).F^i_{down} +$$

$$T_{up2.flat1}.E_{flat}.T_{flat2.down1}.F_{down}.\sum_{i=1}^{h'_{up.down}} (E_{up}.E_{down})^i$$

4.7 APEX

$$F_{up}.\text{gsum}(E_{up},h'_{up}-1) + E_{up}.\text{gsum}(E_{up},h'_{up}-1).T_{up2.flat1}.F_{flat} +$$

$$T_{up2.flat1}.E_{flat}.T_{flat2.down1}.D_{down}.\sum_{i=1}^{h'_{up.down}} E^i_{up}.\text{gsum}(E_{up},h'_{up}-i).E^i_{down} +$$

$$T_{up2.flat1}.E_{flat}.T_{flat2.down1}.F_{down}.\sum_{i=1}^{h'_{up.down}} (E_{up}.E_{down})^i$$

4.8 Kifer-Lozinskii

$$A_{flat} + T_{up2.flat1}.E_{flat}.T_{flat2.down1}.D_{down}.(\sum_{i=1}^{h_{up.down}} (a_{up}(i).E^i_{down}) +$$

$$T_{up2.flat1}.E_{flat}.T_{flat2.down1}.F_{down}.\sum_{i=1}^{h'_{up.down}} (E_{up}.E_{down})^i$$

4.9 Magic Sets

$$F_{up}.gsum(E_{up},h'_{up}-1) + E_{up}.gsum(E_{up},h'_{up}-1).T_{up2.flat1}.F_{flat} +$$

$$T_{up2.flat1}.E_{flat}.T_{flat2.down1}.D_{down}.\sum_{i=1}^{h'_{up.down}} E_{up}^{i}.gsum(E_{up},h'_{up}-i).E_{down}^{i} +$$

$$T_{up2.flat1}.E_{flat}.T_{flat2.down1}.F_{down}.\sum_{i=1}^{h'_{up.down}} (E_{up}.E_{down})^{i}$$

4.10 Counting

$$F_{up}.gsum(E_{up},h'_{up}-1) +$$

$$T_{up2.flat1}.F_{flat}(1+E_{up}gsum(Eu,h'_{up}-1)) +$$

$$\sum_{i=1}^{h'_{up.down}} T_{up2.flat1}.E_{flat}.T_{flat2.down1}.D_{down}.(E_{up}.E_{down})^{i} +$$

$$T_{up2.flat1}.E_{flat}.T_{flat2.down1}.F_{down}.\sum_{i=1}^{h'_{up.down}} (E_{up}.E_{down})^{i}$$

Appendix 2: The Curves

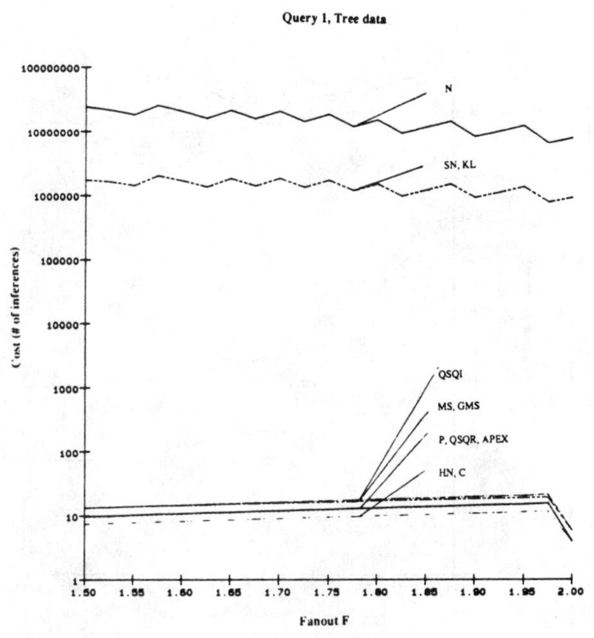

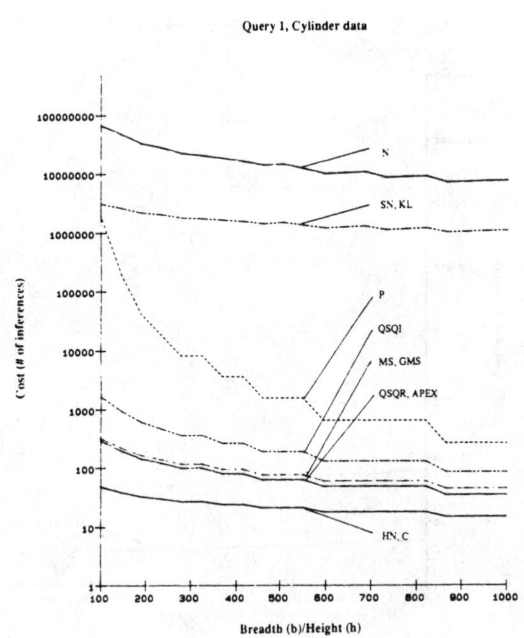

ABF_INV

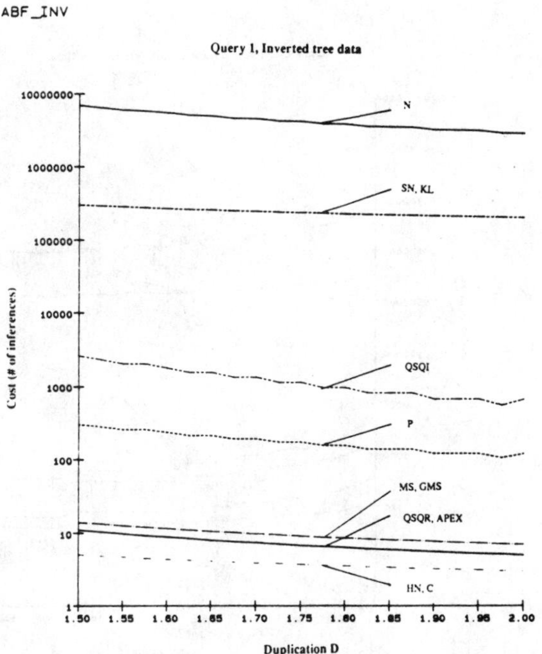

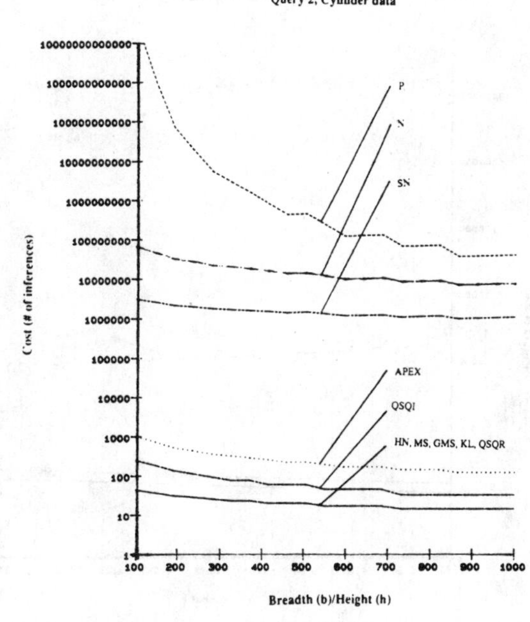

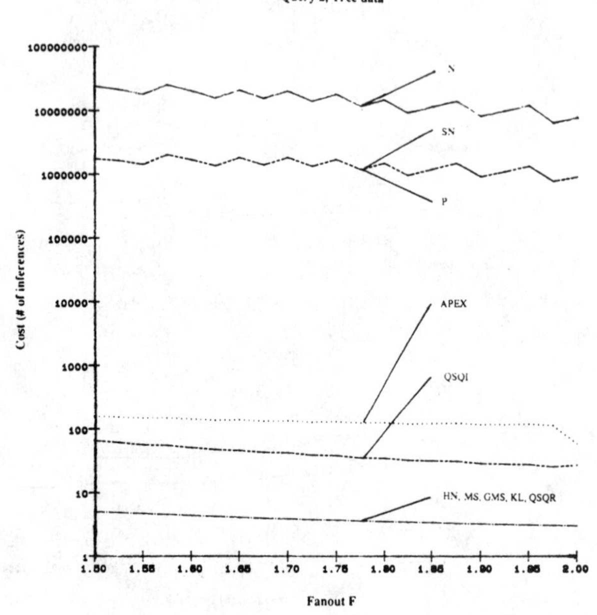
Query 2, Tree data
N
SN
P
APEX
QSQI
HN, MS, GMS, KL, QSQR
Cost (# of inferences)
Fanout F

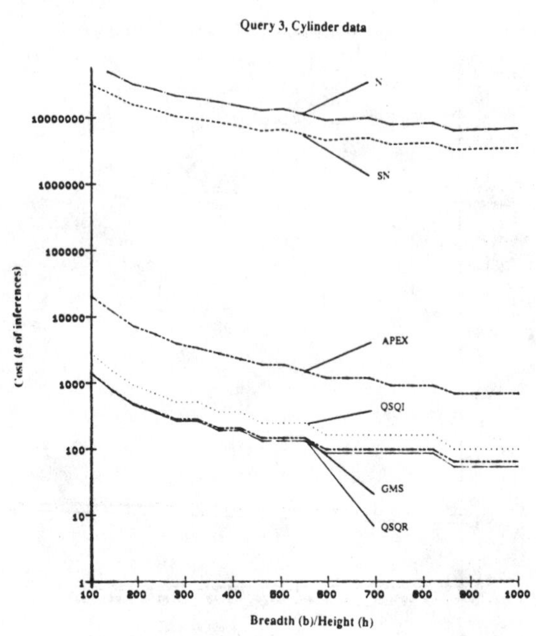
Query 3, Cylinder data
N
SN
APEX
QSQI
GMS
QSQR
Cost (# of inferences)
Breadth (b)/Height (h)

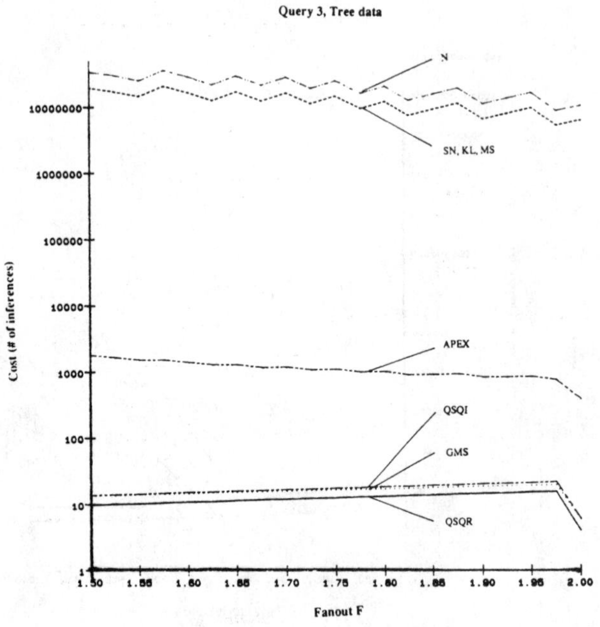
Query 3, Tree data
N
SN, KL, MS
APEX
QSQI
GMS
QSQR
Cost (# of inferences)
Fanout F

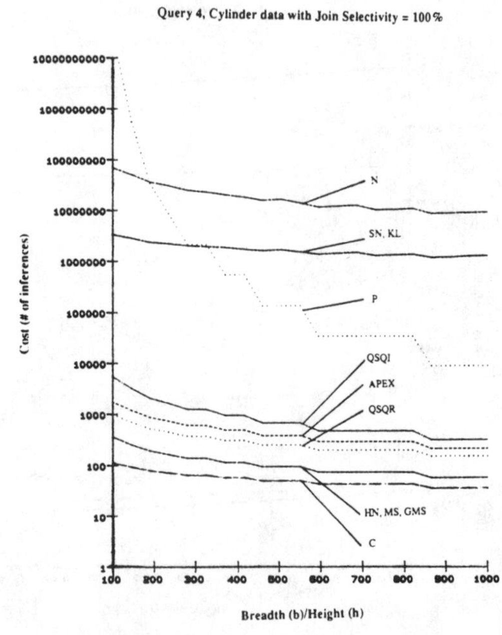
Query 4, Cylinder data with Join Selectivity = 100%
N
SN, KL
P
QSQI
APEX
QSQR
HN, MS, GMS
C
Cost (# of inferences)
Breadth (b)/Height (h)

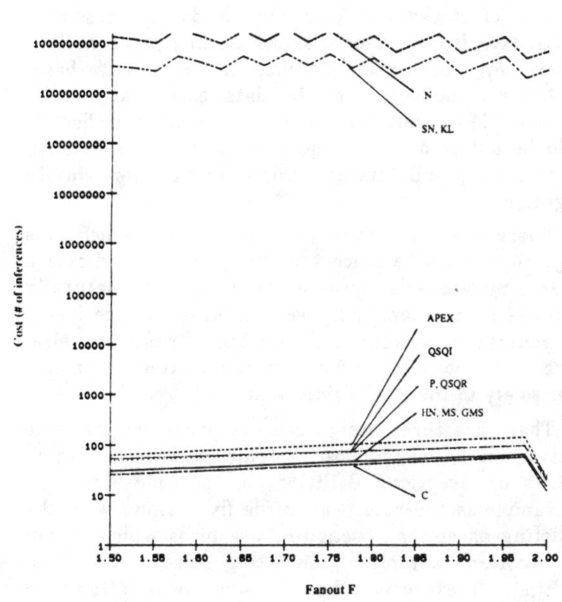
Query 4, Tree data with Join Selectivity = 100%
Cost (# of inferences)
10000000000
1000000000
100000000
10000000
1000000
100000
10000
1000
100
10
1
1.50 1.55 1.60 1.65 1.70 1.75 1.80 1.85 1.90 1.95 2.00
Fanout F
N
SN, KL
APEX
QSQI
P, QSQR
HN, MS, GMS
C

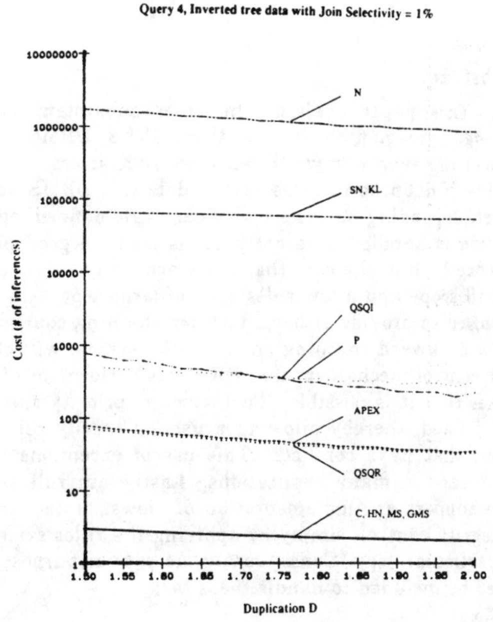
Query 4, Inverted tree data with Join Selectivity = 1%
Cost (# of inferences)
10000000
1000000
100000
10000
1000
100
10
1
1.50 1.55 1.60 1.65 1.70 1.75 1.80 1.85 1.90 1.95 2.00
Duplication D
N
SN, KL
QSQI
P
APEX
QSQR
C, HN, MS, GMS

SG_INV

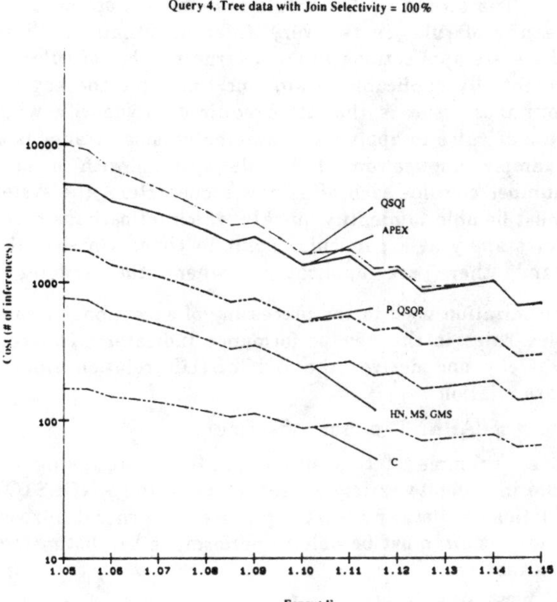
Query 4, Tree data with Join Selectivity = 100%
Cost (# of inferences)
10000
1000
100
10
1.05 1.06 1.07 1.08 1.09 1.10 1.11 1.12 1.13 1.14 1.15
Fanout F
QSQI
APEX
P, QSQR
HN, MS, GMS
C

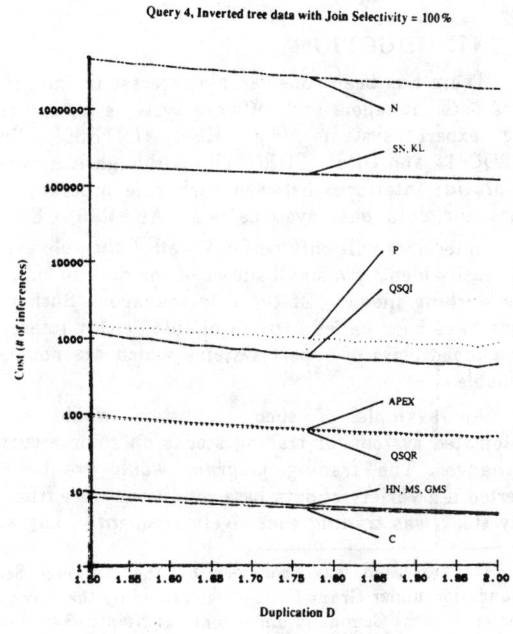
Query 4, Inverted tree data with Join Selectivity = 100%
Cost (# of inferences)
1000000
100000
10000
1000
100
10
1
1.50 1.55 1.60 1.65 1.70 1.75 1.80 1.85 1.90 1.95 2.00
Duplication D
N
SN, KL
P
QSQI
APEX
QSQR
HN, MS, GMS
C

THE DESIGN OF THE POSTGRES RULES SYSTEM

Michael Stonebraker, Eric Hanson and Chin-Heng Hong

EECS Department
University of California, Berkeley, Ca., 94720

Abstract

This paper explains the rules subsystem that is being implemented in the POSTGRES DBMS. It is novel in several ways. First, it gives to users the capability of defining rules as well as data to a DBMS. Moreover, depending on the scope of each rule defined, optimization is handled differently. This leads to good performance both in the case that there are many rules each of small scope and a few rules each of large scope. In addition, rules provide either a forward chaining control flow or a backward chaining one, and the system will choose the control mechanism that optimizes performance in the cases that it is possible. Furthermore, priority rules can be defined, thereby allowing a user to specify rules systems that have conflicts. This use of exceptions seems necessary in many applications. Lastly, our rule system can support an implementation of views, protection and integrity control, simply by applying the rules system in a particular way. Consequently, no special purpose code need be included to handle these tasks.

1. INTRODUCTION

There has been considerable interest in integrating data base managers and software systems for constructing expert systems (e.g. KEE [INTE85], Prolog [CLOC81], and OPS5 [FORG81]). Although it is possible to provide interfaces between such rule processing systems and data base systems (e.g. [ABAR86, CERI86]), such interfaces will only perform well if the rule system can easily identify a small subset of the data to load into the working memory of the rule manager. Such problems have been called ``partitionable'' Our interest is in a broad class of expert systems which are not partitionable.

An example of such a system would be an automated system for trading stocks on some securities exchange. The trading program would want to be alerted if a variety of data base conditions were true, e.g. any stock was trading excessively frequently, any stock or group of stocks was going up or down excessively rapidly, etc. It is evident that the trading program does not have any locality of reference in a large data base, and there is no subset of the data base that can be extracted. Moreover, even if one could be identified, it would be out of date very quickly. For such problems, rule processing and data processing must be more closely integrated.

There are many mechanisms through which this integration can take place. In this paper we indicate a rather complete rules system which is quite naturally embedded in a general purpose data base manager. This next-generation system, POSTGRES, is described elsewhere [STON86a]; hence we restrict our attention in this paper solely to the rules component

There are three design criteria which we strive to satisfy. First, we propose a rule system in which conflicts (or exceptions [BORG85]) are possible. The classic example is the rule ``all birds fly'' along with the conflicting exception ``penguins are birds which do not fly'' Another example of conflicting rules is the situation that all executives have a wood desk. However, Jones is an executive who uses a steel desk. It is our opinion that a rule system that cannot support exceptions is of limited utility.

The second goal of a rule system is to optimize processing of rules in two very different situations. First, there are applications where a large number of rules are potentially applicable at any one time, and the key performance issue is the time required to identify which rule or rules to apply. The automated stock trader is an example application of a rule system with a large number of rules each of narrow scope. Here, the system must be able to identify quickly which (of perhaps many) rules apply at a particular point in time. On the other hand, there are applications where the amount of optimization used in the processing of exceptionally complex rules is the key performance indicator. The rule whereby one derives the ANCESTOR relation from a base relation

PARENT (person, offspring)

is an example of this situation. Here, processing the rule in order to satisfy a user query to the ANCESTOR relation is the key task to optimize. A general purpose rules system must be able to perform well in both kinds of situations.

The third goal of a rules system embedded in a data manager should be to support as many data base services

This research was sponsored by the National Science Foundation under Grant DMC-8504633 and by the Navy Electronics Systems Command under contract N00039-84-C-0039 as possible. Candidates services include views, integrity control and protection. As noted in [STON82], the code needed to perform these three tasks correspond to three small special purpose rules systems. A robust rules system should be usable for these internal purposes, and the POSTGRES rules system is a step toward this goal.

In Section 2 of this paper we discuss the syntax of POSTGRES rules and the semantics desired from a rule processing engine. The general idea is to propose a mechanism that appears to the user as a trigger subsystem [ESWA76, BUNE79]. However the novel aspect of our proposal is that we have two different optimization tactics. First, the time at which triggers are evaluated can be varied. It is clear that triggers can be activated whenever something in their read set changes. However, activation can also be delayed in some cases until somebody queries a data item that they will write. Varying the time of activation will be seen to be a valuable optimization tactic. Secondly, the mechanism that is used to ``fire'' triggers can be used at multiple granularities. This tactic will be usable to optimize separately different kinds of rules. These two optimization tactics will be the subject of Section 3. Then in Section 4 we sketch the algorithms to be run when a trigger is awakened and lastly indicate in Section 5 how our rules system can be used to support protection, integrity control and view subsystems.

2. POSTGRES RULE SEMANTICS

2.1. Syntax of Rules

POSTGRES supports a query language, POSTQUEL, which borrows heavily from its predecessor, QUEL [HELD75]. The main extensions are syntax to deal with procedural data, extended data types, rules, versions and time. The language is described elsewhere, and here we solely indicate the rule component of the language.

POSTQUEL supports the ability to update the salary field for the employee Mike in the EMP relation using a variation of QUEL as follows:

```
replace EMP (salary = E.salary) using E in EMP
where EMP.name = ``Mike'' and
E.name = ``Bill''
```

This command will set Mike's salary to that of Bill whenever it is run.

POSTQUEL also allows any insert, update, delete or retrieve command to be tagged with an ``always'' modifier which changes its meaning. Such tagged commands become **rules** and can be used in a variety of situations as will be presently noted. For example, the following command turns the above update into a rule.

```
replace always EMP (salary = E.salary)
using E in EMP
where EMP.name = ``Mike''
and E.name = ``Bill''
```

The semantics of this command is that it logically must appear to run forever. Hence, POSTGRES must ensure that any user who retrieves the salary of Mike will see a value equal to that of Bill. One implementation will be to wake up the above command whenever Bill's salary changes so the salary alteration can be propagated to Mike. This implementation resembles previous proposals [ESWA76, BUNE79] to support **triggers,** and efficient wake-up services are a challenge to the POSTGRES implementation. A second implementation will be to delay evaluating the rule until a user requests the salary of Mike. With this implementation, rules appear to utilize a form of ``lazy evaluation'' [BUNE82].

If a retrieve command is tagged with ``always'' it becomes an **alerter.** For example, the following command will retrieve Mike's salary whenever it changes.

```
retrieve always (EMP.salary)
where EMP.name = ``Mike''
```

It will be shown that a variety of data base services can be provided utilizing only this ``always'' command. These include backward chaining rules systems, forward chaining rules systems, views, protection control and integrity constraints. Hence, there is great leverage in a simple construct. However the semantics of triggers present a problem as explored in the next subsection.

2.2. Semantics of Rules

Suppose two rules have been defined that provide salaries for Mike, e.g.:

```
replace always EMP (salary = E.salary)
using E in EMP
where E.name = ``Fred''
and EMP.name = ``Mike''

replace always EMP (salary = E.salary)
using E in EMP
where E.name = ``Bill''
and EMP.name = ``Mike''
```

There are several possible outcomes which might be desired from this command collection. The first option would be to reject this collection of rules because it constitutes an attempt to assign two different values to the salary of Mike. Moreover, these two commands could be combined into a single POSTQUEL update, e.g.:

```
replace always EMP (salary = E.salary)
where EMP.name = ``Mike''
and (E.name = ``Bill'' or E.name = ``Fred'')
```

Such updates are **non-functional** and are disallowed by most data base systems (e.g INGRES [RTI85]) which detect them at run time and abort command processing. Hence the first semantics for rules would be to demand functionality and refuse to process non-functional collections.

Of course functionality is not always desirable for a collection of rules. Moreover, as noted in [KUNG84], there are cases where non-functional updates should also be allowed in normal query processing. Hence, we now turn to other possible definitions for this rule collection.

The second definition would be to support **random** semantics. If both rules were run repeatedly, the salary of Mike would cycle between the salary of Bill and that of Fred. Whenever, it was set to one value the other rule would be run to change it back. Hence, a retrieve command would see one salary or the other depending on which rule had run most recently. With random semantics, the user should see one salary or the other, and POSTGRES should ensure that no computation time is wasted in looping between the values.

The third possibility would be to support **union** semantics for a collection of rules. Since POSTQUEL supports columns of a relation of data type procedure, one could define salary as a procedural field. Hence, commands in POSTQUEL would be the value of this field and would generate the ultimate field value when executed. In the salary field for Mike, the following two commands would appear:

```
retrieve (EMP.salary) where EMP.name = ``Bill''
retrieve (EMP.salary) where EMP.name = ``Fred''
```

If Mike's salary was retrieved, both Fred's salary and Bill's salary would be returned. Hence, when multiple rules can produce values, a user should see the union of what the rules produce if union semantics are used.

To support exceptions, one requires a final definition of the semantics of rules, namely **priority** semantics. In this situation, a priority order among the rules would be established by tagging each with a priority. Priorities are floating point numbers in the range 0 to 1, and may appear after the keyword **always**. The Default priority is 0. For example, suppose the priority for the ``Fred'' is .7 and for the ``Bill'' rule is .5. Using priority semantics the salary of Mike should be equal to the salary of Fred.

Since one of the goals of the POSTGRES rules systems is to support exceptions, we choose to implement priority semantics. Hence a user can optionally specify the relative priorities of any collection of tagged commands that he introduced. If priorities are not specified, then POSTGRES chooses to implement random semantics for conflicting rules, and can return the result specified by either of them. However, one of the implementations which we propose is very efficient if union semantics are utilized. Hence, we do not view returning the answers produced by both rules as an error.

In summary, if a user reads a data item for which a collection of rules can produce an answer and some subcollection of the rules have been prioritized using the PRIORITY command, then POSTGRES will return the value produced by the highest priority command from the subcollection. In addition, it may return values specified by some of the unprioritized rules. In the case that the subcollection of prioritized rules is empty, POSTGRES will return at least one value produced by one of the rules and may optionally return more than one. It would have been possible (in fact easy) to insist on functional semantics. However, we feel that this is a less useful choice for rule driven applications.

Notice that collections of rules can be defined which produce a result which depends on the order of execution of the rules. For example, consider the following commands:

```
delete always EMP where EMP.salary = 1000

replace always EMP (salary = 2000)
where EMP.name = ``Mike''
```

If Mike receives a salary adjustment from 2000 to 1000, then the delete would remove him while the replace would change his salary back to 2000. The final outcome is clearly order sensitive. If these commands were run concurrently from an application program, then two outcomes are possible depending on which command happened to execute first. POSTGRES does not alter these semantics in any way. Hence, rules are awakened in a POSTGRES determined order, and the ultimate result may depend on the order of execution.

3. IMPLEMENTATION OF RULES

3.1. Time of Awakening

Consider the following collection of rules:

```
replace always EMP (salary = E.salary)
using E in EMP
where EMP.name = ``Mike''
and E.name = ``Bill''

replace always EMP (salary = E.salary)
using E in EMP
where EMP.name = ``Bill''
and E.name = ``Fred''
```

Clearly Mike's salary must be set to Bill's which must be set to Fred's. If the salary of Fred is changed, then the second rule can be awakened to change the salary of Bill which can be followed by the first rule to alter the salary of Mike. In this case an update to the data base awakens a collection of rules which in turn awaken a subsequent collection. This control structure is known as **forward chaining,** and we will term it **early** evaluation. The first option available to POSTGRES is to perform early evaluation of rules, and a forward chaining control flow will result.

A second option is to delay the awakening of either of the above rules until a user requests the salary of Bill or Mike. Hence, neither rule will be run when Fred's salary is changed. Rather, if a user requests Bill's salary, then the second rule must be run to produce it on demand. Similarly, if Mike's salary is requested, then the first rule is run to produce it requiring in turn the second rule to be run to obtain needed data. This control structure is known as **backward chaining,** and we will term it **late** evaluation. The second option available to POSTGRES is to delay evaluation of a rule until a user requires something it will write. At this point POSTGRES must produce the needed answer as efficiently as possible using an algorithm to be described in Section 4, and a backward chaining control flow will result.

Clearly, the choice of early or late evaluation has important performance consequences. If Fred's salary is updated often and Mike's and Bill's salaries are read infrequently, then late evaluation is appropriate. If Fred does not get frequent raises, then early evaluation may perform better. Moreover, response time to a request to read Mike's salary will be very fast if early evaluation is selected, while late evaluation will generate a considerably longer delay in producing the desired data. Hence, response time to user commands will be faster with early evaluation.

The choice of early or late evaluation is an optimization which POSTGRES will make internally in all possible situations. However, there are three important restrictions which limit the available options.

The first restriction concerns the generality of POSTGRES procedures. A procedure written in POSTQUEL or in an arbitrary programming language can be **registered** with POSTGRES after which it can be used in the query langauge. If arrogance is such a user defined procedure, then the following is a legal rule:

```
retrieve always (EMP.name)
where arrogance (EMP.name) > 10
```

The details of this registration process are contained in [STON86c]. The only issue of concern here is that the definer must specify if the procedure is **cachable.** In the above situation, the answer returned by arrogance does not depend on the time of execution and is thereby cachable. Early or late execution is allowable for rules that contain cachable procedures. Although most procedures are cachable, there are cases where needed information is not available until run time. The following rule contains an uncachable procedure:

```
replace always EMP (salary = 0)
where EMP.name = ``Mike''

and user() = ``Sam''
```

Here, ``user'' is a procedure which makes a system call to ascertain the identity of the user who is currently executing. Hence, the desired effect is that Sam should see Mike's salary as 0. Other users may see a different value. Clearly, this procedure cannot be evaluated early, since needed information is not available. Such rules which deal with protection generally contain uncachable procedures and must be executed late.

A second restriction concerns indexing. Fields for which there are late rules cannot be indexed, because there is no way of knowing what values to index. Hence, a secondary index on the salary column of EMP cannot be constructed if there are any late rules which write salary data. On the other hand, early rules are compatible with indexes on fields which they update.

A third restriction concerns the mixing of late and early rules. Consider, for example, the situation where the Bill-to-Mike salary rule is evaluated early while the Fred-to-Bill salary rule is evaluated late. A problem arises when Fred receives a salary adjustment. The rule to propagate this adjustment on to Bill will not be awakened until somebody proposes to read Bill's salary. On the other hand, a request for Mike's salary will retrieve the old value because there is no way for the Bill-to-Mike rule to know that the value of Bill's salary will be changed by a late rule. To avoid this problem, POSTGRES must ensure that no late rules write any data objects read by early rules.

To deal with these latter two restrictions, POSTGRES takes the following precautions. Every column of a POSTGRES relation must be tagged as ``indexable'' or ``non-indexable''. Indexable columns cannot be written by late rules, while non-indexable columns permit late writes. To ensure that no late rule writes data read by an early rule, POSTGRES enforces the restriction that early reads cannot access data from non-indexable columns. To support this, the POSTGRES parser produces two lists of columns, those in the target list to the left of an equals sign and those appearing elsewhere in the rule. These lists are the write-set and read-set respectively for a rule. If the read-set contains an indexable field, we tag the rule ``read I''. Similarly, a rule that writes an indexed field is tagged ``write I''. For non-indexed fields, the corresponding tags are ``read NI'' and ``write NI'' Table 1 shows the allowable execution times for the various rule tags.

rule status	Time of Awakening
read I write NI	early or late
read NI write I	not permitted
read I write I	early
read NI write NI	late

Time of Rule Awakening

Table 1

The consequences of Table 1 are that some rules are not allowable, some must be evaluated early, some must be evaluated late, and some can be evaluated at either time. This last collection can be optimized by POSTGRES.

To achieve further optimization, POSTGRES can temporarily change the time of evaluation of any late rule to ``temporarily early'' if the rule does not read any data written by a late rule. Similarly, an early rule can be changed to temporarily late if it does not write an object read by an early rule. If at some subsequent time these conditions become false, then the rule must revert from its temporary status back to its permanent status.

An unfortunate consequence of Table 1 is that permanent status of all inserts and deletes is early, since all relations will have at least one indexable field.

There are many examples where late evaluation and early evaluation produce different answers, as noted in the following example:

```
append always to NEWEMP
(name = ``Joe'', salary = EMP.salary)
where EMP.name = ``Mike''
```

If one executes this rule early, then a new tuple will be inserted in the NEWEMP relation each time the salary of Mike changes. On the other hand, temporarily moving the evaluation to late will cause only the last salary of Mike to be available for Joe in NEWEMP. Although we feel that users typically do not wish to specify the time of rule execution, we give them the option to do so. Hence, a rule can be tagged with ``always'' to indicate that POSTGRES can choose the time of execution, ``early'' to specify early execution, or ``late'' to specify late execution. This will allow the user to generate appropriate semantics in the case of commands whose outcome is sensitive to the time of rule awakening. If the user specifies ``early'' or ``late'' awakening, then POSTGRES will comply with the request if possible.

Within these constraints and considerations, POSTGRES will attempt to optimize the early versus late decision on a rule by rule basis. All rules will be inserted with their permanent status, and an arbitrary decision will be made for the ones whose time of awakening is optimizable. Then an asynchronous demon, REVEILLE/TAPS (Rule EValuation EIther earLy or LatE for the Trigger Application Performance System), will run in background to make decisions on which rules should be converted temporarily or permanently from late to early execution and vice-versa.

It is possible for a user to define ill-formed rule systems, e.g.:

```
replace always EMP (salary = 1.1 * E.salary)
using E in EMP
where EMP.name = ``Mike''
and E.name = ``Fred''

replace always EMP (salary = 1.1 * E.salary)
using E in EMP
where EMP.name = ``Fred''
and E.name = ``Mike''
```

This set of rules says Fred makes 10 percent more than Mike who in turn makes 10 percent more than Fred. If the permanent status of these rules is early, then execution of both rules will generate an infinite loop. On the other hand, late execution of the rules will result in a user query to find the salary of Fred or Mike never finishing. In either case POSTGRES must try to detect the infinite loop. How to do this remains to be studied.

3.2. Granularity of Locking

POSTGRES must wake-up rules at appropriate times and perform specific processing with them. In [STON86b] we analyzed the performance of a rule indexing structure and various structures based on physical marking (locking) of objects. When the average number of rules that covered a particular tuple was low, locking was preferred. Moreover, rule indexing could not be easily extended to handle rules with join terms in the qualification. Because we expect there will be a small number of rules which cover each tuple in practical applications, we are utilizing a locking scheme.

When a rule is installed into the data base for either early or late evaluation, POSTGRES is run in a special mode and sets appropriate locks on each tuple that it reads or proposes to write in evaluating the rule. These locks are:

ER (column) : rule read lock by an early rule
LR (column) : rule read lock by a late rule
EW (column) : rule write lock by an early rule
LW (column) : rule write lock by a late rule

These locks differ from normal read and write locks in several ways. First, normal locks are set and released at high frequency and exist in relatively small numbers. When a crash occurs, the lock table is not needed because recovery can be accomplished solely from the log. Hence, virtually all systems utilize a main memory lock table for normal locks. On the other hand, locks set by rules exist in perhaps vast numbers since POSTGRES must be prepared to accommodate a large collection of rules. Secondly, locks are set and reset at fairly low frequency. They are only modified when rules are inserted, deleted, their time of evaluation is changed, or in certain other cases to be explained. Lastly, if a crash occurs one must not lose the locks set by rules. The consequences of losing rule locks is the requirement that they be reinstalled in the data base and recovery time will become unacceptably long. As a result, rule locks must persist over crashes.

Because of these differences, we are storing rule locks as normal data in POSTGRES tuples. This placement has a variety of advantages and a few disadvantages. First, they are automatically persistent and recoverable and space management for a perhaps large number of locks is easily dealt with. Second, since they are stored data, POSTGRES queries can be run to retrieve their values. Hence, queries can be run of the form ``If I update Mike's salary, what rules will be affected?'' This is valuable in providing a debugging and query environment for expert system construction. The disadvantage of storing the locks on the data records is that setting or resetting a lock requires writing the data page. Hence, locks associated with rules are expensive to set and reset.

Like normal locks, there is a phantom problem to contend with. For example, consider the rule to set Mike's salary to be the same as Bill's. If Bill is not yet an employee, then the rule has no effect. However, when Bill is hired, the rule must be awakened to propagate his salary. Setting locks on tuples and attributes will not accomplish the desired effect because one can only lock actual data read or written. To deal with phantoms, POSTGRES also set rule locks on each index record that is read duing query processing and on a ``stub record'' which it inserts in the index to denote the beginning and end of a scan. Whenever a data record is inserted into a POSTGRES relation, appropriate index records must be added to each existing secondary index. The POSTGRES run time system must note all locks held on index records which are adjacent to any inserted secondary index record. Not only must these locks be inherited by the corresponding data record, but also they must be inherited by the secondary index record itself. The above mechanism must be adjusted slightly to work correctly with hashed secondary indexes. In particular, a secondary index record must inherit all locks in the same hash bucket. Hence, ``adjacent'' must be interpreted to mean ``in the same hash bucket''. This mechanism is essentially the same one used by System R to detect phantoms. Although cumbersome and somewhat complex, it appears to work and no other alternative is readily available. Since POSTGRES supports user-defined secondary indexes [STON86d], this complexity must be dealt with by the index code.

Locks may be set a record level granularity as noted above. However, there are situations where lock escalation may be desirable. For example, consider the rule:

```
replace always EMP (salary = avg (EMP.salary))
where EMP.name = ``Mike''
```

This rule will read the salaries of all employees to compute the aggregate. Rather than setting a large number of record level locks, it may be preferable to **escalate** to a relation level lock. Hence, all of the above rule locks can also be set at the relation level. In this case they are tuple level locks set on the tuple in the RELATION relation which exists for the EMP relation.

With this information we can now discuss the actions which must be taken when rules are inserted. If record level granularity is selected, a late rule must set LR locks on all objects which it reads and LW locks on all objects it proposes to write. Similarly, an early rule sets appropriate ER and EW locks. Moreover, an early rule must install values for all data items it writes unless a higher priority command holds an EW or LW lock. It will be efficient to maintain the collection of EW and LW locks in priority order. Hence, when a write lock is set, it will be put in the correct position on the ordered list of EW and LW locks.

When table level locks are utilized, ER, EW, LR and LW locks are set at the relation level on individual attributes and early writes are installed in the data base. If a higher priority command writes the same relation, then the new rule is run but the qualification of the rule is modified to AND on the negation of all higher priority rules. Then the EW lock is inserted in the correct position of an ordered list of EW and LW locks on the appropriate tuple in the ATTRIBUTE relation.

There appears to be no way to prioritize two commands which lock at different granularities. Hence, priorities can only be established for collections of table locking rules or record locking rules.

When a rule locking at either granularity is deleted, its entries in the system catalogs are found and deleted along with any locks it is holding. If a rule holds an EW or LW lock on any object for which a lower priority rule holds a EW lock, then the lower priority rule must be awakened to write its result.

Whenever a user reads a data item he will be returned the stored value if there are no record-level write locks or the highest priority lock is an EW lock. Otherwise, the algorithm in the next subsection is run on the commands holding LW locks in priority order until one produces a value. If none produce a value, then the value of the data item is whatever is stored in the field (if anything). This implements the correct notion of priorities for record locking. Whenever a command writes a data item on which a record level EW lock is held, the write is ignored and the command continues. Whenever, it writes a data item on which an LW lock is held, then the write succeeds normally. Lastly, whenever it writes a data item on which an ER lock is held, then the rule that set the lock is awakened as described in the next section.

If a user writes a relation on which LW locks are held at the relation level, then no special action is taken. On the other hand, if a write is performed on a relation with one or more EW locks, then the corresponding rules must be awakened to refresh the objects they write. The algorithm we use is discussed in the next section. Similarly, when a user reads a relation on which LW locks are held, then an algorithm is performed similar to query modification [STON75] which is also discussed in the next section.

POSTGRES will choose either fine granularity or coarse granularity as an optimization issue. It can either escalate after it sets too many fine granularity locks or guess at the beginning of processing based on heuristics. The current wisdom for conventional locks is to escalate after a certain fixed number of locks have been set [GRAY78, KOOI82].

The decision on escalation in this new context has a crucial performance implication. In particular, one does not know what record level locks will be observed during the processing of a query plan until specific tuples are inspected. Hence, if late evaluation is used, one or more additional queries may be run to produce values needed by the user query. Consequently, in addition to the user's plan, N extra plans must be run which correspond to the collection of N late rules that are encountered. These N+1 queries are all optimized separately when record level locks are used. Moreover, these plans may awaken other plans which are also independently optimized. On the other hand, if all locks are escalated to the relation level, the query optimizer knows what late rules will be utilized and can generate a composite optimized plan for the command as discussed in the next section. This composite plan is very similar to what is produced by query modification [STON75] and is a simplified version of the sort of processing in [ULLM85]. It will often result in a more efficient total execution.

On the other hand, if the rules noted earlier that set Mike's and Bill's salaries are escalated to the relation level, then **ALL** incoming commands will use the rules whether or not they read Mike's or Bill's salary. This will result in considerable wasted overhead in using rules which don't apply.

Like the decision of early versus late evaluation, the decision of lock granularity is a complex optimization problem. Detailed study of both problems in underway.

4. Conflict Processing

4.1. Record Level Locks

A rule is awakened whenever a user writes a data item on which an ER or LR lock is held or reads a data item on which a rule is holding an LW lock. We treat these two cases in turn.

4.1.1. User Writes

There are three different actions which may be taken on user writes. First, the rule must note whether its collection of locks will change as a result of the write. For example, consider the following rule:

```
replace always EMP (salary = 100)
using E in EMP
where EMP.age = E.age
and E.name = ``Mike''
```

This rule holds a read lock on the age of Mike and a conflict will be generated if a user writes a new value for Mike's age. In this case, the collection of employees who receive a salary adjustment changes. In this case the rule must be deleted and then reinstated. A rule which has a join field which is updated by a user must receive this first treatment.

The second action to perform is the conventional case where the set of locks does not change as a result of the update. In this case, there is no action to take for a rule with late evaluation. The third action applies to rules performing early evaluation which must be awakened and run. This can simply occur at the end of a scan of a relation; however, it will usually be faster to apply query modification to the rule to restrict its scope. One simply substitutes the values written by the user command for the current tuple into the rule target list and old values for the current tuple into the rule qualification and then wakes it up.

For example, consider a salary adjustment for Fred and the rule which propagates Fred's salary on to Bill, i.e:

```
replace always EMP (salary = E.salary)
using E in EMP
where EMP.name = ``Bill''
and E.name = ``Fred''
```

If XXX is the proposed salary for Fred, then this rule will be awakened as:

```
replace EMP (salary = XXX)
where EMP.name = ``Bill''
and ``Fred'' = ``Fred''
```

4.1.2. User Reads

When a user reads a data item whose highest priority lock is an LW lock, its value must be obtained from the rule. It is probably wise to call REVEILLE/TAPS to ascertain if one of the LW locks can be profitably turned into a EW lock. If so, the user command can simply continue by utilizing the value written in the record by the early rule. If caching is unprofitable or the rule is uncachable, then the following algorithm should be run.

If the rule is an APPEND which REVEILLE/TAPS changed to temporarily late, then the command is run as a retrieve to materialize one or more tuples which are processed by the run-time POSTGRES system before proceeding. If the rule is a DELETE which was similarly changed to late, then the qualification of the DELETE is tested against the current tuple. If a match is observed, then the run-time system passes over the tuple and continues. If the rule is a REPLACE, then the command is run as a retrieve to provide possibly new values for the current tuple. This modified tuple is then passed to higher level software for further processing.

Note however, that values from the current tuple must be substituted into any such command before it is run. For example consider the following rule:

```
replace always EMP (salary = E.salary)
using E in EMP
where EMP.name = ``Bill''
and E.name = ``Fred''
```

If the user issue a query:

```
retrieve (EMP.salary)
where EMP.name = ``Bill''
```

then the rule will be awakened as:

```
retrieve (salary = E.salary) using E in EMP
where ``Bill'' = ``Bill''
and E.name = ``Fred''
```

If a salary is returned, then it is used in place of a salary in the tuple (if any) before passing the tuple on to higher level software.

If both read and write locks are held on a single field by different rules, then care must be exercised concerning the order of execution. If multiple fields have this property, then the corresponding rules may have to run more than once and infinite loops are possible. Efficient algorithms for this situation are still under investigation.

4.2. Relation Level Locking

Actions must be taken when a user writes a column of a relation on which a rule is holding a ER, LR or EW lock and when a user reads a column of a relation on which a rule is holding an LW lock. We discuss each situation in turn.

4.2.1. User Writes

If a user command, U, writes into a column on which a rule holds a read lock, there are three cases to consider as before. The rule may have to be deleted and reinserted if its collection of locks might change or it might require no action if it is evaluated late and no locks change. The third alternative is that the rule must be awakened to refresh the values which it writes. In this case, it will be profitable to restrict the scope of the rule by substituting values from the target list of U into the rule target list and qualification and then adding U's qualification onto the rule qualification. For example consider the following rule:

```
replace always OLDSAL (salary = EMP.salary)
where OLDSAL.name = EMP.name
```

If a relation level lock is set by the always command, and the following command is run:

```
replace EMP (salary = 1000)
where EMP.name = ``George''
```

then the above algorithm will awaken the rule as:

```
replace OLDSAL (salary = 1000)
where OLDSAL.name = EMP.name
and EMP.name = ``George''
```

The algorithm for the third alternative must also be run if an EW lock is held on an updated column.

4.2.2. User Reads

The query optimizer can discover any relation level write locks held on a relation at the time it does query planning. The following query modification algorithm can be run prior to query compilation and an optimized plan constructed for the composite query.

Query modification for the various POSTQUEL commands is slightly different. Hence individual commands are addressed in turn when awakened by a POSTQUEL retrieve command Q. If the awakened command is an APPEND rule which has been changed to temporarily late by REVEILLE/TAPS, then the APPEND is substituted into Q to form a new command, Q'. Both Q and Q' must be run against the data base. For example, consider

```
append always EMP (NEWEMP.all)
where NEWEMP.age < 40
```

and the query

```
retrieve (EMP.salary)
where EMP.name = ``Mike''
```

The result of query modification is two queries:

```
retrieve (EMP.salary)
where EMP.name = ``Mike''

retrieve (NEWEMP.salary)
where NEWEMP.name = ``Mike''
and NEWEMP.age < 40
```

If the awakened command is a DELETE rule which has been changed to temporarily late, then query modification is run on Q to produce a new command Q' which negates the qualification of the rule and adds it to Q. For example consider:

```
delete always EMP where EMP.salary < 40
```

If the above query to find Mike's salary is run, then it will be modified to:

```
retrieve (EMP.salary)
where EMP.name = ``Mike''
and not EMP.salary < 40
```

If the awakened rule is a REPLACE command, then query modification must construct two commands as follows. The first command will be found by substituting target list values from the rule into Q and appending the rule qualification. The second command is constructed from the user command by appending the negated rule qualification. For example, consider the rule:

```
replace always EMP (salary = 1000)
where EMP.dept = ``shoe''
```

A query to find Mike's salary will result in:

```
retrieve (1000)
where EMP.name = ``Mike'' and
EMP.dept = ``shoe''

retrieve (EMP.salary)
where EMP.name = ``Mike'' and
not EMP.dept = ``shoe''
```

When both read and write locks are held on a column of a relation by different rules, then care must again be exercised in choosing the order of rule evaluation. If multiple columns have this property, recursion and infinite loops are possible, and algorithms for this case are under investigation.

5. DATA BASE SERVICES

5.1. Views

It is possible for the POSTGRES rules system to support two kinds of views, **partial views**, and **normal views**. A normal view is specified by creating a relation, say VIEW, and then defining the rule:

```
retrieve always into VIEW (any-target-list)
where any-qualification
```

This rule can be executed either early or late, if all accessed fields are indexable. Otherwise, the permanent status of the rule is late and REVEILLE/TAPS may temporarily move it to early if no other rule performs late writes on data this rule reads. Late evaluation leads to conventional view processing by query modification, while early evaluation will cause the view to be physically materialized. In this latter case, updates to the base relation will cause the materialization to be invalidated and excessive recomputation of the whole view will be required. Hence, in the future we hope to avoid the recomputation of procedures and instead incrementally update the result of the procedure. The tactics of [BLAK86] are a step in this direction.

Unfortunately normal views cannot be updated using the rules system described so far. Although extensive attempts have been made by the authors to specify the mapping from updates on a view to updates on base relations as a collection of rules, this effort has not yet yielded a clean solution.

On the other hand, partial views are relations which have a collection of real data fields and additionally a set of fields which are expected to be supplied by rules. Such views can be specified by as large a number of rules as needed. Moreover, priorities can be used to resolve conflicts. As a result partial views can be utilized to define relations which are impossible with a conventional view mechanism. Such extended views have some of the flavor proposed in [IONN84].

Moreover, all retrieves to such relations function correctly. Updates to such relations are processed as conventional updates which install actual data values in their fields, as long as all the rules are evaluated late. Propagating such values to base relations becomes the job of additional rules. Specifying all the needed rules is a bit complex, but it can be accomplished.

5.2. Integrity Control

Integrity control is readily achieved by using delete rules. For example the following rule enforces the constraint that all employees earn more than 3000:

```
delete always EMP where EMP.salary < 3000
```

Since this is an early rule, it will be awakened whenever a user installs an overpaid employee and the processing is similar to that of current integrity control systems [STON75]. However POSTGRES may be able to delay evaluation if that appears more efficient. In this case bad data is insertable but it can never be retrieved.

5.3. Protection

Protection is normally specified by replace rules which have a user() in the qualification, so they are non cachable and late evaluation is appropriate. The only abnormal behavior exhibited by this application of the rules system is that the system defaults to ``open access''. Hence, unless a rule is stated to the contrary, any user can freely access and update all relations. Although a cautious approach would default to ``closed access'', it is our experience that open access is just as reasonable.

Notice that this protection system is also novel in that it is possible for the system to lie to users, rather than simply allow or decline access to objects. The example rule discussed earlier, i.e:

```
replace always EMP (salary = 0)
where EMP.name = ``Mike''
and user() = ``Sam''
```

is such an example. This facility allows greatly expanded capabilities over ordinary protection systems.

6. CONCLUSIONS

This paper has presented a rules system with a considerable number of advantages. First, the rule system consists of tagged query language commands. Since a user must learn the query language anyway, there is marginal extra complexity to contend with. In addition, specifying rules as commands which run indefinitely appears to be an easy paradigm to grasp. Moreover, rules may conflict and a priority system can be used to specify conflict resolution.

Two different optimizations were proposed for the implementation. The first optimization concerns the time that rules are evaluated. If they are evaluated early, then a forward chaining control flow results, while late evaluation leads to backward chaining. Response time considerations, presence or absence of indexes, and frequency of read and write operations will be used to drive REVEILLE/TAPS which will decide on a case by case basis whether to use early evaluation. Study of the organization of this module is underway. In addition, the locking granularity can be either at the tuple level or at the relation level. Tuple level locking will optimize the situation where a large number of rules exist each with a small scope. Finding the one or ones that actually apply from the collection that might apply is efficiently accomplished. On the other hand, relation level locking will allow the query optimizer to construct plans for composite queries, and more efficient global plans will certainly result. Hence, we accomplish our objective of designing a rule system which can be optimized for either case. Lastly, the rule system was shown to be usable to implement integrity control, a novel protection system and to support retrieve access to two different kinds of views.

On the other hand, much effort remains to be done. First, the rule system is not yet powerful enough to specify easily all the options desired from referential integrity [DATE81]. It cannot support transition integrity constraints (i.e. no employee raise can be more than 10 percent). Moreover, the rule system generates situations where a rule must be deleted and reinserted. This will be an exceedingly expensive operation, and means to make this more efficient are required. In general, a mechanism to update the result of a procedure is required rather than simply invalidating it and recomputing it. The efforts of [BLAK86] are a start in this direction, and we expect to search for more general algorithms. Lastly, it is a frustration that the rule system cannot be used to provide view update semantics. The general idea is to provide a rule to specify the mapping from base relations to the view and then another rule(s) to provide the reverse mapping. Since it is well known that non-invertible view definitions generate situations where there is no unambiguous way to map backward from the view to base relations, one must require an extra semantic definition of what this inverse mapping should be. We hope to extend our rules system so it can be used to provide both directions of this mapping rather than only one way. Lastly, we are searching for a clean and efficient way to eliminate the annoying restrictions of our rule system, including the fact that priorities cannot be used with different granularity rules, and some rules are forced to a specific time of awakening.

REFERENCES

[ABAR86] Abarbanel, R. and Williams, M., ``A Relational Representation for Knowledge Bases,'' Proc. 1st International Conference on Expert Database Systems, Charleston, S.C., April 1986.

[BLAK86] Blakeley, J. et. al., ``Efficiently Updating Materialized Views,'' Proc. 1986 ACM-SIGMOD Conference on Management of Data, Washington, D.C., May 1986.

[BORG85] Borgida, A., ``Language Features for Flexible Handling of Exceptions in Information Systems,'' ACM-TODS, Dec. 1985.

[BUNE79] Buneman, P. and Clemons, E., ``Efficiently Monitoring Relational Data Bases,'' ACM-TODS, Sept. 1979.

[BUNE82] Buneman, P. et. al., ``An Implementation Technique for Database Query Languages,'' ACM-TODS, June 1982.

[CERI86] Ceri, S. et. al., ``Interfacing Relational Databases and Prolog Efficiently,'' Proc 1st International Conference on Expert Database Systems, Charleston, S.C., April 1986.

[CLOC81] Clocksin, W. and Mellish, C., ``Programming in Prolog,'' Springer-Verlag, Berlin, Germany, 1981.

[DATE81] Date, C., ``Referential Integrity,'' Proc. Seventh International VLDB Conference, Cannes, France, Sept. 1981.

[ESWA76] Eswaren, K., ``Specification, Implementation and Interactions of a Rule Subsystem in an Integrated Database System,'' IBM Research, San Jose, Ca., Research Report RJ1820, August 1976.

[FORG81] Forgy, C., ``The OPS5 User's Manual,'' Carneigie Mellon Univ., Technical Report, 1981.

[GRAY78] Gray, J., ``Notes on Data Base Operating Systems,'' IBM Research, San Jose, Ca., RJ 2254, August 1978.

[HELD75] Held, G. et. al., ``INGRES: A Relational Data Base System,'' Proc 1975 National Computer Conference, Anaheim, Ca., June 1975.

[INTE85] IntelliCorp, ``KEE Software Development System User's Manual,'' IntelliCorp, Mountain View, Ca., 1985.

[IONN84] Ionnidis, Y. et. al., ``Enhancing INGRES with Deductive Power,'' Proceedings of the 1st International Workshop on Expert Data Base Systems, Kiowah SC, October 1984.

[KOOI82] Kooi, R. and Frankfurth, D., ``Query Optimization in INGRES,'' Database Engineering, Sept. 1982.

[KUNG84] Kung, R. et. al., ``Heuristic Search in Database Systems,'' Proc. 1st International Conference on Expert Systems, Kiowah, S.C., Oct. 1984.

[RTI85] Relational Technology, Inc., ``INGRES Reference Manual, Version 4.0'' Alameda, Ca., November 1985.

[STON75] Stonebraker, M., ``Implementation of Integrity Constraints and Views by Query Modification,'' Proc. 1975 ACM-SIGMOD Conference, San Jose, Ca., May 1975.

[STON82] Stonebraker, M. et. al., ``A Rules System for a Relational Data Base Management System,'' Proc. 2nd International Conference on Databases, Jerusalem, Israel, June 1982.

[STON86a] Stonebraker, M. and Rowe, L., ``The Design of POSTGRES,'' Proc. 1986 ACM-SIGMOD Conference on Management of Data, Washington, D.C., May 1986.

[STON86b] Stonebraker, M. et. al., ``An Analysis of Rule Indexing Implementations in Data Base Systems,'' Proc. 1st International Conference on Expert Data Base Systems, Charleston, S.C., April 1986.

[STON86c] Stonebraker, M., ``Object Management in POSTGRES using Procedures,'' Proc. 1986 International Workshop on Object-oriented Database Systems, Asilomar, Ca., Sept 1986. (available from IEEE)

[STON86d] Stonebraker, M., ``Inclusion of New Types in Relational Data Base Systems,'' Proc. IEEE Data Engineering Conference, Los Angeles, Ca., Feb. 1986.

[ULLM85] Ullman, J., ``Implementation of Logical Query Languages for Databases,'' ACM-TODS, Sept. 1985.

Chapter 9

Storage Management Issues

9.1 Introduction

In this section of the book we consider papers that discuss access methods and storage management issues. In the area of access methods, the ubiquitous B-tree remains dominant in the commercial marketplace. Hence the major access method innovations have come in other areas. It should not surprise anyone that traditional static hashing has been improved with the introduction of extendible hashing. Both Fagin at IBM [FAGI79] and Litwin at INRIA independently came up with variations on the same theme. The Litwin paper is included in this collection (9.2) because it expands and contracts more gracefully than the Fagin algorithm. My suspicion is that extendible hashing will gain popularity in the commercial world over the next decade.

In the area of access methods for spatial data, there have been a wide variety of proposals. Traditional multi dimension bin systems have been extensively studied and suffer from poor performance unless the data items are uniformly distributed and the range of item values and the approximate number of items can be predetermined. Alleged improvements include Grid files, Quad-trees, R-trees, R+-trees, and K-D-B-trees. Each structure appears to suffer at least one serious disadvantage. For example Grid files [NIEV84] require a main memory array of pointers to disk blocks plus a vector for each dimension of the structure. If this array becomes large (as it certainly will in production environments with large data sets), space management will become a problem. Quad-trees [SAME84] have the property that their fanout is exactly four. Such structures must be packed carefully into disk pages in order to avoid page faults as the tree is descended. A space management problem of unused pieces of disk blocks will result. R-trees [GUTM84], on the other hand, have a hard-coded page management strategy. Like B-trees they will utilize secondary storage efficiently. However, the R-tree page split algorithm is complex and real-world users of R-trees [GREE88] have reported excessive overlap of rectangles at the top levels of the index. This will cause poor performance on region searches. This overlap can be removed if one moves to R+-trees [FALO87]; however, the tax that must be paid is to split solid spatial objects into multiple pieces that are stored separately. This will consume extra disk space and make the updating of R+-tree objects more complex. Lastly, K-D-B-trees [ROBI81] also have an extremely complex split algorithm that will be difficult to optimize. Moreover, unless the heuristic for page splits is extremely good, K-D-B trees will offer very poor performance on solid data [GREE88].

Overall, one has the sense that there must be better data structures for spatial objects, especially solid ones. Moreover, it would be a great contribution if somebody did a serious performance analysis of the multitude of available spatial access method candidates.

In this section, we use the Grid file paper (9.3) and the R-tree paper (9.4) as representatives of work in this area. However, the interested reader is encouraged to examine the literature cited above for other interesting ideas.

The traditional storage management technique is to store databases entirely on moving-head magnetic disks (DASD). In addition, the DBMS would maintain a small buffer pool of disk blocks in main memory, and disk blocks would be moved back and forth between disk and buffer pool in response to user requests. The log would also be kept on disk and perhaps spooled to tape asynchronously. At least three considerations guarantee that this organization will change over the next few years.

1. The plummeting cost of main memory has made large buffer pools and/or main memory databases a possibility. Not only does this make buffer management even more important, but also it provides new ways of looking at data management services. An early survey of the possible techniques for organizing main memory databases appears in [DEWI84]. This paper discusses group commits and hash-join optimization algorithms. A more definitive study of hash join techniques appeared later in [SHAP86].

   [DEWI84] also argues that specialized main memory databases are a bad idea. Instead one should use main memory as a large buffer pool and not hard code structures that work only in this medium. In my opinion specialized main memory databases will be only 10 to 20 percent faster than general purpose ones that use main memory as a buffer pool for a larger secondary storage system. Building into a software system a limit on database size in exchange for a 10 to 20 percent speedup seems inappropriate. Contrary points of view abound, for example [GARC83, LEHM86].

2. Although the exact use of optical disks will unfold over time, they have a major advantage in that it is essentially impossible to lose data. Hence, they are ideally suited for archival purposes. Moreover, it is not improbable that they will find increasing use as storage media for conventional databases. For example, it is possible to consider systems where indexes are in main memory and the data objects are on an optical disk. In this scenario, DASD has been eliminated.

3. Because of the plummeting cost of 3 1/2 inch magnetic disk drives, they seem especially attractive when significant numbers of them are coupled into arrays with parallel read capabilities. This has the possibility of significantly increasing both the number of arms that can be put into use and the band width of DBMS communication with a DASD system. This might eliminate the "I/O bottleneck" that database machine researchers are fond of complaining about. Moreover, disk arrays present novel possibilities for efficient disk shadowing [PATT88].

In general I expect that innovative storage ideas and architectures will be a very fertile area for research advances over the next few years. The last paper in this section (9.5) is an example of a new storage architecture that makes central use of an optical disk and has the added goal of eliminating crash recovery code.

References

[DEWI84] Dewitt, D. et al., "Implementation Techniques for Main Memory Data Bases," Proc. 1984 ACM-SIGMOD International Conference on Management of Data, Boston, Mass., June 1984.

[FAGI79] Fagin; R. et al., "Extendible Hashing—A Fast Access Method for Dynamic Files," ACM-TODS, Sept. 1979.

[FALO87] Faloutos, C. et al., "Analysis of Object-oriented Spatial Access Methods," Proc. 1987 ACM-SIGMOD Conference on Management of Data, San Fransisco, Calif., June 1987.

[GARC83] Garcia-Molina, H. et al., "A Massive Memory Machine," Princeton Univ., EECS Dept, Princeton, N.J., Tech. Rept. 315, July 1983.

[GREE88] Green, D., "A Comparison of Spatial Access Methods," Electronics Research Laboratory, Univ. of California, Berkeley, Calif., Mermo M88-42, Feb. 1987.

[GUTM84] Gutman, A., "R-trees: A Dynamic Index Structure for Spatial Searching," Proc. 1984 ACM-SIGMOD International Conference on Management of Data, Boston, Mass., June 1984.

[LEHM86] Lehman, T., and Carey, M., "Query Processing in Main Memory Database Systems," Proc. 1986 ACM-SIGMOD Conference on Management of Data, Washington, D.C., May 1986.

[PATT88] Patterson, D. et al., "RAID: Redundant Array of Inexpensive Disks," Proc. 1988 ACM-SIGMOD Conference on Management of Data, Chicago, Ill., June 1988.

[NIEV84] Nievergelt, J., "The Grid File: An Adaptable, Symetric Multikey File Structure," ACM-TODS, Mar. 1984.

[ROBI81] Robinson, J., "The K-D-B Tree: A Search Structure for Large Multidimensional Indexes," Proc. 1981 ACM-SIGMOD Conference on Management of Data, Ann Arbor, Mich., May 1981.

[SAME84] Samet, H., "The Quadtree and Related Hierarchical Data Structures," Computing Surveys, June 1984.

[SHAP86] Shapiro, L., "Join Processing in Database Systems with Large Main Memories," ACM-TODS, Sept. 1986.

LINEAR HASHING : A NEW TOOL FOR FILE AND TABLE ADDRESSING.

Witold Litwin

I. N. R. I. A.
78 150 Le Chesnay, France.

Abstract.

Linear hashing is a hashing in which the address space may grow or shrink dynamically. A file or a table may then support any number of insertions or deletions without access or memory load performance deterioration. A record in the file is, in general, found in one access, while the load may stay practically constant up to 90 %. A record in a table is found in a mean of 1.7 accesses, while the load is constantly 80 %. No other algorithms attaining such a performance are known.

1. INTRODUCTION.

The most fundamental data structures are files and tables of records identified by a primary key. Hashing and trees (B-tree, binary tree,..) are the basic addressing techniques for those files and tables, thousands of publications dealed with this subject. If a file or a table is almost static, hashing allows a record to be found in general in one access. A tree always requires several accesses. However, when the file or the table is, as usually, dynamic, then a tree still works reasonably well, while the performance of hashing may become very bad. It may even become necessary to rehash all records into a new file.

We have shown, however, in /LIT77/ that hashing may be a tool for dynamic files, if the hashing function is dynamically modified in the course of insertions or deletions. We have called this new type of hashing virtual hashing (VH), in contrast to the well known hashing with a static function, which we will refer to as classical. Through an algorithm called VH0 /LIT77/, we have shown that a record in a dynamic file may typically be found in two accessses, while the load stays close to 70 % /LIT77a/. Another algorithm, called VH1 /LIT78/, / LIT78a/, has shown that a record may even be found typically in one access, while the load during insertions oscillates between 45 % and 90 % and is 67.5 % on average. It showed also that the average load during insertions may be always greater than 63 % and almost always greater than 85 %, if we accept that the average successful search requires 1.6 accesses /LIT79a/. Finally, a generalisation of VH1, called VH2, has shown that for a similar load, the average successful search requires very close to one access /LIT79a/. Two other algorithms similar to VH0 have been proposed, Dynamic Hashing (DH) /LAR78/ and Extendible Hashing (EH) /FAG78/. Since trees typically lead to more than 3 or 4 accesses per search and to a load close to 70 % /KNU74/, /COM79/, all these VH algorithms offer better access performance for similar or higher load factors.

VH0, DH and EH require at least two accesses per search because the data structure which represents the dynamically created hashing functions must be on the disk. VH1 and VH2 are faster, because the functions are represented by a bit table which, depending on file parameters, needs 1 kbyte of core (main storage), per file for 7 000 to more than 1 500 000 records. In this paper, we present the algorithm which goes further, only a few bytes of core suffice now for a file of any size. For any number of insertions or deletions, the load of a file may therefore be high and a record may be found, in general, in one access. No other algorithms attaining such a performance are known.

The algorithm is called Linear Virtual Hashing or Linear Hashing in short (LH). The choice of file parameters may lead to a mean number of accesses per successful search not greater than 1.03, while the load stays close to 60 %. It may also lead to a load staying equal to 90 % while the successful search requires 1.35 accesses in the average. Even if the buffer in core may contain only one record, a search in the file needs 1.7 accesses in the average while the load remains at 80 %. This property makes LH probably the best performing tool for dynamic tables as well.

The next section describes the principles of LH. We first show the basic schema for hashing. We then discuss the computing of the physical addresses of buckets, when the storage for them is allocated in a non-contiguous manner. Finally, we present some variants of the basic schema.

Section 3 shows performance of the Linear Hashing. First, we show access and memory load performance of the basic schema. Next, the performance are analysed for a variant with a, so-called, load control.

Section 4 concludes the paper. We sum up the advantages which Linear Hashing brings, we show some application areas and, finally, we indicate directions for further research.

2. PRINCIPLES OF THE LINEAR HASHING.

2.1. Basic schema.

We recall that hashing is a technique which addresses records provided with an identifier called primary key or, simply, key. The key, let it be c, is usually a non-negative integer and, in a work on the addressing by primary key, we may disregard the rest of the record. A simple pseudo-random function, let it be h, called a hashing function, assigns to c the memory cell identified by the value h(c). The hashing by division c /--> c mod M ; M = 2,3,.. ; is an exemple of a hashing function. The cells are called buckets and may contain b records, b = 1,2,.. . The record is inserted into the bucket h(c), called primary for c, unless the bucket is already full. The search for c always starts with the access to the bucket h(c).

If the bucket is full when c should be stored, we speak about a collision. An algorithm called collision resolution method (CRM) is then applied which, typically, stores c in a bucket m such that $m \neq h(c)$. c then becomes an overflow record and the bucket m is called overflow bucket for c. If (i) overflow buckets are not primary for any c,(ii) each of them is devoted to only one h(c) and (iii) a new overflow bucket for an h(c) is chained to the existing ones, then we have a bucket chaining CRM. If, in particular, the capacity b' of an overflow bucket is b' = 1, we call this CRM separate chaining /KNU74/.

A search for an overflow record requires at least two accesses. If all collisions are resolved only by overflow record creations, as it was assumed until recently /LIT77/, then access performance must rapidly deteriorate when primary buckets become full. If the insertion of c leads to a collision and no records already stored in the bucket h(c) should become overflow records, then c may be stored in its primary bucket only if a new hashing function is chosen. The new function, let it be h', should assign new addresses to some of the records hashed with h on h(c) and the file should be reorganized in consequence. If h = h' for all other records, the reorganizing needs to move only a few records and so may be performed dynamically. The new function is then called by us dynamically created hashing function or, shortly, a dynamic hashing function. The modification to the hashing function and to the file is called a split, h(c) is, under the circumstances, split address . The idea in VH in general and so, in particular, in LH is to use splits in order to avoid the accumulation of overflow records. Splits are typically performed during some insertions. All splits result from the application of split functions. For LH, as well as for VH0 and for VH1, the basic split functions are defined as follows /LIT79/, /LIT80/ :

- Let C be the key space. Let $h_0 : C \dashrightarrow \{0, 1,.., N-1\}$ be the function that is used to load the file. The functions $h_1, h_2,.., h_i,..$ are called split functions for h_0 if they obey the following requirements :

$$h_i : C \dashrightarrow \{0, 1,.., 2^iN-1\} \tag{1}$$

(2)

For any c either :

$$h_i(c) = h_{i-1}(c) \tag{2.1}$$

or :

$$h_i(c) = h_{i-1}(c) + 2^{i-1}N \tag{2.2}$$

We assume that, typically, each h_i ; i = 0,1,.. ; hashes randomly. This means that the probability that c is mapped by h_i to a given address is $1/2^iN$. This also means that (2.1) and (2.2) are equiprobable events.

Fig. 1 illustrates the use of split functions. The file is created with h0 : c --> c mod N, where N = 100. The bucket capacity is b = 5 records. For split functions we choose the hashing by division, namely we put :

$$h_i : c \mapsto c \bmod 2^iN.$$

This choice respects (2) since, obviously, for any non-negative integers k, L, either :

$$k \bmod 2L = k \bmod L$$

or :

$$k \bmod 2L = k \bmod L + L.$$

We assume that a collision occurs during the insertion of c = 4900. Instead of simply storing c as an overflow record, we change h_0 to the following h :

$$h(c) = h_1(c) \qquad \text{if } h_0(c) = 0$$
$$h(c) = h_0(c) \qquad \text{otherwise.}$$

We then reorganize the file. We thus have applied h_1 as the split function and we have performed the split for the address 0. The hashing function h results from the split and is a dynamic hashing function.

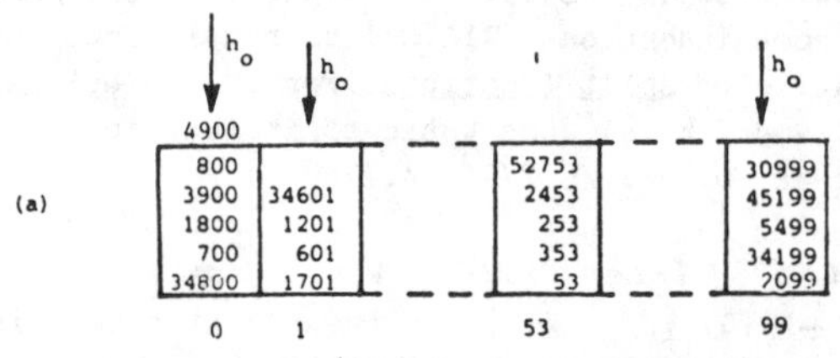

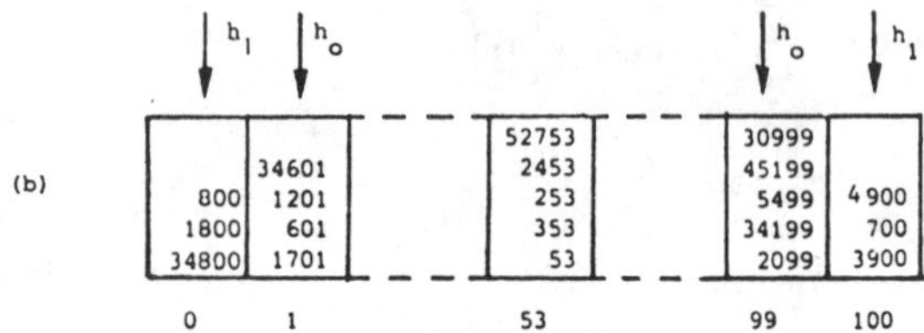

Fig. 1. The use of a split for a collision resolution. (a) - a collision occurs for the bucket 0. (b) - the collision is resolved without creating an overflow record and the address space is extended.

Fig. 1.b shows the new state of the file. Since $h = h_0$ for each address except 0, no records other than these hashed to 0 have been moved. Since $h = h_1$ for the records which h0 hashed to the address 0, for approximatively half the number of these records the address has been changed. It followed from (2) that all these records had the same new address which, under the circumstances, had to be 100. A new bucket has therefore been appended to the last bucket of the file to which all the records have been moved <u>in one access</u>. Since for all these records the bucket 100 is henceforward the primary bucket, they are all accessible in <u>one</u> access. In particular, this is also the case of the new record, i. e., 4 900. On the other hand, the records which remained in the bucket 0 continue to be accessible in one access. In contrast to what could be done if a classical hashing was used, the split has resolved the collision <u>without creating an overflow record</u> and <u>without access performance deterioration</u>.

Let us now assume that the file addressed with h0 undergoes a sequence of insertions which did not yet lead to overflow records. Furthermore, let us assume that a split is performed iff a collision occurs. The natural idea would be to split the bucket which undergoes the collision, this was implicit for all algorithms for VH. However, split addresses must then be random and this must lead to dynamic hashing functions using tables. Dynamic hashing functions which do not need tables may be obtained only if the split addresses are chosen in a predefined order. To perform splits in some predefined order, instead of split the bucket which undergoes the collision, is the main new idea in the linear hashing.

Let m be the address of a collision. Let n be the address of a split to be performed in the course of the resolution of this collision. Since the values of m are random while these of n are predefined, usually $n \neq m$. If so, we assume that the new record is stored as an overflow record from the bucket m through a classical CRM, bucket chaining for instance. Next, we assume that n is given by a pointer which thus indicate the bucket to be split. For the first N collisions, the buckets are pointed in the linear order 0,1,2,..,N-1 and all splits use h_1. (2.2) implies then, that the file becomes progressively larger, including one after another the buckets N+1, N+2,...,2N-1. A record to be inserted undergoes a split usually not when it leads to the collision, but with some delay. The delay corresponds to the number of buckets which has to be pointed while the pointer travels up, from the address indicated in the moment of the collision, to the address of this collision.

With this mechanics, no matter what is the address, let it be m1, of the first collision, LH performs the first split using h_1 and for the address 0. The records from the bucket 0 are then randomly distributed between the bucket 0 and a new bucket N, while, unless m_1=0, an overflow record is created for the bucket m_1. The second collision, no matter what is its address, let us say m_2, leads to an analogous result, except that, first, it splits for the address 1 and appends the bucket N+1. Next, it may constitute the delayed split for the first collision, suppressing therefore the corresponding overflow record. This process continues for each of the N first collisions, moving thus the pointer, step by step, up to the bucket N-1. Sooner or later, the pointer points to each m and the splits, despite of being delayed, move thus most of the overflow records to the primary buckets. We may therefore reasonably expect that, for any $n < N$, only a few overflow records exist.

After N collisions, we have $h = h_1$. (1) implies then that, instead of the hashing on N addresses, we now hash on 2N addresses. (2) implies that h_2 has on the hashing with h_1, the action analogous to that of h_1 on the hashing with $h = h_0$, except that it hashes on 4N addresses. We therefore assume that n = 0 again, that now we split with h_2 and that the upper bound on n is now 2N-1. For further insertions, we use $h_3, h_4, .., h_j, ..$ while the pointer travels each time from 0 to $2^{j-1}N$.

It results from the above principles that, first, the address space increases _linearly_ and is as large as needed. Next, for any number of insertions, most of overflow records is moved to the primary buckets by the delayed splits. On one hand, we may thus reasonably expect that the rate of overflow records remains always small. If $b \gg 1$, the rate should even be neglectable small. Thus, we may expect the linear hashing to find a record usually in one access to the bucket, no matter how few buckets were provided when the file was created and how high the number of insertions finally is.

The highest index of a split function currently used, let it be j ; j=0,1,.. ; is called _file level_. If n=0, we always have $h = h_j$ for some j. Otherwise, first, $h = h_{j-1}$ for the buckets not yet split with h_j, i. e., $n, n+1, .., 2^{j-1}N$. Next, $h = h_j$ for all the others. The algorithm computing the primary address of a c is therefore trivial :

```
(A1)
      if n = 0 : m <-- h_j(c)
      else
            m <-- h_{j-1}(c)
            if m < n : m <-- h_j(c) endif
      endif
endA1
```

2.2. Physical address computing.

The address given by hashing must be transformed into the physical address of the bucket in the memory. The memory for files is usually divided into quanta of let it be q buckets ; q = 1,2,.. Quanta may be all of the same size or different sizes may be available. It then may be particularly worthwhile to use sizes which are 2^i of a certain minimal q (buddy system /KNU74/).

When the file is loaded some quanta are statically allocated. Then, if a file increases dynamically, quanta are sometimes added. If all quanta for a file are contiguous, then the the physical address of a bucket m is as follows :

$$m'(m) = m'(0) + dm \qquad (3)$$

where d is the number of memory elements, i. e., bytes, words or sectors,.. per bucket. Thus the advantage of a contiguous allocation is that only the address of the first quantum is needed and that the computing of the physical address is trivial.

However, if several dynamic files should share a memory, it may be better to allocate non-contiguous quanta. For each file, the addresses of these quanta must then be collected. The address of the i-th quantum may be the value T(i) of a table T. For the quanta of a fixed size, we then have the following formula :

$$i(m) = INT(m/q) \qquad (4)$$

$$m'(m) = T(i(m)) + d(m - i(m)q)$$

where INT denotes the integer part. In particular, if q=1, i. e., if the allocation is totally distributed, then we have simply :

$$m'(m) = T(m). \qquad (5)$$

For the quanta of different sizes, we particularly recommend the following schema :

- let K be a parameter; K = 1,2,.. . The sizes $q_0, q_1, ...$ of successive quanta of the file should be :

$$q_0 = N \qquad (6)$$

$$q_1 = q_2 = ... = q_K = q_0/K$$

$$...$$

$$q_{lk+1} = q_{lk+2} = .. = q_{(l+1)k} = 2^l q_1$$

where l=0,1,.. For instance, if N = 20 and K = 4, then the sizes of the quanta dynamically allocated are 5, 5, 5, 5, 10, 10, 10, 10, 20, 20,.. . Dynamic allocations take thus place when LH starts to use the addresses 20, 25, 30, 35, 40, 50, 60, 70, 80, 100,... Higher is the value of K, smaller is the drop in memory load when a new quantum is allocated, but T is larger. The practical values of K are between 1 and 10.

Let m_i be the smallest logical address in the i-th quantum. Next, let it be ;

$m'' = m - m_{i(m)}$.

Therefore we have :

$$m'(m) = T(i(m)) + dm''. \quad (7)$$

In the case of (6), i(m) and m'' may then be computed by the following obvious algorithm :

```
(A2)
      if m < N : i <-- 0 ; m'' <-- m
      else
           i <-- j-1 ; M <-- 2^i N
           while M > m and i > 0 :
                M <-- M/2 ; i <-- i-1
           endwhile
           i' <-- M/k ; m'' <-- m-M
           i <-- INT(m''/i') +ik +1
           m'' <-- m'' mod i'
      endif
   endA2
```

2.3. Variants of the basic schema.

2.3.1. Split control.

Splits that are performed iff a collision occurs are called uncontrolled. Splits are called controlled if they also depend on other conditions or are performed even if there is no collision. A particularly useful control is called load control. Under this control, a split is performed when a collision occurs, but only if the load factor is superiour to some threshold. This may concern the load factor, let it be â, defined as usual /KNU74/ :

$$\hat{a} = x/bM \quad (8)$$

where x is the number of records in the file, b is the bucket capacity and M is the number of primary buckets. The control may also take in to account the overflow buckets in which case the load factor, let it be â', is defined as :

$$\hat{a}' = x/(bM + b'M') \quad (9)$$

where M' is the number of overflow buckets and b' is the overflow bucket capacity.

In what follows the thresholds are denoted as g and g', respectively. We will show that, when the file undergoes insertions, the load control usually keeps the load factor almost equal to the chosen threshold. A similar control may keep the load factor greater than or almost equal to a threshold, when the file undergoes deletions. Each time a deletion brings the load below this threshold, we may simply perform an operation called grouping which is inverse to splitting. A grouping moves thus the pointer one address backward and so decreases M. If the threshold for deletions is equal to the one for insertions, the load of a LH file usually stays almost constant.

2.3.2. Pointer independent address computing.

It may surprise, but primary address may be computed in fact without the knowledge of the value of n. The following algorithm, analogous to that of VH1 /LIT78a/, proves it :

```
(A3)
     m <-- h_j(c)
     if m >= M : m <-- h_{j-1}(c) endif
endA3
```

If n = 0, then it is obvious that (A3) works. If $n \neq 0$ then, if :

$h(c) = h_j(c)$,

then :

$h(c) < n < M$

or :

$2^{j-1} < n < M$.

Thus (A3) terminates correctly. Else, we have :

$h(c) = h_{j-1}(c)$.

Then, if :

$h_{j-1}(c) = h_j(c)$

then :

$h(c) < 2^{j-1}N < M$.

Thus (A3) also terminates correctly. Else :

$h_j(c) >= M$,

since the bucket h(c) is not yet split. Therefore, in this last case, the algorithm terminates correctly as well.

In particular, we may assume N = 1. The file level j is then a function of M. It follows, first, that the size of address space may be the only one parameter which LH needs for addresses computing. It follows, next, that the parameters of a classical hashing may suffice in order to construct a linear one. For instance, the knowledge of the number of the addresses for the hashing function and of the fact that a hashing by division is used, suffice in both cases.

2.3.3. Other split functions.

Let $b_1, b_2, \ldots, b_i, \ldots$ be a sequence of randomly generated bits, with equiprobability of $b_i=0$ and of $b_i=1$. Such a sequence may be obtained using a random number generator. Let B_i be the integer with binary representation $b_i, b_{i-1}, \ldots, b_1$. The functions h_i defined as follows :

$$h_i : c \mapsto h_0(c) + B_i N \qquad (10)$$

are, obviously, split functions for any h_0. Thus, LH may be constructed not only for a hashing by division, but for any usual hashing function.

Split functions with B_i given by a random number generator may be particularly interesting for $N = 1$. For this value each h_i hashes on 2^i addresses. If the hashing by division is applied, the address of c is, simply, the i least significant bits of c. The hashing by division may then be sometimes rather non-random, while a random number generator may still perform well. The choice of $N = 1$ is particularly useful since, first, there is no more problem to choose among several possible h_0. Next, LH covers all possible address space sizes. Finally, since the file may then be constituted even from only one bucket, a good load factor may be provided even for very few records.

B_i may also result from the multiplication function /KNU74/, let it be h'. If w is the word size and A is an integer relatively prime to w, then the hashing with h' on 2^i addresses is defined as follows :

$$h'_i(c) = \mathrm{INT}(2^i((Ac/w) \bmod 1)). \qquad (11)$$

B_i is in this case constituted from the bits of $h'_i(c)$, taken in the reverse order. In other terms, the most significant bit of h'_i becomes the least significant in B_i etc

Knuth shows that a particularly good choice for A is A = 6 125 423 371. He also shows an algorithm computing (11) in only four instructions of the MIX assembler. Finally, he shows that his algorithm is usually faster than the hashing by division. To compute B_i through the multiplication function may thus be faster than through a random number generator.

In particular, Knuth shows that h' is a scrambling function. This means, first, that its partial result, let it be f(c) ; $f(c) = Ac \bmod w$; is such that if $c' \neq c''$, then $f(c') \neq f(c'')$. Next, this means that the transformation $c \rightarrow f(c)$ tenders to randomize the keys. Therefore, the following split functions may be constructed :

$$h_i(c) = f(c) \bmod 2^i N \qquad (12)$$

which may perform better than the direct hashing by division.

Finally, split functions may also be constructed for alphabetic or variable-length keys. In particular, the individual words of such a key may be simply combined into a single word, to which any of the previously discussed functions may then be applied. Any of the combinations suggested by Knuth may be used, the addition mod w for instance.

2.3.4. General definition of split functions.

LH may be seen as VH1 in which split addresses have been predefined. VH1 may be generalized into an algorithm called VH2. Furthermore, it may be assumed that split addresses are, in fact, predefined for VH2. The conditions (1) and (2) may then be generalized follows ;

- let K be a parameter which value is fixed when the file is created ; K=1,2,.. . Let it be $k_i = K + i \bmod K$. Let N be an integer, $N > 1$. The hashing functions h_i ; i=1,2,.. ; are split functions for a hashing functions h_0, if the following condition are respected :

- for i = 0,1,.. : (13)

$$h_i : C \rightarrow \{0,1,\ldots,N_i-1\}$$

$$N0 = KN$$

$$N_{i+1} = N_i + N_i/k_i$$

(14)

For any c, either :

$$h_i(c) = h_{i-1}(c)$$

or :

$$h_i(c) = N_{i-1} + \mathrm{INT}(h_{i-1}(c) / k_i).$$

For example, if N=5 and K=4, then the successive N_is are : 20, 25, 30, 35, 40, 50, 60, 70, 80, 100,... (note the similarity to (6)).

As previously, we assume that each h_i should hash randomly. It follows that the probability that a key changes the address after a split, let it be p, is now $p_k = 1/(k_i+1)$. If K = 1, then (13) and (14) are, simply, (1) and (2) and $p_k = 0.5$. For greater K, p_k decreases and the distribution of records within LH file becomes more uniform. First, higher load factor obviously results for uncontrolled splits. Next, when the thresnold increases, load control with K > 1 should lead to a better search performance. However, it is easy to see that for such K, to perform a split, usually needs more accesses. Therefore, insertions and deletions will be more costly than for K = 1 as well.

K > 1 implies that the address space doubles not after one, but after K trips of the pointer. Each of K trips may then be called a partial expansion of the address space. Partial expansions may result from formula others than the above, these introduced by /LAR80/ in particular. Performance resulting from (13) and (14) for K > 1 being quite similar to these of the Larson's schema, only the case of K = 1 is discussed in what follows.

3. PERFORMANCE ANALYSIS.

3.1. Address computing.

If the allocation is contiguous, LH is obviously almost as simple and fast as the classical hashing. If the allocation is non-contiguous and (3) or (4) are used, then this is also the case, as long as T may be entirely in core. The use of (6) needs few more instructions, but the computing of (A2) also very fast ; it is quite clear that, for any j, the "while" loop is in the average executed at most twice.

A four byte word allows the values of n and of j to go up to 2^{32}, i. e., allows the LH file to grow up to more than four billions buckets. For any number of insertions, (A1) enters thus even a very small core. If the allocation is contiguous, since (3) is used, the computing of the physical address also needs only a few bytes. If the allocation is non-contiguous, the core is mainly needed for T. If (A2) is used, the size of T is, obviously, not greater than jk+1. For k = 10 which is largely sufficient in practice, 301 words are then sufficient for a file which increases even a billion times. Thus, in practice, no matter if the allocation is contiguous or not, no matter how small is the core and how high is the number of insertions, the computing of a address resulting from LH, never requires a disk access.

However, the disk storage is usually needed if the allocation is totally distributed. (5) shows then clearly that any address is computed in no more than one access. On the other hand, since the disk is required only for T and since T contains only the pointers to buckets, the disk storage required then by LH is the minimal one. It is usually much smaller than that of the index of a VSAM file, since the index contains keys and internal pointers and since its load foactor is lower. It is also several times smaller than the storage required by the tables of VHO, DH and EH, either because of their much lower load factor (VHO, EH) or because of the internal pointers (DH).

3.2. Uncontrolled split.

3.2.1. Access performance.

We now assume that overflow records are addressed through separate chaining and that the file is created by x insertions ; x=0,1,.. . We also assume that each h_i hashes randomly. Finally, we assume (and we have now right to do it) that the computing of an address never requires a disk access. By s', s'', s''' we denote the mean number of accesses per successful search, per unsuccessful search and per insertion. By $\hat{s}$ we denote the mean number of accesses per split. These coefficients will be called costs.

Fig. 2 shows curves of s'(x) obtained through simulations for bucket capacities b = 1,5,10,50. For b =1,5 we have not shown the first splits, since they correspond to x < 10 and to s' practically equal to 1. For b = 5, we have also shown the evolution of the file level j. The curves describe the file which is created with only one bucket and which undergoes $x > 2^{13}b$ insertions. At the end, the number of records in the file is thus more than 8 000 times greater than the number of records which could be found in one access in the initial one. It does not even make sence to compute what would be the deterioration of access performance, if the classical hashing would have been used.

For each b, when x increases, the curve is first irregular and therefore displays the existence of a transient state. After a few insertions, the file reaches a stable state , where the curve is a periodic function of $\log_2 x$. On one hand, it means that in the stable state s' does not depend on x, but on the relative position of the pointer. On the other hand, it means that s' does not increase for whatever the number of

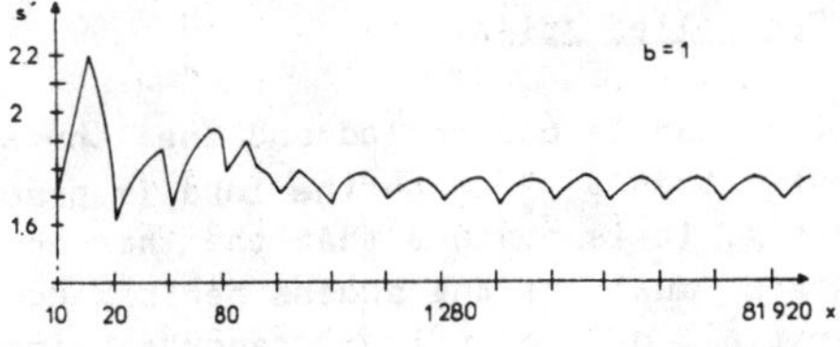

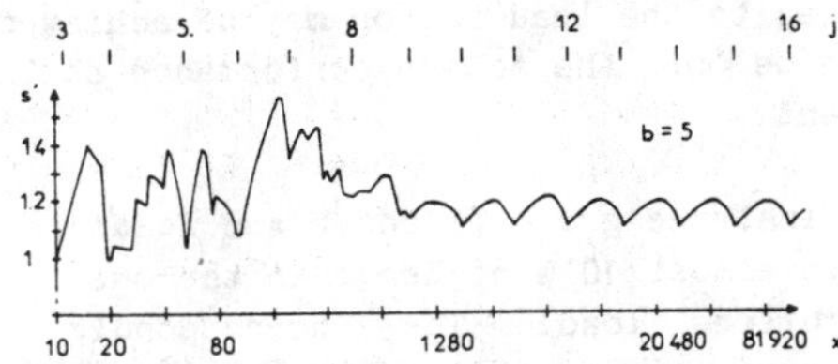

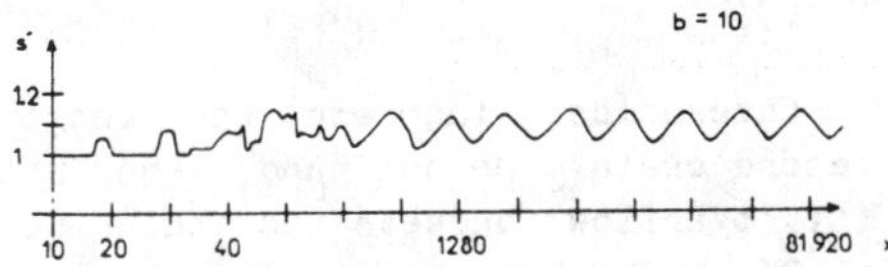

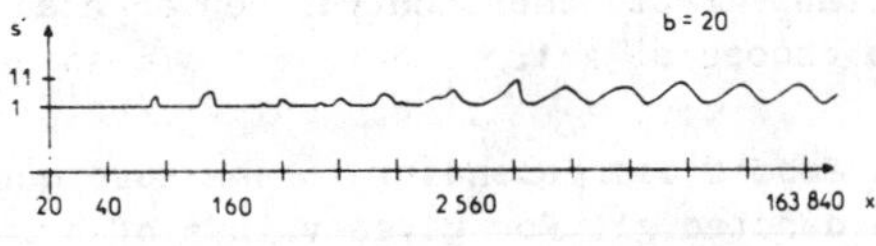

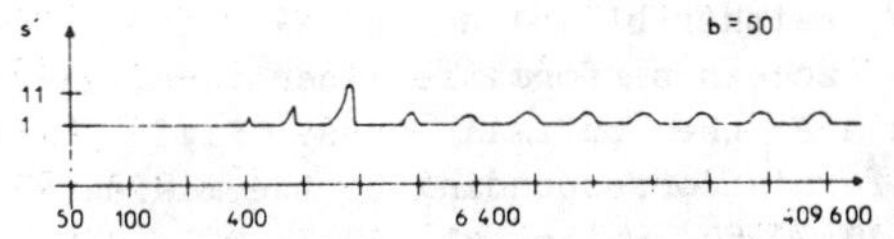

Fig.2. Mean number of accesses per successful search for linear hashing with uncontrolled split.

recall that B-trees need in general 4,5 accesses while binary trees need typically more than 10, since $s'(x) \hat{=} \log_2 x$ /KNU74/.

The transient state may be disregarded, since the performance is good and x is neglectable small. Since the curves in the stable state are periodical, they may be characterized by the values of s'_{min}, s'_{max} and of s'_{ave}, which is the mean value of s' over one period. The values corresponding to the curves are displayed in the table 1.a.

b	1	5	10	20	50	
s'_{ave}	1.73	1.16	1.07	1.02	1.00	
s'_{max}	1.77	1.20	1.11	1.06	1.03	(a)
s'_{min}	1.68	1.10	1.02	1.00	1.00	
s''_{ave}	1.62	1.28	1.19	1.12	1.06	
s''_{max}	1.63	1.32	1.26	1.24	1.23	(b)
s''_{min}	1.6	1.20	1.08	1.02	1.00	
s'''_{ave}	7.91	3.97	3.14	2.67	2.35	
s'''_{max}	8.92	4.07	3.45	3.09	2.71	(c)
s'''_{min}	6.45	3.34	2.48	2.11	2.00	
$\hat{s}_{ave}$	6.94	6.09	5.99	5.98	5.98	
$\hat{s}_{min}$	5.80	5.10	5.00	5.00	5.00	(d)
$\hat{s}_{max}$	8.62	7.45	8.10	8.85	10.85	
$\hat{a}_{ave}$	1.30	0.66	0.61	0.59	0.59	
$\hat{a}_{max}$	1.30	0.67	0.63	0.65	0.70	(e)
$\hat{a}_{min}$	1.30	0.65	0.59	0.55	0.51	
$\hat{a}'_{ave}$	0.8	0.63	0.59	0.59	0.59	

Table 1 - Performance of linear hashing with uncontrolled splits :

(a) successful search,
(b) unsuccessful search,
(c) insertion,
(d) split,
(e) load factor.

insertions could be. We therefore may conclude that for any bucket capacity and any number of insertions, the mean number of accesses per successful search stays close to 1. For large buckets, we may even consider that we have always s'=1 ! LH is thus a very important algorithm, since, first, no other algorithms attaining such an almost ideal performance are known. Next, it performs several times better than trees. We

The analysis of s'' through simulations and through modelling /LIT79/ shows also a transient state and a stable state. Both states correspond of course with these of s'. The performance of unsuccessful search with LH in the stable state are displayed in the table 1.b. As in the case of classical hashing using the separate chaining (see /KNU74/), they are better than the performance of the successful search for b = 1 and poorer for

$b > 1$. However, as before, for any bucket capacity and any number of insertions s'' stays close to 1. The limit value for s''_{max} when b increases is 1.24 /LIT79/.

Table 1.d shows the characteristics of the split cost. Unless split is performed for the address of the collision, this cost is at least five accesses (two accesses in order to store the overflow record for the bucket m, three accesses in order to split the bucket n). The split needs more accesses if the bucket n overflows. This case is obviously the most frequent for $b = 1$; that is why $\hat{s}_{ave}$ is maximal. The number of overflow records on n is obviously the shortest for n close to 0, $\hat{s} = s_{min}$ corresponds to such values of n. Inversely, the longest chains exist for n close to 2^i, $\hat{s} = s_{max}$ corresponds thus to the end of a trip of the pointer. $\hat{s}_{max}$ increases with b, since the chains become longer while the use of the separate chaining implies one access per every record in the chain. However, $\hat{s}_{ave}$ reveals practically independent of b.

Finally, table 1.c lists s''', i. e., the cost of an insertion. For $b = 1$ almost 8 accesses are needed, since split cost is the highest and since a split results from almost any insertion. For larger b, s''' falls down quickly, since the proportion of insertions leading to a split decreases and the others need typically 2 to 3 accesses. If $b >> 20$, which is a typical value for files, s''' oscillates between 2 and 3. Thus, first, as it was the case of the other costs, insertion cost of LH may also stay always close to its theoretical minimum. Next, even in the worst case, i. e., for $b = 1$, the insertion cost is still typically much smaller than for trees, since, for instance, for $x = 10^5$, a binary tree leads to $s''' > 16$ /KNU74/.

3.2.2. Load factor.

The characteristics of load factors $\hat{a}$ and $\hat{a}'$ are shown in the table 1.e. For $b = 1$ the load factor is constantly equal to 80 %. This conjunction of such a good load and of the previously shown access performance makes LH probably the best known tool for dynamic tables. For higher values of b, the load is going down to the average value of almost 60 % and so the load of LH with uncontrolled split may be almost 10 % worse than the load of a B-tree. However, better access performance is usually prefered to a sligtly better use of the increasingly cheaper disk space.

3.3. Controlled split.

If the load is controlled and the threshold g is greater than $\hat{a}_{max}$, then the load is practically equal to g. It is obvious that the higher g is, the worse must be the access performance, since the ratio of overflow records increases. Simulation studies show, however, that substantial increases to the load factor may be achieved while the value of the access performance still stays excellent.

For instance $g = 0.75$ and $b = 5$ leads to a load which is almost 10 % higher than the one for the uncontrolled load. The correspondig access performance is still very good, since $s'_{ave} = 1.25$, $s''_{ave} = 1.43$ and $s'''_{ave} = 3.84$. For $b = 50$, the same g leads to a 16 % improvement, while the access performance becomes : $s'_{ave} = 1.28$, $s''_{ave} = 2.38$ and $s'''_{ave} = 3.46$. For many applications the above trade off may be significant.

Higher thresholds increase the length of overflow record chains. On one hand, the storage occupied by overflow buckets is then no more negligible. On the other hand, larger overflow buckets must lead to better access performance. For higher thresholds, more stable load factor results thus from the control on $\hat{a}'$ and it is better to choose $b' > 1$.

The threshold corresponding to the load control on $\hat{a}'$ is denoted g'. For given values of b and of g', access performance depend on b'. If g' is higher than $\hat{a}_{max}$ of uncontrolled split, then, obviously, neither $b' = 1$ nor $b' >> 1$ can provide the best access performance. Therefore, they are b's which are the optimal ones. Fig. 3 shows curves of s' corresponding to the minimal s'_{ave} for $b = 10,20,50$ while $g' = 0.75,0.9$. It also indicates the corresponding optimal b's. Table 2 displays the performance of the corresponding stable states and the performance for $g' = 0.85$. All these results are obtained through simulations.

It first become apparent from the figure, that if $g' \approx 0.75$, then s' is always almost 1. It is also apparent that s' stays close to one even for $g' = 0.9$! In other words, LH does not only find a record in general in one access independently of the number of insertions, but may also use almost the minimal storage ! In particular LE achieves not only a much better access performance than B-trees but also saves more than 20 % in storage !

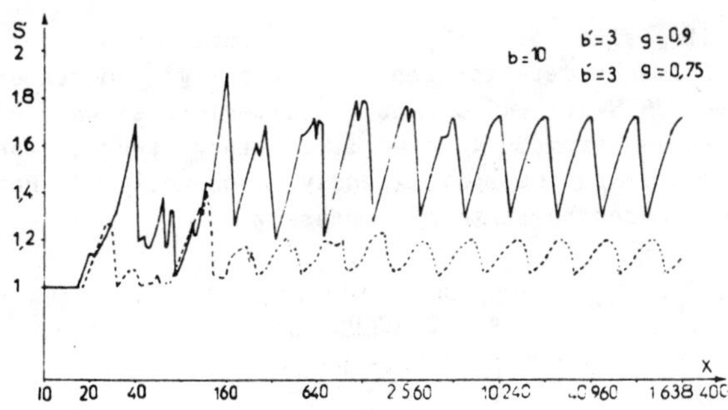

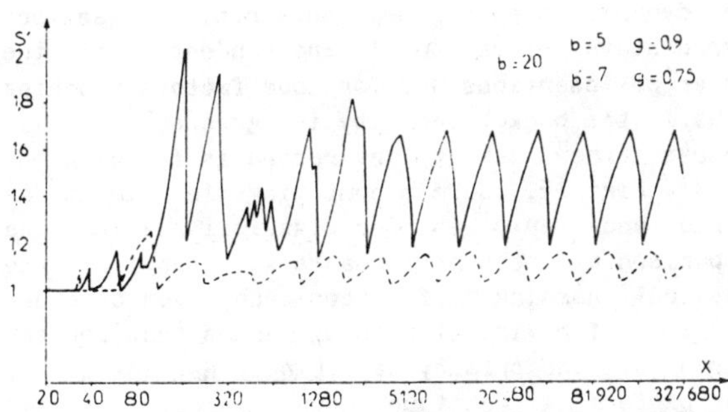

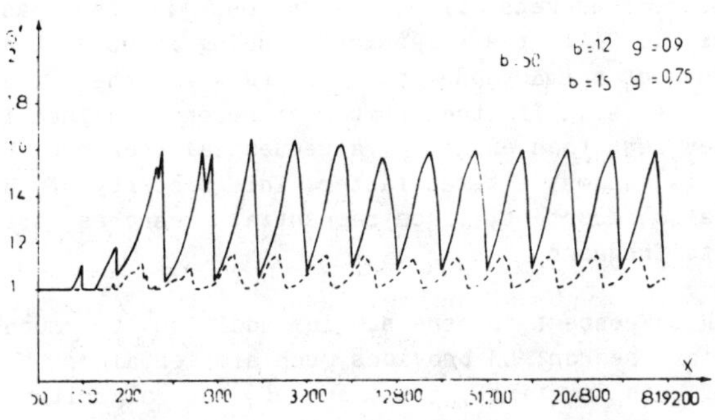

Fig.3. Mean number of accesses per successful search for linear hashing with the load kept equal to 75 % (- -) and to 90 % (——)

Furthermore, with respect to table 1, table 2 shows that it is rather worthwhile to choose a high threshold, even if one seriously cares about performance other than s'. For g' = 0.9, load control improves the load factor up to 31 % in mean and up to 40 % with respect to the worst value. The price to pay for such a significant improvement in load seems rather low, since, first, s''_{ave} increases only by 1.3 accesses. Next, s'''_{ave} increases only by 1.5 accesses. Only $\hat{s}_{ave}$ deteriorates more substantially, since it increases by 3.4 accesses. However, for b = 50 and g' = 0.85, this deterioration stays small, since it not exceed 1.3 accesses. Finally, $\hat{s}_{max}$ may do not deteriorate at all, being, even, for g' = 0.75, better for all each b. For b = 50 the gain is quite important, since it reaches 3.4 accesses. These gains are obviously due to b' > 1.

b	10			20			50			
b'	4	3	3	7	6	5	15	14	12	
â'	0.75	0.85	0.90	0.75	0.85	0.90	0.75	0.85	0.90	
s'_{ave}	1.14	1.33	1.57	1.08	1.24	1.44	1.05	1.20	1.35	
s'_{max}	1.22	1.47	1.73	1.15	1.35	1.65	1.13	1.35	1.59	(a)
s'_{min}	1.06	1.15	1.31	1.02	1.07	1.17	1.00	1.02	1.09	
s''_{ave}	1.37	1.99	2.48	1.29	1.80	2.45	1.27	1.78	2.37	
s''_{max}	1.48	2.15	2.75	1.43	2.11	2.87	1.49	2.19	2.95	(b)
s''_{min}	1.21	1.52	2.06	1.10	1.38	1.85	1.02	1.18	1.66	
s'''_{ave}	3.42	4.05	4.68	2.91	3.42	4.17	2.62	3.10	3.73	
s'''_{max}	3.67	4.71	5.43	3.11	3.60	4.43	2.68	3.38	4.15	(c)
s'''_{min}	2.91	3.29	3.73	2.51	2.82	3.25	2.27	2.43	2.91	
$\hat{s}_{min}$	5.05	5.60	6.15	5.05	5.75	5.9	5.00	5.45	6.20	
$\hat{s}_{ave}$	6.34	7.82	9.48	6.24	7.6	9.47	6.24	7.27	9.02	(d)
$\hat{s}_{max}$	7.10	9.50	11.1	7.35	8.75	11.6	7.15	8.5	10.50	

Table 2 : Performance of linear hashing with controlled load :

(a) successful search,
(b) unsuccessful search,
(c) insertion,
(d) split cost.

Fig. 4 displays s'_{ave} in function of b', with values of b and of g' from table 2 as parameters. It appears that for a file loaded up to 75 %, access performance are almost the same for a large number of values of b'. For these values, performance are, in addition, almost independent of b. For example, s'ave is smaller than 1.2 accesses, for all b' between 2 and 8 when b = 10, for all b' between 2 and 16 when b = 20 and for all b' between 2 and 50 when b = 50 ! Since practical constraints may frequently impose bucket

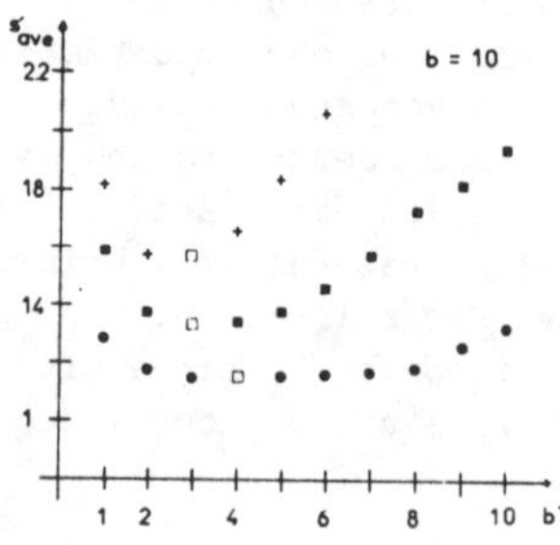

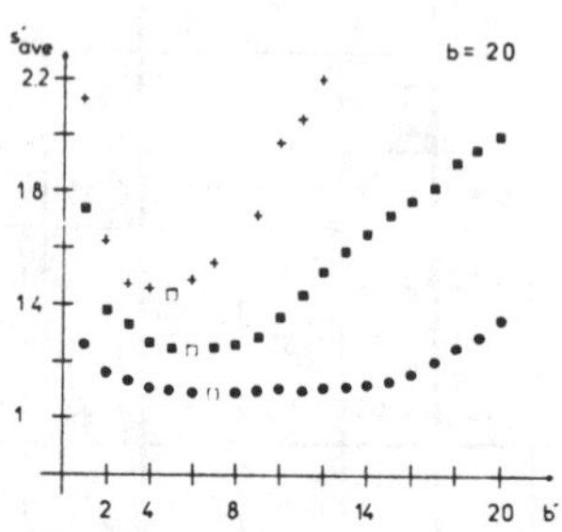

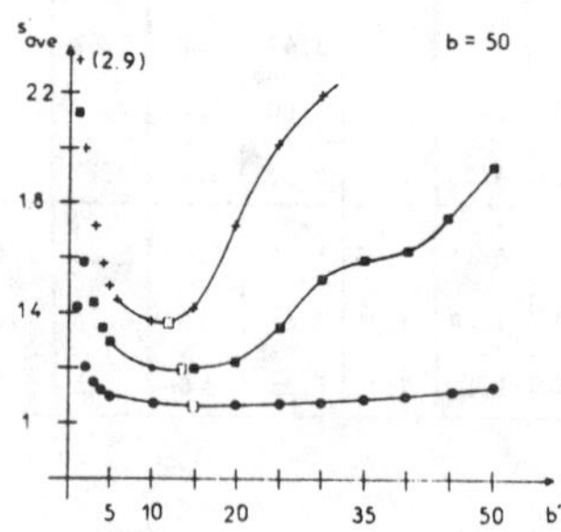

Fig.4. Mean number of accesses per successful search as a function of the size of the overflow bucket.

capacities which are not the optimal ones, this stability of excellent access performance is one more important property of LH.

The figure shows, however, that when the load becomes higher, b' should be kept closer to the optimal one. The practical rule which appears is then :

b/5 =< b' =< b/3.

For b > 20, even if the lower bound is b/7, we stay under a mean of 1.5 accesses.

It also becomes apparent that the access performance deteriorates less when g' increases from 75 % to 85 %, as it deteriorates when g' increases from 85 % to 90 %. In other terms, the last 5 % are the most expensive ones and it is not recommended to further increase g'.

4. CONCLUSIONS.

If a file or a table addressed with LH is static, then the performance is simply that of classical hashing, i. e., the best known. If they are dynamic, then the mean number of accesses per search stays close to 1 independently of the number of insertions and for load factors reaching 90 %. If the bucket capacity is greater than 10 records, then almost any record is found in one access. Finally, address computing is almost as simple and rapid as for classical hashing. The comparison of these performance with those of the classical hashing, of trees and even of other algorithms for virtual hashing, shows that for the search by the primary key, Linear Hashing is the best performing technique known.

High and constant load factor means that LH store records always in an almost minimal storage. A sequential search scans thus an almost minimal number of buckets, i. e., is almost as fast as possible. If the classical hashing is used, the number of primary buckets is fixed when the file is created. If the number of records is then i times less than expected, a sequential search with LH is almost i times faster. This property of LH is also important, since sequential searches are quite frequent.

With respect to trees, in addition to much faster search, LH provides much simpler algorithmic. This is, first, the case of the algorithms for a search, for an insertion and, especially, for a deletion. This is also the case of the algorithms for concurrency control, since only the key and the pointer must be locked, instead of a path in the tree. Also, there is no a problem of an inconsistency which may occur in a tree because of keys duplicated between the file and its index. Thus trees stay more advantageous only when the file must be searched in one order.

LH is, of course, primarly devoted to applications where the file may heavily grow or shrink or where the number of records is unknown when the file is created. It may thus be very useful for compilers and text processing systems. It may avoid the painful estimations of the file sizes in a DBMS, from which files the deleted records are, usually, not physically removed. It may also avoid performance deterioration for such files, rendering thus the very annoying reorganizations of the whole database /SCH73/ unnecessary or less frequent. It is a good tool for the management of working spaces for queries to a DBMS, since the number of records retrieved by a query to a working space is, usually, unknown in advance. It may also be used for a virtual memory management. On the other hand, since it works with very small cores, LH renders dynamic files usable on micro-computers. Clearly, the applications of the Linear Hashing are very numerous.

Research on LH has just started and many possibilities are still open. Other criteria for control may be useful, /SHO79/ for instance shows that the performance may be excellent if we simply split one time for any gb insertions. M. Girault (Institut de Programmation) has suggested to consider splits and groupings as operations which are, finally, completely out of the algorithmic for a record insertion or deletion. He suggests further to leave splits and groupings to the competence of a dedicated processor which task would thus be to take care of performance of all files. This idea obviously leads to a new and interesting type of an associative memory.

Furthermore, methods other than bucket chaining should be explored for overflow record addressing. The first investigations of open addressing show that it may work pretty well /KAR79/. Also, the properties of split functions should be investigated. Finally, much work is needed in modelling, since classical methods do not apply to dynamically created hashing functions. Especially, there is no models for the transient state and for a file with small buckets.

ACKNOWLEDGMENTS.

This work was sponsored by project SIRIUS.

REFERENCES

AHO75 Aho, A.V., Hopcroft, J.E., Ullman, J.D. The design and analysis of computer algorithms, Addison-Wesley Reading Mass. 1975.

BLA77 Blake, I.F., Konhein, A.G. Big buckets are (are not) better! Journal ACM 24, 4 (Oct 1977), 591-606

CAR73 Carter, B. The reallocation of hash-coded tables. Com. ACM 16, 1 (Jan 1973), 11-14

COM79 Comer, D. The ubiquous B-trees. ACM Comp. Surv., 11, 2, (Jun 1979), 121-138.

FAG78 Fagin, R., Nievergelt, J., Pippenger, N., Strong, H. R. Extendible hashing - a fast access method for dynamic files. IBM Res. Rep. RJ2305, (Jul 31, 1978).

GHO75 Ghost, S.P.,Lum, V.Y.Analysis of collisions when hashing by division. Information Systems, 1-B (1975), 15-22

GUI72 Guiho G. Sur l'etude de collisions dans les methodes de hash-coding, CRAS 274 (Feb 14, 1972)

GUI73 Guiho, G. Organisation des memoires, Influence d'une structure et etude d'une optimisation. These de Doctorat d'Etat. Univ. Paris VI, (Jun 1973), 278.

KAR79 Karlsson, K. Resolution de collisions du hachage virtuel lineaire par une methode du type adressage ouvert. Rap. D.E.A. Inf. Institut de Programmation, (Jun 1979), 81.

KNO71 Knott, G. D. Expandable open addressing hash table storage and retrieval. SIGFIDET Workshop on Data Description, Access and Control, ACM, (1971), 186-206.

KNU74 Knuth D.E. The Art of Computer Programing, Vol 3. Addison-Wesley, Reading Mass. 1974

LAR78 Larson, P. Dynamic hashing. BIT 18 (1978), (184,201).

LAR80 Larson, P. Linear hashing with partial expansions. Proc 6-th Conf on Very Large Databases, Montreal (Oct 1980).

LIT77 Litwin, W. Auto-structuration d'un fichier : methodologie, organisation d'acces, extension du hash-coding. Res. Rep 77/11, Institut de Programmation, Paris , (Avr 1977), 102

LIT77a Litwin, W. Methode d'access par hash-coding virtuel (VHAM) : Modelisation, Application a la gestion de memoire. Res. Rep. 77/16, Institut de Programmation, Paris, (Nov 1977), 50.

LIT78 Litwin, W. Une nouvelle methode d'acces par codage decoupe a un fichier. Compte-rendus de l'Academie des Sciences, Paris, t. 286, (Avr 1978), 695,698.

LIT78a Litwin, W. Virtual hashing : a dynamically changing hashing. Proc 4-th Conf on Very Large Databases, Berlin, (Sep 1978), 517-523

LIT79 Litwin, W. Linear virtual hashing : a new tool for files and tables implementation. Res. Rep. MAP-I-021, I.R.I.A , (Jan 1979), 24.

LIT79a Litwin, W. Hachage Virtuel : une nouvelle technique d'adressage de memoires. These de Doctorat d'Etat. Univ. Paris VI, (Mar 1979), 248.

LIT80 Litwin, W. Linear hashing : a new algorithm for files and tables addressing. Proc Int Conf. On Data Bases, Aberdeen, (Jul 1980).

LUM73 Lum V.Y. General performance analysis of key to address transformation methods. Com ACM 16, (Oct 1973).

MAR77 Martin, J. Computer Datbase Organization. Prentice Hall, Inc. Englewood Cliffs, New Jersey, 1977.

ROS77 Rosenberg, A.L., Stockmayer, L.J. Hashing shemes for extendible arrays. JACM 24, 2, (Apr 1977), 199-221.

SCH73 Schneiderman, B. Optimum data reorganization points, Com ACM 16, 6 (Jun 1973), 23-28.

SHO79 Scholl, M. Performance analysis of new file organizations based on dynamic hash-coding. Res. Rep 347, I.R.I.A - Laboria, (Mar 1979), 28.

SPR77 Sprugnoli, R. Perfect hashing functions : a single probe retrieving method for static sets. Com ACM 20, 11 (Nov 1977), 841-850.

The Grid File: An Adaptable, Symmetric Multikey File Structure

J. NIEVERGELT, H. HINTERBERGER
Institut für Informatik, ETH
AND K. C. SEVCIK
University of Toronto

Traditional file structures that provide multikey access to records, for example, inverted files, are extensions of file structures originally designed for single-key access. They manifest various deficiencies in particular for multikey access to highly dynamic files. We study the dynamic aspects of file structures that treat all keys symmetrically, that is, file structures which avoid the distinction between primary and secondary keys. We start from a bitmap approach and treat the problem of file design as one of data compression of a large sparse matrix. This leads to the notions of a *grid partition* of the search space and of a *grid directory*, which are the keys to a dynamic file structure called the *grid file*. This file system adapts gracefully to its contents under insertions and deletions, and thus achieves an upper bound of two disk accesses for single record retrieval; it also handles range queries and partially specified queries efficiently. We discuss in detail the design decisions that led to the grid file, present simulation results of its behavior, and compare it to other multikey access file structures.

Categories and Subject Descriptors: H.2.2 [**Database Management**]: Physical Design; H.3.2 [**Information Storage and Retrieval**]: Information Storage

General Terms: Algorithms, Performance

Keywords and Phrases: File structures, database, dynamic storage allocation, multikey searching, multidimensional data.

1. PROBLEM, SOLUTIONS, PERFORMANCE

A wide selection of file structures is available for managing a collection of records identified by a single key: sequentially allocated files, tree-structured files of many kinds, and hash files. They allow execution of common file operations such as FIND, INSERT, and DELETE, with various degrees of efficiency. Older file structures such as sequential files or conventional forms of hash files were optimized for handling static files, where insertions and deletions are considered to be less important than look-up or modification of existing records. Insertions were usually handled by overflow areas; their growth, however, leads to a progressive degradation of performance, which in practice forces periodic restructuring of the entire file. Modern file structures such as balanced trees or extendible forms of hashing adapt their shape continuously to the varying collection of data they must store, without any degradation of performance. Their discovery was a major advance in the study of data structures.

File processing in today's transaction oriented systems requires file structures that allow efficient access to records, based on the value of any one of several attributes or a combination thereof. The development of file structures that provide multikey access to records repeats the history of single-key structures: earlier schemes, such as inverted files, are extensions of file structures originally designed for single-key access. They do not address the problem of graceful adaptation to highly dynamic files. The design of balanced data structures appears to be significantly more difficult for multidimensional data (each record is identified by several attributes) than for one-dimensional data. This comes as no surprise, since most balanced structures for single-key data rely on a total ordering of the set of key values, and natural total orders of multidimensional data do not exist.

In view of the diversity of file structures for single-key access, one might expect an even greater variety for multikey access. In addition to the traditional inverted file, many other schemes have been proposed: [2, 3, 5, 9, 18, 19, 27, 29, 30, 32] are a representative sample of the techniques known. We review several of these file structures, and their properties, in Section 6: most of them suffer from various deficiencies in a highly dynamic environment. Thus the field is open for improvements, and in this paper we present the grid file as a contribution to the development of balanced multikey file structures.

Consider a file F as a collection of records $R = [a_1, a_2 \ldots, a_k]$, where the a are fields containing attribute values. As an example, consider records with the attribute fields last name, first name, middle initial, year of birth, and social security number, for example [Doe, John, –, 1951, 123456789]. Multikey access means that we reference the records R in file F by using any possible subset of these (key-) fields, as shown in the following examples:

(1) Entire record specified (exact match query, point query)
(2) Doe born in 1951 (a partially specified query)
(3) All records with last name Doe (single-key query)
(4) Social security number 987654321 (presumably unique)
(5) Everybody born between 1940 and 1960 (range or interval query)

Multikey access problems come in two kinds. In information and document retrieval an object (say a book) is characterized by index terms, often chosen from a thesaurus of recommended terms. If we consider each term in the thesaurus to be an attribute, documents become points in a high-dimensional space, but the domain of each attribute is small (perhaps it contains only the two values "relevant" and "irrelevant"). We do not consider this case. We only discuss the other typical case of multikey access, where a record is characterized by a small number of attributes (less than 10), but the domain of each attribute is large and linearly ordered.

For the second case we can specify ranges by expressions r of the form: $l_i \leq a_i \leq u_i$, where l_i and u_i denote lower and upper bounds on attribute value a chosen

A previous version of this paper appeared in *Trends in Information Processing Systems, Proc 3rd ECI Conference.* Lecture Notes in Computer Science 123.

Authors' addresses: J. Nievergelt and H. Hinterberger, Institut für Informatik, ETH, CH-8092 Zurich, Switzerland; K.C. Sevcik, Computer Systems Research Group, University of Toronto, Toronto, Ontario M5S 1A4 Canada.

from its domain S_i. The point specification $l_i = u_i$ and the "don't care" specification l_i = "smallest value in S_i," u_i = "largest value in S_i," are special cases of range specifications that cover exact matches and partially specified queries. The general form of references we consider is $(r_1, r_2, \ldots, r_k)$, where r_i is a value-range of the ith key-field over the attribute domain S_i. If we abbreviate "don't care" specifications as blanks, we can formulate query (2) of the previous example as (last name = Doe , , , year of birth = 1951), or query (5) as (, , , 1940 ≤ year of birth ≤ 1960,). We consider primarily range queries, but the grid file is applicable to other types of queries as well. For example, [31] applies the related technique of "extendible cells" to closest point problems, and [12] studies the problem of executing relational database queries on the grid file.

We approach the problem of designing a practical multikey access file structure by first considering an extreme solution: the *bitmap representation* of the attribute space, which reserves one bit for each possible record in the space, whether it is present in the file or not. Even though the bitmap representation in its pure form requires impractically large amounts of storage, it points the way to practical solutions based on the idea of data compression.

In a k-dimensional bitmap the combinations of all possible values of k attributes are represented by a bit position in a k-dimensional matrix. The size of the bitmap (number of bit positions) is the product of the cardinalities of the attribute domains. Figure 1 shows a three-dimensional bitmap.

FIND$(r_1, r_2 \ldots, r_k)$ reduces to direct access, INSERT/DELETE requires that a position in the bitmap be set to 1 or 0 respectively, and NEXT in any dimension requires a scan until the next 1 is found. If a sufficiently large memory were available, the bitmap would be the ideal solution to our problem. For realistic applications, however, this bitmap is impossibly large. Fortunately it is sparse (almost all zeros), and hence can be compressed. The sparse matrix compression techniques known in numerical applications are inapplicable, since we need a compression scheme that is compatible with file access operations: FIND, INSERT, and DELETE must be executed efficiently in a compressed bitmap. This we can achieve by introducing a dynamic directory. In maintaining a dynamic partition (directory) on the space of all key-values, we approximate the bit map through compression. This dynamic partitioning is treated in more detail in the next section. The result of this approach is a *symmetric*, *adaptable* file structure. *Symmetric* means that every key field is treated as the primary key; *adaptable* means that the data structure adapts its shape automatically to the content it must store, so that bucket occupancy and access time are uniform over the entire file, even though the data may be distributed in a highly nonuniform way over the data space.

The efficiency of a file processing system is measured mainly by response times to multikey access requests. The major component of this response time is the time spent in accessing peripheral storage media. In today's systems these storage media are disks, where the maximal amount of data transferred in one access is fixed (a disk block or page). We will therefore assess efficiency in terms of the number of disk accesses. In particular, we aim at file structures that meet the following two principles.

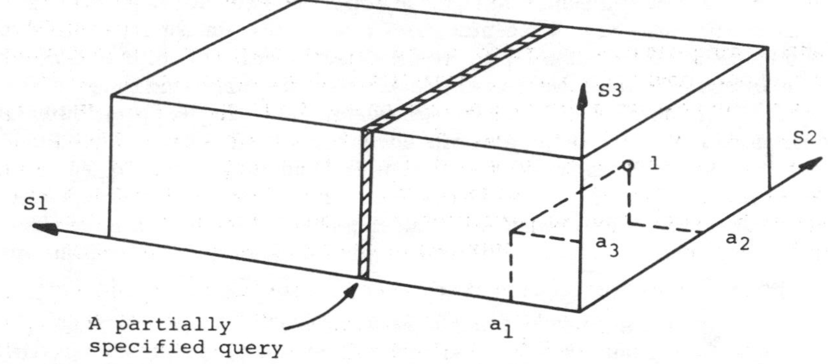

Fig. 1. The three-dimensional bitmap. A "1" indicates the presence of a record with attribute values determined by its position in the map, a "0" indicates absence.

Two-disk-access principle. A fully specified query must retrieve a single record in at most two disk accesses: the first access to the correct portion of the dirctory, the second to the correct data bucket.

Efficient range queries with respect to all attributes. The storage structure should preserve as much as possible the order defined on each attribute domain, so that records that are near in the domain of any attribute are likely to be in the same physical storage block.

Both ideas are as old as disk storage devices: the hope of realizing them led to the traditional index sequential access methods introduced in the late fifties. Since, in a batch processing operation, sequential file access suffices, physical contiguity was dedicated to preserve the order of the primary key alone. And traditional index sequential access techniques find a record specified by a primary key value in one or two disk accesses when the file is newly generated. In practice it turns out, however, that index sequential access techniques, on average, cause more than two disk accesses. This is true for traditional techniques of handling dynamic single-key files by means of chains of overflow buckets. It remained true for balanced trees, which usually require more than two levels for large data collections. The two-disk-access principle for dynamic single-key files was only realized by address computation techniques such as extendible hashing [6]. It was never applied to dynamic multikey files, where each secondary key directory of an inverted file typically introduces an additional disk access.

The reasons why we consider the two principles above important for a modern file system have to do with the expanding spectrum of computer applications:

(1) An interactive system should provide *instantaneous response* to the user's *trivial requests.* In the context of human physiology, *instantaneous* means 1/10th of a second, the limit of resolution of our sense of time. In a typical system 1/10th of a second suffices for a couple of disk accesses, but not for half a dozen. A "trivial request" is often of the form "show me this item," and triggers a fully

specified query. Hence a file system that obeys the two-disk-access principle is a suitable basis for highly interactive applications programs.

(2) Computer-aided design, geographic data processing, and other applications work on geometric objects in two and three dimensions. Complex geometric objects are often decomposed into simple ones, such as rectangles, which can be considered to be points in a higher-dimensional space. Geometric processing generates a lot of intersection and neighborhood queries which translate into range queries along all the dimensions of the space [10].

2. GRID PARTITIONS OF THE SEARCH SPACE

All known searching techniques appear to fall into one of two broad categories: those that *organize the specific set of data* to be stored and those that *organize the embedding space* from which the data is drawn. Comparative search techniques, such as binary search trees, belong to the first category: the boundaries between different regions of the search space are determined by values of data that must be stored, and hence shift around during the life time of a dynamic file. Address computation techniques, including radix trees, belong to the second category: region boundaries are drawn at places that are fixed regardless of the content of the file; adaptation to the variable content of a dynamic file occurs through activation or deactivation of such a boundary. In recent years search techniques that organize the embedding space rather than the specific file content have made significant progress (see [23] for a survey).

Each search technique partitions the search space into subspaces, down to the "level of resolution" of the implementation, typically determined by the bucket capacity. Much can be learned by comparing the partitioning patterns created by different search techniques, regardless of how the partition is implemented. Let us consider three examples, keeping in mind that we only consider the case where the domain of each attribute is large and linearly ordered (for small domains, such as Boolean ones, the space partitioning analogy is not helpful).

Multidimensional trees of various kinds (e.g., [2]) are an example of multikey access techniques that organize the set of data to be stored. The recursively applied divide and conquer principle leads to a partition of the search space as illustrated in Figure 2(a), where region boundaries become progressively shorter. The traditional inverted file, with its asymmetric treatment of primary key and secondary keys, is a hybrid: Values of the primary key determine region boundaries so as to achieve a uniform bucket occupancy, whereas the domain of each secondary key is "partitioned" independently of the data to be stored—to the extreme level of resolution where each value of the secondary key domain is in its own region. Figure 2(b) shows the resulting partition. The grid file presented in this paper is based on grid partitions of the search space illustrated in Figure 2(c). Each region boundary cuts the entire search space in two, but, unlike the inverted file, all dimensions are treated symmetrically. It turns out that the most efficient implementations of grid partitions are obtained by drawing the boundary lines at fixed values of the domain. Hence, grid partitions are an example of techniques that organize the embedding space.

The utility of the different space partitions mentioned above depends on the distribution of data. For the grid partition we assume independent attributes,

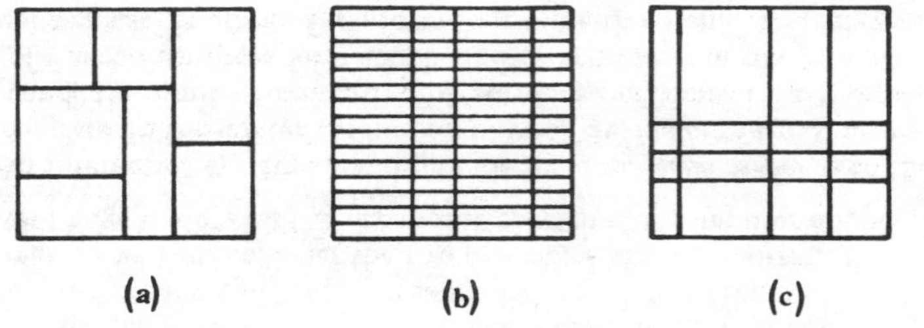

Fig. 2. Space partitions created by different search techniques.

but we do not assume a uniform distribution. Correlated attributes, such as data points that lie on a diagonal, prevent full utilization of a grid partition's discriminatory power. Correlated attributes may mean that attributes are functionally dependent on each other (age and year of birth, for instance), in which case searching becomes more efficient if only some of the attributes are chosen as dimensions of the search space. Or it may mean that we have not chosen the most suitable attributes for searching, and that a transformation of a coordinate system may result in independent attributes (see [10] for an example in the context of a geometric database).

Assuming independent attributes, the grid partition of the search space is obviously well suited for range and partially specified queries. It exhibits some striking advantages over the other types of partitions shown in Figure 2, such as systematic region boundaries and economy of representation (one boundary line of Figure 2(c) does the work of many in Figure 2(a)).

We introduce the following terminology and notation for the three-dimensional case: generalization to k dimensions is obvious. On the record space $S = X \times Y \times Z$ we obtain a grid partition $P = U \times V \times W$ by imposing intervals $U = (u_0, u_1, \ldots, u_l)$, $V = (v_0, v_1, \ldots, v_m)$, $W = (w_0, w_1, \ldots, w_n)$ on each axis and dividing the record space into blocks, which we call grid blocks, as shown in Figure 3.

During the operation of a file system the underlying partition of the search space needs to be modified in response to insertions and deletions. For the grid partition we introduce operations that refine the granularity by splitting an interval, and render it coarser by merging two adjacent intervals.

Partition modification. The grid partition $P = U \times V \times W$ is modified by altering only one of its components at a time. A one-dimensional partition is modified either by splitting one of its intervals in two, or by merging two adjacent intervals into one. Figure 3 shows this for the partition V. Notice that the intervals "below" the one being split or the two being merged retain their index (v in Figure 3), while the indices of the intervals "above" the point of splitting or merging are shifted by +1 or −1, respectively ($v_2 \leftrightarrow v_3$ in Figure 3).

In order to obtain a file system, we will need other operations that relate grid blocks and records to each other, such as: find the grid block in which a given record lies, or list all records in a given grid block. The regularity of the grid partition makes the implementation of such operations straightforward: they are reduced to the separate maintenance of one-dimensional partitions. Thus the

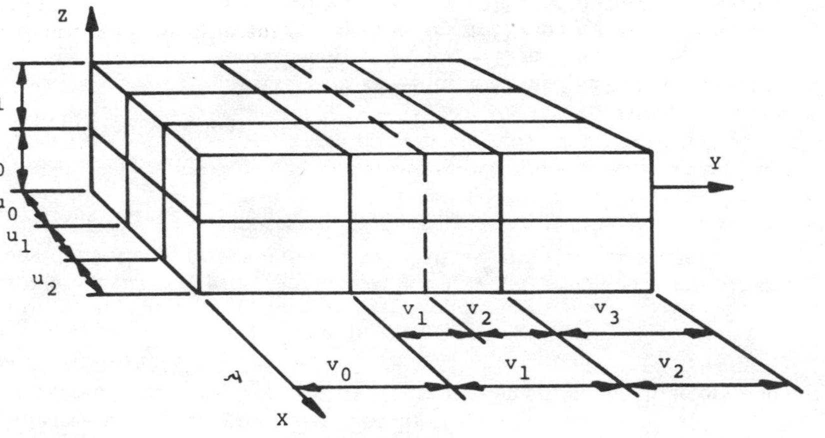

Fig. 3. A three-dimensional record space $X \times Y \times Z$, with a grid partition $P = U \times V \times W$. The picture shows the effect of refining P by splitting interval v_1.

operations that modify the partition emerge as crucial, in the sense that they impose severe constraints on an efficient representation.

3. THE GRID FILE

A file structure designed to manage a disk allocates storage in units of fixed size, called disk blocks, pages, or buckets, depending on the level of description. We use *bucket* for a storage unit that contains records. We assume an unlimited number of them, each one of capacity c records. The case of very small bucket capacities, such as $c = 1$, is not of great interest; other file structures should be designed to handle it. We are interested in the practical range of, say, $10 < c < 1000$, where an entry in the grid directory is tiny compared to a bucket, and where undesirable probabilistic effects such as the "birthday paradox" (high probability that two records cause a bucket to overflow) are less likely. Differences in access time to different buckets are ignored, hence the time required for a file operation can be measured by the number of disk accesses.

The data structure used to organize records within a bucket is of minor importance for the file system as a whole. Often the simplest possible structure, sequential allocation of records within a bucket, is suitable. The structure used to organize the set of buckets, on the other hand, is the heart of a file system. For the grid file, the problem reduces to defining the correspondence betwen grid blocks and buckets: This assignment of grid blocks to buckets is the task of the grid directory, to be described in Section 3.1. In order to obtain an efficient file structure, constraints on access time, update time, and on memory utilization must be met. In particular, we aim at

- the two-disk-access principle for point queries,
- efficient processing of range queries in large linearly ordered domains,
- splitting and merging of grid blocks to involve only two buckets,
- maintaining a reasonable lower bound on average bucket occupancy.

The first three points determine processing efficiency; they are discussed in Sections 3.2 and 3.3, respectively. The fourth point, on memory utilization, is discussed by means of simulation results in Section 5.

3.1 The Grid Directory: Function and Structure

In order to obtain a file system based on the grid partitions described in Section 2, we must superpose a bucket management system onto these partitions. In our case the design of a bucket management system involves three parts:

- defining a class of legal assignments of grid blocks to buckets,
- choosing a data structure for a directory that represents the current assignment,
- finding efficient algorithms to update the directory when the assignment changes.

In this section we discuss the first two points, concerned with function and structure of the directory, respectively.

The purpose of the grid directory is to maintain the dynamic correspondence between grid blocks in the record space and data buckets. Hence we must define the class of legal assignments of grid blocks to buckets before we can design a data structure. Reasons of efficiency dictate that only a subset of all possible assignments of grid blocks to buckets be allowed, characterized by the constraint that bucket regions must be convex.

The two-disk-access principle implies that all the records in one grid block must be stored in the same bucket. Unfortunately, we cannot insist on the converse: if each grid block had its own data bucket, bucket occupancy could be arbitrarily low. Hence it must be possible for several grid blocks to share a bucket: we call the set of all grid blocks assigned to the same bucket B (or equivalently, the space spanned by these grid blocks) the *region* of B. The shape of bucket regions clearly affects the speed of at least the following two operations:

- range queries, and
- updates following a modification of the grid partition.

Given our emphasis on efficient processing of range queries, and given the earlier decision to base the file system on grid partitions of the record space, there appears to be no other choice than to insist that bucket regions have the shape of a box (i.e., a k-dimensional rectangle). We call such an assignment of grid blocks to buckets *convex*. Figure 4 shows a typical convex assignment of grid blocks to buckets. Each grid block points to a bucket. Several grid blocks may share a bucket, as long as the union of these grid blocks forms a rectangular box in the space of records. The regions of buckets are pairwise disjoint, together they span the space of records.

In order to represent and maintain the dynamic correspondence between grid blocks in the record space and data buckets, we introduce the *grid directory*: a data structure that supports operations needed to update the convex assignments

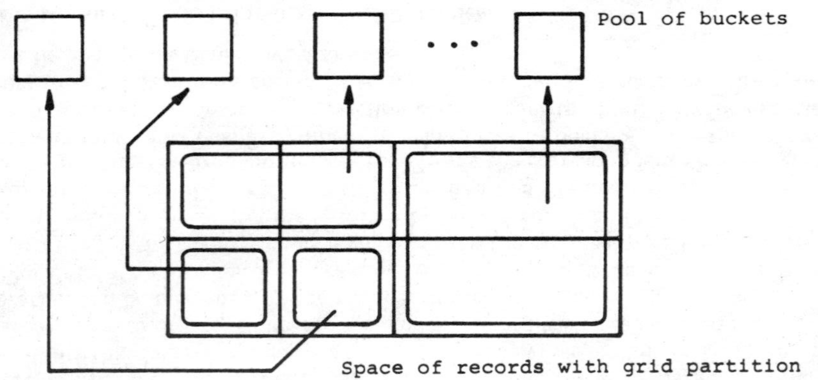

Fig. 4. A convex assignment of grid blocks to buckets.

defined above when bucket overflow or underflow makes it necessary. The choice of just how much to specify about this data structure and how much to leave for later implementation decisions is discussed in Section 4.1. We define the grid directory at a fairly abstract level, fixing only those decisions that appear essential. Different implementations are discussed in Section 4.

A grid directory consists of two parts: first, a dynamic k-dimensional array called the *grid array*; its elements (pointers to data buckets) are in one-to-one correspondence with the grid blocks of the partition; and second, k one-dimensional arrays called *linear scales*; each scale defines a partition of a domain S.

For the sake of notational simplicity we present the case $k = 2$, with record space $S = X \times Y$, from which the general case $k > 2$ is easily inferred.

A grid directory G for a two-dimensional space is characterized by

- Integers $nx > 0$, $ny > 0$ ("extent" of directory).
- Integers $0 \leq cx < nx$, $0 \leq cy < ny$ ("current element of the directory and current grid block").

It consists of

- a two-dimensional array $G(0 \ldots, nx - 1, 0 \ldots, ny - 1)$ ("grid array") and
- one-dimensional arrays $X(0 \ldots, nx)$, $Y(0 \ldots, ny)$ ("linear scales").

Operations defined on the grid directory consist of

- Direct access: $G(cx, cy)$
- Next in each direction

nextxabove: $cx \leftarrow (cx + 1) \bmod nx$
nextxbelow: $cx \leftarrow (cx - 1) \bmod nx$
nextyabove: $cy \leftarrow (cy + 1) \bmod ny$
nextybelow: $cy \leftarrow (cy - 1) \bmod ny$

- Merge

mergex: given px, $1 \leq px < nx$, merge px with nextxbelow; rename all elements above px;
adjust X-scale.
mergey: similar to mergex for any py, $1 \leq py < ny$.

- Split

splitx: given px, $0 \leq px \leq nx$, create new element $px + 1$ and rename all cells above px;
adjust X-scale.
splity: similar to splitx for any py, $0 \leq py \leq ny$.

Constraints on the values. The restriction to convex assignments of grid blocks to buckets is expressed by the following constraints on the values of grid directory elements:

if $G(i', j') = G(i'', j'')$ then for all i, j with $i' \leq i \leq i''$ and $j' \leq j \leq j''$ we have $G(i', j') = G(i, j) = G(i'', j'')$.

Some splitting and merging policies (see Sections 4.2 and 4.3) restrict the set of assignments that may arise during operation of the grid file to some subset of all convex assignments.

3.2 Record Access

The description of the grid directory in Section 3.1, abstract as it may be, suffices to justify a key assumption on which the efficiency of the grid file is based: the array G is likely to be large and must be kept on disk, but the linear scales X and Y are small and can be kept in central memory.

This assumption suffices for the two-disk-access principle to hold for fully specified queries, as the following example shows. Consider a record space with attribute "year" with domain $0 \cdots 2000$, and attribute "initial" with domain $a \cdots z$. Assume that the distribution of records in the record space is such as to have caused the following grid partition to emerge.

$$X = (0, 1000, 1500, 1750, 1875, 2000); \quad Y = (a, f, k, p, z).$$

A FIND for a fully specified query $(r_1, r_2 \ldots,)$, such as FIND [1980, w], is executed as shown in Figure 5.

The attribute value 1980 is converted into interval index 5 through a search in scale X, and w is converted into the interval index 4 in scale Y. For realistic granularities of these partitions, these linear scales are stored in central memory; thus the conversion of attribute value to interval index requires no time in our model, where only the number of disk accesses count. The interval indices 5 and 4 provide direct access to the correct element of the grid directory, where the bucket address is located. Even if only part of the grid directory can be read into central memory in one disk access, the correct page (the one that contains the desired bucket address) can easily be computed from the interval indices. Range queries, including the special case of partially specified queries, are also handled efficiently by the grid file. In information retrieval the following notion of

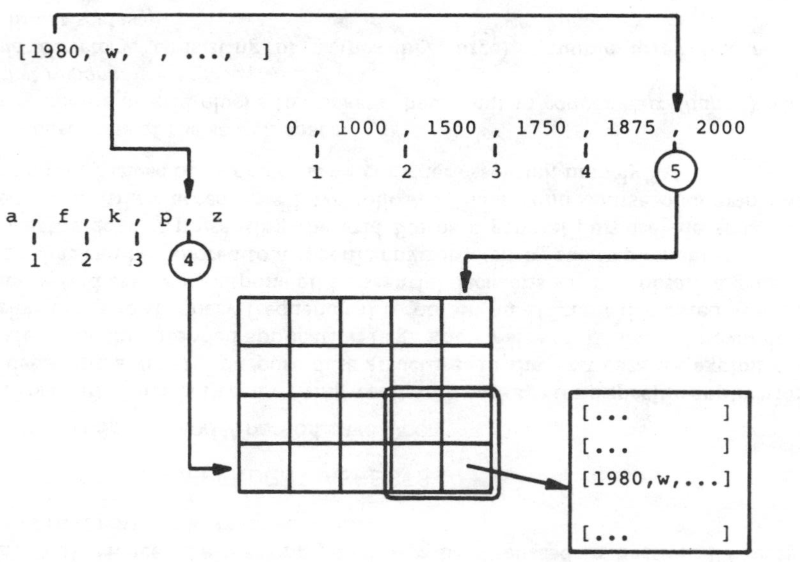

Fig. 5. Retrieval of a single record requires two disk accesses.

"precision" of an answer to a query is well known:

$$\frac{\text{number of records retrieved that meet the query specification}}{\text{total number of records retrieved}}$$

Figure 6 illustrates the fact that the precision of most range queries is high. In particular, precision approaches 1 for queries that retrieve many records (as compared to bucket capacity).

3.3 Dynamics of the Grid File

The dynamic behavior of the grid file is best explained by tracing an example: that is, building up a file under repeated insertions. When deletions occur, merging operations get triggered. In order to simplify the description, we present the two-dimensional case only. Instead of showing the grid directory, whose elements are in one-to-one correspondence with the grid blocks, we draw the bucket pointers as originating directly from the grid blocks.

Initially, a single bucket *A*, of capacity $c = 3$ in our example, is assigned to the entire record space.

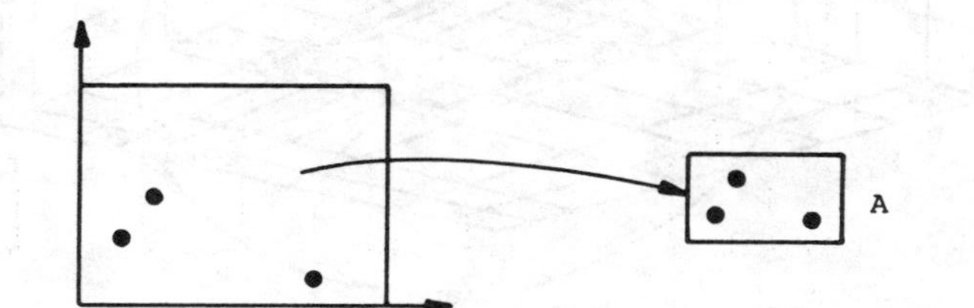

When bucket *A* overflows, the record space is split, a new bucket *B* is made available, and those records that lie in one half of the space are moved from the old bucket to the new one.

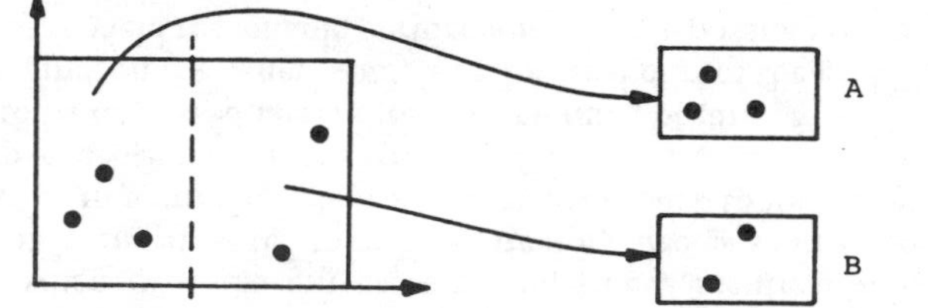

If bucket *A* overflows again, its grid block (i.e., the left half of the space) is split according to some splitting policy: we assume the simplest splitting policy of alternating directions. Those records of *A* that lie in the shaded lower-left grid block of the figure below are moved to a new bucket *C*. Notice that, as bucket *B* did not overflow, it is left alone: its region now consists of two grid blocks. For effective memory utilization it is essential that in the process of refining the grid partition we need not necessarily split a bucket when its region is split.

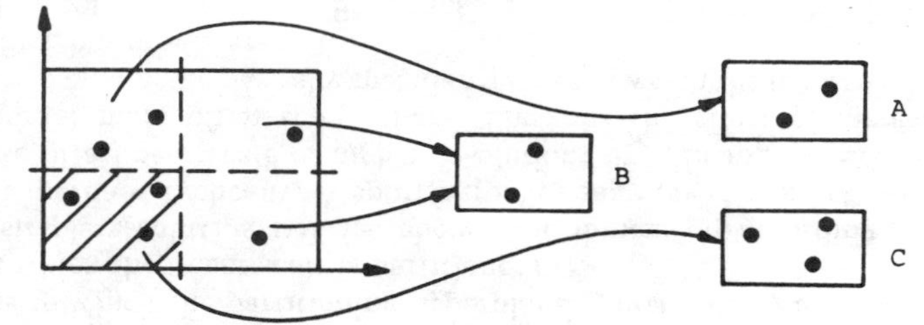

Assuming that records keep arriving in the lower-left corner of the space, bucket *C* will overflow. This will trigger a further refinement of the grid partition as shown below, and a splitting of bucket *C* into *C* and *D*.

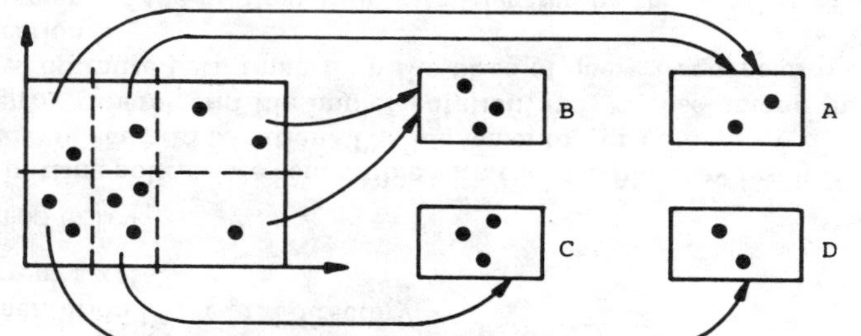

The history of repeated splitting can be represented in the form of a binary tree, which imposes on the set of buckets currently in use (and hence on the set of regions of these buckets) a *twin system*: each bucket and its region have a unique twin from which it is split off. In the picture above, *C* and *D* are twins,

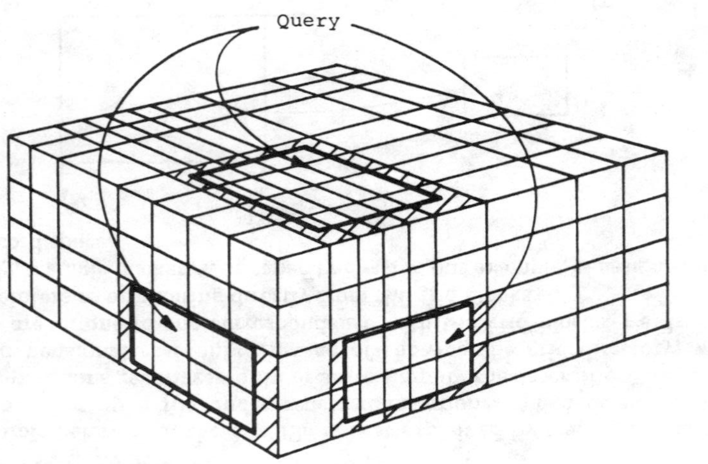

Fig. 6. A range query causes irrelevant records to be retrieved only at the fringes of the answer.

the pair (C, D) is A's twin, and the pair $(A, (C, D))$ is B's twin. Merging, needed to maintain a high occupancy in the presence of deletions, can proceed from the leaves up in the twin system tree. In one-dimensional storage the twin system (also called the "buddy system") created by repeated splits indeed suffices for obtaining a high memory occupancy. In more than one dimension, however, this is not so (in the example above, consider the case where buckets A and B have become almost empty, yet are unable to merge because the pair C and D cannot be merged). Hence, the merging policies to be discussed in Section 4.3 merge buckets that never split from each other.

4. ENVIRONMENT-DEPENDENT ASPECTS

4.1 What to Specify and What to Leave Open

There is a difference between writing a software package for a specific application and designing a general-purpose data structure. In the first case we exploit our knowledge of the intended application (e.g., known size of database, known data distribution, known query frequencies) to obtain an efficient dedicated system. In the second case we postpone all inessential decisions so as to obtain a general design that can be tailored to a specific environment by the implementor.

With the goal of presenting the grid file as a general-purpose file structure suited to multikey access, we have followed the second course of action and specified only those decisions that we consider essential, namely

- *grid partitions* of the search space,
- assignments of grid blocks to buckets that result in *convex* (*box-shaped*) *bucket regions,*
- *grid directory,* consisting of a (possibly large) dynamic array but small linear scales.

Some other important decisions have been left open because we feel that they can be settled in many different ways within the framework set by the decisions above. In this section we discuss the most important open issues, namely

- choice of splitting policy,
- choice of merging policy,
- implementation of the grid directory,
- concurrent access.

4.2 Splitting Policy

Several splitting policies are compatible with the grid file; they result in different refinements of the grid partition. The implementor, or perhaps even the user of a sufficiently general grid file implementation, may choose among them in an attempt to optimize performance on the basis of query frequencies observed in his application.

A refinement of the grid partition gets triggered by the overflow of a bucket, all of whose records lie in a single grid block. Its occurrence is relatively rare: the majority of all overflows involve buckets whose records are distributed over several grid blocks and can be handled by a mere bucket split without any change to the partition. If a partition refinement does occur, there is a choice of dimension (the axis to which the partitioning hyperplane is orthogonal) and location (the point at which the linear scale is partitioned).

The simplest splitting policies choose the dimension according to a fixed schedule, perhaps cyclically. A splitting policy may favor some attribute(s) (in the sense of a linear scale of higher resolution) by splitting the corresponding dimension(s) more often than others. This has the effect of increasing the precision of answers to partially specified queries in which the favored attribute(s) is specified, but others are not.

The location of a split on a linear scale need not necessarily be chosen at the midpoint of the interval, as we have described in Section 3. Little is changed if the splitting point is chosen from a set of values that are convenient for a given application—months or weeks on a time axis, feet or inches on a linear scale used to measure machine parts.

4.3 Merging Policy

Merging occurs at two levels: bucket merging and merging of cross sections in the grid directory. Directory merging is rarely of interest. Although the directory could shrink when two adjacent cross sections have identical values, in most applications, it is unwarranted to reduce directory size as soon as possible, as in a steady-state or in a growing file it will soon grow back to its earlier size. There are only two exceptions: in a shrinking file and in "dynamic weighting of attributes" (to be discussed later) directory merging occurs.

Bucket merging, on the other hand, is an integral part of the grid file. Different policies appear to yield reasonable performance, with a possible trade-off between time and memory utilization. A merging policy is controlled by three decisions: *which pairs* of adjacent buckets *are candidates* for merging their contents into a single bucket; among several eligible pairs, *which one has priority*; and the *merging threshold* that determines at what bucket occupancy merging is actually triggered.

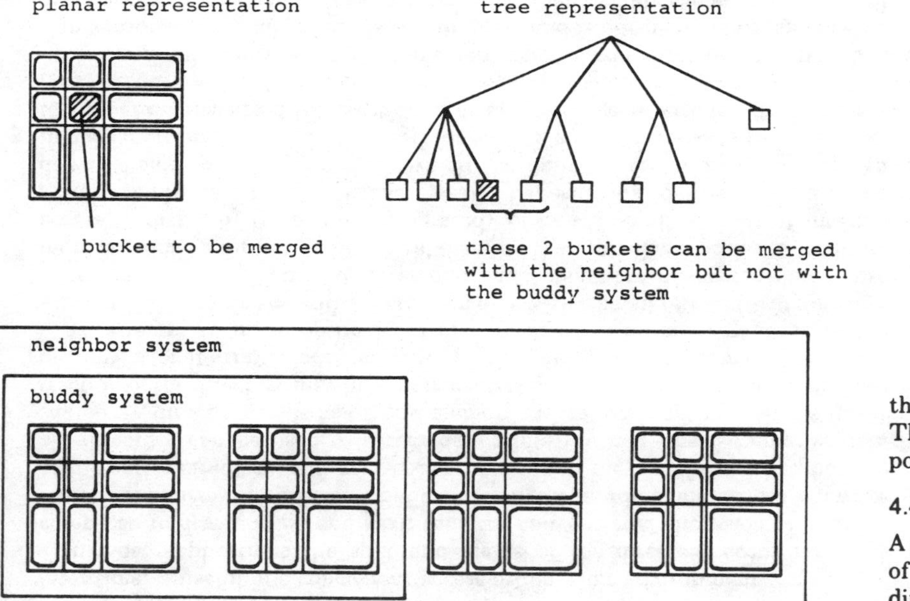

Fig. 7. Possible modifications to the grid directory when merging in the buddy or neighbor systems.

We have used two different systems for determining pairs of buckets that can merge. In the (k-dimensional) "buddy system," a bucket can merge with exactly one adjacent buddy in each of the k dimensions. The assignment of grid blocks to buckets is such that buddies can always merge if the total number of records fits into one bucket. The buddy system is easily implemented, and we recommend it as the standard merging policy. We have also experimented with a more general "neighbor system," in which a bucket can merge with either of its two adjacent neighbors in each of the k dimensions, provided the resulting bucket region is convex. The neighbor system can generate all convex assignments of grid blocks to buckets, whereas the buddy system only generates a subclass that is best described by means of recursive halving and is represented by the "quad tree" in Figure 7. The simulation experiments of Section 5 show that both systems give a reasonable performance.

The second decision, that of which axis to favor when it is possible to merge along several axes, is only relevant when the granularity of the partitions along the different axes happens to be different. For example, if the splitting policy favors some attribute(s) by splitting the corresponding dimension(s) more often than others, the merging policy must not undo this effect by merging more often along these same axes.

The third decision, of setting a merging threshold of p percent, with the interpretation that the contents of two mergeable buckets are actually merged if the occupancy of the result bucket is at most p percent, has a clear answer: Thresholds of around 70 percent are reasonable, those above 80 percent lead to poor performance.

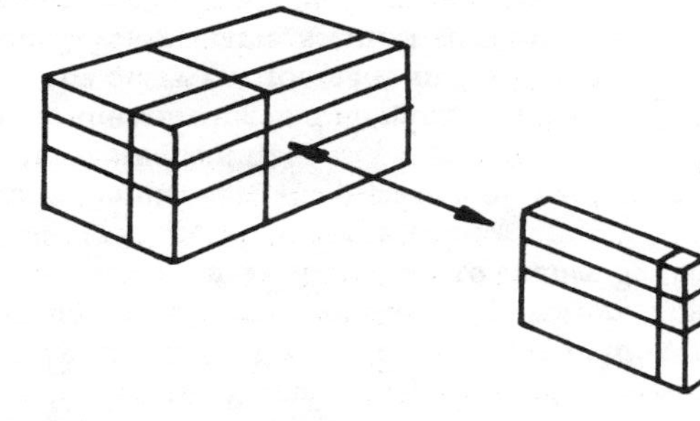

Fig. 8. Insertion and removal of an arbitrary $(k - 1)$-dimensional cross section.

4.4 Implementation of the Grid Directory

A grid directory behaves like a k-dimensional array with respect to the operations of *direct access* and *next*, but the insertion and removal of arbitrary $(k - 1)$-dimensional cross sections (corresponding to hyperplanes in the record space) is an unconventional operation that is difficult to reconcile with direct access (see Figure 8). What data structure should be chosen to implement a grid directory?

It is tempting to design exotic data structures that allow fast insertion and removal of arbitrary $(k - 1)$-dimensional cross sections. Let us mention a few and assess their practicality.

Linked lists are prime candidates for representing any structure where insertions and deletions may occur at arbitrary positions. Since they require the traversal of pointer chains to find a desired element, fast access is only guaranteed if these chains reside within the same page or disk block. A grid directory of several dimensions easily extends over several pages, however. Moreover, a list representation of the directory has the disadvantage of introducing a space overhead of k pointers (one or two for each dimension is the most direct way of representing the connectivity among gridblocks), which is significant compared to the normal content of a directory element (typically, a single disk address and a small amount of status information of the bucket located at that address, such as an occupancy number). It is doubtful whether the overhead caused by pointers is justified for an infrequent operation such as a directory split.

If one is willing to incur a significant space overhead, a better idea might be to represent the grid directory by a k-dimensional array whose size is determined solely by the shortest interval in each linear scale, as shown in Figure 9. This technique is the multidimensional counterpart of the directory used in extendible hashing [6]. A refinement of the grid partition causes a change in the structure of the directory only if a shortest interval is split, in which case the directory doubles in size. This data structure anticipates several small structural updates and attempts to replace them by a single large one. The strategy is successful

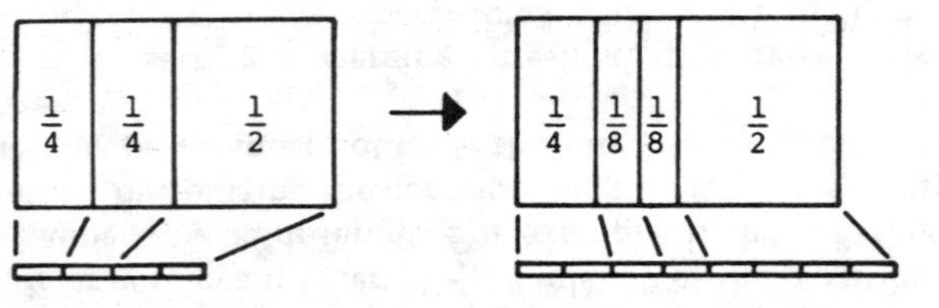

Fig. 9. Representation of the grid directory by an array that occasionally doubles in size.

when data is uniformly distributed, but may lead to an extravagantly large directory when it is not. In extendible hashing the uniformity is provided by a randomizing hash function, even if the data is not uniformly distributed over the record space. Since the grid file is designed to answer range queries efficiently, and randomizing functions destroy order, this approach cannot be used to generate uniformly distributed data. Hence any nonuniformity in the data leads to an oversized directory, and this approach cannot be recommended in general.

An interesting representation of the grid directory that avoids the space overhead of the "doubling array" and yet permits a $(k - 1)$-dimensional update to be written contiguously, rather than being scattered throughout the k-dimensional old array, is described in [12]. A timestamp is attached to the update that allows correct computation of the address of a directory element. Address computation becomes complicated when many such patches are superposed, so the directory must be reorganized periodically. The option of postponing a change to the existing directory, from the moment a partition refinement is needed to some later time, is useful in a concurrent access or real-time environment.

In most applications the split and merge of the directory occur rarely as compared to *direct access* and *next*; thus the conventional allocation of a multidimensional array is sufficient. Split and merge operations may cause a rewrite of the entire directory, and hence take longer than they would in a list, but the old directory can be used to access data while the new one is being written. Moreover, direct access is faster and memory utilization is optimal, thus a larger fraction of the directory may be kept in central memory. We feel these advantages of conventional array allocation outweigh the penalty in processing time.

An attempt to make optimal use of available central memory leads to the scheme of managing the grid directory on disk with a small *resident grid directory* in central memory (Figure 10). Even on a small computer, it is worthwhile to use more auxiliary information in central memory than just linear scales to facilitate access to disk ([8] is an interesting study of how a small amount of internal storage can be used to save disk accesses). The resident grid directory is a scaled down version of the real one, in which the limit of resolution is coarser. An implementation of the grid file used for storing geometric objects uses this fact to answer queries about intersection or distance of objects with few disk accesses [10].

In summary, many ways of implementing the grid directory are possible. Conventional array allocation is the simplest and is adequate, the resident grid directory technique has the best performance when neighborhood relations in all

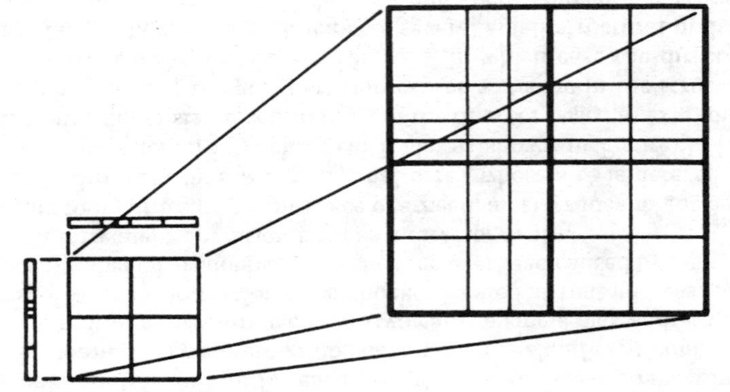
Fig. 10. A small "resident grid directory" manages the large grid directory on disk.

dimensions are important. Regardless of how the grid directory is implemented, it can be supplemented by auxiliary access structures such as directories for attributes not chosen as dimensions of the search space, at the usual cost to be paid in inverted files—directory updates may become a lot more time consuming.

4.5 Extensions: Dynamic Weighting of Attributes, Concurrent Access

Let us mention two possible extensions of the grid file design that appear to be easily incorporated into the structure described so far.

Dynamic weighting of attributes. Transaction environments change. In particular, the query profile that determines access frequencies to individual records in the file may change to such an extent that a new data organization, optimized with respect to the new access frequencies, may enhance the performance of an interactively accessed database. Many multiattribute file organizations have been studied from the point of view of optimal performance of a static file under a fixed access frequency profile (e.g., static multiattribute clustering). Recent efforts aim at extending this clustering to dynamic files, but we are unaware of methods that can adapt to both a dynamic file content and a time-varying query profile.

The grid file permits a dynamic adaptation of its structure to a time-varying access frequency profile by the same technique used to adapt to a varying file content: a dynamic modification of the grid partition. The splitting and merging policies discussed above make it possible to change dynamically the parameters that govern the granularity of the attribute scales. As the granularity of the partition is directly related to the precision of the answers, these parameters can be altered to favor frequent queries.

Adaptation of the splitting and merging parameters can be done automatically by monitoring the query environment and feeding this information into a table-driven grid file. In the extreme, an inactive attribute can be set to a "merge-only" state, whereupon in a dynamic file it will gradually fade away. When its partition has been reduced to a single interval, the corresponding dimension in the grid directory can be removed or assigned to another attribute.

Concurrent access. An increasing number of applications, such as information or reservation systems, require concurrent access to a file system. Concurrency control is complicated in tree structures because the root is a bottleneck shared by all access paths. If a process has the potential of modifying the data structure near the root (such as an insertion or deletion in a balanced tree), other processes may be slowed down by the observance of locking protocols even if they access disjoint data. The grid file (and other structures based on address computation, see [11] and [23]) has the property that access paths to separate buckets are disjoint, thus allowing simpler concurrency control protocols.

5. SIMULATION EXPERIMENTS

The performance of a file system is determined by two criteria: processing time and memory utilization. The grid file is designed to economize disk accesses, and we must show that this overriding concern for speed is compatible with a reasonable utilization of available space. A theoretical analysis of grid file behavior appears to be difficult for two reasons: many of the techniques developed for analyzing single-key data structures do not directly generalize to their multidimensional counterparts, and the grid file has parameters that are complicated to capture in a mathematical model (such as different splitting and merging policies). For these reasons we resort to simulation.

Our experience with grid file performance is based on three programs, two written in Pascal and one in Modula-2. The first program runs on a DEC-10 under the TOPS-10 operating system. It is a simulation program of 600 Pascal lines, implementing both the buddy and the neighbor systems of splitting and merging. The buddy system requires 150 lines of source code for the splitting and 130 lines for the merging operations. The corresponding figures for the neighbor system are 160 and 220 lines respectively. The second program runs on an APPLE III personal computer under UCSD Pascal. It supports a six-dimensional grid file and consists of approximately 1600 lines of Pascal source code. About 300 lines each are required by SPLIT and MERGE, 150 lines are used up by FIND, INSERT, and DELETE, the rest is devoted to dialog and housekeeping operations. The third grid file program, due to K. Hinrichs, is written in Modula-2 and runs on a Lilith personal computer. It has an interactive graphics interface and is used for storing geometric objects and answering intersection queries [10].

5.1 Objectives and Choice of Simulation Model

The simulation runs described below had the following objectives:

(1) estimation of average bucket occupancy,
(2) estimation of directory size,
(3) visualization of the geometry of bucket regions,
(4) evaluation of splitting and merging policies.

Since the grid file is designed to handle large volumes of data, (1) is by far the most important point. Average bucket utilization need not be close to 100 percent, but it must be prevented from becoming arbitrarily small under any circumstances. Point (2) is of greater theoretical than practical importance; we don't know the asymptotic growth rate of directory size, but for realistic file sizes the grid directory tends to require only a fraction of the space required by data storage, as an entry in the grid directory ranges from a few bytes (for a disk address) to a few dozen bytes (if additional information is stored, such as a record count or locking information in a concurrent access environment). Point (3) is merely a confirmation of what one expects from the way the grid file was designed, namely that grid partitions and bucket regions adapt their size and shape to data clusters. Point (4) covers space/time trade-offs and is discussed in Sections 5.3 and 5.4, in which we treat steady-state and shrinking files.

Among the many types of loads that may be imposed on a file, the following are particularly suitable as benchmarks for testing and comparing performances:

- the *growing file* (repeated insertions),
- the *steady-state file* (in the long run there are as many insertions as deletions, so the number of records in the file is kept approximately constant),
- the *shrinking file* (repeated deletions).

We have tested the behavior of the grid file with two simulation programs. One for the three-dimensional case of a growing file, the other for the two-dimensional case (for ease of displaying results graphically) under all three types of loads mentioned above. The justification for restricting our experiments to two and three dimensions is that the bucket occupancy (the primary objective of our simulation) appears to be largely independent of the dimensionality of the record space. For a growing file this is plausible on a priori grounds: buckets are split when they are full, regardless of the nature of their contents and independent of different splitting policies. In fact, the average bucket occupancy for $k = 2$ and $k = 3$ turn out to be the same. With respect to merging, one can readily see that a bucket has more buddies to merge, the more dimensions there are; thus bucket occupancy will not be worse in higher dimensional grid files.

The sample spaces used in the experiments are as follows: attribute values of each record are chosen independently of each other from uniform and piecewise uniform one-dimensional distributions to obtain uniform and nonuniform data distributions over the record space. Two standard, integer-valued random number generators from a program library were used.

5.2 The Growing File

Average bucket occupancy. We observed the average bucket occupancy while inserting 10,000 records from a two-dimensional uniform distribution. Figure 11 shows two typical curves depicting the average bucket occupancy over time, one for bucket capacity $c = 50$, the other for $c = 100$. As soon as the number n of inserted records reaches a small multiple of the bucket capacity c, average bucket occupancy shows a steady state behavior with small fluctuations of around 70 percent. It is tempting to conjecture that it approaches asymptotically the magical value $\ln 2 = 0.6931\ldots$, which often shows up in theoretical analyses of processes that repeatedly split a set into two equiprobable parts (see also [6]).

In Section 4 we mentioned splitting policies that do not necessarily refine a

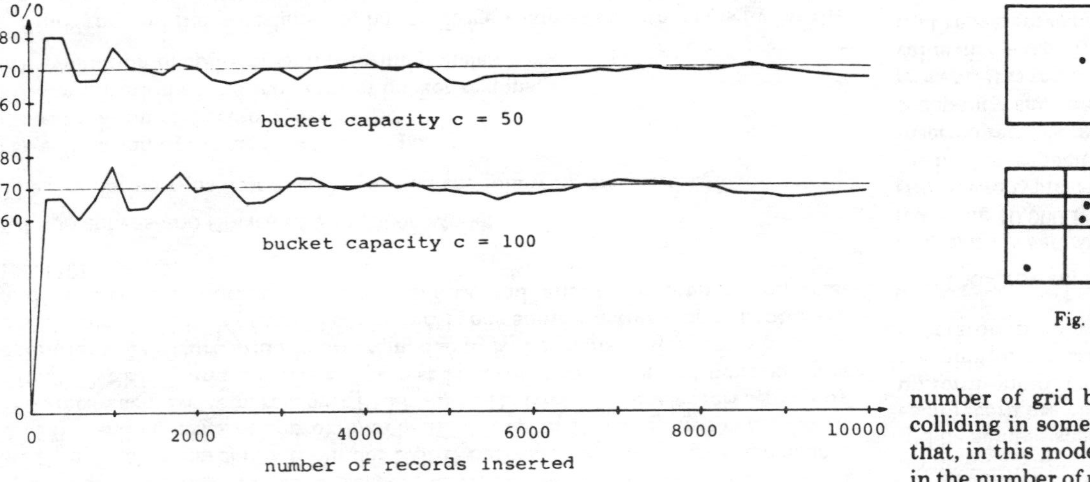

Fig. 11. Average bucket occupancy of a continuously growing grid file.

partition at interval midpoints; for example, a ternary system might always split an interval into three thirds. If such a policy also splits an overflowing bucket into three, then average bucket occupancy drops to 39 percent. Thus the advice: it is possible to use different splitting policies at a moderate increase in the size of the directory, but it is impractical to depart from the rule of splitting one bucket into two.

Growth of the directory. The constant average bucket utilization observed above implies a linear growth of the number of buckets with the amount of data stored. Since a bucket may be shared by many grid blocks, each of which requires its own entry in the grid directory, the question remains open as to how fast the directory grows with the amount of data stored. The number of directory entries per bucket is a good measure of the efficiency of the grid directory.

The assumption of independent attributes is crucial for the size of the directory. Correlated attributes, for example $y = a*x$, are unlikely to significantly affect average bucket occupancy, but they are very likely to increase directory size substantially. Even in the case of independent attributes, the asymptotic growth rate of directory size as a function of the number of records is unknown to us. As an example of the problem, consider random shots into the unit square as illustrated in Figure 12. To model the case of bucket capacity $c = 1$, we divide any grid block that gets hit twice into two halves, alternating directions repeatedly if necessary, until every grid block contains at most one point. The grid file is obviously not immune to the worst-case catastrophe that may strike all address computation techniques, namely that all points come to lie within a tiny area. Conventional practice in hashing ignores this worst case, as it is very unlikely. Another well-known probabilistic effect, however, the birthday paradox, is likely to happen: even if the number of records (people) is much smaller than the number of grid blocks (days in a year), the probability of two or more points colliding in some grid block (having a common birthday) is high. We conjecture that, in this model, the expected number of grid blocks grows faster than linearly in the number of points shot into the unit square. The point at which a superlinear growth rate begins to be noticeable, however, depends strongly on bucket capacity c, and turns out to be sufficiently large so that grid directory size is modest for practical values of n and c.

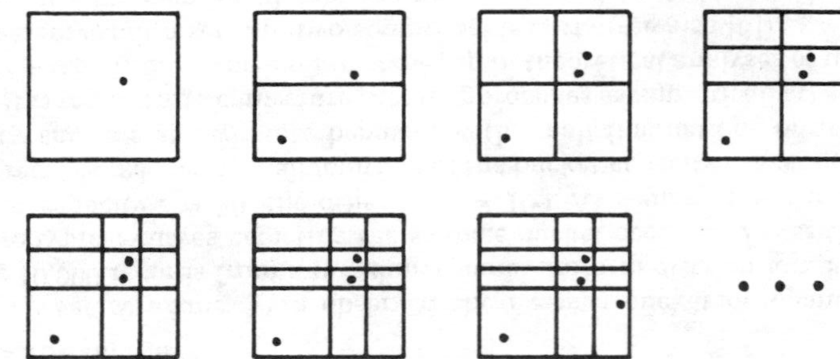

Fig. 12. Random shots into unit square trigger repeated halvings.

Figure 13 shows the number of buckets and the number of grid blocks during insertion of 10,000 records from a two-dimensional uniform distribution into buckets of capacity $c = 100$. The "straight line" depicting the number of buckets has a slope of 70 percent, as expected. The number of grid blocks also appears to grow linearly, but the fluctuations from a straight line (oscillating between one and two directory entries per bucket) have a larger period and amplitude.

This "staircase phenomenon" also occurs in extendible hashing; intuitively, it can be explained as follows. When records are inserted from a space with uniform distribution there are moments when practically all grid blocks have equal size, and almost every grid block has its own bucket. Under the assumption of uniformity (which is essential to this argument!), within a short time span a few buckets whose regions are randomly chosen from the entire record space will overflow; the resulting partition refinements affect all parts of the space, leading to a rapid increase in the number of grid blocks. At this moment the directory has a lot of spare capacity to accomodate further insertions, buckets get split without triggering a partition refinement, until we are back to a "one-grid-block-per-bucket" state, but with a directory that has doubled in size.

Figure 14 shows an experiment to determine the influence of bucket capacity on directory growth by plotting the number of grid blocks per bucket as a function of the normalized number n/c of records. The dashed line connects points where the directory has grown to 40,000 entries. 200,000 records packed into buckets of capacity 20 require a directory with only 2 entries per bucket. Given the small size of a directory entry (small compared to a bucket), we consider an average of 10 directory entries per bucket to be a modest investment. With $c = 1$, the birthday paradox causes this value to be reached with about 100 records. Already, with $c = 2$, a grid directory of 40,000 entries accomodates 9000 records in 6400

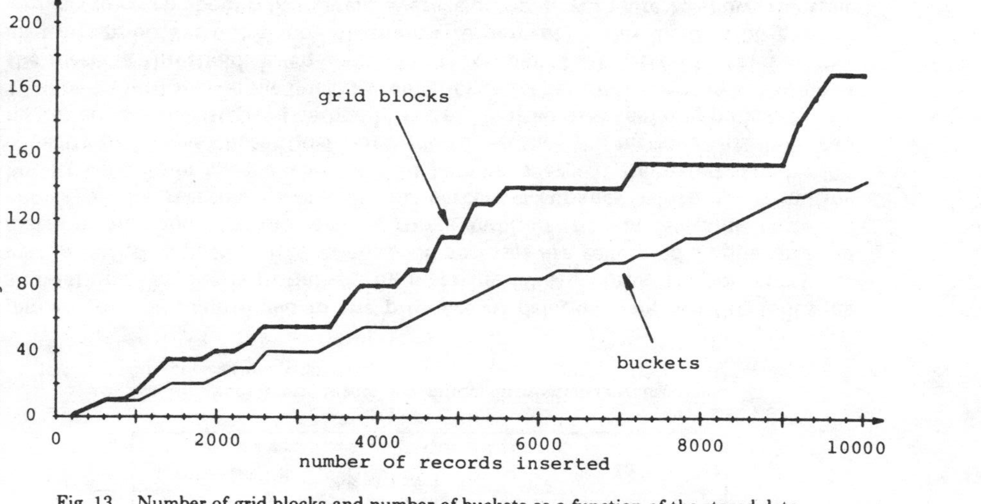

Fig. 13. Number of grid blocks and number of buckets as a function of the stored data.

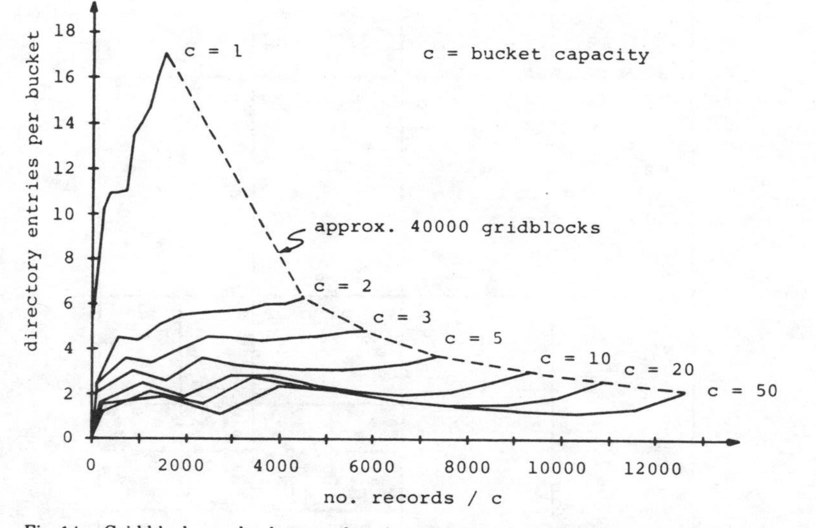

Fig. 14. Grid blocks per bucket as a function of the normalized number n/c of records.

buckets. Such small bucket sizes are only used to demonstrate the effect: we consider 10 or more records per bucket realistic, and for such bucket capacities directory size is no problem.

Visualization of the geometry of bucket regions. Finally, we show how the grid file adapts its shape to the data it must store. Figure 15 shows the bucket regions

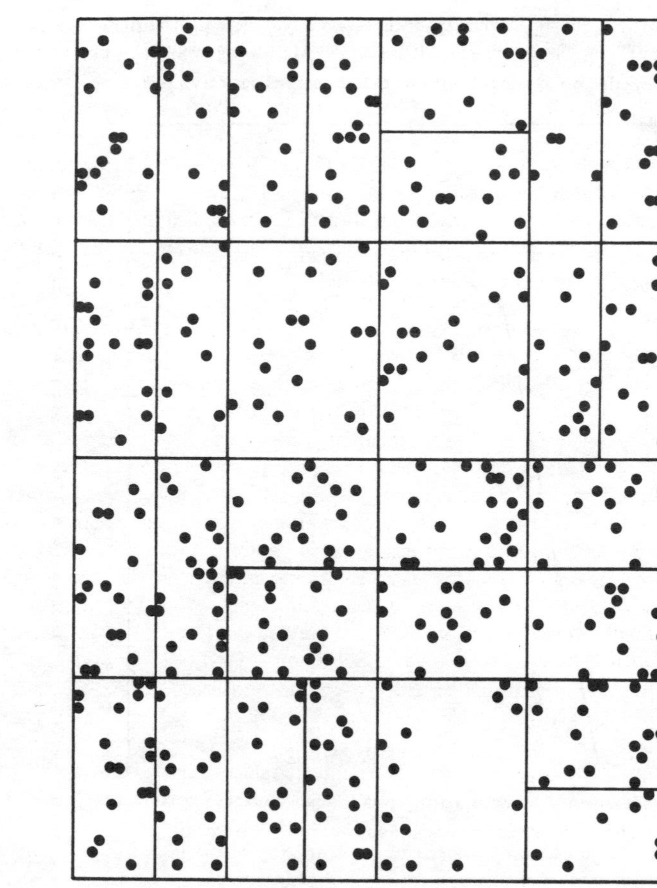

Fig. 15. Bucket regions with uniform record distribution (400 insertions, bucket capacity $c = 20$).

obtained after inserting 400 records from a uniform record distribution and from splitting done at interval midpoints. Figure 16 shows how the grid file "absorbs" a nonuniformity: These bucket regions are obtained from a nonuniform distribution in which the probability is five times greater that a record is drawn from the upper-left quadrant of the space than from the rest.

5.3 Steady-State File

A dynamic file is in a *steady state* if the number of records remains approximately constant, because, in the long run, there are as many insertions as deletions. Whereas a *growing* file is a test for the splitting policy of a file system, a steady-state file tests the interaction between the splitting and merging policies.

In order to determine whether an average bucket occupancy of around 70

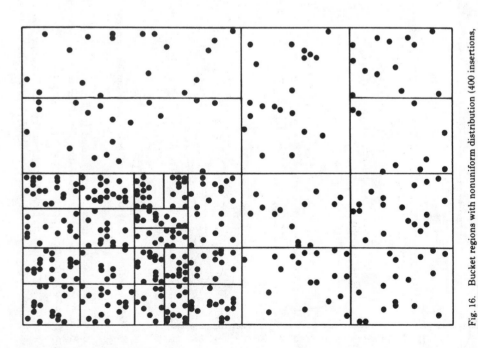

Fig. 16. Bucket regions with nonuniform distribution (400 insertions, bucket capacity $c = 20$).

percent can be maintained in the presence of deletions, we ran the following simulation. The file is initialized by inserting 5000 records into an empty file with a bucket capacity of 16; then, 5000 accesses are generated from a uniform distribution, about half of them insertions and half of them deletions. Different values of the *merging-threshold* (the percent-occupancy which the resulting bucket should not exceed when two buckets are merged) are tested. The bucket capacity of 16 was chosen just large enough so that the merging-threshold can be varied in small steps. The buddy system is used as a merging policy. Figure 17 shows that the average bucket occupancy is rather insensitive to the value of the merging threshold. Even a merging threshold of 100 percent achieves only an average bucket occupancy of around 70 percent, a threshold of 50 percent suffices to reach about a 60 percent average occupancy. Figure 18 shows the time

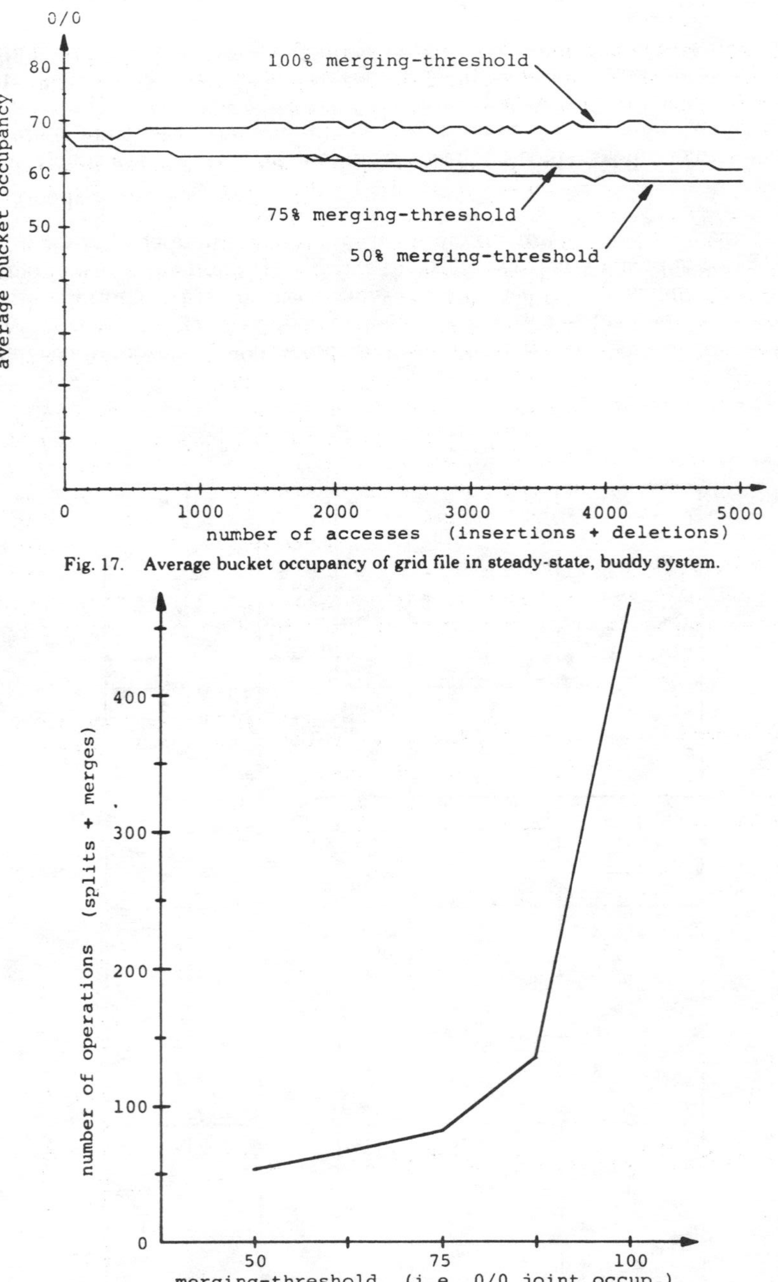

Fig. 17. Average bucket occupancy of grid file in steady-state, buddy system.

Fig. 18. Number of SPLIT and MERGE operations plotted against merging-threshold with 5000 accesses in steady state.

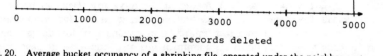

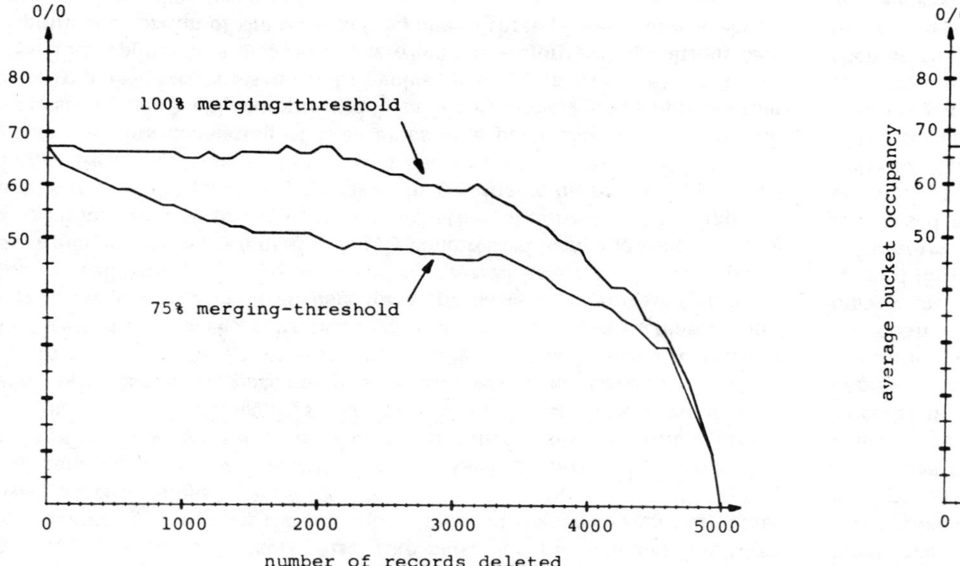

Fig. 19. Average bucket occupancy of a shrinking file, operated under the buddy system with different merging thresholds.

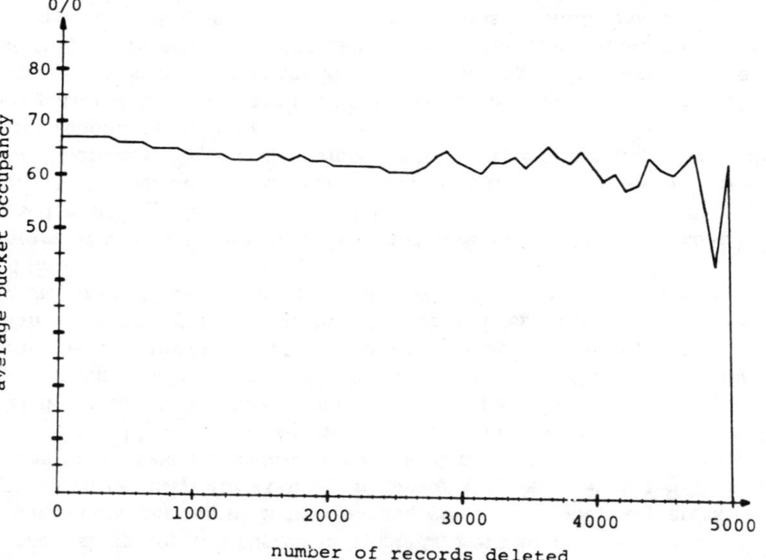

Fig. 20. Average bucket occupancy of a shrinking file, operated under the neighbor system with a merging threshold of 75 percent.

penalty that a high merging threshold entails: if the bucket resulting from a merge is too full, it will soon split again. We recommend a merging threshold of around 70 percent, that is, the average occupancy observed in the growing file.

5.4 The Shrinking File

In order to compare the effectiveness of the merging policies based on the buddy system and the neighbor system, we ran a simulation of a file that shrinks from an initial content of 5000 records down to empty. Figure 19 shows that the buddy system does not guarantee a high average bucket occupancy over a long stretch of deletions. Setting the merging threshold to 100 percent, which may be reasonable if we know the file is in a shrinking phase, helps considerably in the early part. Notice that the merging threshold can easily be adjusted dynamically. In contrast to the buddy system, the neighbor system suffers no degradation in average bucket occupancy, as Figure 20 shows.

In conclusion, we believe that the experiments reported above show that the space utilization of the grid file is good. This is true for a file filling up in its early stages, as well as for a file operating in a steady state or going through brief shrinking phases.

6. REVIEW OF PRIOR MULTIKEY ACCESS TECHNIQUES

In recent years, the increasing usage of databases and integrated information systems has encouraged the development of file structures specifically suited to access by combinations of attribute values. Inverted files were among the earliest such file structures. They have been used pervasively in most applications that require multikey access, and thus have been accepted as a standard against which to evaluate alternative approaches.

Several criteria are of importance in assessing multikey file structures. These include operation speed, space utilization, and adaptability under file growth, among others. The specific context in which the file structure is to be used determines the relative importance of various criteria.

The retrieval time in which to obtain all records that satisfy constraints on the values of a combination of attributes depends on several factors. In an inverted file, for example, the appropriate inverted lists must be accessed and processed in order to locate all relevant records, then the records themselves must be retrieved. In most large information systems, the time to move blocks of data from and to secondary storage (typically disks) dominates the processing time in main memory. Hence the number of required block transfers from secondary storage is frequently used as the measure of efficiency in both retrieval and update operations. For this reason, it is important that the information required to perform any operation be as localized as possible within blocks on secondary storage.

A second performance criterion is the space requirement; it must be discussed separately for data storage and access mechanisms. Some file organizations avoid filling each block of storage in order to permit graceful file growth; the size of such "holes" affects space requirements. Access mechanisms may require significant amounts of storage on disk as well as in main memory. In an inverted file, for example, inverted lists are often so large that they must be stored on disk, but indices to locate the inverted list for each attribute/value pair are retained in main memory.

Inverted files are well suited for accessing records on the basis of Boolean conditions on attributes, but they exhibit drawbacks which have motivated the development of alternate structures. First, retrieval of the inverted lists may require an excessive number of disk accesses. Second, the overhead required for insertions and deletions can become prohibitive in terms of space and time. Finally, in environments where several attributes are equally significant, a file structure that treats all significant attributes symmetrically is appealing.

In the remainder of this section we briefly describe a variety of multikey file structures, each designed to perform better than an inverted file (or other alternatives) in at least some circumstances. Many of the approaches are generalizations of well-known single key file structures. For example, Rothnie and Lozano [29] describe a generalization of hashing in which a bucket address for a record is formed by concatenating the results of hash functions, each of which is applied to the value of one attribute. A critical design decision in setting up such a *multikey hash file* structure is the determination of the number of bits to be allocated to represent the hashed value of each attribute. The more attribute values specified, the smaller the number of buckets that need to be accessed in order to obtain the required records. Because it is difficult to specify a combination of hash functions that lead to a uniform occupancy of buckets, it is necessary to tolerate either a low average bucket occupancy, or a high likelihood that buckets will overflow (more than one storage block is needed to hold the records corresponding to a single bucket). Also, like most hashing schemes, multikey hashing is inappropriate when the selection condition involves ranges of values rather than specific values.

Several generalizations of inverted files have been proposed. Lum describes *combined indices*, in which several attributes are concatenated in various orders and then treated as a single, aggregate key [18]. If more than three attributes are combined, both the storage space and update time become excessive. By combining them in groups of three, however, the number of disk accesses to retrieve inverted lists can be reduced substantially, at the cost of some increased complexity [22]. Bit-encoded inverted lists form the basis of *compressed bitmaps*, described by Vallarino [32]. The bit-encoded inverted lists form a large sparse bit array, which is then represented in highly compressed form and used to locate records specified by a selection condition. Another organization that exploits compression in providing multikey access is the *transposed file* organization, used in ROBOT (Retrieval Organization Based On Transposition) [1, 19]. In this organization, vectors consisting of the values of a particular attribute for all records are stored in a highly compressed form. Thus, retrievals and updates that refer to only a few attributes do not involve memory transfers of irrelevant attributes. This approach is most effective when the majority of operations deal with a significant portion of the records (i.e., one to three percent) and selection conditions involve only a few attributes.

Various generalizations of tree structured indices permit multikey access to files. *Quad trees* [7] are a two-attribute generalization of binary search trees. The straightforward generalization to k dimensions is impractical because the tree nodes become large and contain many nil pointers. These problems are avoided in *k-d trees* [2, 3], which can be thought of as an efficient implementation of the k-dimensional generalization of quad trees. *k-d* trees share many properties with binary search trees.

Similarly, *binary TRIEs* can be generalized to support multikey access [25, 31]. This is achieved by representing each attribute value as a bit string and interleaving these strings. The result is then used as the key in a standard binary TRIE. This organization is particularly effective for handling nearest-neighbor searches [31].

The multiple-attribute tree database organization orders the records lexicographically on the key fields, with the more significant attributes placed toward the higher end of the sorting field [13]. Then the key fields are separated from the records and organized into a doubly-chained tree. The tree can then be used to locate all relevant records for a given query. If both the number of records and the number of attributes are large, several disk accesses may be required to locate records satisfying specified constraints on key values.

Casey describes a complex tree-based multikey access structure in which records are grouped according to the frequency with which they are retrieved together [5]. *Superimposed coding* is used in each node to characterize the records below the node in the tree. Probably because of its complexity, this organization has not been widely used in practice. The importance of this structure is due to the fact that, more than with any other multikey file structure, the selection conditions used in accessing the file influence its organization. A similar, but more practical, approach is suggested by Pfaltz, Berman, and Caglet [26].

Several generalizations of B-trees which would allow multikey access have been proposed recently. For example, Robinson [28] describes *k-d-B-trees*. The leaf nodes of the tree are *pointer pages* that contain pointers to those records which correspond to a "region" (or hyper-rectangle) in k-dimensional space. The internal nodes are *region pages* that reflect the partitioning of a region into nonoverlapping, jointly exhaustive subregions. The root of the tree represents the initial partitioning of the entire k-dimensional space. Efficient utilization of I/O channels is obtained by requiring pointer and region pages to be approximately the size of blocks of secondary storage. Related approaches are taken in [9] and [30].

Quintary trees are a file structure intended to provide faster access than other tree-based multikey file structures, at the cost of requiring more space [15]. Quintary trees consist of k levels, corresponding to the k attributes in decreasing order of importance. Each level resembles a binary tree branching on the values of the corresponding attribute.

Along with *k-d-B*-trees, other multikey file organizations have been proposed recently that are also based on the idea of partitioning k-dimensional space and then storing the records corresponding to each cell of the partition in a single block of secondary storage. One such organization is the *multidimensional directory* suggested by Liou and Yao [17]. Attributes are ordered by priority, and numbers $d_1, d_2, \ldots, d_k$ are chosen such that $B = d_1 \times d_2 \times \cdots \times d_k$ equals approximately the number of blocks of secondary storage required to hold the blocks of the file. The larger d values are associated with the attributes that appear more frequently in selection conditions. Then, each attribute is used in turn to divide each region at one level into d subregions of approximately equal record population. This results in B regions, each containing approximately one block's worth of records. A multidimensional directory, which contains one entry per secondary storage block, is used to locate those blocks that may contain the records that are relevant to a given selection condition.

Multipaging [20] is another organization that uses splitting factors d. In contrast to [17], all attributes are treated alike. The range of values of attribute i is partitioned into d intervals such that approximately the same number of records have values of attribute i in each interval. These partitions impose a grid of hyper-rectangles in k-dimensional space. Unfortunately, correlations among the attributes and statistical variations cause the occupancies of the hyper-rectangles to be quite uneven. When each grid partition corresponds to a single block on secondary storage, either average occupancy in each block is very low or many blocks overflow. Given a k-tuple of attribute values, the corresponding interval in each of the k dimensions can be determined, and a block address for the record can be calculated without using an index.

Dynamic multipaging [21] is an extension designed to overcome the difficulty of handling insertions and deletions in the original multipaging method. Whenever block overflows cause the average number of block accesses per query to exceed some threshold, the partition on one of the attributes is refined by splitting one of the intervals. If attribute i is split, then the fraction $1/d_i$ of the blocks of the file are split, thus increasing the number of blocks by the factor $(d_i + 1)/d_i$. Such reorganizations require substantial effort. Recently, Burkhard presented a multikey access scheme called *interpolation-based index maintenance* [4] which uses a grid partition of the search space, at intervals determined by a radix, similarly to the grid file. This is a multidimensional generalization of Litwin's linear hashing [16], and relates to the grid file as linear hashing relates to extendible hashing [6]—the correspondence between regions (grid blocks) in space and data buckets is given by formulas ("interpolations"), rather than through a directory. The trade-offs involved in the decision of using a directory, as in the grid file, or avoiding it, as in interpolation-based index maintenance, are an interesting topic for research.

7. CONCLUSIONS

Each of the multikey file structures in use today has its strengths and its weaknesses, and also environments for which it is well suited. Nonetheless, for a significant class of environments, there is a need for a file structure that provides a different balance among the performance criteria. The grid file is designed to handle efficiently a collection of records with a modest number (say $k < 10$) of search attributes whose domains are large and linearly ordered. Within this usage environment, it combines several of the better properties of the file structures reviewed above: A high data storage utilization of 70 percent, combined with insensitivity to record clusters; smooth adaptation to the contents to be stored, in particular to file growth; a directory which, up to large but realistic file sizes, is compact by the standards of multikey files; fast access to individual records (two disk accesses); and efficient processing of range queries.

We have presented in detail the reasoning that led to the design of the grid file. In summary:

- range queries demand *grid partitions of the search space*,
- efficient update after modification of a grid partition demands *convex assignments of grid blocks to data buckets*,
- the *two-disk-access principle* demands representation of an assignment by means of the *grid directory*.

We have fixed those decisions that appear to us to be essential, and left others open in order to give the implementor freedom to adapt the file system to his environment. In particular, we have treated the following three aspects of the grid file as parameters to be specified by the implementor:

- splitting policy,
- merging policy,
- implementation of the grid directory.

Simulation results show that the grid file uses space economically over a wide range of operating conditions. Although dynamic space partitioning periodically leads to a rapid increase in the number of grid blocks, the allocation of buckets to grid blocks absorbs these bursts: The number of buckets grows in proportion to the number of records. For independent attributes, the number of directory entries per bucket also appears to grow linearly up to large practical file sizes, although asymptotically it may grow faster. Attribute correlations affect the size of the directory, but do not significantly affect the average bucket occupancy.

ACKNOWLEDGMENT

We are grateful to W. Willinger for writing an early version of the simulation program, and to the following people for communicating to us their experiences about ongoing implementations of the grid file: K. Hinrichs of ETH Zurich (grid file for storing geometric objects); S. Banerjee, S. M. Joshi, S. Sanyal, and S. Srikumar of the Tata Institute for Fundamental Research in Bombay (relational database systems based on the grid file); H. Hickhoff and H. P. Kriegel of the University of Dortmund (performance comparison of grid file and various types of multidimensional trees). We also thank A. B. Cremers, A. Frank, Th. Haerder, J. O. Jesperson, O. V. Johansen, J. Koch, M. Mall, H. Samet, J. W. Schmidt, M. Tamminen, and the referees for helpful comments that have improved this paper. This paper supersedes [24], which describes some early results.

REFERENCES

1. BATORY, D.S. On searching transposed files. *ACM Trans. Database Syst. 4*, 4 (Dec. 1979), 531–544.

2. BENTLEY, J.L. Multidimensional search trees used for associative searching. *Commun. ACM 18*, 9 (Sept. 1975), 509–517.
3. BENTLEY, J.L. Multidimensional binary search trees in database applications. *IEEE Trans. Softw. Eng. SE-5*, 4 (July 1979), 333–340.
4. BURKHARD, W.A. Interpolation-based index maintenance. In *Proc. ACM Symp. Principles of Database Systems* (1983), 76–89.
5. CASEY, R.G. Design of tree structures for efficient querying. *Commun. ACM 16*, 9 (Sept. 1973), 549–556.
6. FAGIN, R., NIEVERGELT, J., PIPPENGER, N., AND STRONG, H.R. Extendible hashing—a fast access method for dynamic files. *ACM Trans. Database Syst. 4*, 3 (Sept. 1979), 315–344.
7. FINKEL, R.A., AND BENTLEY, J.L. Quad trees—a data structure for retrieval on composite keys. *Acta Inf. 4* (1974), 1–9.
8. GONNET, G.H., AND LARSON, P.A. External hashing with limited internal storage. In *Proc. ACM Symp. Principles of Database Systems* (1982), 256–261.
9. GUETING, H., AND KRIEGEL, H.P. Multidimensional B-tree: an efficient dynamic file structure for exact match queries. Forschungsbericht Nr. 105, Informatik, Univ. Dortmund, Dortmund, West Germany, 1980.
10. HINRICHS, K., AND NIEVERGELT, J. The grid file: a data structure designed to support proximity queries on spatial objects. In *Proc. Workshop on Graph Theoretic Concepts in Computer Science* (Osnabruck, 1983).
11. HINTERBERGER, H., AND NIEVERGELT, J. Concurrency control in two-level file structures. Working paper, Informatik, ETH Zurich, 1983.
12. JOSHI, S.M., SANYAL, S., BANERJEE, S., AND SRIKUMAR, S. Using grid files for a relational database management system. Speech and Digital Systems Group, Tata Institute of Fundamental Research, Homi Bhabha Road, Bombay 400 005, India.
13. KASHYAP, R.L., SUBAS, S.K.C., AND YAO, S.B. Analysis of the multiattribute tree database organization. *IEEE Trans. Softw. Eng. 2*, 6 (Nov. 1977).
14. KNUTH, D.E. *The Art of Computer Programming. Vol. 3, Sorting and Searching.* Addison-Wesley, Reading, Mass., 1973.
15. LEE, D.T., AND WONG, C.K. Quintary trees: a file structure for multidimensional database systems. ACM *Trans. Database Syst. 5*, 3 (Sept. 1980), 339–353.
16. LITWIN, W. Linear hashing: a new tool for file and table addressing. In *Proc. 6th International Conference on Very Large Data Bases*, 1980, pp. 212–223.
17. LIOU, J.H., AND YAO, S.B. Multidimensional clustering for database organizations. *Inf. Syst. 2* (1977), 187–198.
18. LUM, V.Y. Multiattribute retrieval with combined indices. *Commun. ACM 13*, 11 (Nov. 1970), 660–665.
19. BARNES, M.C., COLLENS, D.S. Storing hierarchic database structures in transposed form. Datafair, 1973.
20. MERRETT, T.H. Multidimensional paging for efficient database querying. In *Proc. ICMOD* (Milano, Italy, June 1978), pp. 277–289.
21. MERRETT, T.H., AND OTOO, E.J. Dynamic multipaging: a storage structure for large shared data banks. Rep. SOCS-81-26, McGill Univ., 1981.
22. MULLIN, J.K. Retrieval-update speed trade-offs using combined indices. *Commun ACM 14*, 12 (Dec. 1971), 775–778.
23. NIEVERGELT, J. Trees as data and file structures. In *CAAP '81, Proc. 6th Colloquium on Trees in Algebra and Programming*, E. Astesiano and C. Bohm, Eds., Lecture Notes in Computer Science 112, Springer Verlag, 1981, pp. 35–45.
24. NIEVERGELT, J., HINTERBERGER, H., AND SEVCIK, K.C. The grid file: an adaptable, symmetric multikey file structure. In *Trends in Information Processing Systems, Proc. 3rd ECI Conference*, A. Duijvestijn and P. Lockemann, Eds., Lecture Notes in Computer Science 123, Springer Verlag, 1981, pp. 236–251.
25. ORENSTEIN J.A. Multidimensional TRIEs used for associative searching. *Inf. Process. Lett. 14*, 4 (June 1982), 150–157.
26. PFALTZ, J.L., BERMAN, W.J., AND CAGLEY, E.M. Partial-match retrieval using indexed descriptor files. *Commun. ACM 23*, 9 (Sept. 1980), 522–528.
27. RIVEST, R.L. Partial-match retrieval algorithms. *SIAM J. Comput. 5*, 1 (1976), 19–50.
28. ROBINSON, J.T. The k-d-B-tree: a search structure for large multidimensional dynamic indexes. In *Proc. SIGMOD Conference 1981*, ACM, New York, pp. 10–18.
29. ROTHNIE, J.B., AND LOZANO, T. Attribute-based file organisation in a paged environment. *Commun. ACM 17*, 2 (Feb. 1974), 63–69.
30. SCHEUERMANN, P., AND OUKSEL, M. Multidimensional B-trees for associative searching in database systems, *Inf. Syst. 7*, 2 (1982), 123–137.
31. TAMMINEN, M. The extendible cell method for closest point problems. *BIT 22* (1982), 27–41.
32. VALLARINO, O. On the use of bit maps for multiple key retrieval. *ACM SIGPLAN Notices 11*, (Mar. 1976), 108–114.

R-TREES: A DYNAMIC INDEX STRUCTURE FOR SPATIAL SEARCHING

Antonin Guttman
University of California
Berkeley

Abstract

In order to handle spatial data efficiently, as required in computer aided design and geo-data applications, a database system needs an index mechanism that will help it retrieve data items quickly according to their spatial locations. However, traditional indexing methods are not well suited to data objects of non-zero size located in multi-dimensional spaces. In this paper we describe a dynamic index structure called an R-tree which meets this need, and give algorithms for searching and updating it. We present the results of a series of tests which indicate that the structure performs well, and conclude that it is useful for current database systems in spatial applications.

1. Introduction

Spatial data objects often cover areas in multi-dimensional spaces and are not well represented by point locations. For example, map objects like counties, census tracts etc. occupy regions of non-zero size in two dimensions. A common operation on spatial data is a search for all objects in an area, for example to find all counties that have land within 20 miles of a particular point. This kind of spatial search occurs frequently in computer aided design (CAD) and geo-data applications, and therefore it is important to be able to retrieve objects efficiently according to their spatial location.

This research was sponsored by National Science Foundation grant ECS-8300463 and Air Force Office of Scientific Research grant AFOSR-83-0254.

An index based on objects' spatial locations is desirable, but classical one-dimensional database indexing structures are not appropriate to multi-dimensional spatial searching. Structures based on exact matching of values, such as hash tables, are not useful because a range search is required. Structures using one-dimensional ordering of key values, such as B-trees and ISAM indexes, do not work because the search space is multi-dimensional.

A number of structures have been proposed for handling multi-dimensional point data, and a survey of methods can be found in [5]. Cell methods [4, 8, 16] are not good for dynamic structures because the cell boundaries must be decided in advance. Quad trees [7] and k-d trees [3] do not take paging of secondary memory into account. K-D-B trees [13] are designed for paged memory but are useful only for point data. The use of index intervals has been suggested in [15], but this method cannot be used in multiple dimensions. Corner stitching [12] is an example of a structure for two-dimensional spatial searching suitable for data objects of non-zero size, but it assumes homogeneous primary memory and is not efficient for random searches in very large collections of data. Grid files [10] handle non-point data by mapping each object to a point in a higher-dimensional space. In this paper we describe an alternative structure called an R-tree which represents data objects by intervals in several dimensions.

Section 2 outlines the structure of an R-tree and Section 3 gives algorithms for searching, inserting, deleting, and updating. Results of R-tree index performance tests are presented in Section 4. Section 5 contains a summary of our conclusions.

2. R-Tree Index Structure

An R-tree is a height-balanced tree similar to a B-tree [2, 6] with index records in its leaf nodes containing pointers to data objects. Nodes correspond to disk pages if the index is disk-resident, and the structure is designed so that a spatial search requires visiting only a small number of nodes. The index is completely dynamic; inserts and deletes can be intermixed with searches and no periodic reorganization is required.

A spatial database consists of a collection of tuples representing spatial objects, and each tuple has a unique identifier which can be used to retrieve it. Leaf nodes in an R-tree contain index record entries of the form

$$(I, \textit{tuple-identifier})$$

where *tuple-identifier* refers to a tuple in the database and I is an n-dimensional rectangle which is the bounding box of the spatial object indexed:

$$I = (I_0, I_1, \ldots, I_{n-1})$$

Here n is the number of dimensions and I_i is a closed bounded interval $[a, b]$ describing the extent of the object along dimension i. Alternatively I_i may have one or both endpoints equal to infinity, indicating that the object extends outward indefinitely. Non-leaf nodes contain entries of the form

$$(I, \textit{child-pointer})$$

where *child-pointer* is the address of a lower node in the R-tree and I covers all rectangles in the lower node's entries.

Let M be the maximum number of entries that will fit in one node and let $m \le \frac{M}{2}$ be a parameter specifying the minimum number of entries in a node. An R-tree satisfies the following properties:

(1) Every leaf node contains between m and M index records unless it is the root.

(2) For each index record $(I, \textit{tuple-identifier})$ in a leaf node, I is the smallest rectangle that spatially contains the n-dimensional data object represented by the indicated tuple.

(3) Every non-leaf node has between m and M children unless it is the root.

(4) For each entry $(I, \textit{child-pointer})$ in a non-leaf node, I is the smallest rectangle that spatially contains the rectangles in the child node.

(5) The root node has at least two children unless it is a leaf.

(6) All leaves appear on the same level.

Figure 2.1a and 2.1b show the structure of an R-tree and illustrate the containment and overlapping relationships that can exist between its rectangles.

The height of an R-tree containing N index records is at most $\lceil \log_m N \rceil - 1$, because the branching factor of each node is at least m. The maximum number of nodes is $\left\lceil \frac{N}{m} \right\rceil + \left\lceil \frac{N}{m^2} \right\rceil + \cdots + 1$. Worst-case space utilization for all nodes except the root is $\frac{m}{M}$. Nodes will tend to have more than m entries, and this will decrease tree height and improve space utilization. If nodes have more than 3 or 4 entries the tree is very wide, and almost all the space is used for leaf nodes containing index records. The parameter m can be varied as part of performance tuning, and different values are tested experimentally in Section 4.

3. Searching and Updating

3.1. Searching

The search algorithm descends the tree from the root in a manner similar to a B-tree. However, more than one subtree under a node visited may need to be searched, hence it is not possible to guarantee good worst-case performance. Nevertheless with most kinds of data the update algorithms will maintain the tree in a form that allows the search algorithm to eliminate irrelevant regions of the indexed space, and examine only data near the

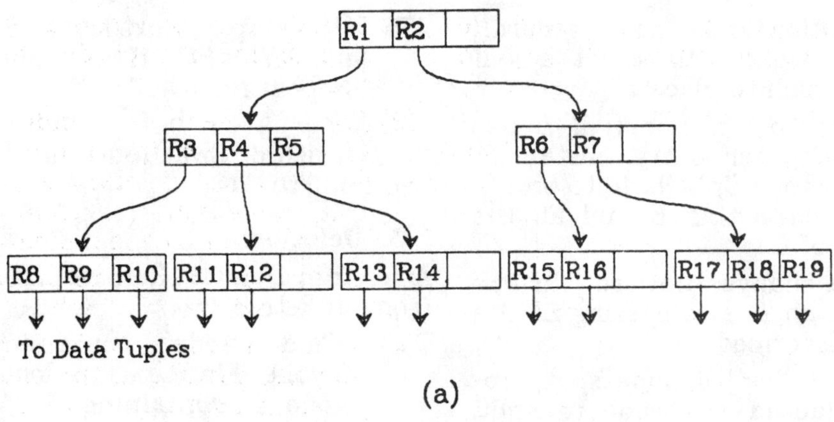

(a)

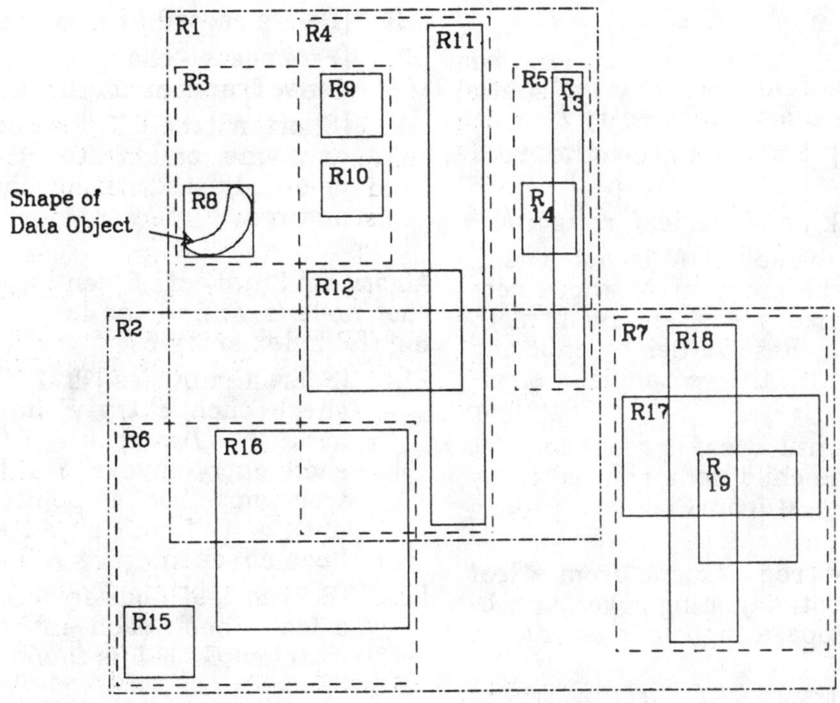

(b)

Figure 3.1

search area.

In the following we denote the rectangle part of an index entry E by $E.I$, and the *tuple-identifier* or *child-pointer* part by $E.p$.

Algorithm **Search**. Given an R-tree whose root node is T, find all index records whose rectangles overlap a search rectangle S.

S1. [Search subtrees.] If T is not a leaf, check each entry E to determine whether $E.I$ overlaps S. For all overlapping entries, invoke **Search** on the tree whose root node is pointed to by $E.p$.

S2. [Search leaf node.] If T is a leaf, check all entries E to determine whether $E.I$ overlaps S. If so, E is a qualifying record.

3.2. Insertion

Inserting index records for new data tuples is similar to insertion in a B-tree in that new index records are added to the leaves, nodes that overflow are split, and splits propagate up the tree.

Algorithm **Insert**. Insert a new index entry E into an R-tree.

I1. [Find position for new record.] Invoke **ChooseLeaf** to select a leaf node L in which to place E.

I2. [Add record to leaf node.] If L has room for another entry, install E. Otherwise invoke **SplitNode** to obtain L and LL containing E and all the old entries of L.

I3. [Propagate changes upward.] Invoke **AdjustTree** on L, also passing LL if a split was performed.

I4. [Grow tree taller.] If node split propagation caused the root to split, create a new root whose children are the two resulting nodes.

Algorithm **ChooseLeaf**. Select a leaf node in which to place a new index entry E.

CL1. [Initialize.] Set N to be the root node.

CL2. [Leaf check.] If N is a leaf, return N.

CL3. [Choose subtree.] If N is not a leaf, let F be the entry in N whose rectangle $F.I$ needs least enlargement to include $E.I$. Resolve ties by choosing the entry with the rectangle of smallest area.

CL4. [Descend until a leaf is reached.] Set N to be the child node pointed to by $F.p$ and repeat from CL2.

Algorithm **AdjustTree**. Ascend from a leaf node L to the root, adjusting covering rectangles and propagating node splits as necessary.

AT1. [Initialize.] Set $N=L$. If L was split previously, set NN to be the resulting second node.

AT2. [Check if done.] If N is the root, stop.

AT3. [Adjust covering rectangle in parent entry.] Let P be the parent node of N, and let E_N be N's entry in P. Adjust $E_N.I$ so that it tightly encloses all entry rectangles in N.

AT4. [Propagate node split upward.] If N has a partner NN resulting from an earlier split, create a new entry E_{NN} with $E_{NN}.p$ pointing to NN and $E_{NN}.I$ enclosing all rectangles in NN. Add E_{NN} to P if there is room. Otherwise, invoke **SplitNode** to produce P and PP containing E_{NN} and all P's old entries.

AT5. [Move up to next level.] Set $N=P$ and set $NN=PP$ if a split occurred. Repeat from AT2.

Algorithm **SplitNode** is described in Section 3.5.

3.3. Deletion

Algorithm **Delete**. Remove index record E from an R-tree.

D1. [Find node containing record.] Invoke **FindLeaf** to locate the leaf node L containing E. Stop if the record was not found.

D2. [Delete record.] Remove E from L.

D3. [Propagate changes.] Invoke **CondenseTree**, passing L.

D4. [Shorten tree.] If the root node has only one child after the tree has been adjusted, make the child the new root.

Algorithm **FindLeaf**. Given an R-tree whose root node is T, find the leaf node containing the index entry E.

FL1. [Search subtrees.] If T is not a leaf, check each entry F in T to determine if $F.I$ overlaps $E.I$. For each such entry invoke **FindLeaf** on the tree whose root is pointed to by $F.p$ until E is found or all entries have been checked.

FL2. [Search leaf node for record.] If T is a leaf, check each entry to see if it matches E. If E is found return T.

Algorithm **CondenseTree**. Given a leaf node L from which an entry has been deleted, eliminate the node if it has too few entries and relocate its entries. Propagate node elimination upward as necessary. Adjust all covering rectangles on the path to the root, making them smaller if possible.

CT1. [Initialize.] Set $N=L$. Set Q, the set of eliminated nodes, to be empty.

CT2. [Find parent entry.] If N is the root, go to CT6. Otherwise let P be the parent of N, and let E_N be N's entry in P.

CT3. [Eliminate under-full node.] If N has fewer than m entries, delete E_N from P and add N to set Q.

CT4. [Adjust covering rectangle.] If N has not been eliminated, adjust $E_N.I$ to tightly contain all entries in N.

CT5. [Move up one level in tree.] Set $N=P$ and repeat from CT2.

CT6. [Re-insert orphaned entries.] Re-insert all entries of nodes in set Q. Entries from eliminated leaf nodes are re-inserted in tree leaves as described in Algorithm **Insert**, but entries from higher-level nodes must be placed higher in the tree, so that leaves of their dependent subtrees will be on the same level as leaves of the main tree.

The procedure outlined above for disposing of under-full nodes differs from the corresponding operation on a B-tree, in which two or more adjacent nodes are merged. A B-tree-like approach is possible for R-trees, although there is no adjacency in the B-tree sense: an under-full node can be merged with whichever sibling will have its area increased least, or the orphaned entries can be distributed among sibling nodes. Either method can cause nodes to be split. We chose re-insertion instead for two reasons: first, it accomplishes the same thing and is easier to implement because the **Insert** routine can be used. Efficiency should be comparable because pages needed during re-insertion usually will be the same ones visited during the preceding search and will already be in memory. The second reason is that re-insertion incrementally refines the spatial structure of the tree, and prevents gradual deterioration that might occur if each entry were located permanently under the same parent node.

3.4. Updates and Other Operations

If a data tuple is updated so that its covering rectangle is changed, its index record must be deleted, updated, and then re-inserted, so that it will find its way to the right place in the tree.

Other kinds of searches besides the one described above may be useful, for example to find all data objects completely contained in a search area, or all objects that contain a search area. These operations can be implemented by straightforward variations on the algorithm given. A search for a specific entry whose identity is known beforehand is required by the deletion algorithm and is implemented by Algorithm **FindLeaf**. Variants of range deletion, in which index entries for all data objects in a particular area are removed, are also well supported by R-trees.

3.5. Node Splitting

In order to add a new entry to a full node containing M entries, it is necessary to divide the collection of $M+1$ entries between two nodes. The division should be done in a way that makes it as unlikely as possible that both new nodes will need to be examined on subsequent searches. Since the decision whether to visit a node depends on whether its covering rectangle overlaps the search area, the total area of the two covering rectangles after a split should be minimized. Figure 3.1 illustrates this point. The area of the covering rectangles in the "bad split" case is much larger than in the "good split" case.

The same criterion was used in procedure **ChooseLeaf** to decide where to insert a new index entry: at each level in the tree, the subtree chosen was the one whose covering rectangle would have to be enlarged least.

We now turn to algorithms for partitioning the set of $M+1$ entries into two groups, one for each new node.

3.5.1. Exhaustive Algorithm

The most straightforward way to find the minimum area node split is to generate all possible groupings and choose the best. However, the number of possibilities is approximately 2^{M-1} and a reasonable value

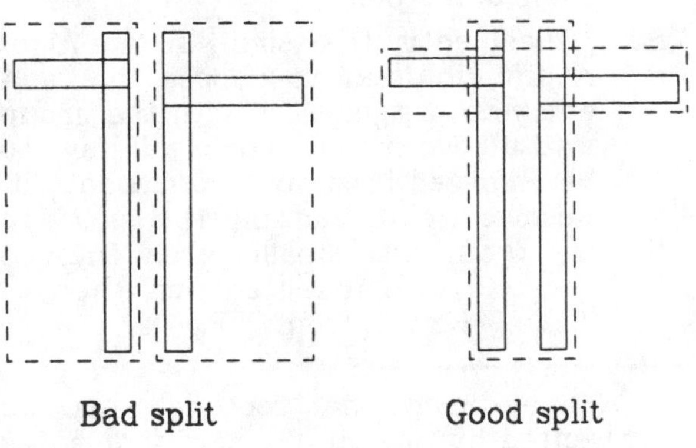

Figure 3.1

of M is 50*, so the number of possible splits is very large. We implemented a modified form of the exhaustive algorithm to use as a standard for comparison with other algorithms, but it was too slow to use with large node sizes.

3.5.2. A Quadratic-Cost Algorithm

This algorithm attempts to find a small-area split, but is not guaranteed to find one with the smallest area possible. The cost is quadratic in M and linear in the number of dimensions. The algorithm picks two of the $M+1$ entries to be the first elements of the two new groups by choosing the pair that would waste the most area if both were put in the same group, i.e. the area of a rectangle covering both entries, minus the areas of the entries themselves, would be greatest. The remaining entries are then assigned to groups one at a time. At each step the area expansion required to add each remaining entry to each group is calculated, and the entry assigned is the one showing the greatest difference between the two groups.

Algorithm **Quadratic Split**. Divide a set of $M+1$ index entries into two groups.

QS1. [Pick first entry for each group.] Apply Algorithm **PickSeeds** to choose two entries to be the first elements of the groups. Assign each to a group.

QS2. [Check if done.] If all entries have been assigned, stop. If one group has so few entries that all the rest must be assigned to it in order for it to have the minimum number m, assign them and stop.

QS3. [Select entry to assign.] Invoke Algorithm **PickNext** to choose the next entry to assign. Add it to the group whose covering rectangle will have to be enlarged least to accommodate it. Resolve ties by adding the entry to the group with smaller area, then to the one with fewer entries, then to either. Repeat from QS2.

---

*A two dimensional rectangle can be represented by four numbers of four bytes each. If a pointer also takes four bytes, each entry requires 20 bytes. A page of 1024 bytes will hold about 50 entries.

Algorithm **PickSeeds**. Select two entries to be the first elements of the groups.

PS1. [Calculate inefficiency of grouping entries together.] For each pair of entries E_1 and E_2, compose a rectangle J including $E_1.I$ and $E_2.I$. Calculate $\boldsymbol{d} =$ area(J) - area($E_1.I$) - area($E_2.I$).

PS2. [Choose the most wasteful pair.] Choose the pair with the largest $\boldsymbol{d}$.

Algorithm **PickNext**. Select one remaining entry for classification in a group.

PN1. [Determine cost of putting each entry in each group.] For each entry E not yet in a group, calculate $\boldsymbol{d}_1 =$ the area increase required in the covering rectangle of Group 1 to include $E.I$. Calculate $\boldsymbol{d}_2$ similarly for Group 2.

PN2. [Find entry with greatest preference for one group.] Choose any entry with the maximum difference between $\boldsymbol{d}_1$ and $\boldsymbol{d}_2$.

3.5.3. A Linear-Cost Algorithm

This algorithm is linear in M and in the number of dimensions. **Linear Split** is identical to **Quadratic Split** but uses a different version of **PickSeeds**. **PickNext** simply chooses any of the remaining entries.

Algorithm **LinearPickSeeds**. Select two entries to be the first elements of the groups.

LPS1. [Find extreme rectangles along all dimensions.] Along each dimension, find the entry whose rectangle has the highest low side, and the one with the lowest high side. Record the separation.

LPS2. [Adjust for shape of the rectangle cluster.] Normalize the separations by dividing by the width of the entire set along the corresponding dimension.

LPS3. [Select the most extreme pair.] Choose the pair with the greatest normalized separation along any dimension.

4. Performance Tests

We implemented R-trees in C under Unix on a Vax 11/780 computer, and used our implementation in a series of performance tests whose purpose was to verify the practicality of the structure, to choose values for M and m, and to evaluate different node-splitting algorithms. This section presents the results.

Five page sizes were tested, corresponding to different values of M:

Bytes per Page	Max Entries per Page (M)
128	6
256	12
512	25
1024	50
2048	102

Values tested for m, the minimum number of entries in a node, were $M/2$, $M/3$, and 2. The three node split algorithms described earlier were implemented in different versions of the program. All our tests used two-dimensional data, although the structure and algorithms work for any number of dimensions.

During the first part of each test run the program read geometry data from files and constructed an index tree, beginning with an empty tree and calling *Insert* with each new index record. Insert performance was measured for the last 10% of the records, when the tree was nearly its final size. During the second phase the program called the function *Search* with search rectangles made up using random numbers. 100 searches were performed per test run, each retrieving about 5% of the data. Finally the program read the input files a second time and called the function *Delete* to remove the index record for every tenth data item, so that measurements were taken for scattered deletion of 10% of the index records. The tests were done using Very Large Scale Integrated circuit (VLSI) layout data from the RISC-II computer chip [11]. The circuit cell CENTRAL, containing 1057 rectangles, was used in the tests and is shown in Figure 4.1.

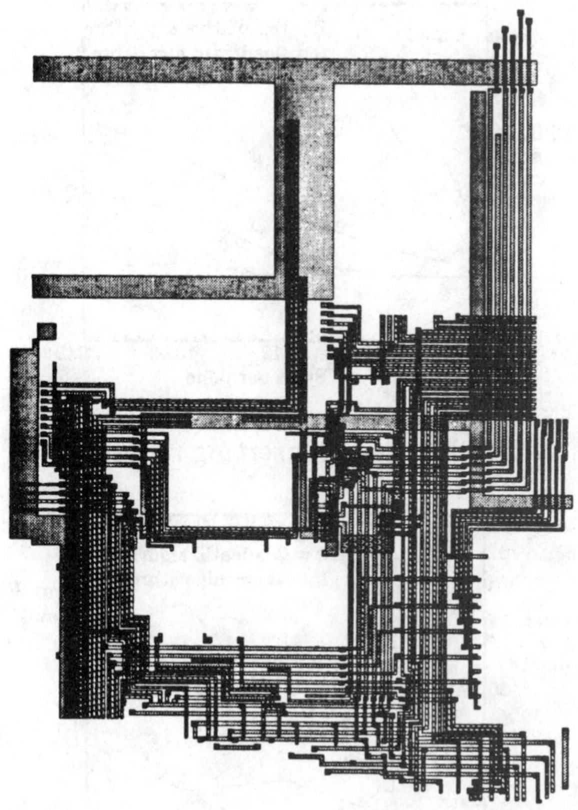

Figure 4.1
Circuit cell CENTRAL (1057 rectangles).

Figure 4.2 shows the cost in CPU time for inserting the last 10% of the records as a function of page size. The exhaustive algorithm, whose cost increases exponentially with page size, is seen to be very slow for larger page sizes. The linear algorithm is fastest, as expected. With this algorithm CPU time hardly increased with page size at all, which suggests that node splitting was responsible for only a small part of the cost of inserting records. The decreased cost of insertion with a stricter node balance requirement reflects the fact that when one group becomes too full, all split algorithms simply put the remaining elements in the other group without further comparisons.

The cost of deleting an item from the index, shown in Figure 4.3, is strongly affected by the minimum node fill requirement. When nodes become under-full, their entries must be re-inserted, and re-insertion sometimes causes nodes to split. Stricter fill requirements cause nodes to become under-full more often, and with more entries. Furthermore, splits are more frequent because nodes tend to be fuller. The curves are rough because node eliminations occur randomly and infrequently; there were too few in our tests to smooth out the variations.

Figures 4.4 and 4.5 show that the search performance of the index is very

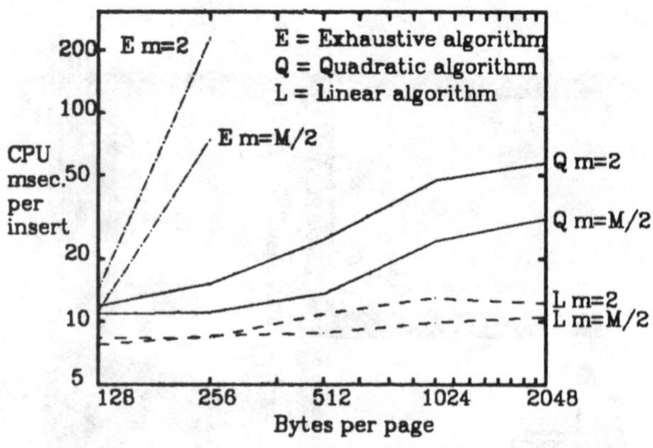

Figure 4.2
CPU cost of inserting records.

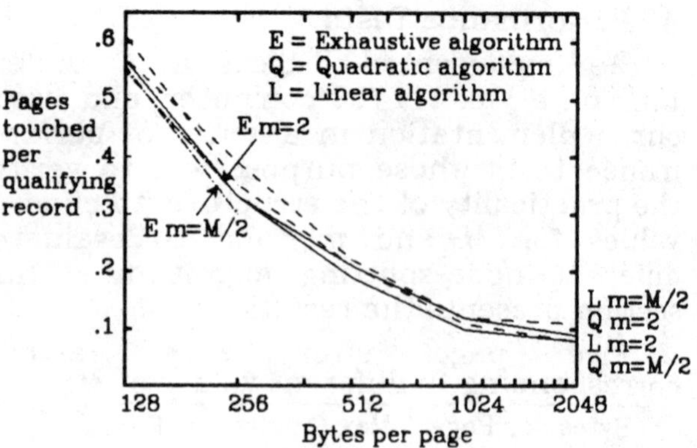

Figure 4.4
Search performance: Pages touched.

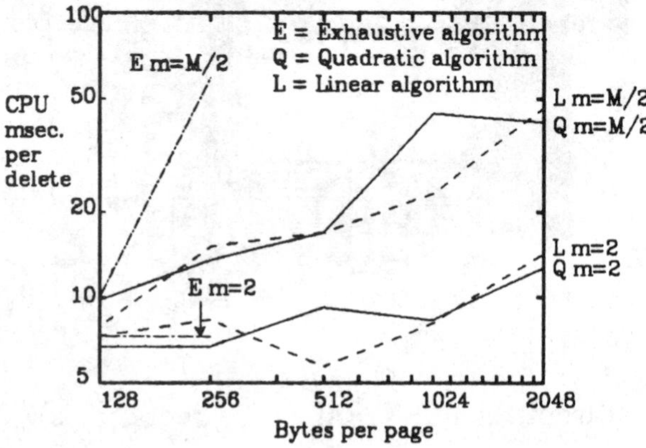

Figure 4.3
CPU cost of deleting records.

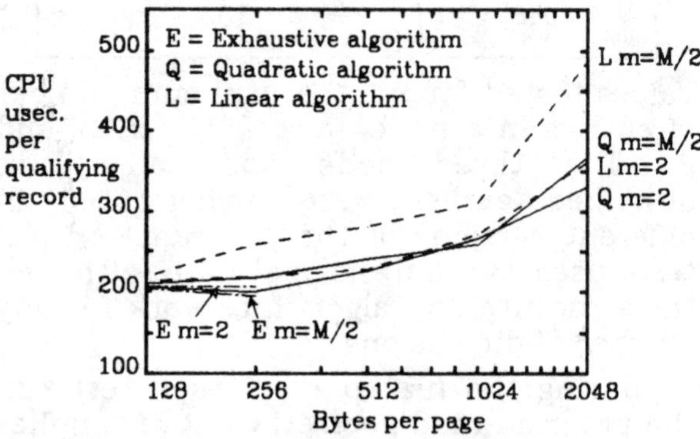

Figure 4.5
Search performance: CPU cost.

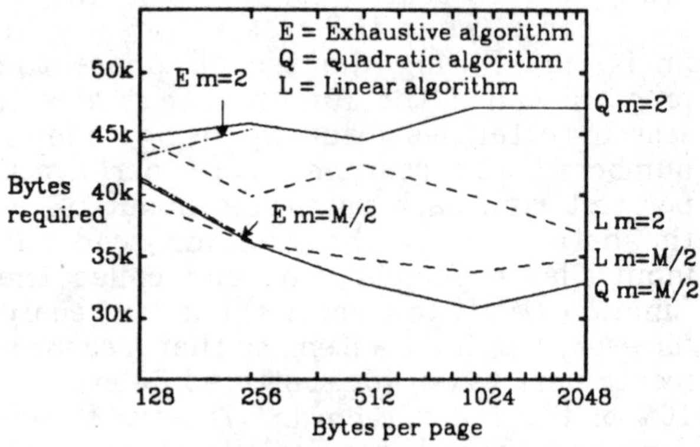

Figure 4.6
Space efficiency.

insensitive to the use of different node split algorithms and fill requirements. The exhaustive algorithm produces a slightly better index structure, resulting in fewer pages touched and less CPU cost, but most combinations of algorithm and fill requirement come within 10% of the best. All algorithms provide reasonable performance.

Figure 4.6 shows the storage space occupied by the index tree as a function of algorithm, fill criterion and page size. Generally the results bear out our expectation that stricter node fill criteria produce smaller indexes. The least dense index consumes about 50% more space than the most dense, but all results for 1/2-full and 1/3-full (not shown) are within 15% of each other.

A second series of tests measured R-tree performance as a function of the amount of data in the index. The same sequence of test operations as before was run on samples containing 1057, 2238, 3295, and 4559 rectangles. The first sample contained layout data from the circuit cell CENTRAL used earlier, and the second consisted of layout from a similar but larger cell containing 2238 rectangles. The third sample was made by using both

CENTRAL and the larger cell, with the two cells effectively placed on top of each other. Three cells were combined to make up the last sample. Because the samples were composed in different ways using varying data, performance results do not scale perfectly and some unevenness was to be expected.

Two combinations of split algorithm and node fill requirement were chosen for the tests: the linear algorithm with $m=2$, and the quadratic algorithm with $m=M/3$, both with a page size of 1024 bytes (M=50).

Figure 4.7 shows the results of tests to determine how insert and delete performance is affected by tree size. Both test configurations produced trees with two levels for 1057 records and three levels for the other sample sizes. The figure shows that the cost of inserts with the quadratic algorithm is nearly constant except where the tree increases in height. There the curve shows a definite jump because of the increase in the number of levels where a split can occur. The linear algorithm shows no jump, indicating again that linear node splits account for only a small part of the cost of inserts.

No node splits occurred during the deletion tests with the linear configuration, because of the relaxed node fill requirement and the small number of data items. As a result the curve shows only a small jump where the number of tree levels increases. Deletion with the quadratic configuration produced only 1 to 6 node splits, and the resulting curve is very rough. When allowance is made for variations due to the small sample size, the tests show that insert and delete cost is independent of tree width but is affected by tree height, which grows slowly with the number of data items.

Figures 4.8 and 4.9 confirm that the two configurations have nearly the same search performance. Each search retrieved between 3% and 6% of the data. The downward trend of the curves is to be expected, because the cost of processing higher tree nodes becomes less significant as the amount of data retrieved in each search increases. The increase in the number of tree levels kept the cost from dropping between the first and second data points. The low CPU cost per qualifying record, less than 150 microseconds for larger amounts of data, shows that the index is quite effective in narrowing searches to small subtrees.

The straight lines in Figure 4.10 reflect the fact that almost all the space in an R-tree index is used for leaf nodes, whose number varies linearly with the amount of data. For the Linear-2 test configuration the total space occupied by the R-tree was about 40 bytes per data item, compared to 20 bytes per item for the index records alone. The corresponding figure for the Quadratic-1/3 configuration was 33 bytes per item.

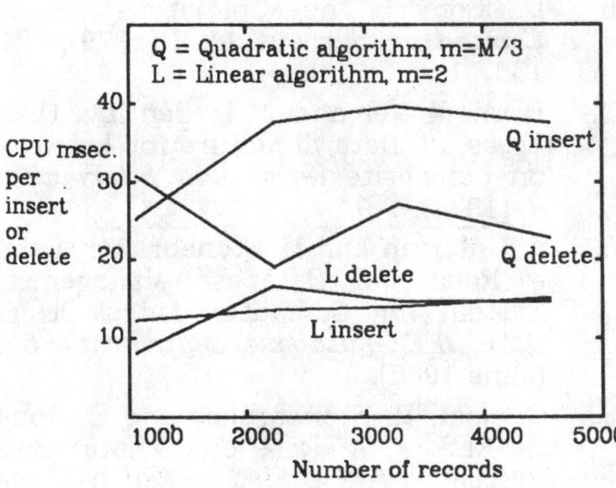

Figure 4.7
CPU cost of inserts and deletes vs. amount of data.

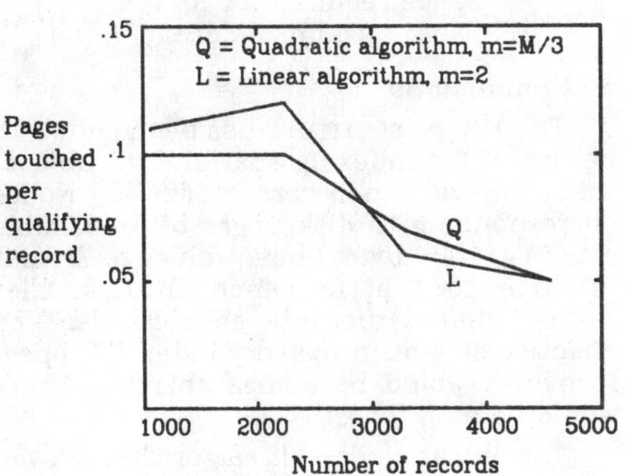

Figure 4.8
Search performance vs. amount of data: Pages touched

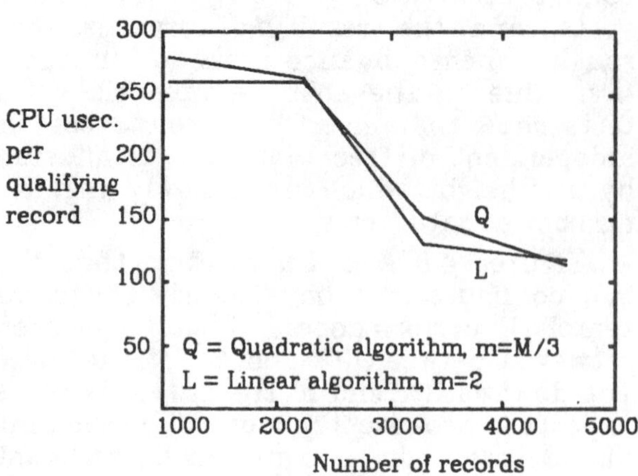

Figure 4.9
Search performance vs. amount of data: CPU cost

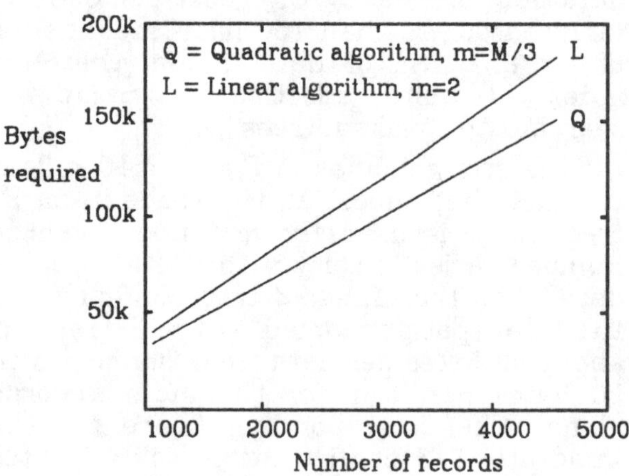

Figure 4.10
Space required for R-tree vs. amount of data.

5. Conclusions

The R-tree structure has been shown to be useful for indexing spatial data objects that have non-zero size. Nodes corresponding to disk pages of reasonable size (e.g. 1024 bytes) have values of *M* that produce good performance. With smaller nodes the structure should also be effective as a main-memory index; CPU performance would be comparable but there would be no I/O cost.

The linear node-split algorithm proved to be as good as more expensive techniques. It was fast, and the slightly worse quality of the splits did not affect search performance noticeably.

Preliminary investigation indicates that R-trees would be easy to add to any relational database system that supported conventional access methods, (e.g. INGRES [9], System-R [1]). Moreover, the new structure would work especially well in conjunction with abstract data types and abstract indexes [14] to streamline the handling of spatial data.

6. References

1. M. Astrahan, et al., System R: Relational Approach to Database Management, *ACM Transactions on Database Systems 1*, 2 (June 1976), 97-137.
2. R. Bayer and E. McCreight, Organization and Maintenance of Large Ordered Indices, *Proc. 1970 ACM-SIGFIDET Workshop on Data Description and Access*, Houston, Texas, Nov. 1970, 107-141.
3. J. L. Bentley, Multidimensional Binary Search Trees Used for Associative Searching, *Communications of the ACM 18*, 9 (September 1975), 509-517.
4. J. L. Bentley, D. F. Stanat and E. H. Williams, Jr., The complexity of fixed-radius near neighbor searching, *Inf. Proc. Lett. 6*, 6 (December 1977), 209-212.
5. J. L. Bentley and J. H. Friedman, Data Structures for Range Searching, *Computing Surveys 11*, 4 (December 1979), 397-409.
6. D. Comer, The Ubiquitous B-tree, *Computing Surveys 11*, 2 (1979), 121-138.
7. R. A. Finkel and J. L. Bentley, Quad Trees - A Data Structure for Retrieval on Composite Keys, *Acta Informatica 4*, (1974), 1-9.
8. A. Guttman and M. Stonebraker, Using a Relational Database Management System for Computer Aided Design Data, *IEEE Database Engineering 5*, 2 (June 1982).
9. G. Held, M. Stonebraker and E. Wong, INGRES - A Relational Data Base System, *Proc. AFIPS 1975 NCC 44*, (1975), 409-416.
10. K. Hinrichs and J. Nievergelt, The Grid File: A Data Structure Designed to Support Proximity Queries on Spatial Objects, Nr. 54, Institut fur

Informatik, Eidgenossische Technische Hochschule, Zurich, July 1983.

11. M. G. H. Katevenis, R. W. Sherburne, D. A. Patterson and C. H. Séquin, The RISC II Micro-Architecture, *Proc. VLSI 83 Conference*, Trondheim, Norway, August 1983.
12. J. K. Ousterhout, Corner Stitching: A Data Structuring Technique for VLSI Layout Tools, Computer Science Report Computer Science Dept. 82/114, University of California, Berkeley, 1982.
13. J. T. Robinson, The K-D-B Tree: A Search Structure for Large Multidimensional Dynamic Indexes, *ACM-SIGMOD Conference Proc.*, April 1981, 10-18.
14. M. Stonebraker, B. Rubenstein and A. Guttman, Application of Abstract Data Types and Abstract Indices to CAD Data Bases, Memorandum No. UCB/ERL M83/3, Electronics Research Laboratory, University of California, Berkeley, January 1983.
15. K. C. Wong and M. Edelberg, Interval Hierarchies and Their Application to Predicate Files, *ACM Transactions on Database Systems 2*, 3 (September 1977), 223-232.
16. G. Yuval, Finding Near Neighbors in k-dimensional Space, *Inf. Proc. Lett. 3*, 4 (March 1975), 113-114.

THE DESIGN OF THE POSTGRES STORAGE SYSTEM

Michael Stonebraker

EECS Department
University of California
Berkeley, Ca., 94720

Abstract

This paper presents the design of the storage system for the POSTGRES data base system under construction at Berkeley. It is novel in several ways. First, the storage manager supports transaction management but does so without using a conventional write ahead log (WAL). In fact, there is no code to run at recovery time, and consequently recovery from crashes is essentially instantaneous. Second, the storage manager allows a user to optionally keep the entire past history of data base objects by closely integrating an archival storage system to which historical records are spooled. Lastly, the storage manager is consciously constructed as a collection of asynchronous processes. Hence, a large monolithic body of code is avoided and opportunities for parallelism can be exploited. The paper concludes with a analysis of the storage system which suggests that it is performance competitive with WAL systems in many situations.

1. INTRODUCTION

The POSTGRES storage manager is the collection of modules that provide transaction management and access to data base objects. The design of these modules was guided by three goals which are discussed in turn below. The first goal was to provide transaction management without the necessity of writing a large amount of specialized crash recovery code. Such code is hard to debug, hard to write and must be error free. If it fails on an important client of the data manager, front page news is often the result because the client cannot access his data base and his business will be adversely affected. To achieve this goal, POSTGRES has adopted a novel storage system in which no data is ever overwritten; rather all updates are turned into insertions.

The second goal of the storage manager is to accomodate the historical state of the data base on a write-once-read-many (WORM) optical disk (or other archival medium) in addition to the current state on an ordinary magnetic disk. Consequently, we have designed an asynchronous process, called the **vacuum cleaner** which moves archival records off magnetic disk and onto an archival storage system.

The third goal of the storage system is to take advantage of specialized hardware. In particular, we assume the existence of non-volatile main memory in some reasonable quantity. Such memory can be provide through error correction techniques and a battery-back-up scheme or from some other hardware means. In addition, we expect to have a few low level machine instructions available for specialized uses to be presently explained. We also assume that architectures with several processors will become increasingly popular. In such an environment, there is an opportunity to apply multiple processors to running the DBMS where currently only one is utilized. This requires the POSTGRES DBMS to be changed from the monolithic single-flow-of-control architectures that are prevalent today to one where there are many asynchronous processes concurrently performing DBMS functions. Processors with this flavor include the Sequent Balance System [SEQU85], the FIREFLY, and SPUR [HILL85].

The remainder of this paper is organized as follows. In the next section we present the design of our magnetic disk storage system. Then, in Section 3 we present the structure and concepts behind our archival system. Section 4 continues with some thoughts on efficient indexes for archival storage. Lastly, Section 5 presents a performance comparison between our system and that of a conventional storage system with a write-ahead log (WAL) [GRAY78].

2. THE MAGNETIC DISK SYSTEM

2.1. The Transaction System

Disk records are changed by data base **transactions,** each of which is given a unique **transaction identifier** (XID). XIDs are 40 bit unsigned integers that are sequentially assigned starting at 1. At 100 transactions per second (TPS), POSTGRES has sufficient XIDs for about 320 years of operation. In addition, the remaining 8 bits of a composite 48 bit interaction identifier (IID) is a command identifier (CID) for each command

This research was sponsored by the Navy Electronics Systems Command under contract N00039-84-C-0039.

within a transaction. Consequently, a transaction is limited to executing at most 256 commands.

In addition there is a **transaction log** which contains 2 bits per transaction indicating its status as:

committed
aborted
in progress

A transaction is **started** by advancing a counter containing the first unassigned XID and using the current contents as a XID. The coding of the log has a default value for a transaction as "in progress" so no specific change to the log need be made at the start of a transaction. A transaction is **committed** by changing its status in the log from "in progress" to "committed" and placing the appropriate disk block of the log in stable storage. Moreover, any data pages that were changed on behalf of the transaction must also be placed in stable storage. These pages can either be forced to disk or moved to stable main memory if any is available. Similarly, a transaction is aborted by changing its status from "in progress" to "aborted".

The **tail** of the log is that portion of the log from the oldest active transaction up to the present. The **body** of the log is the remainder of the log and transactions in this portion cannot be "in progress" so only 1 bit need be allocated. The body of the log occupies a POSTGRES relation for which a special access method has been built. This access method places the status of 65536 transactions on each POSTGRES 8K disk block. At 1 transaction per second, the body increases in size at a rate of 4 Mbytes per year. Consequently, for light applications, the log for the entire history of operation is not a large object and can fit in a sizeable buffer pool. Under normal circumstances several megabytes of memory will be used for this purpose and the status of all historical transactions can be readily found without requiring a disk read.

In heavier applications where the body of the log will not fit in main memory, POSTGRES applies an optional compression technique. Since most transactions commit, the body of the log contains almost all "commit" bits. Hence, POSTGRES has an optional bloom filter [SEVR76] for the aborted transactions. This tactic compresses the buffer space needed for the log by about a factor of 10. Hence, the bloom filter for heavy applications should be accomodatable in main memory. Again the run-time system need not read a disk block to ascertain the status of any transaction. The details of the bloom filter design are presented in [STON86].

The tail of the log is a small data structure. If the oldest transaction started one day ago, then there are about 86,400 transactions in the tail for each 1 transaction per second processed. At 2 bits per entry, the tail requires 21,600 bytes per transaction per second. Hence, it is reasonable to put the tail of the log in stable main memory since this will save the pages containing the tail of the log from being forced to disk many times in quick succession as transactions with similar transaction identifiers commit.

2.2. Relation Storage

When a relation is created, a file is allocated to hold the records of that relation. Such records have no prescribed maximum length, so the storage manager is prepared to process records which cross disk block boundaries. It does so by allocating continuation records and chaining them together with a linked list. Moreover, the order of writing of the disk blocks of extra long records must be carefully controlled. The details of this support for multiblock records are straightforward, and we do not discuss them further in this paper. Initially, POSTGRES is using conventional files provided by the UNIX operating system; however, we may reassess this decision when the entire system is operational. If space in a file is exhausted, POSTGRES extends the file by some multiple of the 8K page size.

If a user wishes the records in a relation to be approximately clustered on the value of a designated field, he must declare his intention by indicating the appropriate field in the following command

cluster rel-name on {(field-name using operator)}

POSTGRES will attempt to keep the records approximately in sort order on the field name(s) indicated using the specified operator(s) to define the linear ordering. This will allow clustering secondary indexes to be created as in [ASTR76].

Each disk record has a bit mask indicating which fields are non-null, and only these fields are actually stored. In addition, because the magnetic disk storage system is fundamentally a versioning system, each record contains an additional 8 fields:

OID	a system-assigned unique record identifier
Xmin	the transaction identifier of the interaction inserting the record
Tmin	the commit time of Xmin (the time at which the record became valid)
Cmin	the command identifier of the interaction inserting the record
Xmax	the transaction identifier of the interaction deleting the record
Tmax	the commit time of Xmax (the time at which the record stopped being valid)
Cmax	the command identifier of the interaction deleting the record
PTR	a forward pointer

When a record is inserted it is assigned a unique OID, and Xmin and Cmin are set to the identity of the current interaction. the remaining five fields are left blank. When a record is updated, two operations take place. First, Xmax and Cmax are set to the identity of the current interaction in the record being replaced to indicate that it is no longer valid. Second, a new record is inserted into the data base with the proposed replacement values for the data fields. Moreover, OID is set to the OID of the record being replaced, and Xmin and Cmin are set to the identity of the current interaction. When a record is deleted, Xmax and Cmax are set to the identity of the current interaction in the record to be deleted.

When a record is updated, the new version usually differs from the old version in only a few fields. In order to avoid the space cost of a complete new record, the following compression technique has been adopted. The initial record is stored uncompressed and called the **anchor point.** Then, the updated record is differenced against the anchor point and only the actual changes are stored. Moreover, PTR is altered on the anchor point to point to the updated record, which is called a **delta record.** Successive updates generate a one-way linked list of delta records off an initial anchor point. Hopefully most delta record are on the same operating system page as the anchor point since they will typically be small objects.

It is the expectation that POSTGRES would be used as a local data manager in a distributed data base system. Such a distributed system would be expected to maintain multiple copies of all important POSTGRES objects. Recovery from hard crashes, i.e. one for which the disk cannot be read, would occur by switching to some other copy of the object. In a non-distributed system POSTGRES will allow a user to specify that he wishes a second copy of specific objects with the command:

```
mirror rel-name
```

Some operating systems (e.g. VMS [DEC86] and Tandem [BART81]) already support mirrored files, so special DBMS code will not be necessary in these environments. Hopefully, mirrored files will become a standard operating systems service in most environments in the future.

2.3. Time Management

The POSTGRES query language, POSTQUEL allows a user to request the salary of Mike using the following syntax.

```
retrieve (EMP.salary) where
EMP.name = "Mike"
```

To support access to historical tuples, the query language is extended as follows:

```
retrieve (EMP.salary) using EMP[T]
where EMP.name = "Mike"
```

The scope of this command is the EMP relation as of a specific time, T, and Mike's salary will be found as of that time. A variety of formats for T will be allowed, and a conversion routine will be called to convert times to the 32 bit unsigned integers used internally. POSTGRES constructs a query plan to find qualifying records in the normal fashion. However, each accessed tuple must be additionally checked for validity at the time desired in the user's query. In general, a record is **valid at time T** if the following is true:

```
Tmin < T and Xmin is a committed
transaction and either:
   Xmax is not a committed transaction or
   Xmax is null or
   Tmax > T
```

In fact, to allow a user to read uncommitted records that were written by a different command within his transaction, the actual test for validity is the following more complex condition.

```
Xmin = my-transaction and Cmin !=
my-command and T = "now"
      or
Tmin < T and Xmin is a committed
transaction and either:
   (Xmax is not a committed transaction and
   Xmax != my-transaction) or
   (Xmax = my-transaction and Cmax =
   my-command) or
    Xmax is null or
    Tmax > T or
```

If T is not specified, then T = "now" is the default value, and a record is valid at time, "now" if

```
Xmin = my-transaction and Cmin !=
my-command
      or
Xmin is a committed transaction and either
   (Xmax is not a committed transaction and
   Xmax != my-transaction) or
   (Xmax = my-transaction and Cmax =
   my-command) or
   Xmax is null
```

More generally, Mike's salary history over a range of times can be retrieved by:

```
retrieve (EMP.Tmin, EMP.Tmax, EMP.salary)
using EMP[T1,T2] where EMP.name = "Mike"
```

This command will find all salaries for Mike along with their starting and ending times as long as the salary is valid at some point in the interval, [T1, T2]. In general, a record is **valid in the interval [T1,T2]** if:

```
Xmin = my-transaction and Cmin !=
my-command and T2 >= "now"
      or
Tmin < T2 and Xmin is a committed
transaction and either:
   (Xmax is not a committed transaction and
   Xmax != my-transaction) or
   (Xmax = my-transaction and Cmax =
   my-command) or
   Xmax is null or
   Tmax > T1
```

Either T1 or T2 can be omitted and the defaults are respectively T1 = 0 and T2 = +infinity

Special programs (such as debuggers) may want to be able to access uncommitted records. To facilitate such access, we define a second specification for each relation, for example:

retrieve (EMP.salary) using all-EMP[T] where EMP.name = "Mike"

An EMP record is in all-EMP at time T if

Tmin < T and (Tmax > T or Tmax = null)

Intuitively, all-EMP[T] is the set of all tuples committed, aborted or in-progress at time T.

Each accessed magnetic disk record must have one of the above tests performed. Although each test is potentially CPU and I/O intensive, we are not overly concerned with CPU resources because we do not expect the CPU to be a significant bottleneck in next generation systems. This point is discussed further in Section 5. Moreover, the CPU portion of these tests can be easily committed to custom logic or microcode or even a co-processor if it becomes a bottleneck.

There will be little or no I/O associated with accessing the status of any transaction, since we expect the transaction log (or its associated bloom filter) to be in main memory. We turn in the next subsection to avoiding I/O when evaluating the remainder of the above predicates.

2.4. Concurrency Control and Timestamp Management

It would be natural to assign a timestamp to a transaction at the time it is started and then fill in the timestamp field of each record as it is updated by the transaction. Unfortunately, this would require POSTGRES to process transactions logically in timestamp order to avoid anomolous behavior. This is equivalent to requiring POSTGRES to use a concurrency control scheme based on timestamp ordering (e.g. [BERN80]. Since simulation results have shown the superiority of conventional locking [AGRA85], POSTGRES uses instead a standard two-phase locking policy which is implemented by a conventional main memory lock table.

Therefore, Tmin and Tmax must be set to the commit time of each transaction (which is the time at which updates logically take place) in order to avoid anomolous behavior. Since the commit time of a transaction is not known in advance, Tmin and Tmax cannot be assigned values at the time that a record is written.

We use the following technique to fill in these fields asynchronously. POSTGRES contains a TIME relation in which the commit time of each transaction is stored. Since timestamps are 32 bit unsigned integers, byte positions 4*j through 4*j + 3 are reserved for the commit time of transaction j. At the time a transaction commits, it reads the current clock time and stores it in the appropriate slot of TIME. The tail of the TIME relation can be stored in stable main memory to avoid the I/O that this update would otherwise entail.

Moreover, each relation in a POSTGRES data base is tagged at the time it is created with one of the following three designations:

no archive: This indicates that no historical access to relations is required.

light archive: This indicates that an archive is desired but little access to it is expected.

heavy archive: This indicates that heavy use will be made of the archive.

For relations with "no archive" status, Tmin and Tmax are never filled in, since access to historical tuples is never required. For such relations, only POSTQUEL commands specified for T = "now" can be processed. The validity check for T = "now" requires access only to the POSTGRES LOG relation which should be contained in the buffer pool. Hence, the test consumes no I/O resources.

If "light archive" is specified, then access to historical tuples is allowed. Whenever Tmin or Tmax must be compared to some specific value, the commit time of the appropriate transaction is retrieved from the TIME relation to make the comparison. Access to historical records will be slowed in the "light archive" situation by this requirement to perform an I/O to the TIME relation for each timestamp value required. This overhead will only be tolerable if archival records are accessed a very small number of times in their lifetime (about 2-3).

In the "heavy archive" condition, the run time system must look up the commit time of a transaction as in the "light archive" case. However, it then writes the value found into Tmin or Tmax, thereby turning the read of a historical record into a write. Any subsequent accesses to the record will then be validatable without the extra access to the TIME relation. Hence, the first access to an archive record will be costly in the "heavy archive" case, but subsequent ones will will incur no extra overhead.

In addition, we expect to explore the utility of running another system demon in background to asynchronously fill in timestamps for "heavy archive" relations.

2.5. Record Access

Records can be accessed by a sequential scan of a relation. In this case, pages of the appropriate file are read in a POSTGRES determined order. Each page contains a pointer to the next and the previous logical page; hence POSTGRES can scan a relation by following the forward linked list. The reverse pointers are required because POSTGRES can execute query plans either forward or backward. Additionally, on each page there is a line table as in [STON76] containing pointers to the starting byte of each anchor point record on that page.

Once an anchor point is located, the delta records linked to it can be constructed by following PTR and decompressing the data fields. Although decompression is a CPU intensive task, we feel that CPU resources will not be a bottleneck in future computers as noted earlier. Also, compression and decompression of records is a task easily committed to microcode or a separate co-processor.

An arbitrary number of secondary indexes can be constructed for any base relation. Each index is maintained by an **access method.** and provides keyed access on a field or a collection of fields. Each access method must provide all the procedures for the POSTGRES defined abstraction for access methods. These include get-record-by-key, insert-record, delete-record, etc. The POSTGRES run time system will call the various routines of the appropriate access method when needed during query processing.

Each access method supports efficient access for a collection of operators as noted in [STON86a]. For example, B-trees can provide fast access for any of the operators:

{=, <=, <, >, >=}

Since each access method may be required to work for various data types, the collection of operators that an access methods will use for a specific data type must be **registered** as an **operator class.** Consequently, the syntax for index creation is:

index on rel-name is index-name
({key-i with operator-class-i})
using access-method-name and
performance-parameters

The performance-parameters specify the fill-factor to be used when loading the pages of the index, and the minimum and maximum number of pages to allocate. The following example specifies a B-tree index on a combined key consisting of an integer and a floating point number.

index on EMP is EMP-INDEX (age with
integer-ops, salary with float-ops)
using B-tree and fill-factor = .8

The run-time system handles secondary indexes in a somewhat unusual way. When a record is inserted, an anchor point is constructed for the record along with index entries for each secondary index. Each index record contains a key(s) plus a pointer to an entry in the line table on the page where the indexed record resides. This line table entry in turn points to the byte-offset of the actual record. This single level of indirection allows anchor points to be moved on a data page without requiring maintenance of secondary indexes.

When an existing record is updated, a delta record is constructed and chained onto the appropriate anchor record. If no indexed field has been modified, then no maintenance of secondary indexes is required. If an indexed field changed, then an entry is added to the appropriate index containing the new key(s) and a pointer to the anchor record. There are no pointers in secondary indexes directly to delta records. Consequently, a delta record can only be accessed by obtaining its corresponding anchor point and chaining forward.

The POSTGRES query optimizer constructs plans which may specify scanning portions of various secondary indexes. The run time code to support this function is relatively conventional except for the fact that each secondary index entry points to an anchor point and a chain of delta records, all of which must be inspected. Valid records that actually match the key in the index are then returned to higher level software.

Use of this technique guarantees that record updates only generate I/O activity in those secondary indexes whose keys change. Since updates to keyed fields are relatively uncommon, this ensures that few insertions must be performed in the secondary indexes.

Some secondary indexes which are hierarchical in nature require disk pages to be placed in stable storage in a particular order (e.g. from leaf to root for page splits in B+-trees). POSTGRES will provide a low level command

order block-1 block-2

to support such required orderings. This command is in addition to the required **pin** and **unpin** commands to the buffer manager.

3. THE ARCHIVAL SYSTEM

3.1. Vacuuming the Disk

An asynchronous demon is responsible for sweeping records which are no longer valid to the archive. This demon, called the **vacuum cleaner,** is given instructions using the following command:

vacuum rel-name after T

Here T is a time relative to "now". For example, the following vacuum command specifies vacuuming records over 30 days old:

vacuum EMP after "30 days"

The vacuum cleaner finds candidate records for archiving which satisfy one of the following conditions:

Xmax is non empty and is a committed
transaction and "now" - Tmax >= T
Xmax is non empty and is an aborted
transaction
Xmin is non empty and is an aborted
transaction

In the second and third cases, the vacuum cleaner simply reclaims the space occupied by such records. In the first case, a record must be copied to the archive unless "no-archive" status is set for this relation. Additionally, if "heavy-archive" is specified, Tmin and Tmax must be filled in by the vacuum cleaner during archiving if they have not already been given values during a previous access. Moreover, if an anchor point and several delta records can be swept together, the vacuuming process will be more efficient. Hence, the vacuum cleaner will generally sweep a chain of several records to the archive at one time.

This sweeping must be done very carefully so that no data is irrecoverably lost. First we discuss the format of the archival medium, then we turn to the sweeping algorithm and a discussion of its cost.

3.2. The Archival Medium

The archival storage system is compatible with WORM devices, but is not restricted to such systems. We are building a conventional extent-based file system on the archive, and each relation is allocated to a single file. Space is allocated in large extents and the next one is allocated when the current one is exhausted. The space allocation map for the archive is kept in a magnetic disk relation. Hence, it is possible, albeit very costly, to sequentially scan the historical version of a relation.

Moreover, there are an arbitrary number of secondary indexes for each relation in the archive. Since historical accessing patterns may be different than accessing patterns for current data, we do not restrict the archive indexes to be the same as those for the magnetic disk data base. Hence, archive indexes must be explicitly created using the following extension of the indexing command:

```
index on {archive} rel-name is index-name
({key-i with operator-class-i})
using access-method-name and
performance-parameters
```

Indexes for archive relations are normally stored on magnetic disk. However, since they may become very large, we will discuss mechanisms in the next section to support archive indexes that are partly on the archive medium.

The anchor point and a collection of delta records are concatenated and written to the archive as a single variable length record. Again secondary index records must be inserted for any indexes defined for the archive relation. An index record is generated for the anchor point for each archive secondary index. Moreover, an index record must be constructed for each delta record in which a secondary key has been changed.

Since the access paths to the portion of a relation on the archive may be different than the access paths to the portion on magnetic disk, the query optimizer must generate two plans for any query that requests historical data. Of course, these plans can be executed in parallel if multiple processors are available. In addition, we are studying the decomposition of each of these two query plans into additional parallel pieces. A report on this subject is in preparation [BHID87].

3.3. The Vacuum Process

Vacuuming is done in three phases, namely:

phase 1: write an archive record and its associated index records

phase 2: write a new anchor point in the current data base

phase 3: reclaim the space occupied by the old anchor point and its delta records

If a crash occurs while the vacuum cleaner is writing the historical record in phase 1, then the data still exists in the magnetic disk data base and will be revacuumed again at some later time. If the historical record has been written but not the associated indexes, then the archive will have a record which is reachable only through a sequential scan. If a crash occurs after some index records have been written, then it will be possible for the same record to be accessed in a magnetic disk relation and in an archive relation. In either case, the duplicate record will consume system resources; however, there are no other adverse consequences because POSTGRES is a relational system and removes duplicate records during processing.

When the record is safely stored on the archive and indexed appropriately, the second phase of vacuuming can occur. This phase entails computing a new anchor point for the magnetic disk relation and adding new index records for it. This anchor point is found by starting at the old anchor point and calculating the value of the last delta that satisfies

"now" - Tmax >= T

by moving forward through the linked list. The appropriate values are inserted into the magnetic disk relation, and index records are inserted into all appropriate index. When this phase is complete, the new anchor point record is accessible directly from secondary indexes as well as by chaining forward from the old anchor point. Again, if there is a crash during this phase a record may be accessible twice in some future queries, resulting in additional overhead but no other consequences.

The last phase of the vacuum process is to remove the original anchor point followed by all delta records and then to delete all index records that pointed to this deleted anchor point. If there is a crash during this phase, index records may exist that do not point to a correct data record. Since the run-time system must already check that data records are valid and have the key that the appropriate index record expects them to have, this situation can be checked using the same mechanism.

Whenever there is a failure, the vacuum cleaner is simply restarted after the failure is repaired. It will re-vacuum any record that was in progress at some later time. If the crash occurred during phase 3, the vacuum cleaner could be smart enough to realize that the record was already safely vacuumed. However, the cost of this checking is probably not worthwhile. Consequently, failures will result in a slow accumulation of extra records in the archive. We are depending on crashes to be infrequent enough that this is not a serious concern.

We now turn to the cost of the vacuum cleaner.

3.4. Vacuuming Cost

We examine two different vacuuming situations. In the first case we assume that a record is inserted, updated K times and then deleted. The whole chain of records from insertion to deletion is vacuumed at once. In the second case, we assume that the vacuum is run after K updates, and a new anchor record must be inserted. In both cases, we assume that there are Z secondary indexes for both the archive and magnetic disk relation, that no key changes are made during these K updates, and that an anchor point and all its delta records reside on the same page. Table 1 indicates the vacuum cost for each case. Notice that vacuuming consumes a constant cost. This rather surprising conclusion reflects the fact that a new anchor record can be inserted on the same page from which the old anchor point is being deleted without requiring the page to be forced to stable memory in between the operations. Moreover, the new index records can be inserted on the same page from which the previous entries are deleted without an intervening I/O. Hence, the cost PER RECORD of the vacuum cleaner decreases as the length of the chain, K, increases. As long as an anchor point and several delta records are vacuumed together, the cost should be marginal.

4. INDEXING THE ARCHIVE

4.1. Magnetic Disk Indexes

The archive can be indexed by conventional magnetic disk indexes. For example, one could construct a salary index on the archive which would be helpful in answering queries of the form:

```
retrieve (EMP.name) using EMP [,] where
EMP.salary = 10000
```

However, to provide fast access for queries which restrict the historical scope of interest, e.g:

```
retrieve (EMP.name) using EMP [1/1/87,]
where EMP.salary = 10000
```

a standard salary index will not be of much use because the index will return all historical salaries

	whole chain	K updates
archive-writes	1+Z	1+Z
disk-reads	1	1
disk-writes	1+Z	1+Z

I/O Counts for Vacuuming
Table 1

of the correct size whereas the query only requested a small subset. Consequently, in addition to conventional indexes, we expect time-oriented indexes to be especially useful for archive relations. Hence, the two fields, Tmin and Tmax, are stored in the archive as a single field, I, of type **interval**. An R-tree access method [GUTM84] can be constructed to provide an index on this interval field. The operators for which an R-tree can provide fast access include "overlaps" and "contained-in". Hence, if these operators are written for the interval data type, an R-tree can be constructed for the EMP relation as follows:

```
index on archive EMP is EMP-INDEX (I with
interval-ops)
using R-tree and fill-factor = .8
```

This index can support fast access to the historical state of the EMP relation at any point in time or during a particular period.

To utilize such indexes, the POSTGRES query planner needs to be slightly modified. Note that POSTGRES need only run a query on an archive relation if the scope of the relation includes some historical records, Hence, the query for an archive relation must be of the form:

```
...using EMP[T]
```

or

```
...using EMP[T1,T2]
```

The planner converts the first construct into:

```
...where T contained-in EMP.I
```

and the second into:

```
...where interval(T1,T2) overlaps EMP.I
```

Since all records in the archive are guaranteed to be valid, these two qualifications can replace all the low level code that checks for record validity on the magnetic disk described in Section 2.3. With this modification, the query optimizer can use the added qualification to provide a fast access path through an interval index if one exists.

Moreover, we expect combined indexes on the interval field along with some data value to be very attractive, e.g:

```
index on archive EMP is EMP-INDEX
(I with interval-ops, salary with float-ops)
using R-tree and fill-factor = .8
```

Since an R-tree is a multidimensional index, the above index supports intervals which exist in a two dimensional space of time and salaries. A query such as:

```
retrieve (EMP.name) using EMP[T1,T2] where
EMP.salary = 10000
```

will be turned into:

```
retrieve (EMP.name) where EMP.salary =
10000
                    and interval(T1,T2) overlaps
                              EMP.I
```

The two clauses of the qualification define another

interval in two dimensions and conventional R-tree processing of the interval can be performed to use both qualifications to advantage.

Although data records will be added to the archive at the convenience of the vacuum cleaner, records will be generally inserted in ascending time order. Hence, the poor performance reported in [ROUS85] for R-trees should be averted by the nearly sorted order in which the records will be inserted. Performance tests to ascertain this speculation are planned. We now turn to a discussion of R-tree indexes that are partly on both magnetic and archival mediums.

4.2. Combined Media Indexes

We begin with a small space calculation to illustrate the need for indexes that use both media. Suppose a relation exists with 10**6 tuples and each tuple is modified 30 times during the lifetime of the application. Suppose there are two secondary indexes for both the archive and the disk relation and updates never change the values of key fields. Moreover, suppose vacuuming occurs after the 5th delta record is written, so there are an average of 3 delta records for each anchor point. Assume that anchor points consume 200 bytes, delta records consume 40 bytes, and index keys are 10 bytes long.

With these assumptions, the sizes in bytes of each kind of object are indicated in Table 2. Clearly, 10**6 records will consume 200 mbytes while 3 x 10**6 delta records will require 120 mbytes. Each index record is assumed to require a four byte pointer in addition to the 10 byte key; hence each of the two indexes will take up 14 mbytes. There are 6 anchor point records on the archive for each of the 10**6 records each concatenated with 4 delta records. Hence, archive records will be 360 bytes long, and require 2160 mbytes. Lastly, there is an index record for each of the archive anchor points; hence the archive indexes are 6 times as large as the magnetic disk indexes.

Two points are evident from Table 2. First, the archive can become rather large. Hence, one should vacuum infrequently to cut down on the number of anchor points that occur in the archive. Moreover, it might be desirable to differentially code the anchor points to save space. The second point to notice is that the archive indexes consume a large amount of space on magnetic disk. if the target relation had three indexes instead of two, the archive indexes would consume a greater amount of space than the magnetic disk relation. Hence, we explore in this section data structures that allow part of the index to migrate to the archive. Although we could alternatively consider index structures that are entirely on the archive, such as those proposed in [VITT85], we believe that combined media structures will substantially outperform structures restricted to the archive. We plan performance comparisons to demonstrate the validity of this hypothesis.

object	mbytes
disk relation anchor points	200
deltas	120
secondary indexes	28
archive	2160
archive indexes	168

Sizes of the Various Objects
Table 2

Consider an R-tree storage structure in which each pointer in a non-leaf node of the R-tree is distinguished to be either a magnetic disk page pointer or an archive page pointer. If pointers are 32 bits, then we can use the high-order bit for this purpose thereby allowing the remaining 31 bits to specify 2**31 pages on magnetic disk or archive storage. If pages are 8K bytes, then the maximum size of an archive index is 2**44 bytes (about 1.75 x 10**13 bytes), clearly adequate for almost any application. Moreover, the leaf level pages of the R-tree contain key values and pointers to associated data records. These data pointers can be 48 bytes long, thereby allowing the data file corresponding to a single historical relation to be 2**48 bytes long (about 3.0 x 10**14 bytes), again adequate for most applications.

We assume that the archive may be a write-once-read-many (WORM) device that allows pages to be initially written but then does not allow any overwrites of the page. With this assumption, records can only be dynamically added to pages that reside on magnetic disk. Table 3 suggests two sensible strategies for the placement of new records when they are not entirely contained inside some R-tree index region corresponding to a magnetic disk page.

Moreover, we assume that any page that resides on the archive contains pointers that in turn point only to pages on the archive. This avoids having to contend with updating an archive page which contains a pointer to a magnetic disk page that splits.

Pages in an R-tree can be moved from magnetic disk to the archive as long as they contain only archive page pointers. Once a page moves to the archive, it becomes read only. A page can be moved from the archive to the magnetic disk if its parent page resides on magnetic disk. In this case, the archive page previously inhabited by this page becomes unusable. The utility of this reverse migration seems limited, so we will not consider it further.

We turn now to several page movement policies for migrating pages from magnetic disk to the

P1 allocate to the region which has to be expanded the least

P2 allocate to the region whose maximum time has to be expanded the least

Record Insertion Strategies
Table 3

archive and use the parameters indicated in Table 4 in the discussion to follow. The simplist policy would be to construct a system demon to "vacuum" the index by moving the leaf page to the archive that has the smallest value for Tmax, the left-hand end of its interval. This vacuuming would occur whenever the R-tree structure reached a threshold near its maximum size of F disk pages. A second policy would be to choose a worthy page to archive based both on its value of Tmax and on percentage fullness of the page. In either case, insertions would be made into the R-tree index at the lower left-hand part of the index while the demon would be archiving pages in the lower right hand part of the index. Whenever an intermediate R-tree node had descendents all on the archive, it could in turn be archived by the demon.

For example, if B is 8192 bytes, L is 50 bytes and there is a five year archive of updates at a frequency, U of 1 update per second, then 1.4 x 10**6 index blocks will be required resulting in a four level R-tree. F of these blocks will reside on magnetic disk and the remainder will be on the archive. Any insertion or search will require at least 4 accesses to one or the other storage medium.

A third movement policy with somewhat different performance characteristics would be to perform "batch movement". In this case one would build a magnetic disk R-tree until its size was F blocks. Then, one would copy the all pages of the R-tree except the root to the archive and allocate a special "top node" on magnetic disk for this root node. Then, one would proceed to fill up

F	number of magnetic disk blocks usable for the index
U	update frequency of the relation being indexed
L	record size in the index being constructed
B	block size of magnetic disk pages

Parameters Controlling Page Movement
Table 4

a second complete R-tree of F-1 pages. While the second R-tree was being built, both this new R-tree and the one on the archive would be searched during any retrieval request. All inserts would, of course, be directed to the magnetic disk R-tree. When this second R-tree was full, it would be copied to the archive as before and its root node added to the existing top node. The combination might cause the top node to overflow, and a conventional R-tree split would be accomplished. Consequently, the top node would become a conventional R-tree of three nodes. The filling process would start again on a 3rd R-tree of F-3 nodes. When this was full, it would be archived and its root added to the lower left hand page of the 3 node R-tree.

Over time, there would continue to be two R-trees. The first would be completely on magnetic disk and periodically archived. As long as the height of this R-tree at the time it is archived is a constant, H, then the second R-tree of height, H1, will have the bottom H-1 levels on the archive. Moreover, insertions into the magnetic disk portion of this R-tree are always on the left-most page. Hence, the pages along the left-side of the tree are the only ones which will be modified; other pages can be archived if they point entirely to pages on the archive. Hence, some subcollection of the pages on the top H1-H+1 levels remain on the magnetic disk. Insertions go always to the first R-tree while searches go to both R-trees. Of course, there are no deletions to be concerned with.

Again if B is 8192 bytes, L is 50 bytes and F is 6000 blocks, then H will be 3 and each insert will require 3 magnetic disk accesses. Moreover, at 1 update per second, a five year archive will require a four level R-tree whose bottom two levels will be on the archive and a subcollection of the top 2 levels of 100-161 blocks will be on magnetic disk. Hence, searches will require descending two R-trees with a total depth of 7 levels and will be about 40 percent slower than either of the single R-tree structures proposed. On the other hand, the very common operation of insertions will be approximately 25 percent faster.

5. PERFORMANCE COMPARISON

5.1. Assumptions

In order to compare our storage system with a conventional one based on write-ahead logging (WAL), we make the following assumptions:

1) Portions of the buffer pool may reside in non-volatile main memory

2) CPU instructions are not a critical resource, and thereby only I/O operations are counted.

The second assumption requires some explanation. Current CPU technology is driving down the cost of a MIP at a rate of a factor of two every couple of years. Hence, current low-end workstations have a few MIPs of processing power. On the other hand, disk technology is getting denser and cheaper. However, disks are not getting faster at a significant rate. Hence, one can still only expect to read about 30 blocks per second off of a standard disk drive. Current implementations of data base systems require several thousand instructions to fetch a page from the disk followed by 1000-3000 instructions per data record examined on that page. As a simple figure of merit, assume 30000 instructions are required to process a disk block. Hence, a 1 MIP CPU will approximately balance a single disk. Currently, workstations with 3-5 MIPs are available but are unlikely to be configured with 3-5 disks. Moreover, future workstations (such as SPUR and FIREFLY) will have 10-30 MIPs. Clearly, they will not have 10-30 disks unless disk systems shift to large numbers of SCSI oriented single platter disks and away from current SMD disks.

Put differently, a SUN 3/280 costs about $5000 per MIP, while an SMD disk and controller costs about $12,000. Hence, the CPU cost to support a disk is much smaller than the cost of the disk, and the major cost of data base hardware can be expected to be in the disk system. As such, if an installation is found to be CPU bound, then additional CPU resources can be cheaply added until the system becomes balanced.

We analyze three possible situations:

large-SM:	an ample amount of stable main memory is available
small-SM:	a modest amount of stable main memory is available
no-SM:	no stable main memory is available

In the first case we assume that enough stable main memory is available for POSTGRES and a WAL system to use so that neither system is required to **force** disk pages to secondary storage at the time that they are updated. Hence, each system will execute a certain number of I/O operations that can be buffered in stable memory and written out to disk at some convenient time. We count the number of such **non-forced** I/O operations that each system will execute, assuming all writes cost the same amount. For both systems we assume that records do not cross page boundaries, so each update results in a single page write. Moreover, we assume that each POSTGRES delta record can be put on the same page as its anchor point. Next, we assume that transactions are a single record insertion, update, deletion or an aborted update. Moreover, we assume there are two secondary indexes on the relation affected and that updates fail to alter either key field. Lastly, we assume that a write ahead log will require 3 log records (begin transaction, the data modification, and end transaction), with a total length of 400 bytes. Moreover, secondary index operations are not logged and thereby the log records for 10 transactions will fit on a conventional 4K log page.

In the second situation we assume that a modest amount of stable main memory is available. We assume that the quantity is sufficient to hold only the tail of the POSTGRES log and the tail of the TIME relation. In a WAL system, we assume that stable memory can buffer a conventional log turning each log write into one that need not be synchronously forced out to disk. This situation (small-SM) should be contrasted with the third case where no stable memory at all is available (no-SM). In this latter cases, some writes must be forced to disk by both types of storage systems.

In the results to follow we ignore the cost that either kind of system would incur to mirror the data for high availability. Moreover, we are also ignoring the WAL cost associated with checkpoints. In addition, we assume that a WAL system never requires a disk read to access the appropriate undo log record. We are also ignoring the cost of vacuuming the disk in the POSTGRES architecture.

5.2. Performance Results

Table 5 indicates the number of I/O operations each of the four types of transactions must execute for the assumed large-SM configuration. Since there is ample stable main memory, neither system must force any data pages to disk and only non-forced I/Os must be done. An insert requires that a data record and two index records be written by either system. Moreover, 1/10th of a log page will be filled by the conventional system, so every 10 transactions there will be another log page which must be eventually written to disk. In POSTGRES the insertions to the LOG relation and the TIME relation generate an I/O every 65536 and 2048 transactions respectively, and we have ignored this small number in Table 5. Consequently, one requires 3 non-forced I/Os in POSTGRES and 3.1 in a conventional system. The next two columns in Table 1 can be similarly computed. The last column summarizes the I/Os for an aborted transaction. In POSTGRES the updated page need not be rewritten to disk. Hence, no I/Os are strictly necessary; however, in all liklihood, this optimization will not be implemented. A WAL system will update the data and construct a log record. Then the log record must be read and the data page returned to its original value. Again, a very clever system could avoid writing the page out to disk, since it is identical to the disk copy. Hence, for both systems we indicate both the optimized number of writes and the non-optimized number. Notice in Table 5 that POSTGRES is marginally better than a WAL system except for deletes where it is dramatically better because it does not delete the 2 index records. We now turn to cases where POSTGRES is less attractive.

	Insert	Update	Delete	Abort
WAL-force	0	0	0	0
WAL-no-force	3.1	1.1	3.1	0.1 or 1.1
POSTGRES-force	0	0	0	0
POSTGRES-non-force	3	1	1	0 or 1

I/O Counts for the Primitive Operations
large-SM Configuration
Table 5

Table 6 repeats the I/O counts for the small-SM configuration. The WAL configuration performs exactly as in Table 5 while the the POSTGRES data pages must now be forced to disk since insufficient stable main memory is assumed to hold them. Notice that POSTGRES is still better in the total number of I/O operations; however the requirement to do them synchronously will be a major disadvantage.

Table 7 then indicates the I/O counts under the condition that NO stable main memory is available. Here the log record for a conventional WAL system must be forced to disk at commit time. The other writes can remain in the buffer pool and be written at a later time. In POSTGRES the LOG bit must be forced out to disk along with the insert to the TIME relation. Moreover, the data pages must be forced as in Table 6. In this case POSTGRES is marginally poorer in the total number of operations; and again the synchronous nature of these updates will be a significant disadvantage.

	Insert	Update	Delete	Abort
WAL-force	0	0	0	0
WAL-no-force	3.1	1.1	3.1	0.1 or 1.1
POSTGRES-force	3	1	1	0 or 1
POSTGRES-non-force	0	0	0	0

I/O Counts for the Primitive Operations
small-SM Configuration
Table 6

	Insert	Update	Delete	Abort
WAL-force	1	1	1	1
WAL-no-force	3	1	3	0 or 1
POSTGRES-force	5	3	3	1
POSTGRES-non-force	0	0	0	0 or 1

I/O Counts for the Primitive Operations
no-SM Configuration
Table 7

In summary, the POSTGRES solution is preferred in the large-SM configuration since all operations require less I/Os. In Table 6 the total number of I/Os is less for POSTGRES; however, synchronous I/O is required. Table 7 shows a situation where POSTGRES is typically more expensive. However, group commits [DEWI84] could be used to effectively convert the results for either type of system into the ones in Table 6. Consequently, POSTGRES should be thought of as fairly competitive with current storage architectures. Moreover, it has a considerable advantage over WAL systems in that recovery time will be instantaneous while requiring a substantial amount of time in a WAL architecture.

6. CONCLUSIONS

This paper has described the storage manager that is being constructed for POSTGRES. The main points guiding the design of the system were:

1) instantaneous recovery from crashes

2) ability to keep archival records on an archival medium

3) housekeeping chores should be done asynchronously

4) concurrency control based on conventional locking

The first point should be contrasted with the standard write-ahead log (WAL) storage managers in widespread use today.

In engineering application one often requires the past history of the data base. Moreover, even in business applications this feature is sometimes needed, and the now famous TP1 benchmark assumes that the application will maintain an archive. It makes more sense for the data manager to do this task internally for applications that require the service.

The third design point has been motivated by the desire to run multiple concurrent processes if there happen to be extra processors. Hence storage management functions can occur in parallel on multiple processors. Alternatively, some functions can be saved for idle time on a single processor. Lastly, it allows POSTGRES code to be a collection of asynchronous processes and not a single large monolithic body of code.

The final design point reflects our intuitive belief, confirmed by simulations, that standard locking is the most desirable concurrency control strategy. Moreover, it should be noted that read-only transactions can be optionally coded to run as of some point in the recent past. Since historical commands set no locks, then read-only transactions will never interfere with transactions performing updates or be required to wait. Consequently, the level of contention in a POSTGRES data base may be a great deal lower than that found in conventional storage managers.

The design of the POSTGRES storage manager has been sketched and a brief analysis of its expected performance relative to a conventional one has been performed. If the analysis is confirmed in practice, then POSTGRES will give similar performance compared to other storage managers while providing the extra service of historical access to the data base. This should prove attractive in some environments.

At the moment, the magnetic disk storage manager is operational, and work is proceeding on the vacuum cleaner and the layout of the archive. POSTGRES is designed to support extendible access methods, and we have implemented the B-tree code and will provide R-trees in the near future. Additional access methods can be constructed by other parties to suit their special needs. When the remaining pieces of the storage manager are complete, we plan a performance "bakeoff" both against conventional storage managers as well as against other storage managers (such as [CARE86, COPE84]) with interesting properties.

REFERENCES

[AGRA85] Agrawal, R. et. al., "Models for Studying Concurrency Control Performance Alternatives and Implications," Proc. 1985 ACM-SIGMOD Conference on Management of Data, Austin, Tx., May 1985.

[ASTR76] Astrahan, M. et. al., "System R: A Relational Approach to Data," ACM-TODS, June 1976.

[BART81] Bartlett, J., "A Non-STOP Kernel," Proc. Eighth Symposium on Operating System Principles," Pacific Grove, Ca., Dec. 1981.

[BERN80] Bernstein, P. at. al., "Concurrency Control in a System for Distributed Databases (SDD-1)," ACM-TODS, March 1980.

[BHID87] Bhide, A., "Query processing in Shared Memory Multiprocessor Systems," (in preparation).

[CARE86] Carey, M. et. al., "Object and File Management in the EXODUS Database System," Proc. 1986 VLDB Conference, Kyoto, Japan, August 1986.

[COPE84] Copeland, G. and D. Maier, "Making Smalltalk a Database System," Proc. 1984 ACM-SIGMOD Conference on Management of Data, Boston, Mass. June 1984.

[DEC86] Digital Equipment Corp., "VAX/VMS V4.0 Reference Manual," Digital Equipment Corp., Maynard, Mass., June 1986.

[DEWI84] Dewitt, D. et. al., "Implementation Techniques for Main Memory Database Systems," Proc. 1984 ACM-SIGMOD Conference on Management of Data, Boston, Mass., June 1984.

[GRAY78] Gray, J., "Notes on Data Base Operating Systems," IBM Research, San Jose, Ca., RJ1879, June 1978.

[GUTM84] Gutman, A., "R-trees: A Dynamic Index Structure for Spatial Searching," Proc. 1984 ACM-SIGMOD Conference on Management of Data, Boston, Mass. June 1984.

[HILL85] Hill, M., et al. "Design Decisions in SPUR," Computer Magazine, vol.19, no.11, November 1986.

[ROUS85] Roussoupoulis, N. and Leifker, D., "Direct Spatial Search on Pictorial Databases Using Packed R-trees," Proc. 1985 ACM-SIGMOD Conference on Management of Data, Austin, Tx., May 1985.

[SEQU85] Sequent Computer Co., "The SEQUENT Balance Reference Manual," Sequent Computers, Portland, Ore., 1985.

[SEVR76] Severence, D., and Lohman, G., "Differential Files: Their Application to the Maintenance of large Databases," ACM-TODS, June 1976.

[STON76] Stonebraker, M., et. al. "The Design and Implementation of INGRES," ACM-TODS, September 1976.

[STON86] Stonebraker, M. and Rowe, L., "The Design of POSTGRES," Proc. 1986ACM-SIGMOD Conference on Management of Data, Washington, D.C., May 1986.

[STON86a] Stonebraker, M., "Inclusion of New Types in Relational Data Base Systems," Proc. Second International Conference on Data Base Engineering, Los Angeles, Ca., Feb. 1986.

[VITT85] Vitter, J., "An Efficient I/O Interface for Optical Disks," ACM-TODS, June 1985.

Author Index

I

J

K

Y

Z

Subject Index

D

T

Morgan Kaufmann Publishers, Inc.

READER'S COMMENT FORM

Your opinion will be helpful in maintaining a useful and up-to-date collection of research:

1. Did you use this book

   □ in a class as recommended or assigned reading?

   □ for personal study?

   □ as a reference volume?

2. Please rate the following chapters:

	Very Important	Worth-while	Non-essential	Unimportant
The Roots	□	□	□	□
Relational Implementation Techniques	□	□	□	□
Distributed Database Systems	□	□	□	□
Performance and Database Machines	□	□	□	□
User Interfaces	□	□	□	□
New Data Models	□	□	□	□
Extendibility	□	□	□	□
Integration of Knowledge and Data Management	□	□	□	□
Storage Management Issues	□	□	□	□

3. Which topics would you most like to see included in the next edition of this book?

____

____

____

____

____

4. Are there any additional papers which you consider essential for including in the next edition of this book? (Please list only three.)

____

____

____

5. Do you have any comments about the author's introduction?

____

____

____

____

____

6. How would you rate the value of this collection?

   □ Excellent □ Above Average □ Average □ Below Average □ Poor

Thank you.

DETACH, FOLD, STAPLE, AND MAIL

NO POSTAGE
NECESSARY
IF MAILED
IN THE
UNITED STATES

BUSINESS REPLY MAIL

FIRST CLASS PERMIT NO. 499 PALO ALTO, CA

POSTAGE WILL BE PAID BY ADDRESSEE

Morgan Kaufmann Publishers, Inc.
ORDER FULFILLMENT CENTER
P.O. BOX 50490
PALO ALTO, CA 94303-9953

Attn: Editorial Dept.